Handbook of Latin American Studies: No. 35

A SELECTIVE AND ANNOTATED GUIDE TO RECENT
PUBLICATIONS IN ANTHROPOLOGY, ECONOMICS,
EDUCATION, GEOGRAPHY, GOVERNMENT AND POLITICS,
INTERNATIONAL RELATIONS, AND SOCIOLOGY

VOLUME 36 WILL BE DEVOTED TO THE
HUMANITIES: ART, FOLKLORE, HISTORY,
LANGUAGE, LITERATURE, MUSIC,
AND PHILOSOPHY

EDITORIAL NOTE

Comments, suggestions, and material intended for review in the *Handbook of Latin American Studies* should be sent directly to the Editor, *Handbook of Latin American Studies,* Latin American, Portuguese, and Spanish Division, Library of Congress, Washington, D.C. 20540.

Advisory Board

Charles Gibson, *University of Michigan,* CHAIRMAN
Cole Blasier, *University of Pittsburgh*
Frank N. Dauster, *Rutgers University, New Brunswick*
Joseph Grunwald, *The Brookings Institution*
Javier Malagón, *General Secretariat, Organization of American States*
Betty J. Meggers, *Smithsonian Institution*
James R. Scobie, *Indiana University, Bloomington*
Kempton E. Webb, *Columbia University*
Bryce Wood, *Social Science Research Council*

Administrative Officers • The Library of Congress

L. Quincy Mumford, *Librarian of Congress*
Paul L. Berry, *Director, Reference Department*
Mary Ellis Kahler, *Chief, Latin American, Portuguese, and Spanish Division*

Representative of the University of Florida

William B. Harvey, *Director, University of Florida Press*

Handbook Editorial Staff

Assistant Editor
    Dolores Moyano Martin
Assistant to the Editor
    Alfredda H. Payne
Editorial Assistants
    Joyce C. Johnson
    Janice M. Herd
    Jane L. Lowe

HANDBOOK OF LATIN AMERICAN STUDIES
No. 35

Prepared by
A NUMBER OF SCHOLARS
for
the Latin American,
Portuguese, and Spanish Division
of
The Library of Congress

•

Edited by
DONALD E. J. STEWART

•

62233

SOCIAL SCIENCES

•

UNIVERSITY OF FLORIDA PRESS
GAINESVILLE
1973

MEMPHIS
THEOLOGICAL SEMINARY
LIBRARY
168 EAST PARKWAY SOUTH
MEMPHIS, TN. 38104

L.C. Card Number: 36-32633

ISBN 0-8130-0442-X

Copyright © 1973 by the State of Florida
Board of Trustees of the
Internal Improvement Trust Fund
printed by rose printing co.
tallahassee, florida

Contributing Editors

Richard E. W. Adams, *University of Texas, San Antonio*, ANTHROPOLOGY
* Earl M. Aldrich, Jr., *University of Wisconsin, Madison*, LITERATURE
Fuat Andic, *University of Puerto Rico, Río Piedras*, ECONOMICS
Suphan Andic, *University of Puerto Rico, Río Piedras*, ECONOMICS
John J. Bailey, *Georgetown University*, GOVERNMENT AND POLITICS
José Fábio Barbosa-Dasilva, *University of Notre Dame*, SOCIOLOGY
* Arnold Bauer, *University of California, Davis*, HISTORY
* Gerard Béhague, *University of Illinois*, MUSIC
Robert L. Bennett, *University of Maryland*, ECONOMICS
* Rolando E. Bonachea, *George Washington University*, HISTORY
Leslie Ann Brownrigg, *Northwestern University*, ANTHROPOLOGY
Ripley P. Bullen, *The Florida State Museum, Gainesville*, ANTHROPOLOGY
* David Burks, *Hunter College*, HISTORY
* E. Bradford Burns, *University of California, Los Angeles*, HISTORY
* David Bushnell, *University of Florida*, HISTORY
Juan J. Buttari, *The Brookings Institution*, ECONOMICS
* Edward E. Calnek, *University of Rochester*, HISTORY
* D. Lincoln Canfield, *Southern Illinois University*, LATIN AMERICAN LANGUAGES
* Thomas E. Case, *San Diego State College*, LITERATURE
* Donald E. Chipman, *North Texas State University, Denton*, HISTORY
Lambros Comitas, *Columbia University*, ANTHROPOLOGY
Michael H. Crawford, *University of Kansas*, ANTHROPOLOGY
* Frank Dauster, *Rutgers University*, LITERATURE
* Ralph E. Dimmick, *General Secretariat, Organization of American States*, LITERATURE
Clinton R. Edwards, *University of Wisconsin, Milwaukee*, GEOGRAPHY
Everett Egginton, *Syracuse University*, EDUCATION
Robert C. Eidt, *University of Wisconsin, Milwaukee*, GEOGRAPHY
Clifford Evans, *Smithsonian Institution*, ANTHROPOLOGY
Yale H. Ferguson, *Rutgers University, Newark*, INTERNATIONAL RELATIONS
* Rubén A. Gamboa, *Stanford University*, LITERATURE
* Naomi M. Garrett, *Dennison College*, LITERATURE
Marion H. Gillim, *Barnard College, Columbia University*, ECONOMICS
* Roberto González Echevarría, *Cornell University*, LITERATURE
* Richard E. Greenleaf, *The Tulane University*, HISTORY
Robert A. Halberstein, *University of Miami*, ANTHROPOLOGY
* Michael T. Hamerly, *University of Northern Colorado*, HISTORY
John R. Hébert, *Library of Congress*, GEOGRAPHY
Pedro F. Hernández, *Loyola University*, SOCIOLOGY
Bruce Herrick, *University of California, Los Angeles*, ECONOMICS
John M. Hunter, *Michigan State University*, ECONOMICS
John M. Ingham, *University of Minnesota*, ANTHROPOLOGY
Thomas B. Irving, *University of Tennessee*, LITERATURE
Quentin Jenkins, *Louisiana State University*, SOCIOLOGY

* Harvey L. Johnson, *University of Houston*, LITERATURE
Seth Leacock, *University of Connecticut*, ANTHROPOLOGY
* Luis Leal, *University of Illinois, Urbana-Champaign*, LITERATURE
Fred D. Levy, Jr., *Syracuse University*, ECONOMICS
* Santiago Luppoli, *New York University*, LITERATURE
* James B. Lynch, Jr., *University of Maryland, College Park*, ART
*Colin MacLachlan, *California State College*, HISTORY
Tom L. Martinson, *Ball State University*, GEOGRAPHY
Betty J. Meggers, *Smithsonian Institution*, ANTHROPOLOGY
* Michael C. Meyer, *University of Arizona*, HISTORY
* Carolyn Morrow, *University of Utah*, LITERATURE
John V. Murra, *Cornell University*, HISTORY
* José Neistein, *Brazilian American Cultural Institute, Washington*, ART
* Betty T. Osiek, *Southern Illinois University*, LITERATURE
* Vincent C. Peloso, *Howard University*, HISTORY
* Humberto M. Rasi, *Andrews University*, LITERATURE
* Daniel R. Reedy, *University of Kentucky*, LITERATURE
* Donald Robertson, *The Tulane University*, ART
* Mario Rodriguez, *University of Southern California*, HISTORY
C. Neale Ronning, *New School for Social Research*, INTERNATIONAL RELATIONS
Gordon C. Ruscoe, *Syracuse University*, EDUCATION
Jorge Salazar-Carrillo, *The Brookings Institution*, ECONOMICS
* Arturo Santana, *Universidad de Puerto Rico*, HISTORY
Hugh H. Schwartz, *Inter-American Development Bank*, ECONOMICS
* James R. Scobie, *Indiana University, Bloomington*, HISTORY
* Merle E. Simmons, *Indiana University, Bloomington*, FOLKLORE
John Strasma, *University of Wisconsin, Madison*, ECONOMICS
Andrés Suárez, *University of Florida*, GOVERNMENT AND POLITICS
Philip B. Taylor, Jr., *University of Houston*, GOVERNMENT AND POLITICS
* Juan Carlos Torchia-Estrada, *General Secretariat, Organization of American States*, PHILOSOPHY
Agnes E. Toward, *University of California, San Diego*, EDUCATION
Alan C. Wares, *Instituto Lingüístico de Verano, Mexico*, ANTHROPOLOGY
J. Benedict Warren, *University of Maryland, College Park*, HISTORY
Kempton E. Webb, *Columbia University*, GEOGRAPHY
Hasso von Winning, *Southwest Museum, Los Angeles*, ANTHROPOLOGY
* Benjamin M. Woodbridge, *University of California, Berkeley*, LITERATURE
* Winthrop R. Wright, *University of Maryland, College Park*, HISTORY

Foreign Corresponding Editors

Hans-Joachim Bock, *Ibero-Amerikanisches Institut, Berlin-Lankwich, Federal Republic of Germany*, GERMAN LANGUAGE MATERIAL
Wolf Grabendorff, *Lateinamerikareferat, Stiftung Wissenschaft und Politik, Ebenhausen/Isar*, SOCIAL SCIENCES
Manfred Kossok, *Karl-Marx-Universitaet, Leipzig, German Democratic Republic*, GERMAN LANGUAGE MATERIAL
Magnus Mörner, *Ibero-Amerikanska Institutet i Stockholm, Stockholm, Sweden*, SCANDINAVIAN LANGUAGE MATERIAL
Daniel Pécaut, *Ecole Pratique des Hautes Etudes, Paris, France*, FRENCH LANGUAGE MATERIAL
R. A. M. van Zantwijk, *Universiteit van Amsterdam, The Netherlands*, DUTCH LANGUAGE MATERIAL

* Contributing Editors to Handbook no. 36 (Humanities), scheduled for publication in 1974.

Special Contributing Editors

T. Stephen Cheston, *Georgetown University,* SLAVIC LANGUAGES
Georgette M. Dorn, *Library of Congress,* GERMAN AND HUNGARIAN LANGUAGES
Hans J. Hoyer, *Department of History, The American University,* GERMAN LANGUAGE
Maurice A. Lubin, *Howard University,* HAITIAN MATERIAL
Carmelo Mesa-Lago, *University of Pittsburgh,* CUBAN MATERIAL
Anita R. Navon, *Library of Congress,* SLAVIC LANGUAGES
Arnold H. Price, *Library of Congress,* GERMAN LANGUAGE
Renata V. Shaw, *Library of Congress,* SCANDINAVIAN LANGUAGES

Contents

	PAGE
EDITOR'S NOTE	x
BIBLIOGRAPHY AND GENERAL WORKS ...*Earl J. Pariseau* and *Donald E. J. Stewart*	3
Journal Abbreviations: Bibl. & Gen. Works	20

ANTHROPOLOGY

GENERAL	21
ARCHAEOLOGY	
MESOAMERICA ... *Hasso von Winning* and *Richard E. W. Adams*	26
THE CARIBBEAN ... *Ripley P. Bullen*	46
SOUTH AMERICA ... *Betty J. Meggers* and *Clifford Evans*	49
ETHNOLOGY	
MIDDLE AMERICA ... *John M. Ingham*	69
WEST INDIES ... *Lambros Comitas*	78
SOUTH AMERICA LOWLANDS ... *Seth Leacock*	94
SOUTH AMERICA HIGHLANDS ... *Leslie Ann Brownrigg*	104
LINGUISTICS ... *Alan C. Wares*	127
PHYSICAL ANTHROPOLOGY ... *Michael H. Crawford* and *Robert A. Halberstein*	139
Journal Abbreviations: Anthropology	152

ECONOMICS

GENERAL ... *John M. Hunter*	157
MEXICO ... *Robert L. Bennett*	168
CENTRAL AMERICA/WEST INDIES (except Puerto Rico) ... *Marion H. Gillim*	173
SPANISH SOUTH AMERICA	
COLOMBIA, ECUADOR, THE GUIANAS, AND VENEZUELA ... *Jorge Salazar-Carrillo* and *Juan J. Buttari*	181
BOLIVIA, CHILE, PARAGUAY, PERU AND URUGUAY ... *John Strasma* and *Bruce Herrick*	194
ARGENTINA ... *Hugh H. Schwartz*	208
BRAZIL ... *Fred D. Levy, Jr.*	217
PUERTO RICO ... *Fuat Andic* and *Suphan Andic*	225
Journal Abbreviations: Economics	231

CONTENTS

EDUCATION

	PAGE
LATIN AMERICA (except Brazil)............*Gordon C. Ruscoe* and *Everett Egginton*	235
BRAZIL .... *Agnes E. Toward*	253
Journal Abbreviations: Education	265

GEOGRAPHY

GENERAL................................*Clinton R. Edwards*	268
MIDDLE AMERICA ....*Tom L. Martinson*	285
SOUTH AMERICA (except Brazil) ....*Robert C. Eidt*	296
BRAZIL....................................*Kempton E. Webb*	315
CARTOGRAPHY ....*John R. Hébert*	330
Journal Abbreviations: Geography	344

GOVERNMENT AND POLITICS

GENERAL ....*Philip B. Taylor, Jr.; John J. Bailey* and *Andrés Suárez*	347
MEXICO, CENTRAL AMERICA, THE CARIBBEAN, THE GUIANAS ....*Andrés Suárez*	362
SOUTH AMERICA: WEST COAST ....*John J. Bailey*	374
EAST COAST ....*Philip B. Taylor, Jr.*	389
Journal Abbreviations: Government and Politics	406

INTERNATIONAL RELATIONS

GENERAL ....*C. Neale Ronning*	409
and *Yale H. Ferguson*	420
MEXICO, CENTRAL AMERICA, THE CARIBBEAN .... *Yale H. Ferguson*	427
SOUTH AMERICA ....*C. Neale Ronning*	432
Journal Abbreviations: International Relations	

SOCIOLOGY

GENERAL ....*Pedro F. Hernández* and *Quentin Jenkins*	434
MEXICO, CENTRAL AMERICA, AND THE CARIBBEAN ....*Pedro F. Hernández*	439
SOUTH AMERICA (except Brazil).............*Quentin Jenkins*	450
BRAZIL.......................*José Fábio Barbosa-Dasilva*	456
Journal Abbreviations: Sociology.............................	464

ABBREVIATIONS AND ACRONYMS	469
TITLE LIST OF JOURNALS INDEXED	473
SUBJECT INDEX	484
AUTHOR INDEX	500

Editor's Note

Users of this series will note that the section introductions to this volume reflect a number of shifts in the orientation of research on Latin America since the publication of *HLAS*.

An increasing segment of the research being carried on in and about Latin America deals with specific subjects and is concerned in great measure with basic data and sources of information and material. It is generally noted that these works are characterized by their high quality and methodological sophistication. Of great significance is the fact that in a number of fields scholarly studies by local Latin American specialists outnumber those by researchers outside Latin America. This shift is a healthy sign, reflecting a further step toward Latin Americans' setting their own development priorities based on their own studies.

Development is the prime concern in most of the fields covered in this volume, and the research is aimed at identifying barriers to development and planning ways to surmount them. In this vein demographic studies are probably the most important. Among the topics covered are census analysis, rural-urban migration which shows relationships between social behavior and peasant migration, the relation of socioeconomic environments and migration patterns, urbanization, and the ecological impact of population dynamics. Labor studies and analyses are also important and deal with unemployment, income distribution, technical training (including adult education and on-the-job training), the importation of technological know-how, etc.

Educational reform is less well represented than in the past but is still of vital interest as a planning factor. The return of foreign-trained Latin Americans to their home countries is reflected not only in the increased number of joint publications in all fields but in the concomitant growth of high quality field research characterized by significant technical ability in the collection and interpretation of data as well.

It is also evident—especially in Mexico and Brazil, which have had stable economies for prolonged periods—that much of the research is being geared toward the direct relevance of the subject to the real, day-to-day requirements of development. This orientation is seen in virtually all of the disciplines and is indicative of the need that has led to the changing character of research from a theoretical to an applied nature.

Persistent gaps are nevertheless evident. For instance, more case studies are required in order to clarify certain concepts and their implications for development, both internally and externally. There is also a clear need for more cross-national studies as well as for severe self-examination.

Over the past decade and a half, the interest of non-American countries in Latin America has been increasing rapidly. This trend in part reflects the erosion of U.S. influence in the hemisphere and in part is a result of "low-profile" diplomacy. Another change is seen in the increasing concern of several Latin American countries with their international position. Regionalism is apparently becoming more and more a means of countering U.S. influence. Brazil is contemplating its role as a future global power, while the rest of the countries are asserting their right to set their own terms for foreign investment and selecting what types of industries are considered best.

Latin America is by no means about to take off into development, but individual countries are progressing rapidly, although unevenly, toward this goal. For those who use the *Handbook* as a starting point in reviewing material concerning Latin America, many of the works in this volume reveal an increasing number of promising signs for the area. Of particular importance among these is the mounting share of significant research on Latin America being performed by Latin Americans themselves.

EDITOR'S NOTE

CHANGES IN VOLUME 35

The bibliographic controls introduced in the past continue to be refined, and the volume of material screened has increased over the past year. Again, to cope with this rising volume, additional Contributing Editors have been appointed and several of the sections have been further subdivided.

In the Anthropology section, Ethnology, South America has been divided into Lowlands and Highlands, with a Contributor for each. The Government and International Relations section has been divided into two separate sections: Government and Politics and International Relations. In the Sociology section Latin America, Except Brazil, was divided into two sections: Mexico, Central America, and the Caribbean and South America, Except Brazil.

The Title List of Journals Indexed, which was discontinued after *HLAS* 29 as a space-saving measure, has been reintroduced in this volume. The expansion of the Subject Index has continued, with additional subdivisions added to major headings.

The practice of adhering to a strict cutoff date for the receipt of material has been continued. In general, items received in the *HLAS* office after May, 1973, have not been included in this volume.

Changes in the roster of Contributing Editors are noted below:

Anthropology: Dr. John M. Ingham (University of Minnesota) prepared the Ethnology Middle America section. Dr. Seth Leacock (University of Connecticut) prepared the Ethnology South America Lowlands section, while Dr. Leslie Ann Brownrigg (Northwestern University) prepared the Highlands section. Dr. Alan C. Wares (Instituto Lingüistico de Verano, Mexico) prepared the Linguistics section. Dr. Michael H. Crawford (University of Kansas), together with Dr. Robert A. Halberstein (University of Miami), prepared the Physical Anthropology section.

Economics: Dr. Robert L. Bennett (University of Maryland) prepared the Mexico section. Dr. Jorge Salazar-Carrillo and Dr. Juan J. Buttari (both of the Brookings Institution) prepared the Colombia, Ecuador, The Guianas, and Venezuela section. Dr. Fred D. Levy, Jr., (University of Syracuse) prepared the Brazil section.

Geography: Dr. John R. Hébert (Library of Congress) prepared the Cartography section.

Government and Politics: Dr. Andrés J. Suárez (University of Florida) prepared the Mexico, Central America, and Caribbean section.

International Relations: Dr. Yale Ferguson (Rutgers University, Newark) prepared the Mexico, Central America, and Caribbean section.

Sociology: Dr. Pedro F. Hernández (Loyola University, New Orleans) prepared the Mexico, Central America, and Caribbean section. Dr. Quentin Jenkins (Louisiana State University) prepared the South America, except Brazil, section. Dr. José Fábio Barbosa-Dasilva (Notre Dame University) prepared the Brazil section.

Administrative changes within the *Handbook of Latin American Studies* section are reflected on the title page of the present volume.

Washington, D.C.
December, 1973

Donald E. J. Stewart

Handbook of Latin American Studies

Bibliography and General Works

EARL J. PARISEAU
Assistant Chief
Latin American, Portuguese,
and Spanish Division

DONALD E. J. STEWART
Editor
Handbook of Latin American Studies

THE PAST THREE YEARS HAVE WITNESSED the convening of a number of important conferences in Latin America, publication of a variety of bibliographies and guides relating to that area, and continuing interest in the development of Latin American studies in both Europe and Japan. This introduction reviews some of the outstanding bibliographical achievements since 1971 and presents an overview of general trends as reflected by the publications noted in the "Bibliography and General Works" sections of volumes 33, 34, and 35 of *HLAS*.

In the field of acquisitions, one of the more surprising developments was the demise of the Latin American Cooperative Acquisitions Program (*LACAP*), sponsored since 1960 by the Stechert-Hafner Company of New York City. A cooperative venture representing more than 40 institutional libraries in the United States, *LACAP* provided current Latin American books and periodicals for the research library community, especially to those institutions with strong Latin American collections. Since the abandonment of the program in January, 1973, many research libraries have reverted to a system of blanket orders, relying upon dealers located in the principal publishing centers in Latin America to fill their acquisitions need. Reduced library book budgets and a relatively high rate of materials returned from some participating institutions were among the principal reasons for termination of the *LACAP* program.

The Seminar on the Acquisitions of Latin American Library Materials (*SALALM*) held its 18th annual meeting in Port-of-Spain, Trinidad, April 29-May 3, 1973. This was the third of the last four annual seminars to have been held outside the United States in an effort to strengthen communication with librarians and documentation specialists throughout the hemisphere, the 15th seminar having been convened in Toronto, Canada, and the 16th in Puebla, Mexico. All were well attended and provided an excellent forum for the exchange of information concerning the acquisition and bibliographical programs of the various institutions represented.

The Association of Caribbean University Research Libraries (*ACURIL*) was established in 1969 with purposes and objectives similar to those of *SALALM*. The need for such an organization had been felt for some time since the area's diverse cultural and linguistic backgrounds had led to bibliographical and acquisitions problems that were peculiarly regional in nature. Representatives from more than 40 institutional libraries from the Caribbean attended *ACURIL* meetings in Caracas, Venezuela, in 1971, San Juan, Puerto Rico, in 1972, and Miami, Florida, in 1973. Among *ACURIL*'s significant achievements have been the initiation of a bilingual *Newsletter* (*Carta Informativa*) in August 1973 and an effort to begin acquiring institutional non-trade publications from the English-speaking countries of the Caribbean for the benefit of its members.

A number of important reference and acquisition guides have also appeared. Several important catalogs of major Latin American collections at U.S. universities were published by G. K. Hall & Co., Boston. Among these distinguished contributions were guides to the Oliveira Lima Library of The Catholic University of America, with rich resources on the Luso-Brasilian world, and to the Latin American collection of Tulane University, exceptionally strong for its resources on the language, history, and archaeology of Middle America (see *HLAS 33*, items 45 and 117). Earlier published catalogs have covered the library of the Hispanic Society of America in New York, the Greenlee collection of the Newberry Library in Chicago, and the George Ticknor collection of the Boston Public Library. Recently published but not yet received for review by the *HLAS* is the catalog of the Latin American collection of the University of Florida Libraries, Gainesville, Florida. Other major reference tools include the second revised edition of the *National Directory of Latin Americanists* (see *HLAS 34*, item 131) and the long-awaited *Latin America: A Guide to the Historical Literature*, edited by Charles C. Griffin and J. Benedict Warren, which contains more than 7,000 annotated references to important publications concerning Latin American history from pre-Colombian times to the present (see *HLAS 33*, item 56a). Another volume devoted to Mexico in the distinguished series entitled *Latin American Serial Documents: A Holding List*, compiled by Rosa Mesa (see *HLAS 33,*, item 85), augments those which have already appeared on Colombia, Brazil, and Cuba.

The third revised and updated edition of *Latin America, Spain, and Portugal: An Annotated Bibliography of Paperback Books*, compiled by Georgette M. Dorn, was published by the Library of Congress in 1971 (see *HLAS 34*, item 45). Other noteworthy contributions in the bibliographical field include Russell H. Bartley and Stuart L. Wagner's *Latin America in Basic Historical Collections: A Working Guide*, published by the Hoover Institution, Stanford University (see *HLAS 34*, item 10); Irene Zimmerman's *National Bibliographies of Latin America: A State of the Art Study*, published by the Center for Latin American Studies of the University of Florida (see *HLAS 33*, item 105), which traces past and recent developments concerning national bibliographies in Latin America; and the American Universities Field Staff's *A Selected Bibliography: Asia, Africa, Eastern Europe, Latin America; Supplement 1971*, the Latin American section of which was prepared by Georgette M. Dorn (see item 1). Guides and surveys describing the Latin American holdings at major U.S. universities are extremely useful research tools, and to this category must be added Joseph W. Bingaman's *A Survey of Holdings at the Hoover Institution on War, Revolution and Peace*, published by Stanford University in 1972 (see *HLAS 34*, item 20).

Another area of particular importance for the reference librarian of Latin American collections are the special subject bibliographies. Garrit Huizer's and Cynthia N. Hewitt's "Bibliography on Latin American Peasant Organizations," although only a section in a larger work, *Latin American peasant movements* edited by Henry A. Landsberger (see *HLAS 34*, item 53), is an important contribution. For literature, Beatriz Alvarez' *Arte y letras en "La Nación" de Buenos Aires: 4 de enero, 1870-30 de diciembre, 1899*, (see *HLAS 34*, item 4); a reprint of Willis Knapp Jones' *Latin American Writers in English Translation: A Classical Bibliography* (see *HLAS 34*, item 59); Carl S. Watson's *Literature of the English and French-Speaking West Indies in the University of Florida Library: A Bibliography* (see *HLAS 34*, item 92); and the *Bibliografía literaria de la revista "Hoy":1931-1943*, which is an index to an important Chilean literary magazine (see item 61), are all welcome additions. Brazil continues to publish its *Bibliografia Brasileira de Educação* (see item 60). Problems of urbanization in Latin America received wide coverage in Martin H. Sable's *Latin American Urbanization: A Guide to the Literature, Organizations and Personnel*, which is an excellent reference tool for specialists in this field (see *HLAS 33*, item 161). Two small but important contributions on agrarian problems are Alain Birou's *Bibliografia reciente (1965-69) sobre problemas agrarios en la America Latina* (see item 63) and *Bibliografia Agricola Boliviana*, compiled by Aliaga de Vizcarra (see item 6841).

Strong interest in Cuban studies continues, and three important resource works were recently published. Nelson P. Valdez and Edwin Lieuwen's *The Cuban Revolution: A Research-Study Guide, 1959-1969* (see *HLAS 33*, item 119), Earl J. Pariseau's *Cuban Acquisitions and Bibliography: Proceedings and Working Papers of an International Conference Held at the Library of Congress, April 13-15, 1970* (see *HLAS 33*, item 95), and the *Cuban Studies Newsletter* (see *HLAS 34*, item 41), published by the Center of Latin American Studies, University of Pittsburgh, for the purpose of fostering communication among specialists, add significantly to the bibliographical resources available for the study of Cuba.

The increasing interest with which Europe and Japan continue to view Latin America is clearly reflected in their recent publishing activities. Since the early 1960's, England has made a major effort to develop its Latin American studies programs. There are now 22 English universities offering advanced degrees to students with a major interest in Latin American studies (see item 56a and item 57). The recently formed Scandinavian Committee for Research on Latin America(NOSALF), has published *Ibero-Americana*, which is designed to promote research and study of Latin America (see *HLAS 34*, item 54); the Instituto de Estudios Ibero-Americanos, established in 1959 in Stockholm, also promotes research on Latin America among Scandinavian universities and institutions, under the able direction of Dr. Magnus Mörner. Spain's strong interest in Latin American studies is reflected in a recent work by Jan Beckman entitled *Documentation der Spanischen Latein Amerika-Forschung* which lists institutions and universities with major interest in Latin America and describes their major archival and library resources (see item 69). The Ibero-Amerikanische Institut in West Berlin and the Karl Marx University in Leipzig, German Democratic Republic, have valuable library resources on Latin America. A new journal entitled *Arbeitsgemeinschaft Deutsche Latein Amerikaforschung*, published in Hamburg, provides information on conferences, symposia, and research projects in progress and covers new publications about Latin America which have appeared in West and East Germany (see item 65). The Latin American Institute of the Soviet Academy of Sciences, founded in 1969, publishes a similar journal entitled *Latinskaia Amerika*. It includes articles on Latin America covering the social sciences and humanities, notes on conferences and seminars, book reviews, and general information on Latin American communist parties. For this and other publications reflecting Russian interest in Latin America, see item 104, item 6066, and *HLAS 34*, item 137.

Japan has long had commercial ties with Latin America. As a result of expanding trade relationships in recent years, there has been a resurgence of interest in Latin American studies in Japan. The Instituto Ibero-Americano, located at Sophia University in Toyko, has published a number of economic and sociological studies on Latin America. The most recent of these, *America Latina na Imprensa do Japão*, prepared by Vendelino Lorscheiter, analyzes the Latin American coverage of six major Japanese newspapers (see item 108).

The Consortium of Latin American Studies Programs (*CLASP*), which is the institutional arm of the Latin American Studies Association, published two important works. *Study Opportunities in Latin America: A Guide to Programs for the U.S. Student*, compiled by Marie L. Rocca (see item 15a) nicely complements an earlier *CLASP* publication entitled *Financial Aid for Latin American Studies*, which was compiled by Franklin Jurado; *Latin America: Sights and Sounds, a Guide to Motion Pictures and Music for College Courses*, compiled by Jane M. Loy, is a major reference and teaching resource that should be well received by students and professors. [E. J. P.]

GENERAL BIBLIOGRAPHY

1. American Universities Field Staff, (firm) Hanover, N.H. A select bibliography: Asia, Africa, Eastern Europe, Latin America; supplement 1971. Hanover, N.H., 1971. 115 p.

Latin American section includes 250 titles in English published since 1969 in the social sciences and humanities. This section was compiled by Georgette M. Dorn, Reference Librarian, Latin American, Portuguese and Spanish Division, Library of Congress. Titles selected were deemed most appropriate for college libraries and students engaged in research on Latin America. Ten-year compilation of the biannual supplements will be forthcoming at the end of 1972.

2. Anuario Bibliográfico Peruano: 1964-1966. Lima, Biblioteca Nacional, 1969. 839 p.

Disinterest of Peruvian publishers and authors in sending copies of their works to the Biblioteca Nacional has caused delays in publishing the *Anuario*, resulting in this three-year accumulation, 1964-66. This is an important bibliography of more than 4,000 books and pamphlets published in and outside Peru. Statistical charts show book publishing by discipline, dept. (state) and by country (for foreign titles published about Perú). Organized by discipline, works are easily accessible through periodical, corporate, author, and individual author indexes. Has separate sections on theses, official publications, periodicals, official government periodicals, and publications concerning Peruvian regions. Also contains useful bio-bibliographical information on recently deceased Peruvian writers.

3. Anuario bibliográfico 1961. México, UNAM, Instituto de Investigaciones Bibliográficas, Biblioteca Nacional, 1971. 804 p.

Contains 3,987 entries covering books, pamphlets, theses, and publishers' and bookdealers' catalogs—all published during 1961. Useful analytical index includes authors, short titles, and some subjects. Introduction states that Mexico now publishes 119 titles per million inhabitants, occupying third place in Hispanic-America.

4. Ardissone, Elena and **Nélida Salvador** *comps*. Bibliografía de la revista *Nosotros*: 1907-1943 (FNA/BAAL, 39/42, 1972, p. 1-700)

Whole issue (700 p.) is devoted to an index of articles that appeared in the important Argentine periodical *Nosotros*, founded by Alfredo Bianchi in 1907. Index covers period 1907-43. Important periodical for understanding cultural, social, and political events of that period. Index is arranged by subject according to universal decimal classification and contains author and subject indexes. Future issue plans similar indexing of Argentine journal *Sur*.

Arze, José Roberto. Acotaciones para una bibliografía selecta sobre sociología boliviana. See item 8416.

5. *Bibliografía Actual del Caribe* [*Current Caribbean Bibliography: Bibliographie Courante de la Caraïbe*]. Biblioteca Regional del Caribe y Norte-Sur, Centro Norte-Sur. Vol. 17, 1967- . Hato Rey, P.R.

One of back volumes covering year 1967. Produced using automated techniques and printed with use of electronic computers. Compiled with cooperation of libraries from Caribbean and US. Organized by general subjects with an alphabetical index of authors and subjects using the KWIC (Key word in Context) method. Extremely useful bibliography for reference and acquisition librarians. Compiled under the direction of María Elena Cardona, Director of the Caribbean Regional Library.

6. ———— [————]. Corporación de Desarrollo Económico del Caribe, Biblioteca Regional del Caribe. Nos. 3/4, marzo/abril, 1971- Hato Rey, P.R.

Bi-monthly supplement to *Current Caribbean Bibliography*. See item 5.

7. *Bibliografía Mexicana.* UNAM. No. 1, enero/feb. 1971 [through] No. 6, nov./dec. 1971- . México.

Bi-monthly listing of current books acquired by the Biblioteca Nacional, arranged by general subjects and containing translations, checklists, books and theses. Analytical index of authors and subjects is appended. (See item 3.)

8. *Bibliotecas 71.* Biblioteca Nacional. Año 9, Nos. 2/4, marzo/agosto 1971- . La Habana.

Official organ of the Dirección Nacional de Bibliotecas, La Habana, includes brief list of recently received reference works, and recent publications of the Biblioteca Nacional. See *HLAS 33:23*.

9. *Boletim Bibliográfico da Biblioteca Nacional.* Ministério da Educação e Cultura, Depto. de Assuntos Culturais. Vol. 18, No. 1, jan./março 1973- . Rio.

Succeeds the *Bibliográfia Brasileira Mensal* (*HLAS 30:13*). Publication will be quarterly. The *Boletim* has been serving as National Bibliography for many years, but bibliography of current Brazilian publications was behind schedule. *Bibliográfia Brasileira Mensal* (see *HLAS 30:13*), published since Nov. 1967 by Instituto Nacional do Livro, provided bibliographical information on current Brazilian books and duplicates much of the information planned for publication in the *Boletim Bibliográfico*. To reduce this duplication of effort, the *Bibliográfia Brasileira Mensal* ceased publication in Dec. 1972 and the Biblioteca Nacional, under the direction of Dr. Jannice Monte-Mor, undertook the responsibility for preparing and publishing the bibliography of current Brazilian books. Since BBM covers publications for period 1968-72 the Biblioteca Nacional decided not to publish its *Boletim* for period 1968-72. Volumes covering 1966 and 1967 are in the press. This issue of the *Boletim* cities only books published during late 1972 and first quarter of 1973. To save time no maps, musical scores or serials were included but will be in subsequent numbers. Organized by subject according to Dewey classification and contains approximately 1200 entries, including children's books, theses, and translations. Titles covering all disciplines in the social sciences and humanities as well as the pure and applied sciences are included. Author index enhances value. Excellent work and a must for all libraries interested in Brazil.

10. Bravo, Enrique R. *comp.* Bibliografía puertorriqueña selecta y anotada. Translated by Marcial Cuevas. N.Y., Columbia Univ., The Urban Center, 1972. 114 p.

Wide-ranging bibliography of Puerto Rican culture, history and life, compiled by professor at the Univ. of Puerto Rico. Includes over 300 titles dealing with Puerto Rican government, economics, education, geography, history, sociology, literature, and religion. Includes works relevant to contemporary Puerto Rico as well as earlier studies now considered classics. Sold at bookstores, but also available free on request to Latin American students at Columbia, from the Urban Center's librarian. Important work fills a void in Puerto Rican bibliography. Highly recommended. [G. M. Dorn]

11. Brazil. Embassy in the United States. Brazilian American Cultural Institute [BACI]. A survey of the Portuguese language Luso-Brazilian and Latin American area studies in institutions of higher learning in the United States. Washington, 1970. 106 p.

Based on results from a questionnaire and information in university catalogs, this is a highly useful guide to Portuguese language, Luso-Brazilian and Latin American studies at approximately 150 US institutions. Universities and colleges are arranged by state with names of Center directors, course offerings and professors teaching in Luso-Brazilian or Latin American field. Good institutional and name indexes. Used in conjunction with National Director of Latin Americanists (see *HLAS 34:131*) it provides librarians and others with current information on institutions and individuals specializing in Latin American affairs.

Brunn, Stanley D. *comp.* Urbanization in developing countries: an international bibliography. See item 7372.

Clermont, Norman. Bibliographie annotée de l'anthropologie physique des Antilles. See item 1135.

12. Díaz-Trechuelo Spínola, María Lourdes. América en la colección de documentos inéditos para la historia de España (EEHA/AEA, 27, 1970, p. 641-732)

Compilation of documents concerning Latin America. Material is divided geographically. Within these sections arrangement is by subject listed chronologically. Identifies sources used by contributors.

Espejo Núñez, Julio. Bibliografía del antiguo Perú: cultura Chavín. See item 943.

13. Exposição da Imprensa Universitária, *I, São Paulo, 1972.* **I (Primeira) exposição da imprensa universitária 1972. Brasília, Ministério da Educação e Cultura, Instituto Nacional do Livro, 1972. 202 p., plates.**

Highly informative bibliography of Brazilian University press publications, exhibited at II Bienal Internacional do Livro, held in São Paulo, in June 1972. Contains 1,500 titles which demonstrate rapid development of university presses in Brazil in recent years. Separate sections on books, pamphlets, and translations; periodical publications, author and title indexes; and theses. Very useful acquisitions guide.

García-Blásquez, Raúl and **César Ramón Córdova.** Bibliografía de los estudios y publicaciones del Instituto Indigenista Peruano: 1961-1969. See item 1408.

Heller, Joyce de. Bibliography of pre-Hispanic goldwork of Colombia. See item 868.

14. *Historiografía y Bibliografía Americanistas.* Escuela de Estudios Hispanoamericanos Consejo Superior de Investigaciones Cientificas. Vol. 16, No. 2, julio 1972- . Sevilla.

Latest edition of this important Spanish bibliographic work on Latin America.

Instituto Euvaldo Lodi, *Rio.* Pesquisa bibliográfica sôbre integração universidade-indústria. See item 6251.

Laberg, Vera B. de *comp.* La guerrilla castrista en América Latina: bibliografía selecta, 1960-1970. See item 7589.

15. Moreira, Eidorfe. Roteiro bibliográfico de Marajó. Belém, Bra., Instituto do Desenvolvimento Econômico-Social do Pará(IDESP), 1969. 67 p. (Cadernos paraenses, 4)

Marajó, island at mouth of Amazon River, has rich pastures for cattle grazing and is interesting to anthropologists for archaeological remains of area's earlier civilizations. Contains 288 annotated references to books and periodical articles on the island's history and culture. Important reference resource for relatively unknown area of Brazilian Amazon.

Olivos, Luis and **Oscar Delgado.** Bibliografía sobre la Iglesia y el cambio social en América Latina. See item 8282.

15a. Rocca, Marie L. Study opportunities in Latin America: a guide to programs for the U.S. student. Prepared under the direction of Kempton E. Webb. Gainesville, Fla., Univ. of Florida, Consortium of Latin American Studies Programs, 1972. 120 p. (CLASP, 4)

Describes opportunities for study in Latin America for US undergraduate students to academic sessions sponsored by US and foreign colleges and other institutions of higher learning. Full information on a particular program may be obtained by writing directly to the sponsoring institution. Useful and much needed compilation. [G. M. Dorn]

16. Santamarina, Estela B. de; Alicia I. García; and Hilda M. Díaz. Nueva bibliografía geográfica de Tucumán. Tucumán, Arg., Univ. Nacional de Tucumán, Facultad de Filosofía y Letras, Depto. de Geografía, 1972. 182 p., map (Serie monográfica, 20)

Earlier similar bibliography prepared by G. Rohmeder and E.B. de Santamarina appeared in 1946 with 573 entries. Pre-1946 titles in addition to those appearing since 1946 form present bibliography of 1,081 entries. Also includes separate section on cartography and aerophotography of Tucumán. Subject and regional indexes. Important resource for geographers.

Twining, Mary Arnold. Toward a working folklore bibliography of the Caribbean area. See item 1211.

Uratsuka, Josefa N.; Lúcia Musenek; and Hermínia Muzanek. Agricultura na América pré-colombiana: bibliografia. See item 532.

17. Wilgus, A. Curtis comp. Doors to Latin America: recent books and pamphlets. Miami Beach, Fla., Inter-American Bibliographical and Library Association in cooperation with the Inter-American Academy, 1972. 16 p. (Vol. 19, No. 4, Oct. 1972)

Brief annotated listing of current books and reprints of older titles on Latin America.

Zapata, Juan Antonio. Economía de los recursos naturales. See item 2411.

COLLECTIVE AND PERSONAL BIBLIOGRAPHY

18. Bibliografia das obras publicadas pelo Exmo. Prof. Dr. Giulo Davide Leoni. São Paulo, Escolas Profissionais Salesianas, 1970. 46 p., plate.

Result of homage to distinguished teacher and citizen of São Paulo, this bibliography is exactly what its title states: a list of 263 items covering everything from Virgil to Molière to Goethe, in translations, plus original works. Leoni was a professor of Italian language and literature in São Paulo, president of the League of Classical Studies of Brazil, a journalist, and a novelist, as well as a teacher. Upon his retirement he was made a citizen of São Paulo in 1964, and volume includes description of that ceremony. [A. E. Toward]

19. Giffoni, O. Carneiro. Dicionário bio-bibliográfico brasileiro de escritores médicos: 1500-1899. São Paulo, Livraria Nobel, 1972. 298 p.

Revealing bibliography of Brazilian medical doctors who published works related to medicine and other fields of interest. It is surprising to note number of poets and prose writers among the medical profession. Arranged alphabetically by author with author index organized by century.

20. Mendonça, Rubens de. Dicionário biográfico mato-grossense. Com um prefácio de Francisco de Aquino Corrêa. 2 ed. Goiás, Bra., Editora Rio Bonito, 1971. 165 p.

Revised and updated edition of work first published in 1953 designed to publicize leading social, political and literary figures of Mato-Grosso and their contributions to Brazilian history and culture. Includes biographical skeches of 19th and 20th century personages.

ACQUISITIONS, LIBRARY HOLDINGS AND CATALOGS

21. Banco Hipotecario de El Salvador, *San Salvador.* Biblioteca. Bibliografia, marzo-abril 1972. San Salvador, 1972. 23 1. (Lista, 30)

Brief index of works catalogued by the Bank's library. Besides titles on economics, labor, accounting, there are also works on geography, history, psychology, literature, and a special section devoted to periodicals received.

22. Bibliografía sobre servicio social. V. 1/2. Montevideo, Organization of American States (OAS), Instituto Interamericano del Niño, 1967. 2 v. 1(424, 207 p.)

Lists complete holdings of the library of the Instituto Inter-Americano del Niño. Designed to promote research in social services for children, it provides readily available information for research purposes. Titles arranged by general subjects and geographical area. Author index. Useful bibliographic resource.

23. Bingham, Marie Ballew. A catalog of the Yucatán collection on microfilm in the University of Alabama libraries. With an introduction by W. Stanley Hoole. University, Ala., The Univ. of Alabama Press, 1972. 100 p., bibl.

"The collection . . . contains many unique items, especially Yucatecan and Mayan imprints, including books, brochures, pamphlets, official documents, manuscripts, and other materials in the broad fields of the social sciences and humanities." Includes "1,760 entries for unique or separate titles, 164 for periodical titles, and 322 cross-reference and holding cards, a total of 2,246, representing 30,000 items." Good reference work which would be enhanced with a subject index.

24. Boletim da Biblioteca. Univ. de São Paulo, Faculdade de Economia e Administração, Instituto de Pesquisas Econômicas. Vol. 3, No. 1, 1972-   . São Paulo.

Brief bibliography of what appears to be recent acquisitions of institute's library. Organized by Dewey classification, it includes titles on pure science, technology, arts, as well as economics.

25. Boletín Bibliográfico. Banco de México, Subgerencia de Investigación Económica, Biblioteca. Vol. 19, No. 1/6, enero/junio 1972-   . Vol. 20, No. 4/6, abril/junio 1973-   México.

Latest number of this monthly bibliography of works received and catalogued by the Banco de México library. References include works in economics and allied disciplines such as demography, statistics, and economic history. Books, pamphlets, reports, and theses are included.

26. Boletín Bibliográfico: lista de obras incorporadas, autores y materias, octubre-diciembre 1969. San Salvador, Administración de Bibliotecas y Archivos Nacionales, Biblioteca Nacional, 1971. 1v. (Unpaged)

Quarterly bibliography of books, pamphlets, and theses added to collections of El Salvador's National Library. Divided into two parts: 1) titles from El Salvador and Central America; and 2) foreign imprints augmenting international section of the collections. Within each of these major sections, titles are organized first by author and then by subject. No index. Because of paucity of material available on Central America this is an especially useful bibliography.

27. Catálogo bibliográfico de la Facultad de Humanidades y Educación, 1948-1968. t. 1, vol. 1. Caracas, Univ. Central de Venezuela, Facultad de Humanidades y Educación, Escuela de Biblioteconomía y Archivos,

1969. 498 p., facsims., (Indice de publicaciones oficiales de la Univ. de Venezuela, 1)

Useful guide to official publications of various departments and institutes within Facultad de Humanidades y Educación. First in a series of indexes to publications of all faculties of the Univ. Central de Venezuela. Includes books, pamphlets, and analytical indexes to periodical publications. Author and title indexes are appended.

Catálogo colectivo de publicaciones periódicas en desarrollo económico y social. See item 2273.

28. Catálogo de la colección cartográfica del Centro Documental. B.A.?, Instituto Nacional de Tecnología Agropecuaria (INTA), Estación Experimental Agropecuaria Pergamino, 1970. 268 p. (Bibliographic series, 52)

Argentina's National Institute for Agricultural Technology (INTA) has developed a valuable cartographic collection. To make this cartographic collection more accessible to researchers in agricultural fields and other allied disciplines is the purpose of this catalog. It contains 2,258 entries to maps and geological charts available at the Pergamino Agricultural Experiment Station. Entries arranged by Argentine provinces and foreign countries. Extremely useful cartographic bibliography.

29. Catálogo de publicaciones periódicas existencias, diciembre 1971. Caracas, Instituto Venezolano de Investigaciones Científicas, Biblioteca, 1972. 335 p.

Though scientific, contains useful journal information for social scientists; e.g., Physical Anthropology, Sociology, Geography.

30. Exposição lançamentos do ano 1969. Rio, Biblioteca Nacional, Divisão de Publicações e Divulgação, Seção de Exposições, 1970. 78 p., bibl.

Each year a book exhibit is held at Tio's Biblioteca Nacional honoring outstanding books published in previous year. This is a bibliography of 592 titles, all published during 1969 and included in the March 1970 exhibition. Also includes translations of foreigners who have written on Brazil.

31. Fundación e Instituto Miguel Lillo, Tucumán, Arg. Biblioteca. Lista de publicaciones periódicas en la biblioteca de la . . . [and] suplemento. Tucumán, Arg., 1971. 2 v. (192, 17 l.)

Approximately 100,000 titles indicating place of publication with open date entry showing earliest edition in collection. Periodicals listed alphabetically by country of publication, each grouped by continent. Styled after "List of Serial Publications in the British Museum (Natural History)." Supplement published in 1972.

Henne, Marilyn Hanson de and **Beth Witt de Studebaker** comps. Bibliografía del Instituto Lingüístico de Verano en Centro América, 1952-1972. See item 1555.

32. Kent, George O. comp. and ed. A Catalog of films and microfilms of the German Foreign Ministry archives, 1920-1945. v. 4. Stanford, Calif., Stanford Univ., Hoover Institution Press, 1972. 978 p.

Final volume completing files from major European missions and consulates with a few from the non-European ones. As evident in this volume, the Latin American files are very poor due to loss or destruction. First three volumes were not seen.

33. Library Bulletin. Inter-American Defense College. 1 April/30 June 1973- . Washington.

Unannotated list of books and periodical articles acquired by IADC Library during April-June 1973. Includes material on Europe and Asia as well as Latin America. No index.

34. Lozano, Eduardo comp. Recent acquisitions in Latin American studies; No. 6, January, 1971-December, 1971. Pittsburgh, Pa., Univ. of Pittsburgh, 1972. 530 p.

The Hillman Library of the Univ. of Pittsburgh maintains a very good collection on Latin America, especially for the Caribbean area. The unannotated acquisition list (No. 6 in the series) contains approximately 4,000 titles, but includes much restrospective material. It includes titles added to their collection during Jan.-Dec. 1971. With similar lists published by Univ. of Texas (strong Mexican collection) and Univ. of Florida (strong Caribbean collection), they represent an excellent resource for acquisition libraries.

35. Museo de América, Madrid. Catálogo de la exposición Argentina en España en el . . . Madrid, Dirección General de Bellas Artes, 1972. 263 p., plates.

Organized into seven chapters on silver works, art and home furnishing, gaucho objects, historical documents, Malaspina memorabilia, documents relating to San Martin, and miscellaneous chapter on items not included elsewhere. Each item is briefly described. Interesting.

36. Reipert, Herman José. História da Biblioteca Pública Municipal Mário de Andrade. São Paulo, Secretaria de Educação e Cultura, Depto. de Cultura, Divisão de Bibliotecas, 1972. 72 p., bibl., facsims., plates.

Municipal library of São Paulo is largest in Brazil. Since its 1926 establishment, collections have grown from 15,000 volumes to more than 850,000 volumes, and services are provided to approximately 2,000 readers daily and recently have been expanded to include 6,000 volume collection of Braille books and a small collection of "Talking Books." Traces history of library to present noting its development under various directors.

37. Seminar on the Acquisition of Latin American Library Materials, XVI, Puebla, Mex., 1971. Final report and working papers. Rapporteur general: Marta V. Tomé. Washington, Organization of American States (OAS), 1973. 2 v. (363, 360 p.) (Reuniones bibliotecológicas, 22)

Provides the summary reports, Seminar's program, resolutions, and first four of the working papers presented during the 16th annual conference which was held in Puebla, Mex. The four papers included in v. 1 are: Marietta Shepard "Progress Report on SALALM, 1971," Jane Garner "Significant Acquisitions of Latin American Materials," Decennial Cumulation 1961/62-1970/71, Gayle Watson "A Report on Bibliographic Activities, 1971," and Suzanne Hogdman "Microfilming Project Newsletter." The second volume contains the working papers.

38. Stephenson, Yvonne comp. A bibliography on the West Indian Federation. Edited by Thomas Kabdebo. Georgetown, Univ. of Guyana Library, 1972. 34 l. (Univ. of Guyana Library Series, 6)

Welcome bibliography on West Indian Federation. Extremely useful compilation limited to books, pamphlets, government documents, and periodical articles available in library of Univ. of Guyana, mostly published from late 1950's to 1968. Entries arranged alphabetically by author.

Tavares, Denis Fernandes. As bibliotecas infanto-juvenis de hoje. See item 6299.

39. Williams, R. J. Luke and **Elmer Broxson.** Manoel de Oliveira Lima: catalogue of the exhibit held in the Mullen Library of The Catholic University of America to commemorate the centenary of his birth, November 13 to December 15, 1967. 15 p., facsim.

Catalog of a book exhibit to commemorate centenary of the birth of Oliveira Lima, noted Brazilian diplomat, and later professor of international law at Catholic Univ.

39a. Tulane University of Louisiana, New Orleans, La. Catalog of the Latin American Library of the . . . First supplement. Introduction [by] Marjorie LeDoux. v. 1, A-I; v. 2, J-Z. Boston, Mass., G. K. Hall, 1973, 2 v. (817, 801 p.), bibl.

Updates original *Catalog* prepared in 1969 (see *HLAS* 33:117) including bulk of Brazilian materials acquired with Ford Foundation grant as well as Mexican codices and early manuscript and ethnographic materials on Middle America. Welcome and valuable reference work.

Wise, Mary Ruth comp. Bibliografía del Instituto Lingüístico de Verano en el Perú, Junio 1946-Junio 1971. See item 1646.

LIBRARY SCIENCE AND SERVICES

40. *Boletín Bibliográfico de COSEBI.* Corporación de Servicios Bibliotecarios. Año 1, No. 4, julio 1973- . Rio Piedras, P.R.

COSEBI was recently created to provide professional library services to institutions with library collections in Spanish. It acts as a central cataloging service for participating libraries which can subscribe to cataloging information on new books and periodicals, available in card form or bibliographical lists. Major cataloging and bibliographical information service for Caribbean libraries. Number one of *Títulos para los cuales se pueden suplir juegos de tarjetas* was published in April 1973. COSEBI president is Paulita M. de la Torre.

41. *Boletín de la Sociedad de Bibliotecarios de Puerto Rico.* enero/junio 1972- . San Juan, P.R.

Includes 18 short articles on various aspects of librarianship and bibliography among which are: Rosa Monclova "Reseña de los Actos de la Décima Convención Anual de la Sociedad de Bibliotecarios de Puerto Rico," Paulita M. de la Torre "Las Bibliotecas Especializadas en Puerto Rico," Robert S. Burgess "What is Information Retrieval?," and Arturo Morales Carrión "Reflexionés sobre la Biblioteca en Puerto Rico."

42. Collings, Dorothy. Library education in the English-speaking Caribbean (UNESCO/BL, 27:1, Jan./Feb. 1973, p. 12-17)

Director of School of Librarianship, Univ. of the West Indies (Kingston, Jam.) examines region's need for libraries and trained librarians and discusses future problems and prospects. Caribbean is viewed as a "microcosm of the world," reflecting in many ways experiences and responses to change of other developing nations. Thus, library developments in this region are important.

43. *Documentación Bibliotecológica.* Univ. Nacional del Sur, Centro de Documentación Bibliotecológica. No. 2, 1971- . Bahía Blanca, Arg.

Centro's information journal. Contains annotated library science bibliography for years 1968-69 followed by author index. Good reference source.

44. Fonseca, Edson Nery da. Precursores da bibliografía brasileira (RIB, 20:3, julio/sept. 1970, p. 265-279)

Professor of library science at the Univ. of Brasília and leading figure in Brazilian library field, traces development of Brazilian bibliography through some of its leading proponents—Ramiz Galvão, Vale Cabral, Sacramento Blake, Alfredo de Carvalho, Simões dos Reis, and Borba de Moraes. Important and informative article.

45. Guía de escuelas y cursos de bibliotecología y documentación en América Latina; pt. 1, Argentina. B.A., Univ. de Buenos Aires, Instituto Bibliotecológico, 1972. 33 l.

Library Science Institute of Univ. of Buenos Aires is gathering information on schools of library science and documentation centers in Latin America. In 1970-71, questionnaires were sent to some 140 institutions asking for information on courses offered on library and information science. Seventy replies were received. This is the first of a series of reports on Latin America. Provides much basic information such as date of library school's establishment, degrees offered, requisites for admission, number of faculty, and curricula. Helpful for evaluating the future needs of library schools and information centers in Argentina.

45a. Juarroz, Roberto. El curso audiovisual de bibliotecología para América Latina; UNESCO, 1969. San Miguel de Tucumán, Arg. Univ. Nacional de Tucumán, Biblioteca Central, 1971. 75 p. (Ciencia de la documentación. Serie 2: La Biblioteca, 9)

Description and evaluation of UNESCO backed projects complete with basic recommendations.

BIBLIOGRAPHY AND GENERAL WORKS

46. Organization of American States. Secretaría General. Planeamiento Nacional de Servicios Bibliotecarios. v. 2, Por países; pt. 4, Colombia. Washington, 1972. 55 p. (Estudios bibliotecarios, 8)

Report of committee of experts—including Paxton Price, Director of St. Louis Public Library, María Teresa Sanz, Director of Libraries, Univ. Católica, Santiago, and William Jackson, Professor of Library Science at Vanderbilt Univ.—on a National Plan for Library Services for Colombia. Provides summary of current facilities, problems areas for library development and specific recommendations for library service development.

47. Seminario de Introducción al Procesamiento de Datos Aplicados a la Bibliotecología y la Documentación, *Buenos Aires, 1971.* Informe. B.A., Univ. de Buenos Aires, Instituto Bibliotecológico, 1972. 101 l.

Report and recommendations of II Seminario held 26 July-6 Aug. 1971 at Instituto Bibliotecológico of Univ. of Buenos Aires, under direction of Dr. Hans Gravenhorst. Divided into five working groups, the Seminar discussed computer technology and its applicability to libraries; user studies; a thesaurus of basic subjects headings; production of catalogs by computer; and user services. Presents summaries and recommendations of each working group.

48. Seminario Interamericano sobre la Integración de los Servicios de Información de Archivos, Bibliotecas y Centros de Documentación en América Latina y el Caribe (SI/ABCD), *Washington, 1972.* Informe final. Compilado por Carlos Víctor Penna en consulta con Eleanor Mitchell y Marietta Daniels Shepard. Washington, 1973. 143 p.

Fiscal report of Seminar which brought together representatives of libraries, documentation center, archives from Latin America and the US to discuss ways and methods of developing integrated information services for Latin America. Three working papers presented during a Seminar are included in this report. Important summary of current programs and improvement plans.

49. Shepard, Marietta Daniels. La infraestructura bibliotecológica de los sistemas nacionales de información, v. 1 (*in* Planeamiento nacional de servicios bibliotecarios. Washington, Organization of American States, Secretaría General, 1972. 136 p. [Estudios bibliotecarios, 8])

Prepared as reference document for Conferencia Especializada sobre la Aplicación de la Ciencia y la Tecnología en el Desarrollo de América Latina (CAETAL), held in Brasília 12-19 May 1972. Report ably reviews problems and stresses need for development of libraries and documentation centers to serve area's economic, scientific and technological development. Should be read in conjunction with item 48.

NATIONAL BIBLIOGRAPHY

50. García, Miguel Angel. Bibliografía hondureña: 1620-1930. v. 1. Tegucigalpa, Banco Central de Honduras, 1971. 203 p.

Monumental work which promises to fulfill the long-awaited hope for a Honduran national bibliography. Draws together the library holdings of such individuals as Jorge Fidel Durón and Rafael Heliodoro Valle as well as such institutions as the Biblioteca Nacional, and Univ. Nacional Autónoma de Honduras. Also provides some biographical information on early authors. Publication suffers to some extent from its division into "private" and governmental sections as well as the arrangement of entries by year of publication rather than alphabetically by author. [T. L. Martinson]

Matos Mar, José and **Rogger Ravines.** Bibliografía peruana de ciencias sociales: 1957-1969. See item 7694.

Minkel, Clarence W. and **Ralph H. Alderman.** A bibliography of British Honduras: 1900-1970. See item 6677.

51. Romero Rojas, Francisco José *comp.* Anuario bibliográfico colombiano Rubén Pérez Ortiz, 1970. Bogotá, Instituto Caro y Cuervo, Depto. de Bibliografía, 1972. 288 p., bibl.

Instituto Caro y Cuervo has published national bibliography since 1951 when it was compiled under direction of Rubén Pérez Ortiz. Organized by major disciplines (social sciences, humanities, and pure and applied sciences), it is limited to imprints of 1970, but richly enhanced by separate sections devoted to Colombian publishers and bookdealers, new periodical titles, list of titles about Colombia translated into Spanish, and list of publications of Instituto Caro y Cuervo. Excellent typography. Author index.

52. Verez Peraza, Elena. Bibliografía colombiana, 1969. t. 14. Coral Gables, Fla., Univ. of Miami, 1971. 144 l., bibl., (Biblioteca del bibliotecario, 84)

Before his death in 1969, Fermín Peraza Sarausa, former director of Biblioteca Municipal de La Habana, compiled the *Bibliografía colombiana* from 1961 to 1968. Mrs. Peraza continues her husband's work on this and other bibliographies including *Revolutionary Cuba: a bibliographical guide.* Of the 1972 titles, the majority of imprints are for the years 1967-69. Arranged alphabetically by author. Combined author-subject index, and list of works published by Fermín Peraza.

52a. Vivó, Paquita *ed.* The Puerto Ricans; an annotated bibliography. N.Y., Bowker, 1973. 299 p.

This comprehensive bibliography was sponsored by the Puerto Rican Research and Resources Center. Includes over 2,600 annotated entries in the humanities and social sciences. Divided into four sections: books, pamphlets, and dissertations; government publications; periodical literature; and audiovisual materials. Useful and up-to-date compilation for librarians, scholars, and researchers studying Puerto Rico. [G. M. Dorn]

REFERENCE WORKS AND RESEARCH

53. *Informaciones.* Univ. Nacional de La Plata, Biblioteca. Año 5, No. 42/43, agosto/sept. 1972- . La Plata, Arg.

Latest in series providing news notes on bibliographical and documentation services of the National Univ. of

La Plata, including titles of important publications published by University and list of works recently received by library.

54. Latin America: economic history and conditions; an annotated bibliography. pt. 1; pt. 2, Monographs. Glendale, Ariz. Thunderbird Graduate School of International Management, Center for Latin American and Iberian Research (CLAIR), 1973. 54 p.

Short but extremely useful annotated bibliography on Latin American economic history. Contains sections on "general reference works," "books," and "periodicals." Bibliography is first in series planned by Thunderbird Graduate School of International Management and represents principally titles in English available in its library. Very useful as a reference or acquisition source for libraries wishing to acquire or update a collection on Latin American economic history. Periodicals are listed only by title and show Thunderbird library holdings.

55. Menezes, Raimundo de. As primeiras e mais antigas livrarias de São Paulo (AM/R, 33:182, 1971, p. 193-218, illus.)

Interesting and informative article on development of book trade in São Paulo from early 19th century. During early history of Brazil, bookdealers performed as a sort of intellectual barometer gauging current intellectual trends in one of Brazil's main cultural centers.

56. *Mensário do Arquivo Nacional.* Año 3, No. 9/10, sept./oct., 1972-   . Rio.

Informative monthly bulletin of National Archives programs and activities on research, publications, visiting dignitaries and announcement of special course on historical research offered to candidates for degrees as teachers of history.

Princeton University, *Princeton, N.J.* Office of Population Research. Population index bibliography: cumulated 1935-1968 by authors and geographical area, geographical index. v. 1, 1935-1954, North America, South America. See item 6585.

56a. Staff research in progress or recently completed in the humanities and the social sciences. London, Univ. of London, Institute of Latin American Studies, 1973. 24 p., (Latin American studies in the universities of the United Kingdom, 5)

Useful guide to research in progress by professors of Latin American studies at British universities. Brings up to date early report, see *HLAS 33:79.*

57. Theses in Latin American studies at British universities in progress and completed: no. 7, 1972-1973. London, Univ. of London, Institute of Latin American Studies, 1972. 1 v. (Unpaged)

Theses include M.A. and Ph.D., arranged by university granting degree. There were 284 degrees granted and in progress during academic year 1972-73, majority of which were at Ph.D. level. Citations contain author, title of thesis and date of completion. Indicative of the increasing interest in Latin American studies at British universities.

58. United Nations. Educational, Scientific and Cultural Organization (UNESCO). Oficina Regional de Educación de la . . . para América Latina y el Caribe. Servicio de Biblioteca y Documentación. Repertorio de publicaciones periódicas de educación de América Latina y el Caribe. Santiago, 1972. 103 p.

Designed to foster an interchange of information among institution and education specialists in Latin America. Besides full title of periodical, each entry includes addresses, periodicity, and date established.

59. Zubatsky, David S. *comp.* Doctoral dissertations in history and the social sciences on Latin America and the Caribbean accepted by universities in the United Kingdom, 1920-1972. London, Univ. of London, Institute of Latin American Studies, 1972. 16 p., bibl.

"Since 1966 the Institute of Latin American Studies has published an annual list of theses in Latin American studies in progress in the universities of the United Kingdom. But no convenient guide exists to dissertations produced before that date." This index fills that gap for history and the social sciences produced from 1920 to 1972.

SUBJECT

Aliaga de Vizcarra, Irma *comp.* Bibliografía agrícola boliviana. See item 6841.

Baesa García, José *comp.* Tenencia de la tierra y reforma agraria: bibliografía. See item 6856.

Berberián, Eduardo E.; Alberto J. Marcellino; and Silva E. Ruete *comps.* Bibliografía antropológica de la provincia de Córdoba, R.A.: años 1874/1969. See item 768.

Bolivia: agricultura, economía y política; a bibliography. Madison, Wis., Univ. of Wisconsin, Land Tenure Center, 1972. 10 p. (Training & methods series, 7) See item 2167.

60. *Bibliografía Brasileira de Educação.* Instituto Nacional de Estudos Pedagógicos, Centro Brasileiro de Pesquisas Educacionais, Serviço de Bibliografia. Vol. 19, Nos. 1/4, jan./dez, 1971-   . Rio.

Valuable guide to current Brazilian books and articles on education. Published since 1953, a hardy reference resource for student and researcher, and a useful acquisition tool for librarians.

61. Bibliografía literaria de la revista *Hoy:* 1931-1943. Prólogo [de] Armando González Rodrígues. Santiago, Dirección de Bibliotecas, Archivos y Museos, Biblioteca Nacional, 1970. 560 p., bibl.

Divided into five sections and author index: General; Creative Writing; Literary Reviews; Non Literary Reviews, e.g. General Works, Social Sciences, etc.; and Non Literary Writing. Excellent reference.

62. *Bibliografía   Venezolana.*   Biblioteca

Nacional, Centro Bibliográfico Venezolano. Año 2, Nos. 5/6, enero/junio, 1971- Caracas.

Prepared with the assistance of the Venezuelan National Council for Technical and Scientific Research (CONICIT). Contains copy of Venezuelan Legal Deposit Law which now has stronger penalty provisions for non deposit–a fine of 50 bolívares for works costing under 20Bs, and triple the cost of the book if it sells for more than 20 Bs. Bibliography includes Venezuelan books and pamphlets, and those about Venezuela: new periodical titles; list of publishers who complied with the Legal Deposit Law; cultural news notes from Biblioteca Nacional; and photoduplication services.

63. Birou, Alain. Bibliografía reciente (1965-69) sobre problemas agrarios en América Latina. n.p., Instituto de Estudios Políticos para América Latina (IEPAL), 1969. 56 l.

Agrarian problems in Latin America continue to receive significant attention by economists, anthropologists, and political scientists. This unannotated bibliography of works published 1965-69 and concerning agrarian and related socioeconomic problems brings together under one cover important resources otherwise difficult to locate.

64. Boletim Bibliográfico. Ministério do Planejamento e Coordenação Geral [and] Fundação IBGE, Instituto Brasileiro de Estatística, Centro de Documentação e Informação Estatística (CENDIE) Vol. 4, No. 1, Jan/Mar 1971- . Rio.

Latest in series containing 914 annotated references to periodical articles and books concerning statistics and socio-economic theses. Printed on perforated 3 x 5 card size entries which are designed to serve as cataloging cards for libraries or documentation centers. Contains combined author and subject index.

Boletín para Bibliotecas Agrícolas. See item 6512.

GENERAL WORKS

65. Arbeitsgemeinschaft Deutsche Latinamerikaforschung. Informationsdienst. Jahrgang 7, Heft 2, Aug. 1972- . Hamburg, FRG.

The Library of Congress has recently subscribed to this useful periodical published quarterly, which informs Latin Americanists on forthcoming international conferences, symposia, and meetings, research projects in progress, as well as listing new publications which have appeared in West and East Germany. This valuable guide is somewhat similar to the *Latin American Research Review* published by LASA. Highly recommended to researchers and librarians specializing in acquisitions of German-language materials. [G. M. Dorn]

66. Armas Alfonzo, Alfredo. Sobre tí, Venezuela. n.p., Ernesto Armitano, 1972. 232 p., facsims., illus., plates.

General work on Venezuela using illustrations to depict the life, people, art, religion, etc. Well done and interesting.

67. Autoridades Brasileiras. Agencia Nacional, Servico de Documentação. No.9, Nov. 1972- . n.p.

List of principal Brazilian government officials in executive, legislative, judicial branches of government; also those in state. governments and private organizations which are national in scope.

68. Azevedo, Fernando de. A cultura brasileira. 5 ed. revista e ampliada. São Paulo, Edições Melhoramentos [and] Editôra da Univ. de São Paulo [USP], 1971. 80 p., bibl., plates, (Obras completas, 13)

In depth cultural history of Brazil, first published in 1943 by an eminent Brazilian social historian. It knots together the diverse ethnic and cultural background and traces these influences in the arts, letters, and sciences. Important work for understanding cultural features, such as ethnic composition, Portuguese tradition and language, and religion, and their impact on Brazilian cultural institutions. An important work.

69. Beckman, Jan D. Dokumentation der spanischen Lateinamerika-Forschung. Hamburg, FRG, Dokumentationsleitstelle der ADLAF, 1971. 311 p. (Schriften der Arbeitsgemeinschaft Deutsche Lateinamerika-Forschung, 3)

Thorough survey of Latin American research carried out in Spain. Study was sponsored by Volkswagen Foundation and Instituto de Sociología y Desarrollo del Area Ibérica. It lists institutes and universities prominent for their interest in Latin America, as well as archives, libraries, and museums with substantial holdings in the field. There is a bio-bibliographical section of Spanish specialists in Latin American studies; a list of Spanish periodicals devoted to Latin America; and a complete list of Spanish publishers specializing in Latin American authors and subjects. Very important contribution, which should be updated every six or seven years. [G. M. Dorn]

70. Bizzarro, Salvatore. Historical dictionary of Chile. Metuchen, N.J., The Scarecrow Press, 1972. 309 p., bibl., maps (Latin American historical dictionaries, 7)

Compilation of biographical, cultural, geographical, governmental, historical, organizational, and political data. Concise, informative and useful reference.

71. Blakemore, Harold. Latin American studies in British universities: progress and prospects. London, The Hispanic and Luso-Brasilian Councils, 1971. 26 p.

Reprint with a few amendments of *HLAS 34:98*.

72. Blomberg, Rolf. Latitud 0°: glimtar fran Ecuador. Stockholm, Almqvist & Wiksell, 1960. 162 p., plates.

Essays by Swedish journalist on various visits to Ecuador, especially to different Indian tribes. The style is breezy, the approach journalistic but the photographs are excellent. [R. V. Shaw]

73. Boletín Bibliográfico de la Secretaría de Hacienda y Crédito Público. Año 18, No. 469, enero 1972- . México.

Despite its title, this is not bibliography of works on Mexico but rather contains informative articles on various themes of Mexican history and culture. Includes: Roberto Villaseñor E. "Los Chilam Balam: Libros Sagrados del Pueblo Maya," Javier Paz Avalos "Vida Indígena: Ayer, Hoy y Mañana," and Ignacio González Polo "Apuntes y Reflexiones Anónimas sobre la Ciudad de México en 1788," and other articles on literature and religion.

74. *Boletín para Bibliotecas Agrícolas.* Organization of American States, Instituto Interamericano de Ciencias Agrícolas. Vol. 9, Nos. 3/4, julio/dic. 1972- Turrialba, C. R.

The Inter-American Institute of Agricultural Sciences (Turrialba, C. R.) maintains a school and agricultural experiment station to train students from all over Latin America. The *Boletín* published by the Inter-American Center for Documentation and Information, provides articles, bibliographical information, book reviews, and general news notes, all designed to foster communications among agricultural specialists and special agricultural libraries. It serves its purpose very well.

75. Bollinger, Armin. Spielball der Mächtigen; Geschichte Lateinamerikas. Stuttgart, FRG, Verlag W. Kohlhammer, 1972. 291 p.

Traces history of Latin America from the Conquest to present giving a succinct overview of social, economic, and cultural developments, as well as the constantly changing political kaleidoscope of the hemisphere. One third is devoted to modern period from Independence to present. Valuable and concise introductory work for German-speaking Latin Americanists or generalists. [G. M. Dorn]

76. Brand, Donald D. and others. The social scientists look at Latin America: six position papers. Austin, Tex., Univ. of Texas, 1967. 174 p., bibl. (Latin American curriculum project. Bulletin, 3)

A collection of six papers prepared by professors of Latin American studies at the Univ. of Texas covering these disciplines: geography (Donald Brand); history (Warren Dean), economics (Calvin Blair); anthropology (Richard N. Adams); sociology (Hurley Browning); and government (Karl Schmitt). Developed as part of Univ. of Texas Latin American Curriculum Project, the papers were written for the "high school graduate or a reasonably literate adult" to promote a basic understanding of Latin American history and culture. Excellent, well organized summary presentations with much information on all disciplines that would benefit the specialist. The beginning student of Latin American studies might also wish to consult Charles Wagley, *ed.*, *Social science research on Latin America* (N.Y., Columbia Univ. Press, 1964) for historiographical articles on the social sciences.

77. Brazil. Ministério das Relações Exteriores. Departmento de Administração. Grupo de Trabalho para a Elaboração do Livro "Brazil." Brasil: Situação, recursos, possibilidades. Préfacio [de] Mário Gibson Barboza. Apresentação [de] F. Gualberto-de-Oliveira. Rio, 1970. 1261 p., maps, tables, illus., etc.

Encyclopedic volume on Brazil. Much statistical information, but also details on tourist spots, military medals, and a great deal more. [P. B. Taylor, Jr.]

78. Bromely, R. J. Sierra of Puebla: by-passed zone of Mexico (GM, 42:10, July 1970, p. 752-761)

Journalistic introduction to the region and problems of the Sierra de Puebla: useful but elementary. [P. H. Hernández]

79. Calvo, Bernardino S. Archivos Municipales: estado actual y perspectivas. Villa María, Arg., Escuela Normal Víctor Mercante, Instituto de Investigaciones Históricas Ramón J. Cárcano, Centro de Documentación e Información Educativas, 1970. 27 p., plates (Cuaderno, 1. Serie: testimonios del pasado)

History of the development of the municipal archive of the city of Villa María, Córdoba prov. Of interest as example for other small municipalities confronted with need to preserve documents.

80. Carvalho, J. and **Vicente Peixoto.** Lisa Pequeno dicionário da língua portuguesa. Supervisão de Alpheu Tersariol. v. 1, A-D; v. 2, E-O; v. 3, P-Z. São Paulo, Lisa–Livros Irradiantes, 1972. 3 v. (1066 p.), facsims., illus., maps, plates, tables.

Attempt to produce low cost, useful and practical dictionary for professors and students of all levels. Includes what is considered basic and essential. Excludes all terms considered useless and archaic, obvious in meaning or to be common use derivatives.

81. Cohen, Martin A. *ed.* The Jewish experience in Latin America: selected studies from the publications of the American Jewish Historical Society. Edited with an introduction by . . . v. 1/w. N.Y., Ktav Publishing House *for the* American Jewish Historical Society, Waltham, Mass., 1971. 2 v. (497, 374 p.)

Two volume selective compilation of studies on Latin American Jewry. Introduction is an overview history concentrating on earliest publications. Short bibliography, divided into Colonial and National periods, supplements articles. Work is a pioneer effort to attract scholars to this untapped field and not intended to be definitive. Cites need for one volume history on subject.

82. Congrès International de l'Université Laval sur les Problèmes Economiques, Sociaux, Culturels, Religieux et Politiques de l'Amérique Latine, *Québec, Canada, 1968.* L'avenir d'un continent, où va l'Amerique latine?: texte integral des conférences et débats. Prologue de Paul Bouchard. Québec, Canada, La Commission Canadienne pour l'UNESCO, Le Ministère des Affaires Culturelles de l'Etat du Quebec, le Conseil Canadien de Recherche en Sciences Sociales, l'Univ. de Sherbrooke [et] l'Univ. de Moncton, 1970. 549 p., tables.

Topics listed below consisted of a paper followed by a critique and a round-table debate which included an average of six participants among whom were: Luis Alberto Sánchez, Miguel Angel Asturias, Germán Arciniegas, François Bourricaud, Paul Verdevoye, César Delgado Barreto, Mariano Zamorano, Alfonso Maldonado Moreleón, Porfirio Muñoz Lego, Olga Pellicer de Brody, Edelberto Torres Rivas, Eugenio Díaz Corvalán, Alejandro del Corro, Gérard Cambron, Georges R. Coulthard, Pierre Monbeig, Frédéric Mauro, and many others.

Paul-Yves Denis and others "L'Avenir de l'Amérique Latine, Ses Richesses: Critique d'une Economie en Retard" p. 57-88

Richard Patee "La Culture de l'Amérique Latine" p. 89-122

Víctor Alfonso Maldonado Moreleón and others "Marchés Communs et Industrialisation en Amerique Latine" p. 123-162

Pierre Monbeig and others "L'Homme de l'Amérique Latine: Critique d'une Société Retardaire" p. 163-202

Víctor Alfonso Maldonado Moreleón and others "L'Amérique Latine: Peut-Elle s'Intégrer?" p. 203-230

Miguel Angel Asturias and others "Vers une Synthèse Culturelle" p. 231-260

César Delgado Barreto and others "Les Mutations d'un Continent en Transition: la Société Rurale et la Société Urbaine" p. 261-302

George R. Coulthard and others "La Vie Spirituelle de l'Amérique Latine" p. 303-330

Yvan Labelle and others "L'Ere des Révolutions: Vers l'Example Mexicain ou Cubain? Vers la Technocracie Capitaliste ou Socialiste"? p. 331-374

Gérard Cambron and others "L'Eglise Post-Conciliaire en Amérique Latine" p. 375-398

Raymond Alexis Comnéne and others "Pour Sortir du Marasme, Que Faire:? p. 399-431

Louis Bérubé and others "Les Rélations Inter-Américaines. l'Amérique Latine et l'Occident" p. 432-492

Paul Bouchard and others "Conclusions de Congrés: Ou Va l'Amerique Latine" p. 493-518

83. **Council on International Educational Exchange,** N.Y. Latin America: study, travel and work opportunities. N.Y., 1971. 29 p., bibl.

Bulk devoted to study and opportunities available—arranged by country showing the sponsoring institution in US. Includes useful basic information on travel and assistance.

Covo, Milena E. Las instituciones de investigación social en la ciudad de México. See item 1917.

84. **Cunha, Raymundo Cyriaco Alves da.** Paraenses ilustres. 3 ed. Belém, Bra., Conselho Estadual de Cultura, 1970. 172 p. facsims., illus. (Col. História do Pará. Série Barão de Guajará)

Revised edition of biographies of important historical and political figures of the 18th and 19th centuries from Paraná state, one of fastest developing states in Brazil. Includes photos of each figure. Important for 18th and 19th century history of Paraná.

85. **Dávila, Mauro.** Arqueo hemerográfico de la ciudad de Mérida: siglo XIX. Mérida, Ven., Centro de Investigaciones Literarias, 1972. 214 p., bibl.

Historical newspapers published in Mérida, Ven., during 19th century. Each entry contains full title, subject focus, founder, editor, date of first issue, periodicity, format, price, and name and address of printer. Pt. 2, lists same newspapers, titles organized chronologically by year of establishment. Pt. 3 lists alphabetically names of the founders, directors, editors, administrators, and writers of all the newspapers. Excellent source for researchers interested in 19th century Venezuelan history. List of printers also appended. For additional information on Latin American newspapers, readers should consult *Latin American newspapers in United States Libraries: a union list,* published by the Univ. of Texas Press, 1968 (see *HLAS 33:47*).

86. Diccionario Porrúa de historia, biografía y geografía de México. t. 1, A-Ll; t. 2, M-Z. 3 ed., corregida y aumentada. México, Editorial Porrúa, 1970-1971. 2 v. (2465 p.) (Continuous pagination) fold. maps.

This edition utilizes 1960 census data, and all measurements are converted to metric system. Place entries include all *municipios* and their *cabeceras* as well as places of historical or geographical interest. There are many entries on territorial divisions and their histories. Contains appendix. [C. R. Edwards]

87. Directorio jurídico biográfico mexicano: 1972. México, Sociedad Mexicana de Información, Biografía Profesional, 1972. 160 p. (Año, 1)

Divided into three parts: alphabetical listing, biographic sketches and location according to states. Useful as potential source of public figures.

88. A experiência do Paraná. Rio, Editôra Laudes, 1971? 280 p., tables.

Encyclopedic description of Paraná state about 1970. Publication emphasizes achievements of state government. [P. B. Taylor, Jr.]

89. **Fernandes, Neusa** and **Sonia Gomes Pereira.** Museus do Rio. Rio, Livraria Francisco Alves Editôra, 1973. 123 p., plates.

Describes 11 Rio museums, their history, holdings and facilities. Useful reference.

90. **Ferreira, Luis Pinto.** Curso de organização social e política brasileira. Rio, José Konfino Editor, 1972. 203 p.

'Textbook' on social and political organization in Brazil. Includes both a survey of more classical discussions and brief materials on contemporary conditions. [J. F. B. Dasilva]

91. **Foster, Dereck H. N.** The Argentines; how they live and work. N.Y. Praeger Publishers, 1972. 150 p., plates.

Not too profound "all about Argentina" directed to the neophyte. Well written and informative.

92. **Franz, Carl.** The people's guide to Mexico. Santa Fe, N.M., John Muir Publications, 1972. 380 p., illus.

Many good points and suggestions on camping, living and eating in Mexico, Guatemala and Belize. Written in a humorous tone that exudes a patronizing contempt for people and things south of the border reminiscent of the highhandedness of a bygone era. Nevertheless, informative and worthwhile.

93. Halkjaer, Eivor. Cuba: beskrivning av ett u-land. Stockholm, Utbildningsförlaget, 1972 130 p., bibl., maps, plates, tables.

Organized like a handbook with short entries, publication covers every aspect of Cuban life from geography, climate and history to the Communist Revolution and the significant changes occurring since then. Author's point of view is neutral and factual. Includes black-and-white photographs. [R. V. Shaw]

Handler, Jerome S. A guide to source materials for the study of Barbados history, 1627-1834. See item 1158.

94. Higuera B., Tarcisio. La imprenta en Colombia, 1737-1970. n.p., Instituto Nacional de Provisiones (INALPRO), 1970. 495 p., facsims., plates.

Besides a history of printing in Colombia, contains chapter on history of leading publications, evolution of technology, printing in America, and its cultural impact. Well illustrated.

95. Holbrook, Sabra. The American West Indies: Puerto Rico and the Virgin Islands. N.Y., Meredith Press, 1969. 273 p., facsims., illus., maps, plates.

Attempt to dispel old notions still prevailing about these territories by tracing earliest history down to present. Current history is interpreted through the eyes of a family in each territory, each of which is a representative composite. Ends with a not unoptimistic look at 1979. A labor of love without footnotes or bibliography.

96. Howell, Thomas A.; Christopher Hunt; and Angelo La Calandra eds. Latin America: 1972. N.Y., Facts on File, 1973. 278 p.

"A comprehensive survey of news developments ... during the year. Most of the material ... was originally published in *Facts on File Weekly . News Digest.*" Arranged by country alphabetically with a regional chapter and other countries chapter which include the so-called smaller countries and dependencies. Handy, worthwhile and informative.

97. Indice general de la *Revista Conservadora del Pensamiento Centroamericano* por materias y autores: números 1 al 100 (RCPC, 20: 100, enero 1969, p. 1-32)

Index of first 100 issues arranged by subject listing authors alphabetically. Also includes list of advertisers.

98. *Informativo LASPAU.* Latin American Scholarship Program of American Universities. Otoño 1972- . Cambridge, Mass.

This is the organ of the Latin American Scholarship Program of American Universities (LASPAU). Purpose and objectives of the journal are now being reviewed by Editor, Donna Laurence, and comments and suggestions from the readership are being solicited. Current issue is devoted to summary of annual meeting of LASPAU, 25-27 Oct. 1972, and a general news and notes section.

100. Kennedy, Paul P. The middle beat: a correspondent's view of Mexico, Guatemala and El Salvador. Edited by Stanley R. Ross. Series note [by] Lambros Comitas. N.Y., Columbia Univ., Teachers College Press, 1971. 235 p., maps, plates (Center for Education in Latin America, Institute of International Studies, 4)

Account of key events between 1954-64. Political and socio-economic trends are brought into focus by brief background histories with the insight of a keen observer. Useful raw data and introduction to countries covered.

101. Kobysh, Vitalii Iavanovich. Braziliia bez karnivala: vpechatleniia zhurnalista [Brazil without carnivals: impressions of a journalist]. Moskva, Polititizdat, 1968. 205 p., plates.

Soviet description of extremes of wealth and poverty in Brazil and of its reactionary and progressive forces, stressing US influence. [A. R. Navon]

102. Lacerda, Carlos *ed.* and **Evanildo Bechara** *comp.* Enciclopêdia século XX. Rio, Libraria J. Olympio Editôra, 1972. 13 v. (v. 1-8, 2391, v. 9-13, 1632 p.)

Divided into two parts: 1) Encyclopedia of eight volumes attempts to condense and summarize basic information considered important to contemporary Brazil: profusely illustrated and oriented toward information on Brazil. International parts based on *Hutchinson's New 20th Century Encyclopedia;* 2) Five volume dictionary which attempts to reflect modern day Brazilian contributions to the Portuguese language in addition to traditional vocabulary conforming to the Luso-Brazilian Accord. Excellent reference work.

103. Latin American studies in the universities of the United Kingdom: 1972-1973; no. 7. London, Univ. of London, Institute of Latin American Studies, 1973. 31 p.

Another in series of short reports on Latin American studies in the universities of the United Kingdom. This lists course offerings and professors of Latin American studies at more than 30 British universities. Useful reference resource.

104. *Latinskaia Amerika.* Nauchnyii obshchest-venno-politicheskii zhurnal: Academiia Nauk SSSR, Institut Latinskoi Ameriki No. 1, 1969- . Moskva.

Latinskaia Amerika is the leading journal devoted to Latin American affairs in the USSR. Founded in 1969 it is published by-monthly by the Institute for Latin America of the Soviet Academy of Sciences. It is broad in scope covering matters of popular as well as scholarly interests: erudite articles on politics, sociology, economics and history; discussion and debates; news of conferences and seminars; book reviews, which include Latin American and US as well as Soviet works; arts and literature; reviews of foreign journals; travelogues; information concerning Latin American communist parties and recent developments in USSR contact with Latin America. [T. S. Cheston]

105. Levy, Owen Lancelott, *ed.* Personalities in the Caribbean: the international guide to who's who in the West Indies, Bahamas, Bermuda. 4. ed. Kingston, Personalities Limited, 1971. 910 p., plates.

Informative compendium of concise biographical sketches of government, business, academic and civic leaders. "A permanent historical record of the men and women of today who have contributed to progress."

106. Lewis, Gordon K. The Virgin Islands: a Caribbean lilliput. Evanston, Ill., Northwestern Univ. Press, 1972. 382 p.

Two part book dealing with the past and present. Pt. 1 covers Danish background, US takeover in 1917, the New Deal and World War II. Pt. 2 deals with the people, economy, politics, culture and religion. Good, sympathetic introduction to the islands. See *HLAS 30:141*.

107. Lisa Enciclopédia Universal. v. 1/3. São Paulo, Lisa—Livros Irradiantes, 1970. 3 v. (1260 p.), facsims., illus., maps, plates, tables.

An adaptation of *Herders Volks-Lexicon* to conform to Brazilian needs and interests. Dictionary portion is selective and readers are referred to standard ones.

108. Lorscheiter, Vendelino. A América Latina na imprênsa do Japão. Tokyo, Sophia Univ. Instituto Iber-Americano, 1968. 13 p., (Estudios Ibero-americanos. Serie A. 4)

Analysis of Latin American coverage in six major Japanese newspapers. Study divided into: pt. 1, Latin American and Japan. Greatest coverage is in economics and sociology, two subjects which are more thoroughly discussed. Countries most written about are Brazil, Mexico, Cuba, Argentina and Panama. Pt. 2 deals exclusively with Brazil, showing topics by subject and discussion of emigration. Interesting.

109. Loy, Jane M. Latin America: sights and sounds; a guide to motion pictures and music for college courses. Amherst, Mass., Univ. of Massachusetts, Consortium of Latin American Studies Programs [CLASP] (Publication No. 5)

Excellent guide divided into nine functional chapters including; How to use Guide; Subject Heading Index, etc. Bulk, 190 p., lists educational and feature films recommended as well as those not recommended. Each is identified: by producer, distributors and cost, length and color. Each is described, appraised and type of audience indicated. Each film has list of suggested readings and overall evaluation—excellent, good or average. Valuable bibliography on film related materials. Excellent and welcome reference and guide.

110. Lynch, Louis. The Barbados book. Preface by Peter G. Morgan. New ed. rev. by E. L. Cozier. N.Y., Coward, McCann & Geoghegan, 1973. 262 p., maps, plates.

General history of culture, economy, geography and education of the island. Discusses for the tourist island's highlights and its character. Interesting chapter on language and folklore. Useful guide.

111. Macapagal, Diosdado. An Asian looks at South America. Manila, Mac Publishing House, 1966. 196 p., map, plates.

Travel notes and reflections by the fifth president of the Philippines made during a trip through 10 South American countries in 1966. [R. C. Eidt]

112. McDowell, Jack *ed.* Mexico. Menlo Park, Calif., Lane Magazine & Book Co., 1973. 255 p., bibl., illus., plates (A Sunset pictorial)

Pictorial story of Mexico. Plates illustrate well the many facets of the culture, including early history. Avoids old, hackneyed stereotypes.

113. Martínez, Rufino. Diccionario biográfico-histórico dominicano, 1821-1930. Santo Domingo, Editora de la Univ. Autónoma de Santo Domingo, 1971. 541 p. (Publicaciones de la Univ. Autónoma de Santo Domingo, 152. Col. Historia y sociedad, 5)

Who's who of historic figures ending with rise of Trujillo to power and published 40 years later. Entries arranged alphabetically. Author index and two page glossary. Useful because many obscure names are included.

Meirinho, Jali. As instituções da cultura catarinense. See item 6265.

114. Meksika: politika, ekonomika, kul'tura (Mexico: politics, economics, culture). Moskva, Nauka, 1968. 353 p., bibl., fold. map, plates, tables.

Fourteen essays by various Soviet authors on: economy, proletariat, peasantry, bourgeoisie, women's democratic movement, international relations, and on various aspects of ethnography and arts. Based on Mexican sources. [A. R. Navon]

115. México: neustra gran herencia. México, Reader's Digest, 1973. 383 p., facsims., illus., maps, plates, tables.

Traces Mexico from earliest times into the future describing major characteristics with an excellent collection of illustrations. Selection of plates and facsimiles is commendable. Useful reference for beginners.

116. Meyer, Harvey K. Historical dictionary of Nicaragua. Metuchen, N. J., The Scarecrow Press, Inc., 1972. 503 p., bibl., illus., maps (Latin American historical dictionaries, 6)

Cross disciplinary compilation of data with information dating from country's earliest times. Concise, useful reference.

117. Miliani, Domingo. Vida intelectual de Venezuela: dos esquemas. Caracas, Ministerio de Educación, Dirección General, Depto. de Publicaciones, 1971. 159 p., bibl. (Cuadernos de prosa, 8)

Elementary discussion of country's social and political thought and literature. Lists Venezuelans who have contributed written work or innovative thought in many subdivisions of the two areas. Lacks systematic discussion of any one person's contributions. [P. B. Taylor, Jr.]

Montemayor G., Felipe. 28 [i.e., Veintiocho] años de antropología: tesis de la Escuela

Nacional de Antropología e Historia. See item 518.

118. Nordeste brasileiro; catálogo da exposição. Rio, Biblioteca Nacional, Divisão de Publicações e Divulgação, 1970. 86 p., bibl.

Divides 546 works by subject, indicating which collection it is in, i.e., Biblioteca Nacional or one of eight others. Patterned after 1969 *Exposição Amazônia Brasileira*.

Organization of American States. Instituto Interamericano de Ciencias Agrícolas. Centro Interamericano de Documentación e Información Agrícola. Indice latinoamericano de tesis agrícolas. See item 6575.

———. ———. ———. Publicaciones periódicas y seriadas agrícolas de América Latina. See item 6576.

119. ———. **General Secretariat.** Statistical compendium of Americas, 1971. Washington, 1971. 119 p., tables.

Pocket sized volume containing standard data, usually for a single year. [J. M. Hunter]

120. Reed, Irving B.; Jaime Suchlicki; and **Dodd L. Harvey.** The Latin American scene of the seventies; a basic fact book. Coral Gables, Fla., Univ. of Miami, Center for Advanced International Studies, 1972. 220 p., illus. (Monographs in international affairs)

Introductory, overview essay and ready reference of basic information for the non specialist, American, arranged by country under the following categories: General Characteristics, Demography and Social Characteristics; Political Conditions; Cultural Panorama; Economic Situation; Foreign Trade; Foreign Relations; U.S. Interests; USSR/East European Interests; and a summary of Key Current Issues and Trends. Excellent reference source.

La reforma de la agricultura en Iberoamérica. See item 6589.

121. Resources for the study of Latin America at Indiana University. Bloomington, Ind., Indiana Univ., Latin American Studies Program, 1972. 92 p. (Latin American studies working papers)

Describes resources available on Latin American subjects at Indiana Univ. including its faculty. Excellent reference.

122. Rippy, Merrill *ed.* Cultural change in Brazil: papers from the Midwest Association for Latin American Studies, October 30 and 31, 1969. Muncie, Ind., Ball State Univ., 1969. 113 p., maps, tables.

Included:
Frank D. McCann "The Military and Change in Brazil" p. 1-12 (see item 7857)
Richard L. Cummings "Transformations in Brazilian Engineering Education: An indicator of Modernity" p. 13-23 (see item 6236)
R. Herbert Minnich "Developing Democrats: Sociocultural Change among the Brazilian Mennonites" p. 24-35 (see *HLAS 33:8578*)
William H. Nicholls "The Agricultural Frontier in Modern Brazilian History: The State of Paraná, 1920-65" p. 36-64
Neale J. Pearson "Small Farmer and Rural Worker Characteristics in the Emergence of Brazilian Peasant Pressure Groups, 1955-1968" p. 65-100 (see item 7869)
Armin K. Ludwig "The Kubitschek Years, 1956-61: A Massive Undertaking in a Big Rush" p. 101-113

Rodríguez Sala de Gomezgil, María Luisa. Las instituciones de investigación científica en México: inventario de su estado actual. See item 6161.

123. Roett, Riordan *ed.* Brazil in the sixties. Nashville, Tenn., Vanderbilt Univ. Press, 1972. 434 p., map, tables.

Twelve chapters by top scholars divided into: The Political Setting: from Kubitschek to Medici; The Economy: Growth versus Development; Social Change in Brazil: The Priorities of a Decade; and Literature in the Sixties. Excellent coverage.

124. Roig, Juan Miguel. El Centro de Documentación e Información Patagónica; bases para su creación y funcionamiento. B.A., Armada Argentina, 1972. 45 p., bibl., illus.

Intent is to create a central point to control collection of all information, published or unpublished, concerning Patagonia. Touches on organization, financing and institutional interest in project.

125. São Paulo yearbook 1972. São Paulo, The American Chamber of Commerce for Brazil, 1972. 261 p., illus., plates.

Devoted entirely to "Communications in Brazil," this issue succinctly summarizes developments in the postal service, telephone service, communication satellite system which links entire coast of Brazil as far as Ceará by microwave radio, progress on new roads for Brazil's interior airline industry and railroads. Excellent summary with color photographs. In English.

126. Saunders, John *ed.* Modern Brazil: new patterns and development. Gainesville, Univ. of Florida Press, 1971. 350 p., maps, plates, tables.

US and Brazilian scholars combine their efforts in an attempt to explain Brazil's modernization process. Included are:
John Saunders "The Modernization of Brazilian Society: (see *HLAS 33:8591*)
Donald R. Dyer "Brazil's Half-Continent"
T. Lynn Smith "The People of Brazil and Their Characteristics" (see *HLAS 33:8594*)
Anisio S. Teixeira "The Changing Role of Education in Brazilian Society" (see *HLAS 33:8596*)
Anyda Marchant "The Political and Legal Framework of Brazilian Life"
J. V. Freitas Marcondes "The Evolution of Labor Legislation in Brazil"
Dorival Teixeira Vieira "Industrial Development in Brazil"
Eric N. Baklanoff "Brazilian Development and the International Economy"

Willaim H. Nicholls "Agriculture and the Economic Development of Brazil"
Sugiyama Iutaka "The Changing Bases of Social Class in Brazil" (see *HLAS 33:8571*)
José Arthur Rios "The Growth of Cities and Urban Development" (see *HLAS 33:8587*)
Earl W. Thomas "The Evolution of Brazilian Literature" p. 289-311
Gerrit de Jong, Jr. "The Evolution of Brazilian Music and Art" p. 312-340

127. Schell, Rolfe and **Lois Schell.** Yank in Yucatán guide to eastern Mexico. Fort Meyers Beach, Fla., Island Press, 1973. 309 p., illus., maps, plates.

Not just a travel guide but also a good description of area with chapters on Mayan ruins and Fidel Castro's sojourn in Mérida. Interesting and readable, but not scholarly.

128. Siefer, Elisabeth *comp.* Neuere Deutsche Lateinamerika-Forschung; Institut und Bibliotheken in der Bundesrepublik Deutschland und in Berlin (West). Hamburg, Dokumentations-Leitstelle der ADLAF *am* Institut für Iberoamerika-Kunde, 1971. 346 p. (Schriften der Arbeitsgemeinschaft Deutsche Lateinamerika-Forschung [ADLAF], 2)

Compilation of research completed and in process on Latin America being done in Federal Republic of Germany (FRG) during 1970. Updating will be done in the "Informationsdienst der Arbeitsgemeinschaft Deutsche Lateinamerika-Forschung." Lists all institutions dealing with Latin America alphabetically by geographic region in FRG. Includes author index, subject index by country and regions and by disciplines. Excellent reference source.

129. Simon, Kate. Mexico: places and pleasures. N.Y., World Publishing, 1971. 368 p.

Something more and deeper than usual guidebook. Through vignettes and historical accounts gives interesting insights about the country and people for the traveller with more than just a passing interest. Revision of 1962 and 1963 editions.

131. Strange, Ian J. The Falkland Islands. Harrisburg, Pa., Stackpole Books, 1972. 256 p., bibl., maps, plates (The Island series)

Basic, informative study of the history, socioeconomic, and administrative aspects on this out-of-way place. While optimistic, future is uncertain due to emigration and other factors brought about by a modernizing world. Useful.

132. Suassuna, Ariano and others. Atlas cultural do Brasil. Rio, Ministério da Educação e Cultura (MEC), Conseho Federal de Cultura (CFC), Fundação Nacional de Material Escolar (FENAME), 1972. 376 p., facsims., maps, plates, tables.

Volume commemorating 150th Independence anniversary. Divided in 21 chapters covering all aspects of Brazil's cultural development graphically from colonial times to present. Richly illustrated with high quality photos and reproductions. Excellent descriptive maps which show distribution of certain assets, i.e., location of libraries and holdings, linguistic maps, distribution and types of industries, etc. Excellent indexes. Excellent reference source.

133. Toro Sugrañes, José A. *comp.* Almanaque boricua: 1972. San Juan, Editorial Cordillera, 1972. 348 p., tables.

Intended for high schools, but contains useful reference information on local and commonwealth government, elections and political parties, education, art and 40 pages of biographic sketches.

135. Varella, Hernani *ed.* and *comp.* Enciclopédia Fortaleza. v. 1, Artes, bibliografias, ciências aplicadas; v. 2, Ciências econômicas e contábeis, ciências puras e naturais, ciências sociais, curiosidades e assuntos gerais educação; v. 3, Filología e lingüística, filosofia, geografia, história; v. 4, História do Brasil, literatura, literatura brasileira; v. 5, Medicina, higiene e farmácia, música, recreação e esportes, religião, seção feminina. São Paulo, Edições Fortaleza, 1971. 5 v. (1600 p.), facsims., illus., maps, plates, tables.

Written in simple up-to-date language with emphasis on Brazilian topics though covering all fields. Five volumes dealing with 20 subjects arranged alphabetically.

136. Vaughan, Denton R. *comp.* Urbanization in twentieth century Latin America: a working bibliography. Austin Tex., Univ. of Texas at Austin, Institute of Latin American Studies, Population Research Center, 1970. 122 p., bibl.

Organized by country including a general section and one on US-Latins in Urban Places. Also includes a supplement, bibliographies and periodicals consulted and a city index. Concentrates on 1965-69 period relying on other bibliographies for earlier coverage. Preface cites additional sources to consult. Useful reference work.

137. Villasis Terán, Enrique M. Elogio del Ecuador. Quito, Ministerio de Defensa, 1972. 336 p., bibl., facsims., illus., maps, plates.

Description of culture, economy, geography, history and arts and crafts. Chapter headings are one for each province, with 11 appendices. Useful for its information on various provinces.

138. Vivó, Paquita *comp.* Sources of current information on Latin America. Washington, Squirrel Publications, 1971. 38 p.

Three part working listing: 1) periodicals on Latin American development, 2) agencies and organizations which at least occasionally publish documents, studies on annual reports on development, and 3) subject index. Also includes how to get information from each country. Valuable reference–cost $3.00.

Volskii, Viktor V. Sovetskaia Latinoamerikanistika: Nekotorye itogi i zadachi (Latin American studies in the USSR: some results and perspectives). See item 6066.

139. Wagley, Charles. An introduction to

Brazil. Rev. ed. N.Y., Columbia University Press, 1971. 341 p., bibl., map, plates.
Updating of useful study. See *HLAS 21:1253*.

140. Wassén, S. Henry *ed.* Göteborg, Etnografiska Museum: Orstryck 1970. Göteborg, Sweden, Elanders Baktryckeri Aktiebolag, 1971. 30 p., bibl., illus., plates.

Annual Report of the Ethnographical Museum, Gothenburg, Sweden lists gifts and new acquisitions for the Latin American Collection. Describes reference library, picture archives, card catalogue additions, phonograph records and film archives. Chapter devoted to museum's activities, other activities and questions concerning personnel. Short bibliography ends report. [R. V. Shaw]

Weil, Thomas E. and others. Area handbook for Paraguay. See item 6944.

141. Ynsfran, Pablo Max. Catálogo de los manuscritos del Archivo de Don Valentín Gómez Farías; obrantes en la Universidad de Texas, Colección Latinoamericana. México, Editorial Jus, 1968. 566 p. (Independent México in documents: independence, empire, and Republic, 3)

Holdings are listed in three categories: by year from 1770 to 1892 though some years are missing; manuscripts signed by Gómez Farías: and other documents. Has author index. Excellent reference.

142. Zepeda Henríquez, Eduardo. Escorzo histórico de nuestra Biblioteca Nacional (RCPC, 20:100, enero 1969, p. 5-6)

Historical highlights of Nicaragua's National Library, founded in 1882. Cites Rubén Darío's association with the institution, as well as other outstanding figures connected with the Library. Informative.

143. Zimmer, Norbert. *comp.* Deutsche in Entwicklungsländern: Erfahrungsberichte von Sachverständigen und Fachkräftern in Afrika, Asien, Lateinamerika. Zusammengestellt von Norbert Zimmer und Alexander Funkenberg. Hofheim/Taunus, FRG, Auslandskurier, 1966. 148 p. (Ausland-Kurier Schriften, 3)

This booklet, designed for German experts going to underdeveloped countries, contains about eight pages of general advice (do not try to bribe officials, and the like) on Brazil and Mexico. [A. H. Price]

JOURNAL ABBREVIATIONS

AM/R	Revista do Arquivo Municipal. Prefeitura do Município de São Paulo, Depto. Municipal de Cultura. São Paulo.
GM	The Geographical Magazine. London.
EEHA/AEA	Anuario de Estudios Americanos. Consejo Superior de Investigaciones Científicas [and] Univ. de Sevilla, Escuela de Estudios Hispano-Americanos. Sevilla.
FNA/BAAL	Bibliografía Argentina de Artes y Letras. Secretaría de Estado de Hacienda, Fondo Nacional de las Artes. B.A.
RCPC	Revista Conservadora del Pensamiento Centroamericano. Managua.
RIB	Revista Interamericana de Bibliografía [Inter-American Review of Bibliography]. Organization of American States. Washington.
UNESCO/BL	Bulletin for Libraries. United Nations, Educational, Scientific and Cultural Organization. Paris.

Anthropology

GENERAL

500. Alcina Franch, José. El Atlántico y América antes de Colón (CH, 256, abril 1971, p. 22-43, bibl., table)

Discussion of history of hypothesis of transoceanic precolumbian contacts and problems of evaluating similarities, in connection with a symposium held in Dec. 1970 in the Canary Islands; participants and their topics are listed. [B. J. Meggers]

501. ———. La producción y el uso de metales en la América precolombina (*in* International Mining Congress, VI, Madrid, 1970. La minería hispana e iberamericana: contribución a su investigación histórica; estudios, fuentes, bibliografía. León, Spain, Cátedra de San Isidoro, 1970, v. 1, p. 307-331, maps)

Summary statement with maps of precolumbian distribution of use of gold, silver, copper, bronze, tumbaga (gold-and-copper alloy), mercury, platinum, and meteoric iron. Bibliography with only 33 entries far from exhaustive. [C. Evans]

501a. Ashcraft, Norman. Developmental economics: some critical remarks (JDA, 7:1, Oct. 1972, p. 3-10)

Critique of the approach taken in developmental economics in the study of underdevelopment. The author, an anthropologist, argues that "economic performance in underdeveloped countries must instead be approached by a method that does not close the system on the basis of some a priori Western theoretical biases which exclude relevant information." [L. Comitas]

Aschmann, Homer. Indian societies and communities in Latin America: an historical perspective. See item 6503.

502. Austral, Antonio G. Método de estudio sectorial de los sitios arqueológicos superficiales (UNC/AAE, 24/25, 1969/1970, p. 77-92)

Recommendations of methods of recovering maximum information from shallow sites and discussion of terminology and classification of significant varieties. [B. J. Meggers]

503. Bate P., Luis F. Material lítico: metodología de clasificación (Noticiario Mensual [Museo Nacional de Historia Natural, Santiago] 16:181/182, agosto/sept. 1971, p. 3-24, bibl., illus.)

Proposal for uniform approach to analysis, classification, description, and nomenclature for use in archeological reports.

504. Bosch-Gimpera, Pedro. L'America precolombiana con 30 tavole fuori testo in nero e a colori. Torino, Italy, Unione Tipografico-Editrice Torinese, 1970. 578 p., bibl., illus., plates, tables.

Review of glaciations and peopling of Americas, "Mesolithic," Eskimo culture, the "Neolithic Revolution," and later North American cultures comprises pt. 1 (260 p.). Pt. 2 describes cultural development in Mesoamerica and the Central Andes. A chart correlates Old and New World glacial chronologies and New World cultural sequences. [B. J. Meggers]

505. Braghine, Alexandre Pavlovitch. Nossa herança da Atlântida: as mais antigas civilizações da terra. Tradução do original russo por Vladimir Malkine. Rio, Livraria Editôra Cátedra *em convênio com o* Instituto Nacional do Livro, 1971. 263 p., bibl.

Totally unreliable reconstruction of New World prehistory based on undocumented and repeated intrusions from the Old World. To be read only as science fiction. [B. J. Meggers]

506. Carter, George F. Precolumbian chickens in America (AAC/AJ, 9:3, 1971, p. 2-5, illus.)

Argues for precolumbian introduction of chickens to America from Asia based on linguistic, ethnographic, biological, and archaeological evidence. [B. J. Meggers]

507. Comas, Juan. Hipótesis trasatlánticas sobre el poblamiento de América: caucasoides y negroides. México, UNAM, Instituto de Investigaciones Históricas, 1972. 32 p., bibl., plates, tables (Cuadernos: serie antropológica, 26)

Critical analysis of existing evidence relating to transatlantic precolumbian immigration, whether from historical, archaeological, or osteological sources, reveals no convincing testimony of the presence of Negroes prior to European contact in the 15th century. [B. J. Meggers]

Denevan, William M. Prehistoric cultural change and ecology in Latin America. See item 6530.

508. Furst, Peter T. ed. Flesh of the gods: the ritual use of hallucinogens. N.Y., Praeger Publishers, 1972. 304 p., bibl., illus., plates.

Discussion of antiquity (probably over 7000 years) of use of hallucinogens for ritual effects. Chapters deal with groups in Venezuela, Colombia, Peru, Mexico, and other parts of the world; an overview is provided for the Western Hemisphere. [B. J. Meggers]

Horst, Oscar H. The study of change in traditional communities. See item 6551.

509. Ibarra Grasso, Dick Edgar. Sobre el origen de las culturas parahistóricas (Pumapunku [Instituto de Cultura Aymara, La Paz] 3 [2. semestre] julio/dic. 1971, p. 74-97)

Comments about origin of cultures in New World and their relationships to Asia, Middle East and Europe. [C. Evans]

510. International Congress of Americanists, XXXIX, Lima, 1970. Actas y memorias. v. 1, Actas, documentos y memorias; v. 2, El proceso de urbanización en América desde sus orígenes hasta nuestros días; v. 3, Proceso y cultura en la Sierra Central del Perú; v. 4; Historia, etnohistoria y etnología de la selva sudamericana; v. 5, Lingüística e indigenismo moderno en América; v. 6, Folklore de las Américas. Edited by Rosalía Avalos de Matos and Rogger Ravines. Lima, Instituto de Estudios Peruanos, 1972. 6 v. (252, 404, 308, 221, 301, 292 p.) bibl., illus., maps, plates, tables.

The following volumes were not available for review at HLAS press time: v. 7, *Prehistoria y arqueología sudamericana: área andina* (Lima, Industrialgráfica, 1972); v. 8, *Problemas étnicos de la sociedad contemporánea* (México, Instituto Indigenista Interamericano, 1970 [Sobretiro del *Anuario Indigenista*, 30]; v. 9, *Historia económica de América Latina*, 2 v. (México, Secretaría de Educación Pública, 1972 [Col., SepSetentas, 37]).

Seven additional volumes are in the planning stage (v. 10 through 16) and will be published only if special funds are made available; their tentative titles are: v. 10, *Formación y proceso de las sociedades americanas* (corresponding to Symposium No. 1 of the Congress); v. 11, *Arqueología del este de Sudamérica* (corresponding to Symposiums 5 and 6 of the Congress); v. 12, tomo 1, *Continuidad y cambio en la cultura araucana desde la prehistoria hasta la actualidad* (corresponding to Symposium 7 of the Congress); v. 12, tomo 2, *Native traditional pictorial source and writing systems in Nuclear America, Mesoamerica and the Andean region* (corresponding to Symposium 14 of the Congress); v. 13, *Arqueología de Norte y Mesoamérica* (corresponding to Section III, Session 2c of the Congress); v. 14, *Historia y etnohistoria americana* (corresponding to Section IV, Sessions 1, 2, 3 and 4 of the Congress); v. 15, *Campesinado contemporáneo* (corresponding to Section V, Sessions 3a and 3b of the Congress; v. 16, *Sociedad contemporánea: movilización, modernización y cambio y psiquiatría social y transcultural* (corresponding to Section V, Session 3c). Tables of contents of the available first six volumes read as follows:

V. 1, *Actas documentos y memorias: pt. 3, Memorias y trabajos científicos:*
Americanística: Niels Fock "Ends and Means in the Study of Man" p. 131-134
M. Jourdan Atkinson "The Import of Archaeology and of Mythology in the Understanding of our Cultural Heritage and a Proposed Chart of Cultural Evolution" p. 135-146
Antropología Física:
Francisco C.H. Devoto "Complejo Racial Dentario de la Población Precolombina de Tastil, Salta, Argentina," p. 147-150
Alejandro Estrada; Dennis McAuliffe; Elena Eritta; and Robert Brumbaugh "Physical Anthropology of the Skeletal Remains from Tombs 25, 26, and 27 from Yagul Oaxaca, Mexico" p. 151-154
R. Brooke Thomas "El Tamaño Pequeño del Cuerpo como Forma de Adaptación de una Población Quechua a la Altura" p. 183-192
Francisco C.H. Devoto and Beatriz M. Perrotto "Frecuencia de los Genes S y S (Incisivos en Pala) en la Población Contemporánea del Valle de Pastos Chicos, Jujuy, Argentina" p. 193-200
H. Fleischhacker "Reflejos de Mestizaje en Características Antropológicas y Genéticas" p. 201-209
Mirtha Sonia Gerber "Nuevas Investigaciones en Serología: los Mapuche" p. 210-212
Andrzej Wiercinski "Interpopulational Differentiation of the Living Amerindian Tribes in Mexico" p. 213-230
Andrzej Wiercinski "Inter and Intrapopulational Racial Differentiation of Tlatilco, Cerro de las Mesas, Teotihuacán, Monte Albán and Yucatán Maya" p. 231-252
V. 2, *El proceso de urbanización en América desde sus orígenes hasta nuestros días:*
Richard P. Schaedel "The City and the Origin of the State in America" p. 15-34
Woodrow Borah "European Cultural Influence in the Formation of the First Plan for Urban Centers that has Lasted to Our Time" p. 35-54
Harley L. Browning "Primacy Variation in Latin America During the Twentieth Century" p. 55-78
Duccio Bonavia Berber "Factores Ecológicos que Han Intervenido en la Transformación Urbana a Través de los Ultimos Siglos de la Epoca Precolombina" p. 79-98
Roberto Cortés Conde and Nancy López de Nisvovich "El Desarrollo Agrícola en el Proceso de Urbanización: Funciones de Producción, Patrones de Poblamiento y Urbanización" p. 99-114
Frédéric Mauro "Preéminence Urbaine et Réseau Urban dans l'Amérique Coloniale" p. 115-132
Alejandro B. Rofman "La Influencia del Proceso Histórico en la Dependencia Externa y en la Estructuración de las Redes Regionales y Urbanas Actuales" p. 133-156
Jorge Enrique Hardoy "Las Formas Urbanas Europeas Durante los Siglos XV al XVII y Su Utilización en América Latina: Notas Sobre el Transplante de la Teoría y Práctica Urbanística de Españoles, Portugueses, Holandeses, Ingleses y Franceses" p. 157-190
Alejandra Moreno Toscano "Economía Regional y Urbanización: Tres Ejemplos de Relación Entre Ciudades y Regiones en Nueva España a Finales del Siglo XVIII" p. 191-218
Marcos Kaplan "La Ciudad Latinoamericana Como Factor de Transmisión de Poder Socioeconómico y Político Hacia el Exterior Durante el Período Contemporáneo" p. 219-256
Barbara J. Price "Population Composition in Pre-Hispanic Mesoamerican Urban Settlements: A Problem in Archaeological Influence" p. 257-270
James R. Scobie "El Impacto de las Migraciones en la Estructura Urbana" p. 271-292
Markos Mamalakis "Urbanization and Sectorial Trans-

formation in Latin America: 1950-65" p. 293-346
Edward E. Calnek "Pre-Columbian Cities: The Case of Tecnochtitlan" p. 347-358
Ralph A. Gakenheimer "The Early Colonial Mining Town: Some Special Opportunities for the Study of Urban Structure" p. 359-372
Graziano Gasparini "La Ciudad Colonial como Centro de Irradiación de las Escuelas Arquitectónicas y Pictóricas" p. 373-386
Edwin Walter Palm "La Ciudad Colonial como Centro de Irradiación de las Escuelas Arquitectónicas y Pictóricas" p. 387-392
Richard M. Morse "The Limits of Metropolitan Dominance in Contemporary Latin America" p. 393-404

V. 3, *Proceso y cultura de la Sierra Central del Perú:*
Rogger Ravines "Grupos de Tradición Cazadora en las Tierras Altas de Huancavélica" (see item 992) p. 17-27
Luis Hurtado de Mendoza and Jesús Ramírez Tazza "Industrias Líticas del Valle de Palcamayo" (see item 955) p. 28-40
Ramiro Matos Mendieta "El Período Formativo en el Valle del Mantaro" (see item 970) p. 41-51
Chiaki Kano "Excavaciones en Shillacoto, Huánuco" (see item 963) p. 52-62
Mario Benavides Calle "Análisis de la Cerámica Huarpa" (see item 916) p. 63-88
William Harris Isbell "Un Pueblo Rural Ayacuchano Durante el Imperio Huari" (see item 959) p. 89-105
Miguel Rivera Dorado "Diseños Decorativos en la Cerámica Killke" (see item 998) p. 106-115
Donald Enrique Thompson "Late Prehispanic Occupations in the Eastern Peruvian Andes" (see item 1005) p. 116-123
José Alcina Franch "El Sistema Urbanístico de Chinchero" (see item 911) p. 124-134
Craig Morris "The Identification in Inca Architecture and Ceramics" (see item 972) p. 135-146
Waldemar Espinoza Soriano "Agua y Riego en Tres Ayllus de Huarochirí, Perú: Siglos XV y XVI" p. 147-166
Lionel Vallée "La Ecología Subjetiva como un Elemento Esencial de la Verticalidad" (see item 1500) p. 167-175
Steven S. Webster "An Indigenous Quechua Community in Exploration of Multiple Ecological Zones" (see item 1503) p. 176-183
Enrique Mayer "Un Carnero por un Saco de Papas: Aspectos del Trueque en la Zona de Chaupiwaranga, Pasco" (see item 1443) p. 184-196
Antonio Días Martínez and others "Contribución al Estudio del Latifundio" p. 197-230
Salvador Palomino Flores "La Dualidad en la Organización Socio-Cultural de Algunos Pueblos del Area Andina" (see item 1459) p. 231-260
Edmundo G. Pinto "Ecos del Warachiku en la Comunidad de Tomanga" p. 261-284
Billie Jean Isbell "No Servimos Más" p. 285-298
Teófilo Altamirano Rúa "El Cambio en las Relaciones de Poder en una Comunidad de la Sierra Central del Perú" (see item 1342) p. 299-308

V. 4, *Historia, etnohistoria y etnología de la selva sudamericana:* Pt. 1: *El Bosque Tropical*
Arqueología
Donald W. Lathrap "Alternative Models of Population Movements in the Tropical Lowlands of South America" p. 13-24
Thomas P. Myers "Sarayacu: Archaeological Investigations at a 19th-Century Franciscan Mission in the Peruvian Montaña" p. 25-38
Etnología
Karl H. Schwertn "Arawak, Carib, Ge, Tupí: Cultural Adaptation and Cultural History in the Tropical Forest, South America" p. 39-58
Robert V. Morey, Jr. "Warfare Patterns of the Colombian Guahibo" p. 59-68
Bernard Nietschmann "Hunting and Fishing Productivity of the Miskito Indians, Eastern Nicaragua" p. 69-88
Scott S. Robinson "Shamanismo entre los Kofan" p. 89-94
André-Marcel d'Ans "Les Tribus Indigènes de Parc National du Manu" p. 95-100
Nicole Maxwell "Actitudes de Cuatro Tribus de la Selva Peruana con Respecto a Plantas Empleadas como Anticonceptivos por Vía Oral" p. 101-110

Pt. 2: *La Montaña Central Peruana*
Jay Lehnertz "Juan Santos, Primitive Rebel on the Campa Frontier: 1742-1752" p. 111-126
Alan K. Craig "Franciscan Exploration in the Central Montaña of Perú" p. 127-144
Marshall S. Chrostowski "The Eco-Geographical Characteristics of the Gran Pajonal and their Relationships to some Campa Indian Cultural Patterns" p. 145-160
William M. Denevan "Campa Subsistence in the Gran Pajonal, Eastern Perú" p. 161-180
Judy Holshouser "Some Aspects of Economic Change Among the Campa of the Western Montaña of Central Perú as Reflected in Land Use Patterns" p. 181-188
Gerald Weiss "Campa Cosmology" p. 189-206
Daniel W. Gade "Comercio y Colonización en la Zona de Contacto entre la Sierra y las Tierras Bajas del Valle del Urubamba en el Perú" p. 207-221

V. 5, *Lingüística e indigenismo moderno en América.* This volume was not available for review. The table of contents will be included in *HLAS 37.*

V. 6, *Folklore de las Américas:*
Dora P. de Zárate "Búsquese una Denominación más Apropiada que 'Folklórico', para Designar la Faena Erudita que Envuelve Proyecciones de Manifestaciones Folklóricas" p. 15-16
Luis Ibérico Más "Folklore, Arte y Cambio Social" p. 17-18
Elmo Ledesma "Análisis y Clasificación de las Adivinanzas" p. 19-20
Miguel H. González "El Fenómeno Folk en el Sur Argentino" p. 21-34
William Bascom "Shango in the New World" p. 37-46
María Angélica Ruiz "Velar el Común: un Mito en Acción" p. 47-58
Alvaro Soto Holguín "Mitos de los Cubeo" p. 59-65
Paul S. Powhson "Tendencias Epicas en la Mitología Yagua" p. 66-86
Thales de Azevedo "Religião Popular e Sentimento de Culpa" p. 89-91
Leslie Ann Brownrigg "El Papel de los Ritos de Pasaje en la Integración Social de los Cañari Quechuas del Austral Ecuatoriano" (see item 1361) p. 92-99
B. June Macklin and N. Ross Crumrine "'Santa' Teresa, el Niño 'Santo' Fidencio, and 'San' Damián: The Structural Development of Three Folk Saints' Movements, Northern Mexico" p. 100-109
Alcira Imazio "Una Hipótesis de Trabajo Referida al San La Muerte" p. 110-116
Vera-Dagny Stahle "Carreras Ceremoniales con Troncos entre Indios Brasileños" p. 117-126
Roswith Hartmann "Otros Datos sobre las Llamadas Batallas Rituales" (see item 1417) p. 125-138
Américo Paredes "El Concepto de la 'Médula Emotiva' Aplicado al Corrido Mexicano 'Benjamín Argumedo'" p. 139-176
Dora P. de Zárate "Sobre la Saloma Panameña: una Manifestación Original de Nuestro Patrimonio Folklórico" p. 177-181
Berta Montero de Bascom "Cecilia Valdés: Sus Interpretaciones Literarias, Folklóricas y Musicales" p. 182-188
Ramón Campbell B. "Romoto Origen de la Música Primitiva de Rapanui" p. 189-205
Dora Ochoa de Masramón "Los Romances en San Luis, República Argentina" p. 206-218

Néstor Lemos "Orígenes de la Cueca Cuyana" p. 219-229
Simeón Orellana Valeriano "Los Huatrillas de Jauja: Folklore del Valle del Mantaro" p. 230-240
Jorge M. Yarrow "Enfoque del Curanderismo en el Departamento de Lambayeque" p. 241-248
Federico Sal y Rosas "Observaciones en el Folklore Psiquiátrico del Perú" p. 249-262
Oscar Santisteban Tello "Folklore de Huarochiri" p. 265-266
David H. Andrews "Los Piropos en Latinoamérica" p. 267
Raúl Martínez Crovetto "Distribución de Algunos Juegos de Hilo Entre los Aborígenes Sudamericanos" p. 268-279
"Bibliografía" p. 280-292.

511. Jeffreys, M.D.W. Some precolumbian trans-Atlantic anomalies (AAC/AJ, 11:1, 1973, p. 2-9)

Detailed commentary on the question of precolumbian maize in Africa, and briefer consideration of problems presented by the occurrence in the Old and New Worlds of various plants and animals whose names carry the prefix "guinea." Also mentioned briefly in the precolumbian transoceanic context are: the peanut, pineapple, cherry tomato, manioc, and the Cape gooseberry. [C. R. Edwards]

512. Katz, Friedrich. The ancient American civilizations. N.Y., Praeger Publishers, 1972. 386 p., bibl., plates, maps (History of civilizations series)

Detailed comparison of Aztec and Inca civilizations, based mainly on written records, including summaries of preceding cultures. Translation of *Vorkolumbische Kulturen* (München, FRG, Kindler, Verlag, 1969). Includes index and glossary. [H. von Winning]

Kemper, Robert V. Bibliografía comentada sobre la antropología urbana en América Latina. See item 6557.

513. Larraín, Horacio. Conceptos básicos y posibilidades del enfoque ecológico en la investigación arqueológica. (Cuadernos de Investigaciones Históricas y Antropológicas [Museo Regional del Iquique, Chile] 1:2, Sept., 1972, p. 1-23)

Good summary of discussions on archaeology and ecology; concludes that culture areas should be defined as cultural ecological areas. [C. Evans]

513a. Lozada, Salvador María. Los indígenas americanos y los regímenes constitucionales (UM/JIAS, 10:2, April 1968, p. 223-231)

Brief survey of how indigenous peoples were treated during colonial period, and of what is said of them in contemporary constitutions in selected national cases. [P. B. Taylor, Jr.]

514. McKern, Sharon S. Exploring the unknown: mysteries in American archaeology. N.Y., Praeger Publishers, 1972. 124 p., bibl., illus., maps, tables.

Popular treatment of selected topics: peopling of the hemisphere; Machu Picchu; trepanation in Peru-Bolivia; Nazca markings on the desert; cause of Maya cultural collapse. Of interest to uninformed layman only. [B. J. Meggers]

515. Marcano, Gaspar. Etnografía precolombina de Venezuela. Caracas, Univ. Central de Venezuela, Instututo de Antropología e Historia, 1971. 366 p., illus.

First edition in Spanish, all in one volume, of Marcano's classic works in French of 1889-91, *Vallées d'Aragua et de Caracas, région des Raudals de l'Orénoque*, and *Indiens Piaroas, Guahibos, Cuicas et Timotes*. Some historically interesting data on archaeology, physical anthopology and ethnology. [C. Evans]

516. Marroquín, Alejandro D. Balance del indigenismo: informe sobre la política indigenista en América. Prólogo [por] Gonzalo Rubio Orbe. México, Instituto Indigenista Interamericano, Sección de Investigaciones Antropológicas, 1972. 300 p., bibl., illus., tables (Ediciones especiales, 62)

Origin and organization of the Instituto Indigenista Interamericano; role of indigenes in Mexico, Guatemala, Ecuador, Peru, Brazil and Bolivia; some positive and negative aspects of current practices. [B. J. Meggers]

517. Meggers, Betty J. Prehistoric America. Chicago, Ill., Aldine Publishing Co., 1972. 200 p., bibl., illus., plates.

Brief introduction to New World archaeology organized by pairs of environmental areas in North and South America. After describing the peopling of the hemisphere and the transition to agriculture, cultural evolution is followed in these areas to the time of European contact. Similarities in environment result in cultural parallels in adaptation, often of a striking nature. The differential access to diffusion from the Nuclear areas helps account for unequal levels of development where local resources are similar. [B. J. Meggers]

517a. Mendieta Alatorre, Angeles. La serpiente: dios protector (UNL/H, 11, 1970, p. 735-742)

Brief non-exhaustive summary of ethnographic and archaeological research on the serpent as symbol, myth and migratory expression of ancient Indo-American cultures. [P. F. Hernández]

518. Montemayor G., Felipe. 28 [i.e., Veintiocho] años de antropología: tesis de la Escuela Nacional de Antropología e Historia. México, Instituto Nacional de Antropología e Historia, 1971. 615 p.

Catalog of 164 dissertations accepted by the Escuela Nacional de Antropología e Historia from 1944-71; table of contents, description, and detailed conclusions are provided. Reference is aided by indexes by subject, author, place names, and general sub-field of anthropology. [B. J. Meggers]

519. O'Brien, Patricia J. The sweet potato: its origin and dispersal (AAA/AA, 74:3, June 1972, p. 342-365)

Sweet-potato originated in northwestern South

America and its domestication is associated with Tropical Forest agricultural villages ca. 2500 B.C. Spanish introduced it to Europe and it spread to China, Japan, Malaysia and the Moluccas. Portuguese carried it to India, Indonesia and Africa. Reexamination of the literature suggests new theories to author. He believes that there was a pre-Magellan accidental introduction of the sweet potato into Polynesia, Samoa area, by about one A.D. and via birds carrying seed or by fortuitous casting of vessel. From there, it spread throughout rest of Pacific. Author, however, does not believe that similarity between Quechua and Polynesian terms for sweet potato (*kumara*) indicates pre-Hispanic contact between Quechua-speaking Indians and Polynesian peoples. [C. Evans]

520. Patterson, Clair C. Native copper, silver and gold accessible to early metallurgists (SAA/AA, 36:3, July 1971, p. 286-321, tables)

Weathered ore deposits no longer in existence are reconstructed by inference to provide estimates of relative abundance of usable nuggets of native copper, silver and gold in precolumbian times. New techniques summarize the metallic impurities in ores. Emphasis on discovery of smelting and melting by Mochica, the inability of New World metallurgists to smelt copper from sulfide ores or silver from lead ores. Sees no transoceanic contacts in metallurgical techniques. [C. Evans]

521. Patterson, Thomas C. America's past: a New World archaeology. Glenview, Ill., Scott, Foresman, 1973. 156 p., bibl., illus.

Comparison of Mesoamerican and Andean prehistory in terms of selected themes: the emergence of food production, settlement pattern, state formation, and influence of environment on cultural development. Emphasis is on inference rather than details of archaeological sequences and remains. [B. J. Meggers]

522. Pedersen, Asbjorn. Aspectos de la metalurgia indígena americana prehispánica: La Huayra y su empleo en el proceso de fundición (MEMDA/E, 14, julio/dic. 1971, p. 5-10, bibl., illus., tables)

Review of chronicle descriptions of metalworking in prehispanic America; suggests probable Asiatic influence. [B. J. Meggers]

523. Persson, Lars. Indianerna i Latinamerika. Stockholm, Utrikespolitiska Instituet, 1970. 36 p., bibl.

Swedish ethnologist, chairman of the IWGIA (International Work Group for Indigenous Affairs), strongly criticizes "integration" policies of Latin American governments towards their Indian populations. He refers to the history of abuse and destruction which has characterized European-Indian relations in South America and recommends that anthropologists be hired to formulate governments' Indian policies. [R. V. Shaw]

524. Price, Barbara J. Prehispanic irrigation agriculture in nuclear America (LARR, 6:3, Fall 1971, p. 3-60, bibl.)

Review of evidence in Mesoamerica and Peru indicates that irrigation alone is not capable of explaining the growth of civilization. Conclusion leads to speculations about the interrelationships of agricultural productivity, population size, and social dynamics under different conditions and their effects on cultural evolution. [B. J. Meggers]

525. Rohr, João Alfredo. Normas para a cimentação de enterramentos arqueológicos e montagem de blocos-testemunha. Curitiba, Bra., Centro de Ensino e Pesquisas Arqueológicas, 1970. 11 p., plates (Manuais de arqueologia, 3)

Method for intact removal of skeletons from archaeological sites for exhibition or detailed examination in laboratory.

Salzano, Francisco M. Genetic aspects of the demography of American Indians and Eskimos. See item 1763.

——. *ed.* The ongoing evolution of Latin American populations. See item 1765.

526. Schwerin, Karl H. Antropología en Sudamérica (*in* Schwerin, Karl H. Antropología social: tres estudios. Cuenca, Ecua., Univ. de Cuenca, 1969, p. 45-67)

Popular review in Spanish of theories concerning the prehistory and cultural typologies as applied in South America. [L. A. Brownrigg]

527. Service, Elman R. Profiles in ethnology. rev. ed. N.Y., Harper and Row, 1971. 521 p., bibl., illus., map, plates.

Modern cultural evolutionary theory underpins the selected synopsis of 21 societies representing differing degrees of socio-economic and political complexity. Latin American examples include the Yahgan (Tierra del Fuego) for band society; the montaña Jívaro (Suara) for tribal organization; Inca and Maya for "primitive states" and Chan Kom (Yucatan, Mex.) as a modern folk society. The past tense is used only in the description of the ancient Mayas, based on Landa, Thompson, Morley, Hay and Villa Rojas, and in the account of the Incas which follows closely Rowe's seriously outdated 1946 reconstruction. Other societies are described in terms of the ethnographic present, more a convention of theory than tense. The Yahgan, who numbered only 40 in 1933, are thus described as though alive and well in a vein similar to Cooper's 1946 reconstruction in the *Handbook of South American Indians* (see *HLAS 12:105*). The Jívaro account reiterates Karsten's errors, though a bow is made to Harner's 1962 cosmology. When first published in 1958, *Profiles* documented a then controversial theory. This 1971 edition is billed as revised, but it ignores both innovations in evolutionary theory (including Service's own) and recent research. It ignores the effect of states stimulating tribe formations, for which the Suara could serve as an example if recent archaeological evidence and ethnohistorical interpretations were used. To classify Inca society as a "primitive state" rather than as an archaic civilization on the imperial level (to use Service's own terminology) is intellectually inadmissible. Both state formation and empires are millenially pre-Incaic in Andean Civilization. Service's *Profiles* has a definite market and usefulness as a text introducing cultural variety in a systematic manner. This reissue, however, represents a fossil of theory, interpretation and research. [L. A. Brownrigg]

Sheck, Ronald C. The persistence of cultural autarchy. See item 6595.

528. Silva Galdames, Osvaldo. Prehistoria de América. Santiago, Editorial Universitaria, 1971. 225 p., bibl., illus., maps, tables (Col. Imagen de América Latina)

Introduction to New World archaeology focusing on Mesoamerica and the Central Andes, after a review of the initial hunting and gathering period. Good for the non-specialist. [B. J. Meggers]

529. Simoni-Abbat, Mireille and **Frédéric Mauro.** Civilisations de l'Amérique Latine. Paris?, Horizons de France, 1971. 286 p., bibl., maps, plates (Hommes et civilisations)

Copiously illustrated overview of Latin American cultures. Simoni-Abbat discusses precolumbian cultures, with emphasis on art and architecture. Mauro divides the postcolumbian civilizations into those of the "conquistadors," the "liberators," and the "gringos," as each impinged on native life and culture. [C. R. Edwards]

530. Struever, Stuart ed. Prehistoric agriculture. Garden City, N.Y., The Natural History Press for the American Museum of Natural History, 1971. 733 p., bibl., illus., maps, tables (American Museum sourcebooks in anthropology)

Well chosen selection of readings that elaborate the following themes: hypotheses to explain the initial shift to agriculture; the beginnings of agriculture and its consequences in various world areas (Mesoamerica, South America, the Near East, and Temperate Europe); the natural scientist views the beginnings of agriculture; the role of agriculture in the development of civilization. Individual papers dealing with Latin America:
Kent V. Flannery "Archaeological Systems Theory and Early Mesoamerica" p. 80-100
Michael D. Coe and Kent V. Flannery "Microenvironments and Mesoamerican Prehistory" p. 131-142
Richard S. MacNeish "Ancient Mesoamerican Civilization" p. 143-156
Kent V. Flannery; Anne V. T. Kirby; Michael J. Kirby; and Aubrey W. Williams, Jr. "Farming Systems and Political Growth in Ancient Oaxaca" p. 157-180
Thomas C. Patterson "The Emergence of Food Production in Central Peru" (see item 984)
Paul C. Magelsdorf; Richard S. MacNeish: and Gordon R. Willey "Domestication of Corn" p. 471-486
Paul C. Mangelsdorf; Richard S. MacNeish; and Gordon R. Willey "Origins of Agriculture in Middle America" p. 487-515

Walton C. Gallinat "The Evolution of Corn and Culture in North America" p. 534-543. [C R. Edwards]

531. Taxay, Don. Money of the American Indians and other primitive currencies of the Americas. N.Y., Nummus Press, 1970. 158 p., bibl., illus., plates.

Summary of materials presumed to have served as currency among North and South American Indians. Unreliable. [B. J. Meggers]

532. Uratsuka, Josefa N.; Lúcia Musenek and **Hermínia Muzanek.** Agricultura na América pré-colombiana: bibliografia (in O hõmem antigo na América. São Paulo, Univ. de São Paulo, Instituto de Pré-Histórica, 1971, p. 123-141)

Bibliography divided into general works on agriculture and specific titles concerning various cultivated plants. Total: 520 references. [B. J. Meggers]

533. von Schuler-Schömig, Immina. Werke indianischer Goldschmiedekunst (Staatliche Museen Preussischer Kulturbesitz, [Berlin] 17, 1972, p. 1-46, bibl., plate, map)

Detailed descriptions of 41 gold ornaments from Mexico, Central and South America, from among 800 artifacts acquired by the Berlin Museum 1880-1910. [H. von Winning]

534. Wassén, S. Henry. The anthropological outlook for Amerindian medicinal plants (in Swain, Toni ed. Plants in development of modern medicine. Cambridge, Mass., Harvard Univ. Press, 1972, p. 1-65, bibl., illus., plates)

Summary of ethnohistorical, archaeological, and ethnographical information on use of tobacco, hallucinogens and other plant drugs by South American Indians. Annotated bibliography. [B. J. Meggers]

Wauchope, Robert ed. The Indian background of Latin American history: the Maya, Axtec, Inca and their predecessors. See HLAS 34:1120.

ARCHAEOLOGY: MESOAMERICA

HASSO VON WINNING

Consultant in Mesoamerican Archaeology
Southwest Museum

RICHARD E. W. ADAMS

Professor of Anthropology
University of Texas
San Antonio

THE FRENZIED OUTPOURING OF PUBLICATIONS has somewhat abated during this reporting period (middle 1971-April 1973), compared with our previous Handbook coverages. In general, relatively short descriptive and interpretative articles predominate. Many of these reflect the growing interest in iconography, particularly in Olmec art. All the cultural areas of Mesoamerica are represented, with greater emphasis on the Central Mexican Highlands and the Maya area. Several important monographs and handbook articles made a welcome, although tardy, appearance.

Information on Current Research

Archaeological research in progress has been reported regularly in *American Antiquity*, as follows: "Guatemala," by Charles A. Hoffman, Jr. (36:2, 1971, p. 236). "Mesoamerica," by Jaime Litvak King (36:4, 1971, p. 488-489; 37:2, 1972, p. 271-272; 38:2, 1973, p. 232-234, the latter comments on the reorganization of INAH and outlines the penalties for infringements of the new law for the protection of archaeological zones and artifacts, see item 580). Publication of the quarterly *Boletín* of the INAH (Instituto Nacional de Antropología e Historia), a useful source of information containing site reports with occasional descriptive notes on sculptural art, was much delayed. Following the Dec. 1970 issue (No. 42), a new series (Epoca 2, No. 1, April/June 1972) was issued in April 1973.

Olmec Civilization

The Olmec have been the subject of numerous contributions. The majority of these are descriptive iconographic and interpretative studies (items 546, 554, 559, 620, 630, 647, and 660). Of particular interest is Joralemon's catalog of Olmec symbols (item 575). Proponents of a Central Highland origin of Olmec civilization presented new arguments (item 555), based, in part, on pre-Olmec ceramic figurines recently discovered near Xochipala, Guerrero (items 648 and 653). Obsidian artifacts, which are indicative of long distance trade relations, received continued attention (items 542, 665, and 706).

Basin of Mexico

A valuable synthesis of Cuicuilco, the dominant Late Preclassic center of the entire Basin, derived from excavations in 1957, made a late appearance (item 661). The second, final, volume of the XI Round Table Conference, concerned with the three, now completed, major Teotihuacan Projects was published in 1972 (item 594). A full report on the ceramics remains a desideratum. Million's first volume on the Teotihuacan Mapping Project is in press and was not available for inclusion in this summary.

West Mexico

In West Mexico, an area in dire need for controlled excavations, significant contributions, on the origin of ceramic figures and on the cultural impact of the area on early Mesoamerican development, were published (items 629 and 670).

Maya Area

Three interpretative monographs of the Altar de Sacrificios Project and a summary contain a wealth of information on artifacts (item 720), hieroglyphic inscriptions (item 725), and skeletal material (item 697). Three major contributions made their appearance after long delays. Eric Thompson completed his monumental trilogy on Maya hieroglyphs with a commentary on the Dresden Codex (item 733) which contains a complete facsimile reproduction in color. The pioneer study of Teobert Maler on Maya architecture, recorded 1886-1905, was edited in German and Spanish by G. Kutscher (item 586). An elegant volume reproducing Merle Greene's superb rubbings of Maya stelae and inscriptions appeared with comments by R. L. Rands and John A. Graham (item 558). The Centro de Estudios Mayas of the National University of Mexico issued a second edition, with addenda, of *El Desarrollo Cultural de los Mayas* and volume eight (1970) of the series *Estudios de Cultura Maya*. The long awaited catalog of the Grolier Exhibition of Maya pottery, by Michael D. Coe, is still in press. It will contain a color reproduction of the fourth Maya codex (see *HLAS 31:82* and p. 29) which is "very Toltec in style," commensurate with its radiocarbon date 720 B.P.±120 A.D. 1230 (personal information M. D. Coe).

General Treatises

General works on Mesoamerican archaeology include college textbooks by Weaver (item 618) and Hedrick (item 571). A comprehensive historiography by Keen (item 576) and a shorter one by Wauchope (see *HLAS 34:1120*) provide a historical perspective of the flow and ebb of viewpoints and theories. Out of print works on Mesoamerican art were made available in revised editions of such classics as Toscano's (item 615), and Kelemen's (item 577) comprehensive treatises. Westheim's and Soustelle's works appeared in English translation (item 619 and *HLAS 31:1141*). Several European museums continued to produce detailed descriptive and well illustrated catalogues of their collections (items 533, 627, 643 and 657). Hopefully, this lead will be followed by American museums. A temporary exhibition on West Mexican anecdotal clay sculpture was catalogued in Los Angeles (item 715). Multi-authored interpretative reports and syntheses include the fourth volume of the Tehuacan Valley Project (item 574), the first volume of the final reports on the Teotihuacan Valley Project (item 696), and two volumes of the *Handbook of Middle American Indians* on the archaeology of Northern Mesoamerica. This area includes the Central Highlands and the regions north of the 18th Parallel and Guerrero (item 550). The proceedings of the XII Round Table Conference on *Religión en Mesoamérica,* held in Cholula 1972, were not available in their entirety for inclusion in this report (see items 599, 601 and 610). The methodology of studies in Transpacific contacts is critically reviewed, with new evidence, by Marschall (item 588) and Asian influence in Codex Laud is pointed out by Barthel (item 721).

Necrology

We regret to report the death of the following scholars: William Rotch Bullard, on 21 May 1972, one of the younger generation Maya archaeologists, known for his work in the Petén and British Honduras. Dudley T. Easby Jr., on 16 March 1973, authority on precolumbian metalwork and secretary (1945-69) of the Metropolitan Museum of Art, N.Y. With his wife, Elizabeth K. Easby, he directed the museum's centennial exhibition "Before Cortés" (see *HLAS 33:657*). James Collier Gifford, 8 Jan. 1973. Founder and editor of *Cerámica de Cultura Maya,* published since 1961. He developed the type-variety system of analysis now widely used in Maya ceramic classification. Paul Kirchhoff, in Mexico, Oct. 1972, who coined the term *Mesoamerica* to designate a large culture area which is distinguished by a set of common traits not shared by neighboring regions. An eminent ethnologist, he also was a great teacher whose publications, although few in numbers, are landmarks in anthropological research. In his later years he initiated research on the origins of Mesoamerican religion as part of a worldwide, Asian derived, system. César Lizardi Ramos, in Mexico, 13 Aug. 1971. As a journalist and Maya epigrapher he published archaeological discoveries and was engaged in Maya hieroglyphic research. Kurt W. Marek, known as C. W. Ceram, in Hamburg, 12 April 1972. Author of *Gods, graves and scholars,* he was highly successful in stimulating popular interest in archaeology. Carlos Samayoa Chinchilla, in Guatemala, 20 Feb. 1973, Director of the Instituto Nacional de Antropología e Historia of Guatemala from 1954 until his retirement in 1967 and a distinguished literary writer. Günter Zimmermann, in Hamburg, 2 Nov. 1972, founder and head of the Hamburg Research Center (Forschungsstelle für Altamerikanische Sprachen und Kulturen der Universität Hamburg) he was active in Otomí, Náhuatl and Maya documentary research. His catalogue of Maya glyphs in the codices became the foundation of Thompson's comprehensive Catalog. (HvW)

GENERAL

535. Adams, Richard E. W. Reply to Haviland (SAA/AA, 37:1, Jan. 1972, p. 140)

Examines Haviland's assertion that cognatic kinship organization is typical of late classic Maya and suggests matrilineal and double descent alternatives. Also suggests lineages as represented in small residential groups at Tikal rather than clans. [REWA]

Alcina Franch, José. La producción y el uso de metales en la América precolombina. See item 501.

Badner, Mino. A possible focus of Andean artistic influence in Mesoamerica. See item 914.

536. Ball, Joseph W. and Jack D. Eaton. Marine resources and the prehistoric lowland Maya: a comment (AAA/AA, 74:3, June/July 1972, p. 772-776, table)

Lange's argument that a large part of classic and post-classic Yucatan depended on marine subsistence resources does not fit with recent data. Preclassic occupations on the coast are heavy while classic and post-classic occupations are scarce. Suggests diverse subsistence pattern as an alternative. Convincing. See item 547. [REWA]

537. Beadle, George W. The mystery of maize (Bulletin [Field Museum of Natural History, Chicago, Ill.] 43:10, 1972, p. 2-11, illus.)

Recent research is summarized and the conclusion presented that a type of *teosinte* is the direct ancestor of maize. Quite different from recently held views and very important. [REWA]

538. Becker, Marshall Joseph. The evidence for complex exchange systems among the ancient Maya (SAA/AA, 38:2, April 1973, p. 222-223)

Comment on Tourtellot and Sabloff hypothesis (item 616) which criticizes the theory on grounds of inaccurate data and lack of logical continuity from data to model building. [REWA]

539. Bordeaux, Edmond S. The soul of ancient Mexico. n.p., Mille Mediations, 1968. 134 p., illus.

Compendium of misinformation with unsubstantiated conclusions to explain Toltec, Aztec and Maya cosmology. [HvW]

540. Braniff, Beatriz. Greca escalonada en el norte de Mesoamérica (INAH/B, 42, dic. 1970, p. 38-41, illus.)

Discusses the stepped fret motif in northwestern Mexico, its origin and distribution. [HvW]

541. Brunhouse, Robert L. Sylvanus G. Morley and the world of the ancient Mayas. Norman, Okla., Univ. of Oklahoma Press, 1971. 353 p., plates.

Creditable, interesting, but not definitive biography of S. G. Morley. Morley was initiator of the Carnegie Institution of Washington's program in Maya archaeology. His principal interest was in Maya hieroglyphic chronology. Brunhouse discusses his life, intellectual achievements, and explorations knowledgeably. [REWA]

Calnek, Edward E. Settlement pattern and Chinampa agriculture at Tenochtitlan. See *HLAS 34:1016.*

542. Cobean, Robert H.; Michael D. Coe; and others. Obsidian trade at San Lorenzo Tenochtitlan, Mexico (AAAS/S, 174:4010, Nov. 1972, p. 666-671, illus., map, tables)

Obsidian imported for manufacture of artifacts could be traced to eight natural sources ranging from Central Highland Mexico to Highland Guatemala. Sharp increase in long-distance trade between San Lorenzo A and B phases is associated with general elaboration of Olmec civilization and supports hypothesis of importance of trade—probably in a ritual context—in the expansion of Olmec influence in Mesoamerica. [HvW]

543. Coe, Michael D. Olmec jaguars and Olmec kings (*in* Conference in Pre-Columbian Iconography, Washington, 1970. The cult of the feline [see item 546] p. 1-12)

Stimulating discussion of certain related aspects in Olmec, Maya and Aztec religion and iconography. Coe postulates that by 1200 B.C. Olmec society was ranked in hereditary classes dominated by royal lineages, and interprets the colossal heads as portraits of Olmec kings. [HvW]

544. Coggins, Clemency. Archaeology and the art market (AAAS/S, 175:4019, Jan. 1972, p. 263-266, illus.)

Documents destructive role of the art market in promoting looting of archaeological sites in Mesoamerica. [REWA]

545. ———. Displaced Mayan sculpture (CEM/ECM, 8, 1970 [i.e., 1972], p. 15-24)

Listing of sculpture robbed from Mexico and Guatemala and presents location of some. Author requests aid in keeping the list up to date. [REWA]

546. Conference in Pre-Columbian Iconography, *Washington, 1970.* The cult of the feline. Elizabeth P. Benson, Editor. Washington, Dumbarton Oaks Research Library and Collections, Harvard Univ. Trustees, 1972. 166 p., bibl., illus.

Contains eight papers on feline (mainly jaguar) motifs in Mesoamerica, see items 543, 560, and 579, and in South America. Each paper followed by discussions. Concluding remarks by Geoffrey H. S. Bushnell (p. 165-166). [HvW]

Cook, Sherburne F. and Woodrow Borah. Essays in population history: Mexico and the Caribbean. See *HLAS 34:1254.*

547. Dornstreich, Mark D. A comment on lowland Maya subsistence (AAA/AA, 74:3, June/July 1972, p. 776-779)

Attacks Lange's marine subsistence thesis on several grounds including lack of quantification, and naiveté in nutritional matters. There is a relatively reliable ecological principle that the larger the population the narrower the range of foods exploited. Therefore, the diversity argued for by Lange, Ball, and Eaton will have to be substantiated by specific data. See item 536. [REWA]

548. Dumond, D. E. Demographic aspects of the classic period in Puebla-Tlaxcala (UNM/SWJA, 28:2, Summer 1972, p. 101-130, bibl., tables)

Re-analysis of recent survey data indicates that parts of Puebla-Tlaxcala rural hinterland must have been depopulated during the classic, concomitant with increasing nucleation of habitation centers. Same situation existed in classic Teotihuacan and some Old World agrarian societies. Neither endemic local warfare, nor commerce and competition for access to resources appear to have spurred nucleation. [HvW]

549. ——— and Florencia Muller. Classic to postclassic in highland Central Mexico (AAAS/S, 175:4027, 17 March 1973, p. 1208-1215, illus.)

A transitional horizon is established between the end of Teotihuacan (Metepec phase) and the arrival of plumbate trade ware. It is marked by a continuation of modified Teotihuacan ceramics, revival of preclassic traits, political fragmentation, and divergent cultural development in the Valley of Mexico, and in Puebla-Tlaxcala, which culminated in Toltec supremacy at Tula in the west and of Cholula in the east. [HvW]

550. Ekholm, Gordon F. and Ignacio Bernal *eds.* Archaeology of Northern Mesoamerica:

pts. 1-2 (HMAI, 10/11, 1972, p. 1-903, bibl., illus., maps, plates, tables)

V. 10 contains following articles:
William T. Sanders "Settlement Patterns in Central Mexico" p. 3-44
Carlos R. Margain "Pre-Columbian Architecture in Central Mexico" p. 45-91
Henry B. Nicholson "Major Sculpture in Pre-Hispanic Central Mexico" p. 92-134
Agustín Villagra Caletti "Mural Painting in Central Mexico" p. 135-156
Román Piña Chan "Preclassic or Formative Pottery and Minor Arts in the Valley of Mexico" p. 157-178
Carmen Cook de Leonard "Ceramics of the Classic Period in Central Mexico" p. 179-205
Carmen Cook de Leonard "Minor Arts of the Classic Period in Central Mexico" p. 206-227
Robert Chadwick "Postclassic Pottery of the Central Valleys" p. 228-257
Eduardo Noguera "Minor Arts in the Central Valley" p. 258-269
Paul Tolstoy "Utilitarian Artifacts of Central Mexico" p. 270-296
Irmgard Weitlaner Johnson "Basketry and Textiles" p. 279-321
Charles E. Dibble "Writing in Central Mexico" p. 279-321
Alfonso Caso "Calendrical Systems of Central Mexico" p. 333-348
Pedro Carrasco "Social Organization of Ancient Mexico" p. 349-375
Charles Gibson "Structure of the Aztec Empire" p. 376-394
Henry B. Nicholson "Religion in Pre-Hispanic Central Mexico" p. 395-446
Miguel León-Portilla "Philosophy in Ancient Mexico" p. 447-451
Miguel León-Portilla "Pre-Hispanic Literature" p. 452-458

V. 11 contains:
Pedro Carrasco "The Peoples of Central Mexico and Their Historical Traditions" p. 459-473
Robert Chadwick "Native Pre-Aztec History of Central Mexico" p. 474-504
José Garcia Payón "Archaeology of Central Veracruz" p. 505-542
William T. Sanders "Cultural Ecology and Settlement Patterns of the Gulf Coast" p. 543-557
Tatiana Proskouriakoff "Classic Art of Veracruz" p. 558-572
Richard S. MacNeish "Archaeological Synthesis of the Sierra" p. 573-581
Guy Stresser-Péan "Ancient Sources on the Huasteca" p. 582-602
Herbert R. Harvey "Ethnohistory of Guerrero" p. 603-618
Robert H. Lister "Archaeological Synthesis of Guerrero" p. 619-631
Donald D. Brand "Ethnohistoric Synthesis of Western Mexico" p. 632-656
Robert Chadwick "Archaeological Synthesis of Michoacan and Adjacent Regions" p. 657-693
Betty Bell "Archaeology of Nayarit, Jalisco and Colima" p. 694-753
Clement W. Meighan "Archaeology of Sinaloa" p. 754-767
Charles Kelley "Archaeology of the Northern Frontier: Zacatecas and Durango" p. 768-801. [HvW]

551. Feldman, Lawrence H. Moluscos mayas: especies y orígenes (CEM/ECM, 8, 1970 [i.e., 1972], p. 117-138, bibl., tables)

Classification and tabulation of shells from all archaeological contexts. Very significant conclusion is that most of the shells in high and continuous demand were from the Gulf of Honduras. [REWA]

552. Flannery, Kent V. The cultural evolution of civilizations (Annual Review of Ecology and Systematics [Palo Alto, Calif.] 3, 1972, p. 399-426, bibl., illus.)

Extremely important paper which examines general theories of cultural evolution and rejects those in the "prime mover" as less explanatory than multivariate theories. Examination of ancient socio-political organizations in Mesoamerica as reflected in settlement patterns is made using R. N. Adams' multivariate theory. Application of central place theory to the Maya lowlands reveals a strikingly uniform settlement lattice which implies a high degree of coherence and community specialization. ". . . the suggested integration is so great that perturbations in one center might have affected other centers strongly, a likely 'precondition' for the much-debated Maya collapse. . .". Comparative material is included from Mesopotamia and other parts of Mesoamerica. [REWA]

553. Folan, W. J. Kukulkan y un culto fálico en Chichen-Itzá, Yucatán, México (CEM/ECM, 8, 1970 [i.e., 1972], p. 77-82, illus.)

Thesis of article is that Kukulkan, the Itzá and the three kings of Chichen Itza were associated with a phallic cult which led to their various expulsions from Yucatan. Ethnohistoric and archaeological evidence cited. [REWA]

554. Fuente, Beatriz de la ed. El arte olmeca (ARMEX, 19:154, 1972, p. 1-102, bibl., illus.)

Contains the following, profusely illustrated (also in color) articles, including English and French translations:
Beatriz de la Fuente "La Escultura Monumental" p. 6-34
Anatole Pohorilenko "La Pequeña Escultura" p. 35-62
Marta Foncerrada de Molina "La Pintura Rupestre" p. 63-68 (a description of the Juxtlahuaca and Oxtotitlan cave paintings, see *HLAS 33:669*)
Jean-Pierre Laporte "La Cerámica" p. 69-82
Francisco Beverido Pereau "Las Ciudades" p. 83-92. [HvW]

555. Gay, Carlo T. E. Chalcacingo. Drawings by Frances Pratt. Graz, Austria, Akademische Druck-und Verlagsanstalt, 1971. 119 p., bibl., illus., plates (Monographien und Dokumentationen: die Amerikanischen Felsbilder)

Interpretative study, with excellent illustrations of 32 pictographs, 11 rock bas-reliefs, 21 bedrock and boulder altars, etc., in Morelos' state. Gay infers that because of their naturalistic style, Chalcacingo reliefs predate more conventionalized sculptures of San Lorenzo and La Venta, and challenges trade route theory that relegates Chalcacingo to more than a colony of the Olmec heartland. Valuable as a definitive and comprehensive record of deteriorating reliefs and rock paintings which Gay ascribes to a yet undetected formative stage of Olmec civilization (which he substantially elaborated in his Xochipala report, see item 648). He also points out comparisons with west European paleolithic cave art. [HvW]

556. Gendrop, Paul. El México antiguo [Ancient Mexico]. México, Editorial Trillas, 1972? 183 p., illus., plates.

General introduction to prehispanic cultures from early beginnings to the Conquest. [HvW]

557. ——. Murales prehispánicos (ARMEX, 18:144, 1971, p. 1-118, bibl., illus.)

Descriptions of content and aesthetic appraisal of mural paintings in Mexico from Olmec rock paintings to native-Hispanic transitional style of early colonial period. Profusely illustrated with many color plates. The most comprehensive coverage published so far. Summary in English and French. Author also published "Estética del Arte Prehispánico" (in *Sandorama*, México, 10, 1971, p. 22-28, illus.; and 11, 1971, p. 22-25, illus.). [HvW]

558. Greene, Merle; Robert L. Rands; and **John A. Graham.** Maya sculpture from the Southern Lowlands, Highlands, and Pacific Piedmont. Berkeley, Calif., Lederer, Street and Zeus, 1972. 432 p., bibl., maps, plates, tables.

Selection from Green's unrivaled series of over 500 rubbings. Indispensable for Mesoamericanists, art historians, art lovers, and archaeology buffs. Professionally of great value for its exact recording of many unpublished sculptures. Knowledgeable, interesting and up-to-date text. Complements Greene's and Thompson's earlier book, *HLAS 29:636a*. Includes 202 plates and endpaper maps. [REWA]

559. Grove, David C. Olmec altars and myths (AIA/A, 26:2, April 1973, p. 128-135, illus.)

Interprets complex symbolism of Altars 4 and 5, La Venta, which depict a person seated in a niche, with reference to Olmec cave paintings and myths of Paez Indians (Colombia). Concludes that Olmec altars are stylized jaguar monsters and that they served as thrones to confirm mythical underworld origin, and right to succession, of Olmec ruler portrayed in the niche. [HvW]

560. ——. Olmec felines in Highland Central Mexico (*in* Conference in Pre-Columbian Iconography, Washington, 1970. The cult of the feline [see item 546] p. 153-164, illus.)

Discussion of jaguar representations on Olmec monumental art with reference to Chalcatzingo rock carvings. [HvW]

561. Guliaev, Valerii Ivanovich. Algunas cuestiones relativas al nacimiento de la primitiva sociedad de clases entre los antiguos mayas (CEM/ECM, 8, 1970 [i.e., 1972], p. 139-159)

Discussion of three defining characteristics of class society and their appearance and features among the Maya. Writing systems, cities, and royal tombs only appear together about the beginning of Christian era, and thus mark initial phase of civilization in Maya lowlands. [REWA]

562. ——. Drevneishie tsivilizatsii Mezoamerikii (The oldest civilizations of Mesoamerica). Moskva, Nauka, 1972. 276 p., bibl., illus., maps, plates.

Survey of Mesoamerican civilizations. Author discusses evolution of a major ethnic group from the Upper Paleolithic through process of settlement and subsequent formation of agricultural cultures to the establishment of an early-class state. Survey ends with comparison between evolution of Old and New World civilizations, indicating that precolumbian America was subject to the "general laws of historical development." Includes Spanish summary (p. 266-267). [A. R. Navon]

562a. ——. Idoly priachutsia v dzhungliakh (Idols hidden in the jungles). Moskva, Molodaia Gvardiia, 1972. 206 p., illus., maps, plates.

Study of Olmec culture by well-known Soviet archaeologist designed for the general public. Discusses individual excavations and debates surrounding origin and development of Olmec culture. [T. S. Cheston]

563. Guzmán Peredo, Miguel. El culto a los dioses del agua en Mesoamérica (ARMEX, 19:152, 1972, p. 8-16, illus.)

Reviews significance of water deities, based mainly on written sources. In same issue, which is entitled *Underwater Archaeology*, author describes explorations of Sacred Cenote at Chichen Itzá, Cenote at Dzibilchaltún, Lake of the Half Moon (San Luis Potosí), and lakes of Nevado de Toluca. These lakes contained large offerings of copal and preclassic clay figurines. Text in Spanish and English. [HvW]

564. Hammond, Norman. Classic Maya music, pt. 1; Maya drums (AIA/A, 25:2, 1972, p. 124-131, illus.)

Presents evidence for use of percussion instruments. The *pax*, *tunkul*, pottery hand-drum, large circular drum, and turtle carapace were all used and produced sound by beating. [REWA]

565. ——. Classic Maya music, pt. 2: rattles, shakers, raspers, wind and string instruments (AIA/A, 25:3, 1972, p. 222-228, illus.)

Knowledgeable and stimulating discussion of individual instruments and their probable combinations. Hammond suggests that music was strong in beat, but lacked tonal delicacy and that the loss of the musical tradition is thus perhaps bearable. [REWA]

566. Hartung, Horst. Die Zeremonialzentren der Maya; ein Beitrag zur Untersuchung der Planungsprinzipien. Graz, Austria, Akademische Bunch-und Verlagsanstalt, 1971. 140 p., bibl., plates, illus.

Presents evidence for the deliberate architectural planning of Maya ceremonial centers, implicit in relationships of key points (door jambs, stelae, altars, etc.) and in the orientation of the buildings. For Piedras Negras and Yaxchilan conclusions agree with Proskouriakoff's glyph interpretations. Visual relationships indicate that similar architectural principles were applied at Uxmal and Chichen Itza. Further data are given for Tikal, Copan and Palenque. Copiously illustrated. [H. Hartung]

567. Hatch, Marion Popenoe. An hypothesis on Olmec astronomy, with special reference to the La Venta site (UCARF/C, 13, June 1971, p. 1-64, illus.)

Following up earlier suggestions that La Venta pyramid could have served as an observatory, author, in carefully reasoned paper, proposes that alignment (eight degrees of true north) is based on observations of certain constellations (Ursa majoris, Cygni). Argues that this discovery provides key for interpretation of iconographic elements in sculptures (upper lip of jaguar, crossed bands, etc.) and glyphs on jade celts. These designs are believed to represent "star maps". [HvW]

568. Haviland, William A. Estimates of Maya population: comments on Thompson's comments (SAA/AA, 37:2, Feb. 1972, p. 261-262)

"The historic Maya habit of abandoning a hut after the occupant's death, and the tendency to move communal sites, may be responses to population decimation and foreign political domination following breakup of the Mayapan hegemony. If so, it is doubtful that they should be projected back to the classic Maya." [REWA]

569. ———. Family size, prehistoric population estimates and the ancient Maya (SAA/AA, 37:1, Jan. 1972, p. 135-139, bibl.)

In attempt to arrive at average household sizes as means of estimating ancient populations, Haviland examines modern Maya communities and 16th-century census data. Concludes that five persons per household is more reasonable estimate than 5.6 figure used and that non-palace populations at Tikal would therefore total about 40,000. [REWA]

570. ———. A new look at classic Maya social organization at Tikal (TU/CCM, 8, 1972, p. 1-16)

Interesting discussion of Tikal data and their social implications. Lineages and sibs were apparently the basic social units, combined with patrilineality. A stratified society was early present and the upper class probably endogamous. Finally, Haviland notes the great diversity in social structure indicated by archaeological data from various Maya sites. [REWA]

571. Hedricks, Basil C.; J. Charles Kelley; and Carroll L. Riley *eds.* The North Mexican frontier: readings in archaeology, ethnohistory and ethnography. Carbondale, Ill., Southern Illinois Univ. Press, 1971. 255 p., bibl., maps.

Reprints of 13 articles, with notes, each prefaced by the editors. Following deal with the archaeology of northern Mexico:
Leopoldo Batres "Visit to the Archaeological Remains of La Quemada, Zacatecas, Mexico" (originally published 1903; translated from Spanish, illustrations deleted) p. 1-20
Donal D. Brand "Notes on the Geography and Archaeology of Zape, Durango" (1939) p. 21-49
Manuel Gamio "The Chalchihuites Area, Zacatecas" (1910, translated) p. 50-72
Agnes M. Howard "Navacoyan: a Preliminary Survey" (1957) p. 73-78
Ales Hrdlicka "The Region of the Ancient Chichimecs, with Notes on the Tepecanos and the Ruin of La Quemada, Mexico" (1903) p. 79-129
J. Alden Mason "Late Archaeological Sites in Durango, Mexico, from Chalchihuites to Zape" (1937) p. 130-143. [HvW]

572. Heyden, Doris. Indumentaria antigua de Oaxaca (Costume of ancient Oaxaca). México, Museo Nacional de Antropología, 1972. 30 p., illus. (Col. Breve, 10)

Explanations of the significance of dress and ornaments depicted in sculptures, clay figures and codices. [HvW]

573. Ivanoff, Pierre. Mayan enigma: the search for a lost civilization. Translated from the French by Elaine P. Halperin. N.Y., Delacorte Press, 1971. 202 p., bibl., plates, tables.

Account of author's "discovery" of Dos Pilas (mistakenly marked Dos Pozos on his map) and his explorations in the vicinity. Pt. 2 deals with visit to the Lacandon (the ever present Bor family). Author tries a not too convincing synthesis of Maya cosmology. Somewhat inaccurate, romanticized, but interesting. [REWA]

574. Johnson, Frederick *ed.* The prehistory of the Tehuacan Valley. v. 4, Chronology and irrigation. Austin, Tex., Univ. of Texas Press, 1972. 290 p., bibl., illus., maps, tables.

Contents: 1) Frederick Johnson and Richard S. MacNeish "Chronometric Dating" (p. 3-55), consists of an elaboration of the Tehuacan chronology described in v. 1-3 (see *HLAS* 33:705) based on stratigraphical sequences, radiocarbon dates and cross-dating with other Mesoamerican regional sequences. 2) Karl A. Wittfogel "The Hydraulic Approach to Pre-Spanish Mesoamerica," (p. 59-80), discusses the theory of "hydraulic society" in the Old World and its application in the New World. 3) Richard B. Woodbury and James A. Neely "Water Control Systems in the Tehuacan Valley," (p. 81-153), is a thorough investigation of the nature and extent of canals, dams and terraces, and of their relationship with changing subsistence systems and settlement patterns. A major feature described in detail is the Purron Dam complex, a series of earth dams with masonry veneer, from 700 B.C. 4) Gorgonio Gil Huerta "History of the Foundation of the Town of San Gabriel Chilacatla" (p. 154-161). 5) Eva Hunt "Irrigation and the Sociopolitical Organization of Cuicatec Cacicazgos" (p. 162-259). [HvW]

575. Joralemon, Peter David. A study of Olmec iconography (Studies in Precolumbian Art and Archaeology [Dumbarton Oaks, Washington] 7, 1971, p. 395, bibl., illus.)

Compilation of 181 Olmec symbols and motifs in profusely illustrated dictionary covering 266 Olmec artifacts, rock carvings, and cave paintings. Defines 10 gods by their attributes and therefore implies a more complex religious system than previously suspected. Very useful handbook. [HvW]

Katz, Friedrich. The ancient American civilizations. See item 512.

576. Keen, Benjamin. The Aztec image in Western thought. New Brunswick, N.J., Rutgers Univ. Press, 1971. 667 p., bibl., plates.

Author presents full account of diverse interpretations of prehispanic cultures of Mexico with emphasis on the Aztecs. The writings of a host of early chroniclers, historians, anthropologists, artists, and novelists are analyzed in the light of the contemporaneous intellectual and artistic climate, from the Renaissance to our days. Leading exponents of successive schools of thought, dissenting viewpoints, and syntheses are presented in their respective social and historical context to highlight causal relationships. This scholarly and well written history is the first comprehensive perspective covering four and a half centuries of historical-archaeological investigations. For colonial historian's comment, see *HLAS 34:1068*. [HvW]

577. Kelemen, Pal. Art of the Americas, ancient and hispanic, with a comparative chapter on the Philippines. N.Y., Thomas Y. Crowell, 1969. 402 p., illus.

Intended for general reader, this survey includes precolumbian horizons (US, Southwest of the US, the

Mexican, Maya, Intermediate, and Andean areas), colonial art and art of the Philippines. Prehispanic art is subdivided into architecture, sculpture, pottery, weaving and metalwork. Organized like his earlier Medieval American art (1943, 1956), the Mesoamerican coverage is shorter but brought up-to-date. Includes appendix. [HvW]

578. Kubler, George. La evidencia intrínseca y la analogía etnológica en el estudio de las religiones mesoamericanas (*in* Mesa Redonda de la Sociedad Mexicana de Antropología, XII, Mexico, 1972. Religión en Mesoamerica. México, Sociedad Mexicana de Antropología, 1972, p. 1-24)

Study of methodology of current problem concerning unitarian versus pluralistic nature of Mesoamerican religion. Kubler contrasts archaeological-iconographic approach (which he favors) with the use of far-ranging ethnographic analogy and with the combination of both methods. [HvW]

579. ———. Jaguars in the Valley of Mexico (*in* Conference in Pre-Columbian Iconography, *Washington, 1970.* The cult of the feline [see item 546] p. 19-49, illus.)

Iconographic study of various jaguar images and of their compound forms. Concludes that the classic Teotihuacan jaguar-serpent-bird motif acquired new meaning under Toltecs and vanished with the coming of the Aztecs when it was replaced by the eagle and jaguar warrior cult. [HvW]

580. Ley federal sobre monumentos y zonas arqueológicos, artísticos e históricos (SSC/K, 8:1, Aug. 1972, p. 1-9)

Transcript of law protecting archaeological zones and monuments enacted in Mexico. Published in *Diario Oficial* (May 6, 1972). [HvW]

581. Lister, Robert H. and **Florence C. Lister** eds. In search of Maya glyphs. Santa Fe, N.M., Museum of New Mexico Press, 1970. 171 p., illus., map.

Selected and edited parts of S. G. Morley's journals dealing with expeditions to Uaxactun, Tulum, Xultun, Piedras Negras, and Calakmul. Knowledgeable introduction sets context for selections. [REWA]

582. Litvak King, Jaime. Las relaciones externas de Xochicalco: una evaluación de su posible significado (UNAM/AA, 9, 1972, p. 53-76, bibl.)

Discusses evidence of abundant extraneous traits present in Xochicalco from the preclassic to Aztec dominance of region. Xochicalco appears to have been situated at crossroads of an early established network over which goods and ideas were exchanged over much of Mesoamerica. Routes changed with shifts in sociopolitical power structures after fall of Teotihuacan. See also *HLAS 33:569.* [HvW]

583. Lizardi Ramos, César. Rito previo a la decapitación en el juego de pelota (UNAM/ECN, 9, 1971, p. 21-46, illus.)

Traces frequent occurrences of kneeling individuals in sculpture and codices. Kneeling position of ball players is interpreted as part of ritual preceding their decapitation. [HvW]

584. Luján Muñoz, Luis. Historia de la arqueología en Guatemala (III/AI, 32:2, abril/junio 1972, p. 353-376, bibl.)

585. MacNeish, Richard Stockton. Speculation about how and why food production and village life developed in the Tehuacan Valley (AIA/A, 24:4, Oct. 1971, p. 307-315, illus.)

Author summarizes information presented in the *Prehistory of Tehuacan* volumes which he co-authored in a pleasant discursive manner. See also item 574. [HvW]

586. Maler, Teobert. Bauten der Maya, aufgenommen in den Jahren 1886 bis 1905 und beschrieben von T.M. Edited by Gerdt Kutscher. Berlin, Gebr.-Mann Verlag, 1971. 120 p., bibl., fold. maps, illus., maps, plates, tables (Ibero-Amerikanisches Institut Berlin. Monumenta Americana, 4)

First German edition, with Spanish translation, of Maler's descriptions of Maya architecture in Usumacinta Valley, the Peten, and Yucatan, which were published so far in English only in the *Memoirs* of the Peabody Museum, 1901-11. Mainly of historical interest, edition nevertheless valuable for facsimile reproduction of large plans and site maps, 14 of which are not included in the *Memoirs*. Prefaced by a biographical sketch of T. Maler (1842-1917). 40 folded maps and plans in portifolio. Second volume is contemplated. [HvW]

587. Marcus, Joyce. Territorial organization of the Lowland Classic Maya (AAAS/S, 180:4089 June 1973, p. 911-916)

Patterns of references to Maya political centers from classic Maya texts, and hexagonal relationships of the centers one to another, indicate that there were probably four at any one time, and these shifted through time. There were probably five tiers of organization within each state. Exceedingly important. [REWA]

588. Marschall, Wolfgang. Transpazifische Kulturbeziehungen: Studien zu ihrer Geschichte. München, FRG, Klaus Renner Verlag, 1972. 292 p., bibl., illus.

Pt. 1 reviews historiography of Old and New World parallels, with critical evaluation of methodology in recent studies. Pt. 2 contains detailed comparisons of four cultural trait complexes (blowgun; house models and death cult; figurines on wheels; weaving and dying techniques) in order to verify and expand previously published research. Pt. 3 deals with processes of cultural transmittal, possibilities of navigational contact, and theoretical considerations. Written from diffusionist viewpoint, author nevertheless withholds final judgment in his strictly factual contribution towards problem of transpacific contacts. Includes index. [HvW]

589. Martí, Samuel. Mudra, manos simbólicas en Asia y América. México, Litexa, 1971. 163 p., bibl., illus.

Reviews significance of symbolic hand movements (mudra) in Hindu religion and points out parallels in Mexican and Maya iconography, citing numerous lengthy quotations. Includes 55 line drawings (by Zita Basich) of hands in Codex Dresden and 30 photographs, none of which are specifically referred to in the text. Data presented merit further elaboration of the precolumbian material. Includes index. For a preliminary version see *HLAS 33:574*. [HvW]

590. Matheny, Ray T. Modern Chultun construction in Western Campeche, Mexico (SAA/AA, 36:4, Oct./Dec. 1971, p. 473-475, illus.)

Modern Chontal Indians in Laguna de Términos area build underground cisterns lined with baked clay. Nearly identical late classic chultuns were found at Aguacatal. [REWA]

591. Matos Moctezuma, Eduardo. Parálisis facial prehispánica. México, Museo Nacional de Antropología, Instituto Nacional de Arqueología e Historia, Depto. de Investigaciones Antropológicas, 1970. 45 p., illus. (Publicación, 25)

Shows unilateral facial distortion on figurines from Central Highland Mexico and Veracruz, beginning in late preclassic. [HvW]

592. ——— *ed.* Miccaihuitl, el culto de la muerte (ARMEX, 18:145, 1971, p. 1-99, illus.)

Contains article by same author entitled "La Muerte en el México Prehispánico" (p. 6-36) with English translation. Consists of brief discussion of prehispanic death cult with numerous illustrations from archaeological sources. Other articles in this issue deal with death cult in colonial times and present-day Mexico. [HvW]

593. ——— and **Luis A. Vargas.** Anomalías del pie en murales y códices prehispánicos (UNAM/AA, 9, 1972, p. 95-103, illus.)

Suggests that deformed feet, represented in mural and codical art, are either portrayals of a pathological condition (*talipes equinovarus*) or attributes of deities. [HvW]

594. Mesa Redonda de la Sociedad Mexicana de Antropología *XI, México, 1966.* Teotihuacán. v. 2. México, 1972. 408 p. (Continuous pagination), bibl., illus., maps.

For v. 1 see *HLAS 31:1140*. Present v. 2 contains:
Clara Millon "The History of Mural Art at Teotihuacan" p. 1-16
Luis Torres Montes "Materiales y Técnicas de la Pintura Mural de Teotihuacán" p. 17-42.
Jorge V. Angulo "Reconstrucción Etnográfica a Través de la Pintura" p. 43-68
George Kubler "La Iconografía del Arte de Teotihuacán" (for a later, comprehensive version see *HLAS 31:1083*) p. 69-85
Arthur G. Miller "Los Pájaros de Quetzalcoatl" p. 87-101
Stephen Tobriner "The Fertile Mountain: an Investigation of Cerro Gordo's Importance to the Town Plan and Iconography of Teotihuacan" p. 103-115
Laurette Sejourné "La Muerte de los Dioses en la Religión Náhuatl" p. 117-124
Eulalia Guzmán "Disquisiciones Acerca de Teotihuacán" p. 125-139
John Paddock "El Ocaso del Clásico" p. 141-147
Jorge R. Acosta "El Epílogo de Teotihuacán" p. 149-156
H. B. Nicholson "The Problem of the Historical Identity of the Cerro Portezuelo/San Antonio Archaeological Site: an Hypothesis" p. 157-200
Evelyn C. Rattray "El Complejo Cultural Coyotlatelco" p. 201-209
John Paddock "Distribución de Rasgos Teotihuacanos en Mesoamérica" p. 223-239
Ignacio Marquina "Influencia de Teotihuacán en Cholula" p. 241-243
Dean R. Snow "Classic Teotihuacan Influences in North-Central Tlaxcala" p. 245-251
José Corona Núñez "Los Teotihuacanos en el Occidente de México" p. 253-256
William R. Coe "Cultural Contact between the Lowland Maya and Teotihuacan as Seen from Tikal, Petén, Guatemala" p. 257-271
Beatriz Braniff "Secuencias Arqueológicas en Guanajuato y la Cuenca de México: Intento de Correlación" p. 273-323
John Paddock "Relaciones de la Sección sobre Extensión de la Cultura Teotihuacana" p. 325-327
René Millon "El Valle de Teotihuacán y su Contorno" p. 329-337
Rosendo Escalante "Tradicionalismo y Modernización en Teotihuacán y su Contorno" p. 339-352
Richard A. Diehl "Contemporary Settlement and Social Organization" p. 353-362
Ignacio Marquina "Clausura de la Mesa Redonda de Teotihuacán" p. 407-408. [HvW]

595. Meyer, Karl E. The Maya crisis: a report on the pillaging of Maya sites in Mexico and Guatemala, and a proposal for a rescue fund. Washington, Center for Inter-American Relations, Maya Rescue Project, 1972. 47p., bibl., plates.

Strong, persuasive presentation of plan to save Maya antiquities from looters by setting up a "Maya Rescue Fund" similar to funds set up for Venice and the UNESCO fund raised for the Abu Simbel temple in Egypt. Tightly reasoned and documented, and important. Argues that action must be taken soon in order to save the cultural heritage of Guatemala. [REWA]

596. ———. The plundered past: pt. 1, The flying façade and the vanishing glyphs (The New Yorker, 24 March 1973, p. 96-121)

Pt. 1 of an excellent series of three articles on the world-wide antiquity trade, deals largely with Mexico and the Maya area. Intimate relationships between museums, art dealers, thieves and smugglers are clearly outlined. Also discusses the ethical ambiguities for the former two and for private collectors and scholars. Thoughtful and of great interest. To be published as a book. [REWA]

597. Michael, Henry N. and **Elizabeth K. Ralph** *eds.* Dating techniques for the archaeologist. Cambridge, The MIT Press, 1971. 226 p., bibl., illus.

This useful handbook explains seven dating methods with advice on selection of samples to be tested. Discussions of archaeomagnetism and obsidian hydration include data from Mesoamerica. [HvW]

598. Nance, C. Roger. Cultural evidence for the altithermal in Texas and Mexico (UNM/SWJA, 28:2, Summer 1972, p. 169-192, illus., tables)

Evaluates archaeological data that indicate periods of adjustment to climatic changes between 5000-2500 B.C. [HvW]

599. Nicholson, Henry B. The cult of Xipe Totec in Mesoamerica (*in* Mesa Redonda de la Sociedad Mexicana de Antropología, XII,

México, 1972. Religión en Mesoamérica. México, Sociedad Mexicana de Antropología, 1972, p. 213-218)

Arcnaeological-iconographic and documentary evidence of origin and expansion of the Xipe cult with critical analysis of interpretative hypotheses. [HvW]

600. Papers on Olmec and Maya archaeology (UCARF/C, 13, June 1971, p. 1-166, illus.)

Contains six papers, see items 567, 665, and 726-728.

601. **Pasztori, Esther.** The historical and religious significance of the Middle Classic ball game (*in* Mesa Redonda de la Sociedad Mexicana de Antropología, XII, México, 1972. Religión en Mesoamérica. México, Sociedad Mexicana de Antropología, 1972, p. 441-455)

Analysis of origin, development, and distribution of the ball game as a major ritual cult in Mesoamerica, based on iconography and documentary sources. [HvW]

602. **Piña Chan, Román.** Historia, arqueología y arte prehispánico. México, Fondo de Cultura Económica, 1972. 215 p., bibl., plates.

Correlation of the Nahua migrations, recorded in Sahagún, with archaeological evidence, selected mainly in terms of art styles, to demonstrate identity of the legendary Tamoanchan with Xochicalco, where the Quetzalcoatl cult, the ritual calendar and other concepts originated. Records of migrations from the Gulf Coast to the Maya area are correlated with the distribution of mainly architectural styles. Concludes that the art style of Tula, Hidalgo, was derived mainly from Chichen Itzá, an unorthodox view expressed earlier by Kubler (see *HLAS 25:147*). [HvW]

603. Precolumbian America: pt. 1, Mesoamerica (OAS/AM, 23:6/7 [Supplement] June/July 1971, p. 1-40, illus.)

Contains "Before Cortés," by Elizabeth P. Benson (A brief review of Mesoamerican art with illustrations of specimens exhibited at the Metropolitan Museum of Art; see *HLAS 33:657*). The five other articles have been adapted from earlier issues of *Americas*. [HvW]

604. **Quirarte, Jacinto.** El juego de pelota en Mesoamerica: su desarrollo arquitectónico (CEM/ECM, 1970 [i.e., 1972] p. 83-96, illus., map)

Extensive study of ballcourts by plans and crossections. Copan court is one of the earliest and may be archetypal. Variations are very small over a vast area and through a thousand years. Summary graphic tables and plates are exceedingly useful in this typological and comparative study. Includes appendix. [REWA]

605. **Riese, Berthold von.** Geschichte der Maya. Stuttgart, FRG, Verlag W. Kohlhammer, 1972. 116 p., maps, plates (Urban Taschenbücher, 148)

"Changes and continuities in social and political situation of the Maya lowlands from the earliest beginning to the present are surveyed. Emphasis is placed on description of the colonial period and the present day. As representative groups, the following are treated: Itzá, Chontal, Chol, Yucatecan, Lacandon, and the (19th-century rebel) Cruzob. The latest research from the fields of archaeology and ethnology are reviewed. These are elucidated by a critical analysis of sources for each chapter and through a detailed bibliography." Subscribes to theory of Old World origins for Maya civilization. [REWA]

606. **Robertson, Merle Greene.** Monument thievery in Mesoamerica (SAA/AA, 37:2, Feb. 1972, p. 147-155, illus.)

Thefts of sculptured stone monuments are accelerating—18 of 50 Maya sites visited by Greene have been looted. Archaeological investigations will be hindered and tourism hurt if the robbery is not stopped. [REWA]

607. **Sabloff, Jeremy A.** and **Robert E. Smith.** Ceramic wares in the Maya area: a clarification of an aspect of the type-variety system and presentation of a formal model for comparative use (CEM/ECM, 8, 1970 [i.e., 1972] p. 97-115, illus.)

Argues that ceramic analysis should start from the ware level and proceed to types and varieties. A rationalistic and methodological model is presented stressing advantages in comparative studies. But notes that there are quite strong arguments against the use of ware as an analytical instead of an integrative device. [REWA]

608. **Sanders, William T.** Hydraulic agriculture, economic symbiosis and the evolution of states in Central Mexico (*in* Anthropological archaeology in the Americas. Washington, Anthropological Society of Washington, 1971, p. 88-107, bibl., maps)

Evolutionary theory on growth of Mesoamerican civilization, based on data from Teotihuacan Valley, attributes growth to interaction of: a) irrigation agriculture which implies supra-community social controls and b) economic specialization with regional markets that led to larger socio-economic groupings ("economic system symbiosis"). As civilization evolved on Central Plateau these symbiotic patterns spread to other ecological zones. [HvW]

609. **Schöndube B., Otto.** Arqueología de occidente: el territorio cultural del occidente y arqueología de Sinaloa. México, Museo Nacional de Antropología, Instituto Nacional de Arqueología e Historia, 1971. 31 p., table (Conferencias)

Up-to-date summary of archaeology and culture history of West Mexico. [HvW]

610. ———. La religión en el occidente de México (*in* Mesa Redonda de la Sociedad Mexicana de Antropología, XII, México, 1972. Religión en Mesoamérica. México, Sociedad Mexicana de Antropología, 1972, p. 357-363)

Religion in early period centered on a death cult embodied in ceramic tomb figures of West Mexico. Author lists 16 categories and discusses possible ritualistic aspects. After 900 A.D. pan-Mesoamerican religious and cosmogonic concepts prevailed and these are outlined for southern Jalisco, Colima and Michoacán. [HvW]

611. **Silva-Galdames, Osvaldo.** Trade and the

concept of nuclear and marginal culture areas in Mesoamerica (TU/CCM, 7 [Supplement] Oct. 1971, p. 74, bibl.)

Interesting and stimulating examination of role of trade in rise of Maya civilization. Internal trade between nuclear and marginal zones of Maya lowlands stimulated and augmented by trade with Teotihuacan, accounts for the rise of Maya high culture. Loss of Teotihuacan as a trading and cultural partner was a factor in the Maya collapse. Afterwards trade routes shifted away from the Petén zone and left it a backwater. [REWA]

612. Stug, David. Manuel Gamio, la escuela internacional y el origen de las excavaciones estratigráficas en las Américas (III/AI, 31:4, Oct. 1971, p. 825-844)

Historical perspective of Gamio's pioneer excavations (1910-20) and of personalities involved in beginning of systematic research to determine ceramic sequence of Valley of Mexico. [HvW]

613. Sturdevant, William D. The world of Aztec sculpture (AIA/A, 26:1, Jan. 1973, p. 10-15, illus.)

Concludes that most Aztec religious sculptures were designed according to a precise planimetric scheme which is absent in secular Aztec and "contemporary Tolteca" sculptures. [HvW]

614. Tibón, Gutierre. El mundo secreto de los dientes. México, Editorial Tajín, 1972. 277 p., bibl., illus.

Discursive elucidation of the symbolic significance of teeth, ornamental tooth mutilation and inlays, in Mexican and Mayan iconography. Includes world-wide ethnographic analogies. Summaries in German, French, English, Italian and Japanese. [HvW]

615. Toscano, Salvador. Arte precolombino de México y de la América Central. Prólogo de Miguel León-Portilla. Edición de Beatriz de la Fuente. 3. ed. México, UNAM, Instituto de Investigaciones Estéticas, 1970. 286 p., bibl., plates, table.

Text remains unchanged from 1952 ed. (see *HLAS 18/100*) and deals with regional styles in architecture, sculpture, painting, pottery, etc. It was updated by inclusion of over 400 notes and a revised bibliography. Several photographs were substituted. [HvW]

616. Tourtellot, Gair and Jeremy A. Sabloff. Exchange systems among the ancient Maya (SAA/AA, 37:1, Jan. 1972, p. 126-135, bibl., map, tables)

Due to relatively uniform environment of Maya lowlands, trade between communities was initially limited to prestige items, while subsistence items were circulated exclusively within communities. This led to development of a ranked society. State development only came under stimulus of already extant Mexican Highland states. Latter developed under stimulus of subsistence trade. Elegant and useful hypothesis. [REWA]

617. Tuggle, H. David. The structure of Tajin world-view (Anthropos [Internationale Zeitschrift für Völkerkunde, St. Augustin, FRG] 67, 1972, p. 435-448, illus.)

Author explores, in a well reasoned sequence, mythical contents of Tajín sculptural art. Concludes that depiction of opposing aspects in ball court panels (e.g., life/death dichotomy, pulque rituals, decapitation, etc.) is related to a dualistic world view, ultimately concerned with maintaining harmony in the universe. [HvW]

618. Weaver, Muriel Porter. The Aztecs, Maya and their predecessors: archaeology of Mesoamerica. N.Y., Seminar Press, 1972. 347 p., bibl., illus., maps, tables.

Well written general introduction, in one volume and in chronological sequence of culture periods, to the archaeology of Mesoamerica as a whole, with a chapter on problems and trends. Includes glossary and index. [HvW]

619. Westheim, Paul and others. Prehispanic Mexican art. Translated from the Spanish edition under the direction of Lancelot C. Sheppard. N.Y., Putnam's Son, 1972. 398 p., bibl., illus., maps, plates, tables.

Panoramic view of artistic creations with excellent photographs (225 in black-and-white, 193 color plates) and line drawings. Most objects are well known from other publications and are only occasionally referred to in text. No bibliographical references after 1960 are cited. Appendix includes chronological charts, maps showing cultural evolution, and architectural drawings. Includes index of illustration. Spanish ed. was published in México, Editorial Herrero, 1969. Contents:

Paul Westheim "Artistic Creation in Ancient Mexico" p. 11-82
Alberto Ruz "The Art of Ancient Mexico in Time and Space" p. 83-186
Pedro Armillas "Volume and Form in Native Art" p. 187-259
Ricardo de Robina "Prehispanic Architecture" p. 261-338
Alfonso Caso "Painting in Mesoamerica" p. 339-396. [HvW]

620. Wicke, Charles R. Olmec: an early art style of precolumbian Mexico. Foreword by Ignacio Bernal. Tucson, Ariz., The Univ. of Arizona Press, 1971. 188 p., bibl., illus., plates, tables.

Reviews history of Olmec research and applies Guttman scale analysis—developed for sociological studies to establish sequential development of colossal heads and votive axes. Develops two solid sequences for Olmec art and concludes that "late Olmec" (Covarrubias' "transitional style") can be tied to later artistic traditions (Classic Veracruz and Maya). Does not include studies after 1967. See also item 575. [HvW]

621. Wilken, Gene C. Food-producing systems available to the ancient Maya (SAA/AA, 36:4, Oct./Dec. 1971, p. 432-448, bibl., illus.)

Article by economist surveying possibilities for ancient intensive cultivation techniques in the Maya area. Wilken surveys highland zones for modern techniques and transposes these as possibilities into the lowland zones. Conclusion is that possibilities of ancient intensive agriculture should be seriously considered and investigated. Correct but somewhat naive in use and analysis of data. [REWA]

622. Williams, Stephen. Ripping off the past (Saturday Review of the Sciences [San Francisco, Calif.] 55:41/44, Oct. 1972, p. 44-53, illus.)

Explains that behind the genteel façade of the antiquities trade is a criminal network of supply. Examples from Maya area are given. Argues that adherence to UNESCO convention by Museums is necessary to cool off market. For more on this, see items 544-545 and 595. [REWA]

EXCAVATIONS AND ARTIFACTS

623. Adams, Richard E. W. Maya highland pre-history: new data and implications (UCARF/C, 16, 1972, p. 1-22, illus., maps, tables)

Data from Cotzal Valley in northern Guatemala indicates late beginning (protoclassic) to human occupation. Further work indicates similar situation elsewhere in north highlands and that therefore the earliest populations of the lowlands did not come from the highlands. But see item 698. [REWA]

624. Aguilera, Carmen. Una posible deidad negroide en el panteón azteca (UNAM/ECN,9, 1971, p. 47-56, illus.)

Describes prehispanic figures with Negroid features and suggests that they are related to the Tezcatlipoca cult. Similar representations appear in the codices. [HvW]

625. Armillas, Pedro. Gardens on swamps (AAAS/S, 174:4010, 12 Nov. 1971, p. 653-661, illus.)

Layout and extension of late postclassic *chinampas* in Valley of Mexico were determined through aerial photography and ground survey. Concludes that creation of highly productive farmland over marshes made region a key economic area that provided base for military expansion. [HvW]

626. Aveni, Anthony F. and Robert M. Sinsley. Mount J. Monte Alban: possible astronomical orientation (SAA/AA, 37:4, Oct. 1972, p. 528-531, illus.)

Investigation of astronomical phenomena in relation to structural details of Mound J indicate that some of the architectural features facilitate observation of certain stars on significant occasions. See also Anthony F. Aveni, "Astronomical Tables Intended for Use in Astro-Archaeological Studies," in same issue cited above, p. 531-540. [HvW]

627. Baer, Gerhard. Figuren und Gefässe aus Alt-Mexico; Keramik, Neuerwerbungen. Basel, Switzerland, Schweizerisches Museum für Völkerkunde, 1972. 1 v. (Unpaged) illus.

Guide to the 1972 exhibition of recent acquisitions with illustrations mainly of figurines from West Mexico. [HvW]

628. Ball, Joseph W. Ceramic sequence at Becan, Campeche, Mexico; Second (final) preliminary report: 1972 (TU/CCM, 8, 1972, p. 34-40, table)

Revision of Rio Bec regional ceramic sequence based on two seasons more of work. Quantities of ceramic complex samples are given. Sequence begins with a Chicanel related complex and ends with a late postclassic complex (Lobo). Becan fortress is early classic in date. Since this was written, a Mamon related, middle preclassic complex has been added. [REWA]

629. Bell, Betty. Archaeological excavations in Jalisco, Mexico (AAAS/S, 175:4027, 17 March 1972, p. 1238-1239, illus.)

First controlled excavation of a pair of "Zacatecas" horned figures indicated that this type originated near Teocaltiche, northeastern Jalisco. [HvW]

630. Benson, Elizabeth P. An Olmec figure at Dumbarton Oaks. Washington, Dumbarton Oaks, 1971. 39 p., bibl., illus. (Studies in precolumbian art and archaeology, 8)

Detailed description of a carved male figurine incised with numerous Olmec symbols. These are analyzed and similar occurrences are noted on a large number of Olmec artifacts. [HvW]

631. Bernal, Ignacio; Pedro Ramírez Vázquez; and Otto Schöndube. Colección arqueológica mexicana de Licio Lagos. México, Ediciones Offset Fersa, 1971. 101 p., plates.

I. Bernal and P. Ramírez V. preface the catalog (by O. Schöndube) of clay and stone sculptures from various areas, illustrated on 100 plates including some in color. Emphasis is on aesthetic impression. [HvW]

632. Blanton, Richard E. Prehispanic adaptation in the Ixtapalapa region, Mexico (AAAS/S, 175:4028, 24 March 1972, p. 1317-1326, illus.)

Offers hypothetical explanations for sociocultural changes in the settlement patterns and demographic data, based on ground survey in the Valley of Mexico. [HvW]

633. Borhegyi, Stephan F. de. Depósitos subterráneos en forma de botella y sonajas de barro del preclásico de Guatemala (CEM/ECM, 8, 1970 [i.e., 1972], p. 25-34, illus.)

Refutation of an interpretation by Rivard that two Las Charcas phase rattles indicate the worship of the death god in the preclassic, Borhegyi illustrates other material from a Las Charcas bottle shaped pit. [REWA]

634. Bray, Warwick. Ancient American metalsmiths (Proceedings [Royal Anthropological Institute of Great Britain and Ireland, London] 1971 [i.e., 1972] p. 25-43, illus., map, plates)

In this study of prehispanic American metallurgy in its wider context (the Curl Lecture for 1971), Bray reviews the technical aspects of metal production and considers the organization of trade. Considerable production was achieved by part-time miners using the simplest technology. Traveling smiths from South America likely introduced the craft to Mesoamerica. The idea is tested against archaeological evidence for metalworking in the Maya area and explains the distribution and peculiarities of style. Includes 21 plates. [REWA]

635. Breiner, Sheldon and **Michael D. Coe.** Magnetic exploration of the Olmec civilization (American Scientist [Burlington, Vt.] 60:5, Sept./Oct. 1972, p. 566-575, illus.)

Magnetic surveying at San Lorenzo was highly successful and resulted in discovery of 17 Olmec monuments, including some of the finest carvings known so far. Methods and results are outlined. [HvW]

636. Castillo Tejero, Noemí. Tecnología de una vasija en travertino (INAH/B, 41, sept. 1970, p. 48-52, illus., plates)

An unfinished ovoid travertine vessel from Tula yields clues for ancient stone working techniques. [HvW]

637. Charlton, Thomas H. El valle de Teotihuacán: cerámica y patrones de asentamiento, 1520-1969 (INAH/B, 41, sept. 1970, p. 15-23, bibl., illus., maps, tables)

Presents new data from excavations to determine changes in Aztec and postconquest occupation sites. [HvW]

638. Corona S., Eduardo. Hallazgo arqueológico en Tiristaran (INAH/B, 42, dic. 1970, p. 31-33, illus.)

Circular altars with upright anthropomorphic sculptures were found near Morelia, Michoacán. [HvW]

639. Davis, Emma Lou. Ancient man in Baja California (SM/M, 45:3, July/Sept. 1971, p. 102-107, illus.)

Stone tools from central peninsula indicate southward extension of the Lake Mojave lithic complex. [HvW]

640. Dyckerhoff, Ursula and **Hanns J. Prem.** Los petrograbados de Tecaltzingo (SSC/K, 7:4, June 1972, Unpaged, illus.)

Preliminary report on 10 rock carvings, reprinted from *Comunicaciones del Proyecto Puebla-Tlaxcala* (4, 1971, p. 1-3, illus.). Some design elements resemble the Olmec Chalcatzingo reliefs, see item 555. [HvW]

641. Eaton, Jack D. A report on excavations at Chicanna, Campeche, Mexico (TU/CCM, 8, 1972, p. 42-61, illus., map)

Very complete, valuable preliminary report on a Rio Bec site. Five groups of structures are late classic in date and have both Chenes and Rio Bec characteristics. A spectacular Chenes style palace with Itzamna doorway was excavated and restored. Eaton also reports extensive hillside terracing and ridged fields in the area. [REWA]

642. Ediger, Donald. The well of sacrifice. Garden City, N.Y., Doubleday, 1971. 288 p., illus., plates.

Journalistic account of the 1967-68 commercial expeditions to the Chichen well. Worthwhile for the 25 color illustrations of some magnificent polychrome painted pottery and gourds. Most skeletal material was of children 10 years and younger. Text is mainly of interest as an adventure story. Speckled with some chestbeating and inaccuracies. [REWA]

643. Eisleb, Dieter. Westmexikanische Keramik. Berlin, Museum für Völkerkunde, 1971. 75 p., bibl., map, plates (N.F. 14)

Well annotated catalog of figural art and pottery from West Mexico in the Berlin Museum, with excellent photographs (four in color) of 261 objects, most acquired before 1912. Chupícuaro and postclassic specimens are not included. [HvW]

644. Enciso, Jorge. Designs from precolumbian Mexico. N.Y., Dover Publications, 1971. 105 l., plates.

Includes publisher's note but no text and 105 plates of 300 designs drawn from decorations on spindle whorls. [HvW]

645. Flores García, Lorenza. Tres figurillas vestidas con piel de desollados (INAH/B, 42, dic. 1970, p. 43-46, illus.)

A male and two female (!) figurines with Xipe attributes from Tlatelolco were mutilated before burial. [HvW]

646. Folan, W. J. Un botellón monopodio del centro de Yucatán, Mexico (CEM/ECM, 8, 1970 [i.e., 1972] p. 67-75, illus.)

Monopod jar from a cave near Sacalum is similar to those claimed by Brainerd and others to be early preclassic in date. Comparative data is presented. But note that newest research indicates that the Yucatan earliest material is chimerical. [REWA]

647. Fuente, Beatriz de la. En torno a las nuevas cabezas olmecas (IIE/A, 10:40, 1971, p. 5-13, bibl., plates)

Discusses style and significance of Olmec colossal heads and reasons for their ritual mutilation. See also Carmen Aguilera de Litvak "Observaciones Acerca del Monumento 64 de La Venta" (*Boletín*, INAH, 2:1, abril/junio, 1972, p. 43, illus.) [HvW]

648. Gay, Carlo T. E. Xochipala, the beginnings of Olmec art. Published for the exhibition at The Art Museum, Princeton University, Jan. 11-13, 1972. Princeton, N.J., Princeton Univ., 1972. 61 p., bibl., illus., map.

First detailed report with a stylistic sequence of a "formative level Olmec" ceramic complex, discovered 1967 in northeastern Guerrero. Middle Xochipala figurines (ca. 1400-1200 B.C.), which were preceded by a remarkably naturalistic early phase portrait types (ca. 1500 B.C.) are suggested to be ancestral to related Central Highland and Gulf Coast ceramic traditions. Two to three centuries precedence of Xochipala over Gulf Coast manifestations revives the argument for a Guerrero origin of Olmec culture, supported by the author. Text is taken from a work in progress on preclassic ceramic figures from Central and Midwestern Mexico, by C. T. E. Gay and Frances Pratt. See also items 555 and 653. [HvW]

649. González Rul, Francisco. El encuentro Cortés-Moctezuma, rectificación histórica (INAH/B, 1 [2.época], abril/junio 1972, p. 15-18, illus.)

Archaeological evidence, obtained from Metro excavations, supplements historical data on the location of buildings in Tenochtitlan and clarifies the site where Cortés met Moctezuma. [HvW]

650. ———. El macuahuitl y el tlatzintepuzotilli: dos armas indígenas (INAH/A, 2 [7. época], 1969 [i.e., 1971], p. 147-152, illus.)

On the characteristics of Aztec obsidian—studded swords and lances. [HvW]

651. Gorenstein, Shirley. Archaeology, history and anthropology in the Mixteca-Puebla region of Mexico (SAA/AA, 36:3, July 1971, p. 335-343, illus.)

Evaluation of postconquest cultural change at Tepexi with consideration of archaeological and ethnohistorical data relating to the late postclassic period. For a comprehensive report, including data on architecture, ceramic and artifact analyses, see: "Tepexi el Viejo: a Postclassic Fortified Site in the Mixteca-Puebla Region of Mexico: pt. 1" (*Transactions of the American Philosophical Society*, 63, Feb. 1973, p. 1-75, bibl., illus., map) [HvW]

652. Graham, John A. and **Rainer Berger.** Radiocarbon dates from Copan, Honduras (UCARF/C, 16, 1972, p. 37-40)

Two dates associated with building phases under the hieroglyphic stairway indicate: a) an early classic midden below the construction (ca. 250 A.D.); and b) dating of construction immediately below stairway as 600 A.D. and compatible with the 11.16 correlation. [REWA]

653. Griffin, Gillet G. Xochipala, the earliest great art style in Mexico (APS/P, 116:4, Aug. 1972, p. 301-309, plates)

Concludes that the stylistic evolution of Xochipala (Guerrero) portrait figurines, which he considered to be "proto-Olmec", progressed from naturalism toward sterile abstraction. See also item 648 [HvW]

654. Grove, David C. and **Louise I. Paradis.** An Olmec stela from San Miguel Amuco, Guerrero (SAA/AA, 36:1, Jan. 1971, p. 95-102, illus.)

Description of a "colonial Olmec" style carved monument, so far the only known Olmec stela in central Mexico. In this context the diffusion of the Olmec art style is explained by a modified trade-route theory which also accounts for the socio-political relationships with local groups under temporary Olmec control. [HvW]

655. Gumerman, George J. and **James A. Neely.** An archaeological survey of the Tehuacan Valley, Mexico: a test of color infrared photography (SAA/AA, 37:4, Oct. 1972, p. 520-527, illus.)

Method and advantages of infrared color photography are detailed. It was found useful in delineation of microenvironments. [HvW]

656. Gussinyer, Jordi. Rescate arqueológico en la presa de la Angostura: primera temporada (INAH/B, 1 [2. época], abril/junio 1972, p. 3-14, illus.)

Preliminary report of salvage operations on the Grijalva River, Chiapas (1971), where 179 sites were located, ranging from early preclassic to 1524. Many indicate architectural remains, some are ceremonial centers and "verdaderas ciudades." [HvW]

657. Haberland, Wolfgang. Die Kunst des Indianischen Amerika; American Indian art. Zürich, Switzerland, Atlantis Verlag, 1970? 408 p., bibl., illus., maps, plates.

Well illustrated and amply commented catalogue of the fine collections in the Swiss Rietberg Museum, ranging from the Arctic to South America. Forty items from Mesoamerica (p. 101-196). Includes charts and index. Text in German and English. [HvW]

658. Hammond, Norman. A minor criticism of the Type-Variety system of ceramic analysis (SAA/AA, 37:3, July 1972, p. 450-452, table)

Argues from experience that types can most usefully be regarded as members of ceramic groups which are polythetically defined. [REWA]

659. Harrison, Peter D. In search of Tzibanche (Rotunda [Bulletin of the Royal Ontario Museum, Toronto] 5:4, 1972, p. 12-21, illus., map)

Well illustrated account of 1972 archaeological survey of southern Quintana Roo. Most sites, including Tzibanche, are classic period, despite Spanish reports of dense population in the 16th century. [REWA]

660. Heizer, Robert F. An unusual Olmec figurine (SM/M, 46:2, April/June 1972, p. 71-74, illus.)

Describes jade figurine of seated hunchback, probably representing a prisoner. [HvW]

661. ———— and **James A. Bennyhoff.** Archaeological excavations at Cuicuilco, Mexico, 1957 (Research Reports: 1955-1960 Projects [National Geographic Society, Washington] 6, 1972, p. 93-104)

Important summary of the prehistory of the Valley of Mexico in which the cultural sequence—from an early preclassic Tlalpan phase, 2000 B.C. to beginning of the classic—is clarified, particularly for the late and terminal preclassic. Cuicuilco dominated the valley during the entire late preclassic (600-200 B.C.) and declined with the emergence of Teotihuacan in the terminal preclassic (200 B.C.-A.D. 250). A preliminary report appeared under the same title in *Science* (127, 1958, p. 232-233). [HvW]

662. Hester, Thomas Roy. Hafted unifaces from southwestern Coahuila, Mexico, (AAHS/K, 36:4, Summer 1971, p. 36-41, illus.)

Two stone scrapers, attached to wooden shafts, from a burial cave near Torreón supply information on ancient hafting techniques. See also by same author "Some Perishable Artifacts from Southwestern Coahuila, Mexico" (*Masterkey*, 45:4, Oct/Dec. 1971, p. 138-145, illus.). [HvW]

663. ————. Notes on large obsidian blade cores and core-blade technology in Mesoamerica (UCARF/C, 14, 1972, p. 95-105, illus.)

Describes four macro-cores; three from Mayapan and one from Villahermosa. Analysis of techniques of blade manufacture. [REWA]

664. ———— and **Robert F. Heizer.** Problems in the functional interpretation of artifact scraper planes from Mitla and Yagul, Oaxaca (UCARF/C, 14, 1972, p. 107-123, plates)

Experimentation with, and technological examination of, obsidian scrapers suggest that they served to extract fibers from agave leaves. [HvW]

665. ————; **Robert N. Jack;** and **Robert F. Heizer.** The obsidian of Tres Zapotes, Mexico (UCARF/C, 13, June 1971, p. 65-131, illus., map, tables)

First technological and chemical analysis of artifacts collected 1939-40. See also in same issue Thomas R. Hester; Robert F. Heizer; and Robert N. Jack "Technology and Geologic Sources of Obsidian Artifacts from Cerro de las Mesas, Mexico, with Observations on Olmec Trade," p. 133-141. [HvW]

665a. ———; ———; and ———. Trace element analysis of obsidian from the site of Cholula (UCARF/C, 16, Oct. 1972, p. 105-110, illus.)

Quarries in Puebla and Hidalgo provided obsidian for blades and flakes from Cholula and Veracruz. See also in the same issue, Robert N. Jack; Thomas R. Hester; and Robert F. Heizer "Geological Sources of Archaeological Obsidian from Sites in Northern and Central Veracruz, Mexico" (p. 117-122, table). [HvW]

666. **Heyden, Doris.** Un adoratorio a Omacatl (INAH/B, 42, dic. 1970, p. 21-24, illus.)

Identifies upper structure of a building, discovered during Metro excavations, as an altar dedicated to Tezcatlipoca. The lower part was devoted to Tlaloc according to Gussinyer, see *HLAS 33:678*. [HvW]

667. ———. Comentarios sobre la Coatlicue recuperada durante las excavaciones realizadas para la construcción del Metro (INAH/A, 2 [7. época], 1969 [i.e., 1971], p. 153-170, illus.)

Iconographic analysis of an Aztec statue of the Coatlicue, discovered 1967, which incorporates numerous dualistic and bisexual traits. It is possibly the first known representation of Ometeotl. English summary. [HvW]

668. **Houston, Margaret** and **Judith Carson Wainer.** Pottery-making tools from the valley and coast of Oaxaca (CER/BEO, 36, julio 1971, p. 1-8, illus.)

On the use of postclassic *azotadores* and similar modern implements for shaping pottery on molds. [HvW]

669. **Johnson, Ann S.** Finger-loops and cruciform objects (SAA/AA, 36:2, April 1971, p. 188-194, illus., map)

Identifies artifacts from Sonora as parts of spear-throwers and reviews their distribution. [HvW]

670. **Kelly, Isabel.** Vasijas de Colima con boca de estribo (INAH/B, 42, dic. 1970, p. 26-30, illus.)

Author identifies, from recent (1970) excavations in Colima, an early preclassic pottery complex which includes a peculiar type (*boca estribo*) known to occur later in Tlatilco and Morelos, but much earlier in Ecuador (Machalilla phase). Considering Colima a probable way station for transmittal by sea of traits from South America to Morelos and Tlatilco, via El Opeño, Kelly challenges the peripheral character traditionally attributed to the West Coast in development of Mesoamerican cultures. [HvW]

671. **Krotser, Paula H.** and **G. R. Krotser.** The life style of El Tajín (SAA/AA, 38:2, April 1973, p. 199-205, maps)

Hypotheses derived from the 1969 season of mapping and excavations concerning the population, sustenance, pottery, and numerous habitation complexes which comprised a city of five km² around the Tajín ceremonial compound. [HvW]

672. **Lee, Thomas A., Jr.** Jmetic Lubton: some modern and prehispanic Maya ceremonial customs in the Highlands of Chiapas, Mexico (New World Archaeological Foundation Papers [Provo, Utah] 29, 1972, p. 1-28, illus., maps)

Report on salvage excavation of eight burials and a stone sculpture at a remote site in Maya Highlands. Modern burial customs and ceremonial patterns still practised by present-day inhabitants of the area are close to ancient ones and indicate a strong continuity with the late classic culture. [REWA]

673. **Leicht, Raymond C.** The Dos Peñas rock paintings: a local art style from the Chilapa region, Guerrero (SSC/K, 8:1, Aug. 1972, p. 58-69, illus.)

Describes four red painted designs, apparently late postclassic, and points out similarities with Hopi art. [HvW]

674. **López Austin, Alfredo.** Instrumental médico de cerámica (INAH/B, 42, dic. 1970, p. 13-17, illus.)

Describes small clay containers with tubular spouts used to administer medicines and refers to pertinent passages in the Florentine Codex. [HvW]

675. **Lorenzo, José H.** and **Lauro González Quintero.** El más antiguo teosinte (INAH/B, 42, dic. 1970, p. 41-43, illus.)

Earliest teosinte at Tlapacoya located with a radiocarbon date 7040 B.C. Teosinte did not occur at Tehuacan. [HvW]

676. **McBride, Harold W.** Teotihuacan style pottery and figurines from Colima (SSC/K, 7:3, Sept. 1969 [i.e., Summer 1971] p. 86-91, illus.)

Censers, moldmade figurines and earrings of Teotihuacan design from Colima indicate sustained late classic contact. [HvW]

677. **Malone, Michael D.** An ancient Mayan cave (CAS/PD, 24:6, 1971, p. 1-8, illus.)

Well illustrated article about discoveries of well preserved pottery, copper, wood and other artifacts in a British Honduras cave. Pottery indicates a date of 600-700 A.D. Ties in well with Pendergast's discoveries in adjacent caves and with the ritual complex of "zuhuy ha" or "pure water" collection. [REWA]

678. **Martí, Samuel.** Alt-Amerika, Musik der Indianer in Präkolumbischer Zeit. Leipzig, GDR, Deutscher Verlag für Musik, 1970. 193 p., bibl., illus., maps (Musik des Altertums, 2, Lieferung, 7)

Pictorial record, with extensive commentaries, of musical instruments in clay, wood, shell, etc., and of representations of musicians, from the entire continent with emphasis on Mesoamerica. Most of these objects were published in his previous works (*HLAS 33:573*). Includes chronological tables and index. For a popular version, see author's *La música precortesiana; Music before Cortés*, (México, Ediciones Euroamericanas Litexa, 1971. 75 p., illus.) [HvW]

679. Martínez del Río de Redo, Marita. Las jícaras de calabaza en el México prehispánico (ARMEX, 19:153, 1972, p. 5-14, bibl., illus.)

Summarizes data on cloisonné decorated gourds and traces survival of this technique through colonial to modern times. With English version. [HvW]

680. Meighan, Clement W. Archaeology of the Morett Site, Colima. Berkeley, Calif., Univ. of California, 1972. 211 p., bibl., illus., plates, tables (Publications in anthropology, 7)

Significant for being the northernmost known preclassic village site on the Mexican west coast, report covers pottery and figurine typologies for an early (300 B.C.-100 A.D.) and a late (150-750) occupation, based on unusually detailed chronologies obtained from radiocarbon and obsidian hidration dates, and ceramic seriation. Resemblances with pottery from Central and northern South America are discussed. Concludes that "the Colima coast was somewhat marginal to the development of Mesoamerican civilizations but by no means isolated and independent." Includes five appendices. [HvW]

681. Minería prehispánica en la Sierra de Querétaro. México, Secretaría del Patrimonio Nacional, 1970. 133 p., illus., maps.

Excavations near mine entrances produced significant preclassic and classic pottery including trade wares and carved stone yokes from Veracruz, which are described and profusely illustrated by José L. Franco Carrasco (p. 23-36). Fibre artifacts are described by Irmgard Weitlaner de Johnson (p. 35-44, illus.). The mines were exploited for cinnabar 500 B.C. (estimated date on account of Olmec traits) through 700 A.D. [HvW]

682. Mountjoy, Joseph B. A dated cruciform artifact? (AAHS/K, 36:4, Summer 1971, p. 42-46, illus.)

Obsidian fragment associated with carbon-dated marine shells (ca. 600-485 B.C.) from San Blas site. Upper stratum contained Early Ixtlán complex ceramics. [HvW]

683. ———; R. E. Taylor; and Lawrence Feldman. Matanchén Complex: new radiocarbon dates on early coastal adaptation in West Mexico (AAAS/S, 175:4027, 17 March 1972, p. 1242-1243)

Non-ceramic complex (ca. 2000 B.C.) in south-central Nayarit represents the earliest known coastal occupation in West Mexico north of Acapulco. [HvW]

684. Navarrete, Carlos. Fechamiento para un tipo de esculturas del sur de Mesoamérica (UNAM/AA, 9, 1972, p. 45-52, illus.)

Recent discovery of a small bearded stone figure on the Chiapas coast suggests a late protoclassic date, 1-100 A.D., for this type which includes men seated on a bench. [HvW]

685. ———. El sitio arqueológico de San Nicolás, Municipio de Ahuachapan, El Salvador (CEM/ECM, 8, 1970 [i.e., 1972] p. 57-66, illus.)

Reports test pitting of a small preclassic rural settlement; occupance from 800 B.C. to 200 A.D. Pottery illustrated, described, and compared. [REWA]

686. ——— and **Ana María Crespo.** Un atlante mexica y algunas consideraciones sobre los relieves del Cerro de la Malinche, Hidalgo (UNAM/ECN, 9, 1971, p. 11-15, illus.)

Stylistic distinctions between Toltec and Mexica sculptural art are outlined. The Tula rock carvings and a warrior statue, believed to be Toltec, are now attributed to the Mexica. [HvW]

687. Noguera, Eduardo. Antigüedad y significado de los relieves de Acalpixcan, D.F.—México (UNAM/AA, 9, 1972, p. 77-94, bibl., plates)

Adds a new interpretation to Beyer's and Krickeberg's of the 17 rock carvings near Xochimilco. Their late postclassic (Mexica) origin is deduced from seriation of surface sherds and written dynastic records. [HvW]

688. ———. Arqueología de la región tetzocana (ARMEX, 19:151, 1972, p. 75-96, illus.)

Description of architectural remains in the vicinity of Tetzcoco (Huexotla, Los Melones), in particular of Nezahualcoyotl's (1402-72) elaborate rock-cut bath installations at Teztcotzingo. Large quantities of Aztec III (Tenochtitlan type) pottery were excavated at Los Melones in 1967. With English translations and French summary. [HvW]

689. Ochoa Salas, Lorenzo. Una representación solar en un plato de la Huasteca (INAH/B, 42, dic. 1970, p. 3-8, illus.)

Description of the Mixteca-Puebla type design on a polychrome plate made in San Luis Potosí. [HvW]

690. ———. Representaciones fálicas de Ehecatl-Quetzalcoatl en el Centro de Veracruz (INAH/A, 2 [7. época] 1969 [i.e., 1971], p. 171-179, illus.)

Description of postclassic figurines, handmodeled in a regional style, with buccal mask and phallic symbols. [HvW]

691. Parsons, Jeffrey R. Prehistoric settlement patterns in the Texcoco region, Mexico. With contributions by Richard E. Blanton and Mary H. Parsons. Ann Arbor, Mich., Univ. of Michigan, 1971. 390 p., bibl., illus., maps, tables (Memoirs of the Museum of Anthropology, 3)

Objectives of the 1967 segment of the Texcoco Region Project, which followed aims and methodology of the Teotihuacan Valley Project (see item 696), were to delineate settlement configurations from the middle preclassic to contact. This first report contains detailed site descriptions in chronological arrangement and comparisons with other regions of the Basin of Mexico. Ceramic analyses and descriptions of the *tlateles* (mounds) are presented in the appendices. Includes glossary and two appendices. [HvW]

692. Pendergast, David M. Altun Ha, Honduras Britanica (Belize): temporadas 1966-1968 (CEM/ECM, 8, 1970[i.e., 1972] p. 35-56, bibl., illus., map)

Data paper giving detailed summary of three season's results. Altun Ha was probably the source of seashells so ritually important to the inland Maya. Middle classic housing is common and of great interest. Teotihuacan presence in the early classic is indicated. Reports series of tombs with sumptuous offerings, including the famous sun-god jade head. Important. [REWA]

693. ———. Evidence of early Teotihuacan-lowland Maya contact at Altun Ha (SAA/AA, 36:4, Oct. 1971, p. 455-460, illus.)

"Discovery of typical Miccaotli phase (150-200 A.D.) offering at Altun Ha, British Honduras (Belize) indicates contact between Teotihuacan and central Maya lowlands in second century A.D., 2. 5 to 3 centuries earlier than previously recognized." Green obsidian human figurines, lance blades and points are included in the cache. [REWA]

694. Piña Chan, Román. Informe preliminar de la reciente exploración del cenote sagrado de Chichen Itzá. México, Museo Nacional de Antropología, Instituto Nacional de Arqueología e Historia, 1970. 24 p., illus., maps (Serie investigaciones, 24)

Report on 1967 INAH/CEDAM project at giant sinkhole used for ceremonial offerings in ancient times. Review of previous work is followed by discussion of project research design and logistics. Excavation of sweatbath on the cenote edge is described. Very summary description and discussion of artifacts recovered is illustrated by general photographs. Most pottery late classic and postclassic in date, and most of skeletal material is of children. For color photos of exquisite painted gourds see Ediger (item 642). [REWA]

695. Robles Ortiz, Manuel and **Francisco Manzo Taylor.** Clovis fluted points from Sonora, Mexico (AAHS/K, 37:4, Summer 1972, p. 199-206, illus.)

Discovery of eight Clovis points and a lithic workshop north of Carbó. [HvW]

696. Sanders, William T.; Anton Kovar; Thomas H. Charlton; and **Richard A. Diehl.** The Teotihuacan Valley Project: final report. v. 1: The natural environment, contemporary occupation and 16th-century population in the valley. University Park, Pa., The Pennsylvania State Univ., Dept. of Anthropology, 1970. 457 p., bibl., maps, plates, tables (mimeo) (Occasional papers in anthropology, 3)

Contains six articles, not all of which are confined to Teotihuacan, but dealing with the larger unit, the Basin of Mexico. Five additional volumes are planned. For "Preliminary Reports" see *HLAS 29:708-709,* also item 637 this volume. [HvW]

697. Saul, Frank P. The human skeletal remains of Altar de Sacrificios. Appendix by Donald Austin. Cambridge, Mass., Harvard Univ., Peabody Museum, 1972. 123 p., illus., maps, tables (Papers of the Peabody Museum, 63:2)

Excellent analysis leading to important conclusions about health status, genetic continuity, longevity and other physical matters. Health status was precarious at all times; anemia, syphilis or yaws, and chronic malnutrition being evident, in addition to traumas. Malnutrition is reflected in the steady decline in stature through time. Saul suggests that health problems were important in the collapse of Maya civilization. [REWA]

698. Sedat, David W. and **Robert J. Sharer.** Archaeological investigations in the northern Maya highlands: new data on the Maya preclassic (UCARF/C, 16, 1972, p. 23-35, illus., maps)

Preliminary work at Sakajut indicates that there was preclassic population about the Coban region. A protoclassic stela found near Salama indicates sophisticated later development. Infers that highlands played a crucial role in development of lowland Maya civilization. [REWA]

699. Sheets, Payson D. An ancient natural disaster (UMUP/E, 14:1, Fall 1971, p. 24-31, illus., map)

Eruption of Ilopango Volcano in the 2d century A.D., probably drove the culturally sophisticated occupants to other lands. Ceramics indicate that people from around the preclassic ceremonial center of Chalchuapa, Salvador, may be responsible for the sudden appearance of protoclassic phases on the peripheries of the Maya lowlands. [REWA]

700. ———. A model of Mesoamerican obsidian technology based on Preclassic workshop debris in El Salvador (TU/CCM, 8, 1972, p. 17-33, illus.)

Analyzes 2500 pieces of obsidian artifacts excavated from a late preclassic deposit for manufacturing techniques. A model, complete with flow chart, is presented of manufacturing steps and the material from which it was derived is presented in detail. [REWA]

701. Siemens, Alfred H. and **Dennis E. Puleston.** Ridged fields and associated features in southern Campeche: new perspectives on the lowland Maya (SAA/A, 37:2, Feb. 1972, p. 228-239, illus., maps)

Important report on evidence for intensive agriculture along the Candelaria River. Canals were used for access from the river to firm ground and as shortcuts. Ridged field complexes are quite extensive, indicate a high population density, and date from terminal classic and postclassic times. This region is the location of the 16th-century province of Acalan crossed by Cortes. [REWA]

702. Simposio del Proyecto Puebla-Tlaxcala, I, Puebla, Mex., 1973. [Papers.] Edited by Wilhelm Lauer and Erdmann Gormsen. Puebla, Mex., Fundación Alemana para la Investigación Científica, 1973. 161 p., bibl., illus., maps, plates, tables (Comunicaciones, 7)

Contains 34 papers to be presented at the symposium of the multi-disciplinary research project, now in its 10th year. Following deal with archaeology:
Bodo Spranz "El Preclásico en la Arqueología del Proyecto Puebla-Tlaxcala" p. 63-64
Florencia Muller "La Extensión Arqueológica de Cholula a Través del Tiempo: Resumen" p. 65
Angel García Cook "El Desarrollo Cultural Prehispánico del Area, Intento de una Secuencia Cultural" p. 67-71
Horst Kern "Estudios Geográficos Sobre Residuos de Poblados y Campos en el Valle de Puebla-Tlaxcala" p. 73-76

E. Seele "Restos de Milpas y Poblaciones Prehispánicas Cerca de San Buenaventura Nealtican, Pue." p. 77-86. [HvW]

703. Sisson, Edward B. First annual report of the Coxcatlan Project. Andover, Mass., Robert S. Peabody Foundation, Phillips Academy, 1973. 108 p., bibl., illus., maps.

Projected four-year multidisciplinary study of postclassic "city state" of Coxcatlan, Puebla, is a continuation of MacNeish's Tehuacan Valley Project. This report, which covers 1971-72 seasons, outlines objectives and describes surveys and excavations of multichambered structures. [HvW]

704. Smith, A. Leydard. Excavations at Altar de Sacrificios: architecture, settlement, burials, and caches. Three appendixes, A and B by Smith and C by Edwin R. Littman. Cambridge, Mass., Harvard Univ., Peabody Museum, 1972. 282 p., illus., maps, tables (Papers of the Peabody Museum, 62:2)

Exhaustive report presenting a mass of fundamental stratigraphic and structural data well illustrated by drawings and photos. Civic architecture was characterized by earthen platforms with stone casings and perishable super structures. Ceremonial groups appear as early as middle preclassic. All 41 domestic house platforms were excavated and 136 burials recovered; these are described and discussed. Caches are compared in their patterns with others from the Maya area. Packed with well organized and cross referenced data. [REWA]

705. Spence, Michael W. Some lithic assemblages of Western Zacatecas and Durango. Carbondale, Ill., Southern Illinois Univ., 1971. 50 p., bibl., illus., tables (Mesoamerican studies. Research records, 8)

Description and classification of chipped stone artifacts with reference to their cultural context. [HvW]

706. ———; Jeffrey R. Parsons; and Mary Hrones Parsons. Miscellaneous studies in Mexican prehistory. Ann Arbor, Mich., Univ. of Michigan, Museum of Anthropology, 1972. 170 p., bibl., illus., tables (Anthropological papers, 45)

Contains: 1) Michael W. Spence and Jeffrey R. Parsons "Prehispanic Obsidian Exploitation in Central Mexico," with appendix by George Fraunfelter, p. 1-43. This is a significant discussion of the location of obsidian quarries and workshops; specialization and preferential utilization of green and gray obsidian for production of cores, blades, etc.; archaeological and ethno-historical evidence of long distance trade and regional redistribution. Some basic characteristics of classic Teotihuacan obsidian industry are evident in the postclassic Aztec period. 2) Mary Hrones Parsons, "Spindle Whorls from the Teotihuacan Valley, Mexico," p. 45-79. Deals with classifications according to size and decoration with observations concerning the use of these mostly postclassic spindle whorls for domestic (maguey) or imported (cotton) fibers. Author's appendix, "A Comparison with Spindle Whorls from the Texcoco Region Survey, 1967." 3) Mary Hrones Parsons "Aztec Figurines from the Teotihuacan Valley, Mexico," p. 81-170. A classification of figurines by functional and iconographic characteristics. Notes that fertility and rain deities, but no celestial gods, are represented. Similarities among figures from marginal areas with those of the Aztec strong-hold suggest mass production in, and distribution from, specialized areas. [HvW]

707. Spores, Ronald. An archaeological settlement survey of the Nochixtlan Valley, Oaxaca. Nashville, Tenn., Vanderbilt Univ., 1972. 206 p., bibl., illus., maps (Publications in anthropology, 1)

Ceramic classification and site descriptions with a developmental interpretative synthesis of sociopolitical, economic and demographic factors. [HvW]

708. Spranz, Bodo. Ergebnisse und Probleme der Erforschung vorspanischer Kulturen Mexicos (SJUG, 4, 1971, p. 326-333, map, illus.)

Summary of results of the German Puebla-Tlaxcala Project excavation of a pyramid at Totimehuacan (1964-70) with a unique interior system of passageways and chambers, carbon-dated 545±50 B.C. Finds include early preclassic Olmecoid pottery (see *HLAS 33:624*); Teotihuacan II pottery in an earlier context than at Teotihuacan; and a local variant of Teotihuacan IV ceramics. [HvW]

709. ———. Nuevas excavaciones en Tlaxcala (INAH/B, 41, sept. 1970, p. 1-3, plates)

Discovery of unusual Teotihuacanoid hollow figurines of females with a child inside. A color plate of these appeared without commentary in INAH's *Boletin* (40, June 1970). [HvW]

710. Stocker, Terrance L. and Michael W. Spence. Trilobal eccentrics at Teotihuacan and Tula (SAA/AA, 38:2, April 1973, p. 195-199, illus.)

Discussion of meaning and distribution of M-shaped obsidian artifacts and related motifs as supporting evidence for cultural continuity between Teotihuacan and Tula. [HvW]

711. Troike, Rudolph C.; Nancy P. Troike; and John A. Graham. Preliminary report on excavations in the archaeological zone of Rioverde, San Luis Potosí, Mexico (UCARF/C, 16, Oct. 1972, p. 69-87, illus.)

Excavations (in 1957) of a site significant for its abundance of stone masonry mounds, with evidence of ball courts and ceramic ties with the Pánuco sequence. [HvW]

712. Tuggle, H. David. El significado del sangrado en Mesoamérica: la evidencia de El Tajín (INAH/B, 42, dic. 1970, p. 33-38, illus.)

Iconographic interpretation of a Ball Court relief panel with reference to Mesoamerican blood-letting rituals and associated symbolism. [HvW]

von Schuler-Schömig, Immina. Werke indianischer Goldschmiedekunst. See item 533.

713. von Winning, Hasso. Keramische Hausmodelle aus Nayarit, Mexiko (MV/BA, 19:2, 1971, p. 343-377, illus.)

Forty-four animated clay house models and several

village scenes from Nayarit are described in detail and it is suggested that the inspiration for their manufacture originated in China. [HvW]

714. ———. Relief-decorated pottery from Central Veracruz, Mexico: Addenda (SEM/E, 36:1/4, 1971, p. 38-51, illus.)

Iconographic interpretation of complex ritualistic scenes on five moldmade relief bowls. See also *HLAS 29:907*. [HvW]

715. ——— and Olga Hammer. Anecdotal sculpture of ancient West Mexico: exhibition sponsored by the Ethnic Arts Council of Los Angeles at the Natural History Museum of Los Angeles County, 1972. Los Angeles, Calif., Ethnic Arts Council, 1972. 96 p., bibl., illus., map, plates, tables.

Catalog illustrating 205 ceramic house models and figurine groups attached to clay slabs. Includes two articles by Hasso von Winning: "Ceramic House Models and Figurine Groups Mounted on Slabs" (p. 17-30), a discussion of house models and of the ceremonial connotation of village, family, ball court, and processional scenes; and "Ritual 'Bed Figures' from Mexico" (p. 31-41) dealing with figures lying supine on a slab, including elaborate forms from classic Veracruz which are related to pulque rituals [HvW]

716. Voorhies, Barbara. Settlement patterns in two regions of the southern Maya lowlands (SAA/AA, 37:1, Jan. 1972, p. 115-126, bibl., maps, tables)

Data from the Izábal zone indicates that no major ceremonial centers existed and that population was sparser than in the Petén. Occupation was along waterways, and began in Chicanel times, terminating with late classic. Flint is scarce in the zone. [REWA]

717. Walter, Heinz. Cerámica preclásica de M. Negrete, Estado de Puebla, México (IAIC/CPPT, 3, 1971, p. 40-54, illus.

Detailed analysis of a surface collection showing relations to Monte Albán and middle preclassic Valley of Mexico ceramics. Reprinted in *Katunob* (7:4, June 1972, p. 40-50, illus) [HvW]

718. Wilkerson, S. Jeffrey K. Un yugo "in situ" de la región del Tajín (INAH/B, 41, sept. 1970, p. 41-45, illus.)

Description of a burial offering consisting of a late classic carved yoke and other artifacts, including a copper tube. [HvW]

719. Willey, Gordon R. The Altar de Sacrificios excavations: general summary and conclusions. Cambridge, Mass., Harvard Univ., Peabody Museum, 1973. 85 p., bibl., maps, tables (Papers of the Peabody Museum, 64:3)

Begins with a recapitulation, followed by phase-by-phase descriptive historical reconstruction. Deals with problems of Thompson's Putun (Chontal) Maya and their possible role in the Maya collapse. Discussion of culture changes and their implications. Contrasts initial orientation of project and its accomplishments. Final section on culture process deals with egalitarian to non-egalitarian social developments in Maya history. Balanced and knowledgeable discussion and capsulized presentation of large bodies of data. Very important. [REWA]

720. ———. The artifacts of Altar de Sacrificios. Cambridge, Mass., Harvard Univ. Peabody Museum, 1972. 312 p., illus. (Papers of the Peabody Museum, 64:1)

"A full description of pottery figurines and miscellaneous ceramic artifacts, and all stone and shell and other artifacts. The report includes the proveniences and phase datings of all these items, and comparative analyses of artifacts at Altar with relation to other Maya lowland artifact collections." Together with the appearance of the *General summary*, this completes the Altar publication series. Includes 233 figures. [REWA]

NATIVE SOURCES, EARLY HISTORY AND EPIGRAPHY

721. Barthel, Thomas S. Asiatische Systeme im Codex Laud (MLV/T, 21, 1972, p. 97-128, illus.)

The first (published) systematic approach to analyze the iconographic structure of Laud, of which only one section (38-33) is paralleled in other codices. Barthel explicitly investigates positional arrangement of icons, calendar signs, numbers (dots), ornaments (eardiscs, gold beads) and elucidates their hidden numerical relationships, planetary associations, and their sequential and directional order. He finds overwhelming substantial evidence of Asiatic prototypes, in some cases perfectly matching concordances, in other cases adaptations to the Mesoamerican tradition. Preliminary conclusions indicate that section 38-33 is based on Hinduistic astronomical concepts. Section 16-9, suggests a mixture with Chinese religious concepts, whereas section 24-17 reveals an Indonesian base. This article will be concluded in the forthcoming issue of *Tribus*, "Informationsverschlüsselungen im Codex Laud" (22, 1973). [HvW]

722. Coe, Michael D. Ancient Maya writing and calligraphy (Visible Language [Cleveland Museum of Art, Ohio] 5:4, 1971, p. 293-307, illus.)

"Maya hieroglyphic writing was carved on stone monuments, written in bark-paper codices, and painted or carved upon funerary pottery. The stone inscriptions . . . contain dynastic histories. The codices treat of ritual matters, while the texts and pictures on the pottery are concerned with the perilous voyage of the soul to the underworld. The script evolved from a highly pictographic system into one that had a strong phonetic-syllabic component. As calligraphy, Maya writing was a basically painterly art." Neat and important. [REWA]

723. Dütting, Dieter. On the inscription and iconography of Kuna-Lacanha Lintel: pt. 1 (DGV/ZE, 95:2, 1970, p. 196-219, illus., tables)

"If the inscription of Kuna-Lacanha lintel 1 is . . . concerned with procreation . . . , then the ceremony with the ceremonial bar must be a rite which has been performed to renew the creative actions of the deities of the earth and the sky. Procreation (renewal) of life, the result of the interaction of the male and the female principle, seems to be the idea behind the ceremonial bar and double headed serpent motifs found so frequently in Maya art . . ." Interesting and significant. [REWA]

724. Escalante, Roberto. Análisis de estructuras en el Códice de Dresde. México, UNAM, Coordinación de Humanidades, Centro de Estudios Mayas, 1971. 90 p., bibl., illus., tables (Cuaderno, 4)

The achievement of a syntactic model of the language used in the Dresden Codex is proposed by means of classification of the parts of glyphs, glyphic compounds, glyph clauses, and other morphological structures. Such a model has been developed and is being compared with the linguistic models derived from such sources as the Chilam Balam texts. Valuable and well illustrated. Compare with the ethnohistorical and ritual interpretative approach of Thompson's recent commentary, item 733. For ethnohistorian's annotation of this volume, see *HLAS 34:1040*. [REWA]

725. Graham, John A. The hieroglyphic inscriptions and monumental art of Altar de Sacrificios. Cambridge, Mass., Harvard Univ., Peabody Museum, 1972. 122 p., illus., map, tables (Papers of the Peabody Museum, 64:2)

Well illustrated final report emphasizing chronological and lunar series information from the Altar monuments. Extensive damage to non-calendrical glyphs precluded much reading of historical data. Such as there is will be presented in the future study of Seibal texts. [REWA]

726. ———. A Maya hieroglyph incised on shell (UCARF/C, 13, 1971, p. 155-159, illus.)

Analysis of a single hieroglyph on a shell "button" indicates that it is likely a name, and possibly a personal name. [REWA]

727. ———. Non-classic inscriptions and sculptures at Seibal (UCARF/C, 13, 1971, p. 143-153)

Preliminary analysis of the 10th-cycle sculptures at Seibal. Non-classic features are seen related to the fine orange pottery in human figures as well as in glyphs. Of particular interest is the apparent surrender of a Maya lord to a Yucatec-appearing warrior in Stela 17. Well illustrated and highly important. Includes appendix. [REWA]

728. ———. Two unusual Maya stelae (UCARF/C, 13, 1971, p. 161-166, illus.)

Ichpaatun Stela 1 is of a schistic stone (phyllonite) probably quarried about 100 miles south in the Maya Mountains. Calakmul Stela 9 is a semi-schist also derived from the same source. Both monuments were likely transported along the coast and one left at Ichpaatun and the other carried 100 miles inland to Calakmul. [REWA]

729. Kelly Owen, Nancy. On the reconstruction of calendarical [sic] sections of the Mayan codices (CEM/ECM, 8, 1970 [i.e., 1972] p. 175-203, tables)

Valuable study on recurrent patterns of day names in the codices. These sets can be used to reconstruct the calendrical section of any page with one day sign and enough numbers to elicit the interval. "An index is (presented) which lists the appropriate sets associated with each page of the Madrid and Dresden Codices, and complete readings of certain calendar sections are presented for the first time." [REWA]

730. Riese, Berthold and Ingeborg Schaumann. Tikal Stele 31: Entzifferung der kalendarischen Daten. Hamburg, FRG, Forschungsstelle für Altamerikanische Sprachen-und-Kulturen, 1972. 17 p., tables (Materialen der Hamburger Maya Inschriften Dokumentation, 1)

Decipherment of the important inscription on Tikal Stela 31. All dates are listed with alternative readings. A proposed Distance Number Introducing Glyph is discussed with incidental observations on the dates. [REWA]

731. Schulz Friedmann, Ramón P. C. El punto cero de la cuenta larga maya y las inscripciones astronómicas de Palenque (CEM/ECM, 8, 1970 [i.e., 1972] p. 167-174)

Study of certain recurrent cycles in Palenque texts and their significance. A short note on Dresden Codex eclipse series of dates ends the article. [REWA]

732. Smiley, Charles H. Los numerales de las serpientes en el Códice de Dresden: un nuevo enfoque (CEM/ECM, 8, 1970 [i.e., 1972] p. 161-165, tables)

Using the Smiley correlation, new moon appearances seem to be the purpose of the "serpent-number" calculations. These link the lunar data to equinoxes, solstices, and to dates of planetary conjunctions with the sun. [REWA]

733. Thompson, J. Eric S. A commentary on the Dresden Codex. Philadelphia, Pa., The American Philosophical Society, 1972. 156 p., facsim., tables (Memoirs, 93)

Dresden is a book of ancient divination mostly consisting of elaborate mechanisms foretelling good or bad luck of particular days. 76 almanacs are arranged into groups; some associated with the Moon Goddess, and the planet Venus, others are Farmers' Almanacs and others miscellaneous. There are also mathematical tables in aid of calculation, prophecies for the 20 year katun periods, the record of a torrential downpour, and a guide to New Years' ceremonies. Probably written ca. 1250 A.D. at Chichen Itza. Filled with new readings of Maya hieroglyphs. Must be used with Thompson's *Maya hieroglyphic writing*, and *A Catalog of Maya hieroglyphs*. Authoritative, perceptive and dogmatic commentary. Facsimile is disappointing in colors and detail, although adequate. Includes appendix and hieroglyphic glossary. [REWA]

734. ———. Maya hieroglyphs without tears. London, The British Museum, The Ethnography Dept., 1972. 84 p., illus., maps.

Updated reprise of the principles of Maya hieroglyphic writing as given in Thompson's *Maya hieroglyphic writing*. Emphasizes calendrics, divination and ritual. Well illustrated. Lacks any discussion of Proskouriakoff's revolutionary discoveries of the historical content of Maya texts. [REWA]

735. ———. Preliminary decipherments of Maya glyphs 6. Essex, England, Ashdon, Saffron Walden, 1971. 2 p.

Final item in the series anticipating the publication of Thompson's commentary on the Dresden Codex (see item 733). [REWA]

736. Thurber, Floyd and Valerie Thurber.

Algunos antiguos conceptos mítico-teológicos mayas expresados jeroglíficamente como componentes del gilfo Kayab (CEM/ECM, 8, 1970 [i.e., 1972] p. 205-215, illus.)

Study of the 19th-Month sign, Kayab, and an attempt to identify its mystical and esoteric values from an ancient Maya scribal viewpoint. [REWA]

ARCHAEOLOGY: CARIBBEAN AREA

RIPLEY P. BULLEN

Curator, Florida State Museum
University of Florida

DURING 1971 AND 1972 the French Archaeological Commission expanded their activities on the Azuero Peninsula of Panama and near Lake Yojoa, Honduras. Olga Linares has continued work in Panama under a National Science Foundation grant and there is also evidence of work by the Associated Colleges of the Midwest. We are sorry to note the damage to the archaeological museum in Guatemala City.

In the Antilles two new museums were under construction in 1972. The first is the Museo del Hombre Dominicano in Santo Domingo, José A. Caro Alvarez director, and was dedicated in Oct. 1973. This large four story museum is devoted to archaeology and ethnology. Its activities include an active program of archaeological research, conservation, and restoration; its first two publications are reviewed below.

The other museum, under the auspices of the newly formed Fundación Arqueológica, Antropológica e Histórica de Puerto Rico, was dedicated 27 Jan. 1973 in San Juan. At the same time a symposium, to be published later, was held on the preceramic cultures of the Caribbean region. The Fundación has started publication of a *Boletín Informativo* of which three numbers have been issued. They include not only items of Fundación business but also short popular articles on unique or important specimens and field work. Mention was made in the last issue of the *Handbook* of the then new Musée Departemental at Fort-de-France, Martinique. Since then exhibits have been completed on the first two floors under the expert supervision of Mario Mattioni, director. These include magnificent examples of Insular and Modified Saladoid vessels dated ca. A.D. 150-600. Artistically these represent the apogee of Antillean ceramic art and compare favorably with any but the highest Mayan attainments. The Musée has continued its work at Vivé, partly in collaboration with the Florida State Museum, University of Florida, and with the Department of Anthropology at the University of Montreal.

We should also mention the 1972 "Caribbean Splendors" exhibit at the University Museum, Philadelphia. Alfredo E. Figueredo has been appointed archaeologist of the Government of the American Virgin Islands. Regrettably, Neville Connell, long time director of the Barbados Museum, recently passed away. The V International Congress for the Study of the Pre-Columbian Cultures of the Lesser Antilles was held on Antigua in July 1973.

CENTRAL AMERICA

737. Baudez, Claude F. and **Pierre Becquelin.** Recherches archéologiques dans la région du Lac de Yojoa, Honduras (SA/J, 57, 1968, p. 135-138).

Brief progress report following period designations presented at the XXXVIII International Congress of Americanists (see *HLAS 33:*825). Gives some ideas of small acropoles and their attendant structures. Hopefully, the full report on this important work will appear in the near future.

738. Contreras, José del C. Importancia de los sitios arqueológicos y sus derivaciones culturales en la prehistoria de Panamá. Bogotá, Ediciones Guadalupe, 1971. 63 p., bibl., illus., plates, tables.

Illustrated 41 stone, tumbaga, and ceramic artifacts from Panama. Presents outline of Panamanian prehistory and lists of important sites. Brief paragraphs cover paleo-Indian, preceramic, and agricultural-ceramic periods (last has a trait list).

739. Dade, Philip L. Archaeology and pre-Columbian art in Panama (SEM/E, 37:1/4, 1972, p. 148-167, bibl., maps, plates)

Author believes polychrome vessels from Veraguas and Coclé, 500-1200 A.D., separable basis paste and shape (Veraguas pedestal plates and loop-leg bowls vs. Coclé ring-base plates and bowl or carafe) and that Indians from former conquered those of latter area about 1200 A.D. ending major Coclé period. Late Coclé graves hence are those of intrusive Veraguans! Such inferences of culture dynamics are stimulating.

740. ———. Bottles from Parita, Panama (AIA/A, 25:1, Jan. 1972, p. 35-43, map, plates)

Describes and illustrates 31 polychrome bottles—stingray and decorated neck types—from Juan Calderón site, Parita, Pan. Includes only stingray vessels exhibiting heads, fins, and separate tails.

741. Haberland, Wolfgang. Doppel-Tecomates im südlichen Mittelamerika (MV/BA, 19:2, June 1971 [i.e., 1972] p. 311-320, bibl., illus., map, plates)

Author compares double *tecomate* bowls to show cultural connections between western Costa Rica and south central Panama. Plates one and two seem to be slightly different views of the same vessel suggesting one of them is in error.

742. Ichon, Alain. La mission archéologique française au Panama (SA/J, 57, 1968, p. 139-143, map)

Presents preliminary results first season's work in Tonosi region, Azuero Peninsula. Apparently, lowest levels of strata-tests relates to an early formative period with incised, punctuated, and simple appliqué decoration. This is followed by apparently negatively painted polychrome pottery and then by grayish pottery having pedestal and annular ring bases. Finally, there is a late "Búcaro" phase which lasts into colonial period.

743. Lange, Frederick W. and Kristin K. Scheidenhelm. The salvage archaeology of a zoned bichrome cemetery, Costa Rica (SAA/AA, 37:2, April 1972, p. 240-245)

Work at a *huaqueros* exploited cemetery (65 out of 80 tombs) produced useful data including limitations of its use to the zoned bicrome period (300 B.C. to 300 A.D.) and discovery of jade amulet. Work was restricted to previously opened tombs. Careful survey failed to reveal a zone bichrome habitation site in the surrounding region.

Linares de Sapir, Olga. Patrones de poblamiento prehispánico comparados con los modernos en Bocas del Toro, Panamá. See item 1071.

744. Stewart, Robert. Evidencias geológicas del hombre primitivo en Panamá (III/AI, 32:1, enero/marzo 1972, p. 31-36)

Interesting article covering rise and rates of rise of sea level off Panama for last 11,000 years. Suggests Clovis point found in Madden Lake dates to more than 6300 before present.

745. Stone, Doris Z. Pre-Columbian man finds Central America: the archaeological bridge. Cambridge, Mass., Harvard Univ., Peabody Museum Press, 1972. 231 p., bibl., illus., maps, plates, tables.

Extremely well illustrated book which presents a semi-popular account of culture change and interaction in Central America. Data is allocated to areas and emphasis is on trade and diffusion. Includes many excellent illustrations not readily available elsewhere.

746. Torres de Araúz, Reina. Culturas prehispánicas del Darién (UNCIA/HC, 2:2, dic. 1971, p. 7-39, bibl., illus., plates)

Good resumé of archaeological work done in Darién province, Pan., including lists of sites investigated. Of interest chiefly to the archaeological historian as findings are not presented.

747. ———. Natá prehispánico. Panamá, Univ. de Panamá, Centro de Investigaciones Antropológicas, 1972. 140 p., bibl., illus., maps, plates (Publicación especial, 3)

Special publication referring to the Nata-Coclé area of Panama and divided into five parts: Ecology of the region; brief description of Conte site with diagrams of tombs 5, 26, 38, and 39; discussion of Nata-Coclé culture; good coverage of early contact period; and a large "Appendix General" covering ethnological matters of early Colonial times. A useful, interesting publication.

Vargas Arenas, Iraida. La fase El Cuartel. See item 1022.

WEST INDIES

748. *Boletín del Museo del Hombre Dominicano.* **Instituto de Cultura Dominicana.** No. 1, 1972- . Santo Domingo.

First issue of this new serial contains introductory material and a note on an exceptional, carved, hump-backed figurine by José A. Caro Alvarez, director, and following articles in Spanish:
Plinio Pina Peña "Las Deformaciones Intencionales del Cuerpo Humano en las Antillas" p. 9-20
Marcio Veloz Maggiolo "Resumen Tipológico de los Complejos Relacionables con Santo Domingo" p. 21-60
Elpidio Ortega; Marcio Veloz Maggiolo; and Plinio Pina Peña "Los Petroglifos de Yabanal, República Dominicana" p. 61-74
Lewis R. Binford "Arqueología como Antropología" p. 75-90.

749. ———. ———. No. 2, 1972- . Santo Domingo.

Second issue includes a methodological introduction by José A. Caro A. and the following reports of archaeological interest, in Spanish:
Elpidio Ortega and Plinio Pina Peña "Un Vaso Inhalador de la Colección del Museo Nacional, República Dominicana" p. 18-24 (similar to ones from Puerto Rico and Grenada in the Lesser Antilles)

Elpidio Ortega "Estudio Tipológico de Diferentes Pipas de los Siglos XVII al XX" p. 45-72
Plinio Pina Peña; Elpidio Ortega; and Marcio Veloz Maggiolo "Informe sobre Reconocimiento Arqueológico en la Casa No. 1 de la Calle Pellerano Alfau, Santo Domingo, República Dominicana" p. 73-104
Marcio Veloz Maggiolo "Algunas Formas de Asa-Estribo en Santo Domingo" p. 121-129
Marcio Veloz Maggiolo and others "El Cementerio de La Unión, Provincia de Puerto Plata" p. 130-156
Marcio Veloz Maggiolo and Elpidio Ortega "Excavaciones en Macao, República Dominicana" p. 157-175
Ethnologists and others will also be interested in the following articles:
Marcio Veloz Maggiolo "Tres Modalidades del Juego de Pelota entre los Aborígenes Americanos" p. 25-32
José Juan Arrom "Manatí: el Testimonio de los Cronistas y la Cuestion de su Etomología" p. 33-38 (author's name omitted in index, p. 33)
Renato O. Rímoli "La Hutia y su Importancia para la Dieta del Indio Antillano" p. 39-44
Manuel E. del Monte Urraca "Capilla del Santísimo Sacramento de la Catedral de Santo Domingo de Guzmán: su Historia y su Restauración" p. 105-119.

750. Bullen, Ripley P. and **Adelaide K. Bullen.** Archaeological investigations on St. Vincent and the Grenadines, West Indies. Orlando, Fla., The William L. Bryant Foundation, 1972. 170 p., bibl., illus., maps, plates, tables (American studies, 8)

Presents and discusses data from site survey with test excavations. Includes revised definitions of ceramic types, 16 new radiocarbon dates, and comparisons with Venezuela and Puerto Rico. Concludes Lesser Antilles and Venezuela form an interacting sphere until ca. 1000 A.D., Ostinoid influences from Puerto Rico then present until ca. 1200 A.D., after which Caribs dominated these islands until well into historic times. To order, write The William L. Bryant Foundation, c/o Library, Florida Technological University, P.O. Box 2500, Orlando, Fla.

751. Easby, Elizabeth Kennedy. Seafarers and sculptors of the Caribbean (UMUP/E, 14:3, Spring 1972, p. 2-10, illus., plates)

Best semi-popular resumé of Antillean prehistory in print. Includes mention of various problems but written too early to reflect results of recent archaeological findings. Monolithic axes are not "prominent" in the US. Small stone balls from graves may be bola weights. Discussion of three-pointed *zemis* neglects classic analyses by Fewkes. Metates and manos are found in the Lesser Antilles. Crescentic stone forms have been found in Carib sites but grooved axes precede petaloid celts, even on St. Vincent. Carib ceramics, based on associated European items and five radiocarbon dates between 1240 and 1580 A.D. and that of the Arawak women they absorbed have been identified. It is found from Grenada to Antigua (but not in the Virgin Islands or Puerto Rico) with the greatest concentration on St. Vincent. See also item 750.

Fewkes, Jesse Walter. The aborigines of Porto Rico and neighboring islands. See item 1145.

752. García del Pino, César. Historia de la arqueología de Vuelta Abajo hasta 1946 (BNJM/R, 13:1 [3. época] enero/abril 1971, p. 59-74)

Rather complete resumé of archaeological work done in Cuba up to 1946.

Handler, Jerome S. An archaeological investigation of the domestic life of plantation slaves in Barbados. See item 1157.

753. Herrera Fritot, René. Exploración arqueológica inicial en Cayo Jurajuría, Matanzas. La Habana, Academia de Ciencias de Cuba, Depto. de Antropología, 1970. 20 p., bibl., maps (Serie antropológica, 6)

Covers survey and tests made in 1951 on Cayo Jurajuría near Playa Menéndez. Food remains, shell celts, chert chips, and red ochre are mentioned but no stone axes or pottery was found except for sherds in the upper half of Test D. Published in honor of Herrera, who died in 1968, his bibliography is presented on p. 5-6.

754. Mattioni, Mario. La culture Arawak aux Antilles (ARCHEO, 45, mars/avril 1972, p. 30-33, map, plates)

Good discussion in French of the Arawak-Carib problem. Suggests ceremonial-symbolic aspects of illustrated Modified Saladoid ceramics. Presents first series of petroglyphs discovered on Martinique in 1970.

755. *Revista Dominicana de Arqueología y Antropología.* Univ. Autónoma de Santo Domingo, Facultad de Humanidades. Año 1, Vol. 1, No. 1, enero/junio 1971- . Santo Domingo.

First issue contains various notes, commentaries, preliminary announcements of field work and ten longer articles and reports, all original Spanish writings or Spanish translations of English articles. The following are of archaeological interest:
Elpidio Ortega "Dos Informes Arqueológicos" p. 21-57
Carlos Morales Ruiz "Informe sobre Tres Grupos Petroglíficos" p. 57-80
Manuel de Jesús Mañón Arredondo; Fernando Morbán Laucer; and Aída Catagena Portalatín "Nuevas Investigaciones de Areas Indígenas al Noroeste de Guayacanes y Juan Dolió" p. 81-133
Betty J. Meggers and Clifford Evans "Especulaciones sobre Rutas Tempranas de Difusión de la Cerámica entre Sur y Mesoamérica" p. 137-149
José M. Cruxent and Irving Rouse "El Hombre Primitivo en las Indias Occidentales" p. 151-163
Plinio F. Pina Peña "Los Períodos Cronológicos de las Culturas Aborígenes en las Antillas Mayores" p. 165-179
José Juan Arrom "El Mundo Mítico de los Taínos: Notas sobre el Ser Supremo" p. 181-200
Marcio Veloz Maggiolo "El Rito de la Cohoba entre los Aborigenes Antillanos" p. 201-216
Manuel Rivero de la Calle "La Estatura en los Aborígenes de Cuba del Grupo no Ceramista" p. 239-249.

756. ———. ———, ———. Año 2, Vol. 2, No. 2/3, julio 1971/junio 1972- . Santo Domingo.

Of the many articles and reports in this issue, six are of special interest to archaeologists:
Elpidio Ortega and Marcio Veloz Maggiolo "Excavación Arqueológica en el Vasto Residuario Indígena de Hatillo Palma" p. 5-27
William J. Kennedy "Comparación de Algunos Diseños de Petroglifos Costarricenses con los de Areas Adyacentes" p. 50-67
Bernardo Vega "Descubrimiento de la Actual Localización del Unico Zemí de Algodón Antillano aún Existente" p. 88-110
Marcio Veloz Maggiolo; Plinio Pina Peña; Elpidio Ortega; and Bernardo Vega "El Quehacer Rupestre

Antillano: Modo de Realización y Patrones Aplicables al Estudio de su Ubicación en el Tiempo" p. 111-127

Carlos M. Raggi "Posibles Rutas de Poblamiento de las Antillas en Paleo-Indio" p. 152-160

Javier Baztan R. "Los Amuletos Precolombinos de Santo Domingo" p. 196-293 (includes a vast number of carved shell illustrations which are most noteworthy).

757. *Serie* **Espeleológica y Carsológica.** 1- . La Habana, Sociedad Espeleológica de Cuba, 1970-

To date 27 monographs have been published of which the following are of archaeological interest: No. 9, by René Herrera Fritot, covers a few artifacts and Pleistocene fossil bones from Soroa, Pinar del Río; No. 10, by José M. Guarch, covers the excavations; No. 11, by Ramón Dacal Moure, the artifacts; and No. 12, by Milton Pino, the diet as revealed at Cueva Funche, also in Pinar del Río. No. 13, by Pastor Terres Valdés and Manuel Rivero de la Calle, discusses the work and skeletal remains at La Cueva de la Santa. No. 16, by Antonio Núñez Jiménez, illustrates pictographs from seven caves. No. 27, by Ernesto E. Tabio, presents a catalog, with brief comments on caves in the provinces of Oriente, Camagüey, Las Villas, Matanzas, La Habana, and Pinar del Río. The series was begun in commemoration of the XXX anniversary of the Sociedad Espeleológica de Cuba.

ARCHAEOLOGY: SOUTH AMERICA

BETTY J. MEGGERS

Research Associate
Department of Anthropology
Smithsonian Institution

CLIFFORD EVANS

Chairman
Department of Anthropology
Smithsonian Institution

THE ACCELERATION OF ARCHAEOLOGICAL INVESTIGATION and publication in South America is clearly evident from a tabulation of publications during the period covered by *HLAS 31, 33, and 35*. Although this coverage is not exhaustive, it contains all of the items available to the contributors and consequently seems likely to be a representative sample. Comparison of the number of entries per country and by nationality of author (domestic versus foreign) provides several interesting observations.

During this period of approximately six years, Peru far outranked all other countries combined in the number of contributions by foreigners, accounting for 63.5, 64.0, and 63.3 percent of the total biennial output (see Table 1). For the continent as a whole, the proportion of foreign to domestic authors shows a slight decline, with foreigners producing 33.4, 29.0, and 28.0 percent of the entries per volume. Noteworthy developments appear to be occurring within several of the countries. Beginning with *HLAS 33*, Peruvian archaeologists authored more articles than foreigners for the first time, and they maintain a slight lead in the current volume. In all other countries except Bolivia, nationals have predominated consistently, and in Argentina, Uruguay, and Venezuela, they account for all but two entries per country during the period reviewed. Only in Colombia has this trend been reversed; there, foreign contributors now lead domestic ones. Although the number of entries is small, it reflects the marked increase in fieldwork in Colombia by North American and European archaeologists during the past several years, which should become more obvious as research in progress reaches publication. Finally, there is a significant decline in the number of publications from Chile, which correlates with the diversion of funding from archaeology to more pressing social and economic fields by the government.

The increased knowledge provided by this expansion of research has made possible the production of general works on New World cultural development. Whereas a few years ago there were no up-to-date, hemisphere-wide summaries, several are now available. Two were included in the previous volume (*HLAS 33:516, 882*) and four have appeared since (item 504, 517, 521, and 528). Theoretical approach, detail and completeness of coverage, and level of technicality vary, but all provide reliable introductions for students and non-specialists.

One form of publication that deserves mention, not only because of its novelty but because of its utility for teaching, is the substitution or supplémentation of text illustrations with 35 mm color slides suitable for projection. Three volumes appeared, one on Colombian gold (item 867) and two on Argentine archaeology (items 782 and 793). Noteworthy major monographs are: *Andes 4* (item 960), which provides additional results of the University of Tokyo excavations at Kotosh in the Peruvian highlands; *Las Aldas* (item 946a), which contains the first detailed descriptions of this important early coastal Peruvian site, and *Tastil* (item 769a), which constitutes the most complete cultural-ecological description of a pre-Inca urban center in northwestern Argentina.

Among new series are the *Boletim do Museu de Arte e História Arqueologia* (Vitória, Bra., No. 1, 1971); *Chungara* (Univ. del Norte, Depto. de Antropología, Arica, Chile, No. 1, 1972); and *Estudios de Arqueología* (Museo Arqueológico de Cachi, Salta, Arg., No. 1, 1972).

Table 1

Country	HLAS 31		HLAS 33		HLAS 35	
	National	Foreign	National	Foreign	National	Foreign
Argentina	71	0	47	2	45	0
Brazil	38	8	65	4	35	2
Bolivia	1	7	4	4	9	7
Chile	37	3	72	8	17	6
Colombia	10	2	9	5	5	8
Ecuador	19	7	18	7	11	4
Peru	25	47	79	57	57	50
Uruguay	3	0	2	2	2	0
Venezuela	17	0	10	0	14	2
	221	74	306	89	195	79
	295		395		274	

GENERAL

758. Bashilov, Vladimir Aleksandrovich. Drevnie tsivilizatsii Peru i Bolivii (The ancient civilizations of Peru and Bolivia). Moskva, Nauka, 1972. 209 p., bibl., illus., maps, tables (USSR Academy of Sciences. Institute of Archaeology)

Archaeological survey, based on published sources, of cultures of the Central Andes from 900 B.C. to 1300 A.D. Sections devoted to: history of research of the Central Andes; mountain regions of Peru and Bolivian altiplano; Peruvian littoral; archaeological data and history of civilizations which existed therein. Author blames difficulties in tracing the development of these societies on bourgeois researchers who have shown little interest in gathering facts on the history of society. Nevertheless, an approximate scheme can be drawn to indicate how Andean societies developed from agricultural cultures to complex civilizations. Author uses term "civilization" to indicate a culture which possesses traits of a class-society. [A. R. Navon]

759. Cardich, Augusto. Hacia una interpretación de la prehistoria de Sudamérica (UNC/AAE, 24/25, 1969/1970, p. 5-32)

Recognizes three principal lithic traditions: pebble industry, biface industry, and point and flake industry, probably representing three waves of immigration reaching South America in relatively rapid succession between 20,000 and 15,000 B.C., after which they continued contemporaneously. Charts show Pleistocene chronology and relative antiquity of various complexes of each tradition.

Conference in Pre-Columbian Iconography, *Washington, 1970.* The cult of the feline. See item 546.

760. Núñez Regueiro, Víctor A. Conceptos teóricos que han obstaculizado el desarrollo de la arqueología en Sud-América (Estudios de Arqueología [Museo Arquelógico de Cachi, Salta, Arg.] 1, 1972, p. 11-35, bibl.)

Failure to use approaches developed principally in the US for making inferences from archaeological data has impeded progress; among examples are ignorance of methods of developing chronological sequences from surface sites, failure to adopt ecological explanations, static rather than dynamic concept of "type".

761. Palavecino, Enrique. Las altas culturas andinas (Relaciones de la Sociedad Argentina de Antropología [B.A.] 6, 1972, p. 7-52, maps)

Views of a leading Argentine archaeologist on the origin and spread of Andean culture over lowland South America: written several years ago and now outdated by new information.

761a. Palavecino, Enrique. Las protoculturas de Sudamérica (Relaciones de la Sociedad Argentina de Antropología [B.A.] 5:2 [nueva serie] 1971, p. 9-34)

Unedited article published posthumously. Only historically interesting.

762. Petersen G., Georg. Minería y metalurgia en el antiguo Perú. Lima, Instituto de Investigaciones Antropológicas, Museo Nacional de Antropología y Arqueología, 1970. 140 p., bibl., plates, tables (Arqueológicas, 12)

Types of rocks and minerals used in prehistoric Andean South America, sources, methods of extraction, preparation and use, types of objects produced, summarized mainly from publications. Peru and Bolivia receive principal emphasis.

763. Szmuk, Peter Raphael. Datação de peças arqueológicas pelo método termoluminescente (MP/R, 18, 1968/1969, p. 57-103, bibl., tables)

Description of method and application to Tupiguarani pottery from sites in the Brazilian state of São Paulo.

ARGENTINA

764. Austral, Antonio Gerónimo. El yacimiento arqueológico Vallejo en el noroeste de la provincia de La Pampa: contribución a la sistematización de la prehistoria y arqueología de la región pampeana (Relaciones de la Sociedad Argentina de Antropología [B.A.] 5:2 [nueva serie] 1971, p. 49-70, illus.)

Reanalysis and new approach to entire Pampa region. Of importance to specialist. Uses the concept of "industries".

765. ———. El yacimiento de Los Flamencos II: la coexistencia del hombre con fauna extinguida en la región pampeana (Relaciones de la Sociedad Argentina de Antropología [B.A.] 6, 1972, p. 203-209, bibl., illus.)

Lanceolate points and other chipped artifacts associated with *Glyptodon*, *Lama*, and *Dolichotis* in a deposit in Buenos Aires province dated geologically in the terminal Pleistocene.

766. Berberián, Eduardo E. Adornos transfictivos labiales en una tumba indígena de la provincia de Córdoba (UNC/R, 12:1/3 [2. serie] enero/junio 1971, p. 334-369, bibl., illus., maps)

Description of the flanged-disk type of labret from a post-500 A.D. site; antecedents are traced to pre-Tiahuanaco period in Bolivian highlands, via El Molle on the Chilean coast.

767. ——— and Dante R. Soria. Investigación arqueológica en el yacimiento de Zárate, departamento de Trancas, Tucumán: informe preliminar (UNT/H, 16:22, 1970, p. 165-176, illus.)

In an area believed to be purely Candelaria culture, both habitation and cemeteries of early Santamariana culture found.

768. ———; Alberto J. Marcellino; and Silvia E. Ruete. Bibliografía antropológica de la provincia de Córdoba, R.A.: años 1874/1969 (ANC/B, 47:2/4, 1970, p. 163-257)

Annotated bibliography containing all works that could be encountered; location of works in public and private libraries in Argentina is also provided.

769. Chiri, Osvaldo C. Acerca de la utilización de valvas de moluscos y la formación de montículos de valvas en yacimientos arqueológicos del nordeste argentino (Relaciones de la Sociedad Argentina de Antropologia [B.A.] 6, 1972, p. 163-172, bibl.)

Review of role of shellfish as food and shell artifacts, with estimates of relationship between size of midden and population. Calculations of daily consumption indicate that accumulation is rapid and population size and length of occupation were much smaller than has been assumed.

769a. Cigliano, Eduardo Mario Tasil, una ciudad preincaica argentina. B.A., Ediciones Cabargon, 1973. 694 p., bibl., illus., plates.

Detailed monograph on a 14th-century urban center in Salta province at 3200 m. elevation, estimated to have had a population of about 2200. Describes structures, artifacts, and skeletal remains and discusses subsistence, environmental adaptation, settlement pattern, and other aspects. A fundamental reference both for factual and theoretical aspects of southern Andean archaeology. Includes 162 illustrations, 30 black-and-white and 32 color plates.

770. ——— and Horacio Calandra. En torno a dos sitios precerámicos en el departamento de Rosario de Lerma, provincia de Salta (Relaciones de la Sociedad Argentina de Antropología [B.A.] 5:2 [nueva serie] 1971, p. 153-162, illus.)

New sites, with projectile points and others with bifaces only, add to picture of lithic, non-ceramic horizon in area.

771. ———; Pedro Ignacio Schmitz; and María Amanda Caggiano. Sitios cerámicos prehispánicos en la costa septentrional de la provincia de Buenos Aires y de Salto Grande, Entre Ríos: esquema tentativo de su desarrollo (SCA/A, 192:3/4, 1971, p. 129-191, illus.)

Detailed analysis of pottery excavated at a variety of sites in northern coast of Buenos Aires province, Isla Martín García and Salto Grande zone. Bases a chronology on carbon-14 dates.

772. ———; **Rodolfo A. Raffino;** and **Horacio A. Calandra.** Nuevos aportes para el conocimiento de las entidades alfareras mas tempranas del noroeste argentino (Relaciones de la Sociedad Argentina de Antropología [B.A.] 6, 1972, p. 225-236, bibl., plates)

Discussion of a ceramic complex with tricolor painting possibly anterior to Condorhuasi-San Francisco, etc., designated as Las Cuevas and estimated to date about 200 B.C.

773. ———; ———; and **María Amanda Caggiano.** Resultados de las investigaciones arqueológicas efectuadas en la zona de Salto Grande, provincia de Entre Ríos (UNLPM/R, 7:43 [Antropología] 1971, p. 79-107, bibl., illus., map, plates, tables)

Tests at two lithic and four ceramic sites revealed four cultural complexes, one preceramic and three ceramic. Two sites with plain pottery are carbon-14 dated 860 and 1180 A.D.; one with Guaraní pottery dates 1545 A.D. Third complex has incised and painted decoration. Lithic sites produced flake and pebble tools.

774. **D'Antoni, Héctor Luis.** Estudio ecológico de dos regiones de contacto cultural (MEMDA/E, 14, julio/dic. 1971, p. 11-19, bibl., illus., tables)

Demonstrates that cultural division between Valliserrana and Selvas Occidentales equates with marked environmental differences and consequently reflects adaptive imperatives.

775. **Di Lullo, Orestes** and **Luis G. B. Garay.** La urna de Uco Pocito (UNT/H, 15:21, 1968/1969, p. 193-202, illus.)

Long resume of Diaguita culture culminating in a brief description of a vessel from Santiago del Estero province.

776. **Dougherty, Bernard.** Las pipas de fumar arqueológicas de la provincia de Jujuy (Relaciones de la Sociedad Argentina de Antropología [B.A.] 6, 1972, p. 83-89, bibl.)

Elbow pipes are abundant in southeastern Jujuy and rare elsewhere in Argentina; they are associated with San Francisco type pottery and carbon-14 dated about 600 B.C. Reviews distribution elsewhere in South America.

777. **Fernández, Jorge.** La recolección de bulbos, rizomas y tubérculos entre los cazadores superiores de la Puna (UNC/AAE, 24/25, 1969/1970, p. 131-142)

Botanical identification of plants collected in excavations in Cueva del Inca and rock shelter of Río Despensas in Puna de Jujuy. Except for maize in upper levels of Incacueva, all were wild examples of root foods.

778. **Fuente, Nicolás R. de la.** Las culturas prehispánicas en la provincia de La Rioja: panorama general. Río Segundo, Arg., Museo Arqueológico Regional Aníbal Montes, 1971. 30 p., bibl., illus. (Museo Arqueológico Regional Aníbal Montes, 2)

Reviews state of archaeological information as of 1971.

779. ———. La fortaleza del Cerro El Toro, provincia de La Rioja (Instituto de Antropología [Univ. Católica de Córdoba, Facultad de Filosofía y Humanidades, Arg.] 1, 1971, p. 1-11, bibl., plates)

Hilltop fortification with pottery belonging to La Aguada culture, first of this type reported in Valliserrana region.

780. ——— and **Gloria I. Arragoni.** Nuevos petroglifos de la región de Talampaya, provincia de La Rioja (Instituto de Antropología [Univ. Católica de Córdoba, Facultad de Filosofía y Humanidades, Arg.] 1, 1971, p. 13-23, bibl., plates)

Anthropomorphic, zoomorphic, and geometric figures, most poorly preserved.

781. **González, Alberto Rex** and **José Antonio Pérez.** Argentina indígena: vísperas de la Conquista. B.A., Editorial Paidós, 1972. 172 p., bibl., illus., maps, plates, tables (Col. Historia argentina, 1)

One of series of eight volumes of Argentine history giving panoramic view of area at eve of Conquest using archaeological and ethnohistorical data. Good generalized popular summary for non-specialist.

782. ——— and ———. Primeras culturas argentinas. B.A., Filmediciones Valero, 1971, 88 p., illus.

Introduction to early ceramic complexes of northwest Argentina illustrated with black-and-white plates and 72 colored slides suitable for projection. Complexes include Tafi, Condorhuasi, Ciénaga, Alamito, Candelaria, Santa María, San José, Belén, Aguada, and Inca.

783. **Gradin, Carlos J.** Noticia preliminar sobre el Cañadón Supaynyieu; la industria lítica de Paso Burgos; provincia de Río Negro (Relaciones de la Sociedad Argentina de Antropología [B.A.] 6, 1972, p. 211-224, bibl., illus.)

Pebble industry emphasizing bifaces from a surface site on a high terrace, related to San Jorgense I and Jacobaccense complexes to south and estimated to date in fifth millennium B.C.

784. ———. Parapetos habitacionales en la Meseta Somuncura, provincia de Río Negro (Relaciones de la Sociedad Argentina de Antropología [B.A.] 5:3 [nueva serie] 1971, p. 171-185, illus.)

Circular to semicircular stone rings at altitude of 1300 meters with stone artifacts suggest use as hunting shelters from Archaic period up to 17th century, located by lakes or old lake beds. Efforts are made to correlate with ethnohistorical data.

785. **Lafon, Ciro René.** Introducción a la arqueología del nordeste argentino (Relaciones de la Sociedad Argentina de Antropología [B.A.] 5:2 [nueva serie] 1971, p. 119-152, illus.)

Summarizes area into three phases of cultural evolution: tradition of hunters and collectors; neolithic; and a generalized Tupiguarani.

786. Lorandi de Gieco, Ana María and **Delia Magda Lovera.** Economía y patrón de asentamiento en la provincia de Santiago del Estero (Relaciones de la Sociedad Argentina de Antropología [B.A.] 6, 1972, p. 173-191, bibl., illus.)

Reconstruction of economy and social organization of prehistoric groups based on archaeological data between 800-1500 A.D. Although there are indications of inter-village food distribution, social integration could not be verified. Matrilocal residence is postulated from continuity of local ceramic typology.

787. Madrazo, Guillermo B. Arqueología de Lobería y Salliqueló, provincia de Buenos Aires (MEMDA/E, 15, enero/junio 1972, p. 1-18, bibl., illus.)

Results of investigations on province coast (Lobería) and western border. Lithic remains abounded in the first area, including fish-tail points; pottery and triangular points were among artifacts from the west.

788. Moreira, María Elena. La cerámica y el material lítico de Laguna del Cristal. Reconquista, Arg., Museo Municipal de Arqueología, 1972. 39 p., illus. (Publicación, 1)

Early lithic occupation and then later pottery bearing cultures of the Laguna del Cristal in Santa Fe province, described as part of the Paraná delta and riverine cultures.

789. Núñez Regueiro, Víctor A. Excavaciones arqueológicas en la unidad DI de los yacimientos de Alumbrera: 1964 (UNC/AAE, 24/25, 1969/1970, p. 33-76)

Habitation construction and burials of the Alamito culture carbon-14 dated between 300-400 A.D. in the Campo del Pucará, Catamarca province.

790. ——— and **Myriam N. Tarragó.** Evaluación de datos arqueológicos: ejemplos de aculturación (Estudios de Arqueología [Museo Arqueológico de Cachi, Salta, Arg.] 1, 1972, p. 36-48, bibl.)

Analysis of evidence for several types of culture contact ranging from objects traded to acculturation in prehistoric complexes of northwestern Argentina.

791. Palanca, Floreal; Leonardo Daino; and **Edgardo Benbassat.** Yacimiento Estancia La Moderna: nuevas perspectivas para la arqueología de la pampa bonaerense (MEMDA/E, 15, enero/junio 1972, p. 19-27, bibl., illus.)

Lithic complex characterized by quartz flakes, a rock not of local origin.

793. Pérez, José Antonio. Arte rupestre de Cerro Colorado, B.A., Filmediciones Valero, 1971. 28 p., illus.

Description of pictographs in northern Córdoba and their possible interpretation. Illustrations include 18 color slides, 35 mm, suitable for projection.

793a. Raffino, Rodolfo A. Agricultura hidráulica y simbiosis económica demográfica en la Quebrada del Toro, Salta, Argentina (UNLPM/R, 7, 1973, p. 297-331, illus.)

Examines potential reasons for a 95 percent decline in area of cultivated land between aboriginal 14th-century occupation and the present. Water shortage appears most crucial, but whether abandonment of conservation and irrigation or climatic change is responsible has not been conclusively ascertained.

794. ———. Las sociedades agrícolas del período tardío en la Quebrada del Toro y aledaños, provincia de Salta (UNLPM/R, 7:45 [Antropología] 1972, p. 157-210, bibl., illus., maps, plates, tables)

Introduction of irrigation during 13-14th centuries caused demographic explosion, followed during mid-15th century by water shortage and population decline.

795. ——— and **José Togo.** El yacimiento arqueológico Cerro del Dique, Quebrada del Toro, provincia de Salta: nota preliminar (Revista [Comisión Municipal de Cultura, Depto. de Antropología y Folklore, Concordia, Arg.] 1:1, 1. semestre 1970, p. 5-11, illus.)

Compares pottery and architecture with finds of Cigliano at Las Cuevas, item 772, and concludes that site belongs to early ceramic period.

796. Rodríguez, Amílcar A. Arqueología del nordeste de Entre Ríos, Río Uruguay medio: nota preliminar. Concordia, Arg., Comisión Municipal de Cultura, Depto. de Antropología y Folklore, 1969. 31 p., illus.

Brief summary statement of principal sites and types of artifacts found in northeastern part of Entre Ríos province.

797. ———. Notas relacionadas con los sitios arqueológicos relevados en Salto Grande, departamento Federación, provincia de Entre Ríos, Argentina: primera nota (Revista [Comisión Municipal de Cultura, Depto. Antropología y Folklore, Concordia, Arg.] 1:1, 1. semestre 1970, p. 12-20, illus.)

Sites have a distinct lithic complex in lower levels, with pottery in upper levels. Compares lithic material to José Vieira in Brazil. Pottery is "Salto Grande Incised" to use the Serrano terminology.

798. Rolandi de Perrot, Diana Susana. Los gorros de Santa Rosa de Tastil, provincia de Salta (Relaciones de la Sociedad Argentina de Antropología [B.A.] 5:2 [nueva serie] 1971, p. 85-93, illus.)

Knotted looping skull cap dating 1349-1430 A.D. Textile experts will find detailed drawings and descriptions.

799. Sanguinetti de Bórmida, Amalia and **Mary Luz Schegel.** Industrias arcaicas del Río

Neuquén (Relaciones de la Sociedad Argentina de Antropología [B.A.] 6, 1972, p. 91-108, bibl., illus.)

Investigations at several sites indicate an initial lithic tradition based on pebble tools, followed by a more specialized flake industry. The former may begin around 10,000 B.C. A chart correlates named complexes from northern Patagonia.

800. **Schobinger, Juan.** Arqueología del valle de Uspallata, provincia de Mendoza: sinopsis preliminar (Relaciones de la Sociedad Argentina de Antropología [B.A.] 5:2 [nueva serie] 1971, p. 71-84, illus.)

Has preceramic, pre-Inca, Inca and Jesuit occupation sites.

801. **Serrano, Antonio.** Líneas fundamentales de la arqueología del Litoral: una tentativa de periodización. Córdoba, Arg., Univ. Nacional de Córdoba, Instituto de Antropología, 1972. 79 p., bibl., illus., plates (Instituto de Antropología, 32)

Review of existing data on the "litoral" region and attempt to place complexes in regional and chronological context composed of three major periods (preceramic, early, late) and four regions (Misionera, Paraná Medio, Uruguay Medio, Déltica). Important as an overview by an archaeologist with long experience in the region.

802. **Sirolli, Amadeo Rodolfo.** ¿Títeres prehispánicos? Salta, Arg., Instituto Antropológico y de Ciencias Afines, 1971. 90 p., illus.

Using pottery figurines from various pre-Spanish cultures of Argentina, argues the possibility that they were used as puppets, manipulated on end of fingertips. Not very convincing argument.

803. **Tarragó, Myriam Noemí** and **Pío Pablo Díaz.** Sitios arqueológicos del Valle Calchaquí (Estudios de Arqueología [Museo Arqueológico de Cachi, Salta, Arg.] 1, 1972, p. 49-61, bibl.)

Site inventory in tabular form, giving site name and number, name of reporter, location, description, cultural affiliation and period.

804. —— and **Víctor A. Núñez Regueiro.** Un diseño de investigación arqueológica sobre el Valle Calchaquí: fase exploratoria (Estudios de Arqueología [Museo Arqueológico de Cachi, Salta, Arg.] 1, 1972, p. 62-85, bibl.)

Description of research design to be applied to the archaeology of the Calchaquí valley in order to reconstruct the ecological dimensions of past cultures. Includes appendices.

805. **Vivante, Armando.** Las estatuitas del Valle de Lerma (Relaciones de la Sociedad Argentina de Antropología [B.A.] 6, 1972, p. 79-82, bibl., illus.)

Possible significance of crude hollow pottery figurines with one or more orifices, from later period graves.

806. **Zetti, Jorge; Eduardo P. Tonni;** and **Francisco Fidalgo.** Algunos rasgos de la geología superficial en las cabeceras del Arroyo de Azul (MEMDA/E, 15, enero/junio 1972, p. 28-34, bibl., illus.)

Description of geological profiles and fauna from Estancia La Moderna (see item 791), raising the possibility of pleistocene date from the site.

BOLIVIA

807. **Avila Salinas, Waldo.** Estudio comparativo por difracción de rayos X de las areniscas de Pumapunku (*in* Procedencia de las areniscas utilizadas en el templo precolombino de Pumapunku, Tiwanaku. La Paz, Academia Nacional de Ciencias de Bolivia, 1971, pt. 3, p. 219-228 [Publicación, 22])

X-Ray diffraction studies of same samples studied by Arturo Castaños Echazu (item 809) and Carlos Ponce Sanginés (item 817). Rio Kausani the probable source.

808. **Bondeson, Wolmar E.** Tobacco from Tiahuanacoid culture period (EM/ES, 32, 1972, p. 177-184, illus.)

Analysis of *Nicotiana* stems from a pouch, part of a medicine-man's equipment (see item 821).

809. **Castaños Echazu, Arturo.** Estudio petrográfico de las areniscas de Pumapunku (*in* Procedencia de las areniscas utilizadas en el templo precolombino de Pumapunku, Tiwanaku. La Paz, Academia Nacional de Ciencias de Bolivia, 1971, pt. 2, p. 209-218, [Publicación, 22])

Detailed petrographic analyses in tabular form of 20 samples from blocks at the temple and 27 samples from various outcrops in area. Demonstrates that valley of Río Kausani, 8.95 kilometers away, is the source rather than the other five geographic areas studied.

810. **Cordero Miranda, Gregorio.** Reconocimiento arqueológico de Pucarani y sitios adyacentes (Pumapunku [Instituto de Cultura Aymara, La Paz] 3 [2. semestre] julio/dic. 1971, p. 7-27, illus.)

Survey of three sites just north of Tiahuanaco area near Pucarani; two showing similarity in ceramics of Inca period, one of Tiahuanaco Expansivo period. No excavation.

811. **Craig, Alan K.** A Tiahuanacoid condor effigy from Cochabamba, Bolivia (SEM/E, 35:1/4, 1970, p. 76-79, plates)

Condor-shaped pottery vessel collected in Cochabamba Valley, possibly associated with a Tiahuanaco cult.

812. **Hjalmarsson, Helge.** Report on examinations of seven yarn samples from a Bolivian archaeological collection (EM/ES, 32, 1972, p. 171-176, plates)

Cotton, alpaca, and unidentified plants are represented in yarn samples from a medicine-man's tomb (see items 813 and 821).

813. —— and **Thomas Liljemark.** Textile fibres in archaeological material from a

Tiahuanacoid tomb in Bolivia (EM/ES, 32, 1972, p. 159-170, plates, tables)

Microphotographs of fibers identified as alpaca and vicuña from textiles in a medicine-man's tomb (see items 812 and 821).

814. Mogrovejo Terrazas, Gerardo. Estudio geológico petrográfico (*in* Acerca de la procedencia del material lítico de los monumentos de Tiwanaku. La Paz, Academia Nacional de Ciencias de Bolivia, 1970, pt. 2, p. 189-258, illus. [Publicación, 21])

Good discussion of area geology, stratigraphy and petrography, especially Tiahuanaco and Iwawe site, and others. Use in conjunction with items 807, 817 and 819.

815. Ponce Sanginés, Carlos. La cerámica de la época I de Tiwanaku. La Paz, Academia Nacional de Ciencias de Bolivia, 1971. 27 p., bibl., plates (Publicación, 28)

Excavations in Kalasasaya sector of Tiahuanaco revealed strata dating from initial occupation of site. Ceramics are described on the basis of complete or restorable vessels. Painting is the most common decorative technique.

816. ———. Examen arqueológico (*in* Acerca de la procedencia del material lítico de los monumentos de Tiahuanaco. La Paz, Academia Nacional de Ciencias de Bolivia, 1970, pt. 1, 11-188, bibl., illus. [Publicación, 21])

Discusses problem of transportation of sandstone blocks to build the temples at Tiahuanaco and how question can be solved, with good illustrations, bibliography. On basis of chroniclers and comparative literature offers ideas on how manpower manipulated to get blocks in place. Use in conjunction with items 807, 817 and 819.

817. ———. Examen arqueológico de las ruinas precolombinas de Pumapunku (*in* Procedencia de las areniscas utilizadas en el templo precolombino de Pumapunku, Tiwanaku. La Paz, Academia Nacional de Ciencias de Bolivia, 1971, pt. 1, p. 15-205, bibl., illus. [Publicación, 22])

Background discussion with good photos and maps of Tiahuanaco site and problem of transporting of stones to the temple of Pumapunku and how this detailed study of petrology of construction blocks would solve the origin of materials. Thorough with detailed citations and complete bibliography.

818. ———. Tiwanaku: espacio, tiempo y cultura: ensayo de síntesis arqueológica (Pumapunku [Instituto de Cultura Aymara, La Paz] 3 [2. semestre] julio/dic. 1971, p. 29-46, tables)

Summary of Tihuanaco with detailed charts on carbon-14 and obsidian dates.

819. Urquidi Barrau, Fernando. Geoquímica de las areniscas de Pumapunku (*in* Procedencias de las areniscas utilizadas en el templo precolombino de Pumapunku, Tiwanaku. La Paz, Academia de Ciencias de Bolivia, 1971, pt. 4, p. 229-240 [Publicación, 22])

Spectrochemical analyses of the same samples handled by Arturo Castaños Echazu, Waldo Avila Salinas and Carlos Ponce Sanginés (items 807, 809 and 817) not as specific in locality as other tests. Sodium is the key element in these studies. Admits the stones from the nearby Tertiary formation of sandstone (Serranía Meridional) but with these tests cannot be as specific as others.

820. von Winning, Hasso. A carved bone from Tiahuanaco (SM/M, 46:4, Oct/Dec. 1972, p. 129-136, illus.)

Carved llama bone bought by Charles F. Lummis while at Tiahuanaco in 1893 and now in Southwest Museum collections, described and illustrated in detail and compared with other typical Tiahuanaco motifs of winged animal figure holding a staff.

821. Wassén, S. Henry. A medicine-man's implements and plants in a Tiahuanacoid tomb in highland Bolivia (EM/ES, 32, 1972, p. 8-114, bibl., plates)

Technical analysis and description of snuff trays and tube, enema syringes, containers (baskets, fruits), bags, plant remains, and a deformed and trephined skull from a burial in the depto. de La Paz carbon-14 dated at around 375 A.D. For ethnohistorian's comment, see *HLAS 34:1236*.

BRAZIL

822. Albuquerque, Marcos. Nota sobre a ocorrência de sambaquis históricos e de contacto interétnico no litoral de Pernambuco (Revista do Instituto de Filosofia e Ciências Humanas [Recife, Bra.] 1, jan./junho 1970, p. 153-158)

Indigenous shell middens located near mollusk beds and European middens located near inland habitations shed light on early period of contact and process of acculturation, little studied on this part of Brazilian coast.

823. ———. O sítio arqueológico PE-16-Cb: um sítio de contacto interétnico. Recife, Bra., Univ. Federal de Pernambuco, Instituto de Filosofia e Ciências Humanas, Setor de Arqueologia, 1971. 37 p., illus.

Excavations at Dutch fort site near Recife, destroyed in 1635, produced aboriginal as well as European types of artifacts.

824. Alvim, Marília Carvalho de Mello e and **Giraldo Seyferth.** Estudo morfológico do número da população do sambaqui de Cabeçuda, Laguna, Santa Catarina (*in* O homem antigo na América. São Paulo, Univ. de São Paulo, Instituto de Pré-História, 1971, p. 25-28, bibl., table)

Summary of measurements and observations on 84 adult skeletons.

825. Beck, Anamaria. Grupos cerâmicos do litoral de Santa Catarina-Fase Rio Lessa e Fase Enseada (Anais do Museu de

Antropologia [Florianópolis, Bra.] 4:4, 1971, p. 25-29, bibl.)

Classifies pottery from sambaquis into two phases attributed to Tupiguarani tradition; description indicates non-Tupiguarani affiliation.

826. ———. Os sambaquis da região do litoral de Laguna, Sta. Catarina (*in* O homem antigo na América. São Paulo, Univ. de São Paulo, Instituto de Pre-História, 1971, p. 69-77, bibl., plates)

Brief resumé of some 55 shell middens dating between 3500 and 1200 before present.

827. Calderón, Valentín. Investigação sôbre arte rupestre no Planalto da Bahia: as pinturas da Chapada Diamantina (Universitas [Univ. Federal da Bahia, Bra.] 6/7, maio/dez. 1970, p. 217-227, bibl.)

Description of pictographs from central Bahia following classificatory framework of traditions and phases (see item 828). Distinguishes two phases in the symbolic tradition and four in the naturalistic tradition.

828. ———. Nota prévia sôbre três fases da arte rupestre no Estado da Bahia (Universitas [Univ. Federal da Bahia, Bra.] 5, jan./abril 1970, p. 5-17, bibl., plates)

Attempt to classify pictographs into two traditions (realistic and symbolic), each subdivided into stylistic "phases," as a basis for making a chronological and geographical framework.

829. Chmyz, Igor. Breves notas sôbre petroglifos no segundo planalto paranaense: sítio PR-UV-5 (Res Facultatis [Faculdade Estadual de Filosofia, Ciências e Letras de Paranaguá, Bra.] 2, 1968, p. 185-193, bibl., illus.)

Crossed and forked, as well as straight lines on a boulder; plain pottery was found in the vicinity.

830. ——— and **Ariete Alice Schmitt.** A cultura payaguá e suas possíveis correlações com a cultura tupiguarani (Boletim do Instituto Histórico, Geográfico e Etnográfico Paranaense [Curitiba, Bra.] 13, 1971, p. 61-76, illus.)

Archaeological phase, called the Icaraima, based on sites excavated along the Rio Paraná, which is Tupiguarani in tradition, is tentatively related to the ethnohistorical data of the Payaguá Indians. Very convincing.

831. Corrêa, Conceição G. and **Mário F. Simões.** Pesquisas arqueológicas na região do Salgado, Pará (MPEG/B [Antropologia] 48, julho 1971, p. 1-30, bibl., illus., plates, tables)

Description of two sites and artifacts on the Pará coast with a distinctive kind of pottery with plain or red-slipped surfaces, designated as the Areão Phase. Griddles imply use of bitter manioc.

832. Cunha, Ernesto de Mallo Salles and **Marília Carvalho de Mello e Alvim.** Contribuição para o conhecimento da morfologia das populações indígenas da Guanabara; notas sôbre a população do sítio arqueológico Cabeça de Indio (*in* O homem antigo na América. São Paulo, Univ. de São Paulo, Instituto de Pré-História, 1971, p. 21-24, bibl., tables)

Detailed metric and observational data on 14 skeltons from a coastal Guanabara site.

833. Dias, Ondemar. A fase Parati: apontamentos sôbre uma fase cerâmica neobrasileira (Universitas [Univ. Federal da Bahia, Bra.] 8/9 jan./agôsto 1971, p. 117-133, bibl., illus., plates)

Remains from 29 sites in different locations (islands, beaches, rock shelters, etc.) permit recognition of a new phase of the neo-Brazilian tradition on the south coast of Rio de Janeiro state. Analysis of the seriated ceramic sequence indicates change in settlement pattern as well as pottery frequencies.

834. ———. As inscrições e as pinturas préhistóricas no Brasil (Boletim do Serviço de Museus [Govêrno do Estado da Guanabara, Rio] 2:3, 1969, p. 7-16, bibl.)

Discussion of misconceptions and erroneous interpretations of pictographs; asserts they must be taken in context of other cultural evidence and seen as part of expression of relatively simple aboriginal cultures of various degrees of antiquity.

835. ———. O GB-3: Gentio, um sítio carioca (Boletim do Serviço de Museus [Govêrno do Estado da Guanabara, Rio] 1:1, 1971, p. 25-36, bibl.)

Description of site and artifacts, which represent the Guaratiba phase of the Tupiguarani tradition.

836. Duarte, Gerusa Maria. Distribuição e localização de sítios arqueológicos tipo sambaqui, na ilha de Santa Catarina (Anais do Museu de Antropologia [Florianópolis, Bra.] 4:4, 1971, p. 31-60, bibl., map)

Brief description of 61 shell middens on Santa Catarina island.

837. Garcia, Caio del Rio and **Albert Thomas de Cornides.** Material lítico do sambaqui de Piaçaguera (*in* O homem antigo na América. São Paulo, Univ. de São Paulo, Instituto de Pré-História, 1971, p. 41-51, bibl., plates)

Preliminary description of axes, anvil stones, pounders, and flakes from a shell midden on the São Paulo coast.

838. Grabert, Hellmut and **Juan Schobinger.** Petroglifos a orillas del río Madeira: N.O. de Brasil (UNC/AAE, 24/25, 1969/1970, p. 93-112)

Geometric and zoomorphic petroglyphs in the state of Rondonia on the Brazil-Bolivia border.

839. Lazzarotto, Danilo; Pedro Ignacio Schmitz; Itala Irene Basile Becker; and **Rolf Steinmetz.** Pesquisas arqueológicas no planalto (*in* O homem antigo na América. São Paulo, Univ. de São Paulo, Instituto de Pré-História, 1971, p. 79-89, bibl., plates)

Description of Taquara tradition sites in the *município* of Bom Jesús, northeastern Rio Grande do Sul.

840. Maranca, Silva. Nota prévia sôbre o sítio José Fernandes, SP-IP-12 (MP/R, 18, 1968/1969, p. 105-118, plates)

Description of 12 pottery vessels and several stone artifacts from the Taquari basin, southern São Paulo, representing the Tupiguarani tradition.

841. Meggers, Betty J. and Clifford Evans. A reconstitução da pré-história amazônica. Belém, Bra., Museu Paraense Emílio Goeldi, 1973. p. 51-69, bibl., illus. (Publicações avulsas, 20)

Recent data indicating fragmentation of the rain forest between 3500 and 2000 years ago may explain linguistic and archaeological evidence for widespread population movements around 1000 B.C.

842. Menezes, Maria José and Margarida Davina Andreatta. Os sepultamentos do sambaqui "B" do Guaraguaçu (*in* O homem antigo na América. São Paulo, Univ. de São Paulo, Instituto de Pré-História, 1971, p. 5-20, bibl., plates)

Description of 28 skeletons from a shell midden on the Paraná coast; all were flexed. Artifacts were rarely associated.

843. Meseses, Ulpiano T. Bezerra de. Arqueologia amazônica: Santarém. São Paulo, Univ. de São Paulo, Museu de Arqueologia e Etnologia, 1972. 32 p., illus.

From an exhibit of 264 Santarem pieces an explanatory catalog with illustrations comments on Santarem culture, and long-range project of Museu to undertake excavations there. Typical material of this culture.

844. Naue, Guilherme and others. Novas perspectivas sôbre a arqueologia de Rio Grande, RS (*in* O homem antigo na América. São Paulo Univ. de São Paulo, Instituto de Pré-História, 1971, p. 91-122, bibl., plates, tables)

Description of remains from sites in the *município* of Rio Grande representing Vieira phase, Vieira-Tupiguaraní mixture, Tupiguaraní tradition, and European contact.

845. Pallestrini, Luciana. Sítio arqueológico "Jango Luís" (MP/R, 18, 1968/1969, p. 25-56, bibl., illus.)

Description of excavations at Tupiguaraní tradition site in southern São Paulo, and pottery and stone artifacts. Two thermoluminescence dates averaged 1210 years ago.

846. ———. Supra-estruturas e infraestruturas arqueológicas no contexto ecológico brasileiro (MP/R, 20, 1972/1973, p. 7-32, bibl., illus., plates)

Comparison of three Tupiguaraní tradition habitation sites in southern São Paulo, dated by thermoluminescence between 1000 and 1200 years ago. "Ecological" comments vague and uninformative.

847. Perota, Celso. Considerações sôbre a tradição Aratu, nos Estados da Bahia e Espírito Santo (Boletim do Museu de Arte e História [Vitória, Bra. Arqueologia] 1, set. 1971, p. 1-11, bibl., illus., plate)

Brief discussion of the Itaúnas phase of the Aratu tradition, with carbon-14 dates of A.D. 870 ± 90 (SI-142) and A.D. 1360 ± 40 (SI-341).

848. ———. Contribuição à arqueologia de Santa Teresa, no Estado do Espírito Santo: pt. 2 (Boletim do Museu de Arte e História [Vitória, Bra.] 2 [Antropologia] set. 1972, p. 1-9, bibl., plates)

Summary of three sites and artifacts of the Cricaré Phase, a Tupiguarani ceramic complex of the painted subtradition, estimated to date between 1000-1200 A.D.

849. ———. O sítio arqueológico "Campus 2" (UFES Revista de Cultura [Univ. Federal Espírito Santo, Vitória, Bra.] 3:1/2, 7 set. 1972, p. 39-45, illus.)

Non-ceramic site on University campus with crudely polished axes and chipped artifacts dating 515 A.D. by carbon-14.

850. Rauth, José Wilson. Nota prévia sôbre a escavação arqueológica do sambaqui do Godo (Res Facultatis [Faculdade Estadual de Filosofia, Ciências e Letras de Paranaguá, Bra.] 2, 1968, p. 149-171, bibl., illus., plates)

Resumé of excavations, burials and artifacts from a shell midden on the Paraná coast.

851. ———. O sambaqui do Gomes, S. 11 B., Paraná, Brasil. Curitiba, Bra., Univ. Federal do Paraná, Conselho de Pesquisas, 1968. 100 p., bibl., illus., plates, tables (Arqueologia, 4)

Detailed description of excavations and artifacts from a shell midden carbon-14 dated about 5000 years ago.

852. Ribeiro, Pedro Augusto Mentz. Inscrições rupestres no vale do Rio Caí, Rio Grande do Sul: nota prévia (UNC/AAE, 24, 1969/1970, p. 113-129, bibl., plates)

Abstract geometric petroglyphs from rock shelters in northeastern Rio Grande do Sul.

853. Rohr, João Alfredo. Os sítios arqueológicos do planalto catarinense, Brasil (IAP/P [Antropologia] 24, 1971, p. 1-56, illus., plates)

Description of 67 sites in west-central part of the planalto of Santa Catarina, including lithic, ceramic, pictographic, and other types of remains.

854. Schmitz, Pedro Ignacio; Itala Irene Basile Becker; Gastão Baumhardt; and José Proenza Brochado. Bolas de boleadeira no Rio Grande do Sul (*in* O homem antigo na América. São Paulo, Univ. de São Paulo, Instituto de Pré-História, 1971, p. 53-68, bibl., plates, tables)

Analysis of 550 bolas from various sites and collections shows greatest similarities with those from Uruguay. Distribution indicates Pampean influence.

855. Silva, Fernando Altenfelder. Un esquema interpretativo de arqueología brasileira (Arqueología y Sociedad [Lima] 4, dic. 1970, p. 45-62, bibl.)

Resumé of Brazilian archaeology in terms of five stages: Lower Lithic, Upper or Advanced Lithic, Archaic, Formative, and Recent.

856. Simões, Mário F. Indice das fases arqueológicas brasileiras: 1950-1971. Belém, Bra., Museu Paraense Emílio Goeldi, 1972. 75 p., illus. (Publicações avulsas, 13)

Alphabetical listing of 169 archaeological phases established in Brazil from 1950-71 of which 45 are preceramic and 124 ceramic with the location, references and absolute dating. Maps and charts valuable for quick reference. An essential report for South Americanists.

857. ———; **Conceição G Corrêa;** and **Ana Lúcia Machado.** Achados arqueológicos no baixo rio Fresco, Pará. Belém, Bra., Museu Paraense Emílio Goeldi, 1973. p. 113-141, bibl., illus., plates (Publicações avulsas, 20)

Pottery from a site in south-central Pará indicates a distinct archaeological complex, designated as the Carapanã Phase, possessing features allying it with the Tupiguaraní tradition of the Brazilian coast.

858. Uchôa, Dorath P. and **Caio del Rio Garcia.** Dentes de animais na cultura do sambaqui de Piaçaguera (*in* O homem antigo na América. São Paulo, Univ. de São Paulo, Instituto de Pré-História, 1971, p. 29-39, bibl., plates, table)

Type (species) and frequency of mammal, fish, and reptile teeth from a shell midden on the São Paulo coast. Majority of mammal and reptile teeth showed evidence of use as ornaments or tools. The site is carbon-14 dated about 5000 B.C.

COLOMBIA

859. Bray, Warwick and **Michael E. Moseley.** An archaeological sequence from the vicinity of Buga, Colombia (IAS/ÑP, 7/8, 1969/1970, p. 85-104, bibl., illus., plates)

Survey in the Cauca valley produced 28 settlements representing three ceramic phases, the earliest dated about 1100 A.D. and characterized by resist-painted or white and red decoration.

860. Bright, A. L. A goldsmith's blowpipe from Colombia (RAI/M, 7:2, June 1972, p. 311-313, illus.)

Description of a ceramic tube tapering toward both ends, found in Pasca, Cundinamarca. It is 23.2 cm long; one end is blackened by fire. Use as a "bellows" for gold working is postulated.

861. Broadbent, Sylvia M. La arqueología del territorio chibcha: pt. 2, Hallazgos aislados y monumentos de piedra. Bogotá, Univ. de los Andes, 1970. 29 p., bibl., illus. (Antropología, 4)

Discusses isolated finds in museums and private collections that appear to be of Chibcha affiliation.

862. Bruhns, Karen Olsen. The methods of Guaquería: illicit tomb looting in Colombia (AIA/A, 25:2, April 1972, p. 140-143, plates)

Methods employed by looters to locate and retrieve objects from Quimbaya tombs.

863. ———. Stylistic affinities between the Quimbaya gold style and a little-known ceramic style of the middle Cauca valley, Colombia (IAS/ÑP, 7/8, 1969/1970, p. 65-84, bibl., plates)

Suggests Brownware Incised defined by Bennett may be associated with the Quimbaya culture because of similarities in style of anthropomorphic treatment.

864. ———. Two prehispanic *cire perdue* casting moulds from Colombia (RAI/M, 7:2, June 1972, p. 308-311)

Two flattened disk-shape moulds from the dept. of Quindío appear to be moulds for production of small objects by the lost-wax process; date is probably Quimbaya, 900-1200 A.D.

865. Duque Gómez, Luis. Cultura quimbaya. Bogotá, Banco Popular, 1971. 16 p., bibl., plates (Catálogos de antropología colombiana, 2)

Brief, well illustrated resumé of origin, religion, goldwork, pottery, and textiles of the Quimbaya culture of the central Colombian highlands.

866. ———. Cultura tumaco. Bogotá, Banco Popular, 1971. 12 p., bibl., plates (Catálogos de arqueología colombiana, 1)

Brief, well illustrated resumé of origin, religion, goldwork, pottery, and textiles of the Quimbaya culture of the central Colombian highlands.

867. Dussán de Reichel, Alicia. Colombia: preHispanic gold objects. Lausanne, Switzerland, Editions Rencontre *published for* UNESCO, 1971. 87 p., plates.

Includes 24 colored slides of precolumbian gold objects from various Colombian cultures, with brief explanatory text in Spanish, English, German, and French.

868. Heller, Joyce de. Bibliography of preHispanic goldwork of Colombia. Bogotá, El Museo del Oro [and] Banco de la República, 1971. 126 p., illus., map (Estudios, 1:1)

Topically arranged annotated bibliography of 842 titles, with author-index.

869. Long, Stanley Vernon and **Juan A. Yánguez B.** Excavaciones en tierradentro (ICA/RCA, 15, 1970/1971, p. 9-127, illus.)

In effort to salvage work begun by Long in 1967 before his death, Yánguez worked up pottery classification from sites of El Tablón, El Volador, Cementerio de Segovia, El Rodeo and El Marne. Site descriptions also given. Of importance to scholars interested in

Colombian archaeology; very specific in comparisons. Sees strong relationships with San Agustín.

870. Reichel-Dolmatoff, Gerardo. The cultural context of early fiber-tempered pottery in northern Colombia (Florida Anthropological Society Publications [Gainesville] 25:6, 1972, p. 1-8, plates)

Brief summary of site, pottery, and other artifacts from the earliest ceramic culture known on the Colombian north coast (Puerto Hormiga). No new data.

871. ———. San Agustín: a culture of Colombia. N.Y., Praeger Publishers, 1972. 173 p., illus. (Art and civilization of Indian America series)

Superbly illustrated, popular volume on San Agustín stone sculptures, pottery found at site, and other features. Lists all radiocarbon dates; divides sequence in region into three periods from 555 B.C. to 1630 A.D.

CHILE

872. Ampuero Brito, Gonzalo and Mario Rivera Díaz. Las manifestaciones rupestres y arqueológicas del Valle El Encanto, Ovalle, Chile (Boletín [Museo Arqueológico de La Serena, Chile] 14, 1971, p. 71-105, illus.)

Detailed discussion with illustration of pictographs and petroglyphs; relates them to one culture—El Molle.

873. ——— and ———. Secuencia arqueológica del alero rocoso de San Pedro, Viejo-Pichasa, Ovalle, Chile (Boletín [Museo Arquelógico de La Serena, Chile] 14, 1971, p. 45-69, illus.)

Excavations in 1968 made in site previously studied in 1949 and 1963 as example of hunters' and gatherers' period now has three carbon-14 dates of 4700, 7050 and 9920 years before present from deposit. Goes from good leafshaped projectile point, stone-chipped horizon into appearance of pottery with grinding stones, etc. (El Molle culture) in upper levels. Preservation good. Basketry. Outside of area related points to Intihuasi in Argentina. Extremely significant.

874. Bauver, Francés Vincent. Noticias etnohistóricas acerca de las ruinas atacameñas de Chiuchiu y Lasana, provincia de Antofagasta, Chile. Iquique, Chile, Museo Regional del Iquique, 1972. 19 p. (Cuadernos de investigaciones históricas y antropológicas, 1:1)

New translation into Spanish of Bauver's (sometimes spelled Bervau) manuscript of travels during 1706-70 along Chile and Peru's coast and which discusses ruins. Designed to replace 1960 poor translation which omitted 19 lines.

875. Berdichewsky S., Bernardo. Excavaciones en la Cueva de los Catalanes (UC/BPC, 1:1, 1968, p. 33-83, bibl., illus., plates)

Excavations in a rock shelter in central Chile revealed five cultural periods beginning with proto-Araucanian and ending with colonial remains. The occupation is estimated to date from about 1200-1600 A.D.

876. ———. Formaciones culturales prehistóricas de la región centro-sur de Chile (Arqueología y Sociedad [Lima] 4, dic. 1970, p. 31-44, bibl.)

Summary of ecology, history of investigation and sequence of cultural development.

877. Dauelsberg, Percy. La cerámica de Arica y su situación cronológica (Chungara [Univ. del Norte, Arica, Chile] 1, nov. 1972, p. 15-26, bibl.)

Review of chronological sequences proposed for the Arica region beginning with Uhle culminating in the author's version as of 1961.

878. ———. Respuesta a Luis G. Lumbreras (Chungara [Univ. del Norte, Arica, Chile] 1, nov. 1972, p. 38-44)

Commentary on Lumbreras (item 884), disputing lack of progress since Bird's 1943 work and some of the other reinterpretations proposed.

879. Iribarren Charlin, Jorge. Instrumentos musicales del Norte Chico chileno (Boletín [Museo Arqueológico de la Serena, Chile] 14, 1971, p. 7-43, illus.)

Description, illustration and drawings of various stone and pottery flutes, whistles, and pan pipes, and ocarinas in Museum's collections taken from archaeological sites and with notations (as appendices) by musicologists Julio Viggiano Essaín and Millapol Gajardo. Musical notes recorded. Most interesting because of indication that many objects previously regarded as elbow and straight pipes might be musical instruments instead, especially if they show no evidence of burning.

880. ———. Una mina de explotación incaica: El Salvador, provincia de Atacama. Potrerillos, Chile, Compañía de Cobre Salvador 1972. p. 53-69, 79, plates (Col. 11 de julio)

Description of variety of artifacts encountered in a copper and turquoise mine associated with the Inca highway in north coastal Chile.

881. ——— and Hans Bergholz W. El camino del Inca en un sector del Norte Chico. Potrerillos, Chile, Compañía de Cobre Salvador, 1972. p. 5-50, 71-78, bibl., illus., plates (Col. 11 de julio)

Survey of Inca highway between the Quebrada Juncal in the north and Copiapó in the south, with description of archaeological remains associated.

882. Laming-Emperaire, Annette. Sites préhistoriques de Patagonie chilienne (MH/OM, 12:2, Été 1972, p. 201-224, bibl., maps, plates, tables)

Inventory of recorded sites, including camps, workshops, mines, burials, and pictographs. Tables indicate environmental setting and state of preservation.

883. ———; Danièle Lavallée; and Roger Humbert. Le site de Marazzi en Terre de Feu (MH/OM, 12:2, Été 1972, p. 225-244, bibl., illus., plates, tables)

Description of lithic artifacts stratigraphically excavated from a rock shelter with an initial carbon-14 date of 9590 ± 200 B.C. Bolas, bifaces, choppers, and flakes were the most common artifact types.

884. Lumbreras, Luis Guillermo. Sobre la problemática arqueológica de Arica (Chungara [Univ. del Norte, Arica, Chile] 1, nov. 1972, p. 27-29)

Decries lack of progress since 1943 in real understanding; "only the names have been changed."

885. Mostny, Grete. Prehistoria de Chile. 3. ed. rev. Santiago, Editorial Universitaria, 1971. 185 p., plates, table.

Completely revised 3. ed. of summary of Chilean cultural development from paleoindian to Spanish times. Contains list of carbon-14 dates and chronological chart divided into five regions.

886. Niemeyer F., Hans. El yacimiento arqueológico de Huana (UC/BPC, 2:2/3, 1969/1970, p. 3-63, bibl., illus.)

Description of salvage archaeology at an Inca-influenced Diaguita site on the south side of the Rio Grande valley, south of La Serena.

887. Núñez A., Lautaro. Algunos problemas del estudio del complejo arqueológico Faldas del Morro, norte de Chile (Abhandlungen und Berichte des Staatlichen Museums für Völkerkunde Dresden [Berlin] 1970, p. 79-109, bibl., illus., plates)

Discussion of content, adaptation, and influences on the Faldas del Morro complex, dated around the Christian era (± ca. 300 years), characterized by hunting, gathering, and incipient agricultural subsistence.

888. ———. Cambios de asentamientos humanos en la Quebrada de Tarapacá, norte de Chile. Antofagasta, Chile, Univ. de Chile, Programa de Arqueología y Museos, 1972. 79 p., bibl., illus. (Serie documentos de trabajo, 2)

Analysis of changes in settlement pattern, exploitation of natural resources and consequences of their exhaustion, and description of the present situation in the lower part of the *quebrada* below 1590 m. elevation.

889. ———. Respuesta a Luis G. Lumbreras (Chungara [Univ. del Norte, Arica, Chile] 1, nov. 1972, p. 30-37)

Commentary on Lumbreras, item 884, pointing out differences in interpretation and problems of unravelling multiple influences from adjacent highlands.

890. ———. Secuencia y cambio en los asentamientos humanos de la desembocadura del Río Loa, en el norte de Chile (UC/B, 112, julio 1971, p. 3-25, illus., plates)

Investigations at 50 sites permits reconstruction of series of stages: hunting, fishing, and gathering (preceramic); maritime economy, incipient agriculture and early pottery; maritime and advanced agriculture; maritime-mining economy (colonial and modern).

891. Orellana Rodríguez, Mario. Excavaciones en la confluencia de los ríos Toconce y Salado Chico (UC/BPC, 2:2/3, 1969/1970, p. 119-136, bibl., illus., plates)

Preliminary description of stone and pottery remains from a rock shelter in north Chile

892. Ortiz Troncoso, Omar R. Excavación arqueológica de la iglesia del poblado hispánico de Rey Don Felipe, Patagonia austral chilena (Anales del Instituto de la Patagonia [Punta Arenas, Chile] 1:1, 1970, p. 5-13, bibl., illus., plates)

Description of architectural remains and burials at a mission founded in 1584 and abandoned before 1587. Spanish artifacts were rare, suggesting their removal by the aborigines after departure of the Europeans.

893. Pollard, Gordon C. Cultural change and adaptation in the central Atacama desert of northern Chile (IAS/ÑP, 9, 1971, p. 41-64, bibl., illus., plate)

Between the introduction of pottery and Spanish Conquest, economy, population growth, and conquest are considered to be the major factors affecting cultural development in the Atacama desert.

894. True, Delbert L. and **Lautaro Núñez A.** Modeled anthropomorphic figurines from northern Chile (IAS/ÑP, 9, 1971, p. 65-86, bibl., illus., plates)

Analysis of all known figures from north Chile suggests at least four styles and two functional classes (mortuary and non-mortuary ritual). Dating does not permit decision whether these differences are chronological.

ECUADOR

895. Alcina Franch, José and **Miguel Rivera Dorado.** Exploración arqueológica en la costa de Esmeraldas, Ecuador (UM/REEA, 6, 1971, p. 125-142, bibl., plates)

Brief description of 16 habitation sites and ceramic remains collected during survey east and west of Esmeraldas.

896. Bischoff, Henning and **Julio Viteri Gamboa.** Pre-Valdivia occupations on the southwest coast of Ecuador (SAA/AA, 37:4, Oct. 1972, p. 548-551, illus.)

27 sherds dug from a cut at G-31, Valdivia site, July 1971, are claimed to prove a pre-Valdivia ceramic horizon which they call San Pedro. Illustrated material plus examination of specimens by Ecuadorians suggests Valdivia material and not another culture. Establishment of such a new horizon should be based on a larger sample, more convincingly different.

897. Bonifaz, Emilio. Microlitos arqueológicos. Quito, n.p., 1972. 37 p., illus., plates, tables.

Large series of obsidian artifacts subjected to hydration measurements gave results between 6000 and 13,000 before present; among the samples is a group of microliths (bifacial ovoid points) of disputed authenticity, measuring seven to 30 mm in length, and not previously reported in the paleoindian assemblage from the central Ecuadorian highlands.

898. Cueva Jaramillo, Juan. Descubrimientos arqueológicos en Ingapirca (Revista de Antropología [Casa de la Cultura Ecuatoriana, Núcleo del Azuay, Sección de Antropología, Cuenca] 3, nov. 1971, p. 215-227)

Analysis of material, mostly pottery, from excavations at site of Pilaloma about 200 meters from the main structure of Ingapirca and in other sites nearby, especially the Quebrada of Intihuaico. Gives percentages of pottery types, etc., to show many occupations from Early Narrío and Chorrera, through the Regional Developmental, and Integration Periods up to Cañari-Inca. Unfortunately no detailed pottery descriptions nor illustrations.

899. Holm, Olaf. Composite or twopiece fishhooks in Ecuador (DEF/F, 13, 1971, p. 37-41, bibl., illus.)

Description of two-piece shell fishhooks from the Bahía culture, Regional Developmental Period. Hypothesizes an evolution from one-piece circular to one-piece straight shank to two-piece to copper wire.

900. Mayer-Oakes, William J. and William R. Cameron. A fluted lanceolate point from El Inga, Ecuador (IAS/ÑP, 7/8, 1969/1970, p. 59-63, bibl., illus.)

Detailed description of obsidian point found by local resident.

901. Piña Chan, Román. Algunas ideas sobre las figurillas de Valdivia—Ecuador—y olmecas (CCE/CHA, 21:38, 1971, p. 151-158, plates)

Suggests Valdivia influence on Olmec figurine style based on head treatment indicative of skull deformation, representation of hair, form of eve, etc.

902. Porras Garcés, Pedro I. Aplicose el sistema Ford en las excavaciones de uno de los concheros más grandes de América, situado en Agua-Piedra, al norte de la Isla La Puna, llamado por los nativos El Encanto (Revista Quitumbe [Pontificia Univ. Católica del Ecuador, Facultad de Pedagogía, Depto. de Historia y Geografía, Quito] 2:2, June 1972, p. 117-124, illus.)

Preliminary statement of excavations at shell mound of El Encanto on Puna Island in Gulf of Guayaquil; 10,000 sherds and 300 stone specimens classify the site as Valdivia Culture. See item 905.

903. ———. Cinco mil años atrás en la costa ecuatoriana: Valdivia, la primera cultura cerámica de América. Quito, Pontificia Univ. Católica del Ecuador, Seminario de Arqueología, 1971-1972. 43 p., illus. (mimeo)

Summary version in Spanish of highlights of Valdivia culture, especially ceramic descriptions, for use in teaching in Ecuador with sketches of artifacts, figurines, and pottery types.

904. ———. Petroglifos del Alto Napo. Guayaquil, Ecua., Edición Huancavilca, 1971? 40 p., illus.

Arty, but with excellent reproductions, presentation of petroglyphs of upper Río Napo, collected by Padre Porras with popularized text.

905. ———. Reseña histórica de las investigaciones arqueológicas en el Oriente ecuatoriano (EANH/B, 54, enero/junio 1971, p. 133-151)

Historical account of archaeological work in eastern Ecuador with commentary by Carlos Manuel Larrea, Director of National Academy of History, Ecuador.

906. ———. Se realizan excavaciones en uno de los concheros más grandes de América, situado en Agua-Piedra, al norte de la isla La Puna, llamado por los pobladores El Encanto (CCE/CHA, 21:38, 1971, p. 189-201, bibl., illus.)

Preliminary statement of investigations then underway at a shell midden of the Valdivia culture. See item 901.

907. Reinoso Hermida, Gustavo. Vestigios arqueológicos en la región occidental del Nudo del Azuay (Revista de Antropología [Casa de la Cultura Ecuatoriana, Núcleo del Azuay, Sección de Antropología, Cuenca] 3, nov. 1971, p. 227-248, illus.)

Important listing and description of a number of ruins in area of mountains known as Nudo del Azuay. Believes that the site of Shungumarca was ordered built by the Inca Túpac Yupanqui during his occupation of Cañari.

907a. Lara, Jorge Salvador. Esquema para el estudio de la prehistoria del Ecuador (UC/A, 26:1/2, enero/junio 1970, p. 157-166, bibl., tables)

Resumé of the major cultural periods by regions, and presentation of a graph showing sequences and temporal correlations.

908. Scheller, Ulf. Joyas de cerámica. Guayaquil, Ecua., Edición Huancavilca, 1970. 53 p., illus.

Arty presentation of Manteño style pottery spindle whorls and beads. Majority appear to be spindle whorls but text calls them all beads. Good representation of the various motifs.

PERU

909. Adovasio, James M. and Thomas F. Lynch. Preceramic textiles and cordage from Guitarrero Cave, Peru (SAA/AA, 38:1, Jan. 1973, p. 84-90, illus.)

55 pieces of cordage and 13 textile fragments from dry cave dating between 9000-6000 B.C. Twining the basic technique from which later ones developed; spiral interlinking and cross-knit looping also found; possibility that simple loom weaving may have longer history in Peru than previously thought.

910. Alcina Franch, José. Excavaciones en Chinchero, Cuzco: temporadas 1968 y 1969 (UM/REAA, 5, 1970, p. 99-122, illus., plates)

Chinchero was founded during the reign of Topa Inca Yupanqui, when the area was greater than that of the modern settlement. Its history can be traced through the colonial into the modern period, from stratigraphic data, superposition of structures and historical documentation.

911. ———. El sistema urbanístico de Chinchero (*in* International Congress of Americanists, XXXIX, Lima, 1970. Actas y memorias [see item 510] v. 3, p. 124-134, bibl., illus.)

Planned town constructed as a "vacation" residence by Inca rulers demonstrated understanding of urban problems by architects and other specialists of the time.

912. Amat Olazával, Hernán. Proyecto Andino de Estudios Arqueológicos; pt. 1: Zona II, Ancash, informe preliminar de exploraciones (Arqueología y Sociedad [Lima] 5, marzo 1971, p. 36-56, bibl.)

Results of survey in Upper Marañón and Mosna basins; 24 sites range from late archaic onward, including 10 with Formative remains.

913. Ascher, Marcia and **Robert Ascher.** Numbers and relations from ancient Andean quipus (Archive for History of Exact Sciences [Berlin] 8:4, 1972, p. 288-320)

Based on study of 54 described and nine new quipus, authors approach problem as more than collection of numbers, but that ideas are shown in form of relations and these can be reduced to algebraic expressions and that quipus could produce astronomical values or other predetermined meanings. Study still underway.

914. Badner, Mino. A possible focus of Andean artistic influence in Mesoamerica. Washington, Dumbarton Oaks, 1972. 56 p., bibl., illus. (Studies in precolumbian art and archaeology, 9)

Evidence for Andean (Chavinoid) influence on Izapa style of Mesoamerica.

915. Belcore, Martha. Idolo de cerámica encontrada en la Huaca Dieciocho, Fundo Pando-Lima (PUCP/BSA, 8, oct./dic. 1970, p. 159-160, illus.)

Description of black pottery female figurine (see item 977).

916. Benavides Calle, Mario. Análisis de la cerámica Huarpa (*in* International Congress of Americanists, XXXIX, Lima, 1970. Actas y memorias [see item 510] v. 3, p. 63-88, bibl., illus., tables)

Description of a ceramic complex from the south Peruvian highlands of uncertain age, but probably not predating 400 A.D. Black on white and tricolor painting are characteristic.

916a. Benson, Elizabeth P. The Mochica: a culture of Peru. N.Y., Praeger, 1972. 164 p., illus.

General summary of Mochica culture, north coastal Peru, ca. 0-800 A.D., based on archaeological excavation and depiction on pottery. Excellent illustrations make up more than half. Useful introduction for non-specialist.

917. Bonavia, Duccio. La ceja de la selva (*in* Bonavia, Duccio and Rogger Ravines *eds.* Pueblos y culturas de la Sierra Central del Perú [see item 922] p. 90-99, illus.)

Colonization in precolonial times into tropical forest area of eastern side of Andes.

918. ———. Factores ecológicos que han intervenido en la transformación urbana a través de los últimos siglos de la época precolombina (*in* International Congress of Americanists, XXXIX, Lima, 1970. Actas y memorias [see item 510] v. 2, 79-97, bibl.)

Inca urban centers on coast follow pre-existing patterns; in ecologically distinct areas, however, they created new forms so different that they are just beginning to be recognized as of Inca origin.

919. ———. Reconocimiento arqueológico en el área del Mantaro (PIIA/A, 14, 1972, p. 11-37, bibl., illus., plates)

Survey conducted in Ayacucho dept. revealed sites between 4000 and 900 m elevation, the majority late, but one possibly dating from the Middle Horizon. Region appears ideal for interdisciplinary studies and testing of hypotheses of verticality and the relation of the *ceja de la selva* to the highlands. A map locates sites, terraces, and other archaeological evidence.

920. ——— and **George Petersen.** Agricultura y minería precolombinas (*in* Bonavia, Duccio and Rogger Ravines *eds.* Pueblos y culturas de la Sierra Central del Perú [see item 922] p. 114-127, illus.)

Precolumbian agricultural techniques and metallurgy and mining.

921. ——— and **Rogger Ravines.** Influence inca sur la côte nord du Pérou (SSA/B, 35, 1971, p. 3-18, bibl., plates)

Description and illustration of 37 vessels from north Peruvian coast showing Inca influence in shape, and/or decoration.

922. ——— and ——— *eds.* Pueblos y culturas de la Sierra Central del Perú. Lima, Cerro Pasco Corp., 1972. 148 p., bibl., illus., plates, tables.

Excellent summary for non-specialist. Volume contains 11 individual contributions. For annotations, see items 917, 920, 945, 957-958, 969, 986, 994-995, 1004 and 1006.

923. Bueno Mendoza, Alberto. Arqueología peruana: Sechín; síntesis y evaluación crítica del problema (BBAA, 33/34, 1970/1971, p. 201-224)

Excellent synthesis of evidence and interpretations concerning nature, origins, and affiliations of the Sechin site in the Casma valley. Current opinion favors a pre-Chavín date; author sees no relationship with Monte Alban in Mexico.

924. Busto Duthurburu, José Antonio. Historia general del Perú: Perú antiguo. Lima, Editorial Universo, 1970. 447 p., illus., plates.

Well illustrated synthesis of Peruvian archaeology, with primary emphasis on Inca culture. Only 132 p. are devoted to earlier cultures.

925. **Campá Soler, Raúl.** Vicús-Pabur (DGV/ZE, 95:1, 1970, p. 78-97, illus.)
Additional information on pottery, metal, and other objects extracted unscientifically from burials on Hacienda Pabur near Vicus on the Peruvian north coast.

926. **Cárdenas Martín, Mercedes.** Adobes asociados al relleno del patio de la plataforma superior de la Huaca Tres Palos (PUCP/BSA, 8, oct./dic. 1970, p. 10-21, bibl., illus.)
Description of various types of adobes used to fill a patio during Inca occupation of site, and comparison with hand-made adobes from other parts of Peru.

927. ———. Ceramio de forma Paracas en una tumba de Tablada de Lurín (PUCP/BSA, 11, julio/sept. 1971, p. 81-87, illus.)
Tomb containing three individuals, numerous pottery, metal, and animal bone fragments. One vessel with Paracas features implies contacts with south coast.

928. ———. Huaca Palomino, Valle del Rímac: fragmentería vidriada fina con decoración en colores (PUCP/BSA, 10, abril/junio 1971, p. 61-67, illus.)
Fragments of glazed decorated pottery indicate prolonged Spanish occupation of site during the 16th-17th centuries.

929. ———. Quenas de hueso en la necrópolis de Tablada de Lurín, Lima Temprano (PUCP/BSA, oct./dic. 1971, 12, p. 12-17, plates, table)
Description of bone flutes with 3-10 perforations; presence in pairs in graves implies two required for complete scale.

930. ———. Tablada de Lurín: objetos de adorno en hueso (PUCP/BSA, 9, enero/marzo 1971, p. 109-111, illus.)
Description of tooth-and-bone beads dating from the early Intermediate period.

931. **Cardich, Augusto.** Un esquema de la prehistoria andina de la crónica de Guamán Poma de Ayala (Relaciones de la Sociedad Argentina de Antropología [B.A.] 5:2 [nueva serie] 1971, p. 35-47)
Demonstrates importance of this chronicler in understanding the prehistory of Andean area.

932. **Cogorno Ventura, Gilda.** Hallazgo último de dos naipes en la Huaca Tres Palos (PUCP/BSA, 9, enero/marzo 1971, p. 84-89, illus.)
Description of two playing cards from excavations at Huaca Tres Palos, from a region adjacent to earlier discoveries of similar post-Spanish objects.

933. **Corbacho Carrillo, Susana.** Mate priograbado de la Huaca Corpus I, Fundo Pando (PUCP/BSA, 8, oct./dic. 1970, p. 1-9, illus.)
Description of a burial containing several offerings, among them a pyro-engraved gourd decorated with human and animal figures. An associated pot showed Chimu influence.

934. ———. Nota sobre Huaca Corpus I, Fundo Pando (PUCP/BSA, 11, julio/sept. 1971, p. 89-94, map)
Excavation of a rectangular stone and clay walled structure revealed remains of burials, a variety of perishable materials, etc., along with carefully placed child bundles possibly representing sacrifices.

935. ———. Piezas de metal de la Huaca Tres Palos (PUCP/BSA, 10, abril/junio 1971, p. 72-75, illus.)
Iron nails and stirrup from post-Spanish occupation.

936. **Craig, Alan K.** and **Norbert P. Psuty.** Paleoecology of shell mounds at Otuma, Peru (AGS/GR, 61:1, Jan. 1971, p. 125-132)
Examination of ecology of shellfish species and evidence for coastal rise leads to interpretation of shell middens around former shoreline as possible intermittent camps for exploitation of shellfish, dating between 3100 and 3600 before present.

937. **Day, Kent C.** Urban planning at Chan Chan, Peru (*in* Ucko, Peter J. and Ruth Tringham. Man, settlement and urbanism. London, G. W. Dimbleby, Duckworth, 1972, p. 927-930)
Chan Chan was a planned city of Chimu empire to orient people, safeguard goods, provide markets and administrative facilities, protect wealthy dead, connect city to countryside and distant parts, and to assure the city's continued commercial prosperity.

938. **Donnan, Christopher B.** Ancient Peruvian potters' marks and their interpretation through ethnographic analogy (SAA/AA, 36:4, Oct. 1971, p. 460-466, illus., maps)
Slash marks and punctates on neck of Moche vessels are suggested to be potter's identifications by analogy with modern central highland practices.

939. ———. Moche-Huari murals from northern Peru (AIA/A, 25:2, April 1972, p. 85-95, illus., map, plates)
Murals on walls of Huaca Facho, 25 km northeast of Chiclayo show blending of Wari and Mochica styles prior to extinction of latter on north coast.

940. **Dwyer, Edward.** A Chanapata figurine from Cuzco, Peru (IAS/ÑP, 9, 1971, p. 33-40, bibl., illus., plate)
Description of a hollow pottery figurine, 20 cm. tall, from Minas Pata, estimated to date between 600-200 B.C.

941. **Earle, Timothy K.** Lurín Valley, Peru: early intermediate period settlement development (SAA/AA, 37:4, Oct. 1972, p. 467-477, maps, tables)
Very important ecologically oriented article showing how the environmental situation of Lurín Valley had a lot to do with the social development of the upper Lurín Valley and the expanding Early Intermediate

Period Lima state. Discusses development of irrigation and population expansion; warfare as a regulator of population. Local social stratification develops but strong centralized political control introduced from outside.

942. Engel, Frederic. Exploration of the Chilca Canyon, Peru (UC/CA, 11:1, Feb. 1970, p. 55-58, bibl.)

Detailed exploration of archaeology of Chilca valley, today one of driest parts of central coast reveals hundreds of sites; gives carbon dates. Specialists should look up article. Shows occupation from 7575 B.C. up to Inca periods.

943. Espejo Núñez, Julio. Bibliografía del antiguo Perú: cultura Chavín (PUCP/BSA, 11, julio/sept. 1971, p. 1-43)

Includes newspaper articles and mimeographed reports as well as published references.

944. ———. Fuentes para el estudio de la cultura Pucara (PUCP/BSA, 9, enero/marzo 1971, p. 78-83)

Bibliography dealing with Pucara culture.

945. Espinoza Soriano, Waldemar. Reducciones, pueblos, y ciudades (*in* Bonavia, Duccio and Rogger Ravines eds. Pueblos y culturas de la Sierra Central del Perú [see item 922] p. 100-113, illus.)

16th-century documents about the area.

946. Friedman, Arnold M.; Edward Olsen; and **Junius B. Bird.** Moche copper analyses: early New World metal technology (SAA/AA, 37:2, April 1972, p. 254-258)

Trace element analysis of 12 Moche copper pedestal cups showed eight to be made from natural ores and four by smelting of oxidized ores.

946a. Fung Pineda, Rosa. Las Aldas: su ubicación dentro del proceso histórico del Perú antiguo (USPMAA/D, 5:9/10, junho/dez. 1969 [i.e., 1972], p. 1-208, bibl., illus.)

Detailed account of cultural stratigraphy at a site south of Casma with preceramic and early ceramic remains (pre-Chavín and Chavinoid). Comparison with other Formative sites leads to the hypothesis that Chavín origins lie on the Central coast rather than in the eastern lowlands, although some elements may be of tropical forest derivation.

947. Gelling, Peter S. Excavation of a cave at Los Castillos in the valley of the Río Huenque in southern Peru (IAS/ÑP, 9, 1971, p. 17-22, bibl., illus., plate)

Potsherds and lithic objects from a rock shelter in south Peruvian highlands, probably resulting from periodic occupation by herders.

948. González Carré, J. E. and **Carlos Chahud.** Arqueología de Naupas (Arqueología y Sociedad [Lima] 4, dic. 1970, p. 1-12, bibl.)

Preliminary description of late pre-Inca site in Ayacucho dept. composed of about 400 houses, probably associated with the Chanka.

949. González del Río Gil, Concepción. Hallazgos arqueológicos en el bajo Madre de Dios (PUCP/BSA, 9, enero/marzo 1971, p. 69-77, illus.)

Description of six stone and one metal ax from a radius of 20 km. from Puerto Maldonado, elevation 250 m.

950. ———. Necrópolis de Tablada de Lurín: área 10,000—hallazgo de una pira funeraria (PUCP/BSA, 12, oct./dic, 1971, p. 1-5, illus.)

Description of an adult cremated after interment in association with preceramic remains dating about 5800 B.C.

951. ———. Necrópolis de Tablada de Lurín: entierro 3 área 15 (PUCP/BSA, 12, oct./dic. 1971, p. 18-22, illus.)

Description of a warrior's grave.

952. Grossman, Joel Warren. A huaquero's discard: eleven associated molds from Huaca Facho, Peru (IAS/ÑP, 7/8, 1969/1970, p. 29-40, bibl., plates)

Molds for casting pottery *adornos*, probably of Chimu affiliation, from the Lambayeque valley.

953. Hoyt, Margaret A. and **Michael E. Moseley.** The Burr Frieze: a rediscovery at Chan Chan (IAS/ÑP, 7/8, 1969/1970, p. 41-57, bibl., plates)

Discussion of an intricate plaster frieze in the Velarde ciudadela, probably dating from just after the Inca conquest of Chan Chan.

954. Huapaya Manco, Cirilo. Manos cruzadas de Kon-Kon (PUCP/BSA, 9, enero/marzo 1971, p. 60-68, illus.)

Discussion of a pottery fragment with crossed hands, from a site in Chillón valley, resembling the architectural representation at Kotosh.

955. Hurtado de Mendoza, Luis and **Jesús Ramírez Tazza.** Industrias líticas del valle de Palcamayo (*in* International Congress of Americanists, XXXIX, Lima, 1970. Actas y memorias [see item 510] v. 3, p. 28-40, bibl., illus., plates)

Surface collections from eight groups of rock shelters produced artifact types corresponding to the Puente, Jaywa, and Piki phases defined by MacNeish in Ayacucho and dated between 8000 and 4500 B.C.

956. Ibarra Grasso, Dick Edgar. La escritura precolombina de los antiguos mochicas sobre pallares o portos (DGV/ZE, 95:1, 1970, p. 98-103)

Interprets symbols on Mochica, Paracas, and other coastal Peruvian objects as a form of hieroglyphic writing that was introduced by transpacific contact through the medium of seals.

957. Isbell, William H. Las culturas intermedias: 200-600 d. de J.C. (*in* Bonavia, Duccio and Rogger Ravines *eds.* Pueblos y culturas de la Sierra Central del Perú [see item 922] p. 44-51, illus.)

Cultures between the Early Formative (Chavín) and the development of Huari.

958. ———. Huari y los orígenes del primer imperio andino (*in* Bonavia, Duccio and Rogger Ravines *eds.* Pueblos y culturas de la Sierra Central del Perú [see item 922] p. 52-65, illus.)

Origins of the first empire—Huari.

959. ———. Un pueblo rural ayacuchano durante el imperio Huari (*in* International Congress of Americanists, XXXIX, Lima, 1970. Actas y memorias [see item 510], v. 3, p. 89-105, bibl., plates)

Excavations at Jargampata, 25 km from Huari, shed light on local way of life under Huari domination.

960. Izmui, Seiichi and **Kazuo Terada** *eds.* Andes 4: excavations at Kotosh, Peru, 1963 and 1966. Tokyo, Univ. of Tokyo Press, 1972. 375 p., bibl., illus., plates, tables.

Detailed description of work subsequent to publication of Andes 2 (see *HLAS 27:660*), with refinement of chronology, revision of ceramic typology, and increased information on the earliest (Mito) period. Conclusions have been amplified rather than altered, except that the Sajara-Patac and San Blas periods have been combined. Liberally illustrated, following the high quality of earlier reports in the Andes series. Includes 107 text figures and 160 plates and figures.

961. ———; **Pedro J. Cuculiza;** and **Chiaki Kano.** Excavations at Sillacoto, Huánuco, Peru. Tokyo, Univ. of Tokyo, University Museum, 1972. 82 p., illus., plates (Bulletin, 3)

Report on excavations at a site near Kotosh, which provided corrobation for the sequence there; Mito, Wairajirca, Kotosh, and Higueras remains were encountered.

962. Jiménez Borja, Arturo and **Alberto Bueno Mendoza.** Breves notas acerca de Pachacamac (Arqueología y Sociedad [Lima] 4, dic. 1970, p. 13-25)

Brief resumé of history of Pachacamac site from founding to Spanish Conquest.

963. Kano, Chiaki. Excavaciones en Shillacoto, Huánuco (*in* International Congress of Americanists, XXXIX, Lima, 1970. Actas y memorias [see item 510] v. 3, p. 52-62, illus.)

Resumé of sequence near Kotosh, verifying the chronology at the latter site.

964. Kelley, David H. Reconocimientos arqueológicos en la costa norte del Perú (Arqueología y Sociedad [Lima] 5, marzo 1971, p. 1-16)

Brief description of 10 new cultures recognized between Boca Virrilá and the mouth of the Río Chira, plus three from other areas.

965. Kirkner, George O. Guijarros de magnetita y de otros materiales en entierros del Peru prehispánico (PIIA/A, 14, 1972, p. 1-9, plate)

Descrption of 28 pebbles (18 magnetite; others hematite, limonite, pyrite, or mixed), some from burials, apparently used for grinding, polishing, or pounding. Absence of the raw material in some regions implies introduction from distant areas.

966. Lumbreras, Luis Guillermo. De los orígenes del estado en el Perú: nueva crónica sobre el viejo Perú. Lima, Editorial Milla Batres, 1972. 153 p., illus.

Discussion of Peruvian prehistory from earliest hunters to Inca Empire with emphasis on development of state, socio-political structure, related religious foundations, etc. Excellently written from an archaeologist's point of view, making a living reconstruction of prehistory rather than dealing only with exotic specimens and ruins.

967. ———. Proyecto de investigaciones arqueológicas en Puno (Pumapunku [Instituto de Cultura Aymara, La Paz] 3 [2. semestre] julio/dic. 1971, p. 58-68)

Explains need to investigate domestication of animals and plants in high Andes from earliest precolumbian times to present, especially use made today by people of area of same plants. Stresses importance of developing region around Puno for tourism in connection with archaeological sites.

968. Lynch, Thomas F. Preceramic transhumance in the Callejón de Huaylas, Peru (SAA/AA, 36:2, April 1971, p. 139-148, bibl., map)

Presence of the same types of stone artifacts in strikingly different proportions at sites in distinct ecological settings suggests seasonal movement for exploitation of varying food resources.

969. Matos Mendieta, Ramiro. Alfareros y agricultores (*in* Bonavia, Duccio and Rogger Ravines *eds.* Pueblos y culturas de la Sierra Central del Perú [see item 922] p. 34-43, illus.)

Beginnings of agriculture and appearance of pottery.

970. ———. El período formativo en el valle del Mantaro (*in* International Congress of Americanists, XXXIX, Lima, 1970. Actas y memorias [see item 510] v. 3, p. 41-51, bibl.)

Five sites were encountered, all of middle or late Formative date judging from ceramic typology.

971. Menzel, Dorothy. Estudios arqueológicos en los valles de Ica, Pisco, Chincha y Cañete (Arqueología y Sociedad [Lima] 6, junio 1971, p. 1-161, bibl., plates, tables)

Summary of results of investigations during 1957-59 under Fulbright auspices.

972. Morris, Craig. The identification of function in Inca architecture and ceramics (*in* International Congress of Americanists, XXXIX, Lima, 1970. Actas y memorias [see item 510] v. 3, p. 135-144, bibl.)

Types of structures and pottery associated with certain functions in imperial centers of Central Highlands, including storage, residence, administration, and religion.

973. Mosley, M. Edward and **Carol J. Mackey.** Peruvian settlement pattern studies and small site methodology (SAA/AA, 37:1, Jan. 1972, p. 67-81)

Objects to Willey's pioneer-settlement pattern study because of a simple site taxonomy that is insensitive to range of human activities that went on at different settlements. Shows that subsequent studies have not recognized problem nor dealt with it. Introduces a small site methodology as one possible solution. Theoretically interesting with good historical resumé of problem.

974. Myers, Thomas P. A seasonal campsite in the Peruvian *montaña:* ethnography and ecology in archaeological interpretation (SAA/AA, 37:4, Oct. 1972, p. 540-545, illus.)

Identifies a site on lower Aguatia River, a tributary of Ucayali River, eastern Peru, as a seasonal turtle harvesting encampment. Evidence presented not convincing; although turtles known to be a basic food supply in area.

975. Neira Avendaño, Máximo and **Vera Penteado Coelho.** Enterramientos de cabezas de la cultura nasca (MP/R, 20, 1972/1973, p. 109-142, plates)

Description of four caches of human heads from cemetery No. 2, Chaviña, associated with Nazca refuse. One carbon-14 date from a textile was 450 A.D.

976. Núñez del Prado Béjar, Juan Víctor. Dos nuevas estatuas de estilo Pucara halladas en Chumbivilcas, Peru (IAS/ÑP, 9, 1971, p. 23-32, bibl., plates)

Description of two stone statues of Pucara style from Chumbivilcas province more than 150 km. from the type site of the culture.

977. Obando, Isolina. Idolo de cerámica encontrado en la Huaca Dieciocho, Fundo Pando, Lima (PUCP/BSA, 8, oct./dic. 1970, p. 161-2, illus.)

Comparison with figurines from Ancón and Pasamayo shows that all possess perforations in the upper part of the head; in other respects the Huaca 18 figurine is unique (see item 915).

978. Olivera de Bueno, Gloria. Blusa de niño y uncu decorado, de la zona arqueológica de Pando, Huaca Tres Palos y Huaca La Luz, Chacra Ríos Sur (PUCP/BSA, 9, enero/marzo 1971, p. 102-106, illus.)

Description of Spanish jacket and aboriginal poncho.

979. ———. Huacas de Pando: una evaluación de sus tejidos (PUCP/BSA, 12, oct./dic. 1971, p. 23-28, illus., plate)

Summary of characteristics of textiles based on examination of more than 500 fragments.

980. ———. Tejidos funerarios de Pando, Lima: una clasificación (PUCP/BSA, 11, julio/sept. 1971, p. 66-80, bibl., illus., plates)

Analysis of 147 textiles from burials of Maranga, Later Intermediate, and Late (16th century) periods.

981. O'Phelan G., Scarlett. Breve comentario sobre idolillos humanos o "cuchimilcos" (PUCP/BSA, 11, julio/sept. 1971, p. 95-102, bibl., illus.)

Figurines of the Late Intermediate period, concentrated in the depts. of Lima and Ica, present sufficient uniformity to suggest existence of a cult involving women, fecundity, earth, rain, and agriculture.

982. Ossa, Paul P. and **Michael E. Mosley.** La Cumbre: a preliminary report on research into the early lithic occupation of the Moche Valley, Peru (IAS/ÑP, 9, 1971, p. 1-16, bibl., illus.)

Stemmed projectile points and other artifacts from a surface site are possibly associated with extinct fauna dated at 8585 B.C.

983. Palacios, Julián. Las pinturas rupestres de las cuevas de Pizocoma (Arqueología y Sociedad [Lima] 5, marzo 1971, p. 57-58)

Painted scenes of guanaco or deer hunting from rock shelters in Puna dept. at an elevation of 3900 meters.

984. Patterson, Thomas C. The emergence of food production in central Peru (*in* Struever, Stuart *ed.* Prehistoric agriculture [see item 530] p. 181-207)

Changes from wild to domesticated food subsistence can be described by a four-factor model composed of interrelationships between population increase, intensity of land utilization, movement of people and/or goods, and location and permanency of settlement. The model does not necessarily apply to other parts of the world, or even other parts of Peru because of variables such as environmental diversity and patterns of exploitation.

985. Proulx, Donald A. Headhunting in ancient Peru (AIA/A, 24:1, Jan. 1971, p. 16-21, illus., map, plates, table)

Review of evidence of head trophies in the Nazca and Ica valleys of south coastal Peru from about 1300 B.C. onward.

986. Pulgar Vidal, Javier. El paisaje (*in* Bonavia, Duccio and Rogger Ravines *eds.* Pueblos y culturas de la Sierra Central del Perú [see item 922] p. 14-23, illus.)

General description of the geographical setting.

987. Ramos de Cox, Josefina. Análisis de materiales, 1960: Facultad de Química de la Universidad Nacional Mayor de San Marcos (PUCP/BSA, 12, oct./dic. 1971, p. 6-11)

Analysis for 13 elements of four metal and four mineral specimens from Tablada de Lurín.

988. ———. Figurines de Lima: posibles arquetipos ocupacionales (PUCP/BSA, 11, julio/sept. 1971, p. 103-108, bibl., plates)

Suggests variations in position of arms and hands on

figurines may symbolize specialized activities, such as agriculture, fishing, weaving, and trading.

989. ———. Implementos de agricultura incipiente—Lima: Tablada de Lurín, 5,880-4,500 A.C. (PUCP/BSA, 8, oct./dic. 1970, p. 129-158, bibl., illus.)

Description of stone tools, with abundant illustration of possible methods of holding for use, with or without hafting.

990. ———. Pando y Tablada, Lima-Perú (PUCP/BSA, 9, enero/marzo 1971, p. 90-101, bibl., illus.)

Some results of 15-year program of research at sites with occupations initially dated at 4500 B.C. and continuing into the Christian era.

991. ———. ¿Transporte pre-hispánico con llamas? (PUCP/BSA, 10, abril/junio 1971, p. 68-71)

Llama corral associated with structures indicative of trade at the Pando site may imply use of llamas for transport of goods.

992. Ravines, Rogger. Grupos de tradición cazadora en las tierras altas de Huancavélica, Perú (*in* International Congress of Americanists, XXXIX, Lima, 1970. Actas y memorias [see item 510] v. 3, p. 17-27, illus.)

Tests in several rock shelters averaging 4600 m elevation produced lanceolate points and pottery of the Initial Period.

993. ———. Introducción (*in* Bonavia, Duccio and Rogger Ravines *eds*. Pueblos y culturas de la Sierra Central del Perú [see item 922] p. 8-13)

Establishes a sequence for precolumbian cultures in central highlands.

994. ———. Los primeros habitantes (*in* Bonavia, Duccio and Rogger Ravines *eds*. Pueblos y culturas de la Sierra Central del Perú [see item 922] p. 24-33, illus.)

Paleo-Indian horizon of hunters and gatherers.

995. ——— and **Duccio Bonavia**. Arte rupestre (*in* Bonavia, Duccio and Rogger Ravines *eds*. Pueblos y culturas de la Sierra Central del Perú [see item 922] p. 128-139 illus.)

Pictographs.

996. Rivera Dorado, Miguel. La cerámica de Cancha-Cancha, Cuzco, Peru (UASD/R, 2:2/3, julio 1971/junio 1972, p. 36-49, illus.)

Site is south of town of Chinchero, Urubamba prov., Cuzco dept. dug by Univ. of Madrid expeditions. Very few Inca sherds found, rest belong to Killke style; classified and described into ten types.

997. ———. La cerámica killke y la arqueología de Cuzco (UM/REAA, 6, 1971, p. 85-24, illus.)

Defines the Killke ceramic style from Cuzco area and gives detailed discussions on the relationships between this culture and Inca, with all the different theories. Of importance to Andean experts since based on recent work of Univ. of Madrid and use of all previous data.

998. ———. Diseños decorativos en la cerámica killke (*in* International Congress of Americanists, XXXIX, Lima, 1970. Actas y memorias [see item 510] v. 3, p. 106-115, bibl., illus., plates)

Description of the Killke painted style based on sherd samples from three sites near Cuzco; the culture fits between the Huari and Inca periods.

999. Roosevelt, Anna. Dolls from the grave (Indian Notes [Museum of the American Indian, N.Y.] 8:1, Jan. 1972, p. 18-25, bibl., plates)

Description and discussion of possible significance of "dolls" from Chancay graves based on examples in Museum of the American Indian. N.Y.

1000. Rowe, John Howland and **Catherine Terry Brandel**. Pucara style pottery designs (IAS/ÑP, 7/8, 1969/1970, p. 1-16, bibl., illus., plates)

Description and illustration of Pucara decorated pottery in the Museo Nacional de Antropología and the Museo Arqueológico of Cuzco.

1001. Samaniego R., Lorenzo Alberto. Chan Chan: la ciudadela "Rivero" (Arqueología y Sociedad [Lima] 4, dic. 1970, p. 26-31)

Brief account of initial work under a program inaugurated 1970 by Casa de la Cultura del Perú for investigation and conservation at Chan Chan. Includes plan.

1002. Spielbauer, Judith. Nazca figures from the Malcolm Whyte collection (AIA/A, 25:1, Jan. 1972, p. 20-25, illus.)

Seven female and three male pottery figurines in Milwaukee Public Museum collections described and illustrated into Lothrop and Mahler classification from Chaviña, Peru burials. One seated figure is most unusual.

1003. Stumer, Louis. Informe preliminar sobre el recorrido del valle de Cañete (Arqueología y Sociedad [Lima] 5, marzo 1971, p. 23-35)

Resumé of results from survey conducted under Fulbright auspices in 1958-59.

1004. Thompson, Donald E. Etnias y grupos locales tardíos (*in* Bonavia, Duccio and Rogger Ravines *eds*. Pueblos y culturas de la Sierra Central del Perú [see item 922] p. 66-74, illus.)

Spanish chroniclers' comments on late period occupations.

1005. ———. Late prehispanic occupations in the eastern Peruvian Andes (*in* International Congress of Americanists, XXXIX, Lima, 1970. Actas y memorias [see item 510] v. 3, p. 116-123, bibl., plates)

Discussion of evidence for the Wamali, a local ethnic group incorporated by the Inca in the dept. of Huánuco.

1006. ———. La ocupación incaica en la Sierra Central (*in* Bonavia, Duccio and Rogger Ravines eds. Pueblos y culturas de la Sierra Central del Perú [see item 922] p. 76-89, illus.)

Inca occupation in Central Sierra.

1007. Tolstoy, Paul. Reconocimiento arqueológico en el valle de Piura (Arqueología y Sociedad [Lima] 5, marzo 1971, p. 17-22)

Work accomplished in 1957-58, together with subsequent investigation by Ford, yielded 234 sites in the lower Piura valley, representing ten chronological complexes.

1008. Valle Quiroga de Corcuera, Rosa del. Antiguas industrias líticas en Tablada de Lurín: continuación (PUCP/BSA, 8, oct./dic. 1970, p. 22-128, bibl., illus.)

Continuation of description of stone implements (see *HLAS 33:1215*), comparison with other South American early lithic complexes, and justification for placing remains in "epiprotolithic" horizon. The earliest carbon-14 date is 9150 ± 120 years.

1009. Van Stan, Ina. Six bags with woven pockets from pre-Columbian Peru (IAS/ÑP, 7/8, 1969/1970, p. 17-27, bibl., illus.)

Six examples (five from Ica) of cloth woven "to provide for small free-hanging pockets that form tabs on the outer faces of the bag."

1010. ———. The wrappings from a child mummy from Ancón, Peru (IAS/ÑP, 9, 1971, p. 87-112, bibl., illus.)

Description of group of textiles in the US National Museum associated with a child mummy; no new techniques were noted.

1011. Wallace, Dwight T. Sitios arqueológicos del Perú: pt. 2, Valles de Chincha y de Pisco (PIIA/A, 13, 1971, p. 1-131, illus.)

List of sites encountered during 1957-58; data include name, location, environment, site description, condition, size, presence of refuse or burials, architecture, culture period, and bibliographical references.

1012. Yde, Jens. Et sydperuansk Paracas-kar i Etnografisk Samling (Nationalmuseets Arbejdsmark [Copenhagen] 1970, p. 103-108, plates)

Color illustration and description of Paracas incised and polychrome anthropomorphic vessel collected in 1847.

1013. Zuidema, R. Tom. Meaning in Nazca art (EM/A, 1971, p. 35-54, bibl., plates)

Effort to demonstrate persistence of religious concepts from Nazca to Huari to Inca based on depictions of deities on pottery vessels.

URUGUAY

1013a. Taddei, Antonio. El Catalanense: un yacimiento precerámico del Uruguay (Revista [Comisión Municipal de Cultura, Dept. de Antropología y Folklore, Concordia, Arg.] 2:2, 1971, p. 6-12, bibl., illus.)

Description of a flake industry represented by some 30,000 artifacts from 34 sites in the Catalán Chico area of northwestern Uruguay; estimated age is 8000 to 9000 years.

1014. ———. Una industria lítica precerámica en Sierras de Acegua, Cerro Largo, Uruguay (MHNM/CA, 1:10, 1972, p. 1-17, bibl., illus.)

213 artifacts from five sites near Brazilian border are classified and described. All are surface collections and include only partially flaked tools, in which attention was given the working edge rather than the overall form.

VENEZUELA

1015. Hall, Robert L. and **Ernest Harburg.** Análisis de unos tiestos de una cueva del Estado Portuguesa, Venezuela (Boletín [Sociedad Venezolana de Espeleología, Caracas] 3:1, marzo 1970, p. 63-71, illus.)

Sherds from Saguas river cave, near Río Saguas' confluence with Río Guanare. Author says they look like River Ranchería (Colombia) material, but in terms of Rouse and Cruzent are Tocuyanoid Series.

1016. Lewis, B.R. and **James Robert Moriarty.** Cave sites in Trujillo, Venezuela (AAC/AJ, 8:3, 1970, p. 2-10, plates)

Figurines, elaborate pottery vessels, and stone "batwing" carvings from caves at high elevations are interpreted as ceremonial caches and burials of distinguished individuals.

1017. Perera, Miguel Angel. Contribución al conocimiento de la espeleología histórica en Venezuela: pt. 2, La arqueología hipógea del Orinoco Medio, Territorio Federal Amazonas (Boletín [Sociedad Venezolana de Espeleología, Caracas] 3:2, nov. 1971, p. 151-163, illus., maps)

Describes archaeological materials from Raudeles area between what is known as Middle and Upper Orinoco and makes comparative comments. Of interest to the expert in northern South America.

1018. ———. Espelelogía histórica: breve relación sobre dos cuevas de interés espeleoarqueológico (Boletín [Sociedad Venezolana de Espeleología, Caracas] 2:1, marzo 1969, p. 49-61, illus.)

Two caves in area of Chichiriviche, estado de Falcón, had archaeological materials. Of importance to specialist.

1019. ———. Espeleologia histórica: notas preliminares acerca de los petroglifos de algunos cuevas del Estado Falcón, Venezuela (Boletín [Sociedad Venezolana de Espeleología, Caracas] 3:1, marzo 1970, p. 51-61, illus.)

See similarities in petroglyphs found in caves of Cabo de Tucacas, Falcón state with those from Aragua, Carabobo, Miranda states and the Distrito Federal.

1020. ———. Notas arqueológicas sobre la alfarería de la Cueva del Toro, estado Falcón,

Venezuela (Boletín, [Sociedad Venezolana de Espeleología, Caracas] 3:1, marzo 1970, p. 73-82, illus.).)

Sees relationships in the material found to the following series of Cruxent and Rouse: Tocuyanoid, Dabajuroid, and Tierroid. Of interest to specialist.

1021. Sanoja, Mario. La fase Zancudo: investigaciones arqueológicas en el Lago de Maracaibo. Caracas, Univ. Central de Venezuela, Instituto de Investigaciones Económicas y Sociales, 1969-1971. 251 p., bibl., illus., plates, tables (Col. Antropología y sociología)

Detailed description of sites, artifacts, faunal remains, and other archaeological evidence for the Zancudo phase; quantitative ceramic analysis permitted construction of a relative chronology and recognition of changes through time in various aspects of the culture. Ecological aspects are discussed. Two carbon-14 dates are 830 and 903 A.D.; estimated duration is between 750 and 1400.

1022. Vargas Arenas, Iraida. La fase El Cuartel (Revista de la Facultad de Ciencias Económicas y Sociales [Univ. Central de Venezuela, Caracas] 12:4, oct./dic. 1970, p. 142-156, illus.)

Description of the complex known as El Cuartel Phase from sites along the coast in Sucre state near city of Carúpano. Relates to Saladoid tradition with interesting difference. Relates it to Ronquín, also showing differences. Of importance to specialist in South American and Caribbean archaeology.

1023. Wagner, Erika. Alte Zeremonialgeräte aus den Venezolanischen Anden (Zeitschrift für Archäologie und Urgeschichte [Berlin] 2:4, 1971, p. 19-27, bibl., plates)

Excellent photographs of figurines and stone amulets from the states of Trujillo and Mérida.

1024. ———. Arqueología de la region de mucuchíes en los Andes venezolanos (UASD/R, 2:2/3, julio 1971/junio 1972, p. 79-87, illus.)

Establishes the Mucuchíes Phase from work in sites of El Mocao Alto and La Era Nueva around the Mucuchíes region, Mérida state. Carbon-dates at 450-1120 before present, or Period IV of Rouse and Cruxent. Relates to Mirinday, Betijoque, Dabajuro and Tierra de los Indios of Venezuela and Chibcha and Tairona of Colombia.

1025. ———. The Mucuchíes phase: an extension of the Andean cultural pattern into western Venezuela (AAA/AA, 75:1, Feb. 1973, p. 195-213, bibl., illus.)

Summary of data previously presented (see *HLAS 33:1271-1272*).

1026. ———. Vasijas multípodas y sus posibles usos en la arqueología americana (IAH/A, 7/8, 1970/1971 [i.e., 1972] p. 441-455, illus.)

Suggests that research in Eastern Colombia and Western Venezuela will give a greater time depth to origin of multipod footed pottery vessels instead of seeing their origin from Middle America to South America.

1027. ——— and **Carlos Schubert.** Prehispanic workshop of serpentinite artifacts, Venezuelan Andes, and possible raw material source (AAAS/S, 175:4024, Feb. 1972, p. 888-890, illus., maps)

Serpentine is not available in Venezuelan Andes and raw materials encountered there must have been acquired from elsewhere; nearest sources are east of Barquisimeto on Venezuelan coast.

1028. Zucchi de Romero, Alberta. Construcciones artificiales en los Llanos Occidentales de Venezuela (IAH/A, 7/8, 1970/1971 [i.e., 1972] p. 401-413, illus.)

Discusses problems of research open in Llanos of Venezuela on artificial constructions of mounds, causeways, ridged fields, canals, moats.

1029. ———. New data of polychrome painting from Venezuela (SAA/AA, 37:3, July 1972, p. 439-446, illus., map, plates)

Description of Caño de Oso polychrome pottery from western Venezuelan Llanos. Although 24 of 26 carbon-14 dates place this complex between 130-600 A.D., author concludes that a single aberrant date of 920 B.C. proves it to be the oldest polychrome pottery from northern South America.

1030. ———. Prehistoric human occupations of the western Venezuelan Llanos (SAA/AA, 38:2, April 1973, p. 182-190, illus.)

Speculations on manioc cultivation and artificial earthworks based upon excavations at Hato de la Calzada, Barinas state.

ETHNOLOGY: MIDDLE AMERICA

JOHN M. INGHAM

Associate Professor of Anthroplogy
University of Minnesota

THE FOLLOWING COMPILATION CONTAINS several innovative analytical pieces and some significant contributions to descriptive ethnography. One may also note with satisfaction that more material is available in Spanish, thanks in part to such outlets as the series SEP/INI (Secretaría de Educación Pública/Instituto Nacional Indigenista).

Recent developments in the study of social symbols and their paradigmatic structures are now being employed to advantage in Middle America, particularly in analyses of religious and cosmological systems. Blaffer's monograph on Mayan spooks and Gudeman's essay on the theology of *compadrazgo* illustrate the strengths of structuralist approaches. Descriptive works on religion outnumber interpretative ones but may nonetheless give rise to theoretical statements; some excellent ethnographic accounts of spiritual life among the Huichol and Totonac, for instance, appear to be amenable to structural analysis. Moreover, the remarkable traditionalism of these cultures should encourage increased attention to indigenous religious patterns in other groups. A more complete ethnographic record of indigenous religious systems may throw important light on the root metaphors and basic paradigms of ancient Mesoamerican religions.

Structural models may be appropriate for religious ideology, but in the Middle American context statistical models frequently seem more germane to the examination of social structures, which are often open-ended and multi-levelled. Advances in network theory and the increasing practicality of multivariate statistical analysis have had an expectable influence on current studies of *compadrazgo*, friendship patterns, socioeconomic change, and urbanization.

American scholars have renewed their interest in acculturation, perhaps in response to its obvious acceleration. The former concerns with general theory and the identification of origins of cultural traits have largely given way to the delineation of sources of change in particular cases by means of historical reconstruction, controlled comparison, or multivariate analysis of survey research data.

Mexican—and to a lesser extent Guatemalan—anthropologists have been engaged in a difficult debate on the ethics of *indigenismo*. The discussion has various facets, but we may observe that indigenistas claim industrialization and incorporation of Indian cultures into national societies are inevitable and that, therefore, anthropologists should participate in government programs to make the unavoidable transitions easier. Their critics note, however, that in some instances indigenistas believe that industrialized society is superior to traditional society and that their writings express ethnocentrism and an outmoded evolutionism. The critics argue further that incorporation merely replaces the colonialist exploitation of Indians with their capitalist exploitation as workers and consumers; they would prefer to see the Indian's radical liberation rather than his economic and cultural integration into the present society. Indigenistas in turn reply that given existing political realities such objections merely lead to inaction. Criticism of indigenismo has indeed been somewhat theoretical, and, despite a plea for relevant research, it has yet to address itself to such concrete issues as the forthcoming removal of the Chinantec from their homeland.

1031. Acheson, James M. Limited good or limited goods? Response to economic opportunity in a Tarascan pueblo (AAA/AA, 74:5, Oct. 1972, p. 1151-1169, map)

Development of mechanized carpentry in the pueblo of Cuanajo suggests that individual acceptance of innovation is better explained in this case by economic variables than by cultural or psychological ones.

1032. Adams, Richard N. A survey of provincial power structure in Guatemala (*in* Goldschmidt, Walter and Harry Hoijer *eds*. The social anthropology of Latin America [see *HLAS 33:508*] p. 157-174, bibl., tables)

Scaling within relative power domains reveals the relationships of local elites and the process of their emergence better than a simple comparative typology.

1033. Arrott, Margaret. A unique method of making pottery: Santa Apolonia, Guatemala (UMUP/E, 14:4, Summer 1972, p. 17-26, illus., plates)

In most Guatemalan pottery-making a coiling technique is employed, but in this community the method can be described as approximating that of the potter who uses the wheel, except that the pot remains stationary and the potter revolves around it. Author describes various refinements of technique and the several types of ware produced.

1034. Baer, Phillip and **William R. Merrifield.** Los lacandones de México: dos estudios. México, Instituto Nacional Indigenista, 1972. 281 p., bibl., illus., map, plates, tables (Col. SEP/INI, 15)

First essay is a history of the southern Lacandon during the last 100 years with attention to family organization, social order, social conflict, and migration, as affected by disease and a shortage of marriageable women. Second describes Lacandon subsistence patterns.

1035. Blaffer, Sarah C. The Black-man of Zinacantán: a Central American legend. Including an analysis of tales recorded and translated by Robert M. Laughlin. Austin, Tex., Univ. of Texas Press, 1972. 194 p., bibl., illus., plates (Texas Pan American series)

Marvelous book offers a structural analysis of various past and present Mayan spooks, particularly the so-called "Black-Man" of Zinacantán, a super-sexed demon with a six-foot-long, death-dealing penis. Insightful analyses of good data suggest that Mayan spooks have anomalous traits and thus mediate such oppositions as life/death and culture/nature. The spooks evidently have the social function of reinforcing proper sex-role behavior among women.

1036. Bonfil, Alicia O. de. La literatura cristera. México, Instituto Nacional de Antropología e Historia, 1970. 115 p., bibl.

Collection of hymns, *corridos*, and speeches from the Cristero rebellion.

1037. Cámara Barbachano, Fernando. Teoría, métodos y técnicas en el rescate etnográfico mexicano (INAH/B, 41, sept. 1970, p. 27-33, bibl., plates)

Demonstrates that in the Mexican context effective salvage ethnography must take account of 1) historical problems, 2) dynamic processes of cultural change and persistence, and 3) the multiple levels of national integration.

1038. Carranza R., Luis Felipe. Costumbres o ceremonias matrimoniales indígenas en el departamento de Totonicapán (GIIN/GI, 6:2/3, abril/sept. 1971, p. 161-171)

Relatively good ethnographic description of courtship, marriage negotiations, and marriage ceremony.

1039. Carrasco, Pedro. La importancia de las sobrevivencias pre-hispánicas en la religión tarasca: la lluvia (*in* International Congress of Americanists, XXXVIII, Stuttgart-München, FRG, 1968. Verhandlungen [see *HLAS 33:510*] v. 3, p. 265-273, bibl.)

Several folktales and beliefs about lightning, rain, and rainbows are presented. While they are partly pre-columbian in origin, they also have folk-Catholic elements; author therefore concludes that they cannot be understood as survivals of a distinct Tarascan religion.

1040. ———. Tarascan folk religion: Christian or pagan? (*in* Goldschmidt, Walter and Harry Hoijer *eds.* The social anthropology of Latin America [see *HLAS 33:508*] p. 3-15, bibl.)

Distinction between folk and church religions is essential. In failing to make this distinction, van Zantwijk has misinterpreted folk Catholic practices as survivals of precolumbian Tarascan religion.

1041. Caso, Alfonso. La comunidad indígena. Prólogo de Gonzalo Aguirre Beltrán. México, Secretaría de Educación Pública, 1971. 246 p. (Col. SepSetentas, 8)

Selection of articles and lectures by leading Mexican anthropologist on various aspects of modern indigenous culture in Mexico. [B. J. Meggers]

1042. Christensen, Bodil and **Samuel Martí.** Brujerías y papel precolombino. México, Ediciones Euroamericanas, 1971. 88 p., bibl., illus., plates.

Description of the ancient art of paper-making in an Otomí village. Uses of paper dolls in curing and fertility rituals are discussed, and some comparative observations are made on precolumbian uses of paper. Bilingual English-Spanish edition.

1043. Correa, Gustavo. Espíritu del mal en Guatemala (GIIN/GI, 6:2/3, abril/sept. 1971, p. 5-110)

Traces the impact of Catholic notions of the Devil and evil spirit, as evidenced in various legendary supernatural figures, superstitions, and witchcraft, on Mayan cultures from the Conquest to the present.

1044. Crumrine, Lynne S. Mayo Santos: a paradigmatic analysis of a sacred symbol (*in* Meeting of the American Ethnological Society, Seattle, Wash., 1969. Proceedings. Seattle, Wash., American Ethnological Society, 1969, p. 134-150, table)

Classes of symbols such as crosses, saints, and flowers consist of allo-symbols which are systematically differentiated. Mayo mechanisms for integrating symbols are illustrated, but the analysis is not paradigmatic; at least, a *system* of opposition and correlation of symbols is not fully delineated.

1045. Fábrega, Horacio, Jr. Begging in a southeastern Mexican city (SAA/HO, 30:3, Fall 1971, p. 277-287)

Begging behavior in the highland town of San Cristóbal, Chiapas, is examined. Social dimensions of begging and begging styles are discussed.

1046. Fábregas Puig, Andrés. El problema del nahualismo en la literatura etnológica mexicana (ICACH, 19:1, [2, época] enero/junio 1970, p. 41-57)

Review of some of the existing ethnographic and theoretical literature concerning *naguales* and *tonales*.

1047. Falla, Ricardo. Hacia la revolución verde: adopción y dependencia del fertilizante químico en un municipio del Quiché, Guatemala (III/AI, 32:2, abril/junio 1972, p. 437-480, bibl., tables)

Detailed report on an introduction of chemical fertilizers in a context of population pressure and *minifundismo*. Degree of acceptance by Indian communities is related to cultural traditions and agricultural practices.

1048. Favre, Henri. Changement et continuité chez les mayas du Mexique: contribution à l'étude de la situation coloniale en Amérique Latine. Paris, Editions Anthropos, 1971. 352 p., bibl., map, tables.

Historical study of change and continuity among the Tzotzil Maya of Highland Chiapas.

1049. Foster, George M. Character and personal relationships seen through proverbs in Tzintzuntzan, Mexico (AFS/JAF, 83:329, July/Sept. 1970, p. 304-317)

Proverbs reveal some aspects of social character and spell out how the prudent villager should cope with his social milieu.

1050. Furst, Peter T. To find our life: peyote among the Huichol Indians of Mexico (*in* Furst, Peter T. *ed.* Flesh of the gods: the ritual use of hallucinogens. N.Y., Praeger Publishers, 1972, p. 136-184, plates)

Detailed and well-crafted description of Huichol use of peyote. Their philosophical and ritual system is essentially pre-European and is predicated on the notion that transformable spiritual energy is imminent and evenly distributed in nature. The symbolic fusion of deer, maiz, and peyote illustrates concern with fertility; and re-birth symbolism is apparent in the ritual pilgrimage to the sacred mountains of *wirikúti*.

1051. ———— and **Salomón Nahmad.** Mitos y arte huicholes. México, Secretaría de Educación Pública, 1972. 171 p., bibl., plates, table (Col. SepSetentas, 50)

Lengthy, detailed essay by Furst on the Huichol conception of the soul, that is, its genesis and composition, maladies related to the soul such as soul loss, the voyage of the soul after death, and the return of souls of the dead as crystals of rock which facilitate a mystical communion between the living and the dead. Shorter paper by Furst examines the yarn paintings of Ramón Medina as they reflect his relation to the supernatural world of the Huichol, his contact with civilization, and the problem of resistance to the commercialization of Huichol art. Twenty colored plates illustrate the yarn painting and are accompanied by explanations of their mythical content. Third paper by Nahmad considers historical, social, and economic dimensions of Huichol artesanry.

1052. Green, Judith Strupp. Archaeological Chihuahuan textiles and modern Tarahumara weaving (SEM/E, 36:1/4, 1971, p. 115-130, plates)

Similarities and continuities are noted between contemporary Tarahumaran and ancient Chihuahuan manufacture of textiles.

1053. Gudeman, Stephan. The *compadrazgo* as a reflection of the natural and spiritual person (*in* Royal Anthropological Institute of Great Britain and Ireland, London, 1971. Proceedings. London, Royal Anthropological Institute of Great Britain and Ireland, 1971, p. 45-71, bibl., illus., tables)

In this fine essay features and variations of godparenthood in Middle America and elsewhere are elucidated by a proportion that follows from the theological antinomy between spiritual and natural birth/baptism; family/*compadrazgo*. It is suggested that the historical reworking of the concepts of spiritual paternity and spiritual relationship is a diachronic unfolding of the antinomy's logic. Data from Veraguas, Panama, further illustrate the argument. For example, ties within the family are said to be profane and private, whereas *compadrazgo* is sacred and public; linkage of separate households through the latter is thus consistent with theology. Cross-cultural permutations of the institution are explained by several principles that presuppose the invariant structure of *compadrazgo* and its relation to the family. Also see item 1108.

1054. Helms, Mary W. Asang: adaptations to culture contact in a Miskito community. Gainesville, Fla., Univ. of Florida Press, 1971. 268 p., bibl., maps, plates, tables.

Descriptive treatment of socioeconomic organization, and a discussion of adaptation to religious missions.

1055. Hernández, Alejandro. Migración de colonos en Darién (UNCIA/HC, 2:1, dic. 1970, p. 81-95, plates, tables)

Examines origins and characteristics of the colonists in Darién and ongoing social, economic. and cultural change in the region.

1056. Herrera, Francisco. La zona indígena del distrito de Las Palmas, Veraguas y el proceso de politización (UNCIA/HC, 2:1, dic. 1970, p. 97-105, bibl., plates)

Cursory survey of Indian groups living in this region, with notes on the adaptation of the indigenous political organization to that imposed by the government.

1057. Hinton, Thomas B. An analysis of religious syncretism among the Cora of Nayarit (*in* International Congress of Americanists, XXXVIII, Stuttgart-München, FRG, 1968. Verhandlungen [see *HLAS 33:510*] v. 3, p. 275-279, bibl.)

Deals with the syncretic nature of a trinity of Cora deities: *Tayaó* (Grandfather Fire, also God and Jesus); *Tati* (Our Mother, also *La Virgen Santísima*); and *Tahás* (Morning Star, also San Miguel). A cycle of Catholic fiestas has few Indian elements, whereas *mitotes,* ceremonies concerned with *maíz,* form a separate cycle which lacks Catholic elements. There follows a reconstruction of the historical development of this pattern of syncretism.

1058. ————. Indian acculturation in Nayarit: the Cora response to mestizoization (*in* Goldschmidt, Walter and Harry Hoijer *eds.* The social anthropology of Latin America [see *HLAS 33:508*] p. 16-35, bibl.)

Rejection of mestizo influence revolves around fear of loss of land and desire to conserve *costumbres,* whereas dwindling population and Cora-mestizo intermarriage, the bracero program, and government schools encourage mestizoization.

1059. ———— and others. Coras, huicholes y tepehuanes. Translations by Carine Joseph de Hernández; Martha Fernández Valdéz; and Silvia Rendón. México, Instituto Nacional Indigenista, 1972. 177 p., bibl., plates (Col. SEP-INI, 11)

Collection of ten previously published papers with

emphasis on descriptive ethnography and acculturation.

1060. Hobgood, John J. The sanctuary of Chalma (*in* International Congress of Americanists, XXXVIII, Stuttgart-München, FRG, 1968. Verhandlungen [see *HLAS 33:510*] v. 3, 247-263, bibl., map)

Article is essentially a diary-like account of a Chalma pilgrimage which author made in the company of Otomi people from Huizquilucan. Concluding remarks discuss the syncretism of Aztec and Catholic traditions at Chalma.

1061. Holloman, Regina Evans. Ritos de pubertad masculina, matrimonio pre-pubertad, y couvade entre los kunas de Panamá: algunas notas etno-históricas. Translated by Reina Torres de Araúz (UNCIA/HC, 2:2, dic. 1971, p. 41-49, bibl.)

Reported here are brief and separate ethno-historical notes on several practices which have disappeared or are in the process of doing so: 1) a male puberty rite which existed until 1850; 2) pre-puberty marriage (i.e., at 12 to 13 years) which allows males to be socialized by their fathers-in-law; and 3) a true couvade which still obtains among the Kunas of the interior of Darién but not among San Blas Kuna.

1062. Horcasitas, Fernando *ed.* Life and death in Milpa Alta: a Nahuatl chronicle of Díaz and Zapata. Translated by . . . Foreword by Miguel Leó-Portilla. Drawings by Alberto Beltrán. Norman, Okla., Univ. of Oklahoma Press, 1972. 187 p., illus.

From the Nahuatl recollections of Doña Luz Jiménez, elderly woman's personal account of life in a Nahuatl-speaking village before the Revolution of 1910. She also tells of her experience during the Revolution. This book has more value as a biographical document than as a source of ethnographic information.

1063. Ichon, Alain. La religión de los totonacas de la sierra. México, Instituto Nacional Indigenista, 1973. 512 p., bibl., illus., maps, plates, tables (Col. SEP-INI, 16)

Significant ethnography of a contemporary Indian religion which preserves a remarkable resemblance to those of the ancient Maya and Aztecs. Included are excellent and copious materials on beliefs, myths, rituals, ceremonies, dances, and medicine which reveal that many Totonac supernatural figures are versions of such Aztec deities as Xipe Totec, Tlaloc, Ehécatl, etc. Analytical treatment of the data bring out the structural properties of religious symbolism, but the social aspects of religion are not given systematic attention.

1064. Ingham, John M. Time and space in ancient Mexico: symbolic dimensions of clanship (RAI/M, 6:4, Dec. 1971, p. 615-629, bibl., illus., map, tables)

Reconstruction of a partially intact barrio-chapel system in the formerly Nahuatl-speaking community of Tlayacapan, Morelos, suggests a model for ideal Aztec social structure (i.e., Tenochtitlan). This model, a four-part divisions of 26 clan-like groups, finds some corroboration in early sources. It is theorized that the solar calendar and 260-day almanac respectively reflected hierarchical and egalitarian aspects of this social structure.

1065. Iwańska, Alicja. Purgatory and utopia: a Mazahua Indian village of Mexico. Foreword [by] Sol Tax. Cambridge, Mass., Schenkman Publishing Co., 1971. 214 p., plates.

Largely descriptive ethnography of a Mazahua community. Emphasis is on world view, especially conceptions of the universe, self, and society as they relate to the somewhat contradictory desires for "progress" and maintenance of Mazahua identity.

1066. Jenkinson, Michael. The glory of the long-distance runner. Photographs by Karl Kernberger (AMNH/NH, 81:1, Jan. 1972, p. 55-65, maps, plates)

Informal description of the rugged Tarahumara country, the role of running in the everyday life of the Tarahumara, and the *rarijipari*, running contests.

1067. Kennedy, John G. Bonds of laughter among the Tarahumara Indians: towards a rethinking of joking relationship theory (*in* Goldschmidt, Walter Hoijer *eds*. The social anthropology of Latin America [see *HLAS 33:508*] p. 36-68, bibl.)

Traditional functional explanations do not adequately account for Tarahumara joking between siblings-in-law and between alternating generations. It is theorized that a more comprehensive approach should consider human needs for play and humor.

1068. ———. Inápunchi: una comunidad tarahumara gentil. México, Instituto Indigenista Interamericano, 1970. 257 p., bibl., illus., maps, plates, tables.

Good treatment of the political and economic organizations of the Tarahumara with emphasis on historical and ecological factors. Of central concern are the social and economic ramifications of the *tesguino* beer-drinking complex in terms of social networks.

1069. Köhler, Ulrich. Gelenkter Kulturwandel im Hochland von Chiapas: eine Studie zur angewandten Ethnologie in Mexico. Bielefeld, FRG, Bertelsmann Universitätsverlag, 1969. 295 p., map, tables (Freiburger Studien zu Politik und Gesellschaft überseeischer Länder: Schriftenreihe des Arnold-Bergstaesser-Institus für Kulturwissenshaftliche Forschung, 7)

Description and analysis of a regional project in the Highlands of Chiapas which aims to integrate Tzeltal and Tzotzil Indians into Mexico's national economy and culture. The project, being carried out by the Centro Coordinador Tzeltal-Tzotzil (CCTT), a dependency of the Instituto Nacional Indigenista, also intends to improve living conditions among the Indians through education, public health, road construction, and economic development.

1070. Leonardo L., Carlos H. Las cofradías de Zacualpa, departamento de El Quiché (GIIN/GI, 6:4, dic. 1971, p. 196-200)

Brief and very descriptive treatment of the organization and obligations of fiesta sponsorship in Zacualpa.

1071. Linares de Sapir, Olga. Patrones de poblamiento prehispánico comparados con los modernos en Bocas del Toro, Panamá (UNCIA/HC, 2:1, dic. 1970, p. 56-67, plates)

Possession of an extensive aboriculture by the Guaymí de Bocas Indians suggests that ecological factors should be taken into account in estimating aboriginal population in this region.

1072. Litzler, Beverly N. A web of land: differential acculturation in southern Oaxaca (*in* Goldschmidt, Walter and Harry Hoijer eds. The social anthropology of Latin America [see *HLAS 33:508*] p. 69-79, bibl.)

Land tenure explains the greater conservatism of one of two Zapotec communities.

1073. Luján Muñoz, Luis. Notas sobre el uso de máscaras en Guatemala (GIIN/GI, 6:2/3, abril/sept. 1971, p. 129-145, bibl.)

Overview of continuities and discontinuities in the uses of ritual masks from precolumbian times to the present suggests that the magical sense of masks is being lost or converted into an expression of play often combined with intoxication.

1074. McGee, W. J. The Seri Indians of Bahia Kino and Sonora, Mexico. Glorieta, N. Mex., Rio Grande Press, 1971. 406 p., illus., maps, plates, tables.

New edition of this classic work, originally the 17th annual report of the Bureau of American Ethnology to the Secretary of the Smithsonian Institution, 1895-96.

1075. Madsen, William and **Claudia Madsen.** A guide to Mexican witchcraft. 2. ed. Commentary by Gonzalo Aguirre Beltrán. México, Editorial Minutiae Mexicana, 1972. 96 p., bibl., illus., plates (Minutiae mexicana series)

Popular and lively account of folk curing, witchcraft, and medical folklore in past and contemporary Mexico which nonetheless deserves professional attention for its rich descriptive material and perceptive reading of ethnographies of Mexican communities. Similarities are noted in seemingly different folk medical practices and the relationship between concern with witchcraft and economic mobility is amply documented with amusing anecdotes. Commentary by Aguirre Beltrán stresses the role of medical beliefs in reinforcing social roles and suggests that practices deemed irrational by modern science tend to persist in areas that have not received the benefits of modern industrialization.

1076. Marroquín, Alejandro D. Panorama del indigenismo en Guatemala (III/AI, 32:2, abril/junio 1972, p. 291-318, bibl., tables)

Reviews current demographic, social, and economic situation of Guatemalan Indians, and evaluates various private and government community development programs. In particular, it offers several constructive criticisms of the Instituto Indigenista Nacional de Guatemala.

1077. Méndez Rodríguez, Alfredo. Una vez más ¿qué es indio? (III/AI, 32:2, abril/junio 1972, p. 337-352)

Considers the merits of substantive and relational meanings of *indio* and similar terms as well as the question of whether Indians comprise a caste or class. Author takes issue with models of dialectical opposition on the grounds that they ignore social complexities.

1078. Mexico. Secretaría de Educación Pública. ¿Ha fracasado el indigenismo?: reportaje de una controversia, 13 de septiembre de 1971. México, 1971. 247 p., bibl. (SepSetentas, 9)

Report on the aims and activities of the Instituto Nacional Indigenista in the presence of President Luis Echeverría Alvarez. Gonzalo Aguirre Beltrán briefly describes *las regiones de refugio* and concludes that a program must include regional economic development as well as social and cultural change among Indian groups *per se*. Specific projects of INI are described in optimistic terms by staff members of INI and other agencies, but Fernando Benítez, an invited speaker, raises disturbing questions about ongoing institutional neglect of Indian communities.

1079. Mielche, Hakon. Maya: Riget, der forsvandt. København, Steen Hasselbalchs Forlag, 1967. 262 p., tables.

Danish travel writer's impressions of countries where Maya culture flourished. Comments on history and archaeology of region and on Maya descendants' plight vis-á-vis the advance of modern technology and education. Includes splendid color photographs of Maya sites. [R. V. Shaw]

1080. Miller, Frank C. Old villages and a new town: industrialization in Mexico. Menlo Park, Calif., Cummings Publishing Co., 1973. 161 p., bibl., plates, tables (The Kiste and Organ social change series in anthropology)

Examines the impact of a planned industrial city on a series of small communities in Hidalgo state. Effects of the Revolution of 1910 on rural Mexico are illustrated in this region by the decline of the *pulque* haciendas, the growth of barley cultivation by *ejidos*, and a shift away from closed-corporate community organization and an ideology of limited good. Recently, a new industrial city has affected traditional inter-village networks, demographic patterns, standards of living, prestige rankings, and educational aspirations. Wealth and education are shown to have had a positive relation to entry into the industrial labor market, whereas the present situation of high educational and occupational aspirations, growing population, and stabilizing labor market leads to a consideration of available adaptive strategies.

1081. Nash, June. The passion play in Mayan Indian communities (CSSH, 10:3, April 1968, p. 318-327, bibl.)

Roles, alliance, and conflict are shown to be symbolized in religious drama. While the social identifications of Jesus and Mary are not always precise, Judas' figure clearly caricaturizes the ladinos' commercial chicanery, sexual license with Indian women, and prerogatives of social dominance. Factions formed around indigenous Catholicism, orthodox Catholicism, Protestantism, and folk religion may clash over the presentation of passion plays, depending on local interpretation of figures in the plays.

1082. Nietschmann, Bernard. The distribution of Miskito, Sumu, and Rama Indians, eastern

Nicaragua (ICUAER/B, 11, 1969, p. 91-102, bibl., map, plates)

Past and present distributions are noted along with the approximate population size and ecological situation of each group. An appeal is made for ethnographic interest in this region, especially with regard to the Sumu, a relatively unstudied and unacculturated people.

1083. Nutini, Hugo A. and Timothy D. Murphy. Labor migration and family structure in the Tlaxcala-Puebla area, Mexico (*in* Goldschmidt, Walter and Harry Hoijer eds. The social anthropology of Latin America [see *HLAS 33:508*] p. 80-103, bibl., map, table)

Agriculture accounts for only 50 percent of a family's subsistence and labor migration accounts for the remainder. Latter is correlated with extended family households, apparently because they provide for the security of and control over the absent laborer's wife and children.

1084. Ordóñez Chipín, Martín. Estudio sobre la poliginia en Santa María Chiquimula, municipio del departamento de Totonicapán (GIIN/GI, 6:2/3, abril/sept. 1971, p. 154-159)

In this community polygyny is a recent phenomenon, having developed in the last 40 years. Marriage practices and household organization are delineated, and polygyny is accounted for in terms of need for female labor and economic ability to support additional wives.

1085. Orozco, Luis Enrique. Los Critos de caña de maíz y otras venerables imágenes de Nuestro Señor Jesucristo. Guadalajara, Mex., The Author, 1970. 522 p., plates.

Contains descriptive and anecdotal material concerning a large number of miraculous images, especially ones relating to fertility, which are found in communities in Jalisco.

1086. Pendergast, David M. The practice of *primicias* in San José Succotz, British Honduras—Belize (SEM/E, 37:1/4, 1972, p. 88-96, bibl., map, plates)

Primicias, ceremonies of thanksgiving to the gods for favors granted, are still held in connection with agriculture and curing, despite Reina's earlier report to the contrary. Rapid acculturation, however, is affecting this and other elements of traditional Mayan culture.

1087. Pennington, Campbell. The Tepehuan of Chihuahua: their material culture. Salt Lake City, Utah, Univ. of Utah Press, 1969. 413 p., bibl., maps, plates, tables.

Covered in this study are physical environment, population, agriculture, hunting, gathering, fishing, animal husbandry, medicinal plants, textiles, and dwellings. Tables illustrate similarities and differences between Tarahumara and Tepehuan cultures, thus establishing the Indian heritage and identity of the Tepehuan.

1088. Pérez Calderón, José A. La población indígena: de la colonia a la época presente (III/AI, 32:3, abril/junio 1972, p. 325-330)

Historical review of Guatemala's Indian population, from colonial times to the present. Briefly comments on the Indians' misfortunes in the colonial period, and with respect to the current situation argues that more should be done to augment the Indian's capacity for production and consumption, while recognizing the social and cultural values of Indian communities.

1089. Plattner, Stuart. Occupation and marriage in a Mexican trading community (UNM/SWJA, 28:2, Summer 1972, p. 193-206, tables)

Marriages in an endogamous barrio of San Cristóbal are related to the socioeconomic ranking of the occupations of both spouses. Spouses tend to match in status, and an application of a Monte Carlo simulation demonstrates that the empirical approximation to perfect matching is highly significant. Occupational status at marriage suggests that higher ranking people achieve benefits of economic integration, whereas lower ranking people may be forced to accept whatever occupations they are capable of entering.

1090. Reed, Karen Barbara. El INI y los huicholes. México, Instituto Nacional Indigenista, 1972. 176 p., bibl., illus., maps, plates (Col. SEP-INI, 15)

Examines the efforts of the Centro Coordinador Cora-Huichol (CCCH) of the Instituto Nacional Indigenista in promoting acceptance of agricultural innovation, formal education, and modern medicine by the Huichol. Sources of Huichol resistance to and acceptance of change are briefly considered, and in conclusion the author asks the question of whether or not INI's aim of raising the Huichol standard of living while encouraging the preservation of some aspects of Huichol culture is realistic.

1091. Reiche Caal, Carlos Enrique. Orfebrería cobanera, estructura y técnicas de producción (GIIN/GI, 6:4, dic. 1971, p. 191-195, plate)

Brief and cursory notes on techniques employed by silversmiths in Cobán.

1092. Rivera Domínguez, Rafael. Revisión antropológica del proceso de cambio sociocultural planificado (UNCIA/HC, 2:1, dic. 1970, p. 69-78)

Makes a number of now hackneyed observations about obstacles to planned community development programs.

1093. Rodríguez Rouanet, Francisco. El licenciado Antonio Goubaud Carrera y la fundación del Instituto Indigenista Nacional (III/AI, 32:2, abril/junio 1972, p. 331-336)

Includes an historical resumé of the founding and activities of the National Indian Institute of Guatemala as well as a brief biography of Licenciado Antonio Goubaud Carrera, its founder.

1094. ———. El maíz y el indígena guatemalteco (GIIN/GI, 6:2/3, abril/sept. 1971, p. 172-186)

According to legends extant in numerous Guatemalan Mayan communities, maíz originated in a cave and was brought to needy humans by animals in a fashion reminiscent of the relevant passage in the *Popol Vuh*. Contemporary offerings and oblations to corn spirits are also described.

1095. Romano Delgado, Agustín. Nueva tendencia ideológica de la antropología mexicana (III/A, 30, dic. 1970, p. 75-100, illus.)

Takes issue with criticisms of Mexican anthropology recently raised by Arturo Warman and others. Comments by Warman and Mercedes Olivera follow. Warman again affirms that the Indian has experienced several centuries of integration and that this is precisely the problem; he argues that what is needed is liberation, a concept radically opposed to integration.

1096. Romanucci-Ross, Lola. Conflict, violence, and morality in a Mexican village. Palo Alto, Calif., National Press Books, 1973. 203 p., bibl., plates.

This well-written book contains some excellent descriptions of kinship, patronage, *machismo*, and social conflict in a mestizo village in the *tierra caliente* of Morelos, Mex. Some readers may find, however, that the author could have made better use of comparative material and recent theoretical literature. As it stands, for example, less informed readers may assume that the village in question is representative of all *mestizo* communities, when it actually serves to illustrate patterns and processes that occur in particular historical and economic conditions.

1097. Rubio Orbe, Gonzalo. Guatemala indígena (III/AI, 32:2, abril/junio 1972, p. 275-290)

This essay, which serves as an editorial introduction to a special issue of *América Indígena* on *indigenismo* in Guatemala, contains a brief review of the demographic and economic situation of Guatemalan Indians and some superficial generalizations on their social and cultural characteristics. Also describes the activities and problems, particularly financial ones, of the Instituto Indigenista Nacional de Guatemala.

1098. Ruiz Franco, Arcadio. La contradicción en la problemática indígena (III/AI, 32:2, abril/junio 1972, p. 319-324)

Analysis of ethnocentric attitudes toward the Guatemalan Indian that have led to contradictory policies of planned change and incorporation.

1099. Sexton, James D. Education and innovation in a Guatemalan community: San Juan La Laguna. Los Angeles, Calif., Univ. of California, Latin American Center, 1972. 72 p., bibl., tables (Latin American studies, 19)

Multivariate regression indicates that external exposure, grade completed in school, and economic status account for 53 percent of the acculturation from Mayan to ladino styles (curiously termed "innovation" by the author). In a Blalock causal model, age negatively affects formal education but positively influences external exposure, which then determines acculturation. These results may be trivial, however, since there was only one school grade when many older men were young.

1100. Sittón, Salomón Nahmad; Otto Klineberg; Peter T. Furst; and Bárbara G. Meyerhoff. El peyote y los huicholes. México, Secretaría de Educación Pública, 1972. 192 p., plates (SepSetentas, 29)

Two brief articles on the general economic, political, cultural situation of the Huichol precede a longer article by Furst and Meyerhoff on myths and rituals connected with Huichol use of peyote and *datura*.

1101. Siverts, Henning. On politics and leadership in Highland Chiapas (*in* Vogt, Evon Z. and Alberto Ruz L. Desarrollo cultural de los mayas. México, UNAM, Coordinación de Humanidades, Centro de Estudios Mayas, 1971, p. 387-407, bibl.)

Analysis of strategies adopted by Indians to check ladino influence in Tzeltal communities. With the advent of the *Ayuntamiento Constitucional* elders have been forced to find Indian candidates for *presidente* to check the power of the ladino secretary. Candidates must have fluency in ladino culture but loyalty to Indian identity (e.g., participation in *cofradías*). The emergence of men with these attributes has in some instances undermined the elders' traditional authority and has encouraged the development of *caciques*, men with great political power who may or may not hold political office.

1102. Sodi M., Demetrio. La literatura maya de Chiapas (ICACH, 19:1 [2. época] enero/junio 1970, p. 59-74)

Spanish translation of 38 Lacandon texts that first appeared in Alfred M. Tozzer, *A comparative study of the Mayas and the Lacandones* (N.Y., 1907). In addition, three Tzotzil curing prayers collected by William R. Holland are published here for the first time.

1103. Spicer, Edward H. Contrasting forms of nativism among the Mayos and Yaquis of Sonora, Mexico (*in* Goldschmidt, Walter and Harry Hoijer *eds*. The social anthropology of Latin America [see *HLAS 33:508*] p. 104-126, bibl.)

Economic and political deprivation have encouraged Mayo and Yaqui nativism, but the millenarian emphasis among the Mayo was further related to disintegration of traditional social and religious organization while Yaqui military nativism was facilitated by intact traditional social organization.

1104. Taggart, James M. The fissiparous process in domestic groups of Nahuatl-speaking community (UP/E, 11:2, April 1972, p. 132-149, bibl., map, tables)

Discussion of the developmental cycle of domestic groups with emphasis on aspects of residential unity and division. Fragmentation of patrilineally extended families is related to the number of married males and to disputes among them over allocation of time and resources.

1105. Tax, Sol. Cultural difference in the Maya area: a 20th century perspective (*in* Vogt, Evon Z. and Alberto Ruz L. Desarrollo cultural de los mayas. México, UNAM, Coordinación de Humanidades, Centro de Estudios Mayas, 1971, p. 353-385, bibl.)

Mayan culture in Yucatan and that in the Chiapas-Guatemalan highlands differ in several respects: 1) lack of "constitutional" ceremonial organization in Yucatan; 2) a singular shaman-priest in Yucatan and separation of shamans and mayordomos elsewhere; and 3) the separation of secular and sacred office in Yucatan and their connection in the highlands. This distributional patterning may be a consequence of a greater preconquest separation of priests and people in the lowlands.

1106. ———— and **Robert Hinshaw.** Panajachel a generation later (*in* Goldschmidt, Walter and Harry Hoijer *eds*. The social anthropology of Latin America [see *HLAS 33:508*] p. 175-195, bibl., tables)

Despite widespread acculturation and economic change, the ethnic distinction between Indian and ladino persists.

1107. Thomas, Norman D. Rotation and synchronic autonomy: alternative expression of social distance in Middle American barrio organization (BBAA, 33-34, 1970-1971, p. 195-200)

Rotation of civil-religious offices through the barrios of a community is compared and contrasted with a system of office rotation within barrios where offices in one barrio parallel those in others. It is argued that antagonistic or factional barrios will resist submission in a hierarchical organization and will prefer, instead, a system of rotation and synchronic autonomy.

1108. Thompson, Richard A. Structural statistics and structural mechanics: the analysis of *compadrazgo* (UNM/SWJA, 27:4, Winter 1971, p. 381-403, tables)

In the Yucatec town of Ticul males who have established patrilocal postmarital residence are less likely to select relatives as godparents for their children than those who have not, and when they do the godparent is more often a kinsman of the husband than the wife. Those who have not experienced such patrilocal residence are more inclined to select a relative, particularly a wife's kinsman. It is suggested that *compadre* selection may be understood in terms of the structural implications of kinship obligations, although this interesting idea remains undeveloped. The selection rules that may account for these patterns are given rigorous formulation, and a sophisticated discussion follows on the relevance of information theory to the analysis of selection structures. Also see item 1053.

1109. Torres de Araúz, Reina. Panorama actual de las culturas indígenas panameñas (UNCIA/HC, 2:1, dic. 1970, p. 7-27, bibl., plates)

Short descriptions of the demography, distribution, and cultural characteristics of the Kuná, Guaymí, and Chocó Indians.

1110. Van Horn, Lawrence. Game theory and the strategies of Mexican cacical politics and political fission (AAC/AJ, 9:3, 1971, p. 6-13)

Survey in game theory jargon of the *cacicazgo* literature. Techniques of winning and holding political office are reviewed.

1111. Villa Rojas, Alfonso. Patrones culturales mayas antiguos y modernos en las comunidades contemporáneas de Yucatán (*in* Vogt, Evon Z. and Alberto Ruz L. Desarrollo cultural de los mayas. México, UNAM, Coordinación de Humanidades, Centro de Estudios Mayas, 1971, p. 333-385, bibl.)

Uneven distribution of aboriginal Mayan culture in Yucatan is interpreted in terms of historical factors, particularly the Caste War and subsequent development of *henequín* haciendas which led to the abandonment of the traditional *milpa* and related practices and beliefs. The influence of modern urban centers is also noted.

1112. Vogt, Evon Zartman. The Zinacantecos of Mexico: a modern Maya way of life. N.Y., Holt, Rinehart and Winston, 1970. 113 p., bibl., illus., map, plates (Case studies in cultural anthropology)

Description of the social, economic, and religious aspects of life in Zinacantan, including brief but interesting analytical treatment of the replication of social and conceptual patterns.

1113. Warman, Arturo and others. De eso que llaman antropología mexicana. México, Editorial Nuestro Tiempo, 1970. 153 p. (Col. La cultura al pueblo)

Separate essays by Arturo Warman; Guillermo Bonfil; Margarita Nolasco Armas; Mercedes Olivera de Vázquez; and Enrique Valencia question the scientific stature and ethical and political consequences of Mexican anthropology. The implications of its situation within the governmental bureaucracy for the range and quality of scientific research are examined, and the government's program of cultural integration of Indian groups into the national culture and the part anthropology has played in this program are subjected to severe criticism. Arguments are made for marxist analyses of the neocolonialist exploitation of Indians and for a political policy of liberating Indians from such exploitation while leaving them the freedom to follow their own cultural inclinations.

1114. Waterbury, Ronald. Urbanization and a traditional market system (*in* Goldschmidt, Walter and Harry Joijer *eds*. The social anthropology of Latin America [see *HLAS 33:508*] p. 126-153, bibl., tables)

Historical trends in Oaxaca's public market include: 1) ongoing viability in the urban economy; 2) rise of wholesalers; and 3) differentiation between the permanent urban market place and the periodic peasant *tianguis*.

1115. Weitlaner, Roberto J. and **Mercedes Olivera de Vázquez.** Los grupos indígenas del norte de Oaxaca. México, Instituto Nacional de Antropología e Historia, 1969. 151 p., bibl., plates.

Collection of 95 excellent photographs of various facets of the lives of the Mazateco, Chinanteco, Cuicateco, and Mixe Indians. Introduction provides a brief ethnographic description of this region.

1116. Woods, Clyde M. and **Theodore D. Graves.** The process of medical change in a Highland Guatemalan town. Los Angeles, Calif., Univ. of California, Latin American Center, 1973. 61 p., bibl., tables (Latin American studies, 21)

Following Blalock, correlational data are used to construct a causal model of the shift from recourse to shamans during illness to recourse to pharmacies and medical doctors: involvement in a cash economy promotes exposure to the outside world which in turn leads to acculturation away from traditional Mayan lifestyles and medical practices. Medical belief systems and practices themselves receive only cursory treatment.

1117. Young, Philip D. Ngwabe: tradition and change among the Western Guaymí of Panama. Urbana, Ill., Univ. of Illinois Press, 1971. 256 p., bibl., illus., maps, plates (Illinois studies in anthropology, 7)

Focuses on social and economic organization, including marital alliance, residence rules, kinship, cooperative labor, inheritance, and the distribution of goods and services. Particular attention is given to the *caserío*, a corporate group of consanguineally related males which is based on residence and bilateral filiation rather than descent.

1118. Zárate, Dora P. de. Especulaciones literarias sobre textos de tamboritos congos en Panamá (CIF/FA, 17/18:16, 1969/1970, p. 261-289, map, plate)

Presentation of a text, along with notes on the use of drums in local musical contests, from Colón province, Pan. [H. A. Selby]

ETHNOLOGY: WEST INDIES

LAMBROS COMITAS

Professor of Anthropology and Education
Teachers College, Columbia University

WHAT FOLLOWS DEPARTS SOMEWHAT FROM THE USUAL introduction by this contributing editor in previous issues of the *Handbook*. Rather than an assessment of publication trends for a very limited time period, this prolegomenon is essentially a personal, albeit partial, view of the state of social and cultural anthropological research in the Caribbean region. It is an attempt to present a perspective of the present firmly placed within the context of efforts in the past—a past that extends back only a few decades but one marked by considerable activity and accomplishment.

For a lengthy period of time before World War II, the obvious value of the Caribbean as a focus of anthropological research was obscured by the then prevailing academic trends and fashions. Some anthropologists of this period argued that the area was one of 'broken' or hybrid cultures too small and insignificant to warrant serious study and therefore of little research interest. Totally transformed as it was by European colonization, the region was, quite naturally, not suited to the traditional ethnographic study of simple societies.

After the war, the Caribbean (mainland littorals controlled by European powers as well as Antillean archipelago) became an important focus of attention for Americans, British, Dutch, Canadian, and West Indian anthropologists, and by 1960, the literature on the area can be said to rival that of many of the larger, longer studied, and better established world ethnographic areas. Furthermore, this anthropology has greatly influenced, if not dominated, other social science efforts in the region.

The underlying reasons for these developments are not difficult to perceive. The Caribbean includes a larger number of politically demarcated societies of relatively small size and population, each different but sharing many commonalities in history and structure and epitomized by cultural, social and racial complexity. Given the nature of anthropological techniques and methods, the Caribbean, particularly the Antilles, presents almost ideal conditions for research into complex societies, a subject which over the past few decades has tended to replace the traditional preoccupations with tribal, homogeneous, and isolated populations. In addition, the abruptness of the original European intrusion into the Caribbean in the sixteenth century and the almost complete extinction of the aboriginal societies at that time has provided the contemporary scholar with an absolute historical baseline from which to work.

During the last quarter century, I would estimate that at least two hundred anthropologists from many nations have carried out field investigations in the Caribbean. Scores of doctoral candidates have received their initial training and field experience in both the Greater and Lesser Antilles as well as in the mainland territories. Presently, no fewer than fifty professional anthropologists actively continue their research interests in the area, adding to an expanding literature on Caribbean social and cultural anthropology. In addition, the discipline has made contributions in archaeology, linguistics, folklore, comparative religion, and in a wide range of applied subject matter.

By the early 1960s, a combination of factors permitted the establishment of a flourishing, often exciting, regional field of anthropological investigation. Among these factors were: the intrinsic research attributes of the Caribbean; the initial ease of access of the region for foreign scholars; the early involvement of major anthropologists such as Melville J. Herskovits, Robert Redfield, Alfred Métraux, Julian Steward, M. G. Smith, George Eaton Simpson, and R. T. Smith among many others; the research stimulation stemming from contact and cross-fertilization of the American traditions in cultural anthropology and the British school of social anthropology; and finally and very importantly for the British Caribbean, the emergence of a resident West Indian research group housed at the Institute for Social and Economic Research in Jamaica which provided continuous, systematic regional study as well as guidelines, advice and critical comment to foreign Caribbeanists for almost a decade.

Anthropological research, by the 1960s, had taken several principal forms: ethnohistorical and synchronic studies of cultural continuities in the Afro-American and East Indian components of the population; functional-structural analyses concentrating particularly on family, domestic, and economic organization; cultural-ecological investigations of regional variations and uniformities; the community study approach; and total society and social stratification analyses stemming from divergent concepts such as levels of sociocultural integration, pluralism, and consensualism. In these thrusts, Caribbean research has had important implications for the study of other world areas and for social science in general. Complexity of society and culture together with manageable conditions of research have permitted the Caribbean to serve as a backdrop for the examination of some of the most significant theoretical developments in contemporary anthropology and sociology.

Limiting myself primarily to research and researchers on the Commonwealth Caribbean and to very few references to work in other parts of the region, I shall first briefly review the major anthropological approaches in Caribbean anthropology and then turn to recent developments and their possible causes.

For purposes of the discussion, the West Indian literature can be conveniently divided into three gross categories: *Continuities,* that is, research and publications dealing with theoretical, methodological, and problem themes, or population segments, which have received considerable attention or development in the past and which have persisted to the present; *Newer Thrusts,* or research which, in terms of problem or subject matter, departs from past experience; and *Consolidations,* or bibliographic work, collections of essays by single authors, and readers.

I. CONTINUITIES

1) *Amerindian-Bush Negro Studies:* with roots into the 19th century, this research continues, in the main, to be the province of French, Dutch, and British anthropologists. Dealing with the relatively isolated peoples of the interior of the Guianas who are generally outside the mainstream of national life, these studies have tended to be primarily ethnographic, social organizational, and ethnohistorical in orientation. Recent work has been marked by considerable methodological and theoretical sophistication, for example, that of Silvia W. de Groot on the ethnohistory of the Djuka and of Peter Rivière on marriage and organization among the Trio. Other important contributions have been made in the past ten years by Audrey J. Butt, Jean-Baptiste Delewarde, D. C. Geijskes, Jean Hurault, Peter Kloos, A. J. F. Köbben, Peter Neumann, Richard Price and Jens Yde. It must be noted, however, that this often meritorious research has often related conceptually more to Tropical Forest anthropology than to the main currents of Caribbean study.

2) *Afro-West Indian Studies:* In the 1930s, Herskovits envisaged a coordinated effort to study the Afro-American in the New World. While his design was never fully implemented and little of his approach and method remains in Caribbean anthropology, Herskovits and his colleagues initiated and stimulated interest and reaction in several areas of black, lower-class, West Indian life, most notably in family organization and religious behavior.

In the former area, the work of R. T. Smith on household developmental cycle, Edith Clarke on variations in household organization, and M. G. Smith on mating patterns and domestic organization provided the parameters for a productive debate on the sociology of West Indian family and household which reached beyond the boundaries of the region. More recently, this interest has continued but has been buttressed by less field work and methodological direction. Sidney M. Greenfield and Keith F. Otterbein have provided monographs on the general subject with the first arguing that the Barbadian family system emanates from English cultural tradition and the second indicating that economic and demographic factors underlie the mating system of Andros islanders. Others who have written on the subject during the last years include Norman Ashcraft, Hyman Rodman, Michael M. Horowitz, William B. Rogers and Guy Dubreuil.

Research on religious behavior and organization of black West Indians has also continued but at a diminished pace and again with less emphasis on sustained field work than in the past and certainly with less explicit grounding in method and theory than studies of domestic organization. George Eaton Simpson, the most productive scholar in this field, has contributed analyses of the Shango Cult, Rastafarianism, and the Shouters and has issued a collection of his essays on religious cults in the Caribbean. A comparison of dissociation states and possession beliefs in Haitian vodun and among the Shakers of St. Vincent has been provided by Erika Bourguignon. J. D. Elder has dealt with a Yoruba ancestor cult in Trinidad and Lydia Cabrera has written on the Abakua, a Cuban secret society. Reviews and descriptions of a variety of Afro-American religious cults have been published by Angelina Pollack-Eltz.

Other post World War II work on the black lower classes, stimulated more by British social anthropology and a growing concern with social problems than by Herskovits and the Afro-American approach, has dealt with the sociocultural parameters of making a living. This genre of anthropological research includes the path breaking studies of Sidney W. Mintz on Jamaican and Haitian marketing; M. G. Smith on rural labor supply; William Davenport and Lambros Comitas on fishing and fishing cooperatives; and Mintz, Elena Padilla, Jerome S. Handler, and Constance Sutton, among others, on plantation life. This thrust, over time, has generated discussion and controversy on the sociocultural attributes and taxonomic classification of rural populations. Concepts such as "rural proletariat," "flux equilibrium," and "occupational multiplicity," have been used with some effectiveness on the analysis of the structure and dynamics of the economic life of working people.

3) *East Indian Studies:* The accumulated research on East Indians, as contrasted with that on Afro-Americans or Amerindians, has been, implicitly or explicitly, the most relevant to what is probably the central concern of Caribbean social science—the nature of regional societies. In part, this orientation is linked to the debate initiated in the late 1950s by Morton Klass and Daniel J. Crowley over whether East Indians were culturally conservative and exclusionist or culturally adaptable and assimilationist. The directions of later studies, limited in number but generally high in quality, were undoubtedly influenced by this debate. In recent years, various elements of East Indian life have been systematically probed: for example, the nature of egalitarian ideology of plantation workers and the institutionalized breaches of this ideology by Chandra Jayawardena; patterns of social control at the village level and family organization by Barton M. Schwartz; reformist Hinduism as a facilitator of participation in national activities and of the incorporation of national values and attitudes by Jayawardena and by Schwartz; the functions, reformulation, or disappearance of caste by Arthur Niehoff, Schwartz, R. T. Smith, Jayawardena, and J. D. Speckmann; and, East Indians in Jamaica by Allen S. Ehrlich.

4) *Total Society Analyses:* The debate on the plural society, as H. Hoetink has indicated in a recent conference paper, has been strongly identified with Caribbean sociology. It should also be stressed that this debate on the nature of West Indian society, with all its ambiguities, has had a subtle and salutary side effect on the field anthropology of the region. At present, even fledgling anthropologists, entering the field for the first time, have been made profoundly aware of the problems and complexities in the alternative explanations of the nature of the society in which they will work. This early awareness, as experience with students demonstrates, has helped improve the initial selection of problem as well as the quality of research. The work of R. A. J. van Lier, Lloyd Braithwaite, M. G. Smith, R. T. Smith, H. Hoetink, and Leo Despres has done much to stimulate this major advance in anthropological perspective.

Anthropology, however, has been remiss in providing studies and data which would directly test the basic tenets in both the pluralist and consensualist positions in this debate. Quite correctly, Hoetink has noted the quasi-systematic neglect by researchers of traditional white groups in the region as well as of Syrians, Chinese and other migrant groups. Only one full-scale anthropological study of white elites exists for the Lesser Antilles, that of Edith Beaudoux-Kovats on the *békés* of Martinique. Few articles have dealt with other minorities, and these often have been limited and dated. Probably more damaging to total society studies in the Caribbean, especially in horizontally stratified social systems, is the virtual lack of anthropological research on the middle classes or segments and on urban areas.

II. NEWER THRUSTS

In recent years anthropologists have ventured into relatively unexplored territories of the Caribbean. There are hopeful signs of anthropological stirrings in Cuba, and, since the death of Trujillo, there has been a significant increase in research by foreign scholars in the Dominican Republic. In the latter country, Malcolm T. Walker studied the source of power in a mountain town, how this power is exercised and the way in which decisions are made. Nancie Solien de González has worked on aspects of rural-urban migration and Glenn Hendricks studied Dominicans in their native land and in New York City utilizing Robert Manners, Richard Frucht and Stuart B. Philpott on remittances, emigration and social field to analyze the Dominican patterns of circulatory migration.

In increasing collaboration with professionals of other disciplines, anthropologists are now contributing to the solution of practical problems and issues. One such project, directed by anthropologists, studied the effects of chronic smoking of cannabis in Jamaica. During the course of this project, the anthropologists who studied ganja users *in vivo,* and the medical clinicians who studied the sample population in the hospital, collaborated productively and effectively and the project report was cited as being instrumental in amending the ganja legislation of Jamaica. As a spinoff of this project, at least three doctoral dissertations are forthcoming on different aspects of the anthropology of ganja. Alcoholism and its sociocultural context is another health area beginning to receive serious attention.

Other recent developments in anthropological activity have been in the area of education. Vera Rubin and Marisa Zavalloni, an anthropologist-social psychologist team, analyzed the attitudes of secondary school students in Trinidad. Nancy Foner, employing traditional anthropological techniques in a study of a Jamaican community, probed into the effects of national education on the local status system, on status aspirations, and on village crises and disputes.

III. CONSOLIDATIONS

Recently, a surprising number of Caribbeanists have turned to research and to publishing efforts that reflect attempts to bring together meaningfully the published data on the region. Some anthropologists have become bibliographers of Caribbeana as, for example, Comitas and Handler; others such as George Eaton Simpson and M. G. Smith have brought together their own articles into single volumes; still others have become editors and annotators of readers on the Caribbean, Jean Benoist, Comitas and David Lowenthal, Michael M. Horowitz, and Richard Frucht.

These developments in publishing have significance. On one level, they indicate some consensus that ample regional scholarship exists which warrants coordination and consolidation in bibliographies, readers, and collections. Probably more importantly, however, these ventures demonstrate a growing interest in Caribbean affairs in the United States (where almost all of this material has been published) fueled by West Indian migrants, by heightened sensitivities of the American public to Cuba, the Dominican Republic, and Puerto Rico, and, by the rise of Black consciousness. In time, this American interest might well have serious repercussions on the conduct and direction of social science in the Caribbean.

IV. SOME ASSESSMENTS

Although it is difficult to support in any quantitative sense, Caribbean anthropology has changed significantly over the past few years. Eschewing judgements, what was once a relatively cohesive disciplinary effort on a limited number of major research foci which heavily emphasized sustained field research has now become a much more eclectic enterprise, somewhat fragmented in its methodological and theoretical orientations, apparently placing less importance on long term field work and more involved with service or applied research.

In my introduction in volume 31 of the *Handbook,* I characterized the period under review as one of consolidation and transition arguing that established Caribbeanists, with some exceptions, were publishing ethnography based on data collected during early field work, or that they were utilizing such data for the formulation or refinement of theory and, on the other hand, a new generation was emerging which had not yet reached full professional status and had yet to publish systematically. I now find this assessment possibly subject to misleading interpretation—that it may carry the implication that the causes for shifts in Caribbean anthropology are to be found within the discipline itself. Certainly it is clear that recent West Indian research has veered from directions followed in the past. However, these shifts in focus and operation appear to me to be the direct result of new pressures and conditions, both within the region and in the home countries of foreign scholars who are specialists on the Caribbean region. The present state of the field can best be understood in these terms.

With reference to regional West Indian conditions, the decrease in publications based on field research, diversification away from an earlier, more coherent effort, and the attempts at "relevance" seem to be linked to 1) the serious brain drain of qualified West Indian social scientists to the United States and the United Kingdom; 2) the promotion of others to high administrative posts away from research; 3) the lack of training facilities for a potential new generation of field oriented West Indian anthropologists; 4) the growing sensitivities to foreign researchers and the growing difficulty of research access to the region. Much of this can be understood in the light of pressures and demands emanating from political independence and self-government, a process that began to take effect, most significantly, in the early 1960s. The possibilities of maintaining a cohesive disciplinary effort have been further exacerbated by the lack of active, resident research units which could take on the vital academic functions assumed by the Institute of Social and Economic Research a decade ago.

Foreign constraints on Caribbean anthropology are coming primarily from the United States. In that country, a belated consciousness of the black population has led, in part, to the introduction of Black Studies programs at many universities. Almost paradoxically, an inordinate number of these programs are staffed and run by West Indian scholars. This has led to heightened interest in Caribbean lifeways and consequently in Caribbean materials (for example, there is almost a reprint explosion of West Indian classics and near classics) but has also contributed heavily to the brain drain and has done little to improve the quality of research on the region. Furthermore, this newly awakened awareness of the Caribbean threatens to compound the long-standing problem of indiscriminately utilizing the region as a dumping ground for the training and for the cross-cultural exposure of large numbers of undergraduate and graduate students. In the past, this has proved to be a burden and irritant to already overworked local professionals with little compensation by way of productive field results.

In sum, Caribbean anthropology still appears to me to be very much in a state of transition. And, given the volatile nature of determining factors external to the discipline, it is likely to remain in flux and uncertainty for some time to come.

I am indebted to Frances Karner Hulser for annotations of Dutch language references in the section which follows.

1119. Abraham-van der Mark, Eva E. Differences in the upbringing of boys and girls in Curaçao, correlated with differences in the degree of neurotic instability (UPR/CS, 10:1, April 1970, p. 83-88)

Brief research note on a survey of school children in Willemstad. Evidence suggests that difference in the degree of neurotic instability of girls and boys is related to differential patterns of upbringing for the sexes and to different social and economic conditions.

1120. Abrahams, Roger D. British West Indian folk drama and the 'life cycle' problem. Austin, Tex., Univ. of Texas, Institute of Latin American Studies, 1972. 265 p. (Offprint series, 112)

Utilizing Christmas plays and tea meetings from the British Leewards as evidence, author argues against the interpretation of these forms in British folk drama as "vestiges of some archetypal 'life-cycle play', through which it is argued, the tradition-oriented peasantry once expressed its agrarian vision of the totality of man's experience in the seasonal cycle and in the interdependence of life and death." This explanation is seen by the author as an urban-rooted, sophisticated, and ethnocentric judgment and not consistent with the facts. This "emphasis on the life-cycle interpretation has simply overshadowed other, equally valid community strategies in the playing of festival drama." The text of a "Bull Play" from Nevis is appended.

1121. Adams, John Edward. Historical geography of whaling in Bequia Island, West Indies (UPR/CS, 11:3, Oct. 1971, p. 55-74, bibl., maps)

Within the context of a physical description and the historical background of Bequia, author describes origins of the whaling industry, its spread to the Grenadines, boat type, the pattern of the hunt, processing the whale, marketing, income, factors in the decline of the industry, and the present struggle to revive whaling. Closes with a short statement as to the contributions of Bequia whaling.

1122. Alleyne, Mervyn. The linguistic continuity of Africa in the Caribbean (*in* Richards, Henry J. *ed.* Topics in Afro-American Studies. Buffalo, N.Y., Black Academy Press, 1971, p. 119-134)

Arguing against the stereotypes that hold that the varieties of Afro-New World speech are sub-standard, deficient and pathological and are indicators of the backwardness and inferiority of their users, the author develops the theme that a fundamental factor "in the communication system from the very inception of European/African contact was the need among Africans to mediate two cultural systems. . . . Creole languages were very effective tools in this mediation, since they allowed a minimum of communication with Europeans on the one hand and on the other hand remained ethnic languages from which Europeans were barred. Creole speakers developed a linguistic capacity which allowed them to shift from an ethnic language comprehensible only to the group to another speech level which allowed some degree of communication with the other group involved in the total system."

1123. Amersfoort, J. M. M. van. Hindostaanse Surinamers in Amersterdam (NWIG, 47:2, April 1970, p. 109-138)

Study of Surinamese of Hindu origin in Amsterdam. Special attention to their migration patterns and adaptive facilities (family, employment, social organization, etc.).

1124. Ashcraft, Norman. Colonialism and underdevelopment: processes of political economic change in British Honduras. N.Y., Columbia Univ., Teachers College Press, 1973. 180 p., bibl., tables.

Based primarily on anthropological research, this volume details the economic history of British Honduras as a case study of underdevelopment and dependence and attacks "conventional approaches to the Third World," specifically the community-study method of anthropology and traditional developmental economics. As an alternative approach, author proposes the use of social field theory which "permits data to be collected and integrated through a combination of historical and ethnographic techniques". In addition to theoretical sections on the meaning and political economy of underdevelopment; substantive chapters are provided on colonization and rise of the British Honduran mono-economy; florescence and depression in the economy; changes in forestry, land tenure, and agriculture; the origins of the rural pattern; the quality of rural life with data on community relationships, household, sources of income, transportation and trade, and schools; small-scale farming in Belize Valley; the internal marketing system; and, the urban consumer.

1124a. ———. Developmental economics: some critical remarks (JDA, 7:1, Oct. 1972, p. 3-10)

Critique of the approach taken in developmental economics in the study of underdevelopment. Anthropologist author urges that "economic performance in underdeveloped countries must instead be approached by a method that does not close the system on the basis of some a priori Western theoretical biases which exclude relevant information."

1125. ———. Economic opportunities and patterns of work: the case of British Honduras (SAA/HO, 31:4, Winter 1972, p. 425-433)

Author argues the essential continuity of contemporary patterns of work and economic opportunities from the monoeconomy patterns of the early colonial period.

1126. Beckford, George. Plantation society: toward a general theory of Caribbean society (Savacou [Caribbean Artists Movement, Kingston] 5, June 1971, p. 7-22)

Modern Caribbean society displays structural forms that are a direct legacy of the slave plantation system. In this section of a longer work, author deals with demographic characteristics of plantation economics, social organization and structure in plantation society, and political organization and distribution of power.

1127. Benoist, Jean. L'archipel inachevé: culture et société aux Antilles fraçaises. Montreal, Canada, Univ. de Montreal, 1972. 354 p., bibl., maps, tables.

Very welcome collection of articles on the French Antilles by members of the center of Caribbean Research of the Univ. of Montreal.
Jean Benoist "L'Étude Anthropologique des Antilles" p. 17-58
Serge Larose "Les Pêcheurs de Marie-Galante" p. 59-74
Jean-Marc Philibert "Les Marie-Galantais à Pointe-à-Pitre: Quelques Problèmes Posés par l'Étude de la Migration Urbaine" p. 75-92
Jean Benoist and Gilles Lefebvre "Organisation Sociale, Évolution Biologique et Diversité Linguistique à Saint-Barthélemy" p. 93-108
Edith Beaudoux-Kovats and Jean Benoist "Les Blancs Créoles de la Martinique" p. 109-132
Joseph Josy Levy "Comparaison des Relations Interpersonnelles dans Trois Communautés Martiniquaises" p. 133-148
Claude Bariteau "Organisation Familiale et Vie Économique à la Désirade" p. 149-162
Lise Pilon-Lé "Les Incidences Sociales de la Parenté Rituelle dans un Bourg Martiniquais" p. 163-178
Micheline Labelle-Robillard "L'Apprentissage du Monde dans un Village Guadeloupéen" p. 179-204
André Laplante "L'Univers Marie-Galantais: Quelques Notes sur la Cosmologie des Marie-Galantais de la Région des Bas" p. 205-232
Dan and Miriam Boghen "Notes sur la Médecine Populaire à la Martinique" p. 233-250
Madeleine Saint-Pierre "Créole ou Française? Les Cheminements d'un Choix Linguistique" p. 251-266
Jean Archambault "De la Voile au Moteur: Technologie et Changement Social aux Saintes" p. 267-292
Georges Létourneau "Régime Foncier et Configuration Domestique: Le Cas de Marie-Galante" p. 293-320
Jean-Claude De l'Orme "Les Transformations Économiques et Sociales d'un Marché Martiniquais" p. 321-336
Jean Benoist "Bilan et Perspectives" p. 337-344.

1128. Boer, M. W. H. de. Report of a contact with stoneage Indians in southern Surinam (NWIG, 47:3, Nov. 1970, p. 248-258)

Incidental description of Akurio Indians' culture and way of life by geologist working in Surinam and French Guiana.

1129. Boodhoo, Ken. Sugar and East Indian indentureship in Trinidad (Caribbean Review, [Hato Rey, P.R.] 5:2, April/June 1973, p. 17-20)

Short description of identured labor in Trinidad and its relationship to the economics of the sugar industry.

1130. Bowen, W. Errol. Rastafarism and the new society (Savacou [Caribbean Artists Movement, Kingston] 5, June 1971, p. 41-50)

Brief review of the historical and ideological background of Rastafarism followed by discussion of the future of the movement.

1131. Brathwaite, Edward Kamau. The contribution of M. J. Herskovits to Afro-American studies (Bulletin of the African Studies Association of the West Indies [Kingston] 5, Dec. 1972, p. 85-94)

An appreciation of the late Herskovits with a review of some of his work in the Afro-American field.

1132. ———. The development of creole society in Jamaica, 1770-1820. Oxford, England, Clarendon Press, 1971. 374 p., bibl., maps, tables.

Author "argues that the people, mainly from Britain and West Africa, who settled, lived, worked and were born in Jamaica, contributed to the formation of a society which developed, or was developing, its own distinctive character or culture which, insofar as it was neither purely British nor West African, is called 'creole'; that this 'creole culture' was part of a wider New World or American culture complex, itself the result of European settlement and exploitation of a new environment; and that Jamaican development (like that of the Caribbean generally), was significantly affected by realignments within this complex caused by the two major upheavals in the area during the period of this study: the American and what may be described as the 'Humanitarian' Revolutions." The posited process of creolization is in sharp opposition to those who have argued plural society in the West Indies. From a historical perspective, this study provides useful Jamaican material for the period 1770-1820, and complements the monographs on Jamaica by Philip D. Curtin, Gisela Eisner, and Douglas Hall which deal with the post-Emancipation period.

1133. Chevannes, Barry. Revival and black struggle (Savacou [Caribbean Artists Movement, Kingston] 5, June 1971, p. 27-39)

Author traces origins and growth of revival in Jamaica and argues that this development was an expression of struggle against the white man's political and cultural control. Data on the Native Baptist Movement, Myal, the Great Revival of 1860-61, and on Alexander Bedward.

1134. Ciski, Robert and **David Mulcahy.** Adaptándose al Soufrière (Ethnica [Barcelona] 4, 1972, p. 27-45, bibl., map)

1135. Clermont, Norman. Bibliographie annotée de l'anthropologie physique des Antilles. Montreal, Canada, Univ. of Montreal, Center of Caribbean Research, 1972. 51 p.

Fully annotated bibliography on the physical anthropology of the Greater and Lesser Antilles.

1136. Comitas, Lambros and **David Lowenthal** eds. Slaves, free men, citizens: West Indian perspectives. Garden City, N.Y., Anchor Press/Doubleday, 1973. 340 p., bibl.

First in a set of four paperback readers on West Indian themes and problems. The total collection contains 72 articles and selections, 45 of which were authored by West Indians. This volume concentrates on the shaping of multiracial West Indian societies and on the nature of the contemporary social order. Includes index. Also, following articles:
C. L. R. James "The Slaves" (1938) p. 4-20
Orlando Patterson "The Socialization and Personality Structure of the Slave" (1967) p. 21-46
John G. Stedman "A Planter's Day" (1806) p. 47-52
Médéric-Louis-Elie Moreau de Saint-Méry "Whites in a Slave Society" (1797) p. 53-74
Edward Long "Freed Blacks and Mulattos" (1754) p. 75-94
C. L. R. James "The Free Colored in a Slave Society" (1938) p. 95-104
Douglas Hall "Absentee-Proprietorship in the British West Indies, to about 1850" (1964) p. 105-136
William G. Sewell "The Ordeal of Free Labor in the British West Indies" (1861) p. 137-150
James Anthony Froude "The Perils of Black Supremacy" (1888) p. 151-160
J. J. Thomas "Froudacity Refuted" (1889) p. 161-173
M. G. Smith "The Plural Framework of Jamaican Society" (1961) p. 174-194
David Lowenthal "The Range and Variation of Caribbean Societies" (1960) p. 195-212
Lloyd Braithwaite "Stratification in Trinidad" (1953) p. 213-240
Edith Kovats-Beaudoux "A Dominant Minority: The White Creoles of Martinique" (1969) p. 241-276
Daniel J. Crowley "Cultural Assimilation in a Multiracial Society" (1960) p. 277-286
Morton Klass "East and West Indian: Cultural Complexity in Trinidad" (1960) p. 287-300
Leo A. Despres "Cultural Pluralism and Nationalist Politics in British Guiana" (1956) p. 301-320.

1137. ——— and ——— eds. Work and family life: West Indian perspectives. Garden City, N.Y., Anchor Press/Doubleday, 1973. 422 p., bibl.

Second in a set of four paperback readers on West Indian themes and problems. This volume concentrates on the problems of making a living and the varying interpretations of domestic organization. Includes index.
Margaret Fisher Katzin "The Jamaican Country Higgler" (1959) p. 3-26
D. T. Edwards "Small Farming in Jamaica: A Social Scientist's View" (1965) p. 27-38
James M. Blaut; Ruth P. Blaut; Nan Harman; and Michael Moerman "A Study of Cultural Determinants of Soil Erosion and Conservation in the Blue Mountains of Jamaica" (1959) p. 39-66
M. G. Smith "Patterns of Rural Labour" (1956) p. 67-94
Jerome Handler "Some Aspects of Work Organization on Sugar Plantations in Barbados" (1965) p. 95-128
R. B. Davison "The Labour Force in the Jamaican Sugar Industry" (1966) p. 129-156
Lambros Comitas "Occupational Multiplicity in Rural Jamaica" (1964) p. 157-174
Colin G. Clarke "The Slums of Kingston" (1967) p. 175-188
Gene Tidrick "Some Aspects of Jamaican Emigration to the United Kingdom 1953-1962" (1966) p. 189-220
William G. Demas "Characteristics of the Caribbean Economies" (1965) p. 221-246
Melville J. Herskovits "Problem, Method and Theory in Afroamerican Studies" (1945) p. 247-272
M. G. Smith "Afro-American Research: A Critique" (1955) p. 273-286
Melville J. Herskovits and Frances S. Herskovits "Retentions and Reinterpretations in Rural Trinidad" (1947) p. 287-294
Dom Basil Matthews "The Plantation and the African Heritage" (1953) p. 295-318
Fernando Henriques "West Indian Family Organisation" (1949) p. 318-334
Edith Clarke "Variations in Jamaican Domestic Patterns" (1957) p. 335-350
Raymond T. Smith "The Family in the Caribbean" (1957) p. 351-364
M. G. Smith "A Survey of West Indian Family Studies" (1966) p. 365-408

1138. Debien, G. and **J. Houdaille.** Les origines africaines des esclaves des Antilles françaises (UPR/CS, 10:2, July 1970, p. 5-29, tables)

Documentary evidence of the ethnic origins of African slaves with much of the data from Saint Dominique.

1139. Dirks, Robert. Networks, groups, and adaptation in an Afro-Caribbean community (RAI/M, 7:4, Dec. 1972, p. 565-585, bibl.)

The relationship of personal networks and groups on Rum Bay, Tortola, a community which totally relies on these two forms of social ties for "its overall organisation." After a discussion of the literature on networks and groups, author presents a description of social relationships in Rum Bay and suggests that it has developed personal networks and group alignments as two adaptations to available resources with unlike characteristics. These adaptations maximize success in both regional markets and government domains. Furthermore, it is suggested that these two organizational forms are in coordinated flux and vary in communal importance in response to economic conditions.

1140. Douyon, Emerson ed. Culture et développement en Haïti. Montreal, Canada, Editions Lemeac, 1972. 233 p.

Papers of the Haiti symposium organized by the Dept. of Anthropology, Univ. of Montreal and the Centre d'Etudes Haitiennes and held 6-9 May 1970.
Emerson Douyon "Introduction" p. 9-22
Georges Anglade "La Signification du Fait de Population en Haïti" p. 23-38
François Latortue "Haïti et sa Main d'Oeuvre: Perspectives d'Avenir" p. 39-49
Mireille Anglade "Commentaire" p. 50-54
Pierre Benoit "Le Défi de Financer la Développement d'Haïti" p. 55-64
Gérard R. Latortue "Haïti et les Institutions Économiques Caraïbéennes" p. 65-92
Fuat Andic "Commentaire" p. 93-96
Gérard Pierre Charles "Interprétation des Faits et Per-

spective du Développement Économique en Haïti" p. 97-120
Rémy Bastien "Idéologie, Recherche et Développement" p. 121-126
Jean Casimir "Commentaire" p. 127-130
Marie Andrée Bertrand "Haïti et les Difficultés de la Recherche Scientifique" p. 131-134
Max Chancy "Education et Développement en Haïti" p. 135-155
Jean Casimir "Commentaire: Education et Instruction en Haïti" p. 156-162
Carlo Sterlin "La Négritude" p. 163-169
Ousmane Silla "Commentaires: Point de Vue d'une Africain" p. 170-173
Stanley Aleong "Négritude et Développement" p. 174-176
Nancy Proter "Point de Vue de la Femme Noire aux Etats-Unis" p. 177-180
Katherine Dunham "L'Evasion par le Folklore" p. 180-186
Emerson Douyon "Sondage d'Opinion sur la Fuite des Cerveaux" p. 187-194
Denis Lazure "Les Pays Sous-Développés et Formation de leurs Cadres" p. 195-200
Roger Bastide "Adaptation des Haïtiens en Pays Etranger" p. 201-210
Jean Benoist "Haïti: Réflexions pour l'Avenir" p. 211-222
Emerson Douyon "Epilogue" p. 223.

1141. Dubelaar, C. N. Het Afaka-schrift in the Afrikanistiek (NWIG, 47:3, Nov. 1970, p. 294-303)

Linguistic comparisons of Surinam script with African systems of notation.

1142. Dunham, Katherine. Island possessed. Garden City, N.Y., Doubleday, 1969. 280 p.

Dunham, anthropologist, dancer and choreographer, relates her fascinating experiences in Haiti. As an anthropologist, she lived close to the peasants, investigating their cultural patterns and traditions and was initiated into their religion. Author's experiences touch all social groups; she reminisces upon her relations with the Haitian elite with the same warmth with which she depicts her friendships with lower classes. Very readable book which should have special interest for students of traditional societies and their religions. [N. M. Garrett]

1143. ———. Journey to Accompong. Westport, Conn., Negro Universities Press, 1971. 162 p., illus.

Originally published in 1946 and reprinted in 1971, this slim volume describes, in almost diary form, the author's short stay among the Maroons of Accompong, Jamaica. While not designed as an anthropological monograph, it does provide glimpses of the social and political organization, work patterns, folklore, and courtship practices of the descendants of a reknown group of escaped slaves.

1144. Elder, J. D. From Congo drum to steelband: a socio-historical account of the emergence and evolution of the Trinidad steel orchestra. St. Augustine, T & T, Univ. of the West Indies, 1969. 47 p., tables.

Description and analysis of development of the steelband placed in the context of folkloric and musical contributions of various ethnic components of Trinidadian society over time.

1145. Fewkes, Jesse Walter. The aborigines of Porto Rico and neighboring islands. N.Y., Johnson Reprint Corp., 1970. 296 p., illus., plates.

Commissioned in 1902 by the Bureau of American Ethnology to visit Puerto Rico "which had lately come into the possession of the United States," author published in 1907 one of the first comprehensive accounts of the prehistory of Puerto Rico and adjoining islands. Now reprinted, it contains archaeological data supplemented by historical and ethnological accounts of the time. Sections are devoted to precolumbian population; present descendants; race and kinship; bodily, mental, and moral characteristics; government; political divisions; house types; secular customs; religion; archaeological sites; and archaeological objects. After weighing the evidence and various arguments, the author accepts the theory of the South American origin of West Indian islanders.

1146. Fletcher, L. P. The decline of friendly societies in Grenada: some economic aspects (UPR/CS, 12:2, July 1972, p. 99-111, tables)

History of the friendly society movement from the first decade of the 20th century to the late 1960s; defense of the proposition that the decline of the movement was primarily due to "inappropriate responses by friendly societies to inflationary conditions and rising real wages;" and finally, conclusions, which argue that this valuable institution will not survive unless the government reverses its policy of neglect and upgrades and modifies its educational system.

1147. Foner, Nancy. Competition, conflict, and education in rural Jamaica (SAA/HO, 31:4, Winter 1972, p. 395-402)

An analysis of the effects of improved educational opportunities on the community level. As education is now considered a prime mechanism for success in Jamaica, competition for secondary education "has become a dominant theme in local disputes. These disputes arise because villagers are sensitive to the slightest indication of superior status from kin or status equals whose children are successful in school. These disputes thus reflect the contradiction between the norms of the local social system and the norms of individual achievement in the wider society." A tentative conclusion is brought forth that local disputes and conflicts may have integrative functions for Jamaican society as a whole as they are alternatives to questioning the values of the total society to "challenging the legitimacy of the institutions which provide only limited channels of mobility."

1148. ———. Status and power in rural Jamaica: a study of educational and political change. N.Y., Columbia Univ., Teachers College Press, 1973. 172 p., bibl., map.

Based on field work in 1968-69, author explores changes engendered by constitution reform in and independence of Jamaica among residents of a community in St. Ann Parish. The monograph is organized into three parts. The first offers a description of the community and an analysis of the local status system (ranking by community members, bases of stratification, occupation and land ownership, life style, leadership, color and education, residence, subjective ranking, local and national status systems). The second part deals primarily with education (history in Jamaica, mobility in the past, past avenues for occupational mobility, recent developments); education and status aspirations (attitudes toward education, changing patterns, child-centeredness); correlates of educational attainment (occupation, education, marital status, family environment, church affiliation, sex role differentiation); disputes and educational mobility (disputes focused on education are seen by the author

1149. Franke, Richard. Economic circuits in a Surinam village (NWIG, 48:2/3, Dec. 1971, p. 158-172, tables)

Exploration of the influence of the external market on the economy of a Creole village in the east-west center of Surinam.

1150. Freilich, Morris and **Lewis A. Coser.** Structured imbalances of gratification: the case of the Caribbean mating system (BJS, 23:1, March 1972, p. 1-19)

Description and analysis of the sex life or "sex-fame game" of Negro peasants based on data collected in 1957-58 in an eastern Trinidadian community located "at an elevation of approximately 5000 feet" which, given the island's topography, would literally place the settlement in the clouds. Authors argue that "a social system . . . based on complementarity between sexual partners nevertheless presents such asymetry that its equilibrium is extremely precarious." Ethnographic detail is preceded by a discussion of equilibrium, disequilibrium, and asymetrical relationships based on Pareto, Merton, Marx, and Alvin Gouldner.

1151. Glasgow, Roy Arthur. Guyana: race and politics among Africans and East Indians. The Hague, Martinus Nijhoff, 1970. 153 p., bibl.

Utilizing the concept of plural society, the author attempts to deal with the "social illness of Guyana" and the distinct ideologies that have shaped patterns of social behavior and politics.

1152. González. Nancie L. Solien de. Black Carib household structure: a study of migration and modernization. Seattle, Wash., Univ. of Washington Press, 1969. 163 p., bibl., maps, plates, tables (The American Ethnological Society, 48)

" . . . the major hypothesis . . . is that the consanguineal household is an alternate type of domestic group that develops during the process of acculturation of neoteric societies [a society whose former cultural identity has been obscured] in which the primary mechanism of Westernization is recurrent migratory wage labor with low remuneration." Data on Black Caribs collected in Guatemala, British Honduras, and Honduras and deal with the development of wage labor and its impact on the social structure of the home villages, with domestic life and with domestic structures.

1153. ———. Peasants' progress: Dominicans in New York (UPR/CS, 10:3, Oct. 1970, p. 154-171)

Description and analysis of the migratory process of rural Dominicans to New York City; conditions of life, aspirations for migration, problems of securing a visa, arranging transportation, obtaining employment in the host country, etc. Description linked to a discussion of the term 'peasant' in the contemporary context.

1154. ———. The sociology of a dam (SAA/HO, 31:4, Winter 1972, p. 353-360)

Case study of the proposed construction of a hydroelectric dam in the northwest of the Dominican Republic. "This paper deals with the frustrations which may arise when the anthropologist attempts to view a problem from the perspective of several different often conflicting, interests. It is suggested, however, that the broadest possible viewpoint is a valuable tool in uncovering many of the elements critical to an overall understanding of the event or institution being examined. The conclusion is that the hydroelectric dam, now being built in the Dominican Republic, is not likely to fulfill the dreams and expectations of the peasants who, nevertheless are fervently in favor of it. Rather, its primary benefits will accrue to the large land holders and to the urban sectors who will receive better electrical service."

1155. Groot, Silvia W. de. Rebellie der Zwarte Jagers: de Nasleep van de Bonni-oorlogen, 1788-1809 (De Gids [Amsterdam] 133:9, 1970, p. 291-304)

Historical account of a Negro revolt and the aftermath of the Boni wars in Surinam.

1156. Hall, Gwendolyn Midlo. Social control in slave plantation societies: a comparison of St. Dominique and Cuba. Baltimore, Md., The Johns Hopkins Univ. Press, 1971. 166 p., bibl.

Author compares 18th-century St. Dominique with 19th-century Cuba "and examines the evolution of significant aspects of both societies from the preplantation period through the emergence of the colonies as the leading suppliers of sugar for the world market. . . . The data . . . indicate a very serious problem of social control in the slave populations . . . which became more acute as prosperity increased. Policy toward the slave population, toward religious conversion and education of slaves, toward slave law, toward emancipation, and toward the free colored population was determined by the urgent needs of the society, especially by the enormous problem of controlling the slaves. The legal and religious traditions, as well as the colonizers' pre-existing attitudes toward race, appear to have been relatively insignificant in determining policy toward the African population, slave or free."

1157. Handler, Jerome S. An archaeological investigation of the domestic life of plantation slaves in Barbados (BMHS/J, 34:2, May 1972, p. 64-72)

Preliminary statement on archaeological research on the social and cultural life of Barbadian slaves.

1158. ———. A guide to source materials for the study of Barbados history, 1627-1834. Carbondale, Ill., Southern Illinois Univ. Press, 1971. 205 p.

Compiled by an anthropologist and West Indianist, this volume is the first, fully annotated, comprehensive bibliography of printed books, pamphlets, broadsheets, parliamentary papers, prints and manuscripts dealing with Barbados. In addition to lengthy annotations, information is provided for each entry as to authorship, place and date of publication, number of volume or pages, and library location. Invaluable to social scientists and others interested in Barbados and in that lengthy period of West Indian history dominated by the slave system. Includes index.

1159. ———. and Charlotte J. Frisbie. Aspects of slave life in Barbados: music and its cultural context (UPR/CS, 11:4, Jan. 1972, p. 5-46, bibl., plates)

Full description of musical ideophones, membranophones, chordophones and aerophones, and dance forms and activities utilized by Barbadian slaves as well as changes from mid-17th century to Emancipation. This data is placed within a sociocultural context including the Barbadian laws and codes affecting musical expression. Contrary to the thesis propounded by Sidney Greenfield that Barbadian slaves were neither able to re-establish African culture nor to develop new independent patterns, authors conclude that, "as a cultural complex, comprised of a number of specific behavioral and material elements, and intimately linked with other highly valued complexes such as recreation and religion, the musical traditions of Barbados slaves were those of Africa in their most essential and characteristic features."

Hicks, Frederick. Making a living during the dead season in sugar-producing regions of the Caribbean. See item 6625.

1160. Higman, B. W. The Chinese in Trinidad, 1806-1838 (UPR/CS, 12:3, Oct. 1972, p. 21-44)

Historical article on the settlement of a small group of Chinese in Trinidad before Emancipation. Of interest to social anthropologists and ethnohistorians, author traces British motivations for the scheme ("A white yeomanry was regarded most favourably, but the climatic factor was thought an insuperable obstacle to its establishment. What was required was a people capable of resisting the debilitation of the tropics, but more civilized than the Africans. As early as 1792 it had been suggested that if the slave trade were to be abolished, the African slaves of the West Indies could be replaced by Chinese servants, 'the Chinese national character being considered as favourable to the scheme of substitution' "); the recruitment process and problems; reception and initial treatment in Trinidad; occupational patterns, particularly in the fishing industry; and assessment of the relative failure of the experiment.

1161. Hoetink, Harmannus. Materiales para el estudio de la República Dominicana en la segunda mitad del siglo XIX: pt. 5 (UPR/CS, 9:2, July 1969, p. 5-26)

Fifth article in the series describes changes in the structure of sanctioning institutions: in the army, navy, public order, and in the formal organization of justice. For pt. 6, see item 1162.

1162. ———. Materiales para el estudio de la República Dominicana en la segunda mitad del siglo XIX: pt. 6 (UPR/CS, 9:4, Jan. 1970, p. 73-103)

Sixth article in the series describes changes in political ideas and structures specifically treating the debate on what is ideal and what is realizable, the political parties, the caudillo politician, and the 'dictadura criolla' of Heureaux. For pt. 5, see item 1161.

1163. Hurault, Jean. Africains de Guyane: la vie matérielle et l'art des noirs refugiés de Guyane. The Hague, Mouton, 1970. 224 p., bibl., plates, tables.

Beautifully illustrated book on Bush Negroes with sections dealing with social structure; the village; woodworking techniques (with particular reference to canoe construction); and with the art of Bush Negroes of Maroni including chapters on style, objects d'art, and motifs and symbols.

1164. Isidoor. Buiten Verantwoordelijkheid. Willemstad, Curaçao, Van Dorp, 1972. 93 p.

Account of Curaçao social structure. (It was not possible to identify the pseudonym "Isidoor" at press time).

1165. Jones, David W. and **Carlyle A. Glean.** The English-speaking communities of Honduras and Nicaragua (UWI/CQ, 17:2, June 1971, p. 50-61, map, tables)

Notes on communities with English-speaking populations with some history and other detail. Specifically deals with Bluefields, the Corn Islands, Puerto Cabezas and the North-East in Nicaragua; the Bay Islands and eastern and northern sections of Honduras.

1166. Jones, Grant D. The politics of agricultural development in northern British Honduras. Winston-Salem, N.C., Wake Forest Univ., 1971. 111 p., bibl., map, tables (Developing nations monograph series, 4)

Analysis of recent economic and political developments in the rural Corozal region in terms of conflicting system of production—large and small scale systems of cash production. Chapters on: haciendas, plantations, and peasant production, 1848-1956; conflict and institutional adaptation; adaptation to peasant cane production; and comparative implications.

1167. Juliana, E. Curaçaosche Pinda's: volkskunde van Curaçao, hekserij, religie, sexuologie, huwelijk, politiek. Willemstad, Lesser Antilles, n.p., 1969. 27 p.

Folklore relating to witchcraft, religion, sexuality, marriage, and politics.

1168. Kätsch, Siegfried; Elke-Maria Kätsch; and **Henry P. David.** Sosua-verheissenes land: eine dokumentation zu adaptionsproblemen Deutsch-Jüdischer siedler in der Dominikanischen Republik. Dortmund, FRG, Sozialforschungsstelle an der Univ. Münster, 1970. 297 p., (Arbeitsunterlage 38/39 zur Lateinamerikaforschung)

Study of the Jewish migrants to Sosua, R.D., including seven long interviews.

1169. Karner, Frances P. The Sephardics of Curaçao; a study of socio-cultural patterns in flux. Assen, The Netherlands, Van Gorcum, 1969. 84 p., bibl.

Socio-historical analysis of the elite Jewish population in Curaçao. Based on questionnaire results and an investigation of social options available to successive generations, author traces social adjustments of group in response to changing economic conditions as Curaçao moved from an agro-mercantile system to an industrial one based on oil refining.

1170. Kloos, Peter. Search for health among the Maroni River Caribs: etiology and medical care in a 20th century Amerindian group in Surinam (KITLV/B, 126:1, 1970, p. 115-141)

1171. Koss, Joan D. El porqué de los cultos

religiosos: el caso del espiritismo en Puerto Rico (UPR/RCS, 16:1, marzo 1972, p. 61-72, bibl.)

Reasons for development of religious cults (when societies are faced with a plurality of conflicting cosmologies in addition to conditions of privation) with special reference to spiritualism in Puerto Rico. Functions of religious cults reviewed, background given on birth of spiritualism in Europe at turn of 19th century and reverberations and developments of this in Puerto Rico from the last decade of the same century.

1172. **Lampe, W. F. M.** Buiten de schaduw van de gouverneurs: een blik op het verleden en het heden. Oranjestad, Aruba, Dewit, 1971. 165 p.

Memoirs present aspects of past and present social organization, customs, and ways of life of Aruba.

1173. **La Ruffa, Anthony L.** San Cipriano: life in a Puerto Rican community. N.Y., Gordon and Breach, 1971. 149 p., plates, tables.

Based on field work in 1963-64, author presents an ethnographic account of a phenotypically black community on the northeastern coast of the island with particular focus on development of and behavior related to Pentecostalism. Data are presented on: spatial and historical setting; economics; structure and organization of community life; life cycle; traditional approaches to the supernatural; Protestantism; and belief, ritual and the Pentecostal religious experience.

1174. **Lavretski, Grigalevich-Lavretski.** Bogi v tropikakh (God is in the tropics). Moskva, Nauka, 1967. 158 p., bibl., illus., plates.

Popularized sketch of religion in the Caribbean area. [T. S. Cheston]

1175. **Lengermann, Patricia Madoo.** Working-class values in Trinidad and Tobago (UWI/SES, 20:2, June 1971, p. 151-163, tables)

Investigation of attitudinal modernity in several working-class groups. Evidence indicates that these populations are "most consistently modern in their orientation to activity. Without exception, they see activity as a means, not of expressing identity or self, but as a method of achieving ends external to self. The data also show a fairly consistent tendency to be individualistic in the approach to everyday problems."

1176. **Louis-Jean, Antonio.** Crise de possession et la possession dramatique. Montréal, Canada, Editions Lémeac, 1970. 1 v. (Unpaged)

Longtemps intéressé au théâtre, l'auteur a constaté une similitude de phénomènes entre la théâtre et la vaudou car les deux se proposent de divertir, de séduire, de servir par la moyen du dédoublement de la personnalité. Il expose ses remarques. La ressemblance ne va pas jusqu'aux extrêmes car dans l'un il y a une question d'art et dans l'autre une question de foi, de croyance. [M. A. Lubin]

1177. **Lowenthal, David.** Black power in the Caribbean context (CU/EG, 48:1, Jan. 1972, p. 116-134)

An analysis of black power and black protest in the West Indies with some comparison to outwardly similar manifestations in the US. Discussion is placed within historical context of colonialism and neo-colonialism; current situation of widening social and economic disparities; economic stress and racial expressions; position of local whites, colored middle class, and the black majority with regard to current societal order; expressions of authoritarianism and repression; black power agitation; négritude and pan-Africanism; black and brown; local criticisms of black power; and, finally, the West Indian search for identity. Unlike situation in US and Great Britain, black power manifestations in West Indies are seen as not essentially racial but rather reflecting general economic and social stress and malaise.

1178. ———. West Indian societies. London, Oxford Univ. Press *for the* Institute of Race Relations, 1972. 385 p., bibl., maps.

Undoubtedly one of the most important works on the non-Hispanic Caribbean in recent years. Utilizing a wide range of materials from the social sciences, history, journalism, and the arts, the author has examined and synthesized many contemporary issues and problems of concern to both West Indians and West Indianists. Divided into six problem oriented chapters bounded by a lengthy introduction and conclusion, the book deals first with the historical dimensions of West Indian development; secondly, with social structure, including sections on homogeneous societies, societies differentiated by color but not by class, societies stratified by both class and color, societies lacking white Creole elites, stratified societies containing additional ethnic groups, pluralism, color, social institutions, family form, religious faith and practice, and social distance, thirdly, with East Indians and Creoles; fourthly with other ethnic minorities which have been analytically divided into ethnic outcasts (Amerindians, Bush Negroes, Javanese) and status-gap minorities (Jews, Portuguese, Chinese, Syrians). These chapters are followed by a review of causes and consequences of dependency, in terms of migration and neo-colonialism; and finally by discussion of racial and national identity. In many ways, the author has come remarkably close to reaching a most difficult objective "to explain how the West Indies and their people became what they are, to show what makes them unique or ordinary, and to describe how they get on with one another and with the world outside."

1179. ———. and **Lambros Comitas** eds. The aftermath of sovereignty: West Indian perspectives. Garden City, N.Y., Anchor Press/Doubleday, 1973, 422 p., bibl.

Fourth in a set of four paperback readers on West Indian themes and problems. This last volume concentrates on issues of freedom and power and on the search for a West Indian identity. Includes index and following articles:
Eric Williams "Massa Day Done" (1961) p. 3-30
Jesse Harris Proctor, Jr. "British West Indian Society and Government in Transition 1920-60" (1962) p. 31-66
Morley Ayearst "A Note on Some Characteristics of West Indian Political Parties" (1954) p. 67-80
Kenneth John "St. Vincent: A Political Kaleidoscope" (1966) p. 81-93
B. A. N. Collins "Some Notes on Public Service Commissions in the Commonwealth Caribbean" (1967) p. 94-120
Gordon K. Lewis "The Trinidad and Tobago General Election of 1961" (1962) p. 121-162
W. A. Domingo "British West Indian Federation-A Critique" (1956) p. 163-188
Hugh W. Springer "Federation in the Caribbean: An Attempt That Failed" (1962) p. 189-214

W. Arthur Lewis "The Agony of the Eight" (1965) p. 215-236
S. S. Ramphal "West Indian Nationahood-Myth, Mirage or Mandate?" (1971) p. 237-264
Frankz Fanon "West Indians and Africans" (1955) p. 265-276
Kerwyn L. Morris "On Afro-West Indian Thinking" (1966) p. 277-282
K. V. Parmasad "By the Light of a Deya" (1971) p. 283-292
W. Arthur Lewis "On Being Different" (1971) p. 293-305
Lloyd Best "The February Revolution" (1970) p. 306-330
Desmond Allum "Legality vs. Morality: A Plea for Lt. Raffique Shah" (1971) p. 331-350
Clive Y. Thomas "Meaningful Participation: The Fraud of It" (1971) p. 351-362
V. S. Naipaul "Power to the Caribbean People" (1970) p. 363-372
C. L. R. James "The Mighty Sparrow" (1962) p. 373-381.

1180. ——— and ——— eds. Consequences of class and color: West Indian perspectives. Garden City, N.Y., Anchor Press/Doubleday, 1973. 334 p., bibl.

Third in a set of four paperback readers on West Indian themes and problems. This volume concentrates on cultural expressions of class and color as well as on education, language, and creativity. Includes index and following articles:
Marcus Garvey "The Race Question in Jamaica" (1916) p. 4-12
C. V. D. Hadley "Personality Patterns, Social Class, and Aggression in the British West Indies" (1949) p. 13-34
Rex Nettleford "National Identity and Attitudes to Race in Jamaica" (1965) p. 35-56
James A. Mau "The Threatening Masses: Myth or Reality?" (1965) p. 57-78
C. L. R. James "The Middle Classes" (1962) p. 79-94
Adrian Espinet "Honours and Paquotille" (1965) p. 95-102
A Young Jamaican Nationalist "Realism and Race" (1961) p. 103-122
H. P. Jacobs "Reality and Race: A reply to 'Realism and Race' " (1961) p. 123-142
Anonymous "The Favored Minorities" (1970) p. 143-147
Eric Williams "Education in the British West Indies" (1951) p. 148-168
H. P. Jacobs "Reality and Race: A reply to 'Realism and Race' " (1961) p. 123-142
Anonymous "The Favored Minorities" (1970) p. 143-147
Eric Williams "Education in the British West Indies" (1951) p. 148-168
Edward P. G. Seaga "Parent-Teacher Relationships in a Jamaican Village" (1955) p. 169-190
M. G. Smith "Education and Occupational Choice in Rural Jamaica" (1960) p. 191-198
Mervin C. Alleyne "Language and Society in St. Lucia" (1961) p. 199-214
Edith Efron "French and Creole Patois in Haïti" (1954) p. 215-240
Lloyd Braithwaite "The Problem of Cultural Integration in Trinidad" (1954) p. 241-262
O. R. Dathorne "Caribbean Narrative" (1966) p. 263-280
W. I. Carr "The West Indian Novelist: Prelude and Context" (1965) p. 281-302
Derek Walcott "Meanings" (1970) p. 303-312

1181. MacDonald, John Stuart and **Leatrice D. MacDonald.** Transformation of African and Indian family traditions in the southern Caribbean (CSSH, 15:2, March 1973, p. 171-198, bibl., tables)

Utilizing census data from Trinidad and Tobago, Barbados, and Grenada, authors argue that "the Negro family ideology of the southern Caribbean was formed *because* of slavery and semi-paternalistic peonage, while the East Indian family ideology was formed *despite* bondage in bureaucratic agriculture. Both drew on the respective principles of family organization from their cultures of origin. The international company agro-factories permit a greater variety of ethnic subcultures than paternalistic or slave plantations."

1182. Mars, Louis. L'ethnopsychiatrie et la schizophrénie en Haïti (Psychopathologie Africaine [Dakar] 5:2, 1969, p. 235-256)

Spécialiste des questions de psychiatrie, l'auteur interroge le vodou et voudrait rattacher ce phénomène constaté en Haïti à l'ethnopsychologie en fixant ses caractéristiques sous l'angle de cette discipline. C'est encore une nouvelle méthode d'approche à l'explication du vodou si dominant en Haïti. [M. A. Lubin]

1183. ———. Temoignages I: essai ethnopsychologique. Madrid, Taller Gráfico Cies Hermosilla, 1966. 77 p.

Mars essaie de situer le vodou dans le cadre d'une discipline scientifique en poussant ses investigations, et il veut créer l'ethnodrame, un phénomène qui est à la fois religion et drame. Il importe de poursuivre les recherches pour asseoir cette nouvelle conception qu'on applique au vodou. [M. A. Lubin]

1184. Martin, Leann. Why Maroons? (UC/CA, 13:1, Feb. 1972, p. 143-144)

In the urgent anthropology section of the journal, author briefly details our knowledge of Jamaican Maroons and indicates need for "good, basic ethnographic material for all the Maroon communities with special attention to the techniques for the preservation of old values and community identity and pride."

1185. Martin, Tony. C. L. R. James and the race/class question (IRR/R, 14:2, Oct. 1972, p. 183-193)

Interesting account "of one black Marxist's quest for a reconciliation of the class and race struggles." Also of use to Caribbeanists is the short but thorough biographical sketch of this important Trinidadian historian and activist.

1186. Métraux, Alfred. Voodoo in Haiti. Translated by Hugo Charteris. New introduction by Sidney W. Mintz. 2. ed. N.Y., Schoken Books, 1972. 400 p., bibl., illus., map, plates, tables.

Second edition of this most useful work on Haitian folk religion with sections on the history of Voodoo; its social framework; the supernatural world; ritual; magic and sorcery; and Voodoo and Christianity. Sidney Mintz provides a new, contextual introduction.

1187. Meyer, A. Engie socio-psychologische opmerkingen over Curaçao (NWIG, 47:1, Sept. 1969, p. 60-66)

Psycho-sociological factors which may obstruct the formation of a true national identity for Curaçaoans.

1188. Midgett, Douglas. Bilingualism and linguistic change in St. Lucia (IU/AL, 12:5, May 1970, p. 158-170, bibl., tables)

Exploration of bilingual development, usage behavior of the two languages (a French-based creole and a variety of Standard English), and a concluding section on directions of change in usage.

1189. Miller, Errol. Education and society in Jamaica (Savacou [Caribbean Artists Movement, Kingston] 5, June 1971, p. 51-70, bibl., tables)

" . . . the educational system because of its relationship to the social order cannot be expected to operate in such a way that it would create radical, revolutionary or even substantial changes in the social order. The best that can be expected is that dysfunctionality will occur, because of tensions between social strata, and that this will result in certain evolutionary changes both in the educational system and the social order. However, one could say that once changes—radical, revolutionary or substantial—begin to occur in the social order one can expect that the educational system will be altered to facilitate and perpetuate these changes."

1190. Nag, Moni. Patterns of mating behaviour, emigration and contraceptives as factors affecting human fertility in Barbados (UWI/SES, 20:2, June 1971, p. 111-133, tables)

The identification of social and cultural factors related to the variation in the fertility level of Barbados during the last few decades.

1191. Nas, P. J. M. Stratifikatie onderzoek in het Caribisch gebied (KITLV/B, 128:2-3, 1972, p. 337-350)

Review of three main approaches to past and present research on social stratification in the Caribbean area. Discussion includes appraisal of the Van Lier and Wooding work on Surinam.

1192. Nath, Dwarka. A history of Indians in Guyana. London, Butler & Tanner, 1970. 281 p., plates, tables.

Originally published in 1950 (see *HLAS 16:1444*) this revised edition updates one of the very few comprehensive works on East Indians in the New World. Author deals with the introduction of the indenture system in British Guiana; the sugar industry; land settlement schemes; a new chapter on the rice industry; treatment of Indians abroad and the cessation of indentured emigration; new material on strikes and disturbances on sugar plantations; the financing of immigration; the Indians' contribution to the country's progress; and, of special interest to social scientists, an expanded section on the progress of Indians and biographical sketches of success stories.

1193. Nettleford, Rex. Manley and the politics of Jamaica. Mona, Jam., Univ. of the West Indies, Institute of Social and Economic Research, 1971. 72 p. (Supplement to *Social and Economic Studies*, 20:3)

Author deals with Norman W. Manley (late Prime Minister of Jamaica) in terms of his personality in relation to that island's politics; with political modernization and development; the strategy of conflict-reconciliation; and Manley in relation to the idea of organized politics, bi-partisan or the two-party system, laborism or labor and politics, socialism, and self-government.

1194. Nicholls, David. Biology and politics in Haiti (IRR/R, 13:2, Oct. 1971, p. 203-214)

Useful examination of the thoughts of Duvalier and other black writers on the question of race and racial difference. The author argues that the group he discusses agreed with Gobineau that there are significant objective differences between the races although rejecting his position that the black races are inferior. This group maintained that specific social characteristics of black people are rooted in psychological peculiarities which themselves are based on biological factors. Duvalier specifically agreed with Gobineau that black people are distinguished by sensibility, subjectivism, and rhythm which are manifested in black accomplishments in poetry, music, and dancing. From this general position, it follows that politicians, such as Duvalier, must understand and undoubtedly use the psychological and biological factors which, they agreed, play a part in setting the culture of the people they lead.

1195. Olien, Michael D. The Negro in Costa Rica: the role of an ethnic minority in a developing society. Winston-Salem, N.C., Wake Forest Univ., Overseas Research Center, 1970. 61 p., bibl., map (Developing nations monograph series, 3)

Four short sections on: the Negro in Costa Rica; social change and the Negro in colonial Costa Rica; pluralism and the study of complex societies, lowland Costa Rica at the turn of the century; and, units of observation in Costa Rican Negro society. Data on the West Indian population of the nation.

1196. Oxaal, Ivar. Race and revolutionary consciousness: a documentary interpretation of the 1970 black power revolt in Trinidad. Cambridge, Mass., Schenkman, 1971. 96 p., plates.

Author sees this short work as an extended final chapter to his earlier study *Black intellectuals come to power* (see *HLAS 33:7853*). He deals with the chronology of events leading to the "February Revolution;" the actions pertinent to that event; and the ideologies utilized during this period of social trauma.

1197. Philpott, Stuart B. The implications of migration for sending societies: some theoretical considerations (*in* Annual Spring Meeting of the American Ethnological Society, Seattle, Wash., 1970. Proceedings: migration and anthropology. Seattle, Wash., Univ. of Washington Press, 1970, p. 9-20)

With specific reference to Montserrat, the author sets out low-level generalizations regarding the relative impact of migration for the sending society. These generalizations are dealt with regard to the pre-existing social structure, the selectivity of migration, type of migration, migrant ideology, and migrant social organization.

1198. Pollak-Eltz, Angelca. The Yoruba religion and its decline in the Americas (*in* International Congress of Americanists, XXXVIII,

Stuttgart-München, FRG, 1968. Verhandlungen [see *HLAS 33:510*] v. 3, p. 423-427)

Description of the religious system of the Yoruba linked to the generalization that most Afro-American cults are based on this system. Followed by brief statements on the state of these cults in Brazil (Candomble, Batuque of Porto Alegre, Shango cult of Recife, the Yoruba-Bantu Macumba of Rio, the Caboclo cults, and Umbanda) and in the West Indies (Shango in Trinidad and Grenada, Shouting Baptists in Grenada, Santería in Cuba, and Vodoun in Haiti). In these short statements, the author traces the progressive process of acculturation.

1199. Pollock, Nancy J. Women and the division of labor: a Jamaican example (AAA/AA, 74:3, June 1972, p. 689-692)

On the basis of a three-month field trip in 1964 to two villages in western Jamaica, it is argued that "reliance on women's support in only a phase in the life cycle of the co-residential family. A male partner will be brought in to share and then carry the economic responsibilities when the couple are middle-aged."

1200. Price, Richard. The Guiana Maroons: changing perspectives in "Bush Negro" studies (UPR/CS, 11:4, Jan. 1972, p. 82-105, bibl., map)

Lengthy review article of Jean Hurault's *Africains de Guyane: La vie materielle et l'art des noirs refugies de Guyane*(item 1163). Substance of this critique of Hurault's analysis of Aluku culture and society and on the art of woodcarving is preceded by a useful review of recent developments in the anthropology of the "Bush Negro" tribes of Surinam and French Guiana.

1201. —— and **Sally Price.** Saramaka onomastics: an Afro-American naming system (UP/E, 11:4, Oct. 1972, p. 341-367, bibl.)

Analysis of the system of personal names and naming among a Bush Negro group in Surinam: types of names; name formation; name giving; name use. Authors explore "the hypothesis that the central features of the Saramaka system are truly 'Afro-American', that they can be found in many Black communities in the Americas." Suggestive and useful article.

1202. Rivière, Peter. The political structure of the Trio Indians as manifested in a system of ceremonial dialogue (*in* Beidelman, T. O. ed. Translation of culture: essays to E. E. Evans-Pritchard. London, Tavistock, 1971, p. 293-311)

An examination as to the extent forms and usages of a type of verbal dueling can be used as evidence of underlying structure. "In summary, the function of ceremonial dialogue is mediation in situations that are likely to give rise to conflict. Such situations are most likely to arise between those who are unrelated, and this fact is recognized by the increasing formality of the ceremonial dialogue in direct proportion to increasing social and physical distance."

1203. Rodgers, William B. Incipient development and vocational evolution in Dominica (SAA/HO, 30:3, Fall 1971, p. 239-254)

Controlled comparison of occupational data collected in 65 communities in Dominica. Utilizing statistical analyses, it is suggested "that with economic development and modernization the vocational structures of communities are changing in a manner which can be explained by operationalized evolutionary theory. Vocational distributions [the number of types of part-time or full-time vocations present in a community] seems to precede vocational specialization [the number of types of full-time vocations] which once it begins seems to advance in a geometric progression." Correlates of vocational distribution are presented.

1204. Romer, R. A. Korsow: een sociologische verkenning van een Caraibische Maatschappij. Willemstad, Curaçao, N.P. 1970. 84 p.

Interesting analysis of social groups constituting present day Curaçao society. Discussion of structural principles.

1205. Salazar Quijada, Adolfo. Ethnología y folklore cubano (UCV/ECS [2. épocal] 12:3, julio/sept. 1970, p. 119-124)

Abbreviated description of anthropological organizations, major figures in anthropology, and anthropological publications in Cuba since 1879. Also included is a more extensive detailing of materials published in *Etnología y Folklore*, the Cuban journal founded in 1966.

1206. Sanders, Andrew. Amerindians in Guyana: a minority group in a multi-ethnic society (UPR/CS, 12:2, July 1972, p. 31-51)

Position of Amerindians in the Guyanese system of social stratification; attitudes, stereotypes, and behavior of Amerindians toward other segments of Guyanese society and the reverse; historical review of colonial and governmental policy with regard to Amerindians, levels of acculturation; present Amerindian organization; developments in Amerindian political activity and organization; and details on the Rupununi insurrection.

1207. Seda Bonilla, Eduardo. Social change and personality in a Puerto Rican agrarian reform community. Evanston, Ill., Northwestern Univ. Press, 1973. 187 p., bibl.

English version of *Interacción social y personalidad en una communidad de Puerto Rico* published in 1964 (see *HLAS 27:1101*). Restudy of a community first researched in 1948, this monograph is based on field work carried out in 1959 and deals with the substantial, and by no means all beneficial changes in the community. Included are chapters on: the second generation; the family; religious changes; sorcery, witchcraft and spiritism; spiritism and psychodrama; the structural context of spiritism; and patronage politics in the welfare commonwealth.

1208. Simpson, George Eaton. Afro-American religions and religious behavior (UPR/CS, 12:2, July 1972, p. 5-30, bibl.)

Survey of Afro-American religions and behavior with particular emphasis on three scientific approaches: the cultural, which includes concepts of history, tradition, and acculturation; the sociological, which includes structural-functional theory; and the psychological, which includes concepts from psychiatry. Attention is paid to the political implications of Afro-American religions over time but with particular reference to the role of clergy in the black nationalism movements of the 1960s.

1209. Staton, Howard R. Social determinants of

housing policy in Puerto Rico: a case study of rapid urbanization (ABS, 15:4, March/April 1972, p. 563-580)

Cursory review of developments in Puerto Rican housing and the social process which determine planning. As an exercise in developmental planning, the author concentrates on housing changes in the coming decade and deals with emerging social conditions (the impending death of agriculture, organization of the urban proletariat, high residential mobility, demand for infrastructure); new public policy; housing industry development; future settlement types in Puerto Rico; and, participation in controversy as a policy.

1210. Twining, Mary Arnold. An anthropological look at Afro-American folk narrative (CLA/J, 14:1, Sept. 1970, p. 57-61)

The folktale, a "vital tradition" among Afro-Americans, draws on both Euroamerican and African sources, and is part of the New World experience.

1211. ———. Toward a working folklore bibliography of the Caribbean area (Black Lines [Pittsburgh, Pa.] 2:1, Fall 1971, p. 69-77, bibl.)

Brief and incomplete review of folkloric as well as social and cultural anthropological research on the Antilles.

1212. Vries, Jan de. Het medisch werk in Suriname's bosland (NWIG, 47:2, April 1970, p. 139-157, bibl.)

Missionary medical activities among Bush Negroes in the interior of Surinam analyzed from a socio-educational perspective.

1213. Walker, Malcolm T. Foreign colonists in a Dominican rural community: the costs of economic progress (UPR/CS, 11:3, Oct. 1971, p. 88-98)

Description and analysis of the impact of the settlement from 1955-57 of 450 Spanish, Hungarian, and Japanese colonists in a mountain community in the Central Cordillera. By 1968, only 144 of the original settlers remained, mostly Spaniards and Japanese, but there is little question that the colonists upgraded agriculture in the area and were a potent innovative force in the economy although unanticipated consequences made the social cost of the experiment high. Cooperation between remaining colonists and Dominicans is minimal and the continued presence of the former in the community, "their relative prosperity, . . . their air of superiority, are a constant source of irritation" to the locals.

1214. ———. Politics and the power structure: a rural community in the Dominican Republic. N.Y., Columbia Univ., Teachers College Press, 1972. 177 p., bibl., maps, plates.

First full-length community study published in English on the Dominican Republic. Primary concerns of the author are with the local power structure and the sources and uses of power in Constanza, a community once favored by Trujillo and the site of an abortive air invasion from Cuba in 1959. Political life in the community is seen as being dominated by men "who, through friendships, familial connections, or ritual kin ties, are able to exploit powerful connections outside the community. These sources, however, whether they rest in the military, in government functionaries, or in the President himself, are not constant but are subject to change." Analysis of power structure and dynamics is placed within the substantive context of community history; economic life in the surrounding countryside (dry farming areas, irrigated valley areas, the agricultural cooperative); economic life in the town (occupational groupings, business men, professionals, civil servants, military and police, and the poor); social activities and social groupings; the life cycle; family relationships and interpersonal relations, formal associations; and finally, the analysis of the local political campaign and municipio elections of May, 1968.

1215. Warner, Maureen. African feasts in Trinidad (Bulletin of the African Studies Association of the West Indies [Kingston] 4, Dec. 1971, p. 85-94)

Brief descriptions of some African feasts found in Trinidad during the latter half of the 19th century up to the first quarter of the 20th. Included are yearly religious feasts (saraka, ebo, vudunu) and secular feasts (birth, initiation, marriage, African dances, funerals and wakes).

1216. ———. Some Yoruba descendants in Trinidad (Bulletin of the African Studies Association of the West Indies [Kingston] 3, Dec. 1970, p. 9-16)

Attitudes of Trinidadian informants to Yoruba culture and to Yoruba language and its use.

1217. Wesche, Marjorie Bingham. Place names as a reflection of cultural chance: an example from the Lesser Antilles (UPR/CS, 12:2, July 1972, p. 74-98, maps, tables)

Through a comparison of maps drawn between 1763-76 and a series issued in the late 1950s and early 1960s, the author deals with "the process by which place names are given, maintained intact, modified, or replaced over a period of time, as related to cultural events and influences throughout that period." Separate sections deal with Tobago, Grenada, St. Vincent, and Dominica with each containing data on 18th-century toponyms, present toponyms, types of name changes, and the historical content of names. Inter-island comparisons and generalizations are offered.

1218. Wilson, Peter J. Crab antics: the social anthropology of English-speaking Negro societies of the Caribbean. New Haven, Conn., Yale Univ. Press, 1973. 258 p., bibl., illus., maps, tables (Caribbean series, 14)

Full scale, sometime polemical, anthropological study of the island of Providencia with comparative data on other English-speaking areas in the Caribbean. Within the framework of materials on problems of living on the land, on social stratification, on "putting on the style" (color, parties, mobility, shaming), and on kinship, and friendship, the author argues the social and theoretical importance of two linked but opposed themes, respectability and reputation, and their dialectical relationship. Also given analytic prominence are men's groups on the island, dubbed "crews" by the author in an earlier article. Contemporary approaches in Caribbean anthropology are strongly critiqued in the concluding section.

ETHNOLOGY
SOUTH AMERICA: LOWLANDS*

SETH LEACOCK

Associate Professor of Anthropology
University of Connecticut

ALTHOUGH THE LITERATURE ON LOWLAND SOUTH AMERICAN ethnology is not expanding as rapidly as that of the highlands (see introduction to *Ethnology, South America: Highlands* (p. 104), it is at least holding its own. In addition to the monographs and articles that have appeared during the last two years, there have been a number of preliminary reports that give promise of significant material to come.

Among the major monographs that have appeared recently, Harner's study of the Jívaro (item 1272), one of the most colorful tribes in South America, will undoubtedly become the best known, both inside and outside of anthropology. Deserving of at least equal attention are the monographs by Arvelo-Jiménez on the Yecuana (item 1224), Rivière on the Trio (see *HLAS 33:1461*), and Kloos on the Maroni River Caribs (item 1279). Somewhat less detailed, but still worthy of note, is Grünberg's material on the Kayabí (items 1269-1271). The appearance of a massive volume on the Tapirapé by the late Herbert Baldus (item 1225) is of somewhat less significance, since most of the material it contains has been published before.

It should be noted that most of these monographs deal with relatively unacculturated tribes. There seems clearly to be an upsurge of interest in relatively independent, functioning societies as objects of study. Since such societies still exist in only a few areas, a large proportion of recent studies tend to cluster geographically, with most work having been done among tribes living in the drainage of the upper Orinoco. In addition to Arvelo-Jiménez' study mentioned above, Coppens has also published on the Yecuana (item 1242), Boglár (items 1229-1230) and Kaplan (item 1277) have published on the Piaroa, Dumont has published a preliminary report on the Panare (item 1254), and Morey (item 1297) and Lucena Salmoral (items 1286-1287) have published on the Guahibo. Moreover, Lizot has begun to publish the results of his two year study of the central Yanomamö (items 1283-1285). This particular area, then, becomes one of the very few in lowland South America where meaningful comparative studies will soon be possible.

An area where some comparative work has already been done, central Brazil, is represented in the present survey only by the outstanding symposium on the Gê tribes organized by Maybury-Lewis (item 1292) for the XXXVIII International Congress of Americanists (see *HLAS 33:510*). However, since it is now five years since this symposium was held, it can be expected that several additional contributions to the understanding of Gê variability are now nearing completion.

As in the past, the majority of studies under review make no pretense of being other than descriptive. Of those in which a theoretical orientation is made explicit, by far the most popular approach is some version of French structuralism. Outstanding examples would be Rivière (see *HLAS 33:1461*), Ingham (item 1276), Melatti (item 1296), and J. C. Crocker (item 1246). However, several other analytical schemes are also employed. Meggers uses an ecological approach to explain differences in institutions among tropical forest tribes (item 1293), and Wilbert uses an evolutionary framework to organize his study of four tribes of Venezuela (item 1335). In two specialized studies of kinship, Scheffler and Lounsbury delve into the underlying principles of Sirionó kinship using the techniques of structural semantics (item 1316), while Suárez uses

* For an explanation of the new division of the ETHNOLOGY: SOUTH AMERICA section, see L. A. Brownrigg's introduction, p. 104.

the alliance theory of Needham to analyze the Warao kinship system (item 1323). A more or less straightforward functional analysis appears in several studies of the Guajiro by Watson (items 1330-1332).

Topically, the most popular subject at the moment seems to be the use of hallucinogenic drugs. One group of studies deals with *ayahuasca* (items 1252, 1272, 1288 and 1300), while a second group deals with various kinds of snuff (items 1235, 1243, and 1329).

There will be a delay in reporting papers given at the XXXIX International Congress of Americanists, since the Proceedings were published too late for review. The contents of volume four, which is devoted to papers on tropical forest tribes, will be found listed under item 510.

I would like to thank Daniel Gross for a very helpful bibliography. It will be greatly appreciated if all interested parties will promptly point out my errors of both commission and, especially, omission.

1219. Alvarez, Ricardo. Los piros: hijos de dioses. Lima, Secretaría de Misiones Dominicas del Perú, 1970. 72 p., plates.

Short, popular account of the culture of the Piro of eastern Peru, written by a Dominican missionary. Deals primarily with material culture and the life cycle.

1220. *América Indígena.* Instituto Indigenista Interamericano. Vol. 32, No. 4, oct./dic. 1972- . México.

Entire issue is devoted to current situation of indigenous populations of Colombia. Articles are very general, in most cases dealing not with specific tribes but all Indians as a unit. There is some useful information on the number and location of existing indigenous groups.

1221. Arnaud, Expedito. A ação indigenista no sul do Pará: 1940-1970 (MPEG/B, 49, 6 out. 1971, p. 1-49, bibl.)

Brief but revealing history of the "pacification" of various Brazilian tribes, written by an ethnologist wih good access to facts. It seems clear that the disastrous results of the program followed primarily from a failure to develop any realistic plan for the future of the Indians once they had been "attracted" and induced to live near an Indian post.

1222. ———. Os índios Oyampik e Emerilon, Rio Oiapoque: referências sôbre o passado e o presente (MPEG/B, 47, 2 fev. 1971, p. 1-28, bibl., map, plates)

Report on a brief visit in 1966. Most useful for bibliography of early sources on these two tribes.

1223. Arnaud, Patrick M. Ressources marines des terres de Magellan: leur utilisation par les Yamana et les Alakaluf (MH/OM, 12:2, eté 1972, p. 107-116, plates, tables)

Algae, molluscs, crustaceans and other useful sea foods are discussed in terms of their use by the Yamana and Alakaluf Indians. [R. C. Eidt]

1224. Arvelo-Jiménez, Nelly. Political relations in a tribal society: a study of the Ye'cuana Indians of Venezuela. Ithaca, N.Y., Cornell Univ., Latin American Studies Program, 1971. 383 p., bibl., map, tables (Dissertation series, 31)

Study of the Carib-speaking Ye'cuana (Makiritare), based on 15 months fieldwork, deals in detail with kinship, village structure, and intervillage relationships. Other topics are treated less thoroughly. Numerous case histories and genealogies give life to descriptive generalizations. One of the best monographs on a Guiana tribe. Also see item 1242.

1225. Baldus, Herbert. Tapirapé: tribo tupí no Brazil Central. São Paulo, Companhia Editôra Nacional [and] Editôra da Univ. de São Paulo, 1970. 510 p., bibl., illus., maps, plates, tables.

Brings together a great quantity of data on the Tapirapé. Much of the material is based on field trips made in 1935 and 1947, and most of it has been published before. In most cases, however, the description has been expanded or made more significant by comparisons based on author's unparalleled knowledge of Brazilian ethnology. Shapiro's recent work on the Tapirapé (see *HLAS 33:1635-1636*) is noted but not discussed.

1226. Bamberger, Joan. The adequacy of Kayapó ecological adjustment (*in* International Congress of Americanists, XXXVIII, Stuttgart-München, FRG, 1968. Vehandlungen [see *HLAS 33:510*] v. 3, p. 373-379, bibl.)

Although early accounts describe the Gê tribes of central Brazil as backward or "marginal," author's research among the Kayapó leads her to stress how well adapted the Gê tribes seem to be. Argues that the utilization of resources by the Kayapó does not depend essentially on their "simple" technology, but rather on their classification of the natural world and its potentialities.

1227. Bartolomé, Leopoldo J. Política y redes sociales en una comunidad urbana de indígenas toba: un análisis de liderazgo y "brokerage" (III/A, 31, dic. 1971, p. 77-98)

Analyzes political power in a *barrio* of an Argentine city occupied primarily by Toba Indians. Leadership in the community is related to the "social network" of the leaders.

1228. Bodard, Lucien. Massacre on the Amazon. London, Tom Stacey, 1971. 335 p., plates.

This book has also been issued in the US with the title *Green hell* (*HLAS 33:1507a*). It is a sensational and often irresponsible account of the tragedy of the

Brazilian Indians. A combination of fact, fiction, and misrepresentation, the book traces the plight of various tribes from first contact through the rubber boom and into the present. Recent atrocity stories are accepted uncritically. There is essentially no documentation. This book should not be used as a primary source. See item 1221.

1229. Boglár, Lajos. Besuch bei den Piaroa/Indianern, T. F. Amazonas, Venezuela (*in* International Congress of Americanists, XXXVIII, Stuttgart-München, FRG, 1968. Verhandlungen [see *HLAS 33:510*] v. 3, p. 24-27, bibl.)

Preliminary sketch, based on seven months fieldwork, of the culture of the Piaroa, a relatively typical tropical forest tribe of southern Venezuela.

1230. ———. Chieftainship and the religious leader (ASH/AE, 20:3/4, 1971, p. 332-337, bibl.)

Brief report on the position of chief among the Piaroa. Chiefs derive their authority from their control of the supernatural, manifested both in curing and in directing rituals. Also see item 1277.

1231. Cadogan, León. Ywyra ñe'ery: fluye del árbol la palabra, sugestiones para el estudio de la cultura guaraní. Prólogo e ilustraciones de Bartomeu Meliá. Asunción, Univ. Católica de Nuestra Señora de la Asunción, Centro de Estudios Antropológicos, 1971. 127 p., bibl., plates.

Rambling presentation of linguistic and mythological material obtained from Mbyá informants living in eastern Paraguay.

1232. Caron, Raymond. Curé d'indiens. Préface [pour] P. et M.-L. Sauchis. Paris, Union Général d'Editions, 1971. 366 p., maps (Série 7:10/18)

Account by Dominican missionary of his herculean efforts between 1966-71 to save the Xikrin from introduced diseases and exploitation by their Brazilian neighbors. Of minor ethnographic interest.

1233. Carrasco Hermoza, Juan R. La tribu machiguenga: algunos aspectos de su cultura (DGV/ZE, 95:2, 1970, p. 231-274, bibl., illus., map, plate)

Notes on the subsistence activities, life cycle, and material culture of the Machiguenga of eastern Peru.

1234. Ceballos, Rita. Les habitants de la Patagonie continentale, Argentine (MH/OM, 12:2, Eté 1972, p. 117-128, bibl., plates)

Brief but fairly thorough account of the history of the Tehuelche of Patagonia.

1235. Chagnon, Napolean A.; Philip Le Quesne; and James M. Cook. Yanomamö hallucinogens: anthropological, botanical, and chemical findings (UC/CA, 12:1, Feb. 1971, p. 72-74, bibl.)

The *ebene* snuff used by the Yanomamö is derived from a number of plants, some wild and some domesticated. The most common plant utilized is a member of the genus *Virola*, but the strongest and preferred snuff is made from the seeds of *Anadenanthera peregrina*. For more on snuffs, see items 1243 and 1329.

1236. Chapman, Anne M. Lune en Terre de Feu: mythes et rites des Selk'nam (MH/OM, Eté 1972, p. 145-158, plates)

Myths and details of initiation rituals collected from some of the last surviving Selk'nam (Ona). In 1970, only ten Selk'nam remained.

1237. Chase-Sardi, Miguel. El concepto nivaklé del alma (UCNSA/SA, 5:1/2, 1970, p. 201-238, bibl., plates)

Although written by a self-proclaimed *aficionado* of ethnography, a quite good account of beliefs about the soul among the Nivaklé (Ashluslay) of western Paraguay. There is also considerable material on shamanism and nine short texts.

1238. ———. Cosmovisión mak'a (UCNSA/SA, 5:1/2, 1970, p. 239-245, bibl., illus., plates)

Brief account of some aspects of Mak'a cosmology obtained from remnants of the tribe living near Asunción.

1239. ———. La situación actual de los indígenas del Paraguay. Presentación de Bartomeu Meliá. Asunción, Univ. Católica de Nuestra Señora de la Asunción, Centro de Estudios Antropológicos, 1972. 111 p., bibl., fold. map, plates, tables.

List of the 18 indigenous populations of Paraguay, giving location and size of every local group, plus comments on current status of each. Includes annotated bibliography of indigenist studies recently published in Paraguay. Detailed map completes this very useful compilation.

1240. Clair-Vasiliadis, Christos. Les Alakaluf de Puerto Edén, 1971 (MH/OM, Eté 1972, p. 197-200, plates, table)

Brief report on the 47 remaining Alakaluf (Wellington Island), who are now living in wooden houses and depending on irregular aid from the Chilean government.

1241. Colson, Audrey Butt. Hallelujah among the Patamona Indians (SCNLS/A, 28, 1971, p. 25-58, bibl., fold. map)

Presents account by participant of circumstances surrounding introduction of Hallelujah religion to the Patamona of Guyana.

1242. Coppens, Walter. Las relaciones comerciales de los yekuana del Caura-Paragua (SCNLS/A, 30, 1971, p. 28-59, bibl., maps, plates)

Deals in some detail with both intratribal and intertribal trade of the Yekuana (Makiritare) of southern Venezuela. The Yekuana exchange their specialities, manioc graters and canoes, with the Pemón and other tribes. For a general account of Yekuana culture, see item 1224.

1243. ——— and Jorge Cato-David. El yopo

entre los cuiva-guajibo: aspectos etnográficos y farmacológicos (SCNLS/A, 28, 1971, p. 3-24, bibl., map, plates, table)

Brief account of the preparation and use of a hallucinogenic snuff (*Anadenanthera peregrina*) by the Cuiva of western Venezuela. For more on snuffs, see items 1235 and 1329.

Cordeu, Egardo Jorge and **Alejandra Sifredi.** De la algarroba al algodón: movimientos milenaristas del Chaco argentino. See *HLAS 34:2692.*

1244. Cossard-Binon, Giselle. La fille de saint (SA/J, 58, 1969, p. 57-78, plates)

Detailed and perceptive description of the role of spirit medium in the Candomblé. Based on observations in one *terreiro* in Rio in 1946. For other studies of Afro-Brazilian religions, see items 1253 and 1282.

1245. Cotlow, Lewis. The twilight of the primitive. N.Y., MacMillan, 1971. 257 p., illus., maps, plates.

Popular and superficial description by well-known explorer of the Jívaro, the Xingú tribes, and various societies in other parts of the world.

1246. Crocker, J. Christopher. The dialectics of Bororo social inversions (*in* International Congress of Americanists, XXXVIII, Stuttgart-München, FRG, 1968. Verhandlungen [see *HLAS 33:510*] v. 3, p. 387-391, bibl.)

Describes intricate organization of moieties, clans, and lineages, and involved patterns of interaction among members of these groups, that make the Bororo of central Brazil the most complex of the Gê-speaking tribes. Some of the details of the system are somewhat obscured by a highly abstract structuralist interpretation.

1247. Crocker, William H. The Canela, Brazil, taboo system: a preliminary exploration of an anxiety-reducing device (*in* International Congress of Americanists, XXXVIII, Stuttgart-München, FRG, 1968. Verhandlungen [see *HLAS 33:510*] v. 3, p. 323-331)

Taboos are said to reduce anxiety by giving the Canela confidence that difficulties can be overcome by carrying out the proper ritual behavior. The pattern of taboo practices is said to probably reflect a basic triadic cognitive orientation.

1248. Denevan, William M. Campa subsistence in the Gran Pajonal, eastern Peru (AGS/GR, 61:4, Oct. 1971, p. 496-518)

Brief description of subsistence techniques, crops grown, and protein intake (for one man during a four-day period) among the Campa. Author, a geographer, appeals for quantified data but provides very little.

1249. Dobkin de Rios, Marlene. Ayahuasca: the healing vine (IJSP, 17:4, Winter 1971, p. 256-267)

Essentially same material as item 1250.

1250. ———. Curanderismo con la soga alucinógena, ayahuasca, en la selva peruana (III/AI, 31:3, julio 1971, p. 576-591)

Condensed version of item 1252.

1251. ———. A note on the use of 'ethno-tests' and western projective tests in a Peruvian Amazon slum (SAA/HO, 30:1, Spring 1971, p. 89-94)

Compares responses to TAT tests with information she obtained while telling fortunes using fortune-telling cards. Concludes that in latter situation she obtained data of "greater thematic richness." For details of research setting, see item 1252.

1252. ———. Visionary vine: psychedelic healing in the Peruvian Amazon. San Francisco, Calif., Chandler Publishing Company, 1972. 161 p., bibl., illus., map, plates, tables (Chandler publications for health sciences)

Highly personalized account of a year's study of folk healing in a slum of Iquitos, Peru. Curers and patients both take the hallucinogen *ayahuasca* to discover the source of illness (usually witchcraft). Author describes her experience after taking the drug, including her visions. Good bibliography on hallucinogenic drugs. Also see items 1272 and 1300.

1253. Dos Santos, Juana Elbein and **Deoscoredes M. Dos Santos.** Ancestor worship in Bahia: the Egun-cult (SA/J, 58, 1969, p. 79-108)

General description of those Afro-Brazilian cult centers in Bahia where the major supernaturals are souls of the dead rather than the *orixás*. It is never made clear when, where, how, or by whom the data were collected. Also see item 1306.

1254. Dumont, Jean-Paul. Compte rendu de mission chez les Indiens Panare (EPHE/H, 11:1, jan./mars 1971, p. 83-88)

Preliminary report of 16 months fieldwork among the Panare (western corner of Bolívar state, Ven.). The ethnographic sketch presented suggests that the Panare are similar to the other bilateral Carib-speaking tribes in this general area. See item 1224.

1255. Eibl-Eibesfeldt, Irenäus. Eine ethologische Interpretation des Palmfruchtfestes der Waika, Venezuela, nebst einigen Bemerkungen über die bindende Funktion von Zwiegesprächen (AI/A, 66:5/6, 1971, p. 767-778, bibl., plates)

Author describes two feasts observed among the Waika (Yanomamö) and presents some information obtained from missionaries. An ethological interpretation is offered to explain why the feasts produce social solidarity. Good photographs. Also see items 1284-1285.

1256. Emperaire, José. Alakaluf 1946-47 (MH/OM, Eté 1972, p. 185-196, bibl., plates)

Brief excerpts from a diary kept by Emperaire during his 18 months with the Alakaluf on Wellington Island. Evocative.

1257. Falk-Rønne, Arne. Massenmord in Mato Grosso: die ausrottung der indianer in Südamerika. Köbenhavn, Bertelsmann Sachbuchverlag, 1970. 220 p., plates.

Danish journalist's sympathetic account of his experiences among jungle tribes of Brazil, Paraguay, Bolivia and Peru. Describes their plight vis-à-vis encroaching 20th century civilization which forces them deeper and deeper into jungle. Points out need for protection of tribes as well as guidance and assistance for those who will incorporate into the modern world. [R. V. Shaw]

1258. Fock, Niels. Authority—its magico-religious, political and legal agencies—among Caribs in northern South America (*in* International Congress of Americanists, XXXVIII, Stuttgart-München, FRG, 1968. Verhandlungen [see *HLAS 33:510*] v. 3, p. 31-34, bibl.)

Describes the authority of the Waiwai headman as being based on his position as head of a large family, his use of the *oho* chant, and usually his status as shaman.

1259. Frikel, Protásio. Dez anos de aculturação tiriyó: 1960-70, mudanças e problemas. Belém, Bra., Conselho Nacional de Pesquisas, Instituto Nacional de Pesquisas da Amazônia, Museu Paraense Emílio Goeldi, 1971. 112 p., bibl., maps, plates, tables (Publicações avulsas, 16)

Detailed account of changes in Tiriyó (Trio) culture induced primarily by missionization. Domination by Protestant missionaries in Surinam and Catholic missionaries across the border in Brazil have produced cultural breakdown and disorientation in both areas, but the Catholics are said to have somewhat better record. For a different perspective, see *HLAS 33:1461*.

1260. ———. Os Kaxúyana: notas etnohistóricas. Belém, Bra., Conselho Nacional de Pesquisas, Instituto Nacional de Pesquisas de Amazônia, Museu Paraense Emílio Goeldi, 1970. 82 p., bibl., map, plates (Publicações avulsas, 14)

Attempt to corroborate an origin story of the Kaxúyana (upper Trombetas river) by tracing uncertain references to them in early historical records.

1261. Fuchs, Helmuth. Some notes on Guajiro research (*in* International Congress of Americanists, XXXVIII, Stuttgart-München, FRG, 1968. Verhandlungen [see *HLAS 33:510*] v. 3, p. 13-22, bibl.)

Argues that some of the material on the Guajiro (Guajira peninsula) in the *Ethnographic atlas* are incorrect. Discusses subsistence, brideprice, and social organization and offers alternative generalizations based on his own research. See items 1330-1331.

1262. Fuerst, René. Une civilisation du palmier (DGV/ZE, 95:1, 1970, p. 114-122, bibl., plates)

Describes many ways in which the Xikrin of central Brazil utilize wood, fronds, and fruit of various palm trees.

1263. ———. Erste Forschungsergebnisse von den südlichen Nambikwara (*in* International Congress of Americanists, XXXVIII, Stuttgart-München, FRG, 1968. Verhandlungen [see *HLAS 33:510*] v. 3, p. 315-321, bibl.)

Preliminary report on three months research among the Nambikwara of central Brazil. The group studied has considerably more horticulture than groups reported by Lévi-Strauss and others.

1264. Gancedo, Omar A. and **Eduardo Mario Cigliano.** Un préstamo cultural entre los guayaquí: la cerámica (UNLPM/R, 7:46 [Antropología] 1972, p. 211-224, bibl., illus., plates)

Pottery made by present-day Guayaquí Indians is a recent adoption and not a degeneration from an aboriginal ancient tradition. [B. J. Meggers]

1265. Gómez Gómez, Antonio. Contactos con la civilización de los indios yuko de la Sierra de Perijá, Colombia. Tunja, Co., Univ. Pedagógica y Tecnológica de Colombia, Fondo Especial de Publicaciones y Ayudas Educativas, 1970. 57 p., bibl. (Ediciones La Rana y El Aguila)

Contains rather superficial data (mostly historical) pertaining to a group of missionized Yuko.

1266. González, Alberto Rex. Une armure en cuir de Patagonie (MH/OM, 12:2, Eté 1972, p. 129-144, bibl., illus., plates)

Detailed description of leather shirt and two leather hats from the Musée de l'Homme. References in the literature make clear that these were worn as armor by the Patagonian tribes. Good bibliography.

1267. González Náñez, Omar E. La antropología aplicada y el desarrollo regional en Venezuela (UCV/ECS [2. época] 12:3, julio-sept. 1970, p. 91-103)

Very general discussion of the role of applied anthropology in future planning for the welfare of the indigenous populations of Venezuela.

1268. ———. Ponencia presentada en la XVIII convención anual de la Asociación Venezolana para el Avance de la Ciencia—División de Sociología y Antropología, Sección de Lingüística—: la mitología baniva reflejada en su literatura oral (UCV/ECS [2. época] 10:3, julio-sept. 1968, p. 87-96)

Purports to deal with the major themes of Baniva mythology. Includes Spanish translations of various myths and parts of myths.

1269. Grünberg, Friedl. Tentativas de análisis del sistema de parentesco de los kayabí, Brasil central (UCNSA/SA, 5:1/2, 1970, p. 227-287, bibl., tables)

Traditional description of kinship terminology (Iroquois type) of the Kayabí, followed by componential analysis of same terminology. Data were collected by Georg Grünberg (see item 1271).

1270. ——— and Georg Grünberg. Die materielle Kultur der Kayabí-Indianer (MVW/AV, 21, 1967, p. 27-89, bibl., illus., plates)

Systematic description, with many illustrations, of items collected from the Kayabí in 1966 which are now in Vienna's Museum für Völkerkunde.

1271. Grünberg, Georg. Beiträge zur Ethnographie der Kayabí Zentralbrasiliens (MVW/AV, 24, 1970, p. 21-186, bibl., illus., facsims., map, tables)

Although based on only eight months of fieldwork, this ethnography deals in reasonable detail with all aspects of Kayabí culture. Formerly living in the headwaters of the Tapajós river, the Kayabí have now been moved to the Xingú National Park. See items 1269-1270.

1272. Harner, Michael J. The Jívaro: people of the sacred waterfalls. Garden City, N.Y., Doubleday *for the* American Museum of Natural History, 1972. 233 p., bibl., illus., maps, plates, tables.

In this long-awaited monograph, author presents straightforward descriptive account of Jívaro culture as it was in 1956-57, when patterns of feuding, drugtaking, and head shrinking were essentially aboriginal. Religion, involving the use of hallucinogenic drugs, is covered very thoroughly, but material on kinship and dynamics of feuding is somewhat disappointing. Final chapter and short epilogue deal with changes in Jívaro culture to 1969.

1273. Harris, David R. The ecology of swidden cultivation in the Upper Orinoco rain forest, Venezuela (AGS/GR, 61:4, Oct. 1971, p. 475-495, map, plates, tables)

Analysis of soil nutrients, acidity, and plant cover for a number of cultivated and recently cultivated plots in the rain forest. Author suggests that the spread of maize may have been inhibited by the need for more efficient clearing.

1274. Hartmann, Günter. Die materielle Kultur de Wayaná—Nord-Brasilien (MV/BA, 19:2, Jun. 1971 [i.e., 1972] p. 379-420)

Detailed, descriptive account of the material culture of the Wayaná Indians in northern Brazil. Includes excellent photographs of items described: weapons, tools and drinking utensils, ceramics, plumes, wood carvings, musical instruments, and toys. [H.-J. Hoyer]

1275. Hermosa Virreira, Walter. Los pueblos guarayos: una tribu del Oriente boliviano. La Paz, Academia Nacional de Ciencias de Bolivia, 1972. 244 p., bibl., plates, tables (Publicación, 27)

Superficial ethnography, supplemented by considerable demographic data, of some 5000 long missionized and highly acculturated Indians of eastern Bolivia.

1276. Ingham, John M. Are the Sirionó raw or cooked? (AAA/AA, 73:5, Oct. 1971, p. 1092-1099, tables)

Yet another interpretation of Holmberg's incomplete data on the Sirionó of eastern Bolivia. In this case a highly abstract model of the kinship system is related to mythology, food taboos, and various symbols supposedly associated with males and females. For a different approach to Sirionó kinship, see item 1316.

1277. Kaplan, Joanna Overing. Cognation, endogamy, and teknonymy: the Piaroa example (UNM/SWJA, 28:3, Autumn 1972, p. 282-297, bibl.)

Unusually lucid analysis of kinship system of the Piaroa of southern Venezuela. Use of teknonymy is seen as functioning to convert affines into kin in a situation of small endogamous villages. "The teknonym . . . is a symbolic statement of the unity of the group and of the artificiality of distinctions within it." Also see items 1229-1230.

1278. Kelm, Heinz. Das Jahresfest der Ayoreo, Ostbolivien (MV/BA, 19[44]: 1, Nov. 1971, p. 97-140, tables)

Detailed descriptive account of activities and myths associated with the most important ceremony of the Ayoreo.

1279. Kloos, Peter. The Maroni river Caribs of Surinam. Assen, The Netherlands, Van Gorcum, 1971. 304 p., bibl., maps, plates, tables (Studies in developing countries, 12)

Based on 18-months fieldwork, this monograph deals in meticulous detail with an acculturated community of Carib-speakers on Surinam's coast. Clearly describes present simple social structure (nuclear families, minimal leadership, avoidance of conflict). Kinship terminology, life cycle rituals, and shamanism have remained more conservative. Discusses increasing integration into the national economy and offers suggestions for future governmental programs. Preliminary annotation appeared in *HLAS 33:1429.*

Lalouel, Jean M. and **Newton E. Morton.** Bioassay of kinship in a South American Indian population. See item 1745.

1280. Laming-Emperaire, Annette. Pêcheurs des archipels et chasseurs des pampas (MH/OM, eté 1972, p. 167-184, bibl., plates, table)

Popular but informed account of the Alacaluf, Yahgan, and Ona, based on standard sources.

1281. Lave, Jean Carter. Some suggestions for the interpretation of residence, descent and exogamy among the eastern Timbira (*in* International Congress of Americanists, XXXVIII, Stuttgart-München, FRG, 1968. Verhandlungen [see *HLAS 33:510*] v. 3, p. 341-345)

On the basis of her research among the Krikatí Brazil), author argues that Nimuendajú was probably not justified in describing the Ramkokamekra (Canela) as matrilineal. Like the closely related Krikatí, the Ramkokamekra were probably matrilocal, but bilateral and without exogamous moieties.

1282. Leacock, Seth and **Ruth Leacock.** Spirits of the deep: a study of an Afro-Brazilian cult. Garden City, N.Y., Doubleday *for the* American Museum of Natural History, 1972. 404 p., bibl., map, plates, tables.

Comprehensive description of the Batuque, a much modified Afro-Brazilian religion practiced in Belém, Bra. Although the belief system, the organization, and the ritual cycle are treated in detail, emphasis throughout is on ways in which the members use their status as a spirit medium to modify their daily lives. Also see items 1244 and 1253.

1283. Lizot, Jacques. Aspects économiques et

sociaux du changement culturel chez les Yanõmami (EPHE/H, 11:1, jan./mars. 1971, p. 32-51, bibl., map, tables)

First detailed report of the central Yanõmami (Yanomamö). Two villages are compared to show how the acquisition of manufactured goods (from missionaries) by one village tended to upset political and economic balances. Enough ethnographic data are presented to indicate that these Yanomamö are much like those studied by Chagnon (*HLAS 31:2086*), except that they are somewhat less violent.

1284. ———. Compte rendu de mission chez les Indiens Yanõmami (EPHE/H, 10:2, avril/juin 1970, p. 116-121)

Brief account of the circumstances of the author's two-year study of the Yanõmami (Yanomamö) of southern Venezuela, together with a sketch of Yanõmami culture.

1285. ———. Remarques sur le vocabulaire de parenté Yanõmami (EPHE/H, 11:2, avril-juin 1971, p. 25-38, bibl., tables)

This brief but lucid description of Yanõmami kinship terminology includes some discussion of kinship behavior and marriage patterns. No comparisons are made with Chagnon's material. See item 1283.

1286. Lucena Salmoral, Manuel. Bardaje en una tribu guahibo del Tomo (ICA/RCA, 14, 1966/1969, p. 261-266)

On the basis of an interview with one informant at a mission, author suggests that the role of *berdache* may be institutionalized among some Guahibo of eastern Colombia.

1287. ———. Notas sobre la magia de los guahibo (ICA/RCA, 15, 1970/1971, p. 130-169)

Systematic description of beliefs and practices associated with the treatment of disease and the life cycle among acculturated Guahibo of eastern Colombia. Limitations of the data are made explicit. Also contains suggestions for government programs affecting the Guahibo. Also see item 1297.

1288. Manganotti, Donatella. I bevitori de veleni (IGM/U, 48:6, nov./dic. 1968, p. 1145-1160, illus.)

Popular article on the nature and use of *ayahuasca* (*Banisteriopsis*), based largely on traveler's accounts. For more detailed studies, see items 1252, 1272, and 1300.

1289. Martínez-Crovetto, Raúl. Introducción a la etnobotánica aborigen del nordeste Argentino (*in* International Congress of Americanists, XXXVIII, Stuttgart-München, FRG, 1968. Verhandlungen [see *HLAS 33:510*] v. 3, p. 91-97)

Preliminary report of an extensive study of plant names and plant utilization among the Guaraní-mbiá, Mocoví, Toba, and Vilela.

1290. Matos Romero, Manuel. La Guajira: su importancia. Caracas, Empresa El Cojo, 1971. 441 p., plates.

Popular and partisan account of the Guajiro, their cul-ture, history, and current problems, by a long-time champion of their cause. More significant as recent history than as ethnography. For more detailed studies of the Guajiro, see items 1330-1331 and 1335.

1291. Matta, Roberto da. Uma breve reconsideração da morfologia social apinayé (*in* International Congress of Americanists, XXXVIII, Stuttgart-München, FRG, 1968. Verhandlungen [see *HLAS 33:510*] v. 3, p. 355-364, bibl.)

Presents a closely reasoned, and reasonable, reconstruction of how Nimuendajú came to describe erroneously Apinayé marriage as being regulated by four *kiyé*. In the process the author discusses in detail the complex way in which names are transmitted among the Apinayé. Data based on 11 months fieldwork.

1292. Maybury-Lewis, David. Some principles of social organization among the Central Gê (*in* International Congress of Americanists, XXXVIII, Stuttgart-München, FRG, 1968. Verhandlungen [see *HLAS 33:510*] v. 3, p. 381-386, bibl.)

Author discusses recent research among the Gê tribes of central Brazil, including work by members of the Harvard-Central Brazil project which he directed between 1962-68. In spite of striking differences among the tribes studied (Kayapó, Bororo, Křikatí, Apinayé, Krahó, Sherente, Shavante), author perceives a number of basic similarities: uxorilocal residence, numerous binary institutions, a public/domestic sphere dichotomy. Explanations of these variations are promised. For studies relating to this summary, see items 1246, 1281, 1291, 1296, and 1325.

1293. Meggers, Betty J. Amazonia: man and culture in a counterfeit paradise. Foreword by Walter Goldschmidt. Chicago, Ill., Aldine-Atherton, 1971. 182 p., bibl., illus., maps, plates, tables (Worlds of man: studies in cultural ecology)

Intended as supplementary reading for undergraduates, this study explains cultural similarities and differences among selected Amazonian tribes in terms of adaptation to the environment. Five *terra firme* tribes (Jívaro, Waiwai, Kayapó, Camayurá, Sirionó) are compared with two tribes that utilized the *varzea* (Omagua and Tapajós). More complex institutions of the latter are attributed largely to superior resources. First chapter provides best available introduction to subsistence patterns in the tropical forest. For geographer's comment, see item 7107.

1294. Melatti, Julio Cezar. Indios do Brasil. Brasília, Coordenada-Editôra de Brasília, 1970. 208 p., bibl., illus., maps, tables.

Popular and rather sketchy introduction to Brazilian Indians.

1295. ———. O messianismo krahó. São Paulo, Editora Herder da Univ. de São Paulo, 1972. 140 p., bibl.

Describes a messianic movement that occurred among the Krahó of central Brazil in 1951. Data are few and conflicting, but the movement seems to have been similar to one reported for the Ramkokamekra, which is also discussed. For a comparative study of messianic movements in Brazil, see item 1315.

1296. ———. Nominadores e genitores: um aspecto do dualismo krahó (*in* International Congress of Americanists, XXXVIII, Stuttgart-München, FRG, 1968. Verhandlungen [see *HLAS 33:510*] v. 3, p. 347-353)

Sketches Krahó (central Brazil) beliefs about procreation, then describes the system of name transmission whereby individuals become members of a variety of ceremonial groups. There is said to be a relation of opposition and complementarity among the ideas involved.

1297. Morey, Robert V. Guahibo time-reckoning (CUA/AQ, 44:1, Jan. 1971, p. 22-36, illus.)

Detailed analysis of those features of the environment that are used as temporal indicators by the Guahibo of eastern Colombia. Because of the fluidity of the social organization, shared social events cannot serve in the same way. Also see item 1287.

1298. ———. Notes on the Sáliva of eastern Colombia (UC/CA, 13:1, Feb. 1972, p. 144-147, bibl., map, tables)

Based on a two-month survey, this brief report gives the location and residence pattern of several villages of Sáliva, with the expressed intention of encouraging someone else to undertake a full-scale study.

1299. Mourão, Noemia. Arte plumária e máscaras de dança dos índios brasileiros. Introdução de Gilberto Freyre. São Paulo, Oficinas de Artes Gráficas Bradesco, 1971. 78 p., bibl., illus.

Large folio volume of paintings by Brazilian artist of ornaments and masks used by tribes of Amazônia and the Mato Grosso. The 69 colored plates are attractive and obviously based on authentic museum specimens, but they are sadly lacking in detail. Captions in Portuguese and English.

1300. Naranjo, Plutarco. Ayahuasca: religión y medicina. Quito, Editorial Universitaria, 1970. 154 p., bibl., illus., plates (Etnobotánica)

Surveys the botanical distribution of *ayahuasca* (*Banisteriopsis*) in western South America, then describes the use of the drug by the tribes of Ecuador, especially the Jívaro and Cofan. Data are derived from the literature. For specific studies of the use of *ayahuasca*, see items 1252 and 1272.

1301. Oliveira, Adélia Engrácia de. Parentesco jurúna (MPEG/B, 45, 16 out. 1970, p. 1-46, bibl., tables)

Description of the Jurúna (central Brazil) kinship system as of 1967. Utilizing early accounts, author shows that the system has not changed over several generations, in spite of a drastic decrease in population and intermarriage with members of several Upper Xingú tribes.

1302. Perrin, Michel. La littérature orale des Guajiro: compte rendu de mission (EPHE/H, 11:2, avril/juin 1971, p. 109-112)

Brief report on a ten month study of oral literature among the Guajiro of the Guajira peninsula. Texts collected include songs, chants used by shamans, and myths.

1303. ———. Introducción a la literatura oral de los indios guajiros (UCV/ECS [2. época] 12:3, julio-sept. 1970, p. 5-20)

Eleven short myths translated into Spanish (the Guajiro text is not given), with a tentative classification intended to facilitate a later structural analysis. Also see item 1335.

1304. Persson, Lars. Flodkällornas folk: Sydamerikas försvinnande indianstammar. Stockholm, P. A. Norstedt & Söners förlag, 1968. 201 p., bibl., illus., maps, plates, tables.

Devoted to travels of author, Swedish ethnographer in the Vaupés-Caquetá region of Colombia in 1966. Persson strongly criticizes policies of Colombian government towards indigenous tribes who are being systematically deprived of their own culture. [R. V. Shaw]

1305. Pessango Espora, Mario A. Los fueguinos. B.A., Comando en Jefe de la Armada, Secretaría General Naval, Depto. de Estudio Históricos Navales, 1971. 237 p., bibl., illus., maps, plates (Cultura náutica general: serie A, 2)

Superficial description of Ona and Yahgan culture, based on the standard sources, by a captain in the Argentine navy.

1306. Pollak-Eltz, Angelina. Der Egungunkult der Yoruba in Afrika und in Amerika (DGV/ZE, 95:2, 1970, p. 275-293)

Compares ancestor worship as practiced in Nigeria (data derived from fieldwork) with what are taken to be survivals of ancestor worship in Cuba and Brazil (data from the literature). Tends to stress similarities and ignore differences. For a recent study of an Egungun cult in Brazil, see item 1253.

1307. ———. Vestigios africanos en la cultura del pueblo venezolano. Caracas, Univ. Católica Andrés Bello, Instituto de Investigaciones Históricas, 1972. 171 p., bibl.

Argues for the presence of African influences in Catholic festivals, musical instruments, burial ritual, and curing, but admits that in some cases the traits described could be of Indian or even European origin. Most of the African elements in the cult of Maria Lionza seem to be recent additions. This work will also be of interest to students of folklore.

Price, Richard and **Sally Price.** Saramaka onomastics: an Afro-American naming system. See item 1201.

1308. Prost, Marian D. Costumbres, habilidades y cuadro de la vida humana entre los chacobos. Riberalta, Bol., Instituto Lingüístico de Verano [and] Ministerio de Educación y Cultura, 1970. 69 p., bibl., map, plates.

Short sketch of the material culture and life cycle of the Chacobo of northern Bolivia by a member of the Summer Institute of Linguistics.

1309. Riester, Jürgen. Die materielle Kultur der

Chiquitano-Indianer, Ost Bolivien, (MVW/AV, 25, 1971, p. 143-230, bibl., illus., map, plates, tables)

Detailed description, with illustrations, of materials collected by the author and others from the Chiquitano.

1310. ———. Uberlieferung und Wandel in der Religion der Chiquitanos (*in* International Congress of Americanists, XXXVIII, Stuttgart-München, FRG, 1968. Verhandlungen [see *HLAS 33:510*] v. 3, p. 65-75)

Brief account of the history of missionization of the Chiquitano (Chiquito) of eastern Bolivia, plus a sketch of their present religious beliefs as a stable blend of aboriginal and Christian elements.

1311. ———. Zur Religion der Pauserna-Guarasug'wä in Ostbolivien (AI/A, 65:3/4, 1970, p. 466-479)

Clear and comprehensive study of the dwindling Guarasug'wa includes a description of their basic beliefs (a grandfather-creator of the tribe, human soul, "masters" or spirits of nature, etc.) and an account of a few myths explaining the beliefs. This Guaraní group lives in the Bolivian dept. of Santa Cruz. [S. C. Caton]

Rivière, Peter. The forgotten frontier: ranchers of North Brazil. See item 7148.

———. Marriage among the Trio: a principle of social organization. See *HLAS 33:1461*.

1312. Rosero, Magdalena. La espiritualidad de los Shuar. Quito, Pontificia Univ. Católica del Ecuador, Facultad de Enfermería, 1972. 57 p., bibl., illus.

Deals with the religious beliefs of the Shuar (Jívaro) of eastern Ecuador, based on interviews with a Catholic priest of 16 years experience. Should be used with caution. Compare with item 1272.

1313. Sanoja O., Mario. Notas sobre los telares y las técnicas de tejidos de los indios guajiros, Venezuela (UCV/ECS [2. época] 10:3, julio-sept. 1968, p. 16-64)

Detailed description, with numerous illustrations, of techniques used in weaving by the Guajiro (Guajira peninsula).

1314. Schaden, Egon. Aculturação e messianismo entre índios brasileiros. 2. ed. São Paulo, Univ. de São Paulo, Escola de Comunicações e Artes, 1972. 16 l., bibl.

Contains essentially the same material as item 1315.

1315. ———. Kulturwandel und Nativismus bei den Indianern Brasiliens (*in* International Congress of Americanists, XXXVIII, Stuttgart-München, FRG, 1968. Verhandlungen [see *HLAS 33:510*] v. 3, p. 35-42, bibl.)

Brief survey of the remarkably few messianic movements that have been reported among Brazilian Indians. Cases discussed include the Baníwa, Tucano, Tukuna, Ramkokamekra (Canela), and Krahó. For a more complete account of the Krahó case, see item 1295.

1316. Scheffler, Harold W. and Floyd G. Lounsbury. A study in structural semantics: the Sirionó kinship system. Englewood Cliffs, N.J., Prentice Hall, 1971. 260 p., bibl., tables.

Primarily of interest to specialists in kinship and formal analysis. Contains an elaborate formal analysis of the kinship terminology of the Sirionó of eastern Bolivia. Some of the structural principles underlying the Sirionó system are said to be present also in the terminologies of the Apinayé, Ramkokamekra, Kayapó, Nambikwara, and Inca. Authors clarify a number of problems raised in earlier studies of these terminologies.

1317. Schultz, Harald and Vilma Chiara. Informações etnográficas dos índios waurá (*in* International Congress of Americanists, XXXVIII, Stuttgart-München, FRG, 1968. Verhandlungen [see *HLAS 33:510*] v. 3, p. 285-308, illus., bibl.)

The late Harald Schultz spent four months in 1964 among the Waurá of the Upper Xingú (central Brazil). Based on his fieldnotes, this article by Vilma Chiara deals in some detail with subsistence activities, the preparation of salt, and the manufacture of pottery.

1318. Silveira, Isôlda Maciel da. Aspectos sócio-econômicos de Oriximiná, sede: nota prévia (MPEG/B, 50, 23 março 1972, p. 48-50, bibl., maps, plates, tables)

Brief sociological description (no data on the political system) of a small town at the juncture of the Trombetas and Amazon rivers.

1319. Spielman, Richard S. and others. The genetic structure of a tribal population, the Yanomama Indians (AJPA, 37:3, Nov. 1972, p. 345-356, map, tables)

Number of measurements (stature, sitting height, head circumference, nose height and breadth, seven others) taken on individuals in 19 Yanomama villages demonstrate "significant heterogeneity in physique," greatly in excess of random differentiation. Differences seem to correlate with geographic distance.

1320. Steinvorth Goetz, Inga. Uriji jami! Die Waika-Indianer in den Urwäldern des Oberen Orinoko. Düsseldorf/Köln, FRG, Eugen Diederichs Verlag, 1971. 216 p., maps, plates.

German original. For Spanish translation see *HLAS 33:1640*.

1321. Stolk, Anthonie. Wegen door de wildernis: mijn ervaringen met de Zuidamerikaanse Jivaro- en Cayapa-Indianen. Wassenaar, The Netherlands, Servire, 1968. 166 p.

Popular account of the experiences of the author (a biologist) among the Jívaro of eastern Ecuador and other tribes.

1322. Suárez, María Matilde. Terminología, alianza matrimonial y cambio en la sociedad warao. Traducción al castellano por Isabel Bacalao. Prólogo por Rodney Needham. Caracas, Univ. Católica Andrés Bello, Instituto de Investigaciones Históricas,

Seminario de Lenguas Indígenas, 1972. 110 p., bibl., map, plates, tables.
Spanish translation of item 1323. In an extensive introduction, Rodney Needham discusses the theoretical significance of the work and provides comparative data on the Guahibo, Piaroa, Yanomamö, and Yaruro.

1323. ———. Terminology, alliance and change in Warao society (NWIG, 48:1, April 1971, p. 56-122, bibl., plates, tables)
Definitive study of the Warao (Orinoco delta) kinship system. Basing her analysis on Needham, the author considers the hypothesis that there has been "a structural change in Warao society from a two-section system of symmetric prescriptive alliance towards a cognatic and preferential system." Current marriage practices interpreted as revealing a high incidence of symmetric alliances are offered as evidence of a former two-section system. See item 1322.

1324. Suárez de Asuaje, M. M. Formas de organización política en sociedades tribales de Venezuela (ACPS/B, 32:50/51, julio/dic. 1972, p. 129-150, bibl.)
Presents a brief sketch of the social structure, especially political institutions, of the Goajiro, Yekuana (Makiritare), Warao, and Bari (Motilone).

Torres de Araúz, Reina. Hábitos dietarios y dieta cuantitativa de los indios chocóes: Panamá. See item 1707.

1325. Turner, Terence S. Northern Kayapó social structure (*in* International Congress of Americanists, XXXVIII, Stuttgart-München, FRG, 1968. Verhandlungen [see *HLAS 33:510*] v. 3, p. 365-371, bibl.)
Presents a structural analysis of some features of Kayapó (central Brazil) social structure. Like other Northern Gê tribes, the Kayapó are bilateral and matrilocal, but they are unusual in having a moiety system based on two men's houses. They share symbolic patrifiliation with the Apinayé. See item 1291.

1326. Varese, Stefano. Investigaciones en la selva (PEMN/R, 36, 1969/1970, p. 282-283)
Brief report of the anthropologists, geographers, and linguists who were carrying out fieldwork in eastern Peru in 1970.

1327. ——— and **Moisés Gamarra.** Dos versiones cosmogónicas campa: esbozo analítico (PEMN/R, 36, 1969/1970, p. 164-177, bibl., tables)
Structural analysis of two apparently dissimilar myths, in both of which the authors claim to discern the same basic themes of Campa thought. For a more detailed account of Campa cosmology, see item 1333.

1328. Villas Boas, Orlando and **Cláudio Villas Boas.** Xingú: os índios, seus mitos. Ilustrações de Poty. 2. ed. rev. Rio, Zahar Editôres, 1972. 211 p., illus.
Primarily collection of 31 myths (Portuguese translation only), this small book also contains the present (1970) roster of tribes living in the Xingú National Park. The recent history of a few of these tribes is included.

Wassén, S. Henry. The anthropological outlook for Amerindian medicinal plants. See item 534.

1329. ———. Einige wichtige, hauptsächlich ethnographische Daten zum Gebrauch indianischer Schnupfdrogen (Ethnologische Zeitschrift Zürich [Switzerland] 1, 1971, p. 47-63, plates)
Useful survey of data on the use of hallucinogenic snuffs by South American Indians. Most early accounts deal with snuff made from the plant *Anadenanthera peregrina*, but more recent studies indicate that plants of the genus *Virola* are also used. The chemical properties of these plants are now well known. For more on snuffs, see items 1235 and 1243.

1330. Watson, Lawrence C. The education of the cacique in Guajiro society and its functional implications (CUA/AQ, 43:1, Jan. 1970, p. 23-38)
Describes the processes whereby the head of a matrilineage trains one of his sister's sons to succeed him. Argues that this training serves a need in Guajiro society, since a strong leader is necessary for the integration of the lineage. Also see items 1261 and 1335.

1331. ———. Sexual socialization in Guajiro society (UP/E, 11:2, April 1972, p. 150-156, bibl.)
Functional analysis of the relationship between socialization of girls and marriage practices. If a bride is found to have had prior sexual experience, her matrilineage is discredited and a large part of the bridewealth must be returned. Severe sexual socialization of girls insures their chastity at marriage.

1332. ———. Urbanization and identity dissonance: a Guajiro case (AAA/AA, 74:5, Oct. 1972, p. 1189-1207, tables)
Study of changes in "self-identity" among Guajiro living in Maracaibo. Interviews, life histories, and TAT responses of urbanized and tribal Guajiro were compared. "Defective socialization in the city is suggested as a possible reason for failure to achieve ideal standards."

1333. Weiss, Gerald. Campa cosmology (UP/E, 11:2, April 1972, p. 157-172, bibl.)
Lucid, detailed account of beliefs about good and evil spirits, "gods," the human soul, and the nature of the universe among the Campa of eastern Peru.

1334. Wiesemann, Ursula. Purification among the Kaingáng Indians today (DGV/ZE, 95:1, 1970, p. 104-113, plates)
Brief description of a ritual (associated with widows) observed by the author (Summer Institute of Linguistics) among a group of acculturated Kaingáng in southern Brazil.

1335. Wilbert, Johannes. Survivors of Eldorado: four Indian cultures of South America. N.Y., Praeger Publishers, 1972. 212 p., bibl., illus., maps, plates, tables.
Presents short ethnographies (50 pages each) of four tribes of Venezuela: Yanoama, Warao, Makiritare (Yecuana), and Goajiro, apparently intended as sup-

plementary reading for ethnology courses. Although there are a few dubious interpretations (e.g., the Yanoama represent hunters and gatherers, the Makiritare are matrilineal), the descriptions are comprehensive and reasonably detailed. Author has first-hand knowledge of all four tribes, and his accounts incorporate most recent research. See items 1224, 1283-1285, 1323, and 1330-1332.

ETHNOLOGY
SOUTH AMERICA: HIGHLANDS

LESLIE ANN BROWNRIGG

Assistant Professor of Anthropology
Northwestern University

This section represents a division of the Ethnology: South America HLAS unit. The terms "highlands" and "lowlands" are used as convenient titles, though neither is precise. No altitudinal lines were drawn to designate each editor's respective responsibilities. In the highlands section are found works which pertain to the sea-level Pacific west coast; in the "lowlands" section, works on tribal groups whose traditional territories are above those occupied by some Andean peoples reviewed. As a rule of thumb, the "highlands" section concerns Andean peoples and the "lowlands," the rest of South America.

One set of criteria for the division of aboriginal peoples between the new sections included size of socio-political units, degree of integration into state organizations and culture. The highland section deals with aboriginal peoples whose socio-economic-political organizations have been successively transformed by and integrated into a series of sophisticated state level organizations: precolumbian states and empires, the Spanish colonial empire and the modern national states of Colombia, Ecuador, Peru, Bolivia, Argentina and Chile. The lowlands section reviews works concerning ethno-linguistic groups which are relatively small and have a more shallow history of integration into state level organizations. By this latter criterion, the peoples of the montaña of Ecuador, Peru and Bolivia, the Amazonian lowland groups of Colombia and transhumant populations of the Guajiro peninsula are reviewed in the lowlands section. In dividing the aboriginal peoples between the sections, similarities in the tradition of ethnological investigations of Amazonian and montaña social structure, religious institutions, ecology and material culture was recognized. No "culture area" is intended or implied. Particularly for the ethno-linguistic groups in the montaña, there exists an intermingling of Andean and Amazonian "traits" and some aspects of contemporary culture are shared by both Andean peoples and clearly Amazonian groups. Were culture traits the basis for this division, the case could be made for including a far larger area as either the Andean or Amazonian hinterland.

An arbitrary geographical division was made regarding the review of the ethnology of non-aborigines. The highlands and lowlands section overlap in subject matters such as peasants, acculturation, urban-based social segments, social change, Afro-American culture, etc. Literature on such subjects from Colombia, Ecuador, Peru, Bolivia and Chile are to be found in this "highlands" section; comparable works from Venezuela, the Guianas, Surinam, (some Guianas items are annotated in the ETHNOLOGY: WEST INDIES section), Brazil, Uruguay, Paraguay and some parts of Argentina are reviewed in the "lowlands" section. There exists both a backlog and an upsurge in the ethnological literature of the Andean area. Previous editors of the South American ethnology section had emphasized the Amazonian and Brazilian literature. Accordingly, some works reviewed in the present section were written as early as 1962 and others from the 1960's will be reviewed in the future. From *HLAS 29* on, the "basic principle of selection [was] concern with groups defined by themselves and by others as Indian and/or with elements of their culture," (see *HLAS 31*, p. 136) although certain accounts of acculturation were reviewed. The present section has lain aside that policy. Entries are not limited to the indigenous cultural sector. For more than a decade, anthropologists have been following highland Indians into the mines, coastal towns and urban centers which have become an important aspect of the life cycle and cultural process of Andean peoples. Urban studies have become an important aspect of Andean anthropological study in their own right. The process of cultural change which in Peru is identified by the special term *cholification* is a central concern of ethnology: the comparative aspect intrinsic in ethnology includes the study of culture change, of before and after ethnography. I leave the documentation of these assertions to some of the works reviewed in this section, particularly: Stein, "Race, Culture, and Social Structure in Peru" (item 1495), Fernando Fuenzalida and others "El Indio y el Poder" (item 1402), Thomas Greaves "The Andean Rural Proletariats" (item 1412), Quijano Obregón "La Emergencia del Grupo Cholo . . ." (item 1473) Doughty "Peruvian Migrant Identity in the Urban Milieu" (item 1384), and Kellert "Culture Change and Stress in Rural Peru" (item 1424). This policy change legitimates the review of studies of such "non-Indian" groups as Afro-American enclaves: Friedemann and Morales "Estudios de Negros" (item 1398), Whittington "Kinship, Mating and Family in the Chaco" (item 1507), and Whitten "Ecología de las Relaciones Raciales" (item 1507); and urban-based groups: Uzzell "Bound for Places . . ." (item 1498), Press "The Urban Curandero" (item 1472), Mangin "Peasants in Cities" (item 1435), Escobar "A Preliminary Analysis . . . of Cuzco . . ." (item 1391), and Middleton "Form and Process: A Study . . ." (item 1445a).

An upsurge in Andean area ethnological literature can be attributed to an increase in research manpower and publication outlets. New publication series now originate from research establishments and religious institutions in the Andean nations.

The tradition of ethnological studies by North American scholars was heavily influenced by Cornell University's involvement in Peru which began in 1951. A generation of American and Peruvian scholars were trained or influenced by the late Allen R. Holmberg's multifold research projects. The emphasis of this "school" were on applied anthropology, Redfieldian community studies, demography, internal migration including urban acculturation, and its theoretical inclination was functionalist. Scholars originally trained in this perspective are now mature and have produced intellectual descendants through their own teaching and research projects as well as through their literature.

New publication outlets are increasing the literature base. The Instituto Indigenista Interamericano of Mexico is making available in inexpensive paper-bound Spanish editions both such classics of Andean literature as Tschopik "Magia en Chucuito" (item 1496) and Faron "Los Mapuche" (item 1393); and new research: Dandler "El Sindicalismo Campesino en Bolivia" (item 1378), Ebersole "La Artesanía" (item 1386), Fuenzalida "La Comunidad Andina," Casillo "Pisac" (item 1370), Montgomery "Ethos y Ayllu en Coasa, Peru" (item 1448), Bourricaud "Cambios en Puno" (item 1358), *HLAS 33: 1513* and *HLAS 31: 2119*.

A major Peruvian source is the Instituto de Estudios Peruanos (item 1421). The Ecuadorian folklore journals and the *Llacta* series of monographs of the Instituto Ecuatoriano de Antropología y Geografía, though not recent innovations, are publishing articles of increasing interest to ethnologists. The new journal, *Estudios Andinos,* of the Instituto Boliviano de Estudio y Acción Social, is a welcome addition. Its articles of ethnological interest are reviewed separately.

A relatively new and steady source of ethnological data concerning religious ideology, ritual and religious social organization originates from institutions and individuals of the Catholic Church and missionary groups active in the Andes. The Instituto de Pastoral Andina, founded by bishops and prelates in the southern Peruvian area to promote and publish anthropological investigations of that area's religious and social customs, publishes an annual journal, *Allpanchis Phuturinqa* (item 1341) and occasional monographs. Other works in this category include: Nordyke "Animistic Aymara and Church Growth" (item 1453), Marzal "El Mundo Religioso de Urcos" (item 1441), Goring "The Antioquians . . ." (item 1411), Monast "On les Croyait Chrétiens" (item 1447), Garr "Cristianismo y Religión Quechua" (item 1409), and Monast, *HLAS 33:1601*.

While the perspective and interpretations of some works on this genre are understandably ideological, commendable attention to principles of anthropological theory and methodology by investigators render these works important data sources.

Some items reviewed are not conventionally published. While an effort was made not to overburden the review with works which circulate only as multilith or mimeograph manuscripts available from their authors, some works in this form are far superior to ephemeral fieldnotes which are published as articles or hodge-podge collations which pass as monographs or ethnological dictionaries. Most certainly the works cited of this form will eventually appear in print. Another unconventional source which this review indicates are those Ph.D. dissertations on Andean ethnology available either through the University Microfilms service (now at fees comparable to university press monographs) or through multilith series.

The total effect of these new publication series and sources is an important increase in materials now available to scholars and which complement such traditional sources as university press monographs, the *Revista del Museo Nacional, América Indígena* and the Proceedings of the International Congress of Americanists (item 510) and occasional articles in non-geographically specialized anthropological journals.

In the last decade, two new important research methodologies have been applied to the analysis of Andean ethnology. Both methodologies represent new theoretical orientations and both were the gift of European-born Inca ethnohistorians to the two America's Andeanists. John Murra has been in the process of a precise identification of the Andean pattern of vertical ecology and altitudinal-climatic "islands" controlled by ancient Andean states. Through publication of research documentation of the concept in Murra's "La Visita de los Chupachu como Fuente Etnológica" (*HLAS 29:2178c*), "An Aymara Kingdom in 1567" (*HLAS 32:1078*), and "El 'Control Vertical' de Un Máximo de Pisos Ecológicos . . ." (*HLAS 34:1195*) and his direct influence on students and members of his mid-1960's Huánuco project, the concept of vertical ecology has moved to a place of central importance. Examples of the application of this perspective include: Custred "Peasant Kinship, Subsistence and Economics . . ." (item 1375), Valle "La Ecología Subjectiva como . . ." (item 1500), Mayer "Un Carnero por un Saco de Papas" (item 1443), Brush "Kinship and Land Use . . ." (item 1362), Burchard "Village Exogamy and Strategies. . . ." (item 1365), Barette "Aspects de l'Ethno-Ecologie . . ." (item 1351), and Webster "The Social Organization of . . ." (item 1505).

R. T. Zuidema is the second Inca ethnohistorian whose theories and methodologies are revitalizing Andean ethnology. Zuidema's original structuralist analysis on the *ceque* system of Cuzco (see *HLAS 29:2156b, 2201a* and *2207*) and his subsequent articles on: "Hierarchy in Symmetric Alliance Systems" (*HLAS 31:2277*) "American Social Systems and their Mutual Similarity" (*HLAS 32:1130*), "El Juego de los Ayllus y el Amaru" (*HLAS 32:1132*), and "El Estudio Arqueológico, Etnohistórico y Antropológico (*HLAS 34:1238*) have advanced his arguments. The structuralist perspective has led to field examinations of Andean kinship, mythology and settlement patterns by younger scholars: Isbell "Kuyaq . . ." (item 1422), Palomino Flores "La Dualidad en la Organización Socio-Cultural . . ." (item 1459), and "Duality in the Socio-Cultural Organization . . ." (item 1460), Javier Albó "Dinámica en la Estructura Inter-Comunitaria de Jesús de Machaca (item 1338) and "Esposos, Suegros y Padrinos . . ." (item 1339) and Belote "The Limitations of Obligation in Saraguru Kinship" (item 1352). Rarely are the structuralist and vertical ecology approaches treated as mutually exclusive. Many of the articles cited above integrate both perspectives.

During the infusion of new theoretical orientation, older traditions of Andean studies were not static. The earlier emphasis on acculturation and rural-urban migration continues with research focused on previously understudied segments such as Lima domestic servants in Smith, "Institutionalized Servitude. . . ." (item 1492a), mine workers in Nash (items 1450-1452), Hichman and Brown, "Adaptation of Aymara and Quechua" (item 1419) and guano diggers, Vásquez (item 1484). Sophisticated analyses of interethnic relations are being developed in Stein "Race, Culture and Social Structure . . ." (item 1495), Weinstock "Ethnic Conceptions and Relations among Otavalo. . ." (item 1506), Fuenzalida "El Indio y el Poder en el Perú" (item 1402), leading to more regionally particular definitions of "Indians" in Casagrande "The Condor and the Bull" (item 1403) a recognition of the fluidity of social race classifications and the process of "cholofication."

Direct applied anthropological research in the Andes has decreased con-commitant with foundations' generosity and the collapse of Alliance for Progress policies. Some studies from that grand tradition are: Maynard "The Indians of Colta" (item 1445), Dobyns "The Social Matrix of Peruvian Indigenous Communities" (*HLAS 27:1329a*), Dobyns "Peasants, Power and Applied Social Change" (item 1382). Andean Indian Community Research and Development Project Indians in Misery: A Preliminary Report of the Colta Lake Zone: McEwen "Rural Bolivia" (item 1432), Bourque "Factions and Faenas. . . ." (item 1357), Burela "Cultura y Muyu-Muyu. . ." (item 1366), Martínez "Enfermedad y Medicina. . . ." (item 1437). A shift of perspective in the application of anthropology from that of the participant interventionist to the analytical observer of governmental social change programs is evident in the more recent literature: Crespi "Changing Power Relations: The Rise of Peasant Unions" (item 1374), Carter "Revolution and the Agrarian Sector" (item 1369), Paulson" Maestros como Agentes del Cambio Comunal" (item 1467), and *America Indígena* (item 1343). An older tradition which continues to thrive is that of the highly politicized analysis, particularly in the Marxist mode. While Mariátegui's standards are not always matched by contemporary imitators (*HLAS 34:2620*) penetrating analyses of the effects of centuries of imperialism and ethnic subordination are being generated particularly by nationals of the Andean countries themselves: Costales "Historia Social del Ecuador" (item 1372), Vásquez "Discriminación Campesina en el Perú" (item 1501), Quintín Lamé "En Defensa de mi Raza" (item 1474), Escobar "Analyse Diachronique d'un Conseil Traditionel" (item 1388) and José Sabogal Wiesse "El Robo a los Andes" (item 1483).

With the rise of research oriented to the documentation of the vertical ecology hypothesis or the structuralist model and to the delineation of directed social change, community studies—the sine qua non of Latin American anthropological research—are changing in character. Though community ethnographies continue to include the prerequisite accounts of each Malinowskian institution, clearly identified in chapter or paragraph titles, appropriate dynamic processes are accounted in all but the earliest cited. The effect of agrarian reform is treated in two Bolivian community studies, Buechler and Buechler "The Bolivian Aymara" (item 1364) and Heyduk "Huayrapampa" (item 1418). The effect of out migration is treated in the Peruvian community studies Hafer "The People Up the Hill" (item 1414), Morris and others "The Social Worlds of Mayobamba" (item 1449). The market changes in community structure with the penetration of cash economy are treated in: Fuenzalida and others "Estructuras Tradicionales. . . de Huayopampa" (item 1401). Less differentiated community studies include: José Arquinio and others "Sociedad, Cultura y Economía en 10 áreas . . ." (item 1347), Rodríguez Pastor "Caqui" (item 1480), Bonilla Mayta "Las Comunidades Campesinas Tradicionales . . ." (item 1358), Galdo Pagaza "Economía de las Colectividades . . ." (item 1405), Galdo Pagaza "El Indígena y el Mestizo de Vilquechico" (item 1406).

A final word. Soon after I assumed the task of reviewing highland ethnology in the fall of 1972, I requested bibliographic suggestions and reprints from colleagues. Their contributions greatly enhanced the breadth of coverage. Bibliographic suggestions from readers of this section will continue to be welcomed. The support of the *HLAS* staff in locating items for review and the guest reviews of articles in German by S. C. Caton are greatly appreciated.

1336. Agüero Blanch, Vicente Orlando. Malargüe, pueblo trashumante (UNC/AAE, 24/25, 1969/1970, p. 209-224, map, plates)

Account of the seasonal migrations in the Andean foothills of Mendoza, Arg., by herders, which reveals a fascination with regional vocabulary and rituals. Includes glossary.

1337. ———. Las remedieras de Malargüe. Córdoba, Arg., Univ. Nacional de Córdoba, 1968. 34 p., map, plates (Instituto de Antropología, 27)

Details native, Pehuenche-influenced ethnomedical practices and a variety of magical cures for anxiety stemming from spinsterhood, female sterility, male couvade symptoms and marital infidelity based on field interviews with 70 practicing curers in the Malargüe dept. of Mendoza. Author identifies the ingredients and processes of each cure. In this Argentina Andean area, the female curers (*remedieras*) enjoy universal prestige. Includes glossary. For other treatment of *curanderos*, see items 1381 and 1508.

1338. Albó, Xavier. Dinámica en la estructura intercomunitaria de Jesús de Machaca (III/AI, 32:3, julio/sept. 1972, p. 773-829)

In this well documented structuralist study, Albó proposes that the hierarchy among communities in the Jesus de Machaca area of La Paz dept. is symbolized by a spatial allegory of their arrangement as parts of two mountain lions facing each other. Their *marka*, or nonpolarized center, is between the two cat's heads, unlike the arrangement of radial structures of the Bororo and possibly Inca Cuzco which locate the *marka* in the center. Rotation of hierarchical offices among communities of the high and low parts is related to the rotation of *aynoqa* dry potato fields. The place of marginal groups such as Urus and haciendas in the aboriginal intervillage structure is explained.

1339. ———. Esposos, suegros y padrinos entre los aymara. Toronto, Canada, n.p., 1972. 47 p. (mimeo)

Fine structural study analyzes the complex of affinal and ritual kinship relationships which surround a married pair among the Aymara. Data is from some 30 communities in La Paz dept. Topics such as patrilineal tendencies, age prestige, terminology of kinship and the concentration of alliances formed among communities through marriage and ritual kinship are included. Paper delivered at Symposium on Andean Kinship and Marriage, American Anthropological Association's meeting in Toronto, 1972.

1340. ——— and others. Religiones nativas y religión cristiana. Oruro, Bol., Editores E. Rodríguez B. y A. Muriel A., 1972. 1 v. (Various pagings) (mimeo)

Uneven scholarship of this set of eight articles on religious syncretism can be illustrated by M. Montaño A.'s contribution. This "anthropologist" provides a useful list of major and minor Bolivian Aymara and Quechua deities and types of native priests, then indulges in a "proof" of the semitic derivation of key terms. Albó's article is a balanced description of religious expression among the Cochabamba Quechua. S. Monast proposes syncretic equivalences: St. James with Llapu-Illapu, Aymara Inti worship in the context of Corpus Cristi, Moon Mother worship at the Annunciation. Other articles are of less interest.

1341. *Allpanchis Phuturinqa.* Univ. de San Antonio de Abad, Seminario de Antropología, Instituto de Pastoral Andina (IPA). Vol. 1, 1969 [through] Vol. 3, 1971-   . Cuzco, Perú.

New annual publication of the Instituto de Pastoral Andina emphasizes religious ethnography. Several articles in v. 1, 1969 (156 p.) are reviewed separately. V. 2, 1970 (255 p., plates) is a collection of articles on southern Peruvian indigenous cosmology. V. 3, 1971 (214 p., plates) is a collection on agricultural ritual in the same area. Latter volumes are studiously descriptive rather then interpretative.

1342. Altamirano Rúa, Teófilo. El cambio en las relaciones de poder en una comunidad de la Sierra Central del Perú (PEMN/R, 37, 1971, p. 299-308, map)

This study of social change in Ongoy district, Andahuaylas, Apurimac, concentrates on the break-up of area haciendas and migration.

1343. *América Indígena.* Instituto Indigenista Interamericano. Vol. 32, No. 3, julio/sept. 1972-   . México.

Special issue entitled a "Panorama of Bolivian Indians." Except for article by Albó (see item 1338) and Ponce Sanginés (a comprehensive account of Tiahuanaco), stress of articles is on social change: the effect on and participation of Bolivian Indian in land reform, educational projects, and thought pieces on community development. There are two articles on Bolivian peasant women ("La Mujer Aymara"; "La Mujer Campesina") and a sample folklore questionnaire used in Bolivia.

1344. Andean Indian Community Research and Development Project. Indians in misery: a preliminary report on the Colta Lake zone, Chimborazo, Ecuador. Ithaca, N.Y., Cornell Univ., Dept. of Anthropology, 1965. 165 p., map, plates (mimeo)

Under AID contract, Cornell Univ. was asked to make an anthropological investigation and report its recommendations to the Ecuadorian Institute for Agrarian Reform for its land reform project on Colta Monjas hacienda. This preliminary report represents a high caliber community study and is supplemented by item 1445.

1345. Arango Cano, Jesús. Aborígenes legendarios y dioses chibchas. Prólogo [por] Silvio

Villegas. Medellín, Col., Movifoto, 1971. 143 p., plates.

Romantic presentation of Colombian folk tales and interpretation of "gods" represented on Chibcha artifacts. Book has little serious foundation but highlights certain themes in Indian legends.

1346. Arnold, Dean E. Native pottery making in Quinua, Peru (AI/A, 67:5/6, 1972, p. 858-872, bibl., map, plate)

Article concerns the material technology of ceramic manufacture in an Ayacucho village. Focuses on utilitarian ceramic articles rather than specialty items which have international distribution.

1347. Arquinio, José and others. Sociedad, cultura y economía en 10 áreas andino-peruanas: Asillo, Chumbao, Chuyas-Huaychao, Huata y Quita, Julcamarca, Layo, Pirapi, Soras, Taraco, Yancao. Lima, Ministerio de Trabajo y Comunidades, Instituto Indigenista Peruano, 1966. 1 v. (Various pagings) tables (Serie monográfica, 17)

Series of regional studies by different authors follows the same format: 1) physical aspect and communications; 2) demography and population; 3) economy (land tenure, agriculture, ranching, commerce, etc.); 4) social organization; 5) political organization; 6) primary necessities (food, housing, clothing); and 7) secondary necessities (education, health, religion, recreation). Each presentation varies in emphasis. Studies co-authored by Humberto Ghersi and José Arquinio (Asillo, Hunata and Quinta, Layo and Taraco) on communities in southern Peru include good statistical information on agricultural production and more detailed description of the institutions of social organization. Six of the "areas" are political districts; Yancao was a legal *comunidad indígena;* Chumbao is a valley in Andahuaylas; Huanta and Quinta are plains (*pampas*) in Cabanillas district, Puno; and Pirapi is a geographical area in Chucuito district. Various definitions of "areas" and uneven quality of some monographs make comparisons difficult.

1348. Barnes de Marshall, Katherine. Cabildos, corregimientos y sindicatos de Bolivia después de 1952 (IBEAS/EA, 1:2, 1970, p. 61-78)

Studies integration of peasants into the national political structure of Bolivia in terms of local peasant political structures and offices. A series of seven charts resumé table of political organization in several specific areas. Not only creation of new institutions such as *sindicatos*, but redefinitions of the function of and qualification for offices in old forms such as the *cabildo* are detailed. Such changes are mentioned in passing in other articles on Bolivia (item 1338) and stand in marked contrast to the erosion of local authority as described in item 1388 for Colombia.

1349. ———. La formación de nuevos pueblos en Bolivia: proceso e implicaciones (IBEAS/EA, 1:3, 1970, p. 23-38)

Overview of new peasant towns in Bolivia based on data drawn from the altiplano, valleys of La Paz, Yungas, Potosí and Chuquisaca. Article describes the internal development of such towns from inception and initial settlement as well as local *sindicato* organizations typical of new towns and their political implication. Concludes that new towns represent one response to new economic opportunities and reflect greater participation in the cash, market-oriented economy.

1350. ——— and **Juan Torrico Angulo.** Cambios socio-económicos en el Valle Alto de Cochabamba desde 1952 (EBEAS/EA, 2:1, 1971, p. 141-171)

Provincial Bolivian towns of Cliza, Punata, Tiraque, Arani, Sacaba and Tarata in Cochabamba valley are analyzed. Social change is measured by the appearance of new markets, new commercial establishments, new local social stratification arrangements and emerging hierarchies of political power.

1351. Barrette, Christian. Aspects de l'ethno-ecologie d'un village andin (Canadian Review of Sociology and Anthropology [Calgary] 9:3, 1972, p. 255-267, bibl., tables)

Excellent article describes native delimitations of three major and two minor named ecological zones with altitudinal parameters and distinct micro-climates used by villagers of Huancaraylla in Ayacucho dept., Peru. Use of these zonal concepts in analyzing marriage patterns, annual dispersions over space, irrigation systems and other elements of socio-cultural organization demonstrates the utility of ethnoscience concepts.

1352. Belote, James, and **Linda Belote.** The limitations of obligation in Saraguru kinship. Toronto, Canada, n.p., 1972. 13 p., tables (mimeo)

Within context of a formally bilateral and ideologically parallel descent system, authors create an analysis of interaction between groups linked through marriage alliance. The analytical categories of "kitchen kin" and "living-room kin" are extracted from behavior at household festivals. Marriage types of cross-cousin, double-cross cousin, sister exchange, brothers marrying sisters and cousins marrying siblings deliminate the formation of kindreds. Paper presented at Symposium on Andean Kinship and Marriage, American Anthropological Association meetings in Toronto, 1972.

1353. Biró de Stern, Ana. Mitos y costumbres relacionados con los animales en la Puna de Jujuy (SRA/A, 105:5, mayo 1971, p. 44-49, plates)

Various rituals which involve animals are described: roundup of donkeys in Carnaval, a dance and *anda* procession of the Virgin Mary image for sheep, festival of dogs which is associated with image of San Roque, sacrifice of a black dog after a human burial, and others.

1354. Bolton, Ralph. Aggression and hypoglycemia among the Qolla. Claremont, Calif., Pomona College, Dept. of Anthropology, 1971. 61 p., bibl., tables (mimeo)

The Qolla (including Aymara) personality trait of aggressivity is documented with case study files from Incawatana, a Quechua-speaking Peruvian village. Males were rated by community members for aggressivity and a sample of 66 were tested for hypoglycemia symptoms through Dextrose Glucose Tolerance Tests. An inverse relationship between levels of blood glucose and involvement in hostile, aggressive behavior is proposed, together with a complex model of biological, social and ecological factors affecting personality. Author glosses all inhabitants of Kollasuyu territory as Qolla. This study received the Stirling Award in Culture and Personality Studies. Revised version appears in *Ethnology* (12:3, July 1973).

1355. ———. La fuente y el sello: patrones cambiantes de liderazgo y autoridad en pueblos peruanos (III/AI, 30:4, oct. 1970, p. 883-927)

Excellent analysis of leadership patterns in the villages of Taracu and Chijnaya.

1356. Bonilla Mayta, Heraclio. Las comunidades campesinas tradicionales del Valle de Chancay. Presentación [por] Rosalía Avalos de Matos. Lima, Museo Nacional de la Cultura Peruana, 1965. 142 p., bibl., fold. maps, plates, tables (Serie: tesis antropológicas, 1)

Portrays distribution of land and population among the Chancay Valley's haciendas, *fundos*, irrigation units and communities. Traces history of several communities (Aucallama, Qupepampa, Lomera de L'achay) through archival records which depict colonial period depopulation and successive sales of communal land. The record of Aucallama, created as a *reducción* in 1551, is especially complete. Examines contemporary social organization, natal origin of families, demographic statistics and movement out of communities into hacienda "yanacona" positions for several communities. Rich source for the analysis of interrelationship of traditional communities and private haciendas.

1357. Bourque, Susan C.; Leslie Ann Brownrigg; Eileen Maynard; and **Henry F. Dobyns.** Factions and *faenas:* the developmental potential of Checras district. Ithaca, N.Y., Cornell Univ., Dept. of Anthropology, Andean Indian Community Research and Development Program, 1967. 173 p., bibl., maps, plates, tables (mimeo) (Socio-economic development of Andean communities: report, 9)

Analysis of a questionnaire administered to the heads of households in the five indigenous communities of Checras district, sierra Chancay, Peru, tests factors such as rate of bilingualism, education, migration experience, internal land distribution, household composition and women's education believed to be influential in communities' orientation to infrastructure development. The communities range from heavily indigenous types with low rates of education, Spanish language and migration experience to their opposite. An important new variable was discovered: communities which had maintained communal land tenure aspects and communal political structure were at once the most successful subsistence agriculturalists and most energetically involved in infrastructure development. Roads and irrigation projects were the principal rivals for communal efforts: the most communally organized village (Capash-Maray) undertook both at once.

1358. Bourricaud, François. Changements à Puno: étude de sociologie andine. Paris, Institut des Hautes Etudes de l'Amérique Latine, 1962. 239 p., map (Travaux et mémoires, 11)

Also available in Spanish as *Cambios en Puno* (México, Instituto Indigenista Interamericano, 1967).

"This extensive and informative monograph is the result of the field work of a French sociologist and his wife carried out over a period of some seven months in 1953-54 in the southern Department of Puno. Focuses of research were the highland city of Puno on Lake Titcaca, the nearby Aymara-speaking Comunidad Indígena of Ichu, and a hacienda of Quechua peones. Bourricaud is most thorough in his analysis of the social structure of the large pueblo of Puno; his comments on the community of Ichu and the hacienda are brief but broad, frankly raising numerous astute questions to which his short and unassisted research was unable to furnish definitive answers. The analysis covers cultural values, pueblo and hacienda systems of economy, political structure, and the syncretism of Indian and mestizo traditions. His emphasis throughout these discussions, founded on the insight of a non-partisan (non-Peruvian), is social structure, stratification, and mobility. He contends that the Indian and his culture are present in the pueblo society of the mestizo. His most detailed and revealing discussions concern the cholo and mestizo." [Peter T. Furst and Karen B. Reed]

1359. Braun, Patrick. Médecins et sorciers des Andes. n.p., Editions et Publications Premiéres, 1971. 232 p., bibl., illus., map.

Collection of ancient and modern medical practices based on chronicle sources, representations in ceramic pieces and observations in the south of Peru. Ch. 6 on birth customs is particularly original and a strong contribution to the literature.

1360. Brisseau, Jeanine. Les communautés indigènes du Pérou (FDD/NED [Problèmes d'Amérique Latine, 21] 3822/3823, oct. 1971, p. 50-64)

Resumé of history, socio-economic, political organization, cultural levels and current problems of the indigenous communities of Peru parallels Dobyn's general remarks in *The social matrix of Peruvian indigenous communities* (see HLAS 27:1329a). Despite its late publication, it is outdated, not taking into account the important legal reforms in the Ley de Comunidades of 1970.

1361. Brownrigg, Leslie Ann. El papel de los ritos de pasaje en la integración social de los cañaris quichuas del austral ecuatoriano (CCE/RA, 3, nov. 1971, p. 203-214)

Examines the ritual exchanges among kinsmen proper to each of the life crisis rites (umbilicus cutting, baptism, marriage, manhood validation and funerals) among a group of Azuayian Quichua (Ecuador). Author interprets the *pukara* (*pucará*) battle of champions to the death as a rite of manhood validation preliminary to the assumption of rank positions in the community, and as boundary-maintaining mechanism. First version is footnoted with references to occurence of described customs elsewhere in Southern Ecuador. Compare with Hartmann's generic description of ritual battles, item 1417. Same article appeared in *Folklore Americano* (19/20:17, 1971/1972, p. 92-99).

1362. Brush, Stephen B. Kinship and land use in a northern sierra community. Toronto, Canada, n.p., 1972. 33 p., bibl., tables (mimeo)

Personal networks as an adaptive response to the ecosystem of Uchucmarca, in La Libertad dept., Peru, are detailed for this legal *comunidad indígena* where mestizo culture prevails. Vertical ecology model is used and what is striking is its adoption by a non-indigenous group. Paper presented at Symposium on Andean Kinship and Marriage, American Anthropological Association meetings in Toronto, 1972.

1363. Buechler, Hans C. Modelos didácticos en el análisis del campesinado boliviano y ecuatoriano (IBEAS/EA, 1:2, 1970, p. 5-18)

Buechler criticizes static and stable equilibrium models and the use of typologies in the analysis of social change. The geographical mobility of many Andean peasants and their dependence on national level decisions pose special problems. Buechler advocates personal networks methodology and the definition of community as that group deliminated by marriage relationships. Author surveys the social structure and migration patterns of two communities to demonstrate his stand: Compi-Llamacachi (item 1364) in Bolivia and Huaytacama, Ecua., a complex "community" with six Indian settlements, seven haciendas, a central town and migrant colonies on the coast and in the eastern jungle region.

1364. ———— and **Judith Maria Buechler.** The Bolivian Aymara. N.Y., Holt, Rinehart and Winston, 1971. 114 p.

Despite its general title, this is a community study of Compi, a village with sub-sections on Lake Titicaca near La Paz. Monograph's strengths include a thorough description of ritual and agricultural cycles, an account of the role of La Paz-based community merchants and of children's activities, but it is weak in regard to social organization. Compi is a post-agrarian reform community, parts of which were under the haciendas' control in various eras. Politics and factionalism is well handled. An excellent introductory text recommended to non-specialists.

1365. Burchard, Roderick R. Village exagamy and strategies of inter-zonal exchange in central Andean Peru: a case study. Toronto, Canada, n.p., 1972. 37 p., bibl., tables (mimeo)

The high exogamy rates of a bilingual community near Huánuco are analyzed as a tactic for establishing trading networks and control of micro-ecological zones from the montaña to the puno over a 130 mile range. Paper presented at the Symposium on Andean Kinship and Marriage, American Anthropological Association meetings, Toronto, 1972.

1366. Burela, Alberto and **Marta Burela.** Cultura y muyu-muyu: el efecto de la enfermedad en el proceso de desarrollo (III/AI, 30:1, 1970, p. 41-60)

Study of three isolated communities on the Bolivian altiplano and the effect of the muyu-muyu disease on their wool-bearing flocks and consequently on the communities' economy. A field study made in connection with a flock improvement project.

1367. Carter, William E. Bolivia: a profile. N.Y., Praeger Publishers, 1971. 176 p., bibl., illus. (Praeger country profile series)

After geographical and historical (including prehistory) surveys, describes Bolivian society in terms of its ethnicities, class cultures and foreign enclaves. Two cantonal centers and the special characteristics of the urban elite and proletariat of the major cities are treated. The economic role and pluralistic integration of such foreign-origin enclaves as Lebanese merchants and Okinawan rice-farmers are commendably included. The sympathetic if moralistic remarks on Bolivia's elite are weakly connected to their direct role in suggested pre-reform suppression of the peasantry. Characterizes mining unions as disruptive. Regards as benign US military aid which built Bolivia's army back into a dominant power contender which replaced the democratic gains of the 1952 revolution with crude *cuartelismo*. The tenor of this weakness of analysis is reflected in a chapter title: "The Puzzle of Poverty". Ends profile's history with Gen. Torres' coup of Oct. 1970. Only in the allegation that violence and betrayal are "themes" of Bolivian history does Carter presage the current repressive Brazilian-style (and Brazilian-influenced) regime. Carter unquestionably knows Bolivian society well. His account constitutes a personalized understanding of its social segments.

1368. ————. Entering the world of the Aymara *(in* Kimball, Solon T. *ed.* Crossing cultural boundaries: the anthropological experience. N.Y., Chandler Publishing Co., 1972, p. 133-150, bibl., plate)

Personal history of Carter's fieldwork and interaction with the Aymara of Bolivia from 1952 to the present, this article details the variety of roles which one fieldworker adopted to further his research and gives an honest presentation of personal reactions in the process of ethnographic discovery.

1369. ————. Revolution and the agrarian sector *(in* Malloy, James M. and Richard S. Thorn *eds.* Beyond the revolution: Bolivia since 1952. Pittsburgh, Pa., Univ. of Pittsburgh Press, 1971, p. 233-268, bibl.)

The effect of agrarian reform in the cantonal capital of "Kachitu" as directly observed by the author opens out into a general description of its nationwide effect.

1370. Castillo Ardiles, Hernán. Pisac: estructura y mecanismo de dominación en una región de refugio. México, Instituto Indigenista Interamericano, 1970. 192 p., illus. (Ediciones especiales, 56)

Pisac, that familiar target of Cuzco tourists for its Sunday market, is studied in the context of Gonzalo Aguirre Beltrán's thesis of indigenous enclaves as refuge zones (see *HLAS 29:2133*). Details the economic dependence of Pisac Indians on haciendas, subordination of their community leaders, ideological aspects of ethnic segregation and the barriers to communication posed by their culture. Appendix by Julio de la Fuente includes earlier survey of Pisac and of near-by Chinchero from the viewpoint of the school *núcleos* program and an essay of interethnic relations and social classes in Cuzco.

1371. Collier, David. Política y creación de pueblos jóvenes en Lima (IBEAS/EA, 2:2, 1971/1972, p. 5-31)

Analyzes detailed data on the creation of 75 "new towns" obtained through questionnaires sent to town directors and from government and newspaper archives. Participation of Peruvian government is judged to have played a significant role and author recommends the study of governments' role in urbanization process. Collier's Ph.D. dissertation, *Squatter settlement formation and the politics of co-optation in Peru* (Chicago, Ill., Univ. of Chicago, 1971) deals in greater depth with the analysis abridged in this article.

1372. Costales Samaniego, Alfredo and **Piedad Peñaherrera de Costales.** Historia social del Ecuador. t. 4, Reforma agraria. Quito, Instituto Ecuatoriano de Antropología y Geografía, 1971. 319 p. (Llacta, 20)

Fourth in a series which has been appearing since 1964 as numbers in the Instituto Ecuatoriano de Antropología y Geografía's Llacta series. (For v. 1-3, see *HLAS 34:2601*.) Like previous volumes, this represents a compilation. Notes primary sources but secondary sources from which they were extracted are not. The Costales' encyclopedic knowledge of Ecuadorian Indians and their gadfly *indigenista* outrage enliven this disorganized account.

1373. Cotler, Julio. Haciendas y comunidades tradicionales en un contexto de movilización política (IBEAS/EA, 1:1, 1970, p. 127-148)

Overview of the politicization of hacienda and *comunidades* in Peru was written before the sweeping changes in the agrarian reform law of June 1970. Its data base is the study of five haciendas in the province of Paucartambo and two *comunidades indígenas* (as the legal community entity was then known) in Canchis province. Prophetically, Cotler predicts the revolutionary potential of their situation.

1374. Crespi, Muriel. Changing power relations: the rise of peasant unions on traditional Ecuadorian haciendas (CUA/AQ, 44:4, Oct. 1971, p. 223-240)

In a short history of labor organization on five haciendas in Cayambe canton, Ecua., author tests theories of Landsberger, Wolf, Coser and Steward concerning peasant movements, social conflict and vertical integration. The haciendas studies have certain special characteristics: the five were owned successively by the religious order of La Merced, the Social Assistance Board (Asistencia Social) (1904-64) and workers' cooperatives, mortgaged and administered by the Ecuadorian Institute of Agrarian Reform and Colonization (IERAC); from the 1920's, urban Marxists were influential in the organization of formal workers' unions. The five have been frequent centers of unrest and strikes.

1375. Custred, Glynn. Peasant kinship, subsistence and high altitude Andean environment. Toronto, Canada, n.p., 1972. 31 p., tables (mimeo)

The Quechua-speaking community of Alccavitoria in Cuzco dept. is dispersed in a territory from 3,920 to 4,890 meters above sea level. 4,000 meters limits agriculture, thus herding predominates the economy, with long-distance trade to obtain maize and cereals. Custred gives a thorough description of the kin terminology, social structure and the use of managing the herding-trading labour organization through lineage-like kin alliances. Paper presented at Symposium on Andean Kinship and Marriage, American Anthropological Association meetings in Toronto, 1972.

1376. Dalle, Luis. El despacho (IPA/AP, 1, 1969, p. 139-154)

This missionary's account of a ritual paying homage to the Pachamama (Earth Mother) in southern Peru may be of interest for its detail.

1378. Dandler-Harnhart, Jorge Erwin. El sindicalismo campesino en Bolivia: los cambios estructurales en Ucureña. México, Instituto Indigenista Interamericano, 1969. 197 p., bibl., illus., maps, tables (Serie antropología social, 11)

Ucureña has been cited in the work of Patch as having played a decisive role in the history of agrarian reform in Bolivia. In this chronicle of events and community study, Dandler traces the land tenure history of Ucureña and the dynamic social processes set in motion by the organization and action of its syndicates. Includes glossary. Also see item 1377.

1379. Deluz, Ariane. Les Embera du bassin Baudo (EPHE/H, 11:4, oct./dec. 1971. p. 84-90)

Brief research report on the Embera of the Colombian Chocó. The cultural influence of other groups, through an exchange of shamanistic expertise, migration, contacts with Catholic missionaries and with Bush Negroes are noted. Author is preparing an ethnographic film on the Embera.

1380. Díaz Martínez, Antonio. Ayacucho y las comunidades del hambre (III/AI, 30:2, abril 1970, p. 307-320)

Contains brief descriptions of a series of freehold communities and haciendas. Chilcas, a freehold community which includes as members persons who serve as *colonos* on the adjoining Apucancha hacienda, is described as exhausted by soil erosion, depopulated by the out-migration of its youth, maintained by labour exchange of the *ayny* and *minka* and plagued by low literacy, high mortality, and no public services. Parallel situations are found in the freehold communities Acco and Qeqra and a more hopeful situation in Tambo, where a federation of farmers exists. The haciendas of Ninabamba and Patibamba are also described. Díaz Martínez, a cultural geographer, seems bemused by the uncaring of the hacendados who occupy the better land and the desperate condition of the adjoining communities, though this serves as good illustration of Eric Wolf's model of the interrelationship of haciendas and freehold communities.

1381. Dobkin de Ríos, Marlene. La cultura de la pobreza y el amor mágico: un síndrome urbano en la selva peruana (III/AI, 29:1, enero 1969, p. 3-16)

Love magic in Iquitos is interpreted as a symptom of the culture of poverty, a manifestation of a perceived lack of control over social relations. Also see items 1337, 1472, and 1508.

1382. Dobyns, Henry F.; Paul L. Doughty; and **Harold D. Lasswell** eds. Peasants, power and applied social change: Vicos as a model. Beverly Hills, Calif., Sage Publications, 1971. 237 p., bibl., map, plates.

Core consists of articles orginally published in a special issue of The *American Behavioral Scientist* (see *HLAS 31:2259*). This ed. also includes articles important for understanding Cornell Univ.'s applied anthropology project in Ancash dept., Peru. Allan R. Holmberg's "Experimental Intervention in the Field," sets forth the general methodological principles of participant intervention; and "The Role of Power in Changing Values and Institutions of Vicos," sets the intervention at Vicos in context of special internal, local, regional,

Peruvian national and international power structures, describing positive and negative transformations at each level as Vicos itself changed; Doughty's "Local and National Power Structure in Relation to Vicos, 1951-1966: An Explanatory Note" (Appendix B) conceptualizes local and national power structure from the Vicos perspective before, during and after the Cornell-Peru Project's intervention; Lasswell's thought-piece on "The Transferability of Vicos Strategy"; J. Oscar Alers' appendix (A) on "Vicos Area and Population Growth" adapted from his demographic Ph.D. dissertation (Cornell, 1966). Many may take exception to editors' introduction and "note to anthropologists" which view Holmberg and Vásquez as revolutionary anthropologists. In its time, Vicos was a splendid example of socially involved, deeply humanitarian anthropology, but the transformation of a community of hacienda serfs into a self-governing and economically-independent freehold peasant community was a special experiment patronized by the Carnegie Foundation and politically influential intellectuals around Carlos Monge Medrano, the Peruvian co-sponsor and co-director. It took a nationalist military regime to instrument a radical agrarian reform in order to offer the opportunity availed to Vicos to similar hacienda communities. The role of former Vicos project members in that regime may indeed prove to be the most influential aspect of the project. This book is highly recommended. Its articles and bibliography should facilitate the instruction of this famous case. For other materials on Vicos, see items 1387, 1435, 1466, and 1494-1495.

1383. Doughty, Paul L. Engineers and energy in the Andes (*in* Bernard, H. R. and P. Pelto eds. Technology and social change. N.Y., MacMillan, 1972, p. 110-133)

Retrospective on the effect of the Santa Corporation's hydroelectric complex at Huallanca on the people of Huaylas district, Peru, this article analyzes regional development from project initiation in 1943 until 1970, just prior to the earthquake. The engineers' only stated goal was to provide electricity for the city and steel mills of Chimbote, never contemplating the "ripple" developmental effects. Among these "ripple effects" were the following: a population boom and secondary service development at Huallanca which transformed a sub-tropical railhead annex of Huaylas (pop. 299 in 1940) into a sophisticated district capital; the learning of a wide variety of technical skills by the 14,000 local workers employed over the years; increased social and geographical mobility for those who acquired technical skills and an independent electrification project in the town and rural areas of Huaylas which changed both domestic and craft work patterns.

1384. ———. Peruvian migrant identity in the urban milieu (*in* Weaver, T. and D. White eds. The anthropology of urban environments. Boulder, Colo., Society for Applied Anthropology, 1972, p. 39-50 [Monograph series, 11])

The best short summary of highland migrant culture in Lima, Doughty emphasizes the vitality of *serrano* urban culture: the institutional and associational contexts and events of regional clubs with their myriad soccer teams, dances and employment networks, the lively expression of traditional cultural themes in the *huayno* and *huaylas* musical forms, the glorification of provincial singers and dancers in the coliseums and the use of the radio (78 percent of Lima's broadcast programs were aimed at serranos by 1966) to unite migrants in a highly personalized communication system.

1385. ———. The social uses of alcoholic beverages in a Peruvian community (SAA/HO, 30:2, Summer 1971, p. 187-197)

The social rituals of alcohol consumption as observed in Huaylas, Ancash, in 1960-61 are analyzed as facilitating social solidarity across moderate stratification lines in the society. Types of alcohol and consumption statistics are given along with contexts for drinking such as bars, religious or secular festivals, during hard physical labor, at civic work parties and in family parties. Translated new version of *HLAS 31:2097*.

1386. Ebersole, Robert P. La artesanía del sur del Perú. Mexico, Instituto Indigenista Interamericano, 1968. 150 p., plates, tables (Serie antropología social, 9)

Based on questionnaire interviews with artisans in 63 districts of southern Peru. Intended as an artesanal survey funded by AID, the emphasis is on generic economic aspects of craft production: source and cost of materials, average incomes, uses and needs for credit, problems of marketing and distribution. Crafts surveyed include carpentry, shoemaking, tailoring, dressmaking, tile-making and other urban-based artisanry as well as more traditional weaving, ceramics, blacksmithery, or straw-weaving. No description of either material technology or social organization of any craft. For folklorist comment, see *HLAS 34:894*.

1387. Edel, Matthew. Funciones y límites del desarrollo de comunidad (IBEAS/EA, 1:3, 1970, p. 39-54)

The cases of Vicos, Peru, and Támesis, a Colombian municipality south of Antioquia, are reviewed to support general conclusions concerning community development programs.

1388. Escobar, María Elvira. Analyse diachronique d'un conseil traditionnel, Colombie (Canadian Review of Sociology and Anthropology [Calgary] 9:3, 1972, p. 268-287)

This study of a peasant political system analyzes the changing role of a particular council of authorities (cabildo) from an interaction mechanism in the colonial era ensuring the tributary exploitation of Indians to a local authority structure confined to the solution of internal disputes and powerless to contend the annexation of its lands by landlords in the early Republican era. Author views even this role as reduced by the greater integration of the community into the national Colombian economy and political structure since 1920. See also item 1348.

1389. Escobar Moscoso, Gabriel. Interacción de la economía y la política en dos comunidades andinas (III/A, 30, 1970, p. 205-212)

Brief comparison of social change in the artesanal community of Sicaya in the Montaro Valley, which is connected to Euro-American models by a railroad and returned migrants, and the community/district of Nuñoa on the southern Peruvian altiplano, a ranching community isolated until its 1950 connection to a railroad. The relative progress and links with service development projects of the Peruvian government experienced by Sicaya is attributed to a generalization of contacts with the outside world and education. All but a minority of mestizos remain ethnocentric in their isolation in Nuñoa.

1390. ———. Organización social y cultural del sur del Perú. Con la colaboración de Richard

P. Schaedel y Oscar Núñez del Prado. México, Instituto Indigenista Interamericano, 1967. 250 p., bibl., tables (Serie antropología social, 7)

Escobar's monograph is a major work on Puno dept., Peru. Its primarily rural perspective complements Dew's urban upper-class focus in *Politics of the altiplano* (see item 7684). The first and strongest chapter (p. 1-81) concerns the political organization of Puno: departmental level political structures and the politico-religious hierarchies of selected local Indian polities in great detail. The central topic of "values" is handled with less sophistication. Concepts of time, knowledge, sex-roles, attitudes, etc., for the cultural levels of Indians, *cholos* and *mistis* are resumed in an impressionistic fashion. "Values" were not researched with any ethno-semantic or ethno-science paradigms. Descriptions of "Attitudes in Social Interaction" (p. 129-163) and "Values, Social Change and Development" (p. 163-184) while still impressionistic, represent dynamic and important hypotheses. A special focus throughout the monograph is on the role of religious organizations—traditional fertility rites, folk Catholicism and the fiesta complex, Maryknoll missionaries' recathechization and cooperative organizing, and Protestant cults—on social change. The macroanalysis of a province does not sacrifice detail. The monograph is recommended as an excellent regional overview.

1391. ———. A preliminary descriptive analysis of the kinship and family organization of the middle class population of the city of Cuzco, Peru. Toronto, Canada, n.p., 1972. 15 p. (mimeo)

The middle class core of Cuzco, identified by 20-30 surnames is described in terms of its kin terms, marriage patterns and extended family. The nicknames which identify lineage fission are an unusual feature. Paper presented at Symposium on Andean Kinship and Marriage, American Anthropological Association meetings in Toronto, 1972.

1392. Esteva Fabregat, Claudio. Un mercado en Chinchero, Cuzco (III/A, 30, dic. 1970, p. 213-254)

The value of this article includes its detailed list of the origin of various products and their vendors, types of market posts, social and physical organization of the market and barter exchange equivalent values of different products. The market analyzed is that of Chinchero outside Cuzco, Peru. The socio-economic function as well as cultural communicative functions of such peasant markets are described.

Fábrega, Horacio, Jr. and **Peter K. Manning.** Health maintenance among Peruvian peasants. See item 1663.

1393. Faron, Louis C. Los mapuche: su estructura social. Prólogo [por] Julian H. Steward. México, Depto. de Antropología, 1969. 284 p., bibl., maps, tables (Ediciones especiales, 53)

Translation of 1961 monograph based on 1950's data with no updating, see *HLAS 25:560*.

1394. Favre, Henri. Tayta Wamani: le culte des montagnes dans le centre sud des Andes péruviennes (*in* Colloque d'études péruviennes, Aix-en-Provence, France, 1966. [Papers] Aix-en-Provence, France, Univ. d'Aix-en-Provence, Faculté des Lettres, 1967, p. 121-140)

Ethnohistorical sources indicate that lineages and even extended families maintained a cult to a particular mountain and that the ranking of these lineages was expressed by the symbolism of the mountain's prestige. Favre describes surviving modern cultism in honor of Wamani—father mountains in south and central Peru. Father mountains remain identified with a particular group of descendants and their cultism involves *illa* ceremonialism, the marking of animals by their owners and sacrifices including human when the Wamani are to be "disturbed" by public works construction.

1395. ———; **Claude Collin-Delavaud;** and **José Matos Mar.** La hacienda en el Perú. Lima, Instituto de Estudios Peruanos, 1967. 395 p., illus., maps, tables (Estudios de la sociedad rural, 1)

Favre analyzes highland hacienda systems of land distribution and human resources in Huancavélica; Collin-Delavaud describes the social conditions, syndicates (labor unions) and wage migration among north coast sugar plantations; and Matos Mar contributes an economic and technological history of Chancay Valley coastal haciendas. For geographer's comment, see *HLAS 31:5662*.

1396. Flora, Cornelia Butler. Mobilizing the masses: the sacred and the secular in Colombia. Ithaca, N.Y., Cornell Univ., Latin American Studies Program, 1970. 285 p., bibl., maps, tables (Dissertation series, 25)

Although properly a dissertation in rural sociology, this history-and-event-analysis chronicle of pentecostalism as a lower class solidarity movement in Colombia, is an excellent cult ethnography. The chapter on the internal structure based on the pentecostal sector of the Palmira intervillage system details the boundary maintaining mechanisms of this social group. Anecdotes, which the author includes to give the study "human dimension," enliven the statistical approach of her interview-survey methodology.

1397. Flores Ochoa, Jorge A. Los pastores de Paratía: una introducción a su estudio. México, Instituto Indigenista Interamericano, 1968. 110 p., bibl., maps, plates (Serie antropología social, 10)

This ethnography of subsistence alpaca pastoralists in a district of western Puno dept. suggests their culture is the survival of an aboriginal pattern. The herders form an endogamous community which follow exact patterns of seasonal migration and depend on trade with agricultural communities at lower altitudes. Paratía communities are located in homelands at 4,300 m. above sea level. For sociologist's comment, see *HLAS 33:838*.

1398. Friedemann, Nina S. and **Jorge Morales Gómez.** Estudios de negros en el litoral Pacífico colombiano (ICA/RCA, 14, 1966/1969, p. 53-70, bibl., plates)

Nina S. Friedemann "Fase 1, Güelbambi: Formas Económicas y Organización Social" and Jorge Morales Gómez "Aspectos Sociales de la Comunidad en un Area Rural de Barbacoas, Nariño" are two preliminary reports of the Instituto Colombiano de Antropología's investigation of Afro-American cultural groups on the west (Pacific) coast of Valle, Cauca and Nariño depts. in Colombia. These reports include general data on the descendants of gold-mining slaves in the settlement of Los Brazos who still follow mining as their primary economic pursuit.

1399. Frites, Eulogio. Los collas (III/AI, 31:2, abril 1971, p. 375-388, bibl., plates)

Very generalized description of customs of the Argentine Colla. The territorial location of these remnant populations of the Apatama, Omoguaca and Diaguita-Calchaquí nations and the bibliography are valuable.

1400. Fuenzalida, Fernando. Santiago y el Wamani: aspectos de un culto pagano (CEA/CA, 5[3]:8, 1966 [i.e., 1968] p. 118-165)

Details cultism to the Wamani also described by Favre (see item 1394) in the guise of ceremonialism associated with Saint James.

1401. ———; **José Luis Villarán; Jürgen Golte; and Teresa Valiente.** Estructuras tradicionales y economía de mercado: la comunidad indígena de Huayopampa. Lima, Instituto de Estudios Peruanos [and] Moncloa Campodónico Editores Asociados, 1968. 301 p., bibl., fold. maps, tables (Proyecto de Estudios Etnológicos del Valle de Chancay: Monografia, 1)

Pioneer study in economic anthropology, this monograph details the non-monetarized (traditional) and monetarized (market economy) aspects of the legal community of Huayopampa in the Central Andes of Peru. Incorrectly reviewed in *HLAS 33:1595* as authored by José Matos Mar.

1402. ——— **and others.** El indio y el poder en el Perú rural. Lima, Instituto de Estudios Peruanos, 1970. 214 p., bibl., illus., tables (Col. Perú problema, 4)

In general, the articles in this collection attack the rigidity of the definition of the Indian in various views of the sociocentric application of this identity. Mayer's contribution must be underscored as one of the most humorous treatments of the subject, a light touch which emphasizes the truth of his sophisticated analysis of the frames of reference, social milieu, and sociocultural indices of "Indians" or peasants, mestizos and cholos or proletariat servile class. Bourricaud's article points to the superficiality of cholification, the expression of traditional social networks through adopted national cultural elements. Each piece is a thoughtful exploration of the ambivalence of Indian status in Peru. Articles include the following:
Fernando Fuenzalida "Poder, Raza y Etnia en el Perú Contemporáneo" p. 15-87
Enrique Mayer "Mestizo e Indio: el Contexto Social de las Relaciones Interétnicas" p. 88-152
Gabriel Escobar "El Mestizaje en la Región Andina: el Caso del Perú" p. 153-182
François Bourricaud "¿Cholificación?" p. 183-198
José Matos Mar "Algunas Consideraciones Acerca del Uso del Vocablo Mestizo" p. 199-201
José Matos Mar "El Indigenismo en el Perú" p. 202-214

1403. Furst, Peter T. and Karen B. Reed *eds.* The condor and the bull: tradition and change in Andean Indian culture. Los Angeles, Calif., Univ. of California, Latin American Center, 1971. 585 p., bibl.

Valuable collection of original articles, some written by former Peace Corps volunteers. William Mangin describes the status of the Indian in Peru and the Vicos experiment. "The Indian and Ecuadorian Society" by Joseph B. Casagrande is one of the first publications of the results of his decade long research on Indian ethnicity and Indo-European relations in Ecuador. The collection also features a long annotated bibliography. Prepared for Peace Corps training; out of print at this writing.

1404. Gade, Daniel W. Ecología del robo agrícola en las tierras altas de los Andes Centrales (III/AI, 30:1, enero 1970, p. 3-14)

Gade describes the basic system of crop guarding with data from villages in Cuzco and Puno (properly the south, not central Andes). He describes the types of observation huts (*chozas de observación*) known generically as *chukllas* and the system of assigning guards (*a rariwa*.) A basic ethnological description of a fairly widespread Andean harvest aspect. Of interest is the spirited though non-ethnological response of José R. Sabogal Weisse, "El Robo a los Andes" (see item 1483), which puts the minor theft of harvest robberies among the marginal poor in the larger context of exploitation of Andean populations by haciendas. international imperialism and American commercialization.

1405. Galdo Pagaza, Raúl. Economía de las colectividades indígenas colindantes con el Lago Titicaca. Lima, Ministerio de Trabajo y Asuntos Indígenas, Plan Nacional de Integración de la Población Aborigen, 1962. 231 p., bibl., illus., map, tables (mimeo) (Instituto Indigenista Peruano: Serie Monográfica, 3)

Distinguished from other monographs in the series by an excellent description of material culture and technology. Detailed description of manufacture and use of a variety of utensils (baskets, querns, ceramics, looms, agricultural implements, musical instruments) and building construction are supplemented by hand-drawn diagrams. Crops and their means of cultivation, herding, hunting, fishing and gathering technology are exactingly detailed. "Magic" is regarded as a technology in its own right.

1406. ———. El indígena y el mestizo de Vilquechico. Lima, Ministerio de Trabajo y Asuntos Indígenas, Plan Nacional de Integración de la Población Aborigen, 1962. 147 p., tables (mimeo) (Instituto Indigenista Peruano: Serie monográfica, 9)

Although the bulk of this study is composed of superficial observations in categories of the Murdock guide for the classification of cultural materials, the descriptions of the local *misti* land-owning class and the traditional textile industry are important contributions.

1407. Gall, Norman. The agrarian revolt in Cautín. Pt. 1, Chile's Mapuches; pt. 2, Land reform and the MIR. Hanover, N.H., American Universities Field Staff Reports, 1972. 2 v. (15, 16 p.) (West Coast South America series: 19:4/5)

Pt. 1 describes the historic background of a contemporary agrarian revolt of Mapuches in Cautín, Chile. Pt. 2 describes the role of the MIR, revolutionary vanguard party, in fomenting land seizures in general and specific interaction with the Mapuche.

1408. García-Blásquez, Raúl and **César Ramón Córdova.** Bibliografía de los estudios y publicaciones del Instituto Indigenista Peruano: 1961-1969 (III/AI, 30:3, julio 1970, p. 761-827)

Readers of this section should take particular note of this bibliography of the publications of the Instituto Indigenista Peruano from 1961-69. Very few of the 265 publications annotated in this list have ever been reviewed in the *HLAS:* this article should be indicated as a supplemental bibliography. Notes on each publication list only the conceptual or chapter divisions of each publication and are not critical. Earlier works in this series (item 1439) are more simplistic ethnographies which use George P. Murdock's *Guía para la clasificación de los datos culturales* (Washington, Unión Panamericana, Oficina de Ciencias Sociales, 1963. 295 p.) as their format. The earlier studies were designed as surveys of the more heavily indigenous zones of Peru. Later works are more problem oriented. Throughout the series are monographs with the pragmatic purpose of investigating reactions of local communities to programs of applied social change: public health, irrigation and potable water projects, government credit, agrarian reform and others. An important series for anyone with an interest in a specific region or in applied anthropology. *HLAS* readers are urged to obtain this article.

1409. Garr, Thomas M. Cristianismo y religión quechua en la prelatura de Ayaviri. Cuzco, Peru, Instituto de Pastoral Andina, 1972. 257 p., map, plates.

Religious ethnography published by the IPA, which details the ritual and belief of Ayaviri, a Catholic jurisdiction in Puno dept., north of Juliaca, Peru. Special emphasis on the economic aspect of the festival complex: costs are accounted to the *sucre*. Although there are certain disproportions (rather than misinterpretations) in some accounts of native customs, Garr's work is a contribution.

1410. Goddard, D.; S. N. de Goddard; and **P. C. Whitehead.** Social factors associated with coca use in the Andean region (ISDA/IJA, 4:4, Dec. 1969, p. 577-590, tables)

Statistical correlation of "factors" associated with coca-chewing in 1966, among 78 rural proletariat males in Jujuy, Arg. (i.e., socio-economic characteristics; attitudes towards women chewing coca; kinship context; users' children's school performance; alcohol consumption; etc.). Authors oppose conclusions that coca-chewers have certain psychological deficits as stated by J. C. Negrete and H. B. Murphy in "Psychological Deficit in Chewers of Coca Leaf," *Bulletin on Narcotics* (19:4, 1967). The small sample and research methodology structure its superficiality. Nevertheless, the conclusion that coca chewing does not indicate a pathology may be applauded.

1411. Goring, Paul. The Antioquians of Medellín (PRAN, 19:4, July/Aug. 1972, p. 145-157)

Pt. 1 is a sociological "tourist guide" description of Medellín; pt. 2, a strategy for evangelical Protestant missionary penetration. Its naiveté becomes apparent reading Flora's far more penetrating analysis, see item 1396.

1412. Greaves, Thomas C. The Andean rural proletarians (CUA/AQ, 45:2, April 1972, p. 65-83, bibl.)

Greaves extends Mintz's definition of the rural proletarian to characterize similar social processes of acculturation and social mobility among Andean wage-earning agricultural workers, miners and oil workers. He makes the significant point that this role category is found in population aggregations rural only in the sense that they are not near so-called "natural" cities or metropoli. Includes a timely analytical review of the literature and an excellent bibliography.

1413. ———. Who lives with whom in Viru? Toronto, Canada, n.p., 1972. 23 p., bibl. (mimeo)

Presents an important new methodology in the analysis of households with data from Viru house-to-house census and genealogies which allows the description of diachronic patterns of the developmental cycle of households from synchronic data. The appendix lists all major bibliographic sources on Viru. Paper presented at Symposium on Andean Kinship and Marriage, American Anthropological Association meetings in Toronto, 1972.

Greene, Lawrence S. Physical growth and development, neurological maturation, and behavioral functioning in two Ecuadorian Andean communities in which goiter is endemic: Pt. 1, Outline of the problem of endemic goiter and cretinism; physical growth and neurological maturation in the adult population of La Esperanza. See item 1694.

1414. Hafer, Raymond Frederic. The people up the hill: individual progress without village participation in Pariamarca, Cajamarca, Peru. Bloomington, Ind., Indiana Univ., 1971. 428 p., bibl. (Ph.D. dissertation)

This study of returned migrants in the context of an individualized northern Peruvian village did not find those with urban experience influential agents for change. Factors which blocked communal efforts and community-wide organizations for mutual benefit goals are examined to explain this atypical phenomena. Available from University Microfilms, Order No. 71-23, 271.

1415. Hartkopf, Herbert. Webkunst und Trachten der Bolivianischen Hochlandindios (MV/BA, 19(44):1, Nov. 1971, p. 73-96, illus., tables)

Superb description of Indian textile art from the dept. of Chuquisaca, Peru, and Potosí, Bol. To preserve the knowledge of textiles, Hartkopf discusses wools, dyes and other materials, weaving techniques, figurations and motifs, clothing and commodities. Estimates of man-hours of weaving and prices are included. [S. C. Caton]

1416. Hartmann, Roswith. Algunas observaciones respecto al trueque y otras prácticas en las ferias de la sierra ecuatoriana (MVW/AV, 25, 1971, p. 43-55, bibl.)

Collection of observations on market practices in Ecuador: pre-columbian money axes, the *yapa* (a little something extra in barter or cash transactions), the colonial and modern use of *cocos* (black seeds) as money, certain regularities in equivalences approaching fixed prices in market place barter and the use of containers for measurement. Text in Spanish, resumé in German. Dr. Hartmann has asserted the importance of precolumbian Andean markets in earlier articles.

1417. ———. Otros datos sobre las llamadas "batallas rituales" (CIF/FA, 19/20:17, 1971/1972, p. 125-135)

This review of the literature concerning so-called "ritual battles" throughout the Andes makes important comparisons. The Cañari *pucará* (see item 1361) is regarded as somewhat of a prototype of similar battles undertaken in a festive context, with the intention of causing injury or death, and imbued with the ideology of influencing natural forces or sacrificing to the earth, which prognosticates the fertility of the subsequent agricultural year.

1418. Heyduk, Daniel. Huarapampa: Bolivian highland peasants and the new social order. Ithaca, N.Y., Cornell Univ., Latin American Studies Program, 1971. 308 p., bibl., maps (Dissertation series, 27)

Details the post-agrarian reform social and economic organization of "Huayrapampa," a Cochabamba-Quechua-speaking ex-hacienda community in highland Chuquisaca, Bol. Heyduk dwells on the institutionalization of status differences in the community, an artifact of land reform. Hacienda tenants (*arrenderos*) were given titles to land tracks but subtenant types (*arrimates* and *vivientes*) were not. *Huayrapampa* is a conventional "community study" with synopses of the local kinship and marriage patterns, kinship terminology, *compadrazgo* patterns, systems of labor exchange, dress customs, ceremonial calendar and the non-material realm of witchcraft beliefs, folk religion, curing and divination. Of particular ethnological interest are Huayrapampa's viable dyadic *ayni* system, first-hair-cutting ceremonial (*rutuy*), regularized trial marriage (*tantanaku*), and aspects of their belief system involving the prehispanic Pachamama diety, fear of ruins (*chullpas*) and disembodied night flying witches. Heyduk's portrait of this physically dispersed and poorly socially integrated community—which lacks any cross-cutting integrative activities, political or religious organizations save the government required union (*sindicato*)—suggests that ecologically mediated settlement patterns require alternative models for close-corporate communities.

1419. Hickman, John M. and Jack Brown. Adaptation of Aymara and Quechua to the bicultural social context of Bolivian mines (SAA/HO, 30:4, Winter 1971, p. 359-366)

Three "modal categories" of acculturation by Bolivian Aymara and Quechua in the context of mines are posited. Written in sociologese to cover the fuzzy data base of 1965 (prenationalization) interviews at the Colquiri tin mine (La Paz province, Bol.) and facile observations. See item 1412 for clearer theory concerning this acculturation context or items 1450-1452 for detailed post-nationalization ethnography and ideology.

1420. Ibáñez-Novión, Martín Alberto. Práctica funeraria en la puna argentina: Cholacor. San Salvador de Jujuy, Arg., Imprenta El Estado, 1970. 1 v. (Various pagings) illus., map, plates.

Fieldnotes describing vigil (*velorio*), burial and ninth-day ceremony (*novena*) of an old woman in the Argentine Andes. Novena practices reported include washing and burning of the deceased's apparel and the sacrifice of a black dog, sheep or llama as a "porter" carrying herbs and spinning materials "to" the deceased.

1421. Instituto de Estudios Peruanos. Lima. Located at Horacio Urteaga 694, Lima 11, Peru, this institute publishes and sponsors the following monographic series: "Serie Perú Problema;" "Serie América Problema;" "Estudios de la Sociedad Peruana;" "Colección de Fuentes e Investigaciones para la Historia del Perú;" "Cuadernos del Instituto de Estudios Peruanos;" "Serie Guías Bibliográficas;" "Serie Teoría;" "Serie Actualidad;" and "Serie Estudios Históricos."

The following monographs are of interest to ethnologists:

Matos Mar, José and others. *Perú problemas: 5 ensayos.* 2. ed. Lima, Instituto de Estudios Peruanos, Moncloa-Campodónico, 1970. 188 p. (Col. Perú problema, 1)

Keith, Robert G. and others. *La hacienda, la comunidad y el campesinado en el Perú.* Lima, Instituto de Estudios Peruanos, Moncloa-Campodónico, 1970. 220 p. (Col. Perú problema, 3)

Fuenzalida, Fernando and others. *El indio y el poder en el Perú rural* (see item 1402)

Delgado, Carlos. *Problemas sociales en el Perú contemporáneo.* Lima, Instituto de Estudios Peruanos, Moncloa-Campodónico, 1971. 185 p. (Col. Perú problema, 6)

Alberti, Giorgio and others. *Aspectos sociales de la educación rural en el Perú.* Lima, Instituto de Estudios Peruanos, Moncloa-Campodónico, 1972. 150 p. (Col. Perú problema, 8)

Favre, Henri; Claude Collin-Delavaud; and José Matos Mar. *La hacienda en el Perú* (see item 1395)

Fuenzalida, Fernando; José Luis Villarán; Teresa Valiente; and Jürgen Golte. *Estructuras tradicionales y economia mercado; la comunidad indigena de Huayopampa* (see *HLAS 33:1595*)

Matos Mar, José and others. *Dominación y cambios en el Peru rural*, Lima, Instituto de Estudios Peruanos, 1969. 375 p. (Estudios de la sociedad rural, 4)

Celestino, Olinda. *Migración y cambio estructural: la comunidad de Lampián.* Lima, Instituto de Estudios Peruanos, 1972. 108 p. (Estudios de la sociedad rural, 5)

Matos Mar, José. *Estudios de las barriadas limeñas.* Lima, Instituto de Estudios Peruanos, 1966. 95 p. (Urbanización, migraciones y cambio en la sociedad peruana, 1)

Matos Mar, José. *Urbanización y barriadas en América del Sur.* Lima, Instituto de Estudios Peruanos, 1968. 405 p. (Urbanización, migraciones y cambio en la sociedad peruana, 2)

Matos Mar, José and others. *Perú hoy.* México, Siglo XXI Editores, 1971. 366 p. (Serie Actualidad, 1)

1422. Isbell, Billie Jean. Kuyaq: those who love me; an analysis of Andean kinship and reciprocity within a ritual context. Toronto, Canada, n.p., 1972. 46 p., bibl., maps, tables (mimeo)

Analysis of kinship structure and reciprocity based on the patterns of cooperation and exchange observed during the cleaning of the irrigation canals (the *Yarqa Aspiy*) in Chuschi, Ayacucho, Peru. *Masa* (and *llumchu*) affinal and *compadrazgo* (ritual kinship) relations to birth-ascribed *ayullus* are dramatized in ritual elements of the event. This study arbitrates many hypotheses concerning Andean kinship structure and relates kinship to the ecological zones of the community. Paper presented at Symposium on Andean Kinship and Marriage, American Anthropological Association meetings, Toronto, 1972.

1423. ———. No servimos más: un estudio de los efectos de disipar un sistema de la autoridad tradicional en un pueblo ayacuchano (PEMN/R, 37, 1971/1972, p. 285-298)

Analyzes the structural rearrangements which led the community of Chuschi in Ayacucho, Peru, to abolish one system of ritual officials—the Hatun Varayoqkuna.

1424. Kellert, Susan; Lawrence K. Williams; William F. Whyte; and Giorgio Alberti. Culture change and stress in rural Peru (MMFQ, 45, 1967, p. 391-415)

Stands as a preliminary report from the massive values study project directed by Whyte and Matos Mar. It correlates indices of psychological strain with individuals' social status and attitudes as obtained in answers to a questionnaire administered in rural communities including several in the coastal Chancay valley, Arequipa, Mantaro Valley and Cuzco areas. The correlations reveal that low indices of psychological stress relate to values accepting the direction of change. The Whyte-Mar project included sending students to study each of the communities where questionnaires were administered as well as a re-study of the same communities and re-administration of the same questionnaire five years after the initial study. In this report, neither the methodology nor the cultural contexts are made explicit: it is an important glimpse of the insights that may eventually emerge from this exceedingly, deliberately long-term and technical study.

1425. Kusch, Rodolfo. Pensamiento aymara y quechua (III/AI, 31:2 abril 1971, p. 389-396)

This attempt to crack the symbolic code of an Aymara *yatiri* ("witch") ritual formulations wanders from the dictionaries of Bertonio (1611) to Canadian Baptist (1963) for basic vocabulary translations and far further afield for inappropriate analogies. Some ethnographic detail on the Aymara of the Chuquichamba, Bol. area (west of Oruro) peep out of the morass.

1426. Landívar U., Manuel Agustín. Contribución a mitos y leyendas en El Azuay y Cañar (CCE/RA, 3, nov. 1971, p. 101-120)

Texts of legends and myths collected from informants in Azuay and Cañar are transcribed with an appendix of Quichua terms. The rainbow myths, and such supernaturals as *gagones* (baby dogs), *carbulcos* (felines) *la Mama Huaca* and *Huacas* (place spirits) are treated. Landívar is the leading amateur folklorist of the southern Ecuadorian region. He collects with a Boasian rigor and although unanalytical, his work can be studiously trusted.

1427. ———. Contribución al folklore poético en El Azuay (CCE/RA, 3, nov. 1971, p. 121-180, tables)

Transcription of verses of folk songs from Azuay and Cañar province and a classification index of their subject matter.

1428. ———. Fiesta del Señor de las Aguas en Girón (CCE/RA, 3, nov. 1971, p. 6-74, illus., plates)

Descriptions, photographs and drawings contributed by a team of trained folklorists who studied the Corpus festival of 5-6 June 1969, comprise the data of this excellent event ethnography. Diagrams of *escaramuza* and dance spatial movements, transcriptions of texts spoken by the *Loa* (a juvenile female orator), and drawings of the fireworks famous in this area add to the data. Landívar himself contributes coverage of the ceremonial sacrifice of a bull and of how the ceremony's sponsors shared in the festival of blood drained from the animal's neck.

1429. Léons, Madeline Barbara. Stratification and pluralism in the Bolivian *yungas* (*in* Goldschmidt, Walter and Harry Hoijer eds. The social anthropology of Latin America [see *HLAS 33:508*] p. 256-282, bibl.)

Analyzes "the impact on the society of the province of Nor Yungas, Department of La Paz, of the social, political and economic changes that followed in the wake of the revolution." The author's reliance on the concept of pluralism jars the interpretations; pluralism usually implies that each ethnic sector has comparable, parallel institutions for education, religion and internal social stratification, a model which is singularly inappropriate for Bolivia.

1430. Lucena Salmoral, Manuel. Informes preliminares sobre la religión de los ijca (ICA/RCA, 14, 1966/1969, p. 223-260)

Origin myths and cosmology of the Ijca, an Arawak Chibcha group nucleated near San Sebastian de Rabago, Co., are related to a reconstruction of their histories. Reports syncretic elements in the belief system (the murder of mountain mother spirits by "civilized" road builders, the location of hell in Cartagena), an alphabetic list of deities and sacred lakes and mountains, ceremonialism at sacred stones, life crisis rituals and the training and ritual status of priestesses ("mama's"). Comparisons with other Colombian religions are made.

1431. Luna Ballón, Milagro; Héctor Huanay Iturrizaga; and Raúl García Blásquez Canales. Algunas artesanías en el distrito de Ocobama, Andahuaylas [and] Algunas artesanías en el distrito de Pacucha, Andahuaylas. Lima, Ministerio de Trabajo, Instituto Indigenista Peruano, 1970. 47 p., bibl., tables (Serie monográfica, 22)

Both short monographs include excellent capsule ethnographies of the districts (physical, demographic, social and political organization, population of major centers). Each monograph contains census of individual artisans and shops (carpenters, blacksmiths, tilemakers, housebuilders) and details tools, physical aspects of shops, source of raw materials and production statistics for typical items. The studies provide insight into artisan economics.

1432. McEwen, William J. and others. Changing rural Bolivia: a study of social and political organizations and the potential for development in six contrasting communities. N.Y., Research Institute for the Study of Man, 1969. 364 p., bibl., illus.

Reports certain results of the Institute's elaborate research project in Bolivia from 1964-67 which had as its objective the study of health and sanitation problems in rural Bolivian communities in diverse ecological zones and the description of the communities' social, political and cultural characteristics. The studies of Coroico, Sorata, San Miguel, Compi, Villa Abecia and Reyes in terms of their reception or rejection of various projects chart each community's developmental priorities and potential to organize to meet its needs. For a resumé of the theory and methodology used in the study, see *HLAS 31:2163*.

1433. ——— and others. El esfuerzo y el águila: la estratificación social en una comunidad provincial (IBEAS/EA, 2:2, 1971/1972, p. 53-65)

Almost a parable of the inner attitudes toward social stratification. Quotes from interviews offer a glimpse of how status is calculated in Bolivia. Study conducted by team from the Research Institute for the Study of Man, N.Y.

1434. Malo de Ramírez, Gloria and others. Pan, panaderías y sistoplástica en la ciudad de Cuenca (CCE/RA, 3, nov. 1971, p. 75-99)

Data description of bread-making technology and economics in the city of Cuenca, Ecua., types of bread and bread molding and sculpture.

1435. Mangin, William *ed*. Peasants in cities: readings in the anthropology of urbanization. Boston, Mass., Houghton Mifflin, 1970. 207 p., bibl., tables.

Six selections reprinted pertain to Andean examples: John C. Turner "Barriers and Channels for Housing Development in Modernizing Countries" (p. 1-19) based on a case study of Lima *barriada* Pampa de Cueva. Mangin "Similarities and Differences between Two Types of Peruvian Communities" (p. 20-29) compares Vicos with a squatter settlement in Lima. Paul L. Doughty "Behind the Back of the City: 'Provincial' Life in Lima, Peru" (p. 30-46) describes *serrano* culture and associations in Lima. Mangin "Urbanization Case History in Peru" (p. 47-54) follows a Quechua-speaking Indian from hacienda to *barriada*. Mangin "Tales from the Barriadas" (p. 55-61) publishes modal responses to Thematic Apperception Tests in Lima. Hans C. Buechler "The Ritual Dimension of Rural-Urban Networks: The Fiesta System in the Northern Highlands of Bolivia" (p. 62-71) describes integration of Compi residents and migrants to La Paz in several levels of festival distribution. See also item 1364.

1436. Manya, Juan Antonio. ¿Temible Ñaqaq? (IPA/AP, 1, 1969, p. 135-138)

Review of ethnohistorical and modern accounts of a monster, the Ñak'aq or Pishtaco in Peru, the Karisiri, in Chile and Bolivia. See also item 900.

Mariátegui, José Carlos. Seven interpretive essays of Peruvian reality. See *HLAS 34:2620.*

1437. Martínez, Héctor. Enfermedad y medicina en Pillapi, Bolivia. Lima, Ministerio de Trabajo y Asuntos Indígenas, Plan Nacional de Integración de la Población Aborigen, 1962. 62 p., tables (mimeo) (Instituto Indigenista Peruano: Serie Monográfica, 10)

Objective of this study was to analyze the ethnomedical practices, health patterns and resistance of Indians to modern health services for the Pillapi Project of Acción Andina in 1955-58. Martínez concludes that the depersonalized character of health services available through the Misión accounted for their reception and recommended a minimal resident staff to encourage clients' confidence.

1438. ———. El indígena y el mestizo de Taraco. Lima, Ministerio de Trabajo y Asuntos Indígenas, Plan Nacional de Integración de la Población Aborigen, 1962. 129 p., tables (mimeo) (Instituto Indigenista Peruano: Serie Monográfica, 8)

Study undertaken to investigate the resistance of Taraqueño Indians to development projects and technical assistance offered through the Puno-Tambopata Mission Andina Project in 1957-58. Martínez concludes with such practical information as the major mestizo land-owners by name, distances between population centers, birth registration statistics, causes of death recorded for 699 persons, out-migration statistics by target and origin and school attendance—in sum, raw data of a type rarely published. Martínez concluded the "resistance" was a myth perpetuated by mestizos and that the Indians were generally unaware of the project and eager to collaborate when informed.

1439. ———. Investigaciones antropológicas por el Instituto Indigenista Peruano, 1966-1969 (III/AI, 30:2, abril 1970, p. 471-491, tables)

Useful review of the establishment of one of the principal research agencies in Peru. See also item 1408.

1440. Martínez-Crovetto, Raúl. Distribución de algunos juego de hilo entre los aborígenes sudamericanos (CIF/FA, 19/20:17, 1971/1972, p. 268-279, illus., maps)

Distribution of "cat's cradle" string games throughout South America is charted with maps and diagrams to illustrate the variations.

———. Introducción a la etnobotánica aborigen del nordeste argentino. See item 6822.

1441. Marzal, Manuel María. El mundo religioso de Urcos: un estudio religioso y de pastoral andina de los Andes. Cuzco, Perú, Univ. de San Antonio de Abad, Instituto de Pastoral Andiana, 1971. 570 p., bibl., plates.

Study made in collaboration with students from the universities of San Antonio de Abad (Cuzco) and La Católica (Lima) on the basis of fieldwork and a standard questionnaire in five sample communities in the Urcos region of Cuzco dept. Emphasizes the more "Catholic" elements of native religion, including the economic organization of local churches and parishes. Clearly intended to instruct clergy but contains important ethnographic information.

1442. Mayer, Enrique. Beyond the nuclear family. Toronto, Canada, n.p., 1972. 31 p., bibl. (mimeo)

Masterful analysis of reciprocal exchanges of labor in the community of Tangor in the Chaupiwaranga area of Pasco dept., Peru. Focuses on the relative (to the married pair) affinal categories of *masha* and *lumtshuy* obligations during a houseroofing ceremony which finalizes married status in the context of other such work-exchange obligations in that society. Paper presented at the Symposium on Andean Kinship and Marriage, American Anthropological Association meetings, Toronto, 1972.

1443. ———. Un carnero por un saco de papas: aspectos de trueque en la zona Chaupiwaranga, Pasco (PEMN/R, 37, 1971, p. 184-196)

Study of the barter system of Tangor in relation to command of ecological zones and market economy, which adds to the growing literature analyzing the vertical ecology pattern of the Andes.

1444. ———. Censos insensatos: evaluación de los censos campesinos en la historia de Tangor (*in* Visita de la provincia de León de Huánuco en 1562. Huánuco, Peru, n.p., 1972, p. 341-365)

Censuses taken at different points in history of Tangor are analyzed for the ethnocentric prejudices which slanted data collection and their faulty survey methodologies. It provides strong documentation for the *dicho* that censuses are the bureaucrat's poetry. Available as a separate paper-bound pamphlet.

1445. Maynard, Eileen *ed*. The Indians of Colta: essays on the Colta Lake zone; Chimborazo, Ecuador. Ithaca, N.Y., Cornell Univ., Dept. of Anthropology, 1966. 153 p., illus., plates, tables (mimeo)

Essays include "Indian-Mestizo Relations" by Eileen Maynard; "Rites of Passage" by Arcenio Revilla C.; "The Indians and the Tules" by Scott S. Robinson (concerning the control of totora reed resources); "Leadership Patterns" by Eileen Maynard; "Clothing and Weaving Techniques" by Carol Robinson; and "Formal Education" by Néstor Solís Y. These essays explore facets of the culture of the Colta Monjas hacienda Indians to serve as baseline studies for cultural change during the land reform process. Data dates to 1965. Includes glossary.

1445a. Middleton, De Wright. Form and process: a study of urban social relations in Manta, Ecuador. St. Louis, Mo., Washington Univ., 1972. 257 p. (Ph.D. dissertation)

Description of social change in a former fishing barrio of Manta "combines quantitative and qualitative data with geographical variables, family developmental cycle and elements of choice and strategy" in its analysis of urban *compadrazgo*. Available from University Microfilms, Order No. 72-24, 232.

1446. Millones, Luis. Deporte y alienación en el Perú: el fútbol en los barrios limeños (IBEAS/EA, 1:2, 1970, p. 87-95)

Millones reports on the *macho* ethos and subculture of *limeño* soccer clubs, interpreted as an institutionalization of alienation, petty rebellion and lost energy.

1447. Monast, Jacques Emile. On les croyait chrétiens: les aymaras. Paris, Les Editions du Cerg, 1969. 493 p.

Complex report of a Canadian missionary priest's discovery of the indigenous system of belief underlying Aymaras' syncretized Catholicism. Account represents a personal odyssey as much as an excellent religious ethnography of the Aymara in the Oruro, Bol. area. For Monast's previous work see *HLAS 33:1601*. This French version is available in Spanish as *Los indios aymarás*. (B.A., Lohle, 1972).

1448. Montgomery, Evelyn Ina. Ethnos y ayllu en Coasa, Peru. México, Instituto Indigenista Interamericano, 1971. 218 p. (Ediciones Especiales, 60)

Translation from publisher's review states: "The thesis of this work consists of determining the ethos—the singular nature of the modern ayllu especially in the south of Peru, measuring the definition not only in terms of the present functions of the ayllu but also in its potential."

1449. Morris, Earl W.; Leslie Ann Brownrigg; Susan C. Bourque; and **Henry F. Dobyns.** Coming down the moutain: the social worlds of Mayobamba. Ithaca, N.Y., Cornell Univ., Dept. of Anthropology, Andean Indian Community Research and Development Program, 1968. 331 p., bibl., maps, illus., plates (mimeo) (Socio-Economic development of Andean communities report, 10)

Details the social worlds of a sierra Chancay indigenous community and its migrant daughter colonies in Lima in interaction with each other and with various Peruvian agencies fomenting public works during the Belaúnde era (e.g., the construction of a road, school formation of various cooperatives, etc.). A sophisticated account, which also reviews research in rural Peru through 1965 and includes an excellent bibliography. Study was made by a rural sociologist and demographic specialist (Morris), political scientist specialized in peasant political change (Bourque), and two anthropologists, each of whose special interests contribute insights, and all of whom were members of an applied anthropology team working closely with the village of *cholos* and Indians.

1450. Nash, June. The devil in Bolivia's nationalized mines (SS, 36:1, Spring 1972, p. 221-233)

Another version of the thesis presented in item 1452 but which goes into greater historical detail.

1451. ———. Devils, witches and sudden death (AMNH/NH, 81:3, March 1972, p. 52-59, plates)

Popular account with photographs of Bolivian tin miners ritual dedication to the "Tio"—a vengeful ogre who is believed to own the mineral resources and control miners' fates.

1452. ———. Mitos y costumbres en las minas nacionalizadas de Bolivia (IBEAS/EA, 1:3, 1970, p. 69-82)

Nash proposes that Bolivian tin miners' ritual and emotional involvement with the Devil Uncle ("Tio," "Huari") dissipated their hositility toward mineowners before nationalization and became a focus of rebellion against the Barrientos military regime which suppressed the propitiatory *ch'alla* ritual.

1453. Nordyke, Quentin. Animistic Aymara and

Church growth. Newberg, Ore., The Barclay Press, 1972. 200 p., bibl.

Contains three major sections: "Aymara Religion," "Aymara Societal Factors Significant to Church Growth," and "Selected Dimensions of Aymara Church Growth." The first compiles identifications and descriptions of Aymara supernaturals, magic, world view and rituals by Tschopik (see item 1496) adding Nordyke's own observations during 10 years as a Quaker missionary to present a balanced religious ethnography. Unlike Catholic writers of this genre, Nordyke concentrates on aboriginal beliefs rather than syncretism. There follows a less thorough overview of Aymara society and personality. Only the final section has the character of a missionary's progress report. Documented with statistics on membership (friends account for 19 percent of the less than five percent total Aymara Protestant community of over 8,000 individuals by 1970), the section on church growth describes Nordyke's culturally sophisticated missionizing methods. Includes index. For a sophisticated study of the inner dynamics of Protestant converts' social organization in Colombia, see item 1396.

1454. Núñez del Prado, Juan Víctor. El mundo sobrenatural de los quechuas del sur a través de la comunidad de Qotobamba (PEMN/R, 36, 1969/1970, p. 143-163)

Description of the cosmology and deities of one southern Peruvian community dwells on the central importance of the *apus*, the spirits of mountains. The grand *apus* are the spirits of remote and prominent peaks, but various local mountains are anthropomorphized and apotheosized. *Aukis* in this account enter as another category of mountain spirits, lower in rank. Núñez del Prado contents himself with a list of supernaturals. Curious readers should compare this account with item 1394.

1455. ——— and **Marco Bonino Nieves.** Una celebración mestiza del Cruz-Velakuy en el Cuzco (IPA/AP, 1, 1969, p. 43-60)

An event analysis of a Day of the Cross festival, a traditional festival with class-culture innovations, held at the Velakuy Cross on Osqollo hill north-northeast of Cuzco on 3 May 1968. The *mayordomo* who organized the festival recruited, among other intellectuals and artists, habitués of the Café Extra, to launch an all-day party with martinis and pisco, instead of chicha, a dance group from the middle-class suburbs and a professional *huayno* dance band. Authors conclude that the adoption of a traditional cholo festival by mestizo intellectuals serves a social function and need to forge a *cuzqueño* identity, without contributing to cross-class solidarity.

1456. Núñez del Prado, Oscar. El hombre y la familia: su matrimonio y organización político-social en Q'ero (IPA/AP, 1, 1969, p. 5-27)

Excellent capsule ethnography of Q'ero in the Cuzco area describes Q'ero's three major ecological zones, the produce and settlement pattern of each, weaving, dyes and clothing, the native marriage ceremony (*warmichakuy*) and the politico-religious hierarchy of *cargos* and male-age stations. Author suggests the kinship system was originally ambilineal, inheritance is based on ultimogeniture and the specific *cargo* system was introduced by Spanish authorities in the 16th century. The data was collected by a field expedition team of nine specialists.

1456a. Núñz del Prado, Oscar. Sicuani, un pueblo grande: reacción social para la colonización de Maldonado. Lima, Ministerio de Trabajo y Asuntos Indígenas, Plan Nacional de Integración de la Población Aborigen, 1962. 50 p., tables (mimeo) (Instituto Indigenista Peruano. Serie monográfica, 7)

Two brief studies emphasizing social stratification and public works infrastructure. Monograph on the colonization area around Puerto Maldonado was completed in 1959 and gives a fascinating glimpse of early processes in this now booming port on the Madre Dios river.

1457. Oblitas Poblete, Enrique. Magia, hechicería y medicina popular boliviana. Prólogo de Antonio Paredes-Candia. La Paz, Ediciones ISLA, 1971. 602 p., illus., plate.

Presents data on popular medicine among the Callawaya (Bolivia) in a series of alphabetically arranged dictionaries: 1) animals, 2) minerals used in curing, 3) typology of illness, 4) significance of dream images, 5) sicknesses and the means of curing them (p. 249-564). Interspersed are essays on medical myths, magical cures, the Chiuchi-Recado magic Callawaya Alphabet and other topics. Good reference material for comparative study of folk medicine. See also *HLAS 34:717*.

1458. Ortiz Vergara, Pedro. Un caso del colonización en la selva alta del Perú: Aucayacu (IBEAS/EA, 1:3, 1970, p. 111-121)

Aucayacu, a colonization center on the eastern slope of the Andes located in Huánuco dept. on the Huallaga river, is taken as a case history. The center is part of the developing montaña area around Tingo María. The effect of governmental policies toward colonization is detailed as are origin of settlers and peasant organization. Jungle colonists are viewed as in the process of creating a new sub-culture.

1459. Palomino Flores, Salvador. La dualidad en la organización socio-cultural de algunos pueblos del área andina (PEMN/R, 37, 1971, p. 231-260)

Reviews the anthropological literature on the topic of "dual organization," the structuralist models of Zuidema and his students and a series of examples of Peruvian dualism in terms of social structure and symbolic oppositions portrayed in ritual. Author arbitrates variations from the limited number of Andean dual organization models posed by Zuidema.

1460. ———. Duality in the sociocultural organization of several Andean populations (DEF/F, 13, 1971, p. 65-88, map, plates)

Shorter English version of item 1459, illustrated with map and plates.

1461. Paredes Candia, Antonio. Diccionario mitológico de Bolivia: dioses, símbolos, héroes. v. 1. La Paz, Ediciones Puerta del Sol, 1972. 192 p., illus.

Dictionary compiles definitions concerning Bolivian supernaturals and legendary heroes from sources including: ethnohistories (cf. Cobo, Cieza de León, Sarmiento, de la Vega, Betanzos); ethnographies (cf. Bandelier, Oblitas Poblete, Métraux); histories; dictionaries; and folklore studies. Individual treatments of terms are adequate but the total selection is thin. Not only Aymara and Quechua divinities are defined but dozens of other ethnicities: Kallawaya, Moxos, Moré, Guarayo, Chiriguano, *et al.*

1462. Patch, Richard W. Agriculture and the supernatural: a case, the altiplano. Hanover, N.H., American Universities Field Staff Reports, 1971. 17 p. (West coast South America series, 18:4)

Describes the agricultural cult and ritual practices of the Aymara-speaking *campesinos* of Manco Capac province bordering Lake Titicaca.

1463. ———. Attitudes towards sex, reproduction and contraception in Bolivia and Peru. Hanover, N.H., American Universities Field Staff Reports, 1970. 10 p. (West coast South America series, 17:11)

Malthusian analysis of Peruvian and Bolivian birthrate concludes that infant mortality is the only check on rising birthrates.

1464. ———. Charazani: center of supernatural beliefs of the Andes. Hanover, N.H., American Universities Field Staff Reports, 1971. 10 p. (West coast South America series, 18:5)

Briefly describes supernatural concepts and religious specialists of the Callawayas of Charazani, Bol.

1465. ———. The concept of luck in indigenous and Hispanic cultures: Alacitas and the Ekeko. Hanover, N.H., American Universities Field Staff Reports, 1970. 16 p. (West coast South America series, 17:4)

Bolivian concepts of luck are illustrated by a description of the Feria de Alacitas.

1466. ———. The Peruvian earthquake of 1970. Pt. 1, Carhuaz; pt. 2, Marcará to Vicos; pt. 3, Huaraz; pt. 4, Yungay. Hanover, N.H., American Universities Field Staff Reports, 1971. 4 v. (21, 11, 13, 14 p.) (West coast South America series, 18:6/9)

Series on the disastrous Peruvian earthquake of 31 May 1970 focuses on three hard-hit settlements (Carhuaz, Huaraz and Yungay) and reviews impact at the well-known former Cornell-Vicos site.

1467. Paulston, Rolland G. Maestros como agentes del cambio comunal: cuatro programas peruanos (III/AI, 30:4, oct. 1970, p. 929-1096)

Analyzes four programs involving teaching for their effect on changing communities: Jesuit *Fe y Alegría* program of vocational instruction and community development planning; the Yarinacocha base of Summer Institute of Linquistics' bilingual education schools among Amazonian groups; CRECER (Campaign for the Effective Reform of Educational Communities in the Republic), an innovative association of primarily rural school teachers and the 1944-61 rural school nucleus system (*núcleos escolares*) which operated in the Cuzco-Puno, Callejón de Huaylas and Tingo María areas. Each program casts teachers in role of promoting social change. *Núcleos* and CRECER, both defunct, are interpreted as primarily interventions based on a North American world view of social mobility and social justice dropped by the Ministry of Education when foreign aid for such projects ended. Paulson predicts the SIL jungle schools would suffer similar fate if not supported directly by the missions. Scores *Fe y Alegría*, a Catholic progressive missionary effort in a Catholic country, free from dependency on, or control by, the Ministry of Education, most viable in preparing schoolteachers as community development leaders.

1468. Peñaherrera de Costales, Piedad and **Alfredo Costales Samaniego.** El Quishihuar o el Arbol de Dios. t. 1-2. Quito, Instituto Ecuatoriano de Geografía e Historia, 1966-1968. 2 v. (560, 505 p.) illus., plates (Serie Llacta, 23)

An elaborate two-volume "dictionary of ethno-cultural survivals" which covers letters A-B-C in v. 1, and Ch-D-E in v. 2 which is clearly modeled after Paulo de Carvalho Neto's *Diccionario del folklore ecuatoriano* (see *HLAS 30:6210*). This treatment includes more texts and diagrams but few references. Presumably other volumes will appear for the remainder of the alphabet.

1469. ——— and ———. Resultados del primer censo indígena de la provincia del Pichincha (III/AI, 30:4, oct. 1970, p. 1039-1096)

A rich source of geographical, demographic and settlement pattern data for the Ecuadorian province of Pichincha which includes the city of Quito. Indians are defined in terms of their membership in ethnic groups located in certain types of settlements (*caseríos*, haciendas, etc.) in particular agricultural labor statuses, in cohesive communities with group conservations of certain "prehispanic" cultural traits such as dress, language, house type, religious belief, etc. The methodology used in the present census is described and further censuses are planned. Little Pichincha cultural data is given and only rural Indian communities are included.

1470. Pesantez de Moscoso, Gloria. Tejas, ladrillos y adobes en la parroquia de Sinincay, Cantón Cuenca (CCE/RA, 3, nov. 1971, p. 181-201)

Description of the technology and types of roof tiles, bricks and adobes produced in Sinincay, a canton in Azuay province, Ecua., which is known for this craft specialty.

1471. Pinto R., Edmundo G. Ecos de Huarachico en la comunidad de Tomanga (PEMN/R, 37, 1971, p. 261-284, bibl., illus., tables)

Author describes and analyzes the politico-religious (*envarado*) offices in the community of Tomanga, Ayacucho, in terms of an age-grading system similar to that described by chroniclers for Inca Peru. Includes glossary.

1472. Press, Irwin. The urban *curandero* (AAA/AA, 73:3, June 1971, p. 741-756)

Stereotype of *curanderos* developed in Latin American peasant literature is broken by case studies of successful urban based *curanderos* (up to US $800 per month) in Bogotá. A "stylistic inventory" and more holistic approach to the phenomena of curanderismo is proposed pointing to the socio-cultural milieus of illness curing behavior. For more on curanderos, see items 1337, 1381, and 1508.

1473. Quijano Obregón, Aníbal. La emergencia del grupo "cholo" y sus consecuencias (*in* Congreso Latinoamericano de Sociología, VII, Bogotá, 1964. Sociología y sociedad en Latinoamérica: estudios sobre su desarrollo. Bogotá, Asociación Colombiana de Sociología, 1965, p. 403-477)

Important study, often referred to, was still unavailable for review at press time but will be annotated in *HLAS* 37. Item included because of significance and publication date.

1474. Quintín Lame, Manuel. En defensa de mi raza. Bogotá, Editorial Editextos *para el Comité de Defensa del Indio, Rosca de Investigación y Acción Social*, 1971. 133 p., plates.

A manuscript originally titled *The thoughts of an Indian self-educated in the Colombian jungle* (1939) by a rebel Indian leader and *indigenista* intellectual constitutes the core of this publication. Introduction and notes by Gonzalo Castillo Cárdenas put the Quitín Lame narrative in perspective.

1475. Ramírez, Juan Andrés. La novena al Señor de Qoyllur Riti. (IPA/AP, 1, 1969, p. 61-88, map, plates)

Folkloric treatment of a festival in honor of an image of the crucified Christ in Mahuayani describes in detail events, processions, songs, dancers, costumes and personal organization. Includes procession and village diagram, four photographs.

1476. Ravines, Rogger. Investigaciones antropológicas en el Perú: 1969-1970, antropología social (PEMN/R, 36, 1969/1970, p. 277-278)

Brief account of research including Favre's on the wamani cult (item 1394) and Núñez del Prado's field studies in Chinchero.

1477. Robinson, J. W. L. and A. R. Bridgman. Los indios noanamá del río Taparal (ICA/RCA, 14, 1966/1969, p. 177-200, plates)

Tantalizing tidbits rather than a formal ethnography, this report on the 1962 expedition to the Noanamá Indians who live above the Afro-American Chocó communities. The account emphasizes material culture (cooking utensils, bow-and-arrow manufacture, adornments, art) though notes on commerce, religion, music, dancing and acculturation are made. The expedition spent only 'several' weeks among this group; better information is found in Reichel-Dolmatoff (1960) who at least spent several months among a related group of Noanamá.

1478. ——— and ———. Notas sobre unos chamíes aculturados (ICA/RCA, 14, 1966/1969, p. 169-176, bibl., plates)

Expedition-style ethnology strikes again, in this article which mercifully only pretends to contain notes on the Chamíes encountered by the Calima valley team.

1479. Robinson, Scott S. El etnocidio ecuatoriano. México, Univ. Iberoamericana, n.d. 1 v. (Unpaged) (mimeo)

Introductory article, "Algunos Aspectos de la Colonización Espontánea de las Sociedades Selváticas Ecuatorianas," details the effects of spontaneous colonization, missionaries and Ecuadorian national agencies on the Ecuadorian montaña peoples. Contains excellent critical bibliography on Ecuadorian tribal groups and a reprint of the Declaration of Barbados. Pamphlet is a reprint of chapter in *La situación actual de los indígenas en América del Sur* (Montivideo, Editorial Tierra Nueva, 1971).

1480. Rodríguez Pastor, Humberto. Caqui: estudio de una hacienda costeña. Lima, Instituto de Estudios Peruanos, 1969. 281 p., bibl., tables (Serie: Estudios del valle de Chancay, 9)

Community study of a hacienda in Chancay includes chapter on the family which owns the hacienda, providing a rare glimpse into the culture of the agrarian elite. Its treatment of the resident worker population is more sociological in orientation, replete with micro-land tenure and demographic statistics.

1481. Ruiz, María Angélica. Velar en común: un mito en acción (CIF/FA, 19/20:17, 1971/1972, p. 47-58, map)

Remarkably sensitive report on an unusual aspect of Andean communality: the concept of the *común* (a group of people integrated by traditional ties and common land worked by their common labor); its symbolic representation as pebbles kept in a gourd, each representing one member; and its ritual enactment in calendrically scheduled vigils, dramatize the integration of the sacred and the secular. The ceremonialism of the ritual vigil is described in full and the communities which enact the rite are sketched.

1482. Saavedra, Alejandro. La cuestión mapuche. Prólogo [por] Enrique Astorga Lira. Santiago, Instituto de Capacitación e Investigación en Reforma Agraria (ICIRA), 1971. 214 p., tables.

Monograph on the Mapuche of Chile with a totally different orientation from Faron's series of studies (item 1393 and *HLAS 31:2104*). Mapuche economy, internal social stratification, power and authority, relations with non-Mapuche and potential for socio-economic development are treated; ritual, kinship and the growing problems of urban Mapuche are ignored. Mapuches are defined by their legal status, the peculiarities of which are made explicit. The data base of the monograph came from a partial census of 453 "reducciones" made by the Chilean Directorate of Indian Affairs in 1966 and from interviews with 46 families and 55 individuals. It is clear that the agrarian reform investigation institute, which sponsored this research and publication, view Mapuche not as people, but as a problem.

1483. Sabogal Wiesse, José R. El robo a los Andes (III/AI, 30:4, 1970, p. 10-19)

Article written in reaction to Daniel W. Gade's "Ecología del Robo Agrícola en las Tierras Altas de los Andes Centrales" (see item 1404), which contrasts the petty harvest thefts accounted by Gade with the massive exploitation of Andean people by a succession of colonial Spaniards, national mestizos and government agencies, and the recent commercialization of cheap imports. The invasions—*los japikusjami*—and thieves of these invasions are given their proper polemic due.

1484. ——— ed. La comunidad andina. México, Instituto Indigenista Interamericano, 1969. 290 p., illus., plates (Ediciones especiales, 51)

General topic of this collection of essays is communal and quasi-communal structures in Peru, Bolivia, Ecuador and Colombia. Matthew Edel interprets the federations of community directorates created in response to Colombia's 1958 program of community action. Social change in specific communities—the Aymara community of Chinchero, Puno (John Hickman) Cañas and Canchis province communities in Cuzco (Hector Martínez), Llica communities in Daniel Campos, Bolivia (Humberto Rodríguez Pastor) and Chacán, near Cuzco (José Sabogal Wiesse)—are the more common subjects treated. Rafael Baraona describes the formation of an agrarian cooperative in the context of nationwide formation of new legal community-types through agrarian reform. Henry F. Dobyns and Paul L. Doughty contribute articles on the general problem of development in Peru. Mario C. Vázquez's article on the seasonal migration of Yungay (Ancash, Peru) laborers to the guano islands off the south central coast provides an interesting model of the capitalization of subsistence agriculture by such unskilled (but in this case jealously guarded) wage migrations.

1485. Sal y Rosas, Federico. Observaciones en el folklore psiquiátrico del Perú (CIF/FA, 19/20:17, 1971/1972, p. 249-262)

Susto (fear, shock) and *mal de corazón* or *sonko-nanay* (a nervous disease here interpreted as prototypical epilepsy) are regarded as psychogenic ailments. Ethnomedical practices used to cure these ills are described. The analysis is pseudo-scientific both in its psychiatric pretenses and its ethnology.

1486. Sanders, Thomas G. The blacks of Colombia's Chocó: race culture, and power in Quibdo. Hanover, N.H., American Universities Field Staff Reports, 1970. 7 p. (West coast South America series, 17:2)

Sanders, a religious historian, has published a number of AUFS reports of interest to ethnologists. This one describes the local Afro-American culture and power structure of the Chocó blacks, a majority in Quibdo, but nationally a minority subject to discrimination.

1487. ———. Economy, education and emigration in the Chocó. Hanover, N.H., American Universities Field Staff Reports, 1970. 12 p. (West coast South America series, 17:9)

Out-migration of the younger generation from the Colombian Chocó area is ascribed to the lack of regional economic development coupled with increased educational aspirations.

1488. ———. Internal migration: Brazil, Colombia, Chile, and Peru. Hanover, N.H., American Universities Field Staff Reports, 1971. 19 p. (West coast South America series, 19:1)

Updated overview of the rural-to-urban migration identifies national level consequences of the trend.

1489. Santisteban Tello, Oscar. Folklore de Huarochiri (CIF/FA, 19/20, 1971/1972, p. 265-266)

1490. Schaedel, Richard P. Patrones de poblamiento del altiplano sur-peruano: una hipótesis sobre la utilización subdesarrollada (MEMDA/E, 10, julio/dic. 1969, p. 1-6)

Characteristics of the diverse population types in the southern Peruvian altiplano. Urbanization process is presented as a general mark of underdevelopment.

1491. Sharon, Douglas G. Eduardo, the healer (AMNH/NH, 81:9, Nov. 1972, p. 32-47, plates)

Popular account focusing on the curandero, Eduardo, with excellent photographs of materials in item 1492. Account of the San Pedro curing session is more detailed and the photographs add an important dimension. For more on the subject, see items 1337, 1472, 1492, and 1508.

1492. ———. The San Pedro cactus in Peruvian folk healing (*in* Furst, Peter T. *ed.* Flesh of the gods: the ritual use of hallucinogens. N.Y., Praeger Publishers, 1972, p. 114-135)

Includes a brief biography of a Trujillo area curandero called "Galváez", a botanical and folk cultural account 'of San Pedro cactus (*Cereus* family, *Trichocereus pachanoi*), a description of the ritual paraphenalia of the *mesa* and curing ritual symbolism, and a brief account of the San Pedro experience. See also items 1337, 1472, 1491, and 1508.

1492a. Smith, Margo Lane. Institutionalized servitude: the female domestic servant in Lima. Bloomington, Ind., Indiana Univ., 1971. 497 p., bibl. (Ph.D. dissertation)

The segment of Lima's population actively engaged in domestic service is estimated to be a quarter million persons at any time. The role of domestic servant is occupied predominantly by unmarried female recent migrants, a category whose urban acculturation deserves careful attention. "The servant's environment is examined in detail in occupational, economic, physical and social terms both in on-the-job life as servants and in their private life as integral members of the urban lower class" (quoted from *Dissertation Abstracts*). This study, based on participant observation of servants in the exclusive San Isidro residential area of Lima adds important data to understanding the urban process. Available from University Microfilms, Order No. 72-10,007.

1493. Solc, Vaclav. Pod chilskými sopkami [Under Chile's volcanoes]. Praha, Orbis, 1969. 174 p., maps, plates.

Account of nine-month tour of Chile by an East German and two Czech ethnographers, chiefly to study the country's Indian groups, e.g., Mapuches, Aymaras, Araucanians, etc. [A. R. Navon]

1494. Stein, William W. Changing Vicos agriculture. Buffalo, N.Y., State Univ. of New York, Council on International Studies, 1972. 69 l. (mimeo) (Special studies, 15)

Based on the virtually untapped gold mine of fieldnotes from the 12-year Vicos project filed at Cornell Univ. In itself, a superb, detailed analysis of the adjustments in agricultural routine and cognitive values upon the introduction of improved potato varieties, this article underscores the potential of the Vicos files for research. Translated quotes from 1952-53 interviews are here published for the first time. Multilith spiral binder available from the university, 107 Townsend Hall, Buffalo, N.Y., 14214.

1495. ———. Race, culture, and social structure in the Peruvian Andes. Buffalo, N.Y., Univ. of Buffalo, Dept. of Anthropology, 1972. 62 p., bibl. (mimeo)

With characteristic insight, Stein attacks a variety of sacred cows: immutable identification of "Indians;" the hacienda as "feudal;" Peru as a "dual society" or even a single stratification hierarchy. He documents the various clues to "Indian" identification which have been published by social scientists who worked in different areas of Peru. Study includes revealing first person statements by: a Carhuasino of medium economic circumstances on his contacts with Indians; various Vicosinos on their negative stereotypes of outsiders in general (potential *pishtacos*, see item 900) and *mishtis* (mestizos), in particular; and on the various Indian cultural clues. Stein concludes that ethnic stratification is a symptom of the unequal distribution of power in Peruvian society, but foresees that no redistribution of power within the Peruvian nation will succeed without a massive international redistribution of power. This article should be required reading for any would-be Andeanist.

1495a. Stuart, David Edward. Band structure and ecological variability: the Ona and Yahgan of Tierra del Fuego. Albuquerque, N. Mex., Univ. of New Mexico, Dept. of Anthropology, 1972. 197 p., bibl. (Ph.D. dissertation)

Band structure is tested against the Ona-Yahgan literature and given the state of that literature, this thesis can be considered more a theoretical treatise on the nature of hunting and gathering economies' social organization critical of the limitations of composite/patrilineal models than a new analysis. Reviews Ona and Yahgan literature, however, an important undertaking. Available from University Microfilms, Order No. 72-30,738.

1495b. Torrico Prado, Benjamín. Indígenas en el corazón de América: vida y costumbres de los indígenas de Bolivia. La Paz, Editorial Los Amigos del Libro, 1971. 284 p., illus., plates, tables.

Indians in the Heart of America is a survey of Indian ethnicities in Bolivia. Cultural descriptions emphasizing folklore (costumes, rituals, legends, folk verses) are balanced by notes on ecology and acculturation, as certain ethnocentric remarks balance generally sympathetic coverage. The chapters on better studied Aymara, Quechua, Bororo, and Siriono groups are comparatively weak, but the inclusion of lesser known groups (Sabaya of Oruro, Lipez, Chayantacas, Sicoya, Jucumanes, and others) contributes to the literature.

1496. Tschopik, Harry. Magia en Chucuito: los aymara del Perú. México, Instituto Indigenista Interamericano, 1968. 382 p., bibl., illus., plates (Ediciones especiales, 50)

Reissue in Spanish of Tschopik's classic monograph (see *HLAS 18:362*) on the function of magical practices among the altiplano Aymara. Allows Spanish readers access to a precise account of witchcraft, sorcery, curing and divination practices.

1497. Urquidi Morales, Arturo. Las comunidades indígenas en Bolivia. Prólogo [por] Abelardo Villalpando R. Cochabamba, Bol., Editorial Los Amigos del Libro, 1970. 278 p., bibl., plates.

This inadequate Marxist overview of Bolivian indigenous communities follows the Morgan-Engels line that the precolumbian kingdoms of Bolivia and the Inca state were mere tribal pharatries. Mariátequi and Haya de la Torre are quoted and applied to Bolivia. Theories and proposals for the future of such communities offer an insight into left-wing academic views. No new data, no new analysis—a lot of old and worn stereotypes.

1498. Uzzell, John Douglas. Bound for places I'm not known to: adaptation of migrants and residence in four irregular settlements in Lima, Peru. Austin, Tex., Univ. of Texas, Dept. of Anthropology, 1972. 372 p., bibl. (Ph.D. dissertation)

Attraction of immigrants to "*pueblos jóvenes*" in Lima and the interaction of the character of the irregular settlements with their resident's urban careers is described with data from four such settlements and interview surveys from others. Available from University Microfilms, Order No. 73-7665.

1499. Vallée, Lionel. Cycle écologique et cycle rituel: le cas d'un village andin (Canadian Review of Sociology and Anthropology [Calgary] 9:3, 1972, p. 238-254)

This intricate analysis related the ecological cycle (in terms of harvests, periods of labor intensity, periods of labor inactivity) to the ritual cycle of a Quechua-speaking community near Ayacucho. Not only time, but space figure in an analysis, as both calendrical cycles mark moments of dispersion to or among special ecological zones and of congregation. Describes social structure with the *ayllu* defined as a patrilineal endogamous group which shares a *marka*, neutral territory between two altitudinally localized moieties. The traditional offices (*varayuqkuna*) and elements of social organization such as institutionalized reciprocity (*ayni, minka, faena*) are briefly described as background. In his description of culturally defined time, Vallée compares Manchiri's ecological cycle with the cultural-ecological annual cycle of the Incas as constructed from ethnohistorical sources. Vallée then proposes a structural model of time and space, territoriality and cycles. An important article, this model combines both the ecological and structural approaches.

1500. ———. La ecología subjetiva como elemento esencial de la verticalidad (PEMN/R, 37, 1971, p. 167-173)

After reviewing the Murra theory of vertical ecology and the ethnoscience hypothesis of Frake, Vallée gives a succinct comparison of the objective ecology of the town of Manchiri including which crops grow in each altitude range and the subjective ecology in terms of the names micro-climatic/crop-zones: Sallqa or puna; Sallga-Keshwa, Keshwa and the river level of Keshwa Baja. Vallée concludes that the study of a people's conceptualization of their ecology is necessary to study the cultural process.

1501. Vásquez, Mario C. Discriminación campesina en el Perú (IBEAS/EA, 1:2, 1970, p. 79-85)

Results of a small significant study among Peruvian university students are reported. The class enrolled in a seminar on social change and a control group in the third year of sociology agreed on a questionnaire that all Peruvians should have equal educational opportunities, but 44 percent designated training as an agricultural technician as the highest educational level proper for Indians. Vásquez concludes that the intellectual status of social scientist is filled by persons bearing the burden of prejudice of their petit-bourgeois dominant mestizo-criollo class backgrounds in Peru.

1502. ———. José María Arguedas, 1911-1969 (III/AI, 30:1, 1970, p. 217-221)

Review by a Peruvian anthropologist of the ethnological and ethnohistorical value of Arguedas work. Interprets Arguedas not so much as a novelist, but as a pioneer fieldworker.

1503. Webster, Steven S. An indigenous Quechua community in exploitation of multiple ecological zones (PEMN/R, 37, 1971, p. 174-183)

Q'ero, small community of 350 is distributed in 12 settlements. Author calculates that inhabitants spend 20 percent of their time moving among settlements. Their staple crops—*auquenidos*, potatoes and corn—occupy four altitudinal zones; the highest devoted to alpaca herding, the nature of which requires frequent movement among several upper valleys. Potato varieties and tubers and grown in middle altitudes (3,400-4,000 m.) and the importance of potatoes and herding leads them to locate their central settlement (usually deserted except during ritual occasions) at the convergence of Q'eros four valleys at 3,400 m. The lowest extreme of the Q'eros region is 2,100 m. (40 km. from upper hamlets) at effluent of the four valleys. Maize, squashes and tropical tubers are grown in this montaña "ecological island." Author remarks that in Q'ero the sophisticated system of exploitation of a highly fragmented ecology of type Murra describes for ancient Andean kingdoms is here done at family level through walking.

1504. ———. Kinship and affinity in a native Quechua community. Toronto, Canada, n.p., 1972. 22 p., bibl. (mimeo)

Describes the Q'ero kinship organization. The community as a whole and the domestic group are judged the only true corporate units, with rights to herds, plots, domiciles, feast houses, camps, and ritual symbols held by domestic groups. The kinship terminology is reported in full and analyzed as a parallel ego-centered kindred. Rules, statistical patterns and strategies of marriage are described. Paper presented at Symposium on Andean Kinship and Marriage, American Anthropological Association meetings, Toronto, 1972.

1505. ———. The social organization of a native Andean community. Seattle, Wash., Univ. of Washington, Dept. of Anthropology, 1972. 384 p., bibl. (Ph.D. dissertation)

Analysis of the interrelationship of ecosystem and social system in Q'ero (Cuzco area) on the eastern cordillera, Peru, is highly representative of the new sophistication in Andean research. Group studied practices a mixed pastoralism and transhumance across several ecological zones and has evolved a flexible kinship system to distribute personnel while maintaining community and lineage integrity. Available from University Microfilms, Order No. 72-28,679.

1506. Weinstock, Steven. Ethnic conceptions and relations among Otavalo Indian migrants in Quito, Ecuador (III/A, 30, 1970, p. 157-168)

Details the out-group terms of reference and attitudes toward out-groups among Otavalo Indians of Ecuador. This ethnic group of above average income and education refer only to themselves as *runa* (men), *naturales* or *indígenas* and they group Indians of other regional Indian ethnicities and *cholos* as *chaupi-runa* (half-Indians) or *chaupi-mishu* (half-white). Otavalos enact respect relationships with true *mishus* (whites) and themselves pass for white by adopting modern dress, Spanish language, and "white" educational and occupational aspirations.

1507. Whitten, Norman E., Jr. The ecology of race relations in northwest Ecuador (SA/J, 58, 1969, p. 223-233)

Analyzes race relations in San Lorenzo on northeast coast of Ecuador as a state of "pre-segregation". Assesses economic, social and political factors precipitating the exclusion of *negros* on the basis of racial phenotype by rivals for "ecological" (economic) roles. Situation is unique in that phenotypic *negro costeños* were the base population in San Lorenzo before the growth of a lumber export industry and consequent population increase through the in-migration of highland mestizos. Based on a 1965-1968 restudy of the town, the subject of Whitten's 1965 monograph (see *HLAS 29:1715*). Also available in Spanish as "Ecología de las Relaciones Raciales al Noroeste del Ecuador" (*América Indígena*, Mexico, 30:2, abril 1970).

1507a. Whittington, James Attison. Kinship, mating, and family in the Chocó of Colombia: an Afro-American adaptation. New Orleans, La., Tulane Univ., Dept. of Anthropology, 1971. 395 p., bibl. (Ph.D. dissertation)

Focus is on kinship patterns in the community of Beté (Río Atrato, Chocó region, northwest Colombian Andes). Includes a componential analysis of the kinship terminology and a description of the legal and consensual mating system including a 20 percent pattern of true polygyny. Available from University Microfilms, Order No. 72-14,209.

1508. Yarrow, Jorge M. Enfoque del curanderismo en el departamento de Lambayeque, Perú (CIF/FA, 19/20:17, 1971/1972, p. 241-248)

Brief description of the crisis-oriented magical rituals and practitioners of Lambayeque, Peru. Lists magical practices and plants, including the hallucinogens San Pedro, ayahuasca and *misha*, a number of alleged aphrodisiacs and other ethnomedical drugs. A curing session is briefly described and a generalized description of the personality of curanderos is made. See also items 1337, 1472, and 1491-1492.

LINGUISTICS

ALAN C. WARES

Bibliographer
Summer Institute of Linguistics

PHONOLOGICAL STUDIES OF INDIAN LANGUAGES ARE represented in about a score of items listed in the linguistics bibliography. A third of these appear in *Sistemas fonológicos de idiomas colombianos: t. I* (item 1640a). A notable exception to the phonemic type of analysis is that of Xavante (item 1514), in which a prosodic analysis seems to the author to be more efficient.

Several items refer to text material in native languages, including Quechua (item 1554), Mixe (item 1559), Maxakalí (item 1604), Mopán Maya (item 1618), and 17 languages of Central America (items 1619-1620). Some studies have been based on historical records (items 1519, 1530, 1581, 1611 and 1622) or on texts transcribed during the colonial period (items 1561 and 1630).

The Summer Institute of Linguistics has published bilingual dictionaries in Huitoto (item 1590) and Ocaina (item 1574) of Peru, Chatino (item 1606) of southern Mexico, and Pima and Papago (item 1614) of northern Mexico and Arizona. Turner's Chontal dictionary (item 1634) could be called trilingual, as the first part of it is Chontal to Spanish and English.

Grammatical studies include D. Bendor-Samuel's monograph on Guajajara (item 1510) and Wiesemann's on Kaingáng (item 1644), both of them with a tagmemic orientation. Wise's Nomatsiguenga monograph (item 1645) also follows the tagmemic model, as does Faust's Cocama article (item 1529) in *Tupí studies I* (item 1511). Harrison's article on Asuriní in the same volume (item 1552) follows the transformational-generative model. Other languages analyzed within the latter framework are Kekchí (item 1536), Cupeño (item 1558), and Quechua (item 1609).

Two entries have to do with the dialect survey of Mexican Spanish currently being carried out by the Colegio de México (item 1523 and 1580). Dialect intelligibility testing carried out in Panama reveals that there are nine mutually unintelligible indigenous languages there, according to the Summer Institute of Linguistics (item 1564). Other dialect studies of recent date include that of Sper in Cakchiquel (item 1623) and of Friedrich in Tarascan (item 1537).

In the area of comparative linguistic studies, two major works have appeared: Girard's *Proto-Takanan phonology* (item 1539) and Matteson's *Comparative studies in Amerindian languages* (item 1587). Among shorter studies might be mentioned Proulx's article on Proto-Quechuan aspirated stops (item 1608) and Lemle's on Tupí-Guaraní (item 1575). Both Hamp (item 1550) and Stark (item 1625) find a relationship between Mayan languages of Mexico and Central America and Araucanian languages of Chile and Argentina. The latter also posits a Yunga-Chipayan proto language in South America that may have been a sister language to Proto-Mayan (item 1624).

Several semantic analyses are listed—in Guaraní (item 1531), Maya (item 1526), Quechua (item 1573), Sirionó (item 1616), Otomí (item 1636), and Nomatsiguenga (item 1648). Finally, two regional bibliographies of the Summer Institute of Linguistics might be mentioned—that for Central America (item 1555) and that for Peru (item 1646), the latter being a partially annotated one.

1509. Bendor-Samuel, David. Hierarchical structures in Guajajara. Norman, Okla., Univ. of Oklahoma, Summer Institute of Linguistics, 1972. 214 p., bibl., illus. (Publications in linguistics and related fields, 37)

Phonology and syntax of Guajajara (a Tupi-Guaraní language of Brazil) are described as separate but related hierarchies. Beginning with the span as the largest phonological unit, author describes its prosodic features and constituents, and compares this analysis with a traditional phonemic statement. Likewise he begins with the sentence as the largest unit of the grammatical hierarchy and describes its syntactic elements. Includes brief analyzed text and index.

1510. ———— ed. Tupí studies I. Norman, Okla., Univ. of Oklahoma, Summer Institute of Linguistics, 1971. 129 p. (Publications in linguistics and related fields, 29)

Collection of five articles on Tupí-Guaraní languages, four of them written by members of the Summer Institute of Linguistics:
Helen Pease and LaVera Betts "Parintintin Phonology" p. 1-14
Carl H. Harrison and John M. Taylor "Nasalization in Kaiwá" p. 15-20
Carl H. Harrison "The Morphophonology of Asurini Words" p. 21-71
Norma Faust "Cocama Clause Types" p. 73-105
Miriam Lemle "Internal Classification of the Tupí-Guaraní Linguistic Family" p. 107-129.

1511. Blair, Robert W. On broadening our capability in Mayan studies (*in* Chicago Linguistic Society Regional Meeting, VI, Chicago, Ill., 1970. Papers. Chicago, Ill., 1970, p. 72-74)

Brief discussion of linguistic studies carried out by Peace Corps volunteers in Mayan Indian languages and a plea for researchers to have a speaking knowledge of the languages they investigate.

1512. Boudin, Max H. Controvérsia sôbre a sintaxe Guaraní: homenagem a León Cadogan (PP/B, 1970, p. 43-60, bibl.)

List of comments upon and emendations by León Cadogan, Paraguayan scholar and student of Guaraní of Antonio Guasch *El idioma guaraní: gramática y antología de prosa y verso* (Asunción, Casa América, 1956).

1513. Bricker, Victoria Reifler. Relationship terms with the usative suffix in Tzotzil and Yucatec Maya (*in* Chicago Linguistic Society Regional Meeting, VI, Chicago, Ill., 1970. Papers. Chicago, Ill., 1970, p. 75-86, bibl.)

Usative suffix -in serves to desubstantivize noun stems in two Mayan languages of Mexico, Tzotzil (Chiapas) and Maya (Yucatán).

1514. Burgess, Eunice. Duas análises das sílabas do Xavante (in Gudschinsky, Sarah C. and others. Estudos sobre línguas e culturas indígenas [see item 1548] p. 96-102)

Compared to a phonemic analysis of Xavante, a prosodic analysis of the same language is simpler and reflects more precisely native reaction, as the author concluded while teaching Xavánte speakers to read their own language. Xavánte is a Jê language of some 3,000 speakers in Mato Grosso, Bra.

1515. Burns, Donald H. Cinco años de educación bilingüe en los Andes del Perú, 1965-1970. Lima, n.p., 1971. 31 p., bibl. (mimeo)

Report on a program of bilingual education among the Quechuas of Ayacucho, Peru, similar to that developed among jungle tribes by the Ministry of Education, with the collaboration of personnel of the Summer Institute of Linguistics. The highland program provided for: teaching reading by the Psychophonemic method in the indigenous language and teaching Spanish by an oral method; the training of bilingual teachers whose mother tongue is Quechua; the development of a three-year curriculum that would prepare the Quechua pupil to continue his education in regular schools where only Spanish is spoken; and the testing and printing of teaching materials to achieve these goals. Program met with unexpected resistance from parents at first for psychological and sociological reasons. Spanish being the language of culture, it was unthinkable that Quechua should be used in school, even though the beginning pupils knew no other language. Report discusses results and makes recommendations for evaluating and improving the bilingual education program.

1516. Cadogan, León. En torno al BAI ETE-RI-VA guayakí y el concepto guaraní de NOMBRE (CIAAP/RS, 1:1, sept. 1965, p. 3-13, bibl.)

Discussion of a Guayakí expression designating a kind of folkloric spirit pertaining to one's name or body (both of these designated by the same word in Guayakí). Cognate words for 'name' from other Guaraní languages (of which Guayakí of Paraguay is one) are listed and reference made to their use.

1517. Campbell, Lyle. Mayan loan words in Xinca (IU/IJAL, 38:3, July 1972, p. 187-190)

Xinca is an unclassified language of Guatemala that seems to be nearing extinction. Many of the words in the Xinca vocabulary have been borrowed from surrounding Mayan languages. Of these, a large number are plant and animal names which suggest that the Xinca were "agriculturally quite improverished until their contact with Mayan speakers."

1518. ————. Nahua loan words in Quichean languages (*in* Chicago Linguistic Society Regional Meeting, VI, Chicago, Ill., 1970, Papers. Chicago, Ill., 1970, p. 1-13, bibl.)

Lists 57 word comparisons between Nahua and the Quichean languages of Guatemala, with several proto-Mayan and proto-Uto-Aztecan reconstructions.

1519. ————. A note on the so-called Alagüilac language (IU/IJAL, 38:3, July 1972, p. 203-207)

Origin of Alagüilac, a dialect spoken in 16th-century Guatemala, has been the subject of speculation for some time. One theory was that it was a dialect of Pipil, a Nahuatl language of Guatemala and El Salvador; another that it was a combination of Pipil and Mayan. Author puts forth argument that it may have been Xinca.

1520. Christian, Diana R. and **Esther Matteson.** Proto Guahiban (*in* Matteson, Esther ed. Comparative studies in Amerindian languages [see item 1587] 1972, p. 150-159)

Field notes on Guahibo, Cuiva, and Guayabero, collected by members of the Summer Institute of Linguistics working in Colombia, provided the basis for this study. Authors list the phonemes of Proto Guahiban and their reflexes in these languages, as well as 217 cognate sets on which they are based.

1521. Crofts, Marjorie. Repeated morphs in Munduruku (*in* Gudschinsky, Sarah C. and others. Estudos sôbre Línguas e culturas indígenas [see item 1548] p. 60-80)

Reduplication in Munduruků functions on three levels of grammatical structure—word, sentence, and paragraph. Munduruků is a Tupí language of about 1,500 speakers living in the state of Pará, Bra.

1522. *Cuadernos de Antropología.* Univ. Nacional del Litoral, Facultad de Filosofía y Letras, Instituto de Antropología, Vol. 1, No. 1, n.d.- . Rosario, Arg.

First issue of this publication dedicated to "Man in Culture" was published under the direction of Germán Fernández Guizzetti, director of the Institute of Anthropology of the National Univ. of the Litoral Entitled "Idiomas, Cosmovisiones y Cultura," it consists of seven articles dealing with language; five of these relate to specific Indian languages of South America, while the other two are more general.

1523. Cuestionario para la delimitación de las zonas dialectales de México. Introducción [por] Juan M. Lope Blanch. México, El Colegio de México, Centro de Estudios Lingüísticos y Literarios, 1970. 86 p., illus.

Questionnaire is used as the basis of research on the number and extent of Spanish dialects spoken in Mexico. Tape recordings of the speech of individuals living in various parts of the country supplement the investigations made by teams of trained linguists in the areas of phonology, grammar, and lexicon.

1524. Derrig, Sandra. Some subcategories of possessed nouns in Yucatec Maya (*in* Chicago Linguistic Society Regional Meeting, VI, Chicago, Ill., 1970. Papers. Chicago, Ill., 1970, p. 87-95, tables)

Four consonant-vowel stem patterns account for 12 basic types of possessed stems in Maya of Yucatán, Mex.

1525. Drumond, Carlos. Caracterização de aspectos da culturado borôro através da língua (Cuadernos de Antropología [see item 1522] p. 55-62)

Borôro tribe of Mato Grosso, Bra., is characterized as a hunting society, a feature that is reflected in plant names and words having to do with various aspects of tribal culture. Many names, even of musical instruments, are related to names of jungle birds and animals with which the speakers of the language are familiar.

1526. Durbin, Marshall. Morphophonemics and semantics (*in* Chicago Linguistic Society Regional Meeting, VI, Chicago, Ill., 1970. Papers. Chicago, Ill., 1970, p. 96-106)

Suggests a correlation of morphophonemics with certain semantic motivations in Yucatecan Maya (Mexico), and presents evidence for the centrality of semantics in natural languages.

1527. Edelweiss, Frederico G. Gûasú e usú, na diacronia das línguas e dialectos tupi-guaranis. VI, Gûasú, usú e asú no livro de João de Léry (USP/RIEB, 8, 1970, p. 51-64, illus., tables)

Continuation of a study of the allomorphs of an augmentative morpheme in Tupí-Guaraní languages of Brazil and Bolivia (see *HLAS 33:1716*). Forms cited are from literature of four centuries ago.

1528. Escobar, Alberto. Notas sobre la fonología del quechua de Lamas (PEMN/R, 36, 1969/1970, p. 190-192)

Brief discussion of the phonemes of the dialect of Quechua spoken in Lamas, on the east of the Andes in northern Peru. There are 17 consonant phonemes and five vowels /i,e,a,o,u/. Neither stress nor vowel length are phonemic.

Fábregas Puig, Andrés. El problema del nahualismo en la literatura etnológica mexicana. See item 1046.

1529. Faust, Norma. Cocama clause types (*in* Bendor-Samuel, David *ed.* Tupí studies I [see item 1510] p. 73-105)

Tagmemic analysis of the syntactic structure of clauses in Cocama, a Tupí-Guaraní language spoken by 10,000 people living mainly in Peru along the Amazon and some of its tributaries.

1530. Feldman, Lawrence H. A note on the past geography of southern Chiapas languages (IU/IJAL, 38:1, Jan. 1971, p. 57-58)

Errors in maps purporting to show distribution and location of Indian languages of Chiapas at the time of initial European contact could be avoided by reference to contemporary documents, some of which are in the Archivo General de Centro América in Guatemala City.

1531. Fernández Guizzetti, Germán. Los determinadores y la cuantificación en el pensar real de los hablantes del guaraní yopará (Cuadernos de Antropología [see item 1522] p. 9-42)

Using concepts of symbolic logic, author makes a semantic analysis of situational quantifiers of the dialect of Guaraní spoken by the urban population of Paraguay. The designation *yopará* 'intermingled' refers to the many Spanish borrowings in this dialect.

1532. ———. La gramática transformacional en la descripción de lenguas indoamericanas (CIAAP/RS, 5:1/2, 1970, p. 247-276, bibl.)

Discussion of the principles of transformational grammar, illustrated by examples of their application to the Guaraní language of Paraguay.

1533. ———. Las marcas aspecto-temporales en el guaraní común del Paraguay (TILAS, 9, juin 1969, p. 501-515, tables)

In several centuries of contact with Spanish, the Guaraní language of Paraguay has developed a tense-aspect system which is here analyzed in terms both of tagmemics and transformational grammar.

1534. Fisher, William M. A study in the reconstruction of proto-Yucatec (*in* Chicago Linguistic Society Regional Meeting, VI, Chicago, Ill., 1970. Papers. Chicago, Ill., 1970, p. 14-19, bibl., tables)

Sketchy study of the Yucatec (Mexico) and Mopan

(Guatemala) dialects of Maya, with transformational rules to account for correspondences.

1535. Foster, Mary LeCron. The Tarascan language. Berkeley, Calif., Univ. of California Press, 1969. 200 p., bibl., map, plates (Linguistics, 56)

Description of the phonology and grammar of a dialect of Tarascan, an unclassified language of the state of Michoacán, Mex.

1536. Freez, Ray. K'ekchi' predicate nominations (*in* Chicago Linguistic Society, Regional Meeting, VI, Chicago, Ill., 1970. Papers. Chicago, Ill., 1970, p. 107-113)

Brief description of transformation rules applied to the syntax of Kekchi, a Mayan language of Guatemala.

1537. Friedrich, Paul. Dialectal variation in Tarascan phonology (IU/IJAL, 37:3, July 1971, p. 164-187, bibl.)

Data from 26 villages of Michoacán, Mex., form the basis for the analysis of dialects of Tarascan (unclassified), which includes a mapping of dialect areas and a taxonomic summary of the phonological processes involved in distinguishing between dialects.

1538. ———. Distinctive features and functional groups in Tarascan phonology (LSA/L, 47:4, Dec. 1971, p. 849-865, bibl.)

Speech sounds of Tarascan (an unclassified language of Michoacán, Mex.) may be defined by the presence or absence of distinctive features, ten of which may be combined into 32 morphophonemes.

1539. Girard, Victor. Proto-Takanan phonology. Berkeley, Calif., Univ. of California Press, 1971. 209 p., bibl., map (Linguistics, 70)

Area in which Tacanan languages are spoken is described as northern Bolivia and southeastern Peru. Tacana, Cavineño, and Ese Ejja are taken as diagnostic of the language family; Mary Key's reconstruction (1968) of Tacanan phonology is considered; and the author's own reconstruction presented. A classification of Tacanan languages is followed by a "dictionary of Proto-Takanan," listing 504 cognate sets and a list of borrowings from Aymara-Quechua, Panoan, and Spanish. In pt. 2, author considers the relation of Tacanan languages to Panoan, and attempts a Proto-Pano-Tacanan reconstruction. Mayoruna, about which little has been published as yet, may be a link between the two families of languages. Pt. 3 is an annotated bibliography of all the literature on Panoan and Tacanan languages.

1540. González Ñáñez, Omar E. Lengua y cultura del grupo guaraquena—familia arahuaca—del Territorio Federal Amazonas (UCV/ECS [2. época] 12:3, julio/sept. 1970, p. 111-118, bibl.)

Guarequena (Arawakan, Ven.) is the only American Indian language known to have voiced aspirated stops, a feature not uncommon to languages of India and Africa. The phonemic system consists of four vowels, 24 consonants, and a phoneme of contrastive stress.

1541. Grimes, James L. A reclassification of the Quichéan and Kekchían—Mayan—languages (IU/IJAL, 37:1, Jan. 1971, p. 15-19)

On the basis of phonological and lexical data, author proposes a modification in the classification of the Mayan languages of Guatemala, of which Quichéan and Kekchían are two main families.

1542. Grimes, Joseph E. Outlines and overlays (LSA/L, 48:3, Sept. 1972, p. 513-524, bibl.)

Repetition of parts of sentences in discourse, which the author terms "overlay," is illustrated by examples from Bororo, a language of Brazil (possibly of the Gê family).

1543. ——— *ed.* Languages of the Guianas. Norman, Okla., Univ. of Oklahoma, Summer Institute of Linguistics, 1972. 91 p. (Publications in linguistics and related fields, 35)

Collection of articles on languages spoken in Surinam: Creole, Cariban and Arawakan.

1544. Grondín N., Marcelo. Método de quechua: runa simi. Oruro, Bol., Imprenta Quelco, 1971. 329 p.

Series of 65 lessons (not linguistically oriented) designed to teach the basic elements of Bolivian Quechua as spoken in the area around Cochabamba.

1545. Gudschinsky, Sarah C. Análisis tagménico [sic] de unidades que combinan componentes verbal y no verbal (Cuadernos de Antropología [see item 1522] p. 43-53, bibl.)

Combinations of verbal and non-verbal communication used by five different indigenous groups of Brazil are cited to show that an analysis of the linguistic component alone is insufficient to describe a complete behavioral situation. The five tribes from which the examples are taken are: Apalaí, Bakairí, Urubú-Kaapor, Kaiwá and Nambikwara.

1546. ———. Ofaié-Xavánte, a Jê language (*in* Gudschinsky, Sarah C. and others. Estudos sôbre línguas e culturas indígenas [see item 1548] p. 1-16, bibl., tables)

Comparison of Ofaié language data with reconstructed Proto-Jê leads to the conclusion that it belongs to the Jê language family. Fifty-five cognate sets are presented as evidence. Ofaié is a language of southern Mato Grosso, Bra., which is now practically extinct.

1547. ——— and Waldo M. Aaron. Some relational post-positionals of Guaraní (*in* Gudschinsky, Sarah C. and others. Estudos sôbre línguas e culturas indígenas [see item 1548] p. 81-95, illus., table)

Describes relational post-positional clitics of Guaraní in terms of the spatial model of the universe they seem to imply. Guaraní is a member of the Tupí-Guaraní language family spoken in Brazil, Bolivia, and Paraguay. Dialect described here is spoken in Paraná, Bra.

1548. ——— and others. Estudos sôbre línguas e culturas indígenas: trabalhos linguísticos realizados no Brasil. Ed. especial. Introdução [por] Sarah C. Gudschinsky. Brasília, Instituto Linguístico de Verão, 1971. 212 p., bibl., illus., plates.

Collection of articles on linguistics (both comparative

and descriptive), folklore, ethnography, and kinship of Indian tribes of Brazil:
Sarah C. Gudschinsky "Ofaié-Xavánte, a Jê Language" (see item 1546)
Edward and Sally Kochn "Fonologia da Língua Apalaí" (see item 1568)
Harold Popovich "The Sun and the Moon, a Maxakalí Text" (see item 1604)
Marjorie Crofts "Repeated Morphs in Munduruků" (see item 1521)
Sarah C. Gudschinsky and Waldo M. Aaron "Some Relational Post-Positionals of Guaraní" (see item 1547)
Eunice Burgess "Duas Análises das Sílabas do Xavánte" (see item 1514)
Protásio Frikel "A Mitologia Solar e a Filosofia de Vida dos Indios Kaxúyana"
Gloria Kindell "Kaingáng Basketry"
Roque de Barros Laraia "A Estrutura do Parentesco Tupí".

1549. Hamp, Eric. P. Maya-Chipaya and typology of labials (*in* Chicago Linguistic Society Regional Meeting, VI, Chicago, Ill., 1970. Papers. Chicago, Ill., 1970, p. 20-22, bibl.)

Relationship of Chipaya (Bolivia) to Maya (Mexico) suggests a hypothesis of an ingressive bilabial stop to account for asymmetry in Mayan labials.

1550. ———. On Mayan-Araucanian comparative phonology (IU/IJAL, 37:3, July 1971, p. 156-159)

Consideration of correspondences between Mayan and Araucanian languages, the former spoken in southern Mexico, and the latter in Chile and Argentina.

1551. Hardman-de-Bautista, M. J. Early use of inclusive/exclusive (IU/IJAL, 38:2, April 1972, p. 145-146)

Earliest documented use of the grammatical terms *inclusive* and *exclusive* was thought to be 1607, but the writer calls attention to the use of these terms in a grammar of Aymara by Ludovico Bertonio which was published in Rome in 1603.

1552. Harrison, Carl H. The morphophonology of Asurini words (*in* Bendor-Samuel, David ed. Tupí studies I [see item 1510] p. 21-70, bibl.)

Presents transformational rules for representing the contrastive pronunciation in slow speech of words of Asurini, a Tupí-Guaraní language of Brazil. Includes short text and analysis.

1553. ——— and John M. Taylor. Nasalization in Kaiwá (*in* Bendor-Samuel, David ed. Tupí studies I [see item 1510] p. 15-20)

Hypothesis attributing intrinsic nasality to certain morphemes of Kaiwá (a Tupí-Guaraní language of Brazil) has proven fruitful in the analysis of nasalization. Four nasalization rules are illustrated by examples in Kaiwá.

1554. Hartmann, Roswith and Udo Oberem. Quechua—Texte aus Ostecuador (AI/A, 66:5/6, 1971, p. 673-718, bibl.)

Ten texts in three dialects of Quechua of eastern Ecuador are presented with interlinear and free translations in German, comments, and notes on grammar, narrative style, and vocabulary.

1555. Henne, Marilyn Hanson de and Beth Witt de Studebaker comps. Bibliografía del Instituto Lingüístico de Verano en Centro América, 1952-1972. Prólogo de David F. Oltrogge. Guatemala, Instituto Lingüístico de Verano, 1972. 40 p.

Bibliography of linguistic, ethnographic, and educational material written by members of the Central America branch of the Summer Institute of Linguistics, or published by that branch during the past 20 years.

1556. Hensey, Fritz G. Otomi phonology and spelling reform with reference to learning problems (IU/IJAL, 38:2, April 1972, p. 93-95)

Considers tone in Otomí (Mexico) a morphological rather than a phonemic feature, and proposes a revision of the phonological analysis, upon which the practical orthography is based.

1557. Hicks, David. A comparative analysis of the Kaingang and Aweikoma relationship terminologies, Brazil (AI/A, 66:5/6, 1971, p. 931-935, bibl., table)

Author presents evidence from relationship terminologies in support of his contention that Kaingang and Aweikoma, Gê-speaking groups of southern Brazil, are two distinct tribes rather than sub-members of the same tribe, as some authorities have believed.

1558. Hill, Jane H. Cupeño lexicalization and language history (IU/IJAL, 38:3, July 1972, p. 161-172)

Discussion, in terms of transformational grammar, of Cupeño, an almost extinct language of southern California.

1559. Hoogshagen, Searle. La creación del sol y la luna según los mixes de Coatlán, Oaxaca (CT/T, 5:4, 1971, p. 337-346)

Mixe legend on the creation of the sun and the moon, with a literal and a free translation into Spanish. Mixe is a Mixe-Zoquean language of southern Mexico.

1560. Hopkins, Nicholas A. Numeral classifiers in Tzeltal, Jacaltec and Chuj—Mayan (*in* Chicago Linguistic Society Regional Meeting, VI, Chicago, Ill., 1970. Papers. Chicago, Ill., 1970, p. 23-35, bibl., table)

Tzeltal (Mexico) numeral classifiers tend to denote states rather than actions, whereas those of Jacaltec and Chuj, (Guatemala) denote the reverse. Author mentions need for more syntactic studies of Mayan languages and suggests a comparison of the classification systems of the three languages to arrive at details of a proto-Western Mayan system.

1561. Horcasitas, Fernando. El entremés del Señor de Yencuictlalpan: una farsa en Náhuatl (UNAM/AA, 9, 1972, p. 125-141, bibl.)

Aztec pilgrims to a shrine in the Federal District of Mexico were entertained by a short farce in their own language. Includes original text with a Spanish translation by article's author and comments on pre-Hispanic theatrical presentations in Aztec.

1562. Howard, Linda. Fonología del camsá (*in* Waterhouse, Viola *ed.* Sistemas fonológicos de idiomas colombianos [see item 1640a] p. 77-92, tables)

Unclassified language of some 2,500 speakers in southwestern Colombia. Camsá has a phonemic system of 21 consonants and six vowels, with free variation occurring among the bilabial consonants /p b ɸ/ Its retroflexed consonants are uncommon among Colombian Indian languages. Speakers of Camsá are largely bilingual and have borrowed many Spanish words into their language.

1563. Huber, Holly. A preliminary comparison of English and Yucatec infant vocalization at nine months (*in* Chicago Linguistic Society Regional Meeting, VI, Chicago, Ill., 1970. Papers. Chicago, Ill., 1970, p. 114-119, bibl., table)

Evidence from Maya of Yucatán, Mex., that the language environment begins to shape an infant's vocalization as early as age four months.

1564. Instituto Lingüístico de Verano, *México.* Las lenguas indígenas de Panamá (III/AI, 32:1, enero/marzo 1972, p. 95-104)

Procedures of dialect intelligibility testing developed by the Summer Institute of Linguistics and used in language surveys in Panama, lead to the conclusion that there are at least nine mutually unintelligible indigenous languages in that country.

1565. Jackson, Frances L. Proto Mayan (*in* Matteson, Esther and others. Comparative studies in Amerindian languages [see item 1587] p. 109-118)

On the basis of linguistic evidence from 21 languages including her own knowledge of Tojolabal (a Mayan language of Mexico), author expands list of Proto Mayan reconstructions begun by Ronald Olson in his "Mayan affinities with Chipaya of Bolivia" (see *HLAS* 29:2304). She lists 118 cognate sets and Proto Mayan reconstructions.

1566. Kaufman, Terrence. El prototzeltal-tzotzil: fonología comparada y diccionario reconstruído. Prólogo [por] Daniel Cazes. Versión española e índice español proto-tzeltal-tzotzil de Daniel Cazes. México, UNAM, Coordinación de Humanidades, Centro de Estudios Mayas, 1972. 161 p., bibl., maps (Cuaderno, 5)

Comparative study of Tzeltal and Tzotzil, closely related Mayan languages of the state of Chiapas, Mex. Includes a vocabulary of 805 reconstructed forms.

1567. Key, Mary Ritchie. Response to Girard on Tacanan (IU/IJAL, 37:3, July 1971, p. 196-201)

Refutation of an unfavorable review of the writer's *Comparative Tacanan phonology* (see *HLAS* 31:2367). She includes a chart of proto-Tacanan phonemes with their reflexes.

1568. Koehn, Edward and Sally Koehn. Fonologia da língua Apalaí. Traduzido por Miriam Lemle (*in* Gudschinsky, Sarah C. and others. Estudos sôbre línguas e culturas indígenas [see item 1548,] p. 17-28, tables)

Phonemic system of Apalaí, a Carib language of Brazil, includes 12 consonants, six oral and six nasal vowels. Speakers of this language number about 100 persons.

1569. Kondo, Victor and Riena Kondo. Fonemas del guahibo (*in* Waterhouse, Viola *ed.* Sistemas fonológicos de idiomas colombianos [see item 1640a] p. 93-102, tables)

Guahibo (of the Guahibo language family), spoken in the eastern plains of Colombia and in Venezuela, has a phonemic inventory of 17 consonants, 12 vowels, and a suprasegmental phoneme of stress. Vowels consist of two series, oral and nasal, with six in each series. The glottal stop is not phonemic, as its occurrence is predictable.

1570. Kroeker, Barbara J. Morphophonemics of Nambiquara (IU/AL, 14:1, Jan. 1972, p. 19-22)

Transformational rules for generating morphophonemic phenomena in Nambiquara, a Brazilian Indian language of the Gê-Pano-Carib phylum.

1571. Langacker, Ronald W. Possessives in classical Nahuatl (IU/IJAL, 38:3, July 1972, p. 173-186, tables)

Variations in Nahuatl possessive constructions are explained with transformational diagrams as resulting from general rules of Aztec syntax.

1572. Lapenda, Geraldo. Estrutura de lingua iatê: falada pelos índos fulniôs em Pernambuco. Prefácio [por] José Cavalcanti Sá Barreto. Recife, Bra., Imprensa Universitária, Univ. Federal de Pernambuco, 1968. 228 p.

Phonemic inventory of Iatê includes seven vowels, three semi-vowels, and 14 consonants. Glottalized, affricated, and aspirated consonants are considered to be combinations of stop plus glottal stop, homorganic fricative, and aspirate respectively. Vowel length, vowel harmony, and five levels of tone add to the complexity of this language spoken by some 1,500 fairly bilingual Indians of the state of Pernambuco, Bra.

1573. Lapidus de Sager, Nejama. El significado de algunos ideogramas andinos, contribución al estudio de la comunicación prehispánica (Cuadernos de Antropología [see item 1522] p. 71-95, bibl.)

Discussion of the prehispanic Quechua sememe "quelca" which referred to engraving, painting, designing, drawing, and later to writing; and of ancient designs and symbols whose meaning is conjectured by author.

1574. Leach, Ilo *comp.* Vocabulario ocaina. Yarinacocha, Peru, Instituto Lingüístico de Verano, 1969. 176 p. (Serie lingüística peruana, 4)

Dictionary of Ocaina, a Huitotoan language spoken by a small group of Indians in the jungles of northern Peru.

1575. Lemle, Miriam. Internal classification of the Tupí-Guaraní linguistic family (*in* Bendor-

Samuel, David ed. Tupí studies I [see item 1510] p. 107-129)

Tentative reconstruction of the phonemic system of proto-Tupí-Guaraní, based on a vocabulary list of 221 cognate sets from ten languages of the Tupí-Guaraní family (the most widespread of any language family in South America). Genetic relationship of the ten languages of the group is illustrated by means of a tree diagram.

1576. Levinsohn, Stephen H. The interrogative in Inga, Quechuan (IU/IJAL, 38:4, Oct. 1972, p. 260-264)

Speakers of Inga, a language of Colombia considered to be the northernmost known member of the Quechuan language family, use the interrogative not only for eliciting information but also as a rhetorical device to express rebuke, puzzlement, hopelessness, etc.

1577. Lindenfeld, Jacqueline. Semantic-categorization as a deterrent to grammatical borrowing: a Yaqui example (IU/IJAL, 37:1, Jan. 1971, p. 6-14)

An analysis of the structure of the comparative degree in Spanish and Yaqui (a Uto-Aztecan language of Sonora and Arizona), with a hypothesis regarding the failure of Yaqui to borrow the words *más* and *menos* from Spanish, even though linguistic borrowing is a common phenomenon in that language.

1578. Lionnet, Andrés. Los elementos de la lengua tarahumara. México, UNAM, Instituto de Investigaciones Históricas, 1972. 104 p., bibl., fold. map (Serie antropológica, 13)

Summary of Tarahumara grammar and vocabulary of the language, including suffixes. Tarahumara is a Utoaztecan language of more than 30,000 speakers living in the state of Chihuahua, Mex.

1579. Loewen, Jacob A. El habla Chocó, 1787-1788 (UNCIA/HC, 2:1, dic. 1970, p. 29-55, bibl.)

Unpublished diary of a Franciscan priest, written in 1787-88, is the earliest source of information about the Chocó Indians of southern Panama and northwest Colombia. Linguistic material contained in the diary, compared with data compiled more recently, shows how the language has changed both phonologically and morphologically over the past two centuries.

1580. Lope Blanch, Juan M. El léxico de la zona maya en el marco de la dialectología mexicana (CM/NRFH, 20:1, 1971, p. 1-63, maps)

On the basis of the results of a dialect study of Mexican Spanish, begun in 1967 and carried out in 50 widely scattered localities throughout the republic, some 17 distinct dialectal zones are posited. One of the most clearly marked is that of the Mayan area, particularly the state of Yucatán.

1581. Lucena Salmoral, Manuel. Gramática chibcha del siglo XVII (ICA/RCA, 14, 1966/1969, p. 203-220)

Publication of number 2922 in the *Catálogo de manuscritos de América del Palacio Real de Madrid* was discussed in an earlier article (see *HLAS 31:2378*). In that, the first three books of a work considered to be by Padre Joseph Dadey were presented; the fourth book consists of questions in Spanish and Chibcha (or Mosca) to be used by priests in the confessional. Questions themselves afford clues to practices and beliefs common among the Chibchas three centuries ago.

1582. Mansen, Richard. Fonemas del guajiro (*in* Waterhouse, Viola ed. Sistemas fonológicos de idiomas colombianos [see item 1640a] p. 53-63, tables)

Arawakan language of some 30,000 speakers in northern Colombia and Venezuela. Guajiro has a relatively simple phonemic system of 15 consonants and six vowels. There is contrast between the flapped and trilled vibrants (as in Spanish) and between the affricated alveopalatal /č/ and the sequence of alveodential stop and palatal sibilant /tš/.

1583. Marschall, Wolfgang. Some notes on the Totonac language of Zihuateutla, Mexico: summary (*in* International Congress of Americanists, XXXVIII, Stuttgart-München, FRG, 1968. Verhandlungen [see *HLAS 33:510*] v. 3, p. 525)

Dialect of Totonac spoken in Zihuateutla, on the western border of the Totonac language area in Mexico, has remained relatively unchanged. This area seems to be a meeting-place of three Totonac dialects.

1584. Martín, Eusebia Herminia. ¿Qué es la investigación lingüística? B.A., Editorial Columba, 1972. 95 p., bibl., tables (Col. Esquemas, 115)

Succinct introduction to the science of linguistics, particularly as it has developed in North America. It is intended as a practical guide to linguistic investigation rather than a textbook on linguistic theory.

1585. Matteson, Esther. Proto Arawakan (*in* Matteson, Esther and others. Comparative studies in Amerindian languages [see item 1587] 1972, p. 160-242)

Arawakan languages are spoken over a wide area extending from Guatemala to Brazil and including Colombia, Peru, and Bolivia. Their classification has generally been made on the basis of geographical location, but with the abundance of language data made available to her by colleagues of the Summer Institute of Linguistics, the author has attempted a classification based on shared linguistic features. The subgroups which she proposes are Proto Shani (based on Kinikinau and Tereno of Brazil, Baure of Bolivia); Proto Harakbut (Wachipayri, Amarakaeri and Sapateri of Peru); Proto Piro-Apuriná (Piro of Peru, Manchineri and Apuriná of Brazil); Proto Ashaninka (Campa, Machiguenga, and Nomatsiguenga of Peru); Proto Madi (Culina of Peru, Paumari of Brazil); Proto Jamamadi-Jaruará (Jamamadi and Jaruará of Brazil), all of the first order; and Proto Newiki (based on reconstructions of Western Newiki and Eastern Newiki; the former includes Piapoco, Cabiyari, and Yucuna of southeastern Colombia; and the latter Tariano, Proto Curipaco-Maniba of Colombia, and Palicur of Brazil) of the second order. Listed in the article are an abundance of cognate sets and reconstructions.

1586. ———. Toward Proto Amerindian (*in* Matteson, Esther and others. Comparative studies in Amerindian languages [see item 1587] 1972, p. 21-89)

"The purpose of this paper is to demonstrate by rigorous application of standard techniques of the comparative method, the genetic relationship of a wide sampling of groups of American Indian languages." Author's discovery of structural similarities between language families of South America came as a result of working successively on a number of languages of Peru, Bolivia, and Colombia. She has gathered language data from many sources including to a large extent field notes of members of the Summer Institute of Linguistics, and lists reconstructions and cognate sets for 974 Proto Amerindian forms.

1587. —— and others. Comparative studies in Amerindian languages. The Hague, Mouton, 1972. 251 p., bibl., (Janua Linguarum. Series practica, 127)

Six articles on comparative reconstruction of Indian languages of the Americas. Each article includes a list of reconstructions and cognate sets based on field notes of members of the Summer Institute of Linguistics currently working in these respective language families. In some cases modifications of traditional classification have been suggested. Individual titles are:
Esther Matteson "Toward Proto Amerindian" (see item 1586)
Alva Wheeler "Proto Chibchan" (see item 1643)
Frances L. Jackson "Proto Mayan" (see item 1565)
Nathan E. Waltz and Alva Wheeler "Proto Tucanoan" (see item 1639)
Diana R. Christian and Esther Matteson "Proto Guahiban" (see item 1520)
Esther Matteson "Proto Arawakan" (see item 1585)

1588. Matthews, P. H. Huave verb morphology: some comments from a non-tagmemic viewpoint (IU/IJAL, 38:2, April 1972, p. 96-118)

Considering a tagmemic analysis unnecessary for the morphology of Huave verbs, author offers an alternative analysis, based on data in the earlier interpretation by Emily F. Stairs and Barbara Erickson Hollenbach (see *HLAS 33:1820*). Huave is an unclassified language of southern Mexico.

1589. Melia, Bartomeu. Fuentes documentales para el estudio de la lengua guaraní de los siglos XVII y XVIII (CIAAP/RS, 5:1/2, 1970, p. 113-161, facsims., plates)

Catalog of early works in or about the Guaraní language of Paraguay, both published and in manuscript.

1590. Minor, Eugene E. and **Dorothy Hendrich de Minor** *comps*. Vocabulario huitoto muinane. Presentación de Martha Hildebrandt. Prólogo de Eugenio E. Loos. Yarinacocha, Peru, Instituto Lingüístico de Verano, 1971. 141 p., illus. (Serie lingüística peruana, 5)

Dictionary of the Muinane dialect of Huitoto, a Huitotoan language of some 3,000 speakers living in Peru and Colombia.

1591. Morena, Alberto. Abstracción y lenguaje. Una mitología (Cuadernos de Antropología [see item 1522] p. 97-101)

In this brief philosophical treatise, the author rejects the use of abstractions and favors the "demythologization" of language.

1592. Mosonyi, Esteban Emilio. Elementos de lingüística arahuaca (UCV/ECS [2. época] 10:3, julio/sept. 1968, p. 77-86)

Arawakan languages are spoken over a large area of northern South America—in Venezuela, Colombia, Brazil, Ecuador, Peru and Bolivia. Many attempts have been made to classify these languages, for the most part using faulty data, the result of superficial analyses. In Venezuela there are three principal groups of Arawakan languages: Arawak in the east; Guajiro and Paraujano in the west; and Baré, Guarequena, Piapoco, Curripaco and Baniva in the south, along the Río Negro. Among phonological features present in these languages are voiced aspirated stops in Guarequena; voiceless nasals and laterals in both Curripaco and Guarequena; significant tone in Baniva; and simple vowel systems and open syllable structure in practically all of them (Guajiro has closed syllables).

1593. ——. Introducción al análisis intraestructural del idioma baniva (UCV/ECS [2. época] 10:3, julio/sept. 1968, p. 65-70)

Baniva, an Indian language of southern Venezuela, is the only Arawakan language in which tone is known to be significant. There are three "tonal accents", four vowels, and contrastive vowel length.

1594. ——. Introducción al análisis intraestructural del idioma yaruro y sus implicaciones para el estudio de la cultura de los hablantes del mismo (UCV/ECS [2. época] 10:3, julio/sept. 1968, p. 71-76)

Phonemic system of Yaruro, an unclassified language of Venezuela, includes voiced unaspirated stops and voiceless stops, aspirated and unaspirated. The nine oral vowels consist of three front vowels (i, e, $\sum$) and six non-front, the latter being unrounded (ü, ö, a) and rounded (u, o, ɔ), in high, mid and low positions respectively. Only the high and the low vowels occur nasalized as well as oral. Grammatical gender depends upon the sex of the speaker and/or that of the referent (whether biological or attributed).

1595. Najlis, Elena. Disambiguation in Selknam (IU/IJAL, 37:1, Jan. 1971, p. 46-47)

Superficial ambiguity, resulting from transformations on different levels of structure, may be avoided by a disambiguating transformation, illustrated by examples of Selknam, a language of Tierra del Fuego, reportedly spoken at present by no more than six people.

1596. ——. Prematoco phonology (IU/IJAL, 37:2, April 1972, p. 128-130)

Note based on a comparative study of several dialects of Mataco, spoken by more than 10,000 Indians of the Argentine Chaco. The writer gives her reconstruction of the phonological system of an earlier stage of the language, which she terms *Prematoco*.

1597. Pacheco Cruz, Santiago. Hahil tzolbichunil tan mayab o Verdadero diccionario de la lengua maya. Prólogo [por] José Díaz-Bolio. Mérida, Mex., The Author, 1969. 438 p.

"True" dictionary of Maya (of the peninsula of Yucatán, Mex.) perhaps in the sense that the entries are in Maya only, with Spanish used only in the introductory and final pages. Since the compiler does not employ the usual linguistic symbols for certain Mayan sounds, but has instead chosen unusual characters such as an inverted c or a "wounded" *h* or *p*, deciphering the pronunciation may be a problem for anyone who is not a native speaker of Maya.

1598. Parker, Gary John. Ayacucho Quechua grammar and dictionary. The Hague, Mouton, 1969. 211 p., bibl., map (Janua linguarum. Series practica, 82)

Ayacucho dialect of Quechua is spoken by about a million people in an area roughly halfway between Lima and Cuzco, Peru. Where other dialects have both a post-velar stop and a post-velar aspirant in their phonological systems, this one has only the latter. The grammatical sketch, which includes categories of verbs and nouns and their derivation, is followed by 115 p. of dictionary.

1599. Pease, Helen and **Vera Betts.** Parintintin phonology (*in* Bendor-Samuel, David *ed.* Tupí studies I [see item 1510] p. 1-14)

Phonological analysis of Parintintín, a Tupí-Guaraní language of Brazil, with text and translation.

1600. Pellizzaro, Siro M. Shuar: apuntes de gramática. Quito, Federación Provincial de Centros Shuar de Morona Santiago, 1969. 96 p., plates.

Traditional type of grammar, in four parts, of Shuar (Jívaro), a Jivaroan language of Ecuador.

1601. Philipson, J. Etnolingüística aplicada (Cuadernos de Antropología [see item 1522] p. 63-69)

Relationship of language to culture, about which Benjamin Whorf wrote three decades ago, is discussed with contrastive examples from Kaiwá and Portuguese.

1602. Pinada Godoy, Fernando. Coba en la ciudad de La Paz (Archivos del Folklore Boliviano [La Paz] 2, 1966, p. 23-50)

Coba, the language of the underworld of La Paz, is a mixture of Spanish, Aymara, and borrowings from the underworld argot of Chile, Argentina, and Peru. Vocabulary is a commentary of Bolivian society as seen from the viewpoint of its shadiest elements.

1603. Podestá, Roberto. Elementos de teoría de los lenguajes (Cuadernos de Antropología [see item 1522] p. 103-145, bibl.)

Discussion of grammar from the point of view of transformational theory, illustrated with rules and tree diagrams.

1604. Popovich, Harold. The sun and the moon, a Maxakalí text (*in* Gudschinsky, Sarah C. and others. Estudos sôbre línguas e culturas indígenas [see item 1548] p. 29-59, table)

Folklore text, with "semi-literal" and free translations, from the Maxakalí tribe of Minas Gerais, Bra.

1605. Powlison, Esther. The suprahierarchical and hierarchical structures of Yagua phonology (LING, 75, Nov. 1971, p. 43-73, table)

Presents phonological structuring of a folktale in Yagua, a major division of the Peba-Yaguan language family, spoken mainly in Peru, but also to some extent in Brazil and Colombia. Analysis is based on eight phonological paragraphs of discourse.

1606. Pride, Leslie and **Kitty Pride** *comps.* Vocabulario chatino de Tataltepec: castellano-chatino, chatino-castellano. México, Instituto Lingüístico de Verano, 1970. 103 p., bibl., illus., maps (Serie de vocabularios indígenas Mariano Silva y Aceves, 15)

Illustrated dictionary of the Tataltepec dialect of Chatino, a Zapotecan language of some 20,000 speakers living in the southern part of the state of Oaxaca, Mex. Includes appendices.

1607. Proulx, Paul. Another y/A correspondence in Quechua (IU/IJAL, 37:1, Jan. 1971, p. 44-45)

Note on historical relationships among dialects of Quechua, with reference to the reconstruction of intransitive person suffixes.

1608. ———. Proto-Quechua /ph/ (IU/IJAL, 38:2, April 1972, p. 142-145, bibl.)

On the basis of cognate sets from four widely separated dialects of Quechua (Ecuador, Peru, Bolivia), the author posits aspirated stops for Proto-Quechua.

1609. Pulte, William. Gapping and word order in Quechua (*in* Chicago Linguistic Society Regional Meeting, VI, Chicago, Ill., 1970. Papers. Chicago, Ill., 1970, p. 193-197, bibl.)

Transformation rules for "gapping" (elision) based on data from the Cochabamba, Bol., dialect of Quechua.

1610. Rendón, Juan José. Relaciones externas del llamado idioma papabuco (UNAM/AA, 8, 1971, p. 213-231, bibl.)

Phonology of Papabuco (of the state of Oaxaca, Mex.) and a study of 100 cognate sets that include Chatino and Zapotec forms as well as Papabuco, leads to the conclusion that this is a language of the Zapotec-Chatino family, but independent of both Chatino and Zapotec.

1611. Rose, Jean. Précis de grammaire du nahuatl classique. México, Institut Français d'Amérique Latine, 1971. 76 p., bibl.

Essentials of the grammar of Aztec as spoken in Mexico at the time of the Conquest, four and a half centuries ago.

1612. Sabet Pebet, Juan Carlos and **José Joaquín Figueira.** Las lenguas indígenas del Uruguay (EMGE/BH, 120/123, 1969, p. 188-220)

Philological discussion of the role of indigenous languages in Uruguayan history and literature.

1613. Salser, J. K., Jr. Cubeo phonemics (LING, 75, Nov. 1971, p. 74-79)

Cubeo (Eastern Tucanoan language family, Colombia) has 11 consonant and 12 vowel phonemes, with two phonemic levels of pitch. Length and stress are predictable.

1614. Saxton, Dean and **Lucille Saxton** *comps.* Dictionary: Papago & Pima to English (O'odham-Mil-gahn), English to Papago &

Pima (Mil-gahn-O'odham). Prologue by Kenneth L. Hale. Tucson, Ariz., The Univ. of Arizona Press, 1969. 191 p., bibl., illus., map, tables.

Dictionary of Papago and Pima, closely related Utoaztecan languages, the former spoken by some 14,000 inhabitants of southern Arizona and northern Sonora, Mex. Pima speakers live on two reservations in Arizona.

1615. Schauer, Stanley and **Junia Schauer.** Fonología del yucuna (*in* Waterhouse, Viola ed. Sistemas fonológicos de idiomas colombianos [see item 1640a] p. 65-76, tables)

Unlike many other Indian languages of Colombia which have six vowels, Yucuna, an Arawakan language of some 450 speakers, has an asymmetric system of only five vowels. There is free variation between the phonemes /s/ and /h/ in 90 percent of the words in which they occur.

1616. Scheffler, Harold W. and **Floyd G. Lounsbury.** A study in structural semantics: the Sirionó kinship system. Englewood Cliffs, N.J., Prentice-Hall, 1971. 260 p., bibl., tables.

In his *Nomads of the long bow: the Sirionó of eastern Bolivia* (published in 1950, see HLAS 16:409), Allan R. Holmberg included a genealogical chart with the native terms used for designating relationships among the Sirionó. It has been argued that what Holmberg designated as a kinship system is in reality an asymmetric prescriptive alliance system of social classification. The present work is an examination of the question and a rather abstruse semantic analysis of the terms used. Sirionó belongs to the Tupí language family.

1617. Schlenterther, Ursula. Etnolinguistische Prozesse der ketschuasprechenden Bevölkerung in den andinen Gebieten (EAZ, 11:2, 1970, p. 283-294, tables)

Quechua language, which in prehispanic era was language of the Inca empire, has become the lingua franca of many Indian groups even beyond the ancient borders of the Inca dominion. Spanish-Quechua bilingualism could be a major factor in the development of some South American nations.

1618. Schumann, Otto. El origen del maíz en maya-mopán (CT/T, 6:4, 1971, p. 305-311)

Text, with a literal and free translation into Spanish, of a legend of the origin of corn in the Mopán dialect of Maya, spoken in Petén, Guat.

1619. Shaw, Mary ed. According to our ancestors: folk texts from Guatemala and Honduras. Illustrated by Patricia Ingersoll. Norman, Okla., Univ. of Oklahoma, Summer Institute of Linguistics, 1971. 510 p., bibl., illus., map (Publications in linguistics and related fields, 32)

Free translation of folklore texts in 17 languages, followed by the texts themselves in the original languages and a literal translation in English. For Spanish version, see item 1620.

1620. ——— ed. Según nuestros antepasados: textos folklóricos de Guatemala y Honduras. Ilustraciones por Patricia Ingersoll. Traducción de Francisco Rodríguez R.; Elcira Herrera; Eugenio Escaler P.; y Lidia Solís Mansilla. Prólogo por Ernesto Chinchilla Aguilar. Presentación de Epáminondas Quintana. Homenaje del Instituto Indigenista Nacional por José Castañeda M. Guatemala, Instituto Lingüístico de Verano *en colaboración con el* Instituto Indigenista Nacional [and] Esso Central America, 1972. 502 p., bibl., illus., map.

Free Spanish translation of folklore texts in 17 languages, followed by the texts themselves in the original languages and a literal translation in Spanish. For English original, see item 1619.

1621. Smith, Richard and **Connie Smith.** Southern Barasano phonemics (LING, 75, Nov. 1971, p. 80-85)

Phonology of Southern Barasano (Eastern Tucanoan language family, Colombia), whose major features are conditioning of variants by contiguous oral or nasalized vowels and the simultaneous occurrence of high pitch and stress.

1622. Solano, Francisco de. Areas lingüísticas y población de habla indígena de Guatemala en 1772 (GIIN/GI, 6:4, dic. 1971, p. 78-140, bibl., maps, tables)

Study of the indigenous languages of Guatemala two centuries ago, based largely upon records kept by parish priests of that era.

1623. Sper, Sheldon A. Results of dialectological research for an atlas of Lake Atitlán Cakchiquel (*in* Chicago Linguistic Society Regional Meeting, VI, Chicago, Ill., 1970. Papers. Chicago, Ill., 1970, p. 36-56, bibl., maps, tables)

Summarizes results of dialect studies begun in 1965 among the Cakchiquel Indians of Guatemala. Two major dialect groups were found.

1624. Stark, Louisa R. Maya-Yunga-Chipayan: a new linguistic alignment (IU/IJAL, 38:2, April 1972, p. 119-135)

On the basis of sets of correspondences between Chol (a Mayan language of Chiapas, Mex.) and Yungas (an almost, if not quite, extinct language of coastal Peru), author considers the latter to have a Mayan affiliation akin to Chipaya (of Bolivia), and suggests that Yunga-Chipayan may have been a sister language to Proto-Mayan.

1625. ———. Mayan affinities with Araucanian (*in* Chicago Linguistic Society Regional Meeting, VI, Chicago, Ill., 1970. Papers. Chicago, Ill., 1970, p. 57-69, bibl.)

Points out similarities between Mayan (Mexico and Guatemala) and Araucanian (Chile and Argentina). Includes 29 consonant and 16 vowel correspondences, with 85 cognate sets (proto-Mayan and Araucanian).

1626. Stolte, Joel and **Nancy Stolte.** A description of Northern Barasano phonology (LING, 75, Nov. 1971, p. 86-92)

Tribal custom of exogamy among the Northern Barasano Indians of Colombia has resulted in multilingualism as members of the tribe speak other Eastern Tucanoan languages as well as their own. Contact with Spanish has been limited. The language has 10 consonant and 12 vowel phonemes as well as two phonemic levels of pitch.

1627. Stout, Mickey and **Ruth Thompson.** Kayapó narrative (IU/IJAL, 37:4, Oct. 1971, p. 250-256, bibl.)

Study of narrative discourse structure in Kayapó, a Jê language of Brazil, with examples from test material in the vernacular.

1628. Stross, Brian. Tzeltal: acquisition and componentiality (*in* Chicago Linguistic Society Regional Meeting, VI, Chicago, Ill., 1970. Papers. Chicago, Ill., 1970, p. 120-128, bibl., table)

Study of how Tzeltal children of Chiapas, Mex., learn their mother tongue. Words learned at an early stage are context determined.

1629. ———. Verbal process in Tzeltal speech socialization (IU/AL, 14:1, Jan. 1972, p. 1-13, bibl.)

Report of a mother-child interaction study in a Tzeltal community (Mayan, Mexico), and the development of the child's verbal environment.

1630. Sullivan, Thelma D. The finding and founding of Mexico, Tenochtitlan, from the Crónica Mexicayotl by Fernando Alvarado Tezozomoc (CT/T, 6:4, 1971, p. 312-336, bibl.)

Aztec legend, written by a grandson of the Aztec emperor, Moctezuma, is described by the translator as "not only a mine of mythico-historical data, but also a saga of true literary merit and heroic dimensions." Possibly the first translation into English of the chronicle of the Aztecs' wanderings.

1631. Susnil, Branislava and **José Sánchez Labrador.** Familia guaycurú: los principales verbos del vocabulario eyiguayegimbayá, orden estructural [and] Vocabulario eyiguayegi, según el manuscrito del siglo XVIII; parte 1ra.: Letra A-LL. Asunción, Museo Etnográfico Andrés Barbero, 1971. 1 v. (Various pagings) (Lenguas chaqueñas, 2)

Two vocabularies of an indigenous language of Paraguay, neither of recent origin. Eyiguayegi (Guaiaqui?), or Mbayá, although here labeled Guaycuruan, may be related to the Tupian languages spoken in eastern Bolivia and western Brazil.

1632. Thomas, Norman D. La posición lingüística y geográfica de los indios zoques (ICACH, 19:1 [2. época] enero/junio 1970, p. 15-39, bibl., tables)

Spoken by more than 30,000 inhabitants of the state of Chiapas in southern Mexico (author cites a 1930 census figure of 20,602). Zoque is one major branch of the Zoquean language family, which also includes Popoluca and Mixe (spoken in the neighboring state of Oaxaca). Classification and distribution of Zoque is discussed, followed by a bibliography of 69 entries covering linguistic and ethnographic works dealing with the Zoque Indians and their language.

Torero, Alfredo. Lingüística e historia de la sociedad andina. See *HLAS 34:1224.*

1633. Trager, Felicia Harben. The phonology of Picuris (IU/IJAL, 37:1, Jan. 1971, p. 29-33)

Sound system of a northern Tiwa language of the Tanoan language family, closely related to Taos. All levels of the language, even the phonology, reflect the social disintegration of the Picuris. Early Spanish loan words have been assimilated, but English words and recent Spanish loans are treated as "foreignisms."

1634. Turner, Paul and **Shirley Turner** *comps.* Dictionary: Chontal to Spanish-English; Spanish to Chontal. Tucson, Ariz., Univ. of Arizona Press, 1971. 364 p., bibl., illus., map, tables.

Chontal, or Tequistlatec, has been classified as a Hokan language spoken by some 5,000 Indians living in the highlands of the southeastern part of the state of Oaxaca, Mex., and by an equivalent number a few miles further south along the coast. This dictionary is of the speech of the highland dialect. Included in the appendixes are a grammatical sketch of the language, map of the area, and historical sketch of the Chontals.

1635. Villagra de García, Sara Delicia. La palabra: sus clases morfológicas en la lengua guaraní (CIAAP/RS, 5:1/2, 1970, p. 163-200, tables)

After listing the phonemes of Guaraní, with comments on analyses of the language during the past four centuries, author makes a morphological and syntactic analysis, resulting in seven basic semantic classes.

1636. Voigtlander, Katherine and **Doris Bartholomew.** Semology and transitivity in Eastern Otomi verbs (LINGUA, 29:1, April 1972, p. 38-53, bibl.)

Participant roles and the relationships between participants in semological constructions are illustrated by examples from the Eastern dialect of Otomi (an Otomanguean language of the state of Hidalgo, Mex.). A need is felt for a link between semological and morphological structures in the lexicon of the language.

1637. Voorhis, Paul H. Notes on Kickapoo whistle speech (IU/IJAL, 37:4, Oct. 1971, p. 238-243, bibl.)

Kickapoos are a Central Algonquian people located in Kansas, Oklahoma, and northern Mexico. The Mexico group has developed a whistle speech typically used for communication between courting adolescents, although the language itself is not tonal.

1638. Walton, James and **Janice Walton.** Fonemas del muinane (*in* Waterhouse, Viola *ed.* Sistemas fonológicos de idiomas colombianos [see item 1640a] p. 41-52, tables)

Muinane (Bora linguistic family) is spoken by a relatively small number of Indians in Colombia and Peru. Its phonology includes a complex consonant system of 22 phonemes; vowel clusters of up to four segments; and two levels of tone.

1639. Waltz, Nathan E. and **Alva Wheeler.** Proto Tucanoan (*in* Matteson, Esther and others. Comparative studies in Amerindian languages [see item 1548] p. 119-149)

Data from 16 languages of the northwestern Amazon basin are used in the reconstruction of Proto Tucanoan on the basis of 278 cognate sets. Examples and details of development are taken largely from seven of these languages, six of them Eastern Tucanoan and one Western.

1640. ────── and **Carolyn Waltz.** Fonología del guanano (*in* Waterhouse, Viola *ed.* Sistemas fonológicos de idiomas colombianos [see item 1640a] p. 29-40, tables)

Guanano, an Eastern Tucanoan language of Colombia, has three series of stops (voiceless aspirated and unaspirated, and voiced), voiceless vowels, strong nasalization, and phonemic stress.

1640a. Waterhouse, Viola *ed.* Sistemas fonológicos de idiomas colombianos. t. 1. Translated by Jorge Arbeláez G. Bogotá, Ministerio de Gobierno, 1972. 102 p., tables.

Translation of phonemic system of Colombian languages, published in 1967 by the Summer Institute of Linguistics. Each of the seven chapters describes the phonology of an Indian language of Colombia, two of them being of the Tucanoan language family, two Arawakan, one Bora, one Guahibo, and one unclassified.

1641. West, Birdie and **Betty Welch.** Sistema fonológico del tucano (*in* Waterhouse, Viola *ed.* Sistemas fonológicos de idiomas colombianos [see item 1640a] p. 13-28, tables)

Segmental phonemes of Tucano (Eastern Tucanoan language family), a trade language of the multilingual Vaupés area of Colombia, consist of 12 consonants and six vowels. Stress, tone, and nasalization are analyzed as suprasegmental phonemes.

1642. Westley, David O. The Tepetotutla Chinantec stressed syllable (IU/IJAL, 37:3, July 1971, p. 160-163)

Although stress in Chinantec (a Chinantecan language of the state of Oaxaca, Mex.) is an element of the word rather than of the syllable, it is necessary to refer to it in describing the latter. Ballistically stressed syllables are of shorter duration than controlled, and exhibit greater variation in pitch and intensity.

1643. Wheeler, Alva. Proto Chibchan (*in* Matteson, Esther and others. Comparative studies in Amerindian languages [see item 1548] p. 93-108)

Data from six languages of northern Colombia were used in the reconstruction of Proto Chibchan: Chibcha, Tunebo, Kogi, Arhuaco, Marocacero, and Motilón.

1644. Wiesemann, Ursula. Die phonologische und grammatische Struktur der Kaingáng-Sprache. The Hague, Mouton, 1972. 211 p., tables (Janua linguarum. Series practica, 90)

Kaingáng, a Jè language of about 7,000 speakers in southern Brazil, is described in terms of tagmemic structure. Its 14 consonant phonemes are analyzed as fortis and lenis stops and continuants, with the nasal series /m n ñ n/ being considered lenis stops (*Verschlusslaute*). There are nine oral vowels and five nasal, as well as a phoneme of length, four phonemes of stress (two of word stress and two of sentence), eight of intonation, four of voice quality, and two of pause. The grammatical hierarchy is described in the second half of the book, with distribution of tagmemes illustrated by matrix displays.

1645. Wise, Mary Ruth. Identification of participants in discourse: a study of aspects of form and meaning in Nomatsiguenga. Norman, Okla., Univ. of Oklahoma, Summer Institute of Linguistics, 1971. 224 p., bibl., tables (Publications in linguistics and related fields, 28)

Nomatsiguenga ('my people') is a Pre-Andine Arawakan language spoken by approximately 1,000 people living on the eastern slopes of the Andes in Peru. An analysis, in tagmemic terms, of the grammatical structure of the language, with particular reference to the variety of forms used for identifying individuals in a narrative.

1646. ────── *comp.* Bibliografía del Instituto Lingüístico de Verano en el Perú, Junio 1946-Junio 1971. Sumarios por Paul Powlison F. Presentación por José Guabloche Rodríguez. Prólogo de Eugenio E. Loos B. Yarinacocha, Peru, Instituto Lingüístico de Verano, 1971. 124 p.

Bibliography of linguistic, ethnographic, and educational works by members of the Peru branch of the Summer Institute of Linguistics, or published by that branch during the quarter century 1946-71. Includes corrigendum.

1647. ────── and **Harold G. Green.** Compound propositions and surface structure sentences in Palikur: Arawakan (LINGUA, 26:3, March 1971, p. 252-280, bibl.)

Consideration of sentence types of deep and surface structure and the relations between them, illustrated by examples from Palikur, an Arawakan language of Brazil.

1648. ────── and **Ivan Lowe.** Permutation groups in discourse (Language and Linguistics: Working Papers [Georgetown Univ., Washington] 4, 1972, p. 12-34, bibl., tables)

Brief text in the Nomatsiguenga dialect of Campa (Arawakan, Peru) serves as the basis for a structural analysis of discourse in terms of participant roles. Lexemic clause types, reflecting the "deep structure" (semantics) of Nomatsiguenga discourse, are derived from grammatical clause types ("surface structure"), and each participant in the action is identified by a specific index, irrespective of the way the person or thing is referred to.

1650. Wolgemuth, Carl. Marriage customs of our forefathers: Nahuat text from Mecayapan, Ver. (CT/T, 6:4, 1971, p. 347-373)

Text in Isthmus Nahuat (of the state of Veracruz, Mex.), with literal and free translation into English.

1651. Ziehm, Elsa. Nahua-Texte aus San Pedro

Jícora in Durango (*in* International Congress of Americanists, XXXVIII, Stuttgart-München, FRG, 1968. Verhandlungen [see *HLAS 33:510*] v. 3, p. 519-524, plates)

Account of the author's visit to towns in Western Mexico in search of the Nahua village where Konrad Theodor Preuss collected some 1,200 pages of text material in the Indian language more than half a century ago.

PHYSICAL ANTHROPOLOGY

MICHAEL H. CRAWFORD
Associate Professor of Anthropology
University of Kansas

ROBERT A. HALBERSTEIN
Assistant Professor of Anthropology
University of Miami

THE BOOKS AND ARTICLES ABSTRACTED IN THIS *HLAS* section on biological anthropology are divided into six subsections entitled: general works; population genetics and demography; human adaptation and acclimatization; growth and nutrition; biomedical studies; and paleoanthropology and osteology. There appears to be an increasing emphasis upon studies dealing with the genetics and evolution of human populations, particularly genetic variability both within and between populations. The development of highspeed computers during the last decade has permitted the calculation of genetic distances utilizing different types of data, such as: anthropometry, serology, dermatoglyphics, and dentition. Another major concern is understanding the relationship between the demographic structure of a population and the action of evolutionary processes. Much attention is currently being devoted to the environmental factors which may affect growth processes. A number of papers treat the nutritional statuses of various Latin American regions and the dietary habits of specific populations. This emphasis has been generated by the increasing realization that the *campesinos* of Latin America suffer malnutrition which may result in long-term effects on future generations. Studies of physiological adaptive mechanisms are mainly concentrated on two topics: high altitude adaptation in the Peruvian Andes, and adaptation to temperature extremes. The International Biological Program has sponsored high altitude adaptation studies in the Highlands of Peru which have produced a wealth of information on the phenotypic effects of hypoxia. The biomedical research has brought an increasing awareness of current need for medical facilities and public health programs. Several articles deal with changing patterns of disease incidence in Latin America and the affects of the public health services on the morbidity of the rural populations.

This section is not exhaustive in regards to all of the possible articles and books on Latin American biological anthropology. The authors have been selective in the choice of articles, limiting this chapter to works of importance to evolutionary theory and to biological anthropology and related subdisciplines. In accordance with the *Handbook* policy, only those publications which seem to have permanent record value are included in this review.

A number of general articles and books of importance to the Latin Americanists have been published in the last two years. The last two biennial review articles by Crawford (1970) and Holloway and Szinyei-Merse (1972) contain discussions of the human biology of Latin America and extensive bibliographies for reference purposes. With the evolution of Siegel's *Biennial Review of Anthropology* to the *Annual Review of Anthropology* is a greater emphasis on the field of Biological Anthropology. For example, the 1972 issue of the *Annual Review of Anthropology* contains two articles of relevance to the readers of this *Handbook*. Baker and Sanders review the recent demographic studies in anthropology, and since both authors have done extensive research in Latin America, many of the field studies cited pertain to the New World. Roberts and Bear present an extensive summary of the recent publications on human genetic and demographic variability.

An important synthesis of human population biology in Latin America, edited by Francisco Salzano, was released in 1971. Entitled *The ongoing evolution of Latin American populations* (see item 1765) is a result of the 1969 Wenner-Gren Foundation Conference at Burg Wartenstein. Significant papers in this volume are abstracted here. The book provides a wealth of original, previously unpublished data.

Two important works were recently published on the demography and ethnohistory of Middle and South American populations. The outstanding compilation by Cook and Borah (see *HLAS 34:1254*) reconstructs the devastating effects of Spanish Conquest and colonization on various Latin American populations. Francisco Salzano, who has been describing and analyzing the demographic structure of Amerindian populations in the Amazon Basin for more than a decade, reviewed the demography of American Indians and Eskimo groups in the volume *The structure of human populations*, edited by Harrison and Boyce (1972).

During the last few years the International Biological Program has exerted considerable influence on the direction and scope of the human biological research in Latin America. Two of the most successful research programs, headed by James V. Neel and Paul T. Baker, have explored problems of genetic microdifferentiation and high altitude adaptation respectively. A large number of articles from these two studies are abstracted in this chapter. Baker and his students have been particularly productive, with approximately 300 publications resulting from this study.

GENERAL

1652. Baker, Paul T. and William T. Sanders. Demographic studies in anthropology (Annual Review of Anthropology [Palo Alto, Calif.] 1, 1972, p. 151-178, bibl., tables)

Importance of demographic data is emphasized for all phases of physical anthropology and archaeology: primatology, reconstruction of prehistoric and ethnohistoric populations, human population genetics, human ecology and micro-evolution, and cultural evolution. Since both authors have done extensive work in Latin America, many of the examples of field studies cited pertain to the New World.

1653. Comas, Juan; Helia de Castillo; and Betty Méndez. Biología humana y/o antropología física: resultados de una encuesta. México, UNAM, Instituto de Investigaciones Históricas, 1971. 125 p., bibl. (Cuadernos: serie antropológica, 24)

Survey of professional physical antropologists as to definition of field, and relationship of physical anthropology to human biology. The 78 replies reveal marked differences between those who regard field as strictly a biological science and those who emphasize importance of cultural behavior. Even greater variability is seen in responses to question of the relationship of physical anthropology and human biology, creating need to delimit and clarify scope and aims of field more precisely.

1654. Crawford, Michael H. Trends in genetics and biological anthropology (Biennial Review of Anthropology [Stanford Univ. Press, Calif.] 1970, p. 191-247, bibl., tables)

Presents a comprehensive review of major recent studies in human biology with primary emphasis upon genetical aspects of human and primate evolution: demography, serological and biochemical genetics, population genetics, cytogenetics, and behavioral genetics. Population studies in Latin American areas are critically discussed, and an extensive bibliography is included.

1655. Holloway, Ralph L. and E. Szinyei-Merse. Human biology: a Catholic review (Biennial Review of Anthropology [Stanford Univ. Press, Calif.] 1972, p. 85-166, bibl., tables)

Attempts to outline recent developments in all subfields of physical anthropology, and this purpose is admirably accomplished. Summarizes wealth of information on following topics: human adaptation and variation, fossil man, biochemical genetics, population genetics, and human behavioral evolution.

1656. Roberts, Derek F. and J. C. Bear. Studies of modern man (Annual Review of Anthropology [Palo Alto, Calif.] 1, 1972, p. 55-112, bibl., tables)

Reviews studies in human biology in contemporary populations for period mid-1969 to mid-1971. Number of topics are critically treated: genetical demography, formal genetic analyses of populations, nutrition and growth, anthropometric and morphological investigations, and adaptation to diverse environments. The 740-item bibliography contains numerous references to Latin American studies.

BIOMEDICAL STUDIES

1657. Allwood Paredes, Juan. Los recursos de

la salud pública en Centro América. 2. ed. San Salvador, Organización de Estados Centroamericanos [ODECA], Secretaría General, 1969. 162 p., tables (Serie monografías técnicas)

Reviews current status of public health facilities in Central America and discusses some specific programs and proposals which may affect the region's future. Following a description of demographic characteristics of Central America, author summarizes available personnel, equipment, etc., in Central America as of 1965. Discusses financial and political matters.

1658. Azeredo Costa, Eduardo; Herman Gonçalves Schatzmayr; Julio de Araújo Mesquita; and Isnard Alves Cabral. Serological studies on an outbreak of smallpox in the state of Bahia, Brazil in 1969 (IOC/M, 70:3, 1972, p. 285-298, tables)

Following outbreak of smallpox in Bahia, Bra., serological studies were conducted for a sample of 99 affected and unaffected individuals. Comparisons were made for hemaglutination inhibition, neutralization, and complement fixation, and significant differences were found among previously affected, recently affected, and unaffected subjects. Antibodies found in different groups were as expected from earlier studies.

1659. Berggren, Warren L. and Gretchen M. Berggren. Changing incidence of fatal tetanus of the newborn: a retrospective study in a defined rural Haitian population (ASTMH/J, 20:3, May 1971, p. 491-494, tables)

In a large sample of women between age 15 and 60 years, tetanus of newborn was discovered to have caused death of 1,148 of their 7,248 liveborn children. This occurred relatively infrequently among younger mothers, but in over half of the older mothers. Frequency of death through tetanus of newborn has diminished over a 30 year period, and this is directly related to a program of immunization and public health.

1660. Camargo, Mario E. Reacciones serológicas y consecuencias sociales de los resultados positivos a la enfermedad de Chagas (OSP/B, 72:6, junio 1972, p. 576-582)

Clinical and serological studies conducted in areas affected by tripanosomic infections reveal that only a limited number of positively reacting individuals shows symptoms of Chagas disease, a trypanosome infection transmitted in excreta of various insects. Positive serological results are often interpreted, however, as evidence of Chagas disease, and these patients are often subject to social segregation as well as exclusion from the labor market.

1661. Camel V., Fayad. Estadística médica y de salud pública. Prólogo [por] Héctor Sequera Palencia. Mérida, Ven., Univ. de los Andes, 1970. 528 p., bibl., tables.

Outlines use of statistics in medicine and public health. Topics include design and set-up of studies, methods of information collection, use of models and practical demonstrations, and presentation and classification of results. Proper use of descriptive and comparative statistics is discussed, as is application of the techniques to demographic data.

1662. Dobkin de Ríos, Marlene. Ayahuasca: the healing vine (IJSP, 17:4, Winter 1971, p. 256-267)

In jungle regions of Peru, Colombia, and Brazil, a woody vine called ayahuasca is used by both horticultural tribes and urbanized mestizos as part of folk healing procedures. Explores relationship of use of this substance, cultural concepts of disease etiology, and curing practices in both urban and countryside settings. Psychedelic drug is used mainly to diagnose magical causes of illness and to neutralize evil magic, rather than as a cure in itself. For more on this topic, see *HLAS 33:1540-1541, 1894.*

1663. Fábrega, Horacio, Jr. and Peter K. Manning. Health maintenance among Peruvian peasants (SAA/HO, 31:3, Fall 1972, p. 243-256, tables)

It was discovered that people of a rural community of highland Peru exhibited a pervasive concern for the functioning of their bodies and maintenance of health. Study examines organized behavioral practices and social use of herbs in this context. 40 adult males were interviewed regarding use of 18 herbs which modify bodily disturbances.

1664. Glanville, E. V. and R. A. Geerdink. Blood pressure of Amerindians from Surinam (AJPA, 37:2, Sept. 1972, p. 251-254, tables)

Analyzes data on blood pressure among hunting-and-gathering Trio and Wajana tribes of Surinam, in relation to age, stature, weight, and sex. Describes differences in diastolic and systolic pressures. Subjects were found to be in good health and there were no cases of clinical hypertension.

1665. Godard, C. and others. A propos d'une expérience de pédiatrie hospitaliére en Bolivie (Courrier [Paris] 21:1, jan./fev. 1971, p. 5-13, bibl., illus., tables)

Authors review installation and development of children's hospital and pediatric clinic in Bolivia. Among 853 hospitalized children, malnutrition is extremely common, as well as diarrheas and dehydrations. Amebiasis is leading type of parasitic disease. Reports treatment procedures for these conditions. Tetanus, pertussis, and diphtheria were found to be quite uncommon. Discusses preventive medication program in terms of training staff.

1666. Golubjatnikov, Rjurik. Prevalence of antistreptolysin O in Mexican and Paraguayan children (ASTMH/J, 21:3, May 1972, p. 345-350, map, tables)

Serologic study was carried out in an isolated population of Mexico in an effort to investigate possible relationship between antistreptolysin O, a diffusable antigen of Group A streptococcus, and the relatively high incidence of rheumatic fever. Results also are compared to similar studies conducted in Paraguay. Relationship of blood groups and rheumatic fever remains questionable. Findings suggest that high altitude, climate, level of sanitation, or crowded living conditions do not by themselves lead to high prevalence of antistreptolysin O in children.

1667. Grases, Pedro J. and Simon Beker G. Veno-occlusive disease of the liver: a case from Venezuela (The American Journal of Medicine [N.Y.] 53:4, Oct. 1972, p. 511-516)

Death by liver disease is normally rare among infants

and young children in Venezuela. Authors here describe clinical features of a case of veno-occlusive disease in a five-year old girl. Child lived in area where certain heptoxic plants are consumed widely, both for medicinal purposes and as foods.

1668. Heredia-Durate, A. El incremento de la mortalidad infantil en México: influencia de diversos factores sociales y de atención médica como causas de la misma (Gaceta Médica de Mexico, 103, 1972, p. 475-493, bibl., tables)

According to 1970 census of Mexico, there has been a nationwide increase in infant mortality rates and a corresponding decrease in expectation of life. Large-scale survey revealed inverse relationships between socioeconomic level and infant mortality, and quality of medical facilities and infant mortality rate. Relationships were found in diverse areas of the country, and were especially marked in Federal District. Article states that large sections of Mexico suffer from poor health and low-life expectancy.

1669. Inter-American Malaria Research Symposium, I, San Salvador, 1971. Proceedings (ASTMH/J, 21:5, Sept. 1972, p. 611-850, bibl., maps, tables)

Collection of papers resulting from conference on presence and control of malaria in Latin America. Problem is comprehensively treated, and following topics are discussed: extent of disease and status of its treatment and eradication; chemical, ecological, and demographic aspects of malaria; and prospects of further progress in the area.

1670. Kumate, Jesus and others. Content of common antigen of Escherichia coli and diarrhea of newborns and infants in a Mexican preindustrial community (NYAS/A, 176, 1971, p. 350-359, bibl., tables)

Follows 34 newborns from rural Tlaltizapan, Mex., from birth to ten months in order to observe clinical episodes of diarrhea. During first five months content of common antigen of E. coli was lower in diarrheal infants than in healthy ones. Level of antigen increased significantly after five months of age in diseased infants but was still lower than in healthy ones.

1671. Mata, Leonardo J. and **J. J. Urrutia.** Intestinal colonization of breast-fed children in a rural area of low socioeconomic level (NYAS/A, 176, 1971, p. 93-112, bibl., tables)

Development of fecal flora and relationship of E. coli infections to diarrheal disease was studied longitudinally in Indian children from Guatemala. Fecal flora showed marked differences among infants with respect to numbers and kinds of bacteria. E. coli level was found to increase throughout first year of life. Breast-fed infants experienced fewer infections with E. coli.

1672. —— and **R. G. Wyatt.** Host resistance to infection (ASCN/J, 24:8, Aug. 1971, p. 976-986, bibl., tables)

Some research has shown that breast-fed infants experience less infectious diseases than those artificially fed, especially evident with respect to gastrointestinal disorders. Mayan children from Guatemala were studied to test hypothesis. All were breast-fed exclusively for three to nine months, after which solids and fluids were introduced. Results suggest that human milk is more effective than cow's milk in protecting newborn infant against infection through a greater concentration of antibodies against pathogenic bacteria.

1673. Mateo de Acosta, O. and others. Prevalencia de la diabetes mellitus en Cuba (Boletín de Higiene y Epidemiología [La Habana] 10, 1972, p. 3-12, bibl., tables)

In large samples from metropolitan Havana and surrounding rural areas of Cuba, prevalence of diabetes mellitus was found to be comparable to other Latin American countries. 2.8 percent of the nearly 8,000 subjects were diagnosed as positive, and 2.3 percent were found to be probable diabetics.

1674. Neel, James V. Genetic aspects of the ecology of disease in the American Indian (in Salzano, Francisco M. ed. The ongoing evolution of Latin American populations [see item 1765] p. 561-590)

Changing incidence of a variety of diseases in Latin American populations is interpreted in terms of genetic and evolutionary effects. Following a discussion of some methodological considerations in study of disease in populations, some specific examples of changing patterns of disease incidence are related to possible implications for natural selection. Author suggests that development of civilized societies and acculturation have created biological pressures in certain populations through impact of new disease vectors.

1675. Peña Gómez, Rosa María. Edad de la menarquía en tres gropos de niñas mexicanas. México, Instituto Nacional de Antropología e Historia, Depto. de Investigaciones Antropológicas, 1970. 84 p., bibl., tables (Publicaciones, 24)

Age of menarche is analyzed for 1,028 Mexican girls aged ten to 15 years, 11 months from Mexico City and rural and urban areas of Tampico state. Group from Mexico City was most heterogeneous. Similarities are seen among three samples when variable of parental occupations are controlled. Mean ages of menarche were found to be 12.19 for Mexico City group, 12.03 years in urban Tampico, and 12.41 years in rural Tampico. These are early ages when compared to other world populations.

1676. Poon-King, Theo and others. Epidemic acute nephritis with reappearance of M-type 55 streptococci in Trinidad (LANCET, 1:7801, March 1973, p. 475-479, bibl., tables)

Fifth epidemic of acute nephritis in South Trinidad within past 20 years was associated with reappearance of group-A streptococci. Disease was preceded and accompanied by outbreak of scabies, a skin condition carried by a mite. Family studies revealed that the scabies probably helped to spread acute nephritis.

1677. Rino, José Bautista. Antropología médica: la persona en su totalidad. Prólogo [por] L. Soria Bermúdez. B.A., Editorial Plus Ultra, 1971. 495 p.

Textbook on historical development of field of medicine from early Greece and Rome to present. Discusses different time periods within anthropological perspective. Although book covers much material, there is neither index nor bibliography.

1678. Roncada, M. J. Hypovitaminosis A:

serum vitamin A content and carotene level in the state of São Paulo, Brazil, seaside population (Revista de Saude Pública [São Paulo] 6, 1972, p. 3-18, bibl., tables)

Nutritional, biochemical, and clinical studies were made of several populations in São Paulo. Concludes that hypovitaminosis A constitutes serious health problem in area.

1679. Sánchez, Otto and **M. J. Moreno de Marval.** Anomalías cromosómicas en reclusos de la cárcel de Ciudad Bolívar (AVAC/ACV, 22:4, 1971, p. 135-137, bibl.)

In a sample of 65 male prisoners from Ciudad Bolívar Jail, two were found to have Klinevelter's syndrome, giving a frequency of three percent. Discusses possibility that abnormal chromosome number may be related to antisocial behavior. Missing are frequencies from general population.

1680. Selections from 1970 (OSP/B [English ed.] 81:1, July 1971, p. 1-52)

Papers contained within present up-to-date accounts of operation of public health programs in various areas of Latin America, as well as an analysis of current trends in nutrition and disease. The following topics are covered:
Ramón Valdivieso D. and Bogoslav Juricie T. "The National Health System in Chile" p. 1-7
Carlos Dávila "Intensive Care Units in Latin America" p. 8-19
Roberto Rueda-Williamson "The Applied Nutrition Program: The Basis of the National Nutrition Plan" p. 20-29
Caribbean Food and Nutrition Institute "Guidelines to Young Child Feeding in the Contemporary Caribbean" p. 30-38
Celso Arcoverde de Freitas "Reflections on the Epidemiology and Prevention of Plague" p. 39-48
Aldo Villas Bôas "The Tuberculosis Problem in the Americas" p. 49-52.

1681. Sousa, Octavio E. and **Carl M. Johnson.** Frequency and distribution of *Trupanosoma cruzi* and *Trypanosoma rangeli* in the Republic of Panamá (ASTMH/J, 20:3, May 1971, p. 405-410, bibl., map, tables)

Comprehensive survey of prevalence of trypanosome parasites in over 10,600 individuals examined, representing all provinces of Panama. Two species of Trypanosoma were detected, and their geographic distributions noted. 75 percent of infected persons were under 16 years of age, and overall condition was most frequent among individuals aged six to ten years. Authors do not treat mortality or possible selective effects.

1682. Torre López, Egidio. Enfermedades venéreas en adolescentes (OSP/B, 72:6, junio 1972, p. 558-564, tables)

Tamaulipas state, Mex., has shown an upward trend in incidence of venereal disease, a problem encompassing the adolescent population. Major precipitating factors are mobility of adolescents, knowledge and use of contraceptives, and ignorance of venereal diseases.

GROWTH AND NUTRITION

1683. *Anais da Comissão Nacional de Alimentação.* Ministério da Saúde, Comissão Nacional de Alimentação. Vol. 4, No. 5, 1970- . Rio.

Issue consists of comprehensive report of dietary and nutritional status of various Brazilian regions. Includes demographic data, relationship of occupational level and habits of consumption, available programs of nutritional improvement, and suggestions and recommendations for further developments.

1684. Ariza Macías, Jaime. Method for evaluation of growth of children, men and women, since birth up to twenty years, for use at national and international level (SLN/ALN, 22, 1972, p. 531-546, bibl., tables)

Discusses different genetic and environmental factors which influence growth process and analyzes limitations of frequently used methods for evaluating growth. Proposes new system for evaluation of growth which takes into account harmonious relationship of height and weight according to different ages.

1685. Beghin, Yvan; William Fougère; and **Kendall W. King.** L'alimentation et la nutrition en Haïti. Paris, Presses Universitaries de France, 1970. 248 p.

Les auteurs dont l'un est haitien, Fougère, et les deux autres les étrangers ayant travaillé en Haïti avec l'Organisation Mondiale de la Santé (WHO) ont dépouillé tout ce qui a été écrit sur l'alimentation et la santé, ont fait des observations basées sur des enquêtes appuées de données statistiques. Excellent travail qui peut aider à appréhender la réalité haïtienne au point de l'alimentation, de la nutrition et de la santé. [M. A. Lubin]

1686. Blanco, Ricardo A. and others. Retardation in appearance of ossification centers in deprived Guatemalan children (WSU/HB, 44, 1972, p. 525-536, bibl., tables)

Analyzes age of appearance of ossification centers of the hand and wrist in 1,409 children aged zero to seven years from rural Guatemala. Compares results with similar studies. Great variability was seen in ossification schedules, especially among male children. Females typically showed earlier ossification. After first year of life, Guatemalan children experience a delay in maturation, and this trend is more marked among males.

1687. Bodenheimer, Thomas S. The political economy of malnutrition: generalizations from two Central American case studies (SLN/ALN, 22, 1972, p. 495-506, bibl., tables)

Author points out that major health problem in Latin America stems from protein deficiencies in childhood which result in many deaths from malnutrition and infections. Problem, however, does not lie in shortage of food or overabundance of people. Real sources of problem, according to author, are facts that countries under-produce food because of land tenure and food-export systems, and also lack of money or land among malnourished people.

1688. Eveleth, Phyllis B. An anthropometric study of northeastern Brazilians (AJPA, 37:2, Sept. 1972, p. 223-232, tables)

Detailed anthropometric measurements were taken from 200 males from a population consisting of a mixture of Portuguese whites, Bantu Negroes, and Brazilian Indians. Subjects were characterized as having short stature and brachycephalic skulls. This hybrid population was found to be more variable in their metric traits than some indigenous Indian populations of Brazil. In several of the characteristics it was found that hybrids are not intermediate between average for parental populations and Brazilian Indians.

1689. Fernández, Nelson A. and others. Nutritional status of the Puerto Rican populations: master sample survey (ASCN/J, 24:8, Aug. 1971, p. 952-965, bibl., tables)

Island-wide survey of nutritional status and dietary habits was conducted in Puerto Rico. 877 families were interviewed, and 142 of the families were examined clinically and biochemically. Sample was stratified by socioeconomic status in order to study relationship of rapid economic growth and nutrition. Patterns of food consumption revealed that higher economic standards do not necessarily improve diet's nutritional value. People from remote rural communities were better fed than people from urban slums in regard to several nutrients.

1690. Frisancho, A. Roberto and **Stanley M. Garn.** Skinfold thickness and muscle size: implications for developmental status and nuritional evaluation of children from Honduras (ASCN/J, 24:5, May 1971, p. 541-546, bibl., tables)

Purpose of study is to determine relationship between skin-fold thickness, muscularity, and stature during childhood and adolescence among rural Honduras children. Standard anthropometric measurements taken of 647 age-matched pairs of children aged zero to 20 years indicated that size of musculature was statistically associated with larger stature. No linear relationship was found, however, between fatness and stature. Findings suggest that muscle measurements may be used as general index of nutritional status, whereas skin-fold measures are useful in this regard only at the extremes of leanness or fatness.

1691. ———; ———; and **Lawrence D. McCreery.** Relationship of skinfolds and muscle size to growth of children (AJPA, 35:1, July 1971, p. 85-90)

Study was made of interrelationships of skinfold thickness, muscle size, and stature in a sample of 2,445 Costa Rica rural children aged zero to 20. Direct relationship was discovered between muscle size and stature during childhood and adolescence. However, fatter children were not significantly taller than leaner children of same age groups. These results conflict with a number of clinical studies which indicate that obese children are taller than average children of same age.

1692. Grantham-McGregor, S. M. and **E. H. Back.** Gross motor development in Jamaican infants (Developmental Medicine and Child Neurology [National Spastics Society, London] 13, 1971, p. 79-87, bibl., tables)

Gross motor and language development in first year of life were studied longitudinally for 300 infants from predominantly poor neighborhoods in Kingston. Authors state that 92 percent of the subjects were of Negro background. Based upon 16 items of gross motor behavior, sample showed marked acceleration compared with white children who are normal according to Gesell schedules. Children lighter at birth were significantly slower in attaining several items. Sex and socioeconomic differences were not significant in age of walking, although high weight at 12 months was beneficial.

1693. ———; Sally M. P. Desai; and **E. H. Back.** A longitudinal study of infant growth in Kingston, Jamaica (WSU/HB, 44, 1972, p. 549-562, bibl., tables)

Growth and development of urban Jamaican children during their first year of life by a longitudinal examination of 271 infants. Children were of predominantly Negro parentage and of low socioeconomic background. Although infants exhibited rapid growth in first three months of life, 20 percent were underweight at some time during year. While growth after first three months was depressed in comparison to US and European standards, Kingston infants appeared to grow faster than control group from rural Jamica.

1694. Greene, Lawrence S. Physical growth and development, neurological maturation, and behavioral functioning in two Ecuadorian Andean communities in which goiter is endemic: Pt. 1, Outline of the problem of endemic goiter and cretinism; physical growth and neurological maturation in the adult population of La Esperanza (AJPA, 38:1, Jan. 1973, p. 119-134, bibl., tables)

Enlargement of thyroid gland is hyperendemic in Ecuador's Andean region and is associated with insufficient intake of iodine. In study of normal and deafmute "cretins", latter showed marked retardation in physical growth and visual motor maturation. 17 percent of controls also exhibited signs of deficient visual motor perception. Goiter may be adaptation to a number of environmental stresses, including geographic isolation, low iodine intake, ingestion of naturally occurring goitrogens, and altitude and temperature stress.

Hey, Nigel. How will we feed the hungry billions?: food for tomorrow's world. See item 6550.

1695. Johnston, Francis E. and others. The anthropometric determination of body composition among the Peruvian Cashinahua (AJPA, 34:3, May 1971, p. 409-415, bibl., tables)

Anthropometric measurements of small, isolated Cashinahua tribe indicate that these people are among shortest of South American Indians. Cashinahua possess stocky body builds at all ages and adequate amounts of body fat, suggesting diet with sufficient caloric intake. Thus, Cashinahua are morphologically similar to other Indians of Peruvian rain forest even though they live in a harsh environment.

Martínez, Héctor. Enfermedad y medicina en Pillapi, Bolivia. See item 1437.

1696. Mata, Leonardo J.; J. J. Urrutia; and **A. Lechtig.** Infection and nutrition of children of a low socioeconomic rural community (ASCN/J, 24:2, Feb. 1971, p. 249-259, bibl., tables)

Study investigates magnitude of infection and its effect upon infant and child growth in small rural village in Guatemala. High levels of infectious disease, malnutrition, morbidity, and early mortality characterize population. In their analyses of growth, diet, and disease, authors were able to determine that deficient growth of children begins quite early in life, and that fetus is likely to be adversely affected by mother's nutritional status and internal infections.

1697. May, Jacques Meyer and **Donna L. McLellan.** The ecology of malnutrition in Mexico and Central America: Mexico, Guatemala, British Honduras, Honduras, El Salvador, Nicaragua, Costa Rica and Panama. Preface [by] L. W. Trueblood. N.Y., Hafner, 1972. 395 p., maps, tables (Studies in medical geography, 11)

Presents demographic, economic, and dietary factors associated with nutrition, for Mexico and each country of Central America, along with appraisals of current nutritional status. Authors discuss history and environment of each geographic region, major means of production, types of foods produced, nutritional level, adequacy of food resources, and patterns of nutritional disease in each area.

1698. Mayer Varela, Romanita and others. Hypovitaminosis A in the sugarcane zone of southern Pernambuco State, Northeast Brazil (ASCN/J, 25:8, Aug. 1972, p. 800-804, tables)

Vitamin A deficiency was found to be a potentially serious health problem in the most densely populated area of Northeast Brazil. Malnutrition is endemic in area, and hypovitaminosis is likely to have its most serious effects upon malnourished preschool aged children.

1699. Meredith, Howard V. Worldwide somatic comparisons among contemporary human groups of adult females (AJPA, 34:1, Jan. 1971, p. 89-132)

Presents worldwide anthropometric data for adult females in tabular form. Notes general trends and makes comparisons. Work represents useful synthesis of diverse and scattered information which should be of value in future comparative investigations.

1700. Mönckeberg, Fernando and others. Malnutrition and mental development (ASCN/J, 25:8, Aug. 1972, p. 766-772, tables)

Study attempts to relate mental development to chronic malnutrition in 220 Chilean children aged one to five years from a Santiago slum area. Results suggest lower psycho-motor development in malnourished group when compared to control group of 90 middle-class Chilean children of same age. Use of US standards for growth, and implication of cultural and biological homogeneity of samples, however, detract from study.

1701. Mullor, Jorge B.. Situación demoalimentaria argentina: problemática y solución (Revista de la Facultad de Ingeniería Química [Santa Fe, Arg.] 39, 1970, p. 95-111, bibl., tables)

After critical appraisal of status of nutrition and diet in Argentina, suggests that serious vitamin and mineral deficiencies presently exist due to shortages of meat and wide discrepancy between ideal and actual dietary practices. In order to alleviate situation, proposes a coordinated plan of dietary balancing and increased educational awareness.

1702. Nammacher, Mark A.; Robert B. Bradfield; and **Guillermo Arroyave.** Comparing nutritional status methods in a Guatemalan survey (ASCN/J, 25:9, Sept. 1972, p. 871-874, tables)

Morphological changes in hair roots have been implicated as possible indicators of protein-calorie malnutrition, and authors compare relationships between two hair-root parameters and standard anthropometric and biochemical measures of malnutrition in a sample of 179 preschool children from Guatemalan highlands. Decrease in hair-root diameter was found to be a consistent sign of inadequate protein intake.

Oblitas Poblete, Enrique. Magia, hechicería y medicina popular boliviana. See item 1457.

1703. Padilla, H. and others. Plasma amino acids in children from Guadalajara with Kwashiorkor (ASCN/J, 24:3, March 1971, p. 353-357)

Changes in levels of plasma amino acids have been found in association with protein malnutrition, but results have been inconclusive. Possible relationship of altered amino acid levels and kwashiorkor was studied in sample of 22 children from Guadalajara being treated for the disease and nine well-nourished children. Results from this small sample indicate that amino acids do exhibit changes in concentration in kwashiorkor patients and that there is possible association between family's eating habits and incidence of kwashiorkor in children.

1704. Robson, J. R. K.; M. Bazin; and **R. Soderstrom.** Ethnic differences in skin-fold thickness (ASCN/J, 24:7, July 1971, p. 864-868, bibl., tables)

1,389 healthy and well-nourished Negro children aged between one month and 11 years from Caribbean Island of Dominica were measured and compared with other ethnic groups. Similarity was found in trends, by age, of skin-fold thickness in males and females of European and Dominican origins. No significant difference was discovered in the Dominican sample with regard to sex. Significant differences were found between Dominican and European samples in one of two sites measured, suggesting that additional reference standards should be developed.

Spielman, Richard S. and others. The genetic structure of a tribal population: the Yanomama Indians. See item 1319.

1705. Stini, William A. Reduced sexual dimorphism in upper arm muscle circumference associated with protein-deficient diet in a South American population (AJPA, 36:3, May 1972, p. 341-352, bibl., tables)

Number of studies have indicated that human growth may be temporarily arrested and muscle tissues resorbed as adaptations to nutritional stress. Author here seeks to ascertain if there are sexual differences in this process. In comparison to some other populations, a sample from Colombia exhibited reduced sexual dimorphism in upper arm circumference. This is attributed to relatively greater reduction of measure in male subjects which is related to reduction in total metabolic demand in muscle tissue.

1706. Sweeney, Edward A.; A. J. Saffir; and R. De Leon. Linear hypoplasia of deciduous incisor teeth in malnourished children (ASCN/J, 24:1, Jan. 1971, p. 29-31, bibl., tables)

Linear hypoplasia is characterized by formation of lesions on labial surface of deciduous incisors which may lead to crown destruction. Since condition is found world-wide in under-developed areas and in people of lower socioeconomic statuses, attempt is made in this study to examine possible relationship of disorder to protein-calorie nutrition in a sample of 254 malnourished Guatemalan children. Linear hypoplasia was detected in 73.1 percent of children recovering from third-degree malnutrition, and in 42.9 percent of the children being treated for second degree, or less severe, malnutrition. Results suggest a significant correlation.

1707. Torres de Araúz, Reina. Hábitos dietarios y dieta cuantitiva de los indios chocóes: Panamá (III/AI, 32:1, enero/marzo 1972, p. 169-178)

Diet of Chocó Indians was investigated as part of complete study on human ecology of region. Bananas and rice comprised majority of consumption in grams in both males and females. This diet reflects close dependence upon agriculture among Chocós, as well as utilization of typical resources of fluvial ecosystem of rainforest they inhabit.

HUMAN ADAPTATION

1708. Baker, Paul T. Adaptation problems in Andean human populations (*in* Salzano Francisco M. *ed.* The ongoing evolution of Latin American populations [see item 1765] p. 475-507)

Author cautions that it is not yet clear to what extent morphological and physiological differences of high altitude peoples are due to heredity, ontogenetic factors, or acclimatization. Reviews available evidence of effects of high altitude upon fertility, infant development, growth, menarche, mortality, aging, metabolism, and temperature regulation as well as studies of upward and downward migrants. Many biological characteristics of Andean populations are related to slow body growth, differences in capacity for oxygen consumption, and various hematological adaptations.

1709. ———— and J. S. Dutt. Demographic variables as measures of biological adaptation: a case study of high altitude human populations (*in* Harrison, G. Ainsworth and A. J. Boyce *eds.* The structure of human populations. Oxford, England, Oxford Univ. Press, 1972, p. 352-378)

With goal of elucidating value of demographic variables as possible indicators of level of adaptation in particular environments, authors discuss marked effects of high altitude upon fertility and mortality. Phenotypic differences among high altitude populations may be product of ontogenetic processes, acclimatization differences, or differences in genetic structure of population. Present knowledge of biological and demographic factors of high altitude populations is well summarized.

1710. Cosío Z., Gabriel. Características hemáticas y cardiopulmonares del minero andino (OSP/B, 72:6, junio 1972, p. 547-557, illus., tables)

Direct relationship was discovered between hemoglobin levels and altitude among miners in the Andes. Studies compatibility of hemoglobin values with life and work at various altitudes. Distinguishes three types of altitude sickness and classifies miners into three groups, based upon their aptitude to carry out intensive physical labor.

Goddard, D.; S. N. de Goddard; and P. C. Whitehead. Social factors associated with coca use in the Andean region. See item 1410.

1711. Hanna, J. Michael. Responses of Quechua Indians to coca ingestion during cold exposure (AJPA, 34:2, March 1971, p. 273-278, bibl., tables)

14 male subjects, used as their own controls, exhibited lower finger and toe temperatures during exposure to cold stress after chewing coca leaves. Other areas of body did not show similar modifications. After ingesting coca, subjects also experienced more gradual decline in core temperature which suggests possible mechanism of heat conservation. One might question small sample size and use of artificial cold stimuli.

1712. Little, Michael A. and others. Population differences and developmental changes in extremity temperature responses to cold among Andean Indians (WSU/HB, 43, 1971, p. 70, bibl., tables)

Two Indian groups investigated maintained warmer skin temperatures than corresponding age groups in white samples. No age differences were noted among white subjects, but older Indians were able to maintain their levels better. This age difference is attributed to combination of developmental acclimatization and genetic adaptation.

1713. Milledge, James S. and Soren C. Sorensen. Cerebral arteriovenous oxygen difference in man native to high altitude (Journal of Applied Physiology [Washington] 32, 1972, p. 687-689, bibl., tables)

Relationship between cerebral arterial and venous oxygen was analyzed in eight subjects residing at high altitude in Peruvian Andes. Cerebral blood flow was less than normal for sea-level samples. Subjects showed increased hematocrits and sharp vascular responses to hypoxia even though they had been exposed throughout their lives to hypoxia.

1714. Peñaloza, Dante and Francisco Sime. Chronic *cor pulmonale* due to loss of altitude acclimatization: chronic mountain sickness (American Journal of Medicine [N.Y.] 50:6, June 1971, p. 728-743, plates, tables)

Studies 10 male subjects with chronic mountain sickness in a population 14,200 feet above sea level, and compares results with data from healthy highland residents. Patients exhibited exaggerated conditions which are also seen in healthy residents—pulmonary hypertension, hypertrophy of right ventricle, and muscularization of pulmonary arteries. Rapid reduction in clinical symptoms was seen in patients moved down to sea level. Conditions described are viewed as normal acclimatization mechanisms, however, small sample obviates firm conclusions.

1715. Rennie, Drummond and others. Renal oxygenation in male Peruvian natives living permanently at high altitude (Journal of Applied Physiology [Washington] 30, 1971, p. 450-456, bibl., tables)

Studied renal oxygenation in six adult males residing at high altitude in Peru. Finds that kidneys of these well-acclimatized individuals were normal with respect to excretion, renal blood flow, and oxygen delivery and uptake. Thus, while no deficiency in oxygenation was discovered, the minute sample size would leave any generalizations open to serious criticism.

1716. —— and others. Urinary protein excretion in high altitude residents (Journal of Applied Physiology [Washington] 31, 1971, p. 257-259, bibl., tables)

Studies urinary protein excretion in 43 Peruvian Indians living at high altitudes and compares results to 30 individuals who had been living at low altitude for at least two years. High altitude sample exhibits increased excretion rates, but cause is uncertain.

1717. Rothhammer, Francisco, and **Richard S. Spielman.** Anthropometric variation in the Aumara: genetic, geographic, and topographic contributions (ASHG/J, 24:4, July 1972, p. 371-380, bibl., tables)

Study of relative effects of genetics, geography, and altitude differences in anthropometric variation of Aymara of northern Chile. Finds anthropometric variability markedly different from that exhibited by serological genetic markers. Employing multivariate analysis of contributions of altitude differences, geographic distances, anthropometric distances, and serologic distances, concludes that altitude differences account for major part of anthropometric variability observed among groups.

1718. Sorensen, Soren C. and **James S. Milledge.** Cerebrospinal fluid acid-base composition at high altitude (Journal of Applied Physiology [Washington] 31, 1971, p. 28-30, bibl., tables)

Examines sixteen male Peruvian subjects for possible relationship between pH of cerebrospinal fluid and hyperventilation. Lower pH values were obtained than in samples of sea-level residents or sojourners to high altitudes. Authors suggest that this may aid hyperventilation even when subjects lack hypoxic peripheral chemoreceptor drive.

1719. Zeballos, Jorge; Bertania Galdós; and **Antonio Quintanilla.** Plasma osmolality in subjects acclimatised at high altitude (LANCET, 1:7797, Feb. 1973, p. 230-231, bibl.)

Plasma osmolality was measured in 80 lowland and 243 highland subjects from Peru. Serum osmolality was found to be lowest among individuals from highest altitude locality. Results support theory that physiological adjustments of high altitude acclimatization do not become pronounced until 3,000 meter level is exceeded.

PALEOANTHROPOLOGY AND OSTEOLOGY

Alvim, Marília Carvalho de Mello e and **Giralda Seyferth.** Estudo morfológico do número da população do sambaqui de Cabeçuda, Laguna, Santa Catarina. See item 824.

1720. —— and ——. O femur na população do Sambaqui de Cabeçuda (BRMN/B, [Nova série. Antropologica] 24, 30 abril 1971, p. 1-14, bibl., plates, tables)

Paper analyzes femoral characteristics of prehistoric population of Sambaqui from Brazil, and compares findings to other prehistoric and historical Indian groups. In certain metrical features, described sample is distinct from other groups, but general morphological patterns are not significantly different from other Amerindian populations. Sexual differences of the femora were marked.

1721. Bárcena, J. Roberto. Estudio antropológico físico sobre un esqueleto de Los Sauces, Tunuyán, Mendoza (UNC/AAE, 24/25, 1969/1970, p. 143-180)

Osteological study of precolumbian skeleton discovered in Argentina. Describes general conformation of specimen and determines age and sex. Estimates stature and notes pathological aspects.

1722. Berger, R. and others. New radiocarbon dates based on bone collagen of California paleoindians (UCARF/C, 12, 1971, p. 43-49, bibl., tables)

Authors present new dates for early man in California: Los Angeles, 23,600 before present; Laguna Beach I, 17,150 before present; Laguna Beach II, 14,000 before present. Calculations support hypothesis that man entered New World much earlier than previously estimated.

1723. Campusano, C. and others. Some dental traits of Diaguita Indian skulls (AJPA, 36:1, Jan. 1972, p. 139-142)

Authors conducted study of dental characteristics of 60 skulls of Diaguita Indians from 10th-century Chile. Results, when compared with those of similar investigations, suggested that population was Mongoloid, and this is concordant with supposed Mongoloid origin of present Diaguitas.

1724. Chapman, Florence Hantschke. Vertebral osteophytosis in prehistoric populations of Central and Southern Mexico (AJPA, 36:1, Jan. 1972, p. 31-38)

Examines 138 skeletons representing five Mexican archaeological sites for presence of osteophytosis, bony lipping which projects from bodies of vertebrae. Describes high frequencies of condition for populations, and compares results with some other groups.

1725. Comas, Juan. La supuesta difusión transatlántica de la trepanación prehistórica (UNAM/AA, 9, 1972, p. 157-173, bibl.)

Survey of literature on causes and origins of trephination reveals following trends: 1) trephining has been quite varied in form, 2) it has been widely diffused throughout the world since Mesolithic times, 3) original centers of trephination are now known, 4) it has occurred in both sexes, and 5) there is no correlation (as has been supposed) between brachycephaly and trephination.

Cunha, Ernesto de Mello Salles and **Marília Carvalho de Mello e Alvim.** Contribuição para o conhecimento da morfologia das populações indígenas da Guanabara; notas sôbre a população do sítio arqueológico Cabeça de Indio. See item 832.

1726. Fastlicht, Samuel. La odontología en el México prehispánico. México, Talleres de Edimex, 1971. 124 p., bibl., plates.

Study of dental practices in Mexico during preconquest times. Describes various types of dental mutilation practices, as well as materials and procedures used in dental inlaying. Finally, methods of oral hygiene and dental diseases are discussed.

1727. Hjortsjö, Carl-Herman. Anthropological investigation of an artificially deformed and trepanned cranium from Niño Korin, La Paz, Bolivia (EM/ES, 32, 1972, p. 145-158)

Artificial deformation is hypothesized from metrical analysis of skull of a 25 year old male from 755 A.D. in Bolivia. Presents technical description on deformation and trepanation seen in skull.

1728. Kunter, Kari. Die entwicklung des schädelderfomationsbrauches im westlichen Südamerika (PMK, 17, 1971, p. 32-38, bibl., illus.)

Reviews development of cranial deformation traditions in South America. Presents history of discoveries and distinguishes three basic types of deformation practices. Offers theories concerning rise and decline of practices.

Menezes, Maria José and **Margarida Davina Andreatta.** Os sepultamentos do sambaqui "B" do Guaraguaçu. See item 842.

1729. Post, Peter W. and **Donald D. Donner.** Frostbite in a pre-Columbian mummy (AJPA, 37:2, Sept. 1972, p. 187-191, plates)

Report on a mummy from precolumbian Chile which shows evidence of frostbite and gangrene. Partial loss of digits on both feet suggests autoamputation.

Rohr, João Alfredo. Normas para a cimentação de enterramentos arqueológicos e montagem de blocos-testemunha. See item 525.

1730. Serrano S., Carlos. Una serie de cráneos procedentes de Campeche, México (UNAM/AA, 9, 1972, p. 175-188, bibl., plates, tables)

Describes a series of 14 skulls from Maya region which have been dated as early 19th century. Comparisons are made with other cranial studies on the Maya. Author supports Comas' contention that peoples of Mayan languages are highly variable in their osteological traits.

POPULATION GENETICS AND DEMOGRAPHY

1731. Benoist, Jean. Population structure in the Caribbean area (*in* Salzano, Francisco M. *ed.* The ongoing evolution of Latin American populations [see item 1765] p. 221-249)

Discusses historical, cultural, and demographic factors involved in development of present population structures in Caribbean and broadly treats evolutionary implications of population dynamics. Variation in gene frequencies are related to diversity of original settlers, culture change, family structure, migrations, community networks, differential fertility, isolating mechanisms, and number of other factors. Same variables have effected opportunity for genetic admixture, drift, and natural selection, and author has placed them in a very useful perspective for future biological studies of region.

1732. Boyd, Monica. Occupational mobility and fertility in metropolitan Latin America (PAA/D, 10:1, Feb./April 1973, p. 1-17, bibl., tables)

Examines relationship between career mobility (defined as occupational change by husband within certain time period) and reproductive behavior in five cities of developing Latin American nations: Bogotá; San José; Caracas; México; and Panamá. In four of the five samples career mobility is not a significant factor in differential reproduction as measured in mean number of live births.

1733. Conway, Donna L. and **Paul T. Baker.** Skin reflectance of Quechua Indians: the effects of genetic admixture, sex, and age (AJPA, 36:2, March 1972, p. 267-281, bibl., tables)

Studies relative effects of hybridization, sex, and age in an analysis of skin color among Quechua Indians, residents of Peruvian highlands. Sample drawn from town of Nunoa was slightly lighter than that from rural areas, and this is partly related to higher levels of European admixture in town. Males were found to be generally darker than females, and trend of gradual darkening was seen from early childhood until about 13 years of age, after which a lightening trend is observed through young adulthood. Early darkening may be related to high activity level of pituitary gland during adolescence.

1734. Crispim, J. and others. Third molar agenesis in a trihybrid Brazilian population (AJPA, 37:2, Sept. 1972, p. 289-292, tables)

Missing third molars were discovered in about eight percent per quadrant in a sample of 490 males in a mixed population of whites, Negroes and Indians of Natal, Bra. Total absence of all four third molars appears in two percent of sample. No significant differences were found between individuals classified as white or Negro. Prevalence of agenesis in this mixed population is similar to that reported for some Caucasian groups.

1735. El-Badry, M. A. Latin American population prospects in the next fifteen years (LSE/PS, 25:2, July 1971, p. 183-192, bibl., tables)

Population projections for Latin America are discussed for period 1965-85 by age and sex. Latin

1736. **Freire-Maia, Newton** and **J. B. C. Azevedo.** The inbreeding load in Brazilian whites and Negroes as estimated with sib and cousin controls (ASHG/J, 23:1, Jan. 1971, p. 1-7, bibl., tables)

Studies inbreeding loads in whites, mulattoes, and Negroes in rural and urban populations of southern Brazil. Investigators previously had hypothesized that inbreeding loads were of different magnitude, but a new approach, utilizing sib and cousin controls in analysis of consanguineous marriages and reproductive wastage and early mortality, failed to confirm earlier findings.

1737. **Gershowitz, H.** and others. The genetic structure of a tribal population: the Yanomama Indians: Pt. 2, Eleven blood group systems and the ABH-Le secretor traits (UCGL/AHG, 35:3, March 1972, p. 261-269, bibl., tables)

Presents analysis of 13 antigenic systems of red blood cell and saliva. Materials represent 2,516 individuals from 46 villages. Lists phenotypic and genotypic frequencies for all polymorphic systems. Great differences were found between villages and within single populations. Values were within ranges previously observed in studies of other South American tribes.

1738. **Halberstein, Robert A.** and **Michael H. Crawford.** Human biology in Tlaxcala, Mexico: demography (AJPA, 36:2, March 1972, p. 199-212, bibl., tables)

Large Indian and mestizo communities are compared demographically as part of wider population genetics study. Resulting similarities and differences in observed patterns of population structure and movement, mate selection, differential fertility, and mortality are interpreted in terms of possible action of genetic drift, natural selection, and hybridization in the two populations. High variance in achieved reproduction and severe childhood mortality suggest the operation of natural selection in both localities. Data on mate selection and mobility indicate that mestizo population is highly hybridized, while endogamous Indian community is a rather well-defined gene pool.

1739. **Iutaka, S.; E. W. Bock;** and **W. G. Varnes.** Factors affecting fertility of natives and migrants in urban Brazil (LSE/PS, 25:1, March 1971, p. 55-62, bibl., tables)

Investigates ways in which immigration affects fertility patterns of urban centers. In six Brazilian cities fertility of migrants was found to be higher than that of natives. Only male subjects were examined for most of measures because investigators attempted to relate fertility level and social status as indicated by occupation. As a result, findings are of limited value biologically.

1740. **Johnston, Francis E.** Microevolution of human populations. Englewood Cliffs, N.J., Prentice-Hall, 1973. 160 p., bibl., illus.

Basic, brief, and introductory treatment of evolutionary processes which affect genetic structure of human populations. Author's own research in Peru provides illustrative examples of action of drift, selection, and hybridization. Bibliographic references are sparse and sometimes not correlated with literature cited in text.

1741. ———— and **K. M. Kensinger.** Fertility and mortality differences and their implications for microevolutionary change among the Cashinahua (WSU/HB, 43, 1971, p. 356-364, bibl., tables)

In calculating Crow's index for potential opportunity of natural selection, the mortality component was found to be about six times that of fertility component. Abortions among Cashinahua occur at high rate with sizable variance. Authors postulate greater selection potential in postnatal than in prenatal mortality.

1742. ———— and others. Albumin Mexico (AlMe) in the Guatemalan highlands (AJPA, 38:1, Jan. 1973, p. 27-30, bibl., tables)

Authors report discovery of variant type of serum albumin, Albumin Mexico, among a sample of 386 Guatemalans. This particular polymorphism had previously been known only in more northern locations. Since populations of Guatemala exhibiting Albumin Mexico are located near Mexican border, its presence in Guatemala is probably the result of gene flow.

1743. **Keyfitz, Nathan** and **W. Flieger.** Population: facts and methods of demography. San Francisco, Calif., Freeman, 1971. 613 p.

Up-to-date and comprehensive compilation of demographic data from all parts of the world along with theoretical conclusions and an account of statistical methods of analysis. Includes many of the recent populational characteristics of Latin American countries.

1744. **Krieger, H.; Newton Freire-Maia;** and **J. B. C. Azevedo.** The inbreeding load in Brazilian whites and Negroes: further data and a reanalysis (ASHG/J, 23:1, Jan. 1971, p. 8-16, bibl., tables)

Investigators present additional data on question of differences in inbreeding load in whites and Negroes from rural and urban populations in southern Brazil. Results of a multivariate analysis of over 51,000 pregnancy terminations support most recent findings based on sib and cousin controls which indicate that inbreeding load is nearly same in whites and Negroes of the area.

1745. **Lalouel, Jean M.** and **Newton E. Morton.** Bioassay of kinship in a South American Indian population (ASHG/J, 25:1, Jan. 1973, p. 62-73, tables)

Kinship and hybridity are measured within and among seven villages of the Makiritare Indians of Venezuela. Degree of relationships of gene pools is examined using 11 polymorphic systems. Rapid decline of kinship with geographic distance is observed with tribes. Results reflect recent history of population migration and exchange with other groups, and these factors affect study of phylogeny of tribes.

1746. **Leser, Walter Sidney Pereira.** Relacionamento de certas características populacionais com a mortalidade infantil no município de São Paulo, de 1950a 1970 (Problemas Brasileiros [São Paulo] 10:109, set. 1972, p. 17-33, illus., plates, tables)

Reviews trends in level of infant mortality (death during first year of life) in *município* of São Paulo for period 1950-70. There was gradual decline until 1961, after which rate shows a rise through 1970. Author relates findings to various demographic and ecological characteristics of population such as distribution patterns, changes in natality, disease incidence, and prevalence of nutritional deficiencies.

1747. Lisker, Rubén; Lesvia Cobo; and Guillermina Mora. Distribution of albumin variants in Indians and non-Indians of Mexico (AJPA, 35:1, July 1971, p. 119-124)

Authors were able to find only a single anomalous albumin (Albumin Mexico) in large samples of Indians and Mestizos. Frequency of variant was similar in both groups, and was found to be fairly evenly distributed throughout the samples. High degree of resemblance of Indians and mestizos may indicate close genetic relationship of two groups. There was no evidence that possession of Albumin Mexico is related to susceptibility to disease.

1748. Morton, Newton E. Genetic structure of northeastern Brazilian populations (*in* Salzano, Francisco M. ed. The ongoing evolution of Latin American populations [see item 1765] p. 251-276)

Much of recent data on microevolution and demographic dynamics in northeastern Brazil is summarized and analyzed theoretically. Interprets genetic consequences of inbreeding, gene flow, and population isolation in terms of various mathematical models of evolutionary change. Considerable local endogamy in Brazil is indicated from migration distances, metrical traits, isonymy, and pedigree analysis. This has produced a coefficient of kinship which is intermediate between "primitive" and industrialized populations.

1749. Neel, James V. The genetic structure of a tribal population: the Yanomama Indians; Pt. 1, Introduction (UCGL/AHG, 35:3, March 1972, p. 225-259, bibl., tables)

Neel relates background and history of Yanomama project which began in 1964. Major purpose of work is to achieve fuller understanding of human population structure and genetic differentiation. The tribe and its culture are described, and some of the logistical problems in administration and conduct of field work are discussed. It is pointed out that studies among Yanomama may provide insights into genetic structure of pre-civilized human populations.

1750. Paolucci, A. M. and others. Taste sensitivity to phenylthiocarbomide (PTC) and endemic goiter in the Indian natives of Peruvian highlands (AJPA, 34:3, May/June 1971, p. 427-430, bibl., tables)

In a Peruvian region where goiter is endemic, very low frequencies of the samples were non-tasters of PTC, a chemical to which sensitivity is thought to be genetically controlled. Data agrees with other reports of South American Indians. Authors postulate that risk of developing goiter is either not associated with PTC tasting, or is greater in the taster class in this population.

1751. Pena, Heloisa F.; Francisco M. Salzano; and F. J. Da Rocha. Dermatoglyphics of Brazilian Cayapó Indians (WSU/HB, 44, 1972, p. 225-241, bibl., tables)

Cayapó, Caingang, and Xavante are shown to differ in several dermatoglyphic features, yet they speak languages which are classified in same linguistic group, indicating a possibly recent genetic relationship. Intratribal dermatoglyphic variability of Cayapó is said to agree closely with the demographic information on recent history of populations which has included population splits and patterned mate exchange. Also there appears to be correlations with blood group distributions and geographic factors, although reader is referred to other publications for the data.

1752. Pinto-Cisternas, J. and others. Genetic structure of the population of Valparaíso (HH, 21, 1971, p. 431-439, bibl., tables)

In a sample of 12 to 18-year-olds, genetic differences were found which relate to geographic and ethnic subgroups within city. Some sub-samples were said to exhibit gene frequencies which resemble "Caucasian" populations, while other subgroups were more similar to non-mixed Chilean Indian populations. Analysis of mate selection patterns might have added depth to the findings.

1753. ——— and others. Preliminary migration data on a population of Valparaíso, Chile (Social Biology [N.Y.] 18, 1971, p. 305-310, bibl., tables)

Analyzes immigration distances and mate-selection in city of Valparaíso. Discovers that individuals with fewest Valparaíso-born parents and grandparents possessed higher frequency of group O. Does not discuss possible evolutionary implications of results, but rather states descriptive conclusions, immediately following data's presentation.

1754. Pujol, Nicole. La raza negra en El Chocó: antropología física (ICA/RCA, 15, 1970/1971, p. 256-292, maps, plates)

Colombia's Chocó region is inhabited by 300,000 individuals representing white, Negro, Indian, and mestizo racial groups. Investigation focuses upon demographic, serological, and anthropometric aspects of Negro population. Although study is purely descriptive, data are often not tabulated, but rather general observations are noted.

1755. Rife, David C. Genetic variability among peoples of Aruba and Curaçao (AJPA, 36:1, Jan. 1972, p. 21-30)

Analyses of dermatoglyphics, skin color, and ABO and MN blood groups are conducted from sample of elementary school students. Subjects from one region are found to be significantly different in all three variables. Historical origins and contemporary relationships of population samples are postulated. Concludes, perhaps prematurely, that people of Curaçao are predominantly of Negro origin with some European mixture, and that Noord region of Aruba possesses significant proportion of American Indian ancestry.

1756. Roberts, Derek F. and others. Dermatoglyphics of Caingang and Guaraní Indians (RAI/M, 6, 1971, p. 61-78, bibl., tables)

Compares digital and palmar dermatoglyphics of sample of 116 Caingang and Guaraní Indians from Paraná state, Bra., to other Latin American populations. Both tribes are distinct in dermatoglyphic patterns, and Guaraní exhibit total ridge counts which are among lowest in the world. Caingang data generally agree with other studies of this group.

1757. Rocha, F. J. da and **Francisco M. Salzano.** Anthropometric studies in Brazilian Cayapó Indians (AJPA, 36:1, Jan. 1972, p. 95-102)

Compares anthropometric measurements with other South American groups. Morphological distances among three Cayapó populations are estimated and found to be smaller than those separating different tribes. These results are placed in context of other genetic and demographic data collected on populations. Authors question value of anthropometric studies in understanding of biological variability among populations.

1758. Roisenberg, I. and **Newton E. Morton.** Genetic aspects of hemophilias A and B in Rio Grande do Sul, Brazil (HH, 21:2, 1971, p. 97-107, map, tables)

Frequency of hemophilia was found to be similar in Caucasian and Negro samples. Frequency of ascertained affecteds in one city (Porte Alegre) was slightly higher than other cities studied. Authors suggest that this may be due to natural selection but do not elaborate. Compares incidence of disease and estimated mutation rates with other reports.

1759. Romain, Jean-Baptiste. L'anthropologie physique des haïtiens. Port-au-Prince, Imprimerie Séminaire Adventiste, 1971. 501 p.

Professeur d'anthropologie et doyen de la Faculté d'Ethnologie de l'Univ. d'Haïti, Romain a étudié anthropologiquement la population d'Haïti ens'arrêtant sur ses composantes raciales, sur le milieu physique, culturel, tout en se basant sur des données morphologiques et anthromorphiques selon l'origine géographique des individus c'est-à-dire selon les grandes divisions administratives du pays (sud, ouest. Artibonite, nord, nordouest) et en établissant des comparaisons. Ces travaux ont été conduits selon les méthodes scientifiques en usage, dans un univers de 19,356 sujets en déterminant leurs caractères: indice cormique, céphalique, nasal, facial, Lefrou, intermembral, etc. Un travail d'envergure fait scientifiquement. [M. A. Lubin]

1760. Rothhammer, Francisco and others. Dermatoglyphics in schizophrenic patients (HH, 21, 1971, p. 198-202, tables)

Compares 97 diagnosed schizophrenic patients from a hospital in Santiago to normal control samples with respect to number of dermatoglyphic characteristics. While significant differences were reported in certain measures, investigators conclude that no particular dermatoglyphic features characterize schizophrenia. Authors state that dermatoglyphics cannot be used as diagnostic tool or as a means of determining genetic influence in etiology of the disorder.

1761. ———and others. The genetic structure of a tribal population, the Yanomama Indians: pt. 8, Dermatoglyphic differences among villages (ASHG/J, 25:2, March 1973, p. 152-166, tables)

As part of an ongoing population genetics investigations of Yanomama Indians of Venezuela and Brazil, dermatoglyphic patterns are presented for a sample of 246 and compared to other South American groups. Yanomama are characterized by high intervillage variability in 15 dermatoglyphic traits and show some significant differences from other populations of region.

1762. Salzano, Francisco M. Demographic and genetic interrelationships among the Cayapó Indians of Brazil (Social Biology [N.Y.] 18, 1971, p. 148-157, bibl., tables)

Cayapó, hunters and gatherers with incipient agriculture, number some 1,500 in eight groups. "Fission-fusion" model of population structure is seen to apply to Cayapó through an analysis of historical information on population splintering. Low rates of fertility and morality, and relatively low fertility variance contribute to low index of opportunity of natural selection, one of lowest in South America.

1763. ———. Genetic aspects of the demography of American Indians and Eskimos (*in* Harrison, G. A. and A. J. Boyce. The structure of human populations. Oxford, England, Oxford Univ. Press, 1972, p. 234-251)

Analyzes archaeological, historical, and demographic data for large number of New World aboriginal populations. Comparisons are made among hunting-and-gathering, agriculture, and fishing populations. Demographic trends and observations are related to possible action of natural selection and other evolutionary forces. Briefly summarizes much literature dealing with genetic variability of New World populations.

1764. ———. Visual acuity and color blindness among Brazilian Cayapó Indians (HH, 22:1, 1972, p. 72-79, tables)

In two tribes of hunters-and-gatherers, only one color blind male was discovered in sample of 269 males and females. Visual acuity was found to be quite high throughout sample. These results lend support to number of studies which indicate that color blindness is rare and visual acuity is strong among hunters-and-gatherers possibly because of natural selection—that is, sharp vision may be an important adaptation in a hunting population.

1765. ———*ed.* The ongoing evolution of Latin American populations. Springfield, Ill., Thomas, 1971. 717 p., maps.

In this collection of original papers, current research is reported by major authorities on ethnohistory, demography and population structure, growth and nutrition, physiological adaptation, disease patterns, and genetic polymorphisms for a broad range of Latin American populations. Presentation of previously unpublished data make this an excellent sourcebook and reference text for those interested in microevolution in New World.

1766. ———; **A. G. Steinberg**; and **Mary A. Tepfenhart.** Gm and Inv allotypes of Brazilian Cayapó Indians (ASHG/J, 25:2, March 1973, p. 167-177, tables)

Analyzes Gm and Inv polymorphisms as part of wider study of genetic variability of Cayapó Indians of Brazil. Reports data from 440 individuals from four different populations and results are generally in accordance with those previously obtained in other South American Indian groups.

1767. ———; **James V. Neel; Lowell R. Weitkamp**; and **J. P. Woodall.** Serum proteins, hemoglobins, and erythrocyte enzymes of Brazilian Cayapó Indians (WSU/HB, 44, 1972, p. 443-458, bibl., tables)

Reports data on 15 genetic systems from a serological study of Cayapó Indians. Discusses presence or absence of polymorphisms, and their genetic implications. Pair-wise genetic distances did not yield clear separation of a Cayapó subgroup from the other, and did not indicate any special pattern of relationship among four populations studied.

Somoza, Jorge L. La mortalidad en la Argentina entre 1869 y 1960. See *HLAS 34:2805a.*

1768. Spielman, Richard S. and others. The genetic structure of a tribal population, the Yanomama Indians; pt. 7, Anthropometric differences among Yanomama villages (AJPA, 37:3, Nov. 1972, p. 345-356, bibl., tables)

Investigates genetic distance among Yanomama through anthropometric evidence and compares results with geographic distances of 19 villages. Generalized distance measure of Mahalanobis was employed, and general correspondence between anthropometric and geographic distance was discovered. Significant anthropometric variability was found both within and across groups studied. Yanomama are generally shorter in stature than most other South American tribes, and have already been shown to be genetically distinct.

1769. Spuhler, James N. Genetic, linguistic, and geographical distances in native North America (*in* Weiner, J. S. and J. Huizinga *eds.* The assessment of population affinities in man. Oxford, England, Clarendon Press, 1972, p. 72-95)

Compares genetic, linguistic and geographical distances for 21 American Indian populations from Mexico, Alaska, Canada and US. Although a significant positive correlation of 0.46 was found between geographical and genetic distances, no significant relationship could be established between genetic distance and glottochronological age.

1770. Ward, Richard H. The genetic structure of a tribal population: the Yanomama Indians; pt. 5, Comparison of a series of genetic networks (UCGL/AHG, 36:1, July 1972, p. 21-43, bibl., tables)

Genetic distances and microevolutionary networks are presented for historical and recent Yanomama populations. Pair-wise genetic distances were calculated, utilizing 23 independent genetic systems based upon a sample of 2,516 subjects from 46 villages. The genetic relationships between villages are discussed. The author has employed the Cavalli-Sforza and Edwards methods of determining genetic relationships.

1771. Weitkamp, Lowell R. and J. V. Neel. The genetic structure of a tribal population: the Yanomama Indians; pt. 4, Eleven erythrocyte enzymes and summary of protein variants (UCGL/AHG, 35:4, April 1972, p. 433-444, bibl., tables)

11 enzyme systems representing 12 genetic loci are studied electrophoretically for Yanomama Indians from 37 villages and are compared with previous reports. With respect to 16 protein systems so far studied, the Yanomama are the least heterozygous of any group which has been described.

1772. ——— and others. The genetic structure of a tribal population: the Yanomama Indians; pt. 3, Seven serum protein systems (UCGL/AHG, 35:3, March 1972, p. 271-279, bibl., tables)

Results of study of seven protein systems are reported, representing 37 Yanomama villages. Findings confirm earlier work by same authors on polymorphic and non-polymorphic traits. Presence and absence of unusual variants are mentioned. Marked inter-village microdifferentiation was discovered.

1773. Zavala, C.; A. Cobo; and **Rubén Lisker.** Dermatoglyphic patterns in Mexican Indian groups (HH, 21:4, 1971, p. 394-401, tables)

Compares dermatoglyphic data from eight Mexican Indian groups with other reported materials and finds few systematic patterns or relationships. Results indicate that dermatoglyphics seem to be more variable among Mexican Indians than many other genetic traits. Investigators question efficiency of dermatoglyphics as genetic markers in characterizing human populations.

JOURNAL ABBREVIATIONS

AAA/AA	American Anthropologist. American Anthropological Association. Washington.
AAAS/S	Science. American Association for the Advancement of Science.
AAC/AJ	Anthropological Journal of Canada. Anthropological Association of Canada. Quebec, Canada.
AAHS/K	The Kiva. Journal of the Arizona Archaeological and Historical Society. Tucson, Ariz.
ABS	The American Behavioral Scientist. N.Y.
AFS/JAF	Journal of American Folklore. American Folklore Society. Austin, Tex.
AGS/GR	The Geographical Review. American Geographical Society. N.Y.
AI/A	Anthropos. International review of ethnology and linguistics. Anthropos-Institut. Posieux, Switzerland.
AIA/A	Archaeology. Archaeological Institute of America. N.Y.
AJPA	American Journal of Physical Anthropology. American Association of

	Physical Anthropologists [and] The Wistar Institute of Anatomy and Biology. Philadelphia, Pa.
AMNH/NH	Natural History. American Museum of Natural History. N.Y.
ANC/B	Boletín de la Academia Nacional de Ciencias. Córdoba, Arg.
APS/P	Proceedings of the American Philosophical Society. Philadelphia, Pa.
ARCHEO	Archeologia. L'archeologie dans le monde et tout ce qui concerne les recherches historiques, artistiques et scientifiques sur terre et dans les mers. Paris.
ARMEX	Artes de México. México.
ASCN/J	American Journal of Clinical Nutrition. American Society for Clinical Nutrition. N.Y.
ASH/AE	Acta Ethnographica. Academiae Scientiarum Hungaricae. Budapest.
ASHG/J	American Journal of Human Genetics. The American Society of Human Genetics. Baltimore, Md.
ASTMH/J	American Journal of Tropical Medicine and Hygiene. American Society of Tropical Medicine and Hygiene. Baltimore, Md.
AVAC/ACV	Acta Científica Venezolana. Asociación Venezolana para el Avance de la Ciencia. Caracas.
BBAA	Boletín Bibliográfico de Antropología Americana. Instituto Panamericano de Geografía e Historia, Comisión de Historia. México.
BJS	British Journal of Sociology. *For the* London School of Economics and Political Science. London.
BMHS/J	Journal of the Barbados Museum and Historical Society. Barbados, W.I.
BNJM/R	Revista de la Biblioteca Nacional José Martí. La Habana.
BRMN/B	Boletim do Museu Nacional. Univ. do Brasil, Oficina Gráfica. Rio.
CAS/PD	Pacific Discovery. California Academy of Sciences. San Francisco, Calif.
CCE/CHA	Cuadernos de Historia y Arqueología. Casa de la Cultura Ecuatoriana, Núcleo del Guayas. Guayaquil, Ecua.
CCE/RA	Revista de Antropología. Casa de la Cultura Ecuatoriana, Núcleo del Azuay. Cuenca, Euca.
CEA/CA	Cuadernos de Antropología. Univ. de San Marcos, Centro de Estudiantes de Antropología. Lima.
CEM/ECM	Estudios de Cultura Maya. Univ. Nacional Autónoma de México, Centro de Estudios Mayas. México.
CER/BEO	Boletín de Estudios Oaxaqueños. Centro de Estudios Regionales. Oaxaca, Mex.
CH	Cuadernos Hispanoamericanos. Madrid.
CIAAP/RS	Revista del Ateneo Paraguayo: Suplemento Antropológico. Ateneo Paraguayo, Centro de Investigaciones Antropológicas. Asunción.
CIF/FA	Folklore Americano. Organización de los Estados Americanos, Instituto Panamericano de Geografía e Historia, Comisión de Historia, Comité Interamericano de Folklore. Lima.
CLA/J	CLA Journal. Morgan State College, College Language Association. Baltimore, Md.
CSSH	Comparative Studies in Society and History. Society for the Comparative Study of Society and History. The Hague.
CT/T	Tlalocan. Revista de fuentes para el conocimiento de las culturas indígenas de México. La Casa de Tlaloc *con la colaboración del* Instituto Nacional de Antropología. México.
CU/EG	Economic Geography. Clark Univ. Worcester, Mass.
CUA/AQ	Anthropological Quarterly. Catholic Univ. of America, Catholic Anthropological Conference. Washington.
DEF/F	Folk. Dansk Etnografisk Forening. København.
DGV/ZE	Zeitschrift für Ethnologie. Deutschen Gesellschaft für Völkerkunde. Braunschweig, FRG.
EANH/B	Boletín de la Academia Nacional de Historia. Quito.
EAZ	Ethnographisch-Archäologische Zeitschrift. Deutscher Verlag Wissenschaften. Berlin, GDR.
EM/A	Arstryck. Etnografiska Museet. Göteborg, Sweden.
EM/ES	Etnologiska Studier. Etnografiska Museet. Göteborg, Sweden.

EMGE/BH	Boletín Histórico del Estado Mayor General del Ejército. Sección Historia y Archivo. Montevideo.
EPHE/H	L'Homme. Revue française d'anthropologie. l'École Pratique des Hautes Études, La Sorbonne. Paris.
FDD/NED	Notes et Etudes Documentaires. Direction de la Documentation. Paris.
GIIN/GI	Guatemala Indígena. Instituto Indigenista Nacional. Guatemala.
HH	Human Heredity. Basel, Switzerland.
HMAI	Handbook of Middle American Indians. Univ. of Texas Press. Austin, Tex.
IAH/A	Anuario. Univ. Central de Venezuela, Instituto de Antropología e Historia. Caracas.
IAP/P	Pesquisas. Instituto Anchietano de Pesquisas. Pôrto Alegre, Bra.
IAS/ÑP	Ñawpa Pacha. Institute of Andean Studies. Berkeley, Calif.
IBEAS/EA	Estudios Andinos. Instituto Boliviano de Estudio y Acción Social. La Paz.
ICA/RCA	Revista Colombiana de Antropología. Ministerio de Educación Nacional, Instituto Colombiano de Antropología. Bogotá.
ICACH	Icach. Instituto de Ciencias y Artes de Chiapas. Tuxtla Gutiérrez, Mex.
ICUAER/B	Bulletin of the International Committee on Urgent Anthropological and Ethnological Research. Wien.
IGM/U	L'Universo. Rivista bimestrale dell'Istituto Geografico Militare. Firenze, Italy.
IIE/A	Anales del Instituto de Investigaciones Estéticas. Univ. Nacional Autónoma de México. México.
III/AI	América Indígena. Instituto Indigenista Interamericano. México.
IJSP	International Journal of Social Psychiatry. London.
INAH/A	Anales del Instituto Nacional de Antropología e Historia. Secretaría de Educación Pública. México.
INAH/B	Boletín del Instituto Nacional de Antropología e Historia. Secretaría de Educación Pública. México.
IOC/M	Memórias do Instituto Oswaldo Cruz. Rio.
IPA/AP	Allpanchis Phuturinqa. Univ. de San Antonio de Abad, Seminario de Antropología, Instituto de Pastoral Andina. Cuzco, Peru.
IRR/R	Race. Institute of Race Relations. London.
ISDA/IJA	The International Journal of the Addictions. The Institute for the Study of Drug Addiction. N.Y.
IU/AL	Anthropological Linguistics. Archives of the Languages of the World. Indiana Univ., Dept. of Anthropology. Bloomington, Ind.
IU/IJAL	International Journal of American Linguistics. Indiana Univ. *under the auspices of* Linguistic Society of America, American Anthropological Association, *with the cooperation of* Joint Committee on American Native Languages. Baltimore, Md.
JDA	The Journal of Developing Areas. Western Illinois Univ. Press. Macomb, Ill.
KITLV/B	Bijdragen tot de Taal-, Land- en Volkenkunde. Koninklijk Instituut voor Tall-, Land- en Volkenkunde. Leiden, The Netherlands.
LANCET	Lancet. London.
LARR	Latin American Research Review. Latin American Studies Association. Univ. of Texas Press. Austin, Tex.
LING	Linguistics. An international review. Mouton. The Hague.
LINGUA	Lingua. North-Holland Publishing Co. Amsterdam.
LSA/L	Language. Journal of the Linguistic Society of America. Baltimore, Md.
LSE/PS	Population Studies. A journal of demography. London School of Economics, The Population Investigation Committee. London.
MEMDA/E	Etnia. Museo Etnográfico Municipal Dámaso Arce. Muncipalidad de Olavarría. B.A.
MH/OM	Objets et Mondes. Revue trimestrielle. Musée de l'Homme. Paris.
MHNM/CA	Comunicaciones Antropológicas del Museo de Historia Natural de Montevideo. Montevideo.

MLV/T	Tribus. Veröffentlichungen des Linden-Museums. Museum für Länder-und Völkerkunde. Stuttgart, FRG.
MMFQ	Milbank Memorial Fund Quarterly. N.Y.
MP/R	Revista do Museu Paulista. São Paulo.
MPEG/B	Boletim do Museu Paraense Emílio Goeldi. Conselho Nacional de Pesquisas, Instituto Nacional de Pesquisas da Amazônia. Belém, Bra.
MV/BA	Baessler-Archiv. Beiträge zur Völkerkunde. Museums für Völkerkunde. Berlin.
MVW/AV	Archiv für Völkerkunde. Museum für Völkerkunde in Wien und von Verein Freunde der Völkerkunde. Wien.
NWIG	Nieuwe West-Indische Gids. Martinus Nijhoff. The Hague.
NYAS/A	Annals of the New York Academy of Sciences. N.Y.
OAS/AM	Américas. Oranization of American States. Washington.
OSP/B	**Boletín de la Oficina Sanitaria Panamericana. Washington.**
PAA/D	Demography. Population Association of America. Chicago, Ill.
PEMN/R	Revista del Museo Nacional. Casa de la Cultura del Perú, Museo Nacional de la Cultura Peruana. Lima.
PIIA/A	Arqueológicas. Instituto de Investigaciones Antropológicas. Museo Nacional de Antropología y Arqueología. Lima.
PMK	Paideuma. Mitteilungen zur Kulturkunde. Deutsche Gesellschaft für kulturmorphologie von Frobenius Institut au der Johann Wolfgang Goethe - Universität. Wiesbaden, FRG.
PP/B	Boletim. Faculdade de Filosofia, Ciências e Letras de Presidente Prudente, Depto. de Ciências Sociais. Presidente Prudente, Bra.
PRAN	Practical Anthropology. Tarrytown, N.Y.
PUCP/BSA	Boletín del Seminario de Arqueología. Pontificia Univ. Católica del Perú. Lima.
RAI/M	Man. The Royal Anthropological Institute. London.
SA/J	Journal de la Société des Américanistes. Paris.
SAA/AA	American Antiquity. The Society for American Archaeology. Menasha, Wis.
SAA/HO	Human Organization. Society for Applied Anthropology. N.Y.
SCA/A	Anales de la Sociedad Científica Argentina. La Plata, Arg.
SCNLS/A	Antropológica. Sociedad de Ciencias Naturales La Salle. Caracas.
SEM/E	Ethnos. Statens Etnografiska Museum. Stockholm.
SJUG	Saeculum. Jahrbuch für Universalgeschichte. München, FRG.
SLN/ALN	Archivos Latinoamericanos de Nutrición. Sociedad Latinoamericana de Nutrición. Caracas.
SM/M	The Masterkey. Southwest Museum. Los Angeles, Calif.
SRA/A	Anales de la Sociedad Rural Argentina. Revista pastoril y agrícola. B.A.
SS	Science and Society. An independent journal of marxism. N.Y.
SSA/B	Bulletin. Société Suisse des Américanistes. Geneva.
SSC/K	Katunob. Southern State College. Magnolia, Ark.
TILAS	Bulletin de la Faculté des Lettres de Strasbourg (TILAS [Travaux de l'Institut d'Etudes Latino-Américaines de l'Université de Strasbourg] subseries). Univ. de Strasbourg. Strasbourg, France.
TU/CCM	Cerámica de Cultura Maya et al. Temple Univ., Dept. of Anthropology. Philadelphia, Pa.
UASD/R	Revista Dominicana de Arqueología y Antropología. Univ. Autónoma de Santo Domingo, Facultad de Humanidades, Depto. de Historia y Antropología, Instituto de Investigaciónes Antropológicas. Santo Domingo.
UC/A	Anales de la Universidad de Cuenca. Cuenca, Ecua.
UC/B	Boletín de la Universidad de Chile. Santiago.
UC/BPC	Boletín de Prehistoria de Chile. Univ. de Chile, Facultad de Filosofía y Educación, Depto. de Historia. Santiago.
UC/CA	Current Anthropology. Univ. of Chicago. Chicago, Ill.
UCARF/C	Contributions of the University of California Archaeological Research Facility. Berkeley, Calif.

UCGL/AHG	Annals of Human Genetics (Annals of Eugenics). Univ. College, Galton Laboratory. London.
UCNSA/SA	El Suplemento Antropológico. Univ. Católica de Nuestra Señora de la Asunción, Centro de Estudios Antropológicos. Asunción.
UCV/ECS	Economía y Ciencias Sociales. Univ. Central de Venezuela, Facultad de Economía. Caracas.
UM/REAA	Revista Española de Antropología Americana [Trabajos y Conferencias]. Univ. de Madrid, Facultad de Filosofía y Letras, Depto. de Antropología y Etnología de América. Madrid.
UMUP/E	Expedition. Bulletin of the University Museum of the Univ. of Pennsylvania. Philadelphia, Pa.
UNAM/AA	Anales de Antropología. Univ. Nacional Autónoma de México, Instituto de Investigaciones Históricas. México.
UNAM/ECN	Estudios de Cultura Náhuatl. Univ. Nacional Autónoma de México, Instituto de Historia, Seminario de Cultura Náhuatl. México.
UNC/AAE	Anales de Arqueología y Etnología. Univ. Nacional de Cuyo, Facultad de Filosofía y Letras. Mendoza, Arg.
UNC/R	Revista de la Universidad Nacional de Córdoba. Córdoba, Arg.
UNCIA/HC	Hombre y Cultura. Univ. Nacional, Centro de Investigaciones Antropológicas. Panamá.
UNLPM/R	Revista del Museo de La Plata. Univ. Nacional de La Plata, Facultad de Ciencias Naturales y Museo. La Plata, Arg.
UNM/SWJA	Southwestern Journal of Anthropology. Univ. of New Mexico and the Laboratory of Anthropology, Santa Fe. Albuquerque, N. Mex.
UNT/H	Humanitas. Univ. Nacional de Tucumán, Facultad de Filosofía y Letras. Tucumán, Arg.
UP/E	Ethnology. Univ. of Pittsburgh. Pittsburgh, Pa.
UPR/CS	Caribbean Studies. Univ. of Puerto Rico, Institute of Caribbean Studies. Río Piedras, P.R.
UPR/RCS	Revista de Ciencias Sociales. Univ. de Puerto Rico, Colegio de Ciencias Sociales. Río Piedras, P.R.
USP/RIEB	Revista do Instituto de Estudos Brasileiros. Univ. de São Paulo, Instituto de Estudos Brasileiros. São Paulo.
USPMAA/D	Dédalo. Revista de arte e arqueologia. Univ. de São Paulo, Museu de Arte e Arqueologia. São Paulo.
UWI/CQ	Caribbean Quarterly. Univ. of the West Indies. Mona, Jam.
UWI/SES	Social and Economic Studies. Univ. of the West Indies, Institute of Social and Economic Research. Mona, Jam.
WSU/HB	Human Biology. A record of research. Wayne State Univ. Press. Detroit, Mich.

Economics

GENERAL

JOHN M. HUNTER

Director
Latin American Studies Center
Michigan State University

FROM THE STEADILY INCREASING FLOW OF MATERIALS on Latin America, some demand recognition either for their quality or topic. One would not want to miss Prebisch's *Change and development* (item 1865), for example. The financial institutions continue the two decade-ending introspection which figured so large in the last biennium: Sidney Dell (item 1798) examines the IDB, and it takes a look at itself (item 1827). White (item 1899) compares it with other regional development banks. The World Bank (item 1832) juxtaposes sectoral papers and performance. Other institutional pieces merit particular mention: the OAS (item 1857-1858) on unemployment and on external financing and ECLA (item 1852) on the mobilization of internal resources. Three individual and team efforts, too, warrant specific attention: Balassa and others on the structure of protection (item 1782), Grunwald and others on Latin American integration and U.S. policy (item 1821) and Armando Samper on agriculture and integration (item 1872).

One of the major developments in the literature is the increasing appearance of empirical research on topics previously treated deductively, speculatively, or not at all. New methodologies are being developed and old ones are being applied to Latin America. The significance of these very solid empirical efforts cannot be overstated. Among the more important of these efforts are: Furtado and Maneschi with a stagnation model (item 1809), Domínguez with a six percent growth model (item 1800), Germidis on tied loans (item 1813), Carnoy on industrialization (item 1791), Cline on income redistribution (item 1794), Bell on tariff profiles (item 1787), Wionczek on cost-benefits of foreign investment (item 1900), and Harberger on aid expectations (item 1824). There are others; this recounting is clearly representative rather than exclusive.

The other major development in the literature is the great attention paid, in one guise or another, to "imperialism" and/or "dependence" including the multinational corporation. This runs the gamut from careless polemic to careful analysis. Much of it is only peripherally economics. Particularly worth noting are the following: Furtado (surely the most quoted) on the concentration of power in the U.S. (item 1808), García who deals particularly with the agricultural sector (item 1810), Sunkel in two long pieces (items 1881 and 1883), Aníbal Pinto with a model which devotes particular attention to the foreign sector (item 1861), Suárez with analysis à-la-Perroux (item 1880), and Gunder Frank's historical analysis (item 1804).

Finally there are a few pieces which do not well fit the categories above but which I want to mention specifically. Barraclough on rural development and employment prospects (item 1785), I found particularly insightful. The volume by Charles R. Frank, Jr. and others (item 1806) attacks four development assistance problems head-on and ought not be overlooked. ECLA's study of energy (item 1802) will surely be much used in the decade ahead with its particular attention to petroleum and electrical energy. There is much to ponder in the volume reporting a joint seminar between Europeans and Latin Americans seeking from the European experience applicability to Latin America (item 1884).

1774. Acuerdos básicos para el comercio en el Grupo Andino. La Paz, Cámara Nacional de Comercio, 1971. 129 p.

Simple reproduction of agreements and resolutions taken at the Third Period of Extraordinary Sessions of the Commission of the Andean Common Market, Dec. 1970. No particular value to foreign scholars, since same materials are more readily available from the Secretariat in Lima, or the *Boletín* of INTAL. [B. Herrick]

1775. Aftalión, Enrique R. Monopolios y sociedades multinacionales. B.A., Sociedad Anónima Editora, 1970. 113 p.

Explores juridical basis of monopoly and multination corporation and their roles in economic integration as well as what may be done to prevent abuses.

1776. Agostino, Vittorio. Integración económica: el Mercado Andino. Lima, Univ. de Lima, 1970. 119 p., bibl., tables.

Booklet reproduces series of author's lectures intended to help university economics students make the transition from the formal study of trade theory to the study of contemporary trade problems and especially the possibilities and problems opened by the Andean Common Market. Skillful summary of foreign literature, including ECLA publications and Belassa's "Theory of Economic Integration." No new data; numerous recommendations as to policies to be followed by member countries if the Andean Common Market is to succeed. [J. Strasma]

1777. Aleixo, José Carlos Brandi. A integração latinoamericana: considerações políticas e históricas sôbre suas bases, processo e significado. Brasília, Coordenana-Editôra de Brasília, 1970. 127 p., bibl.

Essentially historical in approach and literary in form, this essay (a third of the volume is bibliography and collected documents) argues and pleads for increased Latin American integration.

1778. Almeida, Miguel Álvaro Ozório de. O mundo subdesenvolvido persante as sociedades pós-industriais (UMG/RBEP, 32, julho 1971, p. 83-103, table)

General treatment of characteristics of more and less developed nations with special attention to the requirements of larger less developed nations, Brazil in particular.

1779. Andic, Fuat M. and Suphan Andic. El pensamiento latinoamericano de postguerra acerca del papel del sector público (UPR/RCS, 16:1, marzo 1972, p. 123-140, bibl.)

Dispassionate, well-reasoned analysis of *cepalismo* (structuralism), its policy prescriptions, and impact.

1780. Arciniega, Antonio and José Sardón. La crisis mundial del petróleo (ARBOR, 78:303, marzo 1971, p. 43-56)

Straightforward statement of main historical events leading to Teheran agreement of 1971 between producing companies and producer (Third World) countries with respect to pricing. Suggests this could well be considered a model for other products.

Ashcraft, Norman. Developmental economics: some critical remarks. See item 501a.

1781. Avery, William P. and James D. Cochrane. El Mercado Común Andino: un enfoque subregional de la integración (CM/FI, 12:3, enero/marzo 1972, p. 357-372)

Description of provisions of the Andean group agreements comparing them with LAFTA provisions.

1781a. Báez, Mauricio. La productividad por agricultor en los países americanos. Caracas, Ministerio de Agricultura y Cría, 1971? 149 p.

Elementary statistical relationships by country, crop, and other variables. Brings to bear substantial number of data. Special attention devoted to product per operator.

1782. Balassa, Bela and others. Estructura de la protección en países en desarrollo. México, Centro de Estudios Monetarios Latinoamericanos, 1972. 502 p.

Published 1971 by the IBRD and IDB. Brazil, Chile, and Mexico are among seven countries studied. Pt. 1 lays out methodological considerations, and Pt. 2 is the country studies. Fundamental work on this topic. Includes appendices.

1783. Balestrini C., César. La industria petrolera en América Latina. Prológo [por] D. F. Maza Zavala. Caracas, Univ. Central de Venezuela, Ediciones de la Biblioteca, 1971. 311 p., bibl., maps, tables (Col. Ciencias económicas, 1)

Rather superficial treatment most of which describes the industry in each country. Concludes with very brief section about the future.

1784. Barraclough, Solon L. Estrategia de desarrollo rural y reforma agraria (Desarrollo Rural en las Americas [Bogotá] 4:1, enero/ abril 1972, p. 59-79)

Reviews agrarian reform progress for decade and finds

goals not met. Profound changes are required, and they will not occur until vested interests share their power and privileges. Critiques several alternative strategies.

1785. ———. Rural development and employment prospects in Latin America (*in* Field, Arthur J. *ed.* City and country in the Third World: issues in the modernization of Latin America. Cambridge, Mass., Schenkman Publishing Co., 1970, p. 97-135, bibl.)

Twin problems of rural poverty and underemployment are apt to grow more serious in most of Latin America; and the situation has *not* been improving. Dual sector economic models are severely criticized as having little relevance to Latin America. Strategy has to take into account that two generations are probably required to modernize agriculture and to improve agricultural incomes greatly. Alternative strategies for poor, less poor, and industrial countries are explored.

1786. Beckford, George. The dynamics of growth and the nature of Metropolitan Plantation Enterprise (ISER/SES, 19:4, Dec. 1970, p. 435-465)

Historical evolution of trading companies into shipping and then production of tropical commodities. Well-written analysis of internal dynamics that bring about what is sometimes regarded as "imperialism" by countries where such firms have their home offices. A wealth of illustrations, for British firms, makes it clear where, and with what problems, tropical countries may wish to try to seek changes in their relations with such firms. [J. Strasma]

1787. Bell, Harry H. Tariff profiles in Latin America: implications for pricing structures and economic integration. N.Y., Praeger, 1971. 168 p., tables (Praeger special studies in international economics and development)

Solid study of use of tariffs in Latin America. First, a discussion of methodology for measuring tariffs and quasi-tariffs. These levels are then examined with respect to allocation efficiency and corporation advantage, import substitution, integration and location.

1788. Bradbury, Robert W. Economic integration in Latin America: a reappraisal (Annals [Southeastern Conference on Latin American Studies, SECOLAS, Univ. of Georgia, Athens] 3:1, March 1972, p. 60-69)

Paper presented at the 18th Annual SECOLAS Conference held at the Univ. of Georgia, Athens, 15-17 April 1971. It is more of a summary than a reappraisal, a convenient, lucid account of major events and problems of regional and subregional integration.

1789. Brodovich, Boris Nikolaevich *ed.* Eknonomika Latinskoi Ameriki v Tsifrakh: statisticheskii spravochnik (The economy of Latin America in numbers: a statistical handbook) Moskva, Nauka, 1965. 325 p., bibl., tables.

Statistical handbook on Latin American economies covering from the late 1940's to 1962-63. Accurate reproduction of materials drawn from UN, US and Latin American government sources. Preface gives Soviet view of Latin America's economic relationship to the US. [T. S. Cheston]

1790. Calello, Hugo. El modelo marxista en el análisis comparativo de la dependencia: primera parte (UCV/ECS [2 época] 12:1, enero-marzo 1970, p. 43-57)

Interesting but hardly definitive treatment of theme. Part of larger work, probably better read in context.

1791. Carnoy, Martin. Industrialization in a Latin American common market. Foreword [by] Kermit Gordon. Preface [by] Joseph Grunwald. Washington, The Brookings Institution, 1972. 267 p., tables (ECIEL study)

Results of an imaginative, collaborative research effort. Attempts to seek optimal locations for production of six basic commodities within ALALC countries: nitrogenous fertilizers, methanol and formaldehyde, tractors, lathes, powdered milk and cheese, paper and pulp. Separate stages involve demand, cost, and transportation estimates. Carefully done with methodology clearly laid out.

1792. ———. A welfare analysis of Latin American economic union: six industry studies; pt. 1 (JPE, 78:4, July/Aug. 1970, p. 626-654, tables)

Pioneer methodological effort to estimate effects of intra-LAFTA purchases of six industrial product groups: methanol and formaldehyde, nitrogenous fertilizers, tractors, lathes, paper and pulp, powdered milk and cheese. Various alternative assumptions are treated.

Cermakian, Jean. A geografia da ajuda estrangeira à América Latina: problemas de fontes e de método. See item 6522.

1793. Clark, Colin. Requerimientos de bienes de capital de los países en desarrollo. Prólogo por Francisco Carrillo Batalla. Presentación por Ernesto Peltzer. Caracas, Continental de Créditos Mercantiles (CREMERCA), 1971. 79 p., plates, tables.

Memorial lecture with some interesting data on capital/output ratios, housing needs, costs, etc. Includes English version.

1794. Cline, William R. Potential effects of income redistribution on economic growth: Latin American cases. N.Y., Praeger Publishers, 1972. 242 p., bibl., tables (Praeger special studies in international economics and development)

A major work for two reasons: 1) brings together most of what is known about income distribution in Latin America (six countries) and critiques available studies; and 2) examines hypotheses concerning effects of income redistribution on growth both theoretically and empirically. Findings do not support view that increased equity through greater income equality would be a serious deterrent to growth.

1795. Cole, William E. and **Richard Sanders.** A modified dualism model for Latin American economies (JDA, 6:2, Jan. 1972, p. 185-199)

Extending the usual two sector dualism to four (agricultural and urban, both modern and traditional) this study explains why respectable growth rates leave (and will leave) many no better off and why standard policies to increase modern manufacturing will provide little "trickle down."

1796. Córdova, Federico de. El Grupo Andino: mercado subregional del Pacífico (IPI/PI, 7:26, 2. semestre 1969, p. 13-40, table)

Chronology of development of the Grupo Andino including author's view of US imperialistic participation in the countries and the agreement.

1797. Cornblit, Oscar. Factors affecting scientific productivity: the Latin American cases (UN/ISSJ, 22:2, 1970, p. 243-263)

Interesting exploration of characteristics, problems, and prospects of social science research in Latin America. In spite of all difficulties, sees national universities as core of research agencies. Level of frankness is particularly appreciated.

Dagum, Camilo. Universidad y desarrollo económico. See item 6015.

1798. Dell, Sidney. The Inter-American Development Bank: a study in development financing. N.Y., Praeger Publishers, 1972. 255 p., bibl., tables (Praeger special studies in international economics and development)

Careful recounting IDB's evolution with a critical appraisal of its performance. Examines broad developmental issues and some technical financial ones as they relate to the IDB.

1799. Domike, Arthur L. Industrial and agricultural employment prospects in Latin America (in Field, Arthur J. ed. City and country in the Third World: issues in the modernization of Latin America. Cambridge, Mass., Schenkman Publishing Co., 1970, p. 137-163, bibl., tables)

Even optimistic projections suggest massive urban un- and underemployment by 1985. Potentially, agricultural employment may be enormously increased, but political and institutional limits to this growth are formidable. These are particularly related to land-holding systems.

1800. Domínguez, Loreto M. Qué significa para América Latina un meta de crecimiento de 6% en la década de 1970 (BCV/REL, 8:32, 1971, p. 119-141, tables)

Employs model of development in which the capacity to import is critical to sustained growth. Estimates rate of growth necessary in import capacity and assesses difficulties involved in reaching this rate.

1801. Ekelund, Robert B., Jr. Tax reform in Latin America: the ECLA proposals, a critical evaluation (AJES, 28:1, Jan. 1969, p. 93-108)

Heart of article is tax-by-tax impressionistic critique of ECLA's fiscal policy (1962) recommendations.

1802. La energía en América Latina (UNECLA/B, 15:2, 2. semestre 1970, p. 109-193, tables)

Comprehensive study with emphasis on basic trends of 1960's, forecasts of energy needs for 1970's, and anticipation of principal policy problems. Rich in statistical material. Petroleum and electrical energy are treated in particular detail.

1803. Fabbrica Italiana Automobili Torino (FIAT), *Argentina.* **Oficina de Estudios para la Colaboración Económica Internacional.** Mercado ALALC: fundamentos macroeconómicos para su evaluación. B.A., 1971. 365 p., maps, tables.

Compendium of standard economic data on ALALC as a whole (to p. 95) and individual data on 11 countries. Useful reference for data and analytic text.

Francis, Michael J. La ayuda económica de Estados Unidos a América Latina como instrumento de control político. See item 8023.

1804. Frank, André Gunder. Dependencia económica, estructura de clase y política del subdesarrollo en Latinoamérica (BUS, 8:15/17, dic. 1969, p. 129-182)

Tapestry of history (of which only some strands are presented) has determined current role of second-class partnership for Latin America in the scenario of capitalistic imperialism. Although formerly poor, the growing middle class disregards the fact that they derive their income through further impoverishment of the poor, leaving them no hope other than revolution and the development of socialism. Paper presented at IX Congreso Latinoamericano de Sociología.

1805. ———. Lumpenbourgeoisie, lumpendevelopment: dependence, class and politics in Latin America. Translated by Mario Davis Berdecio. N.Y., Monthly Review Press, 1972. 151 p., bibl.

Sweeping Marxist interpretation of history in Latin America with particular attention to the responses of decision-making groups (*lumpenbourgeoisie*) and the results. Only salvation seen is armed revolution and construction of socialism. Spanish original: *Lumpenburguesía, lumpendesarrollo: dependencia, clase y política en Latinoamérica* (Santiago, Ediciones Prensa Latinoamericana, 1971, 177 p. [Col. América nueva]).

1806. Frank, Charles R., Jr.; Jagdish N. Bhagwati; Robert d'A. Shaw; and **Harald B. Malmgren.** Assisting developing countries: problems of debts, burden-sharing, jobs, and trade. Foreword [by] James P. Grant. N.Y., Praeger Publishers, 1972. 482 p., tables (Praeger special studies in international economics and development. Overseas Development Council studies, 1)

Four independent monographs and serious research efforts which deal only incidentally with Latin America: 1) deals with terms of aid and debt servicing outlooks; 2) seeks to assess real value of flow of aid, its burden to donors and distribution among recipients; 3) examines changes in agricultural technology as related to unemployment; and 4) examines increasing trade of Third World countries and their diminishing share and various alternative means of increasing that value.

1807. Furtado, Celso. Analisi strutturale della dipendenza economica (Rassegna Italiana di Sociologia [Bologna] 12:3, luglio/set. 1971, p. 493-508)

Weaves into unsatisfactory neoclassical economics elements of dynamics, dualism, firm size (imperfect competition) for a better understanding of dependency. Not particularly concerned with Latin America.

1808. ———. La concentración del poder económico en los Estados Unidos y sus proyecciones en América Latina (UCV/ECS [2. época] 12:1, enero-marzo 1970, p. 5-18)

Dwells at length on increasing concentration of power among US corporations and growth of the conglomerate. Penetration of latter into Latin American economies will destroy their national character and make managers of Latin American entrepreneurs with prime responsibility to supranational structures.

———. Economic development of Latin America: a survey from colonial times to the Cuban Revolution. See *HLAS 34:1262*.

1809. ——— and **Andrea Maneschi**. Un modèle simulé de développement et de stagnation en Amérique latine (Economies et Sociétés [Geneva] 3:3, mars 1969, p. 624-656, tables)

Three-phase linear programming model for Latin American economies typified by Brazil and Chile. Noted tendency toward stagnation in latter phases is examined under various alternative assumptions.

1810. García, Antonio. Reforma agraria en América Latina. Lima, Instituto de Estudios Peruanos [and] Moncloa Campodónico Editores Asociados, 1970. 268 p., tables (Col. America Problema, 3)

Pt. 1 describes agriculture as a principal problem in Latin America. Pt. 2 puts it in its world market setting and the "strangulation" of Latin American economies through their external relations. Pt. 3 focuses on structural problems and frustrations of "lagging." Pt. 4 analyzes state of reform in the area and by country. Literary rather than statistical in approach.

1811. Geer, Thomas. Price formation on the world coffee market and its implications for the International Coffee Agreement (CAUK/WA, 106:1, 1971, p. 128-152, tables)

Thorough analysis of oligopolistic-oligopsonistic world coffee market. An explanation is described and then analyzed in context of coffee commodity agreement.

1812. Gendell, Murray and **Guillermo Rossel U.** The trends and patterns of the economic activity of women in Latin America during the 1950's (IASI/E, 26:100, sept. 1968, p. 561-576, tables)

One of the early empirical efforts to describe the economic activities of women in Latin America. It is particularly useful in describing faults in data and a base point for later research.

1813. Germidis, Dimitiros A. Los créditos atados: costos adicionales y alternativas ofrecidas a los países beneficiarios (CM/FI, 12:2, oct./dic. 1971, p. 201-220)

Develops a method of estimating costs of "tied" aid and then of choosing between accepting such aid or employing regular financing. This is of increasing significance since some 75 percent of official bilateral aid is some way tied.

1814. Girvan, Norman. Multinational corporations and dependent-underdevelopment in mineral export economies (ISER/SES, 19:4, Dec. 1970, p. 490-526)

Excellent analysis of internal relations of mining companies, which often have divers sources of supply for their refineries and fabricating interests. Result is that one mine is often more important to an underdeveloped country, than to the economy of the parent corporation—yet, as Vaughn Lewis points out in his following comment (p. 527-531)—nationalization of the mine, often attractive to the country, overlooks critical question of marketing and unless that is included somehow, nationalization is likely to leave all concerned worse off than before. [J. Strasma]

1815. Godoy, Horacio H. Argentina y el proceso de integración de América Latina (IESSC/C, 3:9, sept./dic. 1968, p. 115-128)

Recounts factors and circumstances affecting integration at the world, continental, and Argentine levels. Favors participation of Argentina assuring its opponents that the process is in evolution and can and should be made to respond to various criticisms.

1816. González, Alfonso. Castro: economic effects on Latin America (UM/JIAS, 11:2, April 1969, p. 286-309)

Seeks to assess effects of Castro on such variables as domestic budgets (especially military), capital flight, increased aid, tourism, revamped US sugar quotas. Highly speculative but interesting with tabular appendix as support.

1817. Graciarena, Jorge. Las funciones de la universidad en el desarrollo latinoamericano (CPES/RPS, 8. 22, sept/dic. 1971, p. 63-92)

From rough categorization of stages of development, describes role of higher education in each and finishes with a discussion of "brain drain" and need for nationalizing education.

1818. Gramberg, C. B. E. Tien jaar LAFTA (Latin American Free Trade Area) (NGIZ/IS, 25:6, maart 1971, p. 568-573)

Although trade among 11 LAFTA countries shows definite increase, further extension of the free trade area has met with many difficulties. The net winners of LAFTA growth are Argentina, Brazil and Mexico, the Andes countries having concluded a Common Market within LAFTA. Despite many problems that still have to be worked out among member nations, LAFTA is considered to be an important feature in Latin America's overall development. [H. J. Hoyer]

1819. Graziani, Giovanni. América Latina, subdesarrollo e imperialismo. Mexico, Editorial Diógenes, 1971. 70 p., bibl.

From colonial times, metropolitan capitalism has imposed a colonial structure on Latin America and contributed to its class structure. Both ruling classes and imperialism have a mutual vested interest which prevents reform of current feudalism.

1820. Green, María del Rosario. Inversión extranjera, ayuda y dependencia en América Latina (CM/FI, 12:1, julio/sept. 1971, p. 1-26)

External markets, aid, public and private investment, even integration have all contributed to continued stagnation and dependence of Latin American economies. Radical change within the system is sketched as an alternative to armed revolution which, for the present, does not seem a real possibility.

1821. Grunwald, Joseph; Miguel S. Wionczek; and Martin Carnoy. Latin American economic integration and U.S. policy. Washington, The Brookings Institution, 1972. 216 p., bibl.

Excellent survey of the setting, status, and needs for integration. Pt. 2 argues persuasively that US in its own best interests should take initiative in revitalizing the integration movement as it "offers the best immediate hope for Latin American countries to put their economic development on a sounder footing by permitting them to open themselves gradually to international trade without sacrificing their infant industries." Include appendixes.

1822. Grupo Andino: Programa de Liberación; Arancel Externo Mínimo Común. t. 1/2. Lima, Junta del Acuerdo de Cartagena, 1971. 2 v. 614 p. (Continuous pagination) tables.

Official documents concerning program of trade liberalization, common minimum external tariff, initial tariff reductions, lists of exceptions, and related official actions of Andean Common Market organizations. Essential holdings for reference libraries used by scholars interested in the integration movement in Latin America. [J. Strasma]

1823. Guaraldi, Carlos. Aspectos de economía monetaria y financiera en los países latinoamericanos en desarrollo (UBSA/A, 5, 1969, p. 129-138)

Impressionistic, very general set of observations.

1824. Harberger, Arnold C. Issues concerning capital assistance to less-developed countries (UC/EDCC, 20:4, July 1972, p. 631-640)

Even with a hypothetical 10 percent return, calculations show that returns from US aid expenditures seldom are an important proportion of per capita incomes. "Aid" is not the missing link in development as dollars were in post-war European reconstruction. This is not a signal to abandon aid but to improve it—and to expect less of it.

1825. How will multinational firms react to the Andean Pact's decision 24? (IAMEA, 25:2, Autumn 1972, p. 55-65)

Report of an empirical study of attitudes of 20 firms to the Andean Group's decision requiring joint ventures of foreign investors. In general, there was skepticism and reluctance but adaptability.

1826. Ikonicoff, Moisés. Les deux étapes de la croissance en Amérique Latine (UP/TM, 10:37, jan./mars 1969, p. 177-198)

Modestly rigorous attempt at analytic history of economic evolution of Latin American countries. After colonial period, there is pre-1930 stage of integration into world markets and post-1930 stage of industrialization based largely on import substitution. This led to stagnation both because of its nature and as a result of dependance on the demands of five percent of potential buyers.

1827. Inter-American Development Bank. Dez anos de luta pela América Latina. Rio, Fundação Getúlio Vargas, 1971. 723 p., tables.

Useful self-examination by the IDB covering three major topics in about 30 invited papers: structure and functions, IDB and development, IDB and economic integration. Most papers are by Bank officials and are valuable for the insight they give into the philosophy and operations of the institution.

1828. ———. Institute for Latin American Integration. Indicadores de vinculación económica entre los países de la ALALC. B.A., 1971. 73 p., tables (Estudios, 4)

Effort to describe and measure interdependencies of LAFTA countries primarily through scrutiny of trade data, aggregated and by sectors. Includes statement of methodological considerations.

1829. ———. 1971 (i.e., Nineteen hundred seventy-one) annual report; statement of loans: appendix of the annual report. Washington, 1972? 2 v. (128, 69 p.) maps, plates, tables.

Continues to be an authoritative, current statement of the IDB's activities.

1830. ———. Social Progress Trust Fund. Progreso socio-económico en América Latina: informe anual 1971. Washington, 1972? 402 p., maps, tables.

Useful reference. Pt.1: regional analysis including: general economic trends, external sector, integration, development finance, trends in social development. Reports on each individual country follow.

1831. *Inter-American Economic Affairs.* Vol. 23, No. 4, Spring 1970- . Washington.

John P. Powelson "The Terms of Trade Again" p. 3-12 (item 1864)
Fred Miller "Supervised Credit and Agricultural Development: A Peruvian Example" p. 13-22 (item 2287)
Ingo Walter "United States Non-Tariff Measures and Trade Preferences for Latin America" p. 23-46 (item 1896)
John R. Dinkelspiel "Technology and Tradition: Regional and Urban Development in the Guayana" p. 47-80.

1831a. International Bank for Reconstruction and Development. International Finance Corporation. IFC in Latin America. Washington, 1971. 98 p.

Short statement of the purpose of the International Finance Corp., part of the World Bank, and an account of its investments by industrial groups (e.g., textiles and fibers, tourism, etc.). Includes country summaries.

1832. ———. World Bank operations: sectoral

programs and policies. Baltimore, Md., The Johns Hopkins Univ. Press *for the* International Bank for Reconstruction and Development, 1972. 513 p., tables.

Useful compendium of information which consists of a number of World Bank Group sectoral papers (agriculture, industry, transportation, telecommunication, electric power, water supply and sewerage, education, population, tourism, urbanization) juxtaposed with related statistical annexes. Latter include general data as well as those related to Bank operations.

1833. Kaplan, Marcos. Aspectos políticos de la planificación en América Latina (ILARI/A, 20, abril 1971, p. 132-170)

After concluding that there has been little "planning" in Latin America except in the pre-planning of *intervencionismo* and *dirigismo*, author discusses various aspects of planning (as he defines it) in generally abstract terms. Piece essentially concerns planning, not Latin America.

1834. Karadima, Oscar. La planificación económica y social: sus aspectos sociológicos (ILARI/A, 22, oct. 1971, p. 123-150, tables)

The planning process cannot afford to overlook sociological aspects of change: characteristics of society, as to structure, function, and institution; rigidity and flexibility of structure and institution; equilibrium and changing interrelations between the individual and social institutions. This is argument rather than research.

1835. Katz, Sherman E. The tariff preference: a reconsideration (CIDG/O, 14:4, Winter 1971, p. 829-849, table)

Excellent survey of the status of tariff perference in general and for Latin America specifically (subject to becoming dated) and a careful analysis of arguments for and against such preferences.

1836. Kearns, Kevin C. The Andean Common Market: a new thrust at economic integration in Latin America (UM/JIAS, 14:1, Feb. 1972, p. 225-249, maps, tables)

Examines the historical evolution of the Andean Group from the failures of LAFTA. Concentrates particularly on transportation as a Group problem.

1837. Kracmar, John Z. Marketing research in the developing countries: a handbook. Foreword by Jan Tinbergen. N.Y., Praeger Publishers, 1971. 322 p., bibl., illus., tables (Praeger special studies in international economics and development)

Marketing "primer" which specifically eschews sophisticated techniques in favor of the clear and "possible" in developing economies. Of considerable interest is case material and, particularly, the glossary of marketing terms with terms themselves translated into five languages. Case materials include experience in Colombia, Brazil and Peru.

1838. Laso, Luis Eduardo. Evolución de los sistemas monetarios y bancos centrales de América Latina. Quito, Almacenes Editorial Colón, 1972. 85 p.

Includes summary account of central banking in Latin America and its antecedents (p. 1-13) and short history for each country. No bibliographical material.

1839. Latin America (*in* Raffaele, Joseph A. The economic development of nations. N.Y., Random House, 1971, p. 211-265, tables)

Literate and superficial review of development, broadly defined, in Latin America. Two cases, Argentina and Mexico, are discussed in some detail. Suitable for an introductory text.

Levin, Peter J. The development program of the Río de la Plata basin: a new approach to Latin American integration. See item 7428.

1840. Lichtensztejn, Samuel. Programación de corto plazo del comercio exterior (UR/RFCE, 30, dic. 1968, p. 37-57, tables)

Operational, clear approach to problems and means of planning the external sector for the short-run. Concerns itself largely with general procedure rather than specific technique.

1841. Loeb, G. F. ECLA en het tweede ontwikkelingsdecennium (NGIZ/IS, 24:16, sept. 1970, p. 1497-1510)

Outlines plans of the UN Committee for Development Planning and stresses ECLA's part in their execution. Basic causes for underdevelopment in Latin America are: 1) level of economic development, capital formation and the spread of income; 2) low productivity in agriculture; 3) an import-replacing industrialization and 4) how external structural factors form an important bottle neck. According to ECLA a minimun growth of 6 to 7 percent must be realized and an increase of investments to 20 percent of the gross product. According to author, external financial aid will be needed for a long time to come. Author concludes optimistically that, if states cooperate, targets can be attained. [H. J. Hoyer]

1842. Luders, Rolf. Desarrollo del mercado de capitales en América Latina: un programa (ABM/RB, 20:4, abril 1972, p. 11-17, tables)

Level of savings in Latin America is probably adequate, but its allocation is poorly handled. Proposes a program of research, training, technical assistance designed to improve operation of capital markets.

1843. Mansfield, Charles. Tax structure in developing countries: an introduction (AIFLD/R, 3:4, 1971, p. 59-72)

Very general, elementary piece but thoughtful in relating *tax structure* to problems and stages of development. Reprinted from *Finance and Development*.

1844. Márquez, Javier. Promoción fiscal de los mercados de valores en países de América Latina (BHEL/R, 2:2, abril/junio 1967, p. 133-151)

Modern economies require sizeable firms which in turn require large amounts of capital. A securities' market is, then, a requisite of development. Participation of small and medium savers is required which can best be assured by: 1) avoiding tax structures which favor reinvestment of earnings, 2) avoiding progressive tax rates on corporate earnings.

1845. Meeker, Guy B. Fade-out joint venture:

can it work for Latin America? (IAMEA, 24:4, Spring 1971, p. 25-42, tables)

Empirical results of attitudinal study of US firms to "fade-out joint venture." Author finds a surprising degree of open-mindedness in what is very much a live issue.

1846. Milenky, Edward S. Developmental nationalism in practice: the problems and progress of the Andean group (IAMEA, 26:4, Spring 1973, p. 49-68, tables)

Review of the group's first three years by a Boston College political scientist. Useful in the absence of more profound economic analysis. [B. Herrick]

1847. ———. From integration to developmental nationalism: the Andean group, 1965-1971 (IAMEA, 25:3, Winter 1971, p. 77-91)

Optimistic view of the Andean Pact, although the author realizes that its true tests lie in the future. [B. Herrick]

1848. Montrie, Charles; Kenneth J. Fedor; and Harlan Davis. Tax performance within the framework of the Alliance for Progress: a comparative evaluation (NTA/NTJ, 23:3, Sept. 1970, p. 325-334)

Development of a schema for comparing performance in terms of tax collection taking into account such variables as GNP, per capita income, foreign sector size. The system is designed to produce comparisons rather than measurement against some notion of an absolute "capacity."

1849. Moore, Russell Martin. A função das emprêsas internacionais na indústria automotriz da América Latina (FGV/RAE, 11:1, março 1971, p. 53-64, illus., tables)

Analysis, with emphasis on Brazil, of the automobile industry, and ambivalence with respect to regional integration. These ambivalences exist for producers, suppliers, and the respective governments.

1850. Morgan, Robert P. Transfer of technology (PAPS, 30:4, 1972, p. 141-152)

Taking into account criticisms of technology-recipient countries (failure to adapt, restrictive practices, cost), the article considers first-step implications for US policy.

1851. Motta, Fernando C. Prestes. A teoria geral dos sistemas na teoria das organizações (FGV/RAE, 11:1, março 1971, p. 17-33, illus., tables)

Literate, flowing survey of "systems" as a part of organizational theory. Not specifically related to Latin America.

1852. La movilización de recursos internos (UNECLA/B, 15:2, 2. semestre 1970, p. 194-247, tables)

Careful, comprehensive study of *internal* investment in Latin America giving first attention to the processes, capabilities, and problems of *real* capital accumulation. Second major division gives attention to financial aspects, markets, devices, incentives related to stimulation of personal and business savings and its conversion into capital goods of appropriate kinds.

1853. Mustapich, José María. La complementación económica de América Latina en el Mercado Común Europeo (IEP/REP, 163, enero/feb. 1969, p. 149-161)

Plea, largely on the basis of justice and morality, for the European community to take notice of the plight of Latin America and to do something about it.

1854. Nye, J. S. La UNCTAD bajo Prebisch: America (IFSNG/CD, 25/26, Spring 1971, p. 3-22, illus., maps, tables)

Political-structural description and analysis of development and functioning of UNCTAD for five years under Raúl Prebisch.

1855. Odell, Peter R. A European view on regional development and planning in Latin America (IFSNC/CD, 25/26, Spring 1971, p. 3-22, illus., maps, tables)

Geographically and spatially oriented, this interesting article explores regional (intra-national) planning in Latin America. It treats Puerto Rico as a model and special case and then problems of small and large economies. Differences from European planning are emphasized.

1856. Oliver, Covey T. The Andean foreign investment code: a new phase in the quest for normative order as to direct foreign investment (ASIL/J, 66:5, Oct. 1972, p. 763-784)

Perceptive analysis of new foreign investment norms of Andean Common Market, and their conflicts with expectations and habits of transnational corporations, as of 1972. Author sees Andean Code as milestone, as was "Mexicanization," but thinks companies can learn to live with it. [J. Strasma]

1857. Organization of American States. General Secretariat. External financing for Latin American development. Foreword [by] Walter J. Sedwitz. Baltimore, Md., The Johns Hopkins Press, 1971. 248 p., tables.

Very careful study of some aspects of external financing: characteristics, 1961-68; measurement; direct foreign investment; requirements and procedures; problems with external public financing, tied loans. Starting point is the analysis of trends in flow of funds during the 1960's.

1858. ———. El problema del desempleo en la América Latina (RCPC, 25:124, enero 1971, p. 2-14)

Comprehensive review article, particularly valuable for its discussion of the meaning of statistical measures of unemployment in Latin America. Follows with other good sections on causes, outlook and policies.

1859. Oteyza, José Andrés de. Políticas de fomento de los mercados de capitales. Introducción [por] Cecilio J. Morales. México, Centro de Estudios Monetarios Latinoamericanos, 1971. 185 p., tables.

Apparently a highly edited account of seminar sponsored by the IDB in 1969. Coverage is general although there is some specific country experience incorporated. There is less focus on "policy" than title implies and more on "role" and "institutions."

1860. Parra-Peña, Isidro. La transformación de Iberoamérica. Bogotá, Editorial Revista Colombiana, 1971. 102 p. (Populibro, 39)

Critical essay on major concepts (dualism, underdevelopment, dependency, populism) employed by leading Latin American students of development (Jaguaribe, Di Tella, Pinto, Sunkel). [J. J. Bailey]

1861. Pinto, Aníbal. El modelo de desarrollo reciente de América Latina (BCV/REL, 8:32, 1971, p. 89-118, table)

Heavy industry supplants relatively light industry of early import-substitution models. This leads to increased "foreignization" of the dynamic sector. Since there is also structural disequilibrium in the balance of payments, foreign earnings cannot be repatriated and are reinvested in still other sectors leading to still further "foreignization." Concludes with implications of the model of such variables as savings, employment, public finance, income distribution.

1862. Piquet, Rosélia Périssé. A teoria do comércio internacional em face ao subdesenvolvimento econômico (CLAPCS/AL, 13:2/3, abril/set. 1970, p. 70-89)

Re-examination of classical theory of international trade which is found wanting as a basis for liberal trade policy in developing countries (the basic assumptions do not fit). Neither policies to expand exports nor import-substitution policies are likely to be helpful leaving the development of Third-World trading blocks the remaining alternative.

1863. Portnoy, Leopoldo. La economía latinoamericana ante el desarrollo de la ciencia y de la técnica (UNC/R, 9:3/4, julio/oct. 1968, p. 503-520)

Discusses in very general terms the economic problems of Latin America in all its heterogeneity.

1864. Powelson, John P. The terms of trade again (IAMEA, 23:4, Spring 1970, p. 3-11)

Demonstrates that terms of trade do not turn against periphery because of wage policies in the metropole. Prebisch may still be right but for other reasons. Ends with doubts that the issue will be settled.

1865. Prebisch, Raúl. Change and development: Latin America's great task. N.Y., Praeger Publishers, 1971. 450 p., tables (Praeger special studies in international economics and development)

Author, sponsor and topic make this important reading for those interested in the economics of Latin America. Originally an IDB mimeographed study under same title (1970, 235 p.).

1866. Los problemas del financiamiento externo del desarrollo (UNAM/BCRI, 7, junio 1971, p. 21-26)

Brief journalistic review of issues related to 12th annual meeting of IDB.

1867. Quadri, Mario A. La cuenca del Plata como replanteo de la filosofía integracionista latinoamericana (IEP/RPI, 103, mayo/junio 1969, p. 47-64, tables)

Suggests in general terms a union of River Plate countries as a viable alternative to the stagnated LAFTA. More concerned with physical integrations (*i.e.*, infrastructure) than with trading arrangements. Special attention given to an Argentina-Uruguay union.

1868. Romanova, Zinaida Ivanovna. Latinoamerikanskaia integratsiia: Tendentsii razvitiia (Latin American integration: trends in development). Moskva, Nauka, 1970. 134 p., tables.

Examines past decade of economic integration from political-social-economic point of view, stressing that complex, contradictory nature of integration problem precludes painting an entirely white or black picture. Although integration is desirable, capitalist production relationships aggravate the struggle for markets. At same time, combination of positive and negative elements in this process is intensifying and raising the liberation movement to a higher level. Footnotes. [A. R. Navon]

1869. Sachs, Ignacy. The logic of development (UN/ISSJ, 24:1, 1972, p. 37-43)

Post World War II development theory has been struggling with modest success to overcome: 1) Europocentric limitations, b) an unduly narrow conceptualization of development (i.e., growth in GNP), and c) disciplinary fragmentation. Progress has been made; much remains to be done along routes suggested.

1870. Salera, Virgil. Prebisch's change and development (IAMEA, 24:4, Spring 1971, p. 67-79)

Examines Prebisch (item 1865) critically: his attachment to "potential" and to the "big push," the dependence of remedial measures on foreign assistance, failure to examine domestic policy as major inhibiting factors.

1871. Salgado, Germánico. Le développement et l'intégration de l'Amérique latine (ISEA/EA, 22:3, 1969, p. 369-459)

Careful, wise, and realistic monograph-length study. Systematically explores developmental implications of integration with special attention being given localization matters. Preceded by a review of major developmental problems.

1872. Samper, Armando. El sector agropecuario frente a la integración latinoamericana (Desarrollo Rural en las Américas [Bogotá] 4:1, enero/abril 1972, p. 5-32, bibl., tables)

Valuable synthesis which brings together considerable material on problems, institutions, solutions, prospects for integration in Europe and Latin America with careful attention to specifics of agricultural sector. Includes statistical appendices and a useful focused bibliography.

1873. Santos, Milton. L'économie pauvre des villes des pays sous-développés (SGB/COM, 24:94, avril/juin 1971, p. 105-122)

Two-sector (modern, traditional) analysis of urban problems of underdeveloped nations. Not area-specific and only incidental reference to Latin America.

1874. Schydlowsky, Daniel M. Base analítica

para una política nacional de integración económica regional en América Latina (USM/RCEC, 74, enero/junio 1967, p. 14-36, tables)

Conceptual bases for regional integration, with a Latin American example run through a linear program. Basic for an understanding of the inner workings of any international program of complementation. [B. Herrick]

1874a. ———. Latin American trade policies in the 1970's: a prospective appraisal (Quarterly Journal of Economics [Harvard Univ.] 86:2, May 1972, p. 263-289)

Painstaking analysis of data from past decade, for major South American nations, leading author to conclude that economic integration cannot succeed unless most member countries make major changes in their trade policies—and especially in exchange rate structures and mechanisms of adjustment to internal price levels. [J. Strasma]

1875. Sepúlveda Armor, Bernardo. El régimen de la nación más favorecida en el GATT y la ALALC (CM/FI, 12:3, enero/marzo 1972, p. 340-356)

Detailed and rather legalistic analysis of most favored nation requirements of GATT and in particular their relationship with LAFTA provisions.

1876. Sideri, S. Prospectives for the Third World (NGIZ/IS, 25:5, maart 1971, p. 469-498)

Very bleak view of the future of the Third World. Its subordinate position is reinforced by the hierarchical system of nations and the multinational corporation. Views aid and technical assistance as manifestation of the system and as not helpful.

1877. *Statistical Bulletin for Latin America.* United Nations, Economic Commission for Latin America. Vol. 8, No. 2, Oct. 1971- . N.Y.

Periodic reporting of regional and country data on a variety of economic activities.

1878. Stein, L. On the Third World's narrowing trade gap (OUP/OEP, 23:1, March 1971, p. 110-119, tables)

Short but important paper examining surprising reasons why the Prebisch 1964 estimate of a Third World trade deficit of $12 billion failed to materialize and instead the gap lessened and reserves were accumulated.

Stöhr, Walter B. Spatial growth differentials in Latin America, the role of urban and transport investment. See item 6601.

1879. Streeten, Paul and **Diane Elson.** Diversification and development: the case of coffee. N.Y., Praeger Publishers, 1971. 101 p., tables (Praeger special studies in international economics and development)

Tightly reasoned essay touching many of the elements of diversification: exchange policy, joint ventures, relationship of agriculture to industry labor utilization, etc. Prime attention is given to coffee producing countries, but the arguments have far greater applicability.

1880. Suárez, Macrino. Grandes empresas y pequeñas naciones (UNAM/IE, 31:121, enero/marzo 1971, p. 79-155, bibl., tables)

Applies Perroux analysis to the multiple possible relationships between "giant firms" (not clearly characterized) and "small" nations (not clearly defined). Considerable analysis and considerable conjecture in this herculean task. Includes extensive statistical appendix and bibliography.

1881. Sunkel, Osvaldo. Big business and "dependencia:" a Latin American view (CFR/FA, April 1972, p. 517-531)

Import substitution produced an unforeseen, invidious dependency but worse than that has been the penetration of the multinational corporation into the industrial-manufacturing sectors of Latin American economics. The days of seeking "favorable business conditions for direct private investment" are a thing of the past.

1882. ———. Capitalismo transnacional y desintegración nacional (UCIEI/EI, 4:16, enero/marzo 1971, p. 3-61, illus., tables)

An effort to be both interdisciplinary and global in approach to the five major problems: development, underdevelopment, dependency, marginalization, and spatial disequilibria. These are problems generated from "the general process of the international capitalist system" in which the major culprit is the multinational corporation, particularly that of the US.

1883. ———. Desarrollo, subdesarrollo, dependencia, marginación y desigualdades espaciales; hacia un enfoque totalizante (UNAM/IE, 31:121, enero/marzo 1971, p. 23-77, bibl., illus., tables)

Usual, provocative Sunkel article covering, sometimes superficially, items indicated in title. The "general" theory is incomplete with most problems of presently poor nations being attributed to "*el* CONTRA" (conglomerado transnacional). Well worth reading as a thoughtful set of hypotheses.

1884. ——— *ed.* Integración política económica: el proceso europeo y el problema latinoamericano. Santiago, Editorial Universitaria, 1970. 436 p., tables.

Edited papers presented in 1968 to a seminar jointly conducted by the Centre d'Études de Politique Etrangère and the Instituto de Estudios Internacionales (Univ. de Chile). Papers cover specific topics with Europeans addressing themselves particularly to reporting on integration in Europe and their Latin American counterparts seeking further definition of the problem in Latin America.

1885. Switzer, Kenneth A. The Andean group: a reappraisal (IAMEA, 26:4, Spring 1973, p. 69-81, table)

Article focuses on differences among the members of the Andean Pact, and speculates on whether pact will encounter (and founder on) same obstacles that hindered the Latin American Free Trade Association (LAFTA). [B. Herrick]

Taylor, Roselyn G. Desarrollo urbano en América Latina. See item 6604.

1886. Tun Wai, U. Financial intermediaries and national savings in developing countries. N.Y., Praeger Publishers, 1972. 240 p., tables (Praeger special studies in international economics and development)

Defining financial "intermediation" carefully, this study seeks to determine econometrically the relationship between various institutional arrangements and quantity of savings. Available financial instruments and institutions have a positive influence on savings. Latin America is not specifically treated, but Latin American data are important inputs.

1887. United Nations. Economic Commission for Latin America (ECLA). Agricultural policy in the countries signatory to the Andean Subregional Integration Programme (UNECLA/B, 16:2, 2. half 1971, p. 91-119)

Focuses directly on specific countries and commodities. [J. Strasma]

1888. ———. ———. Development problems in Latin America. Austin, Tex., Univ. of Texas Press, 1970. 318 p.

Extraordinarily useful volume consisting of edited ECLA documents related to specific topics (trade theory critique, planning, integration, inflation, etc.) published over two decades. Annex (p. 279-307) lists ECLA publications (1948-67) and their contents.

1889. ———. ———. Economic survey of Latin America, 1970. N.Y., 1972. 351 p., tables.

Special topics in this survey include: Latin America and the second development decade; review of trends and structures in the 1960's; special studies on multinational enterprise; Latin America and the ECC; and Latin America and Japan.

1890. Urquidi, Victor L. Una estrategia tecnológica para América Latina (Gerencia [Lima] nov./dic. 1970, p. 62-65, illus.)

Discussion of long-run strategy alternatives for the technological base in Latin America. Much rests with radically altered education, integration, careful attention to appropriate technologies.

1891. Van Meurs, A. P. H. De toekmst van de petroleum exporterende ontwikkelingslanden (NGIZ/IS, 25:11, juni 1971, p. 1091-1107, tables)

Offers overall-review of situation of oil exporting countries. After pointing out major characteristics of economies dependent on oil export, author draws attention to growing coordination of export policies of these countries as is obvious from recent developments. Finally, author offers outline of future developments and defines influence of rising prices on the position of OPEC countries.

1892. Vanek, Yaroslav. La economía de participación: hipótesis evolucionista y estrategia para el desarrollo. Lima, Instituto de Estudios Peruanos [and] Campodónico*ediciones*, 1971. 156 p., bibl.

Very broad approach to historical development with three main objectives: 1) explanation of meaning and characteristics of a self-managed economy ("participatory economy" in which labor forces rather than owners of capital make decisions); 2) extension of this notion into a still broader one involving social, political, and economic evolution; and 3) examination of "participation" as a development vehicle of interest to Latin America but not specifically about or directed to it.

1893. Véliz, Claudio. Cambio y continuidad: el Pacto Andino en la historia contemporánea (UCIEI/EI, 4:16, enero/marzo 1971, p. 62-92)

Wide ranging historical essay examining factors of continuity which augur success for the Andean Pact. Fewer difficulties exist for it than for other regional integration schemes.

1894. Viñas, Ismael. Capitalismo, monopolios y dependencia. B.A., Centro Editor de América Latina, 1972. 135 p.

Economic history outlining relationships between the "capitalist" countries and their "satellites." Descriptive rather than prescriptive.

1895. Wall, David. The Commonwealth Preference System and its effects on the United Kingdom's imports from Latin America. Milwaukee, Wis., Univ. of Wisconsin, Center for Latin American Studies, 1971. 7 p., tables (Center reprint, 18)

Examines Latin American claim that the 'Commonwealth Preference System discriminates specifically against their exports and that it is biased against their trade, something which does not occur with processed and manufactured goods.

1896. Walter, Ingo. United States non-tariff measures and trade preference for Latin America (IAMEA, 23:4, Spring 1970, p. 23-45, tables)

Attempts to analyze effects of possible preferential tariff treatment to be accorded to Latin America by the US and in particular to analyze effectiveness of non-tariff barriers in offsetting tariff concessions.

1897. ——— and Robert Loring Allen. Los acuerdos preferenciales y los países en desarrollo (ULAFE/E, 7:8, dic. 1970, p. 155-179, tables)

Examines empirically the losses to developing countries (particularly affected in Latin America) of increasing economic integration of the industrial countries. System of preferences could permit developing countries to share in the gains.

1898. Weaver, F. Stirton. The dynamics of U.S. investment in Latin America (SS, 33:1, Winter 1969, p. 20-24, tables)

Essentially Marxist explanation of the role of US capital in Latin America. Although perhaps less obnoxious in its new *industrial* role, it is still invidious since it requires the institutions of private property which, in turn, deter development.

Weisskoff, Richard. Income distribution and economic growth in Puerto Rico, Argentina and Mexico. See item 2528.

1899. White, John. Regional development

banks: the Asian, African and Inter-American Development Banks. N.Y., Praeger Publishers, 1972. 204 p., tables (Praeger special studies in international economics and development)

Particularly insightful analysis of the development of regional banks as new political-economic institutions. Worth reading for account of IDB (ch. 4), comparisons between it and others as well as description of all of their relations with the World Bank.

1900. Wionczek, Miguel S. El grupo andino y la inversión extranjera privada (UNC/REE, 14:1/4, 1970, p. 219-248, tables)

Analysis of US corporate investment in Andean Zone, and a call for measures to ensure that economic benefits of regional integration not accrue mainly to such extrazonal firms. Author was a consultant to Andean Zone secretariat when Andean policy and especially Decision 24 were designed. [J. Strasma]

1901. ———. Inversión y tecnología extranjera en América Latina. México, Joaquín Mortiz, 1971. 189 p., tables (Cuadernos, 14/15)

A needed first step in analyzing the role of foreign capital in Latin America, seeking to approach the truth between exponents of view that foreign investment is at best calamitous and those of the other extreme who view it as a charitable favor to recipients. This is far from the last word since "quantification" with which myths are confronted is itself weak. Coverage, too, is less general than title implies, major attention being given to Mexico.

1902. Worcester, Donald E. The Spanish American past: enemy of change (UM/JIAS, 11:1, Jan. 1969, p. 66-75)

Devotes more attention to the past than to its relation to present Latin American problems of change. Supports usual hypothesis that Spanish colonial heritage is a barrier to development.

1903. Young, Ruth C. The controlled economy and political organization: a cross-national study (JDA, 5:4, July 1971, p. 543-554)

Of interest because it compares results from 17 Middle East and Muslim countries with those reported in item 1904.

1904. ———. The plantation economy and industrial development in Latin America (UC/EDCC, 18:3, April 1970, p. 328-361)

Plantation agriculture is shown to be neither "stunted industry" nor "modern agriculture." It is frequently misunderstood to be one or the other because inappropriate analysis, *i.e.* "economic," has principally been used for the analysis of underdevelopment.

MEXICO

ROBERT L. BENNETT

Associate Professor of Economics
University of Maryland

MEXICO HAS NOW HAD A DECADE AND A HALF of non-inflationary, rapid development. There have been no serious foreign exchange problems and few problems with foreign trade generally. These facts apparently have combined to turn economic policy concerns inward and toward the major areas that were sacrificed earlier in the concern with growth, inflation, and foreign trade. The attention now seems to focus on income distribution and on agriculture. These concerns not only are emphasized by the Echeverría government, but also are becoming more and more the subject of study by economists. Ifigenia M. de Navarrete, of course, has long written on income distribution, and a major addition to the literature this year is her masterful work (item 1940) combining the subjects of income distribution and agricultural development with a plan for action to ameliorate much rural poverty.

The relatively great attention to the national agricultural sector is also evidenced in items 1918-1919, 1930-1931, 1944, 1946, and 1951, among others. Regional studies which include much attention to the agricultural sector are items 1938-1939 and 1942. Furthermore, almost all of the items which are focused on the general current economic situation give substantial attention to agriculture.

Another area in which great strides have been taken in the last two years is pre-Revolutionary history. The Cambridge Latin American Studies include four excellent items on Mexico: Bazant's book on church property during the reform (item 1909); P. J. Blackwell *Silver mining and society in colonial Mexico, Zacatecas; 1546-1700.* (London, Cambridge Univ. Press, 1971, 294 p.) will be reviewed in *HLAS 36,* History, Mexico Colonial section; Brading's book on the Bourbon period (see *HLAS 34:1508*); and Hammett's book on the difficulty of royal supervision of trade in the colonial period (see *HLAS 34:1680*). The reissue or translation of two earlier works increased the availability of good historical material also—Lerdo de Tejada's classic on colonial and pre-reform trade (item 1934) and François Chevalier's *Land and society in colonial Mexico: the great hacienda* (Berkeley, Calif., Univ. of California Press, 1970, 334 p.) which will also be reviewed in *HLAS 36*, History, Mexico Colonial section.

Mexican authors continue to devote major attention to recent economic history and current problems. Noteworthy in the latter category are López Rosado's current edition of the popular *Problemas económicos de México* (item 1936), and the book by Solís and others, *Los problemas nacionales* (item 1949). Perhaps here mention should be made of the 1950-70 reprinted articles in *Cuestiones económicas nacionales* (item 1907). Two good books focus attention on economic dangers of foreign domination or domination of the PRI by the local privileged classes—Carmona de la Peña's *Dependencia y cambios estructurales* (item 1911) and González Navarro's *México: el capitalismo nacionalista* (item 1924).

In this section the reviewer has not included separately several recurring publications which may be of great interest to the researcher. Statistical data are available in the current editions of Banco de México's annual *Asamblea General de Accionistas;* Nacional Financiera's annual *Informe Anual* and bi-weekly *El Mercado de Valores;* Banco Nacional de Comercio Exterior's annual *Comercio Exterior de Mexico* and monthly *Comercio Exterior;* Secretaría de Industria y Comercio's *Anuario de Estadística;* and Banco Nacional de México's quarterly *Review of the Economic Situation of Mexico.* The most comprehensive bibliographical information is found in Banco de México's annual *Bibliografía Económica de México* and bi-monthly *Boletín Bibliográfico.*

Aguilera Gómez, Manuel. Balance de la nueva ley de reforma agraria. See *HLAS 34:1821.*

———. La reforma agraria en el desarrollo económico de México. See *HLAS 34:1821a.*

1905. Arce Cano, Gustavo. Nueva política monetaria y Banco Central para el Desarrollo. México, Ediciones Botas, 1971. 210 p., bibl.

Plea for use of the central bank to promote economic development primarily rather than to promote stability primarily. Author evidences little recognition of the problems or the quantitative importance of doing this.

Avila, Manuel. Tradition and growth: a study of four Mexican villages. See *HLAS 34:1824.*

1906. Baker, Bonnie Lea; Richard A. Wald; and **Rita Zamora.** Economic aspects of Mexican and Mexican-American urban households [Aspectos económicos de la vida urbana mexicana y mexicana-americana: el enganche entre dos mundos]. San José, Calif., San José State College, The Institute for Business and Economic Research, 1971. 150 p., bibl., maps, tables.

There is virtually no merit in this booklet. Disjointed surveys (one of Mexico City families and one of California families) are used ostensibly to point to differences. Differences are not measured well, and if they were, why would they be of importance? Sources are generally from popular US press for general comments on Mexico.

1907. Banco Nacional de Comercio Exterior, México. Cuestiones económicas nacionales: comercio exterior, 1951-1970. México, 1970. 463 p., tables.

Collection of articles by eminent authors originally appearing in *Comercio Exterior* from 1951-1970.

1908. Barkin, David. National institutions and indigenous systems in Mexico: some problems of analysis, a comment (Journal of Economic Issues [Univ. of Massachusetts, Amherst] 4:4, Dec. 1970, p. 82-86)

1909. Bazant, Jan. Alienation of Church wealth in Mexico: social and economic aspects of the Liberal revolution, 1856-1875. Edited by Michael P. Costeloe. Cambridge, England, Cambridge Univ. Press, 1971. 332 p., bibl. (Cambridge Latin American studies, 11)

For comment on the Spanish original, see *HLAS 34:1692.*

Brading, David A. Miners and merchants in Bourbon Mexico: 1763-1810. See *HLAS 34:1508.*

1910. Browning, Harley L. and **Jack P. Gibbs.** Intraindustry division of labor: the states of Mexico (PAA/D, 8:2, May 1971, p. 233-245, tables)

Confusing article using 1950 and 1960 data on the labor force in eight industries in 32 states. Probably of more interest to sociologists than to economists. Also available as offprint No. 113 from the Univ. of Texas, Institute of Latin American Studies.

1911. Carmona de la Peña, Fernando. Dependencia y cambios estructurales: problemas del desarrollo económico de México. México, UNAM, Instituto de Investigaciones Económicas, 1971. 403 p., tables.

Substantial socio-historical work which attributed most of Mexico's current development problems to her present economic and political relations with the rest of the world. Carmona traces the evolution of imperialism from its more flagrant colonial and Porfirian varieties to the more subtle, but equally subordinating, current variety.

1912. Caso Bercht, Jorge. El mercado de acciones en México. México, Centro de Estudios Monetarios Latinoamericanos, 1971. 399 p., tables.

Extraordinarily complete description of the Mexican stock market by an insider. Elaborate statistics. The market is so small that it was described rapidly and many recommendations for improvement are offered. Generally these suggested improvements would virtually guarantee profits to participants on both sides of the market—at government expense, naturally.

1913. Centro de Estudios Económicos del Sector Privado, *México.* Análisis de la potencialidad económica del área metropolitana. Mexico, 1970. 875 p., plates, tables.

Although this large volume of statistics is intended primarily for the use of businessmen in Mexico City, it should prove to be a generally useful source of information on population, production and socio-economic characteristics of the metropolitan area and its 30 subdivisions.

1914. ———, ———. La dinámica de los sectores de la economía mexicana durante las décadas de los cincuentas y sesentas. México, 1971. 229 p., tables.

Group of charts and graphs with economic and demographic data from the Banco de México. *Cuentas nacionales y acervos de capital, 1950-1967.*

Cline, William R. Potential effects of income redistribution on economic growth: Latin American cases. See item 1794.

1915. Cornehls, J. V. and E. Van Roy. Economic development in Mexico and Thailand: an institutional analysis, pts. 1/2 (Journal of Economic Issues [Univ. of Massachusetts, Amherst] 3:3, Sept. 1969, p. 16-32; 3:4, Dec. 1969, p. 21-38)

1916. ——— and ———. Further considerations on Mexico's economic development (Journal of Economic Issues [Univ. of Massachusetts, Amherst] 4:4, Dec. 1970, p. 86-88)

1917. Covo, Milena E. Las instituciones de investigación social en la ciudad de México. México, UNAM, Instituto de Investigaciones Sociales, 1969. 145 p., bibl.

Should be read as an introduction to Mexico City for the social science researcher. Lists principal research organizations, address, phone number and director, as well as brief description of activities and purposes. Also lists publications for 1960-68 approximately. Confusingly organized.

1918. Dovring, Folke. Land reform and productivity in Mexico (UW/LE, 46:3, Aug. 1970, p. 264-274)

1919. Durán T., Marco Antonio. Acotaciones para una definición de la reforma agraria en México (ILARI/A, 22, oct. 1971, p. 6-22, tables)

Good, short history of the institutional characteristics of Mexican agriculture since 1915 and a discussion of some of its current problems.

1920. Friedman, Bruno. To harness what nature gives us (UNESCO/I, 22:1/2, Jan./June 1972, p. 43-53)

Interview with President Echeverría on the subject of the relation of science and technology to Mexican society.

1921. Frietahaler, William O. Mexico's foreign trade and economic development. N.Y., Praeger Publishers, 1968. 160 p., bibl., illus., plates, tables (Praeger special studies in international economics and development)

Study showing how Mexico has avoided major pitfall of developing nations, namely the imbalance of too many essential imports for which exports cannot compensate. Author finds that since 1940 Mexico has been successful in import substitution while at the same time through border trade and tourism it has quadrupled its import capacity, thus preventing usual trade gap. Work's most controversial section is author's suggestion that other countries can do likewise. Offers some worthwhile information, particularly on the economies of northern states and border trade. [R. E. Greenleaf]

1922. Gates, Gary R. and G. Marilyn Gates. Uncertainty and development risk in *pequeña irrigación* decisions for peasants in Campeche, Mexico (CU/EG, 48:2, April 1972, p. 135-152, map, tables)

A methodology (applied to small-scale irrigation projects in Campeche) is illustrated for "pre-design" decision-making incorporating the consideration of uncertainty and risk in technological diffusion.

1923. Gil, Mario [*pseud. for* Carlos M. Velasco Gil]. Los ferrocarrileros. México, Editorial Extemporáneos, 1971. 236 p., plates (Serie: teoría y práctica política, 9)

Short history of Mexican railways and a longer history of the Mexican railway union movement. Strongly nationalistic, working-class, and railroad point-of-view detracts from presentation.

1924. Gonzáles Navarro, Moisés. México: el capitalismo nacionalista. México, B. Costa-Amic, 1970. 333 p., tables.

Collection of 16 articles by author published elsewhere during 1953-70. Evenly divided between pre-Revolution and post-Revolution periods. More recent articles carefully document transformation of PRI from proletarian party to one dominated by the local bourgeoisie.

1925. Gonzáles Salazar, Gloria. Problemas de la mano de obra en México: subempleo, requisitos educativos y flexibilidad ocupacional. México, UNAM, Instituto de Investigaciones Económicas, 1971. 231 p., tables.

Describes current education and training activities in Mexico to improve the quality of the labor supply. Author finds these efforts grossly inadequate for eliminating underemployment now and in the near future in Mexico.

1926. Griffiths, B. Mexican monetary policy and economic development. N.Y., Praeger Publishers, 1972. 174 p., tables (Praeger special studies in international economics and development)

This is primarily a macro-economic econometric model. It is a very good technical job of modeling, but there is little interpretation and use of the model. Writing appears overly hurried and the editing was clearly inadequate. Strongly recommended for those with a special interest in monetary policy and a special competence in econometrics.

1927. Guillén Romo, Arturo. Planificación económica a la mexicana. México, Editorial Nuestro Tiempo, 1971. 143 p., tables (Col. Desarrollo económico)

Traces world planning history very briefly and Mexican planning history at some length. Argues for profound structural changes in Mexico, with planning used to effectuate the changes. He finds Mexico and its Revolution to have come under the dominance of imperialism and national capitalists rather than the Mexican people.

1928. Gutelman, Michel. Reforme et mystification agraires en Amerique Latine: le cas de Mexique. Paris, Maspero, 1970. 259 p.

Hammett, Brian R. Politics and trade in southern Mexico: 1750-1821. See *HLAS 34:1680.*

1929. International Labor Organization, Geneva. The settlement of labour disputes in Mexico (AIFLD/R, 3:3, 1971, p. 32-58)

Comprehensive description of Mexican statutory and case laws concerning labor relations.

1930. Isbister, John. Urban employment and wages in a developing economy: the case of Mexico (UC/EDCC, 20:1, Oct. 1971, p. 24-46, tables)

Good, ingenious analysis of urban employment, growth and wages in the context of a two-sector Lewis-type model. Shows that Mexico has substantially different parameters for the model than most other less developed countries that have been studied.

1931. Jones, William I. Mexico's Puebla project: is there hope for the *minifundistas?* (International Development Review [Washington] 14:2, 1972, p. 21-25, table)

Almost casual discussion of a promising project which has greatly increased agricultural productivity without new seed varieties.

1932. King, Timothy. Mexico: industrialization and trade policies since 1940. London, Oxford Univ. Press *for the* Organization for Economic Cooperation and Development, Development Centre, 1970. 160 p., tables.

1933. Krieger, Ronald A. Mexico: an economic survey. N.Y., First National City Bank, 1971. 40 p., map, tables.

Revision of 1969 *The Mexican economy: performance and prospects.* Unsurprisingly, economic success of the last few decades is attributed to political stability, proximity to US and responsible financial structure.

1934. Lerdo de Tejada, Miguel. Comercio exterior de México: desde la Conquista hasta hoy. Nota preliminar de Luis Córdova. México, Banco Nacional de Comercio Exterior, 1967. 1 v. (Various pagings) bibl., tables.

Reproduction by Banco Nacional de Comercio Exterior of invaluable source book of statistics on Mexican international trade from 1521-1850. Originally published in 1853.

1935. López de la Parra, Manuel. La promoción turística en el estado de México (UNAM/IE, 31:121, enero/marzo 1971, p. 179-215, tables)

After much taxonomy there is a listing of many tourists promotion possibilities in the State of Mexico (surrounding Mexico City) and several methods which could be used to develop these possibilities (such as providing information and building roads).

López Rosado, Diego G. Historia y pensamiento económico de México. v. 1, Agricultura y ganadería; v. 2, Minería e industria; v. 3, Comunicaciones, transporte y relaciones de trabajo; v. 4, Comercio exterior e interior, sistema monetario y de crédito. See *HLAS 34:1759.*

1936. ——. Problemas económicos de México. 3. ed. México, UNAM, Instituto de Investigaciones, 1970. 503 p., bibl., fold. maps, tables (Textos universitarios)

Updates *HLAS 31:3291.*

1937. Martínez le Clainche, Roberto. México: elementos para el estudio estructural de su economía. México, UNAM, Instituto de Investigaciones Económicas, 1972. 136 p., bibl., tables.

Ten p. on the Mexican economy, 24 p. on the Mexican political system. Rest of book is taxonomy and introductions to fields of psychology and political science.

1938. Maturana Medina, Sergio and **Iván Restrepo Fernández.** El azúcar: problema de México; un estudio regional en Michoacán. México, Centro de Investigaciones Agrarias, 1970. 144 p., tables.

Wealth of descriptive statistics of agriculture in three townships of Michoacán. Much historical material, but mainly information from a questionnaire distributed in the mid-1960's. Seems to center on a sugar mill's effects on the region in the last two decades. More description than analysis. Good source of micro-level agricultural information.

1939. Mendoza Berrueto, Eliseo. Planificación regional en México; la experiencia del Plan Lerma (CESN/DE, 24:116, enero/marzo 1971, p. 99-174)

Reasonably thorough description of the process through which the very detailed regional plan for the Lerma-Santiago River Basin was developed in 1963-66. The basin includes about one-sixth of the population and one-16th of the land area of the country, so it is of major importance in the over-all planning. Many data are presented, including a 28x28 input-output matrix. More macro than project planning.

Miller, Frank C. Old villages and a new town: industrialization in Mexico. See item 1080.

1940. Navarrete, Ifigenia N. de *comp.* Bienestar campesino y desarrollo económico. México. Fondo de Cultura Económica, 1971. 337 p., tables.

Seven articles on various aspects of rural welfare, five of which are largely historical and descriptive. One finds a wealth of statistical information—especially in the excellent analytical article by de Navarrete and Arturo Cárdenas Ortega which analyzes the effects of different policies within the context of an econometric model of the agricultural sector with three subsectors. The assumed production functions could probably be improved.

1941. Navarrete, Jorge Eduardo *ed.* México: la política económica del nuevo gobierno. Presentación [por] Francisco Alcalá Quintero. México, Banco Nacional de Comercio Exterior, 1971. 430 p., tables.

Approximately three-fifths of the book are documents such as speeches by the President or cabinet members, decrees, etc. which specify various economic policies (primarily related to foreign trade and investment). The remainder of the book presents an explanation of the plans of the current administration for general development and increased income for rural areas in the 1970's.

1942. Ortiz Wadgymar, Arturo. Aspectos de la economía del Istmo de Tehuantepec. Revisión y presentación [por] Angel Bassols Batalla. México, UNAM, Instituto de Investigaciones Económicas, 1971. 114 p., bibl., fold. map, tables.

Good brief description of the economy of the Isthmus of Tehuantepec—suggesting more rational and concrete planning for the region rather than reliance on foreign interest in it as an alternative to the Panama Canal.

1943. Ramos Garza, Oscar. México ante la inversión extranjera: legislación, políticas y prácticas. México, La Impresora Azteca, 1971. 306 p., facsims., tables.

Paraphrases laws, decrees and policy statements pertinent to foreign investors. Blanks of various permit forms, etc. are provided. Useful for the Mexican lawyer who wants a handy reference book on the subject.

1944. Restrepo Fernández, Iván. El caso de los jornaleros agrícolas en México (ILARI/A, 23, enero 1972, p. 53-61)

Author discusses distressing plight of four million agricultural day laborers (one-half of agricultural labor force)—particularly the three million who have no land.

1945. Reunión Nacional para el Estudio del Desarrollo Industrial en México. *Naucalpán, Mex., 1970.* Reunión nacional para el estudio del desarrollo industrial de México. v. 1, La política del desarrollo industrial [and] Desarrollo de los sectores industriales; v. 2, Los grandes problemas del desarrollo industrial; v. 3/5, La promoción del desarrollo industrial, pts. 1/3; v. 6, Nuevos desarrollos industriales; v. 7, La política del desarrollo industrial; Desarrollo de los sectores industriales [and] Los grandes problemas del desarrollo industrial; v. 8, La promoción del desarrollo industrial; v. 9, Nuevos desarrollos industriales. México, Partido Revolucionario Institucional, Instituto de Estudios Politicos, Económicos y Sociales (PRI-IEPES), 1970. 10 v. (151, 263, 478, 1040[3 v. with continuous pagination], 554, 396, 630, 299 p.) illus., tables (Col. Naucalpán. 1. serie)

Ten-volume study: an introductory one and nine of short papers, all of which resulted from the PRI's presidential candidate suggesting a study. Papers were presented originally on 26-27 June 1970. This is something like a printing of all the background papers developed for a presidential candidate in the US, however, these papers were written for publication.

1946. Revista de la Facultad de Derecho de México. UNAM. Vol. 19, No. 73, enero/marzo 1969- . México.

Issue devoted to four round table discussions on "The Mexican Agrarian Reform." The major discussion papers were presented by Marco Antonio Durán, Ramón Fernández y Fernández, Edmundo Flores, and Fernando Paz Sánchez. Flores' article is especially good—it injects the idea that investment in industry may be more rational in Mexico than investment in agriculture.

Reyes Heroles, Jesús. México y su petróleo. See *HLAS 34:1867.*

————. El petróleo de México. See *HLAS 34:1868.*

1947. Reynolds, Clark W. Changing trade patterns and policy in Mexico: some lessons for developing countries (Food Research Institute Studies [Stanford, Calif.] 9:1, 1970, p. 3-41)

1948. Ross, Stanley R. México: las tensiones del progreso. Austin, Tex., Univ. of Texas, Institute of Latin American Studies, 1971/72. 21 p. (Offprint series, 114)

Short tour of the current Mexican political and economic situation with an optimistic view of Mexico's ability to cope with the problems which material progress brings.

1949. Solis M., Leopoldo and others. Los problemas nacionales. Advertencia [por] Gabriel Careaga. México, UNAM, Facultad de Ciencias Políticas y Sociales, 1971. 201 p., tables (Serie Estudios, 23)

Excellent book on current Mexican economic, political and education problems. Approximately the first two-fifths of the book will be of most interest to economists. There one finds an excellent proposal by Sra. de Navarete for education financing and planning, a general discussion by Solís, and a discussion of taxing and spending policy by B. Retchkinan.

1950. Vázquez Arroyo, Francisco. Presupuestos por programas para el sector público de México. Prefacio [por] Horacio Flores de la Peña. México, UNAM, Coordinación de Humanidades, 1971. 319 p., bibl., tables.

Textbook on "Program Budgeting" written, surprisingly, with no reference to works in the English language. Describes application of the technique in the Mexican budgeting process and presents cases for the National University, the Dept. of Public Works, and Petróleos Mexicanos.

Weisskoff, Richard. Income distribution and economic growth in Puerto Rico, Argentina, and Mexico. See item 2528.

1951. Winkelman, Don and **David Hansen.** Idle land: an anomaly in Mexican resource use (UW/LE, 47:3, Aug. 1971, p. 289-297)

An econometric study of this interesting question. The statistical results were at variance with the hypotheses in many cases and were not adequately explained.

Wionczek, Miguel S. Inversión y tecnología extranjera en América Latina. See item 1901.

1952. Yarza G., Alberto J. El futuro de la política fiscal en México (UNAM/IE, 31:121, enero/marzo 1971, p. 13-22, tables)

Interesting article comparing 1965 and 1969 government spending and income. A projection to 1976 is made and recommendations for reform in the system follow. Compares budget with actual 1969 figures and shows astonishing discrepancies.

CENTRAL AMERICA AND THE WEST INDIES

(EXCEPT PUERTO RICO)

MARION HAMILTON GILLIM

Chairman, Department of Economics
Barnard College
Columbia University

MOST OF THE SAME COMMENTS COULD BE MADE about the works in this section that were made two years ago. Among the changes to be noted are more work by economists from the region and increased attention in the Caribbean to economic integration and CARIFTA.

Most of the publications in the Central American group were prepared by Central Americans. Statistical works and entries treating the Common Market are most frequent. The theme of economic development continues to run through most of the writing. For the past quarter century, the Central American governments have been improving and augmenting their statistical series. This progress can be observed in the statistical entries, including a time series of El Salvador's price index (item 1960), the use of Panama's first commercial census of 1965 in a study of retail trade (item 1966), Guatemala's publication of that country's first commercial census (item 1968), Panama's new series on the immigrants, emigrants, and visitors to the country (item (1974), a Guatemalan study of the expenditures of rural families (item 1973), a sample study of the poor in Managua (item 1980), and two studies of imports using trade statistics (items 1970 and 1977). The post-1969 writings on the Common Market included here do not reflect interest in the economic impact of the Honduran-Salvadorean difficulty. Instead they show some concern with the non-economic aspects of economic integration (items 1964, 1972a and 1981), emphasize its theoretical or legal aspects (items 1956 and 1957), or stop short of 1969 (item 1977). Persons interested in the progress of the Central American Common Market should consult regularly the monthly *Carta*

Informativa of SIECA (Secretaría Permanente del Tratado General de Integración Económica Centroamericana).

The salient feature of the publications in the group of entries from members of the British Commonwealth is the important role of the University of the West Indies in publishing economic works through its Institute of Social and Economic Research and the periodicals *Social and Economic Studies* and the *Caribbean Quarterly*. The chief subject throughout is economic development. In addition, we find economic integration discussed in the early writings on CARIFTA (items 1995-1996), the preoccupation with unemployment as a chronic evil (items 2009 and 2012-2013), and attention to agricultural problems (items 1988, 1999, 2011, 2028, 2030 and 2037). Although the four entries included for the Dominican Republic and three for Haiti are too few to reveal any trend in economic thought in these nations, they suggest a continuing strong interest in economic development as a national goal.

Several Cuban studies already cited in the University of Pittsburgh *Cuban Studies Newsletter* and annotated in this section by its editor, Professor Carmelo Mesa-Lago, reflect Cuban thought and research on the country's economy (items 1986, 1991, 1994, 1997, 2027, 2029, and 2034-2035), other Cuban items listed below are concerned with agricultural production, fishing and the cheese industry (items 2001, 2019, 2022). The writings from the United States on the subject deal largely with explanations of Cuba's failure to achieve the desired rapid economic development or with problems resulting from the breaking of relations between the United States and Cuba. Attention is called both to Professor Mesa-Lago's bibliography in item 2018, which examines Cuba's movement towards reliance on moral incentives and contains many useful references on the country, and to his book *Revolutionary change in Cuba* reviewed elsewhere in this volume (item 7591).

CENTRAL AMERICA

Ashcraft, Norman. Economic opportunities and patterns of work: the case of British Honduras. See item 1125.

1953. Baer, Donald E. The retail sales tax in a developing country: Costa Rica and Honduras (NTA/NTJ, 24:4, Dec. 1971, p. 465-174)

Compares experiences with sales taxes in two economies where many sales are by small vendors and administrative problems are critical. Treats a number of important issues: rates, exemptions, collections, procedures, allocation effects. [J. M. Hunter]

1954. Cappelletti Vidal, Ricardo. Reflexiones en torno a la problemática social de la integración centroamericana. Asunción, Centro Paraguayo de Estudios Sociológicos, 1971. 14 p., tables (Col. de Reimpresiones, 47)

Regrets that sociologists have not participated in planning for the possible important social effects of economic integration. Reprint from the *Revista Paraguaya de Sociología*.

1955. Castrillo Zeledón, Mario. El régimen de libre comercio en Centroamérica. San José, Editorial Universitaria Centroamericana (EDUCA), 1970. 335 p., tables (Col. Integración)

Informative book by an author who was with SIECA during period covered and reports what he observed firsthand of Common Market's development and its problems prior to 1969, with legal analysis of important sections of the General Treaty and Resolutions.

Chilman, Walter J. Isthmian canal demand forecast: an economic analysis of potential tonnage traffic. See item 6705.

1956. Churchill, Anthony; Klaus Huber; Elke Meldau; and Alan Walters. Road user charges in Central America. Washington, International Bank for Reconstruction and Development, 1972. 176 p., bibl., tables (World Bank staff occasional papers, 15)

Case study applying theories of pricing the use of roads with goals of resource allocation and economic growth to the highway system within the Central American Common Market.

1957. Compton Advertising (firm), *San Francisco, Calif.* Compton Economic and Market Development Division. Marketing action plan for the development of tourism in Central America. Guatemala, Delgado Impresores, 1969. 150 p., tables.

Goals and specific recommendations for achieving them prepared by a company selected by SITCA (the Tourism Council of the Organization of Central American States).

1958. Congreso Centroamericano de Economistas, Contadores Públicos y Auditores, *II, San Salvador, 1965.* Compendio de estudios técnicos presentados. San Salvador, 1965. 456 p., tables.

Collection of papers by Central Americans related especially to development and economic integration presented at a meeting in San Salvador.

1959. Cooperativismo en El Salvador: legislación y doctrina. San Salvador, Cooperativa de Abogados de El Salvador, 1971. 200 p., tables.

Includes documents related to lawyers' association and a history of cooperative movement and laws affecting cooperatives in El Salvador.

1960. El Salvador. Ministerio de Economía. Dirección General de Estadística y Censos. Indice de precios al consumidor obrero en San Salvador, Mejicanos y Delgado: 1960-1969. San Salvador, 1970. 103 p., map, tables.

Monthly index based on expenditure survey of working class families made in 1954 with related calculations, including average prices, relative importance of major categories of consumption, and purchasing power of the *colón*.

1961. Fallas, Marco Antonio. La factoría de tabacos de Costa Rica. San José, Editorial Costa Rica, 1972. 249 p., bibl., illus., plates, tables.

Historian looks at leading role played by tobacco in Costa Rica's agricultural development, giving special attention to colonial period both before and after 1766 when Spain established a monopoly.

1962. Fernández, Guido; José Miguel Alfaro; Eduardo Lizano; and Miguel Barzuna. Seminario sobre el Mercado Común Centroamericano. San José, Asociación Nacional de Fomento Económico, 1968. 60 p.

Report of discussion by seminar participants of uniform laws affecting commerce, free movement of labor, convertibility of currencies, and fiscal problems.

1963. Fomenting improvements in food marketing in Costa Rica. East Lansing, Mich., Michigan State Univ., Latin American Studies Center, 1972. 79 p., bibl., map, illus., tables (Marketing in developing communities series. Research report, 10)

Following preliminary analysis, interim report suggests ways to improve marketing including further studies, training programs, central wholesale market, and national system of financing municipal markets.

1964. Galindo Pohl, Reynaldo. Condicionamiento sociopolítico de la integración (UM/JIAS, 12:2, April 1970, p. 159-186)

Examines unfortunate neglect of non-economic aspects of integration and need to identify them and meet problems they raise, with special attention to the Central American situation.

1965. González Fley, Carlos. El sistema cooperativo y nuestro sub-desarrollo socioeconómico (RCPC, 21:105, junio 1969, p. 24-28)

Sees agricultural cooperatives as means of economic improvement in Nicaragua, with examples drawn from Denmark, France, Argentina, Israel, and Mexico.

1966. Greer, Thomas V. The mercantile potpourri called Panama (UM/JIAS, 14:3, Aug. 1972, p. 347-359, bibl., table)

Using data from the first commercial census made in 1965 and observations from personal visits to stores, author describes conditions in both rural and urban trade.

1967. Guatemala. Consejo Nacional de Planificación Económica. La planificación en Guatemala, su historia, problemas y perspectivas. Introducción [por] Oscar del León Aragón. Guatemala, Tipografía Nacional, 1969. 132 p., tables.

Valuable collection of government programs and analysis of why they have not been completely effective.

1968. ————. Ministerio de Economía. Dirección General de Estadística. Censos económicos, 1965. v. 4, II [i.e., Segundo] censo comercial: establecimientos con contabilidad. Guatemala, 1971. 342 p., tables.

Published six years after census, includes: employees, payrolls, sales, stock of goods, and capital of the 2,958 wholesale and retail establishments keeping books.

1969. ————. Ministerio de Hacienda y Crédito Público. Dirección Técnica del Presupuesto. Presupuesto de ingresos y egresos del Estado: ejercicio fiscal 1972. Guatemala, 1971. 1 v. (Various pagings) tables.

1970. Guerra Borges, Alfredo. Evaluación de la política de formento industrial en Guatemala. Prólogo [por] Julio Alfonso Figueroa G. Guatemala, Delgado Impresores, 1971. 150 p., tables.

Statistical study of imports by enterprises operating under development laws and of their production statistics, with critical evaluation of effects of national legislation in promoting industrial growth.

Hoy, Don R. A review of development planning in Guatemala. See item 6693.

1971. Lizano Fait, Eduardo. Comentarios sobre economía nacional. San José, Univ. de Costa Rica, 1971. 355 p., tables (Serie economía y estadística, 35)

Sixteen essays written since 1954 treating agriculture, banking, development and economic integration, 12 were delivered at meetings or published in newspapers, university series and central bank reviews and four appear here for the first time.

1972. McClelland, Donald H. The Central American Common Market: economic policies, economic growth, and choices for the future. N.Y., Praeger Publishers, 1972. 243 p., tables. (Praeger international studies in international economics and development)

Careful study which seeks to evolve the effects of the CACM. Attention is specifically given to effects on GNP, structure, and on such variables as balance of payment, trade diversion, prices, etc. Appendices provide background information. [J. M. Hunter]

1972a. Molina Chocano, Guillermo. Integración centroamericana y dominación internacional: un ensayo de interpretación sociológica. San José, Editorial Universitaria Centroamericana (EDUCA), 1971. 95 p., bibl., tables (Col. Integración)

Examines thesis that Central America suffers increasing dependency with a Common Market and its accompanying industrial growth and offers suggestions for avoiding this dilemma.

1973. Orellana González, René Arturo. Encuesta sobre ingresos y gastos de la familia del campesino asalariado de Guatemala, 1966. Guatemala, Univ. de San Carlos, Instituto de Investigaciones Económicas y Sociales, 1967? 531 p., maps, tables.

After delay of some years in publication, book contains a description of methods used in drawing sample and interviewing 1,800 families in this first study of living conditions of rural wage-earners in Guatamela and tabulation of results.

1974. Panama. Contraloría General de la República. Dirección de Estadística y Censo. Estadística panameña; migración internacional: año 1970. Panamá, 1971. 23 p., tables (Serie, R. Año, 30)

New series showing passengers entering, in transit, and leaving the country, classified by means of transportation, domicile, nationality, length of visit, and age and sex.

1975. Pincus, Joseph. Interim adjustment policy in the CACM [Central American Common Market] (UM/JIAS, 13:2, April 1971, p. 182-196, bibl., tables)

Veteran observer of CACM evaluates San José Protocol of June 1968, as temporary means to counter fiscal and balance-of-payments deficits of 1960's.

Prats, Raymond. Le conflit Honduras-El Salvador: ses conséquences pour la Communauté Centraméricaine. See item 8142.

1976. Sánchez Román, Rodolfo. Consideraciones especiales en torno a la promoción, organización y funcionamiento de las cooperativas de mercadeo (RCPC, 21:105, junio 1969, p. 29-33, tables)

Suggestions with examples of how to organize an agricultural marketing cooperative.

1977. Schiavo-Campo, Salvatore. Import structure and import substitution in the Central American Common Market. Río Piedras, P.R., Univ. of Puerto Rico, College of Social Sciences, Dept. of Economics, 1972. 122 p., tables (Student/faculty seminar series)

Identifies and measures changes in imports during period 1953-68 for each country and for entire Common Market with some consideration of policy.

1978. Siri, Gabriel. El efecto de las carreteras en la integración económica de la América Central (FCE/TE, 38:152, oct./dic. 1971, p. 1081-1098, maps, tables)

Relates changes in transportation costs, price levels, production, and volume of intra-Central-American trade; and recommends an emphasis on highway transportation in planning economic integration.

1979. Soto Jiménez, Rolando A. Some notes on harmonization in the Central American Common Market (Bulletin for International Fiscal Documentation [International Bureau of Fiscal Documentation, Amsterdam] 25:1, Jan. 1971, p. 8-16)

Lawyer and economist analyzes need to harmonize or unify legal systems of Common Market countries and contrasts process in Central America and Europe, with special attention to Central American agriculture, industry, capital markets, and fiscal policy.

1980. Téfel, Reinaldo Antonio. Nicaragua: la economía de los pobres (ILARI/A, 22, Oct. 1971, p. 151-166, tables)

Chapter from longer work prepared by team representing several disciplines set up to learn causes of poverty in capital city with aim of finding how to alleviate problem. This statistical description of group studied includes age, sex, occupation, income, expenditures and savings.

1981. Torres Rivas, Edelberto. Les problèmes sociaux du développement et de l'integration en Amérique Centrale (*in* Congrès International de l'Université Laval, *Québec, Canada, 1968.* L'avenir d'un continent: ou va l'Amérique latine? [see item 82] p. 134-162, tables)

Describes the interaction of economic growth and the Common Market with social changes between 1945-65. Includes a transcript of discussion following presentation of paper.

1982. Villamil, José A. Situación demográfica de Guatemala y sus efectos socio-económicos (UM/JIAS, 13:2, April 1971, p. 197-214, tables)

Disapproving view of rapid growth of population resulting in retardation of economic growth and overcrowding of educational facilities.

WEST INDIES

1983. Adams, Nassau A. Import structure and economic growth in Jamaica, 1954-1967 (UWI/SES, 20:3, Sept. 1971, p. 235-266, tables)

Statistical analysis of the growth of GNP in relation to changes in economy's structure and demand for imports.

Alvarez Díaz, José; Alberto Arredondo; Raúl M. Shelton; and **Juan F. Vizcaíno.** Cuba: geopolítica y pensamiento económico. See *HLAS 34:2046.*

1984. Alvaro Bobadilla, Pedro. Aspectos de la industria y la economía dominicanas en la década del 60. Santo Domingo, Imprenta Nuñez, 1970. 518 p.

Collection of journalist's articles published in his daily column provides useful description of development in the Dominican Republic.

1985. Andic, Fuat; Suphan Andic; and **Douglas Dosser.** A theory of economic integration for developing countries: illustrated by Caribbean countries. London, George Allen and Unwin, 1971. 176 p., tables (Univ. of York studies in economics, 6)

Argues that trade creation and trade diversion are not the appropriate judgment criteria for integration as it applies to *developing* countries. Exchange-saving and industrializing effects are of equal importance. Pts. 2 and 3 concern themselves with description and application of theory to Caribbean countries. Tightly reasoned, well presented. [J. M. Hunter]

1986. *Anuario Azucarero de Cuba.* Ministerio de Comercio Exterior No. 1, 1936 [through] 1962-   . La Habana.

Statistical yearbook includes sugar statistics on output, yields, wages in the sugar sector, prices in the international market, exports, stocks, by-products. [C. Mesa-Lago]

1987. Barkin, David. La estrategia cubana de desarrollo (CM/FI, 12:2, oct./dic. 1971, p. 175-200, tables)

Sympathetic but critical analysis of difficulties of planning for development and carrying out the plans. Also discusses some of the social effects.

1988. Beckford, George L. Análisis económico de la utilización y desarrollo de los recursos agrícolas en las economías de plantación (IDES/DE, 9:35, oct./dic. 1969, p. 349-385, illus., tables)

Translation of article originally published in *Social and Economic Studies* (see *HLAS 33:2837*).

1989. Bhola, Ranal and **Harold Breimyer.** Cuba-U.S. sugar policy and interim suppliers' dilemma (Business & Government Review [Univ. of Missouri, Columbia] 11:6, Nov. Dec. 1970, p. 3-9, tables)

Brief look at the position of countries granted a part of Cuban quota.

1990. Bilkey, Warren J. Public enterprise models and a Caribbean experience (IAMEA, 25:3, Winter 1971, p. 39-55, bibl., tables)

Theoretical structure, goals, and relationship between resources and environment of publicly owned manufacturing and commercial enterprises, with case studies of some actual enterprises.

1991. *Boletín Estadístico (BE).* Dirección General de Estadística, Junta Central de Planificación (JUCEPLAN). 1968 [through] 1970-   . La Habana.

Annual compendium of statistics, originally restricted. Second issue, however, dropped phrase *circulación restringida.* Titles of sections and main topics: 1) Geography and Climate; 2) Population; 3) Global Indicators; 4) Employment and Wages; 5) Agriculture and Livestock; 6) Industry; 7) Construction and Investment; 8) Transportation; 9) Communications; 10) Domestic Trade; 11) Foreign Trade; 12) Education; 13) Cultural Activities; 14) Public Health; 15) Sports and Recreation; and 16) Traffic Accidents. In terms of volume, disaggregation, continuity and accuracy, best data are on: population, education, fishing, sugar, climate, foreign trade and public health, in that order. Poorest data on: global indicators, investment, employment and wages. [C. Mesa-Lago]

Boodhoo, Ken. Sugar and East Indian indentureship in Trinidad. See item 1129.

1992. Brand, W. Hulp aan Suriname en de Nederlandse Antillen (NGIZ/IS, 27:6, feb. 1973, p. 139-144, tables)

Critical evaluation of the Netherlands' development aid to overseas territories (at present 90 percent of total). Author considers this aid excessive and advocates a different orientation. Includes English summary.

1993. *CARIFTA.Economist & Business Post.* Quarterly journal of research information for the Caribbean. No. 1, Nov. 1970- Georgetown.

First issue of quarterly from Guyana addressed to Caribbean businessmen. Not exclusively devoted to economic integration. Lists as a regular feature "CARIFTA Commentary." Articles on economic subjects include: Donald Augustin "Planning for Exports," Clive Thomas "Central Banking in Guyana," and "The Realities of an Incomes Policy in Guyana."

1994. *Comercio Exterior.* Ministerio del Comercio Exterior. No. 1, marzo 1963 [through] sept. 1966-   . La Habana.

Quarterly. Technical articles on foreign trade and sugar market. Discussions on incentives, planning, investment, prices, management, application of mathematical methods for optimal imports. Reports on foreign statistics, including imports and exports by product and trade partners, and commercial agreements. Available at Library of Congress; Harvard Univ.; Univ. of Miami; Univ. of Pittsburgh; and Washington Univ. [C. Mesa-Lago]

1995. Commonwealth Caribbean Regional Secretariat, *Georgetown.* CARIFTA and the new Caribbean. Preface [by] William G. Demas. Georgetown, 1971. 143 p., bibl., maps, tables.

Background, progress, problems, and specific areas of cooperation of this recently established institution for economic integration during its first three years.

1996. ——, ——. Economics of devaluation under West Indian conditions. Foreword [by] William G. Demas. Georgetown, 1972. 20 p., bibl.

Portions of background paper on issues of devaluation prepared for CARIFTA meeting to arrange for stable exchanges within area following international currency re-alignments of late 1971.

1997. Conference of the Food and Agriculture Organization of the United Nations, XVI, Roma, 1971. Delegación de Cuba. Informe presentado por la Delegación de Cuba: la producción agropecuaria en el II Decenio para el Desarrollo. Roma, n.p., 1971. 57 p.

Covers decade of the 1970s. Summarizes Cuban accomplishments, 1966-70 and sets goals, 1971-75. Consists of sections on: 1) infrastructure (irrigation, roads, buildings, electrification, etc.): 2) modernization (soil improvements, mechanization, animal husbandry); 3) research (on agriculture, cattle, poultry, forestry and fishing); 4) education (vocational and higher education schools). Report foresees no changes in rate of output during 1971-75 but expects sharp increases during 1976-80. It acknowledges, however, that all targets for this period are not as yet quantified. [C. Mesa-Lago]

1998. Cumper, G. E. Incomes of upper 2.5 percent and 8.5 percent of income tax payers in relation to national income, Jamaica, 1951-65 (UWI/SES, 20:4, Dec. 1971, p. 362-368, table)

Data based on national accounts and income tax statistics show little change in percentage of national income going to top income groups.

1999. DeCastro, Steve. Operations research [O.R.] and the West Indian sugar industry (UWI/CQ, 17:1, March 1971, p. 23-33, bibl.).

Brief summary of development and use of techniques including linear programming and simulation models, followed by suggested applications of optimizing tools to both the growing and manufacturing stages of sugar production.

2000. Dominican Republic. Banco Central. Oficina Nacional de Estadística. Estudio sobre presupuestos familiares. t. 1, Ingresos y gastos de las familias en la ciudad de Santo Domingo, 1969; t. 2, Metodología para el cálculo del índice de precios al consumidor en la ciudad de Santo Domingo, 1969. Santo Domingo, 1971. 2 v. (133, 422 p.) map, tables.

Expenditure study of sample of 606 households in capital city provides weights for monthly consumer price index to be constructed with 1969 as base year. Includes discussion of the choice of formulae. Study prepared by the Dominican government in cooperation with the USAID mission.

2001. Echeverría Salvat, Oscar A. La agricultura cubana: 1934-66. Miami, Fla., Ediciones Universal, 1971. 116 p., tables.

Pt. 1 consists of comparative analysis of Cuban agricultural worker's standard of living during 1934-66. Main body of work drawn from 1957 survey conducted by Catholic University Assn. (ACU) and National Bank of Cuba, under author's direction. Data include: sociological factors, health and nutritional conditions, housing and living conditions, employment, income and expenditures. Author reconstructs descriptive portion of 1957 survey adding comparisons with investigations carried out in 1934 by Foreign Policy Assn. and by Prof. Lowry Nelson in 1946 (see item 7594). Pt. 2 reviews 1959, Agrarian Reform Law its social objectives and impact on agricultural production. [C. Mesa-Lago]

2002. Estrella, Julio C. La moneda, la banca y las finanzas en la República Dominicana. v. 1, 1492-1947. v. 2, 1948-1970. Santiago, D.R., Univ. Católica Madre y Maestra, 1971. 2 v. (742, 491 p.), bibl., tables (Col. Estudios)

Historical background to 1947, reform in that year of currency and banking, role of international organizations, and financial developments since 1948.

2003. Fiallo, Fabio Rafael. Alternativas de política industrial en la República Dominicana (FCE/TE, 40:157, enero/marzo 1973, p. 159-172, tables)

Questions a protectionist development policy in so small an economy and prefers instead one promoting exports and encouraging investment of domestic capital.

González, Alfonso. Castro: economic effects on Latin America. See item 1816.

2005. Gouré, Leon and Julian Weinkle. Cuba's new dependency (USIA/PC, 2, March/April 1972, p. 68-79, tables)

Anomalies resulting from political character of Soviet Union's interest in Cuba and lack of success in economic development. For Spanish version, see item 2006.

2006. ——— and ———. La dependencia económica de Cuba (USIA/PI, 19:1/2, enero/abril 1972, p. 18-32)

Spanish version of item 2005.

2007. Guyana Journal. Ministry of External Affairs. Vol. 1, No. 4, Sept. 1970- Georgetown.

Publishes data concerning the VI Conference of Heads of Government of Commonwealth Caribbean Countries, development of Free Trade Area agreements (CARIFTA), and establishment of a Caribbean Development Bank.

2008. Haiti. Conseil National de Développement et de Planification. Plan d'action: économique et sociale; 1968-1969. Port-au-Prince, n.p., n.d. 131 p., maps, tables.

Includes changes in laws affecting planning since 1957 statistics of gross domestic product and trade, and program for development by economic sectors.

2009. Harewood, Jack ed. Human resources in the Commonwealth Caribbean. St. Augustine, T. and T., Univ. of the West Indies, Institute of Social and Economic Research, Human Resources Seminar, 1970. 1 v. (Various pagings) tables.

Papers delivered at a seminar held in Mona, Jam., in 1970, and of particular significance in an area troubled both by lack of acceptable employment opportunities and also by shortage of trained persons in labor force.

Hicks, Frederick. Making a living during the dead season in sugar-producing regions of the Caribbean. See item 6625.

2010. Jamaica. Ministry of Finance and Planning. Town Planning Department. A national physical plan for Jamaica: 1970-1990. Kingston, 1971. 116 p., fold. maps, illus., plates, tables.

Special Fund Project presenting a 20-year plan for land use by agriculture, mining, tourism, and manufacturing supported by utilities, housing, recreation, and transportation. Admirable attention devoted to social needs and quality of environment.

2011. ———. Ministry of Rural Land Development. 1st. [First] report. Kingston, 1970. 104 p., map, plates, tables.

Of special interest is new ministry's decentralization of activities for regional development through area land authorities.

2012. Jefferson, Owen. The economic situation of the Commonwealth Caribbean (UWI/CQ, 18:1, March 1972, p. 87-99, tables)

Describes failure of recent development measures to increase employment as well as output. Originally, a paper in item 2009.

2013. ———. The post-war economic development of Jamaica. Mona, Jam., Univ. of the West Indies, Institute of Social and Economic Research, 1972. 302 p., bibl., fold. map, tables.

Examination of Jamaican economy's rapid growth and later tendency to slow down during period 1950-69 and an evaluation of development achieved with particular reference to effects on employment. Author refers frequently to Demas' criteria of development (see *HLAS 29:3458*).

2014. Kuczynski, Jürgen. Probleme de Entwicklung einer sozialistischen Landwirtschaft in Kuba (Jahrbuch für Wirtschaftgeschichte [Deutsche Akademie der Wissenshaften zu Berlin, GDR] 1, 1971. p. 11-43, tables)

Author argues that countries whose economies are underdeveloped because of US imperialistic policies, can only overcome their stagnation by choosing the road to socialism. Selects Cuba as case study because of "her experience of transition from an agricultural to an industrialized society." Concludes with belief that other countries will inevitably follow Cuba's example. Includes preface by Carlos Rafael Rodríguez. [H. J. Hoyer]

2015. Langer, Marshall J. Doing business in the Caribbean. N.Y., Practising Law Institute, 1972. 218 p. (Corporate law and practice course handbook series, 85)

Papers issued prior to seminar on taxation and business using what is described as a "how to do it" approach. Contains compilation of useful information about each country.

2016. Lowenfeld, Andreas F. Act of State and Department of State: First National City Bank vs. Banco Nacional de Cuba (ASIL/J, 66:5, Oct. 1972, p. 795-814)

Purely legal article of interest to economists since it treats decisions affecting protection of private investment abroad.

2017. Marshall, O. R. West Indian land law: conspectus and reform (UWI/SES, 20:1, March 1971, p. 1-14)

Legal analysis of "gap between law and social reality" and suggestion of need for inter-disciplinary research directed towards reforms.

2018. Mesa-Lago, Carmelo. Ideological, political, and economic factors in the Cuban controversy on material versus moral incentives (UM/JIAS, 14:1, Feb. 1972, p. 49-111, bibl., tables)

Important monograph showing wavering development of Cuban attitude towards material rewards and political, economic, and ideological forces influencing it, against background of Marxist-Leninist theory and present situations in principal socialist countries leading to the extreme Cuban position in support of moral incentives. Excellent bibliography. See also author's *Revolutionary change in Cuba*, item 7591.

———. Revolutionary change in Cuba. See item 7591.

2019. Mintchev, Tzoni Velcov. La industria quesera cubana: patagras, gruyere, cheddar, queso-crema, queso proceso; origen, nutrición, producción. La Habana, Empresa Consolidada de Industrias Lácteas, Sección de Capacitación, 1970? 107 p., tables.

Technical work by a consultant on cheese production with applications to Cuba.

2021. Moore, O. Ernest. Haiti: its stagnant society and shackled economy. Jericho, N.Y., Exposition Press, 1972. 281 p. (An exposition university book)

Former UN consultant tells why he believes Haiti has lagged in development and suggests some possible remedies.

2022. Morales, Pedro. 5 [i.e., Cinco] años de Cuba en el mundo pesquero (Mar y Pesca [La Habana] 79, abril 1972, p. 26-35, plates, tables)

Popular article showing increased investment in boats and plants for processing fish and growth in both imports and exports.

2023. Mulchansingh, Vernon C. The oil industry in the economy of Trinidad (UPR/CS, 11:1, July 1971, p. 73-100, map, tables)

Economic geographer continues writing on Trinidad's economic development, concentrating here on dominant industry in its GDP, public revenues, and foreign trade. Description and statistics of background and current importance of petroleum.

2024. Odle, Maurice A. The significance of non-bank financial intermediaries in the Caribbean: an analysis of patterns of financial structure and development. Mona, Jam., Univ. of the West Indies, Institute of Social and Economic Development, 1972. 212 p., tables.

Discusses organization and credit role of insurance companies, building societies, and savings banks, which author finds to be "more 'near-banks' than non-banks." Proposals for their reform. Analysis is limited to institutions in Jamaica, Trinidad, and Guyana.

2025. Pomonti, Bernard. Profil économique d'Haïti (IFH/C, 117, dec. 1971, p. 87-100, tables)

Useful, factual presentation in outline and tabular form of resources, infrastructure, balance of payments, budget, and development policy.

2026. Pujadas, Leo. The outflow of trained personnel from Trinidad and Tobago (*in* United Nations. Social Development Division. United Nations Institute for Training and Research [UNITAR]. The brain drain from five developing countries: Cameroon, Colombia, Lebanon, The Philippines, Trinidad and Tobago. N.Y., 1971, p. 42-66 [UNITAR Research reports, 5]

Describes growing problem, its costs in money, foregone production, and effect on wages; its benefits in form of remittances, return migration, and reduced underemployment; and policies directed at its solution.

2027. *Revista del Banco Nacional de Cuba.* No. 1, enero 1955 [through] marzo 1960- La Habana.

Monthly. Includes articles on national, international and general economic themes, review of economic and financial legislation. Also bibliographic index, tables, graphs, and statistics. Available at Univ. of Pittsburgh. [C. Mesa-Lago]

2028. Richardson, Bonham C. The agricultural dilemma of the post-plantation Caribbean (IAMEA, 26:1, Summer 1972, p. 59-70)

Examines uncertainties facing sugar producers as Britain enters European Economic Community and probable difficulties of adjustment through shift away from colonial institutions and agricultural diversification.

2029. Roberts, C. Paul and **Mukhtar Hamour** eds. Cuba 1968. Los Angeles, Calif., Univ. of California, 1970. 213 p., tables.

Contains 128 statistical tables for 1959-68, drawn largely from JUCEPLAN's *Boletín Estadístico* (see item 1991). Contacts provided by professors Manuel Pedro González and Edward González (who visited Cuba in 1968) made it possible to establish a statistical data exchange with JUCEPLAN's statistical dept. Another trip to Cuba by C. Paul Roberts (July-Aug. 1969) permitted collection of data for later years in addition to clarification of statistical problems. [C. Mesa-Lago]

2030. Rodríguez, D. W. Pimento: a short economic history. Preface [by] W. G. Stuart. Kingston, Ministry of Agriculttre and Fisheries. Agricultural Information Service, 1969? 52 p., bibl., plates, tables (Commodity bulletin, 3)

Production, harvest, and marketing of berries of an indigenous evergreen tree known as "all spice" which ranks fourth among Jamaica's agricultural exports. Data on exports from 17th century to present. Follows two earlier bulletins on bananas and coffee.

2031. Theuns, H. L. Hulpverlening aan de Nederlandse Antillen (NGIZ/IS, 25:5, maart 1971, p. 499-521, tables)

Analyzes financial aid to Netherlands Antilles, describes process of Dutch aid, and reports on necessity and effects of aid. Includes criticisms from Antilles and Netherlands. [H. J. Hoyer]

2032. Thomas, Clive Y. The structure, performance and prospects of central banking in the Caribbean. Mona, Jam., Univ. of the West Indies, Institute of Social and Economic Research, 1972. 77 p., tables.

Organization and operations of central banks of Guyana, Jamaica, and Trinidad-Tobago by professor of economics from area with proposals for reforms to increase their role in economic development.

2033. Trinidad and Tobago. Government of . . . Third five-year plan, 1969-1973, as approved by Parliament. Port of Spain, Government Printery, 1970. 453 p., tables.

Goals of full employment by middle 1980's, diversification of production, and more economic independence in decision-making. Details of sectoral and social programs.

2034. Universidad de La Habana. Centro de Información Científica y Técnica. Centro de Investigaciones de la Caña. Sistema australiano de corte, zafra, 1971. La Habana, 1971. 100 p. (Investigaciones agroindustriales, 8:8)

One of Cuban economy's most serious problems is manpower shortage in sugar harvest, especially in cane cutting stage. In 1970, Center for Research on Sugar Cane began investigation of Australian system of burning cane fields and cutting cane. Here Center reports on system's positive and negative aspects and suggests means for adapting it to Cuban needs. [C. Mesa-Lago]

2035. ———. Equipos de Investigaciones Económicas. Resúmenes de los trabajos terminados y en proceso. La Habana, Centro de Información Científica y Técnica, n.d., 63 p. (Investigaciones económicas, 1:1)

Useful bibliography with descriptions of contents of work at university as of 1968, classified by subject: sugar cane and its derivatives, studies of agriculture and stock raising, industrial studies, and transportation and trade.

Valdés, Nelson P. La diplomacia del azúcar: Estados Unidos y Cuba. See item 7607.

2036. Varlack, Pearl and **Norwell Harrigan.** Anegada: feudal development in the twentieth century (UWI/CS, 17:1, March 1971, p. 5-15, bibl.)

Reports on local opposition to plan to develop this small island (15 square miles with 44 households) by 199-year lease with tax exemptions to stimulate tourism and light industry through construction of an airstrip, hotel, harbor facilities, and roads.

2037. West Indian Agricultural Economics Conference, *IV, Cave Hill, Barbados, 1969.*

Proceedings. Edited by D. T. Edwards. St. Augustine, T. & T., The Univ. of the West Indies, Dept. of Agricultural Economics and Management, 1969. 135 p., tables.

Papers presented by Caribbean specialists on "Diversification, Import Substitution and Regional Economic Integration in West Indian Agriculture."

2038. Williams, R. L. Gross, fixed capital formation in Jamaica, 1948-1966: a constant price series (UWI/SES, 20:4, Dec. 1971, p. 369-377, tables)

Statistical paper examining sources of bias in series and presenting a new series with correction of bias attributed to treatment of labor costs in construction.

COLOMBIA, ECUADOR, THE GUIANAS, AND VENEZUELA

JORGE SALAZAR-CARRILLO
Senior Fellow
The Brookings Institution

JUAN J. BUTTARI
Research Associate
The Brookings Institution

AN INCREASE IN THE ACCESS TO BETTER STATISTICS in Colombia helps to explain the increase in studies using relatively sophisticated econometric techniques. Another salient trait of the literature of Colombia is the growth of interest in applying economic theory to the analysis of economic phenomena.

In order to present a better perspective of the economic literature, an attempt has been made to include works covering as wide a spectrum of topics as possible. Nevertheless, when found to be of low quality or of little interest, works were not annotated.

As is natural in a country troubled by inflation, foreign exchange difficulties, low growth and rising unemployment, these issues, along with regional economic integration, are outstanding in the literature of Colombia. In these areas the works of Nelson and others (item 2072), Musalem (item 2078) and Dunkerley (item 2060) deserve special praise. Likewise, the work by Avramovic (item 2041) is highly meritorious allowing many insights into the Colombian economy. Also commendable are publications based on research conducted at institutions like the Centro de Estudios sobre Desarrollo Económico (Universidad de los Andes), and in governmental centers like the Departamento Administrativo Nacional de Estadística and the Banco de la República.

Although the regrettable dearth of publications on the Guianas still persists, this *HLAS* includes more entries than previous ones. Moreover, the appearance of excellent studies such as David's (item 2107) provides further grounds for optimism. [J. J. B. and J. S. C.]

For the past couple of years the rate of publication of economic works about Venezuela has picked up considerably. Also noticeable is a trend towards more serious publications, with a greater analytical bent and/or empirical content. Yet, in contrast with Latin American countries of similar importance, the quantity and quality of the economic literature on Venezuela is still disappointing. It is also interesting to note that the proportion of foreign economists which have written books, articles, monographs, etc., on Venezuela is lower than that in other comparable Latin American nations.

The contributions have concentrated on certain areas which have been of traditional importance in Venezuela, namely the petroleum and mining sectors and the country's foreign trade. However, it is evident by the relative number of publications, that Venezuelans are increasingly prone to study, retrospectively, their economic development process, and prospectively, their place in the economic integration of Latin America.

Four investigative groups have to be commended by their efforts to upgrade research in Venezuela. These are the Universidad Católica Andrés Bello, the Universidad Central de Venezuela, the Universidad de los Andes in Mérida and the Banco Central de Venezuela. The latter has had a long history of contributions to economic research in that country. A particularly important book among those reviewed is the one by Raymond F. Mikesell and others, *Foreign investment in the petroleum and mineral industries: case studies of investor-host country relations* published by the Johns Hopkins Press for Resources for the Future. Three chapters in this book were devoted to the problem in Venezuela and are annotated below (items 2130, 2133-2134).

Ecuador's economic literature is still scarcer than Venezuela's, even in comparable terms. And evidently, private economic research is still in its infancy there, most publications being generated by the public sector. Nevertheless, the fact that the number of works increased substantially during the period reviewed constitutes a clear indication of research development.

Economic works published in Ecuador in the past two years emphasize two areas: planning and economic integration, the former a recurrent topic in Ecuadorean economics and the latter a welcome newcomer.

In ending we would like to thank Mr. Juan A. Muller of the World Bank for his valuable collaboration, as well as Molly Wainer, Jorge C. Lamas and George Plinio Montalvan for their help in annotating the burgeoning economics literature in the countries covered. Special acknowledgement should go to Ricardo C. Martínez, who apart from contributing with a sizeable number of annotations, provided general organizational help. Of the annotations included in this section, those undertaken by the researchers mentioned above bear their initials at the end, while those unmarked were done by us. [J. S. C. and J. J. B.]

COLOMBIA

2039. Agudelo Villa, Hernando. La política del Ministerio de Desarrollo. Bogotá, Ministerio de Desarrollo Económico, 1972. 52 p.

Brief review of the main policy goals contained in the national development plan. See item 2054.

2040. Arango Londoño, Gilberto. Estructura económica colombiana. Bogotá, El Banco del Comercio, 1972. 374 p., bibl.

Designed as textbook for university students, this work presents a global view of the Colombian economy and describes its financial institutions. Specially useful for noneconomists wishing to obtain a basic understanding of the country's economy. Some salient chapters discuss demographic aspects, agricultural and industrial structures, the coffee sector, balance of payments and exchange control, tariffs, capital markets, budgeting, foreign investment, education and health.

2041. Avramović, Dragoslav. Economic growth of Colombia, problems and prospects: report of a mission sent to Colombia in 1970 by the World Bank. Baltimore, Md., The Johns Hopkins Univ. Press *for the* International Bank for Reconstruction and Development, 1972. 509 p., maps, tables.

Encyclopedic study of Colombia's needs. Employment, investment, public finance, regional and urban development are discussed across sectors in the first chapters. Afterward, the report focuses on problems and prospects for specific sectors such as industry, mining, energy, agriculture, transport, tourism, education and health. Compendium of information highly valuable to students of Latin American development. The report also contains policy suggestions.

2042. Banco de la República, *Bogotá.* El mercado de capitales en Colombia. Prefacio [por] Miguel Urrutia Montoya. Bogotá, 1971. 446 p., tables.

Papers discussing characteristics and growth potential of capital market. Focus is on use of fiscal policy to mobilize savings for public investment and on role of financial intermediaries in promoting private investment. Articles are divided into four parts: analysis of the interrelation between capital markets and development; need to mobilize savings for development; the nature of financial intermediaries; and flow of funds. Includes statistical information of interest to researchers. Indexed.

2043. Bentancourt L., Enrique. Algunos aspectos sobre las exportaciones agrícolas colombianas. Bogotá, Pontificia Univ. Javeriana, 1972. 96 p.

Inquiry into the export potential of agricultural produce traditionally neglected. Author offers suggestions regarding production and marketing of different items.

2044. Bernal V., Carlos; Luis Quiroga C.; and **Jaime Villamizar V.** Análisis de las perspectivas de exportación de Colombia en el Grupo Andino: Bolivia-Ecuador. Bogotá, Asociación Colombiana Popular de Industriales, 1970. 99 l., tables.

Analysis of Colombian export potential to Andean group countries, work offers policy recommendations.

Main contribution is listing of products which Colombia is exporting or might export to Bolivia and Ecuador.

2045. Berry, R. Albert. Farm size distribution, income distribution and the efficiency of agricultural production: Colombia (AFA/AER, 62:2, May 1972, p. 403-408)

Investigates determinants of the skewness of distribution of agricultural income. Focus is on the interrelation between size distribution of farms and productivity.

2046. ———. Presumptive income tax on agricultural land: the case of Colombia (NTA/NTJ, 25:2, June 1972, p. 169-182)

Argues that it is likely that a presumptive income tax on agricultural land would improve land and income distribution and raise agricultural output. It focuses on the framework necessary to evaluate the impact of such a tax.

2047. Bird, Richard M. Taxation and development: lessons from Colombian experience. Cambridge Mass., Harvard Univ. Press, 1970. 277 p., bibl., tables.

Arguing that taxation policy serves to attain greater income equality and growth simultaneously, author outlines a tax strategy for development in Colombia. Appraises performance of the Colombian public sector and discusses aspects of progressive direct taxation, indirect taxes and tax incentive policies, and role of state and local government finance. Important reference for students of public finance in developing countries.

2048. Botero G., Héctor; Luis Javier Jaramillo; and Jairo Serna Silva. Los estudios de transferencia y difusión de tecnología an Colombia. Bogotá, Fondo Colombiano de Investigaciones Científicas (COLCIENCIAS), 1972. 22 l., bibl. (Serie: Estudios, 21)

Quick review of studies about the transfer of technology in Colombia. Focus is on the objectives of the studies; nothing is said about their methodology or relevance.

2049. Chaves, Milcíades. Aproximación al estudio del sistema científico y tecnológico de Colombia: informe de avance sobre los datos de las primeras 22 entidades de la encuesta. t. 1/2. Bogotá, Fondo Colombiano de Investigaciones Científicas (COLCIENCIAS), 1972. 2 v. (102, 71 p.) tables (Serie: Estudios, 17)

Study of the state of science and technology in Colombia. Includes analysis of evolution of science and technology in Colombia and its current standing; an examination of uses of human resources in a sample of research institutions; a model for analysis of diffusion of technology; financing of research activities; and the extent to which physical research facilities are used.

Chu, David S. C. The Great Depression and industrialization in Latin America: response to relative price incentives in Argentina and Colombia, 1930-45. See item 2336.

2050. Colombia. Comisión de Reforma Tributaria. Fiscal reform for Colombia: final report and staff papers of the Colombian Commission on Tax Reform. Edited by Malcolm Gillis. Cambridge, Mass., Harvard Univ., Law School, 1971. 853 p., tables.

Contains final report of commission staff papers and the income and wealth law proposed. First two parts include sections on tax burden distribution, business income tax, indirect taxes and intergovernmental fiscal relations. A quick review of the contents is contained in the works annotated in items 2047 and 2080. The wide spectrum of topics covered makes this study highly useful for economists, tax administrators and development specialists.

2051. ———. Departamento Administrativo Nacional de Estadística (DANE). Encuesta de hogares, 1970; análisis del desempleo. Encuesta de hogares [por] Carlos Becerra and Polibio Córdoba. Análisis de resultados [por] Diego Salazar. Introducción [por] Ernesto Rojas Morales. Bogotá, 1970. 70 p., tables.

Presents results of national survey which took place in 1970 and which sought informatpon on labor force and unemployment. Offers statistics on open and disguised unemployment and underemployment by age, sex, religion and sector.

2052. ———. ———. Encuesta de hogares: Bogotá y Cali, julio 1970. 55 p., tables.

Presents data on employment, education housing conditions and various demographic factors. Information obtained through household surveys, refers to June/July 1970. Includes sample description and methodology.

2053. ———. Departamento Nacional de Planeación. Las cuatro estrategias. Bogotá, 1972. 515 p., maps, plates.

Expands on fundamental aspects and principles of Colombia's development plan. See item 2054.

2054. ———. ———. Plan de desarrollo económico y social: 1970-1973. t. 1, Capítulos del I al VIII. t. 2, Capítulos del IX al XI. Bogotá, 1970. 2 v. (Various pagings) fold. maps, tables.

After a review of the legal framework for planning in Colombia, plan discusses specific policies such as: employment; population; regional and urban development; development of social sectors; development of private sectors; infrastructure; and public investment. Decreasing open employment and underemployment in urban and rural areas respectively, are basic goal of proposed policies. To achieve this goal the plan establishes need for securing, among other objectives: a stable growth rate of GDP; policies encouraging saving and directing savings to productive activities; gradual decrease in the inequality of income distribution; changes in structure of production and technologies used; balanced urban-rural growth.

2055. ———. Ministerio de Agricultura. Comité Evaluador de la Reforma Agraria. Informe: enero 1971. Bogotá, 1971. 168 p., tables.

Appraisal of existing programs for agrarian reform as well as of rural problems and potential solutions.

2056. ———. **Ministerio de Trabajo y Seguridad Social. Servicio Nacional de Aprendizaje (SENA). División de Recursos Humanos.** Clasificación nacional de ocupaciones. Bogotá, 1970. 582 p.

Using five-digit code, it defines and classifies Colombian occupations into following large groups: professionals and technicians, high-level public officers, administrative personnel, tradesmen and truck operators, various and armed forces personnel. Contains chapter explaining its methodology. Classification based on ILO's 1968 occupation classification manual.

2057. ———. ———. ———. ———. **Sección de Estudios.** Estudio sobre las necesidades de formación professional para las ocupaciones especificas de fundición en el departamento de Antioquia: 1967-1971. Bogotá, 1967. 22 l., tables.

Using survey data and applying manpower methods, studies the training needs of foundry workers in Antioquia.

2058. Conferencia Consultiva de Ganaderos, *VII, Cúcuta, Col., 1971.* La rentabilidad ganadera en el país. Trabajo presentado a la ... Cúcuta, Co., Federación Colombiana de Ganaderos, Depto. de Investigaciones Económicas, 1971. 96 l., tables.

Measures returns to different technologies in agriculture. Modern production techniques do not seem to be economically viable. Market size limitations are an important cause of this result. Of methodological and analytical interest.

2059. Dow, J. Kamal. Colombia's foreign trade and economic integration in Latin America. Gainesville, Fla., Univ. of Florida Press, Center for Latin American Studies, 1971. 84 p., bibl., tables (Latin American monographs: 2. series, 9)

Rapid review of main difficulties of Colombian economy and of solution alternative offered by economic integration. Stresses need for increasing export penetration in traditional markets, and benefits Colombia could derive from an Andean subgroup.

2060. Dunkerley, Harold B. Exchange-rate systems in conditions of continuing inflation: lessons from the Colombian experience (*in* Papanek, Gustav F. *ed.* Development policy: theory and practice. Cambridge, Mass., Harvard Univ. Press, 1968, p. 117-174, tables)

Summary of 1960-66 experience in framework of an overall development plan supported by foreign aid. Case study of 1962 and 1965 devaluations is followed by analysis of the choice of exchange-rate systems in conditions of continuing inflation. Interesting discussion of advantages of flexible exchange-rates over a system of fixed rates changed occasionally and abruptly.

2061. Echavarría Olózaga, Hernán. Macro economía de la América cafetera. Bogotá, n.p., 1972. 440 p., tables.

Overflow of macroeconomic theory and policy in a Latin American context. After review of basic concepts, book focuses on development problems. Of general interest.

2062. Eusse Hoyos, Gerardo. The outflow of trained personnel from Colombia (*in* United Nations. Social Development Division. United Nations Institute for Training and Research (UNITAR). The brain drain from five developing countries: Cameroon, Colombia, Lebanon, The Philippines, Trinidad and Tobago. N.Y., 1971, p. 67-82 [UNITAR Research reports. 5])

Review of the brain-drain situation in Colombia during late 1950s and 1960s. Presents estimates of emigration trends, loss of investment in education and training, and losses in potential output and possible gains arising from outflow of trained personnel. Also contains brief analysis of factors contributing to emigration of high-level manpower and of related government policy.

2063. Gómez Riveros, Armando and **Daniel Schlesinger Ricaurte.** Análisis preliminar de la cuentas de flujo de fondos financieros de la economía colombiana: 1962-1969. Bogotá, Banco de la República, Depto. de Investigaciones Económicas, 1971. 127 p., tables.

First attempt in Colombia to present a structured set of statistics for flow-of-funds analysis. Offers tables useful for investigation of sources and uses of funds, and for evolution of financial institutions as well as for their interdependence. Accounts are classified along institutional lines into six major sectors: households; agriculture and business; government; international; financial institutions; central bank. Of interest to national income accountants and planners.

2064. Grunig, James E. Communication and the economic decision-making processes of Colombian peasants (UC/EDCC, 19:4, July 1971, p. 580-597)

Thorough analysis of decision-making setting and of decision processes of Colombian peasants, author argues that communication has little effect in modernizing peasants unless they are faced with structural opportunities. Accordingly, communication plays only a complementary role in development.

2065. *Información Financiera.* Asociación Bancaria de Colombia. Nos. 111/112, julio/agosto 1972- . Bogotá.

Contains changes in financial legislation and presents financial and economic statistics.

2066. Isaza, Rafael B. and **Francisco J. Ortega.** Encuestas urbanas de empleo y desempleo: análisis y resultados. Bogotá, Univ. de los Andes, Centro de Estudios sobre Desarrollo Económico (CEDE), 1972. 172 p., tables.

Presents information on labor force characteristics of entire country and eight major cities; data on unemployment broken down according to family characteristics, sex, industry and occupation. Based on results of 1964 census and 1964 and 1965 surveys.

2067. Junguito, Roberto; Alvaro López; Alvaro Reyes; and **Diego Salazar.** Análisis de la estructura y evolución de la fuerza de trabajo colombiana: 1938, 1951 y 1964, y proyecciones de la población económicamente activa: 1965-1985. Bogotá, Univ. de los Andes, Facultad de Economía, Centro de Estudios sobre Desarrollo Económico (CEDE), 1970. 177 p., tables.

Critical analysis of information contained in 1938, 1951 and 1964 census. Among other aspects, study compares age, sex and urban-rural composition of population in 1951 and 1964, and discusses structural composition of labor force by sector and occupation. Provides valuable demographic statistics.

2068. Lipman, Aaron. The Colombian entrepreneur in Bogotá. Coral Gables, Fla., of Miami Press, 1969. 144 p., bibl. (Hispanic-American studies, 22)

Through interviews with executives of large enterprises and using nonparametric methods, author explores nature of entrepreneurial function and social background and economic milieu of the entrepreneur. Among other conclusions, he finds that a considerable proportion of entrepreneurs are foreign-born; that their educational level is higher than average; and that their outlook is rational and modern.

2069. López, Timoleón. Datos y apreciaciones sobre algunos aspectos de la industria farmacéutica en Colombia. Bogotá, Fondo Colombiano de Investigaciones Científicas y Proyectos Especiales Francisco José de Caldas (COLCIENCIAS) [and] Depto. National de Planeación, 1972. 26 l. (Serie: Estudios, 18)

Presents conclusions of analysis of survey data. Focuses on composition of pharmaceutical firms according to national origin of management and capital, technology use and general characteristics of the industry.

2070. Meneses Olivar, Alvareo. El manejo de la política monetaria en Colombia. Bogotá, Superintendencia Bancaria, 1971. 173 p., tables (Publicaciones superbancaria)

Analysis of monetary policy tools employed during 1960s and review of their respective usefulness. Also contains description of existing monetary institutional structure and its evolution.

2071. Mesa Ospina, Jorge Ernesto. El capital de los bancos extranjeros en Colombia. Bogotá, Pontificia Univ. Javeriana, Facultad de Ciencias Jurídicas y Socioeconómicas, 1969. 91 p., bibl., table.

Descriptive study of legal structure regulating establishment and practices of foreign banks in Colombia.

2072. Nelson, Richard R.; T. Paul Schultz; and Robert L. Slighton. Structural change in a developing economy: Colombia's problems and prospects. Princeton, N.J., Princeton Univ. Press, 1971. 322 p., tables.

Focuses on rapid population growth, urban-rural migration, structure of manufacturing sector and foreign exchange policy. Growth in manufacturing occurs as modern sector expands and replaces traditional sector. Dualism is seen as having important consequences in terms of distribution of income in urban sector as well as on employment. Studying the slowdown of manufacturing development during 1960's, authors trace its causes to modern sector's dependency on imports, falling coffee prices and inadequate foreign exchange policies. Considerable attention is paid to policy making structure which prevented adoption and implementation of adequate policies. Among other policy suggestions, authors recommend distribution of birth-control information and devices, as well as influencing family size goals through expanding school facilities and greater economic opportunities for women. Seeing foreign exchange availability as a key factor for progress, authors argue in favor of a more flexibile exchange rate. Of considerable methodological and theoretical interest to development economists.

2073. Ordóñez Ramírez, Enrique and Guillermo Salcedo Salazar. Bases para la reorganización y desarrollo del transporte de cargo por carretera. Bogotá, Corporación Financiera del Transporte *for the* Banco de la República, Fondo de Promoción de Exportaciones, 1969. 122 p., tables.

Study of existing characteristics and problems of freight transportation by road. Includes proposals for improving and developing transportation systems.

2074. Organization of American States. Department of Economic Affairs. Sectorial Studies Unit. La economía agrícola colombiana. Washington, 1971. 131 p., bibl., tables (333-S-8017)

Survey of state of agricultural sector in Colombia. Focuses on agriculture from a global viewpoint, as well as through analysis of specific crops. Discusses productivity; production techniques; demand for agricultural products; institutional arrangements; agrarian reform. Includes substantial amount of statistical material. Of special interest to agricultural economists.

2075. Poveda Ramos, Gabriel. El fomento industrial en Colombia (ANI/RT, 13, marzo 1972, p. 3-27)

Author analyzes factors affecting industrial growth and suggests policy measures to stimulate industrial expansion and development in Colombia.

2076. Prieto, Rafael; Francisco J. Ortega; and Hernando Guerra. Indice de precios al consumidor: estacionalidad y tendencia. Bogotá, Univ. de los Andes, Centro de Estudios sobre el Desarrollo Económico (CEDE), 1970. 164 p., tables.

Using weights estimated by authors on basis of survey data, study shows that conventional consumer price indexes for four cities are substantially altered. Estimates of seasonal indexes and of growth rates of prices for 11 products are presented. Contains an analysis of the methodology being applied in the estimation of price indexes and offers suggestions for improvement. Of considerable statistical interest.

2077. *Revista Cámara de Comercio de Bogotá.* Año 1, No. 2, marzo 1971-   . Bogotá.

Issue containing articles examining various matters related to the Andean Group; e.g.,

Jorge Mejía Palacio "El Acuerdo sobre Capitales Extranjeros en el Grupo Andino" p. 33-46; and Hugo Palacios Mejía "El Acuerdo Subregional Andino y la Constitución Colombiana" p. 47-56.

2078. Roque Musalem, Alberto. Dinero, inflación y balanza de pagos: la experiencia de Colombia en la post-guerra. Bogotá, Banco de la República, 1971. 189 p., tables.

Quantitative study. Finds a very close correlation between the demand for money and movements in the rate of exchange suggesting the need for coordinating monetary and foreign exchange policies. The results indicate that a positive association between interest rates and deposits in savings accounts exists and that inflation in Colombia basically has not been of the "cost-push" variety. Valuable contribution to the study of monetary policy.

2079. Sheahan, John. Imports, investment, and growth: Colombia (*in* Papanek, Gustav F. *ed.* Development policy: theory and practice. Cambridge, Mass., Harvard Univ. Press, 1968, p. 93-114, tables)

Argues that pattern of import substitution created an excessive dependency on imported production inputs. Instead, emphasis should be on protecting domestic production of materials and equipment, as well as on increasing minor exports through favorable exchange rates. Devaluation and free exchange rates are deemed ineffective.

2080. Tanzi, Vito. Fiscal reform for Colombia: the report of the Musgrave Commission (IAMEA, 26:1, Summer 1972, p. 71-80, table)

Discussion of main recommendations of the Colombian Commission on Tax Reform presided over by Richard A. Musgrave. Proposed measures were geared to increasing tax revenues and alleviating inflation, low growth rate and balance of payment difficulties. Author seems skeptical as to political feasibility of some of the proposals.

2081. Taylor, Lester D. Personal saving in Colombia (IASI/E, 27:103, junio 1969, p. 235-256, tables)

Discusses impact of inflation on personal saving. On the basis of an empirical analysis, author argues that inflation has lowered the rate of personal saving and has discriminated against low income earners. These results are due mainly to the lack of institutional instruments of saving available to low income earners. Increasing the rate of interest on time and savings deposits, and creating a constant value government bond available to the general public are suggested as policy solutions.

Tirado Mejía, Alvaro. Introducción a la historia económica de Colombia. See *HLAS 34:2515*.

2082. Vallejo, César and others. La distribución del ingreso y de la propiedad en Colombia: estudio interdisciplinar. Presentación [por] Jaime Martínez Cárdenas. Bogotá, Centro de Investigaciones y Acción Social (CIAS), 1970. 137 p., tables (Col. Monografías y documentos, 7)

Collection of essays on income distribution; not all of them are related to Colombia. Works reflect social doctrines of the Catholic Church. Salient essay analyses current income distribution situation in Colombia.

2083. Vallejo Arbeláez, Joaquín. A.B.C. de la integración latinoamericana. Bogotá, Ediciones Tercer Mundo, 1971? 75 p., bibl., tables (El Dedo en la herida, 38)

Simple, popular explanation and analysis of integration in Latin America, especially pointed to Colombians and to the Andean groups. [J. M. Hunter]

Villegas, Jorge. Petróleo colombiano, ganancia gringa. See item 7670.

ECUADOR

2084. Cabezas, Rodrigo. El petróleo es nuestro. Quito, Editorial Casa de la Cultura Ecuatoriana, 1972. 166 p., bibl., illus., tables.

Impassioned argument for very close control by Ecuador of its newly found oil riches, and against policies of the international oil companies with respect to the producing countries. [R. C. M.]

2085. Comercio Exterior e Integración. Instituto de Comercio Exterior e Integración. Vol. 1, No. 1, 1970- . Quito.

New journal devoted to problems of foreign trade and economic integration.

2086. El desarrollo económico y social del Ecuador: estructura, proceso y perspectivas (CM/FI, 12:3, enero/marzo 1972, p. 373-385)

Clear, thoughtful essay, written from a Marxist point of view, attempts to integrate economic, social, and political aspects of Ecuador's recent history leading to its present-day problems. [R. C. M.]

2087. Ecuador. Instituto Nacional de Estadística. Encuesta anual de comercio interno: 1969. Quito, 1969? 88 p., tables.

Statistical information about results of a survey on domestic trade during 1969. [M. W.]

2088. ———. Junta Nacional de Planificación y Coordinación. Plan ecuatoriano para el desarrollo de los recursos humanos. Quito, Organización de Estados Americanos [and] Univ. Estatal de Ohio, Centro de Investigaciones de Recursos Humanos, 1970. 2 v. (304 p., Various pagings) tables.

The Ecuadorean Planning Board, with OAS and Ohio State Univ. help, prepared this study on human resources in Ecuador. The study is supposed to be a complementary part of the First Ecuadorean Plan (1964-73). Within a manpower approach, it provides criticism of the targets of the plan. If the latter are extrapolated to 1980, the level of unemployment would grow in Ecuador. An interesting document which appears to come up with useful recommendations even though the data on which they were based were limited.

2089. ———. Junta Nacional de Planificación y Coordinación Económica. Situación y comportamiento del comercio ecuatoriano frente a la A.L.A.L.C. Quito, 1972. 66 p., tables.

Empirical study of the role of international trade as the dominant factor in the recent economic development of Ecuador. Focuses on problems facing that country vis-à-vis other members of LAFTA as the process of economic integration in that group continues. [R. C. M.]

2090. ———. ———. Situación y comportamiento del comercio internacional: análisis pormenorizado del desiquilibrio externo. Quito, 1972. 87 p. tables.

Examination of the export performance of Ecuador during the 1964-70 period. Situation was somewhat bleak, but alas, *oil* later saved the day. Interestingly enough, given the date of publication, that three-letter word is not even mentioned in this pamphlet. The export projections in the first Ecuadorean ten-year plan (1964-73) are examined against the evidence.

2091. ———. Ministerio de Finanzas. Plan operativo de Ministerio de Finanzas. Quito, 1972. 30 l., tables.

After the inauguration of the Rodríguez Lara government, a reorganization of the public finances was sought. This short pamphlet reviews ills plaguing the Finance Ministry from 1965-72, and outlines planned reforms.

2092. ———. Ministerio de la Producción. Dirección General de Planificación. Programa presupuesto de desarrollo agropecuario y forestal. Quito, 1972. 178 l., tables.

An Ecuadorean illustration of the application of the Planning-Programming-Budgeting-system (PPBS) concept. Within the context of the central government.

2093. ———. Secretaría General de Planeación Económica. Junta Nacional de Planificación y Coordinación. Planificación para le integración: sugerencias para una metodología. Quito, 1970. 32 p. (mimeo)

Preliminary research to attain a methodology that would measure the most important economic aggregates of members of the Andean Group. This work is based only on economic grounds, hence, the sociological and political aspects of economic development are left for subsequent studies. [J. C. L.]

2094. Espinel Rivadeneira, Enrique. Ecuador: producción y costos del azúcar. Quito, Congreso Nacional, 1968. 38 p., tables.

This work tries to ascertain: 1) The truth or falsity of allegations made by Ecuador's sugar growers against government interventions; and 2) whether the export tariff, to cover costs of agricultural development, levied on sugar exports is feasible or not. Also, includes an international technical comparison on sugar producing countries to underline the state of the sugar industry in Ecuador. [J. C. L.]

2095. Estrada, Raúl. El problema de la transferencia de tecnología en el Ecuador. Quito, Instituto Ecuatoriano de Normalización, 1971. 70 l., bibl., tables.

Superficial essay covering most important issues on transfer of technology in Ecuador. Some issues revisited are: 1) demand for technology; 2) capacity for innovations; 3) capacity for assimilation of technology; and 4) imperfections of the technology market. [J. C. L.]

2096. Estrategia del desarrollo pesquero dentro del bloque andino. Quito? n.p., n.d. 11 l.

Briefly considers expansion of fishing industry in Ecuador, as prelude to an exploration of its export possibilities within Andean Common Market. Informative but superficial.

2097. Laso, Luis Eduardo. La Banca Central. Guayaquil, Ecua., Almacenes Editorial Colón, 1972. 81 p.

Very interesting series of conferences given by the author in the Centro de Estudios Monetarios Latinoamericanos (CEMLA), Mexico. Clearly related to monetary policy, such as the concept of "money," the role played by the central bank and commercial banks in the economy of a country, different tools for monetary control, etc. Useful to those interested in monetary policy. [M. W.]

2098. Peñaherrera de Costales, Piedad and **Alfredo Costales Samaniego.** Historia social del Ecuador. t. 4, Reforma agraria. Quito, Editorial Casa de la Cultura Ecuatoriana, 1971. 319 p., bibl., tables (Llacta, 18)

Descriptive analysis of history of social laws, starting in the 1920's. Explains process of agrarian reform in Ecuador, within framework of existing laws and presents agrarian structure of Ecuadorian society. Analyses positive and negative aspects of changes in system of land tenure. For vols. 1, 2 and 3, see *HLAS 34:2601*. [M. V.]

2099. Robalino Gonzaga, César Raúl. El desarrollo económico del Ecuador: la ineficiencia de la economía, la evolución de la economía, la estrategia de desarrollo. Quito, Junta Nacional de Planificación y Coordinación, 1968. 382 p., tables.

After presenting an analysis of problems and performance of the Ecuadorean economy during the 1961-66 period using a macroeconomic approach, it proposes a strategy of economic development. Intended as a report to the Congress of Ecuador about the country's economic problems and some proposed solutions, it is somewhat technical for such an audience.

2100. Salgado, Germánico. Ecuador y la integración económica de América Latina. B.A., Banco Interamericano de Desarrollo (BID), Instituto para la Integración de América Latina (INTAL), 1970. 330 p. fold. map, tables (Serie BID-INTAL)

Revised version of background study prepared by senior economist, member of executive Junta of the Andean Common Market, for a month-long seminar in Ecuador in 1969. Begins with analysis of Ecuador's economy and development needs, in a regional economy setting, and shows how integration will influence and facilitate growth. [J. Strasma]

2101. Santos S., Eduardo. Ecuador: década 1960-1970. Quito, Univ. Central, Facultad de Jurisprudencia, Ciencias Sociales y Políticas, Escuela de Psicología, 1970? 17 p.

Interesting lecture by technician from Ecuadorean Planning Board. Considers factors contributing to disappointing performance of Ecuadorean economy in 1960's, even though planning was introduced during that period. Considers future prospects in light of oil findings.

2102. Zuvekas, Clarence, Jr. Economic planning in Ecuador: an evaluation (IAMEA, 25:4, Spring 1972, p. 39-69, tables)
Critical analysis of history of economic planning in Ecuador, with emphasis on 1964-73 plan. Argues that politicians, rather than planners, have been to blame for negligible impact of planning on Ecuador's development. [R. C. M.]

THE GUIANAS

2103. Adamson, Alan H. Sugar without slaves: the political economy of British Guiana, 1838-1904. New Haven, Conn., Yale Univ. Press, 1972. 315 p., bibl., illus., tables (Caribbean series, 13)
Analyzes historical causes that led to survival of sugar as the dominant crop, to plantation economy as the dominant system of production and to sugar planters as the dominant social and political grouping in the former colony.

2104. Arthur D. Little, Inc. (firm), *Cambridge, Mass.* Surinam: a tourism evaluation. Cambridge, Mass., 1970. 57 p.
Study evaluating Surinam's tourism potential with comprehensive appendix on tourism resources. In order to improve the tourist's profile of the country, provides recommendations on tour programs in accordance with existing facilities and limited financial resources available. [J. A. M.]

2105. Becker, Rudolph L. Studies on Surinam agriculture. Paramaribo, U.S. Agency for International Development Mission, 1962-1963. 1 v. (Unpaged)
Discusses agricultural sector focusing on rice, plantain, bacoren and livestock prospects. Includes brief budgetary analysis and labor requirements for small agricultural enterprises devoted to the production of several crops. [J. A. M.]

2106. Chin, H. E. Suriname: ontwikkelingshulp en economische ontwikkeling (NGIZ/IS, 25:15, sept. 1971, p. 1441-1459, tables)
More than 20 years of economic aid did not bring about the economic development hoped for Surinam. Increase of national product in past years is mainly due to autonomous foreign (largely US) private investments especially in mining and processing of bauxite. Therefore an important part of Surinam's domestic product is transported abroad. The unsatisfactory results of economic aid are not only due to Surinam's underdevelopment, but also to the ambivalent attitude of the Netherlands, Surinam's most important donor country, a consequence of a former colonial relationship. One of the most important tasks is to devise and implement adequate education and information programs in order to increase local labour productivity and to improve the underdeveloped political structure. If so, author believes Surinam does have the natural resources to attain a fairly high economic growth rate in the future. [H. J. Hoyer]

2107. David, Wilfred L. The economic development of Guyana: 1953-1964. London, Oxford Univ. Press, 1969. 399 p., bibl., map, tables.
Excellent analysis of development problems facing a small, open and highly dependent economy. Contains chapters on the behavior of national income, population and employment, the agricultural sector, mining, trade, financial aspects, public expenditure and planning. Of special interest to students of Caribbean economies.

2108. ———. Planning from below: local government reform, rural reconstruction, regional decentralization and the ten-year development plan. Georgetown, Ministry of Economic Development, Development Planning Team, 1970. 75 l., tables (DP 27-22770)
A look at the development of the local government system in Guyana and an attempt to present the foundations for a model based on the participation of people at the local level in planning and managing their communities. Of interest to planners of urban development.

2109. Dupont-Gonin, Pierre. La Guyane Française: le pays, les hommes, ses problèmes et son avenir. Geneva, Librairie Droz, 1970. 277 p.
Monograph on French Guiana divided into three parts: Pt. 1 is devoted to discussing territory's natural environment, history and people. Pt. 2 focuses on obstacles to economic development, analyzes public finances pointing out the weakness of the system, and a final chapter examines price mechanism and imbalance income distribution between rural and urban areas. Pt. 3 summarizes fifth economic plan (1971-75). Main recommendation is the implementation of a market economy together with indicative planning "à le style français". [J. A. M.]

2110. Guyana. Ministry of Labour and Social Security. Manpower Research Division. Manpower Reporting Programme. Establishment enquiry report. Georgetown, 1969. 1 v. (Unpaged)
Statistical report attempts to update a 1965 UN survey on manpower requirements and the labor force as of June 1969. Report deals with employment levels and shortages of manpower. Pt. 1 offers a general review of the socio-economic situation while pts. 2 and 3 are devoted to the private and the public sectors respectively. [J. A. M.]

2111. La Guyane Française: les pays, ses problèmes economiques. Cayenne, Departement d'Outre Mer, 1967. 88 p.
This handbook is a complete description of the territory, its natural and human resources and the economy by industrial sector. [J. A. M.]

2112. Surinam. Stichting Planbureau. Tienjahrenplan Suriname: jaarveslag 1965; jaarveslag 1966. Paramaribo, 1967. 2 v. (170, 111 p.)
Economic analysis of industrial sectors, projects and their financing. Published annually by the Planning Office of Surinam. [J. A. M.]

VENEZUELA

2113. Acedo Mendoza, Carlos. América La-

tina; marginalidad y subdesarrollo. Caracas, Fondo Editorial Común, 1973. 440 p.

Study on development of the community in Venezuela, introducing original concepts on marginality and integration. Emphasizes the necessity of structural changes, planning, and utilization of techniques for community development, to improve conditions of marginal sectors in Latin American countries. Also makes thorough description of existing institutions and relevant projects. [M. W.]

2114. ———. Desarrollo comunal y promoción popular. 2. ed. Caracas, Fondo Editorial Común, 1971. 151 p., tables.

Brief monograph addressed to problem of marginality in Venezuela and to how community development can help solve it. Survey-like description of these issues. Of value to those interested in their Venezuelan context.

2115. ———. El desarrollo urbano en Venezuela y la Fundación para el Desarrollo de la Comunidad y Fomento Municipal. Caracas, Gráficas Edición de Arte, 1971. 78 p.

Study presented at "Conference on Urbanism and Development in the Developing Countries," Rehovot, Israel, 1971. Offers general information on process of urban development in several important Venezuelan cities, and also shows the relationship between this process and the overall economic development of Latin American cities. [M. W.]

2116. ———. Doctrina y política. 2. ed. Caracas, Fundacomún, 1971. 332 p., plates, tables.

Collection of speeches, papers and newspaper articles by President of the Foundation for the Development of Communities and Municipalities, covering wide range of topics from community development to regional integration.

2117. ———. Venezuela: Ruta y destino. 2. ed. Prólogo [por] Rafael Caldera. Caracas, Fondo Editorial Común, 1971. 496 p., bibl., tables.

Complete study of economies of Latin American countries with special emphasis on Venezuela, and within a sociological and economic framework. Covers general topics such as: the social conscience, change in political structures, planning and development. Also considers specific problems such as the Alliance for Progress, income distribution, international aid, agrarian reform, etc. [M. W.]

2118. ——— and **Sheila Olmos de Manzo.** El desarrollo de la comunidad. Caracas, Fondo Editorial Común. 104 p.

Analyzes problem of underdevelopment and how community action can be used as an instrument to overcome underdevelopment, marginalism, and dependency. Should be of interest to economists knowledgeable in sociology. [J. C. L.]

2119. **Acosta Hermoso, Eduardo Arturo.** La Comisión Económica de la OPEP. Prólogo por Luis Herrera Campins. Caracas, Editorial Arte, 1971. 185 p., table.

Misleading title. Only one of book's four essays is devoted to Economic Commission of the Organization of Petroleum Exporting Countries (OPEC). Others concern petroleum and mining policies in Venezuela. Prologue adds some comments on OPEC's Economic Commission, the role of which is looming larger in a world where the sources of energy are heavily concentrated in a few countries. Useful and informative statistical appendix includes cost data for major Venezuelan oil companies.

2120. **American Management Association** (firm), *N.Y.* **Executive Compensation Service.** Venezuela. N.Y., 1972. 63 p., tables (Reports on international compensation, 4)

Annual report on compensation paid by local and US companies in Venezuela. Includes information on compensation policies and practices for such firms. Covers primarily the management positions and is limited to the industrial sector. Data presented are useful for international comparisons and time series, given that they are gathered on a yearly basis, and that similar surveys are conducted in other Latin American countries and Europe. However, very little explanation is given of methods used, which limits potential research applications of these data.

2121. **Banco Central de Venezuela,** *Caracas.* Aspectos metodológicos de las cuentas nacionales de Venezuela. Caracas, 1972. 263 p., tables.

Venezuela was among Latin America's leaders in implementing the new System of National Accounts (S.N.A.) developed by the UN. Authors explain how they adapted such methods to their country and present estimates under both old and new national accounting systems. Enlightening publication in view of debate on applicability of new S.N.A. to developing countries.

2122. ———, ———. Estudio sobre presupuestos familiares e índices de costo de vida: área metropolitana de Maracaibo. Caracas, 1972. 198 p., tables.

Careful, scholarly, statistical study of family budgets, consumption patterns, and cost of living indexes in Maracaibo area, one of first of its kind to be undertaken outside a capital city in Latin America. Includes wealth of information useful for a variety of purposes. Study coauthored by Univ. del Zulia, Maracaibo. [R. C. M.]

2123. ———, ———. Informe económico correspondiente al año 1971. Caracas, 1972. 1 v. (Various pagings) tables.

These yearly reviews of conditions and performance of the Venezuelan economy have been undertaken by Central Bank of Venezuela for about 30 years. Covering 1971, this one is carefully executed, as usual. This series offers most useful compendium of economic time series available for Venezuela. A must for the economist working on that country.

2124. ———, ———. Series estadísticas. Caracas, 1970. 210 p., tables.

Basic statistical information on domestic, as well as international, sectors of Venezuelan economy. Includes information on: world economy, monetary liquidity, financial outlook, banking system, price levels, production, and capital formation. [J. C. L.]

2125. **Beyer, John C.** High growth, unemployment, and planning in Venezuela: some observations (UC/EDCC, 18:2, Jan. 1970, p. 267-273)

Comment on paper by M. F. Hassan in July 1967 issue of this same journal. Beyer argues that: 1) despite market imperfections, course of investment in Venezuela has not been inconsistent with its apparent factor proportions; and 2) sustained growth, even if capital-intensive, offers better employment potential for Venezuela in long run than labor-intensive program proposed by Hassan. For Hassan's reply, see item 2135. [R. C. M.]

2126. Casas González, Antonio. La planificación en Venezuela: un ensayo de planificación integral. Caracas, Presidencia de la República, Oficina Central de Coordinación y Planificación, 1972. 16 p.

Thorough explanatory essay of role and structure of economic planning in Venezuela. Issues developed are: plan's methodology; political and economic changes conducive to formal planning; and evaluation of plan's performance. [J. C. L.]

2127. Crazut, Rafael J. El Banco Central de Venezuela: notas sobre la historia y evolución del instituto, 1940-1970. Caracas, Banco Central de Venezuela, 1970. 316 p., bibl., tables (Col. XXX Aniversario)

In-house history of the Central Bank of Venezuela from the time of its establishment. While mostly a narrative account, it also includes chapters which discuss possible role of bank in financing country's economic development as well as bank's views on problems of international financial cooperation. [R. C. M.]

2128. Duque Corredor, Ramón José and others. Política agraria y desarrollo. Valencia, Ven., Univ. de Carabobo, Facultad de Ciencias Económicas y Sociales, Centro de Estudios Agrícolas, 1972. 245 p., tables.

Proceedings of seminar in rural development sponsored by the Univ. of Carabobo's School of Social Sciences. Papers cover four main aspects of agrarian reform in Venezuela: legal, political, sociological and economic. Also, includes general overview of Venezuelan agrarian reform. Very little statistical information is given. [J. C. L.]

2129. *Economía.* Univ. de los Andes, Facultad de Economía, Instituto de Investigaciones Económicas. Vol. 6, No. 7, dic. 1969- Mérida, Ven.

Yearly periodical put out by one of Venezuela's best schools of economics. Authors mostly Venezuelan or Latin American. Articles cover wide range of topics emphasizing policy problems while keeping techniques and analysis at a relatively simple level.

2130. Edwards, Gertrud G. Foreign petroleum companies and the state in Venezuela (*in* Mikesell, Raymond Frech and others. Foreign investment in the petroleum and mineral industries: case studies of investor-host country relations. Baltimore, Md., The Johns Hopkins Press *for* Resources for the Future, 1971, p. 101-128, tables)

Scholarly historical analysis of Venezuelan regulation of its oil industry, with emphasis on present-day conflicts and negotiations between government and international oil companies, as well as on their possible solutions. [R. C. M.]

2131. Gaignard, Romain. Ciudad Guayana: croissance industrielle ou développement régional? (ULIG/C, 15:35, sept. 1971, p. 389-395)

Critical analysis, written on the field, of the Ciudad Guayana industrial development project in Venezuela. Author argues that in order to sustain its considerable success, project must stop functioning as a "development pole" and become more integrated into the surrounding region. [R. C. M.]

2132. Garaicoechea C., Manuel Felipe. El comercio exterior y la estrategia del desarrollo económico de Venezuela. Caracas, Univ. Central de Venezuela, Facultad de Ciencias Económicas y Sociales, Instituto de Investigaciones, 1969. 76 p., bibl., tables (Col. Materiales para el estudio del desarrollo y la planificación económica)

In the context of the country's past experience and present circumstances, examines conditions which would make possible Venezuela's adoption of a development strategy based on promotion of exports of manufactured products, primarily steel and petrochemicals, rather than on import substitution. [R. C. M.]

2133. Gómez, Henry. Venezuela's iron ore industry (*in* Mikesell, Raymond Frech and others. Foreign investment in the petroleum and mineral industries: case studies of investor-host country relations. Baltimore, Md., The Johns Hopkins Press *for* Resources for the Future, 1971, p. 312-344, maps, tables)

Essay evaluating production of iron in Venezuela's Guayana region since early 1950's. Iron industry has been, for all intent and purposes, in hands of foreign capital. However, government has tried to maximize short-run retained value, and in the process has deeply affected development of country's iron production. Future prospects are considered.

2134. Harris, William G. The impact of the petroleum export industry on the pattern of Venezuelan economic development (*in* Mikesell, Raymond Frech and others. Foreign investment in the petroleum and mineral industries: case studies of investor-host country relations. Baltimore, Md., The Johns Hopkins Press *for* Resources for the Future, 1971, p. 129-156, tables)

Examines impact of petroleum industry on Venezuelan economy since 1950 in order to determine why petroleum has not made a greater contribution to economic growth. Attributes this largely to inappropriate government policies and sociocultural attitudes. [R. C. M.]

2135. Hassan, M. F. High growth, unemployment, and planning in Venezuela: a reply (UC/EDCC, 18:2, Jan. 1970, p. 274-277)

Author's reply to item 2125, claims that Beyer misinterprets his views, and that major difference between them is that they probably emphasize conflicting policy objectives, i.e., Beyer, long-term growth and Hassan, short-run elimination of high unemployment. According to Hassan the final decision is a political one. [R. C. M.]

2136. Hochschule St. Gallen für Wirtschafts, und Sozialwissenschaften, *St. Gallen, Switzerland.* Lateinamerikanisches Institut. Venezuela, heute-today-hoy . . . : Wirtschaftliche, soziale, kulturelle und politische aspekte. Zürich, Switzerland, Orell Füssli Verlag, 1968. 179 p., tables.

Series of six lectures given in Switzerland about different aspects of Venezuela and published elsewhere. Four lectures are reproduced in English, one in Spanish, and the other in German. Of particular interest to the economist are the contributions by Machado Gómez, Gustavo Escobar, and Ernesto Peltzer. Book addressed to the lay European reader.

2137. Losada, Benito Raúl. Síntesis monetaria. Prólogo [por] Alfredo Machado Gómez. Caracas, Banco Central de Venezuela, 1971. 159 p., plate (Col. XXX aniversario)

Compilation of speeches and essays by former president of the Central Bank of Venezuela, discussing policies implemented during his presidency, i.e., monetary policy, balance of payments adjustment problems, exchange rate policy and evaluations of economic conditions in Venezuela, 1968, 1969 and 1970.

2138. Machado Gómez, Alfredo. Crisis y recuperación: la economía monetaria venezolana entre 1961-1968. Caracas, Banco Central de Venezuela, 1972. 470 p.

Compilation of essays, speeches, and conferences by author which trace his tenure as president of the Central Bank of Venezuela in 1961-68. Includes documents of obvious historical value. Introductory chapter covers country's monetary history in that period. [R. C. M.]

2139. Mata Mollejas, Luis. Criterios para la selección de inversiones en una área urbana (DPB/RICS, 17, 1971, p. 299-321, tables)

Essay based on application of theories of investment in developing urban areas. Concludes that decision to invest in a developing urban area will depend on the following aspects: 1) comparative advantage of the region where the city is located; 2) its economic base; and 3) city's size. [J. C. L]

2140. Maza Zavala, Domingo Felipe; Héctor Malavé Mata; and Héctor Silva Michelena. Venezuela: economía y dependencia. Caracas, Ediciones Cabimas, 1971. 69 p.

Three essays, commissioned by Venezuelan Cultural Congress on Dependency and Neocolonialism, which reflect its far left-wing point of view. First, analyzes socio-economic development in stages of Latin America from the 16th century. Second, does the same for Venezuela. Third, tries to explain present sociopolitical and economic problems of Venezuela. [R. C. M.]

2141. Mejía Alarcón, Pedro Esteban. El ingreso fiscal y la industria petrolera (UCV/ECS [2. época] 12:1, enero/marzo 1970, p. 19-42, tables)

Argues that some taxes paid by oil companies in Venezuela should not be regarded as such. Bases argument on fact that state is owner of all underground resources in the country. After such government revenues as production and exploration "taxes" are taken out, the tax-profit/split drops below 50/50 in most years of the late 1950s and 1960s.

2142. Mieres, Francisco. El petróleo y la problemática estructural venezolana. Caracas, Univ. Central de Venezuela, Facultad de Ciencias Económicas y Sociales, Instituto de Investigaciones Económicas y Sociales, 1969. 402 p., tables.

Avowedly polemical, Marxist analysis of relation between monopolistic operation of Venezuelan oil industry by international oil companies and the country's economic depression in late 1960s. [R. C. M.]

2143. Montiel Ortega, Leonardo. Petróleo y soberanía. Caracas, Ediciones del Congreso de la República, 1971. 113 p. (Debates)

Record of debates on new petroleum tax legislation (1970) in Venezuela. The text is fragmental, featuring Montiel's portion of the debate. [P. B. Taylor, Jr.]

2144. Morales, Isidro; Paul Irala Burgos; and Jerónimo Irala Burgos. Foro nacional sobre Venezuela y la integración latino-americana; las empresas multinacionales y la integración (AIA/A, 32:47, oct./dic. 1971, p. 83-110, bibl.)

Clearly written essay which systematically examines problems (mostly legal) of organizing Latin-American-owned multinational firms, as well as possible contributions of these firms to region's economic integration. [R. C. M.]

2145. Mueller, Hans J. Venezuela. Washington, U.S. Dept. of Commerce, Bureau of International Commerce, 1969. 60 p., bibl., plates, tables (International Marketing Information Service: country market survey)

Study intended to "help U.S. businessmen meet the competitive challenge in the Venezuelan market." Studies the Venezuelan market in general and explores conditions by industrial category. Very detailed and valuable compendium of hard-to-get information.

2146. Panorama de la economía venezolana en el período enero-setiembre de 1970 (BCV/REL, 8:30, 1971, p. 7-46, tables)

Report on state of Venezuela's economy during stated period. Includes foreign as well as domestic sectors of the economy in addition to statistics on balance of payments and banking system. [J. C. L.]

2147. Panorama de la economía venezolana en el período julio-diciembre del año 1969 (BCV/REL, 8:29, 1970, p. 7-40, tables)

Appraisal by Central Bank technicians of short-run developments in Venezuelan economy in second half of 1969. Emphasizes monetary factors.

2148. Pérez Alfonzo, Juan Pablo. Petróleo y dependencia: prejuicios por contratos de servicio. Caracas, Síntesis Dos Mil, 1971. 247 p., tables (Libros para el desarrollo)

Former Mines and Hydrocarbons Minister argues against recent policy of granting service contracts to international oil companies on basis of effects of oil industry's development, and of oil policy, on Venezuelan economy from 1945 onwards. [R. C. M.]

2149. Pérez Dupuy, Henrique. Opiniones sobre la limitación o expansión en la economía Venezolana. Prólogo [por] Pedro José Lara Peña. Caracas, Trampa-Tip, 1971. 94 p.

Selection of author's brief articles, press interviews and comments related to basic problems of Venezuelan economy: e.g., nationalization of private enterprises, Andean Pact, high tax rates, etc. Believes in free and competitive market system and disapproves of Venezuela's entry into Andean Group. [M. W.]

2150. ———. Recomendaciones sobre economía y el gasto público. Prefacio [por] Vitelio Reyes. Caracas, Tipografía Friulana, 1971. 134 p.

Selection of author's brief articles, press interviews and comments concerning wrong administrative policies of some governments. Opposes state interventionism and advocates a balanced budget, even at the cost of reducing government expenditures. Emphasizes deficits of public enterprises as problem in balancing government budget. [M. W.]

2151. ———. Una sana economía debe privar sobre la política partidista. Prólogo [por] Julio Diez. Caracas, Tipografía Friulana, 1969. 122 p.

Compilation of author's articles, press interviews and comments about the Venezuelan economy. Main topics refer to high tax rates, economic disequilibrium of public enterprises, and his opposition to Venezuela's entry into the Andean Pact. [M. W.]

2152. Pérez Luciani, Rodrigo. Deuda pública externa y balanza de pagos: caso de Venezuela. Caracas, Univ. Católica Andrés Bello, Instituto de Investigaciones, 1971? 134 p., bibl., tables.

Systematic, scholarly, theoretical and empirical analysis of effect of Venezuela's foreign debt policy on: balance of payments, government-spending-multiplier mechanism, general price level, and interest rates. [R. C. M.]

2153. Rangel, Domingo Alberto. Capital y desarrollo. t. 1, La etapa agraria; t. 2, El rey petróleo. Caracas, Univ. Central de Venezuela, Facultad de Ciencias Económicas y Sociales, Instituto de Investigaciones Económicas y Sociales, 1969-1970. 2 v. (370, 417 p.) tables.

V. 1, *La etapa agraria,* analyzes from an historic viewpoint, in its introductory chapter, the process of underdevelopment in Venezuela, which to author is a consequence of Spanish colonial system. Following chapter criticizes ECLA's position with respect to functioning of capitalism before World War I. Points to capitalism as main cause of underdevelopment in its early stages. Examines different economic problems in Venezuela such as relationship between international monetary system and national economy, process of capital accumulation, all during period 1830-1920.

V. 2, *El rey petróleo,* is a Marxist economic history of 1920-50 period, with emphasis on paramount position of oil industry and its consequences for Venezuela. Obscure and tedious. Politically prominent author. [M. W. and R. C. M.]

2154. Rojas R., Iván. El estudio económico de base y la base económica de la región andina (ULAFE/E, 7:8, dic. 1970, p. 131-154, tables)

Fairly pedestrian study of the economic base of Venezuela's Andean region (states of Mérida, Táchira, and Trujillo), done on the basis of data from 1961. [B. Herrick]

2155. San Martín, Julio; Mariluz Cortés de Tadey; and Flavio Aguilar. Prospección industrial, 1970-2000 el modelo prospectivo. Caracas, Comisión del Plan Nacional de Aprovechamiento de los Recursos Hidráulicos, 1970. 43 l., tables (Publicación, 18)

Presents prospective vision of Venezuelan industrial structure by the year 2,000, based on certain assumptions about population, per capita income and industrial development for country in that year based on an outdated cross-section model developed by UN in 1963 to study industrial growth. Of interest for Venezuelan futurologists.

2156. Técnica Agroforestal (firm), *Caracas.* Estudio preliminar de rendimientos y costos de producción de carne de vacuno y leche. Caracas, 1968-1969. 1 v. (Various pagings) plates, tables.

Consulting firm study of costs in production of beef and milk. Nearly half consists of appendixes, mostly reproduced from other sources. Of interest to agricultural specialists.

2157. United Nations. Economic Commission for Latin America (ECLA). Secretariat. The metal-transforming industry in Venezuela: an import substitution development programme (*in* Interregional Symposium on the Development of Metalworking Industries in Developing Countries, *Moscow, 1966.* Reports presented at the United Nations . . . Wien, United Nations Industrial Development Organization, 1969, p. 57-65, tables)

Outlines plan to develop metal-transforming industry in Venezuela, after blueprint for its expansion in the 1963-66 plan failed. New plan for industry recommends more conservative approach with longer lags in development of industry.

2158. Universidad Central de Venezuela, *Caracas.* **Centro de Estudios del Desarrollo (CENDES).** Estilos de desarrollo. t. 1, Análisis comparativo de políticas a largo plazo. Caracas, 1971. 338 p., tables.

Good attempt at comparing and evaluating two different strategies of economic development in Venezuela, through utilization of mathematical model of numerical experimentation. Specifies objectives as well as degree to which society is willing to satisfy them. Alternative ways of reaching proposed goals are evaluated in terms of social effort required. [M. W.]

2159. Universidad de los Andes, *Mérida, Ven.*

Facultad de Economía, Instituto de Investigaciones Económicas. Estudio sobre presupuestos familiares e índices de costo de vida para las ciudades de Mérida, Valera, San Cristóbal y Barinas. Caracas, Banco Central de Venezuela, 1969. 81 p., tables.

Collection of basic information on family consumption. Useful in establishing regional accounts, and in constructing system of weights for elaboration of Cost of Living Index. Includes information on: family structure, housing, features, family income, etc. [M. W.]

2160. ———, ———. ———, ———. Presupuesto de ingresos y gastos familiares de La Fría: Estado de Táchira. Introducción [por] Leocadio Honoria G. Mérida, Ven., 1967. 78 p., tables.

Reports results of income and expenditure/survey, at family level, in an Andean city of Venezuela. Consists mostly of tabulations with little analysis. Complements similar surveys undertaken in other Andean cities in 1966 and 1967. Of interest to empirical researchers.

2161. ———, ———. ———, ———. Sección Economía Urbana. Incidencia de la Universidad de los Andes en el desarrollo urbano de Mérida: crecimiento físico. Mérida, Ven., Talleres Gráficos Universitarios, 1968. 45 p., maps, tables.

Study of university's effects on city of Mérida in the past, with some future projections. Unsophisticated analysis, mainly based on population factors and physical planning.

Van Meurs, A. P. H. De toekmst van de petroleum exporterende ontwikkelingslanden. See item 1891.

2162. **Venezuela. Comisión del Plan Nacional de Aprovechamiento de los Recursos Hidráulicos.** Estructura macroeconómica de Venezuela: una alternativa para el año 2,000. Caracas, 1970. 58 p., tables.

Study investigates design of Venezuela economic structure through the year 2,000. Objective of projection is to determine best strategy for use of hydraulic resources. Study subdivided into: 1) comparative analysis with other Latin American countries; 2) determination of which developed countries to use in this study; and 3) description of the strategy that must be followed by Venezuela to achieve the growth levels of developed countries chosen for this study. [J. C. L.]

2163. ———. **Presidencia. Comisión de Administración Pública.** La reforma administrativa en Venezuela, 1969-1971. Caracas, 1971. 160 l.

Lists the sources of problems in connection with public administration in Latin America, specifically Venezuela. Indicates strategy that must be followed in reform of public administration, describing purpose and methods of the Venezuelan reform of public administration in years 1969-74. Also comments on role of public administration in economic development. [J. C. L.]

2164. ———. ———. **Oficina Central de Coordinación y Planificación.** Primera encuesta nacional de ingresos y gastos familiares en Venezuela, segundo semestre de 1962: descripción de la encuesta y resultados preliminares de ingresos y gastos familiares. 2. ed. Caracas, 1964. 198 p., tables (Documento, 5)

Reports results, for second semester 1962, of first survey of family incomes and expenditures undertaken in Venezuela covering both urban and rural areas. Methodology employed is extensively explained. Valuable source of empirical information about population and economy of Venezuela at the time. [R. C. M.]

2165. **Villalba, Rodrigo.** La industria del gas natural en Venezuela. Caracas, Corporación Venezolana de Petróleo (CVP), 1972. 36 p., map, plates, tables.

Pamphlet attempts to provide general information about natural gas industry in Venezuela. Good summary statement that could be of interest to layman, or used as an introduction by the more serious researcher. Nicely illustrated.

BOLIVIA, CHILE, PARAGUAY, PERU, AND URUGUAY

JOHN STRASMA
Professor of Economics and Agricultural Economics
University of Wisconsin, Madison

BRUCE HERRICK
Associate Professor
University of California
Los Angeles

CHILE AND PERU, AGAIN, ACCOUNT FOR THE BULK of studies from and about these countries. The climate of academic and press freedom which characterized the 34-months government of President Salvador Allende and his Popular Unity coalition is demonstrated in the number and variety of studies of that process. Scholars of the Chilean economy, and others interested in the concept of democratic socialism, will need the publications of both supporters and opponents of Allende. The military junta which overthrew him began silencing critics, and it remains to be seen whether it will permit the sale and circulation of pro-Allende studies, including government documents published between 1970 and 1973.

Beginning in 1972, a University of Chile reorganization produced parallel economic research institutes, each analyzing current problems. Though there were "independents" in both, the work of the Instituto de Economía y Planificación was essentially pro-Allende (item 2252), and the Departamento or Instituto de Economía was in the Opposition (item 2250). At the Catholic University, studies by the Instituto de Economía (ex-CIEUC) and Planning Center (CEPLAN) tended to less polemical and more technocratic approaches to specific problems (items 2185 and 2204).

Apart from the Institutes, current and historical studies were published by various other university and private sources. Insights into events from a pro-Allende viewpoint were published by the Centro de Estudios de la Realidad Nacional (CEREN) at the Catholic University, and the Centro de Estudios Socio-Económicos (CESO) of the University of Chile. For understanding the intellectual rationalization of much Popular Unity policy, the weekly *Chile Hoy* is also helpful (item 2202). The works by CEREN and CESO, which could best be classified as socio-political-economic, ended as abruptly as the constitutional, elected government, and many of the authors of works reviewed in this section were jailed or in hiding (item 2239).

From the Opposition viewpoint, socio-political-economic studies appeared from private sector institutes (see item 2188), and in the new weekly, *¿Qué Pasa?* The venerable *Ercilla* continues as a useful source, as is the *Panorama Económico*, a monthly for informed laymen which specialized in round tables with economists from both the government and the opposition, centering on a current economic policy issue. The weekly international edition of *El Mercurio* is also an excellent source for the chronology of events and for the Opposition viewpoint on Allende. While much of the Opposition literature is polemical, there is an underlying thread which deserves notice. This is that the "structuralist" analysis which supported policies taken by both Frei and Allende had proved inadequate to either explain the Chilean economy or design appropriate policies for economic and social growth. Therefore, this group called for a complete rethinking of the widely-held interpretations of the Chilean economy.

The Allende government itself was also unique in its openness. For instance, early in 1972 the National Planning Office (ODEPLAN) held a week-long Round Table, at which some 50 Chilean and foreign economists discussed the Popular Unity policies, objectives and problems with government planners. Few governments—East or West—would permit, let alone organize, such an extended cross-examination of senior functionaries by foreign economists, many not at all sympathetic. Allende, ODEPLAN and the co-sponsoring Institute of Development Studies (Sussex, England) deserve scholars' thanks for the project, whose proceedings appear here (item 2256).

In Peru, the military government continued pursuit of a "third way," seeking growth, national autonomy, and class harmony rather than class struggle. Published data remain scarce; the English-language weekly *Peruvian Times* remains the best source. The government Planning Institute deserves praise for publishing a five-volume Plan, giving scholars data for recent years and a clearer vision of the government's priorities and economic strategy. The Ministry of Labor also deserves congratulations for its voluminous study on the labor force (item 2293).

Peruvian universities remained a problem for the government, and they produced very little published research. A new journal (*Sociedad y Política*) appeared, but was closed and editors Julio Cotler and Aníbal Quijano deported after only one year (item 2295). Outside Peru, few studies appeared for this *Handbook*, but two major social science anthologies on Peru are to be published soon—one edited by David Chaplin and another by Abraham Lowenthal.

As usual, publications from the smaller countries were few. From Paraguay, the most useful items were on agriculture, population and the capital market, and it may be significant that all were based on research funded by bilateral or regional aid organizations. (Given Paraguay's recently increased political ties to Brazil, it is possible that some items of value appeared there and were overlooked inadvertently.)

There was almost nothing from Bolivia, except for some worthwhile works published outside Bolivia (such as *Estudios Andinos*), and hardly anything of value for Uruguay.

BOLIVIA

Bernal V., Carlos; Luis Quiroga C.; and Jaime Villamizar V. Análisis de las perspectivas de exportación de Colombia en el Grupo Andino: Bolivia-Ecuador. See item 2044.

2166. Bernard, Jean-Pierre. Situation et perspectives de l'économie bolivienne: problèmes et politiques économiques, 1969-1971 (FDD/NED [Problèmes d'Amérique latine, 22] 3847/3848, 27 déc. 1971, p. 5-32, bibl., maps, tables)

Largely descriptive survey, whose main interest lies in analysis of political economy of the Ovando and Torres governments of 1969 and 1970.

2167. Bolivia: agricultura, economía y política; a bibliography. Madison, Wis., Univ. of Wisconsin, Land Tenure Center, 1972. 10 p. (Training & methods series, 7)

Second supplement to Land Tenure Center's bibliography on Bolivia. Like others, it is available upon request and without charge.

2168. Burke, Melvin. Does "Food for Peace" assistance damage the Bolivian economy? (IAMEA, 25:1, Summer 1971, p. 3-19, tables)

Urges the use of PL 480 counterpart funds to finance agricultural improvements that will lessen Bolivia's dependency on food grain imports from the US.

2169. ———. Land reform and its effect upon production and productivity in the Lake Titicaca region (UC/EDCC, 18:3, April 1970, p. 410-450)

Compares Bolivian agriculture, pre- and post-reform, with Peruvian agriculture in the vicinity of the lake. Careful empirical study, with modest aims and modest conclusions. See also item 7720.

2170. ———. El sector privado en la economía boliviana y la necesidad de crédito (IBEAS/EA, 1:1, 1970, p. 114-126)

Reviews size and strength of private sector in Bolivia and argues for its growth through credit expansion.

2171. Chirikos, Thomas N. and others. Human resources in Bolivia: problems, planning and policy. Columbus, Ohio, The Ohio State Univ., Center for Human Resources Research, *in cooperation with* the Division of Social Programming, National Secretariat of Planning and Coordination, Republic of Bolivia, 1971. 382 p.

Data on economy, labor force and market, educational and health systems, with recommendations in all these areas. Alas, data refers mainly to 1966 and proposed program to 1967-80. This final contract report to USAID and the Bolivian Government supercedes earlier unpublished drafts circulated in both languages, dates not specified.

2172. Colegio de Economistas de Bolivia, *La Paz.* Filial Oruro. Evaluación económica del Carnaval de Oruro, 1971. Oruro, Bol., Imprenta Quelco, 1972. 49 p., tables.

Pamphlet presents a benefit/cost study of the Oruran carnival, from its standpoint as a tourist attraction. Largely based on sample survey of 375 persons attending the celebration.

2173. Giménez-Carrazana, Manuel. El Banco Nacional de Bolivia en el centenario de su fundación: 1872-1972. La Paz, E. Burillo, 1972. 124 p., facsims., plates.

Superficial commemorative volume whose main value may be in its architectural photographs and other plates.

2174. Guardia Romero, Jaime and Emil Liebermann. La industria del hierro en Bolivia: consideraciones generales, informe para la Presidencia de la República. La Paz, Ministerio de Industria y Comercio, Instituto Nacional de Inversiones, Oficina de Coordinación de Estudios sobre el Hierro, 1972. 115 l., bibl., maps, plates, tables.

Pre-feasibility study of no apparent scholarly or methodological interest.

2175. Knoerich, Eckart. Los yungas: situación económica y desarrollo. La Paz, Academia Nacional de Ciencias de Bolivia, 1969. 41 p., bibl., maps, plates, tables.

Emphasizes agricultural potential of Bolivia's Amazonian region, northeast of La Paz. Has value as a preliminary survey. Good bibliography.

2176. Lofstrom, William Lee. The promise and problem of reform: attempted social and economic change in the first years of Bolivian independence. Ithaca, N.Y., Cornell Univ., Latin American Studies Program, 1972. 626 p., bibl. (Dissertation series, 35)

Carefully documented history of failure of newly-independent Bolivia to achieve reforms needed to take it from colonial status to nationhood, between 1825-28. Pressures of ideas from and territorial ambitions of neighbours, the lack of modern technology, and other problems have reappeared in more recent decades.

Malloy, James M. and **Richard S. Thorn** eds. Beyond the Revolution: Bolivia since 1952. See item 7720.

2177. Mesa Redonda sobre Plan de Transporte del Algodón, *Santa Cruz, Bol., 1971.* [Actas] La Paz, Banco Agrícola de Bolivia, 1971. 57 p., tables.

Apart from minutes of meeting of cotton growers, bankers and engineers, this is a useful source on rail, highway and water alternative routes from the Eastern lowlands of Bolivia across Argentina, Brazil and Chile to world markets. Background papers include cost and time studies and descriptions of the railroad, roads, ports and bureaucracies involved, all as of 1971.

2178. Ortuño, René. Bolivia y la integración económica de América Latina. B.A., Banco Interamericano de Desarrollo (BID), Instituto para la Integración de América Latina (INTAL), 1969. 168 p., tables.

Assesses Bolivia's prospects for international economic integration on a sectoral level. Given subsequent initiation of the Andean Pact and political nature of bargaining negotations, it is difficult to measure merit of particular point of view represented here.

2179. *Revista Panorama Industrial.* Año 1, No. 1, dic. 1971/enero 1972- . La Paz.

Magazine for Bolivian businessmen. No apparent or immediate scholarly or economic interest.

Smith, Peter Seaborn. Bolivian oil and Brazilian economic nationalism. See *HLAS 34:2832a.*

2180. Velasco S., José Miguel. Mito y realidad de las fundiciones en Bolivia: a la memoria de Mariano Peró A., pionero de las fundiciones de estaño en nuestro país. La Paz, Empresa Industrial Gráfica E. Burillo, 1964. 271 p., tables.

This item, overlooked in previous *HLAS*, reviews economic possibilities of installation of tin refineries in Bolivia. Many of its recommendations have subsequently been acted upon. Wealth of metallurgical detail; less interesting as an economic document.

2181. Whitehead, Lawrence. Estadística básica en países en vías de desarrollo: el caso de Bolivia (IBEAS/EA, 1:3, 1970, p. 83-110)

Spanish translation of *HLAS 33:2899.* No specific mention of its previous appearance in English.

CHILE

2182. Affonso, Almino. Esbozo histórico del movimiento campesino. Santiago, Instituto de Capacitación e Investigación en Reforma Agraria (ICIRA), 1973. 47 p.

Summary of efforts to organize peasant unions, from first stirrings about 1920, through 1970. Too brief for a basic source, but a useful overview, chronology and reference. See also items 2221 and 2224.

2183. Alaluf, David and others. Reforma agraria chilena: seis ensayos de interpretación. Santiago, Instituto de Capacitación e Investigación en Reforma Agraria (ICIRA), 1970. 125 p.

Essays by six Chilean and foreign scholars, on land reform objectives, progress and problems, and related topics such as peasant organization and general agricultural policy, all with reference to the Frei administration (1964-70).

2184. Anderson, Michael B. A model of the small Chilean firm. Ithaca, N.Y., Cornell Univ., Latin American Studies Program, 1972. 155 p., bibl. (Dissertation series, 38)

Theoretical and empirical investigation of role, goals, problems and behavior of small industrial firms in Chile. Based on field work, plus quantitative data from annual reports to a government agency for 1967-71. Fresh evidence for the serious study of the place of small firms in development, and of the government policies which affected them in Chile during that period.

2185. Aninat, U. Eduardo. Nuevas alternativas para el sistema chileno de seguridad social (UCC/CE, 8:25, dic. 1971, p. 79-110, bibl., tables)

Theoretical and empirical study of the creaking social security system, and of the economic and social gains that might be obtained by replacing the payroll taxes that fund it, with direct taxes on personal and company incomes. More extensive statistical series appear in the CEPLAN working papers, see *HLAS 33:2900-2901.*

2186. Aranda, Sergio and **Alberto Martínez.** La industria y la agricultura en el desarrollo económico chileno. Santiago, Univ. de Chile,

Instituto de Economía y Planificación, Depto. de Sociología, 1970. 107 p., tables.

Essays on the structure of manufacturing industry and agriculture, prior to 1970. Most data series stop with 1968, and the intended cross-fertilization of efforts by scholars from two different disciplines failed to produce results of value, perhaps because they were called to responsibilities in President Allende's government.

2187. Baltra-Cortés, Alberto. Le Chili et sa dépendance (ISEA/EA, 24:4, 1971, p. 679-698)

Summary of President Allende's program with regard to reducing Chile's "dependency," written by a senior Chilean economist, once influential in the Popular Unity Front, who later broke with Allende over the role of Baltra's Radical Party in the coalition. Nothing not readily available elsewhere.

2188. Bardon, Alvaro and others. Itinerario de una crisis: política, económica y transición al socialismo. Santiago, Instituto de Estudios Políticos, Editorial del Pacífico, 1972. 192 p.

Essays originally published in magazines and newspapers, by five university economists, former functionaries in the Frei government (1964-70), during first year of President Allende's administration. Useful contemporary source as to what reputable opposition economists thought was good and otherwise, as the Allende policies unfolded. For contrary views, see items 2251 and 2256.

2189. Barkin, David. El consumo y la vía chilena al socialismo: reflexiones en torno a la decisión automotriz. Santiago, Univ. Católica de Chile, Centro de Estudios de la Planificación Nacional, 1971. 29 p. (CEPLAN, 13)

Visiting economist expresses horror that socialist government should invest in an intended expansion of the manufacture of automobiles for individual purchasers. He questions the "new class" image this will create, if the buyers are functionaries of the regime, and points out the externalities—parking problems, air pollution, need to import fuel, etc. Decisive paper in postponing expansion plan.

2190. Behrman, Jere R. Sectoral elasticities of substitution between capital and labor in a developing economy: time series analysis in the case of postwar Chile. (Econometrica [Santiago] 40:2, marzo 1972, p. 311-326)

Member of the ODEPLAN-MIT team applies sophisticated quantitative methods to determine degree to which capital and labor might be substituted for one another in Chile using data from the mid-1940's to mid-1960's. See also item 2275.

2191. ———. Short-run flexibility in a developing economy (JPE, 80:2, March/April 1972, p. 292-313)

On basis of sophisticated quantitative methods and their econometric applications, author concludes that short-run flexibility in Chile is substantial rather than limited as is frequently assumed in the economic literature of underdeveloped countries. Policies that exploit that flexibility are thus indicated. Article combines theoretical and empirical considerations, using data gathered in Chile during late 1960s.

2192. Bitar, Sergio. La inversión extranjera en la industria chilena (FCE/TE, 38:152, oct./dic. 1971, p. 995-1009)

Analysis of foreign investment in Chilean manufacturing industry, mainly to 1968, with reference to current literature and author's own conclusions as to degree to which such investment "benefits" and "costs" a country such as Chile. Professor Bitar (School of Engineering, Univ. of Chile) served as Minister of Mines for about a month in 1973.

2193. *Boletín Mensual*. Banco Central de Chile. Vol. 45, No. 527, enero 1972- . Santiago.

Monthly bulletin continues to provide convenient tables on money, employment, production, prices, and foreign trade. A few items, such as foreign exchange reserves, became embarrassing and were omitted during much of 1972 and 1973. Bank also published annual balance of payments studies with a lag of several years. Reference libraries should order both monthly *Bulletin* and the *Balance of Payments* volumes, as well as the economic studies mentioned in *HLAS 33:2908.*

2194. Cabero, Nora. Análisis del impuesto a las compraventas y otros impuestos a las transacciones internas (UCC/CE, 8:23, abril 1971, p. 44-82)

Analysis of Chilean sales tax as of 1968-69, and of value-added tax alternative then under consideration. Includes useful data and references for specialists.

2195. Cabezón, Pedro. Antecedentes históricos de las importaciones y de la política comercial en Chile (UCC/CE, 8:25, dic. 1971, p. 1-35, tables)

Analysis of Chile's trade policy debate and practices, from Independence to approximately 1965. Accompanied by tables and relevant bibliographical references, with most of data series covering part or all of period 1910-64.

2196. *El Campesino.* Organo oficial de la Sociedad Nacional de Agricultura. Vol. 104, No. 6, junio 1973- . Santiago.

Despite attrition in ranks of landowners, their national society continues to publish its monthly journal, mixing excellent technical articles of intensive production techniques with critical analyses of Popular Unity policies. This issue is especially interesting because it carries sample forms to enable owners to prepare and speedily enter every conceivable appeal to the courts against seizure, intervention or expropriation of their land. If definitive legal transfer of the land could be stalled long enough, the SNA expected (rightly) that the government would be overthrown and the landowner's property thus saved.

2197. Cauas, Jorge. Stabilization policy: the Chilean case; (JPE, 78:4, pt. 2, July/Aug. 1970, p. 815-825)

Description of a price stabilization effort made in Chile during mid-1960's, when author was Vice-President of the Central Bank. Item 2210 covers same material in more depth.

2198. Chile. Instituto de Capacitación e Investigación sobre Reforma Agraria. Instituto de Desarrollo Agropecuario. El minifundio en una política de desarrollo agrícola. Santiago, 1971. 22 p.

Analysis of minifundia problem in a context of agrarian reform that broke up the largest estates but did little or nothing for the peasants who possessed tiny plots of land, too small to earn a living on. Based on extensive field work, study develops a typology, makes quantitative estimates of size of the problem, and recommends specific remedial policies. Concludes with case studies from three provinces.

2199. ———. **Instituto Nacional de Estadísticas.** Evolución de la mano de obra chilena: marzo 1967 a diciembre 1970. Santiago, 1970? 12 p., tables (Serie de investigaciones muestrales)

Summary of nine surveys of labor force during said period. Based on National Survey of Households, and thus provides an independent and somewhat broader base than quarterly surveys of the Institute of Economics of the Univ. of Chile, which refer basically to Greater Santiago.

2200. ———. **Oficina de Planificación Nacional (ODEPLAN).** Aspectos metodológicos de dos planes operativos annuales. t. 1-2. Santiago, 1972. 617 p.

Detailed instructions and working sheets with which planners were to prepare annual economic plans, with emphasis on public sector and "social area," or nationalized part of manufacturing industry. Source for economist trying to see how Unidad Popular technicians actually went about preparing economic plans —whose eventual execution would, nonetheless, depend largely on political events beyond their control.

2201. ———. ———. Chile ante los problemas monetarios y financieros internacionales. Santiago, 1972. 506 p.

Reports and position papers of Chile at UNCTAD III (see introduction to this section). Includes various speeches and essays on international monetary problems as well as trade questions; opens with full text of speeches to Conference by President Allende, and other dignitaries including Robert McNamara, World Bank President.

2202. *Chile Hoy.* Revista semanal. No. 1, julio 1972- . Santiago.

Weekly by intellectuals attempting to articulate clearly policies and perspectives of the Popular Unity Government. Necessary collateral reading, giving the government viewpoint to take alongside newsmagazines such as *Ercilla, ¿Qué Pasa?* and the weekly airmail edition of *El Mercurio,* all less than sympathetic to Allende. Editorial office: Avda. Italia 654, Santiago. Annual subscription in US$ 48.00. Appeared in mid-1972 and presumably disappeared after the Sept. 1973 coup, of which it warned.

2203. Crosson, Pierre R. Agricultural development and productivity: lessons from the Chilean experience. Baltimore, Md., The Johns Hopkins Press, 1970. 198 p.

Economic review of Chilean agriculture during 1950s and 1960s, sponsored by Resources for the Future. Production function analysis, while not the exclusive approach, is used extensively to evaluate alternatives. Data base is of little relevance to Chilean agriculture after 1964.

2204. *Cuadernos de Economía.* Universidad Católica de Chile. Año 8, No. 23, agosto 1971- . Santiago.

The Catholic Univ.'s Institute of Economics continues to put out this excellent journal three times a year. This issue, for instance, contains three translations of articles published abroad (by Schultz, Myint and Selowsky), but also two significant original studies available nowhere else: Pedro Jeftanovic's analysis of household savings in Greater Santiago (based on careful analysis and a major survey in 1969, which includes data on incomes, levels and types of financial assets as a function of family income, etc.). In the other, Norman R. Collins and Peter V. Garrod present results of a detailed study of retail food distribution (relating service, prices, employment, etc. based on 1969 data).

2205. Della Valle, P. A. Diferenciales de salario ocupacional en la minería del cobre en Chile: 1955-1966 (UCC/CE, 8:23, abril 1971, pp. 83-88)

Short essay, but based on data obtained from foreign copper companies and hence of possible use in studies of wage movements in mining enclaves in Chile and elsewhere.

2206. Echeverría, Roberto. Política de precios y redistribución de ingresos agrícolas. Santiago, Instituto de Capacitación e Investigación en Reforma Agraria (ICIRA), 1972. 373 p.

Spanish version of author's Ph.D. thesis (see *HLAS 33:2914*). Refers to redistribution of personal incomes in Chile caused by price fluctuations between 1958-67. Although it was not possible to bring the study up to date, ICIRA published it in Spanish in order to make methodology available to students and others who might wish to apply it to other periods and sectors or countries.

2207. Echeverría Bunster, Andrés. Bases para una visión comunitaria de la economía. Santiago, Instituto de Estudios Políticos, 1972. 107 p.

Handbook for Christian Democratic Party members, seeking to explain to them concept of worker-managed enterprises and relationship of such firms to thought of key ideologues of that party, such as Jacques Maritain. Author also criticizes both liberal capitalist model and collectivist marxist model which the Popular Unity government was attempting to install in its place.

2208. Eckhaus, Richard S. and Paul N. Rosenstein-Rodan eds. Analysis of development problems. Amsterdam, North-Holland, 1973. 425 p.

Series of essays by members of the MIT-ODEPLAN team, covering Chilean economic conditions and development strategies under the political framework present in late 1960s. While many of the *ceteris paribus* assumptions of these quantitatively sophisticated essays have been violated, articles are relevant to planning methods elsewhere and hence their value is little diminished by the changes in government since 1970.

2209. Edwards, Thomas L. Economic development and reform in Chile: progress under Frei, 1964-1970. East Lansing, Mich.,

Michigan State Univ., Latin American Studies Center, 1972. 54 p., tables (Monograph series, 8)

Relatively objective assessment of the degree to which President Frei's government (1964-70) attained its stated objectives during that sexennium. Author concentrates on economic policies and targets, insofar as possible measuring their attainment quantitatively and giving percentage "scores." Useful companion reading to items 2183 and 2256.

2210. Ffrench-Davis, Ricardo. Políticas económicas en Chile: 1952-1970. Santiago, Centro de Estudios de Planificación Nacional (CEPLAN), Ediciones Nueva Universidad, 1973. 350 p.

Systematic analysis of economic policies and their results, followed by Presidents Ibañez (1952-58), Alessandri (1958-64), and Frei (1964-70). Includes stabilization, foreign trade, money and credit, tax and incomes policies. 10 appendices present statistical series revised while the author was Director of Research at the Central Bank. An indispensable reference, more accurate than government publications and more perceptive than previous studies of these periods.

2211. Foxley, Alejandro and Eduardo García. The role of projections in national planning: a methodology for medium-term projections and their application in Chile (Journal of Development Planning [UN, N.Y.] 4, 1972, p. 64-97, tables)

Sophisticated techniques developed while the authors were senior economists at Chile's Oficina de Planificación Nacional (ODEPLAN), 1966-70. Combined consistency and optimization 15-sector model demonstrates tradeoffs for policymakers, 1970-80. Domestic savings, external finance, employment, and changes in the productive structure are analyzed with aid of 1960-68 data base much refined over previously published series. Methodology may interest planners. Others may find it useful primarily as an estimate of what Chile's economy might have done had Allende not been elected in 1970, provided, of course, that the victor had been permitted to govern without having to face first urban terrorism and subsequent military repression.

2212. ——— and Peter B. Clark. Rentabilidad social de nuevas expansiones en la producción de cobre en Chile. Santiago, Univ. Católica de Chile, Centro de Estudios de Planificación Nacional 1972. 44 p. (CEPLAN, 17)

Methodological exercise, using a 15-sector model, to estimate extent to which it would be more profitable to continue expanding copper mining industry, than to devote scarce investment resources to other economic sectors. Relatively sophisticated methods include estimates of future prices, and of the impact of different world price levels on results of study. Follow-up on *HLAS* 33:2918.

2213 ———; Ricardo Infante B; and Mario Gómez P. Desequilibrios de financiamiento en el proceso de desarrollo: resultado para Chile en el decenio 1970-1980 (UCC/CE, 6:19, dic. 1969, p. 1-31)

Technical paper, estimating foreign trade, internal financing, and public sector gaps for possible growth patterns during decade ahead. Item 2211 is a later, more useful version.

Furtado, Celso and Andrea Maneschi. Un modèle simulé de développement et de stagnation en Amérique latine. See item 1809.

2214. Gavilán Estelat, Marcelino. La empresa, el empresario y la explotación en la legislación agraria de Chile (Revista de Estudios Agro-Sociales [Madrid] 20:76, julio/sept. 1971, p. 55-108)

Lengthy discussion of Chilean land reform law of 1967, with emphasis on degrees and variations of ownership-tenancy-management, and other legal problems, that arose in specific cases. Author was an FAO expert in agrarian law, assigned to the Land Reform Research and Training Institute (ICIRA) in Santiago through 1970.

2215. Gimeno, José. Agricultura socialista: Chile y 16 países. Santiago, n.p., 1971. 156 p.

Author, an Uruguayan agricultural expert working for the FAO, assembled material on forms of farm organization, taxation of the rural sector, and other facets of agriculture under socialism, for reference by Chileans considering policy alternatives for Chile. Allende was overthrown before any were implemented.

2216. Gómez, Sergio. Los empresarios agrícolas. Santiago, Instituto de Capacitación e Investigación en Reforma Agraria (ICIRA), 1972. 141 p.

Study of organizations in which landowners and farm operators sought to defend themselves against Popular Unity policies (price policies and land reform), and also illegal land seizures by extreme Left. Descriptive and evaluative material is supported by case study of peasant and owner organizations in Llanquihue province. Valuable, reasonably accurate despite the author's distaste for his subjects, and a useful updating of item 2221.

2217. Goussault, Yves. La réforme agraire au Chili à la veille du gouvernement d'Unité Populaire (IRFDH/DC, 44, juin 1971, p. 3-25)

Summary of analysis, policies and early results of the Frei agrarian reform, through 1968. Item 2247 is a much more complete source.

2218. Huneeus C., Pablo. Fuerza de trabajo y desempleo durante el período 1971-1976 (UCC/CE, 7:22, dic. 1970, p. 56-68)

Sociologist, formerly director of the National Employment Service, urges policy changes to create jobs for the half million Chileans expected to enter the labor force between 1971-76. His proposals, such as not allowing labor-substituting machinery imports and abolishing the ban on firing of workers were apt for the previous regime, hardly addressed the employment question as seen by President Allende. See also the critique and alternative proposals by Ricardo Morán in *Cuadernos de Economía* (Santiago, 8:23, abril 1971, p. 89-107).

2219. International Labour Organisation, Geneva. Creación de empleos y absorción del desempleo en Chile: la experiencia de 1971. Geneva, 1972. 57 p.

Analysis of the employment situation in Chile in 1970, the policies undertaken by President Allende to meet it, and the results. Unemployment fell, but the usual multiplier effect also fell so that the future growth of employment was still somewhat in doubt in late 1971. Objective, accurate work by economists at the ILO office in Santiago. See also work by V. Ramos (*HLAS 33:2933-2936*).

2220. ———, ———. The settlement of labour disputes in Chile (AIFLD/R, 3:3, 1971, p. 59-81)

Description of Chilean labor legislation up to Aug. 1970. During subsequent period of Popular Unity Government (1970-73), legislation changed little but enforcement, implementation and regulations changed greatly.

2221. Kaufman, Robert R. The politics of land reform in Chile, 1950-1970: policy, political institutions and social change. Cambridge, Mass., Harvard Univ. Press, 1972. 321 p., bibl.

Skillful recounting and analysis of process by which reformers moved and landowners resisted enactment and then implementation of agrarian reform legislation in Chile. Compare with item 2247 (for results) and item 2216 (for what the landowners did during the first two years of President Allende's Popular Unity government, 1970-72).

2222. *LTC Newsletter.* Univ. of Wisconsin, Land Tenure Center. No. 35, Dec./March 1971/1972- . Madison, Wis.

Continuing source of research reports on agricultural subjects in Latin America and elsewhere. For example, this issue carries a progress report on field research on effects of land reform in Chile, and a comparative survey of Chilean and Peruvian policies regarding foreign mines and manufacturing companies, under Presidents Allende and Velasco.

2223. Lau, Stephen F. The Chilean response to foreign investment. N.Y., Praeger Publishers, 1972. 118 p., bibl., tables (Praeger special studies in international economics and development)

Assessment of experience under Chilean laws relating to foreign investment, as seen by influential Chileans interviewed in June 1969. Useful background source for understanding policies of both Christian Democrat and Popular Unity governments. Delay in publication is unfortunate; there is virtually nothing on the Allende period, and only two interviewees were in that camp.

Lehmann, David. Political incorporation versus political stability: the case of the Chilean agrarian reform, 1965-1970. See item 7765.

2224. Loveman, Brian. El campesino chileno le escribe a Su Excelencia. Santiago, Instituto de Capacitación e Investigación de la Reforma Agraria (ICIRA), 1971. 552 p.

After brief introduction, author reproduces actual letters and petitions sent by peasants to Chile's presidents, ever since 1938, together with copies of the memos as the bureaucracy responded (or failed to). Demonstrates real vitality of peasant movement, until it was repressed b[,] 1947 outlawing of Communist Party (which landowners used to outlaw labor movements as well). Useful background as many writers had thought land reform movements began with Frei and Allende. See also items 2182 and 7765.

2225. Lüders, Rolf. Una historia monetaria de Chile (UCC/CE, 7:20, abril 1970, p. 4-28)

Summary of author's Ph. D. thesis at Univ. of Chicago, on history of monetary policies and institutions between 1925-58. Valuable chiefly on earlier part of period, and for references. For period after 1952, see instead item 2210.

2226. McCoy, Terry L. La reforma agraria chilena: un análisis político del cambio estructural (CLAPCS/AL, 13:2/3, abril/set. 1970, p. 30-50)

Analysis of causes making agrarian reform possible in Chile, and of the institutions guiding its development through 1969. For serious reference work, scholars would do better to consult author's entire Ph.D. thesis (Univ. of Wisconsin, 1970), based on field work in Chile in 1966, 1967 and 1969.

2227. Mamalakis, Markos. Contribution of copper to Chilean economic development, 1920-67: profile of a foreign-owned export sector (*in* Mikesell, Raymond Frech and others. Foreign investment in the petroleum and mineral industries: case studies of investor-host country relations. Baltimore, Md., The Johns Hopkins Press *for* Resources for the Future, 1971, p. 387-420, bibl., tables)

Painstaking study of foreign exchange and other contributions of foreign-owned copper mines to Chilean development; author demonstrates that government policies, and not only the mining companies, kept copper from contributing its full potential.

2228. Méndez G., Juan Carlos. La carga tributaria de la inflación chilena (UCC/CE, 7:20, abril 1970, p. 69-81)

Theoretical and empirical study of resource transfers produced by inflation in Chile, 1950-68. On average, author estimates that government captured 1.3 percent of gross domestic product and private sector borrowers about 1.5 percent, at the expense of owners of money balances.

2229. Merrill, Robert North. Toward a structural housing policy: an analysis of Chile's low income housing program. Ithaca, N.Y., Cornell Univ., Latin American Studies Program, 1971. 200 p., bibl., tables (Dissertation series, 22)

Painstaking theoretical and empirical analysis of causes of failure in low-income housing plans during 1960s, despite imaginative and innovative efforts to mobilize available labor and self-help potentials, and to apply escalator clauses to savings and debt elements in the financing to guard against inflation. Highly competent analysis of problem, with relevance to study of housing problem in other developing countries as well. Supplants the earlier, draft version. See *HLAS 31:3641*.

2230. Meyer, Richard L. Financing agrarian reform through beneficiary payments: the

Chilean case. Ithaca, N.Y., Cornell Univ., Dept. of Agricultural Economics, 1972. 108 p., bibl., tables (Agricultural economics research, 72:4)

Debt repayment capacity and its possible increase through agrarian reform measures are assessed by this Cornell Univ. doctoral dissertation writer. Case studies of six *asentamientos* 1966-68 are examined. Revised version of *HLAS 33:2925*. See also item 2247.

2231. Mikesell, Raymond Frech. Conflict and accommodation in Chilean copper (*in* Mikesell, Raymond Frech and others. Foreign investment in the petroleum and mineral industries: case studies of investor-host country relations. Baltimore, Md., The Johns Hopkins Press *for* Resources for the Future, 1971, p. 369-386)

Competent history of relations between Chilean governments and foreign copper companies, starting with their arrival in 1904 and ending with partial and gradual nationalization arrangements negotiated with President Frei before 1970.

2232. Molina, Sergio. El proceso de cambio en Chile. Santiago, Editorial Universitaria, 1972. 221 p.

Economic policies during Frei Administration (1964-70) analyzed by economist who served as Finance Minister and then as head of the Development Corporation. Author attempts to analyze, with aid of hindsight, Christian Democratic Party's view of each problem, its policies, and results. Useful source, but no revelations or surprises from a man who may well again hold high office. Book also published in Mexico, Siglo XXI Editores, 1972.

2233. Muñoz G., Oscar. Crecimiento industrial, estructura del consumo y distribución del ingreso. Santiago, Univ. Católica de Chile, Centro de Estudios de Planificación Nacional, 1971. 49 p. (CEPLAN, 8)

Analysis of Chile's industrial growth during 1960s, in relation to changing patterns of consumption and income distribution. Preliminary study, which was to emerge as book-length compendium of studies on income distribution toward end of 1973.

2234. North American Congress on Latin America, *N.Y.* New Chile. N.Y., 1973. 176 p., bibl., illus.

Chronicles Chile's external economic difficulties under President Allende. Even those unsympathetic to basic anti-imperialistic outlook of organization will find chronology and recitation of contracts, credits granted or denied, and even rather weak support of socialist countries, helpful in organizing their own interpretation of the Popular Unity period in Chilean economic history.

2235. Ossandon G., Jorge. Economía de guerra: ¿vía chilena hacia el hambre? Santiago, Instituto de Estudios Políticos, 1973, 128 p.

Essays, most originally published in daily opposition press, by an economist active in the Opposition to President Allende and the Unidad Popular government. While short on hard data, it is a useful view of arguments that were advanced against each step Allende took in implementing his program–and of how the free press aroused alarm as to eventual results of that program. For another view, see items 2221 and 2252.

2236. Panorama Económico. Editorial Universitaria, No. 275, enero/feb. 1973- . Santiago.

In its second incarnation, Chile's economic monthly stresses "round tables" between government economists and others neutral or of the opposition. Topics are both political and economic. For example, this issue had a panel on what could be done with the economy after congressional elections of March, essays on future of the auto industry (see also item 2189), and an essay on meaning of "bosses" strike of Oct. 1972. Statistical tables include copper output, price levels, employment, etc.

2237. Pérez de Arce, Hermógenes. Comentarios escogidos. Santiago, Ediciones Portada, 1973, 432 p.

More essays by an economic commentator outspokenly opposed to the Allende Government, giving an opposition view of the "Chilean Way to Socialism." Useful as contemporary record of slogans, fears and hopes of Allende's opposition, whose publication, in book form, makes available material which was originally delivered over the opposition radio in 1971 and 1972.

2238. Pinto, Aníbal. Tres ensayos sobre Chile y América Latina. B.A., Ediciones Solar, 1971. 154 p., tables (Biblioteca dimensión americana)

Concerned primarily with economic theory (marxism, "cepalismo"). [J. J. Bailey]

2239. Pizarro, Roberto and **Manuel Garretón** *eds.* Transición al socialismo y experiencia chilena. Santiago, Centro de Estudios Socioeconómicos (CESO), [and] Centro para el Estudio de la Realidad Nacional (CEREN), 1972. 191 p.

Texts of speeches presented at public forum in late 1971, organized by the Center for the Study of National Reality (CEREN) and the Center for Socio-Economic Studies (CESO), of the Catholic Univ. and the Univ. of Chile, respectively. Speakers such as Paul Sweezy and Rossana Rossanda discussed theoretical problems of moving into socialism, and Chilean speakers such as Pedro Vuskovic and Marta Harnecker tried to explain (correctly) that foreigners did not fully understand the problem. Valuable record of a "happening" of that period.

2240. Ramos, Joseph R. Inmovilidad en el mercado de capital y la distribución de ingreso (UCC/CE, 8:23, abril 1971, p. 25-43)

Theoretical exploration of impact of immobility of capital in Chile and other less developed countries, due to family or other close economic group control of capital and much of bank credit. Concludes that impact is probably much more adverse to income distribution than to output, and calls for empirical studies of phenomenon.

2241. Ramos, Sergio. Chile ¿una economía de transición? Santiago, Univ. de Chile, Centro de Estudios Socio-Económicos, Editorial Prensa Latinoamericana, 1972. 262 p.

Analysis of Allende's first year in moving Chile toward socialism, from viewpoint that might perhaps best be described as sympathetic, and yet independent of Popular Unity government, by Chilean Marxist economist and professor. One of best general books on what Allende sought to do in economic matters, but slighting of disputes within Chilean Left on pace and style prevent author from adequately foreseeing the disaster ahead.

2242. Romeo, Carlos. Algunos problemas de la economía política del socialismo. Santiago, Univ. de Chile, Instituto de Economía y Planificación, 1972. 119 p. (Serie publicación docentes)

Teaching material prepared by Institute's Director (pro-UP wing) to help apply marxist theory to specific problems of transition from capitalism to socialism, in general and possibly in Chile. Primarily theoretical, with some sound insights into possible problems associated with state property and with international trade among socialist nations, drawing on author's experience in Cuba.

2243. Ruiz-Esquide Jara, Mariano. El socialismo traicionado. Santiago, Instituto de Estudios Políticos, Editorial del Pacífico, 1973. 190 p.

Critical essay by Christian Democratic Deputy, who sees the "betrayal" of title in fact that President Allende's Chilean way turned out to be pretty much like Soviet model. The Left was betrayed by shameless struggle among parties for policymaking posts. Scholars may find value in tables showing names and party affiliation of men assigned to run factories taken over by Allende's government.

2244. Santa María, Domingo. Perspectives on Spanish American legal norms governing mining concessions: "Chileanization," and the "Consensus of Viña del Mar" (The Virginia Journal of International Law [Charlottesville] 11, March 1971, p. 177-191)

Ambassador of Chile to US (1967-70) provides background to enable Anglo-Saxons to understand how Frei's "Chileanization" or forced-buyout of Anaconda's copper interests was well-grounded in Hispanic law and UN resolutions, despite apparent conflict with Anglo-Saxon law systems.

2245. Seton, Francis. Shadow wages in the Chilean economy. Paris, OECD, 1972. (Series on cost-benefit analysis. Case study, 4)

Empirical application of the Little-Mirrlees industrial project analysis method of calculating shadow prices, based on pre-1972 data for Chile. Thorough and craftsmanlike.

2246. *Sociedad y Desarrollo.* Univ. de Chile, Centro de Estudios Socioeconómicos (CESO). Vol. 1, No. 1, enero/marzo 1972- . Santiago.

New quarterly journal, launched by the sociologists and economists working at or with CESO, a multidisciplinary group of scholars that had been working for several years on problems of imperialism and dependency. Fittingly, this first issue is devoted to that theme, with a leading article by Theotonio dos Santos. No. 3, julio/sept. 1972, has good selection of pieces on current state of Chile's agrarian reform. Journal may have been a casualty—along with many of its writers —of Sept. 1973 coup that overthrew President Allende.

2247. Swift, Jeannine. Agrarian reform in Chile. Lexington, Mass., Heath Lexington Books, 1971. 125 p., bibl., tables. (Studies in international development and economics)

Thorough examination of economic arguments favoring agrarian reform in Chile, of laws and actual reform achieved under President Frei, and of available evidence on economic results (costs and benefits) of reform on 17 projects. While data essentially end with 1968, this is a useful source of material otherwise available only in Spanish. See *HLAS 33:2905.*

2248. United Nations. Food and Agriculture Organization (FAO). Chile: producción, industrialización y consumo de leche y productos lácteos; aspectos técnicos y económicos, antecedentes preliminares. Santiago, Corporación de Fomento de la Producción (CORFO), Instituto de Capacitación e Investigación sobre Reforma Agraria (ICIRA), 1972. 134 p., tables.

Compilation of data on Chilean agriculture, with emphasis on dairy herds, forage crop production, dairy management, animal health, and milk production and distribution. Also covers question of nutrition, cost, imports, training of dairy farmers and technicians, foreign aid, etc. Best single source on subject as of 1972, with much data not available in any other published source.

2249. ——. ——. Estudio de nueve predios lecheros del sector reformado de la provincia de Cautín. Santiago, Corporación de Fomento de la Producción (CORFO), Instituto de Capacitación e Investigación sobre Reforma Agraria (ICIRA), 1973. 37 p., tables.

Example of field work undertaken by international dairy development program, in cooperation with the land reform corporation (CORA), to determine practices and resources, problems and possibilities on sample of nine dairy farms that had become land reform projects in southern province. Considerable detail on both reform projects and on dairy management practices and results on those farms, and their interaction with government policies.

2250. Universidad de Chile, *Santiago.* **Instituto de Economía y Planificación,** Comentarios sobre la situación económica. Santiago, 1971- 1972. 1 v. (Unpaged)

Under this title, group of economists (who did not identify with the Popular Unity Government and were employed at the Institute of Economics of the Univ. of Chile) published economic surveys twice a year in 1971 and 1972. With more use of "standard" economic instruments of analysis and less stress on political variables than their ideological opponents' studies, they document the initial boom and then increasing problems of the economy. Basic sources for the analysis of the Allende period, but must be read together with the work of Allende supporters (see items 2251-2252 and 2256) to know what was going on and why.

2251. ———, ———. ———. La economía chilena en 1971. Santiago, 1972. 641 p.

Series of essays by pro-government economists working at the Institute before its division. Volume must be understood as a response to critical studies published by opposition economists in same Institute and elsewhere (see items 2188 and 2250). Quality uneven, but considerable data and insights not available to opposition economists, as to what was going on, and why.

2252. ———, ———. ———. La economía chilena en 1972. Santiago, 1973. 465 p.

Analysis of political and economic developments in second year of President Allende's "Chilean Way to Socialism." Detailed discussion of progress in socializing the economy, and of emerging problems in manufacturing, distribution and prices. Essential counterpoint to the opposition material (see item 2250), and followup to earlier pro-government items 2251 and 2256.

2253. Walker Errasuriz, Francisco and others. The settlement of labour disputes in Chile (ILO/R, 103:4, April 1971, p. 333-350)

Describes in legal rather than economic terms means by which labor disputes could be settled. Unfortunately, authors do not examine empirically application or effects of laws. Describes situation in Chile "as at 31 August 1970," i.e., before Allende's election.

2254. Weeks, John R. Urban and rural natural increase in Chile (MMFQ, 48:1, Jan. 1970, p. 71-89)

Concludes that urban natural increase is greater than rural, on basis of statistics of birth registration data in three urban provinces (Santiago, Valparaíso, Concepción) vs. rest of the country. Ignores existence of rural population in those three provinces or of urban population elsewhere; treats birth underregistration as equal in urban and rural areas; ignores institutional requirements (two witnesses)that discourage registration of rural births. In short, methodologically flawed.

2255. Yver, Raúl E. Dinámica del ajuste de la tasa de inflación: el caso chileno (UCC/CE, 7:20, abril 1970, p. 53-68)

Technical essay on analysis of lags between price changes in money supply, with reference to other sources on subject.

2256. Zammit, J. Ann ed. The Chilean road to socialism. Austin, Tex., Univ. of Texas Press, 1973. 466 pp.

Papers and proceedings of 1972 round table bringing together Chilean planners and distinguished foreign and Chilean economists to review intentions, accomplishments and problems of first year of Allende's Popular Unity Government. Meeting was organized by Sussex Univ.'s Institute of Development Studies (IDS) in England and the Chilean National Planning Office (ODEPLAN). Absolutely essential reference to anyone attempting to assess what Allende sought to do, and how his economists went about it.

2257. Zegers de Landa, Gerardo. El Pacto Andino y la industria subregional de artefactors de la línea blanca (UCC/CE 8:25, dic. 1971, p. 111-147)

Extracts from honors thesis at Catholic Univ.'s School of Economics, this is a study in depth of Chile's ability to compete with Peruvian, Colombian and other Andean Zone makers of refrigerators, stoves, etc., about 1969-70. Useful data on respective industries in these countries, as well as a glimpse of Chilean businessmen's estimates of their situation.

2258. Zylberberg, J. Note sur quelques contradictions du développement national et régional chilien: 1965-1970 (IIDC/C, 21:4, 1971, p. 406-424, tables)

Critique of regional and national planning under Frei. Author concludes that only mass mobilization will allow austerity, savings and work needed to overcome underdevelopment, and that anyhow no progress is possible unless world trade systems are changed in favor of the Third World. No data not readily available from Chilean sources noted in this *Handbook*.

PARAGUAY

2259. Arnold, Adlai F. Foundations of an agricultural policy in Prarguay. N.Y., Praeger Publishers, 1971. 294 p., tables (Praeger special studies in international economics and development)

Analysis of agricultural development, based on study of land resources, population, national history and relevant institutions. Director of an AID agricultural team in Paraguay, 1965-70, author completed this reflective analysis after moving to another assignment. Appendices have agrarian laws and the 1969-73 economic development plan.

2260. Banco Central del Paraguay, *Asunción.* Memoria: 1968. Asunción, 1968? 222 p., tables.

Useful synopsis, especially of monetary and fiscal activities. As in other annual reports, however, few historical series are provided, making difficult any sort of useful analysis about movements over time.

2261. Ceuppens, Henry D. Paraguay: año 2000. Asunción. Artes Gráficas Zamphirópolos, 1971. 285 p.

Written before 1972 census, book surveys country's socioeconomic framework. Despite title, only few projections are made; all seem to be linear extrapolations of trends existing around 1970.

2262. Ibarra, Enrique and others. Implicancias económicas y sociales del crecimiento poblacional paraguayo. Asunción, Instituto de Desarrollo Integral y Armónico (IDIA), 1971? 214 p., bibl., tables (Serie desarrollo y demografía, 1)

AID-sponsored study whose main interest resides in sample survey of 2,000 family units in country as a whole. Family composition, together with various social and economic indicators were surveyed. In addition, makes population projections to end of century.

2263. Mansfield, Charles Y. Elasticity and buoyancy of a tax system: a method applied to Paraguay (IMF Staff Papers [International Monetary Fund, Washington] 19:2, July 1972, p. 425-446)

Paraguayan tax policy between 1962 and 1970 is

examined by member of IMF staff, with focus on automatic response of fiscal revenues to changes in income ("elasticity") and total response, automatic and discretionary, in fiscal revenues to income changes ("buoyancy" or in Spanish, "flexibilidad"). While elasticity during this period was close to unity, revenues rose significantly owing to discretionary changes in indirect taxes and the introduction of a sales tax.

2264. Mitchell, Glen H. Notas sobre hábitos de compra y consumo de comestibles en familias de clase trabajadora en Asunción (CPES/RPS, 8:22, set./dic. 1971, p. 132-161, bibl., tables)

Translation of his original *Food marketing in Asunción*, done under AID auspices. Pilot survey of consumer attitudes and practices in two barrios of Asunción, article's interest is probably limited to marketing practitioners and agricultural economists.

2265. Sánchez Masi, Luis. El mercado de capitales en el Paraguay. Con la colaboración de economistas del CEPADE [Centro Paraguayo de Estudios de Desarrollo Económico y Social]. México, Centro de Estudios Monetarios Latinoamericanos *para el* Banco Interamericano de Desarrollo, 1972. 224 p., tables

V. 14 in series by CEMLA on Latin American capital markets. First such study for Paraguay. Thorough and careful, it forms the basis for all future work in the area.

2266. Sepúlveda Whittle, Tomás. Transporte y comercio exterior del Paraguay. B.A., Banco Interamericano de Desarrollo (BID), Instituto para la Integración de América Latina (INTAL), [and] Asociación Latinoamericana de Libre Comercio (ALALC), 1967. 85 p., tables.

Descriptive study, centered around mid-1960's, of Paraguayan transport in the setting of Latin American economic integration. At this point, probably has little more than historical interest.

PERU

2267. Banco Central de Reserva, *Lima*. Cuentas nacionales del Perú: 1960-1969. t. 2, Anexo estadístico. Lima, 1970. 1 v. (Unpaged) tables (mimeo)

Indexes, monthly and quarterly, of manufacturing output, and estimates of gross value of output at constant prices by sectors. Fiscal, monetary and trade figures. About 200 p. of mimeographed tables.

2268. Bertholet, Christiaan Joseph Leonard. Rural Puno before take-off: an empirical baseline study. Lima, Pontificia Univ. Católica del Perú, Centro de Investigaciones Sociales, Económicas, Políticas y Antropológicas, 1967. 331 p., maps, plates (Publicación CIS-A, 3)

Stratified sample survey, together with a subsequent factor analysis, of 672 families on Peruvian side of Lake Titicaca. Socio-economic variables explored. Extensive tables and explanations of survey method.

2269. Blásquez Canales, Raúl García. Tenencia de la tierra en comunidades del área andina del Peru. Lima, Ministerio de Trabajo, Instituto Indigenista Peruano, 1970. 98 p., bibl., tables (mimeo) (Serie monográfica, 23)

Agrarian reform as an example of Peruvian class struggle. Comparison of pre-reform *hacienda* with post-reform *comunidad,* and of relationships between the two while they co-exist.

2270. Bobbio, Emilio. El mensaje de la CADE '71 en Paracas: gobierno y empresarios dialogaron sobre el "Plan Perú" (Gerencia [Lima] nov./dic. 1971, p. 10-18, plates)

Journalistic report for businessmen on Peruvian Plan for 1971-75. Of limited scholarly value except for students of government-business relations. Fuller version will appear in 1973. See items 2276 and 2277.

2271. Bradfield, Stillman. Mutual obligations between management and workers in Peru (AIFLD/R, 3:4, 1971, p. 73-93, tables)

Attitude survey. Of limited value, except that little else has appeared lately on Peruvian labor.

2272. Brisseau-Loaiza, Jeanine. Le rôle du camion dans les relations ville-campagne dans la région du Cuzco, Pérou (SGB/COM, 25:97, jan./mars 1972, p. 27-56, illus., map, plates)

Points out advantages of road transport as an instrument of economic development in context of highland Peru.

2273. Catálogo colectivo de publicaciones periódicas en desarrollo económico y social. Lima, Grupo de Trabajo para la Integración de la Información, 1972. 185 p.

Union catalog of economic journal holdings of some 20 government and private sector libraries in Lima.

2274. Ceresole, Norberto. Perú: los orígenes del sistema latinoamericano. B.A., Editorial Galerna, 1971. 396 p.

Essays by Argentine writer, attempting to explain (and defend) policies of Peruvian Revolution as led by President Velasco, and refuting assorted critics in Peru and elsewhere. Extensive quotations from decree-laws and speeches. Useful, perhaps, mainly as a "third view" to read along with Peruvian and Anglo-Saxon interpretations of Peruvian process.

2275. Clague, Christopher K. Capital-labor substitution in manufacturing in underdeveloped countries (Econometrica [Menasha, Wis.] 37:3, July 1969, p. 528-537)

Elasticities of substitution are calculated from observed factor proportions in US and Peru. Differences in possible measurement techniques and hence in results are discussed in the comment by Ann D. Witte in this same journal (39:6, Nov. 1971, p. 1053-1054) and in Clague's reply in same issue as Witte's (p. 1055-1056). See also Clague's earlier publications on related topic, *HLAS 31:3707.*

2276. Conferencia Anual de Ejecutivos (CADE), VIII, Paracas, Peru, 1969. El Perú frente al desafío de la integración: áreas críticas y prioridades. Lima, Instituto Peruano de Administración de Empresas (IPAE), 1969. 327 p., plates, table.

Resolutions, background documents and speeches presented at this annual meeting of Peru's leading industrialists and government figures. No mere chamber of commerce effort, these yearly meetings are of interest because they are used by both government ministers and industrialists to announce their concerns, priorities and expectations about behavior of the other party during coming year. Useful documentation to reinforce current reporting in the *Peruvian Times*.

2277. ———, IX, Paracas, Peru, 1970. Perú: nueva sociedad industrial. Lima, Instituto Peruano de Administración de Empresas (IPAE), 1970. 282 p., maps, plates, tables.

Like earlier yearbooks, useful source for verbatim texts of what industrialists said to the government and what the President and some of his ministers said back to the industrialists in their annual encounter. Main topic in 1970, naturally, was the just-announced Industrial Community, which proclaimed the advent of a type of worker participation in management of industries.

2278. Espinoza Uriarte, Humberto and Jorge Osorio Torres. El poder económico en la industria. Lima, Univ. Nacional Federico Villarreal, Centro de Investigaciones Económicas y Sociales, 1972. 201 p.

Serious, painstaking tabulation and analysis of ownership, capital and output of manufacturing industry, in 1968, in an effort to determine not only extent of foreign ownership but also patterns and relations among Peruvian firms. Basic reference for future studies of changes brought about by measures undertaken by the military government under President Velasco.

2279. Frente Nacional de Abogados para la Defensa de la Reforma Agraria, Lima. Reforma agraria peruana: conferencias sustentadas en el Colegio de Abogados de Lima. Lima, Gráfica Labor, 1971. 120 p.

Series of lectures in which pro-reform attorneys attempted to communicate to their colleagues and public in general, that agrarian reform (as promulgated by President Velasco in 1969 and implemented vigorously thereafter) was both legal and reasonable. Aspects such as compensation, size limitations, and role of indigenous communities were treated–often by those who had drafted or who were implementing the relevant legislation.

2280. Gerencia. Organo oficial de IPAE [Instituto Peruano de Administración de Empresas]. Vol. 1, No. 1, dic. 1970- . Lima.

Magazine of Peru's management training institution, particularly useful to scholars interested in knowing how relatively progressive Peruvian businessmen (and managers of foreign-owned firms) see their world. Significantly, this first issue dwells heavily on worker participation in management, with two articles on European experience and attitudes. Other articles discuss Andean Common Market and a technological strategy appropriate for Latin America. IPAE's address: Camino Real No. 111, Oficina 205, Apartado 4075, Lima, Peru.

2281. Jaquette, Jane S. The politics of development in Peru. Ithaca, N.Y., Cornell Univ., Latin American Studies Program, 1971. 276 p., bibl., tables (Dissertation series, 33)

Although ostensibly a thesis in political science, this work provides great detail (based on field work in 1968) on events that shaped the Belaúnde period and set the stage for the military government. Valuable background for scholars interested in the present process, but the user should be careful to update statements as to how far the Junta would go in various directions, with data on what it has in fact done, sometimes more radical than predicted in author's analysis.

2282. Klitgaard, Robert E. Observations on the Peruvian National Plan for Development 1971-1975 (IAMEA, 25:3, Winter 1971, p. 3-22)

Thoughtful description and criticism of the Plan, with emphasis on its political background. See item 2294.

2283. Kressin, Jan and Erich Spiegel. Agrarreform und Produktions-genossenschaften in Peru. Berlin, FRG, Freien Univ., Lateinamerika-Institute, 1973. 86 p.

Survey of Peru's agrarian reform as of early 1972, with accurate perception of potential, problems, and differences with previous efforts. Based mainly on official documents, and substantially same material as items 2269 and 2279.

LTC Newsletter. See item 2222.

2284. La ley de reforma agraria del Perú (Ciencias Económicas [Córdoba, Arg.] 2, 1970, p. 61-64)

Largely a recitation, presumably for the Argentine audience, of 16 titles in the law, together with some skeptical comments about its prospects for success. The law has been modified, and other sources (see item 2279) are more useful.

2285. Llarena G., David and others. La comunidad industrial: naturaleza económica de la empresa industrial en el Perú. Lima, Univ. Nacional Federico Villarreal, Centro de Investigaciones Económicas y Sociales, 1972. 120 p.

Analysis of explicit and implicit reorganization of industrial firms, as a result of labor community laws, with arithmetical examples of operation of these laws to channel part of profits into capital for workers. Concludes with sociological model by Prof. Osvaldo Jorge Gavagnin. While useful as Peruvian interpretations of the new rules, subsequent evolution of laws and their application make this less than a definitive study.

2286. Malpica S. S., Carlos. El mito de la ayuda exterior. Lima, Univ. Nacional Federico Villarreal, Centro de Investigaciones Económicas y Sociales, 1973. 93 p.

Selected chapters from author's book of same title, published almost a decade ago but with tables of foreign investment, credit and aid brought up to 1971. Relates internal US and Peruvian political events with financial movements, from beginning of century until about 1970.

2287. Miller, Fred. Supervised credit and agricultural development: a Peruvian example (IAMEA, 23:4, Spring 1970. p. 13-22, tables)

Explores pitfalls encountered in agricultural credit scheme sponsored by AID in Peru. Concludes, not surprisingly, that creditworthiness rather than poverty alone should be the most important loan criterion if program is to be successful.

2288. Montoya Rojas, Rodrigo. A propósito del carácter predominantemente capitalista de la economía peruana actual. Lima, Ediciones Teoría y Realidad, 1970. 121 p., bibl., tables (Serie: Formación social y estructura económica, 1)

Marxist survey of Peruvian economy.

North, Lisa. Orígenes y crecimiento del partido aprista y el cambio socioeconómico en el Perú. See item 7697.

2289. Ocampo V., Tarsicio comp. Peru International Petroleum Company Limited, 1968-69: reacciones de prensa. Cuernavaca, Mex., Centro Intercultural de Documentación, 1970. 1 v. (Various pagings) (CIDOC: Dossier, 26)

As title indicates, a compilation of (Peruvian) press comments on nationalization of the International Petroleum Company. Valuable for its documentary interest. See item 2298 and account given in *HLAS* 31:3718.

2290. Peru. Ministerio de Agricultura. Dirección de Comunidades Campesinas. División de Estudios Sociales. SAIS [Sociedad Agrícola de Interés Social] Atusparia: datos para el desarrollo. Lima, 1971. 444 p., tables (Zac-Huaylas, 5)

Working document of the Comité Ministerial de Apoyo y Coordinación de Reforma Agraria (COMACRA), reflecting study of Utcuyacu project: 11 large farms which had been managed by one manager, on behalf of one agricultural and livestock enterprise also called Utcuyacu, which was expanded to include four adjacent farms and seven neighboring indigenous communities; the project to be constructed with all of this land was to be called "Atusparia SAIS." Detailed social and economic data on people, land-holdings, crops, income levels, family size, etc.

2291. ———. ———. ———. Pachucutec: datos para el desarrollo. Lima, 1971. 349 p. (mimeo) (*Its* Zac Mantaro, 3)

Another pre-reform study of a particular set of agricultural properties.

2292. ———. ———. ———. ———. ———. Tawantisuyu: datos para el desarrollo. Lima, 1971. 221 p., map, tables (ZA-III Trujillo, 2)

Survey of economic conditions of families on a *hacienda* that was candidate for agrarian reform. Their currently low incomes and needs for future investments are noted; could serve as a benchmark for later restudy.

2293. ———. Ministerio de Trabajo. Dirección General del Empleo. Situación ocupacional del Perú: informe 1971. Lima, 1972? 260 p.

Excellent study of employment patterns by sectors, and of supply and demand for labor, urban and rural, by sex, by education, etc. Includes considerable detail on methodology of study, which was one of basic inputs into planning process (see item 2294). Much of this information, while not confidential, was not readily available to foreign scholars. It is to be hoped that the Ministry will continue this publication on a regular basis. Includes many appendices.

2294. ———. Presidencia. Plan del Perú. Lima, 1971-1972. 11 v. (1400 p.) (Continuous pagination)

V. 1 *Plan global* (223 p.) contains global plan, with succeeding volumes presenting sectoral analyses and projects, concluding with 11, on regional development policies. Valuable source of data and governmental views of needs and priorities; uneven in the extent to which each sector specifies just how goals are to be met, and particularly weak in its lack of proof of overall consistency. That, however, is normally handled in elaboration of biennial budget (at Finance Ministry). Peruvian Government deserves scholars' gratitude for making available what were previously internal documents.

2295. Portocarrero, Felipe. La coyuntura económica: conciliación y lucha de clases (Sociedad y Política [Lima] 1:3, mayo 1973, p. 4-19)

Economic analysis of class struggle in Peru, in 1960-68 and 1969-72. Author believes that conciliatory aims of military will be frustrated by internal contradictions of its economic plans, and that reforms will actually help the dominated classes realize their true class interests and thus escape from the "corporativist" and conciliatory intentions of the military.

2296. Purser, W. F. C. Metal-mining in Peru: past and present. N.Y., Praeger Publishers, 1971. 339 p., bibl., tables (Praeger special studies in international economics and development)

Excellent study, going from pre-Conquest days to 1970, but emphasizing a detailed description of present-day mines, one-by-one, including their associated smelters and refineries. Third section analyzes interrelations between mines and Peruvian economy.

2297. Quijano, Aníbal. Nationalism and capitalism in Peru: a study in neo-imperialism (MR, 23:3, July/Aug. 1971. p. 1-121)

Highly tentative, critical essay (121 p. long) on actions of military junta from its coup of 1968, through early 1971. Accurate, detailed chronology and brilliant use of quotations. The junta has gone further than Quijano predicted in some areas, and the final page is a proforma vision of a socialist uprising, but on the whole this is a stimulating reading for anyone analyzing contemporary Peru. Special issue of *Monthly Review*.

2298. Ramírez Novoa, E. Petróleo y revolución nacionalista: el Perú en su hora histórica. Lima, n.p., 1970. 192 p.

More background material on long legal struggle to restore Peruvian sovereignty to erstwhile domains of International Petroleum Company (subsidiary of EXXON, née ESSO). Useful mainly as a source for documents and declarations by lawyers over decade leading up to Act of Talara, with which President Velasco and the armed forces initiated their revolution in 1968. Complements *HLAS 31:3718*.

2299. Revista de la Academia Nacional de Ciencias Económicas. Año 1, No. 2, 1. trimestre 1972- . Lima.

New journal whose second issue consists essentially of teaching materials, essays on money, and a *ponencia* urging creation of a national technical assistance program for farmers.

2300. Roel, Virgilio. Escritos sobre política económica. Lima, Editorial Gráfica Labor, 1972? 350 p.

Series of 63 essays, some with data or appreciations not readily available elsewhere, written by one of best known (and most controversial) Peruvian professors of economics. Originally published in Sunday editions of *El Comercio*, between Dec. 1968-April 1970, essays reflect actions of Revolutionary Military Government during period. Also includes incursions into economy of Incas, other Peruvian history, and critique of planning process.

2301. Salaverry, José A. Un modelo de programación lineal interregional para el análisis de la política agraria del Perú. Lima, Misión de las Universidades de Iowa *en cooperación con la* Agencia para el Desarrollo Internacional, 1973. 603 p.

Spanish translation of author's Ph. D. thesis.

2302. Smetherman, Bobbie B. and Robert M. Smetherman. Peruvian fisheries: conservation and development (UC/EDCC, 21:2, Jan. 1973. p. 338-351)

Largely descriptive, but recites important facts. Questions of the resolution of property rights disputes with respect to the 200-mile limit and the current diminution in the catch are raised but not dealt with satisfyingly.

2303. Strassmann, W. Paul. Innovation and employment in building: the experience of Peru (OUP/OEP, 22:2, July 1970, p. 243-259)

Technological change in Peruvian construction industry leans toward labor-saving capital-intensive investments. Therefore, traditional role of construction as a labor absorbing sector cannot be confidently projected for the future.

2304. Webb, Richard. Government policy and the distribution of income in Peru, 1963-1973. Princeton, N.J., Princeton Univ., School of Public and International Affairs, 1973. 72 p. (Research program in economic development. Discussion paper, 39)

Long-awaited study by senior Peruvian economist, starting from estimate of earlier income inequalities and attempting to estimate quantitatively impact of reform measures undertaken by Presidents Belaúnde and Velasco over last decade. Discusses literature both on his immediate subject and on options open to Peruvian governments. Essential reading for future studies of Peru.

2305. Yepes del Castillo, Ernesto. Perú, 1820-1920: un siglo de desarrollo capitalista. Lima, Instituto de Estudios Peruanos [and] Campodónico *ediciones*, 1972. 367 p., bibl.

Descriptive economic and sociological history of Peru in century before Leguía. Focuses on displacement of Spain by England as dominant trading partner and on the growth of Peruvian capitalism.

URUGUAY

Astori, Danilo. Latifundio y crisis agraria en el Uruguay. See item 7901.

2306. Azzarini, Mario and others. Producción y comercialización de carnes. Montevideo, Univ. de la República, Depto. de Publicaciones, 1971. 300 p., tables (Col. Nuestra realidad, 12)

Emphasizes agronomic rather than economic considerations. Corrected record of lecture series given in Sept. 1969 at the Dr. Mario Cassinoni Experimental Station.

2307. Bernhard, Guillermo. El problema de la carne. Montevideo, Ediciones de la Banda Oriental, 1971. 47 p. (Col. Conciencia popular, 1)

Pamphlet urges agrarian reform and nationalization of *frigoríficos* and foreign trade in an attempt to stop ravages of oligarchy and imperialism.

2308. Bon Espasandín, Mario. Tenencia, distribución y explotación de la tierra en el Uruguay; sus implicaciones con el desarrollo (BUS, 8:15/17, dic. 1969, p. 3-34)

Author, professor of sociology, engages in rambling and outdated account of Uruguayan agricultural development using Fischer-Clark model from late 1930's. Article's redeeming feature is series of tables taken from agricultural and livestock censuses of 1951, 1956, 1961, and 1966, tables that may not be readily accessible to researchers outside Uruguay.

2309. Fabbrica Italiana Automobili Torino (FIAT), *Argentina*. Oficina de Estudios para la Colaboración Económica Internacional. Uruguay. B.A., 1971. 231 p., map, plate, tables (Síntesis económica y financiera, 3)

Thorough survey of 1960s' Uruguayan economy; similar in tone and construction to *HLAS 33:2898* for Bolivia.

2310. Finch, M. H. J. Three perspectives on the crisis in Uruguay (JLAS, 3:2, Nov. 1971. p. 173-190)

Three perspectives are economic, political, and historical. Economic section contains brief survey from early 1950s to late 1960s.

2311. Fundación de Cultura Universitaria, *Montevideo*. El fin de la estabilización. Montevideo, Univ. de la República, Instituto de

Economía, Facultad de Ciencias Económicas y de Administración, 1971. 115 p., tables (Estudios y coyuntura, 2)

Short-run study of Uruguayan economy in 1970 and pressures that led to recurrence of price inflation thereafter. Both monetary and "real" factors are discussed.

2312. Galeano, Eduardo H. La crisis económica. Montevideo, Univ. de la República, Facultad de Ciencias Económicas y de Administración, Instituto de Economía, 1969. 60 p., plates. tables (Nuestra tierra, 26)

Popularization of 1969 study; scholars will find more value in 1971 edition of full study (item 2315).

2313. Pages, Walter Hugo. Los factores de la producción agropecuaria en el Uruguay y su utilización óptima. Montevideo, Editorial Hemisferio Sur, 1972? 245 p., tables.

Detailed study of Uruguayan agriculture and agricultural policies. See *HLAS 31:3752*.

2314. Trías, Vivian. Imperialismo y rosca bancaria en el Uruguay. Montevideo, Ediciones de la Banda Oriental, 1971. 116 p., tables (Col. Conciencia popular, 3)

Author feels that present Uruguayan crisis will not be overcome, owing to unfavorable foreign influences, unless banking system is nationalized. Book addressed not to a specialized audience, but "a la calle; al trabajador, al estudiante, al vecino."

2315. Universidad de la República, *Montevideo.* **Facultad de Ciencias Económicas y de la Administración. Instituto de Economía.** Estructura industrial del Uruguay. Montevideo, 1971? 1 v. (Various pagings) tables.

First of six projected volumes in series "Estudios sobre la Industria," partly based on industrial survey of 1963. Essentially a statistical complilation.

2316. ——, ——. ——. ——. El proceso económico del Uruguay: contribución al estudio de su evolución y perspectivas. 2. ed. Montevideo, 1971. 476 p., tables (Col. Ciencias, 4)

General survey of Uruguayan economy is followed by more detailed examination of inflationary movements since mid-1968. Lengthy, detailed study worth acquiring.

2317. Uruguay. Comisión Coordinadora para el Desarrollo Económico (COMCORDE). Secretaría Técnica. Remuneración del trabajo: incidencia de las prestaciones en el costo de la mano de obra. Montevideo, 1971. 45 l., bibl., tables (mimeo) (E.ST, 1)

Valuable and hitherto unavailable statistical series, marred only by sometimes unreadable mimeographing on low quality paper.

2318. Vásquez Varini, Felipe S. Formación económica del Uruguay. Montevideo, Escuela Imprenta Don Orione, 1971. 214 p., facsims., plates, tables.

Somewhat mechanical economic history of Uruguay during national period, with 66- p. English summary appended.

2319. Viera, Eduardo. La crisis económica uruguaya: el vaciamiento de la tierra purpúrea; bases materiales de la contradicción pueblo y oligarquía. Montevideo, Ediciones Pueblos Unidos, 1971. 203 p., tables.

On basis of Marxist-Leninist foundations, concludes that revolutionary transformation of the economy is not only possible but "objectively necessary."

ARGENTINA

HUGH H. SCHWARTZ

General Studies Division
Inter-American Development Bank

OF THE PUBLICATIONS DEALING WITH the Argentine economy, five should be particularly noted—all by Argentine authors. Perhaps the most outstanding of these is Jorge Katz' *Importación de tecnología: aprendizaje local e industrialización dependiente* (item 2371), a pathbreaking study of technological change in Argentine industry, prepared at the Instituto Torcuato Di Tella. A second, especially timely work, is Juan Carlos de Pablo's analysis of recent policies employed to cope with inflation (item 2385), which, though of considerable economic sophistication, became available to the public less than half a year after the close of the period being reviewed. De Pablo, a senior economist at the Fundación de Investigaciones Económicas Latinoamericanas (FIEL), also participated in that institution's comprehensive inquiry into the extent and consequences of foreign investment in Argentina (item 2355), directed by A. P. Ribas. Worthy of considerable attention as well are the detailed documentation of technological change in the dairy industry by Herschel, Casares, Nogues and Rotstein (item 2365), and the reexamination of Argentine economic history during the transformation period of 1875-1914 by Vázquez Presedo (item 2406).

Technology and the problems of technological change figure prominently among the topics in the publications examined. In addition to the Katz, Herschel et al studies already mentioned, the Di Tella project also included a report on the availability of university level professionals (Sommer, item 2401), a survey of industrial research and development (Aráoz, item 2321), a study of technological change in the electronics industry (Petrecola and others, item 2386) and a study by two social psychologists on entrepreneurial attitudes towards innovation (Ruth Santu and Catalina Wainerman, *El empresario y la innovación: un estudio de las disposiciones de un grupo de dirigentes de empresas argentinas hacia el cambio tecnológico*). Other pieces on technology included two articles by de Janvry concerning agriculture (items 2366-2367, the latter with Martinez) and a pamphlet of essays by Sábato on technological lag (item 2391). Also in this general area is Gueberoff's critique (item 2362) of the manufacturing analysis of Katz cited in *HLAS 33:3020*.

Industry continued to receive a good deal of attention. Besides the studies dealing primarily with technological change, the major items were two somewhat conflicting works on Argentine industrialization in the period between the two world wars (Chu, item 2336 and Villanueva, item 2410) and a FIEL volume on industrial parks (item 2352). In addition, there were studies of the demand for steel (Loser, item 2374), along with three efforts to grapple with the data recently made available on industrial concentration (Abot and others, item 2320, Givogri, item 2358 and Skupch, item 2397).

Agricultural and agroindustrial studies of note included a major undertaking by FIEL dealing with the livestock industry in the 1960's (item 2353), demand analyses for soybeans (Coscia, item 2341), wine (Reca, item 2345), edible oils (Reca, item 2347) and 23 agricultural commodities (de Janvry and Núñez, item 2345), as well as supply analyses of wine growing (Tomassette and others, item 2388).

Regionally oriented studies have been the focus of more than a dozen authors. The most ambitious efforts are those by Arnaudo, one of which (item 2346) presents a framework for both providing goods and services and allocating taxes among the various levels of government. Other publications in this field include a massive report on Chubut (item 2337) and shorter, more aggregative works on the provinces of Santa Fe (item 2335) and Cuyo (item 2387). Of the fiscal studies, one estimates the income elasticity and stabilizing potential of the income tax (Vega, item 2408) while another provides an overall evaluation of that tax (Oszlik, item 2384). The best of the articles in the somewhat disappointing *Jornadas de Finanzas Públicas* deal with tax burdens and tax evasion (items 2369 and 2370). An unconventional presentation on budget deficits and surpluses is offered by Lascano (item 2372).

Other studies of special interest are the pieces by Mantel (item 2375) and Feldman and Itzcovich (item 2348) on interest rate policy and financial structure; a FIEL volume on non-traditional exports (item 2351); Skupch's analysis of the railway nationalizations of 1947 (item 2399); and a general survey of the Argentine economy since 1930 by Montuschi and Vázquez Presedo (item 2381).

The Central Bank, Ministry of Economics, National Statistical Office, and other government agencies continued to issue their often substantial annual (and, in some cases, quarterly) reports, and to these were added a growing number of special studies. The Ministry of Industry and Commerce, e.g., issued several detailed volumes on individual industries, beginning with textiles and machine tools. Several provincial governments published reports on employment and analyses of the provincial contribution to Gross Domestic Product.

The only note to be added to the report on research institutes in *HLAS 33* concerns the Institute of Economic Research of the University of Buenos Aires, directed by Dr. Julio H. G. Olivera. The members of Dr. Olivera's institute continued to account for a substantial number of theoretical contributions (an area beyond the scope of the *Handbook*), but also became increasingly active in applied work, represented in this report by the publications of Vázquez Presedo, Montuschi, Skupch, and Tow (items 2345, 2369-2370, 2380-2381, 2397-2399, 2406-2407).

To the list of journals and magazines cited in the previous *Handbook* should be added *Ciencias Económicas* (Consejo Profesional de Ciencias Económicas, Córdoba); *Política y Economía; Encuesta de Coyuntura* (FIEL); *Business Conditions in Argentina* (Ernesto Tornquist and Co., Ltd.); the reports of the Oficina de Estudios Para la Colaboración Económica Internacional; the *Anales de la Sociedad Rural Argentina;* and the *Revista de la Cámara Argentina de Comercio.*

2320. Abot, Jorge and others. La concentración en la industria argentina en 1964. B.A., Consejo Nacional de Desarrollo (CONADE), Comisión de Seminarios y Actividades Académicas, 1965? 78 l., tables (mimeo)

The first really substantial documentation concerning industrial concentration.

2321. Aráoz, Alberto. La investigación y el desarrollo de la industria. B.A., Instituto Torcuato Di Tella, Centro de Investigaciones Económicas, 1970. 100 p. (mimeo)

Documents the low volume of technological research in Argentina and the virtual absence of contract investigation or other efforts to transfer results to industrial users.

2322. Argentina. Presidencia. Plan nacional de desarrollo y seguridad, 1971-1975: metas para el mediano plazo. B.A., 1972. 2 v. (Unpaged) tables.

2323. Arnaudo, Aldo A. El desarrollo regional en el plan de desarrollo y seguridad 1971-75 (IDES/DE, 12:47, oct./dic. 1972, p. 495-517, tables)

Critical commentary on the development plan for 1971-75, with particular attention to regional objectives and the consistency of sectoral plans to those regional goals.

2324. Balboa, Manuel. La evolución del balance de pagos de la República Argentina, 1913-1950 (IDES/DE, 12:45, abril/junio 1972, p. 154-172, tables)

First presented in 1952, this still remains a most valuable analysis of Argentine balance of payments from World War I through the first half of the Perón period.

2325. Banco Central de la República Argentina, *Buenos Aires.* La creación del Banco Central y la experiencia monetaria argentina entre los años 1935-43. B.A., 1972. 2 v. (1418 p., Continuous pagination) illus.

Background materials concerning the creation of the Argentine Central Bank; major sections of the Bank's annual reports from 1935-44; an analysis of monetary policy prepared by Raúl Prebisch in 1944; and an introductory essay on characteristics of the financial and economic panorama between the two world wars.

2326. ———, ———. Gerencia de Asuntos Financieros. Departamento de Finanzas Públicas. La experiencia del Banco Central como agente financiero del Gobierno Nacional en la capitación del ahorro interno. B.A., 1971. 24 p., table.

Focuses separately on periods 1935-45, 1946-67, and 1968-70.

2327. Banco de Italia y Río de la Plata, *Buenos Aires.* 100 [i.e., Cien] años al servicio del país, 1872-1972. B.A., 1972. 333 p., tables.

2328. Baumgartner, Jean-Pierre and **Pascual Santiago Palazzo.** Estructura económica del transporte de carga automotor y ferroviario en la Argentina (FCE/TE, 36:143, julio/sept. 1969, p. 381-394)

A model and some empirical results for evaluating highway and railroad transport in Argentina.

2329. Bledel, Rodolfo. La economía argentina, 1952-1972: aplicación constante de la política de la "libre empresa," la confesión de Prebisch. B.A., Juárez Editor, 1972. 123 p., bibl. (Centroplan, 2)

A harsh but not always well-documented criticism of the tendency towards free enterprise in Argentina from the days of the proposed California-Argentina contract in 1954 through 1972.

2330. Bolsa de Comercio de Buenos Aires. Memoria, 1970. pt. 1, Comentario económica; pt. 2, Información estadística; pt. 3, Convocatoria e informe del Consejo, balance general, etc. B.A., 1971. 3 v. (128, 119, 404 p.) tables.

2331. Bonaparte, Héctor M. Subdesarrollo dentro del subdesarrollo (ILARI/A, 20, abril 1971, p. 171-204, tables)

Based on a demographic study of a portion of Santiago del Estero province, Arg. After a quick review of theoretical literature defining underdevelopment, author examines in detail region of study and concludes that is constitutes a useful example of the phenomenon. [P. B. Taylor, Jr.]

2332. Broder, Paulo and others. Desarrollo y estancamiento en el proceso económico argentino. B.A., Ediciones La Bastilla, 1972. 178 p., bibl., tables.

Popularized and nationalistically oriented review of Argentine economic history since 1930.

2333. Cámara de los Frigoríficos Regionales, *Buenos Aires.* Los frigoríficos regionales: su incidencia en la economía nacional. B.A., 1971. 185 p., maps, tables.

Best source of information on Argentina's small- and medium-size slaughterhouses.

2334. Castro Corbat, Marcelo J. Salvar la década del 70: los determinantes económicos. B.A., Editorial El Ateneo, 1972. 99 p., tables.

Popularized exposition of Argentina's major economic difficulties and opportunities.

2335. Cervera, Felipe Justo. Santa Fe: sociedad y economía. Santa Fe, Arg., Ediciones Colmegna, 1970. 183 p., bibl., maps, tables.

A thoughtful and well organized introduction to the economy of Santa Fe.

2336. Chu, David S. C. The Great Depression and industrialization in Latin America: response to relative price incentives in Argentina and Colombia, 1930-45. New Haven, Conn., Yale Univ., Dept. of Economics, 1972. 319 p., tables (Ph.D. dissertation)

Attributes rapid rate of manufacturing in Argentina and Colombia during 1930-45 to changes in relative prices of inputs and outputs brought on by Depression (not to changes in the cost and availability of capital or other factors). Little change in relative prices attributed to tariffs. Essentially in conflict with Villanueva, item 2410.

2337. Chubut (province) *Argentina.* **Gobernación del . . . Asesoría de Desarrollo.** Análisis de la economía del Chubut y sus perspectivas de desarrollo. [Directed by] Oscar Altimir. Rawson, Arg., 1972. 3 v. (Various pagings) tables.

Encyclopedic. Nothing approaching this has ever been prepared on Chubut. Should be of great value to those considering or looking for projects to develop. Only shortcoming, and it is not a small one for such a major effort, is lack of analytical framework to help in selecting from numerous expansion alternatives offered.

2338. Coloquio de Comercialización Internacional, *Buenos Aires, 1970.* La experiencia exportadora argentina. B.A., Univ. Argentina de la Empresa, 1970. 129 p.

Proceedings from a conference on Argentine export experience. Includes presentation by government officials and private businessmen on a variety of topics.

2339. Congreso de los Consorcios Regionales de Experimentación Agrícola, *VI, Rosario, Arg., 1971.* Actas. Rosario, Arg., Asociación Argentina de Consorcios Regionales de Experimentación Agrícola, 1971. 175 p.

2340. *Cooperator.* Revista independiente para la empresa cooperativa. No. 2, dic. 1971- B.A.

Monthly serial directed by Oscar M. Braceras. Distinctly business oriented, although it emphasizes cooperatives. Viewpoint is managerial; contains an insert on management and establishment of cooperatives in the distinctly commercial area. [P. B. Taylor, Jr.]

2341. Coscia, Adolfo. Soja: sus perspectivas económicas en la Argentina. B.A., Instituto Nacional de Tecnología Agropecuaria (INTA), Estación Experimental Regional Agropecuaria Pergamino, 1972. 57 p., bibl., tables (Informe técnico, 112)

Valuable examination of Argentine soybean perspectives with particular attention to the analysis of demand factors.

2342. Cuevillas, Fernando N. Arturo. Prospectiva e integración de la Argentina actual (IESSC/C, 4:10, enero/abril 1969, p. 86-108, tables)

Socio-historical essay, polemic in nature, examining alternative stances for Third World countries, especially Argentina. Conclusions are heavily value-laden. [J. M. Hunter]

2343. Diamand, Marcelo. La estructura productiva desequilibrada argentina y el tipo de cambio (IDES/DE, 12:45, abril/junio 1972, p. 25-47)

Provocative analysis by prominent Argentine industrialist which argues against the use of comparative advantage equilibrium as the norm for determining the country's exchange rates (in part because of the static character of such comparative considerations). Suggests various alternatives amounting to stable, multiple exchange rates to resolve the country's continuing balance of payments crises and the slow rate of economic growth which the crises have been fostering.

2344. DiLella, Eduardo F. Evolución y perspectivas de la industria de paneles a base de madera en la República Argentina. B.A., Secretaría de Estado de Agricultura y Ganadería, Servicio Nacional Forestal, 1970. 29 p., bibl., tables (Planificación del desarrollo forestal, 3)

Short but helpful presentation on the problems and potential of the wood-panel industry.

2345. *Económica.* Univ. Nacional de La Plata, Facultad de Ciencias Económicas, Instituto de Investigaciones Económicas. Año 17, No. 3, sept/dic. 1971-   . La Plata, Arg.

Contains four articles of interest. A. De Janvry and A. Núñez "Análisis de Demanda para Productos Agropecuarios en Argentina," constructs time series of prices and quantities of 23 agricultural products and combines these with cross-section data on consumer expenditures to calculate complete matrix of demand interrelationships. H. P. Llosas "Los Efectos Direccionales de la Protección Aduanera en la Argentina," concludes that tariff protection, the main instrument for industrial promotion in the period 1955-66, stimulated the development of industries producing consumer and intermediate goods for the local market, discriminating against the production of all other tradables. L. G. Reca "La Industria Vitivinícola en la Argentina: Perspectivas de Crecimiento," predicts 1980 wine consumption and projects vineyards expansion requirements based on observed decline in price and income elasticities of wine over 1943-70 period.

F. V. Tow, "Una Comprobación Empírica de Dos Teorías de la Participación del Trabajo: Argentina 1950-63," concludes that income distribution from 1950-63 is better explained by the macro economic theory of Kaldor than by marginalist model using a Cobb-Douglas production function.

2346. ———. ———, ———, ———. Año 18, No. 2, mayo/agosto 1972- . La Plata, Arg.

Contains article by A. A. Arnaudo, "Reformulación de las Relaciones Fiscales entre Nación y Provincias," which establishes and applies to the Argentine economy a framework for both the provision of goods and services and the allocation of taxes among various levels of government.

2347. Estudios sobre la Economía Argen. a. Confederación General Económica de la República Argentina, Instituto de Investigaciones Económicas y Financieras. No. 14, enero 1973- . B.A.

L. G. Reca's "Perspectivas de la Demanda de Aceites Comestibles en la Argentina en 1980" concludes that the price elasticity of edible oils is declining but the income elasticity is rising. A. A. Arnaudo's "El Efecto Escala en la Demanda de Dinero de las Empresas" concludes that bank lending rules lead to discrimination against smaller firms. See also item 2348.

2348. Feldman, Ernesto V. and Samuel Itzcovich. Estructura financiera y concentración bancaria: el caso argentino (UNLP/E, 17:1, enero/abril 1971, p. 43-73, bibl., tables)

Stimulating article which adds another reason to those offered by Mantel (item 2375) and Simone (item 2395) for having more flexible interest rate regulations. Given the institutional impossibility of charging differential rates, banks minimize risk by lending relatively more to large enterprises than they might otherwise do. Moreover, large enterprises are more likely to be foreign and the authors add with equal concern, there is an increasing share of foreign banks in Argentine commercial lending.

2349. Ferrer, Norberto C. and others. Coparticipación provincial en impuestos nacionales. v. 1, Antecedentes. B.A., Consejo Federal de Inversiones, 1965. 317 p., tables.

2350. Ferrocarriles argentinos: plan mediano plazo. B.A., Fundación de Investigaciones Económicas Latinoamericanas (FIEL), 1972? 6 v. (Various pagings)

The economic analysis of the railway's proposed medium-term plan was prepared by FIEL. See especially Ch. 12 of v. 5, "Costos Marginales a Largo Plazo del Transporte Ferroviario y Automotor de Cargas," and v. 6 which is actually Ch. 11, "Resumen y Perspectivas Económicas y Financieras."

Freels, John W., Jr. Industrial trade association in Argentine politics: historical roots and current prospects. See *HLAS 34:2709a*.

2351. Fundación de Investigaciones Económicas Latinoamericanas (FIEL). No. 6, 1971- . B.A.

Principal items of interest concern the export of "nontraditional" products: 1) N. A. Belozercovsky; F. F. Johansen; J. L. Madariaga del Olmo; and M. del P. S. Echart de Bianchi "Asignación de Recursos y Exportaciones No Tradicionales" (p. 173-184), an exposition of the methodology employed in the study and the principal results; 2) N. A. Belozercovsky and others, "Exportación de Productos No Tradicionales: Análisis por Productos y Régimen Vigente" (p. 1-172). Also of note: J. L. Madariaga del Olmo; A. Durini; and Hugo Ziegner "Estimación Preliminar de la Demanda de Cemento: 1970-1974" (p. 211-250); and J. H. Meier and others "Costos Marginales de Transporte a Largo Plazo del Ferrocarril y del Camión" (p. 251-316).

2352. ———. No. 7, 1972- . B.A.

Issue dedicated primarily to industrial parks. J. C. de Pablo; J. L. Madariaga del Olmo; and H. G. Ziegner conclude in "Parques Industriales y Teoría Microeconómica," that the unit cost of providing basic services to small and medium enterprises is less in an industrial park than if the businesses are distributed randomly in either urban or rural areas. In another article of almost 300 p., 12 investigators offer a detailed consideration of the numerous elements to be taken into account in establishing an industrial park in the city of Neuquén. Also of interest is J. C. de Pablo, "Análisis del Balance de Pagos: Argentina 1951-1970."

2353. Fundación de Investigaciones Económicas Latinoamericanas (FIEL), *Buenos Aires*. Análisis de la producción y comercialización de la hacienda y carne vacuna en la Argentina en la década del 60. B.A., 1972. 5 v. (Various pagings) tables (mimeo)

A wealth of data and partial analyses, not really well organized but essential for a serious understanding of livestock and meatpacking plant problems.

2354. ———, ———. Efectos económicos de políticas de regulación de precios. B.A., FIEL *for the* Unión Industrial Argentina (UIA), 1971. 1 v. (Unpaged) tables (Encuestas de coyuntura: 4. serie, 2/3. trimestre 1971)

Judgments on the effects of price controls based on interviews with 300 industrial enterprises.

2355. ———, ———. Las inversiones extranjeras en la Argentina [and] Apéndice 1. B.A., 1971. 2 v. (296, 16 p.) tables.

Outstanding report. A careful and detailed examination of the extent and the recognized and possible consequences of foreign investments in Argentina. Principal conclusions: 1) the contribution of foreign investment to GDP has been positive; 2) foreign investment has contributed, on balance, to improving Argentina's balance of payments; and 3) US investment, approximately half of all foreign investment in Argentina, accounted for 3.5 percent of GDP, approximately 10 percent of manufacturing sales and 40-50 percent of manufacturing exports in 1966, with these proportions tending to rise since that time. Presents excellent data and raises many important questions.

2356. Gallo Mendoza, Guillermo and Clemente Panzone. La utilización de indicadores de producción y el planeamiento (FCE/TE, 36:144, oct./dic. 1969, p. 577-594)

Amplification of author's "Algunos Indicadores Agrícolas y sus Posibilidades de Utilización"

(*Trimestre Económico,* 34:133, enero/marzo 1967, p. 27-145), with an indication of how the data might be used in planning models.

2357. Gelbard, José M. Las organizaciones empresariales en la evolución Argentina. B.A., Confederación General Económica de la República Argentina, 1971. 35 p.

Exposition on Argentine business organizations, particularly the CGE, by the man nominated Minister of the Treasury in the current (as of Sept. 1973) Perón government.

2358. Givogri, Carlos A. La movilidad de las firmas y los cambios en la estructura de la industria manufacturera argentina en el período 1958-67 (UNC/REE, 14:1/4, 1970, p. 115-133, bibl., tables)

Discussion of industrial concentration in Argentina, though at a relatively high level of aggregation. Concludes that the industries most characterized by firm mobility have been those which were most concentrated at the close of World War II.

Godoy, Horacio H. Argentina y el proceso de integración de América Latina. See item 1815.

2359. González Prieto, Pedro. Las industrias de productos alimenticios en la República Argentina: significado y posición dentro del cuadro general de la industria manufacturera, en función de los aportes de materias primas agropecuarias. La Plata, Arg., Univ. Nacional de La Plata, Facultad de Ciencias Económicas, Instituto de la Producción, 1970. 2 v. (122 l., Continuous pagination) tables (mimeo)

Basic data on the foodstuffs industry as of 1970. Compiled by province as well as nationally.

2360. Grupe, Héctor J. and **Aldo A. Arnaudo.** Manufactureros en Córdoba (Economía de Córdoba [Univ. Nacional de Córdoba, Facultad de Ciencias Económicas, Instituto de Economía y Finanzas, Arg.] 9:1, junio 1971, p. 3-27, bibl., tables)

Primarily methodology.

2361. Guadagni, Alieto and **Oswaldo Scheone.** Análisis económico del financiamiento vial argentino (FCE/TE, 36:143, julio/sept. 1969, p. 349-380)

Deals mainly with framework for analyzing financing of a road system, but also contains section evaluating (and critical of) Argentina's instruments for road financing.

2362. Guerberoff, Simón G. Sobre la aplicabilidad del análisis por función de producción para Argentina: análisis de un caso (UNLP/E, 18:1, enero/abril 1972, p. 23-44, tables)

Important criticism of an analysis by Jorge Katz (see *HLAS 33:3020*). Rejects the application of neoclassical production function analysis to Argentina, arguing that change in structural characteristics have had effects similar to those which have been attributed to labor-saving technological change. Emphasizes major changes which have taken place in the relative prices of agriculture and industry, the changes in the product composition of many branches of industry, and the increased degree of market imperfections.

2363. Gutiérrez, Carlos E. La industria editorial argentina. La Plata, Arg., Univ. Nacional de La Plata, Facultad de Ciencias Económicas, Instituto de la Producción, 1970. 52 p., tables (Segunda época. Serie: contribuciones, 212)

Useful descriptive materials.

2364. Herschel, Federico J. and **Julio J. Nogues.** El cambio tecnológico y la aplicación de un método concreto para su análisis en una industria (BCV/REL, 9:34, 1972, p. 161-199)

Taken from the larger work by Herschel, Casares, Nogues, and Rotstein (item 2365).

2365. ———; Vicente Casares; Julio J. Nogues; and **Enrique Rotstein.** Cambio tecnológico en la industria lechera. B.A., Instituto Torcuato Di Tella, Centro de Investigaciones Económicas, n.d. 517 p., table (Documento de trabajo, 61)

Careful study of technological change in an Argentine industry not among those most noted for progressiveness. Attention is given to both methodology and the technical detail of the dairy industry. An evaluation of the present state of technology in the dairy industry is offered, along with recommendations for change.

2366. Janvry, Alain de. Estancamiento tecnológico en el sector agrícola argentino: el caso de la fertilización del maíz (UNLP/E, 17:1, enero/abril 1971, p. 3-28, tables)

Explains the low use of fertilizers in corn production as due to the high price of the former and the low price of the latter, but demonstrates that even with the prevailing price structure it would be profitable to use fertilizer in soils of seriously depleted fertility (more than half the present acreage used for corn). It would be profitable for a still larger area if nitrogen prices were to fall to world market levels. Compare with *HLAS 33:3031a*.

2367. ——— and Juan Carlos Martínez. Inducción de innovaciones y desarrollo agropecuario argentino (UNLP/E, 18:2, mayo/agosto 1972, p. 179-213, bibl., tables)

A model explaining the generation of agricultural innovations and their adoption by rural producers. Maintains that the generation of the innovations is the result of a socioeconomic process of allocating investment funds while their adoption is determined by entrepreneurial behavior. There is a latent and an actual demand for innovations, usually separated by a time lag, the length of which can be reduced by appropriate policy measures affecting relative prices.

2368. Jorge, Eduardo F. Industria y concentración económica: desde principios de siglo hasta el peronismo. B.A., Siglo XXI Editores, 1971. 191 p., tables (Economía)

Outlines the path of Argentine industrialization from

1900 to 1946, drawing on existing studies. Helpful on the importance of political factors in explaining the evolution of the structure of industry but disappointing for its meager commentary on the efficiency or competitiveness of the various branches.

2369. Jornadas de Finanzas Públicas, *II, Córdoba, Arg., 1969.* Trabajos presentados en las . . . organizadas por la Facultad de Ciencias Económicas de la Universidad Nacional de Córdoba. Córdoba, Arg., Ediciones Macchi, 1970. 617 p., maps, tables.

Of special interest are Oswaldo H. Schenone "Un Análisis de Costo-Beneficio del Proyecto Chocón-Cerros Colorados" (p. 121-51) and L. Bobrowski and S. Goldborg "Presión Tributaria por Niveles de Ingreso: un Análisis Comparativo" (p. 389-443). Latter indicates that the tax system was more regressive in 1965 than in 1959. Also of note are, Fernando A. Ibarra, "Costos en la Universidad Nacional de Córdoba" (p. 3-53); Moisés Litwinczuk, "Inversión en Vivienda: Participación del Sector Público (p. 57-110); Walter E. Schulthess, "Análisis del Gasto Publico Provincial" (p. 163-180); and Salvador Treber, "Tendencias a la Inversión Real del Sector Público Argentino" (p. 573-619).

2370. ———, *III, Córdoba, Arg., 1970.* Trabajos presentados en las . . . organizadas por la Facultad de Ciencias Económicas de la Universidad Nacional de Córdoba. Córdoba, Arg., Ediciones Macchi, 1971. 547 p., tables.

Of greatest interest are a symposium on "Reforma Tributaria Para la República Argentina," (p. 501-27) and an article by Fernando V. Tow, "Una Contribución al Estudio de la Evasión al Impuesto a los Réditos Personales en la Argentina," indicating that tax evasion, which had risen from 50 percent in 1952-57 to 75 percent in 1959, rose still further in 1967. Also of note: Ernesto S. Castagnino, "Sugerencias Para un Replanteo de las Transferencias de Recursos Nacionales a las Provincias" (p. 147-166); Salvador Treber, "La Carga Tributaria" (p. 255-72); and "El Empleo en el Sector Gubernamental."

2371. Katz, Jorge. Importación de tecnología, aprendizaje local e industrialización dependiente. B.A., Instituto Torcuato Di Tella, Centro de Investigaciones Económicas, 1972. 1 v. (Various pagings) tables (Documento de trabajo, 59)

One of the most stimulating pieces of research on Argentina in many years, and the most important study of the process of technological change available for any Latin American country. Theoretical chapters reflecting originality and insight. Industrial analyses at a disaggregated as well as aggregated level. Discussion of transfer of technology and of local inventive activity undertaken both by individuals and 80 multinational corporations.

2372. Lascano, Marcelo Ramón. Presupuestos y dinero: la neutralidad del déficit fiscal de crecimiento económico. B.A., EUDEBA, 1972. 252 p., bibl., tables (Biblioteca del universitario. Temas/economía)

Employs theory and reasonable, if casual, empiricism (drawn especially from Argentine experience) to argue that budgetary deficits need not be associated with inflation nor budgetary surpluses with monetary stability. A suggestive presentation, emphasizing the need to focus on real forces rather than the mere character of the budgetary imbalance, but one which unfortunately stops short of attempting to really explain the causal relationships.

Laura, Guillermo Domingo. El capitalismo del pueblo. See item 7960.

2373. Llarena, David I. Demanda de factores productivos Cemento Portland. Mendoza, Arg., Univ. Nacional de Cuyo, Facultad de Ciencias Económicas, 1969. 36 l., tables (mimeo) (Serie Cuadernos. Sección Economía, 38)

2374. Loser, Claudio M. La demanda de acero en la Argentina: un análisis econométrico, 1939-1963 (Revista de la Facultad de Ciencias Económicas [Univ. Nacional de Cuyo, Mendoza, Arg.] 22:64/65, enero/agosto 1970, p. 57-64, bibl., tables)

Findings indicate a high and relatively stable price elasticity of demand for steel in Argentina (from -2.12 to -2.34)

2375. Mantel, Rolf R. Efectos de la política de tasas de interés sobre las empresas en períodos inflacionarios. B.A., Instituto Torcuato Di Tella, Centro de Investigaciones Económicas, 1972. 29 p., tables (Documento de trabajo, 64)

Valuable analysis employing institutional assumptions drawn from Argentine experience to estimate the effects of interest rate policy on business enterprises in periods of inflation. See also item 2395.

2376. Martín, Daniel Fernando. Finanzas públicas en la provincia de Mendoza: recursos. Mendoza, Arg., Univ. Nacional de Cuyo, Facultad de Ciencias Económicas, 1970. 115 p., bibl., tables (Serie Cuadernos. Sección Economía, 82)

Useful analysis of taxes and other sources of revenue in Mendoza province.

2377. Mazzulla, Jorge. Aspectos económicos de la yerba mate. La Plata, Arg., Univ. Nacional de La Plata, Facultad de Ciencias Económicas, Instituto de la Producción, 1971. 34 l., tables (Segunda época. Serie: contribuciones, 213)

Basic data concerning the production, processing and international trade in yerba mate.

2378. Mentz, Raúl Pedro and **Lucía Stella Díaz.** Proyecto: el empleo en Tucumán. Pt. 2: Algunos datos de declaraciones juradas de empleadores. Tucumán, Arg., Univ. Nacional de Tucumán, Facultad de Ciencias Económicas, Instituto de Investigaciones Económicas, 1967. 4 p., tables (Cuadernos, 67:3)

2379. Merkx, Gilbert W. Choques sectoriales y cambio político: la experiencia argentina (CM/FI, 10:2, oct./dic. 1969, p. 149-176)

Spanish translation of *HLAS 33:3026*.

2380. Montuschi, Luisa. Distribución del ingreso y crecimiento económico: análisis neoclásico del caso argentino (FCE/TE, 36:142, abril/junio 1969, p. 287-300)

Concludes that in period 1935-63, the Argentine economy evolved with fixed coefficients calling for use of factors in relatively constant proportions. Couples this conclusion with well-known tendencies of Argentine public policy towards wages and the presumed reactions of entrepreneurs to explain pattern of inflation consistent with model developed by J. H. G. Olivera in his 1964 article in *Oxford Economic Papers*.

2381. ——— and **Vicente Vázquez Presedo.** La experiencia argentina (*in* Montuschi, Luisa and Vicente Vázquez Presedo. Plan y laissez-faire en la economía contemporánea. B.A., Ediciones Macchi, 1970, p. 71-99, tables)

Highly readable survey of Argentine economy since 1930, with an emphasis on government endeavors in field of economic planning.

2382. Moyano Llerena, Carlos. Informe acerca de un política de promoción industrial para la Provincia de Córdoba. Córdoba, Arg., Banco de la Provincia de Córdoba, 1971. 50 p., tables.

Some analysis, but principally basic data (often only through 1964, however) of Córdoba's industrial transformation.

2383. Muscolo, Vicente and **Eugenio F. Corradini.** Unidad económica en agricultura. B.A., Conferencia Nacional sobre Problemas de Subdivisión de la Propiedad Fundiaria, 1970. 51 l., bibl., tables.

Ch. 3 offers an estimation of an "ideal" size exploitation for the dept. of Presidente Roque Saenz Peña, Córdoba prov.

2384. Ozlik, Oscar. Inflación y política fiscal en Argentina: el impuesto a los réditos en el período 1956-1965. B.A., Instituto Torcuato Di Tella, Centro de Investigaciones en Administración Pública, 1970. 77 p., tables (Documento de trabajo, 4)

Thoughtful analysis of the Argentine income tax (with special attention to the effects of inflation on tax collection).

2385. Pablo, Juan Carlos de. Política antiinflacionaria en la Argentina: 1967-1970. B.A., Amorrortu Editores, 1970. 135 p., bibl., tables (Biblioteca de economía política)

Systematic and critical evaluation of official policies to combat inflation in the period March 1967-June 1970. The institutionally relevant details are incorporated into an analysis that is at a high level of economic sophistication, but is not bogged down with extensive technical exposition; the latter, in a number of cases also by de Pablo, are cited where appropriate, however. Study received 1972 award from Fundación Ovidio Giménez.

2386. Petrecola, Alberto; Julio Nogues; Roberto Zubieta; and **Héctor Abrales.** La industria electrónica argentina y cambio técnico. B.A., Instituto Torcuato Di Tella, Centro de Investigaciones Económicas, n.d. 1 v. (Various pagings) tables (Documento de trabajo)

Uses methodology outlined in item 2364 to analyze technological change in electronics industry. Relatively less detailed than comparable study of dairy industry, item 2365.

Quadri, Mario A. La Cuenca del Plata como replanteo de la filosofía integracionista latinoamericana. See item 1867.

2387. Ramlot, Michel Jean Paul. Hacia un porvenir de la región cuyana. Mendoza, Arg., Univ. Nacional de Cuyo, Facultad de Ciencias Políticas y Sociales, Centro de Investigaciones, Instituto de Estudios del Desarrollo, 1972. 261 p., map, tables.

Determined and relatively optimistic view of the economic possibilities of Mendoza and San Juan by the Director General of the Instituto de Estudios Políticos. The emphasis is on the physical endowment of the region—with recommendations taking advantage of its potential and overcoming its limitations. Much good data, some helpful statistical analysis.

2388. *Revista de la Facultad de Ciencias Económicas.* Univ. Nacional de Cuyo, Facultad de Ciencias Económicas. Año 22, No. 66, sept./dic. 1970- . Mendoza, Arg.

Articles include: Angel Ginestar and Adolfo Tripodi, "Polarización de la Región de Cuyo;" Osvaldo Inchauspe, "Región Vitivinícola de Oasis Fluviales: Caracteres Distintivos;" Miguel E. Martínez, "Aplicación de Algunos Indices Derivados de Teoría de Información a la Región de Desarrollo Cuyo;" and Zulema Tomassetti de Piacentini; "Determinación de Costos Marginales para la Industria del Vino." Of considerable value to those interested in the Cuyo region and in dry, wine-growing regions in other countries.

2389. Ricci, Teodoro Ricardo. Algunas consideraciones sobre la economía de Tucumán. Tucumán, Arg., Univ. Nacional de Tucumán, Facultad de Filosofía y Letras, Depto. de Geografía, 1971. 41 p., map, table (Serie monográfica, 19)

Primarily a discussion of sugar cultivation in Tucumán, with a descriptive and qualitative emphasis. No references to economists' discussions cited in *HLAS 33:3002*.

2390. Rijckeghem, W. Van. Políticas de estabilización para un economía inflacionaria (IDES/DE, 12:46, julio/sept. 1972, p. 245-252, tables)

Spanish summary of *HLAS 31:3866*.

2391. Sábato, Jorge A. Ciencia, tecnología, desarrollo y dependencia. Tucumán, Arg., Univ. Nacional de Tucumán, 1971. 61 p.

Three short essays which explore technological aspects of development and especially Argentina's tendency to lag in technological progress. [J. M. Hunter]

2392. Sakamoto, Jorge. Medición de las repercusiones del proceso de industrialización sobre la economía: un análisis crítico del modelo Baer-Kerstenetsky (FCE/TE, 36:142, abril/junio 1969, p. 247-271)

Notes, in passing, that the Baer-Kerstenetsky model of maximizing linkages would have led to a much different pattern of industrialization in the period 1937-39/1948-50, and would have left the country without a metallurgical industry.

2393. Sante Fe (province), *Arg.* **Ministerio de Agricultura y Ganadería de la Provincia de Santa Fe.** Promoción económico-social del norte santafesino: área piloto de la cuña boscosa. Santa Fe, Arg., 1971. 298 p., bibl., fold. maps, illus., maps, plates, tables.

Basic technical and economic data on area in northern Sante Fe prov.

Santillán de Andrés, Selva E. Esquemas de la estructura socioeconómica de la provincia de Tucumán. See item 6830.

2394. Seminario sobre Industria de la Construcción Naval, *Buenos Aires, 1970.* Temas de industria naval argentina. B.A., Fundación Argentina de Estudios Marítimos, 1971. 191 p., tables.

A few chapters contain details on costs unlikely to be found elsewhere.

2395. Simone, Dante. Sobre política monetaria en alta inflación (UNLP/E, 18:1, enero/abril 1972, p. 55-118, tables)

Deals with South Korea and Taiwan as well as Argentina. Notes that Argentine demand for money balances as a percent of real income fell from 1945-60, but has been rising since. This has had an adverse effect on the level of investment and the allocation of resources, author argues. Concludes that in high inflation it is necessary to have an interest rate policy which maintains the real value of monetary assets. See also item 2375.

2396. Simonelli, Jorge. Producción y utilización de la energía eléctrica. San Carlos de Bariloche, Arg., Fundación Bariloche, 1970. 19 1.

Emphasis is on the Chocón project.

2397. Skupch, Pedro Rodolfo. Concentración industrial en la Argentina, 1956-1966 (IDES/DE, 11:41, abril/junio 1971, p. 3-14, tables)

Data indicating that there has been a substantial increase in Argentine industrial concentration since the mid-1960s.

2398. ———. Las consecuencias de la competencia de transportes sobre la hegemonía económica británica en la Argentina: 1919-1939 (UNLP/E, 17:1, enero/abril 1971, p. 119-141, tables)

Outlines the direct and suggests some of the indirect magnitude of British railroad and urban transport investments in Argentina and maintains that decline of British economic hegemony in the country was attributable to the competition resulting from imports of US autos and trucks in the 1920's and the substantial increase in road construction after 1928 (the latter given impulse by the cost pressures facing agricultural producers after the onset of the Depression—as well as by US auto interests). Thesis plausible but needs amplification including elements such as in Villanueva, item 2410. For historian's comment, see *HLAS 34:2802a*.

2399. ———. Nacionalización, libras bloqueadas y sustitución de importaciones (IDES/DE, 12:47, oct./dic. 1972, p. 477-493, tables)

Reexamines Argentina's purchase of the British railroads and associated companies in 1947 and concludes that Argentina did not fare poorly, given the country's industrialization goals, the opportunity the purchase provided to use frozen British sterling, and the fact that a number of facilities other than the railroads were obtained.

2400. Solari Yrigoyen, Hipólito. Participación obrera en las ganancias de las empresas. B.A., Editorial Jorge Alvarez, 1969. 176 p., bibl.

Soldberg, Carl. Rural unrest and agrarian policy in Argentina. See *HLAS 34:2804a*.

2401. Sommer, Juan. La disponibilidad de profesionales universitarios en Argentina. B.A., Instituto Torcuato Di Tella, Centro de Investigaciones Económicas, 1971. 174 p., tables (Documento de trabajo, 57)

Estimates of graduates of Argentine universities are provided for the period 1910-65, along with some analysis of the results. Also see item 8414.

2402. Unión Industrial Argentina, *Buenos Aires.* La región litoral-noreste de la República Argentina. B.A., 1970. 1 v. (Unpaged), tables.

Basic data of the region along with a resumé of the relevant national and provincial industrial promotion laws.

2403. United Nations. Economic Commission for Latin America (ECLA). **Secretariat.** The manufacture of machine-tools in Argentina (*in* Interregional Symposium on the Development of Metalworking Industries in Developing Countries, *Moscow, 1966.* Reports. Wien, United Nations Industrial Development Organization, 1969, p. 67-70)

2404. Universidad Nacional de Rosario, *Arg.* **Facultad de Ciencias Económicas. Instituto de Economía Aplicada.** Estudio de presupuestos familiares para el sector de obreros y empleados de la ciudad de Rosario. t. 1, Esquema conceptual y de organización administrativa del proyecto de investigación. t. 2, Los resultados cuantitativos. Rosario, Arg., Consejo Nacional de Investigaciones Científicas y Técnicas, 1969. 2 v. (82, 73 p.) tables.

Valuable discussion of the methodology of family budget studies and the procedures employed in carrying out such a study in Rosario, as well as the data collected. The empirical analysis scheduled for later publication.

2405. Varsavsky, Oscar A. Proyectos nacionales: planteo y estudios de viabilidad. B.A., Ediciones Periferia, 1971. 332 p. (Col. Ciencia, desarrollo e ideología)

Offers an outline for an interdisciplinary approach to national planning. Author is a former leader of the Mathematical Economics Group of the Instituto de Cálculo of the Facultad de Ciencias Exactas, Univ. de Buenos Aires, but this work is aimed at a less specialized audience, and is, moreover, avowedly political (left-of-center) in orientation. Most sections have references to Argentine characteristics.

2406. Vázquez-Presedo, Vicente. El caso argentino: migración de factores, comercio exterior y desarrollo, 1875-1914. B.A., EUDEBA, 1971. 230 p., bibl., tables (Biblioteca de economía. Temas)

Important work. Examines foreign investment and its effects on the acquisition of basic social capital, presents material on the push-pull forces behind immigration and colonization, and traces the growth of Argentine foreign trade. A wealth of data not previously available, but perhaps somewhat less analysis of that data than might have been desired. For historian's evaluation see *HLAS 34:2819*.

2407. ———. Estadísticas históricas argentinas comparadas: pt. 1, 1875-1914. B.A., Ediciones Macchi, 1971. 114 p., bibl., plates.

The most important compendium of economic data available for the period 1875-1914.

2408. Vega, Juan A. Elasticidad ingreso y poder compensatorio del impuesto a los réditos en la Argentina (Revista de la Facultad de Ciencias Económicas [Univ. Nacional de Cuyo, Mendoza, Arg.] 22:64/65, enero/agosto 1970, p. 85-99, bibl., tables)

Findings indicating low income elasticity and low stabilizing potential of Argentine income tax.

2409. Vilá, María Electra. La Marina Mercante Argentina durante el período, 1959-1969. La Plata, Arg., Univ. Nacional de La Plata, Facultad de Ciencias Económicas, Instituto de la Producción, 1971. 21 p., tables (Segunda época. Serie: contribuciones, 214)

Considerable data and some analysis.

2410. Villanueva, Javier. El origen de la industrialización argentina (IDES/DE, 12:47, oct./dic. 1972, p. 451-476, tables)

Argues that the impetus to modern Argentine industrialization came in the 1920's not the 1930's, contrary to the shift-in-relative-prices explanation often proferred. No acceleration took place in rate of industrial growth, nor in foreign investment or overall industrial investment. Moreover, several areas of notable industrial growth in 1930's are due to: a) anticyclical policy which facilitated use of industrial capacity constructed in 1920's, or b) a foreign exchange policy which discriminated against imports from US. A plausible hypothesis, well presented, disappointing only in failure to discuss adequacy of certain data referred to. Compare with item 2336.

Weisskoff, Richard. Income distribution and economic growth in Puerto Rico, Argentina, and Mexico. See item 2528.

2411. Zapata, Juan Antonio. Economía de los recursos naturales. Mendoza, Arg., Univ. Nacional de Cuyo, Facultad de Ciencias Económicas, 1971. 40 p., bibl., tables (Serie Cuadernos. Sección Economía, 92)

Analytical review of the bibliography on natural resources in Argentina.

2412. Zeni, Enrique R. El destino de la agricultura en la Argentina. B.A., Editorial La Pléyade, 1972. 172 p., tables.

Useful collection of newspaper and magazine articles on topics of agricultural concern by the former president of the Bolsa de Cereales of Buenos Aires.

BRAZIL

FRED D. LEVY, Jr.

Associate Professor of Economics
Syracuse University

THE FOLLOWING PUBLICATIONS WERE SELECTED from among books and articles received through July 1973. Quality, as must be expected, is uneven, but the reviewer is impressed by the rapid growth, in both quantity and analytical quality, of materials from Brazilian sources. Well represented, as in previous years, are works by the outstanding young professionals of the FGV (Fundação Getulio Vargas, Rio de Janeiro); the IPE (Instituto de Pesquisas Econômicas, University of São Paulo); and IPEA (Instituto de Planjamento Econômico e Social, Ministry of Planning). Several new books in the latter's series Coleção Relatórios de Pesquisa arrived too late for inclusion here. Many of the remaining authors are alumni of the University of California/Berkeley and Vanderbilt University technical assistance teams contracted by those institutions.

With Brazil now well into its fifth year of ten percent growth, there is a marked shift in the literature from the earlier concentration on structural inflation and stagnation to the newly perceived concern for the employment and distributional aspects of economic growth. Well reflected are differences of opinion within the Brazilian Government and intellectual community, and among economists worldwide, regarding the extent, if any, to which accelerated growth necessarily conflicts with distributional objectives, and the relative priorities of these ends. The long article by Langoni analyzing 1960 and 1970 census data is a particularly important contribution to this debate.

Another interesting feature of the current batch of articles is the shift of attention from the import-substitution model of earlier years to the present fact of, and future possibilities for, rapid export growth. This, of course, is in response to the very rapid recent growth of Brazilian exports, particularly of manufactures. The aggressive manner in which the Brazilian Government is promoting its exports, on both the supply and demand side, will undoubtedly be reflected in publications reviewed in a later edition of the *Handbook*.

The important role of the foreign entrepreneur in Brazilian development continues to be a preoccupation of the literature. The very large inflow of medium-and long-term portfolio capital—as opposed to direct investments—has not yet attracted the analysis it deserves.

"O Brazil é o pais do futuro, y sempre será (Brazil is the land of the future, and always will be)" is an adage that has long haunted that nation's aspirations to world power status. According to the present Government, "O futuro ja chegou (the future has already arrived)." Much of the literature pertaining to Brazil in the rest of this decade will be devoted to evaluating this assertion and its implications for its own people and for the hemisphere. Comparisons of the "Brazilian model" with other development approaches in Latin America and elsewhere are needed and inevitable.

2413. Adams, Dale W.; Harlan Davis; and Lee Bettis. Is inexpensive credit a bargain for small farmers? The recent Brazilian experience (IAMEA, 26:1, Summer 1972, p. 47-58, table)

Reviews agricultural credit policies over 1960s and very substantial expansion of credit that took place. Authors find, however, that loans have been highly concentrated among few borrowers with little positive impact on small and medium farms. Cause is neither lack of demand on the part of small farmers nor political power of large farmers, but rather the relatively high cost of lending to small farmers and the regulated pricing of credit below its supply price.

Almeida, Miguel Alvaro Ozório de. O mundo subdesenvolvido perante as sociedades pós-industriais. See item 1778.

2414. Andrade, Manuel Correia de. Estrutura fundiária e tipos de explotação agrícola en Pernambuco (CDAL, 2, juillet/déc. 1968, p. 160-172, map, tables)

Uses 1950 and 1960 census data to describe land distribution, tenure, and crop patterns in three major economic zones of northeastern Pernambuco state: the *zona da mata*, the *agreste*, and the *sertão*.

2415. Bacha, Edmar L. El subempleo, el costo social de la mano de obra y la estrategia brasileña de crecimiento (FCE/TE, 38:152, oct./dic. 1971, 1069-1079, tables)

Growing rate of underemployment through 1960s is taken to be the greatest failure of the import-substitution strategy of Brazilian industrialization. Bacha blames this phenomenon on distorted factor prices and the capital-intensive bias of multinational corporations. Argues that faster labor absorption would stimulate faster growth rather than slow it as often assumed.

2416. Baer, Werner and Annibal V. Villela. Industrial growth and industrialization: revisions in the stages of Brazil's economic development (JDA, 7:2, Jan. 1973, p. 217-234, tables)

Divides Brazilian industrial growth into six stages and presents data to support "revisionist" contention of Dean and others that substantial industrial growth occurred prior to World War I. This, however, was industrial growth without industrialization, according to the authors. Not until 1930s did significant structural changes take place from which the industrial sector emerged as the engine of development.

2417. Baklanoff, Eric N. Brazilian development and the international economy (*in* Saunders, John *ed.* Modern Brazil [see item 126] p. 190-214, plates, tables)

Brings together secondary source materials for useful review of Brazil's international finances since the mid-19th century. Takes decidedly positive view of private foreign investment and policies of post-1964 governments.

2418. Brasil Netto, Thomás Pompeu de Souza. Brasil e iniciativa privada. Préfacio de Eugênio Gudin. Rio, APEC Editôra, 1971. 335 p.

Collection of speeches by eminent Northeast industrialist and president of National Contederation of Industry. Topics range from general policies regarding education, economic integration, and income distribution, to problems and progress of particular regions and industries. Useful summary of thoughts of one of Brazil's more influential, articulate, and progressive businessmen.

2419. Brazil. Ministério do Interior. Banco da Amazônia. Departamento de Estudos Econômicos. Amazônia: instrumentos para o desenvolvimento. Belém, Bra., 1969. 215 p., bibl., fold. maps, maps, tables.

Outlines in very summary fashion fiscal incentives and sources of credit to investors in Amazon region as of 1969, and provides instructions regarding how to apply for them.

———. Presidência da República. Metas e bases para a ação de govêrno. See item 7836.

2420. ———. Superintendência do Desenvolvimento do Nordeste (SUDENE). Brasil Nordeste: 10 anos com a SUDENE [Brazil Northeast: 10 years with SUDENE]. São Paulo, Telepress Serviços de Imprensa, 1969. 400 p., maps, plates, tables.

Tenth-anniversary, public relations volume reviewing Northeast's economy and government's plans for regional development. Provides useful institutional reference to agencies involved. Most data provided refer to year 1968.

2421. Brazil: development for whom? N.Y., North American Congress on Latin America (NACLA), 1973. 31 p., map, plates, tables (Latin America & empire report, 7:4)

American radical version of the "Brazilian Economic Miracle." NACLA's readers will know ahead of time that answer to "development for whom?" must be the Brazilian elite and US business. Singled out for study are US mining companies, the foreign aid program, and cotton traders.

2422. Brazil, the Medici administration: performance and prospects (BLSA/QR, 7:76, April 1973, p. 152-163, tables)

Brief and generally laudatory review of government economic policy and performance from 1969-72, and optimistic forecast for medium-term future. Footnotes guide reader to more intensive discussions of particular topics in earlier issues of the *Quarterly Review*.

2423. Campos, Roberto de Oliveira. Função da emprêsa privada. Préfacio por Ermelino Matarazzo. Rio, Gráfica Editôra Rainha Lescal, 1971. 63 p.

Written while author was president of the Inter-American Council of Commerce and Production. Pt. 1, an essay, is a plea for stable rules of the game and an attempt to lay out a pragmatic outline of the division of rights and responsibilities between government and private enterprise, both domestic and foreign. Following essay are transcripts of two press conferences covering variety of topics ranging from foreign investment, to sources of Japanese growth, and economic future of Guanabara state. Not a particularly interesting sample of Campos' extraordinary style and wit.

2424. Carl, Beverly May. A guide to incentives for investing in Brazil. Dallas, Tex., Southern Methodist Univ. Press, 1972. 58 p., map, tables.

Provides brief, optimistic overview of economy, sources of credit, and incentives provided investors by Brazilian government. Also reviews US programs that affect private investment in Brazil.

2425. Cavalcanti, Clóvis de Vasconcelos and Dirceu Murilo Pessôa. Vale do Moxotó: análise sócio-econômica de uma bacia de açude público. Recife, Bra., Instituto Joaquim Nabuco de Pesquisas Sociais [and] Depto. Nacional de Obras Contra as Sêcas, 1970. 272 p., fold. maps, tables.

Socio-economic survey of reservoir and irrigation site in semi-arid *sertão* of Pernambuco state, intended to serve as planning guide for DNOCS, the federal agency responsible for water conservation infrastructure.

2426. Chara, Acir Diniz. Compêndio de índices de correção monetária. Rio, APEC Editôra, 1971. 222 p., tables.

Tables for calculating monetary correction to whole range of financial transactions and assets to which that concept has been applied in Brazil.

2427. Clan S. A. (firm) *Brazil*. Development of the petro-chemical industry in the state of Bahia: resumée. Salvador, Bra., 1970. 164 p., tables.

Summary of pre-project study for Bahia state. Not very useful in this summary form and clumsily translated from the Portuguese.

2428. Cline, William R. Influência das dimensões e relações jurídicas na eficiência produtiva do estabelecimento agrícola (IBE/RBE, 21:1, março 1967, p. 45-60, bibl., tables)

Uses sample data to derive sectoral production functions for various crops in several regions of Brazil in order to compare farm productivity as function of size of cultivated area (as opposed to size of farm unit) and tenure. Efficiency is found not to increase appreciably with size. In two cases where there seemed to be a relationship, non-owners were found to be more efficient than owners.

2429. *Conjuntura Econômica.* Fundação Getúlio Vargas. Vol. 27, No. 1, jan. 1973- . Rio.

Special edition of *Conjuntura* dedicated to development and operation of Brazilian banking and monetary system. Articles devoted, inter alia, to current wave of bank mergers, open market operations, and use of credit cards. Usefulness to North American reader somewhat reduced by amount of space given to description of US system. See also the Sept. 1972 issue devoted to capital market growth.

2430. Costa, Ronaldo. Mercado internacional de produtos de base (IBRI/R, 12:51/52, set./dez. 1970, p. 7-15)

Highlights, in brief and simplistic fashion, importance of export sector to development. Notes that despite rapid growth of manufactured exports, Brazil will continue to depend heavily on primary exports for some time to come. Hence, urgency of improving productivity and entering international agreements to offset price instability and other well-known disadvantages of primary goods in international markets.

2431. Dean, Warren. The industrialization of São Paulo 1880-1945. Austin, Tex., Univ. of Texas Press, Institute of Latin American Studies, 1969. 263 p., bibl., tables (Latin American monographs, 17)

Analyzes origin and growth of São Paulo industry and its leaders. Incomes and externalities generated by coffee sector provide motive force; author refutes conventional wisdom that protectionism forced by Depression and world wars was major stimulus to domestic industrialization.

2432. Donnelly, John T. External financing and short-term consequences of external debt servicing for Brazilian economic development, 1947-1968 (JDA, 7:3, April 1973, p. 411-429, tables)

Analyzes rapid growth and deteriorating structure of external debt built up over the Kubitschek years and resulting squeeze on imports, particularly of intermediate goods. Combined with import limitations imposed by lagging exports, result was the early 1960s economic slowdown. Author relates these foreign exchange constraints to austerity measures being demanded by the IMF and AID as conditions for new loans and debt relief, and to the political turmoil of the early 1960s.

2433. Dória, Antônio Roberto Sampaio *ed.* Incentivos fiscais para o desenvolvimento. São Paulo? José Bushatsky Editor, 1971? 324 p.

Superficial but useful review of part of Brazil's elaborate system of fiscal incentives to promote development of particular regions or sectors.

2434. A experiência do Paraná. Rio, Editôra Laudes, 1971? 280 p., tables.

Details plans, policies, and accomplishments, during 1965-70, of Paraná's state government, one of Brazil's southern and more prosperous states. Particular attention is given to FUNDEPAR, the state's educational planning agency.

2435. Faissol, Speridião. Um modêlo preditivo de desenvolvimento econômico do Brasil: um estudo utilizando a cadeia de Markov (IBGE/B, 30:224, set./out. 1971, p. 3-21, maps, tables)

Computer simulation of demographic growth and migration in response to rising incomes and changing economic structure. Interesting primarily for its clear and simple discussion and illustration of a useful analytical method. Includes graphs.

2436. Fajnzylber, Fernando. Sistema industrial e exportação de manufaturados: análise da experiência brasileira. Rio, Ministério do Planejamento e Coordenação Geral, Instituto de Planejamento Econômico e Social (IPEA), Instituto de Pesquisas (INPES), 1971. 334 p., tables (Relatório de pesquisa, 7)

Provides wealth of data, albeit preliminary, broken down by sectors, regarding size of firms, industrial concentration, foreign investment, productivity, export performance, importation of technology, and analyzes interrelationships of these variables.

2437. Figueiredo, Nuno Fidelino de. A transferência de tecnologia no desenvolvimento industrial do Brasil. Rio, Instituto de Planejamento Econômico e Social, Instituto de Pesquisas (IPEA/INPES), 1972. 360 p., tables (Monografia, 7)

Examines in detail process of technological transfer between foreign and Brazilian-based companies. Eschewing an ideological approach, author argues that Brazil must expand still further its rate of importation of industrial technology but within a carefully designed plan of sectoral priorities, diffusion of know-how, and development of indigenous scientific establishment. Some of the current issues *re:* imported technology—e.g., factor proportions, income distribution—are not analyzed.

2437a. Fishlow, Albert. Brazilian size distribution of income (AEA/AER, 62:2, May 1972, p. 391-402, bibl., tables)

Estimates income distribution and its determinants from 1960 and preliminary 1970 census data. High concentration found is similar to that found in other Latin American countries, and appears to have worsened over the decade. Author attributes this retrogression more to stabilization than to growth policies but expects it to continue as result of government's propensity to ignore distributional effects of its chosen policy mix.

Foland, Frances M. A profile of Amazonia: its possibilites for development. See item 7065.

2438. Frederick, Kenneth D. Production controls under the international coffee agreements (UM/JIAS, April 1970, p. 255-270, tables)

Useful, albeit brief, history of the International Coffee Agreement and Brazil's stop-and-go eradication and diversification programs in the coffee sector through 1968. Repeated frosts and coffee rust have thus far kept Frederick's foreboding of growing surpluses from being realized. However, in the face of tight world markets, the government has again shifted to an expansive policy, and surpluses may again be coming on line before the decade is out.

2439. Fundação IBGE, *Rio.* Instituto Brasileiro de Estatística. Sinopse estatística, Paraná:1970. Rio, 1971? 113 p., map, plates, tables.

Statistical tables up to 1968, summarize demographic, economic, and social dimensions of Paraná state.

2440. ———, ———. ———. Sinopse estatística, Piauí: 1970, Rio, 1971. 91 p., plates, tables.

Statistical tables, ending 1967-68, summarizing demographic, economic, and social data for Piaui state, poorest in Brazil's Northeast.

2441. Furtado, Celso. Agricultura y desarrollo económico: consideraciones sobre el caso brasileño (FCE/TE, 39:153, enero/marzo 1972, p. 13-36)

Furtado describes Brazil as only country of the Americas created from the initial conquest on the basis of commercial capitalism in the form of large agricultural enterprise. Control given the large landlords has carried down to present day and limits agrarian masses to minifundia cultivation, direct exploitation by enterprises (as sharecroppers, wage laborers, etc.), or sub sistence farming at the outer frontier. Incomes become ever more concentrated as output expansion is based on expanded land use, an elastic labor supply, and a primitive technology. Dependence of urban wages and demand patterns on rural income distribution leads to sweeping conclusion that this heritage of powerful agricultural enterprises determines country's entire economic and social structure. True development for benefit of the masses, both urban and rural, is impossible without a well-planned restructuring of the agricultural sector. This is vintage Furtado and provides provocative contrast to the Nicholls version of Brazilian development, see item 2457.

2442. ———. Análise do "modelo" brasileiro, Rio, Editôra Civilização Brasileira, 1972. 122 p. (Col. Perspectivas do homen, 29. Serie Economia)

Book composed of two essays, title essay and a discussion of agrarian structure similar to item 2441. Furtado's themes are by now familiar, but as always the discussion is provocative. Briefly, the model, according to the author, flows from post 1964 government's purposeful diversification of pattern of demand away from traditional manufactures toward the technologically dynamic consumer durables sectors, a direction also promoted by international capitalist corporations that dominate these sectors. This transformation must necessarily been supported by fiscal, monetary, wage and price, subsidy, etc. policies that shift income distribution in favor of the upper-middle class. Result is rapid growth but at the cost of increasing inequality in income distribution and ever greater control over the domestic economy by multinational corporations. Local entrepreneurs acquiesce in latter phenomenon because, rightly or wrongly, they have been trained to equate their own interests–and indeed national interest–with that of international capitalism.

——— and **Andrea Maneschi.** Un modèle simulé de développement et de stagnation en Amérique latine. See item 1809.

2443. Goodman, David E.; Júlio F. Ferreira Sena; and **Roberto Cavalcanti de Albuquerque.** Os incentivos financeiros à industrialização do Nordeste e a escolha de tecnologias (IPEA/PP, 1:2, dez. 1971, p. 329-365, table)

Reviews and evaluates financial incentives designed to promote investment in Northeast prior to 1970. Despite announced goal of labor asborption, and substantial increase in investment in the area that did occur, little progress was made in reducing unemployment. On the basis of econometric analysis, authors conclude that failure partly derives from relative factor prices that favored excessive capital intensity, a distortion exacerbated by the incentives themselves. Suggests corrective measures.

2444. Goulart, Rina Norma Tosello. A intervenção do estado no domínio econômico (Boletim [da] Faculdade de Filosofia, Ciências e Letras de Presidente Prudente, Depto. de Ciências Sociais [Presidente Prudente, Bra.] 1970, p. 67-71)

Slays straw man of laissez faire and affirms the need for some governmental intervention in the economy. So what else is new?

Graham, Douglas H. Divergent and convergent regional economic growth and internal migration in Brazil: 1940-1960. See item 8507.

2445. Hess, Geraldo and others. Investimentos e mercado de capitais. Rio, Forum Editôra, 1971. 509 p., tables (Estante de economia e finanças)

Textbook on Brazilian capital market, mixing capital theory, monetary data, and description of legislative and institutional framework. Authors are members of the faculty of Rio's Catholic Univ.

2446. Huddle, Donald L. Essays on the economy of Brazil: the Berkeley group (UC/EDCC, 20:3, April 1972, p. 560-574)

Critical review of essays contained in Ellis' *The economy of Brazil* (see *HLAS 33:3060*). Drawing heavily on his own previously published work, Huddle devotes particular attention to sources of Brazilian inflation, strategy of import substitution, and agricultural policies.

2447. Ianni, Octavio. Ideologia e prática do planejamento durante o Estado Nôvo (FGV/RAE, 11:1, março 1971, p. 7-15)

Briefly traces evolution of ideology and practice of governmental intervention in the economy up to 1945. Growing role of government and importance of technocrat is attributed to economic crisis created by the war and increasing complexity and development potential of the industrial economy.

2448. Lafer, Celso. El planeamiento en el Brasil: observaciones sobre El Plan de Metas, 1956-1961 (IDES/DE, 10:39/40, oct./dic. 1970 [and] enero/marzo 1971, p. 309-330, tables)

Speculates on nature of political and intellectual evolution that led to use of comprehensive planning as a decision-making tool by the Kubitschek government, and the administrative difficulties of plan implementation. Examines goal achievement sector by sector and concludes that the very success of the Plan de Metas was the most difficult legacy left to subsequent governments. Largely theoretical discussion.

2449. Langoni, Carlos Geraldo. Distribuição da renda e desenvolvimento econômico do Brasil (USP/EE, 2:5, out. 1972, p. 5-88, tables)

Most intensive analysis available thus far of changes in income distribution and its causes over 1960s. Based on 1960 and 1970 census data, Langoni finds clear increase in inequality but somewhat smaller than estimated in other studies. Educational level is found to be a major determinant, but author disputes Fishow's contention that blame can be attributed to unequal educational opportunities. Instead, Langoni points to exaggerated demands for high skills partly caused by capital and skill intensity of imported technology. Argues that purpose of growth is elimination of poverty and not equalization of incomes, and that these two objectives are not consistent in short and medium terms.

2450. Levy, Fred D., Jr. Planejamento simulado: documentos para projetos de planejamento. N.Y., Inter-American University Foundation, 1971. 294 p., tables.

44 background papers on the Brazilian economy prepared for a simulated five-year planning exercise, covering agriculture, education, urban, health, and infrastructure sectors.

2451. Lima Filho, Alberto de Oliveira and Andrew Foster Powell. Pesquisa mercadológica no Brasil: estágio atual e tendências (FGV/RAE, 11:1, março 1971, p. 65-74, tables)

Surveys state of the art of market research in Brazil and factors underlying growth of its use. Research is casual and presents no surprises.

2452. Mikesell, Raymond Frech. Bethlehem's joint venture in Brazilian manganese (*in* Mikesell, Raymond Frech and others. Foreign investment in the petroleum and mineral industries: case studies of investor-host country relations. Baltimore, Md., The Johns Hopkins Press *for* Resources for the Future, 1971, p. 365-368)

Much too brief treatment of an apparently successful joint venture in Brazilian mining, in which US investor has from the beginning accepted junior partner status.

2453. ———. Iron ore in Brazil: the experience of the Hanna Mining Company (*in* Mikesell, Raymond Frech and others. Foreign investment in the petroleum and mineral industries: case studies of investor-host country relations. Baltimore, Md., The Johns Hopkins Press *for* Resources for the Future, 1971, p. 345-364, map)

Traces politically and legally troubled history of Hanna Mining in Brazil. Author blames Hanna's problems largely on rising Brazilian nationalism in late 1950's and tangled legal background of mining concessions. Problems might be alleviated by joint venture arrangement. Item 2452 on Bethlehem Steel provides a contrast in this regard.

Moore, Russell Martin. A função das empresas internacionais na indústria automotriz da América Latina. See item 1850.

2454. Moreira, Marcílio Marques. Indicações para o projeto brasileiro. Rio, Edições Tempo Brasileiro, 1971. 218 p. (Biblioteca Tempo universitário, 29)

Collection of previously published essays by prominent Brazilian businessman and civil servant. Topics include education, foreign aid, developmental role of the military, and capital market development. Treatment is generally historical and theoretical.

2455. Morley, Samuel A. and Gordon W. Smith. The effects of changes in the distribution of income on labor, foreign investment and growth in Brazil. Houston, Tex., Rice Univ., 1971. 28 p., bibl., tables (Program of development studies paper, 15)

Using estimates of consumption patterns by income class and an input-output growth model, authors test relationship between income distribution and pattern of demand. Assumptions regarding this relationship are fundamental to analyses of Brazilian growth offered by Furtado and others. Data are weak and results tentative, but study finds surprisingly little relation between income distribution and overall growth rates, the structure of growth, the size of the foreign share, or the rate of labor absorption. These results would suggest that both those who argue that growing inequality is essential to the continued viability of the "Brazilian model," and those who anticipate imminent stagnation from the same source, are wrong.

2456. ——— and ———. Import substitution and foreign investment in Brazil (OUP/OEP, 23:1, March 1971, p. 120-135, tables)

Provides sectoral estimates of import substitution between 1949 and 1962, taking into account increased domestic production of intermediate goods used in substitute industry. High correlation is found between sectoral growth rates and extent of import substitution. Authors conclude, however, that this "forced" import substitution strategy unduly benefitted foreign enterprise rather than domestic entrepreneurs.

Mota, Fernando de Oliveira *comp.* Recursos e necessidades do Nordeste: um documento básico sôbre a região nordestina. See item 7114.

2457. Nicholls, William H. Agriculture and the economic development of Brazil (*in* Saunders, John *ed.* Modern Brazil [see item 126] p. 215-256, tables)

Comprehensive survey of the historical development of Brazilian agriculture, as contrasted with US experience, and factor uses and productivities by region. Describes early landowner of Northeast as conspicuous consumer when compared with São Paulo investor, but asserts that present landowning class throughout country is profit-oriented and responding rapidly to market incentives. Argues that the need is for greater integration into the market rather than for administrative land reform. Major shortcomings in agricultural development are derived from government's failure to provide infrastructure, adequate research and other services, and the capital-intensive bias of industrialization policy. Not everyone will agree with all of Nicholl's conclusions, but this is an excellent article with which to begin one's study of Brazilian agriculture.

Oliveira, Décio Rufino de. Recursos naturais, fatores determinantes na ocupação do território brasileiro. See item 7122.

2458. Rattner, Henrique. Industrialização e concentração econômica em São Paulo. Rio, Fundação Getúlio Vargas, Instituto de Documentação, 1972. 215 p., bibl., tables.

Analysis of industrial concentration in city of São Paulo and its economic and social impact on it, surrounding towns, countryside, and nation as a whole. Views consequences in terms of accumulating sectoral, regional, and social disequilibria leading to rising political tension and social conflict. The solution: planned decentralization of industry and population in order to widen and integrate the national market.

2459. Las realizaciones de la nueva política económica del Brasil (Política y Economía [B.A.] 4, julio 1971, p. 12-17, tables)

Brief and enthusiastic outline of economic policy since 1964 revolution. Characterizes pursuit of social objectives as attempting "a balance between political stability, social tranquility, and economic growth."

Riegelhaupt, Joyce F. and Shepher Forman. Bodo was never Brazilian: economic integration and rural development among a contemporary peasantry. See *HLAS 34:2924.*

2460. Rocca, Carlos Antônio and José Roberto Mendonça de Barros. Recursos humanos e estrutura do comércio exterior (USP/EE, 2:5, out. 1972, p. 89-109, bibl., tables)

Refutes Tyler's contention (item 2473) that Brazil is exporting a mix of products with higher relative labor skill content than justified by the comparative advantage dictated by its human resource endowment. Tyler's use of sectoral skill coefficients was based on estimates made for the US and overstates skill coefficients of Brazilian exports. When correction is made, authors conclude that Brazil indeed reflects the Heckscher-Ohlin model, exporting goods of relatively low skill intensity and importing goods of high skill intensity consistent with its current factor endowment.

2461. Rondon, J. Lucídio N. Recursos econômicos de Mato Grosso. São Paulo, Gráfica Urupês, 1972. 236 p., bibl., plates.

Combination travelogue-resource survey of the vast and rapidly growing frontier state of Mato Grosso. In both its facets, book is too summary to be very satisfying.

Rosenbaum, J. Jon and William G. Tyler. Contemporary Brazil: issues in economic and political development. See item 7881.

2462. Sá, Jayme Magrassi de. Aspectos da economia brasileira. Rio, Editôra Alba, 1970. 198 p., tables.

Collection of author's newspaper and magazine articles ranging from difficulties of implementing birth control programs, to development of domestic capital markets, to quantity theory of money.

2463. Salera, Virgil. Brazil and Japan: economic parallels or contrasts? (IAMEA, 26:2, Autumn 1972, p. 3-17)

Simple minded polemic against nationalistic limitations on private foreign investment. Suggests that Brazil's high growth rate will outlast Japan's, if Brazil avoids latter's restrictions on the multinational corporation.

2464. Santiago, Alberto Alves and others. Brasil potência. São Paulo, Editôras Unidas, 1971. 431 p., maps, tables.

Series of essays assembled to celebrate 50th anniversary of São Paulo's Institute of Engineering. Most provide brief surveys of industrial sector—e.g., steel, hydroelectric power, food processing, coffee—while a few examine government policy in education, economic integration of the Northeast and Amazon regions, oil, etc. In one essay, Finance Minister Delfim Netto outlines his export strategy.

Silva, Fernando A. Rezende da. A evolução das funções do govêrno e a expansão do setor público brasileiro. See item 7887.

2465. Silva, Luiz Octávio Souza e; Washington Land; and Luiz Pereira Barroso. Petróleo, derivados e gás combustível: evolução recente e perspectivas (IPEA/PP, 1:2, dez. 1971, p. 283-327, map, tables)

Reviews growth of supply and demand for petroleum products and gas from 1964-70 with projections to 1974, and suggests implications for investment in exploration, refining capacity, and transport and distribution facilities. Does not discuss important implications for Brazil's growing import needs and likelihood of a widening trade deficit. Includes graphs.

2466. Slater, Charles and others. Processos de mercado no Recife: área do Nordeste brasileiro. 2. ed. Recife, Bra., Ministério do Interior, Superintendência do Desenvolvimento do Nordeste, Depto. de Agricultura e Abastecimento, 1972. 1 v. (Various pagings) maps, plates, tables.

Comprehensive survey and analysis of agricultural marketing systems of Brazil's Northeast, undertaken by a technical assistance team from Michigan State Univ. in cooperation with SUDENE.

Smith, Peter Seaborn. Bolivian oil and Brazilian economic nationalism. See item 8238.

2467. Soares, José Teodoro. O papel do estado no campo econômico no Brasil (Revista de Ciências Sociais [Fortaleza, Bra.] 2:2, 2. semestre 1971, p. 114-136, bibl., tables)

Short history of growing role of government in Brazilian development. Matter-of-fact style; offers little new insight.

2468. Strachan, Lloyd W. A survey of recent agricultural trends in northwestern Paraná (LTC Newsletter [Univ. of Wisconsin, Land Tenure Center, Madison] 40, April/June 1973, p. 19-29, tables)

Describes economic and demographic boom beginning in 1940 that converted northwestern Paraná into major coffee-producing area of Brazil, and analyzes social and economic problems that had emerged as a consequence by early 1960s.

2469. Tintner, Gerhard; Isabella Consiglieri; and José T. M. Carneiro. Um modêlo econométrico aplicado á economia brasileira (IBE/RBE, 24:1, jan./março 1970, p. 5-17, bibl., tables)

Presents a highly aggregated (five-equation) econometric model of Brazilian economy from which crude projections are made of effects of a one-percent change in employment, wages, government spending, and other variables.

2470. Torres, José Garrido. O papel da empresa privada e da empresa pública no desenvolvimento sócio-econômico (Carta Mensal [Rio] 17:206, maio 1972, p. 3-11)

Banal statement on role of private enterprise, complemented by, but not substituted by, wise government policy. Calls also for sense of social responsibility on part of entrepreneur because of necessary interrelationship between social and economic development.

2471. Trubek, David M.; Jorge Hilário Gouvêa Vieira; and Paulo Fernandes de Sá. O mercado de capitais e os incentivos fiscais. Préfacio [de] Marcílio Marques Moreira. Rio, TN-APEC, 1971. 265 p., tables.

Empirical study of interrelationships between law, government policy, and economic development. Specifically examines use of fiscal incentives in period 1964-69 as stimulus to stock market development in Brazil. After outlining theoretical framework, based on Gurley and Shaw's work, for choosing among alternative techniques of mobilizing domestic savings, authors review and evaluate objectives and legal history of subject incentives.

2472. Tyler, William G. A combinação de fatôres de produção nas exportações industriais no Brasil (IBE/RBE, 24:1, jan./março 1970, p. 109-128, tables)

Attempts to explain apparent fact that, despite capital scarcity, Brazil's manufactured exports tend to be concentrated along the relatively capital intensive side of its manufacturing spectrum. Chief explanations offered are: price distortions resulting from government policies, Brazil's position in LAFTA, and raw material endowment. Highly aggregated nature of the data, lack of capital stock data at all, and substantial idle capacity in the year analyzed make conclusions difficult to reach.

2473. ———. O comércio de manufacturas e a participação do trabalho especializado: o caso brasileiro (USP/EE, 2:5, out. 1972, p. 129-153, bibl., illus., tables)

Sets out to test Heckscher-Ohlin theory in Brazilian case, as expanded by Keesing to take account of human capital. Confirms that, as expected, Brazilian exports are less intensive in use of labor skills than Brazilian imports. However, skill composition of exports is found to be higher than that of several developed countries with much higher per capita incomes and skill endowments. Author explains this "paradox" by the high proportion of exports going to other lower-skill LAFTA countries, regional income and skill disparities within Brazil, natural resource endowment, and factor market distortions. Concludes that export growth could be enhanced if its composition were shifted toward lower skill-intensive products. Tyler's analysis is refuted in item 2460.

2474. United Nations. Economic Commission for Latin America. Secretariat. The manufacture of machine tools in Brazil (*in* Interregional Symposium on the Development of Metal-working Industries in Developing Countries, *Moscow, 1966.* Reports presented at the United Nations . . . Wien, United Nations Industrial Development Organization, 1969, p. 71-87, tables)

Evaluates current (1961) status of machine tool industry in Brazil in light of projected demands over 1960s. Unfortunately, study was out of date before publication date.

2475. Valla, Víctor. Os Estados Unidos e a influência estrangeira na economia brasileira: um período de transição–1904-1928; II (USP/RH, 43:87, 1971, p. 169-185 tables)

Describes shift in direction of Brazilian trade from Europe to the US that occurred during World War I. Article provides useful quick review of secondary sources but offers nothing new.

2476. Viacava, Carlos. Os bons frutos do café flexível (CDEP/R, jan./fev. 1971, p. 31-40, tables)

Outlines too briefly to be very useful recent modifications in domestic coffee policy made possible principally by tightened world market on one hand, and progressive diversification of Brazilian exports on the other.

2477. Vieira, Dorival Teixeira. O comerciário e o desenvolvimento econômico (Problemas Brasileiros [São Paulo] 8:87, nov. 1970, p. 5-21, plate, tables)

Brief review of state of commerce in Brazil and defense of social utility of merchant and his role in the development process.

2478. ———. Industrial development in Brazil (*in* Saunders, John ed. Modern Brazil [see item 126] p. 156-189, tables)

Disorganized hodgepodge of data of varying reliability on industrial growth since colonial period. Offers nothing new analytically, and most recent data are for 1963.

2479. Vieira, Francisca Isabel Schurig. O japonês na frente de expansão paulista: o processo de absorção do japonês em Marília. São Paulo, Editôra da Univ. de São Paulo, Livraria Pioneira Editôra, 1973. 270 p., bibl., maps, tables (Biblioteca Pioneira de ciências sociais: antropologia)

Pt. 1 traces history of Japanese immigration in Brazil in contexts both of Japanese economic development and expansion of coffee and cotton culture in São Paulo. Pt. 2 is an anthropological study of Japanese culture in Paulista city of Marília. For more on subject of Japanese in Brazil, see items 8513 and 8516.

2480. Weiss, Joseph S. The benefit of broader markets due to feeder roads and market news: Northeast Brazil. Ithaca, N.Y., Cornell Univ., Latin American Studies Program,

1971. 187 p., bibl., maps, tables (Dissertation series, 24)
Describes in detail farming and food marketing patterns in selected area in southern part of Pernambuco state and evaluates regional programs for construction and maintenance of rural roads and improved market information systems.

SPECIAL ARTICLE
AN ANNOTATED BIBLIOGRAPHY ON THE ECONOMY OF PUERTO RICO, 1969-1972

FUAT ANDIC and SUPHAN ANDIC

Professors of Economics
University of Puerto Rico, Río Piedras

THE PRESENT BIBLIOGRAPHY COVERS ESSENTIALLY the period 1969-72. The reader will note a few entries referring to earlier years. These are studies which have come to the attention of the compilers after the Puerto Rican section was published in *HLAS 31*, covering 1954-69. Again, the bibliography does not include any articles or books which aim at popular consumption, statistics, and official speeches. However, we have included this time, under separate listing, unpublished Ph.D. theses submitted to various U.S. universities from 1960 onwards.* Our justification in doing this is that they deal with very interesting aspects of the Puerto Rican economy (sometimes more so than the published works) and are usually accessible to the interested scholar from University Microfilms. (These entries have not been annotated.) We have also included a few mimeographed studies, some of which were at the pre-publication stage, and the others may never appear in black and white, simply because neither the professional journal world nor the book world is unfortunately commercially interested in specialized economic problems relating to very special economies. Most of the entries in this current bibliography are local publications.

The literature since 1968 reveals that the most popular topic is the problems afflicting the agricultural sector, especially the declining sugar industry, where the number of sugar mills has been reduced drastically, and where the government has taken over the administration of the majority of mills still remaining in operation. The literature is mainly dedicated to the rehabilitation program of the sugar industry and the effectiveness of the various types of subsidies and incentives that are given to increase productivity, sugar yield, and to maintain the level of income of sugar cane growers so as to prevent a mass exodus to the urban areas and the aggravation of the unemployment problem. In this sense Puerto Rico is not unique in the Caribbean region where other islands are going through a similar dismal experience.

Despite the existence of relatively high level of unemployment in the economy, especially aggravated by the developments in the agricultural sector, the past recession in the U.S. economy, and the structural changes that are taking place in the world economy which cause the relocation of industries with different degrees of labor intensity, there is no serious attempt at a critical analysis of the problem. The few entries relating to the area are descriptive, being brief explanations based on statistics compiled by the Department of Labor. There is, however, serious attention given to the consequences of the discrepancy between the availability and need for skilled human resources as required by the industrial development of the island. There is also some attention given to education and human capital formation, but not, in the eyes of the compilers, as much as the subject matter deserves.

* These are taken from: Enid M. Baa *comp*. Theses on Caribbean topics: 1778-1968. San Juan, Univ. of Puerto Rico, Institute of Caribbean Studies, 1970 (Caribbean Bibliographic Series, 1), and brought up to date till 1971.

Development and the role of financial institutions in such development still receive some attention. But it may not be too wrong to predict a change of emphasis from financial institutions towards subjects dealing with fiscal, budgetary and tax reform and cost-effectiveness of the various programs of government agencies. One such entry is the study of Keller of government-operated birth control clinics. There are two good studies on the regulation of the transportation industry, one dealing with land and the other with maritime shipments. (There are others that the compilers are aware of, such as the CAB report on airlines, and the study on cement industry of the island, but they are unfortunately not made public.) The inflationary developments of the past years and the present concern with the maintenance of price levels of basic consumer items, we hope, will be sufficient incentive for scholars to have an analytical look into the workings of market structures and their implications for public intervention.

DOCTORAL DISSERTATIONS
1960-1971

Ason, Elías Raúl. An econometric model of the Puerto Rican banking sector. Univ. of California, Berkeley, 1970.

Bonnick, Gladstone C. The United States Sugar Acts: effects on Puerto Rican sugar cane output. Univ. of Chicago, 1965.

Bothwell, Lynn Dutton. Capital formation in Puerto Rico, 1950-60. George Washington Univ., 1964.

Carey, George Warren. The application of vectors and correlation analysis to the study of the urban economic geography of Mayagüez, Puerto Rico. Columbia Univ., 1964.

Carpenter, Bruce Rogers. Puerto Rico's planned development of tourism. American Univ., 1964.

Coley, Basil Glasford. A comparative analysis of some factors affecting economic growth in Jamaica and Puerto Rico, 1959-1967. Univ. of Illinois, Urbana-Champaign, 1971.

Collins, Jerome Fiske. An investigation and multivariate analysis of industrial location: Puerto Rico, a case study. New York Univ., 1970.

Di Paolo, Gordon Anthony. The marketing planning for industrial promotion of the Economic Development Administration of Puerto Rico. New York Univ., 1970.

Díaz-Rojas, Armando. Financing economic development in Puerto Rico, 1942 to date. New York Univ., 1964.

Drass, Robert E., Jr. Industrialization and stratification change in Puerto Rico. Northwestern Univ., 1970.

Ellison, John Neil. The impact of tax exemption and minimum wage policy on industry structure in an inter-regional setting: the case of Puerto Rico and the U.S. mainland. George Washington Univ., 1969.

Estrella, Arturo. Anti-trust law in Puerto Rico: a study on the interplay of federal and local legislation. George Washington Univ., 1967.

Fleisher, Belton Mendel. Some economic aspects of Puerto Rican migration to the United States. Stanford Univ., 1962.

Fuerst, Alfred Meir. Economic development with special attention to the role played by human capital: the cases of Israel and Puerto Rico. New York Univ., 1970.

Goldsmith, William Woodbridge. The impact of the tourism and travel industry on a developing regional economy: The Puerto Rican case. Cornell Univ., 1968.

González, Luis Manuel. The economic development of Puerto Rico from 1898 to 1940. Univ. of Florida, 1965.

Gosfield, Amor. Input-output theory and its application, with special reference to an underdeveloped economy: the case of Puerto Rico. Univ. of Pennsylvania, 1965.

Gray, Lois S. Economic incentives to labor mobility: the Puerto Rican case. Columbia Univ., 1966.

Griffith, Rosemary Coward. Factors affecting continental United States manufacturing investment in Puerto Rico. Radcliffe College, 1961.

Harrison, Kelly Max. Agricultural market coordination in the economic development of Puerto Rico. Univ. of Michigan, 1966.

Hernández, Nicolás. The entrepreneurial role of the government in the economic development of Puerto Rico. Rutgers Univ., 1965.

Imus, Harold R. The Mayagüez area: a study in farm economy analysis. Northwestern Univ., 1966.

Lange, Irene Lydia. Marketing institutions in the economic development of Puerto Rico, 1950-1964. Univ. of Illinois, 1968.

Lee, Hy Sang. The entrepreneurial activities of the government in the economic development of Puerto Rico. Univ. of Wisconsin, 1965.

McElheny, John Richard. Puerto Rico: industrial education, 1948-1958; a descriptive and evaluative report on the program in "Operation Bootstrap." Ohio State Univ., 1960.

Macisco, John J., Jr. Internal migration in Puerto Rico, 1955-1960. Brown Univ., 1966.

Mingo, John Jerald. Labor mobility, capital importation and economic growth: the case of post-war Puerto Rico. Brown Univ., 1970.

Mings, Robert Charles. The role of the Commonwealth government in the growth and development of the Puerto Rican tourist industry. Ohio State Univ., 1966.

Pringle, George Edward. A temporal-spatial analysis of sugar production and marketing in Puerto Rico. The Univ. of Wisconsin, 1969.

Ramírez Pérez, Miguel A. Functional distribution in Puerto Rico: 1947-1966. Rutgers Univ., 1970.

Sáenz, Michael. Economic aspects of church development in Puerto Rico. Univ. of Pennsylvania, 1961.

Sánchez Aran, Frank. Financial aspects of economic development in Puerto Rico. New York Univ., 1963.

Schlenker, Robert Erwin. Health improvements and economic growth: neo-classical theory and Puerto Rican experience. Univ. of Michigan, 1968.

Segarra Ortiz, Hilda. Relationship of non-economic variables of saving of farm families in a Puerto Rican county. Cornell Univ., 1969.

Seplowin, Virginia M. Training and employment patterns of Puerto Ricans in Philadelphia. Univ. of Pennsylvania, 1967.

Silva Recio, Luis Fernando. Public wage fixing and its effect on collective bargaining and the labor movement in Puerto Rico. Univ. of Wisconsin, 1962.

Stahl, John Emery. Economic development through land reform in Puerto Rico. Iowa State Univ. of Science and Technology, 1966.

Weller, Robert Hubert. Female work experience and fertility in San Juan, Puerto Rico; a study of selected lower and middle income neighborhoods. Cornell Univ., 1967.

Wisdom, Harold Walter. Public forestry investment criteria for Puerto Rico. Syracuse Univ., 1967.

Zalduondo, Baltazara Colón de. The saving and consumption variables in the growing Puerto Rican economy. Rutgers Univ., 1971.

2481. Andic, Fuat M. Phases of fiscal reform: the case of Puerto Rico (Finanzarchiv [Tübingen, FRG] 31:2, 1972, p. 310-325, tables)

There has been no serious attempt to study, review, evaluate and reform the fiscal system despite the revolutionary changes in the structure of the Puerto Rican economy. Article makes a case for a continuous process of comprehensive reviews of the fiscal system as socio-politico-economic terms of reference change.

2482. Andic, Fuat; Luz M. Torruellas; and Suphan Andic. Economic and fiscal implications of the presidential vote (*in* Six special studies requested for the Ad Hoc Advisory Group on the Presidential Vote for Puerto Rico. Washington, GPO, 1971, p. 1-43)

Analyzes—within the existing set of political-economic relationships and considering way in which these have shaped the island's economic growth and determined amount of her fiscal resources—economic and fiscal implications of the possibility of voting for the US President on said relationships.

2483. Bagué Ramírez, Jaime. Movimientos de reforma agraria en Puerto Rico (Revista de Agricultura de Puerto Rico [San Juan] 55:12, enero/dic. 1968, p. 1-133)

History of agrarian reform in Puerto Rico from 1510 to 1961.

2484. Cappalli, Richard B. Federal financing in the Commonwealth of Puerto Rico (UPR/RJ, 39:1, 1970, p. 7-146)

Comprehensive examination and analysis of federal aid, its impact and effect on local politics and government and its significance for the economic development of the island.

2485. ———. The potential impact of the presidential vote on Puerto Rico's participation in Federal Aid Programs (*in* Six special studies requested for the Ad Hoc Advisory Group on the Presidential Vote for Puerto Rico. Washington, 1971, p. 44-55)

Evaluation of the effect of the presidential vote in Puerto Rico's participation in federal aid programs in terms of quantity of aid as well as its effectiveness and efficiency.

2486. Castañeda, Rolando and José A. Herrero. La no-planificación y la planificación de Puerto Rico a lo Picó (UPR/RCS, 15:1, marzo 1971, p. 135-141)

The economic growth of Puerto Rico is due not to integral planning but to the special situation of its economic relations with the US.

2487. Chenery, Hollis B. Comparative advantage and development policy (AEA/AER, 51:1, March 1961, p. 18-51)

In passim: reference to the application of dynamic comparative advantage theory in the promotion of industrial development of Puerto Rico.

2488. Choudhry, Parimal. Let's save the sugar industry (Industrial Puerto Rico [San Juan] 8:6, Winter 1971/1972, p. 14-16)

2489. Corrado, Rafael. Hacia una estrategia de desarrollo urbano para Puerto Rico (Plerus [Graduate School of Planning, Univ. of Puerto Rico, Río Piedras] 5:1, junio 1961, p. 15-40)

Compares actual population distribution with one which would be required by the predictable development of Puerto Rico. Planning of population distribution according to development requirements has serious ideological difficulties. Nevertheless, such a strategy, together with other planning instruments, would prevent or correct socio-economic maladjustments which would be provoked if population distribution were not to coincide with the distribution of industrialized regions.

2490. Dam, Kenneth. Implementation of import quotas: the case of oil (The Journal of Law and Economics [Chicago, Ill.] 14:1, April 1971, p. 1-60)

In passim: a very brief description of the special deal granted to Puerto Rico in a general discussion of the US mandatory oil import quota program.

2491. Duke, Keith S. and others. Development of tourism in the Commonwealth of Puerto Rico. Prepared for the Economic Development Administration of Puerto Rico. South Pasadena, Calif., Stanford Research Institute, 1968. 7 v. (144, 108, 178, 76, 85, 41, 25 p.) tables.

Study on tourism's role in and its long-range impact on the economy with emphasis on evaluation of alternative development programs for the sector. Extensive reliance is based on survey methods for data gathering and as the basis of interpretive analysis. Three appendices discuss the sources of unpublished material, data collection and analysis, and a mathematical model of simulation.

2492. Dutta, M. and P. L. Sharma. Alternative estimators and predictive power of alternative estimators: an econometric model of Puerto Rico. New Brunswick, N.J., Rutgers Univ., 1972. 50 l. (Bureau of Economic Research. Discussion paper 13)

Title of paper is misleading: the study is not an econometric model of Puerto Rico but a statistical exercise in testing the predictive power of various estimators using data from Puerto Rico.

2493. Echenique, Miguel. La problemática del desempleo en Puerto Rico (Revista del Trabajo [San Juan] 1:3, julio/agosto 1968, p. 13-26)

2494. Espinet Colón, Gabriel R. Producción y estructura del mercado de cítricas en Puerto Rico. Río Piedras, P.R., Univ. de Puerto Rico, Estación Experimental Agrícola, 1969. 52 p. (Boletín, 215)

Analyzes practices, problems and market structure of the citrus fruits of major economic importance in Puerto Rico. Three phases of the distribution channels are studied in more detail: a) sales by trucker-vendors; b) sales at supermarkets; and c) sales at the main fresh-produce markets.

2495. Freyre, Jorge F. Comentarios en torno a la capacidad de absorción de capital externo de la economía puertorriqueña (UPR/RCS, 10:2, june 1966, p. 167-195, tables)

Critique of J. Baquero's "La Importación de Fondos Externos y la Capacidad Absorbente de Nuestra Economía" in *Revista de Ciencias Sociales* (Univ. de Puerto Rico, 7:1/2, marzo/junio 1963, p. 79-90). Author tries to demonstrate that the formula Baquero uses to measure the excess funds with regard to Puerto Rico's absorptive capacity leads to results which lack analytical meaning and proposes alternative methods of measuring the efficiency in the utilization of external capital.

2496. ———. Possible effects of the presidential vote on the inflows of external capital to

Puerto Rico (*in* Six special studies requested for the Ad Hoc Advisory Group on the Presidential Vote for Puerto Rico. Washington, GPO, 1971. p. 56-73)

Extraordinary growth rates attained by the Puerto Rican economy during the post-war period have been induced largely by a substantial influx of external investments. Although economic analysis cannot provide a categoric answer, it can be expected that the presidential vote will have an overall favorable impact upon such investments, if it is assumed that other aspects of the present institutional, political and economic environment are not altered by such a political action.

2497. Gil-Bermejo García, Juana. Panorama histórico de la agricultura en Puerto Rico. Sevilla, Escuela de Estudios Hispano-Americanos [and] Instituto de Cultura Puertorriqueña, 1970. 381 p.

2498. González Tejera, Efraín. Transportation in Puerto Rico: a search for new regulatory philosophy. Río Piedras, P.R., Univ. de Puerto Rico, Instituto de Investigaciones de Problemas del Consumidor, 1971. 306 p.

Considering the highly "competitive" nature of the industry, absence of barriers to entry, existence of excess capacity, and lack of economies of scale (which imply inefficient use and allocation of resources, according to author) book calls for regulation of transport industry in Puerto Rico only with respect to safer equipment and operation, adequate financial responsibility, protection of roads and minimizing traffic congestion in the community interest. Concludes that rate fixing, entry control etc., are not in the public interest and that market place competition premised on costs and quality of service is a more appropriate vehicle to resolve issues than government regulation.

2499. Gonzalez Villafañe, Edgardo and others. Costos e ingresos relacionados con la producción de plátanos. Puerto Rico, 1966-67. Río Piedras, P.R., Univ. de Puerto Rico, Estación Experimental Agrícola, 1970. 17 p. (Boletín, 220)

Determines costs, returns and marketing problems related to production of plantains in Puerto Rico. Most important marketing problems faced by farmers were lack of stability in selling prices, difficulty in finding buyers for their product, and lack of proper transportation facilities.

2500. Haszard, Frank K. The taxation of capital gains in Puerto Rico (Bulletin for International Fiscal Documentation [Amsterdam] 23:5, Oct. 1969, p. 488-490)

Synopsis of 1966 changes in the taxation of capital gains and their complexity.

2501. Hernández-Alvarez, José. Migration, return, and development in Puerto Rico (UC/EDCC, 16:4, July 1968, p. 574-587, tables)

Two factors largely explain the return migration to the island in the late 1950s: the push factor of mechanization and automation in tasks performed by Puerto Ricans in the US, and the pull factor of demand created for professionals, managers, and skilled workers by the establishment in Puerto Rico of industries based on the secondary elaboration of imported materials. For a version of ch. 5 see *HLAS 31:9067*.

2502. Herrero, José A., and Rolando Castañeda. Efectos de la legislación sobre salario mínimo en las tasas de crecimiento y empleo en la economía de Puerto Rico (Plerus [Graduate School of Planning, Univ. of Puerto Rico, Río Piedras] 5:2, dic. 1971, p. 87-117)

Using an econometric model specifically constructed for the purpose, it is found that present policy of raising minimum wages has led to price increases resulting from oligopolistic structure of local production. Nevertheless, economy has succeeded in achieving a real per capita growth rate of six percent in GDP. Article notes that labor protectionism of minimum wage legislation also leads to a less equitable distribution of income.

2503. Huetz de Lemps, Christian. La place des plantations dans l'économie portoricaine (SGB/COM, 24:96, oct./déc. 1971, p. 329-393, plates, tables)

History of the development of sugar plantations accompanied by discussion of the economic problems facing them, their reasons, and of public policy for rehabilitation. Such public policy also extends to the areas of coffee and tobacco.

2504. Kelly, William J. A cost-effectiveness study of clinical methods of birth control: with special reference to Puerto Rico. N.Y., Praeger Publishers 1972. 150 p., bibl., tables (Praeger special studies in international economics and development)

Presents a general method of calculating the marginal cost of birth prevention with different method-user combinations and applies it to a program in several government-operated clinics in Puerto Rico. Determines relative costs of different method-user combinations, the least-cost combination of labor and capital inputs, and the optimal clinic capacity.

2505. Maldonado, Rita Marinita. The role of the financial sector in the economic development of Puerto Rico. n.p., Federal Deposit Insurance Corporation, 1970. 1152 p.

Attempt to analyze and evaluate role played by financial institutions, both private and public, in the economic development of Puerto Rico. Main emphasis is on significance of saving-investment process that takes place through these intermediaries. Concludes that banking system has been successful in eliciting savings from a public reluctant to save at all, but that it has not played as prominent a role in financing industrial capital formation.

2506. Meléndez, Jaime Santiago. Política económica pública en Puerto Rico (Revista de Administración Pública [Univ. de Puerto Rico, Río Piedras] 5:1, marzo 1972, p. 157-162)

2507. Mihaly, Z. M. Tax aspects of Puerto Rican manufacturing operations. Oxford, N.H., Equity Publishing Corp., 1968. 149 p.

Description and explanation of the tax rules applicable to profits from manufacturing operations in Puerto Rico.

2508. National Academy of Sciences. National Academy of Engineering. The report on Puerto Rico's agriculture to the Governor (Industrial Puerto Rico [San Juan] 5:5, Sept./Oct. 1968, p. 47-51)

Odell, Peter R. A European view on regional development and planning in Latin America. See item 1855.

2509. Picó, Rafael. La estrategia de planificación en Puerto Rico (Revista de la Sociedad Interamericana de Planificación [Cali, Co.] 2:7, sept. 1968, p. 50-56)

2510. Puerto Rico. Junta de Planificación. Informe de recursos humanos al gobernador. San Juan, 1971, 224 p., tables.

Review of population characteristics, labor migration, employment and unemployment, human resources, health, education and housing.

2511. The Puerto Rican Sugar industry: rehabilitation providing design for future (Sugar y Azúcar [N.Y.] 65:5, May 1970, p. 31-32; 53-54)

Includes English version, p. 31-32; Spanish, p. 53-54.

2512. Ramírez Pérez, Miguel A. Los gastos en educación en Puerto Rico como inversión en capital social (Pedagogía [Río Piedras, P.R.] 17:2, julio/dic. 1969, p. 131-142)

2513. ———. Government investment, fixed and human capital, and economic growth in Puerto Rico. Río Piedras, P.R., Univ. of Puerto Rico, Center for Educational Research, 1969. 72 l., tables.

Brief examination of process of economic growth as can be inferred from secular magnitudes and trends present in statistical data on prices, capital accumulation, investment in human capital, external trade, labor productivity, and output levels.

2514. ———. Inferencias sobre economía gubernamental en el estudio de economía del Departamento de Salud (UPR/RCS, 12:2, junio 1968, p. 173-193)

Main constraint on the performance of the Dept. of Health of the Government of Puerto Rico is its archaic system of operations. This antiquated organization is caused by the absence of systematic economic studies of government performance.

2515. ———. El informe de economía en el gobierno y la ausencia del estudio sistemático de la economía gubernamental en Puerto Rico (UPR/RCS, 11:2, junio 1967, p. 147-160)

Criticism of 1967 Report of the Citizen's Committee on Efficiency in Government and discussion of basic guide-lines for a systematic economic analysis of public sector activities. The paper is in very general terms.

2516. Riollano, Arturo. A progress report on the rehabilitation of the Puerto Rican sugar industry (Sugar y Azúcar [N.Y.] 65:11, Nov. 1970, p. 34-35; 60-61)

English version, p. 34-35; Spanish, p. 60-61.

2517. Rivera Brenes, Luis. Puerto Rico moves back to sugar (Sugar y Azúcar [N.Y.] 64:11, Nov. 1969, p. 40-42; p. 74-76)

Outline of the new rehabilitation program for the sugar industry. English version, p. 40-42; Spanish, p. 74-76.

2518. Stahl, John E. The economic performance of proportional profit sugar farms in Puerto Rico, 1950-62. Washington, U.S. Dept. of Agriculture, Economic Research Service, 1971. 35 p., bibl., tables.

Econometric study of the economic performance of proportional-profit sugar farms, where net income is distributed to farm labor in proportion to wages received. Concludes that such farms were not able to maintain efficient performance levels over the 13-year period: losses increased and total net returns declined. One of the most important reasons for the poor performance was the use of more capital and labor than economically justified when measured in terms of operating efficiency. However, total sugar output was maintained and employment opportunities were provided in a period of substantial unemployment. Thus, the social impact of the program was considered more important than the maintenance of efficient production, the achievement of which was made further difficult by the mandatory distribution of profits to workers. Since wages on farms were the same as in sugar industry as a whole, workers would have suffered no relative welfare decline without profit sharing. However, the program would have been politically unacceptable without this feature, which very likely had a dampening effect on growth in total income during the period since labor income has a high marginal propensity to consume. This may be an acceptable price for achieving a distribution of income more heavily weighted to labor.

2519. Tirado, Irma G. Programme budget proposals for the Department of Education in Puerto Rico (UPR/CS, 11:4, Jan. 1972, p. 60-72)

Develops a program-oriented structure for the presentation of the budget of the Dept. of Education, reflecting the allocation of resources to objectives adopted.

2520. Torruellas, Luz María. Necesidades presentes y futuras de recursos humanos en ocupaciones técnicas, diestras y clericales (UPR/RCS, 16:2, junio 1972, p. 263-284)

Surveys conducted among employers in different industrial sectors and among teachers of vocational schools and analysis of statistics on vocational training programs and job openings as registered by employers reveal that as economic growth continues Puerto Rico will be facing an ever increasing demand for human resources with specialized skills. Present vocational and training programs will not suffice to meet this demand unless steps are taken taken to expand them substantially.

2521. ———. Puerto Rico's present and prospective technical, skilled and clerical manpower and training needs, 1968-1975. San

Juan, Univ. de Puerto Rico, Social Sciences Research Center, 1971. 342 p., tables (mimeo)

Full version of the report to the Area for Vocational and Technical Education of the Commonwealth Dept. of Education. Report forms basis of item 2520. Includes appendices.

2522. United States. Federal Maritime Commission. Bureau of Domestic Regulation. Puerto Rican-Virgin Islands trade study. Washington, GPO, 1970. 251 p.

An analysis primarily concerned with ocean transportation, terminal, and trucking services; their costs and economic effects in the two trade areas. The high degree of competition in transportation has led to capital intensive technological advances and an efficient pattern of services. Possibilities of regulation over entry to an exit from the trade should be examined in the public interest, especially in view of expected expansion in demand as a function of growth in population, production and incomes. There appears to be an increasing need for more efficient rate structures to accomodate the large containerships which are altering traffic patterns in trade. Adherence to traditional rate structures may restrain the ultimate efficiencies inherent in containerization, the evolution of through rates, as well as inhibit the ultimate simplification of rate structures. Flat dollar charges per container rates potentially offer greater efficiencies, but will have to allow for differentials according to the importance of goods. Freight rate charges do not appear to be as significant as other factors in the final selling price of most essential foods, but have a substantial effect on the selling price of many intermediate goods of extreme importance to the industrialization process. The distribution of goods within Puerto Rico is dominated by one-truck operators, many of which are unregulated. The latter makes difficult the prescription and enforcement of accounting and reporting requirements, determination of appropriate rate levels, the policing of tariff requirements, and inspection and enforcement of safety requirements. This also has contributed to inefficiency, underutilization of equipment, and rate cutting below economically justifiable levels.

2523. Vázquez Calcerrada, Pablo B. and **J. Belcher.** La vivienda y el cambio social en un municipio en el sur de Puerto Rico (UPR/RCS, 15:1, marzo 1971, p. 5-59)

Study indicates that the improvement of housing conditions was chief interest of both urban and rural population. Thus, social change must be based on housing improvement as an initial phase of development

2524. Vilches, Rubén A. Comentarios sobre la situación de desempleo en Puerto Rico (Revista del Trabajo [San Juan, P.R.]3:13/14, enero/junio 1971, p. 1-80)

2525. ———. Empleo y subempleo en Puerto Rico (Revista del Trabajo [San Juan] 1:3, julio/agosto 1968, p. 1-12)

2526. Villar Roces, Mario. Puerto Rico y su reforma agraria. Río Piedras, P.R., Editorial Edil, 1968. 196 p., tables.

2527. Wagenheim, Kal. Puerto Rico: a profile. N.Y., Praeger Publishers, 1970. 416 p., bibl., illus., maps.

Ch. 5 presents in 35 p. a journalistic journey into all the aspects of the economy over the past 70 years. Includes chronology and index.

2528. Weisskoff, Richard. Income distribution and economic growth in Puerto Rico, Argentina, and Mexico (The Review of Income and Wealth [New Haven, Conn.] 16:4, Dec. 1970, p. 303-332, bibl., tables)

Following a brief review of advantages and deficiencies of several traditional measures of income distribution, article examines evidence in three countries. Income shares received by the lower half and by the top five percent of families in Puerto Rico have declined from 1953 to 1963. The rising Gini ratio and standard deviation of the logs of income, coefficient of variation. All the summary measures indicate that there was greater equality within agriculture than non-agriculture in 1953. By 1963 the distribution in both broad sectors had become more unequal. One reason for greater inequality in agriculture is believed to be the decline in the importance of sugar cane, the contraction of the marginal cane farmer, and higher negotiated enforced wages in contrast to other agricultural activities. The results of any statistical analysis are as good as the statistics themselves. A look at the 1950 and 1960 census data would have shown results contrary to those found by author. The 1970 census data should shed further light on the problem.

2529. Wish, John Reed and **Kelly M. Harrison.** Marketing, one answer to poverty: food and marketing and economic development in Puerto Rico, 1950-1965. Eugene, Ore., Univ. of Oregon, 1969. 191 p. (Business publications, 3)

Statistical analysis of innovative behavior among food retailers and farmers helping to explain the variables associated with those persons or firms most likely to bring about change.

JOURNAL ABBREVIATIONS

ABM/RB	Revista Bancaria. Asociación de Banqueros de México. México.
AEA/AER	American Economic Review. American Economic Association. Evanston, Ill.
AIA/A	Archaeology. Archaeological Institute of America. N.Y.
AIFLD/R	A.I.F.L.D. Review. American Institute for Free Labor Development. Washington.
AJES	The American Journal of Economics and Sociology. N.Y.
ANI/RT	Revista Trimestral. Asociación Nacional de Industriales. Medellín, Co.
ARBOR	Arbor. Revista general de investigación y cultura. Madrid.

ASIL/J	American Journal of International Law. American Society of International Law. Washington.
BCV/REL	Revista de Economía Latinoamericana. Banco Central de Venezuela. Caracas.
BHEL/R	Revista del Banco Hipotecario de El Salvador. San Salvador.
BLSA/QR	See BLSAL/QR.
BLSAL/QR	Quarterly Review. Bank of London and South America. London.
BUS	Boletin Uruguayo de Sociología. Montevideo.
CAUK/WA	Weltwirtschaftliches Archiv. Zeitschrift des Instituts für Weltwirtschaft an der Christians-Albrechts-Univ. Kiel. Kiel, FRG.
CDAL	Cahiers des Amériques Latines. Paris.
CDEP/R	Revista Paranaense de Desenvolvimento. Companhia de Desenvolvimento Econômico do Paraná (CODEPAR). Curitiba, Bra.
CESN/DE	De Economía. Revista de temas económicos. Consejo Económico Sindical Nacional. Madrid.
CFR/CA	Foreign Affairs. An American quarterly review. Council on Foreign Relations. N.Y.
CIDG/O	Orbis. Bulletin international de documentation linguistique. Centre International de Dialectologie Générale. Louvain, Belgium.
CLAPCS/AL	América Latina. Centro Latino-Americano de Pesquisas em Ciências Sociais. Rio.
CM/FI	Foro Internacional. El Colegio de México. México.
CPES/RPS	Revista Paraguaya de Sociología. Centro Paraguayo de Estudios Sociológicos. Asunción.
CU/EG	Economic Geography. Clark Univ. Worcester, Mass.
DPB/RICS	Revista del Instituto de Ciencias Sociales. Diputación Provincial de Barcelona. Barcelona, Spain.
FCT/TE	El Trimestre Económico. Fondo de Cultura Económica. México.
FDD/NED	Notes et Études Documentaires. Direction de la Documentation. Paris.
FGV/RAE	Revista de Administração de Empresas. Fundação Getúlio Vargas, Instituto de Documentação. São Paulo.
IAMEA	Inter-American Economic Affairs. Washington.
IASI/E	Estadística. Journal of the Inter-American Statistical Institute. Washington.
IBE/RBE	Revista Brasileira de Economia. Fundação Getúlio Vargas, Instituto Brasileiro de Economia. Rio.
IBEAS/EA	Estudios Andinos. Instituto Boliviano de Estudio y Acción Social. La Paz.
IDES/DE	Desarrollo Económico. Instituto de Desarrollo Económico y Social. B.A.
IEP/REP	Revista de Estudios Políticos. Instituto de Estudios Políticos. Madrid.
IEP/RPI	Revista de Política Internacional. Instituto de Estudios Políticos. Madrid.
IESSC/C	Comunidades. Instituto de Estudios Sindicales, Sociales y Cooperativos, Centro de Prospección Social. Madrid.
IFH/C	Conjonction. Revue franco-haïtienne. Institut Français d'Haïti. Port-au-Prince.
IFSNC/CD	Community Development. International Federation of Settlements and Neighborhood Centres. Roma.
IIDC/C	Civilisations. International Institute of Differing Civilizations. Bruxelles.
ILARI/A	Aportes. Instituto Latinoamericano de Relaciones Internacionales. Paris.
ILO/R	International Labour Review. International Labour Office. Genève.
IPEA/PP	Pesquisa e Planejamento. Instituto de Planejamento Econômico e Social. Rio.
IPI/PI	Política Internacional. Ministerio de Relaciones Exteriores, Instituto de Política Internacional. La Habana.
IRFDH/DC	Développement et Civilisations. Institut de Recherche et de Formation en vue du Développement Harmonisé. Paris.
ISEA/EA	Économie Appliquée. Archives de l'Institut de Science Économique Appliquée. Vendôme, France.
JDA	The Journal of Developing Areas. Western Illinois Univ. Press. Macomb, Ill.
JLAS	Journal of Latin American Studies. Centers or institutes of Latin American

	studies at the Universities of Cambridge, Glasgow, Liverpool, London and Oxford. Cambridge Univ. Press. London.
JPE	Journal of Political Economy. Univ. of Chicago. Chicago, Ill.
MMFQ	Milbank Memorial Fund Quarterly. N.Y.
MR	Monthly Review. An independent Socialist magazine. N.Y.
NGIZ/IS	Internationale Spectator. Tijdschrift voor internationale politiek. Het Nederlandsch Genootschap voor Internationale Zaken. The Hague.
NTA/NTJ	National Tax Journal. National Tax Association [and] Fund for Public Policy Research. Washington.
OUP/OEP	Oxford Economic Papers. Oxford Univ. Press. London.
PAA/D	Demography. Population Association of America. Chicago, Ill.
PAPS	Proceedings of the Academy of Political Science. The Academy of Political Science [and] Columbia Univ. N.Y.
RCPC	Revista Conservadora del Pensamiento Centroamericano. Managua.
SGB/COM	Les Cahiers d'Outre-Mer. Publiée par l'Institut de Géographie de la Faculté des Lettres de Bordeaux, par l'Institut de la France d'Outre-Mer, par la Société de Géographie de Bordeaux *avec le concours* du Centre National de la Recherche Scientifique et de la VIième Section de l'École Pratique des Hautes Études. Bordeaux, France.
SS	Science and Society. An independent journal of Marxism. N.Y.
UC/EDCC	Economic Development and Cultural Change. Univ. of Chicago, Research Center in Economic Development and Cultural Change. Chicago, Ill.
UCC/CE	Cuadernos de Economía. Univ. Católica de Chile. Santiago.
UCIEI/EI	Estudios Internacionales. Univ. de Chile, Instituto de Estudios Internacionales. Santiago.
UCV/ECS	Economía y Ciencias Sociales. Univ. Central de Venezuela, Facultad de Economía. Caracas.
ULAFE/E	Economía. Univ. de Los Andes, Facultad de Economía. Mérida, Ven.
ULIG/C	Cahiers de Géographie de Québec. Univ. Laval, Institut de Géographie. Québec, Canada.
UM/JIAS	Journal of Inter-American Studies and World Affairs. Univ. of Miami Press *for the* Center for Advanced International Studies. Coral Gables, Fla.
UMG/RBEP	Revista Brasileira de Estudos Políticos. Univ. de Minas Gerais. Belo Horizonte, Bra.
UN/ISSJ	International Social Science Journal. United Nations Educational, Scientific, and Cultural Organization. Paris.
UNAM/BCRI	Boletín del Centro de Relaciones Internacionales. Univ. Nacional Autónoma de México, Facultad de Ciencias Políticas y Sociales. México.
UNAM/IE	Investigación Económica. Univ. Nacional Autónoma de México, Escuela Nacional de Economía. México.
UNC/R	Revista de la Universidad Nacional de Córdoba. Córdoba, Arg.
UNC/REE	Revista de Economía y Estadística. Univ. Nacional de Córdoba, Facultad de Ciencias Económicas. Córdoba, Arg.
UNECLA/B	Economic Bulletin for Latin America. United Nations, Economic Commission for Latin America. N.Y.
UNESCO/I	Impact of Science on Society. United Nations Educational, Scientific and Cultural Organization. Paris.
UNLP/E	Económica. Univ. Nacional de La Plata, Facultad de Ciencias Económicas, Instituto de Investigaciones Económicas. La Plata, Arg.
UP/TM	Tiers Monde. Problèmes des pays sous-développés. Univ. de Paris, Institut d-Étude du Développement Économique et Social. Paris.
UPR/CS	Caribbean Studies. Univ. of Puerto Rico, Institute of Caribbean Studies. Río Piedras, P.R.
UPR/RCS	Revista de Ciencias Sociales. Univ. de Puerto Rico, Colegio de Ciencias Sociales. Río Piedras, P.R.
UPR/RJ	Revista Jurídica de la Universidad de Puerto Rico. Univ. de Puerto Rico. Río Piedras, P.R.
UR/RFCE	See UR/RFCEA.
UR/RFCEA	Revista de la Facultad de Ciencias Económicas y de Administración. Univ. de la República. Montevideo.

USIA/PC	Problems of Communism. United States Information Agency. Washington.
USM/RCEC	Revista de la Facultad de Ciencias Económicas y Comerciales. Univ. Nacional Mayor de San Marcos. Lima.
USP/EE	Estudos Econômicos. Univ. de São Paulo, Instituto de Pesquisas Econômicas. São Paulo.
USP/RH	Revista de História. Univ. de São Paulo, Faculdade de Filosofia, Ciências e Letras, Depto. de História [and] Sociedade de Estudos Históricos. São Paulo.
UW/LE	Land Economics. A quarterly journal of planning, housing and public utilities. Univ. of Wisconsin. Madison, Wis.
UWI/CQ	Caribbean Quarterly. Univ. of the West Indies. Mona, Jam.
UWI/SES	Social and Economic Studies. Univ. of the West Indies, Institute of Social and Economic Research. Mona, Jam.

Education

LATIN AMERICA
(Except Brazil)

GORDON C. RUSCOE

Professor
School of Education
Syracuse University

With the Assistance of Everett Egginton and Terry Bullitt
(Research Assistants, School of Education)

THERE SEEMS TO BE NO SINGLE DESCRIPTOR by which to categorize this year's collection of items on education. As might be expected, a major part of the items deal with higher education and with education and development, but even in these two cases there is little to tie the various items together. In general, the surge of "hard data" of four years ago and the CIDOC-inspired arguments of two years ago have largely disappeared. Instead, many of the items are rather humdrum, conventional pieces that do not do much to advance our knowledge or understanding of education in the region. Be that as it may, we will discuss briefly some of the major kinds of items available.

Among the items which deal in general with Latin America, La Belle's anthology (item 6038) and Silvert's survey (item 6054) deserve mention. Case studies of Ecuador (item 6143), Peru (item 6174), the West Indies (item 6195) and Central America (item 6104) add to our knowledge of these areas, as do somewhat less ambitious studies of El Salvador (item 6095), Costa Rica (item 6100), Argentina (item 6072), Paraguay (item 6167), Colombia (item 6134), and Puerto Rico (item 6196).

As usual, the largest single group of items deals with higher education, particularly university education. Indeed, these account for approximately one-third of the items examined for this volume. Among the specific pieces on universities, the King and others (item 6155) in-depth study of Mexican provincial universities is unusual in its provision of extensive data on these institutions. Chilean universities continue to be a focus of attention and a source of data (items 6110, 6113, 6116-6118, and 6122). In particular, documents on recent university reform movements (items 6105 and 6119) and Lechner's critique of Sunkel (item 6040) merit reading. Colombia, too, has received a good deal of attention (items 6026, 6123, 6125, 6131, 6133, 6138, and 6185 for example), and "crisis" would seem to be the most commonly applied term to describe the situation in that country. Of particular note is Rama's (item 6132) contention that elite recruitment is increasingly from private universities and on social rather than pedagogical bases; and appeals by private education for greater government assistance (items 6130 and 6139).

Peru (items 6171 and 6176) and Uruguay (item 6182) offer some debate on the government's role in higher education; while Uzcátegui's (item 6103) account of his role as UNESCO advisor in El Salvador is worth examining.

Individuals concerned with the role of universities offer a variety of remedies. Two well-known thinkers, Risieri Frondizi (item 6020) and Leopoldo Zea (item 6164), argue that the university must change. Frondizi urges that the university become one of the primary agents of radical reform but that internal reform must come first. Zea, looking principally at Mexican education, argues that the mission of the university has changed from one of service to the individual to one of service to the society. Wright (item 6070) stresses the difference between those who favor reforms to upgrade academic quality and those who favor continued Córdoba-type reforms. Perhaps representative of the latter group are Giner de los Ríos (item 6027), Mendoza (item 6185), Ikonicoff (item 6035) and Tolentino (item 6059), all of whom argue for a politically active university.

Of particular interest, as might be expected, has been the role of students in university affairs, especially in Chile (items 6112 and 6120), Mexico (items 6162 and 7520), and Colombia (item 6126). Graciarena's (item 6077) excellent defense of the thesis that the Argentine student movement has succeeded or failed in relation to its correspondence to middle class aspirations; and Suchlicki's (item 7484) general survey of the literature on student violence make good collateral reading to the contemporary case studies.

Almost as popular a topic as universities has been the topic of education and development. Lacking, however, in discussions of this topic is "hard data" necessary to reach any firm conclusions about the role of education. Carnoy's studies of Puerto Rico (items 6192-6193), Paulston's studies of Cuba (items 6199-6200), Bachhus' study of Guyana (item 6144), and Balan's and Contreras' studies of Mexico (items 6146 and 6149) provide some data on the subject. Generally, however, most of the items are largely speculative, and some simply assume that there is a relationship (for example, item 6179).

Skepticism about schooling continues. Illich (item 6036) and Reimer (item 6049) continue their arguments against schooling. Few seem to have joined their group, however. (See as an exception item 6086). Rather, the questioning seems to lead more to skepticism than to outright abolishment. Zanotti (item 6071), for example, contends that mass communications have replaced schools as the major educative process. Palerm (item 6159), speaking for the Mexican National Commission of Integral Educational Planning, seriously questions the assumed causal relationship between schooling and economic and social development. Alleyne (item 6188) questions manpower planning in Trinidad. Bolland (item 6191) raises provocative questions about the meaning of and training for functional literacy in Jamaica. Tarso Santos (item 6057) argues that at least in part schooling is conservative. And Avalos (item 6108) argues that schools tend to enslave rather than to liberate.

Largely using empirical data, Barkin (item 6147) documents disparities in Mexican education. Woodhall (item 6140) and Arrigazzi (item 6106) question the assumptions used in specific rate-of-return studies. And Beirn and others (item 6005) review worldwide data on wastage in schooling.

As in the past, little specifically about day-to-day operations in schools seems to be written. Gyarmati and others (item 6114) provide a very good account of the professionalization of Chilean secondary teachers. Argudin (item 6003) provides, in diary form, an account of an "open" kindergarten in Mexico; and Gonima gives us some insights into the daily operations of Colombian schools in her autobiographical novel. In addition, programs of study for Argentine secondary education (item 6081), health conditions and their effects on learning (items 6010 and 6023), and infant education in Grenada, Jamaica and Barbados (item 6205) receive some attention. Of some interest is Ramírez' biography of Mariano Fiallos, former Minister of Education and Rector of the national university in Nicaragua, which paints a vivid if discouraging picture of educational administration.

Rural education (items 6047, 6145, and 6168), agricultural education (item 6084) and adult education (items 6008, 6019 and 6178) receive some attention, which is not usual. Finally, mention should be made of the Blanksten-Wolpin debate (items 6006-6007 and 6067-6068) which, while concerned with Latin American studies in the United States, is refreshing. It would be most useful to see more of this type of debate among the authors of other topics related to Latin American education.

GENERAL

6000. Albornoz, Orlando. Obstáculos para la planificación universitaria en América Latina (CPES/RPS, 7:18, mayo/agosto 1970, p. 53-60)

Problems of university planning arising from lack of political stability, from autonomy and from public-private disparities. [G. R.]

6001. América Latina. Centro Latino Americano de Pesquisas em Ciências Sociais. Ano 3, No. 1, jan./março 1970- . Rio.

Issue includes articles by Albornoz, Graciarena, Labbens and Germani, among others, on engineering education, Uruguayan desertion rates at the university level, and modernism in the Univ. of Chile. All worth reading. [G. R.]

6002. Aparicio, Luis. Pasos previos del planeamiento integral de la educación (ESME/C, 52, abril/junio 1969, p. 30-36)

Excerpts from earlier book on planning, in which Aparicio attempts to outline *all* steps necessary to educational planning. Better seen as an agenda for research than as a how-to-do-it manual. [G. R.]

6003. Argudín de Luna, Yolanda. Diario vivo de una escuela activa. México, New American Kinder, 1970. 118 p., illus., plates.

Lesson plans and daily activities of an "open" kindergarten teacher in diary form. [G. R.]

6004. Aspectos de la enseñanza de la demografía en la universidad latinoamericana (UC/B, 101, mayo 1970, p. 25-26)

It is argued that, with the limited exception of medical and public health schools, Latin American universities have been reluctant to incorporate demography into their curricula, despite the fact that demography as a scientific discipline has gained worldwide recognition. [E. E.]

6005. Beirn, Russell; David C. Kinsey; and **Noel F. McGinn.** Antecedents and consequences of early school leaving: an analytical survey of research activities. Paris, UNESCO, 1972. 116 p., bibl., tables (Occasional papers in education and development, 8)

Excellent review of worldwide research on wastage, including sections on Latin America. [G. R.]

6006. Blanksten, George I. Latin American studies: radicalism on the half shell (JDA, 5:3, April 1971, p. 330-336)

In rebuttal to item 6068 author argues that Wolpin's radicalism is nothing more than a collection of arguments, some of which are valid, but not a separate ideology or a separate approach to social science research. [E. E.]

6007. ———. The second civil disquisition (JDA, 5:4, July 1971, p. 521-522)

Continuation of the Wolpin-Blanksten debate (items 6006, 6067-6068). After briefly commenting on Wolpin's charges, which he largely agrees with in a "so what?" manner, Blanksten asks the readers to make their own judgment on the basis of the arguments already spelled out. [E. E.]

6008. Buitrón, Aníbal. Problemas y perspectivas de la educación de adultos (III/AI, 31:3, julio 1971, p. 641-660, bibl.)

Examining problems of adult education programs in Latin America, author concludes that, though there have been such programs for years, there have been no notable successes. Though the author does claim that he cannot generalize to all of Latin America, this is precisely what he does in an unconvincing manner. [E. E.]

6009. Capitanelli, Ricardo G. La geografía en las facultades de humanidades: communicación presentada a las Primeras Jornadas Universitarias para el Fomento de las Humanidades, Córdoba, 1962 (UNT/H, 15:21, 1968/1969, p. 177-191)

Brief history of the development of geography from the time of Homer to the present, emphasizing changes in meaning and methodology. Author concludes that geography is a combination of humanistic and scientific study. [E. E.]

6010. Cervera Andrade, Alejandro. El niño en la escuela: charlas de un médico (UY/R, 12:71, sept./oct. 1971, p. 66-77)

Physician addresses himself to the need for good health and sound nutrition among school age children. He implores educators to consider medical or nutritional explanations for "intellectual laziness" and suggests changes based on medical evidence to improve learning. [E. E.]

6011. Ciencia Interamericana. Organization of American States, Dept. of Scientific Affairs. Vol. 12, Nos. 1/2, enero/junio 1971- . Washington.

Issue devoted to science and technology in Latin America. Includes reports on national and regional developments. Obvious educational implications. [G. R.]

6012. La ciencia y la tecnología al servicio de los pueblos de América: Programa Regional de Desarrollo Científico y Tecnológico de la OEA (PAU/CI, 11:3/6, mayo/dic. 1970, p. 10-21, illus., tables)

Final report of the Regional Program for fiscal year ending June 1970, including money and man hours invested in each of Program's research areas. Projects are briefly described and classified by area of inquiry. [E. E.]

6013. Congreso Iberoamericano de Promoción Profesional de la Mano de Obra, *l, Madrid, 1967.* [Actas] v. 1, Convocatoria, circulares, congresistas, reglamento, actas y conclusiones; v. 2, Ponencias y comunicaciones. Madrid, 1967. 2 v. (283, 841 p.) tables.

Extensive report of conference, including papers by participating countries and organizations. Valuable information here for the digging. [G. R.]

Cornblit, Oscar. Factors affecting scientific productivity: the Latin American case. See item 1797.

6014. Costa, Roberto B. da and **Délia V. Ferreira.** Intercâmbio de informação em física na América Latina (IBBD/N, 4:3, jul./set. 1970, p. 253-257)

Description of growth of the Latin American community of physicists. Authors argue for continued development of regional system of information exchange. [E. E.]

6015. Dagum, Camilo. Universidad y desarrollo económico (UNAM/IE, 30:118, abril/junio 1970, p. 255-267)

Summary of economic development theory and recommendations for university participation in development. Dagum's two major strategies for university involvement would seem to be to challenge the status quo and to produce better economists. [G. R.]

6016. Delobelle, André. Die katholische Universität in Lateinamerika. Cuernavaca, Mex., Centro Intercultural de Documentación, 1968. 98 p., tables (CIDOC: Cuaderno, 16)

Discussion of historical origins of Latin American, particularly Catholic, universities and investigates possibilities of increasing role of Catholic universities in educating intellectuals and in bringing about a "more just society" through education of the masses. [T. B.]

6017. Drouet, Pierre. Evaluación sistemática de programa de formación profesional. Montevideo, Centro Interamericano de Investigación y Documentación sobre Formación Profesional (CINTERFOR), 1971. 126 p., bibl., tables (Estudios y monografías, 8)

ILO consultant presents detailed account of the methods and aims of school evaluation, with emphasis on statistics. [G. R.]

6018. Fernández del Valle, Agustín Basave. Ser y quehacer de la universidad: estructura y misión de la universidad vocacional. Monterrey, Mex., Univ. Autónoma de Nuevo León, Centro de Estudios Humanísticos, 1971. 496 p.

Extensive discussion of university development, structure and objectives in Europe, US and Latin America. Includes sections on student rebellion, university reform, types and methods of scientific investigation, democratization, and the new university humanism. [T. B.]

6019. La formación de adultos y el desarrollo socio-económico. San José, Fundación Friedrich-Ebert-Stiftung [and] Centro de Estudios Democráticos de América Latina (CEDAL), 1969. 102 p., bibl. (Col. Seminarios y documentos)

Useful collection of papers on the role of adult education in national development, including speculations on how to improve adult education and reports on adult education in several of the countries of the region. [G. R.]

6020. Frondizi, Risieri. La universidad en un mundo de tensiones: misión de las universidades en América Latina. B.A., Editorial Paidós, 1971. 337 p., bibl. (Serie mayor, 23)

Author argues that Latin American universities should become one of the primary agents of radical reform and that internal changes in objectives, teaching and research must occur first. Extensive bibliography. [T. B.]

6021. Fuenzalida Faivovich, Edmundo. La dependencia de América Latina en el saber superior (CPES/RPS, 7:18, mayo/agosto 1970, p. 98-114, tables)

Using survey of 292 Chilean university professors, author argues that Latin America is too dependent on foreign sources of training and knowledge and that such dependence is at least as dangerous as economic or political dependence. [G. R.]

6022. García Jiménez, Jesús. Televisión educativa para América Latina. Prólogo de Alvaro Gálvez y Fuentes. México, Editorial Porrúa, 1970. 358 p., bibl.

6023. García Maldonado, Leopoldo. Educación y salud pública. Caracas, Ediciones Ministerio de Sanidad y Asistencia Social, Oficina de Publicaciones, Biblioteca y Archivo, 1970. 697 p.

Extensive but unclearly organized and poorly annotated collection of García Maldonado's writings on education and public health from 1927-70. Some insights into the health of school children and into health education might be laboriously and painfully extracted. [G. R.]

6024. Gelsi Bidart, Adolfo. El hombre concreto en la enseñanza de las ciencias normativas (UNAM/RFD, 21:83/84, julio/dic. 1971, p. 425-435)

Appeal for greater humanism in the teaching of law. [G. R.]

6025. Gil Arántegui, Malaquías. Los períodos evolutivos de la pedagogía contemporánea

(Aula [Santo Domingo] 1:1, abril/junio 1972, p. 13-26, bibl.)

Attempt to outline modern (1890 to present) pedagogical thinking around such individuals as Dewey and Vasconcelos and around such stages as "scientific pedagogy" and "educational internationalization." [G. R.]

6026. Gillon, Philip and **Hadassah Gillon** eds. Science and education in developing states. Foreword by Abba Eban. N.Y., Praeger Publishers in cooperation with the Continuation Committee of the Rehovot Conference, 1971. 288 p. (Praeger special studies in international economics and development)

Of interest is Marcelo Alonso "Integration of Science and Education in Latin America," in which author argues that lack of scientific and technological training and research is being overcome by increased attention to science education at all levels, including curriculum development, and to educational technology. [G. R.]

6027. Giner de los Ríos, Francisco. Ensayos. Selección edición prólogo de Juan López-Morillas. Madrid, Alianza Editorial, 1969. 236 p. (El Libro de bolsillo. Sección clásicos, 187)

Giner, a Spanish pedagogue and influential figure in the Latin American university reform movement, writes on his philosophy of teaching, his conception of education and his judgments about university development. He speaks out strongly on dangers he perceives in centralized or state control of universities. [E. E.]

6028. González Pedrero, Enrique. Universidad, política y administración. México, UNAM, Facultad de Ciencias Políticas y Sociales, 1970. 168 p. (Serie estudios, 22)

Principally a collection of addresses by a current Senator and former director of the Escuela Nacional de Ciencias Políticas y Sociales. Despite title, there is no apparent theme in the collection, and topics range from mass culture to the UN, from loyalty to the university to prospects for employment in public administration. [G. R.]

6029. Graciarena, Jorge. Las funciones de la universidad en el desarrollo latinoamericano (CPES/RPS, 8:22, set./dic. 1971, p. 63-92)

Intriguing analysis of role of universities in modernizing countries, with stress on postgraduate studies and research as necessary parts of this development. Well worth reading. [G. R.]

6030. Gutiérrez Pérez, Francisco. El lenguaje total en el proceso de la educación liberadora. Introducción [por] Luciano Metzinger. Lima, Editorial Venus-Offset, 1970. 127 p., bibl.

Appeal to schools to adopt "total language" instruction in order to allow students to live in a world where communications include not only books but the mass media and computers. [G. R.]

6031. Hernández Sánchez-Barba, Mario. El problema de la univeridad actual hispano-americana (ARBOR, 80:312, dic. 1971, p. 87-100)

Looking at the Latin American university as a microcosm of Spanish-American civilization, author argues that 1918 Córdoba Reforms have failed because the university still remains largely isolated from Latin American life and has not contributed appreciably to social and economic development. Author's arguments, and his assumptions about the university, warrant consideration. [E. E.]

6032. Herzfeld, Ana; Barbara Ashton Waggoner; and **George R. Waggoner** eds. Autonomía, planificación, coordinación, innovaciones: perspectivas latinoamericanas. Lawrence, Kan., Univ. de Kansas, Escuela de Artes Liberales y Ciencias, 1972. 220 p.

Collection of essays presented at Seminar on Higher Education in the Americas (1972). Primary topic is the Latin American university in relation to autonomy, planning, coordination and innovation. [T. B.]

6033. Hori Robaina, Guillermo. Antecedentes del adiestramiento y de la capacitación (MSTPS/R, 16:2 [6 época] abril/junio 1970, p. 29-36)

Call for greater training to reduce industrial accidents, to increase productivity, and to better prepare workers. [G. R.]

6034. Ibero-Amerikanska Institutet i Stockholm. La reorganización del Instituto Iberoamericano de Estocolmo en 1969 y actividades durante el año laboral de 1969-1970. Stockholm, 1970. 24 p.

Description of reorganization of the institute as well as its activities, in the form of an annual report. Issue yearly. [M. Mörner]

6035. Ikonicoff, Moïses. Rôle de l'Université et des étudiants dans le développement de l'Amérique Latine (UP/TM, 11:41, jan./mars 1970, p. 169-182)

Well-argued explanation of the centrality of the Latin American university in regional politics and a warning that a "de-politicized" university cannot play a major role in area development. Well worth reading. [G. R.]

6036. Illich, Ivan D. The dawn of Epimethean man and other essays. Cuernavaca, Mex., Centro Intercultural de Documentación, 1970. 1 v. (Various pagings) (CIDOC: Cuaderno, 54)

Continuation of the deschooling theme. Most of the pieces have appeared elsewhere and are also collected in Illich's *Deschooling society* (N.Y., Harper & Row, 1971, 116 p.). [G. R.]

6037. Jaramillo Uribe, Jaime. *La universidad latinoamericana:* observaciones a Atcon. Caracas, Comisión de Reforma Universitaria, Ediciones del Congreso de la República, 1971. 195 p.

In a rather misleading publication Jaramillo Uribe has taken Atcon's controversial 1961 report (see *HLAS 29:4019a*), and used it as an introduction to his own reaction to it, which accounts for only 15 p. of the publication. [G. R.]

6038. La Belle, Thomas J. ed. Education and development: Latin America and the Caribbean. Los Angeles, Calif., Univ. of California, Latin American Center, 1972. 732 p., tables (Latin American Studies Series, 18)

Multidisciplinary anthology addressed to complexities in meeting individual and national goals through schooling and containing theoretical frameworks, empirical studies and methodological approaches. [T. B.]

6039. Leaños Navarro, David. Los fundamentos de la reforma educativa. México, n.p., 1970. 59 p.

Retired educator's speech to educational conference in which author questions too great stress on education for national development and calls for greater concern with spiritual and political values. [G. R.]

6040. Lechner, Norbert. La reforma universitaria y el "optimismo burgués" (UC/B, 101, mayo 1970, p. 4-12, bibl.)

In a critique of Sunkel's *Reforma universitaria, subdesarrollo y dependencia* (Santiago, Editorial Universitaria, 1969) author argues that Sunkel's position is immediately suspect because he has not taken into account political and economic realities and thus naïve in calling for universities to assume an intellectual role. Lechner, in contrast, concludes that the university can only serve the interests of the state monopolistic and capitalistic society. [E. E.]

6041. Lopes, Juarez R. B. A pesquisa educacional em paises em desenvolvimento: abordagem histórico-estrutural (SBPC/CC, 23:6, déz. 1971, p. 717-720)

Argument for importance of history in educational research, in sense that consideration of "historical-structural interpretation" of educational systems and processes is essential for better understanding of role of education in development. Lopes claims that usual research of sociologists and economists fails to offer guidelines for action, in terms of how and where to invest in education and how to effect change in the system. His conclusion: "In order to obtain more adequate theories and programs in education (adequate in the sense of appropriate to our needs), it will be necessary to analyze, in much greater detail, the processes and relationships among education, the labor force, and development." [A. E. Toward]

6042. Loughlin, Lidia N. C. de. Profesores y alumnos: ¿comunicación o conflicto? B.A., Librería del Colegio, 1972. 299 p., illus. (Biblioteca nueva pedagogía, 15)

Analysis of interpersonal relations between teachers and students with emphasis on the psychology of adolescence. Author also discusses different types of leadership used by educators in working with adolescents. [T. B.]

6043. Mena Soto, Joaquín. La experiencia de las clásicas y modernas instituciones universitarias (UCE/FLCE, 35, 1968, p. 19-28)

Attempting to draw parallels between the problems of medieval European and modern Latin American universities, Mena Soto urges reform to make universities more responsive to public needs. His criticisms of reforms already undertaken are at times puzzling. [G. R.]

6044. Muñoz de Suárez, María Angeles and J. Armando Suárez Huízar. El método del seminario en la enseñanza media. Guadalajara, Mex., Editorial Trillas, 1971. 92 p., bibl., tables.

Description and explanation of seminar method of teaching, with exemplary topics and plans. [G. R.]

6045. Myers, Robert G. The changing face of education in Latin America (PAPS, 30:4, 1972, p. 50-64, tables)

Wide-ranging but well-done essay on current education in Latin America, with stress on the extent to which currently available and "financeable" programs tend to determine educational purposes, rather than vice versa. Many of the points discussed merit further investigation and refinement. [G. R.]

6046. Newbry, Burton C. and Kenneth L. Martin. The educational crisis in the lesser developed countries (JDA, 6:2, Jan. 1972, p. 155-162)

Authors argue that present evaluation of education in developing countries is based on quantitative growth and that this criterion is inadequate because education should be judged according to what a society feels it ought to do and what contribution education ought to make. If evaluation were changed to qualitative measures, authors contend, basic educational assumptions would begin to be questioned and alternatives to traditional educational programs to be considered. [E. E.]

6047. Organization of American States. Department of Social Affairs. Preliminary report on the situation and needs in the field of rural vocational training in Latin America (AIFLD/R, 2:2, 1970, p. 57-94, tables)

OAS-ILO report on rural and vocational training in Latin American, with special attention to Chile, Costa Rica, Ecuador and Venezuela. Although noting country variations, report concludes that throughout Latin America illiteracy is high and skill levels low in rural areas. Many data supporting this conclusion are included. [G. R.]

6048. ———. Inter-American Council for Education, Science, and Culture, *III, Panama, 1972*. Final report. Washington, 1972. 124 p., tables (EA/Ser. C/V. 12)

6049. Reimer, Everett W. An essay on alternatives in education. 2. ed., rev. and amplified. Cuernavaca, Mex., Centro Intercultural de Documentación, 1971. 1 v. (Various pagings) (CIDOC: Cuaderno, 58)

Actually a series of essays in which Reimer argues for alternative educational processes. Analysis is at times clear and compelling, as when the role of ritual in schooling is described, but unfortunately Reimer treats schools in terms which allow for no exception. Also, author blames schools for many of society's ills but does not show that schools have either the power or the responsibility for these ills. [E. E.]

Reis, Fábio Wanderley. Educação, economia e contestação política na América Latina. See item 7463.

EDUCATION: GENERAL

6050. Reunión de Ministros de Educación de la Región Andiana, *I, Bogotá, 1970.* [Actas] Bogotá, Ministerio de Educación Nacional, Oficina de Relaciones Públicas, 1970? 109 p., illus., plate.

Important document in the development of cooperative programs in education among Andean nations. Includes 11 resolutions approved at this first meeting. [G. R.]

6051. Reunión Extraordinaria del Consejo Interamericano para la Educación, la Ciencia y la Cultura, *II, Washington, 1972.* Informe final. Washington, Organización de los Estados Americanos, Secretaría General, 1972. 46 p., tables.

Various documents of the meeting. [G. R.]

6052. Ribeiro, Darcy. La universidad latinoamericana. Santiago, Editorial Universitaria, 1971. 314 p., illus. (Col. Imagen de América Latina, 13)

Exploring role of universities in emerging nations, author maintains that Latin American universities are in turmoil as a result of students rebelling against and privilege. There is a sense of urgency, the author argues, to restructure the university, not as a "guardian and transmitter of knowledge" but as an active participant in creating a more just society. Concluding chapter describes a theoretical framework for an alternative model to the traditional university. [E E.]

Sábato, Jorge A. and **Natalio Botana.** La science, la technique et l'avenir de l'Amérique Latine: analyse et stratégie. See item 7469.

6053. Seminario Regional Interamericano de Educación Profesional para Adolescentes y Jóvenes, *III, São Paulo, 1966,* [Actas]. Montevideo, Instituto Interamericano del Niño, 1967. 52 p.

Report of seminar on vocational education held in Brazil, for delegates from Argentina, Bolivia, Brazil, Chile, Paraguy, Peru, and Uruguay. Includes two protocol speeches and list of representatives and of votes and recommendations. [A. E. Toward]

6054. Silvert, Kalman H. Introducción a la educación en América Latina (CPES/RPS, 7:18, mayo/agosto 1970, p. 5-41, tables)

Survey of education in Latin America, including historical development (particularly in Chile) and current problems. Useful general picture. [G. R.]

6055. Sito, Nilda. Educación y desarrollo: los países latinoamericanos (CPES/RPS, 7:18, mayo/agosto 1970, p. 115-128, tables)

Provocative attempt to analyze role of education in social change, particularly distinguishing between political and economic effects of education. [G. R.]

Student activism and higher education: an inter-American dialogue. See item 7483.

Suchlicki, Jaime. Sources of student violence in Latin America: an analysis of the literature. See item 7484.

6056. Tabra Chávez, Emilio. Evaluación estadística y orientación del educando. 3. ed., ampliada. Lima, Editorial Ensayos Pedagógicos, 1970. 317 p., bibl., illus., tables.

Intended as a statistics text for normal school students. [G. R.]

6057. Tarso Santos, Paulo de. Educación y cambio social. La Paz, Ministerio de Educación, Fundación Rosa Agramonte, 1970. 53 p., plate (Col. Nuevos caminos, 1)

Examination of premise that Latin American education is both conservative and revolutionary: conservative as a socialization process oriented toward traditional ways of thinking and acting; revolutionary as preparation of students to take part in the building of a new society. Reforms of education are proposed. [G. R.]

6058. Tiller, Frank M. Structural reform in Latin American universities (*in* Johnson, Harvey L. ed. Contemporary Latin America: a selection of papers presented at the Third Annual Conference on Latin America, April 11-13, 1968. Houston, Tex., Univ. of Houston, Office of International Affairs, 1969, p. 42-48)

Appealing for university reform in Latin America, author calls for modernization. Unfortunately, call is couched in rhetoric terms and the assumption is made that existing "modern" universities ought to be the model for Latin American universities of the future. [E. E.]

6059. Tolentino, Hugo. Papel de la universidad en la sociedad latinoamericana contemporánea. Santo Domingo, Editora Nuevo Mundo, 1970. 31 p.

Searching for the elusive Latin American university, author argues for a reformed but politically active university. [G. R.]

6060. Torres Sánchez, Isabel. Interpretación de programas. Bogotá, Voluntad, 1970. 131 p., bibl., illus. (Biblioteca del Ecuador, 5)

Discussion of doctrines and planning of educational programs and their often unrealized importance and development. [T. B.]

6061. Trejos Dittel, Eduardo. Educación y desarrollo en América Latina. Prólogo de Ethel M. Manganiello. B.A., Librería del Colegio, 1971. 207 p. (Biblioteca nueva pedagogía, 12)

Critical analysis of Latin American education with emphasis on importance of socioeconomic and cultural development of the masses. [T. B.]

6062. Uhia Pinilla, Agustín. Dinámica de la supervisión. Bogotá, Voluntad, 1970. 143 p., bibl. (Biblioteca del Ecuador, 8)

Essentially a "textbook" review of modern supervision theory and practices, with little reference to Colombia or Latin America. [G. R.]

6063. *Universidades.* Unión de Universidades de América Latina. Año 12, No. 48, 2. serie, abril/junio 1972- . México.

In addition to the usual reports on UDUAL activities, this issue contains Frondizi's analysis of universities and society, Tunnermann's arguments on the relationship between planning and autonomy, and a review of university legislation in Peru. [G. R.]

6064. Vásquez, Emilio. Historia de la educación. Lima, Editorial Universitaria, 1969. 307 p., bibl.

World history of education, based largely on the "great men" in the field and intending to show education's role in culture, progress and civilization. Includes 20 p. on Peru and another 35 p. on the rest of Latin America. As might be expected by the scope of the work, it is rather superficial. [G. R.]

6065. Velasco Letelier, Eugenio. La Facultad de Ciencias Jurídicas y Sociales en la integración latinoamericana (UC/B, 78/79, sept./oct. 1967, p. 12-14)

Complete speech of Dean of the Faculty given at the opening of the VI Chilean Congress of Public Law pleading for total integration of Chile, Peru and Bolivia as the only solution common to all Latin American nations. The "united we stand, divided we fall" theme is not new, and author's proposed use of the judiciary as a means toward integration is not clear. [E. E.]

6066. Volskii, Viktor V. Sovetskaia Latinoamerikanistika: Nekotorye itogi i zadachi (Latin American studies in the USSR: some results and perspectives) (SSSR/LA, 3, May/June 1971, p. 6-16)

Reviews impressive growth and development of Latin American studies in the USSR emphasizing methodological advantage the Soviets have in using Marxist-Leninist analysis in studying Latin America. Contends that US social science studies of region are based on narrow class interests and cannot be objective. Article should be read in conjunction with Al'perovich's book on Soviet historiography of Latin America (see *HLAS 34: 1438*) and V. N. Komissarov "Latinskaia Amerika v Sovetskoi bibliografii i istoriografii" (Latin America in Soviet Bibliography and Historiography) in *Latinskaia Amerika* (3, May/June 1971, p. 202-208). [T. S. Cheston]

6067. Wolpin, Miles D. Latin American studies: for a radical approach (JDA, 5:3, April 1971, p. 321-329)

"Call to arms" for all radical social scientists to reveal the extent to which academic freedom does not exist when it comes to Latin American research. [E. E.]

6068. ———. Latin American studies: half-baked nonradicalism (JDA, 5:4, July 1971, p. 517-520)

Reply to Blanksten (item 6006), in which Wolpin charges Blanksten with using an unsavory reductio ad absurdum approach in criticizing Wolpin's earlier article (item 6067). It is unfortunate that Wolpin's rebuttal is replete with ad hominum arguments because otherwise it does indeed point to certain misunderstandings on the part of Blanksten. [E. E.]

6069. Wood, Bryce. Scholarly exchanges between Latin America and the United States (PAPS, 30:4, 1972, p. 123-140)

Useful summary of changes in scholarly exchange, stressing current attempts to encourage us scholars to collaborate with Latin American colleagues. [G. R.]

6070. Wright, Freeman J. The Latin American university at the crossroads (IAMEA, 24:4, Spring 1971, p. 81-91)

Clear but general account of Latin American universities, with stress on differences between those who favor continued Córdoba-type reforms and those who favor reforms to upgrade academic quality. [G. R.]

6071. Zanotti, Luis Jorge. Etapas históricas de la política educativa. B.A., EUDEBA, 1972. 127 p. (Biblioteca cultural cuadernos, 192)

Intriguing attempt to show that the school, which only this century became the heart of the educative process, is now losing its place to mass communications. Careful study of Zanotti's thesis is warranted. [G. R.]

ARGENTINA

Allende, Andrés R. Ricardo Levene, presidente de la Universidad de La Plata. See *HLAS 34:2646a.*

6072. Bravo, Héctor Félix. Bases constitucionales de la educación argentina: un proyecto de reforma. B.A., Editorial Paidós, 1972. 217 p., bibl., table (Biblioteca del educador contemporáneo. Serie menor, 174)

Well-done examination of historical and current constitutional bases for Argentine education and carefully developed argument and proposals for reform through constitutional change. [G. R.]

6073. Cauwlaert, Isabel Haydée van. Bases de una real planificación educacional en el municipio (DPB/RICS, 17, 1971, p. 197-202)

Most sketchy attempt to show that each metropolitan area in Argentina should plan its own education. [G. R.]

6074. Cirigliano, Gustavo F. J. Universidad y proyecto nacional. Tucumán, Arg., Univ. Nacional de Tucumán, 1971. 64 p., (Serie: mensaje)

Reflections on Argentina, its role in the world and its universities. [G. R.]

6075. Delfino, Pedro. Administración y desarrollo: la institucionalización de la enseñanza de la ciencia de la administración al servicio del desarrollo. La Plata, Arg., Taller de Impresiones Bellas Artes, 1970. 210 p.

Essentially course materials of Facultad de Ciencias Económicas of Univ. de La Plata outlining current research and training programs in administration worldwide. [G. R.]

6076. Devoto, Raúl A. Sobre una nueva universidad: discursos y conferencias. B.A., EUDEBA, 1968. 146 p., illus.

Discussion of functions and objectives of Argentine university, with detailed proposal for restructuring the Univ. of Buenos Aires. [T. B.]

6077. Graciarena, Jorge. Clases medias y movimiento estudiantil: el reformismo argentino, 1918-1966 (UNAM/RMS, 33:1, enero/marzo 1971, p. 61-100)

Excellent defense of the thesis that the Argentine student movement has succeeded or failed in relation to its correspondence to middle-class aspirations and programs. [G. R.]

6078. Misiones (province), *Arg.* **Dirección General de Estadística.** Educación en área de frontera. Posadas, Arg., 1971. 54 l., tables.

Excellent collection of data on schooling in the "frontier" area of Misiones province, including comparisons with both general provincial and national data. [G. R.]

6079. Pérez Duprat, Rodolfo. Vidas educadoras. La Plata, Arg., Editora Platense, 1970. 126 p.

Brief biographies of 20 Argentine educators and their contributions to the field of education. [T. B.]

6080. Ray, Víctor. Como rendir examen. B.A., Compañía Argentina de Editores, 1966. 105 p.

Directed both to students and to their parents, book attempts to explain how to prepare for and take examinations successfully and to examine those factors, particularly in the home, which might hinder examination success. Includes examples of questions used in IQ tests. [G. R.]

6081. Revista de Educación. No. 31, oct. 1971- . Santiago.

Issue devoted to programs of study adopted in the scientific-humanistic section of Argentine secondary education. Includes goals, lesson plans and bibliographies. [G. R.]

6082. Sastre de Cabot, Josefa Margarita. La formación del profesor de enseñanza media. Tucumán, Arg., Univ. Nacional de Tucumán, Facultad de Filosofía y Letras, 1967. 96 p. (Cuadernos de humanitas, 24)

Author advocates slow, cautious reform of Argentine secondary education professorate and cites need for more and better reformist educators in the system and for systematization of educational goals to serve as guidelines for the elevation of educational standards. [T. B.]

BOLIVIA

6083. Bolivia. Ministerio de Educación. Política educativa, cultural y científica del gobierno revolucionario de Bolivia. La Paz, Fundación Rosa Agramonte, 1970. 63 p., plates (Col. Documentos fundamentales, 1)

38 policies of the revolutionary government listed without explication. Brief introduction by Minister of Education. [G. R.]

6084. Cosío, Carlos. La educación agrícola en Bolivia. Lima, Instituto Interamericano de Ciencias Agrícolas, Zona Andina, 1971. 189 p., tables.

Detailed description of agricultural education, including curriculum, enrollments and budgets. Problems discussed intelligently. [G. R.]

6085. Gumucio, Mariano Baptista. Pido la paz y la palabra: para una pedagogía del hombre nuevo. La Paz, Cooperativa de Artes Gráficas E. Burillo, 1970. 153 p., plate.

Reprints of Minister of Education's speeches and letters during 1970. Some useful comments on the educational plans and objectives of the revolutionary government. [G. R.]

6086. ———. Salvemos a Bolivia de la escuela. La Paz, Editorial Los Amigos del Libro, 1971. 220 p., bibl., facsim.

No conventional exhortation but a serious discussion of the would-wide school crisis and a call for alternative schooling, with some special reference to Bolivia. [G. R.]

6087. Hacia la revolución cultural: escuelas populares de educación agropecuaria. La Paz, Ministerio de Educación y Cultura, 1970. 50 p., plates (Col. Nuevos caminos, 7)

Extremely brief, limited description of structure and objectives of new agricultural school, stressing Bolivia's need for more trained skilled workers and fewer "professionals." [T. B.]

6088. Luna P., Nazario. Enfoque de la alfabetización funcional. Presentación [por] Bernabé Ledesma. La Paz, Empresa Editora Universo, 1971. 205 p., bibl., illus., table.

Very good discussion of meaning of and ways to eliminate functional illiteracy, with special reference to Bolivia. [G. R.]

6089. Medinaceli, Carlos. El huayralevismo: o la enseñanza universitaria en Bolivia. La Paz, Editorial Los Amigos del Libro, 1972. 368 p. (Biblioteca clásicos bolivianos)

Works of Bolivian educator Medinaceli on such topics as Bolivian education and literature. [T. B.]

6090. Payne, Ruth and **Emma Violand de Ponce.** Guía de la educación vocacional y profesional en Bolivia. La Paz, Cooperativa de Artes Gráficas E. Burillo, 1971. 193 p., bibl.

Vocational education handbook. Description and data of various programs offered in Bolivia. [T. B.]

6091. Taborga, Huáscar. Mito y realidad de la universidad boliviana. La Paz, Editorial Los Amigos del Libro, 1970. 101 p., tables.

Essentially the same analysis as reported in item 6092. [G. R.]

6092. ———. La universidad boliviana conflictiva (ILARI/A, 19, enero 1971, p. 125-161, tables)

Interesting attempt to analyze Bolivian universities both horizontally (in terms of stages of development) and vertically (in terms of internal structure and function). Although both data used and model developed are useful, author has not succeeded in effecting a bond between these two methods of analysis. [E. E.]

CENTRAL AMERICA

6093. *Apuntes Universitarios.* Año 8, No. 37, abril 1971- . Guatemala.

Articles and news generally about higher education in Guatemala. Of interest in the issue is Edgar Godoy's arguments for universities to get involved in literacy training. [G. R.]

6094. El Salvador. Ministerio de Educación. Dirección General de Cultura. Plan quinquenal de educación: julio 1967-junio 1972. San Salvador, 1970. 61 p., tables (Documentos de la reforma educativa, 2)

Limited outline of plans to improve education during the five-year period, including building projects, budgets and enrollment projects. An evaluation of the success of the plan would now be appropriate. [G. R.]

6095. ———. ———. ———. El sistema educativo: fundamentos doctrinarios, estructuras, planes y programas. San Salvador, 1970. 75 p. (Documentos de la reforma educativa, 3)

Description of Salvadorean educational system, including brief history of educational reform from 1939 and basic plan of existing programs at primary and secondary levels. [T. B.]

6096. Gamboa, Emma. Omar Dengo. San José, Ministerio de Cultura, Juventud y Deportes, Depto. de Publicaciones, 1971. 307 p., plates (Serie ¿Quién fue y qué hizo?)

Biography of Costa Rican educator Dengo (1888-1928), with selections from his writings on education, philosophy, literature and politics. [T. B.]

6097. Gámez Solano, Uladislao. Planeamiento integral de la reforma de la educación de Costa Rica. San José, Imprenta Nacional, 1970. 59 p., plate.

Short history of Costa Rica and parallel development of educational system. Summary of a national plan for educational development and improvement of instruction to integrate educational system with necessities of the country, to be implemented by March 1972. Focus of plan is on social demands of education, educational opportunities and better utilization of human, financial and physical resources. [T. B.]

Gutiérrez, Carlos José. Student participation in the government of the University of Costa Rica. See item 7547.

6098. Juárez Toledo, Luis Adolfo and **Reinaldo Alfaro Palacios.** El programa de castellanización socio-educativo rural: una fórmula feliz para la educación del indígena monolingüe guatemalteco (III/AI, 32:2, abril/junio 1972, p. 377-390)

Description of the Programa Nacional de Castellanización designed to teach Spanish to the indigenous population of Guatemala. It is estimated that 67 percent of the population speak only a native dialect. [E. E.]

6099. Márquez V., Marcela. La televisión y sus efectos en la conducta de los niños (LNB/L, 16:189, agosto 1971, p. 47-54)

Author looks at some data on TV exposure in Panama, but stops short of analysis. Argues that sheer power of TV begs for more systematic and structured inquiry into its effects on the behavior and motivation of children. [E. E.]

6100. Pérez, Humberto. Educación y desarrollo: reto a la sociedad costarricense. Presentación [por] María Eugenia Dengo de Vargas. San José, Editorial Costa Rica, 1971. 112 p., tables.

Critical analysis of present Costa Rican education. Author maintains that although Costa Rica's educational system is regarded as one of the best in Latin America, there is still great disparity between theory and reality. [T. B.]

6101. Ramírez, Sergio. Mariano Fiallos: biografía. León, Nic., Univ. Nacional Autónoma de Nicaragua, 1971. 203 p., bibl., plates (Col. Ensayo, 4)

Intriguing biography of Fiallos, erstwhile appointee of Somoza, who later became one of the representatives of the government in exile and finally became rector of the national university until his death. First half of book reads like a political novel, second half recounts Fiallos' fight for university autonomy. [G. R.]

6102. Soto Blanco, Ovidio. La educación en Centroamérica. San Salvador, Organización de Estados Centroamericanos (ODECA), Secretaría General, 1968. 144 p., bibl., tables (Serie monografías técnicas)

Comparison of Central American and Panamanian educational systems, based on 1966 study by Curso Centroamericano de Planeamiento de la Educación, with emphasis on primary level. Objective is to facilitate future programming to achieve integration of Central American educational systems. Extensive use of detailed charts. Some chapters incomplete due to lack of specific or reliable data. [T. B.]

6103. Uzcátegui, Emilio. Una verdadera reforma, la de la Universidad de El Salvador (UCE/FLCE, 35, 1968, p. 57-73, tables)

Reminiscences of a UNESCO advisor to Salvadorean university reform. Uzcátegui comments favorably on stronger central administration, increased student financial assistance, more full-time professors, and clearer curricula. [G. R.]

6104. Waggoner, George R. and **Barbara Ashton Waggoner.** Education in Central America. Lawrence, Kan., Univ. of Kansas Press, 1971. 180 p., tables.

Well-written, concise accounts of school systems of Guatemala, El Salvador, Honduras, Nicaragua, Costa Rica and Panama; plus a general historical introduction and a concluding section on regional cooperation. Essentially school-oriented and cautious in examining educational problems. [G. R.]

CHILE

6105. *Anales de la Universidad de Chile.* Año 126, No. 146, abril/junio 1968- . Santiago.

Always interesting collection of documents pertaining to the university's governance and problems. Special reference is made to the difficulties of student participation in university reform. [G. R.]

6106. Arrigazzi, Lucila. Chile: evaluating the expansion of a vocational training program (*in* Coombs, Philip H. and Jacques Hallak eds. Educational cost analysis in action: case studies for planners. v. 1-3. Paris, UNESCO, International Institute for Educational Planning, 1972, v. 1, p. 331-360, tables)

Excellent reanalysis of the 1965 International Bank for Reconstruction and Development cost-benefit study of vocational training. Author carefully examines the assumptions made by the Bank and points out how different assumptions, perhaps more realistic, would have yielded different results. See also items 6107 and 6140. [G. R.]

6107. ——— and **José de Simone.** Chile: improving efficiency in the utilization of teachers in technical education (*in* Coombs, Philip H. and Jacques Hallak eds. Educational cost analysis in action: case studies for planners. v. 1-3. Paris, UNESCO, International Institute for Educational Planning, 1972, v. 2, p. 271-301, bibl., tables)

Analysis of consequences of 1968 decision to maintain technical education budgets at 1967 levels and improve teacher efficiency. Authors maintain that up to 35 percent increase in efficiency was achieved. See also items 6106 and 6140. [G. R.]

6108. Avalos D., Beatrice. La educación en Chile: perspectivas (UCC/CE, 7:22, dic. 1970, p. 3-13)

Questioning some commonly accepted assumptions about schooling, author argues that truly liberating education runs counter to industrialization and that schools, as presently constituted, enslave rather than liberate. [E. E.]

6109. Carreño Silva, Luis. Realizaciones y programas de la Junta Nacional de Auxilio Escolar y Becas (UC/B, 76/77, julio/agosto, 1967, p. 15-17, tables)

Description of selection processes employed by Junta to provide financial aid to students. Established in 1964, the Junta replaces an earlier board which was concerned only with primary education. New board provides assistance at all levels of schooling. [E. E.]

6110. La expansión de los centros universitarios de la Universidad de Chile (UC/B, 78/79, sept./oct. 1967, p. 15-18, tables)

Descriptive rather than evaluative report on the Univ. of Chile's university centers. Data included are: enrollments by center and by program of study. [E. E.]

Friedman, Bruno. Science in Chile's development programme. See item 7747.

Fuenzalida Faivovich, Edmundo. La dependencia de América Latina en el saber superior. See item 6021.

6111. Giliberto de Guevara, Ninfa. Rendimiento estudiantil en la Escuela de Salubridad de la Universidad de Chile: análisis preliminar (UC/B, 104, agosto 1970, p. 10-19, tables)

Attempt to evaluate public health program in terms of levels of student achievement and factors which affect learning. Author argues that such evaluations are necessary throughout the university. Model used might be of interest to others engaged in evaluation of this nature. [E. E.]

6112. Glazer, Myron and **Penina Migdal Glazer.** Estudiantes y profesores en la reforma universitaria de Chile (ILARI/A, 23, enero 1972, p. 101-119)

In an analysis of the Chilean university reform movement of 1967-69—parts of which appeared in *Student politics in Chile* (see *HLAS 33:4625*)—authors argue that societal and internal, university goals are often in conflict. Latter leads to tension and prolonged strikes, problems not likely to be solved by current reform, which has destroyed the university's old bureaucracy but has not created a new body with the power to effect change. [E. E.]

6113. González, Eugenio. La universidad y su responsabilidad nacional: limitaciones y perspectivas (UC/B, 82, abril 1968, p. 4-11)

Description of quantitative and qualitative changes which have taken place at the Univ. of Chile since 1957. Outlines services and programs available at the university and includes budgetary figures. [E. E.]

6114. Gyarmati, Gabriel; Pelagia Ortúzar; and **Luz E. Cereceda.** El nuevo profesor secundario: la planificación sociológica de una profesión. Santiago, Ediciones Nueva Universidad, 1971? 293 p., table.

Excellent analysis of Chilean secondary teachers' professionalization, based in part on questionnaire data. Theoretical considerations well-developed and clear. [G. R.]

6115. Hawkes, Nigel. Chile: trying to cultivate small base of technical excellence (AAAS/S, 174:4016, Dec. 1971, p. 1311-1313)

Brief, clear account of Chile's needs in technology and of problems encountered in developing this technology. [G. R.]

6116. Informe estadístico acerca del alumnado de la Universidad de Chile en 1968 (UC/B, 93/94, junio/julio 1969, p. 11-14, tables)

Statistical profile of university students at all levels and in all fields in Chile. There is no attempt to analyze the data. The profiles are aggregated according to sex and grade level within the university, specialization, and enrollments within the different university locations. Also see item 6117. [E. E.]

6117. Informe estadístico acerca del alumnado de la Universidad de Chile en 1969 (UC/B, 101, mayo 1970, p. 13-21, tables)

See item 6116.

6118. Ponce, Lautaro. Necesidad de un mayor intercambio entre las universidades de la URSS y la de Chile (UC/B, 80/81, nov./dic. 1967, p. 16-17)

Argument for greater exchange of students between Chile and the USSR, particularly Univ. of Moscow. Opportunities available to Chilean and other Latin American students for study in the Soviet Union are described. Ponce's belief that increased exchange programs will undoubtedly lead to greater understanding between the two nations is rather unconvincing. [E. E.]

6119. Proyecto de Estatuto Orgánico de la Universidad de Chile emanado del Congreso Universitario Transitorio (UC/B, 102/103, junio/julio 1970, p. 3-21)

Complete document of propositions and articles approved by the Chilean University Congress and the entire university community in a plebiscite, 7 July 1972. Important source of information. [E. E.]

6120. Reca, Inés Cristina. El movimiento estudiantil y el proceso de reforma de la Universidad de Chile (CPES/RPS, 6:16, sept. /oct. 1969, p. 63-104)

Lengthy and involved account of the 1968 student reform movement, with stress on competition among student groups for control of the movement. [G. R.]

6121. Sater, William F. The hero as a force for change in Chilean education (JDA, 7:1, Oct. 1972, p. 89-103, bibl.)

Examination of treatment of Arturo Prat in Chilean textbooks as national hero, with some comments on the use of heroes in other Latin American countries. [G. R.]

Silvert, Kalman H. Introducción a la educación en América Latina. See item 6054.

6122. Universidad de Chile, *Santiago.* Servicio de Bienestar Estudiantil. Alumnos universitarios no deben interrumpir sus estudios por falta de recursos (UC/B, 76/77, julio/agosto 1967, p. 12-14)

Describing the functions of the Student Welfare Service of the Univ. of Chile, author argues that no student should be deprived of the opportunity to study or subjected to interrupting his studies for lack of financial resources and that student financial aid must be the foremost concern of the Service. [E. E.]

COLOMBIA

6123. Asociación Colombiana de Universidades, *Bogotá.* **Fondo Universitario Nacional. Comité de Planeación.** Plan básico de la educación en Colombia; sintesis de politicas y normas, pt. 1. Bogotá, 1968. 34 l. (Uninorte, 2, oct./ dic. 1971, p. 5-16, tables)

Straightforward description of statutes, objectives and criteria for higher education in Colombia. [T. B.]

6124. Castro, Julio. Tasas internas de retorno social y privado a la educación universitaria en Colombia (Uninorte, 2, oct./dic. 1971, p. 5-16, tables)

Initial calculations of rates of return which suggest that university expansion in Colombia has been understandable. [G. R.]

6125. Cohen, Lucy. Las colombianas ante la renovación universitaria. Bogotá, Ediciones Tercer Mundo, 1971. 149 p., tables (Col. Tribuna libre, 4)

Anthropologist discusses role of women in rennovating Colombian universities. Author argues that cultural identity of professionals in contemporary Latin American society ought to be understood in relation to historical perspective, cultural values and social structure. [T. B.]

6126. Crisis universitaria colombiana 1971: itinerario y documentos. Bogotá, Ediciones El Tigre de Papel, 1971. 319 p.

Account of 1970-71 student conflicts, including a chronology, documents and commentaries. Well worth examining. [G. R.]

6127. Díaz Borbón, Rafael. La universidad colombiana: una crisis institucional. Bogotá, Sociedad Universitaria de Editores, 1972. 88 p., bibl.

Brief history and description of Colombian universities and their present crisis. Author also discusses university's role in Colombian society, politics and economic development. [T. B.]

6128. Gónima, Ester. Una maestra, una vida, un destino. Prológo [por] Luis Gutiérrez. Medellín, Co., Luis Martel Editor, 1969. 333 p.

Autobiographical novel written by Colombian teacher. Some insights into daily operations of schools. [G. R.]

6129. Low-Maus, Rodolfo. Compendium of the Colombian educational system. Bogotá, The Ford Foundation, 1971. 139 p., bibl., illus.

Comprehensive description of Colombian educational system from pre-school to adult and non-school education. Although approach is descriptive, much unanalyzed information is included. Useful source. [E. E.]

6130. Observaciones sobre la reforma universitaria. Bogotá, n.p., 1972. 1 v. (Various pagings)

Interesting collection of nine statements made by rectors of Colombian private universities as regards university reform and increased aid and freedom for private institutions. See also item 6139. [G. R.]

6131. Pelczar, Richard S. University reform in Latin America: the case of Colombia (CIES/CER, 16:2, June 1972, p. 230-250, tables)

Traces Colombian university reform movement from 16th and 17th centuries to the 1970's. Pelczar concludes that universities tend to reflect society more than to shape it and thus are not solutions to serious political and socioeconomic problems of Colombia. Forecasts a period of revolutionary change within the universities. [T. B.]

6132. Rama, Germán W. Educación universitaria y movilidad social: reclutamiento de élites en Colombia (ITT/RLS, 6:2, julio 1970, p. 230-261, tables)
Extensive analysis of growth of higher education and the tendency to recruit elite members from the growing private institutions on the basis of social rather than pedagogical factors. [G. R.]

6133. ———. El sistema universitario en Colombia. Bogotá, Univ. Nacional de Colombia, Dirección de Divulgación Cultural, 1970? 256 p., tables.
Analysis of the Colombian university, its relation to global society, distribution of power, and role played in the formation of human resources for social change. Extensive use of charts. [T. B.]

6134. Renner, Richard R. Education for a new Colombia. Foreword [by] Robert Leestma. Washington, GPO, 1971. 199 p., bibl., map, plates, tables.
Comprehensive description of the educational system, including historical, geographical and cultural background; development of the system; and detailed descriptions of administration, planning and operations at all levels of education. Data are drawn from a wide range of sources, and the book is well-organized and clearly and concisely presented. An indispensible reference. [G. R.]

6135. Rodríguez, Humberto Angel. Actividades extraescolares. Bogotá, Voluntad, 1969. 141 p., bibl., tables (Biblioteca del educador, 3)
Inventory of such extracurricular activities as Red Cross, sports clubs, civic associations and discussion of their social, cultural and educational value. [T. B.]

6136. Uhía Pinilla, Agustín. Lectura y escritura. Bogotá, Voluntad, 1969. 117 p., bibl., illus. (Biblioteca del educador, 2)
Intended as a guide for normal school teachers in Colombia, author attempts to put together recent research and thought on teaching methods, motivation, behavioral objectives. Perhaps more useful to outsiders interested in seeing how methods are taught than to those being taught the methods. [G. R.]

6137. Universidad Nacional de Colombia, *Bogotá.* **Oficina de Planeación. División de Programación Económica.** Análisis del censo del personal docente. Bogotá, 1970. 61 p., tables.
Report of questionnaire study of professors at the national university and includes both demographic and pedagogical information. Although not truly an analysis of the results, the report is a useful beginning. [G. R.]

6138. Villarreal, Juan F. Consideraciones sobre la crisis universitaria. Bogotá? Instituto Colombiano para el Fomento de la Educación Superior (ICFES), 1971. 44 p. (Serie universidad hoy, 1)

Description of Colombian university crisis: structure, politics, autonomy, external aid and relations with community. [T. B.]

6139. Vivas Dorado, Raúl. Diagnóstico de la educación privada. Introducción [por] P. Rodrigo Díaz. Bogotá, Confederación Nacional de Centros Docentes (CONACED), 1971. 94 p., tables.
Attempt to show that private education, at all levels, plays an important role in Colombia and that the government ought to aid private education more. See also item 6130. [G. R.]

6140. Woodhall, Maureen. Colombia: the use of cost-benefit analysis to compare the rates of return at different educational levels (*in* Coombs, Philip H. and Jacques Hallak *eds.* Educational cost analysis in action: case studies for planners. v. 1-3. Paris, UNESCO, International Institute for Educational Planning, 1972. v. 2, p. 247-271, tables)
Reanalysis of earlier AID cost-benefit study, calling into question both the specific assumptions of that study and the assumptions of cost-benefit analysis in general. See also items 6106-6107. [G. R.]

ECUADOR

6141. Miranda Ribadeneira, Francisco. La primera escuela politécnica del Ecuador: estudio histórico e interpretación. Quito, Ediciones FESO, 1972. 391 p., bibl., facsims., plates (Col. Desarrollo y paz)

6142. Murgueytio, Reinaldo. Bosquejo histórico de la escuela laica ecuatoriana, 1906-1966. Quito, Editorial Casa de la Cultural Ecuatoriana, 1972. 300 p., tables.
Attempt to document and analyze the development of lay education. Unfortunately, the book is a hodgepodge of materials and thus hard to follow. [G. R.]

6143. Wilson, Jacques M. P. The development of education in Ecuador. Coral Gables, Fla., Univ. of Miami Press, 1970. 169 p., bibl., tables (Hispanic-American studies, 24)
A good summary of Ecuadorian education, with special reference to the reforms instituted between 1963 and 1966 by the military junta. The author perhaps places too much emphasis on the junta's educational accomplishments but does suggest that long-run change cannot occur simply because of this four year reform movement. [G. R.]

GUYANA

6144. Bacchus, M. K. Patterns of educational expenditure in an emergent nation: a study of Guyana 1945-65 (UWI/SES, 18:3, Sept. 1969, p. 282-301, tables)
Two-part study dealing with changes in patterns of educational expenditures in Guyana between 1945-65 and with those groups in Guyana society which influenced these changes. Significantly, while both real expenditures and expenditures as a percentage of

national budget rose during the period, the percentage of the budget allocated to education at the primary level decreased from 84 percent to 72 percent. Valuable study both for its findings and for its method of analysis. [E. E.]

MEXICO

6145. Aguilera Dorantes, Mario and **Isidro Castillo.** Santiago Ixcuintla: un ensayo de educación básica. México, Secretaría de Educación Pública, 1970. 319 p., maps, plates.

Description of the work of the Ensayo Piloto Mexicano, a community development group dedicated to the development of rural educational opportunities in a small Mexican village. Written 23 years after the project began, this is the story of its success in arranging community facilities and in inspiring residents to participate in educational and developmental opportunities. [E. E.]

6146. Balán, Jorge. Determinantes del nivel educacional en Monterrey, México: un análisis multivariado (ITT/RLS, 6:2, julio 1970, p. 262-292, tables)

Using data from adult Monterrey males, author finds that amount of schooling is dependent principally on respondents' parents' education and on respondents' ages. Worthwhile data and explication. [G. R.]

6147. Barkin, David. Acceso de la educación en México: un enfoque regional (UNAM/RMS, 33:1, enero/marzo 1971, 33-50, bibl., tables

Excellent review of the disparities in Mexican education by region, socioeconomic status and finance, despite proclaimed equality and growth. [G. R.]

6148. Brown, William F.; Eduardo García Hassey; and **Fernando García Cortés.** Adaptabilidad transcultural de la orientación de estudiante a estudiante para el ajuste académico (SIP/RIP, 4:3/4, 1970, p. 203-214, bibl., tables)

Comparative study of effects of counseling on student achievement in an American (Southwest Texas State Univ.) and a Mexican (Univ. Nacional Autónoma de México) university. Findings indicate that in both settings achievement was increased through counseling and authors conclude that the counseling techniques employed do have cross-cultural adaptability. [G. R.]

6149. Contreras S., Enrique. La adecuación-ocupación: un estudio sobre la educación técnica mecánica a nivel medio en el Distrito Federal (UNAM/RMS, 31:1, enero/marzo 1969, p. 93-107, tables)

Small but useful survey of technical school students and graduates which suggests that students are not being well trained for existing occupations and that graduates are not being well employed, business and governmental claims to the contrary. [G. R.]

6150. Cowart, Billy F. La obra educativa de Torres Bodet: en lo nacional y lo internacional. Traducción de Arturo Cantú Sánchez. México, El Colegio de México, 1966. 53 p. (Jornadas, 59)

Discussion of the works of Mexican educator Torres Bodet and his contributions to Mexican education and to the world. [T. B.]

6151. Díaz y de Ovando, Clementina and **Elisa García Barragán.** La Escuela Nacional Preparatoria: los afanes y los días, 1867-1910. v. 2. México, UNAM, Instituto de Investigaciones Estéticas, 1972. 593 p.

6152. García Ramos, Domingo. Planificación de edificios para la enseñanza. Presentación [por] Ramón Torres Martínez. México, UNAM, Escuela Nacional de Arquitectura, 1970. 98 p., illus.

Interesting attempt to coordinate architectural and pedagogical aims with special reference to Mexican culture and needs. [G. R.]

6153. Ivie, Stanley D. *ed.* Mexican education in cultural perspective. Tucson, Ariz., Univ. of Arizona, College of Education, 1971. 73 p., tables (Monograph series, 5)

Six papers presented at comparative education conference, 1970, focusing on Mexican education. Although common theme is the way in which education reflects society, papers range from Valenzuela's statistical analysis to Romanell's conceptual analysis of social philosophy and educational aims. [G. R.]

6154. Jones, John Maxwell and **Ralph E. Stout.** Operatión [sic] educación, México: a contemporary study. n.p., The Authors, 1971. 84 p., bibl.

Primarily description of the Mexican educational system with discussion of student revolts and their effect on future development and quality of Mexican education. [T. B.]

6155. King, Richard G.; Alfonso Rangel Guerra; David Kline; and **Noel F. McGinn.** The provincial universities of Mexico: an analysis of growth and development. N.Y., Praeger Publishers, 1971. 234 p., bibl., tables (Praeger special studies in international economics and development)

Based principally on questionnaire data, a report on nine provincial universities which deals with responsiveness to regional needs, instructional capacity, administrative support and measures of growth. The analysis of data is useful and is supported by many tables. Authors maintain that data contradict the negative picture commonly held of Latin American universities. In part this seems true, particularly as regards concern for program and teaching reform and for meeting regional needs. But even in these universities data on library facilities, incentives for research and planning, and selection of professors paint a rather bleak picture. [G. R.]

Liebman, Arthur. Student activism in Mexico. See item 7520.

6156. Mebane, Donata and **Dale L. Johnson.** A comparison of the performance of Mexican boys and girls on Witkin's cognitive tasks (SIP/RIP, 4:3/4, 1970, p. 227-239, bibl., tables)

Testing hypothesis that in a highly sex-role differentiated society boys differ from girls in cognitive learning performance, authors conclude that such differences do exist and attempt to relate these differences to child rearing practices. Although the research is systematic, one might question the randomness of the sample and the reliability of the measuring instrument. [E. E.]

6157. Modiano, Nancy. Teaching personnel in the Indian schools of Chiapas (Newsletter [Council on Anthropology and Education] 2:2, May 1971, p. 9-11)

Arguing that Chiapas represents the problems of rural education in the extreme, the author describes conditions of living and teaching which prevent the adequate supply and improvement of teachers. [G. R.]

6158. Moshinsky, Marcos. La développement scientifique (Revue des Deux Mondes [Paris] 1, jan. 1973, p. 109-112, plate)

Brief review of scientific developments in Mexico, with emphasis on university research units. [G. R.]

6159. Palerm, Angel. Planeamiento integral de la educación en México. México, Ediciones Productividad, 1969. 118 p. (Col. Recursos humanos)

Final report of the Mexican National Commission of Integral Educational Planning. Unlike many quantitatively oriented educational plans, this report seriously questions the assumption of a causal relationship between schooling and economic and social development, although it does conclude that schooling does contribute something to economic growth and social mobility. The view of education as a "right of youth to instructional and cultural opportunity" is refreshing. [E. E.]

6160. *Revista del Centro de Estudios Educativos.* Vol. 1, No. 2, 2. trimestre 1971- . México.

In addition to book reviews and reports on education throughout the region, issue contains articles on Mexican primary school output and Peruvian university education. [G. R.]

6161. Rodríguez Sala de Gomezgil, María Luisa. Las instituciones de investigación científica en México: inventario de su estado actual. México, UNAM, Instituto Nacional de la Investigación Científica [and] Instituto de Investigaciones Sociales, 1970. 1 v. (Various pagings), tables.

Reference book of Mexican institutions of scientific investigation. Extensive use of charts and tables. [T. B.]

6162. Wences Reza, Rosalio. El movimiento estudiantil y los problemas nacionales. México, Editorial Nuestro Tiempo, 1971. 151 p., tables (Col. Pensamiento político de México)

Although openly radical, author presents some valuable questionnaire data on university student opinions in 1964 and 1970. Necessary reading in understanding recent Mexican events. [G. R.]

6163. Yáñez, Agustín. La educación se dirige al futuro (MSEP/LP, 66, julio 1970, p. 4-15, illus.)

Complete 1970 speech by Minister of Public Education listing advances made in education under the Díaz Ordaz administration. Accomplishments in vocational education, literacy, and in use of radio and television are stressed; but Yáñez tends to deemphasize the many problems remaining. [E. E.]

6164. Zea, Leopoldo. Misión de la universidad (UY/R, 12:71, sept./oct. 1970, p. 11-19, illus.)

Well-known Mexican thinker argues that mission of the university has changed from one of service to the individual to one of service to the community and society. Failure of the Mexican university to fulfill its new function explains the "Crisis of 1968." Although Zea's distinction between instruction for the individual and education for society is useful, the essay is rather poorly organized and repetitive. [E. E.]

PARAGUAY

6165. Gutiérrez, Asir P. Educational planning for the National University of Asunción, Paraguay. Washington, The Catholic Univ. of America, Education and Manpower for Development Seminar, 1970. 41 1., bibl. (mimeo)

Review of planning definitions, models and procedures; a general description of Paraguay; and some recommendations for the development of the national university. Superficial as a paper on planning but does contain some useful information on the national university. [G. R.]

6166. Kreider, L. Emil. Crecimiento de la población: un aspecto en la educación primaria en el Paraguay (CPES/RPS, 7:18, mayo/agosto 1970, p. 129-142, tables)

Author argues that currently proposed reforms cannot be realized, given the rapid increase in the school age population. Data on costs are included. [G. R.]

6167. Salcedo Cáceres, Epifanio and Margarita Ortiz de Salcedo. Perfiles de la educación paraguaya (CPES/RPS, 7:18, mayo/agosto 1970, p. 143-191, tables)

Conventional but useful and rather complete description of the Paraguayan educational system. Includes basic data on enrollment, administration and teachers. [G. R.]

Solís M., Leopoldo and others. Los problemas nacionales. See item 1949.

PERU

6168. Alberti, Giorgio and others. Aspectos sociales de la educación rural en el Perú. Lima, Instituto de Estudios Peruanos [and] Campodónico*ediciones,* 1972. 149 p., bibl., tables (Col. Perú-problema, 8)

Useful collection of articles on rural education problems, including mobilization, urban migration and value change. Other collaborators are: Julio Cotler, Dennis Chávez, Peri Paredes, and Luis Soberon. [T. B.]

6168a. Boggio, Ana; Carmen Lora; Gustavo Ríofrío; and **Rafael Roncagliolo.** ¿Cuesta arriba o cuesta abajo? Lima, Centro de Estudios y Promoción del Desarrollo (DESC) [and] Campodónico ediciones, 1973. 160 p.

Critical analysis of textbooks most commonly used in Peruvian primary schools. Authors demonstrate that upper-class life style of families depicted in texts bears little resemblance to what most pupils will ever know or be able to afford. Title itself a jibe at the title of one of most widely-used texts. [J. Strasma]

6169. Castro Harrison, Jorge. Prologómenos del planeamiento integral y administración de la educación. Lima, Depto. de Impresiones Tawa, 1971. 649 p., tables.

Extensive review of educational planning, both worldwide and Peruvian, including summaries of laws, meetings and seminars in the field. [G. R.]

6170. Epstein, Erwin H. Education and peruanidad: "internal" colonialism in the Peruvian highlands (CES/CER, 15:2, June 1971, p. 188-201, tables)

Documentary and questionnaire study of Peruvian Indian acculturation. Although the questionnaire data are interesting, the argument falters in many places. [G. R.]

6171. Joworski, Helam. La nueva ley universitaria: universidad y sociedad en el Perú (IESSC/C, 5:14, mayo/agosto 1970, p. 7-28)

Examining the 1969 Peruvian university reform law, author points out that law both takes governance power away from students and deemphasizes university's social role, apparently to make it a political tool of government. Joworski implores government to debate with university in order to reexamine university's essential functions. [E. E.]

6172. Morales, Emilio Felipe. Organización y administración escolar: la reforma de la educación en el Perú. Lima? Ediciones Escuela Peruana, n.d. 118 p.

"How to" book for elementary school teachers explaining fundamentals of organization and administration of schools. [T. B.]

6173. Paulston, Rolland G. Education and community development in Peru: problems at the cultural interface (CAE/N, 2:2, May 1971, p. 1-8, tables)

Attempts to determine conditions under which teachers in rural areas could be used as community developers. Although data available for such an analysis are limited, author raises questions which merit further study and consideration. [G. R.]

———. Maestros como agentes del cambio comunal: cuatro programas peruanos. See item 1467.

6174. ———. Society, schools and progress in Peru. N.Y., Pergamon Press, 1971. 312 p., tables.

Background chapters on history and culture; description of school system, its development, administration and organization; and examination of nonformal education, teacher preparation and planning. Although largely descriptive, with little hard data, book is useful addition to general literature on Latin American education. [E. E.]

6175. ———. Sociocultural constraints on educational development in Peru (JDA, 5:3, April 1971, p. 101-106)

Examines consequences of attempts to develop universal schooling and sociocultural stratification and concludes that, without a new *cholo* culture, efforts at educational modernization will likely not succeed. For political scientist's comment, see item 7698. [T. B.]

6176. Pérez Alba, Simón. ¿Es San Marcos una universidad de masas? (UC/B, 91, abril 1969, p. 20-21)

Author argues that indeed San Marcos is a university of the masses (citing a figure of 70 percent of the students from lower and lower-middle classes but not footnoting this figure), but as a consequence there has been a tragic lowering of standards. The university, he concludes, must raise its standards and must also assist those who enter without the necessary academic preparation by providing them with some remedial work. [E. E.]

Revista del Centro de Estudios Educativos. Vol. 1, No. 2, 2. trimestre 1971 . See item 6160.

Vásquez, Emilio. Historia de la educación. See item 6064.

URUGUAY

6177. Cernuschi, Félix. Educación, ciencia, técnica y desarrollo. Montevideo, Univ. de la República, Facultad de Humanidades y Ciencias, Depto. de Astronomía y Física, 1968. 124 p., tables (Publicación, 39)

Attempt to delineate causes of stagnation in the educational, scientific and industrial development of Uruguay and to suggest structural changes to alleviate stagnation. [T. B.]

6178. Iglesias, Enrique; Abner Prada; Guillermo Savloff; and **Julio de Santa Ana.** Conceptos de extensión universitaria. Montevideo, Fundación de Cultura Universitaria, 1972. 137 p.

Four essays on university extension in Uruguay, covering goals, programs and problems. [G. R.]

6179. Otero, Mario H. El sistema educativo y la situación nacional. Montevideo, Editorial Nuestra Tierra, 1969. 72 p., bibl., plates, tables (Nuestra tierra, 7)

In this account of the Uruguayan educational system, author begins by assuming that education is necessary for economic growth and also creates opportunities for the growth of man and his civilization. Although this assumption is not fully examined, author concludes that, in general, demographic growth within the school system is impressive, with the exception of technical education, which he describes as "lethargic." [E. E.]

6180. Ribeiro, Lidio. Compromiso en la educación: sentido y alcance de una experiencia educativa. Montevideo, Editorial Ejido, 1972. 154 p.

Emotional discussion of 1968 uprising in small rural Uruguayan pilot high school, its causes and implications for education. Some knowledge of Uruguayan politics useful in reading this. [T. B.]

6181. Sosa, Ademar. Gratuidad/obligatoriedad: evolución histórica y situación actual. Montevideo, Fundación Editorial Unión del Magisterio, 1971. 39 p.

Detailed review, principally legal, of historical and present situation as regards free, compulsory education in Uruguay. [G. R.]

6182. La universidad ante la intervención de secundaria. Montevideo, Univ. de la República, Depto. de Publicaciones, 1970. 39 p.

Detailed attack on the 1970 decree which allowed for government intervention in the Consejo Nacional de Enseñanza Secundaria, including legal opinions and more general criticisms on the government's entire educational policy. [G. R.]

VENEZUELA

6183. Arnove, Robert F. Student alienation: a Venezuelan study. Foreword by Kalman Silvert. N.Y., Praeger Publishers, 1971. 209 p., bibl., tables (Praeger special studies in international economics and development)

Empirical study of student attitudes at Univ. de Oriente in which author maintains that technical competence must be coupled with social commitment to achieve dynamic participation in social change. [E. E.]

6184. Chal Baud Zerpa, Reinaldo. La universidad y la reforma educativa en América Latina (UNAM/RMS, 33:1, enero/marzo 1971, p. 17-32)

Conventional account of university growth and need for reform, with special reference to Venezuela. Includes useful data on socioeconomic bias in higher education. [G. R.]

6185. Mendoza Angulo, José. Por la democracia universitaria. Mérida, Ven., Univ. de los Andes, 1970. 210 p., bibl.

An examination of the 1968 university law, current university problems, and proposals for making universities more democratic. Although Mendoza claims that the 1968 law, because it is vague, does not help universities to beeome more democratic, it is not clear how his proposals will accomplish this aim. [G. R.]

6186. Pérez Olivares, Enrique. Desarrollo de la educación y política científica en Venezuela. Caracas, Ministerio de Educación, 1971. 188 p., tables.

Official ministerial document for regional meeting containing discussion of Venezuelan educational progress, with supporting data. Useful if not critical. [G. R.]

6187. Quintero, Rodolfo. El Estudio de Caracas, un estilo nuevo en las investigaciones científicas nacionales (UCV/CU, 94/95, enero/junio 1967, p. 23-33)

Description of purposes and structure of Estudio de Caracas, a research center affiliated with UCV and an interesting, if at times polemical, discussion of the need for more rigorous inquiry in social research. Quintero points out that much so-called scientific research in Venezuela is really nothing more than simple accumulation of data or lists of facts and lacks systematic inquiry. [E. E.]

WEST INDIES

6188. Alleyne, Michael. Educational planning in Trinidad and Tobago (UPR/CS, 11:4, Jan. 1972, p. 73-81)

Director of educational planning argues that manpower planning puts too much emphasis on quantitative growth and thus fails to work in underdeveloped countries, where greater stress is needed on qualitative, particularly curricular, changes. [G. R.]

6189. Babín, Maria Teresa. Los estudios puertorriqueños en los Estados Unidos (UTIEH/C, 18, 1972, p. 29-41)

Intriguing account of problems author encountered in directing Puerto Rican Studies at CUNY, including lack of facility in Spanish of many students of Puerto Rican background and lack of professors, either American or Puerto Rican, to teach. [G. R.]

6190. Benn, Bernard W. Metropolitan standards and their effects on Carribbean teaching (UPR/CS, 11:2, July 1971, p. 85-89)

After examining effects of externally imposed examination and syllabus standards on teaching of English in West Indies, author argues that most teachers blame narrowness of Cambridge syllabus for their authoritarian, traditional teaching methods and that teachers, without constraints of the syllabus, would engage in more discussions, debates and public speaking. Although author suggests that syllabus is not totally at fault, he does raise some important issues. [E. E.]

6191. Bolland, O. Nigel. Literacy in a rural area of Jamaica (UWI/SES, 20:1, March 1971, p. 28-51, tables)

Surveying two rural communities, author finds that literacy is valued largely for social reasons or for purposes of urban migration but seldom for rural economic reasons. Raises provocative questions about the meaning of and training for functional literacy. [G. R.]

6192. Carnoy, Martin. The quality of education, examination performance, and urban-rural income differentials in Puerto Rico (CES/CER, 14:3, Oct. 1970, p. 335-349, tables)

Attempt to relate educational quality to income differentials between urban and rural workers. Although the calculations are interesting, the many assumptions made raise some serious questions about the applicability of the findings. [G. R.]

6193. ———. The rate of return to schooling and the increase in human resources in Puerto Rico (CES/CER, 16:1, Feb. 1972, p. 68-86, tables)

Computations of private rates of return to investments in schooling for period 1940-60, with comparisons of males and females and urban and rural dwellers. [G. R.]

6194. Cross, Malcolm and **Allan M. Schwartzbaum.** Social mobility and secondary school selection in Trinidad Tobago (UWI/SES, 18:2, June 1969, p. 189-207, tables)

Questionnaire study of secondary students. Authors find that selection to secondary schools is influenced most significantly by socioeconomic factors but that regional and ethnic factors also affect selection. See also item 6203. [G. R.]

6195. Figueroa, John J. Society, schools and progress in the West Indies. N.Y., Pergamon Press, 1971. 208 p., tables.

Examination of schooling in the former British holdings in the Caribbean, including historical background and current problems. [G. R.]

Foner, Nancy. Competition, conflict, and education in rural Jamaica. See item 1147.

———. Status and power in rural Jamaica: a study of educational and political change. See item 1148.

6196. Gómez Tejera, Carmen and **David Cruz López.** La escuela puertorriqueña. Sharon, Conn., Troutman Press, 1970. 262 p., bibl., plates (Puerto Rico: realidad y anhelo, 11)

Principally a history of Puerto Rican education from precolumbian to present times, but also includes some speculation on future of Puerto Rican education. Although a comprehensive and well-written history, author unquestioningly accepts certain assumptions about schools, such as efficacy of schools to "provide the knowledge necessary for its people to think and act intelligently."

6197. Levin, Lillian and others. U-bildning: skola och samhälle i Kina, Kuba, Tanzania och Vietnam. Stockholm, Rabén & Sjögren, 1970. 335 p.

Study of "socialist" education in poor countries entitled: *Education in less developed countries: school and society in China, Cuba, Tanzania and Vietnam.* Devotes 60 p. to Cuba. [M. Mörner]

Miller, Errol. Education and society in Jamaica. See item 1189.

6198. Nuestro experimento en la educación universitaria (HU/U, 32:190, abril/junio 1968, p. 63-67)

Brief, pro-Castro description of the role of the revolutionary university in the socio-economic development of Cuba, after which underdeveloped nations "ought" to model their universities. Basic premise is that to achieve university reform, change in the social order must first occur. [T. B.]

6199. Paulston, Rolland G. Cambios en la educación cubana (ILARI/A, 21, julio 1971, p. 61-82, tables)

Primarily interested in the relationship of education to social development, author explores changes in Cuban education through analysis of pre- and post-revolutionary periods. His arguments are based largely on quantitatives data. Although his contention that there is perhaps a quantitative problem is weak, it does not adversely affect his overall analysis as much as it begs for an accurate and open investigation of present day Cuban education. [T. B.]

6200. ———. Cultural revitalization and educational change in Cuba (CIES/CER, 16:3, Oct. 1972, p. 474-485, tables)

Paulston's basic premise is that comparative educators should become more knowledgeable consumers of and contributors to social science theory. Presents extreme case of Cuba to explain how process of rapid growth and educational change is intricately bound up in the process of radical social reconstruction, drawing heavily on Wallace's revitalization theory. [T. B.]

6201. Portorreal, Juan E. La reforma de la educación media en la República Dominicana (Aula [Santo Domingo] 1:1, abril/junio 1972, p. 27-32)

Brief description of reforms in Dominican secondary education, with suggestions for further restructuring of the Dept. of Education. Author stresses importance of community involvement. [T. B.]

Preiswerk, Roy. The teaching of international relations in the Caribbean. See item 8175.

6202. Ronceray, Hubert de. Où va notre système d'éducation? (IFH/C, 117, déc. 1971, p. 101-110, tables)

Attempting to answer question posed by title, author defines a philosophy of education for his country within framework of strong Haitian traditions and ancient beliefs. Describes current primary and secondary education situation and makes some proposals for improving it. [E. E.]

6203. Schwartzbaum, Allan M. and **Malcolm Cross.** Secondary school environment and development: the case of Trinidad and Tobago (UWI/SES, 19:3, Sept. 1970, p. 368-388, tables)

Authors find significant relationship between students' orientation toward mobility and socioeconomic composition of secondary schools they attend. See also item 6194. [G. R.]

6204. Tirado, Irma G. Programme budget proposals for the Department of Education in Puerto Rico (UPR/CS, 11:4, Jan. 1972, p. 60-72, tables)

In attempting to transform the Puerto Rican education budget into a program budget, author points out defects in present budgeting and presents several alternative programming methods. It is not clear, however, how the proposed budgeting solves the current defects. [G. R.]

6205. Walters, Elsa H. Some experiments in training personnel for the education of young children in the British Caribbean (UNESCO/IRE, 16:1, 1970, p. 110-119)

Examining approaches to and problems in infant education in Grenada, Jamaica and Barbados, author argues for improved teacher training consistent with local needs and resources. Proposals do not seem very convincing or even helpful, but description of conditions is illuminating. [G. R.]

BRAZIL

AGNES E. TOWARD

*Director of Education
Program for Extension
University of California, San Diego*

6206. Abreu, Jayme. Produtividade dos sistemas de ensino em geral e no Brasil (INEP/RBEP, 54:120, out./dez. 1970, p. 274-279)

Differences of opinion exist between economists and educators concerning best method by which to measure efficiency in education. The IPEA effort to measure educational efficiency has been based on: enrollment vs. graduates, utilization of resources, student-teacher ratios, decrease in qualified staff, percentage of dropouts or repeated courses of study, and unit costs. While preliminary findings are still unsophisticated and rudimentary, they do provide a starting point for further study in this area.

6207. Almeida, Fernando Bessa de. A experiência de orçamento por programas no nordeste. Salvador, Bra., Univ. Federal da Bahia, Escola de Administração, 1970? 93 p., tables,

Summary of seminar co-sponsored by universities of Bahia and Ceará on funding of programs to train state employees. Participants were from Ceará, Bahia, Maranhão, Pernambuco, and Minas Gerais, and from federal and state administrations. One of the principal reasons for the seminar was to bring about policy regarding the implementation of a new law, 4.320 (of March 1964) regarding distribution and control of funding. For a three-day seminar, the report is quite detailed (93 p.).

6208. Almeida Júnior, Antônio F. de. A escola pitoresca e outros estudos. Rio, Ministério da Educação e Cultura, Instituto Nacional de Estudos Pedagógicos, Centro Brasileiro de Pesquisas Educacionais, 1966. 276 p. (Série 11: Os grandes educadores brasileiros, 2)

First published in 1934, this book is now re-issued by the *Centro* as second in its series of Almeida works (for first, see item 6209). Full of anecdotes and informal observations ("why do children smoke? surely not for the taste, at the beginning . . ."), author gives us best description of his book in his preface to first edition, in which he states that it is ". . . from the comic in solemn things and the seriousness of funny truths, that one tries to derive the educational precept." Almeida, Jr., after an outstanding career of over 50 years in education, has a wealth of material to draw from this and other books.

6209. Amaral, Maria Lúcia. Criança é criança: literatura infantil e seus problemas. Petrópolis, Bra., Editôra Vozes *em convênio com o* Instituto Nacional do Livro, 1971. 118 p.

Author has had extensive and successful career, not only as writer of children's books, but as journalist and scriptwriter for films. As journalist she edited children's section and "Daily Scholar" column, also was contributor to several magazines. This book is outcome of successful series of classes offered at the National Historical Museum for parents, librarians, and teachers. Her preface states she intends book to serve as guide for teachers and especially parents who do not have time to attend a class but need guidance in literature for children. Her style is forthright and clear and her topics are: books for children, fantasy in children's literature, folklore in this literature, poetry for children, theatre for children, theatre in school, comic books (references to those of US), a children's newspaper, space literature, literature as recreation, and a bibliography, all in 116 solid p. of practical, and thoughtful information. Highly recommended.

6210. Angelini, Arrigo Leonardo. Educational technology and television in Brazil (SIP/RIP, 4:1, marzo 1970, p. 59-68)

Writing from point of view of Educational Psychology Dept. at the Univ. of São Paulo, author begins by noting changes within that dept. in terms of research interests and activities. He then gives an exciting capsule review of developments in educational TV that provides average readers with comprehensive picture of present situation, future plans, and priorities. Cites lack of qualified technical personnel as one of greatest problems, lists priorities determined by Brazilian Center of Educational Television, and emphasizes that in Brazil educational television is viewed as a substitute medium for schools, rather than as a supplement, as in US. Educational TV is also regarded as a powerful medium for teacher training, and as an answer to problems presented by vast geographical distances, large groups of illiterates, and high percentage of school dropouts. Of particular interest to some readers is his discussion of violence on television in a section dealing with commercial TV. Rich, readable source of information.

6211. Arquivos Brasileiros de Psicologia Aplicada. Fundação Getúlio Vargas. Vol. 21, No. 2, abril/junho 1969- . Rio.

Contribution of some substance in terms of seniority, offering articles on psychotheraphy, case studies, and social behavior. There is also a news notes section and a section of book reviews.

6212. Azevedo, Thales de. As ciências sociais no Bahia: notas para su história. Salvador, Bra., Univ. da Bahia, 1964. 81 p. (Univ. da Bahia. Instituto de Ciências Sociais, 1)

Book appeared in 1964, but Thales de Azevedo's credentials as a sociologist and a *bahiano* merit attention of his work, particularly since there have not been any other recent reviews. Reading Thales de Azevedo is both nourishing and frustrating, and this slim effort is no exception. He is very generous with references to Brazilian and non-Brazilian sources (there is no bibliography here) which keeps the reader jumping from century to century, from language to language (German, French, Spanish, and occasional use of Latin), and from discipline to discipline. Furthermore, his style is extremely difficult, featuring sentences of paragraph length and words not easily found in a pocket dictionary. In this particular work he cites sources from 1500 forward, moves comfortably from ethnography to anthropology, to medicine, to spiritualism, to history, and back again, and provides a veritable resource book for anyone seeking bibliographical guidance. 81 p. of high density information for the persevering reader or researcher.

6213. Barros, Roque Spencer Maciel de. Ensaios sôbre educação. São Paulo, Editôra da Univ. de São Paulo [and] Editorial Grijalbo, 1971. 305 p.

Author of several books including a detailed analysis of the Law of Directives and Guidelines presents heterogeneous collection of essays—everything from "Positivism and Education" to "Batman and Robin Hood" (the latter a discussion of folk heroes and other matters). Some were written as early as 1962; some were first presented as speeches. He expects a well-read audience; in return he delivers some wide-ranging thoughts related to education.

6214. Benathar, Roberto Levy. Supervisão escolar no ensino fundamental (SBPC/CC, 24:5, maio 1972, p. 444-447)

Originally a speech delivered at the XI Meeting of State Supervisors of Instruction in Goiás, April 1971, article concerned primarily with recent changes in Brazilian education, particularly impact of new commitment to educate much larger portion of population. Author, Director of Basic Education, Ministry of Education, describes new role of educational administrator whose major responsibility is productivity, rather than planning. Also explores new supervisory relationships among school personnel, evolution of comprehensive secondary schools, opportunities for experimentation in Goiás and "reform" goals for Brazilian secondary schools.

6215. Bernard, Philippe. Le rôle de l'université dans un pays en voie de développement: un exemple dans le Nordeste brésilien (Revue d'Historie Moderne et Contemporaine [Paris] 19, oct./déc. 1972, p. 654-666)

Thorough exposition of particular view of this topic. After Bernard introduces what he calls "the problem of the Northeast," he presents history of development programs therein, beginning in 1908 and leading up to the establishment of SUDENE in 1959. His interest seems to be in recounting ways in which these programs failed to realize their objectives, and why, particularly in the case of the UCLA-USAID-Asimow Project in the 1960's. After some small praise for the transformation of the Asimow project into PUDINE (Programa Universitário de Desenvolvimento Industrial), which he considers more attuned to local needs because it is more "Brazilianized", Bernard then considers problems PUDINE will face in future. Regards government policy and student attitudes to be most significant potential influences on future programs.

6216. Betting, Joelmir. Brazil: the take-off is now. São Paulo, American Chamber of Commerce for Brazil, 1971. 47 p., maps, plates.

Once told that this is a publication, in English, of the American Chamber of Commerce in Brazil, this glossy magazine no doubt assumes an immediate bias for the reader. Apparently written and/or edited by the Editor of Economic and Financial Matters of the newspaper *Folhas de São Paulo* (Joelmir Betting), first title heading gives a clue to the orientation and approach to the subject of Brazil in the 70's—"The Great Transformation." With spectacular photographs of almost all of the principal cities (where is Fortaleza?) this is a very interesting publication for anyone who knew Brazil before 1964.

6217. Bibliografia Brasileira de Educação. Centro Brasileiro de Pesquisas Educacionais. Vol. 17, No. 4, out/dez 1969- . Rio.

Excellent bibliography which deserves mention in every review of Brazilian educational publications and materials because it is compact, yet thorough and prepared by knowledgeable professionals. Individual items listed in the *Bibliografia* are frequently listed separately in this section. Comprehensive coverage for researcher.

6218. Boletim do IESPE. Instituto de Estudos Sociais, Políticos e Econômicos da PUCRGS [Pontifica Univ. Católic do Rio Grande do Sul]. No. 14, junho 1972- . Pôrto Alegre, Bra.

Excellent summary of this catholic university's social science sector—very thorough listing of demographic and pedagogical data: enrollments, percentage of students working, method of admission, events each month at Social Science Institute, news notes, etc. Could be useful for someone examining student populations in higher education.

6219. Brazil. Ministério da Educação e Cultura. Conselho Federal de Educação. Ensino de 1.° e 2.° graus. Rio, 1971. 293 p.

As principal source of legislative interpretation, and therefore of considerabld policy, the Federal Education Council has been producing reports and opinions since 1961. This most recent effort is a thorough treatment of regulations pertaining to primary and secondary education. To be specific (and quote from the preface supplied by Julia Azevedo of the Secretariat) "The material . . . prepared originally for the Seventh Joint Meeting of Education Councils was supplemented in this edition, by the results of that meeting and by options formulated by His Excellency, the Minister of Education, Jarbas Gonçalves Passarinho." The Council regularly publishes *Documenta*, a monthly report of Council deliberations and opinions, but this volume is a separate publication detailing work done on implementing recent law governing primary and secondary education. Comprehensive material for the specialist.

6220. ———. ———. Documentário estatístico sobre a situação educacional no Espírito Santo. Vitória, Bra., Univ. Federal do Espírito Santo, 1968. 116 p., tables (mimeo)

Statistical data, including graphs, tables and figures comparing Espírito Santo's development with rest of Brazil and with other Latin American nations. Provides comments on number and percentage of dropouts, proportion of expansion in school enrollment in relation to population. Covers following: 1) "Demanda e Oferta de Educação no Espírito Santo," 2) "Prestação de Serviços do Sistema Educacional," 3) "Perda dos Efetivos Discentes," 4) "Corpo Docente," 5) "Despesas com a Educação," 6) "Aspectos Demográficos, Econômicos e Ocupacionais," and 7) "Conclusões."

6221. ——. ——. **Instituto Nacional de Estudos Pedagógicos. Centro Brasileiro de Pesquisas Educacionais (MEC-INEP-CBPE).** Melhoria do rendimento do ensino no primeiro ano. Rio, 1971. 71 p., tables (Publicações: série 8. Pesquisas e monografias, 7)

INEP research project designed to investigate causes for high rate of failure between first and second years of primary school students in Brazil. Drop between first and second years is one of greatest obstacles facing Brazilian efforts to reduce illiteracy and expand education. In this preliminary study several factors were examined, including: changes in methods and resources, teacher expectations, maturation theories, and reading readiness. Research will continue, but this first report merits careful reading.

6222. ——. ——. Plano setorial de educação e cultura, 1972/74. Brasília, Secretaria Geral, 1971. 250 p., tables.

In compliance with Law No. 9 of 11 Dec. 1970, concerning the First Economic and Social Plan and the Budget of Investments, the Ministry of Education and Culture prepared this proposal, which will be submitted to the Dept. of Planning for integration and revision as needed. Developed before the new law governing primary and secondary education, this proposal will be revised to comply with its provisions. Index reveals a very thorough coverage—from construction of buildings, equipment, and financing, to research, administrative reform, personnel considerations, and special programs.

6223. Britto, Luiz Navarro de. Sous-développement et programmation de l'éducation: une expérience dans l'état de Bahia (UP/TM, 13:49, jan./mars 1972, p. 85-101)

Report on attempts to install a new educational approach in Bahia (begun in 1967 with election of new governor who used young university graduates as a team to renovate the educational program) and the opposition to its implementation.

6224. Brum, Hélio de Almeida. A integração universidade—indústria. Rio, Instituto Euvaldo Lodi (IEL), 1970. 32 1., bibl., map, tables.

In a speech delivered at Seminar on University and Business, co-sponsored by Associação dos Diplomados da Escola Superior de Guerra (ADESG) and Instituto Euvaldo Lodi (IEL) from 28 July to 9 Nov. 1970, Professor Brum, technical specialist on IEL's staff, begins with historical development of Brazil and origins of the university therein before discussing modern times. His attention to history is both compact and helpful and would be of interest to those unfamiliar with Brazil. He then presents observations on: role of political, educational, and economic leaders, difficulties in implementing an integration program, and integration as a factor in mobilization. Provides enrollments (by state) at elementary, secondary, and higher education levels, and concludes with a description of IEL itself and projects (of national scope) that it sponsors. Limited bibliography.

6225. *Cadernos de Jornalismo e Comunicação.* Edições Jornal do Brasil. No. 28, jan./fev. 1971- . Rio.

Issue devoted to television, specifically education. Contributors include: representative of National Institute of Pedagogical Studies (INEP); president of Brazilian Center for Educational Television, Cilson Amado; member of the National Commission for Space Activities; and several staff members from TV, Channel 2 (an educational TV outlet in São Paulo). Regular features in this issue are section of book reviews and page of news notes. Publication of Rio's *Jornal do Brasil.*

6226. *Cadernos Região e Educação.* Centro Regional de Pesquisas Educacionais do Recife. Vol. 11, No. 22, dez. 1971- . Recife, Bra.

Always of value, as indication of current research trends in Northeast and as source of information about local programs in that area. Despite its poor format, *Cadernos Região e Educação* is the official publication of the Regional Center for Educational Research in Recife. Articles of interest are reviewed individually elsewhere in this section. Topics vary widely. Present volume contains two: "The Situation of Normal Schools in the Northeast" and "The Teaching of Mathematics in the Primary Schools of Recife."

6227. Cantídio, Walter de Moura. Universidade em reexame. Fortaleza, Bra., Univ. Federal do Ceará, Imprensa Universitária, 1972. 41 p. (Col. Pensamento universitário, 3)

Three speeches by new (as of 1971) Reitor of Univ. of Ceará, in Brazil's Northeast. First, delivered in Brasília, on occasion of his acceptance of assignment, in Minister of Education's office (theme: Mission and Commitment) is very brief and especially idealistic. Second, delivered at university upon assuming role, (theme: goals and plans for the university), is much more pragmatic, specific, and lengthy. Last, during Minister's visit to university in 1972, (theme: overview of year's accomplishments) reviews events of first year of his administration.

6228. Carneiro, José Fernando Domingues; Laerte Ramos de Carvalho; Osmar Ferreira; and Rubens d'Almada Horta Pôrto. Relatório da Equipe de Assessoria ao Planejamento do Ensino Superior (EAPES); Acôrdo MEC-USAID. Rio, Ministério da Educação e Cultura, Directoria do Ensino Superior, 1969. 648 p., plate, tables.

Report of team of Brazilian education experts appointed to work with AID consultants on a major project to reform higher education in Brazil. Much more detailed than necessary, report begins with complete history of project, discusses education vis-à-vis development, includes sections on resources, general culture vs. professional culture, and history of higher education in Brazil, then finally approaches some of major questions confronting higher education in Brazil. Essays, lectures, and other presentations of AID consultants appear in English and in translation.

6229. Carvalho, Joaquim Montezuma de. O ensino da filosofia nas universidades brasileiras (RIB, 20:3, julio/sept. 1970, p. 318-324)

Author from Moçambique, Africa, argues that modern universities are merely collections of departments unless they offer their students opportunity to study philosophy. Begins with a response to article by José Antônio Tobias on same subject but finds fault with Tobias' suggestions, first, because he reduces philosophy to "a science of truth" or metaphysics, and second, because Tobias wants students to *begin* their university years with the philosophy course. Author advances arguments of Manuel Sacristan, professor at the Univ. of Barcelona, whose definition of philosophy is much broader and who suggested that philosophy be studied towards end of student's career. Also see item 6302.

Castelo, Plácido Adelraldo. História do ensino no Ceará. See *HLAS 34:2903a*.

6230. Castro, Cláudio de Moura. Desenvolvimento econômico: educação e educabilidade. Rio, Edições Tempo Brasileiro, 1972. 82 p., tables (Univ. do Estado da Guanabara)

Impressive biographical sketch describes Moura Castro as fast-rising star of Brazilian economics: obtained degree from Univ. Federal de Minas Gerais, 1962; took Master's Yale, 1964; doctorate Vanderbilt, 1970; and postgraduate study at Berkeley and Harvard; published articles; secured professorship in economics at Getúlio Vargas Foundation and with this study, won first annual Union of Brazilian Banks' Award for best essay stimulating improved relations between private enterprise and university. Nevertheless, little fresh insight or so-called innovative thinking in this effort. His thoughts about "preparation for the future" are so compatible with elitist tradition, and possibly with present political priorities, that one wonders if bank award was won on that basis rather than on originality of thought or quality of scholarship. Opposes expanded enrollments and greater access to education, concluding that he sees little justice or viability in educational reforms that emphasize expanded enrollments (he would certainly oppose open admissions) and his major thesis, that there are "educogenic families" which provide intellectual stimuli and socialization appropriate to formal study, favors providing education to upper-class citizens who are most likely to succeed, both in school and in adult life. Moura Castro appears to be very ambitious. Delves into much else, including relationship between nutrition and intelligence, but his treatment of economics of education is superficial, his explanations are simplistic and condescending to the reader (e.g., see his definition of scientific method) and his conclusions are at odds with findings and data he reports.

6231. Coelho, Celso Barros. Universidade em causa. Teresina, Bra., TAL, 1969. 66 p.

Old material, revived in order to "awaken in students greater interest in their participation in the task of creation of our University." Material originally published as newspaper columns then gathered into book. Topics are brief: "O Universal pelo Regional," "Presença da Universidade," "A Universidade e o Desenvolvimento," "A Universidade e o Poder Jovem," "A Problemática Universitária," "Universidade e Humanismo," "Concepção da Reforma Universitária," "Lição Proveitosa."

6232. Constituição da República Federativa do Brasil: emenda constitucional no. 1, de 17 de outubro de 1969. Contendo índice alfabético e remissivo organizado pelo Dr. Carlos Eduardo Barreto. São Paulo, Edição Saraiva, 1970. 312 p. (Col. Legislação brasileira)

Título IV—"Da Família, Da Educação, e Da Cultura" (comprising Articles 175-180). As in previous constitutional provisions, this version provides for: civil marriage, official aid to private schools, compulsory schooling for ages seven to 14, support from commerce and industry for education (salary-education provision).

6233. Côrrea, Arlindo Lopes. Applicability of advanced educational technologies in Brazil. Rio, Ministerio de Planejamento e Coordenação Geral, Centro Nacional de Recursos Humanos, 1971. 11 l.

Reader is deprived of some of the most interesting and provocative observations about education in this commentary by a totally inadequate translation. Author has been firsthand witness and participant of planning for Brazilian education and in final pages of this work he alludes to several major developments in what he calls "patterns for handling the educational sector in Brazil". His approach to educational planning and investment and his view of the future value of education in relations to human resources deserve a better translator.

6234. ——— and Edson Machado de Souza. Metodologia para avaliação do desempenho da rêde de ensino industrial. Rio? Ministério da Educação e Cultura, Depto. de Ensino Médio, 1971. 85 p., bibl., tables.

At request of Dept. of Industrial Education of Ministry of Education, two economists undertook to define approach or method for evaluation of industrial education. Their choice was quite traditional—productivity in relation to investment. First phase of their work, described in this volume, was to define the method. Second phase would be to conduct a field experiment applying the method. Third, to extend results to national level. Bibliography is particularly cosmopolitan.

6235. A crise do ensino: coletânea de artigos de revista *El Correo* de la UNESCO, de abril de 1969 e janeiro de 1970. Tradução de Rui Berford Dias. Apresentação [de] Irene Estevão de Oliveira. Rio, Fundação Getúlio Vargas, Instituto de Documentação, Serviço de Publicações, 1971. 96 p., plates (Série Informação & Comunicação, 3)

Despite slim appearance, a heavy book to skim or read, since selections cover wide range of topics and areas. As Director of Dept. of Education at Getúlio Vargas Foundation states in her preface, these ideas, expressed in articles selected from a UNESCO education publication, are gathered together by the Foundation in this publication in order to circulate, in Portuguese, the developments in education that are occurring beyond Brazil's borders. She also states that she hopes both adults and young people, as teacher or student, will have access to this material. Authors of the various sections are: Marcel Hicter "Theoretical Questions of Education"; John I. Goodlad "The Future of Instruction"; René Habachi "From An Explosive Civilization to an Integrated Education;" and Paul Lengrad "A Complete System to Reform"

6236. Cummings, Richard L. Transformations in Brazilian engineering education: an indicator of modernity (*in* Rippy, Merrill *ed.* Cultural change in Brazil [see item 122] p. 13-23. tables)

Returns to 1808 to trace development of industrialization and technical training in Brazil. After presenting historical background, discusses sources of engineers in the 1940's, 1950's, and early 1960's, including immigrants, military school graduates, and self-taught practitioners. Sees a marked change in both status and form of engineeriing education with last 30 years.

6237. Cunha, Maria Auxiliadora Versiani. Didática fundamentada na teoria de Piaget. 1. ed. Rio, Forense, 1972. 66 p., bibl., tables.

Lauro de Oliveira Lima's preface expresses admiration for author's ability to compress Piaget's extensive research and writing into brief 66 p. Praise is well founded, for author provides excellent source of information about Piagetian theory and pedagogy that teachers in US might profitably read. Discusses not only theories, but also their relationship to teacher training, curricula, and other facets of classroom activities. Includes appropriate bibliography.

6238. *Educação.* Ministério da Educação e Cultura, Depto. de Apoio, Diretoria de Documentação e Divulgação. Ano 1, No. 2, julho/set. 1971- . Brasília.

New publication (1971) to be issued on a trimester basis, *Educação* is of a superior quality, with excellent photographs and illustrations. This issue's lead article is by President of the Federal Education Council, Roberto Figueira Santos. Range of topics and contributors is broad and representative of all segments of education community. Most useful section of summaries of articles in French, Spanish, and English appear in back.

6239. *Educação.* Orgão da Federação Nacional dos Establecimentos de Ensino. Ano 8, No. 46, julho 1970- . Rio.

Good, up-to-date newspaper source on events from private school sector, (political events, particularly). This issue provides reprint from the *Diario de Notícias* of May 29 on topic of university students' failure to respond to Minister Passarinho's attempts to win their support. Other items include Federal Council Resolution on moral and civic education, and interview with president of Federation on "Perspectives of the Private School" reprinted from *Tribuna do Ceará*. Subscription could be a worthwhile investment for anyone following current events, if delivery could be assured.

6240. Encontro Brasileiro sôbre Introdução ao Estudo da História, *1, Nova Friburgo, 1968.* Anais. Niteroi, Bra., Univ. Federal Fluminense, Instituto de Ciências Humanas e Filosofia, 1970. 377 p.

Report of I Brazilian Conference on Study of History is noteworthy for first lecture, in which José Honório Rodrigues attacks present structure of higher education history courses in Brazil, focusing on problems created by *cátedra* or lifetime professorship, when system is abused by unqualified individuals dominating few key positions. Makes numerous references to actual situations and in many instances compares Brazilian and American universities when giving examples of areas in need of improvement in Brazilian universities. While not all of his examples are entirely accurate (he describes fate of tenured professor in US who fails to continue publishing as "professional ruin"), his arguments in favor of curricular reform are well founded. Conference was attended by representatives from nine states and 37 universities or faculties, as well as some professors from abroad. List of participants appears on p. 369-374.

6241. Ensino técnico industrial em Minas Gerais. Belo Horizonte, Bra., Univ. do Trabalho de Minas Gerais, Instituto de Pesquisa do Trabalho, 1970. 21 p.

Raw data on: Minas Gerais' secondary education, industrial type, including *colegios técnicos, ginasios industriais, escolas de aprendizagem, fundação universidade de trabalho.* Summary chapters on *síntese das matrículas* and *sínteses do número de estabelecimentos.* Of possible interest to someone wanting to examine vocational education in a particular state.

6242. Fachin, R. C. Brazil: costing an espansion programme for secondary education in Rio Grande do Sul (*in* Coombs, Philip H. and Jacques Hallak *eds.* Educational cost analysis in action: case studies for planners. Paris, UNESCO, International Institute for Educational Planning, 1972, v. 2, p. 193-215, tables)

Quite accurate title for material in article. R. C. Fachin is identified as staff member for State Secretariat in Rio Grande do Sul, but this report is not based solely on his efforts. In Rio Grande do Sul, one of four states selected to participate in a USAID project, the State Secretariat and the State Council of Education began developing a comprehensive educational plan. Report presents case study illustrating techniques followed in preparing state plan. To quote from introduction: "The purpose of the study is to show how, in a concrete situation, a group of experts has costed an educational project with very limited and inadequate data, and related it to the general educational plan." An attempt at evaluation of methods used can be found in final section, "Concluding Remarks."

6243. Freyre, Gilberto. Gilberto Freyre e as universidades do nordeste. Ceará, Bra., Directorio Central dos Estudantes, 1960. 27 p. (DCE, 1)

Graceful rebuttal to an article in *O Cruzeiro* written by Gilberto Freyre in which he defends idea of regional university for Northeast, thus implying abolishment of state universities. Original Freyre article is presented, followed by seven replies rejecting his thesis. Published in magazines or newspapers, all are short and easily read.

6244. Gevertz, Rachel. Da estrutura de material pedagógico de ciências naturais e exatas (SBPC/CC, 24:3, março 1972, p. 218-222)

Miss Gevertz, science educator active in innovative programs of instruction in sciences in Northeast, is capable of offering much more than she does in this article, which is nothing more than an enumeration of material she acquired while participating in a special summer course at Harvard Univ. Subheads are: diagnostic instrument: for the appreciation of the logical structure of mathematics; for the appreciation of the philosophical structure of science; for the appreciation of behaviorism; and for the appreciation of gestalt, followed by a bibliography. Publication unworthy of author's experience and background, based on material from 1964.

6245. Goldberg, Maria Amélia Azevedo. O pesquisador educacional e o mercados de trabalho (SBPC/CC, 23:6, dez. 1971, p. 754-758)

Discussion of need for research that could provide data in three areas: 1) total number of qualified professionals available in educational research; 2) productive capacity of professional institutions, i.e., number of openings for graduate study in the field; and 3) potential employment market, followed by analysis of distribution of talent presently conducting research. Goldberg's contribution here is to sketch a sort of "map" of educational research and research resources.

6246. Gondim, Maristella de Miranda Ribeiro. Crianças escrevem para criança. Belo Horizonte, Bra., Imprensa Oficial, 1971. 295 p.

Interesting collection of children's writing, drawn from a fourth year class at the *Grupo Escolar Barão do Rio Branco,* in Minas Gerais. While a better attempt could have been made to identify authors by age, level, and background and to explain context in which collection developed, material itself is very well presented; in fact, selections read so well that one is tempted to cavil and ask, do children really write so fluently? Fourth in a series, this book suggests possible projects for classes concerned with writing, literature, self-expression, and language elsewhere.

6247. Graciarena, Jorge. As prioridades da pesquisa em sociologia da educação (SBPC/CC, 23:6, déz. 1971, p. 721-727)

Comments from UNESCO researcher who suggests three areas for study: 1) post-graduate training; 2) Brazil's technological system as a nation; and 3) methods used by industry and business in acquiring technological expertise. Includes further and very important area for investigation: national policies for science and technology.

Guerra, C. Vianna. Pequeno inquérito sôbre o conhecimento de 100 palavras da língua portuguêsa aplicado a 361 estudantes. See item 8509.

6248. Harrell, William A. The Brazilian educational system: a summary. Washington, US Dept. of Health, Education, and Welfare, 1970. 26 p.

Companion pamphlet to earlier Harrell publication, *Educational Reform in Brazil: the Law of 1961* (See HLAS 33:4797). Contains outline of organization of education program, enrollment data for all levels, and limited discussion of recent changes. Harrell deals very gently with realities, e.g., on the Federal Education Council (Conselho Federal de Educação): "Less vulnerable than is the Ministry to change of members with each political change, the Council has considerable autonomy in most respects. Nevertheless, when making decisions it is influenced by the Minister and when attempting to have its decisions implemented is held back until it is certain that he approves. This pattern . . . obviously gives much authority to the Minister."

6249. Haussman, Fay. A giant begins to stir (Saturday Review [N.Y.] 53, 17 Oct. 1970, p. 62-63)

Haussman, who lived in Brazil for several years, is free-lance journalist who describes herself as "realistic leftist" commentator on Brazilian affairs. She seems neither realistic nor leftist in her optimistic and enthusiastic overview of large-scale changes in Brazilian education. Praises the GOT program (Ginásios Orientados para o Trabalho) as most promising reform for past, highly selective and unrealistic programs, yet has no difficulty reconciling praise for programs to teach needlework with her own allegation that middle-level technical training is present top priority. Comments are superficial and thereby misleading—some measures she selects for praise are repeats of various failures, as case of higher quotas for enrollments and adaptation to regional needs, both of which were part of 1961 reform effort. It is a pity that writing for layman has apparently affected accuracy and depth of her report, a disservice to American readers hoping to learn about Brazilian education.

6250. *Informativo.* Fundação Getúlio Vargas. Vol. 4, No. 1, jan. 1972- . Rio.

News bulletin and monthly magazine of the Getúlio Vargas Foundation, center for research, training, and publications in the areas of administration and, more recently, social sciences. Among items in this issue are: reports of new research to be funded by FGV, book reviews, news of FGV activities and courses, an editorial, and a chronological summary of FGV events for the previous year.

6251. Instituto Euvaldo Lodi, *Rio.* Pesquisa bibliográfica sôbre integração universidade-indústria. Rio, 1970. 61 p.

Sponsoring agency for this bibliography (Euvaldo Lodi Institute) is an outgrowth of cooperation among three organizations: National Industrial Confederation (CNI), Industrial Social Service Organization (SESI), and National Industrial Apprenticeship Service (SENAI). Institute is intended to function by means of network of regional centers which work closely with local industries, promoting optimum use of resources by both industry and higher education. Regional centers undertake studies, of which the present work (completed at the headquarter's office in Guanabara) is one. There are presently 17 regional IEL centers. Covering only Guanabara, work will be expanded to other states through studies at regional centers. Team of four visited six libraries, eight Ministries, the Ford Foundation and USAID, the morgues of three newspapers, and four research centers from which they list 138 entries with variable length annotations. Perhaps most useful (or thoughtful) aspect of this limited work is indication of its location with each item, so that anyone consulting bibliography can find item in proper library, Ministry, or research center. Another feature of possible interest is list of periodicals consulted.

6252. Integração universidade-indústria hoje: IEL-ADESG. Rio, APEC Editôra, 1971. 252 p., bibl., tables.

For review of Ch. 4, see item 6224. Large volume has 12 contributors of established credentials in worlds of business, education, and government. Roberto Campos, former Minister of Planning from 1964-67, writes on education for development. Final article deals with "Professional Frustration" and was written by a psychologist. Generous supply of graphics and statistical data, as well as other material of interest to economists, social planners, and social scientists.

Jackson, William Vernon. Fifty million books for Brazil. See *HLAS 34:57.*

6253. Lacerda, Roberto Mündell de. O ciclo básico: 1º ciclo geral de estudos.

Floranópolis, Bra., Univ. Federal de Santa Catarina, 1971. 102 p., tables.

Prepared by committee composed of university administrators. Attempts to explain Basic Course developed as part of reform effort begun 1970 at Santa Catarina. Provides as much information as possible from detailed course outlines to a guide list of references.

6254. Lacombe, Laura Jacobina. L'éducation préscolaire au Brésil (UNESCO/IRE, 16:1, 1970, p. 100-106, tables)

Lacombe begins with history of pre-school and kindergarten programs in Brazil, describes first kindergartens (1896, São Paulo) and brings history up to now. Stresses changes in society with last 20 years. Provides two tables, one showing development of preschool education from 1946-62 (number of kindergartens, enrollments, number of maternal health courses, and enrollments); other showing distribution of pre-school education by state (number of units, number of teachers, and enrollments).

6255. Lenhard, Rudolf. Um dilema da administração escolar (CRPE/PP, 12, out. 1970, p. 141-160)

Long discussion of generalities precedes topic: identification of three kinds of administrators in education: those completely bureaucratized and submissive to the administration; those exercising professional leadership, capitalizing on bureaucracy to gain their objectives; and those who establish paternalistic regime. Educational administration is compared to other types, particularly in terms of alienation and related problems.

6256. Levy, Samuel. As prioridades da pesquisa em economia da educação (SBPC/CC, 23:6, déz. 1971, p. 728-730)

Levy begins by discussing over-emphasis on economic planning for education and need for integrated, multidisciplinary planning. Then discusses pressure placed on higher education by marked increase (300 percent) in enrollments at that level and resulting shortage of qualified instructors. Provides brief statistical summary of higher education enrollment picture and some figures related to expenditures. After identifying major points (proportion of resources devoted to higher education, high cost, and pressure caused by need to expand), he asks: What are the most important questions, analyses, and kinds of information that an educational planner should try to obtain from an economist?

6257. Lima, Maria Nayde dos Santos. O ensino de matemática na Escola Primária do Recife (CRPER/CRE, 11:22, dez. 1971, p. 31-88, tables)

Education programs throughout Brazil, particularly at primary level, are in transition period due to legislation and subsequent plans for its implementation. Research team in Recife investigated area of mathematics instruction in primary school during new program's first year. Objectives listed indicate interest in discovering if staff members are properly qualified and prepared to implement math programs; if problem areas were clustered in public rather than private schools; and similar questions. Questionnaire composed of 14 questions (article provides sample) was circulated to 51 Recife schools. Discussion of results accompanies tables, lists, or graphics.

6258. Lima, Revira Lisboa de Moura. Sugestões de atividades baseadas num mesmo texto para a primeira série ginasial (Letras de Hoje [Pontifica Univ. Católica de Rio Grande do Sul, Pôrto Alegre, Bra.] 5, dez. 1970, p. 31-39, tables)

Unit of lesson plans for classes in Portuguese. After brief reading selection, there are questions and answers based on reading, followed by structural drills on verb forms and pronouns. Article begins with reading selection, without prior information about source or purpose of unit, and without explanation of its place in any larger framework.

6259. Lopes Côrrea, Arlindo. Applicability of advanced educational technologies in Brazil. Rio, I. Contece, 1971. 11 p. (mimeo)

As Executive Secretary of National Center for Human Resources of Ministry of Planning, author has first-hand, authoritative view of educational policy formation in Brazil. In this commentary, subtitled "The Great Contemporary Questions on Education," he advances theory that education is in a pre-industrial stage and must suffer a revolution in order to meet expanding demands of modern society. After reviewing general situation of education worldwide, in terms of priorities, resources, and expectations, he provides brief overview of Brazilian case. For readers seeking an introduction to Brazilian education during last decade, this would be an excellent source.

6260. Lourenço Filho, Manuel Bergström. Organização e administração escolar: curso básico. 6. ed. São Paulo, Edições Melhoramentos, 1972. 314 p., tables (Obras completas, 6)

Sixth ed. of classic first published 1963 (see *HLAS 27:2651*). Lourenço Filho, distinguished educator who has held every prominent appointment in education in Brazil, is eminently qualified to analyze and describe educational administration. Intended as general survey of topic, so only last section (p. 211-301) is concerned with Brazilian education where he provides excellent description of the system and knowledgeable review of recent education legislation. No bibliography.

6261. O Magistério. Orgão de Divulgação da C.P.P.B. [Confederação dos Professores Primários do Brasil]. Ano 5, No. 12, julho/set. 1970- . Curitiba, Bra.

Pamphlet of Federation of Primary Teachers of Brazil, member of World Confederation of Teacher Organizations, emphasizes business: concentrates on legislative action of Federation: news of local, branch organizations; and areas of concern (early retirement, delinquent salaries, federal legislation, etc.). Despite narrow focus and limited format, informative. Reveals increased unified interests of teachers, trend toward unionization.

6262. Maia, Newton da Silva. Apontamentos para a história da Escola de Engenharia de Pernambuco. Recife, Bra., Impresa Universitária, 1967. 78 p., plates, tables.

Collection of notes on history of Pernambuco's School of Engineering now part of Univ. of Recife, prepared by former student of school who later became its president. Small "history" is much better than average attempt of this kind. Photographs of five buildings occupied by School in course of its growth and development, are very revealing and add to book's value.

6263. Marquez, Rubens Murillo. A linguagem computacional e a formação do pesquisador educacional (SBPC/CC, 23:6, déz. 1971, p. 752-753)

Originally contribution to meeting of researchers concerned about effective use of computers, this discussion covers considerable ground. Beginning with a quote from Aparecida Joly Gouvea, established sociologist and survey research specialist (in which she is sharply critical of current research efforts as "descriptive, over-ambitious, and vague"), Marquez goes on to discuss fear, tension, and dissatisfaction many researchers experience in trying to use computers. Stresses need for communication, in-progress, with computer, need to intervene, interrupt, or otherwise modify calculations, and benefits now derived from simplified language (APL) introduced in 1966. While commentary may not present anything new or surprising to researchers in US, it is revealing of Brazilian attitudes in this area.

6264. Mascaro, Carlos Corrêa. Brésil: la mouvement éducatif en 1967 (UNESCO/AIE, 30, 1968, p. 82-91, table)

Resume of report presented to the XXXI International Conference on Public Instruction by the Brazilian delegate. Provides thorough synopses of all phases of education program including: administration, planning, school construction, personnel, auxiliary services (health, nutrition, scholarships, and cultural activities), adult education, and literacy programs.

6265. Meirinho, Jali. As instituições da cultura catarinense. Florianópolis, Bra., Secretaria de Educação e Cultura, Depto. de Cultura, 1970. 30 p., bibl. (mimeo)

Author is Director of the Science Division of the Dept. of Culture for the State Education Dept. and in that capacity has put together this guide to cultural institutions in Santa Catarina. In his preface he notes that he has included libraries, museums, theatres, official agencies, private institutions, as well as the media. Very succinct treatment in which each topic is given about 2 p., this could prove quite useful, particularly the bibliography.

6266. Menezes, Eduardo Diatay B. de. A influência dos métodos de ensino sôbre as relações interpessoais dos alunos (Revista de Ciências Sociais [Fortaleza, Bra.] 2:2, 2. semestre 1971, p. 15-51, bibl., tables)

Outcome of a training seminar for educational researchers, sponsored by UNESCO at São Paulo Regional Research Center, this article was originally presented as a report of research performed as part of the seminar, in 1962. Author spends so much time apologizing for, explaining, or otherwise qualifying limitations and shortcomings of the research, that very little is said about the investigation itself. One tentative conclusion is offered: that traditional teaching methods produce superior work.

6267. Le mouvement éducatif dans 75 pays, rapports nationaux: Brésil (UNESCO/AIE, 31, 1969, p. 29-31)

Identification of principal changes in policy on part of federal government is keynote of this Ministry of Education report. Highlights are: new emphasis on planning, with attention to development of human resources; "Operation School," heightened effort to increase elementary enrollments; major revisions in first cycle of secondary education which will require establishment of comprehensive secondary schools; and reform of higher education, begun in 1968. All of these measures can be examined in greater detail through other sources reported in this *Handbook* section.

6268. Nina, Afonso Celso Maranhão. Notas sôbre a origem do Colégio Estadual do Amazonas. Manaus, Bra., Editôra Fink, 1969. 25 p., bibl., facsims.

Precise pamphlet full of careful notes tracing *colegio*'s origin and early development. Includes loving detail such as remodeling costs of old buildings, decrees modifying administration, changes in staff, etc. Originally 19-p. article in *A Notícia* (14 Dec. 1969).

6269. Octávio, José. Nilo Peçanha e o ensino industrial na Paraíba. Paraíba, Bra., Escola Técnica Federal da Paraíba, 1970. 26 p.

Selection of short articles (average length, 3 p.) written in 1968 by aide to Secretary of Education of Paraíba. Interesting reading for historians, perhaps more than for educators, because of references to political context within which education changed and developed. Not for the casual reader, since author's style demands ability to follow casual references to major historical events in relation to education.

6270. Palermo, Alfredo. Estudo de problemas brasileiros: educação moral e cívica; nível superior. São Paulo, LISA-Livros Irradiantes, 1971. 241 p., bibl.

After the 1964 revolution, the Brazilian government decreed that certain textbooks on "moral and civic education" be required reading at all school levels (see item 6293). This one is addressed to university students. [J. F. B. Dasilva]

6271. Pará (state), *Bra.* Secretaria de Estado de Educação. Departamento de Educação Primária. Currículo e programas do curso primário. Belém, Bra., n.d. 88 p., tables.

Curriculum guide for all subjects at elementary level. Format is that of a horizontal chart listing objectives, resources and activities, and content. Subjects include: math, Portuguese, social studies, science, civic education, and physical education. No index or bibliography. Intended as teachers' workbook, it provides blank pages in back.

6272. Peçanha, Wolga and **Duarte Aracy Bezerra.** O ensino agrícola e desenvolvimento integrado do pais (INEP/RBEP, 54:120, out./dez. 1970, p. 338-349)

1960 census showed that only 29.39 percent of Brazil's total land area was in use and of that proportion only 3.38 percent was cultivated, and much of that in small farms that are not productive for national needs. Agricultural education programs need to be expanded, both to help improve the general situation of agriculture and to keep pace with technological improvements. According to data gathered by the FAO, Brazil needs five times as much agricultural produce. Since farmer's low level of productivity and lack of technical and cultural background have been found to be major factor determining the present difficult situation, education is viewed as most important area for reform and expansion.

6273. Peeters, Francisca and **Maria Augusta de Cooman.** Pequena história da educação. 10. ed. São Paulo, Edições Melhoramentos, 1971. 154 p. (Biblioteca de Educação. Serie grandes textos)

Tenth edition of work first published in 1936. Its strong religious bias (Catholic) is forthrightly identified on inside cover by publisher. Authors are two nuns who regard advent of Christianity as most important event in history, and in history of pedagogy. They are certainly not modest—they begin with education in China and India (551 B.C.), include every prominent philosopher of education from Socrates to Montessori, and even attach a short sketch of history of woman which concludes: "As for the poor young girl, nothing is more precious to her than the acquisition of those virtues and domestic skills that will make of her a humble but very useful worker for social peace."

6274. Pereira, José Severo de Camargo and **Nancy das Garças Cardia.** A formação estatística do pesquisador em educação (SBPC/CC, 23:6, déz. 1971, p. 747-751)

After historical note regarding earliest use of statistics, authors move on to discuss examples of statistical research and stress value of statistics in educational investigations. After describing problems created by those who do not fully understand applications of statistics, especially researcher who seeks the statistician's help, asking: What can I do with my data? (after it is already collected), they indicate needs for better provision of "statistical literacy" among researchers. Article concludes with summary of a very limited survey of educational research journals to determine extent to which statistics are used and most common techniques employed.

6275. Peres, Janise Pinto. Situação das escolas normais do Nordeste (CRPER/CRE, 11:22, dez. 1971, p. 3-29, tables)

Study undertaken to improve planning for distribution of resources to normal schools, major thrust being to up-date all available data. Questionnaire of 47 items was administered to directors of normal schools, focus of study. Hypothesis established by research team was that quality of leadership for schools had a great influence on course of study offered. Results were tabulated and, with commentary, comprise remainder of article.

6276. Pfromm Neto, Samuel. As prioridades da pesquisa em tecnologia da educação (SBPC/CC, 23:6, dez. 1971, p. 733-738)

Strongly influenced by US sources which he cites frequently, author begins with a now-customary criticism of current status of research in Brazil, then moves on to describe scope of his own statements in this article, i.e., confined to technology but not including any attempt to discuss methodologies, theories, or models. His broad definition of educational technology embraces everything from programmed instruction to classroom movies. Far from listing priorities, Pfromm rambles in his discussion of goals, but concludes by suggesting long-range plan for development and establishment of Educational Technology Centers at Brazilian universities. Reader suspects that he would be only too happy to direct such a project.

6277. Piauí (state), *Bra.* **Govêrno do Estado do . . . Coordenação do Desenvolvimento do Estado (CODESE).** Evolução e situação atual do sistema de ensino do Estado do Piauí: pesquisa socio-educacional. v. 1, t. 1-2, Ensino primário: estabelecimentos e matrículas; v. 2, t. 1-4, Ensino primário: corpo docente; v. 1, Ensino médio: estabelecimentos e matrículas; v. 2, t. 1, Ensino médio: corpo docente; v. 3, Ensino superior: estabelecimentos, matrícula e corpo docente. Teresina, Bra., 1970. 10 v. (Various pagings) maps, tables.

Marked increase in appetite for data and need for more self-knowledge as fundamental to planning are evident in this massive effort by Piauí state. Ten volumes of statistics, graphics, and analysis of educational system constitute one of most ambitious attempts to acquire self-knowledge and prepare for future development by one of smaller, less well-known states. Surely, traditional complaints of researchers concerning lack of data will diminish in the face of this and similar efforts. Outline calls for: pt. 1, Organization of primary, secondary, and higher education (7 v.); pt. 2, Enrollment and attendance problems; pt. 3, Education and the Community (3 v.). All material is based on period 1964-70.

6278. Pinto, Myrthes da Fonseca. Disciplina: um problema de pais e mestres (Boletim [Faculdade de Filosofia, Ciências e Letras de Presidente Prudente, Depto. de Ciências Sociais, Bra.] 1970, p. 61-66, bibl.)

Discipline, an old treatment of an old topic. Latest source listed in the bibliography is 1957 and no fresh insights are offered by the author.

6279. Pontes, Salvador Pires. A escola e a valorização do menino brasileiro: alimentação, saúde, instrução, educação. Belo Horizonte, Bra., Imprensa Oficial, 1971. 262 p., bibl.

Titles of selections include: "The Nutrition of Children," "The Big Ought to Help the Small," "The Punishment of Making a Student Stand," "Homage to Professor Machado Soubrinho," "Poetry of Humberto Campos," etc. In short, potpourri of many short topics, majority related to nutrition and health. Book-jacket describes author as combination pharmacist and school inspector.

6280. Poppovic, Ana Maria. As prioridades da pesquisa em psicologia da educação (SBPC/CC, 23:6, dez. 1971, p. 731-732)

After arguing great dearth of trained researchers in educational psychology, partly due to lack of requirements and courses in educational psychology, author proceeds to identify priorities for research: attention to national rather than comparative or international questions, application of scarce resources to real needs identified in a responsible and professional manner, and an emphasis on pragmatic rather than theoretical projects. Also urges greater attention to cultural context within which programs must operate, criticizing popularity of imported models and techniques poorly adapted to Brazilian realities.

6281. Prado, J. Leal. Opinião sôbre a pós-graduação na área biomédica (SBPC/CC, 24:4, abril 1972, p. 329-332)

Prado's basic message seems to be: "scientific research is not learned in the classroom," or as he expands it, "one learns to conduct research through active participation in research projects." His preference for post-graduate study would be to have a group of actively practicing researchers with whom graduates might work on research projects, rather than any formal "course of study," and he speculates that the entire process may require up to ten years. Issues warning against danger of allowing "theorists ... who consider themselves qualified in scientific research, but who never produce any data" to acquire positions of influence.

6282. Quirino, Tarcízio Rêgo. Educação e profissionalização na área rural do Nordeste (INEP/RBEP, 54:120, out./dez 1970, p. 313-337, tables)

Report of research conducted in rural Northeast, to study changes occurring in rural society. Through questionnaires filled out by parents, it was possible to identify their goals for their children. General results indicated that: 1) inhabitants of rural areas are increasingly attracted to urban areas; 2) desire to improve social status is related to obtaining better education and better job for their children; 3) standards of feminine behavior appear to follow tradition more closely than those for masculine behavior; 4) economic situation is greater handicap to children's education than any lack of schools; and 5) most inhabitants are optimistic that their social status can be improved.

6283. ———. Obstaculos sociais ao uso da televisão como veículo educacional. Recife, Bra., Univ. Federal do Pernambuco, Instituto de Filosofia e Ciências Humanas, 1970. 209 l., bibl., tables (Tese apresentada à Escola Pos-Graduada de Ciências Sociais da Fundação Escola de Sooiologia e Política de São Paulo)

Thorough study of current status of educational TV in Recife, prepared by author as his master's thesis. Bibliography includes reference and general sources as well as those useful to persons seeking information on educational TV. Also lists questionnaires, one of which produced some interesting results concerning status symbols and consumerism. Readers would do better to consult any of several other more compact sources on educational TV (a popular topic in last few years), since four chapters of this work are devoted to discussion of research methodology employed. Includes graphs, tables, and statistics.

6284. Rachid, Cora Bastos de Fritas. Perspectivas do ensino técnico comercial (INEP/RBEP, 54:120, out./dez. 1970, p. 350-364)

Recommends that public education sector increase its participation in commercial education by: 1) providing financing for improvement and equipping of schools; 2) encouraging articulation among school-industry-community areas; and 3) developing vocational orientation services.

6285. Reforma do ensino no Estado da Guanabara: ensino de 1. e 2. graus. Rio, Conquista, 1971. 135 p., tables.

Complete report from Task Force appointed to implement Law of Instruction (No. 5.692, of 11 Aug. 1971), for Guanabara's elementary and secondary education. Text of law appears in back of book in original form, as decreed by President Medici. Task Force was thorough—covering everything from reorganization of Secretariat to detailed plans for resolving articulation problems between old and new programs. Editor has chosen to present flow charts and US-style graphics instead of usual charts of numbers. Of interest to someone examining change at these levels.

6286. Reforma universitária: 1968-1969. v. 4, Leis, decretos-leis, decretos, portarias, pareceres, resoluções. Rio? Ministério da Educação e Cultura, 1968. 1969. 174 p.

From the Costa e Silva government (Tarso Dutra, Minister of Education), comes a collection of laws, decrees, documents, reports, and other materials pertinent to educational reform during 1968-69. These 174 pages are useful in identifying some of policy makers, they also provide (p. 70, 111) information on state aid agreements and material from Federal Education Council as well as from the President and Minister. No commentary or illustrations.

6287. Réis, Arthur Cézar Ferreira. Manoel da Nóbrega e a pedagogia jesuítica (CFC/RBC, 3:7, jan./março 1971, p. 85-92)

Skirts edges of some very interesting questions regarding role of Jesuits in colonial Brazil, wandering instead among general observations of period and recounting familiar efforts to catequize Indians, establish schools, and cooperate with the governors. Although he refers to "a political accusation of the greatest gravity", and mentions the Indianization of religious ceremonies, he is only teasing reader, for he concludes coyly: "Where is the truth in this rosary of accusations?" Instead of exploring his questions, he is content to conclude that: "Nóbrega, statesman, civilizer, initiated that heroic enterprise" (of colonization).

Reis, Fábio Wanderley. Educação, economia e contestação política na América Latina. See item 7875.

6288. Revista Brasileira de Estudos Pedagógicos. Vol. 54, No. 119, julho/set. 1970- Rio.

Regular publication of national research center offers balanced selection of articles by authors from national and state organizations and programs. This particular issue is concerned with financing education. Includes world-wide bibliography on economics of education and detailed report on federal expenditures for education that should be of interest to many, economists as well as educators.

6289. ———. Vol. 54, No. 120, out./dez. 1970- Rio.

General topic for this issue is technical education, of various kinds. Lead article on measurement of educational efficiency; others discuss: aspects of secondary education; professionalization in the rural Northeast; agricultural instruction and national development; and perspectives of technical commercial education. Bibliography includes all of recent legislation pertaining to technical education.

6290. Ribeiro Neto, Adolpho. A pesquisa e o planejamento educacional (SBPC/CC, 23:6, dez. 1971, p. 715-716)

Difficult reading, thanks to author's turgid style. Main points have been made before—a great lack of rigor in the little research done in education to date, and need for research as a sound basis for planning. Others have already said same things, much more eloquently.

6291. Rio Grande do Norte, (state) *Bra.* Secretaria de Estado de Educação e Cultura do . . . Programa do ensino primário elementar. v. 1, Primera série; v. 2, Segunda série; v. 3, Terzeira série; v. 4, Quarta série. Natal, Bra., Edições Walter Pereira, 1968. 4 v. (153, 144, 171, 201 p.) bibl., illus., tables.

Complete set of curriculum guides, planned, prepared, and published in accordance with requirements of 1961 National Law of Directives (see *HLAS 33:4797*). Each volume lists teachers who formed team of contributing editors, and provides general breakdown of subject matter schedules. Also serves as teacher's guide or manual in which philosophy of each program is described, followed by suggested lesson plans and activities. Each volume contains recommendations for: Language, Social Studies, Mathematics, and Natural Sciences.

6292. Sant'Anna, Flávia Maria and Isolda Holmer Paes. Formação intensiva do professor: micro-experiência de ensino como modalidade de treinamento. Pôrto Alegre, Bra., Ministério da Educação e Cultura, Instituto Nacional de Estudos Pedagógicos, Centro Regional de Pesquisas Educacionais, 1970. 207 p., tables (Série, 1. Pesquisas e monografias, 13)

In response to growing concern for better teacher preparation, Rio Grande do Sul state undertook this project, which was heavily based on programmed instruction. As described in rationale section: "a new technology of training based on cybernetic principles (feedback) and applied psychology in education" was focus of project. Double outcome for project is suggested: 1) to discover better data about teacher training; 2) to identify better methods for training. Includes various examples of programmed exercises in appendix and bibliography. Authors view this approach or "micro-experience" as means to accelerate teacher preparation and develop an instructional model responsive to contemporary demands on the educational system.

6293. Scantimburgo, João de. Tratado geral do Brasil. São Paulo, Companhia Editôra Nacional [and] Editôra da Univ. de São Paulo, 1971. 595 p., maps, tables.

Intended as textbook and source for civic and moral education courses—now mandated at every level of instruction in Brazil (see item 6270)—this weighty volume of over 500 p. is subtitled: *Study of Brazilian problems, moral and civic for use in higher education courses,* in accordance with the official program. Chapters discuss evolution of Brazilian nation and its people; political institutions; culture; national security; international relationships; and the future. Journalist-author is professor and member of many organizations.

6294. Senise, Paschoal E. Américo. A função da pos-graduação na formação de pesquisadores (SBPC/CC, 23:6, dez. 1971, p. 739-740)

Definitions and discussion of post-graduate study, particularly of its value in preparation of researchers. Very dry style.

6295. Silva, Ady Raul da. Observações e sugestões sobre o desenvolvimento da pos-graduação no país (SBPC/CC, 24:4, abril 1972, p. 333-338)

Comments on present situation and future possibilities of postgraduate study. Researcher with Ministry of Agriculture, author describes various ways in which individual strengths on university staff might be combined to provide balanced post-graduate program of study. Seems to have confused American university policy of not hiring its own graduates with practice of doctoral candidates being examined by committees from outside of their university. Discusses program of Escola Superior de Agricultura Luis de Queiros da Univ. de São Paulo (located in Piracicaba) as good example of application of resources.

6296. Silva, Benedicto. Entrosamento entre as instituicoes especializadas em ciências sociais (Noticias [Rio] 4:3, julho/set. 1970, p. 259-269)

Verbose discussion of value and importance of human, particularly intellectual, resources and appreciation of technology and cultural exchange. Author goes so far as to suggest that cultural exchange is "the magic remedy that can establish permanent peace and banish war from the history of Humanity." He also predicts an increase in information of over 800 percent based on a geometric progression, by year 2020. His goal is consolidation of all entities that teach, conduct research, publish, or transmit social science data into national information system. For example, center for Cultural Anthropology in Pôrto Alegre might serve an entire region better than several small collections throughout southern states. Concludes with his outline for development of a nationally coordinated information system.

6297. Sodré, Roberto Costa de Abreu. Desenvolvimento e educação tecnológica. São Paulo, Serviço de Publicações da Federação e Centro das Indústrias do Estado de São Paulo, 1970. 24 p.

Speech given by Governor Sodré at founding of Center for Technological Education. Sodré quotes Maritain (on poetry and art), and cites big steps forward such as hydroelectric power development and increased access to *ginásio*. His picture of technology includes ". . . a figura do técnico superior saiu da penumbra que encobria a zona had nossas intuições, para se tornar cada vez mais nítida, com sua silhueta sobressaindo do pano de fundo das novas exigências do progresso tecnológico e industrial, até se concretizar na recente legislação federal, e em resoluções definitivas do Conselho Federal de Educação e do Conselho Estadual de Educação." Views creation of schools of applied technology as secret to industrial development and cites need to satisfy graduates of secondary level courses who seek university education when universities cannot accept them. Hopefully, opening new channels will reduce strong appeal of academic study and diplomas.

6298. Subsídios para o estudo do ginásio polivalente. Rio, Ministério da Educação e Cultura, Diretoria do Ensino Secundário (EPEM), 1969. 96 p., bibl.

Group of writings (some as old as 1953) on secondary education, selected by Planning Team for Secondary Education to serve as sources for personnel involved in training programs for new *ginásios* created by Program of Improvement and Expansion of Secondary Education. Authors: all prominent educators, Anísio Teixeira "A Escola Secundária em Transformação;" Newton Sucupira "Princípios da Educação da Escola Media com a Superior;" and Gildásio Amado "Ginásio Orientado para o Trabalho." First three, members of Federal Education Council and leaders in education both in Northeast and at federal level, have had considerable influence on policy. Fourth, Amado, was Ministry's Director of Secondary Education for several years. Since these articles were selected rather than written for this purpose, it is very likely that anyone who is well read in education will have read them previously, in which case the preface, with its description of the new dimensions of secondary education, will have more interest. Short bibliography.

6299. Tavares, Denise Ferandes. As bibliotecas infanto-juvenis de hoje. Salvador, Bra., Biblioteca Infantil Monteiro Lobato, 1970. 52 p.

Report written for architectural conference covers: concept, children's libraries in Brazil, audience, scope, skills of librarians, organization, community role, installation, personal suggestions, and bibliography. Author presents description, in outline form, of Monteiro Lobato library—25,000 books, records, tapes, slides, a reference section, and a collection of Lobato material. Thanks to thorough treatment of problems of libraries, their clients and needs, this is really a "how-to" guide.

6300. Teixeira, Anísio. Cultura e tecnologia. Rio, Fundação Getúlio Vargas, Instituto de Documentação, 1971. 70 p., plates.

Essays by late, well-known educational leader on culture and technology. Continues with his discussion of the place and role of "integrated" education in the process of social development.

6301. Thebaud, Annie. Aspirations des étudiants de psychologie (CLAPCS/AL, 13:2/3, abril/set. 1970, p. 3-29)

Report based on data compiled 1968-69 among psychology students in Rio, São Paulo, and Recife. Describes present state of teaching and research in psychology and professional status and image it enjoys. Findings suggest that upper-class students tend to study psychology, but do not usually practice after graduation. To date there has been very little research, and teaching is concerned principally with clinical psychology. Investigation based on questionnaires.

6302. Tobias, José Antônio. O ensino da filsofia nas universidades brasileiras. Washington, Organização dos Estados Americanos, Secretaria Geral, 1968. 82 p.

Tobias is a purist—argues that "philosophy" and "university" are synonymous. Wants everyone to organize the university on this basis and insists that all students study philosophy, with occupational or professional studies as secondary objective. He has his critics (see Moura Castro's comments in item 6230) and his position is not compatible with development or current expansion of Brazilian universities, as he freely concedes. Or, as he explains: "não existe, propriamente, tradição universitária brasileira." Apart from his thesis in favor of philosophy, Tobias provides an interesting treatment of history and present state of Brazilian higher education, moving from chapters on Dom João VI and the First Brazilian Faculty, the First University, and the Vestibular, to suggestions about the future. He concludes with a particularly interesting section on "Brazilian University Myths." This might prove of special interest to reformers, planners, and theorists, since it deals with: 1) luxurious buildings, 2) recognized universities only in capital cities, 3) anything imported is better, 4) the trilogy of occupations (doctor, lawyer, priest), and 5) professionalization in response to the pressing need for trained manpower.

Identified as a neothomist, Professor Tobias currently teaches History and Philosophy of Education in Marília. Contrary to what his arguments might suggest, he is a young scholar whose essays began appearing in print in 1960. Also see on same subject, item 6229.

6303. Torres Neto, Pedro. Educação pela tevê. Rio, Edições O Curzeiro, 1971. 184 p., plates.

Basic book intended for use in schools of Journalism or Communications. Jacket credits author with being one of pioneers of Brazilian educational TV, as well as specialist in education. Chapter headings reveal approach: "Panorama of Communications," "Educational TV," "Possibilities of Educational TV," "Description of a TV System," and "Organization and Control of Reception." Very interesting bibliography.

6304. Uchoa, Júlio Benevides. Flagrantes educacionais do Amazonas de ontem. Prefácio de Arthur Cézar Ferreira Réis. Manaus, Bra., Edições Govêrno do Estado do Amazonas, 1966. 201 p., bibl. (Série Euclides da Cunha, 7)

Dedicated historian and retired professor, Júlio Uchoa, writes in detail of panorama of Amazonian education, from first schools, in 1800, to Republic's beginning. Some of material may have appeared first in Manaus's newspapers.

6305. Universidade Católica do Paraná, Curitiba, Bra. Anuário III, 1968. Curitiba, Bra., Reitoria, 1969. 100 p., plates, tables.

University's annual report, crowded with data of particular interest to administrators or to investigators seeking state data. Shows that medicine, philosophy, and letters still attract most students (in order of preference). One problem, as far as casual reader is concerned, is that there is no effort made to cross-reference illustrations with text so some tables and charts are less informative than they might have been. Over years, Anuarios have developed in scope and depth, from perfunctory listings of faculty and programs, to reports providing considerable data.

6306. Universidade do Estado de Guanabara, Rio. Mandamentos básicos. Rio, 1971. 111 p.

Compilation of all legislation, statutes, general regulations, and related correspondence, beginning with provision for state university in the state constitution and concluding with the general regulations governing the Univ. of the State of Guanabara. Includes list of all courses offered (with titles conferred), several organization charts, and index to articles of regulations. For more on subject, see item 6307.

6307. ———, ———. Mandamentos universitários. v. 1-2. Rio, 1971. 2 v. (373, 452 p.) bibl., tables.

In addition to item 6306, these are volumes of resolutions, deliberations, and recommendations concerning Univ. of the State of Guanabara. V. 2, contains a marvelously immodest and overblown preface by Rector João Lyra Filho. V. 3 is forthcoming: general university catalog.

6308. Universidade Federal de Santa Catarina, Florianópolis, Bra. Catálogo de pós-graduação, 1972. Florianópolis, Bra., 1972. 84 p., plates (*Its* Catálogo, 1)

Beginning with brief history of development of post-graduate study at Univ., catalogue outlines guidelines and special features of post-graduate programs available.

6309. ———, ———, ———. Elementos para o planejamento universitário. Florianópolis, Bra., 1971. 1 v. (Unpaged), tables.

University which was founded in 1932 as faculty of law began acquiring other schools from 1946-69. Team report on data related to planning includes: charts showing increases in enrollments and projected increases for future; architectual planning and distribution of space; flow charts and other graphics showing all phases of organization; and marvelous amoeba-like graphic (in three stages) intended to reveal "campus" aesthetic development.

6310. **Universidade Federal do Ceará,** *Fortaleza, Bra.* Administração Fernando Leite. Fortaleza, Bra., Depto. de Educação e Cultura, 1971. 39 p.

Summary of accomplishments of the Leite Administration at the Federal Univ. of Ceará. Emphasis on changes made, ideas advanced by Leite, and results achieved.

6311. **Universidade Federal do Rio Grande do Norte,** *Natal, Bra.* Faculdade de Ciências Econômicas. Grupo Universitário de Pesquisas Econômicas. Quantos irão a universidade? Natal, Bra., 1969. 1 v. (Various pagings), tables.

Pragmatic, rather than philosophical approach to title question in this case. Group of students developed and administered questionnaire to determine probable number of candidates for university courses in 1970. Report of results obtained from 1,146 interviews and replies obtained in 1968 from secondary level students.

6312. **Universidade Federal do Rio Grande do Sul,** *Pôrto Alegre, Bra.* Regimento geral da Universidade. Pôrto Alegre, Bra., Comissão Central de Publicações, 1970. 76 p. (*Its* Documentos, 4)

Official regulations of university, as approved in 1970 by University Council, Federal Education Council, and Ministry. Titles I to XII spell out university's organization and various functions.

6313. **Velloso, João Paulo dos Reis.** Ensino técnico de nivel médio: aspectos de sua programação (INEP/RBEP, 54:120, out./dez. 1970, p. 280-289, tables)

Begins with overview of period 1955-65 in secondary technical education. Remainder devoted to describing present and planned changes for this type and level of education. Provides some statistical estimates for labor market demands and suggests some areas where improvement can be expected.

6314. **Viana, José de Alencar Carneiro.** Planejamento universitario (UMG/R, 18, dez. 1968/1969, p. 69-100, tables)

Fragmented approach to general topic of university planning. Speech divided into short sections corresponding to slides shown at VII Reunião Anual da Associação de Escolas de Agronomia e Veterinária do Brasil, 1967, Belo Horizonte. Result makes for very strange reading, since reader does not have benefit of slides and total experience of exchange during original presentation. Topics include: planning phases; new responsibilities and planning; educational planning and socio-economic development; university models; land-grant colleges; institutional research, etc.

6315. **Witter, G. P.** and others. Realizações e atitudes de estudantes universitários num programa ramificado (SBPC/CC, 24:1, jan. 1972, p. 32-35, bibl., table)

Research project to determine efficacy of programmed learning in two subject areas: history and psychology. After introductory section providing necessary evidence that authors have done their homework and can cite reputable sources on programmed learning, there is description of project and summary of findings.

JOURNAL ABBREVIATIONS

AAAS/S	Science. American Association for the Advancement of Science. Washington.
AIFLD/R	A.I.F.L.D. Review. American Institute for Free Labor Development. Washington.
ARBOR	Arbor. Revista general de investigación y cultura. Madrid.
CES/CER	Comparative Education Review. Comparative Education Society. N.Y.
CFC/RBC	Revista Brasileira de Cultura. Ministério da Educação e Cultura, Conselho Federal de Cultura. Rio.
CIES/CER	See CES/CER.
CLAPCS/AL	América Latina. Centro Latino-Americano de Pesquisas em Ciências Sociais. Rio.
CPES/RPS	Revista Paraguaya de Sociología. Centro Paraguayo de Estudios Sociológicos. Asunción.
CRPE/PP	Pesquisa e Planejamento. Centro Regional Prof. Queiroz Filho. São Paulo.
CRPER/CRE	Cadernos Região e Educação. Centro Regional de Pesquisas Educacionais do Recife. Recife, Bra.
DPB/RICS	Revista del Instituto de Ciencias Sociales. Diputación Provincial de Barcelona. Barcelona.

ESME/C	Cultura. Ministerio de Educación. San Salvador.
IAMEA	Inter-American Economic Affairs. Washington.
IBBD/N	Notícias. Conselho Nacional de Pesquisas, Instituto Brasileiro de Bibliografia e Documentação. Rio.
IESSC/C	Comunidades. Instituto de Estudios Sindicales, Sociales y Cooperativos, Centro de Prospección Social. Madrid.
IFH/C	Conjonction. Revue franco-haïtienne. Bulletin de l'Institut Français d'Haïti. Port-au-Prince.
III/AI	América Indígena. Instituto Indigenista Interamericano. México.
ILARI/A	Aportes. Instituto Latinoamericano de Relaciones Internacionales. Paris.
INEP/RBEP	Revista Brasileira de Estudos Pedagógicos. Instituto Nacional de Estudos Pedagógicos. Rio.
ITT/RLS	Revista Latinoamericana de Sociología. Instituto Torcuato Di Tella, Centro de Sociología Comparada. B.A.
JDA	The Journal of Developing Areas. Western Illinois Univ. Press. Macomb, Ill.
LNB/L	Lotería. Lotería Nacional de Beneficencia. Panamá.
MSEP/LP	El Libro y el Pueblo. Secretaría de Educación Pública, Depto. de Bibliotecas. México.
MSTPS/R	Revista Mexicana del Trabajo. Secretaría del Trabajo y Previsión Social. México.
OAS/CI	Ciencia Interamericana. Organization of American States, Dept. of Scientific Affairs. Washington.
PAPS	Proceedings of the Academy of Political Science. The Academy of Political Science [and] Columbia Univ. N.Y.
PAU/CI	See OAS/CI.
RIB	Revista Interamericana de Bibliografía [Inter-American Review of Bibliography]. Organization of American States. Washington.
SBPC/CC	Ciência e Cultura. Sociedade Brasileira para o Progresso da Ciência. São Paulo.
SIP/RIP	Revista Interamericana de Psicología (Interamerican Journal of Psychology). Sociedad Interamericana de Psicología (Interamerican Society of Psychology). Austin, Tex.
SSSR/LA	Latinskaia Amerika [América Latina]. Akademia Nauk SSSR, Institut Latinskoi Ameriki [Academia de Ciencias de la URSS, Instituto Latinoamericano]. Moskva [Moscú].
UC/B	Boletín de la Universidad de Chile. Santiago.
UCC/CE	Cuadernos de Economía. Univ. Católica de Chile. Santiago.
UCE/FLCE	Filosofía, Letras y Ciencias de la Educación. Univ. Central del Ecuador. Quito.
UCV/CU	Cultura Universitaria. Univ. Central de Venezuela, Dirección de Cultura. Caracas.
UH/U	Universidad de La Habana. La Habana.
UMG/R	Revista da Universidade Federal de Minas Gerais. Belo Horizonte, Bra.
UNAM/IE	Investigación Económica. Univ. Nacional Autónoma de México, Escuela Nacional de Economía. México.
UNAM/RFD	Revista de la Facultad de Derecho. Univ. Nacional Autónoma de México. México.
UNAM/RMS	Revista Mexicana de Sociología. Univ. Nacional Autónoma de México, Instituto de Investigaciones Sociales. México.
UNESCO/AIE	Annuaire International de l'Education. United Nations Educational, Scientific and Cultural Organization, Bureau International d'Education. Geneva.
UNESCO/IRE	International Review of Education. United Nations Educational, Scientific and Cultural Organization, Institute for Education. Hamburg, FRG.
UNT/H	Humanitas. Univ. Nacional de Tucumán, Facultad de Filosofía y Letras. Tucumán, Arg.
UP/TM	Tiers Monde. Problèmes des pays sous-développés. Univ. de Paris, Institut d'Étude du Développement Économique et Social. Paris.
UPR/CS	Caribbean Studies, Univ. of Puerto Rico, Institute of Caribbean Studies. Río Piedras, P.R.

UTIEH/C	Caravelle. Cahiers du monde hispanique et luso-brésilien. Univ. de Toulouse, Institute d'Études Hispaniques, Hispano-Americaines et Luso-Brésiliennes. Toulouse, France.
UWI/SES	Social and Economic Studies. Univ. of the West Indies, Institute of Social and Economic Research. Mona, Jam.
UY/R	Revista de la Universidad de Yucatán. Mérida, Mex.

GEOGRAPHY

GENERAL

CLINTON R. EDWARDS
Professor of Geography
University of Wisconsin-Milwaukee

INTEREST AMONG MANY UNITED STATES GEOGRAPHERS in various economic and social problems of Latin American countries has become focused in the recently organized Conference of Latin Americanist Geographers (CLAG), see item 6526. Conceived originally in mid-1969 as a means of defining "problems for geographic research during the coming decade and [relating] these problems to current needs," CLAG has evolved into an emphasis on what geographers in the United States call "development geography," that is, the use of geographic expertise to examine and make recommendations on various economic, social, political, technological and environmental problems, the amelioration of which is referred to generally as "development." It is somewhat analogous to "action anthropology."

Plans for a first national conference were made, and a tentative agenda was sent to potentially interested geographers. The agenda reflected very strongly the apparent feeling of the organizing group that the major orientation of geographical research efforts as they pertain to Latin America should be toward the direct application of findings to development. The substantive part of the program included "1) Research problems in ecological research in Latin America. The role of ecological research in resource evaluation, agricultural geography and geographic aspects of planning; 2) Agricultural geography: Indian and peasant cultures; 3) Agricultural geography: commercial agriculture; 4) Data collection: Opportunities and problems; 5) Population geography; 6) Urban, industrial and transportation geography; 7) The role of geographic research in regional planning of economic development; 8) Exploration of the role of numerical analysis in geographic research in Latin America."

The theme of the conference was "The Future of Geographic Research in Latin America: An Agenda for the Seventies." In response to the reactions of a number of geographers who were contacted as potential participants, the program was broadened somewhat to include settlement geography, physical geography and social geography. The former was lumped with population geography, while the latter two were entered under the heading of "neglected fields."

The proceedings of the first conference (30 April-3 May, 1970) have now been published (item 6560) and reviewed in *Annals of the Association of American Geographers* (63:2, June 1973, p. 269-270). All papers except those dealing with individual countries or regions are reviewed in this section.

The second general meeting, held on 17 April 1971 during the annual meetings of the Association of American Geographers, featured population studies and resulted in the second number in CLAG's publication series, *Population Dynamics of Latin America: A Review and Bibliography* (Robert N. Thomas, *ed.*, East Lansing, Mich.,

CLAG Publications, 1973). CLAG *Newsletter* (7, 15 March 1973) announced its release: "The publication presents timely articles concerning contemporary population research by geographers working in Latin America. Donald J. O'Brien (U.S. Bureau of Census) lists all published census volumes for Latin America and indicates where they are available. He also discloses 1) the addresses of national census offices, 2) the present directors of these institutions, and 3) provides a status report for the 1970 census.

"The increasing use of computers and computerized-related techniques makes Gustavo Antonini's (University of Florida) discussion of Latin American data banks particularly appropriate. He discloses what census and socioeconomic data are on tapes and how and where they can be obtained.

"Alfonso Gonzalez (University of Calgary) sets the stage for the substantive papers by providing a survey of population geography research in Latin America. As for the research papers, Stanley D. Brunn and Robert N. Thomas (Michigan State University) employ over 30 variables in order to define the socioeconomic environments related to the migration system of Tegucigalpa, Honduras. Whereas Brunn and Thomas worked on a macro-scale, Richard W. Wilkie (University of Massachusetts) considers microspace while investigating the relationship between social behavior and the migration of peasants in Argentina. The final paper, contributed by James Nance and Robert N. Thomas (Michigan State University) discusses the role that the rural-urban continuum plays in the spatial variation of fertility levels in Honduras. The volume also includes an extensive bibliography (over 1100 citations) of population research numbers relating to Latin America."

On 2-4 December 1971, the Second National Conference, later called the "third general session," was held, and the agenda shows that the original thrust had not lost momentum. The theme was "Latin American Development Issues," with sections entitled 1) Urbanization and Industrialization; 2) Ecological Impact of Development; and 3) Regional Development Planning. Publication of the papers was announced in CLAG *Newsletter*, (8, 15 June· 1973) as *Latin American Development Issues*, (A. David Hill, ed., East Lansing, Mich., CLAG Publications, 1973). The contents as listed in the *Newsletter* are "*Keynote Address:* Geography and Development in Latin America (Rafael Picó). *Urbanization and Industrialization:* Economic Growth and Polarized Space in Latin America: A Search for Geographic Theory? (Howard L. Gauthier); Growth Poles, Diffusion, and Development: Comments on Interrelated Work (Lawrence A. Brown); Spatial Investment Strategies: A Balanced View (Barry Lentnek); Development Versus De-Pollution: Brazil Cannot Afford Both (Armin K. Ludwig); General Discussion; Electoral Development in Latin America: Spatial Problems and Policy Alternatives (Orin C. Patton); Latin American Cities: Nodes of Political Action (Stanley D. Brunn); General Discussion. *The Ecological Impact of Development:* Development and the Imminent Demise of the Amazon Rain Forest (William M. Denevan); Development and Ecological Reality in Latin America (Charles F. Bennett); Geographic Aspects of Soil Use Considerations in Latin America (Gerald W. Olson); General Discussion; Sewage as a Pollutant in Central America (Carl L. Johannessen); The Conflict Between Accelerating Economic Demands and Regional Ecological Stability in Coastal El Salvador (Howard E. Daugherty); Protein Flight from Tropical Latin America: Some Social and Ecological Considerations (Joshua C. Dickinson, III); General Discussion. *Regional Development Planning:* A Geographic Assessment of Regional Education Patterns: Turrialba Cantón, Costa Rica (Paul A. I. Cox); Rural Population Potential and Regional Planning (Pierre A. D. Stouse, Jr. and Betty Holtzman); Difficulties with Planned Agricultural Change in the Post-Plantation Caribbean (Bonham C. Richardson); General Discussion; Regional Development in the CACM: Too Many Realities and Not Enough Myths; Ptolemy to the Rescue (James E. McConnell); The Rise and Decline of Geography in Brazilian Development Planning: Some Lessons to be Learned (Paul I. Mandell); Northeast Brazilian Development Studies: Practices and Problems (Richard P. Momsen, Jr.); General Discussion."

The fourth general session was held 28-30 June 1973, with a theme related closely to that of the third: "Geographical Analysis for Development in Latin America." The sections were entitled 1) Evaluating Rural Development Potentials; 2) Special Opportunities for Resource Use and Development; 3) Political Geography and Regional Development; and 4) Special Problems of the Commonwealth and French Caribbean. There was also a special session for "presentations by geographers from Latin America on methodological issues and current research needs and priorities."

The organizers of CLAG sessions thus maintain emphasis on development geography, and research on other aspects of the geography of Latin America continues to be reported in a variety of journals rather than becoming concentrated in the CLAG series. Participation by geographers from Latin America has so far been slight, but for each major session CLAG has subsidized visits by a few Latin American scholars. Current membership is about 240, including about two dozen from Canada and various Latin American countries.

Many of the data and much of the commentary on economic development and related social change in Latin America are contributed by non-geographers; a representative sample is reviewed in this section as of interest to geographers concerned with these themes. Urban problems, rural-urban migration, agrarian reform, and changes in systems of land tenure continue to occupy the attention of many scholars, and the contributions of Latin Americans, including geographers, are on the increase. Suggestions for augmenting the role of geographers in these spheres are made by Dickenson and Crist (item 6532).

Among bibliographic and reference items, the availability of the results of agricultural research has been increased significantly by the work of the Centro Interamericano de Documentación e Información Agrícola at Turrialba, Costa Rica (items 6575-6576 and 6512). Progress on another bibliographic effort, of use in studies of population, is manifested in item 6585. Legal data for the question of Latin American countries' territorial waters and the controversial 200-mile limit are provided in item 6608.

Historical geography, both physical and cultural, are represented in discussion of South America's place in the theory of continental drift (items 6523 and 6556), in two new reprints of voyages and travels (items 6504 and 6513) and in continuing commentary on Alexander von Humboldt's life and letters (items 6502, 6509-6510 and 6561). The perennial question of precolumbian transoceanic dispersals and cultural contacts continues in items 511 and 6541.

6500. Adams, Dale W. Aid agencies and land reform in Latin America: a suggested change in policy (UW/LE, 46:4, Nov. 1970, p. 423-434)

Discussion focuses on "the merits of several economic arguments often cited against land reform: 1) decreases production, 2) urbanization is more practical than parcelization, and 3) colonization is more feasible than land reform." All three are found wanting as reservations against land reform, although they are commonly expressed as such by "aid agency personnel." Suggested change in policy is to develop ways to encourage or contribute to land reform, and several are described.

6501. Agricultural trade of the Western Hemisphere: a statistical review. Washington, U.S. Dept. of Agriculture, Economic Research Service, 1972. 124 p., tables (ERS-Foreign, 328)

From the forward: "This publication provides, for the first time, a historical series showing US agricultural trade with countries and regions of the Western Hemisphere by major Standard International Trade Classification (SITC); trade of Western Hemisphere countries by major SITC groups, and trade of leading Western Hemisphere countries by destination and origin as well as by principal commodities (SITC groups). Data for US trade with countries of the Western Hemisphere are for 1962-70; data for countries of the Western Hemisphere are for 1962-68 or 1962-69; and data for Canada, Argentina, Brazil, Chile, Colombia, Mexico, Peru, and Venezuela are for 1965-69."

6502. Arias de Greiff, Jorge. El diario inédito de Humboldt (ACCEFN/R, 13:51, dic. 1969, p. 393-398, facsims.)

Discussion of manuscript notes from which derived Humboldt's scientific works and the reports of his travels. Notebooks contain combined intercalated fragments of his observations which can be identified as an "astronomical diary," barometric observations, travel journal, and scientific memoirs of observations and experiments during his travels. Lack of order in notes is reflected in nine books into which they have been collected together with the many notes on loose sheets inserted over the years. Since Humboldt did not realize full publication of travel results, notes comprised valuable addition to his published works. Article traces their vicissitudes after Humboldt's death. They were used by Schumacher in composing his biographical work on Mutis, Caldas, and Codazzi, then were forgotten for many years. During World War II they were taken to Moscow, then returned to Berlin where they now reside in the Deutsches Staatsbibliothek. Reproduces index of nine books as it appeared in 1859 together with detailed list of part referring to travels in northern South America. Also includes facsimiles of portions of manuscript and a commentary on Humboldt's relations with Caldas.

6503. Aschmann, Homer. Indian societies and communities in Latin America: an historical perspective (*in* Conference of Latin Americanist Geographers, *I, Muncie, Ind., 1969.* Geographic research on Latin America [see item 6526] p. 124-137)

The myriad of native Indian cultures of Latin America provide bases for many practically and theoretically oriented studies by geographers. Although diminished from aboriginal times, number of cultures, often in juxtaposition either with other Indian groups or with advanced technological societies, provide abundant opportunity for varied studies ranging from man-land relationships to questions of kinds and rates of assimilation. Past research and recommendations for the future are discussed in context of historical concerns—destruction, survival in densely settled areas, survival as fugitives, semi-acculturated societies, and the assimilated Indian or mestizo—and programmatic concerns. Latter includes question of survival of Indian cultures, insights of ecological perspective combined with ethnography, community and local regional studies, and various topical studies (e.g., domesticated plants and animals) that depend on data from Indian cultures. Lastly, there is the concern with social process, social theory, and value systems, with which geographers have done little. However, approach through studies of cultural perception seems promising. Such studies are necessary for full understanding of Latin America's cultural landscapes.

6504. Atkins, John. A voyage to Guinea, Brasil, and the West-Indies; in his majesty's ships, the *Swallow* and *Weymouth*. Foreword by Blyden Jackson. Northbrook, Ill., Metro Books, 1972. 254 p.

Reprint of London 1735 ed. Although account concerns mostly Guinea coast, there is an interesting hodgepodge of notes on history, natural history, politics, economics, and other aspects of Barbados and Jamaica, with shorter treatment of other Caribbean islands. Atkins was a surgeon in the Royal Navy, with an active curiosity that moved him to observe and comment upon such diverse natural phenomena as hurricanes and internal geography of pelicans as well as upon various aspects of the human condition in foreign lands. There is almost no commentary on Brazil, but on the passage thence from Africa. Atkins reflected upon the problem of determining longitude, revealing perhaps the extent of the knowledge of an educated man of the times on this subject. West Indian material covers about fifty pages, but well worth a glance for scattered and miscellaneous details of interest to historical geographers. Atkins' visit was in the latter half of 1722.

6505. Augelli, John P. Future research in Latin America: changing professional viewpoints and issues (*in* Conference of Latin Americanist Geographers, *I, Muncie, Ind., 1969.* Geographic research on Latin America [see item 6526] p. 428-434)

Summary statement on first Conference of Latin Americanist Geographers.

6506. Barraclough, Solon. Alternate land tenure systems resulting from agrarian reform in Latin America (UW/LE, 46:3, Aug. 1970, p. 215-228)

"What land tenure institutions should replace the traditional *latitundia-minifundia* systems that remain dominant in most of Latin America and that nearly everyone agrees are outdated and undesirable?" The question is first discussed in context of constraints and objectives in planning tenure alternatives. Some alternatives are private land holdings, communal and cooperative holdings, and state farms. Each has advantages and disadvantages, as demonstrated in brief descriptions of past experiences in various parts of Latin America. Concludes that most workable alternative cannot be answered in abstract terms. This "depends on the time, the place, on what one wants and on what is politically possible."

6507. Bataillon, M. C. Rôles et caractères des petites villes (AGF/B, 382/383, juin/nov. 1970, p. 185-191, table)

Author's summary: "Texto establecido a partir de ocho informes con referencia principalmente a regiones de poblamiento antiguo y tupido, salpicadas con numerosas ciudades pequeñas. La repartición de las ciudades corresponde a un planteamiento inicialmente administrativo en los países de habla española y al contrario son la consecuencia de un poblamiento pionero para Brasil. Los servicios mínimos que ofrecen las pequeñas ciudades se asemejan entre las regiones, para satisfacer a las necesidades de clases acomodadas semejantes; sin embargo difieren también según los ambientes naturales (transportes), según las jerarquías nacionales (enseñanza) y sobre todo según los niveles economicos. Con aquellos servicios corresponden varios tamaños de las ciudades, según la agrupación y densidad de la población rural y según los niveles de la economía regional, que también determina la intensidad de las relaciones con el campo. Las pequeñas ciudades se presentan finalmente como un reflejo directo de aquel campo."

6508. Bennett, Charles F. Animal geography in Latin America (*in* Conference of Latin Americanist Geographers, *I, Muncie, Ind., 1969.* Geographic research on Latin America [see item 6526] p. 30-40)

Author's summary: "Although animal geography in Latin America has not received major attention from geographers it has long been accorded some interest by the discipline. There are many aspects of animal geography which will yield useful results to those geographers trained to work in this broad area. The most promising aspects of zoo geography are those in which attention is focused upon interactions between man and other animals. This human dimension gives geography and the geographer the most obvious raison d'être for undertaking research in animal geography in Latin America. Further, it is just this human dimension that is so glaringly missing from much of the work that has been done in the past by non-geographers."

6509. Biermann, Kurt-R. Der Brief Alexander von Humboldt's an Wilhelm Weber von Ende 1831: ein bedeutendes Dokument zur Geschichte der Erforschung des Geomagnetismus (DAWB/M, 13:3, 1971, p. 234-242)

Text and explication of Humboldt's letter demonstrating his contribution to geomagnetic research, with informative scholarly annotation.

6510. ———. Die "Memoiren Alexander von Humboldt's" (DAWB/M, 13:4/5, 1971, 382-392)

Examines the authorship question of the *Memoiren* and their value for research on Humboldt.

6511. Blase, Melvin G. ed. Institutions in agricultural development. Ames, Iowa, The Iowa State Univ. Press, 1971. 247 p., tables.

Although none deal specifically with Latin America, these papers will be of interest to geographers concerned with agricultural development. Institutions receiving individual treatment are: land tenure, factor markets, product markets, planning, graduate and undergraduate teaching, research, extension, agricultural credit, rural governing institutions, and legal systems. The project leading to this collection of readings was undertaken in 1967 by the International Rural Institutions Subcommittee of the North Central Land Economics Research Committee.

6512. *Boletín para Bibliotecas Agrícolas.* Organización de los Estados Americanos Instituto Panamericano de Ciencias Agrícolas, Centro Interamericano de Documentación e Información Agrícola. [Vol. 9,] No. 1, marzo 1972- . Turrialba, C. R.

Information bulletin for regional agricultural libraries in Latin America. Useful bibliographic information for agricultural geographers.

6513. Brackenridge, Henry Marie. Voyage to South America, performed by order of the American government in the years 1817 and 1818, in the frigate *Congress*. N.Y., AMS Press, 1971. 2 v. in 1 (317 p.), tables.

Reprint of London 1820 ed. From the preface: "I have undertaken to give a narrative of a voyage of nearly twenty thousand miles, with all that I saw and heard, or could collect from authentic sources, at the places where I touched . . . What is wanted at present, is not so much a work embracing the necessary information on the subject of South America generally, as one that should create a desire to be informed." As secretary to the mission, Brackenridge visited Rio de Janeiro, Montevideo, and Buenos Aires. There are detailed descriptions of these cities, of potential interest to historically minded urban geographers. The main contribution is the record of reactions of a man of arts and letters to the Latin American wars of independence from Spain.

6514. Brown, Lawrence. Diffusion of innovation in Latin America: a geographer's perspective (*in* Conference of Latin Americanist Geographers, *I, Muncie, Ind., 1969.* Geographic research on Latin America [see item 6526] p. 324-332)

Reviews research on diffusion in Latin America at macro-scale and within a single urban field, with example of diffusion analysis from Aguascalientes, México.

6515. Brunn, Stanley D.; John J. Ford; and **Terry L. McIntosh.** The state of political geography research in Latin America (*in* Conference of Latin Americanist Georgraphers, *I, Muncie, Ind., 1969.* Geographic research on Latin America [see item 6526] p. 265-287)

Reviews studies in political geography by geographers and other social scientists, and suggests lines of future research.

6516. Brunnschweiler, Dieter. The study of the physical environment in Latin America (*in* Conference of Latin Americanist Geographers, *I, Muncie, Ind., 1969.* Geographic research on Latin America [see item 6526] p. 220-231)

Output of North American geographers on this subject has been extremely meager in comparison with Europeans, particularly Germans, and Latin Americans. Partly due to relatively stronger position of physical geography in Europe and among Latin Americans, most of whom have been taught in European rather than the North American geographical tradition. Instruction in physical geography of Latin America is subject to gross over-generalizations; some new departures allowing more precision are noted. Recommends shift "from our past empirical and descriptive research orientation to a more dynamic, problem-oriented approach . . ."

6517. Calle Restrepo, Arturo and **Jorge Vélez O.** Demografía: ¿controla el mundo sus nacimientos? Bogotá, Tercer Mundo, 1971. 218 p., bibl., tables.

Detailed treatment of static and dynamic demography, followed by political demography—the search for population legislation, possible solutions to population increase, and moral issues. Many tables of population data from various Latin American countries.

6518. Cardona Gutiérrez, Ramiro. Mejoramiento de tugurios y asentamientos no controlados: los aspectos sociales (IFSNC/CD, 25/26, Spring 1971, p. 129-148, tables)

Commentary on policy in relation to social aspects of urbanization, and on processes involved in rural-urban migration, with special reference to spontaneous development of urban slums. Describes general and specific characteristics of various measures implemented in reaction to influx of migrants to urban areas. Following is attempt to contribute to theory concerning possibilities of effective participation in economic and political spheres by "lowest strata" of society, using Colombian data. List of recommendations includes formulation of official policy on urbanization; establishment of reception and orientation organizations; improvement of education; realization that spontaneous settlements are integral parts of cities rather than separate from them; extension of existing public health, educational, and recreational services to these settlements rather than creation of separate sets of services that help to preserve their marginality; and the encouragement of fundamental changes in the legal system.

6519. Carter, William E. Agrarian reform in Latin America (PAPS, 30:4, 1972, p. 1-14)

Relates recent past history of concern over agrarian reform, with brief description of historical development of conditions leading up to modern insistence on redistruction of land ownership. By beginning of Alliance for Progress, several models for agrarian reform had been operating for some time. Alliance engendered much study and debate, and fomented reform, but by and large it has so far fallen short of goals. Basic reason is lack of knowledge and investigation at local level. Mere titling of land is often ineffective—it does not necessarily increase amount of land available to farmers where *minifundia* are prevalent. Often, reform has meant decrease in production partly because of native farmers' ignorance of or disinclination to use modern techniques. However, in long run production is increased through introduction of new systems of production and marketing. Details of how this is accomplished are not known well at all. Another question concerns adaptability of farmers belonging to various cultures to cooperative and collective ventures. A deterrent to understanding has been common myth that native communities readily accept cooperative organization because of deeply entrenched collectivist traditions. Agrarian reform tends to increase magnitude of rural-urban migration, a paradox never explained satisfactorily. Another seeming paradox is that agrarian reform has not resulted generally in a more equitable distribution of wealth and power. Except in Cuba, "elite" groups seem to "have weathered [reform] very well indeed." One thesis is that since reform laws are promulgated mainly by members of the elite it is not surprising that they are "couched in such ambiguous phraseology" and call for redistribution on an estate-by-estate basis, a cumbersome process with ample warning to owners of hearings for which they may prepare strong cases favorable to themselves. Despite recent legislation and increasing pressure for reform, control of agrarian sector in a number of countries remains in hands of small minority of large landholders. At same time the US is supporting reform in Latin America, "agribusiness is driving small American farmer into oblivion," the justification being efficiency of production. This is the same argument used by the "landed elite" of Latin America, who must react to the clamor for redistribution. "One wonders how many years will pass before the same clamor is heard in the United States."

6520. Casimir, Jean. Definición y funciones de la ciudad en América Latina (UNAM/RMS, 32:6, nov./dic. 1970, p. 1497-1511)

Commentary on original functions, evolution leading to changes in character and function, and the modern definition of the city reflecting these changes. Latin American cities are defined in terms of their exterior roles and as centers for the organization of national territories.

6521. Centro Internacional de Agricultura Tropical (CIAT), *Cali, Co.* Annual report, 1969. Cali, Co., 1969. 72 p., maps, plates, tables.

Reports on center's basic commodity programs with beef cattle, swine, rice, corn, food legumes, and tropical root crops; and on supporting programs in agricultural economics, soils, agronomic systems, crop protection, agricultural engineering, training and communications, and establishment of a center library.

6522. Cermakian, Jean. A geografia da ajuda estrangeira à América Latina: problemas de fontes e de método (IBGE/B, 216:29, maio /junho 1970, p. 29-39, bibl., maps, tables)

Data concerning foreign aid are neither sufficiently precise nor detailed for comparative purposes among countries of "third world." Describes various sources of data and analyzes their relative usefulness. Because of fragmentary nature of many data, it is impossible to study many aspects of foreign aid, such as private investment. Describes system for estimating foreign aid by international financial organizations. Series of tables and maps show distribution of aid in Latin America in terms of financial resources put at disposal of various countries.

6523. Colbert, Edwin H. Antarctic fossils and the reconstruction of Gondwanaland (AMNH/NH, 81:1, Jan. 1972, p. 67-73, maps, plates)

Discovery of fossilized remains of mammal-like reptile *Lystrosaurus* and other elements of *Lystrosaurus* fauna in Triassic formations of Antarctica and their identification with same elements in Africa and India support theory of former existence of a Gondwanaland continent and continental drift that accounts for present separation of these areas.

6524. Colombo, Oscar Juan Héctor and others. República Argentina: informe a la IX Asamblea General y Reuniones Panamericanas de Consulta sobre cartografía, geografía, historia y ciencias geofísicas. B.A., Instituto Panamericano de Geografía e Historia, Sección Nacional [Argentina], 1969. 211 p., fold. maps, maps, tables.

Reports of the commissions on cartography, geography, history and geophysical sciences. Geography section includes reports by the committees on regional geography, basic natural resources, geomorphology, urban geography, geographical terminology, teaching and texts, and the application of geography to development plans.

6525. Comisión de Integración Eléctrica Regional (CIER). **Secretaría General.** Recursos energéticos de los países de la CIER: informe de la Secretaría General. Montevideo, 1970. 1 v. (Various pagings) maps, tables.

Data by countries (Argentina, Bolivia, Brazil, Colombia, Chile, Ecuador, Paraguay, Peru, Uruguay, Venezuela) on sources of electrical energy, consumption, and projections of demand.

6526. Conference of Latin Americanist Geographers, *I, Muncie, Ind., 1969.* Geographic research on Latin America: benchmark 1970. Proceedings of the . . . Edited by Barry Lentnek, Robert L. Carmin and Tom L. Martinson. v. 1. Muncie, Ind., Ball State Univ., 1971. 438 p.

From the preface: "This volume of proceedings has been designed to serve a number of purposes, among which are: 1) an inventory of current research in Latin American geography by North Americans, 2) identification of some of the major research themes characterizing the geographic literature, and 3) a beginning attempt to identify some of the needs for further research." As an introduction, Preston E. James contributes "Studies of Latin America by Geographers in the United States," (see item 6554) and John P. Augelli concludes with "Future Research in Latin America: Changing Professional Viewpoints and Issues" (see item 6505). Body of collection is divided into nine parts: 1) ecology; 2) population and settlement; 3) aboriginal and peasant cultures; 4) commercial and primary activities; 5) physical geography; 6) political and social geography; 7) urban, transportation, and industrial geography; 8) spatial factors in development planning; and 9) research methodology. Individual contributions are reviewed in this section under authors' names. For individual reviews of articles see items: 6503, 6505,

6508, 6514-6516, 6529-6531, 6535, 6540, 6549, 6551, 6554-6555, 6560, 6562-6563, 6568-6570, 6573-6574, 6581, 6586, 6591, 6595, 6597-6598, 6600-6602, 6605-6606, 6611, and 6614.

6527. Congreso de la Emigración Española a Ultramar, *III, Madrid, 1965.* La emigración española a ultramar. Madrid, Ministerio de Trabajo, Instituto Español de Emigración, 1966. 223 p., plates.

Acts, papers, and recommendations concerning relationships between Spaniards and Latin Americans, and on problems of immigration to the Americas and repatriation of Spaniards.

6528. Costa Villavicencio, Lázaro. Diccionario de geografía. Lima, n.p., 1970? 573 p., tables.

More than 100,000 entries, some superficial and others compendious and informative, on geography, cosmography, hydrography, orography, and economy. Contains the Peruvian agrarian reform law of 1969, and a list of political subdivisions of Peru.

6529. Daugherty, Howard E. Climate and ecology in Latin America (*in* Conference of Latin Americanist Geographers, *I, Muncie, Ind., 1969.* Geographic research on Latin America [see item 6526] p. 47-71)

Modes of climatic study treated are macroclimatology, including descriptive, dynamic, and energy balance climatology; bioclimatology, study of microclimates that affect directly plants and animals; and climatic change and weather modification. Macroclimatology is subject to lack of data as well as noncomparability of data. Reviews research on descriptive and dynamic climatology, along with commentary on recent work and possibilities for improvement in study of global energy balance. Standard weather observations are largely unsuitable for bioclimatic analysis, thus "bioclimatic systems" based upon them are of limited value. Reviews attempts to construct and implement kinds of observations relevant to bioclimatic studies, with recommendation for future work. Climatic change in prehistoric times has had attention, but previous studies generally lack time depth and do not extend over large areas. Short-term, modern changes have obvious ramifications for agricultural planning. Effects of man's activities on local weather are largely unknown; burning of vegetation and forest removal may have significant consequences. Research on intentional weather modification such as cloud seeding to induce precipitation has just begun; much needed are studies of its possible impact on agricultural development and on the activities of native cultures.

6530. Denevan, William M. Prehistoric cultural change and ecology in Latin America (*in* Conference of Latin Americanist Geographers, *I, Muncie, Ind., 1969.* Geographic research on Latin America [see item 6526] p. 138-151)

Anthropologists have taken over the task, perhaps by default, of elucidating Latin American prehistory through "ecological approach." Their "cultural ecology" overlaps geographer's concern with man-land relationships, and latter can make significant contributions to this field. Theme is elaborated by reviewing previous work by geographers, ecological studies by archaeologists, and commentary on future role of geographers, methodology, and rationale. Geographers could contribute insights to questions of technological change, population growth and its effects, dietary patterns, the role of humid lowlands in the development of civilizations, and prehistoric urban geography. New applications of statistical methods can contribute to demographic studies that must perforce use incomplete data. New techniques of remote sensing allow quicker survey work and detection of relic features unidentifiable otherwise. Spatial viewpoints are of potential value to research in palaeocology, biogeography of the past, and prehistoric settlement analysis. For rationale, there is need for historical perspective on questions of how and why cultures change; need for knowledge of former settlement patterns and land use in areas now sparsely populated which are about to be reoccupied by land-hungry peasant farmers; and factors of fundability and scholarly and public interest.

6531. Dickenson, Joshua C., III. Research on forests an man in Latin America (*in* Conference of Latin Americanist Geographers, *I, Muncie, Ind., 1969.* Geographic research on Latin America [see item 6526] p. 215-219)

Despite its importance for "any ecologically and economically viable development plan for the area," forestry has received little attention from Latin Americanist geographers. Uses of forests are listed with commentary, and suggestions are made for geographic research on forestry. Perceptions and uses differ among cultures. Introduced species need attention as to success, failure, and their roles in local economies. Integrated forest industries have been established in different kinds of environments, providing opportunities for comparisons. Charcoal is still a significant fuel, with social, dietary, and other interesting implications. Population pressure impinges on humid lowland forests, with consequences for future of shifting field agriculture. Latin American forests are rapidly being modified or eradicated, with drastic ecological results. Geographers can contribute to the discovery and implementation of environmentally and economically rational use of forested land.

6532. ———. and Raymond E. Crist. Geographic and economic scholarship (*in* Esquenazi-Mayo, Roberto and Michael C. Meyer *eds.* Latin American scholarship since World War II [see *HLAS no. 33,* item 137] p. 299-311)

Insufficient effort by specialists in developed countries has been devoted to amelioration of problems, especially food supply, in underdeveloped areas. Discusses ways and means of correcting this and suggests various potential contributions by geographers.

6533. Dollfus, M. O. Colloque sur le rôle des villes dans la formation des régions en Amérique Latine (AGF/B, 382/383, juin/nov. 1970, p. 183-184, table)

Brief report on studies in Guadalajara, Mexico; Medellin, Colombia; Cuzco, Peru; and in Ecuador, by geographers, historians, and sociologists.

6534. Dorner, Peter *ed.* Land reform in Latin America: issues and cases. Madison, Wis., *Land Economics for* Univ. of Wisconsin, Land Tenure Center, 1971. 276 p., bibl., tables (Land economics monographs, 3)

Land Tenure Center at Univ. of Wisconsin (Madison) continues its dissemination of information and results of research with this useful collection of readings: Peter Dorner "Needed Redirections in Economic Analysis for Agricultural Development Policy"

GEOGRAPHY: GENERAL

Don Kanel "Land Tenure Reform as a Policy Issue in the Modernization of Traditional Societies"
Peter Dorner and Don Kanel "The Economic Case for Land Reform"
William C. Thiesenhusen "Employment and Latin American Development".
Selected case studies include a contribution on "Agrarian Reform Legislation: Chile," by Joseph R. Thome, and commentary on agrarian reform in Chile (William C. Thiesenhusen), Bolivia (Ronald J. Clark), and Colombia (Herman Felstehausen). Supplementary reform measures are discussed by: Marion Brown, "Peasant Organizations as Vehicles of Reform," William C. Thiesenhusen "Colonization: Alternative of Supplement to Agrarian Reform in Latin America," Joseph R. Thome, "Improving Land Tenure Security" and Marion Brown, "Private Efforts at Reform," and Peter Dorner, "Policy Implications."

6535. Dozier, Craig L. Geography and the emergent areas of Latin America (*in* Conference of Latin Americanist Geographers, *I, Muncie, Ind., 1969.* Geographic research on Latin America [see item 6526] p. 86-94)

"Emergent areas" are settlement frontiers comprising newly occupied or reoccupied lands, formerly sparsely inhabited by agriculturalists or, if thickly populated at one time, virtually abandoned during recent centuries. Regional syntheses generally have failed to keep pace with changes in these lands caused by recent migrations and introduction or reintroduction of various agricultural technologies. Pioneer works are cited, with a call for more attention to the field. Work of quality can result only from broad approach, drawing data and methods from other disciplines, without hindrance by narrow concepts of what comprises "proper" geography. Four recommendations are made as to directions future research might take: 1) studies in depth of the past; 2) human attitudes and their roles in change; 3) environmental impacts of new or renewed agricultural or other activity; and 4) land use and market studies. A number of specific areas are pointed out as eminently suitable for this research.

6536. Dozo, Salvador Ramón Manuel and Miguel García Firbeda. Tratado de geografía económica. pt. 1. B.A., Ediciones Macchi, 1972. 694 p., fold. maps, illus., maps, plates, tables.

First of two parts of a basic text, by a geographer and an economist. Definitions, principles, relationship of physical geography to economic activity, production, finances, energy, water, transport, and communications. Pt. 2, in preparation, will deal with agriculture, forestry, livestock, fishing, hunting, mining, and industry.

6537. Driver, Edwin D. The social sciences and population (NYAS/A, 172, 27 Oct. 1971, p. 441-478, bibl., tables)

Brief note on geography states that it is second only to sociology in its commitment to population studies. However, consideration of population policy *per se* does not seem to be widespread in geographical instruction in the US.

6538. Dumont, René. Menaces de famine et "révolution verte" (IRFDH/DC, 47/48, mars/juin 1972, p. 24-33)

General public must be alerted to disproportionate increases in population and food supply in underdeveloped areas. Less spectacular but more insidious than outright famine is lack of protein in diets of many of world's peoples. More effective distribution of "upgraded" crop plants and domestic animals, such as tropical cereals and cattle, would seem advisable, but a major difficulty lies in their adaptation to different environments. Other difficulties occur in the effects of localized developments in increasing regional disparities in economic opportunities and unemployment. Economic and social limitations on agricultural improvements and dependence on developed countries hinder rational development and distribution of the means of subsistence in underdeveloped countries. "Common front" of the "Third World" should be effort to become economically independent. Examples are drawn from several parts of the world including Latin America.

6539. Eichler, Arturo. El problema del medio ambiente. Merida, Ven., Univ. de los Andes, Facultad de Economía, Instituto de Investigaciones Económicas, 1972. 45 p., table.

Describes a number of elements of "environmental crisis," and offers a strategy for amelioration involving criteria and standards, observation and control, planning, and education.

El-Badry, M. A. Latin America population prospects in the next fifteen years. See item 1735.

6540. Gauthier, Howard L. Geography, transportation, and regional development (*in* Conference of Latin Americanist Geographers, *I, Muncie, Ind., 1969.* Geographic research on Latin America [see item 6526] p. 333-342)

Notes attention of social scientists since World War II to "development." Discusses nonspatial relationships between transportation and economic development; transportation and unbalanced economic development, and transportation as a spatial system in development process.

6541. Genovés, Santiago. *Ra,* una balsa de papyrus a través del Atlántico. México, UNAM, Instituto de Investigaciones Económicas, 1972. 88 p., bibl., plates, tables (Cuadernos: serie antropológica, 25)

Account by a participant of Thor Heyerdahl's transatlantic voyages in papyrus floats, with commentary on implications for problem of precolumbian transoceanic dispersals of culture traits. Also commentary on oceanic pollution and human behavior under difficult conditions in limited space.

6542. George, Pierre. Aspects méthodologiques avec référence à l'Amérique Latine (IRFDH/DC, 45/46, sept./déc. 1971, p. 12-21)

Essay comprises first part of Ch. 2, "Géographie: Ecologie et Environnement" in the set of readings titled *Développement & Civilisation.* Methodological aspects concern physical factors, of human environment, and effects of industrialization. "The route from geomorphology to urban geography is a long one," but each subdiscipline has something to offer in an effective approach to problems of underdevelopment in Latin America.

6543. Goff, Nollie R. USAF [i.e., United States Air Force] satellite triangulation in the Western Hemisphere (PAIGH/RC, 18:18, 1969, p. 101-112, table)

Describes method of satellite triangulation using geodetic stellar cameras. In 1967 a program of connecting isolated locations and filling in existing survey networks was begun in northern South America. The North American Datum has been extended through Trinidad and Curaçao to South America, and five of the stations coincide with PAGEOS world-wide network, allowing all world datums to be tied in with a high degree of accuracy.

6544. González, Alfonso. Population, agriculture and food supply in Latin America (ULIG/C, 15:3, Sept. 1971, p. 333-343, tables)

Presents various data concerning role of agriculture in the economy of Latin American countries, comparing them with other parts of the world. After discussing such factors as gross domestic product, export trade, pressure on arable land, and trends in productivity, concludes on an optimistic note concerning the "green revolution" role in providing the necessary time lag between reduction of death rate and control of birth rate.

6545. Goode, Judith Granich. Latin American urbanism and corporate groups (CUA/AQ, 43:3, July 1970, p. 146-167, bibl.)

Author's abstract: "Traditional agrarian societies tend to develop corporate groups as important structural components. These groups are ascriptive and are formed on such bases as kinship, occupation and ethnicity among others. They pervade many areas of life and are significant to both the identity and activity of the individual. Traditional Latin American society, however, was not characterized by such groups. Both prehispanic corporate kin groups and medieval Spanish groups such as the *gremio* disintegrated after the Conquest. Traditional Latin American society is characterized by flexible ego-centered networks, a strong ideological emphasis on an individualistic self-concept and a preference for individual autonomy in activity. Despite this lack of emphasis on collectivities, recent urbanization in Latin America has been characterized by widespread proliferation of voluntary associations as corporate groups. This process is less an outgrowth of traditional patterns or a spontaneous response to new needs than it is a result of the diffusion of Euro-American group models. Because of a general lack of experience with collectivities, certain kinds of activity and function are emphasized in Latin American voluntary associations while others are less successful. Participation varies according to class, age, sex and nationality. More data is needed to test the hypothesis that while voluntary associations follow modernization in Latin America they are weaker there than elsewhere in such aspects as proportion of population affiliated, importance of group membership to the individual and longevity of groups. Such weakness might be related to the lack of experience with groups in traditional society."

6546. Hambleton, Hugues-Georges. La modernisation de l'agriculture en Amérique Latine (ULIG/C, 15:35, sept. 1971, p. 115-169, table)

Author's abstract: "During the last 20 years agricultural production has increased annually by 4 to 5 percent. This growth is indicative of a 'young' agriculture, based on large capital investment from both private and community sources. Modern and high capital outlay agricultural enterprises are situated in the north west of Mexico, in Venezuela (rice near Calabazo), in Colombia (sugar in the Cauca Valley), in the north of Peru (sugar), in the south of Brazil, at Belize (citrus fruits), in Paraguay (quebracho). In the future, agriculture must face an increased demand in both quality and quantity. This demand will be better met by a developing agriculture which allows a better integration of production and a reduction of costs, and which increases its productivity. However, a too great and too sudden modernization could lead to unemployment and a low productivity per acre compared to the high productivity of family farms. It is, therefore, essential to develop a plan aimed at increasing the size of plots of land, at favouring the entry of latifundia into the commercial market and at developing food industries which would in turn absorb the surplus of the rural labor force."

6547. Hammerly Dupuy, Daniel. Bajo el signo del terremoto: los sismos ante la historia, la ciencia y la religión. Lima, Ediciones Peisa, 1971. 616 p., illus., maps, plates, tables.

Pt. 1 describes the great Peruvian earthquake of 31 May 1970 and its consequences. Pt. 2 deals with hypotheses about causes of earthquakes, recent advances in seismology, possibilities of predicting earthquakes, and the seismic nature of Peru. Pt. 3 reviews various religious aspects of earthquakes. Appendices contain eyewitness reports of the destruction of Yungay in the Huascarán avalanche, and of the earthquake in southern Peru that occurred on 13 Aug. 1868.

6548. Harris, Walter D., Jr. The growth of Latin American cities. In collaboration with Humberto L. Rodríguez-Camilloni. Athens, Ohio, Ohio Univ. Press, 1971. 314 p., bibl., maps, plates, tables.

Author's summary: "There is no doubt that the urban place must be considered as a major element in the social and economic development of the Latin American region. In writing this book the concern has been less with a country-by-country description of the growth of specific cities than with the patterns of urban growth in the various regions of the Latin American continent. Because these patterns have in many cases been influenced by the preexisting urban systems dating back to pre-columbian and Colonial times, the book begins with a survey of the geographic setting and historical development of Latin American cities from pre-columbian days to the present. "The single most significant factor in the expansion of urban and metropolitan areas in Latin America in recent decades has been the phenomenal increase in the rate of population growth through most of the southern hemisphere, and the projections of the continuation of this trend in the future. A profile of population distribution and its relation to urban growth is presented next, followed by an evaluation of the role that rural-urban migration and industrialization have played in this development in Brazil, Costa Rica, Ecuador, Honduras, and Mexico. The rate of urbanization and some of the socioeconomic problems associated with it are discussed with reference to Chile and Perú, and this is followed by a description of urban systems within a regional context as manifested in the cluster of countries which constitute the region of Central America—the regional setting here being more significant than national boundaries. Associated with the growth of cities has been a startling expansion of metropolitan areas. This is illustrated by a discussion of seven metropolitan areas that have been selected both because they share certain similarities and at the same time demonstrate some unique characteristics. The focus in Chapter 7 is narrowed to an evaluation of the effect of population growth and the proliferation of peripheral settlements on urban structure in Latin America, with a detailed description of the evolution and character of the barriadas in Lima, Perú. The book concludes with some generalized observations on the physical structure of cities in Latin America, including a discussion of trends in residential patterns by income groups; of the location of industry and commerce; and of the nature and form of city centers."

6549. Hegen, Edmund E.; Don R. Hoy; and Ernst Griffin. Commercial agriculture (*in* Conference of Latin Americanist Geographers, *I, Muncie, Ind., 1969.* Geographic research on Latin America [see item 6526] p. 182-208)

Describes past characteristics and trends of research by US geographers in Latin American agriculture, as well as contributions by Latin Americans and Europeans. Major contributors among latter have been French and Germans. Cites publications of various organizations and individuals as examples of nongeographic sources on subject. Suggests number of research deficiencies and lists research subjects, with commentary. Recommendations include application to agricultural studies of analytic techniques used in other subfields; linking of studies existing now in isolation; realization of commercial agriculture's important and broad scope; and appreciation of human aspects of this study. Includes tabular summary of research published in *Annals of the Association of American Geographers, Geographical Review, Economic Geography, Professional Geographer* and by US geographers in *Revista Geográfica*.

6550. Hey, Nigel. How will we feed the hungry billions?: food for tomorrow's world. N.Y., Julian Messner, 1971. 191 p., bibl., plates.

Although not devoted specifically to Latin America, much data is included in discussions of food and nutrition problems and their possible solutions.

6551. Horst, Oscar H. The study of change in traditional communities (*in* Conference of Latin Americanist Geographers, *I, Muncie, Ind., 1969.* Geographic research on Latin America [see item 6526] p. 152-160)

Study of traditionally oriented communities dates from the 1920's, and has been dominated by anthropologists who up to the 1950's contributed mainly descriptive works. Since then, due largely to rapid growth of urbanization, members of other disciplines, including geographers, have been drawn to community studies, but these tend more to be concerned with "developed" areas and assimilated cultures than with traditional societies. Remainder of commentary describes need for and impediments to research, and problems of obtaining data. Under latter heading there are several suggestions as to topics for research by geographers.

6552. Humboldt, Alexander von. Relation historique du voyage aux régions équinoxiales du nouveau continent fait en 1799, 1800, 1801, 1803, et 1804 par . . . et A. Bonpland. Stuttgart, FRG, F. A. Brockhaus, 1970. 688 p., tables (Quellen und Forschungen zur Geschichte der Geographie und der Reisen, 8)

Reprint of v. 3, published originally by J. Smith et Gide Fils, Paris, 1814-25. Contains Venezuelan material not covered in v. 2; various shorter essays on other regions; the Antilles; the "Political Essay on the Island of Cuba"; and northern Colombia. Useful index by Hanno Beck has been added to this handsome reprint.

6553. James, Preston E. On geography: selected writings of . . . Edited by D. W. Meinig. Introduction by Richard Hartshorne. Syracuse, N.Y., Syracuse Univ. Press, 1971. 407 p., bibl., illus., maps, plate, tables (Syracuse geographical series, 3)

Contains six of James' writings on Latin America: "Studies of Latin America by Geographers in the United States" (see item 6554); "Some Geographic Relations in Trinidad"; "Changes in the Geography of Trinidad"; "Belo Horizonte and Ouro Prêto, a Comparative Study of Two Brazilian Cities"; "The Problem of Brazil's Capital City"; and "General Introduction to Latin America," from his widely used textbook.

6554. ———. Studies of Latin America by geographers in the United States (*in* Conference of Latin Americanist Geographers, *I, Muncie, Ind., 1969.* Geographic research on Latin America [see item 6526] p. 1-12)

Reviews past contributions, beginning with first decade of 20th century. Highlights before World War I were: contributions of Isaiah Bowman and American Geographical Society, with inputs by G. M. McBride and Mark Jefferson; and work of Bailey Willis and Wellington D. Jones as land-use surveyors. After war, geographic research took on more individual flavor, with pioneers like Carl O. Sauer, Robert S. Platt, Clarence F. Jones, and Preston E. James. James describes number of interdisciplinary programs, formal and informal, that resulted in fruitful cooperation among scholars and the beginning of such durable publications as *Ibero-Americana* (in 1932) and the *Handbook of Latin American Studies* (in 1936).

6555. Jorgenson, Harold T. Basic issues in the process of development in Latin America: food, land, employment, income, environment (*in* Conference of Latin Americanist Geographers, *I, Muncie, Ind., 1969.* Geographic research on Latin America [see item 6526] p. 402-411)

Discusses population increase, food supply, misuse of land, problems of underemployment and unemployment, incomes, and needs for geographic research on settlement of new lands, colonization, environmental preservation, and growth of urban areas.

6556. Keast, Allen; Frank C. Erk; and Bentley Glass *eds.* Evolution, mammals, and southern continents. Albany, N.Y., State Univ. of New York Press, 1972. 543 p., illus., maps.

Pt. 2 discusses now widely accepted theory of continental drift, with commentary on historical development of concept, plate tectonics, sea-floor spreading, recent reconstruction of continental movements in southern hemisphere and biotic relationships. Includes index.

6557. Kemper, Robert V. Bibliografía comentada sobre la antropología urbana en América Latina (BBAA, 33/34, 1970/1971, p. 85-140)

Includes works in social anthropology published since 1940; omits theses, papers, and unedited articles; and the annotations are informative rather than critical. Organization: 1) general studies; 2) works listed accord-

Keyfitz, Nathan and **W. Flieger.** Population: facts and methods of demography. See item 1743.

6558. Killer, Peter. Alexander von Humboldt. Das Reisewerk (Du. Kulturelle Monatschrift [Zürich, Switzerland] 30:9, Sept. 1970, p. 616-653, illus., plates)

Short description of Humboldt's travels in South and Central America, illustrated with beautiful plates from his early works "Vues des Cordilleres" and "Plantes Equinoxiales." [César Caviedes]

6559. Lands and peoples. v. 6, South and Central America. N.Y., Grolier, 1972. 346 p., maps, plates.

Nicely illustrated compendium of generalities and particular facts, organized by country each with different author. Subjects in most descriptions are organized in sections entitled "people, land (and cities), economy, history." Each treatment of a country is accompanied by a map and a list of "facts and figures".

6560. Lentnek, Barry. Latin American peasantry in transition to modern farming (*in* Conference of Latin Americanist Geographers, *I, Muncie, Ind., 1969.* Geographic research on Latin America [see item 6526] p. 161-166)

Due to rapid changes taking place in Latin America, much of previous geographic research is irrelevant. "Precolumbian and other historical studies by geographers are a nicety well worth preserving for a handful of our colleagues and their academic audiences." Most Latin Americanist geographers should devote attention to modern problems. Under heading "Some Views on the Peasant," a summary by Clifton R. Wharton, Jr. (ed. of *Subsistence agriculture and economic development*, Chicago, Ill., Aldine, 1969) of papers in an agricultural development council conference is "paraphrased and discussed from a spatial perspective." Remaining section comments on "spatial perspectives of selected aspects of the transition to modern farming."

6561. López Sánchez, José. Humboldt y su época: en homenaje al bicentenario de Alejandro de Humboldt. La Habana, Academia de Ciencias de Cuba, Museo Histórico de las Ciencias Carlos J. Finlay, 1969. 151 p., bibl., plates.

Cuba's contribution to the Humboldt anniversary, commemorating the "Political Essay on the Island of Cuba" as well as Humboldt's contributions to natural history and geography. After brief sections on Humboldt's times, science and technology in the industrial revolution, his formative years, and his voyages to the New World, major part of the book comprises a chronological scientific history of Humboldt era and brief biographies of his associates, acquaintances, and other scientists, scholars, and travelers.

6562. McNulty, Michael L. Urbanization and economic development: research directions and needs (*in* Conference of Latin Americanist Geographers, *I, Muncie, Ind., 1969.* Geographic research on Latin America [see item 6526] p. 343-349)

Suggests directions of future research, data collecting, and research priorities.

6563. Marasciulo, Edward. Quasi-economic political units in Latin America (*in* Conference of Latin Americanist Geographers, *I, Muncie, Ind., 1969.* Geographic research on Latin America [see item 6526] p. 412-414)

Suggests that geographers study the motivations for creation of new organizations based on production areas, financial cooperation, and other possibly logical criteria. Examples include the economic role of San Pedro Sula, Honduras, and the new attention to river basins and colonization areas that do not conform to national boundaries.

6564. Mashbits, Iakov Grigor'evich. Latinskaia Amerika: problemy ekonomicheskoi geografii [Latin America: problems of economic geography]. Moskva, Mysl', 1969. 254 p., bibl., maps, tables (Institut Geografii Akademii Nauk SSSR)

Pt. 1, "Population, Economic Development and Use of Natural Resources"; pt. 2, "Geography of the Economy and of the Population." Cuba is mentioned only in the concluding pages. Includes chapters on: Latin America within the capitalist division of labor; urbanization; and the creation of economic regions within each country. Footnotes. The basic bibliography includes only books in all languages. [A. R. Navon]

6565. Mazo, Gabriel del. Gran canal fluvial de integración sudamericana (USM/RCEC, 74, enero/junio 1967, p. 66-86)

Recommends implementation of the mid-19th century idea of joining the Amazon, Orinoco, and La Plata river systems by canals to promote economic development of interior South America.

6566. Menz, John A. Some aspects of land-use planning in peasant cultures (UW/LE, 47:1, Feb. 1971, p. 46-54)

In underdeveloped countries the constraints on indiscriminate or irrational use of forested lands are ineffective or non-existent, affecting lands where quick-return alternatives to timber production are possible. Article is "concerned with few of more important aspects of land-use planning for agrarian reform and colonization projects in Latin America in which forestry is one of the viable alternatives." Theses advanced are 1) it may be in best interests of colonizers or beneficiaries of agrarian reform to leave land in forest or to reforest; 2) cooperatives or unions of such people can be important in convincing them to look to the future; 3) after initial exterior aid has helped to establish such people on new holdings, long term projects such as reforestation may be financed internally; 4) forest resources should be pooled into cooperative ventures; 5) the state should participate in and encourage such ventures because there are broader social values associated with management of forest lands.

6567. Mesa Redonda sobre Recursos Naturales, *II, México, 1969.* Recursos naturales. Editado por N. Bernardes. Revisión de M. Ruiz Elízetui. Rio, Instituto Panamericano de

Geografía e Historia, Comisión de Geografía, 1972. 213 p., maps, plates, tables (Publicación, 329)

Papers:
Reynaldo Börgel O. "Alocución del Presidente del Comité de Recursos Naturales"
Sergio Padilla Guzmán "El Espectro: Realidades e Implicaciones en la Percepción Remota"
Carlos Elizondo A. "Desarrollo de los Estudios sobre Percepción Remota y su Aplicación a la Evaluación Básica de Recursos Naturales"
Fernando García Simo "Plática sobre Nuevas Técnicas de Percepción Remota con las Películas Blanco y Negro y Color"
Tema general "Evaluación de los Recursos para el Desarrollo en la América Latina: Instrumentos de Investigación Metodológica para la Integración Regional"
Raul Higuerra Mota "Técnicas de Barrido y Formación de Imágenes en la Región Infrarroja"
Carlos Elizondo A. "El Programa de Percepción Remota en México"
Alfonso de la Torre Cavazos "Aplicaciones de la Película Infrarroja en la Evaluación de Recursos"
Tema general "Evaluación de los Recursos para el Desarrollo en la América Latina: Instrumentos de Investigación Metodológica para la Integracion Regional"
B. N. Koopmans "Un Enfoque Dinámico de la Fotointerpretación en Levantamientos Costeros"
Daniel Deagostini, "Métodos Fotogramétricos para la Construcción del Mapa Base de Fotointerpretación"
Gerardo Sicco Smith "Sistema de Fotointerpretación Recomendado para los Bosques Húmedos Tropicales de Colombia"
Orris C. Herfindahl "Algunos Problemas en el Uso de los Inventarios de Recursos Naturales por Países en Vías de Desarrollo"
Enriqueta García de Miranda "Correlaciones en Vegetación y Clima según dos Sistemas Climáticos"
Angel Ramos S. and Efraim Hernández X. "Cálculo de Productividad Pecuaria en las Regiones Ganaderas de México"
Javier Chavelas Pólito; Efraim Gernández Xolocotzi; Arturo Gómez Pompa and Roberto Villaseñor Angeles "Metodología Seguida en la Elaboración de Mapas de Vegetación para la Evaluación de los Recursos Naturales y Conservación de los Mismos"
G. W. Elbersen and E. Nieuwenhuis "Terrazas del Rio Pamplonita"
Ambrosio González C. "Evaluación de Programas en Materia de Conservación de Recursos Naturales en la Enseñanza Superior en México"
Enrique Beltran "Medios de Comunicación y Conservación"
A. Barrera and A. Laguerenne "Cursillos de Extensión en el Museo de Historia Natural"
J. M. Montoy Maquin "Una Experiencia en Enseñanza Postgraduada en Inventarios y Evaluación de Recursos para la Planificación del Desarrollo Agricola."

6568. Mings, Robert C. Research on the tourist industry in Latin America: its present status and future needs (*in* Conference on Latin Americanist Geographers, *I, Muncie, Ind., 1969.* Geographic research on Latin America [see item 6526] p. 315-323)

Review of informational sources and recommendations for research.

6569. Minkel, Clarence W. Latin America in the sixties: the geography of minerals (*in* Conference of Latin Americanist Geographers, *I, Muncie, Ind., 1969.* Geographic research on Latin America [see item 6526] p. 209-214)

The dearth of publications by geographers on mineral production, processing, and transport in Latin America is offset partly by contributions of other disciplines. Reviews few articles, theses, and dissertations by geographers and presents research needs and opportunities. Latter include inventories; impact of mineral-related activities on landscape; development of theory, methodology, and application of quantitative techniques; contribution of master's theses if more widely disseminated; with part of the way shown by Homer Aschmann ("The natural history of a mine," *Economic Geography*, 46:2, 1970, p. 172-189).

6570. Momsen, Richard P. Mapping spatial factors for development planning (*in* Conference of Latin Americanist Geographers, *I, Muncie, Ind., 1969.* Geographic research on Latin America [see item 6526] p. 397-401)

Except in Brazil, geographers have generally not become involved in mapping of spatial factors for purposes of development planning. Natural resources, land use, and population distribution constitute only small part of data that need mapping for this purpose. Suggests various data should be brought to same level of detail, and that geographers return to "concept of the region as the sum total of all its measurable, mappable parts" for purposes of development planning.

6571. Müller, Paul. Ausbreitungszentren in der Neotropis (*Naturwissenschaftliche Rundschau* [Stuttgart, FRG] 25:7, Juli 1972, p. 267-270, bibl., illus.)

After recognizing 40 diffusion centers for fauna of Middle and South America, author discusses mobility of species which seems to have been directly related to climatic-vegetational changes of post-glacial period. Routes of particularly high migration activity were peripheral zones of Amazonia, Central American Cordilleras and southern coast of Brazil. [César Caviedes]

6572. Myers, George C. Demographic surveys in Latin America (IRFDH/DC, 45/46, sept./déc. 1971, p. 50-58, bibl.)

Description and analysis of demographic sample survey in Latin America as used for collecting data on mortality, fertility, and migration. Instruments discussed are population census, registration of vital statistics, both less than ideal means of providing needed statistics, and social demographic surveys of fertility, mortality, and migration which often supplement more traditional efforts in providing insights into problems attending rapid population increases. Points made in summary are: 1) "The demographic survey has been an important source of population information for a region that suffers many deficiencies in its census and vital statistics systems." There is a recommendation to extend these surveys into conventional systems of data gathering; 2) activities like those of CELADE (Latin American Demographic Center in Santiago) should be extended to other areas to provide more comparative data; and 3) the demographic survey has potential as an "important tool for the planning of social, economic, educational and health services."

6573. Nietschmann, Bernard. The substance of subsistence (*in* Conference of Latin Americanist Geographers, *I, Muncie, Ind.,*

1969. Geographic research on Latin America [see item 6526] p. 167-181)

Introduces subject by suggesting that there are many false conceptions about people living at "subsistence" level and that we know little about content or structure of subsistence. Effective research will employ quantitative methods to measure components, inputs, and outputs of subsistence systems. Characteristics of these systems are then described and analyzed in terms of productivity, time and labor, distance from residences to farm sites or hunting and gathering areas, carrying capacity, use of data on diet and nutrition, and the potentials of aerial photography and remote sensing. Recommends long-term measurements and standardization where feasible for comparability.

6574. Nunley, Robert E. Two aspects of quantitative methodology: uniform areal data units and analog simulation (*in* Conference of Latin Americanist Geographers, *I, Muncie, Ind., 1969.* Geographic research on Latin America [see item 6526] p. 415-420)

The number of Latin American studies employing statistics and mathematics has increased significantly in last decade, as result of search for more objective analysis and more coherent body of theory. Discusses problem of uniform area data units, and describes applications of analog simulation.

6575. Organization of American States. Instituto Interamericano de Ciencias Agrícolas. Centro Interamericano de Documentación e Información Agrícola. Indice lationamericano de tesis agrícolas. Turrialba, C. R., 1972. 718 p.

7,242 entries with indices of key words and authors, for the period 1957-67.

6576. ——. ——. ——. Publicaciones periódicas y seriadas agrícolas de América Latina. Turrialba, C.R., 1971. 69 p. (Bibliotecología y documentación, 19)

Arranged alphabetically with geographical (by country) and subject indices. Entries include title, date, editor, place of publication, form of distribution, and information concerning bibliography and languages in which summaries are presented.

6577. ——. Instituto Interamericano de Estadística. América en cifras 1972: situación física. Washington, 1972. 86 p., tables (312-S-6221; Fascículo, 1)

Identification of frontiers by cardinal points, geographical positions of extreme points, altitudes of principal heights, data on political divisions; climatic data include temperature and precipitation.

6578. ——. Instituto Panamericano de Geografía e Historia. Acta final de la IX Asamblea General y Reuniones de Consulta Conexas. Washington, 1969. 105 p., tables.

Contains resoluciones and recommendations of committees on cartography, geography, history, and geophysical sciences.

6579. ——. Instituto Panamericano de Geografía e História. Grupo de Trabalho para o Vocabulário de Geografia Urbana. Vocabulary of urban geography. Rio, 1971. 156 p. (Publicação, 328)

232 basic terms and definitions in English, Spanish, Portuguese, and French.

6580. Papvero, Nelson. Essays on the history of neotropical dipterology, with special reference to collectors: 1750-1905. v. 1. São Paulo, Univ. de São Paulo, Museu de Zoologia, 1971. 216 p., bibl., fold. maps, maps, plates.

Title hardly suggests interest to geographers, but they will find accounts of collectors' itineraries, some accompanied by maps, of great use in tracing routes of exploration and survey by such as Humboldt, Spix and Martius, and others whose works have been consulted by historical geographers.

6581. Parsons, James J. Ecological problems and approaches in Latin American geography (*in* Conference of Latin Americanist Geographers, *I, Mucie, Ind., 1969.* Geographic research on Latin America [see item 6526] p. 13-32)

Parsons sees new interest in "ecology" as golden opportunity to return to "fundamental concern with earth as home of man or, stated a bit more grandly, with man-environment systems;" this after retrenchment into more conventional approaches involving "scientific" techniques and concepts such as "spatial interaction, locational analysis, landscape perception," etc. Geographers generally have been slow to appreciate possibilities in "ecological approach." Describes possibilities in sections on ecologic crisis in Latin America; study of vegetation as geographic factor much closer to man in its relationship to human activity than in temperate regions; tropical agricultural systems, of which there is so much still to be learned, especially about soils and soil fertility; and opening of new lands. Historical demography is an indispensable element along with knowledge of past human movements and their relationships to habitats. A significant opportunity for development of the ecological approach lies in cultural-historical-ecological studies of resource base. Other opportunities are in spheres of land use planning and case studies of local areas for evaluation of ecologic consequences of development schemes. Parsons concludes with persuasive challenge to Latin Americanists: "It may lie in the hands of the area specialists among the geographers to bring the subject back into the mainstream of human concern—the manner of man's occupance and use of the habitable earth. Ecologic research in the Latin American tropics provides an unexcelled opportunity to demonstrate this potential."

6582. Patiño, Víctor Manuel. Plantas cultivadas y animales domésticos en América equinoccial. t. 5, Animales domésticos introducidos. Cali, Co., Imprenta Departamental, 1970. 381 p.

Very useful series continues with historical syntheses, for regions and individual countries, of the introductions of insects, fish, birds, cats, dogs, horses, cattle, pigs, and camels.

6583. Polidoro, Nicola. Presenza dell'Italia nell'America Latina. v. 1. Roma, Edizione Il Gabbiano, 1971. 268 p., illus., maps, plates.

Organized by country, listing and description of Italian business interests in Latin America, with geographical, historical, and economic notes. Contains chapters on Mexico, Central America including Panama, Cuba, Haiti, and the Dominican Republic.

6584. Un predicamento del hombre: la población (Boletín de Población [Bogotá] 2:6, oct. 1971, p. 1-45, tables)

Spanish edition of the *Population Bulletin's* general article on the origin and significance of the world's "demographic explosion."

6585. Princeton University, *Princeton, N.J.* **Office of Population Research.** Population index bibliography: cumulated 1935-1968 by authors and geographical area, geographical index. v. 1, 1935-1954, North America, South America. Boston, Mass., G. K. Hall 1971. 797 p.

Arranged by country, with entries for many classified by topics.

6586. Psuty, Norbert P. Contributions of the coastal geomorphology of Latin America (*in* Conference of Latin Americanist Geographers, *I, Muncie, Ind., 1969.* Geographic research on Latin America [see item 6526] p. 250-264)

Review of contributions and subject matter, prognosis and recommendations concerning gathering of data, construction of maps and application of geomorphological knowledge to such fields as land use planning, identification of hazards, and archaeology.

6587. Ramos, Manuel M. La energía como problema ambiental en las ciudades (OAS/CI, 13:1/2, enero/abril 1972, p. 5-14, tables)

Effects and problems of the production and use of energy in cities, with special emphasis on air pollution and concentrations of use. Data on consumption and production in various Latin American countries, US and Canada.

6588. Ravines, Eudocio. El desastre de la reforma agraria en la América Latina (SRA/A, 105:6, junio 1971, p. 10-11, 53)

The disastrous type of agrarian reform permeating Latin America, characterized by expropriation of large landholdings and their division into small ones, is attributable to three influences: communist infiltration and marxist brainwashing; the Mexican Revolution; and the pressure exerted by the Alliance for Progress. The general philosophy is that of the French revolution of the late 1700's, inapplicable to modern times and conditions. The example of the Mexican revolution is also inappropriate because it was essentially a revolution against the Church rather than one against the large private landholder. Parceling leads to diminution of productivity because it works against the application of modern agricultural technology. Economic crises will not be solved in terms of numbers of landholders, but in terms of methods by which each hectare is made more productive. The best chance for increased productivity lies not in parceling land to thousands of smallholders, but in the application of modern agricultural technology to large holdings.

6589. La reforma de la agricultura en Iberoamérica (Revista de Estudios Agro-Sociales [Madrid] 21:80, julio/sept. 1972, p. 9-154, bibl.)

Closing statements of the seminar on "La Reforma de la Agricultura en Iberoamérica." Includes the "Informe del Comité Especial sobre Reforma Agraria de la FAO;" information on the "Seminario Latinoamericano de Reforma Agraria y Colonización" organized by the FAO and the Peruvian government; and a bibliography of agrarian reform since 1960.

6590. Reunión Latinoamericana de Fitotecnia, *VIII, Bogotá, 1970.* Resúmenes. Bogotá, Canal Ramírez Antares, 1970. 250 p.

420 resumés of articles on scientific and technological advances in agriculture. Sections include agroclimatology, communications, education, statistics, entomology, fertilizers, genetics, herbicides, economic planning, agricultural chemistry, and soils, as well as many on major types of crop plants and individual species.

6591. Richardson, C. Howard. American research on the political geography of Latin America (*in* Conference of Latin Americanist Geographers, *I, Muncie, Ind., 1969.* Geographic research on Latin America [see item 6526] p. 288-298)

Reviews research in political geography and political science referring to Latin America, and identifies problems for research in the future.

6592. Robinson, D. J. Historical geography in Latin America (*in* Baker, Alan R. H. *ed.* Progress in historical geography. Cambridge, England, Wiley-Interscience, 1972, p. 168-186, illus.)

A number of "indigenous impediments and imperfections" hinder the development of geography as a discipline in Latin America: it lacks literary stylists, and scientific writing, to be acceptable, must be elegant in the literary sense; in the majority of Latin American universities the primary role of the geography department is to train secondary school teachers, predominantly female; univeristy salaries are low, the libraries are poor, age is equated with wisdom and thus seniority; and there is little time for research since most instructors must work part-time at other jobs. There has been in the past a concentration on physical geography, partly because of the culturally determined difficulties of eliciting information concerning local history and other matters essential to cultural or human historical geography. The author's term "intellectual colonialism" refers to the fact that ideas and traditions have come mainly from Europe and North America. Examples are the French in Brazil and at the Univ. of Cuyo, Argentina; and the Germans in Colombia, Chile, Argentina, Mexico, and Brazil. These influences operated both through the introduction of ideas from French and German scholarship and long-term presence of scholars from these countries in Latin American universities and institutes. The North American influence has been in terms of research of scholars who came to investigate, not to remain and teach Latin Americans; thus it is relatively slight. A section on "scales, areas, and themes of research" contains brief critical reviews of work of individuals and "schools" of historical geography. Comments on competition from allied disciplines imply strongly that historical geography lags behind history and anthropology in providing rationales for various approaches and the application of modern research techniques. Robinson concludes with an "outline for the future," suggesting four major time periods within which many subjects could be treated systematically: 1) the aboriginal; 2) the colonial; 3) the period of penetration of non-Iberian culture; and 4) the period (up to the present) of modernization, rapid population increase, and urbanization.

6593. Robinson, Harry. Latin America. 3. ed. London, MacDonald & Evans, 1970. 509 p., bibl., maps, plates, tables.

First published in 1961, with a second edition in 1965, this text for "advanced level" or Sixth Form British students is now offered in an updated edition that brings numerical data to 1967. Expanded sections include those on urbanization, iron and steel industry, Peruvian irrigation, and colonization in Paraguay.

6594. Robirosa, Mario C. Internal migration, human resources, and employment within the context of urbanization (IFSNC/CD, 25/26, Spring 1971, p. 49-65, tables)

Rural-urban migration has caused disproportionate pressure on urban employment opportunities, unemployment, and lowering of productivity and standards of living. This is in marked contrast to 19th century situation in presently developed countries where there was a large demand for labor. Modern trends in redistribution of Latin America's people and effects on the labor market are described.

6595. Sheck, Ronald C. The persistence of cultural autarchy (in Conference of Latin Americanist Geographers, I, Muncie, Ind., 1969. Geographic research on Latin America [see item 6526] p. 350-355)

Reviews research on cultural minorities in Latin America in context of "geography and the cultural interface." Suggests themes of investigation and describes national and minority cultural systems and their areas of interaction.

6596. Silveira, Estanislau Kostka Pinto da. Preservação dos ambientes naturais e comunidades bióticas (IBGE/B, 29:219, nov./dez 1970, p. 52-61, bibl., plate, table)

General statement and series of recommendations on pollution, preservation of natural areas or ecosystems, and various ways of designating areas for purposes of conservation or preservation, by a member of the Instituto de Conservação da Natureza.

6597. Simkins, Paul D. Contributions by geographers to Latin American population studies (in Conference of Latin Americanist Geographers, I, Muncie, Ind., 1969. Geographic research on Latin America [see item 6526] p. 72-85)

Despite widespread concern since World War II over Latin America's burgeoning population, geographers have contributed relatively little to population studies. This is especially true of US geographers, very few of whom combine expertise in population with interest in Latin America. Major contributions have come from other disciplines, and from scholars outside Latin America. Field is thus wide open, with such basic tasks as compilation of maps of population distributions of many areas yet to be done. Concepts of demographic transition and population pressure need study from geographer's viewpoint. Demographers have provided much insight on interrelationships between demographic and other variables, but not much has been done on spatial aspects. Especially rewarding might be study of relationship between economic development and population characteristics.

6598. Soja, Edward W. The geography of modernization: some comments on the relevance to Latin America of recent research in Africa (in Conference of Latin Americanist Geographers, I, Muncie, Ind., 1969. Geographic research on Latin America [see item 6526] p. 299-308)

Discusses modernization, modernization surfaces, and spatial integration in context of possible approaches to geographical analysis in Latin America, following example of recent research in Africa.

6599. Steinhardt, Ricardo J. M. Geografía en marketing, problemas de comercialización: criterios para zonificar y evaluación de vendedores. B.A., Ediciones Macchi, 1971. 123 p., illus., tables.

Commentary on markets, zoning, planning and control of rational distribution of vending activities.

6600. Stillwell, H. Daniel. Recreational geography in Latin America (in Conference of Latin Americanist Geographers, I, Muncie, Ind., 1969. Geographic research on Latin America [see item 6526] p. 309-314)

Review of recent research, including theses and dissertations, summary of "major research questions raised in the past decade," and current research objectives.

6601. Stöhr, Walter B. Spatial growth differentials in Latin America, the role of urban and transport investment (in Conference of Latin Americanist Geographers, I, Muncie, Ind., 1969. Geographic research on Latin America [see item 6526] p. 367-377)

Author's summary: "Spatial growth differentials in Latin America have been defined at four levels; interregional, interurban, urban-rural and international. Policies to influence these growth differentials have relied considerably on urban and transport investment. Very little is known to date about the impact of these two types of investment on regional growth and the results of these policies have therefore often been disappointing. As a basis for clarifying the potential role of these two policy instruments, the paper reviewed relevant decision criteria and analyzed the functional relationship between urban/transport investment and spatial growth differentials via their influence on the mobility of such growth determinants as production factors, commodities and external economics."

6602. Stouse, P. A. D., Jr. Settlement geography in Latin America (in Conference of Latin Americanist Geographers, I, Muncie, Ind., 1969. Geographic research on Latin America [see item 6526] p. 95-103)

Defines field, then reviews literature under headings "settlement form" and "settlement process." Justification of settlement as focus of study is presented as well as brief commentary on uses to which such studies may be put.

6603. Taylor, Philip B., Jr. and **Sam Schulman** eds. Population and urbanization problems of Latin America. Houston, Tex., Univ. of Houston, Office of International Affairs,

Latin American Studies Committee, 1971. 124 p., tables.

Papers and transcription of discussions of conference at Univ. of Houston, April 2-3, 1971. Contents:
T. Lynn Smith "Urban Growth and Urban Problems in Latin America"
J. Mayone Stycos "Population Dynamics and Population Problems in Latin America"
Thomas Merrick "Population Pressures for the 1970's: Lessons for Development Planning"
Robert Black "Options for Latin Parents—Through Family Planning"
Antonio Ordóñez P. "A Case Study in Population: Colombia"
Marta Cehelsky "A Case Study in Urbanization: Brazil"
Benjamin Viel "Efforts of Private Organizations in Population Control in Latin America"
Victor Urquidi "The Latin American University and Urban Problems"
Ralph W. Conant "The North American University and Urban Problems."

6604. Taylor, Roselyn G. Desarrollo urbano en América Latina (UC/B, 100, abril 1970, p. 37-40)

Based on an International Development Bank report of 1969 in which various factors surrounding problem of urbanization in Latin America are discussed. Rapid rate and magnitude of urbanization are seen as obstacles to well-ordered social and economic development. Presents data on the dimensions of urbanization, describes "push" and "pull" factors in migration to cities, and unemployment. Trends in distribution of labor force among major sectors of economic activity indicate that by 1980 there will be a preponderance of workers in tertiary sector; that is, many more workers engaged in service-oriented activities than in primary production or manufacturing, a situation considered by most economists to be at odds with economic improvement. Projections for city sizes and concentrations in 1980 are not encouraging.

6605. Thomas, Robert N. Internal migration in Latin America: an analysis of recent literature (*in* Conference of Latin Americanist Geographers, *I, Muncie, Ind., 1969.* Geographic research on Latin America [see item 6526] p. 104-118)

Discusses number of definitions of "internal migration," then reviews literature with respect to directional bias, incentives for migration, distance and spatial mobility, migration differentials (age, sex, education), step-wise migration, and consequences of migration. Thomas concludes with some guidelines for future research, based mainly on Edward Ackerman's recommendations and strictures in his "Where is a Research Frontier?" (*Annals of the Association of American Geographers,* 53, 1963, p. 229-239). Substantive recommendations include research on consequences of out-migration for centers of origin, intra-urban mobility, and use of behavioral approach.

6606. ———. Survey research design: a case of rural-urban mobility (*in* Conference of Latin Americanist Geographers, *I, Muncie, Ind., 1969.* Geographic research on Latin America [see item 6526] p. 421-427)

Describes sampling procedure employed in Guatemala and the use of a gravity model.

6607. United Nations Industrial Development Organization, *Wien.* Fertilizer demand and supply projections for South America, Mexico and Central America. N.Y., United Nations, 1971. 80 p., bibl., tables (Fertilizer industry series; monograph, 6)

Analysis by country; basic data of use to agricultural geographers.

6608. Uruguay, Presidencia de la Republica. Secretaría. America Latina y la extensión del mar territorial: régimen jurídico. Montevideo, 1971. 440 p., bibl., fold. maps, maps, tables.

Contains texts of and commentary on legislation of Latin American countries concerning the 200-mile limit of territorial waters, published on occasion of Uruguay's establishment of the limit. Uruguay's case is discussed in detail, followed by a chapter on other countries and chapters dealing with conferences and conventions among Latin American nations, interamerican agreements and conferences, and international documents concerning the law of the sea.

6609. Violich, Francis and Juan B. Astica. Desarrollo de la comunidad y el proceso de planificación urbana en la América Latina. Traducido por Sergio Seelenberger. Revisado por Winston C. Estremadorio. Los Angeles, Calif., Univ. of California, Latin American Center, 1971. 107 p.

Discussion of problems in Latin American urban planning, role of the community and its development, and importance of combining community development with urban planning. Translation with supplementary notes. First published in 1966 (Univ. of Calif. Latin American studies series, 6).

6610. Volskii, Viktor V. Economic geography (UN/ISSJ, 24:1, 1972, p. 132-148)

Commentary on economic geography as social science and its relationship to problems of economic development and development planning, by director of the Institute for Latin American Studies of the Academy of Sciences of the USSR in Moscow and head of the Dept. of Foreign Economic Geography at Moscow Univ. Because nature remains sole basis of subsistence and creation of material wealth for mankind, its rational and efficient use depends upon knowledge both of nature itself and of social laws that determine this use. Non-scientific and spontaneous direction of economics, catering to special interests, is generally destructive of natural resources and leads to misuse of human resources. Present economic inequalities among nations cannot be rectified through ordinary evolution; disproportions are increasing, as shown in the Latin America example. Three stages in the formulation of "development targets" are described, followed by commentary on economic geography's potential contributions to implementation of development programs. International comparisons are necessary for identifying structural, sectorial, and geographic inequalities. The "economic geography method" can be used to identify workable economic regions. In appraisals of economic potentials or regions, economic geography can contribute estimates of resource requirements, exploration and surveys to identify resources, resource inventories, suggestions for rational regionalization, and other studies in connection with development planning.

6610a. ———. I.A. Vitver: odin iz osnovatelei Sovetskoi Latinoamerikanistiki (I. A. Vitver:

one of the founders of Soviet Latin American studies) (SSSR/LA, 5, Sept./Oct. 1971, p.160-172)

Vitver was first Soviet economic-geographer to undertake serious study of Latin America. Article offers insight into limited resources for academic study of region available in USSR prior to World War II. [T. S. Cheston]

6610b. ———. and **K. S. Tarasov.** Problemy narodona-seleniia i puti ikh resheniia (Population problems and ways to solve them) (SSSR/LA, 4, July/Aug. 1970, p. 6-26)

Article discusses wide differences between the Soviet and western approaches to solving the problems of the population explosion in Latin America. [T. S. Cheston]

6611. Wagner, Philip L. Latin American vegetation: work by American geographers in the sixties and prospects for the seventies (*in* Conference of Latin Americanist Geographers, *I, Muncie, Ind., 1969.* Geographic research on Latin America [see item 6526] p. 41-46)

Despite fact that there are many important interrelationships of man and vegetation in American tropics, research on vegetation here and in Latin America generally has been sparse in past decade. Vegetation mapping is particularly subject to difficulties of scale; the larger the area mapped, the thornier is the problem of assigning workable units of classification. "Model building" and "imposition of discrete categories of some kind upon a sort of natural continuum" yield less than satisfactory results, especially in attempts to determine what vegetation might be in unvisited areas or what "ideal" type is for a given climate. Modern trend is toward concentration on local situations; if these are to be combined eventually into broader picture and if man's relationships with and effects on vegetation are to be more fully understood, some new schemes of general vegetation analysis must be developed. Newly revitalized biogeography and more thorough local and regional studies of man-land relationships provide context in which next advances in geography of vegetation are likely to be made.

6612. Webb, Kempton E. Geography of Latin America: a regional analysis. Foreword [by] Phillip Bacon and Lorrin Kennamer. Englewood Cliffs, N.J., Prentice-Hall, 1972. 126 p., maps, plates, tables (Foundations of world regional geography series)

Topical and regional treatments are about equally balanced. Former includes chapters on European antecedents of New World discovery and exploration, process of colonization in Latin America, physical geography, population, economic activities, and transport and communication. Regional divisions are "Andean America," the La Plata countries and Chile, Brazil, Middle America, and Caribbean (subtitles placed inadvertently under Middle America in the contents). Main context into which descriptive and historical material fits is evolution of landscapes as results of imposition of different cultures and of cultural choices that vary through time.

6613. Weller, Robert H.; John J. Macisco, Jr.; and George R. Martine. The relative importance of the components of urban growth in Latin America (PAA/D, 8:2, May 1971, p. 225-232)

Author's abstract: "Four generalizations are made: 1) Despite the varying interpretations made by the respective authors, previous studies indicate that urban growth in Latin America is caused by both rural-urban migration and a positive rate of urban natural increase. Thus, to ascribe Latin American urban growth to a single prime causal factor is a misleading oversimplification; 2) Net in-migration apparently plays a larger role in determining the rate of growth of large metropolitan centers than is the case with smaller urban areas; 3) A significant portion of urban growth in a given intercensal period may be attributed to the growth of localities previously too small to be classified as "urban"; 4) urban natural increase is the weighted sum of the natural increase of in-migrants (after their arrival) and urban natives. Improper recognition of this last point may lead to an overstatement of the relative importance of urban natural increase as a component of urban growth."

6614. Williams, Lynden S. The population concept and the Latin Americanist geographer (*in* Conference of Latin Americanist Geographers, *I, Muncie, Ind., 1969.* Geographic research on Latin America [see item 6526] p. 119-123)

Overpopulation should be viewed in context of relationship between population and available resources. Discusses geographer's role in studies of this relationship in terms of widely accepted symptoms of overpopulation: per capita living space, resource depletion, environmental pollution, and poverty. These symptoms are not always coexistent with overpopulation. Williams takes issue with opinion that many environmental ills can be attributed to single cause of overpopulation; it has "become a catchall for any human/resources problem which cannot be easily explained away by some other factor."

6615. Yudelman, Montague; Gavan Butler; and Ranadev Banerji. Technological change in agriculture and employment in developing countries. Paris, Organization for Economic Cooperation and Development, Development Center, 1971. 204 p., tables (Development Center studies; Employment series, 4)

Pt. 1 contains discussion of employment in traditional agriculture, with appendix on land distribution in Latin America; of process of technological change on structure of traditional agriculture and pre-emptive structural change. Pt. 2 offers case studies of technological change and labor utilization at farm level and aggregate analysis of technological change, agricultural development, and labor absorption. Pt. 3 is concerned with international transfer of agricultural technology and offers conclusions and possible inferences for policy.

6616. Zsilincsar, Walter. Städtewachstum und unkontrollierte Siedlungen in Lateinamerika (GR, 23:12, Dez. 1971, p. 454-461, tables)

General observations on urbanization, population growth, and expansion of cities, followed by discussion of relationships between urbanization and migration, socio-economic basis of urbanization, and problem of unregulated suburban settlements.

MIDDLE AMERICA

(CARIBBEAN ISLANDS, CENTRAL AMERICA AND MEXICO)

TOM L. MARTINSON

Associate Professor of Geography
Director
Institute of International Studies
Ball State University

ECONOMIC TOPICS DOMINATE THE SCHOLARLY GEOGRAPHICAL literature and books for the traveler dominate the popular geographical literature on Middle America this year. Among the scholarly geographical works those on resources, population, and applied science prevail. Biogeographical studies by Kellman and Adams (item 6676) and Johannessen, Wilson, and Davenport (item 6663) deserve special recognition, while geomorphological investigations edited by Ayala-Castañares and Phleger (item 6670) and Yarza de la Torre (item 6758) and a water resources survey by Ruth (item 6695) are outstanding as well. Excellent geographical studies of population include those on colonization by Sawatzky (item 6753), community studies by Falcon de Gyves (item 6729), population dynamics by several scholars in El Colegio de México (item 6719), urban form by Sandner (item 6708), migration by Thomas (item 6697), and Lewis (item 6655), and a study of the new city of Belmopan by Furley (item 6674). Works on agricultural change are especially apparent in the applied science field, with fine local field investigations such as that by Alfaro (item 6678) balanced by an admirable three-volume survey of Mexican agriculture produced by the Centro de Investigaciones Agrarias (item 6717). Especially important are the three analyses of subsistence agriculture by Ballance (item 6713), Maturana Medina and Sánchez Cortés (item 6743) and Fonck (item 6699).

Many good additions to the travel and descriptive literature of this area include standard guidebooks such as Clark's (item 6620) and fine compositions by Crow on Mexico (item 6721) and Severin on the Caribbean area (item 6630).

Both the scholarly and popular geographical inquiries provide rich fare for the reader this year. Geography students who digest all the works in this section will find their efforts rewarded by ample professional growth.

GENERAL

6617. Adams, John Edward. Historical geography of whaling in Bequia Island, West Indies (UPR/CS, 11:3, Oct. 1971, p. 55-74)

Whaling, an alternative to the declining cash crop agriculture, became an important local economic activity on Bequia from 1875 to 1925. Recently, interest in whaling has revived and author relates that although whaling will never become a leading activity, it will survive as long as there are whales to hunt and markets for whale oil and meat.

6618. Besancenot, J.-P. Introduction à l'étude géographique du bioclimat humain des Petites Antilles françaises (AGF/B, 382/383, juin/nov. 1970, p. 167-179, maps, tables)

According to author, Guadeloupe and Martinique suffer from an undeserved reputation as climatically undesirable islands; actually, their temperature and moisture conditions vary with altitude and direction of prevailing winds.

6619. Cazes, Georges. Problèmes de population et perspectives économiques en Martinique et en Guadeloupe, avec 17 figures dans le texte (SGB/COM, 23:92, oct./déc. 1970, p. 379-424)

Population census conducted in Martinique and Guadeloupe in 1967 shows slowing of population growth which may be attributed to out-migration as well as a degenerating economic situation.

6620. Clark, Sydney and Margaret Zellers. All the best in the Caribbean: including Puerto Rico and the Virgin Islands. N.Y., Dodd, Mead & Co., 1972. 420 p., maps, plates.

Travelers to the West Indies (except Cuba) will find this volume of historical vignettes and contemporary peripatetics just as valuable as the 23 preceding versions.

6621. Edwards, D. T. The development of small scale farming: two cases from the Commonwealth Caribbean (UWI/CQ, 18:1, March 1972, p. 59-71, bibl.)

Jamaican small farming has responded little to government efforts toward improvement, while gardening in Aranjuez, Trinidad, has expanded without direct assistance and in spite of fierce competition. It appears that in Jamaica agricultural innovations are discouraged, whereas in Trinidad, they are quickly adopted.

6622. Ellis, Bengt. Glodande oar i Karibien. Stockholm, P. A. Norstedt & Soners, 1972, 206 p., bibl., plates.

Author, Swedish painter, bases book on three visits in 1966, 1968 and 1971 to "glowing islands of the Caribbean." Trinidad and Tobago, Grenada, Mustique, St. Vincent, St. Lucia and Dominica. Although basically travel writer, author tries to penetrate behind glossy façade of tourist picture of islands and discusses contemporary problems of industrial development, tourist trade and black power movement. Excellent color and black-and-white photographs. [R. V. Shaw]

6623. Freeland, George L. and **Robert S. Dietz.** Plate tectonic evolution of Caribbean-Gulf of Mexico region (NWJS, 232:5305, July 1971, p. 20-23, maps)

Plate tectonics provides new method for synthesizing data from land field work and marine surveys. The evolution of this region apparently is related to former plate junctions between North America, South America and Africa, and to strike-slip, extensional, and compressional motions as the New World drifted westward.

6624. Giacottino, Jean-Claude. Les petites Antilles britanniques, avec 2 planches hors-texte et 9 figures dans le texte (SGB/COM, 23:91, juillet/sept. 1970, p. 307-334, maps, plates, tables)

Tourism is replacing agriculture as the primary economic resource in the Lesser British Antilles, but continuing importation of food and industrial products results in serious deficits in their balance of payments.

6625. Hicks, Frederick. Making a living during the dead season in sugar-producing regions of the Caribbean (SAA/HO, 31:1, Spring 1972, p. 73-81, bibl.)

Seasonal rhythm of *zafra* and *tiempo muerto* in Caribbean sugar cane production requires workers to find other employment during the slack season. Author's survey of literature identifies three alternative occupations.

6626. Hummelinck, P. Wagenaar and **P. J. Roos.** Een natuurweten-schappelijk onderzoek gericht op het behoud van het Lac op Bonaire (NWIG, 47:1, Sept. 1969, p. 1-28, bibl., maps, plates)

Lac Bonaire, the Netherlands Antilles' largest and as yet almost unspoiled lagoon, will soon be involved in development plans. Scientific survey of lagoon reveals that area is ecologically vulnerable and requires expert management if it is to retain its distinctive flora and fauna.

6627. Hunte, George. The West Indian islands. N.Y., Viking Press, 1972. 246 p., bibl., maps, plates.

Whirlwind tour of Antilles which includes only French, Dutch, British, and US dependencies. Good companion to standard travel guide in that it offers some historical insight.

6628. Robertson, C. J. Bitter-sweet challenge to the Six (GM, 43:11, Aug. 1971, p. 793-798)

Instability of Caribbean sugar market has been aggravated by trade agreements of a political as well as an economic nature, the narrow market, increasing amount of sugar grown behind tariff walls, the dumping of surpluses, and now the impending renegotiation of major international trade agreements.

6629. Schaw, Janet. Journal of a lady of quality: being the narrative of a journey from Scotland to the West Indies, North Carolina, and Portugal, in the years 1774 to 1776. Edited by Evangeline Walker Andrews, in collaboration with Charles McLean Andrews. 3. ed. Spartanburg, S.C., The Reprint Co., 1971. 351 p., facsim., maps, table.

This lively journal, now carefully annotated, provides clear picture of perils in crossing the Atlantic as well as manners and customs, climate and scenery, and also the social and political life of 18th century West Indies and Carolinas.

6630. Severin, Timothy. The golden Antilles. London, Hamish Hamilton, 1970. 336 p., bibl., plates, map.

Authoritative and skillfully written, volume singles out exploits of Raleigh, Gage, and Wafer as examples of hucksterism and raw courage which were elements in the North European intrusion of the early Spanish Caribbean.

6631. Sjörgen, Bengt. Oarna Kring vinden. Stockholm, Tidens Bokklubb, 1970. 234 p., maps, plates.

Swedish author, a naturalist whose chief interests are the Caribbean flora and fauna, describes his travels in 24 of its islands. Includes descriptions of little-known settlements of native Indian groups as well as Bush Negroes and religious sects of every persuasion. Deeply interested in conservation education, author hopes that international organizations will step in to save rain forests, exotic birds and other wildlife of area from total extinction. Illustrations consist of black-and-white photographs. [R. V. Shaw]

6632. Vedder, John G. and others. USGS-IDOE [United States Geological Survey-International Decade of Ocean Exploration] Leg 2 (Geotimes [Washington] 16:2, Dec. 1971. p. 10-12, illus., maps)

Geophysical and geological reconnaissance east of the Yucatan reveals that this continental margin may be in an early stage of evolution and thus is of considerable interest to scholars.

6633. Weeks, Morris, Jr. Hello, West Indies. N.Y., Grosset & Dunlap, 1971. 209 p., bibl., map, plates.

Perpetuating some of the worst cliches on tropical climate and land tenure, volume serves as poor companion to a tour guidebook.

BARBADOS

6634. Leemann, Albert. Barbados (GH, 25:3, 1970, p. 130-135, plates)
Thumbnail sketch of Barbados, with emphasis on those factors in the British heritage which distinguish the island from others in the West Indies.

CUBA

6635. Müller, Fritz Paul. Beiträge zur Kenntnis der Blattlausfauna von Kuba; *Homoptera: Aphidina* (UR/WZ, 17:4/5, 1968, p. 439-448, bibl.)
Authors collected more than 240 samples of aphids in Cuba during 1956-66, some hitherto unreported there. Some aphids in great abundance are highly efficient virus vectors and therefore are of considerable economic importance.

6636. Mulville, Frank. In *Granma's* wake: Girl Stella's voyage to Cuba. London, Seafarer Books, 1970. 301 p., fold. maps, plates.
Extremely well-written tale of a British family's love for the sea and for Castro's Cuba. Provides insights into the depth of the Cuban revolution and its impact on rural communities.

6637. Wylie, Kathryn H. A survey of agriculture in Cuba. Washington, U.S. Dept. of Agriculture, Economic Research Division, Foreign Regional Analysis Division, 1969. 30 p., bibl., maps, tables (ERS—foreign, 268)
Author relates that problems in the overall economy together with inefficient and scarce farm labor have resulted in short-term decreases in Cuban agricultural output. Documents the re-emphasis on sugar in the agricultural economy of the country.

CURACAO

6638. Dupuis, Jacques. Les paradoxes de Curaçao: à travers les provinces de l'empire Shell (SGB/COM, 22:85, jan./mars 1969, p. 63-74, maps, plates)
Curaçao has prospered despite a fragile economic base, but increasing reliance on international commerce has made the island perhaps more vulnerable to economic reverses.

6639. Leemann, Albert. Curaçao (GH, 25:3, 1970, p. 136-140, plates, table)
Thumbnail sketch of Curaçao, with emphasis on the recent impact of tourism and oil refining.

DOMINICAN REPUBLIC

6640. Berges, Roberto L. Procesos de urbanización en la República Dominicana (AuLa [Santo Domingo] 1:1, abril/junio 1972, p. 122[133])
Accepting the premise that the city of Santo Domingo is in crisis, author illuminates the problems and calls for a comprehensive urban plan.

6641. Buck, Wilbur F. Agriculture and trade of the Dominican Republic. Washington, US Dept. of Agriculture, Economic Research Service, 1972. 41 p., maps, plates, tables (ERS-Foreign, 330)
Short-term outlook for Dominican agriculture is optimistic because market prospects are favorable, but some arable land remains underutilized.

6642. Dorner, Peter; C. W. Loomer; Raymond Penn; and Joseph Thome. Agrarian reform in the Dominican Republic: the views of four consultants. Madison, Wis., Univ. of Wisconsin, Land Tenure Center, 1967. 46 p. (mimeo) (LTC, 42)
Brief evaluation of the Dominican Republic's agrarian reform program in 1966, this series of papers reviews status of land for agrarian reform, legal aspects of the agrarian reform program, and procedures to determine and record land titles. Consultants conclude that although land picture is clouded by unreliable statistics and unclear laws, machinery exists for implementing basic reform.

6643. García Bonnelly, Juan Ulises. Sobrepoblación, subdesarrollo y sus consecuencias socio-económicas: ensayo de biogeografía dominicana. Santo Domingo, Editora Cultural Dominicana, 1971. 481 p., tables (Sociedad Dominicana de Geografía, 2. Biblioteca dominicana de geografía y viajes)
More useful for its data on population and migration than its analysis, volume's author advocates education and hard work to overcome the overpopulation problem in the Dominican Republic.

6644. Gardiner, C. Harvey. The Japanese and the Dominican Republic (IAMEA, 25:3, Winter 1971, p. 23-37, tables)
Reorientation of sugar trade, disillusionment among Japanese immigrants, growing prosperity in Japan, and ill-treatment by Dominican authorities have made the Dominican Republic less attractive as a migration site, but trade interest continues high. Although containing much valuable information, article is remarkably disjointed and stylistically marred.

GUADELOUPE

6645. Guide to Guadeloupe. Paris, Editions de la Pensée Moderne, 1971. 182 p., maps, plates.
As one small remnant of the once-vast French territories in the New World, Guadeloupe requires further geographical study. This tourist guide offers not only the usual information but also piques the scholar's curiosity.

HAITI

6646. Bitter, Maurice. Haïti. Paris, Editions du Seuil, 1970. 189 p., illus., plates.
This French-language historical and social survey includes brief mention of the Duvalier era, but concentrates on folklore and the occult.

6647. Lohier, Gérard. Bref aperçu sur les sols rouges d'Haïti (IFH/C, 108, 2./3. trimestres 1968, p. 37-43, bibl.)

Field investigation suggests that red soils of Haiti are developed from volcanic materials which lie atop calcareous substrata.

6648. Rémy, Raoul. Etude socio-économique sur Ça-Ira. Port-au-Prince, Presses Nationales d'Haïti, 1971. 214 p.

C'est le mémoire que l'auteur avait soumis en 1969 à la Faculté d'Ethnologie. Il concerne Ça-Ira, une localité située près de la ville de Léogane et il a été étudié du point de vue historique, social, économique avec, accompagnant le texte, des tableaux statistiques comme suite d'une enquête faite. Ce travail donne aux étudiants l'habitude de saisir la réalité haitienne à l'aide de chiffres. [M. A. Lubin]

JAMAICA

6649. Adams, C. D. Flowering plants of Jamaica. Mona, Jam., Univ. of the West Indies, 1972. 848 p., tables.

This compendium of information on 3,000 species of flowering plants occurring in Jamaica again underscores fact that this island is one of great variety and contrast. Contains painstakingly comprehensive descriptions of the flora, with general statement of habitat for most species.

6650. Eyre, L. Alan. Geographic aspects of population dynamics in Jamaica. Boca Raton, Fla., Florida Atlantic Univ. Press, 1972. 172 p., maps, plates, tables.

Population study based on solid field investigation of selected areas in Jamaica presents a broad picture of options available to growing populations on the island.

6651. Floyd, Barry. Planning for rural development in Jamaica: spatial systems analysis (UWI/CQ, 18:1, March 1972, p. 5-13, illus.)

Spatial systems analysis, or the synthesis of agricultural strategies adopted by both planners and scientists in many fields, is urgently required to analyze man/rural land relationships in the Caribbean.

6652. Worthington, E. B. Ecology and conservation: Jamaica (UNESCO/NR, 7:1, March 1971, p. 2-8)

Review and justification of ecological study of the ancillary impacts of selected development schemes in Jamaica. The country is at a stage when prevention of pollution is still possible, but there is already some cause for concern with regard to water resources.

PUERTO RICO

6653. Boehm, David Alfred. Puerto Rico in pictures. Prepared by Robert V. Masters. N.Y., Sterling Publishing Co., 1969. 64 p., map, plates (Visual geography series)

Encyclopedic accumulation of lists and photographs of little value to travelers or scholars.

6654. González, Ricardo Raúl ed. Puerto Rico de hoy: 1956-1970. Bayamón, P.R., Gual, 1971? 134 p., illus., plates, tables.

6655. Lewis, Lawrence A. The spatial properties of population mobility within Puerto Rico (USM/JTG, 29, Dec. 1969, p. 33-38, bibl., maps, table)

In Puerto Rico, population mobility is inversely related to distance from urban areas, with the direction and magnitude of movements affected by the relative sizes of urban areas. While conclusion is not particularly striking, the argument is well supported by principal components and trend surface analysis.

6656. Picó, Rafael; Zayda Buitrago de Santiago; and Héctor H. Berrios. Nueva geografía de Puerto Rico: física, económica y social. San Juan, Editorial Universitaria, 1969. 460 p., bibl., maps, plates, tables.

Basically an update of the principal author's two earlier volumes, book contains an abundance of appropriate detail, good maps, and an extensive bibliography. Probably the best general geographical compendium on Puerto Rico now available.

ST. LUCIA

6657. Leitch, Adelaide. St. Lucia: island in transition (RCGS/CGJ, 85:6, Dec. 1972, p. 210-215, plates)

Brief sketch of "Saint Loosha" with no apparent emphasis.

TRINIDAD & TOBAGO

6658. Clarke, Colin G. Residential segregation and intermarriage in San Fernando, Trinidad (AGS/GR, 61:2, April 1971, p. 198-218)

Racial and religious divisions of second largest town in Trinidad mirror those of the island as a whole. There appears to be considerable racial and religious integration at the community level, but little at the household level.

CENTRAL AMERICA

GENERAL

6659. Dickinson, Joshua C., III. Alternatives to monoculture in the humid tropics of Latin America (AAG/PG, 24:3, Aug. 1972, p. 217-222, illus., table)

High diversity agricultural system appears desirable in the tropics, where high population density and low levels of industrialization are common, and where biological competition is the major limiting factor in agricultural production.

6660. Harroy, Jean-Paul. Les parcs nationaux en Amérique Centrale (SMHN/R, 30, dic. 1969, p. 147-153)

Brief justification for establishment of several parksites in Mexico, Guatemala, Nicaragua, and Costa Rica.

6661. Helbig, Karl. Von Belice bis Panamá (HGG/M, 111:2/3, 1969, p. 193-220, maps, plates)

Supported by several extended journeys leading from Mexico to far beyond the Panama canal, author draws a regional geographic picture of Central America. Shows contrast between uniform cultural development and political separation resulting from Spanish administration, local rule and foreign influence. Reasons for century-lasting elimination of land connection as traffic connection between North and South America are demonstrated. Discusses recent development and connection by Pan America highway and lack of sufficient cross connections. Points out cooperation of national institutions in this development. [H. J. Hoyer]

6662. Heyerdahl, Thor. Ra II erreicht das Ziel: mit einem Papyrusboot von Afrika nach Amerika (WM, 2, Feb. 1971, p. 44-53, plates)

Heyerdahl's voyage provides some evidence that communication was possible between the ancient civilizations on either side of the Atlantic.

6663. Johannessen, Carl.; Michael R. Wilson and **William A. Davenport.** The domestication of maize: process or event? (AGS/GR, 60:3, July 1970, p. 393-413)

Authors view domestication of maize as a process focusing on the human actions that caused plant modifications. Further research on domestication processes must begin soon, before traditional agricultural practices disappear.

6664. Karen, Ruth. The land and peoples of Central America. 2. ed. rev. Philadelphia, Pa., J. B. Lippincott, 1972. 159 p., maps, plates (Portraits of the nations series)

Marred by one poor frontispiece map and some outdated information, book nevertheless offers an adequate country-by-country survey of contemporary economic, social, and political conditions in Central America.

6665. Kearns, Kevin C. A transisthmian sealevel canal for Central America: proposals and prospects (NCGE/J, 70:4, April 1971, p. 235-246, illus., maps, plates, table)

With about ten years remaining before work should begin on a new transisthmian canal, studies indicate that the most suitable site at present is directly west of the original canal. Article ably summarizes many points of contention on building a new canal, including the effects of nuclear excavation, tidal currents, and threats to marine ecology, all of which pose especially difficult questions.

6666. Maldonado-Koerdell, Manuel. Informe sobre la situación de los trabajos geofísicos en los países centro-americanos. México, Instituto Panamericano de Geografía e Historia, 1966. 71 p., (mimeo) bibl.

Discussion of the general aspects of geophysical work now being conducted in Central America, with recommendations for specific projects including expansion of the gravimetric network, measuring the terrestrial magnetism, establishing a regional program of seismic research, and creating a vulcanologic observatory in the Nicaraguan Depression. Report takes on special significance in the wake of the Managua earthquake of Dec., 1972.

6667. Markun, Patricia Maloney. The first book of Central America and Panama. N.Y., Franklin Watts, 1963. 90 p., map, plates.

Primarily descriptive historical approach to understanding the Central American republics. Contains too many hasty generalizations and inaccuracies to impress the expert.

May, Jacques Meyer and **Donna L. McLellan.** The ecology of malnutrition in Mexico and Central America: Mexico, Guatemala, British Honduras, Honduras, El Salvador, Nicaragua, Costa Rica and Panama. See item 1697.

6668. Minkel, Clarence W. Programs of agricultural colonization and settlement in Central America (PAIGH/G, 66, junho 1967, p. 19-53, bibl., maps)

Outlines historical development of land reform and tasks of contemporary land reform agencies in the Central American republics as well as British Honduras and Panama. The old land problems being attacked through colonization and settlement may yield to solution if decisive action is taken now.

6669. Payne, Horace. The role of miniresearch stations in increasing farm productivity in the Caribbean (UWI/CQ, 18:1, March 1972, p. 24-28)

Author contends that small research stations operated on the land of the traditional farmer stimulate increases in yield and farm income.

6670. Simposio Internacional sobre Lagunas Costeras, UNAM-UNESCO, *México, 1967.* Memoria: origen, dinámica y productividad [Memoir: origin, dynamics and productivity]. Edited by Agustín Ayala-Castañares and Fred B. Phleger. México, UNAM, Instituto de Biología, 1969. 686 p., fold. map, illus., maps, plates, tables.

Contains papers presented at international scientific conference on coastal lagoons (held Nov. 20-28, 1967). Papers are believed fair representation of the state of knowledge on coastal lagoons, so volume contains a wealth of information on such general topics as physical hydrology, chemistry, biology, economic value, and history of these features. Volume deserves most serious attention from beginning and advanced scholars in this area. Bilingual English-Spanish edition.

6671. Urban, Francis S. Agricultural prospects in Central America. Washington, US Dept. of Agriculture, Economic Research Service, 1969. 7 p., tables (ERS-foreign, 270)

Booklet one of a series designed to evaluate the long-term potential supply and demand for Central American agricultural products. The total demand is expected to increase substantially because of increases in population growth.

6672. Villanueva, Benjamín. The case of the United Fruit Company in Central America. Madison, Wis., Univ. of Wisconsin, Land Tenure Center, 1971. 10 p. (Latin American research briefs, 13)

Study designed to determine development potential of the United Fruit Company as a privately-owned enterprise on the regional economy of Central America versus its potential as a regionally-owned one. If the viability of the company could be retained, the Central American republics may benefit from regional ownership.

Wesche, Marjorie Bingham. Place names as a reflection of cultural chances: an example from the Lesser Antilles. See item 1217.

BELIZE

6673. Carpenter, Allan and Tom Balow. British Honduras. Chicago, Ill., Childrens Press, 1971. 95 p., maps, plates (Enchantment of Central America)

Illustrates panorama of British Honduras in a manner not only comprehensible to children but also interesting and informative for adults.

6674. Furley, Peter. A capital waits for its country (GM, 43:10, July 1971, p. 713-720)

Despite the few social amenities, unfamiliar housetypes, and rural atmosphere, Belmopan's population is growing. Author believes Belmopan must be a success, because this project will reveal how well the government can organize itself for more complex tasks related to the country's independence.

6675. Jones, David. Belize hovers on the brink of independence (GM, 43:10, July 1971, p. 708-712)

General review of the basic economic resources of Belize (British Honduras) as it faces the complex problems of independence.

6676. Kellman, M. C. and C. D. Adams. Milpa weeds of the Cayo district, Belize, British Honduras (CAG/CG, 14:4, Winter 1970, p. 323-343, illus., map, tables)

Statistical study revealing that Belizian milpa weed flora is extremely rich and taxonomically diverse. An appreciable number of weed species encountered showed tendencies to associate together.

6677. Minkel, Clarence W. and Ralph H. Alderman. A bibliography of British Honduras: 1900-1970. East Lansing, Mich., Michigan State Univ., 1970. 93 p. (Latin American Studies Center research report, 7)

This invaluable guide is perhaps the most comprehensive bibliography on British Honduras, with over 1,000 references.

COSTA RICA

6678. Alfaro, Gregorio. Problemas que afectan el desarrollo agropecuario en cuatro cantones de la península de Nicoya. San José, Ministerio de Agricultura y Ganadería, Oficina de Planeamiento y Coordinanción, 1966. 64 p., maps, plates, tables.

Survey of distribution, use and tenancy of land and principal occupation of family-head as well as income, costs, capital, labor force, and efficiency of resource use in the agricultural economy of the Nicoya peninsula. Presents highly valuable local planning information. Should be repeated in other parts of Costa Rica.

6679. Carpenter, Allan. Costa Rica. Chicago, Ill., Childrens Press, 1971. 96 p., maps, plates (Enchantment of Central America)

Unusually attractive and accurate survey is recommended as a good introduction to Costa Rica for young people.

6680. Chaves Camacho, Jorge. Evolución demográfica de la población de Costa Rica (UCR/R, 27, dic. 1969, p. 37-42, bibl.)

Traces, census by census, changes in Costa Rican population which have made country's growth rate nearly the highest in the world.

6681. Dufour, Jules. La crue du Reventazón, Costa Rica, en avril 1970 (ULIG/C, 15:35, sept. 1971, p. 370-379, maps, plates, tables)

An unusual *temporal* storm in ordinarily dry April created a flood which was destructive of the natural as well as the cultural features of the upper Reventazon basin. Author pleads for a flood control scheme to minimize losses due to this hazard.

6682. Harris, Stuart A. Quaternary volcanicity in the Talamanca range of Costa Rica (CAG/CG, 15:2, Summer 1971, p. 141-145, illus.)

Separation of the two active volcanic belts of Costa Rica (the Central American Volcanic axis and the Panamanian volcanic axis) appears to be post-glacial in age.

6683. Lizano F., Eduardo. La organización institucional de la agricultura nacional. Ciudad Universitaria Rodrigo Facio, C.R., Univ. Nacional de Costa Rica, 1969. 80 p. (Serie Economía y estadística, 28)

Pt. 1 of this source stresses need to augment production factors and to reduce uncertainty of social equilibrium in Costa Rica. Pt. 2 discusses decision-making and strategy to achieve desired ends. [R. C. Eidt]

6684. Trejos Quirós, Juan. Geografía ilustrada de Costa Rica: con un vocabulario geográfico. 22. ed., rev. San José, Trejo Hermanos Editores, 1968. 146 p., map, plates.

Traditional and encyclopedic, volume still contains much valuable information on Costa Rica.

6685. Weyl, Richard. Magnetitsande der Küste Nicoyas: Costa Rica, Mittelamerika (Neues Jahrbuch für Geologie und Paläontologie, Monatschefte [Stuttgart, FRG] 8, 1969, p. 499-511, bibl., illus., maps, tables)

The coast of the Nicoya Peninsula of Costa Rica is covered by beach sands apparently derived not from local basalts but from the Quaternary Bagaces formation and the volcanics of the Guanacaste highlands.

6686. ———. Die Morphologisch-Tektonische Gliederung Costa Ricas, Mittelamerika: Bericht über neue Karten und ihre Interpretation (UBGI/E, 25:3, Sept. 1971, p. 223-230, illus., plates, maps)

New relief and geological maps allow production of a new map of Costa Rica's morpho-tectonic regions. Author examines each new region in detail.

EL SALVADOR

6687. Reyes Ramírez, José Ricardo. Evaluación de los censos de población de El Salvador de 1950 y 1961 a nivel de los Departamentos según la declaración de la edad (UES/ES, 17:37/38, enero/dic. 1968, p. 59-72, tables)

An estimate of the ability of the census to indicate a "national consciousness" by determining the relationship between reliable census figures and selected socio-economic factors in Salvadorean *departamentos*.

6688. *La Universidad.* Universidad de El Salvador. Vol. 95, No. 1, enero/feb. 1970- . San Salvador.

Presents papers and resolutions of first national conference on agrarian reform in El Salvador. A landmark volume in that it contains statements from a wide variety of sources and offers concrete suggestions for implementing agrarian reform through legislation.

6689. Zéndegui, Guillermo de *comp.* Image of El Salvador (OAS/AM, 25:2, Feb. 1973, p. S-1-S-24, plates)

First-time tourists will find this article valuable for its information on cultural tradition and contemporary landscape even though its tone and substance is obviously promotional.

GUATEMALA

6690. Bechtol, Bruce E. A matter of perception: locational considerations of industrialists in Guatemala (CCGT/CG, 11, 1970, p. 15-20, map, table)

Market appears to be major factor affecting development of industry in Guatemala. Although it is true, as author relates, that important locational considerations are not necessarily found in economic models, a model as well as maps containing the information gained in interviews may have elucidated some points.

6691. Camisa, Zulma C. Guatemala: proyecciones de la población total: 1965-2000. San José, Centro Latinoamericano de Demografía (CELADE), 1970. 36 p., tables (CELADE Serie AS, 3)

Filled with 27 tables of valuable data on population estimates as well as population growth, age, and sex, this volume provides information enough for several significant studies.

6692. Carpenter, Allan. Guatemala. Chicago, Ill., Childrens Press, 1971. 93 p., maps, plates (Enchantment of Central America)

Although designed for children, this well-illustrated, comprehensive volume may be one of the best nontechnical introductions to Guatemala.

6693. Hoy, Don R. A review of development planning in Guatemala (UM/JIAS, 12:2, April 1970, p. 217-228)

Author relates that the limited success of planning in Guatemala is the result of intragovernmental politics, reticence to change, government instability, and lack of trained personnel.

6694. Organization of American States. Comité Interamericano del Desarrollo Agrícola. Tenencia de la tierra y desarrollo socioeconómico del sector agrícola en Guatemala. Guatemala, Editorial Universitaria, 1971. 395 p., bibl., tables (Col. Realidad nuestra, 2)

Essentially same as 1965 ed. published by the Pan American Union, work is exhaustive with scholarly treatment of general agricultural situation, principal land tenure types, these tenure types in relation to economic and social development, and nature of agricultural change in Guatemala. Contains a great deal of late 1950's and early 1960's data in table form.

6695. Ruth, James M., Jr. The administration of water resources in Guatemala (PU/PIA, 5:1, Spring 1967, p. 249-278)

Non-technical and sympathetic analysis of the efficiency of the Guatemalan government's water resource activities. Valuable for illuminating points of potentially fruitful cooperation among government agencies.

6696. Soza, José María. Monografía del Departamento del Petén. 2. ed., rev. t. 1-2. Guatemala, Editoral José Pineda Ibarra, 1970. 2 v. (666 p., continuous pagings) fold. maps, illus., maps, plates, tables (Col. Monografías, 9)

Massive but encyclopedic treatment of Peten, containing wide variety of information on this *departamento* ranging from rainfall to notable personalities to ancient Maya ceremonial sites, with many appropriate maps.

6697. Thomas, Robert N. The migration system of Guatemala City: spatial inputs (AAG/PG, 24:2, May 1972, p. 105–112, illus., map, tables)

Stepwise migration, undertaken mostly by *ladinos* in larger towns close to the capital, is one of the most important internal migration processes occurring in Guatemala. Article is a model of lucidity.

―――. Survey research design: a case of rural-urban mobility. See item 6606

HONDURAS

6698. Carpenter, Allan and **Tom Balow.** Honduras. Chicago, Ill., Childrens Press, 1971. 95 p., maps, plates (Enchantment of Central America)

Comprehensive and well-illustrated volume deserves praise because of its skillful combination of past and current social, political, and economic trends, generalization and detail, and children's stories and scholarly narrative.

6699. Fonck, Carlos O'Brien. Modernity and public policies in the context of the peasant sector: Honduras as a case study. Ithaca, N.Y., Cornell Univ., Latin American Studies Program, 1972. 148 p., bibl., tables (Dissertation series, 32)

Careful and incisive study based on general hypothesis that the peasant sector, almost exclusively responsible for foodgrain production in Honduras, is practically excluded from the process of social problem identification. Concludes that agricultural policies aim at expanding farm output to benefit large landowners and at the peasant's expense.

6701. **Honduras. Instituto Nacional Agrario** [INA]. 3 [i.e., Tres] años de labor: 1968, 1969, 1970. Tegucigalpa, 1971. 1 v. (Unpaged) illus., maps, plates, tables.

More than a record of accomplishments, volume contains a full program for land redistribution including financial support, land acquisition, technical assistance, development of cooperatives, and organization of the Instituto Nacional Agrario. Invaluable to students of agricultural change in Honduras.

Marasciulo, Edward. Quasi-economic political units in Latin America. See item 6563.

6702. **Mejía, Medardo.** Historia de Honduras. v. 2, El descubrimiento, la mundialización de Honduras. Tegucigalpa, Editorial Andrade, 1970. 129 p., bibl., maps.

Broad, primarily descriptive work concentrating on Columbus' voyages with some introduction to earliest explorers of Central America.

NICARAGUA

6703. Ferrocarriles, vapores: lo que va de ayer a hoy en Nicaragua (RCPC, 26:128, mayo 1968, p. 59-73, plates)

Detailed descriptive account of growth, extent, and equipment of Nicaraguan railways and steamships.

6704. **Patten, George F.** Dairying in Nicaragua (AAG/A, 61:2, June 1971, p. 303-315, plates, tables)

Author investigates factors which have accelerated or retarded development of dairying in Nicaragua, emphasizing temporal variations in supply, demand, production efficiency, and degree of farm specialization.

PANAMA

6705. **Chilman, Walter J.** Isthmian canal demand forecast: an economic analysis of potential tonnage traffic. Washington, Dept. of Transportation, 1970? 79 l., tables.

Presents results of an economic analysis that develops an estimate of tonnage demand for commercial traffic through an isthmian canal. Presents linear correlation as a tool allowing the analyst to vary the independent variable (the regional product) to derive a new dependent variable (tonnage generated). Because study is based on past economic growth and commerce, marked changes in trade relationships and growth will distort the forecast.

6706. **Edwards, Ernest Preston** and **Horace Loftin.** Finding birds in Panama. 2. ed., rev. and enlarged. Sweet Briar, Va., Ernest P. Edwards, 1971. 97 p., bibl., maps.

Arranged in two parts: treatment of ornithological study areas located along various highways and a full checklist but no illustrations of the birds of Panama.

6707. **Glynn, Peter W.; Robert H. Stewart;** and **John E. McCosker.** Pacific coral reefs of Panama: structure, distribution and predators (GV/GR, 61:2, 1972, p. 483-519, maps, plates, tables)

In spite of earlier observations to the contrary, large and growing coral reefs are found in the Pacific coastal waters of Panama, and coralivores have significant effects on coral reef growth in this location.

6708. **Sandner, Gerhard.** Panamá: Strukturmerkmale und Leitlinien der sozialräumlichen Desintegration einer lateinamerikanischen Grosstadt (GEB/E, 101:4, 1970, p. 265-283, illus., tables)

There has been a decrease in the number of identifiable residential areas in Panama City, but their structural complexity is increasing. Slum areas are especially difficult to categorize, for there are growing differences in types or levels of economic activity and integration into urban life among the inhabitants.

6709. **Tesh, Robert B.; Byron N. Chaniotis; Mark D. Aronson;** and **Karl M. Johnson.** Natural host preferences of Panamanian phlebotomine sandflies as determined by precipitin test (ASTMH/J, 20:1, Jan. 1971, p. 150-156, bibl., plate, tables)

Sandflies have been implicated as vectors of several diseases. Analysis presents information of the host range of several Panamanian sandflies, indicating that some are potentially good vectors of human disease.

MEXICO

6710. **Baillon, Claude** and others. Las zonas suburbanas de la ciudad de México. México, UNAM, Instituto de Geografía, 1968. 55 p., bibl., maps, plates, tables.

Purely geographic study, complementing studies in other disciplines, which focuses on demography, housing, industry, and agriculture in Mexico City suburbs. Many good maps.

6711. Baja California norte: beginning the peninsular journey. Los Angeles, Calif., Automobile Club of Southern California, 1972. 80 p., maps, plates, tables.

Short guide, with highway maps and mileage meter, provides information on major cities and their tourist accommodations as well as lesser-known attractions.

6712. **Baker, Charles Laurence.** Geologic reconnaissance in the eastern cordillera of Mexico. Boulder, Col., Geological Society of America, 1971. 82 p., bibl., fold. maps, maps, plates, tables (Special paper, 131)

Reprint of 1920's geological investigation in Mexico,

valuable for detailed information on a region whose geology is still incompletely known.

6713. Ballance, R. H. Mexican agricultural policies and subsistence farming (AJES, 31:3, July 1972, p. 295-306, tables)

There is a tendency to overlook traditional agriculture while supporting new commercial agriculture in Mexico. This policy has, to some extent, precluded the possibility of modernizing traditional farms.

6714. Ballesteros, Juan; Matthew Edel; and **Michael Nelson.** La colonización en la Cuenca del Papaloapan: una evaluación socioeconómica. Presentación [por] Sergio Reyes Osorio. México, Centro de Investigaciones Agrarias, Comité Interamericano de Desarrollo Agrícola, 1970. 148 p., bibl., maps, tables.

Colonization as a solution to population pressure often ignores potential of those areas colonized. Study incorporates a number of inquiries to conclude that both natural resources and entrepreneurial talent are necessary to growth of such successful projects as the Papaloapan.

6715. Bloomgarden, Richard. The easy guide to Oaxaca and environs. 2. ed. México, Ammex Asociados, 1971. 66 p., illus., maps, plates.

Short, folksy guide with complete tourist information on Oaxaca and nearby points of interest.

Brown, Lawrence. Diffusion of innovation in Latin America: a geographer's perspective. See item 6514.

6716. Carter, George F. Impressions of Mexico (AAC/AJ, 9:4, 1971, p. 2-4)

An informal recording of field impressions of crop, housing, and poultry diffusion in Mexico.

6717. Centro de Investigaciones Agrarias, *México.* Estructura agraria y desarrollo agrícola en México. México, Aquiles Serdán, 1971? 3 v. (673, 512, Various pagings) tables.

Written on proposition that agrarian reform has been central to development of modern Mexico and dedicated to defining characteristics of the agricultural sector and its interrelationships with other aspects of Mexican economic, social, and political life, these volumes contain perhaps the most comprehensive qualitative and quantitative treatment ever afforded modern Mexican agriculture.

6718. Civeira Taboada, Miguel. Benito Juárez en la Sociedad Mexicana de Geografía y Estadística. México, B. Costa-Amic Editor, 1968. 100 p., facsims.

Documents from the Society's archives reveal Juárez' role in and correspondence with the organization during its formative years.

6719. El Colegio de México. Centro de Estudios Económicos y Demográficos. Dinámica de la población de México. México, 1970. 291 p., tables (Publicaciones del Centro de Estudios Económicos y Demográficos, 3)

Volume ably meets objective of investigating recent Mexican population growth and characteristics of variables which influence it. Includes studies of mortality, fecundity, internal migration, urbanization, the economically active population, and future tendencies of the population. Especially valuable is the appendix, which lists nature and type of data gathered in Mexican population censuses during 1895-1970.

6720. Corona Rentería, Alfonso. Economía y planeación urbanas (UNAM/IE, 30:118, abril/junio 1970, p. 317-339)

Latin American cities, because of their rapid and complex growth, are not always best explained by the tools of traditional economics. Author outlines the need for a new interdisciplinary "urban economics" in Mexico.

6721. Crow, John Armstrong. Mexico today. Rev. ed. N.Y., Harper & Row, 1972. 369 p., plates.

Observations of a famous author whose tales of Mexican history are as vivid as his impressions of the contemporary land which is "so far from God, so close to the United States."

6722. Cserna, Zoltan de. Precambrian sedimentation, tectonics, and magmatism in Mexico (GV/GR, 60:4, dez. 1971, p. 1488-1513, bibl., maps)

Concise review of the Mexican Pre-cambrian, with maps and descriptions of the areas in which outcrops were studied as well as an analysis of the geotectonics of the area.

6723. David, L. Irby. A field guide to the birds of Mexico and Central America. Color plates by F. P. Bennett, Jr. Austin, Tex., Univ. of Texas Press, 1972. 282 p., plates, table (John Fielding and Lois Lasater Maher series, 1)

Beautifully illustrated guide identifies thousands of birds by name, range, and voice. Author relates that many vocalizations are presented here for the first time.

6724. Dovring, Folke. Land reform and productivity in Mexico (UW/LE, 46:3, Aug. 1970, p. 264-274)

New data as well as re-evaluation of older works indicates that Mexican *ejido* land reform contributes to general agricultural development. The land reform effort appears to have channeled more of Mexico's resources into labor intensive growth in agriculture at the right time in the nation's economic development.

6725. Dozier, Craig L. Agricultural development in Mexico's Tabasco lowlands: planning and potentials (JDA, 5:1, Oct. 1970, p. 61-72, map)

Mexico's efforts to develop its wet tropical lowlands are less recognized than its accomplishments in arid areas but the Tabasco lowlands, plagued by floods, have been reclaimed by integrated development which includes modification of the traditional *ejido* and new commercial orientation.

6726. Edwards, Ernest Preston. A field guide to the birds of Mexico: including all birds occurring from the northern border of Mexico to the southern border of Nicaragua. Illustrated by Murrell Butler, Ernest P. Edwards, John O'Neill and Douglas Pratt. Spanish descriptions by Miguel Alvarez del Toro and Ernest P. Edwards. Sweet Briar, Va., The Author, 1972. 300 p., maps, plates.

Contains descriptive sketches and color plates of over 1,000 Mexican birds, arranged by family, with information on color, size, voice, habitat, range, and other features.

6727. Enjalbert, Henri. Le peuplement de Mexique (SGB/COM, 24:93, jan./mars 1971, p. 5-15)

An unprecedented population explosion has occurred in Mexico between 1940-70, but author believes that Mexican standard of living has improved. Important sites of unusual growth are the large cities of the central plateau and the desert cities of the northern frontier.

6728. Falcón de Gyves, Zaida. Análisis de los mapas de distribución de la población del estado de Tabasco. México, UNAM, Instituto de Geografía, 1965. 54 p., bibl., fold. maps, tables.

Study devoted to analysis of distribution and evolution of population clusters in Tabasco from 1900-60. Includes much background information on physical and economic patterns, and is full of maps, tables, and graphs.

6729. ———. Chilpancingo, ciudad en crecimiento. México, UNAM, Instituto de Geografía, 1969. 58 p., bibl., fold. map, illus., plates, tables (Serie Cuadernos)

Based on principle that small-scale studies are necessary to rank and solve problems of small, rapidly-growing cities in developing areas, survey includes physical and cultural characteristics of Chilpancingo and its surroundings. Text and its many fine maps make a significant contribution to local geography of Mexico, indicating that this study bears repeating elsewhere.

6730. Falegeau, Xavier. Mexique: cité du soleil (Revue de Défense Nationale [Paris] 27, avril 1971, p. 566-577, map, table)

Thumbnail sketch of Mexican cultural history designed to illuminate capital city's image as a utopia.

6731. Flores, Edmundo. Rural development in Mexico (*in* Weitz, Raanan *ed.* Rural development in a changing world. Cambridge, Mass., The MIT Press, 1971, p. 515-531, bibl., tables)

Mexico is the only Latin American country virtually self-sufficient in food. Distinguished agricultural economist asserts that main components of Mexican rural development are land reform, expansion of agricultural acreage, more intensive crop production and cattle breeding, and increases in productivity.

6732. Gann, Thomas William Francis. In an unknown land. Freeport, N.Y., Book for Libraries Press, 1971. 263 p., facsims., illus., map, plates.

More than an explorer's journal, relates the success of an archaeological expedition which discovered several new, important Mayan sites, developed the method of dating used in the Yucatan, and deciphered a number of new dates in the Mayan occupance of the peninsula. Reprint of 1924 ed.

6733. Girault, Christian A. Les villes de l'état de Morelos, Mexique (ULIG/C, 15:35, sept. 1971, p. 213-232, maps, plates, tables)

Cuernavaca and Cuautla, tributary to Mexico City, are strongly influenced in their city form by tourism. Thesis of study is that physical attractions contribute to an unbalanced growth which undermines simplistic assumptions about urban hierarchies in Mexico.

6734. González Navarro, Moisés. La tenencia de la tierra en México (UTIEH/C, 12, 1969, p. 117-134)

Descriptive survey of trends in landholding and agricultural labor force from middle 1800's to the present, with emphasis on data from the first four agricultural censuses (1930-60).

6735. Gutiérrez de MacGregor, Maria Teresa. Geodemografía del estado de Jalisco. México, UNAM, Instituto de Geografía, 1968. 100 p., bibl., maps, tables.

Study designed to determine why Jalisco's people are distributed in their present pattern. Useful for planners, this study may serve as a model for similar studies elsewhere. Large section of graphs and maps.

6736. Irigoyen Rosado, Renan. Bajo el signo de Chaac (UY/R, 10:57/58, mayo/agosto 1968, p. 30-42)

Author believes that water has been the principal factor in the distribution as well as the quality of cultural processes in the Mayan, Spanish, and Mexican settlements on the Yucatán peninsula. Also available as monograph: Renán Irigoyen. Bajo el signo de Chaac: monografía del agua potable en Yucatan. Mérida, Mex., Editorial Zamna, 1970. 135 p., bibl., maps, plates, tables.

6737. Klaus, Dieter. Zusammenhänge Zwischen Wetterlagen-Häufigkeit un niederschlagsverteilung im Zentramexikanischen Hochland (UBGI/E, 25:2, Juni 1971, p. 81-90, illus., maps, tables)

Scholarly study indicates that occurrence of rainfall is associated with high altitude stream line movements over the Puebla basin of Mexico.

6738. Leander, Birgitta. Mestizaje ecológico en México: algunas frutas, legumbres y semillas (SA/J, 59, 1970, p. 65-89, bibl.)

Brief survey of agricultural plants both indigenous and imported by Spanish into Mexico, with supporting bibliographical citations of the historical record.

6739. Lemus García, Raúl. Panorámica actual de la reforma agraria en México. México, Editorial Limsa, 1968. 81 p., tables.

Reviews progress of agrarian reform in Mexico from colonial times through the Díaz Ordaz administration; especially valuable for its specific references to legislation.

López de la Parra, Manuel. La promoción

turística en el estado de México. See item 1935.

6740. MacDougall, T. The Chima wilderness de México. 2. ed., rev. México, M. Aguilar Editor, 1971. 237 p., bibl., illus., maps, plates, tables.

Scholarly yet attractive to popular readers, this volume is divided into three parts: vulcanology, vulcanism in Mexico, and a description of major volcanoes of Mexico. Contains good maps and excellent photographs.

6740. ———. The Chima wilderness (EJ, 49:2, June 1971, p. 86-103, bibl., maps, plates)

Record of a botanical expedition to a small, isolated section of Oaxaca in southern Mexico. Replete with information on the local flora and fauna, particularly the former.

6741. Maderey Rascón, Laura Elena. Estudio preliminar sobre las aguas subterráneas en México. México, UNAM, Instituto de Geografía, 1967. 75 p., bibl., illus., maps, plates, tables.

Locates sources of subterranean water in Mexico and indicates some potential uses. Supplemented by good photos and maps.

6742. Marett, Robert. Mexico. London, Thames and Hudson, 1971. 208 p., bibl., maps, plates.

Primarily a brief and informal historical background to modern Mexico and augmented by a "who's who" and selected bibliography, this book should serve as a good companion for Mexico-bound travelers.

6743. Maturana Medina, Sergio and **José Sánchez Cortés.** Las comunidades de la Meseta Tarasca: un estudio socioeconómico. México, Centro de Investigaciones Agrarias, Comité Interamericano de Desarrollo Agrícola, 1970. 124 p., map, tables.

Rare study of indigenous communal agriculture designed to investigate development of one such enclave in highland southern Mexico. Data derived from intensive field investigation reveal much rural underemployment, and authors recommend it be diverted to development projects.

6744. Menéndez, Arturo. Una interpretación socioeconómica de Yucatán (UY/R, 11:63/64, mayo/agosto 1969, p. 45-55, table)

Summarizes physical environment, population growth, cultural change, communications, and public health of Yucatan as an introduction to a discussion of the present economic crisis resulting from reverses in the henequen industry.

6745. Mesas Redondas sobre Problemas de Ecología Humana de la Cuenca del Valle de México, *México, 1970.* Problemas de ecología humana en la cuenca del valle de México. México, Instituto Mexicano de Recursos Naturales Renovables, 1971. 206 p.

Results of discussion by a number of Mexican specialists on environmental pollution in the Mexico City area, where this problem has reached alarming proportions. Offers suggestions for alleviating the worst of the problems.

6746. Mihelic', Dusan. Note sui punti franchi nel Messico (SGI/B [Serie 9] 12:1/3, gen./marzo 1971, p. 137-149)

Mexico's response to the opening of the Panama Canal was the establishment of preferential trade ports, Coatzacoalcos on the Gulf of Mexico and Salina Cruz on the Pacific, but the effort proved largely unsuccessful.

6747. Moor, Jay *ed.* Guanajuato: an analysis of urban form. Seattle, Wash., Univ. of Washington, College of Architecture and Urban Planning, Dept. of Urban Planning, 1968. 72 p., illus., maps (Urban planning development series, 5)

Publication results from a field trip by Washington urban design students for five days in Dec. 1966. An investigation of the urban form of Guanajuato for purpose of developing insights that will help in the formulation of design principles. Lack of time and language facility make this a rather superficial study, but one with many well-recorded visual impressions.

6748. Mori, Alberto. Colonie agricole tradizionali italiane nel Messico (IGM/U, 49:4, luglio/agosto 1969, p. 569-586, illus., maps)

Outlines extent of Italian colonization in Mexico, with special reference to those colonies in the temperate highlands of central Mexico.

6749. Navarrete, Jorge Eduardo *ed.* México 1970: hechos, cifras, tendencias. México, Banco Nacional de Comercio Exterior, 1970. 246 p., bibl., plates, tables.

Fifth ed. of this compendium, a comprehensive introduction to the contemporary social and economic life of Mexico. Extremely valuable as an introduction to basic development measures in industry, population, and agriculture.

6750. Norman, James. Terry's guide to Mexico. A completely revised edition of T. Philip Terry's standard guidebook to Mexico. Garden City, N.Y. Doubleday, 1972. 833 p., illus., maps.

Informative but sometimes patronizing guidebook. Separate guides to each major section of Mexico, with special attention given to well-travelled transportation routes.

Puente Leyva, Jesús. Recursos y crecimiento del sector agropecuaria en México: 1930-1967. See *HLAS 34:1865.*

6751. Rojas, Manuel. Pasé por México un día. Santiago, Editora Zig-Zag, 1965. 285 p., illus., map (Col. Historia y documentos)

Novelist's travel diary contains not only personal observations from a 10-month's trip to Mexico but also a sympathetic vision of Mexicans.

6752. Ross, Patricia Fent. Mexico. Grand Rapids, Mich., Fideler, 1971. 192 p., plates.

Straightforward and instructive, with much opportunity for creative expression, this text is recommended for elementary social studies classroom use.

6753. Sawatzky, Harry Leonard. They sought a country: Mennonite colonization in Mexico with an appendix on Mennonite colonization in British Honduras. Foreword [by] Carl Sauer. Berkeley, Univ. of California Press, 1971. 387 p., bibl., maps, tables.

Scholarly and energetic study outlines survival and apparent success of Mennonite colonies while analyzing their diminishing capability to find remedies for their growing economic and social ills.

6754. Söderlund, Siv and **Börje Söderlund.** I Cortés spar genom Mexico. Stockholm, Natur Øch Kultur, 1967. 206 p., illus., maps, plates.

Popular travel account by two Swedish tourists who visited Mexico following in Cortés' footsteps. [R. V. Shaw]

6755. Soto Mora, Consuelo and **Luis Fuentes Aguilar.** El uso del suelo en la región Huejotzingo San Martín Texmelucan, Puebla. México, UNAM, Instituto de Geografía, 1969. 79 p., bibl., fold. maps, plates, tables.

Northern part of valley of Puebla is studied in order to offer practical recommendations on agricultural land use.

Venezian, Eduardo L. and **William K. Gamble.** The agricultural development of Mexico: its structure and growth since 1950. See *HLAS 34:1877.*

6757. Weckstein, R. S. Evaluating Mexican land reform (UC/EDCC, 18:3, April 1970, p. 391-409).

Presents new approach to measuring efficiency of landholding institutions using a two-sector model of the Mexican agricultural economy in which land is distinguished from other resources and is assigned in accordance with specific administrative rules. When comparing efficiency of private and public sugar cane farming enterprises, it is seen that *ejidos* are relatively inefficient primarily because of the lower value of their land in production.

6758. Yarza de la Torre, Esperanza. Volcanes de México. 2 ed., rev. México, M. Aguílar editor, 1971. 237 p., bibl., illus., maps, plates, tables.

Scholarly yet attractive to popular readers, this volume is divided into three parts: vulcanology, vulcanism in Mexico, and a description of major volcanoes of Mexico. Contains good maps and excellent photographs.

SOUTH AMERICA

(EXCEPT BRAZIL)

ROBERT C. EIDT

Professor of Geography
University of Wisconsin, Milwaukee

AN ANALYSIS OF THIS HANDBOOK SECTION REVEALS that the greatest number and diversity of entries pertain to the Argentine section as in most previous years. That this is true even for entries in the last *Handbook* in which Dr. César Caviedes López, a specialist in Chilean geography, concentrated efforts on his homeland, speaks for the great vitality of Argentine geography. Some items from Dr. Caviedes' contributions last year have been saved for the present *Handbook*. Chile is, therefore, runner up, although the balance of topics is not as even, there being a much greater emphasis on physical geography and a lack of some aspects of human geography compared with Argentina. Venezuela occupies third position for total entries, and Colombia, Bolivia, Peru, and Ecuador have the only other significant places in that order. Perhaps the unexpected decline in entries from Colombia and Peru and the increase from Bolivia reflect anomalous conditions rather than a trend.

Topically, research on geology-geomorphology, regional development, agriculture, general economic and settlement (rural and urban) themes predominated. Although the divisions used must necessarily be arbitrary, they nevertheless illustrate that great attention has been given to research of an economic nature, which in turn indicates that South American geography has a strong applied character. That this is likely to continue is to be expected from the developmental nature of conditions in the countries represented.

Numerous articles and books written by foreigners have been reviewed for this *Handbook*. German entries dominate European contributions and these deal frequently with settlement geography and economic development. French research seems, as usual, to focus on geology-geomorphology and on urban problems. Examples of outstanding foreign investigations are those of R. Wesche on migration to the Peruvian *montaña* (item 6957), C. V. Delavaud on urban population in northern Peru (item 6951), R. Vollmar on pioneer settlement in Santo Domingo de los Colorados, Ecua. (item 6938) and M. S. Taylor's regional study of the Falkland Islands (item 6834).

GENERAL

6759. Baker, R. E. and **I. McReath.** 1970 [i.e., Nineteen seventy] volcanic eruption at Deception Island (NWJS, 231:18, May 1971, p. 5-9, maps, plates, tables)

Volcanic activity at Deception Island (63°S) has created a new strip of land and is likely to occur again. Ejected material is analyzed for mineral content.

6760. Caffera, Rodolfo. *Triticum timopheevi* zhuk. interacciones genéticas con *Triticum aestivum L.* para la obtención del trigo híbrido. B.A., Ministerio de Agricultura y Ganadería de la Nación, Dirección Nacional de Fiscalización y Comercialización Agrícola, Servicio Nacional de Fiscalización de Semillas, Depto. de Programación y Desarrollo, 1971. 20 p., bibl., plates, tables.

Describes contribution of *Triticum timopheevi*, Zhuk., a tetraploid wheat with primitive features, to hybridization of wheat.

6761. Casamiquela, Rodolfo M. Faune terrestre présente et passée (MH/OM, 12:2, Eté 1972, p. 97-106, illus., plates)

Terminal period of Andes' uplift in the Quaternary resulted in different biological evolution on the west and east sides of the mountains. These differences are discussed for southern South America and related to man's presence.

6762. Clapperton, Chalmers M. Antarctic link with the Andes (GM, 44:2, Nov. 1971, p. 124-130, illus., maps)

Examines island of South Georgia, 58 percent covered by permanent snow and ice, from physical-geographical point of view. Describes complex oscillations of glaciers and suggests that useful appreciation of trends in world-wide changes in climate may result from observations of the glaciers.

6763. Condarco Morales, Ramiro. El escenario andino y el hombre: ecología y antropogeografía de los Andes centrales. La Paz, Imprenta y Libería Renovación, 1971. 596 p.

Interesting book begins with a 75-page introduction to field of geography which includes discussion of wide-ranging topics such as determinism, development of human geography, etc. Pt. 1 commences with discussion of central Andes; Pt. 2 with geographical factors such as relief, water, and climate in the Andes. Pt. 3 deals with ecology and economies within the Andes. Emphasizes pastoral life and discusses vestiges of nomadism as well as prehispanic habitations.

6764. D'Andrea, Héctor. Aprovechamiento hidroeléctrico del Río Paraná en la zona de las islas Yaciretá y Apipé. Corrientes, Arg., Comisión Mixta Técnica Paraguayo-Argentina del Apipé, 1969. 27 p., maps, tables.

Report of Argentine-Paraguayan technical commission, to make Paraná river more navigable between Ituzaingó and Posadas, presents plan for construction of locks which will bypass the Apipé rapids. Present navigation is restricted to boats which draw less than four feet, whereas river could be accessible to those drawing up to 10 feet. Some 800,000 tons of cargo and almost 800,000 passengers yearly move along the Upper Paraná.

6765. Enne, Giuseppe. Prime osservazioni sulle prove di incrocio delle razze bovine da carne italiane con razze dell'America Latina (IAO/RAST, 66:1/3, gen. marzo 1972, p. 3-21, bibl., plates, tables)

Reports on production, weight-gain, and other indices from Paraguay and Brazil, with description of cross-breeding experiments in Brazil. Other countries involved in programs of interchange are Argentina and Uruguay. [C. R. Edwards]

6766. Ferguson, John Halcro and others. The River Plate republics: Argentina, Paraguay, Uruguay. N.Y., Time-Life Books, 1971. 160 p., bibl., illus., maps, plates (Life world library)

Presents these three nations in an interwoven manner linked by great rivers with common destinies. Although popularly written, book attempts to outline life and problems in a fair way.

6767. Garrido, Manuel I. Levantamiento del Río de la Plata (PAIGH/RC, 19:19, 1970, p. 213-230, illus., map, plates)

Reports nautical survey of the Río de la Plata carried out in 1963-64. Includes influence of tides on surveys and lists of nautical charts published as result of investigations.

6768. Jacobs, Charles R. and **Babette M. Jacobs.** South America travel digest. 7. ed. Los Angeles, Calif., Paul Richmond, 1971. 144 p., illus., maps, plates, tables.

Travel comments on what to see in South America with more than usual tourist information

6769. Kane, Robert S. South America A to Z. Garden City, N.Y., Doubleday, 1962. 370 p., plates.

Unusual travel book with comments both negative and positive about countries of South America, their living conditions, people, customs, and politics.

6770. Laugenie, Claude. La structure et l'orogenèse des Andes Chiléno-Argentines (ULIG/C, 15:35, sept. 1971, p. 267-287, maps, tables)

Chilean-Argentine sector of Andes is distinguished by its great rigidity, structural combinations of various forms, and vulcanism. It was formed primarily from continental sediments which were interrupted twice during the Andean geosynclinal cycle by marine transgressions. The Tertiary, or last period of building, was characterized by some subsidence.

6771. Machado, Emilio A. Un problema de desarrollo de áreas: la elección de cultivos en una región en vias de irrigación (ANC/B, 47:2/4, 1970, p. 147-161)

Presents mathematical proposals for most economical crop production in given areas. Argues that such methods are essential to regional planning.

6772. Martínez Montero, Homero and others. La cuenca del Plata. Palabras liminares [por] Juan Carlos Pedemonte. Montevideo, Ministerio de Relaciones Exteriores, Instituto Artigas del Servicio Exterior, 1969. 126 p. (Libertad Republicana)

Presents series of talks ranging from historical to economic and legal to political regarding development of the Cuenca del Plata by Argentina and Uruguay.

6773. Nelson, Joan M. Migrants, urban poverty and instability in developing nations. Cambridge, Mass., Harvard Univ., Center for International Affairs, 1969. 81 p., bibl., tables (Occasional papers in international affairs, 22)

Many observers believe that rapid and sizeable influx of migrants to South American cities constitutes a major source of political instability. Author contests this notion by citing studies which show that migrants do not necessarily support extremist parties or partake in riots.

6774. Organization of American States. Secretaría General. Departamento de Asuntos Económicos. Unidad de Recursos Naturales. Cuenca del Río de la Plata: estudio para su planificación y desarrollo, inventario de datos hidrológicos y climatológicos. Washington, 1969. 272 p.

Cooperation among Argentina, Bolivia, Brazil, Paraguay and Uruguay since accord of 1967 has proceeded slowly. This is one of the first studies on development of common drainage sheds and puts into perspective some of the enormous problems faced by developing nations of South America.

6774a. Ostrovskii, Viktor. Zhizn'Bolskoi Reki (Life on the Great River). Moskva, Izdatel'stvo Mysl', 1971. 206 p., illus., maps.

Travelogue of adventures of Polish writer-traveler on the Río de la Plata and its tributaries. Much information on geography and ethnography of area as well as on plant and animal life. [T. S. Cheston]

6775. Pedersen, Owe and **Walter Stöhr.** Economic integration and the spatial development of South America (ABS, 12:5, May/June 1969, p. 2-12, bibl., maps, tables)

Demonstrates thesis of a peripheral development of traffic flows and trade patterns for South America. Studies in hinterlands reveal that they often reach beyond national frontiers. Among regions with potential development in the near future are South Brazil, the River Plate and Central Chile. [César Caviedes]

6776. Pimstein C., Rainer. Aspectos de la vegetación andina: condiciones de desarrollo y aprovechamiento (UC/B, 100, abril 1970, p. 54-66)

Considers vegetation of Andean zone (10°N-55°S) in various environments: upper Andean level, puna, páramo, ceja de montaña, and dry eastern valleys. Discusses introduced species and native plants and includes detailed morphology of Andean plants.

6777. Rawls, Joseph. East of the Andes (OAS/AM, 23:8, Aug. 1971, p. 15-24, map, plates, table)

Offers account of Inca activities in eastern Andean area by means of analysis of historical documents. Interesting references to the two areas of resistance to Inca invasions, namely Chachapoyas and Vilcabamba. Speculates that Incas operated as far east as Puerto Maldonado. Inca genealogical table with dates of interest.

6778. Rox-Schulz, Heinz. Verrückter Gringo; ein Sudamerikanisches Abenteuer. Baden-Baden, FRG, Signal-Verlag, 1971. 200 p., illus.

Describes interesting trip through tropical South America. Author, young German traveler and journalist, visited jungles of Brazil, Colombia, Ecuador, Peru, Bolivia, and Paraguay in search of Indian tribes to learn about their life-styles, beliefs, and modes of survival. Written with verve and a sense of humor. Of interest to generalists. [G. M. Dorn]

6779. Torre, Antonio de la. El mundo mágico de los Andes: viaje por Chile y Perú. B.A., Librería Hachette, 1969. 184 p.

Coloridas impresiones de viaje acompañada de algunas poesías del autor. [H. M. Rasi]

6780. Zahl, Paul A. Seeking the truth about the piranha (NGS/NGM, 138:5, Nov. 1970, p. 715-732)

Discussion of a fish which Humboldt labeled as one of the great scourges of South America. Presents distribution, habits, and effects on everyday life.

ARGENTINA

6781. Altimir, Oscar. La configuración espacial del Chubut y su inserción en el sistema regional argentino (UNLP/E, 18:2, mayo/agosto 1972, p. 123-155, maps, tables)

Examination of transportation poles in Argentina with special reference to Patagonia and Chubut province. Discusses hierarchical areas of influence in Chubut's economy and includes tables of localization of industrial and service activities.

6782. **Argentina. Consejo Agrario Nacional. Instituto Geominero Argentino (INGEMAR).** Investigaciones hidrogeológicas en Los Cerrillos, pcia. de Córdoba. B.A., 1969. 106 l., bibl., fold. maps, maps, tables.

In 1968, Córdoba province transferred some 5,000 ha. of fiscal lands to the Consejo Agrario Nacional for colonization. Since surface water in area is already utilized, the Consejo has produced this investigation of subsurface water available. Study makes positive recommendation about colonization possibilities.

6783. ———. **Consejo Nacional de Desarrollo. Instituto Nacional de Estadística y Censos.** Censo nacional de población, familias y viviendas, 1970: resultados provisionales. B.A., 1970. 105 p., maps, tables.

This analysis of Argentine population statistics will be useful to all social scientists. Presentation of maps of provinces with individual department boundaries accompanied by population data of several varieties enables reader to compare different parts of country at a glance.

6784. ———. ———. Programa sobre instalación de nuevas praderas consociadas permanentes; mejoramiento de las existentes, y conservación de forraje. Región Pampeana, Arg., 1963. 125 l., maps.

Program for installation of new pasture on the pampa which is designed to augment Argentine beef production for export. First stage of the program is designed to cover 60 million hectares of the pampa; later it is hoped to extend pasturage to other places.

6785. ———. **Dirección Nacional del Turismo.** Comahué, la tierra del pasado legendario y del maravilloso porvenir. B.A., 1963. 39 p., map, plates.

Development hopes for tourist region in northern Patagonia.

6786. ———. **Fondo de Integración Territorial (FIT).** FIT en las provincias: San Juan. B.A.?, n.p., n.d. 55 p., plates, tables.

Discusses housing, transportation, farm and storage facility improvement, and urbanism for region around San Juan, Argentina.

6787. ———. **Presidencia de la Nación. Secretaría General.** Energía atómica. B.A., 1970. 36 p., maps, plates.

Contains a map of distribution of outcrops of nuclear minerals in Argentina, treatment plants, and principal nuclear districts.

6788. **Armero Sixto, Carlos.** Estudio económico de la fruticultura argentina: 1967. Bahía Blanca, Arg., Corporación de Productores de Fruta de Río Negro [CORPOFRUT], 1968. 159 p., bibl., illus., maps, plates, tables.

Views Argentine fruit production in light of world production. Devotes special attention to European and Brazilian markets.

6789. **Barba, Fernando E.** Indice de mapas, planos y fotografías de la sección Ministerio de Obras Públicas: 1885-1910. La Plata, Arg., Ministerio de Educación, 1968. 149 p., illus. (Publicaciones del Archivo Histórico de la Provincia Dr. Ricardo Levene. Catálogo de los documentos del archivo, 2)

Archival holdings of Ministry of Public Works (1885-1910) on Buenos Aires province with annotations.

6790. **Bergmann, John F.** Soil salinization and Welsh settlement in Chubut, Argentina (ULIG/C, 15:35, sept. 1971, p. 361-369, maps, plates)

Welsh influence has steadily declined during last 50 years in Chubut Valley. Of the 40,000 ha. surveyed for the original 400 farms, 18,000 ha. were under cultivation in 1966. By end of 1960's, author estimates that 25 percent decline had taken place. Problem partly due to salinization of soils because of poor irrigation practices as well as refusal to change farming methods.

6791. **Besil, Antonio C.** Análisis de las causas del actual cambio en la estructura del sector agrícola en la provincia del Chaco. Resistencia, Arg., Univ. Nacional del Nordeste, Facultad de Ciencias Económicas, 1969. 120 p., bibl., tables.

Discusses difficulties with cotton production in Argentine Chaco. Small holdings, inefficient farm practices, competition from synthetic products, and mediocre fibre results have prompted recommendations such as diversification, attention to farm practices and cotton types, and industrialization of zone in question so that use can be made of existing transport facilities.

6792. ——— and **Ernesto A. Martina.** El nordeste argentino: evaluación de su situación económica y social. Resistencia, Arg., Univ. Nacional del Nordeste, Depto. de Extensión Universitaria y Ampliación de Estudios, 1968. 35 p. (Serie extensión universitaria, 3)

Statistical representation and analysis of population, land tenure, production, and some economic problems in northeastern Argentina.

6793. **Billard, Jules B.** and **Winfield Parks.** Buenos Aires, Argentina's melting-pot metropolis (NGS/NGM, 132:5, Nov. 1967, p. 662-695)

Up-to-date discussion of Buenos Aires' problems, including pressing need for housing, rising numbers of *villas miserias*, political difficulties, and social customs.

6794. **Borrello, Angel V.** Los geosinclinales de la Argentina. B.A., Ministerio de Economía y Trabajo, Dirección Nacional de Geología y Minería, 1969. 188 p., bibl., maps, plates (Anales, 14)

During geological development of southern-most extreme of South America, geosynclines shifted gradually from east to west, the Andes being last of geosynclines whose layers were upfolded during the Mesozoic Age. [César Caviedes]

6795. ———. Sobre el volcanismo embrionario en el ciclo neoídico de los Andes

Patagónico-Fueguinos (ANC/B, 47:1, 1969, p. 21-26, bibl., table)

Describes existence of embryonic volcanism related to Jurassic tuffs, lavas and agglomerates in Austral Andes between latitudes 44° and 55° south. [César Caviedes]

6796. Buenos Aires (province), *Arg.* **Ministerio de Asuntos Agrarios. Asesoría Ministerial de Desarrollo.** Diagnóstico agropecuario por áreas geográficas. B.A., 1968. 106 l., bibl., fold. maps, maps, tables.

Presents: land-use maps of agricultural products such as alfalfa, cereals, and cattle; detailed information concerning land tenure in regional subdivisions; physical geography and other facets of geography.

6797. ——. Ministerio de Educación. Subsecretaría de Cultura. Indice de mapas, planos y fotografías del Ministerio de Obras Públicas. Prepared by Fernando E. Barba. La Plata, Arg. 1969. 149 p., plates (Publicaciones del Archivo Histórico Dr. Ricardo Levene. Catálogos de los documentos del archivo, 2)

Annotated list of documents, books, maps, etc., pertaining to Buenos Aires province. Maps of a cadastral scale are listed and should be useful to social scientists.

6798. Bünstorf, Jurgen. Entwicklungsprobleme in Nord-Argentinien (GR, 23:1, Jan. 1971, p. 31-35, maps, table)

In Argentina, as in other countries of the world, rail traffic has declined while road traffic has increased. Buildup of road network in Argentina since 1960 is discussed in connection with other communication developments for northern part of country.

6799. Cafferata, Juan Daniel. Vocabulario geográfico correntino. Corrientes, Arg., Ediciones Temas, 1965. 38 p. (mimeo).

Useful lexicon of Corrientes province, Arg., with maps and statistics.

6800. Centro de Industriales Siderúrgicos, *Buenos Aires.* La siderurgia argentina en 1968. B.A., 1969. 122 p., illus., maps, tables.

Economic geographers will find rich source of information on Argentine iron and steel production in this well-illustrated volume.

6801. Daus, Federico A. Fisonomía regional de la Argentina. 3. ed. B.A., Editorial Nova, 1971. 195 p., bibl., map (Col. Enseñar)

Geographers will find this small volume useful for clear picture presented of eight regions selected by author: La Pampa, Las Sierras Pampeanas, Cuyo, El Noroeste, El Chaco, La Mesopotamia, La Estepa, and La Patagonia. Analyzes each section according to physical and human geographical characteristics and presents series of color land use maps for each region.

6802. Delich, Francisco José. Tierra y conciencia campesina en Tucumán. B.A., Ediciones Signos, 1970. 160 p., maps, plates (Ensayos)

Sociological work discusses problems of interest to geographers such as technological obsolescence in production of sugar in Tucumán, economic difficulties, growth of Tucumán as an industrial center which has outgrown its reliance on the monopoly of sugar production and the social system involved.

6803. Denis, Paul Yves. San Rafael: la ciudad y su región. Mendoza, Arg., Univ. Nacional de Cuyo, Facultad de Filosofía y Letras, 1969. 432 p., illus., maps, tables.

Vivid impression of life and development of an agricultural city in arid piedmont of the Argentine Andes is gathered from this comprehensive dissertation. Pt. 1 which deals with physical environment is followed by colonization phases in southern part of Mendoza province and development of San Rafael as a secondary urban center. Growth of city has been due to wine industry and dry fruit processing plants. San Rafael still suffers from a kind of underdevelopment, a consequence of its location in the shadow of city of Mendoza. [César Caviedes]

6804. Di Lullo, Orestes and **Luis G. B. Garay.** La vivienda popular de Santiago del Estero. Tucumán. Arg., Univ. Nacional de Tucumán, Facultad de Filosofía y Letras, 1969. 88 p., bibl., illus., plates (Cuadernos de humanitas, 32)

Settlement geographers will welcome this comprehensive little volume on vernacular housing in Santiago del Estero. Discusses historical development of the rancho, its evolution, and future with illustrative material.

6805. Durán, Eva Arcidiácono de; Alberto Lüthers; and **Bernabé J. Quartino.** Actividad granítica y kinetometamorfismo en calizas, anfibolitas y gneises según dos localidades de las sierras de Córdoba; diseminación asimilativa (ANC/B, 47:2/4, 1970, p. 283-314, bibl., illus., plates)

Examines in detail geological deformation of materials in the Sierra de Córdoba, Arg. Investigates two localities and analyzes and compares processes of deformation.

6806. Erb, H. H. and others. La inmigración japonesa en la República Argentina: estudio preliminar (UNCIG/B, 15:58, 1968, p. 1-54, maps, plates)

Examines colonization and immigration by Japanese in Argentina and concludes that in 67 years of legal Japanese emigration original colonists and nisei have adapted quickly to country's customs and entered favorably into its economy.

6807. Eriksen, Wolfgang. Der argentinische Nationalpark Nahuel Huapi als Wirkungsfeld raumdifferenzierender Kräfte und Prozesse (GR, 23:1, Jan. 1971, p. 24-30, maps)

Argentina is among first American nations to reserve land for national parks. Over 26,000 km² are now set aside for this end. Largest and most visited is Nahuel Huapi in northwest Patagonia, dating from 1904. Author describes it and its development as settlement center over the years. Over-settlement, even to extent of appearance of *villas miserias* in Bariloche, indicates need for better planning.

6808. Escalante, Rodolfo. Aves marinas del Río de la Plata y aguas vecinas del Océano Atlántico. Ilustrado por Víctor García Espiell. Montevideo, Barreiro y Ramos, 1970. 199 p., bibl., illus., plates, tables.

Morphological descriptions of birds living on Atlantic coast near the mouth of the River Plate. Considers their customs and their geographical distribution. [César Caviedes]

6809. Escardó, Florencio. Nueva geografía de Buenos Aires. B.A., Editorial Américalee, 1971. 177 p.

Humorous account of habits of *porteños* and of the way they live, including vivid descriptions of city of Buenos Aires. For historian's comment, see *HLAS 34:2700*.

6810. Federación Argentina de Cooperativas Agrarias, *Buenos Aires.* Memoria y balance general correspondiente al XXIII° ejercicio económico cerrado el 31 de diciembre de 1970. B.A., 1971. 78 p., tables.

General summary of activities of the Argentine Federation of Agrarian Cooperatives with list of member organizations.

6811. Fidalgo, Francisco; Eduardo P. Tonni; and **Jorge Zetti.** Algunas observaciones estratigráficas en la Laguna Blanca Grande (MEMDA/E, 14, julio/dic. 1971, p. 1-4, illus., plate)

Climatic and faunistic correlations present problems in stratigraphic correlations for the Quaternary at a lagoon in Buenos Aires province.

Fuente, Francisco de la and others. Manual de historia y geografía de La Rioja. See *HLAS 34:2711*.

6812. Fundación Bariloche, *San Carlos de Bariloche, Arg.* **Departmento de Sociología.** Datos comparativos de las provincias argentinas. v. 1, Indicadores demográficos, económicos, políticos y sociales: 1947-1960. San Carlos de Bariloche, Arg., 1970. 150 l. tables (mimeo)

First in planned series of publications to make available quantitative information about Argentine society. Compilation of data from provinces after fashion of *World handbook of political and social indicators* (Yale Univ. Press, 1964). Data, from 1947 and 1960, include subjects such as surface area and population with numerous variables such as growth of population, density, infants, etc.

6813. Galmarini, Alfredo G. and **José M. Raffo del Campo.** Rasgos fundamentales que caracterizan el clima de la región chaqueña. B.A., Presidencia de la Nación, Consejo Nacional de Desarrollo, 1964. 178 p., maps, tables.

Presents climate of the Chaco in detail with summary maps in the Thornthwaite and Koeppen systems. Concludes that Koeppen system and first Thornthwaite system give best results from practical viewpoint. Second Thornthwaite system is too complex and does not consider what authors call "geographic criterion" which is essential in good climatic classification.

6814. Goicoechea, Helga Nilda. El Instituto Geográfico Argentino: historia e índice de su *Boletín*, 1879-1911-1926-1928. Resistencia, Arg., Univ. Nacional del Nordeste, Facultad de Humanidades, Instituto de Historia, 1970. 96 p., facsims. (Publicaciones e impresiones, 15)

Summary of people and events associated with development of Argentina's Geographic Institute. Includes expeditions sponsored by Institute, and index of materials and authors of its *Boletín*.

6815. González Carbalho, José. Estampas de Buenos Aires. B.A., Centro Editor de América Latina, 1971. 112 p., illus., plates (La historia popular: vida y milagros de nuestro pueblo, 17)

Popular account of life in Buenos Aires, past and present.

6816. Hidronor (firm), *Buenos Aires.* El Chocón-Cerros Colorados: síntesis del proyecto. B.A., 1968. 13 l., fold. maps.

Large scale (310,000 km²) water control project studies in northern Patagonia, at the headwaters of the Río Negro (Río Limay), for irrigation possibilities.

Ibáñez, Francisco M. Toponomía de Entre Ríos: la tierra, el hombre y los hechos. See *HLAS 34:2733a*.

6817. Instituto de Estudios Investigaciones [IDEI], *Buenos Aires.* Algunos aspectos básicos de la integración de la Cuenca del Plata. B.A., 1967. 157 p., illus., maps, tables.

Seven articles concerning historical development of Cuenca del Plata project idea, availability of water for human use, energy problem, river network and navigability, coordination of diverse methods of transport, economic structure of region, and frontier aspects.

6818. Laming-Emperaire, Annette. Paysages de Patagonie et de Terre de Feu (MH/OM, 12:2, eté 1972, p. 79-96, bibl., plates)

Discusses climate and vegetation structures of the island region at southern tip of South America, the lake region, and the pampas to the north.

6819. La Pampa (province), *Arg.* **Ministerio de Economía y Asuntos Agrarios. Dirección General de Geodesia y Catastro.** Geonimia: obra mapa de La Pampa. Santa Rosa de Toay, Arg., 1968. 84 p., bibl. (Biblioteca pampeana; serie libros, 3)

Attempt to correct spelling of indigenous names on maps of La Pampa. Includes meanings of names.

6820. Luxardo, José D. Los caminos en la República Argentina. B.A., Consejo Nacional de Desarrollo, 1966. 65 p. (mimeo) maps.

Historical survey of development of roads in Argentina, with discussion of problems such as fuel prices and highway management, and recommendations concerning national plans for various transportation systems.

6821. Maeder, Ernesto J. A. La Revista de la Sociedad Geográfica Argentina, 1881-1890: descripción e índice. Resistencia, Arg., Univ. Nacional del Nordeste, Depto. de Extensión Universitaria y Ampliación de Estudios, 1968. 27 p. (Serie humanidades, 4)

Annotated bibliography of a host of subjects and places dealing with Argentine investigations and explorations.

Maroni, José Juan. Breve historia física de Buenos Aires. See *HLAS 34:2753.*

6822. Martínez-Crovetto, Raúl. Introducción a la etnobotánica aborigen del nordeste argentino (*in* International Congress of Americanists, XXXVIII, Stuttgart-München, FRG, 1968. Verhandlungen [see *HLAS 33:510*] München, FRG, 1971, v. 3, p. 91-97, tables)

Analysis of terms used by various Indian groups for plant and vegetation forms in northeast Argentina. Linguistic rules are developed concerning the nomenclature for plant life.

6823. Mendoza (province), *Arg.* **Dirección de Estadísticas e Investigaciones Económicas.** Esto es Mendoza, 1971. Mendoza, Arg., 1971. 1 v. (Unpaged) maps, plates, tables.

General regional description of Mendoza with economic, political and other data.

6824. Misiones (province), *Arg.* **Dirección General de Estadística.** Censo nacional de población, familias y viviendas. 1970: cifras provisorias. Posadas? Arg., 1970. 28 p. (mimeo) tables.

Provisional census data for 1970 tabulated according to population densities, totals, sexes, foreigners, etc.

6825. Orrego Aravena, Reynaldo. Vertebrados de La Pampa. Santa Rosa de Toay, Arg., Gobierno de La Pampa, Consejo Provincial de Difusión, 1970? 31 p., maps (Biblioteca pampeana, serie folletos, 13)

Maps and lists of fauna of La Pampa province presented systematically. May be of use to geographers.

6826. Pronsato, Domingo. Patagonia año 2.000: reflexiones de una experiencia. Bahía Blanca, Arg., Panzini Hermanos, 1971. 151 p., maps, plates.

Discussion of problems of Patagonia with chapters on economic development, water problems in Bahía Blanca and diverse notes on tourism, physical geography and origins of American man.

Randle, Patricio. Estructuras urbanas pampeanas. See *HLAS 34:2784.*

6827. Río Negro (province), *Arg.* **Departamento Provincial de Agua.** Canal Pomona-San Antonio. Viedma? Arg., 1970. 18 p., fold. map, plates, tables.

Discussion of the 165km canal which will supply water to the San Antonio Oeste zone of Río Negro province.

6828. Santa Cruz (province), *Arg.* Mensaje pronunciado por el Gobernador de la Provincia Comodoro Carlos A. Raynelli reseñando cuatro años de gobierno de la Revolución Argentina en Santa Cruz. Río Gallegos, Arg., 1971. 127 p., maps, tables.

Report by the administration of Santa Cruz province. Consists of general regional presentation of data about schools, transportation, energy, labor, banking, and planning. Province has a number of problems which need solution: poor demographic distribution, low population density, lack of transportation lines and communications.

6829. Santamarina, Estela B. de; María A. Moreno; and Enrique de Jesús Setti. Al área jurisdiccional del Tucumán, su representación cartográfica y sus derroteros. Tucumán, Arg., Univ. Nacional de Tucumán, Facultad de Filosofía y Letras, 1968. 80 p., fold. map, maps (Cuaderno de humanitas, 27)

Three articles concerning the limits of Tucuman province, evolution of region's cartographic representation and geographic aspects of urban traffic in Tucuman city.

6830. Santillán de Andrés, Selva E. Esquemas de la estructura socioeconómica de la provincia de Tucumán. Univ. Nacional de Tucumán, Facultad de Filosofía y Letras, Depto. de Geografía, 1969. 37 p., bibl., maps, tables (Serie monográfica, 18)

Analysis of Tucuman province economy, which calls for intensification of industrialization process according to the development of poles or areas of influence united by urban centers. Land use maps and others are helpful.

6831. Shell Compañía Argentina de Petróleo (firm), *Buenos Aires.* La relación entre el consumo energético y el producto bruto interno: el caso argentino y un muestreo mundial. B.A., 1969? 16 p. (Notas informativas)

Explanation of consumption of energy in different countries along with notions about planning for use of energy. Comparison of energy usage among many countries shows Argentina relatively low on the list. This is explained by placing Argentina with countries whose industry is mainly light, service sector is well developed, and agriculture is the mainstay of the economy.

6832. Sociedad Rural Argentina, *Buenos Aires.* **Instituto de Estudios Económicos.** La población rural (SRA/A, 106:6, junio 1972, p. 8-14, illus., plates, tables)

Rural population of Latin America in 1950 was some 53 percent of the total. It is estimated this percentage will decline to 38 by 1975. Portion of Argentine population active in agricultural occupations was 16.5 in 1969. Similar decrease is noted for the country in forecasts.

6833. **Tabbush, Berta de** and **Carlota Boero de Izeta.** Desde el camino. Rosario, Arg., Editorial Biblioteca, 1970. 210 p., bibl., map, plates (Col. Imagen)

Descriptive route analysis along roads traversing the Argentine nation from south to north. Color photographs.

6834. **Taylor, Margaret Stewart.** Focus on the Falkland Islands. London, Robert Hale, 1971. 191 p., plates.

Well written, up-do-date account of Falkland islanders which sheds light on latest attempts by Argentina to assume sovereignty.

6835. **United Nations. Comisión Económica para la América Latina.** Los recursos hidráulicos de América Latina: Argentina, análisis y programación tentativa de su desarrollo. 2. ed. rev. B.A., Consejo Federal de Inversiones, 1970. 419 p. (ECN. 12/917)

Revised and abridged edition of original seven-volume study prepared by CEPAL in cooperation with Argentina's Consejo Federal de Inversiones. Includes statistical presentation of hydroelectric potential and actual production in country. Provides information on many aspects of water potential such as river navigability, international cooperation, evaluation of river projects, planning concepts, and economic effects of planning. Useful maps summarize technical data.

6836. **Universidad Nacional de Buenos Aires. Instituto de Investigaciones de la Vivienda.** Tipos predominantes de vivienda rural en la República Argentina. B.A., 1971? 132 p., illus., maps, plates.

Contains analysis of 22 types of dwellings in rural areas of Argentina. Maps of types and country-wide distribution are most useful. Vernacular dwellings are classified according to materials of construction.

6837. **Urban, Francis S.** Agricultural prospects in Argentina. Washington, U.S. Dept. of Agriculture, Economic Research Service, Foreign Regional Analysis Division, 1972. 11 p., tables (ERS-Foreign, 331)

Argentina is expected to increase exports of most farm products through 1980, with largest increase in grain exports. Beef exports are projected to remain at same base period level because of continued high domestic demand. Country will remain, however, as world's largest beef exporter.

6838. **Vainstok, Arturo.** La Confederación Cooperativa de la République Argentina: COOPERA (IESSC/C, 4:11, mayo/agosto 1969, p. 76-84)

Brief review of 71 years of cooperatives in Argentina, beginning with first, called El Progreso Agrícola de Pigüé, and leading to federation of cooperatives begun in 1962. Discusses various types of cooperatives.

6839. **Vapñarsky, Cesar A.** La población urbana argentina: revisión crítica del método y los resultados censales de 1960. B.A., Instituto Torcuato Di Tella, 1969. 190 p., tables (Serie celeste: planeamiento regional y urbano)

Analyzes Argentine census data of 1960 for urban phenomena. Nation's population is 72 percent urban. Official statistics are contested and different urban population data are employed for numerous items such as towns with over 10,000 people. Official statistics give 2,778 as population of Eldorado, Misiones, for example, whereas 13,000 is used here.

6840. **Winsberg, Morton.** Una regionalización estadística de la agricultura en la pampa argentina (PAIGH/G, 71, dez. 1969, p. 45-60, bibl., illus., tables)

Labor input applied to a given agricultural surface unit is main criterion used in approach to Pampa's regionalization problem. Data processing confirms importance of some dairy areas already established intuitively and points out other less conspicuous areas. Also shows the low impact of oilseed crops and hog and sheep breeding on region's economy.

BOLIVIA

6841. **Aliaga de Vizcarra, Irma** *comp.* Bibliografia agrícola boliviana. La Paz, Ministerio de Agricultura, 1969. 44 p. (Suplemento, 1)

Continuation of a bibliography containing 1691 citations about Bolivian agriculture up through 1966. Annotated.

6842. **Barnes de Marschall, Katherine.** La formación de nuevos pueblos en Bolivia: proceso e implicaciones (IBEAS/EA, 1:3, 1970, p. 23-38)

Article explains findings of a study of settlements in Bolivia founded since the 1952 revolution. Most are located at boundaries of former haciendas and old community sites, formerly used for freight transfer. Disappearance of hacienda facilities has attracted transport agents, buyers, sellers, etc., to these centers and they have become important new market hubs. However, they have arisen mainly near the city of La Paz and are still lacking significance in other parts of the country.

6843. **Barth, Walter.** Das Permokarbon bei Zudán, Bolivien, und eine Übersicht des Jungpaläozoikums im zentralen Teil der Anden (GV/GR, 61:1, März 1972, p. 249-270, maps, tables)

Geological study of Permo-carboniferous, and of Paleozoic materials in region east of Sucre, Bol. Compares latter with those in central Andes; investigates Gondwana ice mass extension on western and eastern boundary of marine sedimentation (Permian).

6844. **Bolivia. Ministerio de Minas y Petroleo** Yacimientos de hierro de la Serranía del Mutún. La Paz, 1965. 39 p., maps.

Report on iron deposits 27km from Puerto Suárez in southeastern Bolivia. Purported to be among largest in the world, Bolivia is seeking active exploitation of reserves first explored in 1845 by Belgian Fracis Castelnau. Discusses colonization possibilities. Could bring economic impulse to Santa Cruz area.

6845. **Caccia, Angela.** Beyond Lake Titicaca. London, Hodder & Stoughton, 1969. 221 p., illus., map, plates.

Interesting account by a diplomat's wife of her experiences in Bolivia during the 1960's.

6846. Cárdenas, Martín. Manual de plantas económicas de Bolivia. Cochabama, Bol., Imprenta Icthus, 1969. 421 p., illus.

Useful to geographers and others interested in land development and characteristics. Introduction traces various studies made in Bolivia from time of N. I. Vavilov and his emissary to Bolivia, S. V. Juzepczuk, to modern period, and 15 chapters deal with useful plants making up a sizeable volume. Bibliography is short but welcome.

6847. Cevallos Tovar, Walter. El trigo. Cochabamba, Bol., Editorial Universitaria, 1967. 62 p.

Booklet designed to familiarize Bolivian farmers with wheat, its origins, its possibilities as a crop in Bolivia, and ways to raise it.

6848. Clark, Ronald J. Reforma agraria e integración campesina en la economía boliviana (IBEAS/EA, 1:3, 1970, p. 5-22)

Deals with some changes resulting from agrarian reform in Bolivia: campesino participation in marketing, rechanneling of marketing procedures, and formation of new farm settlements. Compares southern regions with northern regions and shows that success of reform measures depends heavily on market possibilities, transport routes, and conditions of transportation.

6849. Griffin, Margaret. Tiquimani. Foreword by Roger Wilson. Stellenbosch, South Africa, Kosmo Publishers, 1965. 164 p., plates.

Popular account of a seven man climbing expedition from South Africa to Bolivia.

6850. Gúzman Velasco, Lucio; Felix Soruco; and Rafael Morato Vargas. Aprovechamiento del gas natural en Bolivia. La Paz, n.p., 1967. 40 p., map, tables.

This study of gas available to Bolivians for industrial development concludes that there will be no shortage of natural gas in Bolivia, even in the long run consideration of expanded mining and other activities, and that it should be exported to neighboring countries.

6851. Hastenrath, Stefan. Beobachtungen zur Klima-Morphologischen Höhenstufung der Cordillera Real, Bolivien (UBGI/E, 25:2, Juni 1971, p. 102-108, maps, tables)

Compares radiosonde observations on the west coast and above the Bolivian altiplano. Warmer conditions above the altiplano may indicate heating effect of this mass of land on atmosphere above. Discusses turf exfoliations in vicinity of 0°C level along with other phenomena of geomorphologic interest at high altitudes. This model field report should be read by all geographers.

6852. Marden, Luis and Flip Schulke. Titicaca, abode of the sun (NGS/NGM, 139:2, Feb. 1971, p. 272-294)

Popularized article about life in Lake Titicaca shore areas. Some items of interest to economic geographers.

6853. Preston, David A. New towns: a major change in the rural settlement pattern in Highland Bolivia (JLAS, 2:1, May 1970, p. 1-27)

Geographer examines spontaneous nucleated settlements that have developed since 1952 in northern altiplano and Yungas' subtropical valleys. Concludes they represent real break with past patterns. [J. R. Scobie]

CHILE

6854. Antonioletti, Rodrigo and Orlando Peña. Caracterización del régimen pluviométrico en las cuencas de los ríos Valdivia y Bueno (UCIG/IG [Número especial] 1970, p. 39-53, bibl., illus., tables)

Basins of Valdivia and Bueno rivers represent dry islands within the humid climate of Southern Chile. Reasons for this are briefly explained. [César Caviedes]

6855. Aschmann, Homer. The natural history of a mine (CU/EG, 46:2, April 1970, p. 171-190, bibl., illus.)

Explains the development of activities around a mine. First stage in the history of a mine is the phase of prospects and investment with a second stage following, where mining operations start to produce and expand. In a third stage, stable operation of deposits and their profits are shared by investors and labor force; however, signs of exhaustion may be noticeable already. In the last stage, maintenance becomes uneconomical as a consequence of ore depletion and high demands of the mining companies. Many traits of the model developed by the author are found in the reality of Chilean mining industry. [César Caviedes]

6856. Baesa García, José. Tenencia de la tierra y reforma agraria: bibliografía. Santiago, Centro para el Desarrollo Económico y Social de América Latina, 1968. 220 p.

Annotated bibliography of land reform materials in Chilean libraries. Geographical and author indexes.

6857. Bermúdez, Oscar. Las oficinas salitreras adyacentes la linea del ferrocarril de Antofagasta a Bolivia (AGECH/B, 1:3, dic. 1967, p. 13-19, illus., tables)

Between 1880 and 1925 more than 15 nitrate works were exploited along railway connection between Antofagasta and Oruro, Bol. [César Caviedes]

6858. Berry, Brian J. L. Relações entre o desenvolvimento econômico regional e o sistema urbano: o caso do Chile (AGB/BCG, 21, 1971, p. 13-51)

Deals in part with the case of Chile and analyzes structure of communities over 15,000 in population; 59 social, economic, political and demographic variables for 80 urban communities; and some of the aspects of communication for 94 urban localities. In general, no new light is shed on problems of urban Chile.

6859. Borde, Jean. Les Andes de Santiago et leur avant-pays: étude de géomorphologie. Bordeaux, France, Union Francaise d'Impression, 1966. 560 p., bibl., illus., maps, plates, tables.

Maipo Valley, Central Chile, was shaped by uplifting of Andes, accompanied by very active volcanism, and by Quaternary glaciations. In coastal region, diastrophism and sea-level variations were responsible for marine terraces, which are characteristic of the area. [César Caviedes]

6860. Calvo, Gilberto. Antecedents para la creación de un centro de ecología de zonas áridas en La Serena (UC/B, 108, dic. 1970, p. 27-33)

Presents initial and follow-up correspondence regarding establishment of a center of ecology and arid zones at Univ. of Chile. Center is result of international conference on arid lands held in Chile in 1970.

6861. Casamiquela, Rodolfo and others. Convivencia del hombre con el mastodonte en Chile Central (Noticiario Mensual [Museo Nacional de Historia Natural, Santiago] 11:32, 1967, p. 1-6, map)

Finding of fossil giant sloth in Middle Chile seems to prove existence of man and of a dense forest some 6,000 years ago in the present subtropical shrub region. [César Caviedes]

6862. Caviedes, César. Geomorfología del Cuaternario del Valle del Aconcagua, Chile Central. Freiberg, FRG., n.p., 1972. 153 p., bibl., maps, plates, tables (Freiburger Geographische, 11)

Comprehensive study of Upper Aconcagua Valley from the upper limits of glaciation to the sea. This valley was shaped by three glacial advances during Pleistocene. In the Middle Valley, denudation modeled the slopes, whereas in coastal region main features of geomorphology are due to glacio-eustatic sealevel changes.

6863. ———. On the paleoclimatology of the Chilean littoral (The Iowa Geographer [Cedar Falls, Iowa] 29, Spring 1972, p. 8-14, bibl., illus.)

Climatic changes frequently occurred along Chilean coast during the Pleistocene as proved by geomorphological, paleontological, and paleobotanical evidence.

6864. Cunill G., Pedro. Chile meridional criollo: su geografía humana en 1700 (Cuadernos Geográficos del Sur [Concepción, Chile] 1:1, 1971, p. 21-63, illus., maps)

Excellent study on historical geography of "Old Chile" shows clearly progressive racial integration between creoles and Indians and origin and development of dispersed rural settlements in buffer zone of "La Frontera" during the 18th century. [César Caviedes]

6865. Desierto lunar en el norte de Chile (UC/B, 108, dic. 1970, p. 33-34)

Investigations in Atacama desert conducted in connection with US space program reveal that soils are so dry in places that they contain perchlorate, and that these soils have a lower concentration of microorganisms (or none) when there is a higher concentration of nitrates. Bacteria resemble those found in Antarctica.

6866. Flores, Eusebio and others. Estudios geográficos: homenaje de la Facultad de Filosofía y Educación a don Humberto Fuenzalida Villegas, Santiago, Univ. de Chile, Facultad de Filosofía y Educación, 1966. 233 p., illus., maps, plates.

Collection of papers written by friends and colleagues of the late Professor Humberto Fuenzalida. They include:
R. Borgel "Geomorfología Cuaternaria de la Cuenca de Santiago"
M. Concha "Establecimientos Humanos en el Altiplano Chileno"
J. Galdames "Una Hacienda del Valle de Rio Clara: Tres Curces"
D. McPhail "El Gran Lahar del Laja"
R. Paskoff "Premier Résultats de l'Étude Morphométrique des Cailloutis de la Formation Las Chilcas"
R. Santana "Evolución Geomorfológica del Litoral Guipuzcoano. País Vazco Español"
S. Sepúlveda "Interpretación Geográfica del Ultimo Censo General de Población"
W. Weischet "Solifluxión Periglacial en el Sur de Chile"
W. Zeil "Perfil Geológico del Sector Medio de la Cordillera de los Andes: Chile-Bolivia". [César Caviedes]

6867. Geografía económica de Chile. Santiago, Corporación de Formento de la Producción, 1966. 369 p., bibl., illus., maps, tables.

Concise treatise on the geography of Chile written with scientific understanding as a complement to the "Geografía Económica de Chile, Corfo," which first appeared twenty years ago. [César Caviedes]

6868. González-Bonorino, Félix. Series metamórficas de la Cordillera de la Costa, Chile Central. Santiago, Univ. de Chile, Depto. de Geologia, 1970, 68 p., bibl., illus., maps, plates, tables (Publicación, 37)

Metamorphic rocks of Cordillera de la Costa are main subject of this article. Formed during the Late Paleozoic, they were changed partially by uprising of Chilean coastal batholith. [César Caviedes]

6869. Grenier, Philippe. Observations sur les taffonis du désert chilien (AGF/B, 364/365, juin/sept. 1968, p. 193-211, bibl., maps, table)

Special form of rock weathering known as taffoni appears on north Chilean littoral as consequence of alternate action of coastal drizzle and drying winds. Discusses in detail petrographic and further climatic conditions for the formation of taffonies. [César Caviedes]

6870. Guerrero, Raúl. Estructuras agrarias, despoblamiento y trama urbana en la Frontera: reflexiones a propósito de un estudio reciente (Cuadernos Geográficos del Sur [Concepción, Chile] 1:1, 1971, p. 65-75, illus., tables)

Decaying latifundia and minifundia characterize land tenure pattern in this part of Central Chile, where small central places keep losing their importance against rise of an active major city, Temuco. [César Caviedes]

6871. Gunckel, Hugo. De cómo el abate Molina vió y describió los chilenos (UC/B, 80-81, nov/dic 1967, p. 41-44)

Discussion of writings of Juan Ignacio Molina, Fraile de Ocopa y Chiloé, with particular reference to his descriptions of Chilean lakes.

6872. Instituto de Investigación de Recursos Naturales, *Santiago.* Algunas características de los recursos climáticos de la región de Cautín (Los Recursos Naturales de la Provincia de Cautín [Santiago] 2:29, 1970, p. 72-100, bibl., illus., maps, tables)

Temperate semi-humid climate of Cautín province, South Chile, is characterized in all of its parameters. [César Caviedes]

6873. Jornadas Forestales de la Asociación Chilena de Ingenieros Forestales, *V, Santiago, 1969.* Actas de las . . . Santiago, 1969. 120 p., illus., tables.

Papers discussed deal mostly with ecology, management and forest policy of exotic species, especially pines (*Pinus radiata,* D. DON). This issue represents a good cross-section of Chilean research on forestry. [César Caviedes]

6874. Kubanek, Florian and **Werner Zeil.** Beitrag zur Kenntnis der Cordillera Claudio Gay: Nordchile (GV/GR, 60:3, Juni 1971, p. 1009-1024, illus., maps, plates)

Geological examination of section of pre-Cordillera of north Chile. Also discusses dating problems.

6875. Lauer, Wilhelm. Die Glaziallandschaft des Sudchilenischen. Seengebietes (Acta Geographica [Helsinki] 20:16, 1968, p. 215-235, bibl., illus., plates)

Glacial geomorphology of Lago Ranco-La Union, in Chilean Lake District, shows traces of three major Pleistocenic glaciations. In coastal zone of Valdivia, littoral deposits corresponding to sea-level heights between three glaciations mentioned can be clearly differentiated. [César Caviedes]

6876. Laugénie, Claude. Elementos de la cronología glaciar en los Andes chilenos meridionales (Cuadernos Geográficos del Sur [Concepción, Chile] 1:1, 1971, p. 7-20, bibl., illus., plates)

By studying glacial modeling and forms of deposition in northern part of Chilean Lake District, author recognizes traces of three glaciations contemporaneous with those of northern hemisphere. [César Caviedes]

6877. Llaumett P., Carlos and **Enrique Viteri A.** Zonación de elementos y minerales en el distrito minero El Volcán. Santiago, Univ. de Chile, Facultad de Ciencias Físicas y Matemáticas, Depto. de Geología, 1969. 19 p., bibl., maps, tables (Publicaciones del Depto. de Geología, 36)

Mining district, El Volcan, is considered as an example of zonal distribution of chemical and mineral materials arranged around granitic intrusives. Fe, Cu, Zn, Bb, and Ag are found.

6878. Lomnitz, Cinna. Acerca de una curiosidad geológica chilena: los orígenes del lago Budi (UC/B, 82, p. 37-41)

Explanation of Tertiary formations next to preCambrian rocks and combination of faulting and seawater intrusion in evolution of local lake.

6879. Markham, Brent J. Reconocimiento faunístico del área de los fiordos Toro y Cóndor, Isla Riesco, Magallanes (Anales del Instituto de la Patagonia [Punta Arenas, Chile] 1:1, 1970, p. 41-59, bibl., maps, plates, tables)

Faunal survey of the fiord Toro and Cóndor area of Magallanes in which species and subspecies of birds were observed. Nine mammal specimens were collected, showing a much poorer variety than the avifauna of the area.

6880. Olivares, Reynaldo Börgel. Las glaciaciones cuaternarias al oeste del lago Llanquihue, en el sur de Chile (PAIGH/G, 67, dez. 1967, p. 101-108, table)

By means of a profile drawn from E to W, author characterizes the Riss and Wurm glaciation affecting Chile's lake district. Regrettable is absence of bibliography on contributions of other geomorphologists who worked in same area or nearby, such as W. Lauer, W. Weischet, H. Illies. [César Caviedes]

6881. Paskoff, Roland. Antecedentes generales sobre la evolución del litoral de Chile del norte durante el Plioceno y el Cuaternario (AGECH/B, 1:3, dic. 1967, p. 11-12, bibl.)

Transgressions of sea, diastrophism and climatic changes occurred several times on coast of Northern Chile during Quaternary. [César Caviedes]

6882. ———. Los cambios climáticos plio-cuaternarios en la franja costera de Chile semiárido (AGECH/B, 1:1, abril 1967, p. 11-13)

Climatic changes that occurred in semi-arid coast of Chile during the Quaternary are reflected particularly by traces left in the geomorphology, soils and vegetation. [César Caviedes]

6883. ———. Etat résumé des acquisitions récentes sur le quartenaire Chilien (ULIG/C, 15:35, sept. 1971, p. 289-314, bibl., maps, tables)

Lengthy article attempts to explain some phenomena of Chilean Quaternary. Discusses climatic change, tectonic movements, sea level variations, and relation between marine and continental formations. Good bibliography.

6884. ———. Recherches géomorphologiques dans le Chili semi-aride. Bordeaux, France, Biscaye Frère Imprimeurs, 1970. 420 p., bibl., illus., maps, plates, tables.

After more than eight years of work in Chile, author offers complete study on relief and geomorphology of "Norte Chico". The bordering Cordillera was affected by at least two glaciations of arid character, whereas in coastal region, forms were shaped by glacio-eustatic sea-level changes. [César Caviedes]

6885. Péfaur, Jaime. Consideraciones sobre el problema de la conservación de mamíferos silvestres chilenos (UC/B, 93/94, junio-julio 1969, p. 4-10, tables)

Chilean wild life has never been adequately protected by laws or conservation policy, therefore a large number of species is threatened with extinction by epidemics and excessive hunting. [César Caviedes]

6886. **Peña A., Orlando.** Temperatuas en Chile Central: influencias del océano y el relieve sobre su comportamiento medio (UCV/RG, 4:1/2, 1970, p. 43-63, illus., tables)

Amplitudes of temperatures in Middle Chile are studies in their linkage to the sea and to the relief features. Littoral and mountain-stations are characterized by low amplitude and thermal homogeneity all year round, whereas in valleys that pepetrate into the Cordillera as well as in some piedmont basins, temperature-variations show continentality. [César Caviedes]

6887. **Pisano Valdés, Edmundo.** Vegetación del área de los fiordos Toro y Cóndor y Puerto Cutter Cove (Anales del Instituto de la Patagonia [Punta Arenas, Chile] 1:1, 1970, p. 27-40, bibl., plates, tables)

Attributes vegetational differences in the Toro Fiord and Cóndor and Cutter Cove area of Magallanes to slope and drainage differences as well as to rocky substrata. Discusses reasons for peat bog association.

6888. **Rodriguez, José.** Circulación y desarrollo de la Panamericana en Osorno (UCIG/IG, 18/19:1, 1970, bibl., map, tables)

As consequence of bad planning, city of Osorno was faced with urban problems and socio-economic implications after construction of Pan American Highway in South Chile. [César Caviedes]

6889. **Salinas, René.** La población de Valparaíso en la segunda mitad del siglo XVIII: estudio preliminar del empadronamiento de 1779. Valparaíso, Chile, Univ. Católica de Valparaíso, 1970. 35 p., illus., tables (Serie monografías, 15)

Reconstructs social and cultural status of Valparaíso's population in 18th century with data provided by local census from 1779. For historian's comment, see *HLAS 34:2307*. [César Caviedes]

6890. **Salinas, Rolando.** Un ejemplo de valorización pesquera del litoral norte de Chile: la industria de harina de pescado de Iquique (AGECH/B, 1:2, agosto 1967, p. 8-15, bibl., illus., maps, tables)

From 1960-67, a fish-meal production brought an unexpected flourishing to many coastal towns of northern Chile which had declined after the nitrate boom at beginning of century. [César Caviedes]

6891. **Santana-Aguilar, Rómulo.** El rio Salado y el sector oriental de la cuenca de Calama (AGECH/B, 1:3, dic. 1967, p. 21-28, bibl., illus.)

During humid periods of the Quaternary, rivers coming down from the Andes dug deep canyons into volcanic and limestone layers deposited in the Basin of Calama. [César Caviedes]

6892. ———. Les cendres volcaniques de la vallée du Cachapoal-Rapel: Chili (ULIG/C, 15:35, sept. 1971, p. 315-332, bibl., illus., plates)

Volcanic material deposited along the Cachapoal and Rapel Rivers, Middle Chile, was expelled from the Maipo volcano. Fluid flow of cinder, ashes and mud (lahar) spread to the vicinity of the coast at a distance of about 90 miles. [César Caviedes]

6893. **Schneider, Hans.** El clima del Norte Chico. Santiago, Univ. de Chile, Depto. de Geografía, 1968. 132 p., bibl., illus., maps.

Transitional region of Norte Chico is characterized climatically. Author pays special attention to determination of the limit between semi-arid region of Norte Chico and semi-humid region of Middle Chile. [César Caviedes]

6894. ———. Tipos de tiempo de Chile Central (Cuadernos Geográficos del Sur [Concepción, Chile] 1:1, 1971, p. 77-93, bibl., illus., tables)

Most of dominating weather types that influence Central Chile depend upon predominance of subtropical high pressure cell located in South Pacific. Bad weather is associated with depressions and fronts whose extent and action is limited by high pressure center. Graphically illustrates several typical weather situations. [César Caviedes]

6895. **Spinner, Julius.** Gehäuftes Vorkommen von Taurodontismus in prähistorischen und rezenten Populationen in Nord- und Mittel-chile (DGV/ZE, 95:1, 1970, p. 42-77, illus., plates)

Frequent appearances of taurodontism in former and present population of Northern and Central Chile is used by author to prove that Neanderthaloids, coming probably from Asia, were first to populate South America. [César Caviedes]

6896. **Stiefel, Jörg.** Zur tektonischen Entwicklung Chiles im Känozoikum (GV/GR, 61:3, 1972, p. 1109-1125, maps)

Presents tentative explanations of recent tectonic developments of middle and south Chilean coastal regions by synthesis of dating estimates from available sources. In spite of numerous apparent differences in rock formations, the tectonics of development are comparable for the Cenozoic.

6897. **Torres, Manuel.** El terremoto de Tacna y Arica (ACH/B, 37:83/84, 1./2. semestres 1970, p. 159-184)

Account of violent earthquake in Tacna and Arica during mid-August, 1868. Quotes from an eye-witness whose descriptions, though not always elegant, are realistic. Partly reviews copious notes from Frederick James Stevenson's diary which has been published under title *A traveller of the sixties* (London, Constable, 1929).

6898. **Wadhams, Peter.** Ocean surveyors in the Chilean fjords (GM, 44:8, 1972, p. 563-567)

First oceanographic survey of Chilean fjord region since 1833 was made in 1970 by a Canadian icebreaker named Hudson. Descriptions of conditions of settlements as well as coastal phenomena are up-to-date and useful for the geographer.

Weischet, Wolfgang. Chile: Seine laenderkundliche Individualitaet und Struktur. See *HLAS 34:2867.*

6899. Wormald Cruz, Alfredo. Frontera norte. Santiago, Editorial Orbe, 1968. 195 p., bibl., facsim., plates, tables.

Account of region of Arica, Chile which is divided into two parts: "History," and "Man and the Land." Useful economic and statistical data.

COLOMBIA

6900. Bateman, Alfredo D. Vocabulario geográfico de Colombia: letras S, T, U, V, W, X, Y, Z (SGS/CGC, 24, 1969, p. 3-260)

Final volume of study commenced in 1955 (see *HLAS 21:1970*) which presents numerous place names, physical feature names, political entities, etc., for entire country. Essential source material for those studying details of Colombian landscape.

6901. Cardona Gutiérrez, Ramiro. Las invasiones de terrenos urbanos: elementos para un diagnóstico. Bogotá, Ediciones Tercer Mundo, 1969. 105 p., bibl., plates, tables (El dedo en la herida, 33)

Divided into three parts: Pt. 1 deals with process of urbanization with reference to marginal groups, especially in Colombia. Pt. 2 examines socio-demographic characteristics of two types of marginal city dwellers, *inquilinos* and *invasores*. Data taken from two censuses of *barrios de invasión* in Bogotá. Pt. 3 attempts to illustrate how these types of spontaneous settlements are manifestations of urban development.

―――. Mejoramiento de tugurios y asentamientos no controlados: los aspectos sociales. See item 6518.

6902. Carvajal, Manuel. Realidades de la electrificación en el Valle del Cauca. Cali, Co., n.p., 1969. 39 p.

Basis for two new hydroelectric projects in Cauca Valley region. Some useful statistics and developmental assessment.

6903. Colombia. Instituto de Crédito Territorial. Departamento de Vivienda y Desarrollo Urbano. Vivienda y desarrollo en Colombia. Bogotá, 1970. 95 p., tables.

In 1970, there was a shortage of 539,944 houses in Colombia. Rapid population growth and unemployment make the deficiency even more critical. As a solution, author proposes: 1) lifting of educational levels, 2) greater engagement of governmental agencies in financing of popular housing. Statistical appendix concludes report. [César Caviedes]

6904. ―――. **Instituto Geográfico Agustín Codazzi. Oficina de Estudios Geográficos.** Monografía del Departamento de Sucre. Bogotá, 1969. 60 p., bibl., maps, plates, tables.

Physical and human geography of Sucre dept. including special section on economic development.

6905. ―――. **Ministerio de Agricultura. Oficina de Planeamiento, Coordinación y Evaluación.** Programas para el desarrollo agropecuario en el departamento de Sucre: 1968-1971. Bogotá, 1968. 70 p., tables (mimeo)

Program for the development of rural economy in Sucre dept. Recommends organization of campesinos, discusses productivity, problems and solutions with intragovernmental agency help; proposes creation of an organization which will orient, supervise, and evaluate programs.

6906. Córdoba G., J. Rodrigo and **Alberto Villegas V.** Estudio preliminar para el uso y manejo de la cuenca de captación del embalse La Fe. Bogotá, Instituto Geográfico Agustín Codazzi, 1966. 79 p., maps, plates, tables (Departamento agrológico, II:2)

One of series of studies on conservation of natural resources in Colombia distributed by the Instituto Geografico Augustín Codazzi. Geographers and others will find it of much interest for the serious attempt to recommend rational use of land in an area south of Medellín. Land-use and potential-use maps in colors.

6907. Corporación Autónoma Regional del Cauca, Cali, Co. La energía eléctrica y el progreso del valle. Cali, Co., Litolenis, 1971? 1 v. (Unpaged) maps, plates, tables.

Useful maps of growth of installed electrical energy in the Valle del Cauca dept. during 1948-68.

6908. ―――. Programa de desarrollo eléctrico: sinopsis. Cali, Co., 1970. 8 l., (mimeo) maps, plates, tables.

Electrification of rural areas in Valle del Cauca, Co., by Corporación del Valle del Cauca (CVC).

6909. Currie, Lauchlin Bernard. El manejo de cuencas en Colombia: estudio sobre el uso de las tierras. Bogotá, Ediciones Tercer Mundo, 1965. 84 p. (Col. Aventura del desarrollo. Documentos, 4)

Deterioration of natural resources has prompted proposal of specific programs for Colombia's development. Suggestions regarding Sierra Nevada de Santa Marta include regeneration of forests now being destroyed.

6910. Edel, Matthew. Funciones y límites del desarrollo de comunidad (IBEAS/EA, 1:3, 1970, p. 39-54)

Describes organization of a community action program in a municipio (Támesis) near Antioquia, Co. Community activities have not been extended to agricultural area. General frustration is felt over inadequacy of reform.

6911. Felstehausen, Herman. Planning problems in improving Colombian roads (UW/LE, 47:1, Feb. 1971, p. 1-13)

In 1968, Colombia had 18,000km of national highways of which some 4,000 were paved, and 16,000km of departmental roads. Between roads and the 3,436km of railway track, Colombia has become one of the few developing countries to have made such rapid strides. However, it may actually have invested too heavily in transportation neglecting other important projects such as education. Discusses plans for national-highway network and special problems such as providing rural access roads. Of much interest to geoscientists.

6912. Fondo Ganadero de Santander, *Bucaramanga, Co.* 25 [i.e., Veinticinco] años: 1945-1970. Bucaramanga, Co., Talleres Graficos Salesianos, 1970. 1 v. (Unpaged), facsim., plates, tables.

Historical survey of life of cattle organization presented with statistics.

6913. Forero, Manuel José. Reseña histórica de la geografía de Colombia. Bogotá, Instituto Geográfico Agustín Codazzi, 1969. 138 p.

Summary of discoveries, expeditions, settlement foundings, and other facts about Colombian geography.

6914. Herrmann, Reimer. Die zeitliche Änderung der Wasserbindung im Boden unter verschiedenen Vegetations-formationen der Höhenstufen eines Tropischen Hochgebirges: Sierra Nevada de Sta. Marta/Kolumbien (UBGI/E, 25:2, Juni 1971, p. 90-102, illus., maps, tables)

Measures soil moisture potential under several vegetation formations along sloping profile in western Sierra Nevada, Santa Marta, Co. Changes in soil moisture catena indicate soil moisture tension, pF, above conventional wilt point (4.2) in areas below the páramo and tropical montaña forest levels. Isopleths of pF and a vegetation-pF profile from sea level to 3000m, and detailed discussion of each vegetation association enhance this valuable contribution to geographical literature.

6915. Instituto Latinoamericano de Mercadero Agrícola, *Bogotá.* Análisis técnico de la industrial arrocera en Colombia. Bogotá, 1968. 87 p. (mimeo) (Informes sobre comercialización)

Booklet offers information on rice production in Colombia and economic statistics along with installation data on rice mills.

6916. Martínez Caicedo, Alejandro *comp.* El zarpazo: andanzas del INCORA [Instituto Nacional de la Reforma Agraria] en el Valle del Cauca. n.p., n.p., 1970? 1 v. (Unpaged) illus.

Pamphlet presents objections to activities of INCORA in Valle del Cauca. It is claimed that INCORA has expropriated land under purview of Corporación del Cauca (CVC) causing social problems among different classes of people and general pessimism among private farmers.

6917. Pérez Arbeláez, Enrique. Amazonia. Bogotá, Instituto Geográfico Agustín Codazzi, 1969. 163 p., bibl., plate (Documentación Geográfica)

Well-known botanist, Pérez Arbeláez, presents collection of newspaper articles dealing with Amazon, especially Colombian parts. He favors rational colonization but recognizes its problems.

6918. ———. La fauna colombiana amenazada (SMHN/R, 30, dic. 1969, p. 139-146)

Discussion of causes of depredation of Colombia's fauna. Hunting by Indians and for sport are main problems, although collecting animals for zoos, laboratories, private reasons, etc., are also significant. Heading list of most threatened animals are: condor, manatí, various turtles, crocodiles, deer, etc.

6919. Ramírez, Jesús Emilio. Historia de los terremotos en Colombia. Bogotá, Instituto Geográfico Agustín Codazzi, 1969. 218 p., bibl., fold. maps, plates, tables (Documentación geográfica)

Begins with explanatory section about earthquakes, theories of explanation, and classification. Second longer section, deals with Colombian seismology and presents chronology of earthquakes with map and detailed comments.

6920. Rodríguez Mariño, Tomás. Críticas al urbanismo. Tunja, Co., Univ. Pedagógica y Tecnológica de Colombia, 1971. 58 p., bibl.

Historical resumé of urbanization processes, followed by discussion of principal relationships between city and hinterland as they affect urban development in underdeveloped countries, using Colombian example. [C. R. Edwards]

6921. Simmons, Alan B. and **Ramiro Cardona G.** La selectividad de la migración en una perspectiva histórica: el caso de Bogotá, Colombia, 1929-1968 (CPES/RPS, 7:18, mayo/agosto 1970, p. 61-79, tables)

Investigation of type of people migrating to Latin American cities and who make up the so-called *cinturones de miseria.* Level of economic development of nation concerned determines social status for most migrants. Offers Bogotá as example of migratory phenomenon. Over 70 percent of male population (1964) between 15 and 64 years of age is migratory. Women dominate the short-distance migratory group.

6922. Shlemon, Roy J. and **L. Barry Phelps.** Dredge-tailing agriculture on the Río Nechí, Colombia (AGS/GR, 61:3, July 1971, p. 396-414)

Reports effects of gold-dredging activities on lower Río Nechí in Antioquia, Co. Seventy percent of tailings created in 15 years prior to the investigation are used for raising plantain, the remainder for cattle grazing, or nothing at all. Interesting reconstruction of dredging on river from colonial times to present, and evolving ecosystem.

6923. Torre, Antonio de la. Viaje al Orinoco en 1782 (SGC/B, 26:100, 4. Trimestre 1968, p. 349-389)

Transcription of travel report written by Antonio de la Torre in 1782, during journey from Bogotá to junction of the Meta and Orinoco rivers. [César Caviedes]

6924. Wood, Walter A. Recent glacier fluctuations in the Sierra Nevada de Santa Marta, Colombia (AGS/GR, 60:3, July 1970, p. 374-392)

Concludes that northerly exposure, i.e., orientation, is important in number and area covered by glaciers on Santa Marta, and that gradient seems to be major factor in mass wasting. The steeper the slope the less the mass wastage.

ECUADOR

6925. Acosta Solís, Misael. Lucha contra la sequía y la erosión en la mitad del mundo (SMHN/R, 30, dic. 1969, p. 155-191, map, plates)

Estimates that over 1,000,000ha. of arable land have been lost in the Sierra of Ecuador because of erosion. Selects zone in northern Río Guayllabamba Valley and investigates its climate and causes of erosion. Includes discussion of reforestation, with types of plants, conditions of growth, and results, covering a 20-year period.

6926. Baird, D. M. Sands of the Galápagos (RCGS/CGJ, 84:3, March 1972, p. 92-97, plates)

Discusses organic débris beaches and those made of rock and mineral particles.

6927. Ballesteros Guerrero, Carlos. Desarrollo en el Napo ecuatoriano: la precooperativa agropecuaria y de consumo y mercados San José de Puerto Quinche (IESSC/C, 2:5, 1967, p. 81-124)

Literary remarks on ethnography, agriculture, and natural resources of a community near the Napo River, Ecua. [César Caviedes]

6928. Blomberg, Rolf. Imbabura: bergsindianernas land. Stockholm, Bok Och Bild, 1967. 102 p., maps, plates.

Account of mountain Indians of Imababura province. Author is Swedish film-maker who provides superficial description of world of high Andes. [R. V. Shaw]

6929. Borrero Vintimilla, Antonio. Geografía económica del Ecuador (UC/A, 27:1-2, enero/junio 1971, p. 15-120)

Contribution on geography of Ecuador includes position, major physical divisions, climates, vegetation, and introduction to human geography. Country is divided into traditional Costa, Sierra, and Oriente. Useful statistical data and literature.

6930. ———. Geografía económica del Ecuador (continuación) (UC/A, 28:3-4, julio/dic. 1971, p. 9-104)

Summary section deals with Ecuador's demography. Also reviews bibliography, sociology, economy, populations, locations and other aspects of Indian life. Presents general population census data from first census (1780) to 1962 along with urban-rural relationships, migration tendencies, and sociological phenomena. Physical geography discussed in terms of geology and soils.

6931. Dalmasso, E. and P. Fillon. Influences comparées de Quito et Guayaquil, Equateur (AGF/B, 382/383, juin/nov. 1970, p. 213-219)

Costal and Sierran contrasts in Ecuador are exemplified by differences in migratory movements. Sierran city of Quito attracts only residents from Sierra, whereas Guayaquil receives migrants from entire country. Observations about banking and commerce are similar. Quito maintains its position with regard to industry because of hard-goods manufacturing and reinforcement from new oil fields in the Oriente.

6932. Ecuador. Ministerio de Agricultura y Ganadería. Plan nacional de political cafetera del Ecuador, 1970 a 1973. Quito, 1970, 99 l., tables.

In 1968, coffee plantations covered 170,000ha. and made 19 percent of total export of Ecuador's agrarian products. About 325,000 people found work on these plantations. Fertilizers and improvements in marketing should raise present coffee production, which produces 57 percent of Ecuador's coffee. [César Caviedes]

6933. Ellis, Bengt. Landet närmast solen: en resa i Ecuador. Stockholm, P.A. Norstedt & Söners, 1967. 133 p., map, plates.

Swedish traveler's report of excursion through almost impenetrable jungles beyond Andes into interior of Ecuador. Some settlements in these remote regions are still outposts of civilized world where travelers from Europe see a life not much different from the 16th century. [R. V. Shaw]

6934. Kahrer, Wilhelm. Die eozänen Konglomerate von San Lorenzo in Manabí: West-Ecuador (Neues Jahrbuch für Geologie und Paläontologie [Stuttgart, FRG] 6 Juni 1971, p. 345-347)

Describes large block conglomerates 15km southwest of Manta in Manabí province, Ecua. Supposedly transported some 130km from the Cordillera Occidental by means of water and earth movements.

Loor, Wilfrido. Manabí desde 1822. See *HLAS 34:2594.*

6935. Momsen, Richard P., Jr. Priorities for the Guayas basin (GM, 43:3, Dec. 1970, p. 167-176)

Northern part of the Guayas Basin, Ecua., has greater natural advantages for development than the rest, but is only now being settled. Northern section is therefore recommended for future development.

Peñaherrera de Costales, Piedad and **Alfredo Costales Samaniego.** Resultados del primer censo indígena de la provincia del Pichincha. See item 1469.

6936. Sanchéz Baron, Ricardo. La vía marginal en la zona de la selva amazónica ecuatoriana: la via interoceánica de la selva amazónica; Guayaquil, Cuenca, Gualaceo, Limón, Río Morona. Guayaquil, Ecua., Univ. de Guayaquil, Depto. de Publicaciones, 1967. 29 p.

Student report published by the Univ. of Guayaquil which concludes that the *via marginal* is not desirable for Ecuador. On the other hand, the highway from the Pacific to Amazonian region is considered desirable.

6937. Temme, Mathilde. Entwicklungsprobleme in den südamerikanischen Anden (GR, 23:12, dez. 1971, p. 472-480, maps)

Eight small basins and valleys constitute main physical components of farm locations in Loja province. Discusses one of them, Valle de Catamayo, at 1275m above sea level, with approximately 7,000 inhabitants. Low population level, abnormal movement of population, and drought characterize the valley. Agrarian reform and industrialization are both occurring, although author feels progress is hindered by unharmonious economic and social activities.

6938. Vollmar, Rainer. Die Entwicklungsregion von Santo Domingo de los Colorados, Ecuador (GEB/E, 102:2/3, 1971, p. 208-226, illus., tables)

Investigation of pioneer settlement of Santo Domingo de los Colorados, according to geographical conditions, migration aspects and socio-economic bases. Santo Domingo is situated at a crossroad where three major highways intersect. Although in 1940 only 40 huts were there, in 1970 the settlement had some 15,000 people. Economy consists of agriculture, wood production, and small industry. Settlers come mainly from the highlands. Most of them have holdings between 20 and 50ha. The latter are laid out in strips (250m × 2500m) parallel to each other and extending from road frontage inland to the forest.

GUYANA

6939. Aubert, Michel Cl. Paradis en enfer: la Guyane française. Paris, Editions Robert Laffont, 1972. 300 p., bibl., map, plates.

Adventure-oriented introduction to French Guyana with emphasis on Indian inhabitants of the Amazon rainforest. [T. L. Martinson]

6940. Berrangé, Jevan P. and **Richard L. Johnson.** A guide to the upper Essequibo River, Guyana (RGS/RJ, 138:1, March 1972, p. 41-52)

Geologists from Overseas Division of London's Institute of Geological Sciences, made canoe journeys on the upper Essequibo River and report in this article on falls, navigation problems and limits, and corrected locations of various physical phenomena. A new map of upper Essequibo drainage basin has been produced as a result of this investigation which took place in 1969.

6941. Donner, R. W. Suriname en de E.E.G. Paramaribo, n.p., 1962. 119 p.

Presents and discusses purchase of tropical agricultural products from Surinam by Europe and US, and position of Surinam in confrontation with economic blocks in the New and Old World. [César Caviedes]

6942. Fletcher, Alan Mark. The land and the people of the Guianas. Foreword [by] L. F. S. Burnham. Philadelphia, Pa., J. B. Lippincott, 1972. 149 p., map, plates (Portraits of the nations series)

Largely historical account of the growth of present social, economic and political systems of all the Guianas. Much editorializing on author's part. [T. L. Martinson]

6943. Richardson, Bonham C. Guyana's "green revolution:" social and ecological problems in an agricultural development programme (UWI/CQ, 18:1, March 1972, p. 14-23)

Modern rice development programs are being applied in various parts of the world. Article deals with aspects of the Green Revolution in Guyana. Large holdings are deemed fundamental to use of modern techniques of water control, but consolidation into government estates is not recommended. Support of small-scale village producers is considered mandatory for any program.

PARAGUAY

6944. Weil, Thomas E. and others. Area handbook for Paraguay. Washington, The American Univ., Foreign Area Studies, 1972. 316 p., bibl., maps, tables (DA-PAM, 550-156)

Part of well-known series dealing with countries of the world. Social, political, economic, and national security chapters give quick summaries of current conditions with some historical interpretation. Lack of sufficient maps and neglect of non-English sources except for some from Paraguay are weaknesses.

PERU

6945. Alers, Oscar J., and **Richard P. Appelbaum.** La migración en el Perú, un inventario de proposiciones. Lima, Instituto de Estudios Peruanos, Centro de Estudios de Población y Desarrollo, 1968. 43 p., bibl., tables (Serie original, 2)

This study emphasizes impact of urban environment on migrants coming from Sierra to Lima, Peru. Vivid image of socio-economic aspirations of newcomers. [César Caviedes]

6946. Amiran, David H. K. El Desierto de Sechura, Peru: problems of agricultural use of deserts (PAIGH/G, 71, dez. 1969, p. 7-12, illus.)

Agricultural use of Desert of Sechura, especially at lower course of Río Chima, is illustrated by example of cotton-growing Hacienda of Mallares. [César Caviedes]

6947. Brisseau, J. Aspects de l'influence du Cuzco dans sa région (AGF/B, 382/383, juin/nov. 1970, p. 203-212, map)

Population of Cuzco has doubled since 1940 as result of new roads and increased tourism. Development of industry has also stimulated growth, although urban market is not large enough to absorb all production. City demands for fresh vegetables, fruit, and dairy products are slowly changing urban-rural relationships near city.

6948. Clapperton, Chalmers M. and **Patrick Hamilton.** Peru beneath its eternal threat (GM, 43:9, June 1971, p. 632-639)

Describes mountain areas east of Chimbote, and summarizes recent earthquakes, pointing out dangers of poor construction of settlement structures as well as poor location.

6949. Cobbing, E. J. and **W. S. Pitcher.** Plate tectonics and the Peruvian Andes (NWJS, 240:99, Nov. 1972, p. 51-53, map, table)

Discusses geological evidence which does not accord with plate tectonic models of development of Peruvian and Bolivian Andes. Believes that true oceanic rocks are absent along Peruvian continental margin. Assumption that this is an active subduction zone between plates would mean that oceanic materials have been carried under the continent—an order of events not depicted by evidence on the land.

6950. Cortázar, Pedro Felipe. Departamento de San Martín. Lima, Ioppe, 1971? 158 p., maps, plates (Col. Documental del Perú, 22)

Part of series dealing with Peruvian departments. Discusses tourism, folklore, history, colonization, agriculture, industry, and politics, with photographs and some elementary maps.

Costa Villavicencio, Lázaro. Diccionario de geografía. See item 6528.

6951. Delavaud, Claude Collin. Les rapports entre villes et campagnes dans les départements nord-côtiers du Pérou (ULIG/C, 15:35, sept. 1971, p. 233-250, maps, plates, tables)

Analysis of urban population in three departments on Peru's north coast. Cities are inhabited by rural folk and only some 30 percent are economically active. Except for three capital cities, only four agglomerated settlements may be called urban. Others are agricultural villages. By contrast, sugar plantations are highly urbanized. Absence of real urban network is accentuated by centralized administration. Result is an urbanization of rural areas and a ruralization of cities.

6952. Deler, Jean-Paul. Croissance accélérée et formes de sous-développement urbain à Lima, avec 4 planches hors-texte et 4 figures dans le texte (SGB/COM, 23:89, jan./mars 1970, p. 73-94)

Phenomenal growth-rates of Lima are closely related to city's under-development. Since 1940 total population has almost tripled because of large-scale migratory movements from smaller group settlements to capital. (1941-45: 88,356 people; 1961-65: 400,000) Barriadas are spreading to Callao along road from Lima, and to seaside resorts, now comprising half the dwellings in greater Lima.

6953. Jätzold, Ralph. Luftbild der verschüttete Stadt Yungay, Peru (GEB/E, 102:2/3, 1971, p. 108-117, illus., plates)

Compares destruction of Yungay, Peru in May, 1970, with that of Pompey and Martinique and analyzes causes. Utilizes air photo map interpretation effectively.

6954. Ortiz Vergara, Pedro. Un caso de colonización en la selva alta del Peru: "Aucayacu" (IBEAS/EA, 1:3, 1970, p. 111-122)

Description of settlement proceedings near Aucayacu, second population center of importance after Tingo María, downstream along Huallaga river. Federation of campesinos has resulted in strife with system of cooperatives fostered by agrarian reform agency.

6955. La reforma agraria: realizaciones y proyectos (IESSC/C, 5:14, mayo/agosto 1970, p. 124-133, tables)

Peruvian land reform has affected only 4.8 percent of total cropland which is being worked. From total population of 13,500,000, land has been distributed to only 34,019 families. Figures show slow progress of land reform in that country. [César Caviedes]

6956. Salazar L., Arturo. Lima: teoría y práctica de la ciudad. Lima, Campodónico*ediciones*, 1968. 166 p., illus., plates.

All the experience gained by author as alderman in city of Lima is condensed in this book, which is quite recommendable as an introduction to sociological, urban and geographical studies of Peru's capital. Underscored are problems related to overgrowth and insufficient city planning. [César Caviedes]

6956a. Suchl, Jan. Cresta konči pod Huascaranem (The path ends below Huascaran). Praha, Olympia, 1972. 104 p., plates.

Story of Czech mountain-climbing expedition in Peru in 1970, in which all 15 members of the expedition lost their lives, 14 as a result of the May 31 earthquake. Includes photographs taken during expedition and biographies of members. [A. R. Navon]

Varese, Stefano. Investigaciones en la selva. See item 1326.

6957. Wesche, Rolf. Recent migration to the Peruvian montaña (ULIG/C, 15:35, sept. 1971, p. 251-266, illus., maps)

Analyzes settlement in Peruvian Montaña by presenting issues in national demographic and economic contexts, by discussing extent and nature of colonization to date, and by detailed analysis of types of migration (seasonal labor, suitcase farming, and permanent relocation). Reference is made to population flows into and out of Montaña. Excellent maps.

URUGUAY

6958. United States. Department of Agriculture. Economic Research Service. A survey of agriculture in Uruguay. Washington, GPO, 1970. 52 p., bibl., maps, plates, tables (ERS-foreign, 299)

More than nine-tenths of Uruguay's agricultural area is pasture. Production of livestock for beef and wool is leading farm enterprise. Wheat and oilseed are principal cash-crops. Production of grain fluctuates because of weather anomalies. Since 1950, stagnation characterizes Uruguay's agriculture. Reasons are: low international prices for beef and wool, unreasonable export taxes created for support of high cost industries, social services and bureaucracy. Agricultural improvement policies undertaken since 1965. These policies regard pasture management, only an unclearly stated land reform and improvement on farm practices. Not until 1968, however, did government make a serious effort to implement them. Future of Uruguay's agriculture will depend on degree of economic and political stability country may attain; both goals seem, however, very far in the future.

VENEZUELA

6959. Aristeguieta, Leandro. Arboles ornamentales de Caracas. Dibujos de Harijs Ebersteins. Caracas, Univ. Central de Venezuela,

Consejo de Desarrollo Científico y Humanístico, 1962. 218 p., illus.

Poor landscape planning in Caracas' parks, plazas, gardens and avenues has inspired this systematic look at types of trees cultivated by city authorities. Offers suggestions for the improvements of landscaping.

6960. Armas Alfonso, Alfredo. ¡Qué de recuerdos de Venezuela! Fotos [por] Graziano Gasparini. Caracas, Ediciones Armitano, 1970. 1 v. (Unpaged) plates (Serie de libros de arte de Ediciones Armitano)

Poetic text accompanies impressive color photographs of Venezuela.

6961. Carpio Castillo, Rubén. El Golfo de Venezuela: mar territorial y plataforma continental. Caracas, Ediciones del Congreso de la República, 1971. 140 p., maps.

Discussion of off-shore jurisdiction and of continental shelf in Gulf of Venezuela.

6962. Congreso Geológico Venezolano, *IV, Caracas, 1969.* Memoria. t. 1, Acta final; Resúmenes; Guía de las excursiones; Geología general y estatigrafía; Geología minera y petrolera. Caracas, Ministerio de Minas e Hidrocarburos, Dirección de Geología, 1971. 552 p., bibl., fold. maps, maps, tables (Boletín de Geología; publicación especial, 5)

Valuable volume offers resumés of numerous papers presented in four commission meetings. Subjects are: general geology and stratigraphy; tectonism, rock formation, and geochemistry; mineral geology and petroleum; and geohydrology, geotechniques, and geophysics. Geographers will find interesting discussion of Andean geology, especially the Barquisimeto Trough.

6963. Contreras, Agustin. Resumen climatológico y mareográfico 1968 Punta de Piedras, Estado Nueva Esparta, Venezuela (SCNLS/M, 30:86, mayo/agosto 1970, p. 75-101, tables)

Surprisingly high annual range of temperature on Margarita island (17.7°C) is established from climatological data for period 1962-66. Also discusses solar radiation, insolation, humidity and evaporation.

6964. Coppens, Walter and others. Pegoncito, estado de Aragua, Venezuela: un estudio de desarrollo rural local (SCNLS/M, 31:88, enero/abril 1971, p. 5-113, illus., maps, plates, table)

Informative eight-day anthropological-sociological investigation of group of 102 persons whose families know no marriage customs but who otherwise follow precepts of Catholic Church. Community bases its economy on production of maize, beans, and cotton in spite of fact that region's principal agricultural items are tobacco and beef cattle. Part of maize is sold, but group's economy is near subsistence level. Overpopulation is cited as basic. Suggests substitution of maize by milo along with larger holdings.

6965. Eden, Michael J. Scientific exploration in Venezuelan Amazonas (RGS/GJ, 137:2, June 1971, p. 149-156)

Describes expedition by hovercraft in 1968 along the Río Negro-Orinoco route following the Casiquiare canal. Purpose of expedition was to demonstrate ability of hovercraft along rivers intermittently obstructed by rapids, and to gather scientific data. Hydrological studies, vegetation analysis, and ethnobotanical investigation were carried out.

6966. Gallovich, Eugenio and **Luis Aguilera L.** Ensayos sísmicos de refracción efectuados en la Isla Aves (SCNLS/M, 30:87, sept./dic. 1970, p. 206-212, map, tables)

Geological expedition to Aves Island, off north coast of Venezuela. Records refraction seismograph readings.

6967. Glynn, Peter W. A systematic study of the sphaeromatidae, crustacea: isopoda, of Isla Margarita, Venezuela, with descriptions of three new species (SCNLS/M, 30:85, enero/abril 1970, p. 5-48, bibl., illus., map, tables)

Discusses *sphaeromatidae* (Crustacea) with reference to surface currents moving northwesterly along the Brazilian coast and entering Caribbean Sea near Margarita. Stresses importance of biological factors in limiting migrations.

6968. Harris, David R. The ecology of Swidden cultivation in the Upper Orinoco rain forest, Venezuela (AGS/GR, 61:4, Oct. 1971, p. 475-495)

Examines swidden agricultural plots along the Casiquiare and Orinoco rivers during hovercraft expedition from Manaus to Trinidad via the Río Negro. Monocultural swiddens seem to be less stable but are less influenced in their moves by weeds than polycultural ones. Suggests great modification of rain-forest by such farming methods. Maize plantings seem to be more dependent than manioc on efficiency of clearing and burning. Thus ecological barriers may influence spread of maize agriculture in rainforest areas.

6969. Herranz M., Julián. Estudio sobre el mercado del coco en Venezuela. Valencia, Ven., Univ. de Carabobo, 1968. 94 p.

Ten chapters include: uses of coconut, cultivation, markets, and conclusions. Present production satisfies only 22 percent of Venezuelan needs.

6970. Koch, Conrad. La Colonia Tovar: Geschichte und Kultur einer alemannischen Siedlung in Venezuela. Basel, FRG, Pharos-Verlag Hansrudolf Schwabe, 1969. 336 p., maps, plates, tables.

Colony of Tovar was one of first foreign settlements in Venezuela, and dates from 1842. Whereas other colonies failed, Tovar has the distinction of surviving to become well-known tourist attraction not far west of Caracas. It has grown to municipio size and importance and has an expanding economy involving agricultural products and small industries. Thorough account of much interest to geographers.

6971. López, José Eliseo. La segunda excursión pedagógica de la Escuela de Geografía

(ULA/RG, 8:19, julio/dic. 1967, p. 167-176, illus., maps)

Observations on Las Mesas area where cultivation of peanuts and oil-extraction are the predominant economic activities. Includes notes on iron mining of Guayana and rise of new industrial center of Ciudad Guayana. [César Caviedes]

6972. Maloney, Neil J. Geología de la Isla de La Blanquilla y notas sobre el Archipiélago de Los Hermanos, Venezuela Oriental (AVAC/ACV, 22:1, 1971, p. 6-10, maps)

Islands, whose geology is studied here, are on a platform some 125km north of the Venezuelan coast. La Blanquilla is a low island only 11km wide. Discusses terraces and elaborates upon composition of bedrock. Los Hermanos represents a group of seven islands with mountainous topography. Highly fractured rocks are present.

6973. Monasterio, Maximina; Guillermo Sarmiento; and Juan Silva. Reconocimiento ecológico de los Llanos Occidentales. Pt. 3, El sur del estado de Barinas (AVAC/ACV, 22:5, 1971, p. 153-169, illus., maps, tables)

Ecological survey of part of Barinas State, western Venezuela, in a forested area. Rapid deforestation of savana forest and replacement by grasslands and crops characterize this region. Soil descriptions and lists of natural vegetation varieties are especially useful in this series. Good bibliography.

6974. Ojeda Olaechea, Alonso and Jorge Santana. Situación actual del campo venezolano. Caracas, Editorial Cantaclaro, 1970. 183 p., bibl., plates, tables.

Communist's interpretation of investigation of the National Agrarian Institute by the Centro de Estudios de Desarrollo (CENDES). Contains usual diatribes and negative conclusions which make it impossible to consider it as a scholarly work.

6975. Robinson, David J. Evolución en el comercio del Orinoco a mediados del siglo XIX (PAIGH/G, 71, dez. 1969, p. 14-43, illus., tables)

Between 1830-60, the lower course of the Orinoco river was opened to international trade, especially with the US and English colonies in Caribbean. Export items were hides, furs and cattle, while clothes, manufactured goods and food were among the principal imports. [César Caviedes]

6976. Sarmiento, Guillermo; Maximina Monasterio; and Juan Silva. Reconocimiento ecológico de los Llanos Occidentales. Pt. 1, Las unidades ecológicas regionales (AVAC/ACV, 22:2, 1971, p. 52-60, bibl., map, tables)

Western Llanos vegetation is grouped into four main types: forests, humid savannas, dry savannas and swamps. Seven landscapes and 31 land-systems are recognized in this area. Color map illustrates various subdivisions of ecological factors.

6977. ———. Reconocimiento ecológico de los Llanos Occidentales: pt. 4, The western part of Apure State (AVAC/ACV, 22:5, 1971, p. 170-180, maps, tables)

Ecological study of an area mostly covered with humid savannas along the Colombian border. Analyzes present and potential land use according to an integrated consideration of land forms, soils, and principal plant communities. Concludes that physical geofactors limit production of commercial crops and that agriculture is possible only on soils of forested zones where drainage is better.

6978. Silva, Juan; Maximina Monasterio; and Guillermo Sarmiento. Reconocimiento ecológico de los Llanos Occidentales. Pt. 2, El norte del Estado Barinas (AVAC/ACV, 22:2, 1971, p. 60-71, maps)

Continuation of item 6976. Northern part of Barinas state, Ven. was investigated applying same methods to determine five landscapes and 16 land-systems in which ecological dynamics and land potentiality are discussed.

6979. Texier, Jean Marie. Acción colectiva en Venezuela (IESSC/C, 7, enero/abril 1968, p. 121-151)

After reviewing structure and function of various cooperative societies in the world, author takes closer look at coffee-plantations in Caldera, Barinas state, where, as a result of collective action, production has grown, savings increased, and the individual's sense of responsibility has strengthened. [César Caviedes]

6980. Universidad de los Andes. Facultad de Economía. Los márgenes de comercialización de los productos agropecuarios en los Andes venezolanos. Mérida, Ven., 1969. 1 v. (Unpaged) (mimeo)

Mimeographed work presents an analysis of the vending of agricultural products in Venezuela. Data are from the early 1960's. Minimization of commercialization occurs because of market fluctuations and small holdings, largely, and because of ignorance of modern agriculture. Includes analysis of the margin of commercialization.

6981. Valladeres, Licia de Prado. Au Vénézuela: les villes du diamant: la naissance de San Salvador de Paul (ULIG/C, 15:35, sept. 1971, p. 396-402)

Analyzes development of new settlement based on diamond mines. Predicts that San Salvador de Paul will become a permanent settlement because of its favorable situation with respect to Ciudad Bolívar and Ciudad Guayana, as well as its good airport.

6982. Vareschi, Volkmar. Flora de los páramos de Venezuela. Mérida, Ven., Univ. de los Andes, Ediciones del Rectorado, 1970. 429 p., bibl., illus., maps, plates, tables.

Useful compendium of *páramo* plant life with color photographs, drawings, and soil associations.

6983. ———. Helechos. t. 1, *Lycopodiaceae-Aspidiaceae;* t. 2,*Aspleniaceae-Salviniaceae.* Caracas, Ministerio de Agricultura y Cría, Dirección de Recursos Renovables, Instituto Botánico, 1969. 2 v. (1032 p.) bibl., illus., tables (Flora de Venezuela, 1)

Two volumes fill gap in Venezuelan literature and will be welcomed by social scientists. Drawings and descriptions will facilitate field identification of plant types and permit comparison with sources like Decker for Brazil and Pérez Arbeláez for Colombia.

6984. Venezuela. Corporación Venezolana de Guayana. Electrificación del Caroní (CVG/EDELCA). Informe anual. Caracas, 1971. 73 p., illus., maps, plates, tables.

Annual report of the CVG electrification program for Venezuela states that the Guri dam, 75km south of Ciudad Guayana, stores enough water to supply electricity even in the dry season. Lake created occupies some 800km² and will be extended to 3,200km² in the third stage. Installed potential of Guri is 525 megawatts. When completed potential will reach 2,065 megawatts. System of transmission is being constructed. Total cost of project will be over 100 million dollars.

6985. ———. Oficina Central de Información. La reforma agraria en Venezuela. Caracas, 196?. 1 v. (Unpaged)

Resumé of agrarian reform activities in Venezuela during 1959-66 gathered from the Instituto Agrario Nacional, Banco Central, and national census data.

BRAZIL

KEMPTON E. WEBB

Professor of Geography
Director, Institute of Latin American Studies
Chairman, Department of Geography
Columbia University

METHODOLOGICAL INNOVATIONS ASSOCIATED WITH THE "new geography" practiced by European and North American colleagues, are making inroads upon Brazilian geography.

Markov chain applications applied to Brazil (item 7038) show the population in the year 2001 to be 180 million people with a per capita income of $1060 dollars. Functional analysis à la Ullman and Dacey (item 7103) has been applied to the cities of Santa Catarina State. Other items by Faissol (items 7058 and 7060) interpret skillfully the ideas of Berry, Harvey, James and Hartshorne and proclaim the usefulness of new concepts and techniques to Brazil's planning.

The Amazon boom associated with the trans-Amazon Highway and the new northern Perimetral Highway has produced several studies (items 7000, 7009, 7023-7024, 7107 and 7117).

Northeast Brazil, which formerly lacked basic inventory data, now abounds with studies ranging from water deficit (item 7114) to irrigation potential (item 7174), to food supply (item 7033) and sugar cane (item 7047).

The development process is the single most persistent theme in Brazil in the mid-1970's (item 7156), and all phases of development are considered relevant to geographical study. The two themes of most significant importance are those of urban planning (item 7109) and environmental problems. The awareness of the hazards of environmental destruction is heightening as studies of flooding and its causes (item 7045) and deforestation (item 7166) and landscape preservation (item 7171) are written.

The next *Handbook* will document the revolutionary changes in Brazilian food supply and marketing systems which are the result of extensive research since 1956 and the incredible network of CEASA (Centrais de Abastecimento, S.A.) installations which have been built within the last year. Most middlemen are being eliminated, and the efficiency of the system is having a salutory effect in the interior upon small independent farmers.

6986. Abreu, Alcides. Planejamento integral do desenvolvimento local no Centro-Oeste: um depositivo para a ação. Brasília, Companhia do Desenvolvimento do Planalto Central (CODEPLAN), 1967. 1 v. (Various pagings) tables (Série Estudos para o desenvolvimento, 1)

Broad conceptualization of the role of West Central Brazil. Too general and abstract to be of much use.

6987. Ackermann, Fritz Louis. Geologia e

fisiografia da região bragantina: Estado do Pará. Manaus, Bra., Conselho Nacional de Pesquisas [and] Instituto Nacional de Pesquisas da Amazônia, 1964. 90 p., bibl., illus., map, plates, tables (Cadernos da Amazônia)

Sketch of physiography of zone between Belém and Bragança. Comments on ground water and sandy soils of the area (up to 98 percent silica).

6988. Agroplan-Planejamento Agrícola Limitada, São Paulo. São João da Boa Vista. v. 1-2. São Paulo, 1970? 2 v. (Various pagings) maps, tables.

Poorly documented but typical example of a municipal inventory and planning document within which much useful information, of interest to geographers, may be obtained. Town located in hilly northeastern São Paulo state.

6989. Alagoas (state), Bra. Secretaria de Planejamento. Estado de Alagoas: diagnóstico geo-sócio-econômico. Introdução [por] Luíz Fernando de Oiticia Lima. Brasília?, n.p., n.d. 112 p., maps, tables (Micro relião programa, 5)

Superficial but useful profile of little-studied state of Northeast Brazil.

6990. Alegre, Marcos. Aspectos do fato urbano no Brasil: análise quantitativa pelo método cartográfico. Presidente Prudente, Bra., Faculdade de Filosofia (Ciências e Letras de Presidente Prudente, 1970. 290 p., bibl., fold. maps, maps, tables.

French doctoral thesis dealing with cartographic representation of quantitative urban analysis in Brazil. Lavishly illustrated. Substantive work.

6991. Alameida, Fernando Flávio Marques. Origem e evolução da plataforma brasileira. Rio, Ministério das Minas e Energia, Depto. Nacional da Produção Mineral, Divisão de Geologia e Mineralogia, 1967. 36 p., bibl., fold. map (Boletim, 241)

Tectonic history of the Brazilian Highlands, with extensive bibliography.

6992. Alvim, Paulo do T. and Milton Rosário. Cacau ontem e hoje. Bahía, Bra., Comissão Executiva do Plano de Recuperação Economico-Rural da Lavoura Cacaueira (CEPLAC) [and] Centro de Pesquisas do Cacau, 1972. 83 p., bibl., maps, plates, tables.

Basic data; little analysis. Useful maps and photos.

6993. Amábile, Francisco Walter and others. Mercado para transporte hidroviário no Médio Tietê. São Paulo, Secretaria de Transportes, Hidrovias, 1964. 1 v. (Various pagings) maps, tables.

Evaluation of possibilities for water transport along middle Tietê river. Results are inconclusive since success depends upon alternative systems of rail and road transport which are changing rapidly.

6994. Amazônia: tipos e aspectos; excertos de *Tipos e aspectos do Brasil*. Edição do Conselho Nacional de Geografia. Illustrações de Percy Lau. Prefácio de Leandro Tocantins. 2. ed. Rio, Superintendência do Desenvolvimento da Amazônia (SUDAM). 1966. 89 p., illus., maps.

Percy Lau's exquisite pen-and-ink drawings of life and livelihood in the Amazon North. Excerpted from the larger *Tipos e aspectos do Brasil* (see *HLAS 15:1289*).

6995. Amora, Manuel Albano. Pacatuba: geografia sentimental. Fortaleza, Bra., Editôra Henriqueta Galeno, 1972. 135 p., map, plates.

Sentimental.

6996. Anais da Associação dos Geógrafos Brasileiros. Vol. 14, 1960/1962 [i.e., 1968]- . São Paulo.

Major papers, proceedings and discussions pertaining to the Associação dos Geógrafos Brasileiros annual meetings in Londrina, Paraná state (1961) and Penedo, Alagoas state (1962). Includes brief history of the association founded in São Paulo in 1934 by Pierre Defontaine.

6997. ———. Vol. 15, 1962/1964 [i.e., 1969]- . São Paulo.

Proceedings and papers of the 18th and 19th general assemblies of the Associação dos Geógrafos Brasileiros (AGB) in, respectively, Jequié (1963) and Poços de Caldos (1964).

6998. Andrade, Manuel Correia de Oliveira. Geografia, região e desenvolvimento: introdução ao estudo do "aménagement du territoire." 2. ed. São Paulo, Editôra Brasiliense, 1971. 95 p., bibl.

Senior geographer of Northeast Brazil compares observations of Europe and Israel with Brazil regarding the role of geography in development.

6999. ———. Latifúndio, cana-de-açúcar e côco no norte de Alagoas (AGB/BPG, 45, junho 1968, p. 16-58, bibl., maps, plates, tables)

Interrelationships between land, man, and economic activities in the coastal area north of Maceió, backwater of Brazil.

7000. ———. Monte Alegre e a indústria de papel e celulose no Paraná. São Paulo, Associação dos Geógrafos Brasileiros, 1968. 64 p., fold. maps, maps, plates, (Avulso, 6)

Study of pulp-and-paper industry of the Klabin group concludes that profits of company did not benefit local populace very much. Area of Slavic colonization in Paraná Pine area.

7001. Andritzky, Georg. Baugeschechte des prä-Bambui-Kristallins im Gebeit Caratacá; Bendegó, Distrikt Uauá, Nord-Bahia, Brasilien (GV/GR, 60:3, Juni 1971, p. 1050-1061, illus., map)

Detailed evolutionary sequences in the Brazilian shield (northern Bahia state) are reconstructed for an area about 300 km^2 in extent. [R. C. Eidt]

7002. Araujo Filho, José Ribeiro de. O sítio e a vocação portuaria de Santos. São Paulo, Univ. de São Paulo, Instituto de Geografia, 1969. 23 p., bibl., fold. map (Geografia urbana, 5)

Observations on Santos' port function related to site and situation.

7003. Aspectos econômicos da mandioca. Rio, Ministério da Agricultura, Serviço de Informação Agrícola, 1967. 37 p., tables (Estudos brasileiros, 25)

Concise and useful presentation of the facts of production and industrialization of manioc in Brazil. It requires modernization of its production.

7004. Associação de Crédito e Assistência Rural de Mato Grosso, (ACARMAT) *Cuiabá, Bra.* Plano de trabalho. Cuiabá, Bra., 1970. 89 1., fold. maps, maps, tables.

The government of Mato Grosso recognizes the threat which the state's slow development in agricultural sector poses to the states whole growth. The key is to raise productively. Useful data.

7005. Associação de Crédito e Assistência Rural do Espírito Santo (ACARES), *Vitória, Bra.* Programa estratégico, 1970. Vitória, Bra., 1969. 156 p., maps, tables.

Basic agricultural facts of life for little-studied Espírito Santo state. ACAR programs have been successful in raising welfare levels in other states of Brazil.

7006. Astiz, Lilia Veirano de. Geografía de Brasil: lineamientos generales para su enseñanza. Montevideo, Instituto de Cultural Uruguayo-Brasileño, 1969. 63 p., bibl., fold. maps, tables (Publicaciones, 18)

Short regional geography of Brazil written by an Uruguayan for Uruguayan students.

7007. Azevedo, Aroldo de. O Brasil e suas regiões; Brasil, país de contrastes: Brasileira, Nordeste Brasileiro, Sudeste do Brasil, Sul do Brasil, Centro-Oeste Brasileiro. São Paulo, Companhia Editôra Nacional, 1971. 391 p., maps, plates, tables.

Respectable regional geography of Brazil written for junior high school students by the dean of paulista geographers.

7008. Balhana, Altiva Pilatti and others. Campos Gerais: estruturas agrárias. Curitiba, Bra., Univ. Federal do Paraná, Faculdade de Filosofia, 1968. 268 p., bibl., maps, tables.

Excellent study of Witmarsun, Paraná, by a team of social scientists who examined the transformation of agrarian structures in a Mennonite community. Well documented.

7009. Banco da Amazônia (firm), *Manaus, Bra.* Desenvolvimento econômico da Amazônia: redação preliminar. Apresentação [por] Armando Dias Mendes. Belém, Bra., Editôra da Univ. Federal do Pará, 1966. 290 p., tables.

An economist's and banker's assessment of Amazon's resources and prospects. Analysis attacks myth that area is good only for low productive extractive activities such as rubber gathering. Recommends improvement of access by building roads and increasing competition.

7010. Banco do Nordeste do Brasil (firm), *Fortaleza, Bra.* **Departamento de Estudos Econômicos do Nordeste (ETENE). Divisão de Agricultura.** Aspectos econômicos da suinocultura no Nordeste. Fortaleza, Bra., 1970. 83 p., fold. map, tables.

Statistics which present a profile of growing hog industry in Northeast Brazil. Conclusions recommend integration of hog production with use of feed by products of other industries.

7011. Barbosa, Getúlio V. and **David Marcio Santos Rodrigues.** Guadrilátero ferrífero. Belo Horizonte, Bra., Univ. Federal de Minas Gerais, Instituto Central de Geo-Ciências, 1967. 130 1. (mimeo) fold. maps, tables.

Introduction to other aspects as well as the all-important geology of this iron-rich zone. Land forms and economic history are described. There are a number of United States Geological Survey professional papers cited on the area.

7012. Barros, Ernani Thimóteo de. Aplicações dos resultados do censo demográfico (IBGE/RBE, 32:126, abril/junho 1971, p. 191-201)

More summary census results with emphasis on sex, age structure, education, alphabetization, and internal migration.

7013. Bernardes, Nilo. A geografia e o planejamento regional. São Paulo, Univ. de São Paulo, Instituto de Geografia, 1969. 27 p., bibl. (Geografia e planejamento, 2)

Brief explanation of how geographers can and have contributed to regional planning.

7014. Brasil/açúcar. Apresentação [por] Sylvio Pélico Filho. Rio, Ministério da Indústria e Comércio, Instituto do Acúcar e do Alcool, Divisão Administrativa, Serviço de Documentação, 1972. 243 p., illus., plates, tables (Col. Canavieira, 8)

General history and description of sugar in Brazil.

7015. Braun, Oscar P. G. Contribuição à geomorfologia do Brasil Central (IBGE/R, 32:3, julho/set. 1970, p. 3-39, bibl., illus., maps, plates, tables)

Updating of landform history of central Brazil. Excellent air photos.

7016. Brazil. Centro de Coordenação Industrial para o Plano Habitacional. Instituto de Desenvolvimento de Guanabara. A construção habitacional no Brasil. Rio, Banco Nacional de Habitação, 1971. 160 p., tables.

Analytical history of residential construction in Brazil of interest to urbanists and historians.

7017. ———. Congresso. Câmara dos Deputados. Comissão Especial do Polígono das Sêcas. Palestras dos Secretários de Agricultura dos Estados da região Nordeste, proferidas no Plenário da Comissão, no período de agosto a setembro de 1971. Brasília, 1971. 262 p. (Serie Comissões especiais, 4)

Unedited transcription of a conference of all secretaries of agriculture of northeastern states. Lack of structure makes comments less useful.

7018. ———. Departamento Nacional de Obras Contra as Sêcas. Compilação dos dados hidrológicos do Nordeste. Brasília, 1970? 327 p., tables.

Gold mine of monthly stream gauge readings of all eleven river basins in states of Ceará, Rio Grande do Norte and Paraiba. Hard evidence of water deficit condition of most of the interior of Northeast Brazil.

7019. ———. Instituto Brasileiro de Reforma Agraria (IBRA). Area prioritaria de Brasília: síntesis. Brasília, 1966. 24 p., maps, plates.

Focus on problems and areas of greatest need lying within about 300 kilometers of Brasília. Air photos used.

7020. ———. Cadastro de imoveis rurais: resultados. Rio, 1967. 1 v. (Unpaged) tables (Cadernos, serie 8:13/14)

Summary of cadastral survey of rural properties in Sergipe taken in 1965.

7022. ———. Marinha. Diretoria de Hidrografia e Navegação. Evoluções típicas do tempo no Brasil. Rio, 1970. 1 v. (Various pagings) maps.

Synoptic weather maps showing at large scale development of air mass patterns through time. Traces advance of polar air mass northward over Brazil.

7023. ———. Ministério da Agricultura. Instituto Nacional de Colonização e Reforma Agraria (INCRA). Secretaria de Planejamento e Coordenação. Projeto de colonização Sidney Girão. Brasília, 1971. 161 p., illus., maps, tables.

Operational plans for a colonization project located along the Guajara-Mirim-Sburña highway.

7024. ———. Ministério das Minas e Energia. Departamento Nacional da Produção Mineral. 5[i.e., Quinto] Distrito—Norte: contribuição do Departamento Nacional da Produção Mineral no desenvolvimento geo-econômico da região norte; documento básico. Rio, 1969. 105 p., bibl., fold. maps (Publicação especial, 7)

Preliminary inventory of mineral resources in the Amazon North and 10-year plan for development of selected deposits. Maps of occurrences; geology and air photo coverage. El Dorado lives!

7025. ———. Relatório das atividades de 1970: programa de realizações para 1971. Brasília, 1971. 72 p., maps, plates, tables.

Vivid cartographic portrayal of distribution of thermal and hydroelectric power sources in Brazil as well as information on all aspects of mining and energy production.

7026. ———. Plano Decenal de Desenvolvimento Econômico e Social. Agricultura e abastecimento. t. 4[v. 2]: Abastecimento: versão preliminar. Rio? 1967? 140 p., tables.

This preliminary study is only one of seven large projects attempting to lay out an inventory of problems and a conceptualization of goals for Brazil's military government. There exists much data on food supply in Brazil. It remains for someone to really do something with the information.

7026a. Brazil: land tenure conditions and socioeconomic development of the agricultural sector. Washington, Organization of American States, Inter-American Committee for Agricultural Development (CIDA), 1966. 609 p., bibl., maps, tables.

Extremely worthwhile and detailed examination of single most important topic of rural Brazil. Includes case studies of 11 municipios representing diverse land tenure situations. Conclusions stress private benefits and social waste of the *latifundio;* distinction of power versus law in social relations. First rate contribution. Chapter headings: "Introduction;" "Agriculture and the Brazilian Economy;" "The Monopolization of Land Resources in Brazil;" "Definitions and Methods Used to Classify Farms;" "Economic and Social Aspects of Brazil's Land Tenure Systems with Special Emphasis on the Latifundio-Minifundio Complex;" "The Economic Consequences of Brazil's Tenure System;" "Concluding Remarks."

7027. Brinkman, W. L.; M. N. Goes Ribeiro; and J. B. Pate. Soil temperatures in the tertiary region of Central Amazonia (Acta Amazônica [Instituto Nacional de Pesquisas da Amazonia, Manaus, Bra.] 1:1, abril 1971, Unpaged)

Actual daily soil temperatures were taken at three depths (30, 50, and 70 cm) at Km 26 of the Manaus-Itacoatiara Road. Diurnal ranges are less than 0.3°C. Period July 1968-July 1969.

7028. Canteiro, João Ruy. Construções: seus custos de reprodução na capital de São Paulo de 1939 a 1970 [and] Terrenos: subsídios à técnica da avaliação. 2. ed. São Paulo, Editôra Pini, 1971. 80 p., bibl., illus., tables.

Nuts-and-bolts presentation of urban building costs of construction and of land appraisal procedures in São Paulo city 1939-70. This period was a roller coaster of soaring costs and inflation and urban sprawl. Practical guide on how to bid construction jobs and estimate all costs depending on age, style and location of site.

7029. Cardoso, Lamartine. Geografia econômica do Brasil. 5. ed. rev., ampliada e atualizada. São Paulo, Edições Fortaleza, 1972. 231 p., bibl., fold. maps, illus., maps, tables.

Conventional superficial sketch of Brazil. Most interesting part deals with national integration of Amazon into total effective territory.

7030. Carta da produção de Minas Gerais. Belo

Horizonte, Bra., Secretaria de Estado da Agricultura, Depto. de Estudos Rurais, 1967. 31 p.

True summary of plans and projects being undertaken by Minas Gerais state in farming and livestock areas.

7031. Carvalho, Carlos Miguel Delgado de and **Therezinha de Castro.** Geografia humana: política e econômica. 2. ed. Editado pelo Conselho Nacional de Geografia. Rio, Instituto Brasileiro de Geografia e Estatística, Serviço Gráfico, 1967. 332 p., maps, plates, tables.

Founder of modern geography in Brazil between two World Wars has added another volume to his long list of published works. Major sections are human groups, habitat, productive use of soil, and industry, commerce and communications. Methodological treatment reflects an older, more European orientation.

7032. Cavalcanti, Clóvis de Vasconcelos. Mercados para a pesca em Aracajú. Recife, Bra., Superintendência do Desenvolvimento do Nordeste (SUDENE) [and] Instituto Joaquim Nabuco de Pesquisas Sociais (IJNPS), 1971. 119 p., tables.

Straight study of demand potential for fish in Sergipe's capital city.

7032a. Cavalcanti, Mário de Barros. Da SPVEA a SUDAM: 1964-1967. Belém, Bra., Imprensa Universitária do Pará, 1967. 705 p., tables.

Major general Cavalcanti reports in considerable detail on efforts to open the Amazon basin as well as to link Brasília to the coast. [P. B. Taylor, Jr.]

7033. Ceará Pescas, S. A. (CEPESCA), Fortaleza, Bra. Programa integrado de pescado do Estado do Ceará. Fortaleza, Bra., Governo do Estado do Ceará, 1971? 1 v. (Unpaged) maps, tables.

Fish supply possibilities for the entire state of Ceará with aim of stimulating production and marketing.

7034. Ceron, Antônio Olívio and **José Alexandre Felizola Diniz.** Tipologia da agricultura: questões metodológicas e problemas de aplicação ao Estado de São Paulo (IBGE/R, 32:3, julho/set. 1970, p. 41-71, bibl., tables)

Application of methodology of International Geographic Union (IGU) Agricultural Typology Commission characterizing São Paulo agriculture.

7035. Chaves, Jonas Leite. Uma política agrícola para o desenvolvimento da Paraíba: estudos preliminares. João Pessôa, Bra., Associação dos Engenheiros Agrônomos da Paraíba, 1970. 64 p., fold. maps.

Good overview of Paraíba state, with priority suggestions for agriculture.

7036. Chaves, Maria Paula Ramos. Belém: onde se afirman as promessas da Amazônia; aspectos históricos e modernos. Belém, Bra., Grafisa, 1970. 1 v. (Unpaged) bibl., illus., plates.

Photos and description of Belém, largest city and water-gateway to the Amazon.

7037. Coelho, Francisco Ananias de Paula and **Raúl Suárez Inclán.** Considerações preliminares das condições agrícolas e do uso atual dos solos da zona fisiográfica de Baturité. Fortaleza, Bra., Superintendência do Desenvolvimento Econômico e Cultural (SUDEC), Divisão de Biblioteca e Documentação, 1967, 36 p., bibl., fold. map.

Extract from authors' study (item 7173). Physical characteristics of one of the important "serras" or highland oases 50 miles south of Fortaleza. Includes detailed soils map. Paper delivered at the XI Congresso de Ciência do Solo, held in Brasília, June 1967.

7038. Cole, John P.; Speridião Faissol; and **M.J. McCullagh.** Projeção da população do Brasil: aplicação do método Cadei de Markov (IBGE/R, 32:4, out./dez. 1970, p. 173-207, maps, tables)

Markov chain statistical application projects Brazil's population in the year 2001 to be 180 million with a per capita income of $1,060 dollars. Also presents regional variations.

7039. Companhia Agrícola Imobiliária e Colonizadora (CAIC), São Paulo. Projeto de colonização da Fazenda Pirituba. São Paulo, 1969. 1 v. (Various pagings) fold. maps, maps, tables.

Basic plan of a colonization project including specifications of house types, administration, land use, etc., and of land evaluation before colonization. Good for a before/after study.

7040. Companhia do Desenvolvimento do Planalto Central (CODEPLAN), Brasília. Estudo da população e da renda no Distrito Federal. Apresentação [por] Octavio Odílio de Oliveira Bitencourt. Brasília, 1972. 122 p., tables.

Projection of population in federal district (Brasília) in 1980 is around one million.

7041. Congresso Brasileiro do Cacau, I, Itabuna, Bra., 1967. Anais do . . . Bahía, Bra., Federação da Agricultura do Estado da Bahía, Confederação Nacional da Agricultura, 1967? 407 p., plates, tables.

Proceedings of first Brazilian congress on cacau provides insights into problems and prospects of the cacau "establishment," which is basic to the economic health of southern coastal Bahía especially.

7042. Conselho de Desenvolvimento de Extremo Sul (CODESUL), Florianópolis, Bra. Cultura e aproveitamento da mandioca en Santa Catarina. Florianópolis, Bra., 1972. 76 1., maps, tables.

How the "bread of the tropics" is grown, processed and marketed in Santa Catarina, an important source of production outside of Northeast Brazil and the Amazon North.

7043. ———. Utilização e renovação de recursos florestais em Santa Catarina. Florianópolis, Bra., 1971. 79 l., bibl., maps, tables.

Global view of forest resource situation in southern Brazil with emphasis upon modern forest management needs and technology benefits. Devastation of the araucaria conifer forests is alarmingly rapid.

7044. Consultoria e Planejamento de Hidráulica e Saneamento (firm), *São Paulo*. Guarujá: plano diretor e projeto do sistema de água e sistema de esgôto sanitário da Ilha de Santo Amaro. São Paulo, Secretaria dos Serviços e Obras Públicas, 1970. 123 l., fold. maps, maps, plates, tables.

Comprehensive planning document for piped water system and sewer network at popular coastal resort city.

7045. Costa, Gerson Teixeira da; Abelardo Cordoso Montenegro; Antônio Barreto Coutinho Neto; and **Antônio Figueiredo de Lima.** As enchentes de Capibaribe: preliminar visão global do problema. Recife, Bra., Govêrno do Estado de Pernambuco, Secretaria de Viação e Obras Públicas, 1967. 20 p., fold. maps, plates.

Approximately half of the built-up area of Recife (population one million) was flooded in 1966. This study documents floods and attempts to pose some remedial steps. Difficult to be optimistic.

7046. Costa, Rubens Vaz da. Population growth and economic development. Fortaleza, Bra., Banco do Nordeste do Brasil, 1970. 28 p., tables.

Bold clear voice speaking sense. Author is now President of national housing bank.

7047. Costa Filho, Miguel. A cana-de-açúcar em Minas Gerais. Rio, Instituto do Açúcar e do Alcool, 1963. 415 p., bibl., illus., plates.

Serious book on history of sugar cane in Minas Gerais. Extensive bibliography.

7048. Dados preliminares gerais do censo agropecuário, região Sul: VIII recenseamento geral, 1970. Rio, Ministério do Planejamento e Coordenação Geral [and] Fundação IBGE, Instituto Brasileiro de Estatística, Depto. de Censos, 1972. 47 p., fold. maps, tables.

Data and colored maps with information on agriculture and livestock in Southern Brazil.

7049. Dantas, Humberto da Silveira. Complexo sortivo dos principais solos do Estado de Pernambuco. I, Zona litoral—Mata. Recife, Bra., Instituto de Pesquisas e Experimentação Agropecuárias do Nordeste (IPEANE), 1967. 116 p., bibl., fold. maps, tables.

Samples analyzed from the most productive *zona da mata* area of Pernambuco.

7050. Davidovich, Fany. Formas de projeção espacial das cidades na área de influência de Fortaleza (IBGE/R, 33:2, abril/junho 1971, p. 39-101, bibl., fold. map, maps, tables)

Detailed data and maps showing nature and extent of Fortaleza's influence spatially over Northeast Brazil. Serious, substantive study using sophisticated techniques.

7051. ———. Relaçoes da indústria com o espaço geográfico (IBGE/B, 216:29, maio/junho 1970, p. 61-69)

Describes uneven distribution of industrial activity and discusses some problems attending its concentration in only a few centers, with Brazil as example. [C. R. Edwards]

7052. Delaney, Patrick J. V. Fisiografia e geologia de superfície da Planície Costeira do Rio Grande do Sul. Porto Alegre, Bra., Univ. do Rio Grande do Sul, Escola de Geologia, 1965. 105 p., bibl., fold. maps, maps, tables (Publicação especial, 6)

Portuguese edition of author's thesis published in 1963, see *HLAS 27:2914a*.

7053. Dicionário geográfico brasileiro. 2. ed. Pôrto Alegre, Bra., Editôra Globo, 1972. 619 p., bibl., fold. map, map, plates.

Straightforward geographical dictionary with data from 1970 census. Reference volume with much of the information contained in its "Enciclopédia dos municipios brasileiros" minus the valuable analytical introductions.

7054. Divisão territorial do Brasil em grandes regiões e micro-regiões homogêneas, com suas nominatas (IBGE/RBE, 32:125, jan./março 1971, p. 33-86, maps)

New official regional division of Brazil proposed by the Instituto Brasileiro de Geografia and approved by the National Planning Commission. North is everything north and west of Mato Grosso and Goias, which comprise the Central West; Northeast includes Maranhão and Bahia and everything in between. South is the southernmost three states and the Southeast is the remainder.

7055. Duarte, Aluízio Capdeville and others. Aracajú e sua região (IBGE/B, 30:220, jan./fev. 1971, p. 3-130, maps, tables)

Fundamental regional monography about this little-known urban center between Recife and Salvador. Gold mine of basic data and maps.

7056. Eletrificação do Paraná. Curitiba, Bra., Companhia Paranaense de Energia Elétrica (COPEL), 1971. 1 v. (Unpaged) fold. maps, plates, tables.

Vivid photographic record of why Paraná will follow São Paulo state on the road to prosperity.

7057. A extensão rural no Brasil. Rio, n.p., 1970. 129 p., tables.
History of aims and achievements of rural extension services globally and in Brazil.

Enne, Giuseppe. Prime-osservazioni sulle prove di incrocio delle razze bovine da carne italiane con razze dell'America Latina. See item 6765.

7058. Faissol, Speridião. As grandes cidades brasileiras: dimensões básicas de diferenciação e relações com o desenvolvimento econômico: um estudo de análise fatorial (IBGE/R, 32:4, out./dez. 1970, p. 87-130, maps, tables)
Factoral analysis of 50 Brazilian cities using 30 variables. Clear distinctions appear between urban hierarchies of the developed Central-South and the difficient urban networks of the developing Northeast.

7059. ———. Pólos de desenvolvimento no Brasil: uma metodologia quantitativa e uma exemplificação empírica (IBGE/R, 34:2, abril/junho 1972, p. 52-80, tables)
Application of "optimal origin point" methodology to analysis of development poles in Brazil. Indices plotted but not mapped.

7060. ———. Teorização e quantificação na geografia (IBGE/R, 34:1, jan./março 1972, p. 145-164)
Explanation of basic ideas of the "new geography" to Portuguese readers. Skillful attempt to bring together ideas of Berry, Harvey, Hartshorne and James in a statement which proclaims the usefulness of new concepts and techniques of geography to practical planning in Brazil.

7061. Fernandes, Eurico. A contribuição do índio á economia da Amazônia. Apresentação de Arthur Cézar Ferreira Reis. Manaus, Bra., Edigraf, 1966. 29 p.
Listing of cultural traits and artifacts, such as the *rede* (hammock) which have been accepted into general use from the Indians of the Amazon area.

7062. Fernandes, Liliana Laganá. Aspectos da organização do espaço no bairro rural dos Pires, município de Limeira, Estado de São Paulo (AGB/BPG, 45, junho 1968, p. 72-123, bibl., fold. map, maps, plates, tables)
Geographical "community study" of small village in São Paulo state.

7063. ———. O bairro rural dos Pires: estudo de geografia agrária. São Paulo, Univ. de São Paulo, Instituto de Geografia, 1971. 90 p., bibl., plates, tables (Série teses e monografias, 5)
Traditional masters thesis; a community regional geography.

7064. Ferreira, Carlos Mauricio de Carvalho. Um estudo de regionalização do Estado de Minas Gerais por meio de um modêlo de potencial. Belo Horizonte, Bra., Univ. Federal de Minas Gerais, Centro de Desenvolvimento e Planejamento Regional (CEDEPLAR), 1971. 391., fold. maps, tables (Monografia, 3)
Interesting map using a gravity model to divide Minas Gerais into a network of urban-focused regions.

7065. Foland, Frances M. A profile of Amazonia: its possibilities for development (UM/JIAS, 13:1, Jan. 1971, p. 62-77)
General review article with emphasis on current efforts to develop the Amazon. [E. B. Burns]

7066. Foury, A. Paul. As matas do Nordeste brasileiro e sua importância econômica (IBGE/B, 31:227, março/abril 1972, p. 14-221)
First half of two-part transcription of long study dealing with economic aspects of forest and pasture lands in Northeast Brazil. Detailed comments on vegetation characteristics of each zone. Originally published in SUDENE's *Boletim de Recursos Naturais* (4, jan./dez. 1966).

7067. Freyre, Gilberto and others. Cana e reforma agrária. Pt. 1, Transformação regional e ciência ecológica: o caso do Nordeste brasileiro; pt. 2, O problema agrário na zona canavieira de Pernambuco: conderências, comentários e debates em tôrno do assunto. Recife, Bra., Ministério da Educação e Cultura, Instituto Joaquim Nabuco de Pesquisas Sociais, 1970. 369 p.
Multidisciplinary symposium on the theme of sugar cane and land reform by prominent nordestine scholars and activists.

7068. Fundação Getúlio Vargas. Instituto Brasileiro de Economia. Centro de Estudos Agrícolas. Variações estacionais de preços, ao nível dos agricultores, de alguns produtos selecionados, anos de 1966 a 1969. Rio, 1971. 210 p., tables.
Seasonal price fluctuations plotted for agricultural commodities during 1966-69.

7069. Galvão, Marília Velloso and **Speridião Faissol.** A révolução quantitativa na geografia e seus reflexões no Brasil (IBGE/R, 32:4, out/dez. 1970, p. 5-22)
The rallying cry of the quantitative revolution has come to Brazilian geography.

7070. Gardner, George. Travels in the interior of Brazil, principally through the northern provinces, and the gold and diamond districts, during the years 1836-1841. N.Y., AMS Press, 1970. 562 p., map, plate.
Fascinating botanist's account of itinerary from Ceará through Piaui, Goiás and Minas Gerais to Rio in the early 19th century. Travels and observations on every subject from climate to diseases.

7071. Gehlen, Iegle. Significado do fluxo de passageiros na vida de relação (IBGE/B, 30:222, maio/junho 1971, p. 51-59, map, tables)

Passenger flow data linking major cities of Rio Grande do Sul.

7072. Geiger, Pedro Pinchas. Cidades do Nordeste: aplicação de "factor analysis" no estudo de cidades nordestinas (IBGE/R, 32:4, out/dez. 1970, p. 5-22)

Classification of Northeast's cities into a hierarchy based upon area of influence and variables. Excellent extension of former studies by Geiger on all Brazil.

7073. —— and R. Lobato Corrêa. De Vitória a Belo Horizonte pelo Vale do Rio Doce. Rio, Comissão para os Aspectos Regionais do Desenvolvimento, União Geográfica Internacional 1971, 84 p., maps.

Analysis by geographers of urban networks within the Southeast of Brazil. Good maps. Legends in English.

7074. George, Pierre. Aire metropolitaine, conurbation ou région industrielle?: le cas de São Paulo. São Paulo, Univ. de São Paulo, Instituto de Geografia, 1969. 16 p. (Geografia das indústrias, 2)

Methodological discussion of definition of urban regions. The spread and growth of São Paulo is so rapid that a dynamic definition focusing upon the industrial functions (and increasing power needs) is needed.

7075. Gilmore, Norman and Dilson Cosme Ramos. Minas Gerais, 1971-75: perspectivas; transportes. Belo Horizonte? Bra., Conselho do Estado de Minas Gerais [and] Funcação João Pinheiro, 1971? 123 l., maps, tables.

Extension of the national transportation philosophy down to the state level; i.e., the rational deployment of lines of communication in order to valorize areas and integrate the national territory effectively. Good history of transportation in Minas Gerais. We have seen the transition from pack trains to railroads to highways and now the fuller integration of all modern means including fluvial transport on the São Francisco river.

7076. Gioja, Rolando I. Planeamiento urbano y regional en Brasil. La Plata, Arg., Univ. Nacional de La Plata, Facultad de Arquitectura y Urbanismo, 1972. 59 p., maps (Ciencias del hombre)

Brief history of Brazilian urban and regional planning efforts by an Argentine architect who studied in Brazil.

7077. Goes, Terezinha de Jesus M. Noções de geografia e história do Município de Cruzeta. Rio Grande do Norte, Bra., n.p., 1971. 98 p., plates.

Compilation of information about a município in Rio Grande do Norte presented in the old style with little analysis.

7078. Goiás (state), *Bra.* **Secretaria do Planejamento e Coordenação.** Goiás: 1967. Goiânia? Bra., 1967? 153 p., maps, tables.

Inventory of the sparse data on physical conditions and economic activities in this state which lies squarely in the path of Brazil's modernization.

7079. Gomes, Raymundo Pimentel. Corografia dinâmica do Ceará. Fortaleza, Bra., Depto. de Imprensa Oficial, 1968? 308 p., bibl.

Old fashioned rambling compedium. Not analytical. Few data.

7080. Gradvohl, Roberto Gerson; Haroldo José Sousa Costa Lima; and José Alexandre Robatto Orrico. Produção e mercado de fumo do Nordeste. Fortaleza, Bra., Banco do Nordeste do Brasil, Depto. de Estudos Econômicos do Nordeste (ETENE), 1970. 67 p., tables.

Handy description of the details of tobacco production, demand patterns, and commercialization inside and outside of Brazil. Especially useful is a "chronogram" or calendar of tobacco cultivation in Arapiraca, Bahía, a center of production.

7081. Hasui, Yociteru and Fernando Flávio Marques de Almeida. Geocronologia do Centro-Oeste brasileiro (SBG/B, 19:1, set. 1970, p. 5-26, bibl., fold. map, tables)

Recent updating of the sequence of tectonic events shaping Central Brazil.

7082. Hochtief-Montreal-Deconsult (firm), *São Paulo.* Metro de São Paulo. v. 1, Estudos sócio-econômicos, de tráfego e de viabilidade econômico-financeira. São Paulo, Sistema Integrado de Transporte Rápido Coletivo da Cidade de São Paulo, 1968. 248 p., fold. maps, illus., maps, plates, tables.

Basic planning document of São Paulo's projected subway system. For art critic's comment, see *HLAS 34:612*.

7083. Hunnicutt, Benjamin Harris. Brazil: world frontier. N.Y., Greenwood Press, 1969. 387 p., illus., plates, tables.

An exact copy of the 1949 Van Nostrand edition (see *HLAS 15:62*), complete with the same photographs. It is a reminder of how quality of writings has improved and expanded in 20 years.

7084. Iglesias, Dolores and Maria de Lourdes Meneghezzi. Bibliografia e índice da geologia do Brasil: 1962-1963. Rio, Ministério das Minas e Energia, Depto. Nacional da Produção Mineral, Divisão de Geologia e Mineralogia, 1969. 134 p., (Boletim, 244)

Supplement to earlier bibliography on the geology of Brazil. See *HLAS 27:2934*.

7085. Indice dos topônimos contidos na Carta do Brasil 1:1000.000 do IBGE [Instituyo Brasileiro de Geografia e Estatística] São Paulo, Fundação de Amparo à Pesquisa do Estado de São Paulo (FAPESP), 1968. 197 p.

Gold mine for the place name geographer. See also item 7121.

7086. Inventário cafeeiro: pesquisa com fotografias aéreas nas regiões cafeicultoras do Estado de São Paulo, a Este de 48° W. Rio, Ministério da Indústria e do Comércio,

Instituto Brasileiro do Café, Grupo Executivo de Racionalização da Cafeicultura, Serviço de Fotointerpretação, 1968. 66 p., bibl., maps, tables.

Impressive survey showing technique of air photo interpretation applied to a diversified agricultural area of eastern São Paulo state. High quality maps, overlays, and air photographs.

7087. Japanese Cultural Association, *São Paulo.* Brazil. São Paulo, 1967. 56 p., illus., maps, plates, tables.

Portrait, in Japanese, of Brazil with emphasis on numbers and concentrations of Japanese-Brazilians. Excellent maps show the great concentration in São Paulo and northern Paraná. Thirty paulista and three Paraná municipios have more than 10 percent Japanese.

7088. Jurema, Aderbal. O sobrado no paisagem recifense. 2. ed. Recife, Bra., Univ. Federal de Pernambuco, 1971. 127 p., bibl., plates.

Definitive treatment of distinctive 19th-century house type. Good photos.

7089. Kampen, Anthony van. Het land dat God vergat. Hilversum, The Netherlands, Uitgeverij C. de Boer jr, 1967. 255 p., maps, plates.

Popular account of recent travels through West Central Brazil to Cruzeiro do Sul and then downriver to Manaus. Emphasis on health problems.

7090. Keller, Elza Coelho de Souza. Tipos de agricultura no Paraná, uma análise fatorial (IBGE/R, 32:4, out./dez. 1970, p. 41-86, maps, tables)

Results of factor and cluster analyses of agriculture in southern Paraná show concentrations in: 1) the older Portuguese-Brazilian colonization zone of the east, and 2) the recent pioneer frontier of the west.

7091. Kohlhepp, Gerd. Standortbedingungen und räumliche Ordnung der Industrie im brasilianischen Santa Catarina (GR, 23:1, Jan. 1971, p. 10-23, maps, tables)

Most of the manufacturing industries of Santa Catarina, Bra., are oriented toward the labor force of the German-Brazilian region of this state, not at mineral resources, energy supply, transportation facilities or population centers. This situation is the result of the immigration, in several phases, of Germans since the second half of the 19th century and of the present stable social milieu of the skilled labor force. [H. Hoyer]

7092. Lambert, Jacques. Os dois Brasisl. 7. ed. São Paulo, Companhia Editôra Nacional, 1971. 277 p., tables.

New edition of a well known interpretation of Brazil by French sociologist. It rings more of the past than the present Brazil.

7093. Langenbuch, Juergen Richard. Os núcleos de colonização oficial implantados no planalto paulistano em fins do século XIX (ABG/BPG, 46, dez. 1971, p. 88-108, bibl., map, tables)

Map and details showing mainly Italian colonies established within 50-60 km. of São Paulo City at end of the 19th century.

7094. ———. Organização urbana do Estado de São Paulo analisada pela circulação de ônibus intermunicipais (IBGE/B, 29:219, nov./dez. 1970, p. 26-52, maps, tables)

Application of British method to identify urban networks by analysis of inter-city bus traffic sharpens zones of influence of smaller cities whose communication function is greater than suspected. Example of use of modern methods in Brazilian geography.

7095. ———. O sistema viário da aglomeração paulistana: apreciação geográfica da situação atual (IBGE/R, 33:2, abril/junho 1971, p. 3-38, bibl., maps, plates)

Street layout variations in Greater São Paulo City and attendant problems of transport and communications.

7096. Leão, Antônio Carlos and João Baptista Soares Gouvêa. Uso atual das terras da região cacaueira do Estado da Bahía: folhas itabuna, una, potiraguá, mascote e canavieiras. Bahia, Bra., Comissão Executiva do Plano de Recuperação Econômico-Rural da Lavoura Cacaueira (CEPLAC), 1971? 22 p., bibl., fold. maps, tables (Boletim técnico, 8)

Detailed land use maps in Bahia cacau region based upon air photo interpretation.

7097. Leite, Eraldo Gueiros. Pernambuco está mudando. Recife, Bra., Companhia Editôra de Pernambuco, 1972. 27 p., fold. map.

Present government is as committed to improving life in the Northeast as was the Goulart government. This one is having more success on the whole.

7098. Leite, José Ferrari. A Alta Sorocabana e o espaço polarizado de Presidente Prudente. Presidente Prudente, Bra., Faculdade de Filosofia, Ciências e Letras de Presidente Prudente, 1972. 249 p., bibl., fold. maps, maps, plates, tables.

Regional monograph about the hinterland or zone of influence of a western São Paulo city.

7099. Leonardos, Othon Henry. Geociências no Brasil: a contribução britânica. Prefácio de Pedro Calmon. Rio, Forum Editôra, 1970, 343 p., bibl., maps, plates, tables.

Basic volume in the history of science and exploration in Brazil. Dean of Brazilian geologists relates the British travellers' accounts and how they influenced the course of scientific growth. Emphasis is expectedly upon mineral discoveries. From meteorites and gold to diamonds, coal, iron and manganese.

7100. Lima, Afonso Augusto de Albuquerque and others. Problemática da Amazônia. Apresentação [por] Waldir da Costa Godolphim. Rio, Biblioteca do Exército-Editôra, 1971. 405 p., plates, tables (Col. General Benício, 90)

Essays by specialists on all aspects of the Amazon North, from physical geography to participation by the armed forces and religious organizations to raw material reserves.

7101. Lima, Gelson Rangel. Solos (IBGE/B, 29:216, maio/junho 1970, p. 44-60, fold. map, plates, tables)

1:10,000,000 scale map of Brazilian soils with 20 categories related to vegetation and other characteristics.

7102. Machado, Renato Rodrigues. Carmo do Paranaíba, Minas Gerais: situação sócio-econômica. Belo Horizonte? Bra., Associação de Crédito e Assistência Rural (ACAR), Extensão Rural e Crédito Educativo, 1967. 24 p., illus., tables.

Data for socio-economic profile of a municipio near Patos de Minas, Minas Gerais. A small gold mine of information in an area which has been little-studied. Author is an economist with ACAR.

7103. Magnanini, Ruth Lopes da Cruz. As cidades de Santa Catarina: base econômica e classificação funcional (IBGE/R, 33:1, jan./março 1971, p. 85-121, bibl., maps, tables)

Application of Ullman and Dacey methodology of functional analysis to the cities of Santa Catarina.

7104. Mato Grosso (state), Br . Sugestões para os problemas de reforma agrária em Mato Grosso. Cuiabá? Bra., n.p., 1968? 32 l., maps, tables.

Short valuable discussion of the recent land boom in forested frontier areas of Mato Grosso since 1950 and especially since 1960. Government's goal is a rural middle class.

7105. Mattsson, Ake. Vatten över huvet. Stockholm, P. A. Norstedt & Söners förlag, 1971. 187 p., illus., map, plates.

True adventure story by Swedish sailing enthusiast who sailed alone from Rio to Bahia, Recife and Fortaleza. Without a word of Portuguese, he managed to communicate with helpful Brazilians in every port and was finally saved from the ocean where he spent 50 hours after being shipwrecked. [R. V. Shaw]

7106. Medidas e propostas para o desenvolvimento do Nordeste e sua integração à economia nacional. Brasília, Aliança Renovadora Nacional (ARENA) [and] Comissão Coordenadora de Estudos do Nordeste (COCENE), 1971. 333 p., maps, tables (Estudo, 1)

Inventory of problems and recommendations for solutions in Northeast.

7107. Meggers, Betty Jane. Amazonia: man and culture in a counterfeit paradise. Chicago, Ill., Aldine Atherton, 1971. 182 p., bibl., illus., maps, plates, tables (Worlds of man. Studies in cultural ecology)

Fundamentally important analysis of challenge which the Amazon and its inhabitants are experiencing in the face of "modernization." For ethnologist's comment, see item 1293.

7108. Mente, Alberto; Geraldo A. Gusmão; and **Waldemir B. Cruz.** Estudo hidrogeológico da região de São João do Piauí (SUDENE, 4:3/4, julho/dez. 1966, p. 325-370, illus., maps, tables)

Scientific study of ground water resource possibilities in a part of the Northeast.

7109. Minas Gerais (state), Bra. **Conselho Estadual do Desenvolvimento.** Identificação de um núcleo urbano polarizador no Sul de Minas. Belo Horizonte? Bra., Fundação João Pinheiro, 1971. 85 l., maps, tables.

Bold and brilliant plan for identifying urban-industrial centers throughout Minas Gerais which could receive extra inputs to create polarizing centers and subcenters in order to disperse urban growth away from hydrocephalic Belo Horizonte.

7110. ———. Diretrizes para aplicação do crédito rural em Minas Gerais. Belo Horizonte? Bra., Fundação João Pinheiro, 1971. 329 p., maps, tables.

Interesting maps of agricultural land potential for several crops based upon multiple criteria. Essentially a geographical assessment of the crop carrying capacity of Minas Gerais as a basis for extending rural credit to farmers.

7111. ———. Secretaria de Estado da Agricultura. Circunscrições agropecuárias. Belo Horizonte, Bra., Diretoria Agropecuária, 1970. 60 p., maps, tables.

Proposal to establish agricultural assistance posts jointly by state and municipal governments. Fees charged to users of services provided.

7112. Moçoró: um centro regional do Oeste Potiguar. Rio, Ministério do Planejamento e Coordenação Geral [and] Fundação IBGE, Instituto Brasileiro de Geografia, Depto. de Geografia, 1971. 45 p., fold. maps, tables (Subsídios ao planejamento da área nordestina, 11)

Excellent balanced study of zones of influence of Moçoro (Rio Grande do Sul) as a preliminary step to a master plan document. Abundant detailed maps. One of a series of 11 studies on planning in Northeast Brazil.

7113. Monteiro, Mário Ypiranga. O sacado: morfo-dinâmica fluvial. Manaus, Bra., Conselho Nacional de Pesquisas, Instituto Nacional de Pesquisas da Amazônia, n.d. 53 p., plates (Cadernos da Amazônia, 3)

Good description of how curves or meanders of the Amazon and its tributaries especially become cut off leaving ox-bow lakes.

7114. Mota, Fernando de Oliveira comp. Recursos e necessidades do Nordeste: um documento básico sôbre a região nordestina.

Recife, Bra., Banco do Nordeste do Brasil, Escritório Técnico de Estudos Econômicos do Nordeste (ETENE), 1964. 666 p., bibl., fold. maps, maps, tables.

Basic studies by authorities in diverse fields based upon research done between 1962-67. Some sections are more useful and up to date than others. Two-thirds pertains to structures and trends in the Northeast's economy.

7115. Muller, Doris Maria and others. Anatomia de bairro: Menino Deus, para a Prefeitura Municipal de Pôrto Alegre. Pôrto Alegre, Bra., Univ. Federal de Rio Grande do Sul, Gabinete de Planejamento Urbano e Regional, 1969. 200 l., illus., maps, tables.

Urbanists' plan for a barrio of Porto Alegre tries to fulfill the needs of its residents. Much basic data and illustrations.

7116. Neves, Gervásio Rodrigo. Contribuição as estudo da rêde urbana do Rio Grande do Sul (IBGE/B, 30:222, maio/junho 1971, p. 19-50, bibl., maps, tables)

Introduction to urban network analysis of Rio Grande do Sul based upon recent American and European writings.

7117. Nimer, Edmon. Climatologia da região Nordeste do Brasil: introdução à climatologia dinâmica; subsídios à geografia regional do Brasil (IBGE/R, 34:2, abril/junho 1972, p. 3-51, bibl., maps, tables)

Excellent substantive contribution to our understanding of the complex climatology of Northeast Brazil. Brilliantly colored maps of high cartographic quality enhance the presentation. Validity of several small scale maps based upon too few stations is debatable. Insufficient reference is made in text or bibliography to previous excellent work by others such as Gilberto Osorio de Andrade (see *HLAS 29:5221*) and others.

7118. ———. Ensaio de um novo método de classificação climática: contribuição à climatologia intertropical e subtropical, especialmente do Brasil (IBGE/B, 31:227, março/abril 1972, p. 141-153)

New climatic classification is explained, but no maps provided.

7119. ———; Arthur Alves Pinheiro Filho; and **Elmo da Silva Amador.** Análise da precipitação no região do Cariri cearense: contribuição ao estudo da climatologia dinâmica no Nordeste brasileiro (IBGE/R, 33:1, jan./março 1971, p. 3-37, map, tables)

Analysis of the wet Cariri, dry Cariri and transition Cariri points to ground water variations accounting for primary discontinuities in moisture, not rainfall.

7120. ———; and **Mário Diniz de Araújo Neto.** Climatologia da região Sudeste do Brasil: introdução à geografia regional do Brasil (IBGE/R, 34:1, jan./março 1972, p. 3-48, bibl., maps, tables)

Heterogeneous climate of the Southeast (Minas Gerais, São Paulo, Espírito Santo and Guanabara) ranges over greatest extremes within Brazil; from super humid to semi-arid and from hot to mesothermic climates. Rainfall is largely the product of a clash between tropical highs and polar highs.

7121. Oliveira, Cêurio de. As origens psicos-sociais dos topônimos brasileiros (IBGE/B, 29:215, março/abril 1970, p. 61-70, tables)

Brief but absolutely fascinating cross referencing of place names in terms of type: religion, vegetation, hydrography, optimism, animals, relief, trees, nimerals, quadrupeds, birds, fruits, fish. Major regions are ranked according to relative frequency of each type name. Excluding places named for individuals which comprise 19 percent of total, the rest, in order of importance, refer to religious themes, to optimistic expressions, to vegetation, and to animals and to trees in particular. Based upon Brazil's 1:1,000,000 maps, see item 7085.

7122. Oliveira, Décio Rufino de. Recursos naturais, fatores determinantes na ocupação do território brasileiro. Rio, Editôra Gondwana, 1971. 198 p., tables.

Introduction to global view of Brazil's resources and role they play in development process.

7123. Oliveira, Guarino Alves d'. A costa setentrional do Brasil na carta de navegar de Alberto Cantino: *charta del Navichare*. Fortaleza, Bra., Editôra Fortaleza, 1968. 98 p., bibl., maps, tables.

Coast of northern Brazil is compared in charts of Cantino and other contemporary maps. Relevant to historical geographers.

7124. Paraíba (state) *Bra.* **Comissão Estadual de Planejamento Agrícola.** Plano agropecuário de Paraíba: metas para 1971. João Pessôa, Bra., 1971. 121 l., maps, tables.

Programs stressing productivity, infrastructure and services are proposed to strengthen Paraíba's agricultural sectors.

7125. Um passo de gigante em 4 anos: Rio Grande do Sul. Pôrto Alegre, Bra., Sociodade Nacional de Promoções (SNP), 1970. 144 p., plates, tables.

Photographic record of impressive gains made recently in paved highway and hydroelectric construction in Rio Grande do Sul.

7126. Pébayle, Raymond. A área rural do Distrito Federal brasileiro (IBGE/R, 33:1, jan./março 1971, p. 39-83, map, plates, tables)

Classification and description of rural activities around Brasília.

7127. Peixoto, Dídima de Castro. Geografia fluminense. Niterói, Bra., Newton Mattoso, 1968. 299 p., bibl., fold. maps.

Encyclopedic compendium of facts which have no theme or development. No evidence of professional training.

7128. Peixoto, Enaldo Cravo. O problema do abastecimento no Brasil. Rio, Ministério da Agricultura, Superintendência Nacional do Abastecimento, 1967. 61 p., maps, tables.

Sanitary engineer addresses the War College regarding Brazil's food supply problems. Each administration must apparently rediscover pressing national problems and restructure and re-create administrative devices to attack them. Results vary.

7129. Peluso Júnior, Victor Antônio. Latifúndios e minifúndios no Estado de Santa Catarina. Florianópolis, Bra., Univ. Federal de Santa Catarina, 1971. 37 p., tables.

Concise presentation by experienced native geographer.

7130. Pereira, Osny Duarte. A Transamazônica: prós e contra. Rio, Civilização Brasileira, 1971. Prefácio [por] Arthur Cézar Ferreira Reis. 368 p., bibl., maps (Col. Retratos do Brasil, 81)

Much heat, but little light on the Trans-Amazon debate. With the speed of road building in Brazil, everything on the subject is soon out of date.

7131. Petróleo Brasileiro, S.A. (PETROBRAS), Rio. Departamento de Exploração e Produção. Coletânea de relatórios de exploração. Pt. 1. Rio, Depto. Industrial (DEPIN), Dentro de Pesquisas e Desenvolvimento (CENPES), Setor de Documentação e Patentes, 1967. 2 v. (Various pagings) fold. maps, maps, tables (Ciência-técnica-petróleo. Secção: Exploração de petróleo. Publicação, 3-4)

Broad panorama of the scope and quality of the exploration work carried out by Petrobras in search for petroleum. Many maps and sections.

7133. Pina, Hélio. A agro-indústria açucareira e sua legislação. Rio, APEC Editôra, 1972. 364 p., bibl., tables.

Documents how sugar cane production has been affected by discriminatory legislative acts which maintain the inefficient northeastern production despite cheaper São Paulo production.

7134. Pompeu Sobrinho, Thomaz. Esbôço fisiográfico do Ceará. 3. ed. Fortaleza, Bra., Imprensa Universitária do Ceará, 1962. 219 p., plates, tables.

The most recent edition of a traditional treatment of Ceará's physical geography. Does not reflect recent advances in the field.

7135. Prado Júnior, Caio and others. A agricultura subdesenvolvida. Petrópolis, Bra., Editôra Vozes, 1969. 275 p., tables (Col. Caminhos brasileiros, 2)

Assemblage of previously published essays on general theme of Brazilian agriculture.

7136. Programa de desenvolvimento da pecuária de Corte. Belo Horizonte, Bra., Banco de Desenvolvimento de Minas Gerais, 1970? 250 p., fold. maps, illus., maps, plates, tables.

Inventory study financed partly by the Interamerican Development Bank for purposes of raising rate of reproduction of livestock and lowering age at slaughter.

7137. O projeto Rondon. Rio, Instituto Nacional do Livro [and] Bloch Editôres, 1972. 64 p., plates, tables (Col. Brasil hoje, 9)

A Brazilian "Vista" or domestic Peace Corps program to encourage students to serve in Brazil's interior.

7138. Queiroz Neto, José Pereira de and **Antônio Cristofoletti.** Ação do escoamento superficial das águas pluviais no Serra de Santana, E. S. Paulo (AGB/BPG, 45, junho 1968, p. 59-71, bibl., tables)

Details of sheet wash and deposition of sediments in the valleys of the Serra de Santana.

7139. Quinn, L. R.; G. O. Mott; and **W. V. A. Bisschoff.** The effect of diethystilbestrol upon the performance of pasture-fed Zebu steers. N.Y., IRI Research Institute, 1971. 47 p., bibl., tables (Bulletin, 34)

Impressive documentation of how a small investment in diet supplement costing less than the price of 2 kg. of liveweight of beef will produce an additional 40 kg. of liveweight. One of a series of technical studies, numbering through No. 37, illustrating the possibilities of technology applied to agriculture in Brazil. Titles are: No. 35, W. V. A. Bisschoff; L. R. Quinn; G. O. Mott; and G. L. da Rocha "Supplemental Feeding of Steers on Pasture with Protein-Energy Supplements" (47 p.)
No. 36, G. O. Mott; L. R. Quinn, W. V. A. Bisschoff; and G. L. da Rocha "Molasses as an Energy Supplement for Zebu Steers Grazing Nitrogen-Fertilized and Unfertilized Colonial Guinea Grass Pasture" (54 p.)
No. 37, M. B. Jones; L. M. M. de Freitas; and K. H. Mohrdieck "Differential Responses of Some Cool Season Grasses to N, P, and Lime" (24 p.)

7140. Reis, Arthur Cézar Ferreira. A Amazônia e a integridade do Brasil. Manaus, Bra., Edições Govêrno do Estado do Amazonas, 1966. 309 p. (Série Alberto Tôrres, 4)

The Amazon's best known scholar presents a history of area which is undergoing radical transformation under modern planning methods which will link remote North to rest of Brazil.

7141. ———. O impacto amazônico na civilização brasileira: a Transamazônica e o desafio dos trópicos. Rio, Editôra Paralelo [and] Instituto Nacional do Livro, 1972. 181 p., maps.

The Amazon invites still more analysis of the impact of modernization by region's elder historian.

7142. *Revista Industrial do Amazonas.* Federação das Indústrias do Estado do Amazonas. No. 3, Janeiro 1971- . Manaus, Bra.

The face of industrialization in the Amazon area.

7143. Ribeiro, Sylvio Wanick and others. Salários, preços de terras e serviços no meio rural: anos de 1966 e 1967. Rio, Fundação Getúlio Vargas, Instituto Brasileiro de Economia, Centro de Estudos Agrícolas, 1968. 48 p., tables.

Valuable data on salaries and the prices for land and services in each state and for each sub-region within each Brazilian state.

7144. ———. 22 [i.e., Vinte dois] anos de evolução da agricultura: 1947 a 1968. Rio, Fundação Getúlio Vargas, Instituto Brasileiro de Economia, Centro de Estudos Agrícolas, 1970. 96 p., tables.

Documents fact that agriculture has grown at just about half the rate of industry during 1947-68.

7145. Rio Grande do Norte (state), *Bra*. **Comissão Estadual de Planejamento Agrícola.** Estudos básicos para a formulação de programas de desenvolvimento agropecuário no Estado do R. G. N. Natal, Bra., Depto. Estadual de Imprensa, 1970. 3 v. (137, 113, 227 p.) bibl., fold. maps, maps, tables.

Basic inventory of information relevant to planning of programs necessary to promote the agricultural and livestock sectors. V.1 is physical, demographic and economic aspects. V. 2 is land capability, water and soil resources. V. 3 is land tenure characteristics. Written by group of agronomists, not geographers.

7146. Rio Grande do Sul (state), *Bra*. **Grupo Executivo do Desenvolvimento da Indústria da Pesca (GEDIP).** Planejamento integrado da pesca industrial no Rio Grande do Sul. Pôrto Alegre, Bra., 1970. 5 v. (Various pagings) fold. maps, maps, tables.

Massive feasability study on rational planning of a modern fishing industry in Rio Grande do Sul. V. 1 treats the present fish industry. V. 2 discusses trends and port considerations. V. 3 deals with port administration and costs-benefits analyses and distribution and commercialization of fishing. V. 4 summarizes oceanographic research carried out to locate fish and on modern fishing techniques needed. V. 5 is a synthesis of study. Done in association with Engenharia e Planejamento Ltda. (PLANAVE), Escritório Técnico de Planejamento (ETEPE), Planejamento e Assessoria Ltda. (PLANO), and Centro de Projectos Industriais S.A.R.L. (PROABRIL).

7147. ———. Projeto grande Rio Grande. Diretrizes para ação do Govêrno do Estado Quadriênio, 1971-74: Síntese. Pôrto Alegre, Bra., 1970? 40 l., maps, tables.

Terse statement of large state goals of development consistent with national goals. Emphasis on hard work, elimination of privilege, austere control of costs and planning and uppermost is the pursuit of higher yields from labor, from capital, and from land.

7148. Rivière, Peter. The forgotten frontier: ranchers of North Brazil. N.Y., Holt, Rinehart and Winston, 1972. 127 p., bibl., maps, plates (Case studies in cultural anthropology)

Valuable anthropologist's analysis of the cattle culture of Roraima. Area has been little-studied.

7149. Rocque, Carlos. Antologia da cultura amazônica [see *HLAS 34:135*]. v. 5, Narrativas de viagens e estudos geográficos. Belém do Pará, Bra., Amazônia Edições Culturais (AMADA), 1970. 304 p. (Grande enciclopédia da Amazônia. Estante de obras subsidiárias)

Vignettes of the Amazon region, people and activities by famous travellers whose brief biographies precede the selections from their writings. For other volumes of this *Antologia*, see *HLAS 34:135*.

7150. Rodrigues, Carlos ed. Belém: 350 anos. Belém, Bra., 1966? 64 p., map, plates.

Informative colored photos of the new Belém and life in its surrounding area. Looks like most other Brazilian booming metropolises.

7151. Rodrigues, David Márico Santos and **Fabiano Marques dos Santos.** Região setentrional de Belo Horizonte. Belo Horizonte, Bra., VI Semana da Geografia, 1968. 57 p., bibl., map, tables.

The vast area to the north of Belo Horizonte poses interesting problems.

7152. Rondon, J. Lucídio N. Tipos e aspectos do pantanal. São Paulo, Livraria Nobel. 1972. 160 p.

A native of the annually flooded Pantanal of western Mato Grosso tells of life and livelihood in a water world.

7153. Rondônia (territory), *Bra*. **Ministério do Interior. Serviço de Geografia e Estatística.** Flagrantes de Rondônia. Pôrto Velho, Bra., 1971. 20 l.

Brief factual portrayal of the remote territory (formerly named Guaporé) whose capital of Pôrto Velho has 50,000 people and a few paved streets.

7154. St. Clair, David. The mighty, mighty Amazon. N.Y., Funk & Wagnalls, 1968. 304 p., bibl., maps, plates.

Readable profile of people and events of the Amazon Basin. Already out of date because of highway developments since 1968.

7155. Saint-Hilaire, Auguste de and others. As fabulosas aguas quentes de Caldas Novas. Antologia organizada pelo editor T. Oriente. n.p., Oriente, n.d. 125 p., bibl.

Thermal waters and commercialized thermal baths have been an important aspect of Brazilian life.

7156. Santiago, Alberto Alves and others. Brasil potência. São Paulo, Editôras Unidas, 1971. 432 p., maps, tables.

Authorities on Brazil's economic and technological capacities present essays which exhibit strong conviction that Brazil intends to become a ranking world power among all nations.

7157. São Paulo (state), *Bra.* **Secretaria de Economia e Planejamento. Departamento de Estatística. Divisão de Estatísticas Demográficas.** Situação demográfica do Estado de São Paulo. 2. ed. 1971. 138 p., tables.

São Paulo's population projections for 1980! Would you believe 12 million?

7158. ———. Grupo Executivo da Grande São Paulo (GEGRAN) [and] Secretaria de Transportes. Assessoria Técnica de Coordenação e Planejamento (ATCP). PAITT: Programa de Ação Imediata de Transportes e Tráfego. Pt. 1, Relatório institucional; Pt. 2, Relatório intermediário. São Paulo, Grupo de Planejamento Integrado (GPI) [and] Planning and Development Collaborative International (PADCO), 1971. 94 p., maps, tables.

São Paulo has a plan to relieve traffic congestion if they can keep ahead of dizzying growth of population and automobiles.

7159. ———. Secretaria dos Serviços e Obras Públicas. Companhia de Saneamento da Baixada Santista. Plano diretor de esgostos das cidades de Santos e São Vicente. São Paulo, 1970? 158 l., fold. maps, maps, plates, tables.

Master plan for sewer network for Santos and São Vicente has many interesting air photos showing current pollution patterns. Relevant to urban planning.

7160. Seabra, Manoel. A cooperativa Central Agrícola sul-Brasil e o abastecimento da cidade de São Paulo. São Paulo, Univ. de São Paulo, Instituto de Geografia, Setor de Pesquisas, 1966. 25 p., tables (mimeo) (Geografia economica, 5)

Mimeographed preliminary results of large food supply study of São Paulo by the paulista geographers. Precise data are tabulated.

7161. ———. Vargem Grande: organização e transformações de um setor do cinturão-verde paulistano. São Paulo, Univ. de São Paulo, Instituto de Geografia, 1971. 229 p., bibl., fold. map, tables (Série teses e monografias, 4)

Famous Japanese cooperative COTIA and its general area of Vargem Grande is analyzed as Greater São Paulo has spread outward toward it.

7162. Sergipe (state), *Bra.* Plano de emergencia para o setor primário. Governo Paulo Barreto de Menezes. Aracajú, Bra., 1971. 1 v. (Unpaged) maps, tables.

This drought emerging plan includes some basic data on the economy of Sergipe and an expression of what sectors are most valuable.

7163. Serra, Adalberto B. Chuvas intensas na Guanabara (IBGE/B, 29:218, set./out. 1970, p. 24-48, maps, tables)

Author relates disastrous and killing torrential rains of 1966 and 1967 to air mass movements. He pleads for the reestablishment of radiosonde baloon network which has been discontinued.

7164. ———. Clima da Guanabara (IBGE/B, 29:214, jan./fev. 1970, p. 80-111, tables)

Evidence of considerable climatic variation within the former federal district: Greater Rio de Janeiro. Tallies of hot and cool nights by month for various stations.

7165. Silva, Hilda da and others. Maceió e sua área de influência (IBGE/B, 30:225, nov./dez. 1971, p. 3-75, maps, tables)

Another hinterland study.

7166. *Silvicultura em São Paulo.* Estado de São Paulo, Secretaria da Agricultura, Serviço Florestal. Vol. 6, No. único, 1967- . São Paulo.

Collection of articles emphasizing the maximization of forest productivity, reforestation, and answering demand for Parana Pine softwood and railroad trees. São Paulo state is facing up to the problems caused by 400 years of forest devastation.

7167. Simpósio sobre Poluição Ambiental, *1. Brasília, 1971.* Anais. v. 3, Comissão de poluição do solo. Brasília, 1971. 253 p., plates, tables (Série Comissões especiais, 3)

Proceedings of a conference on environmental pollution. Recommendations include 1) making a natural resource of the São Francisco limestone formation known as the Bambu of Minas Gerais and Bahia and 2) the careful planning of Amazon settlement. V. 1-2 not available for review.

7168. Sinopse preliminar do censo demográfico, Brasil: VIII recenseamento geral, 1970. Rio, Ministério do Planejamento e Coordenação Geral [and] Fundação IBGE, Instituto Brasileiro de Estatística, Depto. de Censos, 1971. 256 p., fold. map, tables.

Excellent summary volume of basic population characteristics. One of every three Latin Americans was Brazilian in 1970. Now the 100 million Brazilians number 10 times the number counted in the first national census in 1872. The birth rate peaked out at 3.0 percent in 1950-60 and has dropped slightly to 2.90 in 1960-70.

7169. Souza, Maria Adélia Aparecida de. Paraná: o quadro geográfico, histórico e economico do processo de urbanização (AGB/BPG, 46, dez. 1971, p. 38-87, bibl., maps, tables)

Useful background for analysis of urbanization in Paraná state.

Spix, Johann Baptist von and **Carl Friedrich Philipp von Martius.** Reise in Brasilien in den Jahren 1817-1820: Unveränderter Neudruck des 1823-1831 in München in 3 Text bänden und 1 Tafelfand erschienenen Werkes. See *HLAS 34:2966a.*

7170. Strang, Harold Edgard. Panorama da

botánica brasileira (IBGE/B, 29:217, julho/agôsto 1970, p. 71-102, map, plates)
Excellent, concise, illustrated description of Brazilian vegetation types, the useful plants, and how man and institutions have affected them.

7171. ———— and **Henrique Pimenta Veloso.** Parques nacionais e reservas equivalentes no Brasil: relatório com vistas a uma revisão da política nacional nesse campo. Rio, Ministério da Agricultura, Instituto Brasileiro de Reforma Agrária (IBRA) [and] Instituto Brasileiro do Desenvolvimento Florestal (IBDF), 1969. 100 p.
The national parks provide a starting point for a conservationist outlook which is badly needed in Brazil.

7172. ————; **Ari Délcio Cavedon;** and **Sayuri Shibata.** Principais fitofisionomias do extremo sul de Mato Grosso (IBGE/R, 32:3, julho/set. 1970, p. 73-84, plates)
Brief description and photos of vegetation types in southern Mato Grosso state.

7173. **Suárez Inclán, Raúl** and **Francisco Ananias de Paula Coelho.** Diagnóstico sócioeconômico da zona fisiográfica de Baturité. v. 1, Aspectos fisiográficos. Fortaleza, Bra., Superintendência do Desenvolvimento Econômico e Cultural (SUDEC), Setor de Biblioteca e Documentação, 1967. 71 p., bibl., fold. maps.
Hydrography, relief, vegetation, climate and soils of the 800-meter high Baturité oasis area. For an abridged version of this study, see item 7037.

7174. **Tahal Consulting Engineers,** *Rio.* **Sondotécnica Engenharia de Solos.** Programa plurianual de irrigação, 1971. v. 1, Relatório de síntese. Brasília, Minstério do Interior, Grupo Executivo de Irrigação para o Desenvolvimento Agrícola (GEIDA), 1971. 1 v. (Various pagings) fold. maps, maps, tables.
This series of volumes is the first comprehensive evaluation of irrigation potential and priorities for much of Brazil. Sophisticated assessments of not only production potential but also social benefits. As of 1971 only about 70,000 hectares in the Northeast were irrigated. Brazil has a possible irrigated area of 1,300,000 ha. of which half is located in the Northeast.

7175. **Tamer, Alberto.** Nordeste, os mesmos caminhos: reforma agrária, afinal? Apresentação [por] Frederico Heller. Rio, APEC Editôra, 1972. 187 p., plates, tables.
Journalist's enthusiasm for everything that is happening in Northeast Brazil lessens his credibility.

7176. ————. Transamazônica: solução para 2001. Préfacio [por] Roberto de Oliveira Campos. 2. ed., rev. e aumentada. Rio, APEC Editôra, 1971. 311 p., plates.
An informed plea to complete the land evaluation studies for national colonization projects before the highway is built. Author questions the haste of road construction. He approves of emphasis on agricultural gains in Northeast Brazil.

7177. **Tanaka, T.; E. Lobato; W. V. Soares;** and **G. E. de França.** Comparisons of sweet corn varieties in "cerrado" soils. N.Y., IRI Research Institute, 1972. 21 p., tables (Bulletin, 40)
Another experiment proving that if the sterile acidic cerrado soils are prepared with three to six tons of limestone per hectare, and several hundred kilograms of fertilizer per hectare, and if insect control is practiced, US-type yields of eight to 12 tons of corn per hectare can be realized. Key question: How does this information relate to the average Brazilian farmer?

7178. **Tarifa, José Roberto.** Estudo preliminar das possibilidades agrícolas da região de Presidente Prudente, segundo o balanço hídrico de Thornthwaite: 1948-1955 (IBGE/B, 29:217, julho/agôsto 1970, p. 34-54, bibl., tables)
Application of Thornthwaite to western São Paulo state detailed data on water balance, rainfall and crop needs.

7179. **Taveira, Carlos Cesar Guterres.** Problemas brasileiros: geografia do desenvolvimento no Brasil. Introdução [por] . . . São Paulo, Lisa-Livros Irradiantes, 1971. 245 p., fold. map, maps, plates, tables.
School text which goes beyond history and geography to comprise an economic geography of Brazilian development. Good introduction.

7180. **Universidade de São Paulo. Instituto Oceanográfico.** Primeira pesquisa oceanográfica sistemática do Atlántico Sur entre Tôrres e Chuí. v. 1-2. Pôrto Alegre, Bra., Gôverno do Estado do Rio Grande do Sul, Grupo Executive do Desenvolvimento da Indústria da Pesca (GEDIP), 1969. 2 v. (58, Unpaged) maps, tables.
V. 1 is a survey of fish populations on the continental shelf off Rio Grande do Sul. V. 2 is temperature/salinity profiles and other oceanographic data relevant to fishing prospects.

7181. **Universidade Federal do Ceará,** *Fortaleza, Bra.* **Instituto de Pesquisas Econômicas.** Mercado de pescado de Fortaleza. Fortaleza, Bra., Superintendência do Desenvolvimento do Nordeste (SUDENE), Depto. de Agricultura e Abastecimento, Divisão de Abastecimento, 1967. 122 l., fold. maps, maps, tables.
Comprehensive "fish supply" study in tradition of other food supply studies done in Northeast since 1957.

7182. **Valverde, Orlando.** Fundamentos geográficos do planejamento de município de Corumbá (IBGE/R, 34:1, jan./março 1972, p. 49-144, bibl., maps, plates, tables)
Comprehensive, in-depth analysis of the physical,

social and economic components of the pantanal, the flooded area of western Mato Grosso of which Corumbá is a primary urban center.

7183. Vasconcelos Sobrinho, João de. Problemática ecológica do Rio São Francisco: conferência pronunciada na Assembléia Legislativa do Estado de Pernambuco, em 6 de julho de 1971. Recife, Bra., Univ. Federal Rural de Pernambuco, 1971. 34 p., map.

Eloquent plea to increase stream flow by reforesting the watershed slopes and decrease dam construction which loses much water by evaporation.

7184. ―― and others. As regiões naturais do Nordeste: o meio e a civilização. Recife, Bra., Conselho do Desenvolvimento de Pernambuco (CONDEPE), 1971. 441 p., maps, plates, tables.

Collection of essays on Northeast Brazil by specialists. Lacks the cohesion of a study which is by a single author.

7185. Veirano de Astiz, Lilia. Geografia de Brasil: lineamientos generales para su enseñanza. Presentación [por] Albino Peixoto. Montevideo, Instituto de Cultura Uruguayo-Brasileño, 1969. 63 p., bibl., fold. maps (Publicación, 18)

Woman geographer who studied at Rio's federal university has written this brief textbook for Uruguayan readers.

7186. Veloso, Henrique Pimenta and **Harold Edgard Strang.** Alguns aspectos fisionômicos da vegetação do Brasil (IOC/M, 68:1, 1970, p. 9-76, map, plates)

Regional characterizations of vegetation associations in Brazil observable in the national parks. Excellent photography.

7187. ―― and ――. Aspectos da fitofisionomia do sul do Estado de Mato Grosso (IOC/M, 68:1, 1970, p. 77-88, plates)

Brazilian Institute for Agrarian Reform is promoting research on soil fertility in southern Mato Grosso, complemented by survey of main types of vegetation. Many photos in this article were taken to permit the identification of important species.

7188. Veríssimo, José. A pesca na Amazônia. Prefácio [por] Arthur Cézar Ferreira Reis. Belém, Bra., Univ. Federal do Pará, 1970. 130 p., illus. (Série José Veríssimo. Col. Amazônica)

Informative and almost poetic description of fishing in Amazon region with all its economic, social and environmental aspects. Unusual sketches of a way of life and activity few people have written about.

7189. Vianna, A. J. Barbosa. Recife: capital do Estado de Pernambuco. Apresentação [por] Orlando de Cunha Parahym. Recife, Bra., Govêrno de Pernambuco, Secretaria de Estado de Educação e Cultura, Depto. de Cultura, 1970. 173 p., plates, tables.

New ed. of an 1899 portrait of Recife with interesting facts and photos on the details of urban life.

7190. Wallace, Alfred Russell. A narrative of travels on the Amazon and Río Negro. 2. ed. With a new introduction by H. Lewis McKinney. N.Y., Dover Publications, 1972. 363 p., illus., maps, plates (Dover classics of travel, exploration, true adventure)

New (paperback) edition of an old classic travel account.

7191. Westphalen, Cecília Maria; Brasil Pinheiro Machado; and **Altiva Pilatti Balhana.** Nota prévia ao estudo da ocupação da terra no Paraná moderno. Curitiba, Bra., Univ. Federal do Paraná, Depto. de História, Conselho de Pesquisas, 1968. 52 p., bibl., maps, table (Boletim, 7)

Good for historical geography.

CARTOGRAPHY

JOHN R. HÉBERT

Geography and Map Division
Library of Congress

THE TWO YEAR PERIOD SINCE THE LAST REPORT of cartographic items in the *HLAS* has witnessed the retirement of J. Douglas Hill as contributor. The work of compiling a list of materials will be carried on, however, from the same source, the Geography and Map Division of the Library of Congress, as it was previously.

Since we realize that this section's list has been used by scholars and institutions as a guide to the purchase of maps, we have tried to maintain the standards of availability and timeliness on all current maps and atlases included. Only printed maps and atlases are listed. Ozalid or photostatic reproductions of current maps received through special procurement arrangements will not be listed. We will attempt not to list any items older than the previous edition of the *HLAS,* unless that item is still available, is significant and has not been previously included.

Noteworthy atlases that have been reviewed by this contributor include Jorge Quargnolo's *Atlas del potencial argentino* (item 7229) and the planning atlas for Buenos Aires province prepared by the provincial Asesoría Provincial de Desarrollo (item 7222). Both of these Argentine works contain a wealth of information on various economic and geographic factors affecting the nation's and Buenos Aires' growth and development. Additional interesting atlases are the *Atlas de la República de Chile* (item 7281), *Atlas de Colombia,* 2. ed. (item 7285) by Colombia's Instituto Geográfico Agustín Codazzi, the *National atlas of Jamaica* (item 7306) and the *Atlas de Venezuela,* 2. ed. (item 7346) by Venezuela's Dirección de Cartografía Nacional. The 1972 appearance of the *Atlas nacional de Guatemala* (item 7300), prepared by the Instituto Geográfico Nacional, is an outstanding contribution to that nation's cartographic materials and of value to the understanding of current geographical and economic factors in Guatemala.

Various mapping firms in Brazil, Colombia, and Mexico provided the largest selection of state maps of the various Latin American nations. The Sociedade Comercial e Representações Gráficas (items 7266-7268) and the Instituto Brasileiro de Geografia (items 7249-7253) published useful Brazilian state maps. Hector Esparza Torres' state maps (items 7313-7314) provided complete coverage of the Mexican states and districts.

We have tried to provide a representative list of plans for the major Latin American cities. Some of the entries, undoubtedly, are later editions of previously mentioned city plans. One that has not been mentioned, however, is the plan of British Honduras' new capital city, Belmopan (item 7276). While not cartographically distinctive, it is unique. Regarding the general listing of city plans, where a choice was available between a plan of the city with an index and a key or one without, we chose naturally only the one with the aids.

The difficulty of reporting completed series maps for the Latin American nations persists. However, it is a pleasure to report the completion of Costa Rica's nine sheet mid-scale (1:200,000) series prepared by the Instituto Geográfico Nacional (item 7291). This series should be included in any map library specializing in Central American studies. It is also our understanding that most of the Central American nations have been mapped at the scale of 1:50,000.

We call the reader's attention to the transparencies (for use in overhead projectors) of all the areas of Latin America prepared by the General Drafting Company (item 7211). A supportive text accompanies each of the 12 sets. This format should provide ease in usage over the more cumbersome wall maps.

In addition to maps and atlases, the reviewer has included articles and cartobibliographies relating to the cartographic record of Latin America. Obviously some noteworthy written contributions are missing from this list due to the necessity yet to establish a thorough search technique for such articles. Regarding those articles included in this edition, the cartobibliographies in the Map Collectors' Circle (items 7199-7201, 7207-7208) should be interesting to the historical cartographer especially those involved in Caribbean studies.

Since this Cartography section constitutes our initial effort for the HANDBOOK, some future plans are suggested. We hope to devise a more efficient way to report general city plans by shortening the entries and yet conforming to the editorial demands of the *HLAS* staff. The format may change to accomodate increased listings of such maps. A more thorough survey of journal articles and cartobibliographies is contemplated. It is the belief of this contributor that the previous cartographical listings in *HLAS* contained mainly current information. We wish to widen our scope. Regarding that, we will improve our lists of articles of interest to the historical cartographer in future contributions. Also, the inclusion of a few entries of significant historical maps and the collections in which they are contained is contemplated. Although the historical maps to be listed will no longer be available in original form to the scholar or institution, a determination whether or not facsimile copies can be made will be indicated. By increased journal articles and the listing of historical maps we hope to entice historical cartographers and geographers, historians, sociologists, etc., to peruse our entries and find them useful. With these innovations we hope to provide a more rounded listing of cartographic items and related materials to Latin Americanists.

ARTICLES AND CARTOBIBLIOGRAPHIES

7192. Cline, Howard F. The Oztoticpac lands map of Texcoco, 1540 (*in* Ristow, Walter W. A la carte; selected papers on maps and atlases. Washington, Library of Congress, 1972, p. 5-33)

Reprint of Howard Cline's article on the Oztoticpac map (contained in the Geography and Map Division, Library of Congress) which appeared in the *Quarterly Journal of the Library of Congress* (April 1966). Excellent study on an Aztec land litigation map.

7193. Colombia. Instituto Geográfico Agustín Codazzi. Indice de publicaciones cartográficas y zonas aerofotografiadas. Bogotá, Centro de Información Geográfica, 1971. 1 v. (Unpaged)

Seven page index to mapping done by Agustín Codazzi of Colombia at the scales of 1 : 100,000/ 1 : 50,000/1 : 25,000/1 : 10,000/1 : 60,000/1 : 40,000/1 : plastic overlay showing divisions of individual states is useful in determining mapping of specific areas. 20,000.A

7195. Ferreira Sobral, Eduardo F. and others *comps.* Catálogo de la colección cartográfica del Centro Documental [Catalogue of the Documental Center's cartographic series]. Prólogo [por] Armando L. De Fina. B.A., Instituto Nacional de Tecnología Agropecuaria (INTA), Estación Experimental Agropecuaria Pergamino, 1970. 268 p. (Serie bibliográfica, 52)

Checklist of holdings of Argentine Estación Experimental de Tecnología Agropecuaria. Maps are mainly current.

7196. Galráo, María José *comp.* Indice de mapas existentes en la Biblioteca Conmemorative Orton: preliminar. Turrialba, C.R., Organización de los Estados Americanos. Instituto Interamericano de Ciencias Agrícolas, Centro de Enseñanza e Investigación, 1969. 195 p.

Lists general and thematic maps (20th century) contained in Orton Library's collections. Majority relate to Latin America. Includes index.

7197. Hébert, John. Maps by Ephraim George Squier; journalist, scholar and diplomat (Quarterly Journal of the Library of Congress [Washington] 29:1, Jan. 1972, p. 14-31)

Discusses Squier's activities in Central America and Peru during mid-19th century as US diplomat and scholar. Article is preceded by a cartobibliography of 38 manuscript maps attributable to Squier contained in the Library of Congress' Geography and Map Division. Maps relate primarily to Squier's 1853 venture to build a railroad through Honduras.

7198. ———. Population maps of the Western Hemisphere; a list of national and regional population maps from 1960 in the Geography and Map Division, Library of Congress. Washington, Library of Congress, Geography and Map Division, March 1971. 21 p., maps.

Lists population maps of US, Canada, and Latin American nations.

7199. Kapp, Kit S. The early maps of Colombia up to 1850. London, Map Collectors' Circle, 1971. 32 p., maps (Map collectors' series, 8:77)

Useful list of maps and illustrations of pre-1850 Colombia maps.

7200. ———. The early maps of Panama up to 1865. London, Map Collectors' Circle, 1971. 31 p., maps (Map collectors' series, 8:73)

Useful listing of pre-1865 Panama maps.

7201. ———. The printed maps of Jamaica up to 1825. London, Map Collectors' Circle, 1968. 36 p., maps (Map Collectors' series 5:42)

Lists in cartobibliography 153 maps of Jamaica, from Bordone's 1528 map of island to that of Weimar Geographisches Institut of 1825; 33 maps are illustrated. Useful survey of early mapping of Jamaica.

7202. León Tello, Pilar *comp.* Mapas, planos y dibujos de la Sección de Estado del Archivo Histórico Nacional. Madrid, Dirección General de Archivos y Bibliotecas, 1969.

Entries of 386 maps, plans and drawings contained in the collections of la Sección de Estado of the historical archive. Materials are mainly of the 18th and 19th centuries and include 124 printed and manuscript maps relating to America.

7203. Martin, Lawrence and **Walter W. Ristow.** John Disturnell's map of the United Mexican States (*in* Ristow, Walter W. *comp.* A la carte: selected papers on maps and atlases. Washington, Library of Congress, 1972, p. 204-221)

Lawrence Martin's article, edited and revised by Walter Ristow, appeared initially in V. 5 of *Treaties and other international acts of the United States of America* (1937). Current article compares the 24 editions of the Disturnell map, editions 12 and seven of which were used by the Mexican and US governments as the treaty map for the 1848 Treaty of Guadalupe-Hidalgo.

7204. ———— and ————. **South American historical maps** (in Ristow, Walter W. *comp*. A la carte: selected papers on maps and atlases. Washington, Library of Congress, 1972, p. 189-203)

Dr. Ristow has revised and expanded Lawrence Martin's general article which appeared in the *Library of Congress Quarterly* Journal of Current Acquisitions (1944). Particular maps discussed are the Spanish maps prepared to show boundaries between Spanish and Portuguese possessions in South America following 1 Oct. 1777 Treaty of San Ildefonso.

7205. Melli, Oscar Ricardo. Atlas geográficos de la República Argentina; 1869-1892 (PAIGH/RC, 17:17, 1968, p. 51-87)

Excellent article on Argentine atlases ranging from Martin de Moussy's 1869 Atlas to the scientifically prepared Atlas of the Instituto Geográfico Argentino (1882-92). Includes description of the contents of these Atlases as well as various comparisons of the material.

7206. Smith, Thomas R. Cruz Cano's map of South America, Madrid, 1775: its creation, adversities and rehabilitation (IM, 20, 1966, p. 49-78)

Outstanding article on famous map of South America by Cruz Cano. Smith compares map's various states and editions pinpointing with illustrations the variations noted.

7207. Tooley, R. V. The printed maps of Antigua. London, Map Collectors' Circle, 1969. 12 p., maps (Map collectors series, 55)

Describes 102 maps of Antigua issued from 1689 to 1899. Works contain clear illustrations useful to both researcher and map collector.

7208. ————. Printed maps of Dominica and Grenada. London, Map Collectors' Circle, 1970. 15 p., maps (Map collectors' series, 7:62)

Describes 64 maps of Grenada from 1717 to 1874; 36 maps of Dominica dated 1745 to 1898. With 12 illustrations.

7209. United States. Board on Geographic Names. Dominican Republic: official standard names. 2 ed. Prepared by the Defense Mapping Agency Topographic Center. Washington, 1972. 477 p.

Extensive gazetteer of the Dominican Republic.

GENERAL

7210. Comisión de Integración Eléctrica Regional (CIER), *Montevideo.* Atlas del desarrollo energético de América del Sur. 3. ed. Montevideo, 1971. 43 l., 9 colored maps, 55 × 76 cm.

Maps indicate electricity, power distribution, power resources, petroleum and power plants in South America. Good source of information on continent's energy development.

7211. General Drafting Company (firm), Convent Station, N.J. Latin America, set 2. Prepared by Bertrand P. Boucher. Convent Station, N.J.? 1969. 49 maps (part colored) in 12 folders (World regional geography transparencies)

Transparencies of South America, Mexico, Central America, West Indies, Colombia, Venezuela, The Guianas, Brazil, Bolivia, Ecuador-Peru, Paraguay-Uruguay, Argentina-Chile. Each set includes climatic, political, population density, outline, relief, industrial, agricultural, and transportation maps. Sets include from 4 to 5 maps and are ideal for presentation with an overhead projector. Text with supporting information and questions accompanies the transparencies.

7212. Hueck, Kurt and Paul Seibert. Vegetationskarte von Südamerika. Stuttgart, FRG, Gustav Fischer Verlag, 1972. Colored 96 × 68 com. Scale 1 = 8,000,000.

Well-presented map of South America's vegetation. Separate explanatory text accompanies map. All material presented in German.

7213. Lonardi, Alberto G. and **Maurice Ewing.** Bathymetric chart of the Argentine Basin, the Rio Grande Rise, Malvinas Plateau, Scotia Arc, and Scotia Sea. Oxford, Pergamon Press, c1971. Colored map. 105 × 122 cm. Scale ca. 1 : 2,900,000.

Depths shown by gradient tints and contours. Descriptive text of this chart is published in "Sediment Transport and Distribution in the Argentine Basin.—Pt. 4—Bathymetry of the Continental Margin, Argentine Basin and other related Provinces—Canyons and Sources of Sediments"—by Alberto G. Lonardi and Maurice Ewing, in vol. 8 of *Physics and Chemistry of the Earth* (Pergamon Press, London), Authors are associated in the Lamont Geological Observatory, Columbia Univ.

7214. MacMillan Education Limited (firm), *Kingston.* The Caribbean. Kingston, Jamaica Publishing House, 1971. Colored. 87 × 112 cm. Scale 1 : 3,500,000.

Wall maps. All show roads, cities and towns, capitals, boundaries, sea and air routes, oil bunkering stations, oil pipelines and Satellite Earth station. Insets: British Honduras, Jamaica, Trinidad, Puerto Rico, Guadeloupe, Barbados, hurricane tracks.

7215. National Geographic Society. South America. Washington, 1972. Colored. 74 × 56 cm. Scale 1 : 10,700,000.

Thematic maps on verso are perhaps more useful than general map of the continent: physical map; climate; land use and population density; mining and industry; before Columbus; discovery and conquest; wars for Independence. Map is supplement to *National Geographic* (142:4, Oct. 1972, p. 445-A).

7216. Stevenson, Merritt R.; Oscar Guillén G.; and José Santoro de Ycaza. Marine atlas of the Pacific coastal waters of South America [Atlas de las Aguas Costaneras del Oceano Pacifico en la America del Sur]. Berkeley, Calif., Univ. of California Press, 1970. 1 v. (Unpaged)

Atlas is presented in English and Spanish. Charts showing temperature, salinity, density, oxygen, surface circulation, surface winds and barometric pressure are included.

7217. **Stuart, George F.** Archeological map of Middle America: land of the feathered serpent. Washington, National Geographic Society, 1972. Colored. 47 × 62 cm. Scale 1: 2,250,000.

Map is indexed, has a comparative table of development of Oaxaca, Central Mexico, Gulf Coast, Maya and Old World, and contains short historical sketches. Map covers the area from Mexico City to Tegucigalpa and locates various archeological sites or findings. Insets: Teotihuacán, Monte Albán, Chichén Itzá, Tirac. On verso: the Valley of Mexico.

7218. **United Nations. Food and Agriculture Organization.** Soil map of the world. V. 4, South America. Paris, UNESCO, 1971. Colored.2sheets(IV-1,IV-2)each76 × 108cm. Scale 1 : 5,000,000.

Colorful, useful maps of the variant soil types of South America accompanied by explanatory texts.

ARGENTINA

7219. **Automóvil Club Argentino,** *Buenos Aires*. [Maps and provinces] B.A., 1971. 81 × 69 cm. Scale 1 : 1,140,480; Corrientes, 1971. 47 × 43 cm. Scale 1 : 1,140,480; Entre Ríos, 1971. 48 × 46 cm. Scale 1 : 1,140,480; La Rioja, 1971. 59 × 43 cm. Scale 1 : 1,064,448; Mendoza, 1971. 65 × 48cm. Scale 1 : 988,416; Neuquén, 1971. 59 × 44 cm. Scale 1 : 988, 416; Santa Fe, 1971. 71 × 54 cm. Scale 1 : 1,140,480. Buenos Aires, Zona Centro, 1972. 40 × 59 cm.

General reference maps with types of roads, towns, streams, and administrative boundaries given. Each provincial map contains insets of province's major cities, e.g., Santa Fe (city), Neuquén, Mendoza, Junín, La Rioja, Paraná, Corrientes, and La Plata.

7220. ———, ———. República Argentina: carta turística. B.A., 1971. Colored. 8 sheets, ea. 79 × 70 cm. Scale 1 : 1,140,480.

Major concern of these maps are auto travel conditions in nation. Includes all classes of roads, town, administrative boundaries and other cultural features.

7221. **Buenos Aires** (city), *Arg*. **Oficina Regional de Desarrollo. Area Metropolitana.** Región metropolitana de Buenos Aires organización del espacio urbano, esquema directa, año 2000. B.A., Consejo Nacional de Desarrollo, Secretaría, 1971.

Map of land usage and population density of Buenos Aires projected to 2000 A.D. Shows air and auto lines, park lands, residential and commercial areas.

7222. ——— (province), *Arg*. **Asesoría Provincial de Desarrollo.** Atlas de planeamiento de la provincia de Buenos Aires. Ejecutor del trabajo base: Remus Tetus. Elaboración de los cómputos y textos definitivos: Asesoría Provincial del Desarrollo. Texto y composición del atlas: Emilio L. Díaz y Adolfo O. Cambre. La Plata, Arg., Dirección de Impresiones del Estado, 1971. (Publicación, 18)

Planning atlas which furnishes statistics, graphs, seven transparencies used as overlays (regarding climate, electric energy, paved roads, railroads, hydrography erosion, and geomorphology) and 74 statistical maps of province divided into *municipios*. Detailed study of economic and geographical factors affecting Buenos Aires province's growth and development.

7223. ———, ———. **Dirección de Geodesia.** Alrededores de Buenos Aires. La Plata, Arg., Ministerio de Obras Públicas, 1972. Colored. 84 × 115 cm. Scale 1 : 100,000.

General map of Buenos Aires province surrounding B.A. city. Shows roads, streams, transportation lines and towns. Also gives district and *circunscripción* boundaries.

7224. **Bugarín, Antonio Alberto.** Primer mapa de la Patagonia y zona de influencia de Bahía Blanca. Técnico asesor: León Saucnier. [Printed by Instituto Geográfico Militar] Bahía Blanca, Casa Muñiz-Adelino Gutiérrez 1970? Colored. 106 × 74 cm. Scale 1 : 2,000,000.

Map of region which shows general cultural features, i.e., roads, towns, administrative boundaries.

7225. **Chivelekian, Juan C.** Zona lacustre argentina. B.A., Autómovil Club Argentino, 1972. Colored. 44 ½ × 63 cm. Scale 1 : 950,400.

General map of Argentina's Andean lake region, especially Bariloche area. On verso: description of region with particular reference to national parks, San Martín de los Andes and San Carlos de Bariloche. Insets on verso: map of San Carlos de Bariloche and distance from various Argentine cities.

7226. **Editorial Mapa** (firm), *Buenos Aires*. Zona urbana del Gran Buenos Aires. Cartógrafo: E. Mario Menconi. B.A., 1972. Colored map. 79 × 116 cm. Scale 1 : 40,000.

Oriented with north toward lower right. Accompanied by 47 p. guide entitled: "Guía de las Calles del Plano de la Zona Urbana del Gran Buenos Aires."

7227. **Kapelusz** (firm) *Buenos Aires*. Coloratlas Kapelusz; República Argentina; físico-político-económico-estadístico. B.A., 1971. 4 p., illus; 3 p. of colored maps; 9 p.

Presents Argentina in nine geographical sectors. Each includes population density, physical-political-geological structure and vegetation.

GEOGRAPHY: CARTOGRAPHIC MATERIALS

7228. Peuser Jacobo (firm), *Buenos Aires*. Departamento de Cartografía. Plano de la ciudad de Buenos Aires. B.A., 1972. Colored map. 87 × 101 cm. fold. in cover 27 × 17 cm. Scale 1 : 20,000.

Current general city plan of Buenos Aires. Indexed.

7229. Quargnolo, Jorge. Atlas del potencial argentino. B.A., Angel Estrada [and] Aula, 1972.

Excellent work. Presents 36 maps including over 30 thematic maps covering various subjects including population distribution, administration, rainfall, natural vegetation, energy, electrical, transportation, grain, fruit, cattle and fish. Maps are complemented by information in tabular form on themes presented.

7230. ———. República Argentina: recursos agricolas. Información geográfica, cartografía, diseño gráfico y tipografía realizado por Aula. B.A., Editorial Estrada, 1972. Colored. 130 × 90 cm. Scale 1:3,000,000.

Sixty-five symbols are used to show agricultural products and general land types. One of a number of useful thematic maps prepared by Aula. Inset: map of Argentine Antarctica.

7231. ———. República Argentina: recursos energéticos. Información geográfica, cartografía, diseño gráfico y tipografía realizado por Aula. B.A., Editorial Estrada, 1972. Colored. 130 × 90 cm. Scale 1 : 3,000,000.

Colorful map which appeared in reduced form in Quargnolo's *Resource atlas* (item 7229). Includes and indicates by symbolization various forms of energy resources. Inset: map of Antártida Argentina. Scholars will find this map as well as other Aula thematic maps (items 7230 and 7232) excellent visual aids.

7232. ———. República Argentina: recursos ganaderos y pesqueros. Información geográfica, cartografía, diseño gráfico y tipografía realizado por Aula. B.A., Editorial Estrada, 1972. Colored. 130 × 90 cm. Scale 1 : 3,000,000.

Various types of fish and livestock shown by location and symbol. Inset: map of Antártida Argentina.

7233. Ricci, Susana M. Provincia de La Pampa: mapa minero 1971. Con la colaboración de la Dirección de Minas de la Provincia de La Pampa. B.A., Dirección Nacional de PromociónMinera,1971.Colored.69 × 75cm. Scale 1 : 750,000.

Numbered key indicates mines in province and code indicates mineral used. Active and inactive mines are shown. Other general features, road, towns, departments, etc., are given.

7234. ———. Provincia de San Luis: mapa minero, 1971. Con la colaboración de la Dirección General de Minería de la Provincia de San Luis. B.A., Dirección Nacional de PromociónMinera,1971.Colored.70 × 43cm. Scale 1 : 760,320.

Numbered key indicates mines in province and code indicates mineral mined. Active and inactive mines are are shown. Other general features—roads, towns, departments etc., are given.

7235. ——— *comp.* Provincia del Neuquén: mapa mineral 1970-1971. Con la colaboración de la Dirección General de Minería de la provincia del Neuquén. B.A., Dirección Nacional de Promoción Minera, 1970-1971. Colored. 79 × 55 cm. 750,000.

Numbered key indicates mines in province and code indicates mineral mined. Active and inactive mines are shown. Other general features, road, towns, departroads, towns, departments, etc.

BARBADOS

7236. Barbados. The Town and Country Development Planning Office. Protection of water resources, restrictions on development. Bridgetown, Barbados Water Board, 1970. 28 × 25 inches. Scale 1 : 50,000.

Map shows areas where development is allowed and restricted (five categories) as a measure to conserve water and to avoid its pollution. Accompanying 4 p. text explains restrictions.

BOLIVIA

7237. Ayalaz, Alfredo. Atlas escolar de Bolivia: mapa general de Bolivia y departamentales en colores. 6. ed. La Paz, Colegio Don Bosco, 1969. 27 p.

An atlas of small scale colored maps of nation and its departments, divided by provinces. Maps show roads, railroads, towns, and streams. General information includes provincial capitals and products of particular departments. Last map is of Bolivia's Littoral department which is now under Chile-Antofagasta province.

7238. Bolivia. Instituto Geográfico Militar. Plano guía de la ciudad de Sucre, 1971. La Paz, 1971. Photo map. 62 × 42 cm. Scale 1 : 10,000.

Includes road types, railroads, street names, and location of major buildings. On verso: numbered key to building locations, short note on Sucre, and an inset map of the Chuquisaca department.

BRAZIL

GENERAL

7239. Almeida, Fernando Flávio Marques de. Mapa geológico do Brasil. Compilação por G. R. Derge e C. A. G. da Vinha, 1970. Planejamento cartográfico pela S. de Cartografia Geológica, D.G.M. Brasília, Depto. Nacional de Produção Mineral, 1971. Colored. 93 × 104 cm. Scale 1 : 5,000,000.

Geologic map of Brazil enhanced by clear legend which explains color and symbolization coding used. Insets: Atol das Rocas, Rochedos de São Pedro e São Paulo, Ithada Trindade, Arquipélago de Fernando de Noronha, Ithas Martin Vaz.

7240. Brazil. Departamento Nacional de Estradas de Rodagem. Sistema rodoviario federal 1970. Brasília. 1970. Colored. 46 × 46 cm. Scale 1 : 10,000,000.

Shows road system of Brazil including planned, under construction and paved roads. Shows major roads of area above Brasília, roads of the Program of National Integration. Accompanying map is report "Transamazonian Highways," subtitled "A Report on the Transamazonian and the Cuiabá-Santarem Highways" presented by Ministry of Transportation of Federative Republic of Brazil to the VI World Meeting of the International Road Federation held in Montreal, Canada, Oct. 1970. Map highlights two major Amazonian roads, Transamazonian Highway and Cuiabá-Santarém Highway.

7241. ———. Instituto Brasileiro de Geografia. Departamento de Cartografia. República Federativa do Brasil. Rio, 1972. Colored. 92 × 99 cm. Scale 1 : 5,000,000.

General reference map showing various cultural and geographical features. Relief is indicated by colored tints. Inset: Distrito Federal. [1 : 5,000,000]

7242. ———. ———. ———. Atlas nacional do Brasil. pt. 2, Regional. Mapa físico; Sul, Sudeste, Norte, Nordeste, Centro, Oeste. Rio, 1970-1972. Colored. 54 × 74 cm. Scale 1 : 4,000,000.

General physical map of country which employs layer tints to express altitude.

7243. ———. ———. ———. Brasil: população, densidade demográfica. Rio, 1971. Colored. 92 × 99 cm. Scale 1 : 5,000,000.

This population density map uses layer tints to illustrate its purpose. This and item 7244 are companion distinctive maps.

7244. ———. ———. ———. Brasil: população; população urbana, população rural. Rio, 1972. Colored. 92 × 99 cm. Scale 1 : 5,000,000.

Population map of the nation which used graduated spheres to indicate variant populations. A distinctive thematic map.

7245. Cartobrás (firm), *Rio*. República Federativa do Brasil: edição comemorativa do sesquicentenário do Independéncia. 1822-1972. Rio, 1972. Colored. 100 × 119 cm. Scale 1 : 4,500,000.

Useful general reference map showing 200-mile limit of Brazil and indicating trans-Amazonica and transcontinental highways. As title indicates map was prepared for 150th anniversary of Brazil independence. Insets: Brasil Regiões Geográficas; Brasil Superintêndencias de Desenvolvimento; Distrito Federal.

Cortesão, Jaime. História do Brasil nos velhos mapas. See *HLAS 34:2906*.

7246. Ferreira, Evaldo Osório and others. Mapa tectônico do Brasil. Brasília, Ministério das Minas e Energia, 1971. 32 p. Colored. 93 × 104 cm. Scale 1 : 5,000,000.

Colorful and well prepared map of Brazil accompanied by 32-p. text in Portuguese and English. Insets: Atol das Rocas, Rochedos de São Pedro e São Paulo, Ilha de Trindade, Arquipélago de Fernando de Noronha, Ilhas Martin Vaz.

7247. Geomapas Editôra de Mapas e Guias (firm), *São Paulo*. Brasil, 1972: 2° semestre. São Paulo, 1972. Colored. 94 × 89 cm. Scale 1 : 5,000,000.

General reference map which employs a dot system to indicate range of urban population from 50,000 to 500,000.

STATES AND REGIONS

7248. Brazil. Companhia do Desenvolvimento do Planalto Central. Distrito Federal: mapa rodoviário, 1971. Brasília, 1971. Colored. 45 × 56 cm. Scale 1 : 200,000.

Road map of Federal District, Brasília.

7249. ———. Instituto Brasileiro de Geografia. Departamento de Cartografia. Mapa de bacia Amazônica. Rio, 1971. Colored map. 167 × 211 cm. on 4 sheets 89 × 113 cm. Scale 1 : 1,500,000.

Excellent map of region showing state boundaries, streets, towns, roads. Existing and proposed roads are especially noted. Map's one failing is lack of legend.

7250. ———. ———. Estado de Paraíba. Rio, 1970. Colored map. 60 × 96 cm. Scale 1 : 500,000.

General reference map of state indicating roads, streams, towns, and municipio boundaries. Relief shown by contour lines and spot heights.

7251. ———. ———. Estado do Acre. Rio, 1970. Colored map. 61 × 88 cm. Scale 1 : 1,000,000.

Good general reference map. Relief indicated by contour lines.

7252. ———. ———. Estado do Piauí. Rio, 1970. Colored. 99 × 68 cm. Scale 1 : 1,000,000.

General map of state indicating municipal boundaries and relief by contour lines.

7253. ———. ———. Território de Roraima. Rio, 1970. Colored map. 81 × 70 cm. Scale 1 : 1,000,000.

General map which includes legend. Relief is shown by contours.

7254. Editôra Presidente Limitada (firm) *Rio*. Estado da Guanabara: geográfico, didáctico, rodoviário, turístico. Rio, 1972. Colored. 64 × 117 cm. Scale 1 : 60,000 (Mapa Schoeffer, 5)

No index. Names only major thoroughfares. Indicates limited land use. Shows relief ortographically.

7255. ———, ———. Estado do Rio de Janeiro. 10. ed. Rio, 1972. Colored. 61 × 91 cm. Scale 1 : 500,000 (Mapa Schneffer, 6)

Legend in Portuguese, Spanish and English. Gives various grades of towns and highways and specific information for tourists including locations of gasoline stations, service centers, hotels and restaurants. Uses orthographical relief.

7256. Geocarta (firm), *Rio*. Situação da cafeicultura em 1965: estado de São Paulo. Rio, Instituto Brasileiro do Café, Grupo Executivo de Racionalização da Cafeicultura, Serviço de Fotointerpretação, 1970. Colored. 77 × 116 cm. Scale 1 : 800,000.
Locates areas of coffee growth in state by municipal areas.

7257. ———, ———. Situação de cafeicultura em 1965: estado do Paraná. Rio, Instituto Brasileiro do Café, Grupo Executivo de Racionalização da Cafeicultura, Serviço de Fotointerpretação, 1971. Colored. 77 × 110 cm. Scale 1: 600,000.
Locates areas of coffee growth in state by municipal areas. Text contained in separate booklet.

7258. ———, ———. Situação do cafeicultura em 1970: estado do Paraná. Rio, Instituto Brasileiro do Café, Grupo Executivo de Racionalização da Cafeicultura, Serviço de Fotointerpretação, 1971. Colored. 77 × 110 cm. Scale 1 : 600,000.
Shows new coffee areas in state and those already established. Top portion of state divided into 400-hectare divisions and color coded as to level of production on new and established coffee plantations.

7259. Geomapas (firm), *São Paulo*. Mapa do Estado de São Paulo: divisão política. São Paulo, 1972. Colored. 68 × 95 cm. Scale 1 : 1,000,000.
General and colorful map of state with roads, towns, streams, and municipio boundaries. Includes inset map of Greater São Paulo, scale 1:500,000.

Lima, Gelson Rangel. Solos. See item 7101.

7260. Minas Gerais (state), *Bra*. **Departamento Geográfico.** Estado de Minas Gerais, mapa geográfico. Belo Horizonte, Bra., 1970. Colored map. 100 × 122 cm. Scale 1 : 1,000,000.
Map includes information on transportation networks, administrative boundaries, towns by population. Includes insets on hydrography, climate and vegetation.

7261. Nönoya Fieno, José. Grande região Nordeste: político, econômico, rodoviário. São Paulo, Geomapas, 1972. Colored. 97 × 82 cm. Scale 1 : 2,000,000.
General map of northeast with products and minerals indicated by a keyed symbol.

7262. Paraná (state), *Bra*. **Departamento de Geografia, Terras e Colonização, Divisão de Geografia.** Mapa do estado do Paraná, 1971.

Curitiba, Bra., 1971. Colored. 82 × 115. Scale 1 : 600,000.
Main map shows towns, roads, streams, individual municipios, railroad lines, spot heights, airports. Relief shown by hachuring. Well executed map. Inset maps show states, climate, geology and judicial division.

7263. Santa Catarina (state), *Bra*. **Departamento Estadual de Geografia e Cartografia.** Estado de Santa Catarina. Florianópolis, Bra., Secretaria do Desenvolvimento Econômico, 1972. Colored. 56 × 76 cm. Scale 1 : 750,000.
General map showing each municipio.

7264. São Paulo (state), *Bra*. **Secretaria de Economia e Planejamento.** São Paulo, desenvolvimento: atlas, 1970. São Paulo, 1971. 10 plates in portfolio. 43 × 60 cm.
Very colorful maps cover: political administrative divisions; demography; agriculture; industry; education; and energy. Political maps divide states into *região, sub-região* and *municipio*. Each map is at a scale 1:200,000. A translucent sheet with the political breakdowns divided by black lines can be used to give the subject info in demography, agriculture, for each municipio, region or subregion desired. Each subject has accompanying graphs. Useful portofolio of maps.

7265. Serviços Aerofotogramétricos Cruzeiro do Sul (firm), *São Paulo*. Mapa rodoviário do estado da Guanabara. Preparado por: Depto. de Estradas de Rodagem. São Paulo, 1971. Colored map. 66 × 120 cm. Scale ca. 1 : 60,000.
Road map of state with relief shown by contours and spot heights.

7266. Sociedade Comercial e Representações Gráficas Limitada (firm), *Curitiba, Bra*. Brasil. Curitiba, Bra., Impressora Paranaense, 1972. Colored. 102 × 97 cm. Scale 1:4,500,000.
General map of country indicating relief by colored tint and bathymetric information. Insets: 1) Ilhas Oceânicas Brasileiras. 2) Thematic maps; Divisão Regional; Tipos de Clima; Vegetação; and Relêvo. 3) Distrito Federal de Brasília.

7267. ———, ———. Mapa do Nordeste do Brasil. Curitiba, Bra., Impressora Paranaense, 1972. Colored. 95 × 110 cm. Scale 1 : 1,500,000.
General map of northeast region including states of Maranhão, Paiauí, Ceará, Rio Grande do Norte, Paraíba, Pernambuco, Alagoas, Sergipe and parts of Bahia, Goiás, and Pará. Indicates roads, towns, streams, airports and bathymetric depths off-shore.

7268. ———, ———. [Maps of states] Bahia, 1969-70, 94 × 88 cm. Scale 1 : 1,200,000; Ceará, 1972, 118 × 96 cm. Scale 1 : 500,000; Mato Grosso, 1972, 120 × 85 cm. Scale 1 : 1,600,000; Minas Gerais, 1971, 83 × 106 cm. Scale 1 : 1,250,000; Paraná(Norte), 1972, 76 × 117 cm. Scale 1 : 450,000; Paraná, 1972,

61 × 89 cm. Scale 1 : 1,000,000; Rio Grande do Sul, 1971, 102 × 122 cm. Scale 1 : 750,000; Rio de Janeiro, 1970, 77 × 112 cm. Scale 1 : 400,000; Santa Catarina, 1970, 81 × 115 cm. Scale 1 : 500,000; Santa Catarina, 1971, 41 × 58 ʻcm. Scale 1 : 1,000,000. Curitiba, Bra., 1971-1972.

General reference maps of states with municípios in various colors, populated places, roads, railroads, and indicating hydrography, when it applies. Several of the maps, e.g., those of Paraná, Rio de Janeiro, Mato Grosso, contain insets of geographical locations in state or thematic maps furnishing information on geology and climate.

7269. Universidade de São Paulo. Instituto de Geografia. Atlas do Estado de São Paulo. São Paulo, 1972? 21 p.

Atlas covered: geophysical, hydrography, population, agriculture and industry. Good useful atlas.

CITIES

7270. Blanco, Flaliero. Município de São Paulo e seus arredores. 5. ed. São Paulo, Casa Especializada em Mapas, 1972. Colored. 82 × 99 cm. Scale 1 : 100,000.

General map of São Paulo municipio showing only major roads as well as future circumferential road around São Paulo.

7271. Curitiba (city) *Bra.* **Instituto de Pesquisa e Planejamento Urbano de Curitiba.** Curitiba: Zoneamento de USO do Solo. Curitiba. 1971. Colored. 89 × 62 cm. Scale 1 : 20,000.

Colorful land-use map of city. No index.

7272. Editôra Presidente Limitada (firm), *Rio.* Guia Schaeffer: Rio, cidade do Rio de Janeiro, Estado da Guanabara. Rio, 1972. Colored. 86 × 122 cm. Scale 1 : 25,200.

General street map of city with index on verso. Relief ortographically presented.

7273. Natividade Filho, Osny. Planta dos logradouros públicos de Florianópolis. 3. ed. Florianópolis, Bra., 1972. Colored. 49 × 75 cm. Scale 1 : 8,500.

City plan with street names listed in key.

7274. Oliveira, Luiz Gonzaga de. Planta parcial da cidade do Recife. Elaborada e desenhada por . . . Recife? Bra., 1972? Colored. 39 × 59 cm. Scale ca. 1 : 10,000.

Some buildings shown pictorially. Map is oriented with north toward the upper right. Tourist information on verso.

7275. Rohrbach, Paulo Carlos. Planta de Curitiba. Curitiba, Bra., Sociedade Comercial e Representações Gráficas, 1972. Colored. 88 × 61 cm. Scale 1 : 20,000.

General city plan of Curitiba with street index. Includes inset of Santa Felicidade.

BRITISH HONDURAS

BELIZE

7276. British Honduras. Belmopan in the heart of Belize, 1972. 21 × 29 cm. Scale not given.

Map of new capital of British Honduras. Although very simplistic, it is only plan of city seen by this contributing editor.

7277. United Kingdom. Ministry of Defense. Directorate of Military Survey. British Honduras town plan: Belize. Belize, Crown Copyright, 1970. Colored. 95 ×57 cm. Scale 1 : 500,000.

Used UTM grid photographic map with streets and major buildings printed over in red and black. Effective presentation.

BRITISH VIRGIN ISLANDS

7278. United Kingdom. Ministry of Defense. Directorate of Military Survey. British Virgin Islands. London, 1969. 6 sheets. Colored. 63 × 77 cm. Scale 1 : 25,000. (Series, E-803)

Excellent topographical series which updates previous Directorate of Military Survey series (DOS 346, E837).

CAICOS ISLANDS

7279. United Kingdom. Ministry of Defense. Directorate of Military Survey. Turks and Caicos Islands. London, 1971. 90 × 73 cm. Scale 1 : 10,000 (Series, E-8113)

Large scale topographical series of Turks and Caicos Islands. Large scale mapping of the British possessions and former British possessions are a nceessary addition to any facility interested in the Caribbean area.

CAYMAN ISLANDS

7280. United Kingdom. Directorate of Overseas Surveys. Cayman Islands. Compiled, drawn and photographed by . . . 2. ed. London, 1972. Colored. 2 maps on 1 sheet: 21 × 32 cm. [and] 12 × 32 cm. (DOS, 928)

Map shows principal roads, tracks, district boundaries, subdistricts and towns. Altitude given in feet.

CHILE

7281. Chile. Ministerio de Defensa Nacional. Instituto Geográfico Militar. Atlas de la República de Chile; Atlas of the Republic of Chile; Atlas de la République du Chili. Santiago, 1970. 244 p., illus. Part colored, colored coats of arms, colored maps. 41 cm.

Atlas contains topographical maps of country by section running north to south at a scale of 1 : 1,000,000. In addition, atlas contains 15 thematic maps indicating climatic conditions, population density, geology, fish distribution, and tourism, etc. Gazetteer appears at end of volume. In topographic maps, color tints are used to indicate altitude. Geographic synthesis of Chile by provinces appears at front of volume and shown by region, principal mountains, lakes, rivers, islands, ports, airports, railroad stations, roads, chief production, schools, and communications media. While not filled with outstanding and large scale topographical maps, atlas has useful thematic maps and pages of photographs of cities and regions in Chile. In Spanish, English and French.

COLOMBIA

7282. Acevedo Latorre, Eduardo. Atlas de mapas antiguos de Colombia, siglos XVI a XIX. Bogotá, Litografía Arco, 1971. 1 v. (Unpaged)

Historical collection of maps of Colombia from 1500 to 1889. The maps are clearly and handsomely presented but with little explanation as to their significance. Included are general maps of the country and city plans.

7283. Colombia. Dirección General de Conservación. Red de carreteras nacionales en conservación. Bogotá, Ministerio de Obras Públicas, 1970. 67 × 49 cm. Scale 1 : 3,041, 280.

Shows road conditions with paved, unpaved, under construction and projected roads listed.

7284. ———. Federación Nacional de Cafeteros. Investigaciones Económicas. Mapa de utilización actual de la tierra de la zona cafetera de Colombia, 1971. Bogotá, 1971. Colored. 129 × 93 cm. Scale 1 : 1,500,000.

Indicates various areas of coffee production in Colombia and types of coffee plantations. Map appeared in *Atlas cafetero de Colombia* and now issued separately.

7285. ———. Instituto Geográfico Agustín Codazzi. Atlas de Colombia. 2. ed. Bogotá, 216 p.

Essentially same material as in first edition, 1967. Contains departments and major city maps, numerous thematic maps and photographs of various portions of country. Excellent atlas, one of the few good national atlases produced in Latin America. Includes index.

7286. ———. ———. [Maps of Departments] Bogotá, 1969-70. Caldas, 1970. 54 × 69 cm. Scale 1 : 250,000. César, 1970, 2 sheets each 77 × 74 cm. Scale 1 : 250,000. Chocó, 1970. 55 × 109 cm. Scale 1 : 250,000. Magdalena, 1969. 115 × 75 cm. Scale 1 : 250,000. Sucre, 1970. 104 × 74 cm. Scale 1 : 250,000.

Essentially these maps offer same type of information. roads, towns, streams, municipio boundaries. Relief is given in contour lines and in hypometric tints. Includes inset maps of the major cities in the departments, e.g., Manizales, Valledupar, Quibdó, Santa Marta and Sincelejo.

7287. ———. ———. Plano de la ciudad de Bogotá. Bogotá, 1971. Colored. 68 × 99 cm. Scale 1 : 25,000.

General maps with index to sites of interest and barrios. Verso includes inset of map of center city.

7288. ———. ———. Plano de la ciudad de Medellín. Bogotá, 1971. Colored. 47 × 99 cm. Scale 1 : 25,000.

Map of city and vicinity indicating location of churches, schools, hotels, theatres, consulates, hospitals, sites of interest and cemeteries. Relief showing contour lines. On verso: map of central portion of Medellín.

7289. ———. ———. República de Colombia: mapa físico político. Bogotá, 1972. Colored. 131 × 93 cm. Scale 1 : 1,500,000.

Main maps show administrative boundaries, roads, towns, streams, and classes of ports. Relief shown by contour lines. Excellent general map of nation. Insets of Colombia's island possessions also appear.

7290. ———. Ministerio de Minas y Petróleos. Instituto Nacional de Investigaciones Geológico-Mineras. Mapa geológico de la Península de la Guajira, Colombia. [Preparado] con la colaboración del United States Geological Survey. Compilación por Earl M. Irving. Bogotá, 1972, Colored. 91 × 131 cm. Scale 1 : 100,000.

Contour intervals of 100m. On verso: "Cuadro comparativo de la Leyenda Estratigráfica de las Diferentes Areas de la Guajira."

COSTA RICA

7291. Costa Rica. Instituto Geográfico Nacional. Costa Rica. San José, 1968-1971. 9 sheets, 48 × 68 cm each. Scale 1 : 200,000.

Excellent topographical map of the country. Each sheet has a legend. Complete in nine sheets.

CUBA

7292. Cuba. Instituto Cubano de Geodesia y Cartografía. Mapa turístico Cuba. La Habana, 1972. 63 × 94 cm. Scale ca. 1 : 1,500,000.

General information map with relief shown by shading and spot heights. Includes inset maps of 10 principal cities, tourist information, a distance chart, explanatory notes and indexes.

DOMINICA

7293. United Kingdom. Overseas Development Administration. Roseau and Environs, Dominica, Lesser Antilles. London, 1972. Colored. 77 × 63 cm. Scale 1 : 5,000 (D.O.S. series, 151)

Detailed city plan with major locations indexed.

DOMINICAN REPUBLIC

7294. Dominican Republic. Oficina Nacional de Estadística. Mapa de la República Dominicana. Santo Domingo, ONE, 1971. 19 × 25 cm. Scale 1 : 1,900,800.

Administrative map of country to the municipal level.

7295. ———. **Universidad Autónoma de Santo Domingo. Instituto Geográfico Universitario.** Plano de la ciudad de Santo Domingo. Santo Domingo, 1972. Colored. 38 × 69 ½ cm. Scale ca. 1 : 30,400.

General city plan, but without index.

ECUADOR

7296. Ecuador. Dirección General de Geología y Minas. Departamento de Cartografía. Mapa geológico detallado del Ecuador. Quito, 1970. Scale 1 : 100,000.

Geology map series with contour lines. Locates construction materials: gravel, stone. Includes index to adjoining sheets and locational map. Maps and tectonic profiles are given on verso. Explanatory sheets accompany map.

7297. Granado G., U.M. Santiago de Guayaquil. Guayaquil, Ecua., Artes Gráficas Senefelder, 1972. Colored. 80 × 60 cm. Scale 1 : 15,200.

General city plan, but no index.

EL SALVADOR

7298. El Salvador. Instituto Geográfico Nacional. Zacatecoluca. San Salvador, Instituto Geográfico Nacional, 1972. Pictomapa. 60 × 69 cm. Scale 1 : 5,000.

Pictomap including key to interesting sites.

GUADELOUPE

7299. France. Institut Géographique National. Guadeloupe: carte touristique et routière. Paris, 1972. Colored. 88½ × 98 cm. Scale 1 : 100,000.

General map with legend indicating spot heights, road grades and vegetation. Map includes insets of Saint-Martin and Saint Barthélémy.

GUATEMALA

7300. Guatemala. Instituto Geográfico Nacional. Atlas nacional de Guatemala. Guatemala, 1972. 1v. (Unpaged)

Eight section atlas with maps on physical resources, human resources, economic activities, industry, tourism, and public services. Maps, graphs, photographs and text make this atlas a real contribution to Guatemala's cartographic record.

7301. ———. ———. Ciudad de Guatemala. 2. ed. Washington, US Army Topographic Command, 1971. Colored map. 96 × 100 cm. Scale 1 : 12,500.

Excellent map of city and vicinity giving contour lines in 10 meter intervals.

7302. ———. ———. Mapa preliminar de la República de Guatemala. 4. ed. Guatemala, 1971. Colored. 57 × 55 cm. Scale 1 : 1,000,000.

General map indicating departamental boundaries. Map claims Belize [British Honduras] belongs to Guatemala.

GUYANA

7303. Guyana. Lands Department. Cartographic Division. Map of Guyana. Georgetown, 1971. Colored. 54 × 36 cm. Scale ca. 1 : 600,000.

List of references including symbols for transportation, vegetation, types, major crops, minerals, Indian settlements, population distribution and streams. Simplistic, informative pictographic map.

7304. ———. ———. ———. Survey Department. Map of the seacoast of Guyana. Georgetown, 1971-1972. Colored, 3 sheets, each 52 × 67 cm. Scale 1 : 250,000.

Map indicates land ownership, roads, trails, railroads, airports, streams, towns, municipal boundaries, and Amerindian reservations.

JAMAICA

7305. General Drafting Company (firm), *Convent Station, N.J.* Jamaica. Convent Station, N.J., 1972. Colored. 27 × 71 cm. Scale 1 : 356,000.

Main maps show roads, towns, streams, parishes, and lists principal points of interest. Index locates communities, hotels, public beaches, points of interest and bauxite plants. Includes six inset city plans and a street index to Kingston. Prepared for Esso Standard Oil.

7306. Jamaica. Ministry of Finance and Planning. Town Planning Department. National atlas of Jamaica. Kingston, 1971. 1v. (Unpaged)

National atlas supported by funds from United Nations Special Fund Project "Assistance in Physical Development Planning". Contains 47 maps, most of which are thematic showing geology, climate, minerals, population statistics, agriculture and manufacturing products distribution, health and educative statistics, and tourism. Written information related to maps and charts appear on companion pages. Maps are uncolored. Presents useful information on country.

7307. ———. [National Electoral Board?]. General elections, 1972. Kingston, Golding Printing Service, 1972. Colored. 41 × 58 cm. Scale not given.

Country outline with parishes and political districts delineated. Majority party (People's National Party or Jamaica Labour Party) is indicated by color in each election area. Lists members of the Jamaican cabinet on left side below the map. Interesting political map for observers of Caribbean politics.

MARTINIQUE

7308. France. Institut Géographique National. Martinique. Paris, 1972. Colored. 66 × 66 cm. Scale 1 : 100,000.

General reference map with relief indicated by spot

heights and shading. Includes inset maps of Saint-Pierre and Fort-de-France.

MEXICO

7309. Asociación Nacional Automobilística, Mex. Ciudad de México [Mexico City]. 3. ed. Copyright Carlos Encinas. México, 1973. Colored. 84 × 65 cm. Scale ca. 1 : 40,000.

Spanish and English. Indexed for points of interest, streets and subway stations.

7310. Bowen, Emanuel. A new and accurate map of Mexico or New Spain together with California, New Mexico, etc., drawn from the best modern maps and charts and regulated by astronomical observations, 1747 (*in* Bowen, Emanuel. A complete system of geography. London, W. Innys, 1747, v. 2, plate 57, Colored facsimile. 35 × 42 cm. Scale 1 : 10,500,000)

Facsimile of Bowen's maps prepared by Graham Historical Maps, 1114 Waynewood Boulevard, Alexandria, Va. 22308. Price $5.00. Nice map for framing. Covers area from Panama to New Mexico, Florida to California.

7311. Ediciones Ing. Behn, *Guadalajara, Mex.* Plano de Guadalajara. Guadalajara, Papelería Fregoso, 1972. Colored. 67 × 91 cm. Scale 1 : 20,000.

Map includes street portions in Tlaquepaque and Zapopán. Includes postal zones and street index.

7312. English, William P. Tenochtitlan—Mexico City—1519. 1972. 40 × 55 cm. Scale 1 : 12,672.

Map shows the appearance of Tenochtitlan in 1519 with streets, bridges, parks, pyramids, docks, built up areas and water indicated. Map represents the city at the time of Cortes' conquest.

7313. Esparza Torres, Héctor F. Guanajuato: mapas de los estados. Mexico, Librería Patria, 1972. Colored. 54 × 83 cm. Scale 1 : 400,000.

Map contains index to towns, percentage breakdown of state production and statistics on age groups, demography, education and town populations. Insets on verso: maps of Guanajuato (city) and León.

7314. ———. [Maps of States]. Mexico, 1972. Aguascalientes, 46 × 67 cm. Scale 1 : 200,000; Baja California (terr.), 67 × 46 cm. Scale 1 : 1,200,000. Campeche, 46 × 66 cm. Scale 1 : 800,000; Coahuila, 67 × 46 cm. Scale 1 : 1,000,000, Colima, 46 × 67 cm. Scale 1 : 200,000; Chiapas, 46 × 67 cm. Scale 1 : 900,000; Durango, 67 × 46 cm. Scale 1 : 1,000,000; Hidalgo 46 × 66 cm. Scale 1 : 400,000; Oaxaca, 46 × 67 cm. Scale 1 : 800,000; Puebla, 66 × 46 cm. Scale 1 : 600,000; Quintana Roo (terr.), 67 × 46 cm. Scale 1 : 600,000; Tamaulipas, 66 × 46 cm. Scale 1 : 1,000,000; Yucatán, 46 × 67 cm. Scale 1 : 600,000; Zacatecas, 67 × 46 cm. Scale 1 : 800,000.

Maps include text, index and statistics. Each is general reference map of state. Includes inset maps of major city or cities of each state.

7315. García de Miranda, Enriqueta and Zaida Falcón de Gyves. Atlas: nuevo atlas Porrúa de la República Mexicana. México, Editorial Porrúa, 1972. 197 p.

Contains state maps: thematic maps on: geology, altitude, soils, climate, vegetation, hydrolic, language, and graphs.

7316. Guía Roji (firm), *Mex.* Ciudad de Monterrey. México, 1972. Colored. 80 × 113 cm. Scale 1 : 20,000.

City plan with street index. General map of state of Nuevo León, measuring 81 × 49 cm. appears on verso.

7317. ———, ———. Plano de la ciudad de México. México, 1972. Colored. 115 × 81 cm. Scale 1 : 30,413.

General city map includes street and *colonia* index; and vicinity map of Mexico City on verso.

7318. Jáuregui O., Ernesto. Mesomicroclima de la ciudad de México. México, UNAM, Instituto de Geografía, 1971. 87 p. 28 cm.

Published by UNAM's Institute of Geography, includes 42 maps giving monthly maximum and minimum temperatures in centigrades, days of ice, rain, intensity of rain, electrical storms, annual precipitation, humidity, concentration of sulfur bioxide, concentrations of smoke and dust, in city of Mexico. Includes graphs and text.

7319. McMahan, Mike. Baja California, Mexico. 3. ed. Los Angeles, Calif., McMahan Brothers Desk Company, 1972. 144 × 84 cm. Scale ca. 1 : 850,000.

Map on parchment-like paper. Current map of state gives roads, missions, airports, resorts, Indian cave paintings and hotels in cities. Cost: $7.50. Order from: McMahan Brothers Desk Company, 313 South Figueroa Street, Los Angeles, Calif. 90007.

7320. Mexico. Comision de Estudios del Territorio Nacional y Planeación. Carta de climas. México, 1970. Colored. 58 × 71 cm. Scale 1 : 500,000.

Classification of climates according to Koppen, modified by E. García, in 1964. Includes index to adjoining sheets. Only limited number of sheets have been seen by this compiler.

7321. ———. ———. Carta geológica. México, 1970. Colored. 58 × 71 cm. Scale 1 : 50,000.

Universal Transverse Mercator projection. Each sheet has an index to adjoining sheets. Useful series of which this compiler has seen only a few sheets.

7322. ———. ———. Carta uso del suelo. México, 1970. Colored. 58 × 71 cm. Scale 1 : 50,000.

UTM projection. Includes index to adjoining sheets. New series of land use maps. This compiler has seen only one of the sheets and no index to determine the plan of coverage.

7323. ———— ————. **Estados Unidos Mexicanos, carta topográfica.** México, 1970? Colored. 58 × 71 cm. Scale 1 : 50,000.

New series of maps of Mexico only a few of which this compiler has seen. Includes relief, vegetation and cultural information. Drawn on a UTM projection.

7324. ————. **Comisión Federal de Electricidad. Red nacional eléctrica y centrales generadoras en la República Mexicana.** México, 1971. 10 l. 20 × 39 cm.

Section maps of Mexico showing transmission lines—existing and planned; 400 KV lines existing and planned; hydroelectric; thermal electric, diesel and gas electrical generating plants.

7325. Departamento de Turismo y Petróleos Mexicanos. Maps turístico de carreteras. México, Secretaría de Obras Públicas, 1972. Colored 63 × 85 cm. Scale 1 : 3,500,000.

General road map which includes city index. Insets of major cities of Mexico appear on map's recto and verso.

7326. ————. **Dirección de Obras Públicas. Plano de la ciudad de Urapán, Michoacán.** Impresión autorizada por el Gobernador del

General city plan without index.

7327. ————. **Dirección General de Estadística. Estados Unidos Mexicanos: división municipal, 28 de enero de 1970.** México, Secretaría de Industria y Comercio, 1970. 82 × 102 cm. Scale not given.

Map shows municipal divisions and state boundaries.

7328. ————. **UNAM. Instituto de Geografía. Plano de la ciudad de Urapán, Michoacán.** Impresión autorizada por el Gobernador del Estado José Servando Chávez Hernández. Formó: Carlos Garcia de León. México, 1972. Colored. 81 × 59 cm. Scale 1 : 12,000.

Land-use map of city. Indicates vegetation, location of buildings and future development sites. Key, text and index appear.

7329. ————. ————. ————. **Plano de la ciudad de Zitacuaro, Michoacán.** Impresión autorizada por el Governador del Estado José Servando Chávez Hernández. Formó: Carlos García de León. México, 1971. Colored. 60 × 81 cm. Scale 1 : 5,000.

Land-use map similar to one of Uruapan by same authority. Text and index accompany map.

7330. Palacios Roji G., Agustín. Plano de la ciudad de Guadalajara. 2. ed. México, Guía Roji, 1971-1972. Colored. 80 × 114 cm. Scale 1 : 20,000.

City plan includes street index. On verso state map of Jalisco measuring 77 × 81 cm. with general information.

7331. Sinaloa (state), *Mex.* **Mapa moderno de Sinaloa.** Culiacán, Mex., 1972. Colored. 71 × 56 cm. Scale 1 : 800,000.

General reference map of state.

NICARAGUA

7332. Nicaraguan Private Enterprise, *Managua.* Map of the City of Managua, Nicaragua, Central America. Managua, 1972. Colored. 45 × 58 cm. Scale not given.

Tourist map of Managua shows city prior to earthquake of late 1972.

PARAGUAY

7333. Ponte, Alberto da. Mapa de la República del Paraguay 1972. Asunción, Instituto Geográfico Militar, 1972. Colored. 58 × 46 cm. Scale 1 : 2,000,000.

General reference map of nation which is fairly simplistically presented but only one of few maps from that country to be seen by this compiler.

7334. ————. **Plano de la ciudad de Asunción.** Asunción, Estudios da Ponte, 1972. 35 × 56 cm. Scale 1 : 20,000.

General city plan with key to 31 locations.

PERU

7335. Góngora Perea, Amadeo. Plano de la ciudad de Lima metropolitana. Lima, Cartográfica Nacional, 1973. Colored. 60 × 87 cm. Scale 1 : 24,000.

City plan which includes street index, but no legend.

7336. Peru. Ministerio de Guerra. Instituto Geográfico Militar. Departamento de Puno, 1971: mapa físico político. Lima, 1971. Colored. 77 × 56 cm. Scale ca. 1 : 670,000.

General reference map. Indicates altitude by hypsometric tints in provinces of department.

SURINAM

7337. Surinam. Centraal Bureau Luchtkartering Kaart Van Suriname [Map of Surinam]. Paramaribo, 1971. Colored. 67 × 58 cm Scale 1 : 1,000,000.

General reference map which shows towns, airfields roads, railways, and physical features. Elevatior shown by color tints. Legend in English and Dutch

TRINIDAD and TOBAGO

7338. Trinidad and Tobago. Surveys Division Port of Spain. Port of Spain, 1971. Colored 70 × 77 cm. Scale 1 : 10,000.

GEOGRAPHY: CARTOGRAPHIC MATERIALS

Indexed city plan. Public buildings, schools, places of worship, consulates and other places of interest are keyed.

7339. ———. ———. Trinidad. 2. ed. Port of Spain, 1971. Colored. 63 × 80 cm. Scale 1 : 150,000.

General reference map including country and ward boundaries. Ten symbols indicate various facilities: location of bathing beaches, hunting sites, filling stations and telephone call boxes.

URUGUAY

7340. Mapasy Guias Eureka (firm), *Montevideo.* Mapa: guía de Montevideo "Eureka." Montevideo, 1972. Colored 53 × 78 cm. Scale not given.

General map of city with street index. Inset maps of Santiago Vázquez, La Paz, Abayuba and Las Piedras appear.

7341. Montevideo (city), *Uru.* **Intendencia Municipal de Montevideo. Departamento de Montevideo.** Montevideo, Ministerio de Defensa Nacional, Servicio Geográfico Militar, 1962. Colored. 39 sheets, each 67 × 44 cm. Scale 1 : 10,000.

Detailed map of department. Percentage of building density indicated by shading; width of sheets indicated. Excellent large scale map of Montevideo department not previously listed in *HLAS.*

7342. Uruguay. Ministerio de Defensa Nacional. Servicio Geográfico Militar. Carta del Uruguay al millonésimo. Montevideo, 1971. Colored. 74 × 80 cm. Scale 1 : 1,000,000.

General map. Elevation in meters; color tints for altitude.

7343. ———. **Ministerio de Transporte, Comunicaciones y Turismo.** Uruguay. Montevideo, 1973. Colored. 57 × 50 cm. Scale ca. 1 : 1,050,000.

General reference map. Relief shown pictorially. Includes "Mapa de la Zona Balnearia," Montevideo map, index and 18 local route maps on verso.

VENEZUELA

7344. Bellizzia, Alirio; Domingo Rodriguez; and A. Zambrano. Recursos minerales del Estado Yaracuy. Caracas, Ministerio de Minas e Hidrocarburos, 1970. Colored. 46 × 70 cm. Scale 1 : 265,000.

Mineral map of state, colored coded with descriptive text on each mineral.

7345. Drenikoff, Iván. Mapas antiguos de Venezuela, grabados e impresos antes de 1800 con la reproducción del primer mapa impreso en Venezuela y de mapas antiguos [por] Iván Drenikoff. Caracas, Ediciones del Congreso de la República, 1971. 57 p., illus.

Useful collection of pre-1800 maps of Venezuela.

7346. Venezuela. Dirección de Cartografía Nacional. Atlas de Venezuela. 2. ed. Caracas, 1972. 210 p.

Revised edition of 1969 national atlas. New maps, boundary changes and new thematic maps appear. Charts, graphs, and illustrations add to this very useful work.

7347. ———. ———. Barcelona. Caracas, 1971. Colored. 94 × 64 cm. Scale 1 : 12,500.

Lists buildings and sites of interest. Contour lines at 10 meter intervals. An inset of Lechería appears.

7348. ———. ———. Barquisimeto. Caracas, 1971. Colored. 64 × 94 cm. Scale 1 : 15,000.

Detailed city plan, with residential and commercial buildings indicated. Contour lines at 20 meter intervals. Indexed.

7349. ———. ———. Coro. Caracas, 1970. Colored. 63 × 94 cm. Scale 1 : 10,000.

City plan with index to buildings and interesting sites.

7350. ———. ———. Puerto La Cruz. Caracas, 1971. Colored. 64 × 94 cm. Scale 1 : 12,500.

General city plan. Key to sites of interest and buildings. Contour lines at 10 meter intervals.

7351. ———. **Dirección de Vialidad.** Mápa vial con otros datos de comunicaciones terrestres, marítimas y aéreas de la República de Venezuela. Caracas, 1970. Colored. in 4 sheets, each 27 ½" × 40". Scale 1 : 1,000,000.

Map includes index to populated places and inset maps, scale 1 : 500,000, of vicinity of Caracas, San Cristóbal, Maracaibo, Ciudad Bolívar and Cumaná-Isla Margarita. Map includes symbols for population of towns from 100 to over 100,000. Indicates all classes of roads including those under construction. Locates railroad lines, ferry boat routes, airports (international, national and secondary), national parks, tourist sites, spas, oil fields and refineries, mines. Altitude shown by color tints. Map compiled May 1970.

WEST INDIES

7352. Coronelli, Vincenzo. Archipelague du Mexique sont les Isles de Cuba, Espagnole, l'Amaique, etc. Avec les isles Lucayes, et les isles Caribes, connues sous le nom d'Antilles. Paris, Chez I.B. Nolin, 1688. [Ithaca, N.Y., Historic Urban Plans, 1972?] Colored. Facsimile map 36 × 48 cm. Scale ca. 1 : 6,500,000.

Reproduction of Coronelli's 1688 map of West Indies made by Historic Urban Plans, Ithaca, N.Y.

7353. USSR. Glavnoye Upravleniye Geodezii i Kartografi Tsentral' Naya Amerika i Vest-Indiya. Moscow, Glavnoye Upravleniye Geodezii i Kartografi pri Sovete Ministrov SSSR, 1972. Colored. In 2 sheets, each 94 × 79 cm. Scale 1 : 2,500,000.

General map of region, in cyrillic, giving administrative boundaries and other general information.

JOURNAL ABBREVIATIONS

AAC/AJ	Anthropological Journal of Canada. Anthropological Association of Canada. Quebec, Canada.
AAG/A	Annals of the Association of American Geographers. Lawrence, Kan.
AAG/PG	Professional Geographer. Association of American Geographers. Washington.
ABS	The American Behavioral Scientist. N.Y.
ACCEFN/R	Revista de la Academia Colombiana de Ciencias Exactas, Físicas y Naturales. Bogotá.
ACH/B	Boletín de la Academia Chilena de la Historia. Santiago.
AGB/BCG	Boletim Carioca de Geografia. Associação dos Geógrafos Brasileiros, Secção Regional do Rio de Janeiro. Rio.
AGB/BPG	Boletim Paulista de Geografia. Associação dos Geógrafos Brasileiros, Secção Regional de São Paulo. São Paulo.
AGF/B	Bulletin de l'Association de Géographes Français. Paris.
AGS/GR	The Geographical Review. American Geographical Society. N.Y.
AJES	The American Journal of Economics and Sociology. N.Y.
AMNH/NH	Natural History. American Museum of Natural History. N.Y.
ANC/B	Boletín de la Academia Nacional de Ciencias. Córdoba, Arg.
ASTMH/J	American Journal of Tropical Medicine and Hygiene. American Society of Tropical Medicine and Hygiene. Baltimore, Md.
AVAC/ACV	Acta Científica Venezolana. Asociación Venezolana para el Avance de la Ciencia. Caracas.
BBAA	Boletín Bibliográfico de Antropología Americana. Instituto Panamericano de Geografía e Historia, Comisión de Historia. México.
CAG/CG	Canadian Geographer. Le Géographe Canadien. Canadian Association of Geographers. Toronto, Canada.
CCGT/CG	The California Geographer. California Council of Geography Teachers. Long Beach, Calif.
CPES/RPS	Revista Paraguaya de Sociología. Centro Paraguayo de Estudios Sociológicos. Asunción.
CU/EG	Economic Geography. Clark Univ. Worcester, Mass.
CUA/AQ	Anthropological Quarterly. Catholic Univ. of America, Catholic Anthropological Conference. Washington.
DAWB/M	Monatsberichte der Deutschen Akademie der Wissenschaften zu Berlin. Berlin.
DGV/ZE	Zeitschrift für Ethnologie. Deutschen Gesellschaft für Völkerkunde. Braunschweig, FRG.
EJ	Explorers Journal. N.Y.
GEB/E	Die Erde. Zeitschrift der Gesellschaft für Erdkunde zu Berlin. Walter de Gruyter & Co. Berlin.
GH	Geographica Helvetica. Schweizerische Zeitschrift für Länder- und Völkerkunde. Kümmerly & Frey, Geographischer Verlag. Bern.
GM	The Geographical Magazine. London.
GR	Geographische Rundschau. Zeitschrift für Schulgeographie. Georg Westermann Verlag. Braunschweig, FRG.
GV/GR	Geologische Rundschau. Internationale Zeitschrift für Geologie. Geologische Vereinigung. Ferdinand Enke Verlag. Stuttgart, FRG.
HGG/M	Mitteilungen der Geographischen Gesellschaft in Hamburg. Hamburg, FRG.
IAMEA	Inter-American Economic Affairs. Washington.
IAO/RAST	Rivista di Agricoltura Subtropicale e Tropicale. Istituto Agronomico per l'Oltremare. Firenze, Italy.
IBEAS/EA	Estudios Andinos. Instituto Boliviano de Estudio y Acción Social. La Paz.
IBGE/B	Boletim Geográfico. Conselho Nacional de Geografia, Instituto Brasileiro de Geografia e Estatística. Rio.
IBGE/R	Revista Brasileira de Geografia. Conselho Nacional de Geografia, Instituto Brasileiro de Geografia e Estatística. Rio.

IBGE/RBE	Revista Brasileira de Estatística. Ministério do Planejamento e Coordenação Geral, Instituto Brasileiro de Geografia e Estatística. Rio.
IESSC/C	Comunidades. Instituto de Estudios Sindicales, Sociales y Cooperativos, Centro de Prospección Social. Madrid.
IFH/C	Conjonction. Revue franco-haitienne. Bulletin de l'Institut Français d'Haiti. Port-au-Prince.
IFSNC/CD	Community Development. International Federation of Settlements and Neighborhood Centres. Roma.
IGM/U	L'Universo. Istituto Geografico Militare. Firenze, Italy.
IM	Imago Mundi. London.
IOC/M	Memórias do Instituto Oswaldo Cruz. Rio.
IRFDH/DC	Développement et Civilisations. Institut de Recherche et de Formation en vue du Développement Harmonisé. Paris.
JDA	The Journal of Developing Areas. Western Illinois Univ. Press. Macomb, Ill.
JLAS	Journal of Latin American Studies. Centers or institutes of Latin American studies at the Universities of Cambridge, Glasgow, Liverpool, London and Oxford. Cambridge Univ. Press. London.
MEMDA/E	Etnia. Museo Etnográfico Municipal Dámaso Arce. Municipalidad de Olavarría. B.A.
MH/OM	Objets et Mondes. Revue trimestrielle. Musée de l'Homme. Paris.
NCGE/J	Journal of Geography. National Council of Geographic Education. Menasha, Wis.
NGS/NGM	National Geographic Magazine. National Geographic Society. Washington.
NWIG	Nieuwe West-Indische Gids. Martinus Nijhoff. The Hague.
NWJS	Nature. A weekly journal of science. Macmillan & Co. London.
NYAS/A	Annals of the New York Academy of Sciences. N.Y.
OAS/AM	Américas. Organization of American States. Washington.
OAS/CI	Ciencia Interamericana. Organization of American States, Dept. of Scientific Affairs. Washington.
PAA/D	Demography. Population Association of America. Chicago, Ill.
PAIGH/G	Revista Geográfica. Instituto Panamericano de Geografia e História, Comissão de Geografia. Rio.
PAIGH/RC	Revista Cartográfica. Instituto Panamericano de Geografía e Historia, Comisión de Cartografía. B.A.
PAPS	Proceedings of the Academy of Political Science. Columbia Univ., N.Y.
PU/PIA	Public and International Affairs. Princeton Univ., Woodrow Wilson School of Public and International Affairs. Princeton, N.J.
RCGJ/CGJ	Canadian Geographical Journal. Royal Canadian Geographical Society. Ottawa.
RCPC	Revista Conservadora del Pensamiento Centroamericano. Managua.
RGS/GJ	The Geographical Journal. Royal Geographical Society. London.
SA/J	Journal de la Société des Américanistes. Paris.
SAA/HO	Human Organization. Society for Applied Anthropology. N.Y.
SBG/B	Boletim da Sociedade Brasileira de Geologia. Univ. de São Paulo, Instituto de Geociências e Astronomia. São Paulo.
SCNLS/M	Memoria de la Sociedad de Ciencias Naturales La Salle. Caracas.
SGB/COM	Les Cahiers d'Outre-Mer. Publiée par l'Institut de Géographie de la Faculté des Lettres de Bordeaux, par l'Institut de la France d'Outre-Mer, par la Société de Géographie de Bordeaux *avec le concours* du Centre National de la Recherche Scientifique et de la VIième Section de l'Ecole Pratique des Hautes Etudes. Bordeaux, France.
SGC/B	Boletín de la Sociedad Geográfica de Colombia. Academia de Ciencias Geográficas. Bogotá.
SGC/CGC	Cuadernos de Geografía de Colombia. Sociedad Geográfica de Colombia, Academia de Ciencias Geográficas. Bogotá.
SGI/B	Bollettino della Societá Geografica Italiana. Roma.
SMHN/R	Revista de la Sociedad Mexicana de Historia Natural. México.
SRA/A	Anales de la Sociedad Rural Argentina. Revista pastoril y agrícola. B.A.

SUDENE	Sudene. Boletim de Recursos Naturais. Superintendência do Desenvolvimento do Nordeste. Recife, Bra.
UBGI/E	Erdkunde. Archiv für Wissenschaftliche Geographie. Univ. Bonn, Geographisches Institut. Bonn.
UC/A	Anales de la Universidad de Cuenca. Cuenca, Ecua.
UC/B	Boletín de la Universidad de Chile. Santiago.
UC/EDCC	Economic Development and Cultural Change. Univ. of Chicago, Research Center in Economic Development and Cultural Change. Chicago, Ill.
UCIG/IG	Informaciones Geográficas. Univ. de Chile, Facultad de Filosofía y Educación, Instituto de Geografía. Santiago.
UCR/R	Revista de la Universidad de Costa Rica. San José.
UCV/RG	Revista Geográfica de Valparaíso. Univ. Católica de Valparaíso. Valparaíso, Chile.
UES/ES	Economía Salvadoreña. Univ. de El Salvador, Instituto de Estudios Económicos. San Salvador.
ULA/RG	Revista Geográfica. Univ. de Los Andes. Mérida, Ven.
ULIG/C	Cahiers de Géographie de Québec. Univ. Laval, Institut de Géographie. Quebec, Canada.
UM/JIAS	Journal of Inter-American Studies and World Affairs. Univ. of Miami Press *for the* Center for Advanced International Studies. Coral Gables, Fla.
UN/ISSJ	International Social Science Journal. United Nations Educational, Scientific, and Cultural Organization. Paris.
UNAM/IE	Investigación Económica. Univ. Nacional Autónoma de México, Escuela Nacional de Economía. México.
UNAM/RMS	Revista Mexicana de Sociología. Univ. Nacional Autónoma de México, Instituto de Investigaciones Sociales. México.
UNCIG/B	Boletín de Estudios Geográficos. Univ. Nacional de Cuyo, Instituto de Geografía. Mendoza, Arg.
UNESCO/NR	Nature and Resources. United Nations Educational, Scientific and Cultural Organization. Paris.
UNLP/E	Económica. Univ. Nacional de La Plata, Facultad de Ciencias Económicas, Instituto de Investigaciones Económicas. La Plata, Arg.
UPR/CS	Caribbean Studies. Univ. of Puerto Rico, Institute of Caribbean Studies. Río Piedras, P.R.
UR/WZ	Wissenschaftliche Zeitschrift der Universität Rostock, Gesellschafts- und sprachwissenschaftliche Reihe. Rostock, GDR.
USM/JTG	The Journal of Tropical Geography. Univ. of Singapore [and] Univ. of Malaya, Depts. of Geography. Singapore.
USM/RCEG	Revista de la Facultad de Ciencias Económicas y Comerciales. Univ. Nacional Mayor de San Marcos. Lima.
UTIEH/C	Caravelle. Cahiers du monde hispanique et lusobrésilien. Univ. de Toulouse, Institut d'Etudes Hispaniques, Hispano-Americaines et Luso-Brésiliennes. Toulouse, France.
UW/LE	Land Economics. A quarterly journal of planning, housing and public utilities. Univ. of Wisconsin. Madison, Wis.
UWI/CQ	Caribbean Quarterly. Univ. of the West Indies. Mona, Jam.
UY/R	Revista de la Universidad de Yucatán. Mérida, Mex.
WM	Westermann Monatshefte. Georg Westermann Verlag. Braunschweig, FRG.

Government and Politics

GENERAL

PHILIP B. TAYLOR, JR.
*Professor of
Political Science
Director
Latin American
Studies Center
University of Houston*

JOHN J. BAILEY
*Assistant Professor
of Government
Director
Latin American
Studies Program
Georgetown University*

ANDRES SUAREZ
*Professor of
Political Science
Center for
Latin American Studies
University of Florida*

POLITICAL SCIENCE RESEARCH AND WRITING ON LATIN AMERICA have increased apace over the biennium since *HLAS 33*. In order to deal with the materials more efficiently, an areal division of labor—which has been the practice in other sections of the social sciences—has been effected. There has been no attempt, however, to compartmentalize the efforts strictly; rather, contributors have maintained flexibility in locating and abstracting literature pertaining to all of the region. The general intent of the reorganization is to permit a greater in-depth concentration on the literature of a region of the area. We concede, in effect, the difficulty in maintaining an expertise on all aspects of the entire region, and trust that the reorganization will enhance the coverage. Substantive comments on characteristics of the literature preface each of the sections: 1) Mexico, Central America, The Caribbean and the Guianas; 2) South America: West Coast (Colombia, Ecuador, Peru, Bolivia, Chile); and 3) South America: East Coast (Venezuela, Brazil, Paraguay, Uruguay, Argentina).

Some general comments on the uses and limits of the Government and Politics section are in order. The *Handbook* may most usefully be used by specialists as a somewhat comprehensive compilation of the more significant (in our estimation) contributions to the field. As a research tool, the volume should be viewed as a beginning point which provides a detailed overview of recent literature. Obviously, the researcher should consult other sections of the *Handbook* relevant to his interests, since many items are not cross-referenced. We emphasize that it is virtually impossible (and unnecessary) to report on all of the literature of interest to political scientists. Broadly speaking, government documents (e.g., ministerial reports) and news-oriented journalistic pieces have been excluded. Unhappily, important materials which were received late, or which might have been missed in our normal search processes, further limit the extent of the coverage. These materials must wait the two-year interlude for their appearance in *HLAS 37*.

Clearly, the most obvious development during the period here reported has been the rising level of intellectual nationalism/regionalism, and the rejection of influence from the north by highly articulate (if not strident) young writers. Not all that has been written in recent years is in this tone or has this approach; and not all that partakes of either is necessarily worth the attention of the specialist. But it is a kind of writing on the wall, based on the conviction of Latin American intellectuals and scholars that the specialists of Anglo-American background have not been sufficiently sensitive to the unique qualities and values of the national societies of the region.

Despite harsh views of certain extreme writers from both North and Latin America, this school of thought cannot but command the attention of serious students, in light of the severe self-examination of the American political system that has been going on during the past decade.

7354. Agor, Weston H. *ed.* Latin American legislatures: their role and influence; analyses for nine countries. N.Y., Praeger Publishers, 1971. 511 p., bibl., tables (Praeger special studies in international politics and public affairs)

Compiled in response to the dearth of modern institutional studies on legislatures in Latin America (due in part to dominance of a narrowly interpreted behavioralism in US political science in the 1960's). Considers the legislatures of Chile, Costa Rica, and Uruguay as "relatively influential on a world scale," those of Argentina, Brazil, Guatemala, and Peru as transitional cases of increasing or decreasing decisional influence, and those of Colombia and Venezuela as structures with weak decisional influence. Inevitably the 11 chapters vary in quality, but overall effort constitutes an important contribution and a basic reference work. [J. J. Bailey]

7355. —— and **Andrés Suárez.** The emerging Latin American political subsystem (PAPS, 30:4, 1972, p. 153-166)

Assesses factors (e.g., economic integration) militating for more intensive interaction as well as emerging points of conflict among Latin American nations. Raises questions for US foreign policy in relation to emerging subsystem. [J. J. Bailey]

7356. Aguilar, Luis E. Political traditions and perspectives (USIA/PC, 20:3, May/June 1971, p. 62-69)

How could a leftist-socialist government, tending toward communism, grow logically out of a Latin American country? This brief historical survey offers reasons. Conclusion suggests, in broad generalization, what could happen in the future to the political system. [P. B. Taylor, Jr.]

7357. Agundez Fernández, Antonio. Justicia agraria en Iberoamérica (Revista de Estudios Agro-Sociales [Madrid] 21:79, abril/junio 1972, p. 169-184)

Reviews briefly legal provisions on agrarian reform procedures in 11 Latin American countries and suggests possible improvements. Legalistic in tone. [J. J. Bailey]

7358. Alexander, Robert J. Latin American political parties. N.Y., Praeger Publishers, 1973. 537 p., bibl. (Praeger special studies in international politics and government)

Like so many other political scientists, Alexander makes an effort to establish some order among the multitude of parties of Latin America. Unlike other writers, however, he has received the support to put it into a massive (and excessively costly) volume. His description is by programmatic or ideological policies, rather than by countries. His emphasis is on names and dates rather than on detailed analysis. He indicates in his introduction his hope that this can be a kind of reference book for students and specialists. Unfortunately, it cannot be regarded as such because it is still too small, too sketchy, and too historical. Moreover, in light of the velocity with which positions and policies are changing throughout the region, it is too dated. Alexander has scarcely used the available bibliography in English, not to speak of Spanish language sources. [P. B. Taylor, Jr.]

7359. ——. El trotskismo en la América Latina (USIA/PI, 19:3, majo/junio 1972, p. 15-31, plate)

Historical overview of Fourth International, its early development in Latin America, with some attention to Mexico and Bolivia, and recent relationships with Castroism. Useful summary by a leading student of Communism in the region. [J. J. Bailey]

7360. América Latina en armas. B.A., Ediciones M.A., 1971. 127 p.

Anonymously written piece (and "anonymously" sponsored, as well) describes in detail all revolutionary/terrorist movements operating in Latin America and "suppressed" as to news coverage by *yanqui* imperialism and the CIA, of course. Discusses movements in Argentina, Bolivia, Brazil, Chile, Nicaragua, and Uruguay. Some of the material is summary in nature and written by observers; some is documentary, by the movements' spokesmen. [P. B. Taylor, Jr.]

7361. Andronova, V. P. Revoliutsiia monsen'orov? (The revolution of monsignors?) (SSSR/LA, 2, March/April 1971, p. 76-91)

Study of the rebelling clergy in the Catholic church in Latin America and some of the dilemmas they present to communists. [T. S. Cheston]

7362. Apunen, Osmo. Vaihtoehtona vallankumous: Latinalaisen Amerikan kehitysongelmien historiaa. Helsinki, Otava, 1971. 1 v. (Unpaged)

Entitled *The revolution as an alternative: the history of development problems in Latin America* and by a Finnish political scientist who is well-read on the subject. [Magnus Mörner]

7363. Arnáiz Amigo, Aurora. Soberanía y potestad. v. 1, De la soberanía del pueblo. México, UNAM, Facultad de Ciencias Políticas y Sociales, 1971. 355 p., tables (Serie Estudios, 20)

Extended treatise on theory of sovereignty in historical and contemporary settings. Explores questions of federalism, imperialism, religion, administration and economics. Consistent attempts to define, classify, and generalize. [J. J. Bailey]

7363a. ——. Soberanía y potestad. v. 2, De la potestad del estado. México, UNAM, Facultad de Ciencias Políticas y Sociales, 1971. 305 p., bibl. (Serie Estudios, 21)

V. 2 extends analysis to consider characteristics of modern nation-state: liberal, welfare interventionist, socialist. [J. J. Bailey]

7363b. *Aus Politik und Zeitgeschichte.* Beilage zur Wochenzeitung Das Parlament. No. 8, 1971 [through] No. 11, 1972- . Boon, FRG.

Following issues include articles on Latin America:
No. 48 (1971) Dieter Nohlen "Politischer Wandel durch Wahlen: der Fall Uruguay" p. 3-22.
Ernest-J. Kerbusch "Die Bedeutung von Wahlen in Lateinamerika am Beispiel der'demokratischen Wiederwahl ehemaliger Kiktatoren" p. 23-36.
Boris Goldenberg "Chiles Weg zum Sozialismus" p. 37-53.
No. 11 (1972) Rudolf Schloz "Kirche un Sozialismus in Chile" [W. Grabendorff]

7364. Bambirra, Vania and others. Diez años de insurrección en América Latina. t. 2. Santiago, Ediciones Prensa Latino-americana, 1971. 218 p. (Col. América nueva)

Essays on leftist revolutionary groups in four Latin American countries:
Silvestre Condoruma "Las Experiencias de la Ultima Etapa de las Luchas Revolucionarias en el Perú" (1965) p. 11-71
Carlos Núñez "MLN Tupamaros: los Combatientes no se Improvisan" (1970) p. 73-112
Ruy Mauro Marini "La Izquierda Revolucionaria Brasileña y las Nuevas Condiciones de la Lucha de Clases" p. 113-166
Antonio Zapata "Etapas y Coyunturas de la Lucha Guerrillera en Colombia" p. 167-218. [J. J. Bailey]

7365. Barneix, Atilio J. La ciencia política: su objeto. B.A., Abeldo-Perrot, 1969. 101 p., bibl. (Monografías jurídicas, 128)

Brief primer on epistemology and methodology of scientific study of politics. [J. J. Bailey]

7366. Baudouin, Renée Lescop. La guerra de guerrillas en América Latina entre 1960 y 1969: el refuerzo de una ideología y el debilitamiento de un movimiento (BUS, 10:19/20, feb. 1972, p. 105-126)

Reviews theoretical work of Ernesto Guevara and Régis Debray on guerrilla war and describes tactical, organizational, and leadership problems encountered by guerrilla movements in various Latin American countries. [J. J. Bailey]

7367. Benoit, Emile. Growth effects of defense in developing countries (SID/IDR, 14:1, 1972, p. 2-10, table)

Drawing on data from 44 developing countries covering 1950-65, author balances off adverse as against positive effects of national defense programs. Offers model of causation and concludes that growth patterns are by no means adversely affected by defense expenditures. Followed by comments by Robert Dorfman and Everett Hagen, and a rejoinder by the author (p. 10-15). [P. B. Taylor, Jr.]

7368. Black, Robert J. A change in tactics? the urban insurgent (AF/AUR, 23:2, Jan./Feb. 1972, p. 50-58, illus.)

Descriptive analysis, drawing in part on Latin America, of factors accounting for a perceived shift in guerrilla activity from rural to urban settings. [J. J. Bailey]

Blanksten, George I. Latin American studies: radicalism on the half shell. See item 6006.

7369. Boersner, Demetrio; Alberto Baeza Flores; Jorge Selser; and **Luis Alberto Monge.** América Latina y el socialismo democrático. San José, Centro de Estudios Democráticos de América Latina (CEDAL), 1970. 81 p. (Col. Seminarios y documentos)

Papers prepared for two seminars held by CEDAL in 1970. First two authors each write lengthy comparative papers; last two write, respectively, on Argentina and Costa Rica. Quality of detail varies, although each is usefully provocative. [P. B. Taylor, Jr.]

7370. Boizard, Ricardo. La América que no habla: panorama político de la América Latina. Santiago, Editorial Orbe, 1970. 232 p.

Not a scholarly contribution, but a combination travelogue, history, and political commentary by a Chilean journalist-diplomat-politician. Remarks on a tour through Central America, Mexico, and the Andean countries (1968?) during which interviews were held with leading politicians, journalists, Church and government officials. Frank, insightful, and entertaining. [J. J. Bailey]

7371. Borón, Atilio Alberto. Clases populares y políticas de cambio en América Latina (CPES/RPS, 7:19, sept./dic. 1970, p. 67-88)

Wide-ranging and interesting theoretical essay which elaborates on previous work (e.g., by Almond and Apter) to suggest new elements for a typology of Latin American regimes. Focuses on problem of institutionalizing mobilized masses into viable political structures. [J. J. Bailey]

7372. Brunn, Stanley D. *comp.* Urbanization in developing countries: an international bibliography. East Lansing, Mich., Michigan State Univ., 1971. 693 p. (Latin American Studies Center research report, 8)

Arranged by region and country, contains 2753 entries on Latin America. Essential research aid. [J. J. Bailey]

7373. Büntig, Aldo J. and **Carlos A. Bertone.** Hechos, doctrinas sociales y liberación: ensayo de exposición sistemática del Magisterio Social de la Iglesia en su contexto sociológico e ideológico. B.A., Editorial Guadalupe, 1971. 275 p., tables.

Very comprehensive survey of the social doctrine of the Church, in general, and in Latin America, in light of major documents of last 15 years. While some attention is paid to Argentina, most of this extensive study relates to Latin America. An essential piece. [P. B. Taylor, Jr.]

7374. Burnell, Elaine H. *ed.* One spark from holocaust: the crisis in Latin America. Santa Barbara, Calif., The Center for the Study of Democratic Institutions, 1972. 234 p., tables.

Reprints papers developed from meetings held in Mexico in 1969, sponsored by Center for the Study of

Democratic Institutions and chaired by Justice William O. Douglas and Raúl Prebisch. Contents: Helio Jaguaribe "The Politics of Military Domination" p. 15-31
Jacques Chonchol "Neo-Liberal Capitalism: Formula for Failure in Latin America" p. 32-38
Israel Wonsewer "Failures, Frustrations, and Forces for Change" p. 39-44
Roger Vekemans "Traditionalism and Polarization: Colonial Foundations for a Society in Conflict" p. 51-62
Aldo Solari "The Social Constraints on Progress" p. 63-73
Luis Ratinoff "The Non-Receptive Culture" p. 74-80
David M. Helfeld "Law and Politics in Mexico" p. 81-92
Manuel Balboa "The Legacy of the Sixties" p. 100-110
Germánico Salgado "Reforms to Fit the Objectives" p. 111-122
Carlos Manuel Castillo "Reflections of a Skeptic: Some Notes in Partial Dissent" p. 123-132
Wayne Morse "The Obligation and the Opportunity: a Hemispheric Approach in a Time of Transition" p. 139-149
Gustavo Romero Kolbeck "The Plight and the Plea: a Third World View" p. 151-154
Paul N. Rosenstein-Rodan "The Crossroads and the Choice: Economic Alternatives for Full-Employment Growth" p. 155-167
Cândido Mendes de Almeida "The Potential and the Promise: A Challenge to the Intelligentsia" p. 160-175
Frank Church "The Image and the Ideal: a New Role for the United States" p. 176-186
Roger Vekemans "Epilogue" p. 187-188
Robert M. Hutchins "Memorandum in Retrospect" p. 189-192 [J. J. Bailey]

7375. Câmara, Hélder. Revolution through peace. Translated from the Portuguese by Amparo McLean. N.Y., Harper & Row, 1971. 149 p. (World perspectives, 45)

Thoughts on peaceful change by the Bishop of Recife. [P. B. Taylor, Jr.]

7376. Cardoso, Fernando H. and Francisco Weffort eds. América Latina: ensayos de interpretación sociológico-política. Santiago, Editorial Universitaria, 1970. 384 p., tables (Col. Tiempo latinoamericano, 4)

Intended primarily to be a university-level text, reprints 17 major articles on political sociology by such Latin American authors as Antonio Garcia, Aníbal Quijano, and Pablo González Casanova. Useful collection marking the emergence of a Latin American political sociology. [J. J. Bailey]

7377. Carril, Bonifacio del. El problema político proposición para su solución. 2. ed., aumentada. B.A., Emecé Editores, 1970. 173 p.

Revised second edition of work originally published in 1967 fully develops writer's thoughts on nature and possible resolution of country's economic and social problems. Pt. 1 contains text of first edition. Pt. 2 contains eight additional essays. [P. B. Taylor, Jr.]

7378. Carvajal, Rafael Tomás and others. América Latina: movilización popular y fe cristiana. Montevideo, ISAL, 1971. 172 p.

Essays elaborating a radical Catholic indictment of capitalism and imperialism and defining alternative means of political and social development. Reprints documents from 1971 continental meeting of ISAL (Church and Society in Latin America) held in Peru. [J. J. Bailey]

7379. Carvalho, José Murilo de. Três abordagens da política latino-americana (UMG/RBEP, 31, maio 1971, p. 91-116, tables)

Critical comparative discussion of three models for analysis of Latin American change, as presented by Merle Kling, Charles Anderson and Peter Heintz. Author finds Anderson's work more promising than the others. [P. B. Taylor, Jr.]

7380. Castelnuovo, Elías. Jesucristo: montonero de Judea. B.A., La Técnica Impresora, 1971. 137 p.

Was Jesus a revolutionary or, better, are all good Christians morally committed to being revolutionaries for the furtherance of justice? Distinctly polemic answer, growing out of current inner doubts and clashes within the Catholic Church in Latin America. Piece has very little to say about latter, but much about the human condition. [P. B. Taylor, Jr.]

7381. Cavarozzi, Marcelo J. Mechanisms of political power in Latin America: suggestions for a new conceptual framework (IFSNC/CD, 25/26, Spring 1971, p. 149-174, bibl.)

Stimulating neo-marxist critique of basic concepts developed by Easton and Almond. Suggests analysis of politics in terms of differential access of groups to various arenas of policymaking. [J. J. Bailey]

7382. Cerda, Carlos. El leninismo y la victoria popular. Santiago, Editora Nacional Quimantu, 1971. 273 p. (Col. Camino abierto, 1)

Presents statements and doctrine of Chilean Communist Party, after long analysis of the viability of Lenin's thought as a tool or strategy for political victory. Very useful summary of literature and ideas emphasizing the 1960s. [P. B. Taylor, Jr.]

7383. Chalmers, Douglas. Parties and societies in Latin America (RU/SCID, 7:2, Summer 1972, p. 102-128)

Author rejects typologies of parties in Latin America as essentially inappropriate for understanding these institutions in their context. Instead, he offers his own typology which consists of four principal interrelated characteristics. On this basis, author suggests that the unique Latin American party type can be combined with unique types of other regional cultures. Author's typologies will be used in projected major study of national political systems. [P. B. Taylor, Jr.]

7383a. Chile, Perú, Bolivia: documentos de tres procesos latinoamericanos. B.A., Centro Editor de América Latina, 1972. 174 p. (Biblioteca fundamental del hombre moderno)

Contains text of speeches by Juan José Torres (Bolivia), Juan Velasco Alvarado (Peru), Salvador Allende (Chile) and others giving their views on economic nationalism and social reforms. [C. N. Ronning]

7384. CIDOC Informa: enero/junio 1970.

Cuernavaca, Mex., Centro Intercultural de Documentación, 1970. 223 p. (CIDOC: Cuaderno, 10:49)

Majority of 23 articles reprinted here deal with contemporary Church in Latin America and aspects of educational reform. Contributors include Ivan Illych, Ralph Abernathy, Helder Câmara, and Thomas Sanders. [J. J. Bailey]

7385. Clissold, Stephen. Latin America: New World, Third World. N.Y., Praeger Publishers, 1972. 394 p., bibl., map, tables.

Sketches precolumbian civilizations, Conquest and colonial period. Includes capsule histories of the 20 republics and chapters on society, economy, and politics. Well written introduction for beginning student or interested public. [J. J. Bailey]

7386. Conference on the Western Hemisphere, *N.Y., 1970.* Issues for the 1970's. N.Y., Center for Inter-American Relations, 1971. 138 p.

Seven papers presented at conference held 29 April-2 May 1971. Authors include Mariano Grondona (Arg.), Fernando Henrique Cardoso (Bra.), Gert Rosenthal (Guat.), Colin I. Bradford, Jr. (OAS), Sergio Bitar (Harvard Univ.), David Bronheim (The Center), and Felipe Paolillo (Uru.). The scope is multi-disciplinary, and papers touch all aspects of economic, social and political questions. [P. B. Taylor, Jr.]

7387. *Confirmado.* No. 375, 22 agosto 1972- B.A. Weekly newsmagazine, with most of the characteristics of the genre. Generally good; advertising indicates it is directed principally toward business and middle-class (upper) clientele. Contains good political commentary and analysis, some useful articles on development plans and problems in provinces, etc. [P. B. Taylor, Jr.]

7388. Cornelius, Wayne A. The cityward movement: some political implications (PAPS, 30:4, 1972, p. 27-41)

Systematically summarizes research findings on political attitudes of low-income urban immigrants in Latin America. Useful beginning point for future research in that findings are stated in form of testable hypotheses. [J. J. Bailey]

7389. Correa, Jorge. Los jerarcas sindicales. B.A., Editorial Polémica, 1972. 108 p.

Who are the elite leaders of labor, and how and why have they been corrupted? Book is dedicated to "those leaders who have not been corrupted"! Despite polemic tone, includes valuable detail. [P. B. Taylor, Jr.]

7390. Cuéllar, Oscar. Un esquema para el análisis de los aspectos políticos de la reforma agraria (CPES/RPS, 8:21, mayo/agosto, 1971, p. 60-83, tables)

Attempts to synthesize aspects of pluralist and marxist analysis in a general consideration of social change (of which agrarian reform is a component). Abstract analysis of a middle-range phenomenon. [J. J. Bailey]

7391. David, Donald E. Marxism and people's wars (CIDGO/O, 15:4, Winter 1972, p. 1194-1205)

Since Lenin's doctrine of the Peking Road, "people's wars" in developing areas have assumed greater importance in Marxian theory, despite implicit contradiction with classical Marxism. Describes contributions to the doctrine by such theorists as Mao Tse Tung, Lin Piao, and Che Guevara. [J. J. Bailey]

7392. Drekonja, Gerhard. Religion and social change in Latin America (LARR, 6:1, Spring 1971, p. 53-72, bibl.)

Quite useful synthesis of research and thinking on role of the Church in post-1968 period. Points out range of positions taken within the Church and poses central questions for further research. [J. J. Bailey]

7393. Dumas, Benoit A. Los dos rostros alienados de la Iglesia: ensayo de teología política. B.A., Latinoamérica Libros, 1971. 255 p.

Based on three years' service in Montevideo, a French lay brother writes of the crisis of the Church in Latin America. Largely theological piece with interesting spin-offs into politics. [P. B. Taylor, Jr.]

7394. Ebel, Roland H. Governing the city-state: notes on the politics of the small Latin American countries (UM/JIAS, 14:3, Aug. 1972, p. 325-346, tables)

Useful interpretive essay which questions the nation-state assumption which influences North American research and suggests the city-state perspective as more applicable in certain instances. Advances specific hypotheses interrelating size of political unit and distribution of political power and policymaking. [J. J. Bailey]

7395. Fals Borda, Orlando. Subversión y desarrollo: el caso de América Latina (JLAIS/CS, 9:26/27, 1971, p. 39-51)

Synthesizes author's previous work (see *HLAS 33:7896*) on anti-establishment movements in a general historical and contemporary Latin American context. Notes impact of Latin American subversives on other regions of world. [J. J. Bailey]

7396. Fitzgibbon, Russell H. Components of political change in Latin America (UM/JIAS, 12:2, April 1970, p. 187-204, tables)

Eminent Latin Americanist rightly points out that "Latin American politics must be measured, not against what prevails in United States . . . but against what Latin America offered a century and a half ago." But his article is too short, and data too scarce, to generate something else than vague generalizations. [A. Suárez]

7397. Fossum, Egil. Latin-Amerika mellom revolusjon og kontra revolusjon. Oslo, Gyldendal Norsk Forlag, 1970. 142 p.

Norwegian social scientist, at the Peace Research Institute, addresses the general public in this volume entitled *Latin America: between revolution and counterrevollution.* Clearly states his belief in a "revolutionary" rather than a "reformist" transformation of Latin America, a viewpoint which does not prevent him from sharply criticizing Cuban weaknesses (e.g., excessive centralization; bureaucracy; lack of popular participation; exaggerated dependence on the USSR). Knowledgeable and very readable book. [Magnus Mörner]

7398. Francis, Michael J. Revolutionary labor in Latin America: the CLASC (UM/JIAS, 10:4, Oct. 1968, p. 597-616)

CLASC represents a novel and possibly very effective challenge to the ORIT for the role of principal labor representative in Latin America. In order to explain CLASC's effectiveness, author examines its "unique ideological base" and its operations and programmatic positions. Concludes with mixed generalizations concerning possible future strengthening of the organization. [P. B. Taylor, Jr.]

7399. Frei Montalva, Eduardo. The second Latin American revolution (CFR/FA, 50:1, Oct. 1971, p. 83-96)

Former Chilean president suggests that the new context of Latin American politics is one of mass mobilization and participation, which in turn has created a need for greater political creativity. Calls for continued US concern with and openness to Latin America during this period of transition. [J. J. Bailey]

7400. Frutkin, Arnold W. and Richard B. Griffin, Jr. Space activity in Latin America (UM/JIAS, 10:2, April 1968, p. 185-193)

An alternative title might be "The Latin American Relations of the National Aeronautics and Space Administration." Very brief recounting by two NASA officials of how Latin American countries became interested in space, and the degree to which they have made commitments. [P. B. Taylor, Jr.]

7401. Fulchi, Gustavo Adolfo. Algunas consideraciones sobre el rol de las fuerzas armadas en las sociedades intermedias (ILARI/A, 15, enero 1970, p. 164-173)

Review article of works dealing with the armed forces' political role in both the developed and less developed societies. Concludes with discussion of characteristics of military establishments with political-action goals. Includes useful bibliographic footnote. [P. B. Taylor, Jr.]

7402. Galeano, Eduardo H. Las venas abiertas de América Latina. Montevideo, Univ. de la República, Depto. de Publicaciones, 1971. 391 p. (Col. Historia y cultura, 16)

Veins of Latin America are open to the suction of the developed countries, from colonial times onward. Useful to the devotée of this interpretation. [P. B. Taylor, Jr.]

7403. Gall, Norman. Latin America: the Church militant (AJC/C, 49:4, April 1970, p. 25-37)

Describes contemporary crisis in Latin American Church resulting from emergence of militant reformist and revolutionary leaders and groups. Stresses somewhat cases of Brazilian Church and Jesuit order and explores possibility of internal dissolution of Church structure and discipline. Perceptive overview. [J. J. Bailey]

7404. ———. Teodoro Petkoff: the crisis of the professional revolutionary: pt. 1, Years of insurrection. N.Y., American Universities Field Staff Reports, 1972. 19 p., plates (East Coast South America series, 16:1)

First-person recounting of Petkoff's experiences, based on ten hours of taped interviews with Gall, covering period from youth through 1963 when he escaped from the military hospital after capture by police. [P. B. Taylor, Jr.]

García, Antonio. Dialéctica de la democracia. See item 7652.

7405. Gavi, Philippe. Che Guevara. Paris, Editions Universitaries, 1970. 170 p., bibl., plates (Les justes)

Biographical narrative on Guevara from youth in Argentina to death in Bolivia. Based on secondary sources for most part. [J. J. Bailey]

7406. Gavilán Estelat, Marcelino. Las nuevas tendencias de la reforma agraria en Iberoamérica (Revista de Estudios Agro-Sociales [Madrid] 21:79, abril/junio 1972, p. 53-70)

Discusses evolution of agrarian reform legislation in Mexico and Andean countries. Comparative legal analysis with some attention to cooperatives as a policy instrument. [J. J. Bailey]

7407. Gil, Federico G. Instituciones y desarrollo político de América Latina. B.A., Instituto para la Integración de América Latina (INTAL), 1966. 201 p., bibl.

Introductory survey of Latin American politics with an institutional approach. Chapters on colonial background, political and social organization, government institutions, parties, and pressure groups. [J. J. Bailey]

7407a. Goldenberg, Boris. Kommunismus in Lateinamerika, Stuttgart, FRG, Kohlhammer, 1971. 639 p., bibl.

Major work by one of the best-known German experts on Latin America consists of three parts: communism in Latin America between 1951-58; the most important communist parties in Latin America and their historical and ideological development; communist development in Latin America from the Cuban revolution to 1968. Goldenberg stresses his intention to give an inside view of Latin American communism without being concerned for the real or imaginary threat it may offer. He has used a tremendous amount of Latin American and Soviet sources for his scholarly analysis which can probably be regarded as a standard work of its kind. [W. Grabendorff.]

7408. Gott, Richard. Guerrilla movements in Latin America. N.Y., Doubleday, 1971. 626 p., bibl., maps, plates.

Extraordinary work, based on personal experience, reporting, and on research in available literature. Book has long sections on Guatemala, Venezuela, Colombia, Peru and Bolivia. Also includes valuable long series of appendices, and often exceptional photographs. [P. B. Taylor, Jr.]

7409. Grabendorff, Wolf ed. Lateinamerika: Kontinent in der Krise. Hamburg, FRG, Hoffman und Campe Verlag, 1973, 413 p., bibl.

West German sociologist and TV commentator as well as *HLAS* Foreign Contributing Editor has assembled

here articles by Latin American and German specialists, highlighting contemporary political problems of the region. Topics range from study of theories of dependence to industrialization, experiments in socialism, and search for new formulas. Very readable and important contribution. Includes:
Wolf Grabendorff "Einführung" p. 7-15
Marco Aurelio Garcia de Almeida and Thomas Amadeo Vasconi "Entwicklung der in Lateinamerika vorherrschenden Ideologien" p. 16-47
Hans-Jürgen Puble "Nationalismus in Lateinamerika" p. 48-77
Manfred Wöhlcke "Wirtschaftliche, soziale und politische Aspekte der interethnischen Beziehungen in Lateinamerika" p. 78-98.
Heinrich W. Krumwiede "Katholische Kirche und soziopolitischer Wandel in Lateinamerika" p. 99-130
Klaus Lindenberg "Politische Parteien in Lateinamerika" p. 131-178
Marcos Kaplan "Politische Aspekte der Planung in Lateinamerika" p. 179-205
Sergio Bagú "Industrialisierung, Gesellschaft und Abhängigkeit in Lateinamerika" p. 206-243
Ricardo Ffrench-Davis "Auslandsinvestitionen in Lateinamerika" p. 244-279
Manfred Nitsch "Außenhandel und Entwicklung in Lateinamerika" p. 271-298
Félix Peña "Perspektiven der wirtschaftlichen Integration Lateinamerikas" p. 299-314
German Kratochwil "Entwicklungshilfe der Industrieländer und Abhängigkeit Lateinamerikas" p. 315-339
Wolf Grabendorff "Außenpolitische Emanzipation Lateinamerikas" p. 340-378
Octavio Ianni "Epilog: Soziologie der Dependencia in Lateinamerika" p. 379-399 [G.M. Dorn]

Grayson, George W. El viaje de Castro a Chile, Perú y Ecuador. See item 8031.

7410. Grote, Bernd ed. América Latina; Lateinamerika: der erwachende Riese. Herausgeber [von] Bernd Grote. Texte [von] Franz Dülk, Paul Hoffacker, Hildegard Lüning und Gernot Schley. Hamburg, FRG, Rowholt, 1971. 140 p., illus., map (Rororo tele)

Up-to-date, incisive analysis of Latin America as a breeding ground for revolution by four young West German TV and newspaper correspondents. Despite brevity, accurately reflects Latin America's social and economic problems. [G.M. Dorn]

7411. Guillén Martínez, Fernando. Planeación y participación social en América Latina (ILARI/A, 21, julio 1971, p. 16-29)

Planning has been regarded, abstractly, as a way to solve problems. But since no one has examined the notion honestly, it is a shibboleth without content. Author seeks to reexamine the term and to ask rigorous questions as to who, what, how, why, etc. Modest contribution to the discussion. [P.B. Taylor, Jr.]

7412. Gutiérrez-Girardot, Rafael. Lateinamerika: Abschied von der Revolution? (MDZED, 26:1, Jan. 1972, p. 29-44)

Definition of and critical look at the notion of "revolution" in Latin America. What motivates it, how do its actors conceive it, and what is likely to be the outcome? Postulates that revolutionary movements of the past decade have been outcries against the fascism of technology. [P.B. Taylor, Jr.]

Heare, Gertrude E. Trends in Latin American military expenditures, 1940-1970: Argentina, Brazil, Chile, Colombia, Peru and Venezuela. See *HLAS* 34:2989a.

7413. Herrera, Amílcar Oscar. Ciencia y política en América Latina. México, Siglo XXI Editores, 1971. 206 p., tables (El mundo del hombre: economía y demografía)

Analyzes factors which account for underdeveloped state of science and technology in Latin America. In a kind of corollary to the structuralist analysis of inflation, suggests that development of science requires prior socioeconomic changes. Prescribes strategy for planning in science policy, with attention to instruments, goals, and international cooperation. Useful in consideration of social, economic, and political aspects of science and technology policy. [J.J. Bailey]

7414. Hodara, Joseph. La dependencia en la dependencia (ILARI/A, 21, julio 1971, p. 6-15)

"Dependence" has caught on in Latin American jargon as a modish notion, and has clearly lost some of its conceptual integrity as a tool of analysis. It has, as a result, all sorts of cheapened implications, many of them profoundly anti-intellectual. Thus, redefinition and precision are in order. Author makes the effort to provide these concepts. [P. B. Taylor, Jr.]

7415. Horowitz, Irving L. La ideología política de la economía política (ILARI/A, 14, Oct. 1969, p. 80-102)

US policy concerning the development of underdeveloped countries and regions tends to assume these units are incapable of free growth and thus in need of a kind of economic therapy. As a result, application of specifics has tended to preclude free choice by these countries and change has strengthened US control of them. Paper concludes with seven suggestions directed as much toward the US as toward the developing countries. [P.B. Taylor, Jr.]

Houtart, François and **André Rousseau.** The Church and revolution: from the French Revolution of 1789 to the Paris Riots of 1968; from Cuba to Southern Africa; from Vietnam to Latin America. See item 7587.

7416. Huizer, Gerrit. Peasant organizations in the process of political modernization: the Latin American experience (*in* Field, Arthur J. ed. City and country in the Third World: issues in the modernization of Latin America. Cambridge, Mass., Schenkman Publishing Company, 1970, p. 49-62, bibl.)

Draws on experiences of peasant organization and agrarian reform in Mexico, Bolivia, Venezuela, Peru and Colombia. Develops middle-level generalizations on circumstances which activate peasant organizations and shape tactics on agrarian reform issues. Interesting interpretive essay. [J. J. Bailey]

7417. Hyman, Elizabeth H. Soldiers in politics: new insights on Latin American armed forces (APS/PSQ, 87:3, Sept. 1972, p. 401-418)

In an essentially extended and selective review article, writer argues that not until the 1960's did social scientists begin to examine the armed forces of Latin America in realistic terms. Compares value of published works, establishes series of observations about what soldiers are and are not in Latin America, and concludes that for the most part they reflect with some accuracy the environments of their individual countries. [P.B. Taylor, Jr.]

7418. Iglesias, Enrique V. Cambio estructural en América Latina (BID/T, 7:12, abril 1971, p. 5-23, illus., plates)

Models and theories of change have been discussed at great length, and in recent years it appears that many of them have been incorrect to some degree. Adjustments thus seem in order. Writer, a noted Uruguayan economist, also asks if it will be possible for the upper class leaders of Latin America to assume more courageous and far-sighted roles concerning change and development. [P.B. Taylor, Jr.]

7419. Jaguaribe, Helio. Political development: a general theory and a Latin American case study. N.Y., Harper & Row, 1973. 603 p., tables.

On the basis of operational models carefully defined and evaluated for the analysis of the phenomenon of political development, writer seeks to answer why Latin America has not experienced development. He feels this can be both answered and remedied. Enormously ambitious work and clearly one of the most sophisticated efforts yet made by any social scientist. [P. B. Taylor, Jr.]

7420. Kaplan, Marcos. Aspectos políticos de la planificación en América Latina (ILARI/A, 20, abril 1971, p. 130-170)

Has there really been any planning for development in Latin America? There has been much interventionism and *dirigismo* by governments. But certain essential elements of planning have been absent. Long and perceptive essay defines general terms and specific qualities in detail. [P. B. Taylor, Jr.]

7421. Kloppenburg, Boaventura. A eclesiologia do Vaticano II. Petrópolis, Bra., Editôra Vozes, 1971. 291 p.

Examination of developments and implications of results reached at the II Vatican Council. [J. F. B. Dasilva]

7422. Kowalewski, Z. Martin and **Miguel Sobrado.** Antropología de la guerrilla: hacia la ciencia social del Tercer Mundo. Caracas, Editorial Nueva Izquierda, 1971. 118 p. (Col. Monografías)

Three essays attempt to integrate anthropological concepts of culture to theories and practice of guerrilla war. Identifies the problem as that of penetrating beliefs and customs of supportive communities. Reaffirms the insurrectional path to form new socialist institutions. [W. H. Agor]

7423. Lambert, Jacques. Structure sociale dualiste et administration publique en Amérique Latine (Bulletin de l'Institut International d'Administration Publique [Paris] 2, avril/juin 1967, p. 23-35)

Thoughts on the dual structure of Latin American society and its effect on public administration. Rather shallow think-piece, but provocative nevertheless.

Includes separate sections on rural and urban problems, etc. [P.B. Taylor, Jr.]

7424. Lambert, Roberto F. Consideraciones concluyentes en torno a las guerrillas castristas en Latinoamérica (ILARI/A, 25, julio 1972, p. 107-118)

Thirteen brief hypotheses are offered to explain why Castro's guerrilla movements never succeeded in revolutionizing whole region. This is a brief critical typological essay on errors. [P. B. Taylor, Jr.]

7424a. *Lateinamerika.* Probleme, Perspektiven. Vol. 16, No. 2, 1972- . Berlin, GDR.

Entire issue (307 p.) of official foreign policy periodical of the GDR devoted to recent developments in Latin America. Includes documents, statistics, conference reports, maps, following articles:
Manfred Uschner "Lateinamerika: ein wichtiger Abschnitt des revolutionären Weltprozesses" p. 9-21
Adalbert Dessau "Der antiimperialistische Kampf der Völker Lateinamerikas in den sechziger Jahren" p. 22-39
Dieter Kulitzka "Die Beziehungen der DDR zu den Staaten Lateinamerikas" p. 40-46
Peter May "Eine neue Etappe des sozialistischen Aufbaus in Kuba" p. 47-52
Siegfried Körner "Chile im Aufbruch" p. 52-60
Werner Strauss "Entwicklung und Politik der Militärregierungen in Peru und Bolivien" p. 61-74
Erich Ducke "Zur Rolle und Entwicklung der Arbeiterklasse Lateinamerikas" p. 75-89
A.F. Schulgovski "Der ideologische Kampf in Lateinamerika in der gegenwärtigen Etappe" p. 90-106
Max Zeuske "Zur Struktur der Landwirtschaft in Lateinamerika und zur Rolle der Bauernschaft" p. 107-118
Manfred Kossok "Kirche und Armee: zur Krise traditioneller Machtinstitutionen in Lateinamerika" p. 118-149
Alfred Hoege and Bernd Hütte "Der Antiyankeeismus in Lateinamerika" p. 149-156
Klaus Bollinger and Renate Petrahn "Ziele und Möglichkeiten der Lateinamerikapolitik der USA" p. 156-171
Werner Hintzke "Die Lateinamerika-Politik Westdeutschlands" p. 171-183
Paul Halpap "Die Wirtschaftsexpansion der japanischen Monopole nach Lateinamerika" p. 183-200
Klaus Rudolph "Hauptwidersprüche in der Entwicklung der kapitalistischen Produktionsweise in Brasilien" p. 201-210. [W. Grabendorff]

Latin America: the quest for change. See item 8048.

7425. *Latinskaia Amerika.* USSR Academy of Sciences, Latin American Institute. No. 2, March/April 1970- . Moskva.

Entire issue devoted to Leninism and Latin America on the 100th anniversary of Lenin's birth. For a concise summary of the highlights of Leninist theory regarding Latin America see in this issue, V.V. Vol'skii "Leninizm i Problemy Revoliutsionnogo Protsessa v Latinskoi Amerika" (Leninism and Problems of Revolutionary Process in Latin America). [T. S. Cheston]

7426. ———. ———, ———. No. 4, July/August 1971- . Moskva.

Entire issue devoted to the military in the political life of Latin America. Of special note for those interested in the changing role of the military in recent years is: N.S. Lenonov "Peru: Novaia rol'Voennykh" (Peru: the New Role of the Military). [T. S. Cheston]

7426a. Lehner, Gunthar *ed.* Lateinamerika heute: ein Subkontinent im Umbruch. München, FRG, Kösel, 1972. 167 p.

Collection of ten essays on various topics and of varying quality originally written for a radio series. Some of the articles serve as quite acceptable introductions to the subjects:
German Kratochwil "Explosion des Elends: Wirtschaftliches Wachstum und Familienplanung" p. 7-21
Egloff Schwaiger "Geschäft unter dem Kreuz des Südens: Wirtschaftliche Strukturen und Interessen" p. 22-34
Boris Goldenberg "Von Bolívar bis Allende: Revolutionäre Modelle" p. 35-49
Friedhelm Merz "Der katholische Kontinent: Paternalismus-Reform-Revolution?" p. 50-59
Walter Hanf and Klaus Dressel "Reform in Uniform: Sozialmilitarismus in Lateinamerika" p. 60-80
Udo Reiter "Kulturrevolution als Lösung? Die umstrittenen Thesen des Ivan Illich" p. 81-95
Karl Brugger "Che Guevara-welche Folgen? Revolutionäre Praktiken in Lateinamerika" p. 96-130
Hugo Loetscher "Präsidenten und Exilierte: Literatur als gesellschaftspolitisches Engagement" p. 115-130
Oriana Fallaci "Der rote, der schreckliche Bischof: Interview mit Dom Helder Câmara" p. 131-152
Gunthar Lehner "Zwischen Atlantik und Pazifik." p. 153-167 [W. Grabendorff]

7427. Lenkersdorf, Karl. Iglesia y liberación del pueblo (JLAIS/CS, 9:26/27, 1971, p. 52-64)

The way out of a repressive state requires elimination of those conditions that enslave. Author acknowledges long road between liberation on behalf of the people and liberation by the people themselves. Suggests that the role of the Church can be much stronger in reconciling those differences. [A. Suárez]

7428. Levin, Peter J. The development program of the Río de la Plata basin: a new approach to Latin American integration (JDA, 6:4, July 1972, p. 493-522)

Argentina, Bolivia, Brazil, Paraguay and Uruguay have been involved since 1967 (when a joint program was agreed upon) in development of this river basin. Paper examines details of the plan: objectives, possible achievements, and legal/institutional obstacles and problems to be surmounted. Writer suggests this form of joint action may become a model for later similar efforts elsewhere. [P. B. Taylor, Jr.]

7429. Llano Cifuentes, Rafael. La actuación del cristiano en la vida política (ISTMO, 77, nov./dic. 1971, p. 32-44, plates)

Based on Church teachings and scholarly writings, argues for an active role for Catholics in politics. Suggests broad guidelines to orient political activity for Catholics in various social roles. [J. J. Bailey]

7430. López Oliva, Enrique *ed.* El camilismo en la América Latina. Introducción, compilación y notas [de] . . . La Habana, Casa de las Américas, 1970. 97 p. (Cuadernos Casa, 10)

Anthology of documents and speeches by Catholic activitists in Chile, Argentina, Uruguay, and Brazil sympathetic to teachings and example of Camilo Torres, the Colombian priest whose gradual radicalization led him to join the guerrilla and who was subsequently killed by units of the Colombian army in 1965. [J.J. Bailey]

7431. McDonald, Ronald H. Party systems and elections in Latin America. Chicago, Ill., Markham Publishing Co., 1971. 324 p., tables.

Employing parties and elections as the institutional analytical tool, author offers a text that features a sustained and thoroughly tested thesis. Based on both exhaustive use of previously-published materials by other political scientists and extensive personal research. Useful teaching tool for college level work as well as a more than satisfactory first selection for beginning students. [P.B. Taylor, Jr.]

7432. Maduro, Otto. Revelación y revolución. Mérida, Ven., Univ. de los Andes Depto. de Publicaciones, Ediciones del Rectorado, 1970. 133 p.

Philosophical-interpretive essays on Christian love, violence, justice, and political action by young Catholic activist. Seeks in Christian teachings the moral basis of political revolution. [J.J. Bailey]

7433. Mallin, Jay. Terrorism as a political weapon (AF/AUR, 22:5, July/Aug. 1971, p. 45-52, illus., table)

Casual consideration of uses of terror with recommendations on combating it. Draws on Latin American examples to illustrate. [J.J. Bailey]

7434. *Marcha.* Año 33, No. 1559, sept. 4, 1971 [through] Año 33, No. 1570, nov. 19, 1971- Montevideo.

Among the more thoughtful and informative leftist publications in Latin America, *Marcha* is a non-partisan weekly, directed by Carlos Quijano. Other contributors: Eduardo Galeano, María Ester Gilio, Roque Faraone, Marcos Gabay, Raúl Gadea, etc. Some of their foreign correspondents: *Argentina:* Rogelio García Lupo, Gregorio Selser, Rodolfo Walsh; *Bolivia:* Augusto Céspedes; *Cuba:* Roberto Fernández Retamar, Carlos María Gutiérrez; *Ecuador:* Benjamín Carrión; *México:* Luis Cardoza y Aragón Gilly, Mario Guzmán Galarza; *Perú:* José Miguel Oviedo; *Puerto Rico:* Manuel Maldonado Denis; *Venezuela:* Ugo Ulive, Daniel Waksman Schinca; *Spain:* Juan Goytisolo, Mario Vargas Llosa, Juan García Grau; *United States:* James Petras, Antonio Frasconi, etc. [D. M. Martin]

7435. Mariscal, Nicolás. La renovación de la Iglesia latinoamericana (CJ/RF, 886, nov. 1971, p. 351-362, table)

Optimistic assessment of reform tendencies in the Church since Vatican II. [J. J. Bailey]

7436. Marsal, Juan Francisco *ed.* and *comp.* Los intelectuales políticos. Introducción y selección de . . . B.A. Ediciones Nueva Visión, 1971. 341 p. (Cuadernos de investigación social. Serie: Textos fundamentales)

The intellectual, in general and in Latin America, as perceived by 14 writers. Some of the pieces are based on behavioral or sociological research, while others (Lenin, for example) take a different approach. [P. B. Taylor, Jr.]

7437. Martínez Sáez, Santiago. Teología y liberación (ISTMO, 74, mayo/junio 1971, p. 9-21, plates)

Conservative critique of political and economic emphases over orthodox interpretations of Christian concept of liberation. [J. J. Bailey]

7438. Martz, John D. Democratic political campaigning in Latin America: a typological approach to cross-cultural research (SPSA/JP, 33:2, May 1971, p. 370-398, tables)

Author does not really demonstrate that this is a subject sufficiently important to warrant "spadework" for theory building. Rather scientistic in tone. [J. J. Bailey]

7439. ———. Political science and Latin American studies: a discipline in search of a region (LARR, 6:1, Spring 1971, p. 73-99)

Regional specialist re-writes the generally adverse earlier comments by others about the state of the art. This exercise in flagellation is partially justified, but the art is not therefore advanced. [P. B. Taylor, Jr.]

7440. Matthews, Herbert Lionel. A world in revolution: a newspaperman's memoir. N.Y., Charles Scribner's Sons, 1971. 462 p.

Title states the essentials. Three chapters are devoted to Latin America, one specifically to "Cuba and *The New York Times*." [P. B. Taylor, Jr.]

7441. Max, Alphonse. Guerillas in Lateinamerika. Zürich, Switzerland, Schweizerische Handelszeitung, 1971. 62 p.

Journalist who lived in Latin America for many years and had first-hand knowledge of some of the events he describes, analyzes here the comparatively recent phenomenon of guerrilla activities. He concentrates on the kidnapping of the Swiss envoy, Giovanni Bader, in Brazil and on the Uruguayan guerrillas. Journalistic but very informative. [G. M. Dorn]

7442. Micklin, Michael. Demographic, economic and social change in Latin America: an examination of causes and consequences (JDA, 4:2, Jan. 1970, p. 173-195, tables)

Somewhat experimental article, seeks to develop relationships among demographic, social and economic areas of change in Latin America—as representative of "the third world." Data are extracted from previously published sources, and submitted to mathematical analysis. [P. B. Taylor, Jr.]

7443. Morales, Víctor Hugo. Del porteñazo al Perú. Caracas, Editorial Domingo Fuentes, 1971. 271 p., bibl., maps, plates (Col. Estos días)

Author, a naval officer often involved in political acts, was imprisoned for six years for his role in the uprising at Puerto Cabello (Ven.) in June 1962. This is his case for the action. Last part discusses Peruvian military government that seized power in 1968 claiming that the Venezuelan armed forces were trying to do the same. Offers useful detail concerning court martials, but in general it is a case of special pleading by an uniformed politician. [P. B. Taylor, Jr.]

7444. Morelli, Alex. Libera a mi pueblo. Prólogo de Sergio Méndez Arceo. México, Ediciones Carlos Lohlé, 1971. 130 p., bibl. (Cuadernos Latinoamericanos)

Essentially philosophical tract keyed by the attitudes of the Church as expressed at Medellín. Morelli is a priest and the volume bears the imprimatur. Pt. 2 struggles with the problem of violence by the non-violent, citing King, Ghandi, and others. [P. B. Taylor, Jr.]

7445. Moreno, Francisco José and Barbara Mitrani eds. Conflict and violence in Latin American politics: a book of readings. N.Y., Thomas Y Crowell, 1971. 452 p.

Posits political instability as "the cornerstone on which any knowledge of the area's politics must rest." Organizes essays into historical, psychocultural, political, and socioeconomic approaches. Useful collection of 27 articles and essays. [J. J. Bailey]

7446. Morse, Richard M. Trends and issues in Latin American urban research: 1965-1970 (LARR, 6:1, Spring 1971, p. 3-52; 6:2, Summer 1971, p. 19-75)

Exhaustive descriptive and analytical examination of literature on the subject, arranged topically. [P. B. Taylor, Jr.]

7447. Moss, Robert. Urban guerrillas: the new face of political violence. London, Temple Smith, 1972. 288 p., bibl.

General analysis of causes of urban political violence in developing and industrialized nations. Besides cases drawn from Europe and North America, provides brief chapters on Cuba, Venezuela, Guatemala, Brazil, and Uruguay. Useful contribution. [J. J. Bailey]

Nelson, Joan M. Migrants, urban poverty and instability in developing nations. See item 6773.

7448. Nelson, Michael A. The Latin American military: positive roles (AF/AUR, 23:5, July/Aug. 1972, p. 57-64)

American air force officer accentuates the positive. His opening paragraphs indicate his wish to counter old stereotypes. [P. B. Taylor, Jr.]

7449. Oszlak, Oscar. Agrarian reform in Latin America: a political approach (IFSNC/CD, 25/26, Spring 1971, p. 109-128)

Analyzes factors which tend to weaken political power of landed groups and thus facilitate agrarian reform. Interesting attempt at middle-range theory. [J. J. Bailey]

7450. Owens, Gene M. Approaches to the study of political parties in the Latin American milieu (The Journal of International and comparative Studies [Washington] 5:1, Winter 1972, p. 78-109, bibl.)

Review essay on central problems in the study of political parties and an assessment of recent trends. [J. J. Bailey]

7451. Palacio Ruedas, Alfonso. Los columnas del

cofrade, 1966-1970. Ibagué, Col., Univ. del Tolima, 1971. 328 p.

Collection of author's weekly columns in *El Espectador* of Bogotá from Nov. 1966 to Aug. 1970. Writer also is national Senator from the Tolima dept. [P. B. Taylor, Jr.]

7452. Paligorić, Ljubomir. Politicke doktrine levice u Latinskoj Americi (Political doctrines of the Left in Latin America). Beograd, Institut za Medunarodni Radnicki Pokret (Institute of the International Labor Movement), 1972. 464 p., bibl.

After an analysis of the crisis in the socio-economic system, author examines development of political ideas on the continent, classifies the various political movements, and describes the alternatives they offer. Emphasizes socialist concepts and the question of their viability in underdeveloped environments. Main hypothesis is that political concepts of Latin America were shaped by foreign ideologies and indigenous political movements have not been attuned to the real needs. Socialist movements in the region are not keeping up with the growing role of the working class because of fragmentation and dependence on European models. The Cuban Revolution tried to create its own original transformation, but, because of the same basic dependence, became dogmatic. This is a further demonstration that orthodox theory must be adapted; in brief, that there are no "models" for socialist transformation. [A. R. Navon]

7453. Paz, Ida. Contraofensiva ideológica en la nueva ciencia social latinoamericana (PC, 48, enero 1971, p. 206-223)

Sketches recent origins of dependency school and describes principal tenets through a review of examples of dependency literature. Argues that dependency theory is more appropriate for Latin American social science than models derived from foreign experience. [J. J. Bailey]

7454. Pérez, Javier. Cuba, Paraguay, Uruguay y la Iglesia (Actualidad Pastoral [B.A.] 4:42, junio 1971, p. 123-126, plate, tables)

Short series of statements, including many quotes, concerning conditions under which clergy have sought to remedy adverse official policies. Names of clergy imprisoned in these countries or otherwise sanctioned as a result are detailed. [P. B. Taylor, Jr.]

7455. Petras, James. Politics and social structure in Latin America. N.Y., Monthly Review Press, 1970. 382 p., tables.

24 papers (and fragments), some co-authored, some previously published. Petras emerges as one of the more effectively articulate radical North American social scientists. His work contrasts with the humbuggishness of some publications on the subject. [P. B. Taylor, Jr.]

7456. ———— *comp.* América Latina: economía y política. B.A., Ediciones Periferia, 1972. 458 p., tables (Col. Estados Unidos y América Latina)

Compilation of essays on general theme of nature of dependency in Latin America. Contents: James Petras and Marcelo Cavarozzi "Conflicto Político y Dependencia Económica en Chile;" Jorge I. Tapia Videla and Luis Quirós Varela "El Gobierno de la Unidad Popular: El Difícil Camino de Transición hacia el Socialismo;" Bolivia. Ministerio de Planificación "Bolivia: Estrategia Socioeconómica del Desarrollo Nacional 1971-1999;" René Zavaleta Mercado "Bolivia: de la Asamblea Popular al Combate de Agosto;" María C. Tavares and José Serra "Más Allá del Estancamiento: Una Discusión sobre el Estilo de Desarrollo Reciente del Brasil;" Alberto Couriel "Uruguay: Las Causas Económicas de sus Transformaciones Políticas e Ideológicas." [J. J. Bailey]

7457. ———— *ed.* Latin America: from dependence to revolution. N.Y., John Wiley & Sons, 1973. 274 p., bibl., tables.

Essays apparently are original. Contents:
James Petras "Political and Social Change in Chile" p. 9-40
James Petras "Chile: Nationalization, Socioeconomic Change, and Popular Participation" p. 41-60
M. C. Tavares and José Serra "Beyond Stagnation: a Discussion on the Nature of Recent Developments in Brazil" p. 61-99
José Serra "The Brazilian 'Economic Miracle' " p. 100-142
James Petras and Thomas Cook "Dependency and the Industrial Bourgeoisie: Attitudes of Argentine Executives toward Foreign Economic Investments and U.S. Policy" p. 143-175
James Petras and Thomas Cook "Politics in a Nondemocratic State: the Argentine Industrial Elite" p. 176-195
James Petras and Robert LaPorte, Jr. "U.S. Response to Economic Nationalism in Chile" p. 195-231
James Petras; H. Michael Erisman; and Charles Mills "The Monroe Doctrine and U.S. Hegemony in Latin America" p. 231-272. [J. J. Bailey]

7458. Pinto, Luis de Aguiar Costa and **Sulamita B. de Costa Pinto.** La crisis latinoamericana: fundamentación de un modelo teórico para su análisis sociológico (ILARI/A, 18, oct. 1970, p. 6-15)

Modest effort to define terms and to suggest theoretical model that can be employed for research in specific cases. Doubtless the purpose is desirable, but the exercise seems a bit passé at this time. [P. B. Taylor, Jr.]

7459. Plaza, Galo. Latin America: today and tomorrow. Washington, Acropolis Books, 1971. 229 p., illus., plates.

CAS Secretary General makes some essential points about the hopes, frustrations and achievements as well as future problems of the region. Work is not uncritical and reflects new, statesmanlike style of American policy in the area. [P. B. Taylor, Jr.]

7460. Powelson, John P. El radicalismo estudiantil en las Américas (USIA/PI, 19:1/2, enero/abril 1972, p. 1-8)

While North and Latin American student radicals adopt similar political tactics, their goals are basically different. Points out contrasts in student attitudes toward economic growth and the role of government. [J. J. Bailey]

7461. Ranis, Peter. Five Latin American nations: a comparative political study. N.Y., Macmillan, 1971. 337 p., tables.

Comparative topical analysis of Mexico, Argentina, Chile, Brazil, and Peru intended as an introductory text and general essay on modernization and political development. Idea of book is sound; execution, however, is disappointing. [J. J. Bailey]

7462. Ratinoff, Luis. Población y desarrollo en América Latina; evolución de las doctrinas (BID/T, 7:12, abril 1971, p. 24-35, plates, table)

General review of theory and fact concerning relationship of population growth (via natural means and migration) and national economic development. Typology of Latin American countries is offered, with sociodemographic indicators suggested in a quadripartite arrangement. [P. B. Taylor, Jr.]

7463. Reis, Fábio Wanderley. Educação, economia e contestação política na América Latina (UMG/RBEP, 31, maio 1970, p. 9-52, tables)

Secondary analysis of cross-national data seeking to establish levels of correlation between status (economic and educational levels) and political responsiveness. Principally useful as one author's exercise with numbers. [P. B. Taylor, Jr.]

Richardson, C. Howard. American research on the political geography of Latin America. See item 6591.

7464. Riemens, H. Latijns-Amerikaanse kroniek (NGIZ/IS, 24:16, sept. 1970, p. 1485-1496)

Chronicle which examines many aspects of Latin American politics, chiefly the guerrilla movement. Discusses Uruguayan and Guatemalan guerrillas and their victims. Also treats OAS, its charter and the election of Galo Plaza as Secretary General; President Nixon's speech on Latin America; and various sociopolitical and economic aspects of Latin American countries. [H. J. Hoyer]

7465. Rojas Rodríguez, Marta Tania. La guerrilla inolvidable. La Habana, Instituto del Libro, 1970. 355 p., facsims., map, plates.

Extensive compilation of letters, photos, interviews, and documents covering life of Tamara Bunke from her birth in Argentina in 1938 to her death in Bolivia in 1967. Skillfully edited. [J. J. Bailey]

7466. Rouquié, Alain. Révolutions militaires et indépendance nationale en Amérique Latine: 1968-1971 (FNSP/RFSP, 21:5, oct. 1971, p. 1045-1069)

Peru, Bolivia and Panama—locales of military seizures of power in the period indicated—are examined. Why did the military act, and for what purposes? What internal or external factors can be distinguished? Have the claims of *nationalist* revolutions, for freedom from foreign dependency, been achieved? [P. B. Taylor, Jr.]

7467. Ruddle, Kenneth and **Philip Gillette** *eds*. Latin American political statistics: supplement to the statistical abstract of Latin America. Los Angeles, Calif., Univ. of California at Los Angeles, Latin American Center, 1972. 128 p., tables.

Useful reference work which compiles electoral data on 20 Latin American countries from the early 1940s to, in some cases, 1971. Also useful is a section which summarizes changes in governments over basically the same time period. [J. J. Bailey]

7468. Russell, Charles A. and **Robert E. Hildner.** Urban insurgency in Latin America: its implications for the future (AF/AUR, 22:6, Sept./Oct. 1971, p. 54-64, illus.)

Policy oriented essay which summarizes factors accounting for the transition of guerrilla insurgency from rural to urban setting. Stresses role of urban police forces in reacting to this development and recommends necessary steps to be taken, particularly in areas of organization and intelligence, to develop an effective counterinsurgency force. [J. J. Bailey]

7469. Sábato, Jorge A. and **Natalio Botana.** La science, la technique et l'avenir de l'Amérique Latine: analyse et stratégie (UP/TM, 12:47, juillet/set. 1971, p. 579-594)

Two Argentines, one a physicist and the other a political scientist, make the case for joint government and private enterprise support for science and technology in the development of Latin America: the only hope, as they put it. The paper is long on theory and short on specific analysis as applied to the region. [P. B. Taylor, Jr.]

7470. Sáez Iglesias, Hernán and **José A. Vieragallo Quesney.** Investigaciones para un estudio de la revolución en América Latina. Santiago, Editorial Jurídica de Chile, 1970? 325 p., bibl.

Three-part book (social history of Latin America, beginning with the discovery; the nature of developed industrial society; and notes on humanism), an interpretive survey of ideas about where society *should* be as opposed to where it is. Scholarly, and worth examination. [P. B. Taylor, Jr.]

7471. Santos, Theotonio dos. Dependencia económica y cambio revolucionario en América Latina. Caracas, Editorial Nueva Izquiera, 1970. 152 p., tables (Col. Monografías)

Descriptive statement of the theory of dependency in underdevelopment. Ch. 3, which discusses revolutionary movements in a number of countries, offers new (i.e., not previously collected) material. [P. B. Taylor, Jr.]

7472. Sanz de Santamaría, Carlos. Revolución silenciosa. México, Fondo de Cultura Económica, 1971. 264 p., maps, tables.

Examines sources of misunderstanding between US and Latin American nations and relates such to difficulties encountered in the Alliance for Progress and US aid. Contains far-ranging considerations of trade, commerce, planning, administration, and economic integration. Valuable as the personal recollections and impressions of a noted Colombian politician and international public official who participated in much of the recent historical development of inter-American economic institutions. Stresses positive steps taken to promote economic development and regional independence. Reiterates a commitment to political democracy and international cooperation. [J. J. Bailey]

7473. Schmitter, Philippe C. Desarrollo retrasado, dependencia externa y cambio político en América Latina (CM/FI, 12:2, oct./dic. 1971, p. 135-174)

Two-fold contribution: 1) explores item 7475 further, the distinctiveness of Latin American development in a theoretical context; 2) attempts to test with aggregate data hypotheses on dispersion of participation and concentration of authority in relation to patterns of development. Interesting both theoretically and methodologically. [J. J. Bailey]

7474. ———. New strategies for the comparative analysis of Latin American politics (LARR, 4:2, Summer 1969, p. 83-110, tables)

Aggregate data is the topic of discussion. Is it available, how valid is it, and how can it be employed and for what purposes? Schmitter urges establishment of adequate data banks, and use of these materials for methodological exactness and sounder conclusions. [P. B. Taylor, Jr.]

7475. ———. Paths to political development in Latin America (PAPS, 30:4, 1972, p. 83-105, illus.)

Useful review and summary of theorizing on political development in Latin America. Suggests that regime characteristics and development sequences are more complex than hitherto interpreted. Discusses corporatist-authoritarian regimes and raises pertinent questions for further research. [J. J. Bailey]

7476. Schump, Walter. Las guerrillas en América Latina: el principio y el fin. B.A., Punto Crítico, 1971. 124 p. (Informes, 4)

Primer about movements of political violence in Colombia, Venezuela, Guatemala, Uruguay, Brazil and Peru. Marginal. [P. B. Taylor, Jr.]

7477. Semenoy, Sergeĭ Ivanovich. Khrstianskaía Demokratiía i Revoliustionnyi Protsess v Latinoskoĭ Amerike (Christian Democracy and the revolutionary process in Latin America). Moskva, Nauka, 1971. 301 p.

Study of the Christian Democratic movement in Latin America with special attention to parties in Chile, Venezuela and El Salvador. Compares Latin American Christian Democrats with their European counterparts and with conservative and reformist parties within Latin America. Concludes that Christian Democracy is an all inclusive movement with the potential to go to the extreme right or left. [T. S. Cheston]

7478. Seminario de Profesores de Ciencia Política, *I, Bogotá, 1969.* Ensayos de ciencia política. Introducción [de] Diego Uribe Vargas. Bogotá, Fundación para la Nueva Democracia, 1970. 166 p.

Ten essays on the definition, scope, methods, and teaching of political science. Considerations of political parties, public opinion, public administration, international relations, and theory. Indicative of increasing disciplinary self-awareness. [J. J. Bailey]

7479. Sigmund, Paul E. Latin American Catholicism's opening to the left (UND/RP, 35:1, Jan. 1973, p. 61-76)

Useful overview interpretation which describes sources of change over the past two decades in Church doctrine and group activity by lay members and priests which have resulted in a closer alignment between elements of the Church and the marxist left. [J. J. Bailey]

7480. ——— *ed.* The ideologies of the developing nations. 2. ed. N.Y., Praeger Publishers, 1972. 438 p., bibl.

Useful collection of excerpted papers and speeches by leaders of selected countries in Asia, the Islamic World, Africa and Latin America. Editor has written a long comparative introductory essay that tends to slight Latin America, although the selections are more balanced as to number and length. All authors are nationalists, usually radicals, and about evenly divided among officials and theoreticians. [P. B. Taylor, Jr.]

7481. Sloan, John W. Three views of Latin America: President Nixon, Governor Rockefeller, and the Latin American consensus of Viña del Mar (UP/O, 14:4, Winter 1971, p. 934-950)

Contrasts economic nationalism of the Special Latin American Coordinating Committee's 1969 report with the Cold War rhetoric of the Rockefeller mission recommendations and stress on trade expansion in President Nixon's "Action for Progress" speech. Criticizes assumption underlying all three statements that major impetus for Latin American development is external, and draws attention to internal requirements for socio-economic change. [J. J. Bailey]

7482. Smith, Carlos J. Introducción a la ciencia política. pt. 1, Fundamento y desarrollo del poder. Río Piedras, P.R., Editorial San Juan, 1972. 190 p., bibl. (Cuadernos de ciencias sociales, 2)

Introductory text with institutional-sociological emphasis. Exception to general trend toward "dependency" interpretation. [J. J. Bailey]

7482a. Steger, Hanns-Albert *ed.* Die Aktuelle Situation Lateinamerikas Frankfurt, FRG, Athenäum, 1971, 463 p. (Beiträge zur Soziologie und Sozial-kunde Lateinamerikas. COSAL, 7)

Proceedings of the II Academic Overseas Colloquium of the Universities of West Germany and West Berlin held at Münster (FRG) in Nov. 1967. Divided into four main sections: methodological problems of social science; cultural and social change in Latin America; social scientific aspects of university problems; problems of the political relations between Latin America and Germany.
Contributions of interest are: Hanns-Albert Steger "Soziologie in und über Lateinamerika" p. 25-35
Florestan Fernandes "Klassengesellschaft und Unterentwicklung" p. 95-162
Gilberto Freyre "Gibt es eine brasilianische Revolution?" p. 163-178
Norbert Lechner "Ideologie und Entwicklung" p. 178-186
Dankwart Danckwerts "Funktionale Interventionen der Industrieländer" p. 186-191
Fernando Henrique Cardoso "Die sozialen Träger des Wandels und der Beharrung in Lateinamerika" p. 200-222
Roger Vekemans "Integrationsprobleme der lateinamerikanischen Gesellschaften" p. 223-231
Juan Carlos Agulla "Das Schicksal der Eliten in Lateinamerika" 231-243
Jose Matos Mar "Herrschaft, ungleiche Entwicklung

und Pluralismen in der peruanischen Gesellschaft und Kultur" p. 244-273

Siegfried Kätsch "Sosua: Adaptionsprobleme deutscher jüdischer Siedler in der Dominikanischen Republik" (see HLAS 34:2111) p. 274-286

Celso Furtado "Probleme der Industrialisierung in Lateinamerika" p. 286-290

Vamireh Chacon "Soziale Gegensätze in der brasilianischen Entwickling Entwicklung" p. 290-297

Carlos M. Rama "Aktuelle Probleme der Industrialisierung in Uruguay" 297-303

Edgar Castellanos "Hindernisse bei der Plangung und Entwicklung Boliviens" p. 303-309

Jaime Jaramillo Uribe "Funktion der Universität in der lateinamerikanischen Gesellschaft der Gegenwart" p. 366-371

Felix Martinez Bonati "Die Universität s-situation Lateinamerikas am Beispiel Chiles" p. 371-378

Luis Molina Piñeiro "Die Studentenbewegung an der UNAM im Jahre 1966" p. 379-397

Günther Kahle "Grundzüge der deutschmexikanischen Beziehungen bis zum Ersten Weltkrieg. p. 431-442 [W. Grabendorff]

7483. Student activism and higher education: an inter-American dialogue. Introduction by James F. Tierney. N.Y., Council on Higher Education in the American Republics, 1970. 100 p., bibl.

Edited transcript of a four-day conference held by CHEAR at Bogotá, 23-28 Feb. 1969. 34 participants attended (US, 16; Colombia, 11; seven other countries, one each) including government officials, presidents and rectors of universities, and research specialists. [P. B. Taylor, Jr.]

7484. Suchlicki, Jaime. Sources of student violence in Latin America: an analysis of the literature (LARR, 7:3, Fall 1972, p. 31-46)

Summarizing categories of present research, author finds that little is known about historical background of student organizations. Other topics which need to be investigated are: influence of outside groups, role of generational conflict, personality of student leaders, and comparison of student violence to other forms of violence. [A. Suárez]

7485. Taylor, Philip B., Jr. and Sam Schulman eds. Population and urbanization problems of Latin America. Houston, Tex., Univ. of Texas, Office of International Affairs, 1971. 124 p.

Papers delivered at a conference held under the auspieces of the Univ. of Houston's Committee on Latin American Studies in 1971:

T. Lynn Smith "Urban Growth and Urban Problems in Latin America" p. 1-19

J. Mayone Stycos "Population Dynamics and Population Problems in Latin America" p. 20-39

Thomas Merrick "Population Pressures for the 1970s: Lessons for Developmental Planning" p. 40-42

Robert Black "Options for Latin Parents—Through Family Planning" p. 43-49

Antonio Ordóñez P. "A Case Study in Population: Colombia" p. 50-55

Marta Cehelsky "A Case Study in Urbanization: Brazil" p. 56-74

Benjamin Viel "Efforts of Private Organizations in Population Control in Latin America" p. 75-94

Víctor Urquidi "The Latin American University and Urban Problems" p. 95-102

Ralph W. Conant "The North American University and Urban Problems" p. 103-112. [P. B. Taylor, Jr.]

7486. Turner, Frederick C. Catholicism and political development in Latin America. Chapel Hill, N.C., The Univ. of North Carolina Press, 1971. 272 p., bibl., tables.

Analyzes perceptions of political and economic change by Catholic leaders in Latin America. Stresses diversity in the Church and examines orientations toward major policy issues such as education, birth control, and Church-state relations. Well researched and useful general study. [J. J. Bailey]

7487. Vallier, Ivan. Radical priests and the revolution (PAPS, 30:4, 1972, p. 15-26)

Sees appearance of radicalism in clergy as product of systemic difficulties in channeling radical impulses, resulting in political polarization and religious definition of social conflicts. Denouncing "clerical radicalism" as effectively retrogressive, author sees positive change possible through "pastoral radicalism." Latter abandons the two level "ins" and "outs" model of the former for a multi-level casual model of society and acts within normative pattern of the Church to bring about cultural change. [W. H. Agor]

7488. Vekemans, Roger. La prerevolución latinoamericana. Santiago, Centro para el Desarrollo Económico y Social de América Lahina (DESAL), 1969. 88 p. (Cuadernos de discusión, 2)

Three related essays, examining the psychological basis for revolution. Highly provocative and useful piece. [P. B. Taylor, Jr.]

7489. Verner, Joel G. Patterns of presidential recruitment in Latin America, 1930-1970: a research note (International Review of History and Political Science [Meerut, India] 9:1, Feb. 1972, p. 45-68, tables)

Reports gross data on age and recruitment patterns of Latin American presidents since 1930 (N=269). Lacks theoretical orientation and data presented in summary form, which hinders trend or individual country analysis. [J. J. Bailey]

7489a. Vierteljahresberichte. Forschungsinstitut der Friedrich-Ebert-Stiftung, Probleme der Entwicklungsländer. No. 44, Juni 1971 [through] No. 52, Juni 1973- . Hannover, FRG.

The following issues include articles on Latin America:

No. 44(1971) Heinrich W. Krumwiede "Die kolumbianische Agrarreform: Analyse des Scheiterns einer Sozialreform"

No. 46(1971) Karl-Heinz Stanzick "Elcobre es chileno: Eine Untersuchung zur Nationali sierung des chilenischen Kupferbergbaus" p. 345-364.

Hans J. Wendler "Perus Cooperación Popular: Eine Möglichkeit für sozioökonomischen Wandel?" p. 365-394.

No. 49(1972) Klaus Dressel "Argentinien: Politik und Parteien, 1955-1972"

No. 49(1972) Aldo Ferrer "Auslandsunternehmen: Bemerkungen zu den Erfahrungen in Argentinien"

Fernando Cepeda Ulloa and Mauricio Solaun "Direct Private Foreign Investment in Colombia: a Socio-Political Perspective"

No. 51 (1973) Reinhard von Brunn "Chile: Mit altem Recht zur neuen Wirtschaft?" p. 11-39

No. 52 (1973) Caio Kai Koch-Weser "Zwölf Jahre Entwicklungsplanung der SUDENE im brasilianischen Nordosten: Analyse einer verhinderten Reformpolitik." [W. Grabendorff]

7490. Vitalis, Hellmut Gnadt. The significance of changes in Latin American catholicism since Chimbote 1953. Cuernavaca, Mex., Centro Intercultural de Documentación, 1969. 342 p., bibl. (CIDOC: Sondeos, 51)

Overview description which marks Chimbote, Peru, conference of 1953 as a turning point in reform of Latin American Church. Describes contributions of Council of Latin American Bishops (CELAM), Catholic Action, and Vatican II in reform process. Optimistic in tone. [J. J. Bailey]

7491. Von Lazar, Arpad. Latin American politics: a primer. Foreword by Federico G. Gil. Boston, Mass., Allyn and Bacon, 1971. 157 p., tables (The Allyn and Bacon series in Latin American politics)

Introductory essay for Allyn-Bacon country series. As is perhaps inevitable in a brief overview of entire region, many assertions seem oversimplified. [J. J. Bailey]

7492. ———. Multi-national enterprises and Latin American integration: a sociopolitical view (UM/JIAS, 11:1, Jan. 1969, p. 111-128)

What can bring about effective integration of the Latin American regional economy? Argues that multi-national enterprises are part of a possible answer. But notes that this will succeed only on the basis of thechnocratic and entrepreneurial leadership and in terms relevant to the socio-political *ambiente*. [P. B. Taylor, Jr.]

7493. Waldmann, Peter. Política y violencia en Iberoamérica (ZPKW/A, 7:2, 2. semestre 1971, p. 169-178)

In the absence of political legitimacy and universally accepted norms of democratic governance, multiple capabilities, including violence, structure political bargaining among groups. Author stresses the generally symbolic and communications functions of violence. [J. J. Bailey]

7494. Weaver, Jerry L. Expectativas de los funcionarios latinoamericanos en relación con la administración pública (ILARI/A, 25, julio 1972, p. 119-146, tables)

Secondary analysis of data drawn from several surveys in a systematic attempt to test propositions on sources of role expectations. Available in English as "Role Expectations of Latin American Bureaucrats: Hypotheses and Data" (*Occasional Papers*, American Society for Public Administration, Washington, 2:3, 1972). [J. J. Bailey]

7495. Whitaker, Arthur P. The new nationalism in Latin America (UND/RP, 35:1, Jan. 1973, p. 77-90)

Identifies anti-imperialism and structural revolution as defining elements of the "new nationalism" and discusses some implications of this variant for South American and international politics. [J. J. Bailey]

7496. Wiarda, Howard J. The Latin American development process and the new developmental alternatives: military "Nasserism" and "dictatorship with popular support" (UU/WPQ, 25:3, Sept. 1972, p. 464-490)

Will either of these two newly-devised strategies succeed in advancing Latin America's development —especially since the Alliance for Progress failed so badly? Analysis is both theoretical and practical, and set within the context of possibilities and obstacles to development. Concludes that "Nasserism" is most congenial to the region's values. [P. B. Taylor, Jr.]

7497. ———. Law and political development in Latin America: toward a framework for analysis (The American Journal of Comparative Law [Berkeley, Calif.] 19:3, Summer 1971, p. 434-463)

Elaborates author's view of Latin American politics and society as corporatist, thus basically conservative and adaptive. Only cursory attention given to the role of law in political development. [J. J. Bailey]

7498. ———. Toward a framework for the study of political change in the Iberic-Latin tradition: the corporative model (PUCIS/WP, 25:2, Jan. 1973, p. 206-235)

Perhaps strongest statement of themes of historical continuity and cultural uniqueness in the corporatist nature of Latin American politics. Trenchancy in such a general statement will likely draw criticism. [J. J. Bailey]

Wolpin, Miles D. Latin American studies: for a radical approach. See item 6067.

———. Latin American studies: half-baked nonradicalism. See item 6068.

7499. Yglesias, José. Down there. N.Y., World, 1970. 181 p.

Skillful and often unexpectedly gutsy if somewhat carefree short piece. Product of short stays in Brazil, Chile and Peru by a working US journalist and author of Cuban-Galician extraction. For his experiences in revolutionary Cuba, see item 7611. [P. B. Taylor, Jr.]

MEXICO, CENTRAL AMERICA, THE CARIBBEAN AND THE GUIANAS

ANDRES SUAREZ

Professor of Political Science
Center for Latin American Studies
University of Florida

INCREASING RESEARCH AND PRODUCTIVITY have led to a geographic division of the field, as stated in the introduction to the Government and Politics: General section of the *Handbook,* p. 347. Initially, Professor Weston H. Agor was appointed as Contributing Editor for the subsection: Mexico, Central America, the Caribbean and The Guianas. However, professional obligations prevented him from completing the assignment and this author took on the responsibility at a late date. It is hoped that any flaws apparent in this section and due to the latê change in authorship, will be avoided in future *Handbooks.*

The persistent interest in the Revolution is reflected in the great number of Cuban items. Among them, special mention must be made of *Revolutionary change in Cuba* edited by Carmelo Mesa-Lago (item 7591). This is a judicious and balanced analysis of eleven years of Revolutionary Government using the available sources, and only lacking a sense of immediate contact with Cuban reality, a privilege granted to very few foreign scholars by the Cuban government. Mexico is second to Cuba in number of items. Although some significant omissions are noticeable they are chiefly due to recent publication dates. Two works by Roger D. Hansen and José Luis Reyna (items 7516 and 7534) attest to the growing sophistication in the analysis of Mexico's political system. The suggestive essay by the great Mexican poet, Octavio Paz (item 7529) must not be overlooked. The smaller number of selections on Central America and the non-English Caribbean, excepting Cuba, reflects the well-known scarcity and weakness of research in the first two areas. But the under-representation of the Caribbean Commonwealth can be attributed to the omission of significant ongoing research at the University of West Indies, particularly the Jamaica Campus. References to studies by scholars such as Norman Girvan, Trevor Munroe, Owen Jefferson, Charles Beckford, and Carl Stone, among others, will be included in future volumes.

Although the area covered by this section seems to offer ideal conditions for comparative political research, efforts aimed at generating it have been few and barely significant. It is hoped that in the future, political scientists will realize the potential of cross-national studies of the countries in this area.

MEXICO

7500. Adie, Robert. Cooperation, cooptation, and conflict in Mexican peasant organizations (IAMEA, 24:3, Winter 1970, p. 3-25)

Traces growth and development of Independent Peasant Central (CCI) and concludes that its function was to gain political advantage rather than to help the peasants. Further contends that tolerance of the CCI by the PRI under Cárdenas may have been to release the PRI from the pressure of peasant organization. [W. H. Agor]

7501. Alcazar, Marco Antonio. Las agrupaciones patronales en México, México, El Colegio de México, Centro de Estudios Internacionales, 1970. 130 p., tables (Jornadas, 66)

Descriptive and historical study of the most important groups representing business interests. Based on legal sources and newspapers published by those organizations. Although a chapter discusses policies of these groups concerning national issues, there is no attempt to evaluate their influence upon the decision-making process. No use is made of the literature on interest groups.

7502. Albores Guillén, Roberto. La dinámica de los partidos políticos en México (Pensamiento Político [México] 3:9, enero 1970, p. 69-90)

Very ameliorative to criticism of the PRI, traces evolution of parties in Mexico from freemasonry to institutionalized government. Contends that popular vote in current multi-party elections proves the PRI to be a party of social mobilization. Does not broach issues of effectiveness in meeting social demands. [W. H. Agor]

Alexander, Roberto J. El trotskismo en la América Latina. See item 7359.

7504. Asamblea Nacional Ordinaria del Partido Revolucionario Institucional, *VI, México, 1971.* Documentos fundamentales: declaración de principios, estatutos, programas de acción. México, Comisión Nacional Editorial, 1972. 594 p., plates.

Although documents contained herein are abbreviated and selected, it is nonetheless a useful compendium. Plates provide an interesting photographic history of the PRI.

7505. Baker, Richard D. Judicial review in Mexico: a study of the *amparo* suit. Austin, Tex., Univ. of Texas Press, Institute of Latin American Studies, 1971. 304 p., bibl. (Latin American monograph, 22)

Purpose of study is "to determine, primarily through analysis of cases, established precedents, and relevant statutes, the adequacy of *amparo* and various subsidiary institutions for the function of constitutional defense both in legal theory and practice." Thorough research, meticulous analysis. [J. J. Bailey]

7506. Blough, William J. Political attitudes of Mexican women: support for the political system among a newly enfranchised group (UM/JIAS, 14:1, Feb. 1972, p. 201-224, tables)

Since enfranchisement in 1953, Mexican women hold parallel opinions to those of men, although a smaller percentage are willing to voice them. Study based on survey of urban men and women.

7507. Buve, R. Th. J. Van anarchisme tot staatssyndicalisme: de ontwikkeling van de Mexicaanse vakbeweging 1860-1960 (NGIZ/IS, 24:16, sept. 1970, p. 1511-1542)

Author stresses three factors to explain development of Mexican trade union movement: 1) pluralistic character of Mexican society; 2) the harsh hacienda system and its repercussions in the industrial field; 3) the impact of events in Western Europe and North America on Mexican society. Author traces history of Mexican labor movement from Porfiriato to present. Notes influence of Hungarian immigrant Rhodakanaty and the Asociación Internacional del Trabajo, among many others. [H. Hoyer]

7508. Camp, Roderic A. The cabinet and the *técnico* in Mexico and the U.S. (Journal of Comparative Administration [Beverly Hills, Calif.] 3:2, Aug. 1971, p. 188-214, bibl., tables)

Reports data on Mexican cabinet members since 1933. Explores associations between ministers' education and political activity as well as type of ministry headed and tenure in office. Some vagueness on sources of information and procedures employed. [J. J. Bailey]

7509. Careaga, Gabriel. Los intelectuales y la política en México. México, Editorial Extemporáneos, 1971. 140 p., bibl., plates (Serie A pleno sol)

Sketches contrasting views of the intellectual's role in the liberal and marxist perspectives. Examines causes of political weakness and alienation among leftist intellectuals in Mexico, and considers briefly sources of antiintellectualism. Marxist humanist bias, but generally a well balanced treatment. [J. J. Bailey]

7510. Cosío Villegas, Daniel. Labor periodista: real e imaginaria. México, Ediciones Era, 1972. 405 p.

Contains articles published by Mexico's noted historian in the daily Excelsior during 1968-71. As subtitle indicates, these are original versions, free of newspaper's editorial changes. Presented chronologically, articles are divided into five topics: new regime, political system, student rebellion, personalities, and small series. Relevant not only as a portrait of contemporary Mexican politics, but also for what they reveal about author.

Craig, Richard B. The bracero program: interest groups and foreign policy. See item 8112.

7511. Cuadra, Héctor. Algunos obstáculos políticos al desarrollo de México (UNAM/RMS, 32:6, nov./dic. 1970, p. 1527-1539)

Paper presented at the IX Latin American Congress of Sociology. In only 12 p. author offers "a theory on the political institutions required to overcome underdevelopment." Also criticizes some obstacles interposed by present institutions. Final result seems to be total failure.

7512. Dávila, Gerardo and **Manlio Tirado** *comps.* Como México no hay dos: porfirismo, revolución, neoporfirismo. Proyecto y supervisión [por] Editorial Nuestro Tiempo. Recopilación y arreglo del material [por] . . . México, Editorial Nuestro Tiempo, 1971. 227 p., illus. (Col. Reportajes documentales)

First in series of documentary reports, selected press clips, sponsored by Editorial Nuestro Tiempo. This issue demonstrates the resurgence of Porfiriato tendencies within current regime regarding national objectives and foreign capital. Fascinating and often clever presentation by spokesman of the Mexican left.

7513. Fernández, Julio A. Political administration in Mexico. Boulder, Colo., Univ. of Colorado, Bureau of Governmental Research and Service, 1969. 80 p., bibl., tables.

Draws on the theoretical work of the SSRC (Social Science Research Council, Princeton, N.J.) comparative politics group to provide an overview of public administration in a transitional political culture. Author stresses importance of relationship between the PRI organization and the president in order to understand Mexican administration. Includes tables on ministerial recruitment. [J. J. Bailey]

Gavilán Estelat, Marcelino. Las nuevas tendencias de la reforma agraria en Iberoamérica. See item 7406.

7514. González, Carlos Hank and others *comps.*

Caminos y voces: Luis Echeverría, discursos. México, Editorial Imprenta Casas, 1970. 409 p., plates.

Speeches on various topics from the Mexican presidential campaign of 1969-70. [J. J. Bailey]

7515. ——— and others comps. Todos con México: reuniones nacionales de estudio; discursos de Luis Echeverría. México, Editorial Imprenta Casas, 1970. 170 p., plates.

Campaign speeches on diverse topics from 1969 and 1970. [J. J. Bailey]

7516. **Hansen, Roger D.** The politics of Mexican development. Baltimore, Md., The Johns Hopkins Press, 1971. 267 p., bibl., tables.

Seeks to understand the "miracle" of Mexican economic development. Analyzes sources of economic growth and focuses on the phenomenon of gross maldistribution of wealth. Suggests that "the economic development strategy which has emerged in Mexico over the past four decades is best understood as a reflection neither of official party interests nor of the sectoral demands within the PRI but rather in terms of the interests and value-orientations of the country's self-renewing political elite." Emphasizes that an important dynamic in Mexican politics is political activity as an avenue of social mobility, which is rooted in the mestizo heritage in 19th-century politics. [J. J. Bailey]

7517. **Hernández, Salvador.** El PRI y el movimiento estudiantil de 1968. México, Ediciones El Caballito, 1971. 126 p., bibl.

Leftist account which collates the best of North American scholarship to demonstrate the increasing political rigidity of the PRI since 1930. Hernández attempts to prove the hypothesis that political rigidity necessitates repressive methods. Includes chronology of events of 1968 leading to the Oct. confrontation in the Zócalo, but reveals little not available from press sources. [W. H. Agor]

7518. **Huizer, Gerrit.** La lucha campesina en México. México, Centro de Investigaciones Agrarias, 1970. 111 p., plates.

Brief historical overview of principal peasant leaders and organizations and major policy developments in agrarian reform from the Revolution to the early 1960s. [J. J. Bailey]

7519. **León Ossorio y Agüero, Adolfo.** ¡Secuestro!: historia de una gran infamia. México, The Author, 1971. 109 p.

On 4 March 1969, Gen. León Ossorio was summoned to the Mexcian Ministry of Defense. Once in the building's elevator he was disarmed, arrested, and sent to an isolated island in the Pacific, Socorro, 380 miles from the Mexican coast. Here he tells the story of his sufferings until his liberation, which was as unexpected as his detention.

7520. **Liebman, Arthur.** Student activism in Mexico (AAPSS/TA, 395, May 1971, p. 159-170)

Suggests that causes of the July 1968 student rebellion lay in a widespread alienation from the PRI regime, student antagonisms toward the Summer Olympics, and situational-tactical blunders by Mexican authorities in dealing with minor student disorders. Concludes that the 1968 events produced a qualitative change in Mexican student politics but does not specify the form or direction of the new orientation. [J. J. Bailey]

7521. **Madrazo, Carlos A.** Madrazo: voz postrera de la Revolución; discursos y comentarios. Prólogo y epílogo [por] L. Darío Vasconcelos. México, B. Costa-Amic, 1971. 295 p., tables.

After his dismissal as head of the official party in 1966, Madrazo began his public criticism of the Mexican regime. Later, he died in a suspicious airplane accident. In this compilation of his speeches prepared by his friends, he strongly denounces the PRI but is rather timid in proposing solutions. It is difficult to envisage him as "voz postrera de la revolución."

7522. **Margaín, Hugo B.** Documentos económicos de la administración pública: intervenciones del Señor Licenciado . . . , Secretario de Hacienda y Crédito Público, ante el Poder Legislativo. México, Dirección General de Prensa, Memorias, Bibliotecas y Publicaciones, 1971. 111 p. (Col. Documentos económicos de un sexenio, 3)

Former Ambassador to the US explains the government's proposal to create the Instituto Mexicano de Comercio Exterior. In response to rather gentle questioning, describes related aspects of economic policy. Very useful insight into economic policymaking in Mexico. [J. J. Bailey]

7523. **Medina Valdés, Gerardo.** Operación 10 de junio. México, Ediciones Universo, 1972. 270 p., plates.

Representative of a number of works about the contemporary student movement. Although it raises the issue of governmental responsibility concerning Tlatelolco and the incident of 10 June 1971, it fails to provide a satisfactory answer.

7524. **Molina Piñero, Luis.** Investigación de Críticas al Partido Revolucionario Institucional (P.R.I.) de México (IESSC/C, 4:11, mayo/agosto 1969, p. 33-41)

Lists criticisms of party as enumerated by selected groups of students at UNAM; criticisms broken into categories but no indication given as to either strength or accuracy of criticism. [W. H. Agor]

7525. **Navarrete, Alfredo.** Alto a la contrarevolución. México, Testimonios de Atlacomulco, 1971. 502 p., plates.

Veteran labor leader looks back on his life and on the movement toward readjustment of the Mexican society that was planned by the Revolution. Result is a detailed but mixed evaluation. Author warns against peril of counterrevolution. Ends with appeal to return to basics of Mexican Revolution. [P. B. Taylor, Jr.]

7526. **Needler, Martin C.** Política y carácter nacional: el caso mejicano (IOP/REOP, 23, enero/marzo 1971, p. 141-146)

Stresses linkages between child-rearing patterns and perceptions of politics. Arbitrary paternal authoritarianism produced a "Mexican [who] is a rebel and a potential dictator, but not a fanatical piece in a state apparatus." For English version, see item 7527. [J. J. Bailey]

7527. ———. **Politics and national character: the case of Mexico** (AAA/AA, 73:3, June 1971, p. 757-761, bibl.)

English version of item 7526.

7528. ———. **Politics and society in Mexico.** Albuquerque, N. Mex., Univ. of New Mexico Press, 1971. 143 p., bibl., tables.

Chapters on the PRI, elections, presidency, economic policy, military, and political culture are integrated by the theme that Mexican politics have evolved from open conflict to constitutional procedures. Somewhat eclectic collection. [J. J. Bailey]

7528a. Nickel, Herbert J. Die Campesinos zwischen Marginalität und Integration. Düsseldorf, FRG, Bertelsmann, 1971. 294 p., bibl. (Materialien des Arnold-Bergstraesser-Instituts für kulturwissenschaftliche Forschung, 29).

Book based on intensive field research of agrarian structure and role campesino's in Mexico. Author offers theory of differentiation and integration in marginal sub-societies. [W. Grabendorff]

7529. Paz, Octavio. The other Mexico: a critique of the pyramid. Translated by Lysander Kemp. N.Y., Grove Press, 1972. 147 p.

Outstanding work by Mexico's eminent poet and critic who once again analyzes the country since his 1950 classic *The labyrinth of solitude* (N.Y., Grove Press, 1962). Author draws parallel between ritual of the Aztec pyramid and contemporary bureaucracy. Essays envision a more human path towards development, independent of either Eastern or Western models, a subject inexorably linked to the search for a Latin American identity. Translation of *Posdata* (México, Siglo XXI Editores, 1970, 149 p.)

7531. Pellicer de Brody, Olga. México y la Revolución cubana. Prólogo de Jorge Castañeda. México, El Colegio de México, Centro de Estudios Internacionales, 1972. 131 p., tables (Publicaciones, 7)

Under the cloak of a "leftist" policy towards the Cuban Revolution, the Mexican government hid internal concessions to the Mexican right and US interests. Thoughtful book explores national determinants of foreign policy and linkages between domestic and international politics.

7532. Poitras, Guy E. and Charles F. Denton. Bureaucratic performance; case studies from Mexico and Costa Rica (Journal of Comparative Administration [Beverly Hills, Calif.] 3:2, Aug. 1971, p. 187-196, bibl., tables)

Based on survey data, finds a positive relationship between bureaucrats' perception of their effectiveness in pursuing developmental goals and their perception of external (particularly political party) support. [J. J. Bailey]

7533. Poniatowska, Elena. La noche de Tlatelolco: testimonios de historia oral. México, Editorial Era, 1971. 282 p., plates (Biblioteca Era: testimonios)

Scores of interviews with persons who participated in or were affected by the violence at Tlatelolco in 1968. Vivid impressions. [J. J. Bailey]

7534. Reyna, José Luis. An empirical analysis of political mobilization: the case of Mexico. Ithaca, N.Y., Cornell Univ., Latin American Studies Program, 1971. 213 p., bibl., tables (Dissertation series, 26)

"What accounts for differences among the Mexican states in political mobilization." Attempts to establish linkages between electoral participation and level of opposition voting and aspects of economic development. Explicitly comparative; theoretically interesting; sophisticated use of aggregate data. Useful contribution to the political sociology of Mexico. [J. J. Bailey]

7535. Sánchez Cárdenas, Carlos. Disolución social y seguridad nacional. México, Ediciones Linterna, 1970. 189 p.

Contains argumentation by the long congressional opponent of attempts to legislate stronger penalities for civil disobedience in the context of official reaction to the disturbances of 1968. Criticizes the servility of the Chamber of Deputies. Illustrates well the clash between the ideal of constitutional democracy and the reality of an authoritarian regime in Mexico. [J. J. Bailey]

7536. Schmitt, Karl M. Congressional campaigning in Mexico: a view from the provinces (UM/JIAS, 11:1, Jan. 1969, p. 93-110, tables)

Short report of the off-year congressional campaign in Yucatán state: candidacies, campaign techniques, voting procedure, etc. [P. B. Taylor, Jr.]

7537. Sepúlveda, César. Student participation in university affairs: the Mexican experience (AJCL, 17:3, 1969, p. 384-389)

Author finds that student participation in university affairs in Mexico has not had any noticeable positive impact. He also observes that "this execution of a chaotic power . . . not only has provoked a heavy repression by the public power but also the natural resentment of the latter against the educational institution." [C. N. Ronning]

7538. Solís Mimendi, Antonio. Jueves de Corpus sangriento: sensacionales revelaciones de un halcón. México, Imprenta Argo, 1972. 155 p., plates.

The *Halcones* is, or was, a vigilante group officially or semi-officially organized to combat the student movement. Here an ex-member of the *Halcones* describes the activities of the group. If authentic, this document is revealing of the violence and corruption of Mexican politics, especially the student movement.

7539. Stevens, Evelyn P. Legality and extralegality in Mexico (UM/JIAS, 12:1, Jan. 1970, p. 62-75)

The Mexican system has several devices for handling institutionalized protest by groups or individuals not part of the official political system. One is the law of social dissolution, and another is the cooption of the protestors into the official system and their subsequent nullification by the bureaucracy. A third, more generally used, is the mix of threat, pressure and violence so very possible in an authoritarian regime. [P. B. Taylor, Jr.]

7540. Suárez Valles, Manuel *comp.* Lázaro Cárdenas: una vida fecunda al servicio de México. Compilación, biografía y epílogo de . . . México, B. Costa-Amic Editor, 1971. 533 p., illus.

Extraordinary collection of short articles by some 80 authors, of all viewpoints, concerning Cárdenas. Rather than a researched volume, this is a broad-scale declaration of the importance of the man for his times and country. [P. B. Taylor, Jr.]

7541. Womack, John, Jr. The spoils of the Mexican Revolution (CFR/FA, 48:4, July 1970, p. 677-687)

Traces the development of the Mexican Revolution in terms of government's attitude toward development and concludes that the contemporary standard of progress evolved in spite of government direction. The business of the Mexican Revolution is now business. The PRI is now the organ of the national capitalists. [W. H. Agor]

CENTRAL AMERICA

General

Bodenheimer, Thomas S. The political economy of malnutrition: generalizations from two Central American case studies. See item 1687.

7542. Torres-Rivas, Edelberto. Procesos y estructuras de una sociedad dependiente: Centroamérica. Santiago, Ediciones Prensa Latinoamericana, 1969. 210 p., bibl., tables (Col. América nueva)

Historical interpretive essay on Central America from independence to present which stresses linkages of economic dependence with advanced industrial nations, particularly England and the US, as the dominant explanatory factor. Relates patterns of finance and commerce to evolution of domestic society and politics in the Central American nations. Emphasizes impact of the Depression in creating forces for change in the region, and analyzes prospects for Central American economic integration. Consistent efforts to muster data in support of the argument. Contribution to the growing "dependency" literature. [J. J. Bailey]

COSTA RICA

7543. Arias Sánchez, Oscar. Grupos de presión en Costa Rica. Preámbulo [por] Alberto Cañas. San José, Editorial Costa Rica, 1971. 130 p., bibl.

Brief but useful thesis which covers structure, resources, and tactics of major interest groups in Costa Rican politics. Well grounded in relevant literature on pressure groups. Rather strong dose of normative preference woven into description and analysis. Stresses role of political parties and a disinterested state in mitigating dysfunctional consequences of interest group activity. [J. J. Bailey]

7544. Bodenheimer, Susanne. The social democratic ideology in Latin America: the case of Costa Rica's Partido Liberación Nacional (UPR/CS, 10:3, Oct. 1970, p. 49-96)

Despite a rather casual use of class as an analytical concept, a quite good analysis of the content of PLN ideology, structure of the Party, and its governing performance. Suggests that social composition of the PLN acted to constrain the Party to policies of moderate reform. Concludes that social democratic ideology is appropriate only for a past era in Latin American politics, and that it does not reflect current aspirations of the lower class. [J. J. Bailey]

7545. Edwards, Harold T. Power structure and its communication behavior in San José, Costa Rica (UM/JIAS, 9:2, April 1967, p. 236-247, tables)

Interesting study of community power structure, employing models of methodology devised by Floyd Hunter. The product of this suggestive study (by a professor of *English*!) is a sociogram. [P. B. Taylor, Jr.]

7546. English, Burt H. Liberación Nacional in Costa Rica: the development of a political party in a transitional society. Gainesville, Fla., Univ. of Florida Press, 1971. 185 p., bibl., tables (Latin American monographs: 2. series, 8)

Student of Harry Kantor investigates origin and development of political party in a transitional society. Uses elaborate survey questionnaire and analysis. Concludes that establishment of successful party in Costa Rica was due to opportunity (crisis period), personality (Figueres), and chance (cadre of workers was available). [W. H. Agor]

7547. Gutiérrez, Carlos José. Student participation in the government of the University of Costa Rica (AJCL, 17:3, 1969, p. 390-394)

Although student participation in Costa Rica follows general patterns in Latin America, it is nevertheless unique. One of the unique features mentioned here is the non-involvement in political (non-university) affairs. [C. N. Ronning]

Poitras, Guy E. and **Charles F. Denton.** Bureaucratic performance; case studies from Mexico and Costa Rica. See item 7532.

7548. Saxe-Fernández, John. The militarization of Costa Rica (MR, 24:1, May 1972, p. 61-70)

Commentary documented from Senate hearings and AID releases that the police of Costa Rica are being converted into a military organization with antiguerrilla capabilities through USAID police-training program and their participation in the Central American Defense Council. [W. H. Agor]

EL SALVADOR

7549. Barón Ferrufino, José René. Comunismo y traición. San Salvador, 1971. 459 p., illus., plates, tables.

Title page includes the line "Fariseísmo, filosofismo, iluminismo, liberalismo, democratismo, socialismo, y comunismo, son la mismo." It should be added that author also is down on Masons, the US, and the UN. All this within a Salvadorian context! [P. B. Taylor, Jr.]

7550. Membreño, María B. de. ¿Porqué fuimos a la guerra. . . ? San Salvador, Editores La Nación, 1969. 1 v. (Unpaged) plates.

Quasi-official defense of El Salvador's military and diplomatic actions in the 1969 "soccer war" with Honduras. Numerous photos. [J. J. Bailey]

7551. Sánchez Hernández, Fidel. Discursos del Señor Presidente de la República, General . . . t. 1, julio 1º, 1967-junio 30, 1968. San Salvador, Casa Presidencial, Publicaciones del Depto. de Relaciones Públicas, 1968? 114 p.

Unannotated compilation of 27 speeches arranged chronologically. [J. J. Bailey]

HONDURAS

Arellano Bonilla, Robert. ¡Basta . . . ; para los hondureños únicamente! See *HLAS 34:1979*.

7552. Cruz, Ramón Ernesto. Discursos del Presidente: año de 1971. Tegucigalpa, Ediciones Oficina de Relaciones Públicas, 1972. 11 p.

Patriotic speeches by the President of Honduras, recently deposed by a military coup.

7553. ———. Discursos del Presidente Cruz: primer semestre, año 1972. Teguciagalpa, Ediciones Oficina de Relaciones Públicas, 1972. 175 p.

More speeches by the deposed President of Honduras

GUATEMALA

7554. Aguilera Peralta, Gabriel Edgardo. El proceso de terror en Guatemala (ILARI/A, 24, abril 1972, p. 116-136)

Conceptual model from Eugene Victor Walter, *Terror and resistance* applied to Guatemalan situation. Author is most knowledgeable writer on subject of Guatemalan violence; has completed thesis at Univ. of San Carlos on subject, see item 7555. Particularly valuable in revealing complexity of right-wing terrorism. [W. H. Agor]

7555. ———. La violencia en Guatemala como fenómeno político. Presentación [por] Carlos López. Cuernavaca, Mex., Centro Intercultural de Documentación, 1971. 1 v. (Various pagings) bibl., tables (CIDOC: Cuaderno, 61)

Thesis presented for degree of licenciado at the Univ. of San Carlos, Guat. Without doubt the best published treatment of the topic, it attempts to explain violence in terms of Guatemalan political conflict. Concludes that Guatemala is not in a revolutionary situation and that the source of terror is the reactionary right. Includes article "El Proceso de Terror en Guatemala," see item 7554.

7556. Johnson, Kenneth F. The 1966 and 1970 elections in Guatemala: a comparative analysis (APS/WA, 134:1, Summer 1971, p. 34-50, tables)

Based on aggregate data, notes sharp decline of pro-civilian and commensurate rise in pro-military voting patterns. Offers several hypotheses to account for the shift. Reasoning and conclusions go beyond data presented. [J.J. Bailey]

7557. Melville, Thomas and **Marjorie Melville.** Guatemala: the politics of land ownership. N.Y., The Free Press, 1971. 120 p., tables.

Concentrates for most part on agricultural policies of regimes during 1945-70 period. Authors were Catholic missionaries in Guatemala from mid-1950s until forced to leave in 1967. On balance, a rather restrained critique of agrarian reform policies and US foreign policy vis-à-vis Guatemala and Central America. [J.J. Bailey]

7558. Petersen, John H. Student political activism in Guatemala (UM/JIAS, 13:1, Jan. 1971, p. 78-88, tables)

Using 1967 survey data and enrollment information from the registrar (Univ. de San Carlos) students' background is compared by faculty—law, economics, and humanities considered to be "most active." Statistics too gross to establish any significant findings about either activism or Guatemala. [W. H. Agor]

7559. Sloan, John W. Electoral power contenders in Guatemala (UPR/CS, 11:3, Oct. 1971, p. 19-34)

"Temporary coherence of interest" concept applied to Guatemalan politics since 1944. Concludes that elections have weak legitimacy due to lack of cohesion in political parties. Contends that larger parties, as required by new electoral law, will force party leaders to conciliate internal factions. [W. H. Agor]

7560. Thesing, Josef. La política en Guatemala (ILARI/A, 21, julio 1971, p. 30-59)

Macro-level interpretive essay in the "pathology of democracy" tradition. Juxtaposes conditions necessary for political democracy with conditions extant in Guatemala. Finds, not surprisingly, wide disparities between is and ought. [J.J. Bailey]

7562. Verner, Joel G. Characteristics of administrative personnel: the case of Guatemala (JDA, 5:1, Oct. 1970, p. 73-85, tables)

Tests hypothesis that a bottleneck in national development is due to the comparative incapacity of senior members of the public administration. Uses Guatemala to illustrate point: 327 members of comparatively senior rank were asked to respond to a questionnaire administered in 1967. [P.B. Taylor, Jr.]

7563. ———. Socialization and participation in legislative debates: the case of the Guatemalan Congress (UPR/CS, 11:2, July 1971, p. 45-73, tables)

Reviews general literature on legislative studies and examines relationships of personal background to participation in the Guatemalan Congress. Data on legislators collected from published sources and from personal interviews: place of birth, age, residence, education, occupation matched to degree of participation determined by number of times engaged in debate.

Article evades any evaluation of importance of congress vis-à-vis other institutions such as the military. [W. H. Agor]

THE CARIBBEAN

General

Lowenthal, David. Black power in the Caribbean context. See item 1177.

——. West Indian societies. See item 1178.

—— and **Lambros Comitas** eds. The aftermath of sovereignty: West Indian perspectives. See item 1179.

7564. Nettleford, Rex. Caribbean perspectives: the creative potential and the quality of life (UWI/CQ, 17:3/4, Sept./Dec. 1971, p. 114-127)
Describing the plantation system as the cultural model of the Caribbean, Nettleford suggests that search for a new model to meet racial demands should identify with the human element rather than the diffuse past cultural heritage. New prototype however, is not delineated. [W. H. Agor]

CUBA

7565. Aguilar León, Luis E. Cuba: conciencia y revolución, el proceso de una reflexión sobre el problema cubano. Miami, Fla., Ediciones Universal, 1972. 188 p. (Col. Cuba y sus jueces)
Avatars of exile have made the Cuban Aguilar into a historian. But at his best he continues to be an essayist in the Spanish American tradition. Here he has collected some of his essays from 1954-68. Very well written, as is usual with Professor Aguilar. Particularly relevant for his fellow citizens.

Alvarez Díaz, José; Alberto Arredondo; Raúl M. Shelton; and **Juan F. Vizcaíno.** Cuba: geopolítica y pensamiento económico. See HLAS 34:2046.

7566. Amaro V., Nelson. Las fases de la Revolución cubana (ILARI/A, 13, julio 1969, p. 81-101, tables)
Young Cuban sociologist in exile applies to the Cuban Revolution a model of five stages: democratic, humanist, nationalist, socialist, and marxist-leninist. Although he is fortunately free of any bias, and shows an acceptable familiarity with Cuban developments, it is highly doubtful that his scheme contributes something new to the understanding of the Revolution.

Bekarevich, A. D. Kuba: vneshneekonomicheskie otnosheniia (Cuba: foreign economic relations). See item 8153.

——. SSSR-Kuba: Leninskie printsipy proletarskgo internatsionalizma (USSR-Cuba: Leninist principles of proletarian internationalism). See item 8154.

7567. Bernardo, Robert M. The theory of moral incentives in Cuba. Introduction by Irving Louis Horowitz. University, Ala., Univ. of Alabama Press, 1971. 159 p., tables.
The attempt to abandon material rewards and introduce non-material (symbolic) incentives for increased productivity and loyalty represents perhaps the key to the Cuban experiment in terms of regime survival and formation of the communist man. Clearly drawn and concise analysis of origins and significance of the ideal of moral incentives. [J.J. Bailey]

7568. Betancourt Roa, Gilda. Revolución cubana y cambio social (BUS, 8:15/17, dic. 1969, p. 119-128)
Chairman of Sociology dept. of the Univ. de la Habana writes a short, doctrinnaire piece on change in general in Cuba, and changes in agriculture. [P.B. Taylor, Jr.]

Bonachea, Rolando E. and **Nelson P. Valdés** eds. Revolutionary struggle, 1947-1958: volume 1 of the selected works of Fidel Castro. See HLAS 34:2049.

7569. Cardenal, Ernesto. En Cuba. B.A., Ediciones Carlos Lohlé, 1972. 370 p., illus.
Nicaraguan priest and poet visited Cuba and wrote this book of hopes and dreams, more than facts. Very little that is useful to social scientists.

7570. El caso Padilla (Mensaje [Santiago] 20:199, junio 1971, p. 229-239, illus.)
In light of Heberto Padilla's self-criticism, *Mensaje* requested comments of Chilean writers who knew him and had visited Castro's Cuba for substantial periods. Cristian Huneeus transcribes interview held 19 Feb. 1971; Enrique Lihn, Mauricio Vázquez, Carlos Ossa, Huneeus, Germán Marín and Lisandro Otero offer short statements of opinion. Many other writers were asked but declined to comment for publication. For more on the Padilla case see HLAS 33:7806a, 7824. [P. B. Taylor, Jr.]

7571. Castro, Fidel. Fidel in Chile: a symbolic meeting between two historical processes; selected speeches of Major Fidel Castro during his visit to Chile, November 1971. N.Y., International Publishers, 1972. 234 p.
Collection of 15 of the most important speeches delivered by Fidel Castro during his visit to Chile from 10 Nov. to 4 Dec. 1971. Not all texts appear in full. [R. E. Bonachea]

7572. ——. Socialismo y comunismo: un proceso único. Selección y notas de Carlos Varela. Santiago, Ediciones Prensa Latinoamericana, 1970. 218 p. (Col. América nueva)
Fragments of 85 speeches by Fidel between Jan. 1965-March 1969. Appendices contain more speeches, editorials, and miscellaneous documents. Unindexed grab bag. [J. J. Bailey]

7573. Castro Hidalgo, Orlando. Spy for Fidel. Miami, Fla., E.A. Seeman Publishing, 1971. 110 p.
Member of the Cuban Intelligence who defected at the end of the 1960's tells some of his experiences.

No exciting revelations. One appendix, "A Brief History of D.G.I." (Dirección General de Inteligencia) describes, for the first time, the Cuban C.I.A.

7574. Cuba. Fuerzas Armadas Revolucionarias. Dirección Política. Curso de instruccíon política. v. 1, El capitalismo en Cuba. La Habana, n.d. 173 p., plates.

One of the political education textbooks used by Cuban Armed Forces. Deals lightly with development of Cuba's economy, frustrated revolution of 1933, Batista's 1952 military coup and the Cuban Revolution, as well as several Marxist-Leninist concepts. Also includes Second Declaration of Havana (1962) and Ernesto Che Guevara's Message to the Tricontinental. [R. E. Bonachea]

7575. Domínguez, Jorge I. Sectoral clashes in Cuban politics and development (LARR, 6:3, Fall 1971, p. 61-87, tables)

Discusses aspects of contemporary Cuban politics and economics up to 1969 from point of view of theory of sectoral clashes of Markos Mamalakis, focusing on those aspects of theory which attempt to explain conflict and policy-making. Uses published statistics where applicable. Concludes that Mamalakis' theory is one of sectoral pre-eminence useful in the Cuban case but only if modified through other social and political theories. [W. H. Agor]

7576. Dumont, René. Cuba: socialism and development. Translated by Helen R. Lane. N.Y., Grove Press, 1970. 240 p., bibl.

Translation of original French edition published in 1964, with two afterwords written in 1968 and 1969. Dumont has been an adviser to the Cuban government, and is one of the few western experts really familiar with the country's rural economy. Indispensable for all those interested in Cuba.

7577. Espin, Vilma. O zhenskom dvizhenii na Kube (The women's movement in Cuba) (SSSR/LA, 4, 1972, julio/agosto 1972, p. 126-132)

Interview held by Prensa Latina with Ms. Espín, head of the Federation of Cuban Women, where she discusses the importance of the women's movement as part of the class struggle and liberation movements in general. She also describes efforts to improve the status of women in Cuba. [A. R. Navon]

7578. Fagen, Richard R. Continuities in Cuban revolutionary politics (MR, 23:11, April 1972, p. 24-48)

Behind frequent changes in policies of the Revolution there are some continuities. The first one, of course, is the presence of Fidel Castro. But there are others analyzed by the author, a political scientist in this lucid but unconvincing article.

7579. Furtak, Robert K. Cuba: pts. 1/2 (*in* Kernig, C. D. *ed.* Marxism, communism and Western society: a comparative encyclopedia. N.Y., Herder and Herder, 1972, v. 2, p. 262-269, bibl.)

Good brief introduction to study of the Cuban Revolution followed by an even briefer analysis of the October crisis.

7580. Gall, Norman. How Castro failed (COMMENT, 52:5, Nov. 1971, p. 45-57)

Intertwines themes of René Dumont, Hugh Thomas, and K. S. Karol to demonstrate that Castro failed because he permitted no institution to give the revolution a life of its own separate from himself. [W. H. Agor]

Gavi, Philippe. Che Guevara. See item 7405.

7581. Gorbachev, B. V. and A. I. Kalinin. Kuba: Nekotorye sotsial'noekonomicheskie i politicheskie aspekty revoliutsii (Cuba: some socio-economic and political aspects of the revolution) (SSSR/LA), 3, 1969, p. 21-41)

Reviews successes and problems in Cuban revolutionary process. Notes need of Cuban Communist Party to strengthen its contact with the masses. [T. S. Cheston]

7582. Grigulevich, Iosif Romul'dovich. Ernesto Che Gevara. Moskva, Izdatel'stov. Tsk Vlks. Molodaia Gvardiia, 1972. 350 p., bibl., illus., maps.

Sympathetic biography of Che Guevara by Soviet expert on Cuba. Attacks those who claim that Guevara was anything other than a Communist and friend of the Soviet Union. Contains a 1971 interview with Anastas Mikoyan about his reminiscences of his contact with Cuban leaders. Mikoyan said Guevara was a romantic revolutionary and that the two of them had exactly opposite opinions on a number of questions though in a friendly way. [T. S. Cheston]

7583. ———. Kul'turnaia revoliutsiia no Kube (The Cultural Revolution in Cuba). Moskva, Nauka, 1965. 302 p., bibl., illus.

Study of the cultural revolution in Cuba from 1959-64. The term "cultural revolution" should be understood in the traditional Marxist rather than Maoist sense; that is, the transformation of a bourgeois culture into a socialist one instead of the revitalization of an existing socialist culture. Contends that the leaders of pre-revolutionary Cuba could not have enriched the culture of the working classes because their subordination to the US did not allow them to raise the economic level to underwrite it. The Revolution freed Cuba from such bondage and allowed it to launch a massive literacy campaign, open its private schools and universities to the workers, orient school curriculums to the technical needs of the economy and instill Marxist-Leninist philosophy. Literature, the arts and sports were stimulated with, for example, Cuba producing award winning films for the first time. Most important, however, was the establishment of a new attitude in which workers saw their labors were for the common good rather than the enrichment of others. The USSR assisted in many ways such as sending 140 technical specialists and 100 language teachers to teach in Cuban schools. [T. S. Cheston]

7584. Guevara, Ernesto Che. Pasajes de la guerra revolucionaria. Medellín, Co., Editorial Prisma, 1971. 166 p.

New Colombian ed. of Che's memoirs of guerrilla activities in Cuba, covering principally 1957. See *HLAS 29:6665*. [J. J. Bailey]

7585. Häger, Olle and Hans Villius. Rebellernas rike: Cuba och Castros Revolution. Stockholm, Sveriges Radios förlag, 1970. 37 p., bibl., maps, plates.

Short history of recent political events in Cuba comprising period 1933-70. Presentation is factual without any political viewpoint stressed. [R. V. Shaw]

7586. Halperin, Maurice. The rise and decline of Fidel Castro: an essay in contemporary history. Berkeley, Calif., Univ. of California Press, 1972. 380 p., map, plates.

Author stayed from 1962-68 teaching at the Univ. of Havana. Unfortunately, instead of using observations and impressions acquired through such a rare experience, he settled for this prolix work that could have been written without even going to Cuba. Despite title, this is an historical account of the Cuban Revolution's foreign relations using almost only Cuban and Western printed sources. More speculation than analysis. Author seems unaware of work that is being done in the field of International Relations.

7587. Houtart, François and André Rousseau. The Church and revolution: from the French Revolution of 1789 to the Paris Riots of 1968; from Cuba to Southern Africa; from Vietnam to Latin America. Translated by Violet Nevile. Maryknoll, N.Y., Orbis Books, 1971. 371 p.

Subtitle suggests scope of the book. Contains brief chapter on role of the Church in the Cuban Revolution and aftermath under Castro. Chapter on Latin America contains capsule descriptions of recent developments in selected countries and a longer discussion on Camilo Torres. Overview based on primary and secondary sources. [J. J. Bailey]

Khronologiia vazheneishikh sobytii istorii sovetsko-Kubinskikh otnoshenii: 1960-70 (Chronicle of the most important events in the history of Soviet-Cuban relations: 1960-70). See item 8167.

7588. Kurland, Gerald. Fidel Castro: communist dictator of Cuba. Charlotteville, N.Y., SamHar Press, 1972. 32 p., bibl. (Outstanding personalities, 36)

Biography of Fidel Castro for beginners.

Lamberg, Roberto F. Consideraciones concluyentes en torno a las guerrillas castristas en Latinoamérica. See item 7424.

7589. Lamberg, Vera B. de. La guerrilla castrista en América Latina: bibliografía selecta, 1960-1970 (CM/FI, 12:1, julio/sept. 1971, p. 95-111)

Annotated bibliography of 132 works relevant to study of the propagation of guerrilla warfare in Latin American countries other than Cuba. Covers works published in Europe, Latin America, and US. Compilation intended to cover many points of view. [W. H. Agor]

7590. Malloy, James M. La Revolución cubana: apoyo político y distribución de costos (USIA/PI, 19:5, sept./oct. 1972, p. 17-30, plates)

Spanish translation of chapter from item 7591. Interesting approach by political scientist to study of the Cuban Revolution, in terms of political support, social costs, and political mobilization. Although in need of further refinement, such an approach deserves the attention of those interested in the study of revolutionary phenomena.

Matthews, Herbert Lionel. A world in revolution: a newspaperman's memoir. See item 7440.

'7591. Mesa-Lago, Carmelo ed. Revolutionary change in Cuba. Pittsburgh, Pa., Univ. of Pittsburgh Press, 1971. 544 p., bibl., tables.

Sixteen specialists in the field contribute essays never published before. This valuable collection is divided into three sections: polity, economy, and society. After analyzing the Cuban, Chinese, Yugoslavian, and Soviet socialist alternatives, editor concludes that the most probable for Cuba is some type of compromise between Castro and the Soviets.

7592. ———— **and Roberto E. Hernández.** La organización del trabajo y el sistema salarial en Cuba (IEP/RPS, 95, julio/sept. 1972, p. 5-53, tables)

Once again and with the collaboration of a junior scholar, Carmelo Mesa Lago shows his well recognized expertise in the study of the Cuban economy under Castro. Highly recommended.

7593. Mikoiam, S. A. Vstrechi s Che Gevaroi (Meetings with Che Guevara) (SSSR/LA, 5, sept./oct. 1972, p. 161-164)

Reminiscences of two meetings between the author and Guevara, in particular one at Geneva, first UNCTAD conference. In the conversations between Guevara and Soviet delegates and journalists, there was much warmth and common ground despite some disagreements as to whether there is a need for material incentives in communist societies. Author notes that Guevara's not feeling this need constitutes one indication of his truly heroic character. [A. R. Navon]

Mulville, Frank. In *Granma's* wake: Girl Stella's voyage to Cuba. See item 6636.

7594. Nelson, Lowry. Cuba: the measure of a revolution. Foreword by Moses L. Harvey. Minneapolis, Minn., Univ. of Minnesota Press, 1972. 242 p., bibl., tables.

Author of an excellent book, *Rural Cuba* (Minneapolis, Minn., Univ. of Minnesota Press, 1950, 285 p., bibl.), based on field work, Nelson found his request for a visa denied by the Cuban government. Nevertheless, he decided to go ahead with this second volume using the available published sources. He honestly admits in the preface that this work is solely designed to provide general information. As such, it deserves some attention even though most of the information is taken from sources highly critical of the present Cuban regime. This is understandable given Nelson's viewpoint that "revolutions are messy, bloody, irrational, and destructive . . ."

7595. Omskriven revolution: fakta och asikter om Kuba, 1959-1971. Stockholm, Latinamerika-instituet & Arbetarrörelsens Arkiv, 1971. 32 p., bibl., tables.

Booklet entitled: *Much discussed Revolution: facts and opinions about Cuba, 1959-1971*, issued by Sweden's Institute of Latin American Studies and Swedish Labour Movement in connection with an exhibition on Cuba which they organized in 1971. Includes statistics and bibliography. [Magnus Mörner]

Paligorić, Ljubomir. Politicke doktrine levice u Latinskoj Americi (Political doctrines of the Left in Latin America). See item 7452.

7596. Partido Unido de la Revolución Socialista de Cuba (PURSC). Dirección Nacional. Comisión de Orientación Revolucionaria. Relatos del asalto al Moncada. La Habana, Empresa Consolidada de Artes Gráficas, 1964. 166 p., map, plates.

On the occasion of the 11th anniversary of the assault on the Moncada Fortress, volume reprints from speeches and previously published sources, accounts by participants. Includes descriptions by Raúl, Fidel, Pedro Miret, Haydée Santamaría, and others. Interesting collection of photos. [J. J. Bailey]

7597. Ruiz, Leovigildo. Diario de una traición. Miami, Fla., The Indian Printing, 1970. 398 p., illus.

Privately printed day-by-day chronicle of 1960, written by a Cuban exile and vigorous opponent of Castro. Offers no discussion, but only a highly partial chronology whose detail is useful, even though only one man's view. [P. B. Taylor, Jr.]

7598. Silverman, Bertram ed. Man and socialism in Cuba: the great debate. Edited and with an introduction by . . . N.Y., Atheneum, 1971. 382 p.

Translation of most important articles published from 1962-65 in Cuba, during so-called "great debate" between the "economists" and those in favor of moral incentives. Castro's *guevarista* speech of 26 July 1968 is included as an epilogue. Editor's brief preface has been written with more devotion than acumen. Available as paperback, by Atheneum, 1971.

7599. Sokolova, Z. I. Kubinskaia revoliutsiia i krest'ianskie organizatsii (The Cuban Revolution and the peasant organizations) (SSSR/LA, 4:3, 1972, p. 97-103, tables)

History of Cuban peasant labor organizations is traced from their beginnings in the 1920's to the creation of a single peasant organization in 1961, coinciding with the Revolution. An important victory was the establishment, under communist leadership, of the National Association of Peasants in 1941. After it was forced to disband as "communist," leftist organizations began working within trade associations. Author focusses attention on history and tactics of Cuban peasant movement. [A. R. Navon]

7600. Solaun, Mauricio. El fracaso de la democracia en Cuba: un régimen "patrimonial" autoritario, 1952 (ILARI/A, 13, julio 1969, p. 57-80)

Stresses structural and cultural factors to explain the downfall of Batista. Syndrome of dishonesty and corruption in politics had produced popular alienation, which undermined the possibility of effective democracy and legitimized widespread use of extra-legal tactics. Batista failed due to: 1) his symbolic commitment to democracy, which limited the coercive capacity of the regime; and 2) the socioeconomic complexity of Cuban society. [J. J. Bailey]

7601. Suárez, Andrés. The Cuban revolution: the road to power (LARR, 7:3, Fall 1972, p. 5-29)

Discusses literature on the Cuban insurrection and points out conflicting versions of events and major gaps in our knowledge of the period. Divided along major themes: Moncada Barracks attack; *Granma* expedition; origins of the guerrillas; April strike; sierra-llano conflict; foreign influences; and studies providing insights into Fidel Castro. This thoroughly researched essay constitutes required reading for those interested in the state of the research on the Cuban Revolution. [R. E. Bonachea]

7602. Suchlicki, Jaime. La Revolución cubana: retrospectiva y perspectiva (USIA/PI, 19:5, sept./oct. 1972, p. 1-16, plates)

Young historian tries to summarize Cuban developments since 1968. Sees a growing militarization, more dependence on the Soviet Union, and does not expect an opening toward the US from Castro. Today, probably first and third assertions would require some qualifications.

7603. Sundell, Jan-Olof. Revolutionens Kuba. Stockholm, Almqvist & Wiksell, 1970. 156 p., bibl., map, tables.

Calm and serious reassessment of the Cuban Revolution by a nonsocialist Swedish social scientist. Relies heavily on Mesa-Lago's analysis of Cuban statistics. [Magnus Mörner]

7604. A travers les livres et les revues: a la recherche d'un communisme sans larmes (CEDN/R, 26, août/sept. 1970, p. 1361-1373, map)

Useful review article of recent major pieces on Cuba. [P. B. Taylor, Jr.]

Tretiak, Daniel. Cuba and the Communist system: the politics of a Communist independent, 1967-1969. See item 8179.

7605. Tutino, Saverio. L'octobre cubain. Traduit de l'italien par Jean Dufflot. Paris, François Maspero, 1969. 315 p. (Cahiers libres, 143/144)

Long piece, originally written in Italian: *L'ottobre cubano* (1968). Missile crisis of 1962 is point of departure, but book's text is a history of Castro, Cuba's problems that led to his takeover, and policies since that time through 1967. [P. B. Taylor, Jr.]

7606. Valdés, Nelson P. Cuba: ¿socialismo democrático o burocratismo colectivista? (ILARI/A, 23, enero 1972, p. 25-52)

Traces process of conversion to socialism; Stalinist methods and militarization of the work force seen as consequences of low level of socialist consciousness. Visualizes that a break from these methods will be hard if possible at all. Author suggests solution is to divide power among workers, but state will not permit itself to be diluted. [W. H. Agor]

7607. ———. La diplomacia del azúcar: Cuba y Estados Unidos (CM/FI, 22:1, julio/sept. 1971, p. 46-65, tables)

Since the spring of 1960, the Cuban sugar quota in

the American market was used as a weapon to prevent the Revolution from developing an independent foreign policy. Cubans were forced to look for Soviet support. Shows a good grasp of available sources.

7608. —— and **Rolando E. Bonachea.** Fidel Castro y la política estudiantil de 1947 a 1952 (ILARI/A, 22, oct. 1971, p. 23-40)

Two young historians explore interactions between Fidel Castro and "grupos de acción" active for several decades in Cuban student politics. For this purpose they profusely use Cuban newspapers and magazines. But they do not try to analyze the real nature and role of these peculiar entities, which suggest some analogies with contemporary urban guerrillas. Much work remains to be done both on this subject and Castro involvement in "grupos de acción."

7609. Welch, Claude E., Jr. and **Mavis Bunker Taintor** eds. Revolution and political change. North Scituate, Mass., Duxbury Press, 1972. 313 p., tables.

Anthology of 18 selections, plus introduction by editors, dealing with subject. One deals directly with Cuba, and another touches on it along with sketchy reference to other Latin American cases. A college text-reader, much more concerned with paradigms and sophisticated (overly so?) analytical schemes than with detailed reporting. Not a source. [P. B. Taylor, Jr.]

7610. Wilson, Desmond P., Jr. Alternative futures in the Cuban Revolution (CIDGO/O, 15:3, Fall 1971, p. 842-855, tables)

Wilson sees three possibilities: 1) Castro model of dependence on USSR; 2) Batista model of dependence on US; or 3) Tito model of independent socialism. Concludes that dependence is necessary and does not foresee a rapprochement with US. [W. H. Agor]

Wolpin, Miles D. Cuban foreign policy and Chilean politics. See item 8184.

——. La influencia internacional de la revolución cubana: Chile, 1958-1970. See item 7789.

——. Revolutionary Cuba's impact upon Chilean politics. See item 7790.

7611. Yglesias, José. In the fist of the Revolution: life in a Cuban country town. N.Y., Pantheon Books, 1968. 307 p.

In 1967, author stayed at Mayari, a village on northern coast of Oriente province. Without any jargon he tells his impressions and experiences, offering the unusual opportunity of a look at daily life in a small Cuban town under Castro. For author's recent account of his experiences in Latin America, see item 7499.

7612. Zorina, A. M. Kamilo S'enfuegos [Camilo Cienfuegos]. Moskva, Nauka, 1966. 70 p., map, plates.

Popularized biography. Includes footnotes. [T. S. Cheston]

DOMINICAN REPUBLIC

7613. Despradel, Fidelio. Santo Domingo: ¿evolución o revolución? Santo Domingo, Editora Nacional, 1970? 71 p.

Written for the "Dominican fighters, in first place the Marxist-Leninists . . ." Author strongly criticizes "leftism", and rejects relevance of Mao's thoughts to the Dominican situation. He seems to have in mind Marxist-Leninists who follow the Soviet line. Same arguments can be found in Soviet publications.

7614. Espinal, Andrés Julio. Trujillo, Bosch y yo y . . . el desafío. Santo Domingo, Editora Arte y Cine, 1970. 151 p.

Representative example of works originating in the Dominican Republic, more concerned with poetic justice than politics. Entirely lacking in objectivity.

7615. Lamarch Henríquez, Carlos M. Por que la democracia al servicio de la patria. Santo Domingo, Secretaría de Estado, Educación, Bellas Artes y Cultos, 1967. 134 p.

Two part book. Pt. 1, composed of articles previously published discussing nature of democracy. Pt. 2 consists of letters sent by the author to the US State Department, while in exile, requesting a meeting to explain his own formula for the elimination of Trujillo and reestablishment of democracy in the Dominican Republic. He was never granted the meeting.

7616. La Souchère, Elena de. Crime à Saint-Domingue: l'affaire Trujillo-Galíndez. Paris, Editions Albin Michel, 1972. 254 p., bibl.

Journalistic account of Jesús de Galíndez' disappearance in 1957 and Trujillo's assasination four years later. Although some new documentary sources are offered, "l'affair Galíndez" continues to be an unsolvable mystery.

7617. Sasson, Lil Despradel. Introducción al estudio de los sindicatos de la industria azucarera en la República Dominicana (UPR/RCS, 15:3, sept. 1971, p. 317-338)

Traces sugar industry from its colonial origins and organized labor from the American occupation through the Trujillo era to the present. Identifies the problem of labor as that of social identity of the Haitian work force and critical nature of the industry itself. [W. H. Agor]

Walker, Malcolm T. Politics and the power structure: a rural community in the Dominican Republic. See item 1214.

HAITI

7618. Dynastic republicanism to Haiti (PQ, 44:1, Jan/March 1973, p. 77-84)

Interesting but unfortunately too brief an account of events in Haiti after the death of Duvalier. We know so little about contemporary Haitian politics that even bits of journalistic information such as these are welcome.

7618a. Fleischmann, Ulrich. Aspekte der sozialen und politischen Entwicklung Haitis. Stuttgart, FRG, Klett, 1971. 100 p., bibl. (Schriftenreihe des Instituts für Iberoamerika-Kunde, 17)

Historical overview of economic and social development in Haiti with special emphasis on racial and religious problems. Author concludes that all structural deficiencies of present Haiti derive from her colonial situation which in fact has changed very little after independence. [W. Grabendorff]

Nicholls, David. Biology and politics in Haiti. See item 1194.

7619. ———. Embryo-politics in Haiti (Government and opposition [London] 6:1, Winter 1971, p. 75-85)

Compares political trends in Haiti to theoretical totalitarianism. Identifies three currents of ideology in Haiti: *négritude*, technocratism, and fascism, but concludes that, although despotic, Haiti is not totalitarian in that it contains no total prescription for internal policies. [W. H. Agor]

JAMAICA

Foner, Nancy. Status and power in rural Jamaica: a study of education and political change. See item 1148.

Jamaica [National Electoral Board?] General elections, 1972. See item 7307.

7620. Manley, Michael. Overcoming insularity in Jamaica (CFR/FA, 49:1, Oct. 1970, p. 100-110)

Argues that the compelling forces of nationalism in an economically dependent area ties the bargaining power of the Caribbean nations to Third World politics. Nonetheless Jamaica has rejected collectivism in government. Author argues against this policy to bring about changes such as joint ownership of Jamaican industry. [W. H. Agor]

Nettleford, Rex. Manley and the politics of Jamaica. See item 1193.

———. Norman Washington Manley and the new Jamaica: selected speeches and writings, 1938-68. See *HLAS 34:2146.*

7621. Rodney, Walter. The groundings with my brothers. With an introduction by Richard Small. London, The Bogle-L'Oouverture Publications, 1969. 68 p., map.

Series of lectures given in Jamaica by a young black lawyer and professor at the Univ. of the West Indies. Militant series, geared to the theme that in a country of blacks, discrimination in all its aspects, is still a reality. [P. B. Taylor, Jr.]

PUERTO RICO

7622. Agrait, Luis E. Las elecciones de 1968 en Puerto Rico (UPR/RCS, 16:1, marzo 1972, p. 17-60, bibl., tables)

Explains overthrow of Partido Popular Democrático by means of analysis of election returns by area. Concludes that Partido Nuevo Progresista victory rested with urban and youth vote, but represented vote over basic issues, such as statehood, and issues of personality as well. [W. H. Agor]

7623. García-Passalacqua, Juan M. Puerto Rico: whither Commonwealth? (CIDGO/O, 15:3, Fall, 1971, p. 923-942)

García-Passalacqua asserts that rising social tensions in Puerto Rico—stemming mainly from the generation gap—doom the Commonwealth as a long-term "solution" to the problem of the island's status. He says Commonwealth "has always been preached as a value of the stomach. This is the hour of the heart." He proposes a Constitutional Convention representing all major parties in Puerto Rico as a first step either toward statehood or independence. [Y. Ferguson]

Maldonado Denis, Manuel. Puerto Rico: una interpretación histórico-social. See *HLAS 34:2162.*

7624. ———. La situación política de Puerto Rico (UTIER/C, 18, 1972, p. 7-20)

Thesis of this article is that Puerto Rico is not a semicolony, like the Dominican Republic or Haiti, "but a colony in the classical sense of the word." Author has repeatedly stated arguments supporting this characterization in several other publications, see *HLAS 33:150.*

7625. Morales Otero, Pablo. Comentarios alrededor del desarrollo político de Puerto Rico. San Juan, Biblioteca de Autores Puertorriqueños, 1970. 294 p.

Outline of political development in Puerto Rico. Historical discourse by Puerto Rican author devoid of critical analysis.

7626. Pabón, Milton. Los partidos políticos en el régimen colonial (UPR/RCS, 15:3, sept. 1971, p. 339-347)

Professor of political science at Univ. of Puerto Rico examines Puerto Rican political system finding it to be one of schizophrenic hybridism with regard to the US. He sees parties as servants of colonial economic interests rather than of the majority of citizens. One sided directing efforts for change toward the electoral system itself, but well written. [W. H. Agor]

7627. Wells, Henry. The modernization of Puerto Rico; a political study of changing values and institutions. Cambridge, Mass., Harvard Univ. Press, 1969. 440 p., tables.

Draws on theoretical work of Clyde Kluckhohn, Harold Lasswell and Abraham Kaplan to analyze the transformation of values in Puerto Rico in the 19th and 20th centuries. Stresses impact of US occupation and public policies under Muñoz Marín. Successfully integrates political and sociological perspectives in a well researched study. An important book by a leading scholar of Puerto Rican politics. [J. J. Bailey]

ST. KITTS-NEVIS-ANGUILLA

7628. Clarke, Colin G. Political fragmentation in the Caribbean: the case of Anguilla (CAG/GG, 15:1, Spring 1971, p. 13-29, illus., maps)

On 30 May 1967, Anguilla, with about 6,000 inhabitants, declared independence from the associated state of St. Kitts-Nevis-Anguilla. Excellent descriptive study of those events, including due consideration to the social and economic structure as well as geopolitical factors involved in the process of fragmentation.

7629. Forbes, Urias. The Nevis local council: a case of formalism in structural change (UPR/CS, 11:2, July 1971, p. 21-32, table)

Outlines process of decentralization following statehood and difficulties experienced by the Nevis local council (of the St. Kitts-Nevis-Anguilla associated state) regarding expenditure and composition. Concludes that devolution of power by law must be accompanied by sense of partnership between central and local government. [W. H. Agor]

Marten, Neil. Their's not to reason why: a study of the Anguillan operation as presented to Parliament. See *HLAS 34:2152*.

TRINIDAD AND TOBAGO

7630. Ferkiss, Barbara and **Victor C. Ferkiss.** Race and politics in Trinidad and Guyana (APS/WA, 134:1, Summer 1971, p. 5-23)

Asks how and why race dominates politics in Guyana as well as in Trinidad and Tobago. Cities patronage, general economic interests, desire for a positive self-image and need for physical and psychic security as central factors. Stresses pork-barrel aspect of government as source of ethnic-racial conflict. Suggests that political conflict is not a matter of domination by one racial group over another, but rather a desire to protect or promote specific, identifiable interests. [J. J. Bailey]

7631. Hooker, James R. Anatomy of a mutiny. Hanover, N.H., American Universities Field Staff Reports, 1972. 7 p. (Mexico and Caribbean area series, 7:1)

Report of events that began with student and worker demonstrations, and culminated in a military mutiny. Though the 1970 mutiny in Trinidad was quelled, repercussions from the events are still evident.

Martin, Tony. C. L. R. James and the race/class question. See item 1185.

Oxaal, Ivar. Race and revolutionary consciousness: a documentary interpretation of the 1970 black power revolt in Trinidad. See item 1196.

THE GUIANAS

Guyana

7632. Burnham, Forbes. A destiny to mould: selected discourses by the Prime Minister of Guyana. Compiled by C. A. Nascimento and R. A. Burrowes. Port-of-Spain, Longman Caribbean, 1970. 255 p., plates.

39 speeches on topics ranging from parties and elections to administration and foreign policy over period 1955-69. Brief introduction provides background on recent political developments in Guyana. Speeches arranged by topic and annotated to provide a context for understanding. [J. J. Bailey]

Ferkiss, Barbara and **Victor C. Ferkiss.** Race and politics in Trinidad and Guyana. See item 7630.

Glasgow, Roy Arthur. Guyana: race and politics among Africans and East Indians. See item 1151.

7633. Jagan, Cheddi. The truth about bauxite: nationalisation. Georgetown, n.p., 1971. 16 p.

Short pamphlet of press articles by Jagan explaining different types of nationalization and confrontation between imperialisms. Distinction raised herein can be read with profit by left and right scholars alike.

7634. Lutchman, Harold A. The co-operative Republic of Guyana (UPR/CS, 10:3, Oct. 1970, p. 97-115)

Discusses symbolic, ideological, partisan, and related factors in Guyana's transition from monarchy to republic. [J. J. Bailey]

7635. Premdas, Ralph R. Elections and political campaigns in a racially bifurcated state: the case of Guyana (UM/JIAS, 14:3, Aug. 1972, p. 271-296, tables)

Campaigns in Guyana fail to resolve political and social differences. Racially, the society is divided very deeply and parties reflect these divisions. Thus, elections are bitter, outcomes are not accepted, and with each election tension increases. Party tactics in several elections are reported, and the outcome as of 1964 described. [P. B. Taylor, Jr.]

SOUTH AMERICA: WEST COAST

(COLOMBIA, ECUADOR, PERU, BOLIVIA, CHILE)

JOHN J. BAILEY

Assistant Professor of Government
Director, Latin American Studies Program
Georgetown University

THE GREAT BULK OF THE LITERATURE REPORTED HERE (roughly two-thirds) pertains to Peru and Chile, with the quantity of items on the latter more than doubling over *HLAS 33*. As one might expect, considerable attention is devoted to examining the historical-political sources of the Chilean marxist regime and the Peruvian nationalist-military regime and evaluating the significance of these governments in their national setting as well as for development strategies throughout the region. Of the 25 or so general essays on the Chilean case, a pluralist position is stated by Arturo Valenzuela (item 7787) while examples of marxian interpretations may be found in the contributions by James Petras (item 7772), Paul M. Sweezy (item 7783), and Gustavo Canihaunte (item 7738). Several contributions by participants in the Chilean experiment in socialism are also of particular significance, especially the speeches by and the interviews with Salvador Allende (item 7730-7731, 7741 and 7748), and documents and papers by pro-regime (item 7732) and anti-regime (item 7767) partisans. In the Peruvian case, a marxian defense of the regime is presented in Ismael Frias' book (item 7687), while an insightful critique from the same ideological perspective is provided by Aníbal Quijano (item 7700). A useful brief overview of the Peruvian government, from a policy-making perspective, is Jane Jaquette's article (item 7692). To note especially the contributions by political scientists and activists is not to deny the merit of interpretive essays by perceptive observers such as Eric J. Hobsbawn (item 7690). A safe prediction is that, given the intense interest aroused by these governments, the next biennium should produce an even greater number of scholarly assessments of their performance. Undoubtedly, the September 1973 coup d'etat against President Allende's government will intensify research on topics of military and other forms of authoritarian regimes throughout Latin America.

On the whole, rather conventional emphases persist in this literature, with considerable attention to agrarian reform, political parties and elections, military involvement in politics, guerrilla movements, and the Catholic church. The behavioral approach in comparative analysis is represented in studies of political socialization and voting. Unfortunately, the persistent gaps remain as well, with insufficient attention to legal and governmental institutions and processes. Exceptions to this would include the studies by Dale Furnish, Joseph Thome, and Weston Agor. One hestitates to single out particular works as exceptionally meritorious for fear of relegating the remaining contributions to a "residual" category. It is appropriate, however, to call the reader's attention to innovative or otherwise outstanding work. In regard to agrarian reform, conceptual and theoretical interest mark the contributions by David Lehmann (item 7764), F. LaMond Tullis (item 7703), and José Matos Mar and others (item 7695), while Robert R. Kaufman (item 7759) has added a solid case study to the already substantial literature on Chile. The collaborative effort by Luigi R. Einaudi and Alfred C. Stepan on the military regimes of Peru and Brazil (item 7685), and the interpretive monograph on Chile (which stresses conceptual as well as comparative foci) by Alain Joxe (item 7758) should be noted by beginning students of the military as well as specialists. Logically enough, interesting analyses of electoral behavior are particularly associated with Chile and Colombia, with noteworthy contributions by Atilio A. Borón (item 7736), Steven W. Sinding (item 7782) and Lars Schoultz (item 7669). Readers with an interest in theory-relevant quantitative techniques should note particularly the exercise in secondary analysis by Alejandro Portes (item 7773).

While marxian analysis has only recently become significant in U.S. political interpretations of Latin America (as seen particularly in the dependency school) one finds the continuing dominance of this perspective among Latin American social scientists. Since the 1920s and 1930s, varieties of marxism have been significant as an intellectual force in the area and are amply reflected in the present literature (items 7652-7653).

Apparently, as the Development Decade comes more to be defined as the failure of liberal-evolutionary development strategy, non-liberal and non-incremental alternatives have become more predominant. One might speculate that, in turn, political debate will move further into the context of varieties of socialism, e.g., marxian, Christian, and populist. Of potential interest to students of intellectual history is the confluence of an emerging Latin American social science and the contemporary emphasis on economic determinism. The most active intellectual ferment at present is centered in the still rather loosely defined dependency school (see, for example, items 7376, 7453, 7456, and 7695) and the next biennium should witness a further elaboration of this approach as well as the emergence of a critical evaluation of it.

COLOMBIA

7636. Arenas, Jaime. La guerrilla por dentro: análisis del E.L.N. colombiano. Bogotá, Ediciones Tercer Mundo, 1971. 204 p. (Col. Tribuna libre, 5)

Describes origins of the youth branch of MRL (Movimiento Revolucionario de Liberación) and ELN (Ejército de Liberación Nacional). Discusses participation by Camilo Torres in ELN, problems in coordinating the urban and rural guerrilla, and ideological-tactical disputes within movement over the period 1963-69. Arenas, a leader in the movement, has written an intelligent and reflective memoir.

7637. Bermúdez, Luis A. Colombia hacia la revolución. Caracas, Editorial Domingo Fuentes, 1971. 128 p., plates (Col. Estos días)

General critical essay whose central thesis is that the unviable nature of social and political institutions in Colombia is due to oligarchical domination in a setting of rapid change and rising popular demands.

7638. Betancur, Belisario. ¡Despierta, Colombia! Prólogo [por] Jorge Eliecer Ruiz. Bogotá, Ediciones Tercer Mundo, 1970. 329 p. (Col. Documentos politicos)

Speeches from Betancur's unsuccessful presidential campaign of 1969-70 during which he ran against the National Front candidate, Misael Pastrana.

7639. Caballero Calderón, Eduardo. Yo, el alcalde: soñar un pueblo para después gobernarlo. Bogotá, Banco de la República, 1971. 308 p., plates.

Memoir by one of Colombia's leading essayists and public figures on his stint as mayor of Tipacoque, Boyacá, during 1969-71. Insights on frustrations of governance.

7640. Cataño, Gonzalo *ed.* Colombia: estructura política y agraria. Selección y prólogo [por] . . . · Bogotá, Ediciones Estrategia, 1971. 276 p., tables (Sección sociología y economía colombianas)

Collection of previously published essays from the Colombian left. Contents: Darío Mesa "Treinta Años de Historia Colombiana" (1957); Rafael Baquero "La Economía Nacional y la Política de Guerra" (1951; Rafael Baquero "Un Plan de Colonización Imperialista: El Programa de la Misión Currie al Desnudo" (1951); Hernán Toro Agudelo "Planteamiento y Soluciones del Problema Agrario" (1957); Estanislao Zuleta "Claves para el Debate Electoral" (1962); Estanislao Zuleta "Introducción a un Debate sobre la Política Revolucionaria" (1963).

7641. Corr, Edwin G. The political process in Colombia. Denver, Colo., Univ. of Denver, Graduate School of International Studies [and] The Social Science Foundation, 1972. 149 p., bibl., tables (Monograph series in world affairs, 9:1/2)

Useful overview of Colombian politics which stresses political culture, social structure, groups and elites in relation to capacity of government to achieve development and satisfactory levels of welfare.

7642. Dávila Ortiz, Alfonso. Minifundio rural: latifundio urbano; un enfoque liberal sobre las reformas agraria y urbana. Bogotá, Editorial Revista Colombiana, 1971. 176 p., tables (Populibro, 45)

Discussion, rather technical in parts, of problems of agricultural production, land tenure, and unemployment in Colombia. Evaluates agrarian reform and tax laws with suggestions for modifications. Rejects socialist strategy as inappropriate and defines problems and solutions in liberal-reformist framework.

7643. Deas, Malcolm. Colombian Aprils (CUH, 64:378, Feb. 1973, p. 77-80, 88)

Emphasizes political interplay of ANAPO (Alianza Nacional Popular) and factions of the traditional parties in preparation for post-National Front period beginning 1974. Properly stresses ambiguities of the April 1972 elections.

7644. Delgado, Oscar. La organización de los campesinos y el sistema político (ILARI/A, 25, julio 1972, p. 83-106, tables)

Campesinos can be organized for a variety of purposes, and by a variety of techniques. Where and why have organizations appeared? What costs are involved? Specific data from Chile and Colombia base the study for the most part, although a table offers estimates for other countries of Latin America as well. [P. B. Taylor, Jr.]

7645. Escobar Sierra, Hugo. Las invasiones en Colombia. Bogotá, Ediciones Tercer Mundo, 1972. 125 p., tables.

Vitriolic attack by a Conservative politician on communist subversion and the Asociación Nacional de Usuarios in promoting land invasions and apparent inability or unconcern of the Colombian government in stopping them. Provides data on locations of invasions and number of participants.

7646. Ferrero Calvo, César. Los sindicatos obreros colombianos (ESC, 4:15/16, julio/dic. 1970, p. 32-78)

Narrative synthesis of Colombian labor movement from colonial period to 1970. Emphasizes centrality of government support and consequences of such support for political behavior of unions.

7647. Flora, Jan Leighton. Elite solidarity and land tenure in the Cauca Valley of Colombia. Ithaca, N.Y., Cornell Univ., Latin American

Studies Program, 1971. 195 p., bibl., tables (Dissertation series, 30)

Thesis examines ". . . the concrete facts of land distribution in the Cauca Valley of Colombia, the solidary (sic) structures that are tied to land tenure and to the occupational situation in general, and third, the wider social policies of the nation and of the part of the world to which Colombia is tied economically and politically."

7648. Galán, Miguel A. ¿A donde vais Colombia, patria mía? Bogotá, n.p., 1971. 407 p.

Satirical critique of Lleras Restrepo administration (1966-70). Point of view defies classification. Perhaps classical liberal comes closest.

7649. Gally, Héctor *ed.* and *comp.* Camilo Torres: con las armas en la mano. Prólogo y selección de . . . México, Editorial Diógenes, 1971. 183 p.

Fragments of speeches, letters, and published works arranged according to such topics as "the priest," "the sociologist," "the revolutionary ideologue." Selections are unannotated and sources of many are not noted.

7650. Garcés, Joan E. La continuidad del sistema a través del cambio: el sistema bipartidista de Colombia (ITT/RLS, 6:1, marzo 1970, p. 7-59, tables)

Despite important socioeconomic change, the Colombian party system remains elitist and pragmatic with no significant differences on policy. Reasons for persistence of party system and weakness of antiestablishment movements (MRL, Gaitán, ANAPO) are analyzed, using voting and survey data.

7651. ———. Structural obstacles to the development of revolutionary political forces in Colombia (Government and Opposition [London] 6:3, Summer 1971, p. 303-332, tables)

Works from Easton's systems model to analyze anti- and pro-system political forces in Colombia. Not consistently rigorous in developing analysis.

7652. García, Antonio. Dialéctica de la democracia. Bogotá, Ediciones Cruz del Sur, 1971. 334 p.

Extended interpretive essay on contemporary crisis of democracy and capitalism in world, Latin America, and Colombia. Outlines a socialist alternative to bourgeois democracy. Author is economics professor at National Univ. of Colombia and leader of the Socialist Party. This is a much more sophisticated treatment of themes discussed in item 7653.

7653. ———. Una vía socialista para Colombia. Bogotá, Ediciones Cruz del Sur, 1972. 89 p. (Col. América andina)

Analyzes failure of capitalist strategy and policies of National Front in solving key development problems in Colombia. Outlines a socialist alternative in straightforward fashion directed to nonspecialist public. Interesting attempt at simplification.

Guzmán Campos, Germán. Camilo Torres. See *HLAS 34:2493a.*

7654. ———. El padre Camilo Torres. México, Siglo XXI Editores, 1968. 321 p., plates, tables.

Close friend, professional colleague at the Sociology Dept. of the National Univ., and fellow-priest, offers best biography to date on Camilo Torres, the defrocked revolutionary priest who joined ELN and was killed in 1966. Author pointedly notes that the book is not intended as an "objective" analysis, but rather is an attempt to communicate his understanding of Camilo Torres, priest, scholar, and political activist in the context of Colombian reality. Draws on interviews, published sources, private papers, and personal recollections. Essential for one who seeks an understanding of revolutionary movements in Latin America. The gradual and consistent radicalization of Camilo Torres, who moved from participation in the administration of agrarian reform to join the guerrilla, is a fascinating story in itself.

7655. Hernández de Ospina, Bertha. El tábano. Prólogo [por] Abelardo Forero Benavides. Bogotá, Instituto de Estudios Socio-Políticos, 1970. 426 p.

Compilation of articles which appeared in *La República* (1961-70) by prominent Conservative party leader, former Senator, and wife of former President Mario Ospina Pérez.

7656. Hornman, Wim. De rebel: roman over Camilo Torres. Haarlem, The Netherlands, J. H. Gottmer, 1968. 320 p.

Fictionalized account of the life and death of Camilo Torres the Colombian guerrillero-priest by a Dutch novelist. Action takes place in the South American republic of Conciencia. Book succeeds in capturing the revolutionary mood of Latin American youth today. [G. M. Dorn]

7657. Jaramillo, Francisco de Paula. Camilo: 8 ensayos apasionados. Bogotá, Editorial Revista Colombiana, 1970. 139 p. (Populibro, 35)

Essentially a eulogy of Camilo Torres by a personal friend and activist in the Colombian Christian Democratic Party. Contains some interesting anecdotes and remembrances.

7657a. Kerbusch, Ernst-J. Kolumbien vor dem Ende eines, "Regierungsystems auf Zeit" (Zeitschrift für Politik [Berlin] 19:2, 1972, p. 130-149)

Detailed analysis of Colombia's Frente Nacional and its effects on the party system. [W. Grabendorff]

7658. Lleras Restrepo, Carlos. Mensaje presidencial. t. 4, 1970; anexo primero, v. 2: discursos del doctor . . . sobre los programas y realizaciones de la Transformación Nacional. Bogotá, [1971]. 534 p.

Selected speeches and papers of Lleras, 1963-70, concerning national problems. A number of these pre-date his presidency, and presage the plans he offered after his 1966 election. On the whole a more than normally-useful volume of presidential papers.

7659. López, Francisco. Proceso al poder religioso en Colombia. Bogotá, Editorial Hispana, 1968. 245 p.

Polemical attack on the political role of the Roman Catholic Church in Colombia. Refers to the Church as the "fundamental pillar" of the status quo. Calls for complete separation of Church and state. Includes the complete text of the Concordat. [W. R. Wright]

7660. López Michelsen, Alfonso. Posdata a la alternación: intervenciones políticas de 1964 a 1970. Bogotá, Editorial Revista Colombiana, 1970. 458 p., plates (Populibro, 36)

33 speeches, letters, and interviews by leader of MRL and Minister of Foreign Relations in the Lleras Restrepo Administration. Prefaced with a lengthy description of party politics by López over the period 1964-70, documents evolution of MRL from opposition to the Officialist Liberal party in 1965-67 to its subsequent coalition with the dominant wing. Interesting here is speech by López in defense of coalition. Useful documents for study of party politics and government policymaking in Colombia.

7661. Losada, Rodrigo. Perfil socio-político típico del congresista colombiano. Bogotá, Univ. de los Andes, Depto. de Ciencia Política, 1972. 158 l., tables.

Based on survey data, analyzes attitudinal and demographic characteristics of Colombian legislators in comparison with other national elite groups (e.g., upper level bureaucrats) in 1958-66 time frame.

7662. ——— and **Miles W. Williams.** Colombia política: estadísticas, 1935-1970. Bogotá, Depto. Administrativo Nacional de Estadística (DANE), 1972. 398 p., tables (DANE/72/004—UANDES)

Reports findings from survey and voting studies by researchers at universities of Los Andes and del Valle on presidential elections of 1970 and electoral abstention in 1968 in Cali. Reprints time series voting data on congressional and presidential elections for period 1935-1970 collected and analyzed by DANE. Quite useful data source.

7663. Mutchler, David E. The Church as a political factor in Latin America, with particular reference to Colombia and Chile. N.Y., Praeger, 1971. 460 p., bibl. (Praeger special studies in international politics and public affairs)

Emphasizes internal disintegration of the Catholic Church in recent years in contrast to the Vallier thesis of reform and adaptation. Author makes useful theoretical and descriptive contribution, the latter enhanced by access to confidential materials in both countries. Provides particularly useful information on internal organization and decision-making of the Church.

7664. Parra Sandoval, Rodrigo ed. Dependencia externa y desarrollo político en Colombia. Bogotá, Imprenta Nacional, 1970. 222 p., tables.

Critiques concepts and frameworks of North American and European sociologists for failure to account sufficiently for conditions of external dependency which affect Colombian institutions and social processes. Offers a series of essays by sociologists of National Univ. which attempt to correct this deficiency.

7665. Pérez Ramírez, Gustavo. Planas: las contradicciones del capitalismo. Bogotá, Ediciones Tercer Mundo, 1971. 253 p., bibl., map, plates (Col. Tribuna libre, 6)

Condemns brutalization of Colombian Indians in Eastern plains area by white colonists and military units. Links brutality to values of capitalist-imperialism and external-internal dependency.

7666. Pinto, Luiz de Aguiar Costa. Clase, partido, y poder: el caso colombiano (ILARI/A, 22, oct. 1971, p. 96-122)

Contribution here is an interpretation of the origins of populism (*rojismo*) and its limitations as a political movement in the Colombian context.

7667. ———. Voto y cambio social: el caso colombiano en el contexto latinoamericano. Bogotá, Ediciones Tercer Mundo, 1971. 92 p.

Analyzes Colombian election of 1970 in theoretical context of limits of social modernization (institutional transformation) in a reconciliation regime. Examines hypothesis that Colombian democratic institutions maintain social and economic conditions which prevent attainment of viable democracy. Interesting contribution by leading Brazilian sociologist.

7668. Rama, Germán W. El sistema político colombiano: Frente Nacional y ANAPO (CPES/RPS, 7:19, sept./dic, 1970, p. 5-53)

Far-ranging interpretive study of consequences of the National Front with regard to politics and socioeconomic change since 1958. Analyzes class and occupational composition of the mass and elite elements of Rojas Pinilla's Anapista movement, and interprets ANAPO as an anti-oligarchical counter-elite.

7669. Schoultz, Lars. Urbanization and changing voting patterns: Colombia, 1946-1970 (APS/PSQ, 87:1, March 1972, p. 22-45, tables)

Reviews theory of urbanization and political change and posits two contrasting positions. Analyzes presidential vote, controlling for urban-rural variables. Concludes that "as urbanization has accelerated, the development of an increasingly large urban radical voting bloc has, as yet, failed to materialize. Nevertheless, it is clearly evident that radical candidates obtain a disproportionate amount of their electoral strength from urban areas." Quite competent analysis.

Taylor, Philip B., Jr. Thoughts on comparative effectiveness: leadership and the democratic left in Colombia and Venezuela. See item 7826.

7670. Villegas, Jorge. Petróleo colombiano, ganancia gringa. Bogotá, Ediciones El Tigre de Papel, 1971. 166 p., plates, tables.

Historical interpretation of Colombian oil policies over the period 1900-64. Quite critical of excessively generous concessions in oil matters by succeeding administrations, which are seen to be controlled by the "oligarchy." Polemical in style, but draws on diplomatic correspondence and other evidence to support the argument.

ECUADOR

7671. Atkins, George Pope. La Junta Militar Ecuatoriana 1963-1966; los militares latinoamericanos de "neuvo tipo" (ILARI/A, 24, abril 1972, p. 6-21)

Describes events leading to 1963 coup and evaluates subsequent performance of junta. Suggests that junta conforms neither to traditional notion of military guardian of status quo nor to revisionist notion of modernizing military.

7672. Crespi, Muriel. Changing power relations: the rise of peasant unions on the traditional Ecuadorian haciendas (CUA/AQ, 44:4, Oct. 1971, p. 223-240, bibl.)

Historical interpretation of causes (market forces, new political groups) and consequences (unionization, strikes) of changing role perceptions of highland peasantry. Suggests that "unions emerge as a new basis for communication between disparate powerholders when previous rules regulating the use of power cease to be operable."

Mena Soto, Joaquín. Enfoques universitarios de la dictadura militar al quinto velasquismo: hombres y proyecciones. See *HLAS 34:2596*.

PERU

7673. Alisky, Marvin. Peru's SINAMOS: governmental agency for coordinating reforms (Public Affairs Bulletin [Arizona State Univ., Institute of Public Administration, Tempe, Ariz.] 11:1, 1972, p. 1-4)

Describes SINAMOS (Sistema Nacional de Apoyo a la Movilización Social), its position in the reform-oriented bureaucracy and wide variety of its activities. Useful fact-sheet. [P. B. Taylor, Jr.]

7674. Andrews, Frank M. and **George W. Phillips.** The squatters of Lima: who they are and what they want (JDA, 4:2, Jan. 1970, p. 211-223, table)

Preliminary report of a 1967 study directed by Andrews, with 350 respondents in *barriada* households providing useful data. Briefly outlines schedule and offers data as to needs and expectations of this sample of city's slum population. [P. B. Taylor, Jr.]

7675. Astiz, Carlos Alberto. La Iglesia Católica en la política: el caso peruano. Traducción por Graziella Corvalán. Asunción, Centro Paraguayo de Estudios Sociológicos, 1971. 16 p., tables (Col. De reimpresiones, 36)

Descriptive note on reformist tendencies in the Peruvian Church and problems of Church adjustment to competing secular ideologies and political groups. Suggests that basis of reformist ideology exists in a reinterpretation of existing Papal encyclicals. Also published by *Revista Paraguaya de Sociología* (Asunción, 8:20, enero/abril 1971, p. 101-114, tables).

7676. ———. The Peruvian military: achievement orientation, training, and political tendencies (UU/WPQ, 25:4, Dec. 1972, p. 667-685, tables)

Questions applicability of North American concept of achievement in relation to officer corps. Notes disproportionate weight assigned to conduct (obedience) over academics in officer training and explores implications of this on political role of military. Useful clarification of an important assumption.

7677. Baines, John M. Revolution in Peru: Mariátegui and the myth. Introduction by Juan Mejía Baca. University, Ala.; The Univ. of Alabama Press *for the* Latin American Studies Program, 1972. 206 p., bibl., illus.

Integrates biographical data, intellectual history, and political analysis in interpreting the seminal theorist, José Carlos Mariátegui. Contains chapters on *Amauta, Siete ensayos* (see *HLAS 34:2620-2621*), ideological and tactical conflicts within the Peruvian left during the 1920s. Useful bibliography on Mariátegui's writings.

7678. Bourque, Susan Carolyn. Cholification of the campesino: a study of three Peruvian peasant organizations in the process of societal change. Ithaca, N.Y., Cornell Univ., Latin American Studies Program, 1971. 286 p., bibl., map, tables (Dissertation series, 21)

Examines three peasant organizations as agents of political socialization and social mobilization. Compares measures of political efficacy of organized with unorganized peasant.

7679. Bourricaud, François. Los militares: ¿por qué y para qué? (ILARI/A, 16, abril 1970, p. 13-55)

Very long paper deals largely with Peru, where author finds data for an extended analysis, against a backdrop of detailed reporting of Peruvian politics. Occasionally compares Peru's armed forces to those of other Latin American countries. Concludes that the soldiers cannot control nor resolve national problems except under unique circumstances. [P. B. Taylor, Jr.]

7680. Castro Contreras, Jaime. Perú: implicancias políticas del conflicto bancario de 1964 (ILARI/A, 24, abril 1972, p. 67-100)

Analyzes leadership factions and strategies in the Peruvian Federation of Bank Employees within context of the general labor confederations, press, and political institutions. Skillfully executed case study which relates the bank conflict to general considerations of class fragmentation and value dissensus.

7681. Ceresole, Norberto. Perú o el nacimiento del sistema latinoamericano. B.A., Editorial Galerna, 1971. 397 p.

Develops thesis that: 1) Peruvian junta is indeed revolutionary, and 2) nationalist-military regimes constitute a viable institutional strategy of development for other Latin American nations. Interesting interpretation of Peruvian phenomenon from point of view of Argentina as an actor in the future inter-American system.

Chile [e] Perú: democracia, marxismo, militarismo. See item 7739.

Choy, Emilio and others. Lenín y Mariátegui. See *HLAS 34:2610*.

7682. Clinton, Richard Lee. APRA: an

appraisal (UM/JIAS, 12:2, April 1970, p. 280-297, tables)

Evaluates APRA's performance in terms of its 1926 maximum plan. Reinforces new orthodox, i.e., critical, interpretation of party and leader.

7683. Cordera, Rolando and **Salvador Hernández.** Recent developments in Peru: an interview with Aníbal Quijano (FRBNY/MR, 24:11, April 1973, p. 53-61)

"As a whole, the reformist measures of the military regime are laying the basis for a new capitalist structure in Peru." Updates author's previous critique of the regime, see item 7700.

Costa Villavicencio, Lázaro. Historia cronológica del Perú. See *HLAS 34:2611.*

Davies, Thomas M., Jr. The indigenismo of the Peruvian Aprista party: a reinterpretation. See *HLAS 34:2612.*

7684. Dew, Edward M. Politics of the altiplano. Austin, Tex., Univ. of Texas Press *for the* Institute of Latin American Studies, 1961. 216 p., bibl., maps (Latin American monographs, 16)

Analyzes politics in two cities in Puno dept., southern Peru, with emphasis on early and mid-1960's. In interpreting socioeconomic change in the region, suggests that altiplano may be viewed as a plural society, or one which ". . . consists in the coexistence of incompatible institutional systems. . . " Political conflict is structured by coexisting Indian and mestizo cultural systems. Describes dimensions of conflict (regional, class, cultural) with specific attention to development programs and agrarian reform. Useful case study in attempt to interrelate city and regional politics and with national and international systems and awareness of theoretical concerns.

7685. Einaudi, Luigi R. and **Alfred C. Stepan, III.** Latin American institutional development: changing military perspectives in Peru and Brazil. Santa Monica, Calif., Rand Corp., 1971. 132 p., tables (R-586-DOS)

Comparative analysis of military institutions in context of Peruvian and Brazilian societies. Bulk of policy-oriented essay deals with Peruvian case. Stepan reports interesting career data on Brazilian general officers. Both stress the transition of the military from role of political arbiter to that of policymaker, and both emphasize the socialization role of superior war colleges in that transition. Insightful contribution. For historian's comment, see *HLAS 34:2983a.*

7686. Fairlie Fuentes, Enrique. Grandes reportajes. Lima, n.p., 1970. 386 p., tables.

Interviews with leading Peruvian political figures, journalists, and novelists over period 1961-71, including President Velasco, Prime Minister Montagne, and Interior Minister Artola.

7687. Frías, Ismael. La revolución peruana y la vía socialista. Lima, Editorial Horizonte, 1970. 277 p.

Defense of the military regime as authentically revolutionary by a leading marxist activist.

7688. Furnish, Dale B. The hierarchy of Peruvian laws: context for law and development (AJCL, 19:1, Winter 1971, p. 91-120)

Descriptive overview of types of law and processes of rule adjudication in Peruvian political context. Essential reading for an understanding of policy implementation.

7689. Grayson, George W. Peru's revolutionary government (CUH, 64:378, Feb. 1973, p. 61-65, 87)

Summarizes recent reform policies and reviews present economic and political (foreign and domestic) conditions. Sympathetic treatment.

7690. Hobsbawm, Eric J. Peru: the peculiar "Revolution" (The New York Review of Books, 17:10, 16 Dec. 1971, p. 29-36, illus.)

Describes sources of support and opposition as well as recent public policies in an attempt to characterize the Peruvian regime. Balanced and perceptive.

7691. Jaquette, Jane S. The politics of development in Peru. Ithaca, N.Y., Cornell Univ., Latin American Studies Program, 1971. 276 p., bibl., tables (Dissertation series, 33)

Which model, coalition (pluralist) or clientelist (elitist), more usefully explains economic policy-making in Peru in 1960s? Establishing existence of oligarchy, which is central to author's position, is unsatisfactory (Payne's critique of concept, see *HLAS 31:7508,* is ignored). Nonetheless, thesis defines an interesting topic and develops it competently.

7692. ———. Revolution by fiat: the context of policy-making in Peru (UU/WPQ, 25:4, Dec. 1972, p. 648-666)

Succinct and insightful analysis of historical emergence and present policy orientations of the Peruvian regime. Reasons from process and content of recent policies to suggest that the junta is a "watershed event in Peruvian and Latin American history."

Kumm, Björn. Gerillans ansikte: Latinamerika i hunger och revolt. See item 7717.

7693. Listov, Vadim Vadimovich. Veter peremeny, Peru vybiraet put (The wind of change, Peru chooses a way). Moskva, Izdatel'stvo Mezhdunardnye Otnosheniia, 1971. 255 p., illus.

Report by *Pravda* correspondent of his visit to Peru in 1971 to study changes since the Velasco military takeover of 1968. Generally sympathetic treatment envisions Peruvian junta as first of a new kind of Latin American military, technically trained and imbued with "progressive tendencies" which are anti-US "imperialism," and interested in land reform. [T. S. Cheston]

7694. Matos Mar, José and **Rogger Ravines.** Bibliografía peruana de ciencias sociales: 1957-1969. Lima, Instituto de Estudios Peruanos [and] Campodónico *ediciones,* 1971. 453 p.

Cites some 2,000 items published in Peru from various social science fields including sociology, economics, education, anthropology, and government. Provides information on Peruvian research institutions, social

7695. ———— and others. Dominación y cambios en el Perú rural: la micro-región del Valle de Chancay. Lima, Instituto de Estudios Peruanos, 1969. 377 p., bibl., illus., plates.

Comparative studies of six villages in Chancay Valley organized around theme of internal domination and unbalanced development. Contents:
José Matos Mar "El Pluralismo y la Dominación en la Sociedad Peruana: una Perspectiva Configuracional" p. 23-59
Julio Cotler "Actuales Pautas de Cambio en la Sociedad Rural del Perú" p. 60-79
Lawrence K. Williams "Algunos Correlatos Sicosociales de los Sistemas de Dominación" p. 80-94
J. Oscar Alers "Procesos de Desarrollo Socio-Económico: un Modelo Analítico" p. 95-114
José Matos Mar "Micro-Región y Pluralismo" p. 115-134
José Matos Mar; Fernando Fuenzalida V.; and William F. Whyte "Dimensión Diacrónica del Pluralismo" p. 135-222
Julio Cotler "Alternativas de Cambio en Dos Haciendas Algodoneras" p. 223-241
J. Oscar Alers "Pasos al Desarrollo en Dos Comunidades Costeñas" p. 242-284
Giorgio Alberti and Fernando Fuenzalida V. "Pluralismo, Dominación y Personalidad" p. 285-325
William F. Whyte "Consideraciones Generales Sobre una Teoría de los Procesos Sociales" p. 326-344
William F. Whyte "Hacia una Nueva Metodología para los Estudios de Campo" p. 345-360.

7696. Moretić, Yerko. José Carlos Mariátegui: su vida e ideario, su concepción del realismo. Santiago, Ediciones de la Univ. Técnica del Estado, 1970. 269 p., bibl.

Originally submitted as a doctoral dissertation for Caroline Univ., Prague. Perspective is one of Mariátegui's contributions to marxist thought and focus is on concept of realism in interpreting art and literature.

7697. North, Lisa. Orígenes y crecimiento del partido aprista y el cambio socioeconómico en el Perú. Translated by Mario Dos Santos (IDES/DE, 10:38, julio/sept. 1970, p. 163-214, tables)

What relationships obtain between socioeconomic change (concentration of land, foreign investment, migration) and support for radical parties (APRA)? Employs voting, census, and economic data in comparative analysis of departments giving high and low support to APRA in 1932 and 1963. Explores interesting theoretical question with methodological skill.

7698. Paulston, Rolland G. Sociocultural constraints on education development in Peru (JDA, 5:3, April 1971, p. 401-415, tables)

Does universal education bring about greater upward mobility and development for both individuals and nation states in search of modernization? The article tests hypotheses to this effect. [P. B. Taylor, Jr.]

7699. Pratt, Raymond B. Community political organization and lower class politization in two Latin American cities (JDA, 5:4, July 1971, p. 523-542, tables)

Based on 1965 survey data on four lower class urban settlements in Lima and Santiago, reports, among other findings, that "in terms of general organizational participation, political activism increased with the number of memberships." Accounts for findings partially in terms of social and political characteristics of Peruvian and Chilean systems.

————. Parties, neighborhood associations, and the politicization of the urban poor in Latin America: an exploratory analysis. See item 7775.

7700. Quijano, Aníbal. Nationalism and capitalism in Peru: a study in neo-imperialism. Translated by Helen R. Lane. N.Y., Monthly Review Press, 1971. 122 p., tables.

While the ruling Junta is acting to break up "traditional" imperialism (US dominance in an extractive, enclave economy), it is facilitating the creation of neo-imperialism (multiple foreign and domestic participation in an urban industrial economy). Reviews recent innovations in economic policy from this perspective. Quite interesting marxist critique of the Peruvian regime.

Ribeiro, Darcy. Nuevos caminos de la Revolución Latinoamericana. See item 7778.

7700a. Sonntag, Heinz Rudolf, ed. Der Fall Peru: 'Nasserismus' in Lateinamerika zur Überwindung der Unterentwicklung? Wuppertal, FRG, Hammer, 1971. 187 p.

Consists mainly of Julio Cotler's famous analysis "Political Crisis and Military Populism in Peru" (see HLAS 33:8010). Also offers translation of 1969 agrarian reform law and president Velasco's message to the nation that year. Editor introduction is a rather balanced overview of Peru's nationalist government. [W. Grabendorff]

7701. Stephens, Richard H. Wealth and power in Peru. With an introduction by Harold D. Lasswell. Metuchen, N.J., The Scarecrow Press, 1971. 219 p., bibl.

Posits existence of historical landed elite and reasons from this to nature of politics in Peru. Relies principally on impressions drawn from Peruvian participants in several seminars held at the Brookings Institution (Washington). Rather lacking in demonstrating existence of elite and channels of political influence.

7702. Trias, Vivian. Perú: fuerzas armadas y revolución. Montevideo, Ediciones de la Banda Oriental, 1971. 175 p. (Col. Las voces libres, 5)

Rather wide-ranging essay on Peruvian history, economics, politics, and ideology, which attempts to explain emergence of nationalist military. In a marxist framework, compares Peruvian process with other socialist countries and suggests that Peruvian military may carry out "original socialist accumulation" as a stage of socialist revolution.

7703. Tullis, F. LaMond. Disquietude in Central Peru or how peasants may overcome a rigid environment and introduce themselves into the national, economic, political and social fabric of their country (in Tullis, F.

LaMond ed. Politics and social change in Third World countries. N.Y., John Wiley and Sons, 1973, p. 227-307, bibl.)

Compares process of peasant politicization and agrarian reform in two villages during the 1960s. Attempts to move from case studies to model to explain origin and intensity of new peasant social forces. Interesting interplay between cases and middle-range theory.

7704. United States. Comptroller General. Allegations of mismanagement of a Peruvian highway project financed with United States assistance funds; Agency for International Development, Export-Import Bank, Department of Transportation: Comptroller General's report to the Honorable William Proxmire, United States Senate. Washington, General Accounting Office, 1971. 81 p., maps, plates, tables (B-172661)

Report on GAO investigation of Tarapopo road construction project in Peru, 1967-70. Useful case study of problems in implementation of assistance programs.

7705. Villanueva, Víctor. El CAEM [Centro de Altos Estudios Militares] y la revolución de la Fuerza Armada. Lima, Instituto de Estudios Peruanos [and] Campodónico*ediciones*, 1972. 249 p., bibl.

Chapters on historical background of CAEM, development of military thinking and reflections of this in Center's curricula, and impact of Center on Peruvian politics and development policy. Data on enrollment, curricula, lecture topics, faculty, and graduates in appendices. Important contribution by leading student of the Peruvian military.

7706. Visser, J. D. Peru 150 jaar onafhankelikl (NGIZ/IS, 25:6, maart 1971, p. 602-615)

The integration of the Peruvian Indian into a modern industrial society remains unresolved in 150 years of country's existence. New military government is concerned with this problem and no longer serves as the protector of the oligarchy, which today is made up chiefly of sugar and cotton plantation owners in the coastal area, instead of the highland landowners of the past. The military policy is to develop and modernize the country without violence or repression and without adhering to either the capitalist or communist models. One of their compromises in this regard has been to decree that basic industries in foreign hands must sell out the majority of their holdings to Peruvians. [H. J. Hoyer]

7707. Wils, F. C. M. Peru's militaire revolutionaire junta, radicaal nieuwe variant van de militaire factor in Latijns-Amerika (NGIZ/IS, 25:21, dec. 1971, p. 2025-2039)

Characterizes general trends of public policy in Peru and discusses political problems (domestic and international) in strategy's implementation.

BOLIVIA

7708. Alvarado, Julio. El balance de la experiencia socialista boliviana, 1952-1964: ensayo sobre la política económica contemporánea de Bolivia. Madrid, Artes Gráficas y Ediciones, 1969. 462 p., tables.

Detailed indictment of MNR's mismanagement of Bolivian economy and politics during 1952-64. Program by program, author (exiled since 1951) systematically amasses evidence of failure. Plausibly argued with substantial documentation.

7709. Añez Pedraza, David and others. La dramática lucha por los hidrocarburos. Cochabamba, Bol., Univ. Mayor de San Simón, Editorial Universitaria, 1971. 174 p., plates.

Speeches and documents from a university forum on petroleum policy held in Cochabamba in aftermath of nationalization of Bolivian Gulf Oil Company. Arguments advanced against compensation for the expropriation.

7710. Antezana E., Luis. La reforma agraria campesina en Bolivia: 1956-1960 (UNAM/RMS, 31:2, abril/junio 1969, p. 245-321, tables)

Based on a two-volume study, summarizes history of agrarian reform in Bolivia from mid 19th century to 1960. More emphasis on political and military events than policy analysis, although data on agricultural production are provided in an appendix. For geographer's annotation, see *HLAS 33:5234*.

7711. ———. La táctica nacionalista en la Revolución boliviana. La Paz, Editora Popular, 1969. 56 p.

Journalistic critique of Bolivian leftist parties (Bolivian Communist Party, Revolutionary Leftist Party) for failure to support sufficiently what author perceives as democratic and nationalist government which came to power in Sept. 1969.

Barnes de Marshall, Katherine. Cabildos, corregimientos y sindicatos de Bolivia después de 1952. See item 1348.

7712. Bedregal, Guillermo. Los militares en Bolivia: ensayo de interpretación sociológica. La Paz, Editorial Los Amigos del Libro, 1971. 176 p., bibl.

Bulk of work is an historical-sociological discussion of the period 1904-64, which is rather more objective and analytical than latter chapters, which deal with military interventions since 1964.

7713. Camacho Peña, Alfonso. Los militares en la política boliviana (ILARI/A, 22, oct. 1971, p. 41-95, bibl.)

Periodizes Bolivian history from 1825 to 1970 in terms of military and civilian ascendancy. Historical description for most part, but includes insights on international factors and recruitment and socialization of military officers in explanation sketches of military behavior, particularly since 1952. Useful interpretive essay.

7714. Diarios de Bolivia: diarios de campaña de compañeros del Che no divulgados hasta ahora en nuestro idioma. Por: Rolando, Pombo, Braulio. B.A., Ediciones Fuerte, 1971. 162 p.

Pirate edition of the previous publication of these diaries by Stein and Day, see *HLAS* 33:7719.

7715. Galeano, Eduardo. Siete imágenes de Bolivia. Caracas, Fondo Editorial Salvador de la Plaza, 1971. 91 p. (Cuadernos Rocinante, 9)

Extends Leninist perspective in a discussion of economic colonialism and dependency in Bolivia. Applies argument in a rather vivid journalistic style to problems of foreign control over Bolivian oil, iron, and tin.

7716. Justo, Liborio. Bolivia: la revolución derrotada; del Tahuantisuyu a la insurrección de abril de 1952 y las masacres de mayo y septiembre de 1965—raíz, proceso y autopsia de la primera revolución proletaria de América Latina. 2. ed. B.A., Juárez Editor, 1971. 321 p.

First published in 1967, a marxist history of Bolivia from pre-columbian times to 1971. Depicts Paz Estensorro and MNR as anti-revolutionary. Anti-Trotskyist theme throughout.

7717. Kumm, Björn. Gerillans ansikte: Latinamerika i hunger och revolt. Stockholm, Rabén & Sjögren, 1968. 179 p. (TEMA serien)

Discusses political situation in Bolivia and Peru, both of which were almost feudal until recently. Traces 1952 revolution in Bolivia and its aftermath and explains lack of a revolution in Peru. Based on a thorough knowledge of region. [R. V. Shaw]

7718. Malloy, James M. Bolivia: the uncompleted revolution. Pittsburgh, Pa., Univ. of Pittsburgh Press, 1970. 396 p., plate.

Analyzes Bolivia as case study of revolution from latter 19th century to 1960 "in terms of the interaction among incumbent elites, counter-elites and those sectors of the society which are actively drawn into the central conflict (mobilizable publics)." Develops thesis that Bolivia is an unfinished revolution in sense that MNR was unable to construct a new regime capable of generating economic development and satisfying demands of mobilized groups. Useful country study interestingly interwoven into general theories of revolution.

7719. ———. El MNR [i.e., Movimiento Nacional Revolucionario] boliviano: estudio de un movimiento popular nacionalista en América Latina (IBEAS/EA, 1:1, 1970, p. 57-92)

Analyzes MNR and Revolution of 1952 in framework of national popular movements advanced by Torcuato Di Tella. Demonstrates how circumstances which may bring a change-oriented elite to power may also hinder its ability to govern.

7720. ——— and Richard S. Thorn eds. Beyond the revolution: Bolivia since 1952. Pittsburgh, Pa., Univ. of Pittsburgh Press, 1971. 402 p., tables.

Product of an interdisciplinary seminar on Bolivia undertaken at Univ. of Pittsburgh in 1966. Includes: Carter Goodrich "Bolivia in Time of Revolution" p. 3-24

Herbert S. Klein "Prelude to the Revolution" p. 25-51
Cole Blasier "The United States and the Revolution" p. 53-109
James M. Malloy "Revolutionary Politics" p. 111-156
Richard S. Thorn "The Economic Transformation" p. 157-216
James W. Wilkie "Public Expenditure Since 1952" p. 217-231
William E. Carter "Revolution and the Agrarian Sector" p. 233-268
Madeline Barbara Leons and William Leons "Land Reform and Economic Change in the Yungas" p. 269-299
Melvin Burke "Land Reform in the Lake Titicaca Region" p. 301-339
Murdo J. MacLeod "The Bolivian Novel, the Chaco War, and the Revolution" p. 341-365.

7721. Peña Bravo, Raúl. Hechos y dichos del General Barrientos. n.p., Bol., n.p., 1971. 168 p.

Series of vignettes critical of the former Bolivian president. Whether these ironic commentaries on Barrientos' public and private life are accurate is not known. They constitute, however, an interesting psychological profile and an insight into Bolivian politics.

7722. Ponce García, Jaime. El sindicalismo boliviano: resumen histórico y perspectivas actuales (IBEAS/EA, 1:1, 1970, p. 28-56)

Narrative sketch which describes principal organizations and ideologies of labor groups and patterns of relations with governments over the period 1854-1968.

7723. Romero Pittari, Salvador. Bolivia: sindicalismo campesino y partidos políticos (ILARI/A, 23, enero 1972, p. 62-100)

Reports on 1969 survey of peasants in Chochabamba. Attempts to interrelate information on and attitudes toward parties and peasant organizations with patterns of participation. Nature of sample not clearly indicated, but results interestingly developed.

7724. Russe, Jean. Bolivia 1970. Potosí, Bol., Editorial Universitaria, 1970. 115 p.

Strong polemical attack on imperialistic (CIA) subversion and an account of labor, student, and military activities from leftist point of view.

7725. Sandoval Rodríguez, Isaac. Nacionalismo en Bolivia: ensayo histórico-político. La Paz, Cooperativa de Artes Gráficas E. Burillo, 1970. 277 p., bibl.

Views nationalism historically in terms of strengthening the state vis-à-vis internal and external economic interests. Straightforward narrative account of independence movements, Chaco War, MNR accession in 1952, and 1964 "counterrevolution." Apparently well researched, with useful details on cabinets and major personalities.

7726. Vázquez-Viaña, Humberto. Acerca de la publicación de *Mi campaña junto al Che* atribuída a Inti Peredo. La Paz, n.p., 1971. 32 p.

An ELN militant attempts to refute authenticity of a memoir attributed to Guido Alvaro Peredo Leigue, "Inti" (see *HLAS* 33:7707). Bases the attack on portrayal of Inti's thought and writing style, and suggests that the counterfeiters are concerned with sowing discord in the Bolivian left and profiting from a tenuous association with Che and Inti.

CHILE

7727. Agor, Weston H. The Chilean Senate: internal distribution of influence. Austin, Tex., Univ. of Texas Press, Institute of Latin American Studies, 1971. 206 p., bibl., tables (Latin American monograph series, 23)

Reports extensive data (interviews with almost all senators and unpublished legislative data) on internal structures and processes of Chilean Senate largely over period 1965-69. Substantial treatment of committees, with some attention to party and Senate leadership. Useful institutional analysis.

7728. Aguilar, Luis E. Tradiciones políticas y perspectivas (USIA/PI, 20:3, mayo/junio 1971, p. 14-21)

Brings an historical perspective to a consideration of possible future directions for the Allende regime. Points to a long democratic tradition and pluralism (or fragmentation) in the marxist left as factors supporting the continuance of political democracy. Concludes that forces within the governing coalition and a possible confrontation with the MIR, will soon force a basic choice of strategy upon Allende.

7729. Allemann, Fritz René. Chile: Revolution auf dem Prüfstand (WM, März 1972, p. 36-46, plates)

Short but balanced analysis of political, social and economic problems facing the Allende regime. Despite grounds for optimism during initial two years, author contends that government will face increasing difficulties, because of both the constitutional framework within which it must operate as well as army's role in maintaining this framework. [H. J. Hoyer]

7730. Allende Gossens, Salvador. Nuestro camino al socialismo: la vía chilena. Selección de Joan E. Garcés. B.A., Editorial ECASA, 1971. 185 p. (Ediciones Papiro: Col. Política)

Contains inaugural address, messages to Congress, and other speeches over the period Nov. 1970 to May 1971. Useful documents for assessing Allende's foreign and domestic policies during his first months in office.

7731. ———. Speech delivered by Dr. . . . . President of the Republic of Chile before the General Assembly of the United Nations, December 4, 1972. Washington, Embassy of Chile in the United States, 1972. 39 p., illus.

Text of speech. In some respects a formalization of Chilean allegations against the US government, as well as a statement of Chilean views on other international questions. [P. B. Taylor, Jr.]

7732. ——— and others. El pensamiento económico del Gobierno de Allende. Santiago, Editorial Universitaria, 1971. 354 p., maps, tables.

Collection of 28 statements and documents by seven members of the Allende government and two organizations. Documentary record of the planning and intentions of the Allende government and its supporting coalition. 13 chapters deal with all aspects of domestic and foreign economic problems, popular participation in formulating policy in the future, and development.

7732a. Ammon, Alf and **Heino Froehling.** Die Christliche Demokratie Chiles: die Spaltung der Christdemokratischen Partei 1969. Bonn, FRG, Neue Gesellschaft, 1971. 159 p., bibl.

In pt. 1 Alf Ammon deals with organizational development of the Christian Democratic Party in Chile as well as with this movement's ideological foundations. Also includes selection of various party declarations in Spanish and German. Heino Froehling offers a rather short explanation of the party's split in 1969. [W. Grabendorff]

7733. Angell, Alan. Politics and labour movement in Chile. London, Oxford Univ. Press, 1972. 289 p.

Outlines the historical development of Chilean labor, the size and structure of the movement, and its role in the industrial relations system. Second part of book examines efforts of Socialists, Communists, Christian-Democrats, and Radical parties to organize and co-opt the labor movement. Net result has been that labor as a power contender is stronger in Chile than most Latin American countries, which is in turn correlated with Chile's election preference for President Salvador Allende in 1970. [W. H. Agor]

7734. ———. Problems in Allende's Chile (CUH, 64:378, Feb. 1973, p. 57-60, 86)

Emphasizes interrelations between short-run economic difficulties (inflation, balance of payments) and their political repercussions.

7735. Barría S., Jorge. Historia de la CUT [Central Unica de Trabajadores]. Santiago, Ediciones Prensa Latina, 1971. 156 p. (Col. Doctrinas Sociales)

Labor activist and academic specialist on labor problems, the author here presents first half of a longer work on the CUT. Essentially a history, this volume discusses period 1946-70, with the period 1946-52 covered sketchily. [P. B. Taylor, Jr.]

7735a. Boris, Dieter; Elisabeth Boris; and **Wolfgang Ehrhardt.** Chile auf dem Weg zum Sozialismus. Köln, FRG, Pahl-Rugenstein Verlag, 1971. 296 p., tables.

Important study of Chile's historical and socio-economic development from Marxist viewpoint. Presentation of political participation during Frei period is not entirely convincing and treatment of the first year of the Allende government seems rather euphorical. [W. Grabendorff]

Borón, Atilio Alberto. El estudio de la movilización política en América Latina: la movilización electoral en la Argentina y Chile. See item 7924.

7736. ———. Movilización política y crisis política en Chile: 1920-1970 (ILARI/A, 20, abril 1971, p. 41-69, tables)

Closely reasoned analysis interweaving census, survey, and electoral data since 1912 to account for quantitative increases as well as a leftward shift in voting patterns. Raises possibility that increased electoral participation, further extended by 1970 reforms, may lead to political crisis.

7737. Brown, Marion R. Agricultural "extension" in Chile: a study of institutional transplant (JDA, 4:2, Jan. 1970, p. 197-210, table)

Short study of methods and programs designed to improve technical knowledge and processes of Chilean farmers and farm workers. Examines transplant of US "extension" practices and philosophy to Chile together with its modification under different prevailing circumstances. Offers some details of both institutions and practices. [P. B. Taylor, Jr.]

7738. Canihuante, Gustavo. La revolución chilena. México, Editorial Diógenes, 1972. 278 p.

Discusses origins and significance of Allende regime in marxist-leninist context. Describes regime response to social, economic, and political problems encountered in 1971. Sympathetic interpretation by a self-styled "independent-leftist", yet one which confronts major questions in a serious fashion.

Cerda, Carlos. El leninismo y la victoria popular. See item 7382.

7739. Chile [e] Perú: democracia, marxismo, militarismo. Salvador, Bra., Centro de Estudos e Ação Social, 1971. 92 p., tables (Cadernos do CEAS, 13)

Overview description of Chilean politics, position of Catholic Church, and evaluation of policies pursued in first eight months of Allende administration. Analyzes separately nature of Peruvian junta and reform policies since 1968.

7740. Corvalán Lepe, Luis. Camino de victoria. Santiago, Sociedad Impresora Horizonte, 1971. 427 p., plate.

Speeches, interviews, and essays by General Secretary of the Chilean Communist Party over period 1961-71. Deals largely with Chilean domestic politics.

7741. Debray, Régis. The Chilean revolution: conversations with Allende. Postscript by Salvador Allende. Translated by Ben Brewster and others. N.Y., Vintage, 1971. 201 p., illus.

In lengthy introduction, Debray attempts to reconcile the Chilean case with marxism-leninism. Explores problems of ideology and statecraft with Chile's marxist president in skillful and sympathetic interviews. Extensive notes make the *Conversations* intelligible to non-specialists.

7742. ———. Entretiens avec Allende sur la situation au Chili. Paris, François Maspéro, 1971. 176 p. (Cahiers libres, 202)

French translation from the Spanish edition. For English version, see item 7741.

Delgado, Oscar. La organización de los campesinos y el sistema político. See item 7644.

7743. Esser, Klaus. Chile en el camino hacia el socialismo (ZPKW/A, 7:2, 2. semester 1971, p. 151-159)

Descriptive overview of economic development policies pursued by the Alessandri, Frei, and Allende administrations.

7743a. Durch freie Wahlen zum Sozialismus oder Chile Weg aus der Armut. Reinbek, FRG, Rororo, 1972. 158 p.

Probably the best analysis of Chile's political development published in German so far. Author traces Chile's economical problems and her dependency from abroad througout her history. He offers a very balanced view of the Revolution in Liberty and analyzes not only the domestic implications of the socialist alternative but also the effect on Chile's foreign policy. [W. Grabendoroff]

7744. Evangelio, política y socialismos. Santiago, Conferencia Episcopal de Chile, 1971. 91 p. (Documento de trabajo)

Report of the Plenary Assembly of Chilean Bishops held in April 1971. Attempts to define a Christian humanist position for Catholics vis-à-vis theories of marxism and socialism and the concrete political setting of Chile at the outset of the Allende government. Valuable document.

7745. Evans de la Cuadra, Enrique. Relación de la Constitución Política de la República de Chile. Santiago, Editorial Jurídica de Chile, 1970? 193 p.

Textual analysis of and commentary on Constitution of 1925 and subsequent reforms. Intended as a textbook, but useful as comprehensible introduction to Chilean constitutional law.

Foxley, Alejandro and others. Chile: búsqueda de un nuevo socialismo. See *HLAS 34:2919*.

7746. Francis, Michael J. and **Hernán Vera-Godoy.** Chile: Christian Democracy to Marxism (UND/RP, 33:3, July 1971, p. 323-341)

Perceptive analysis of candidates, issues, and voting of 1970 presidential elections. Evaluates various explanations of electoral outcome and suggests alternative scenarios for the Allende administration.

7747. Friedman, Bruno. Science in Chile's development programme (UNESCO/I, 22:1/2, Jan./June 1972, p. 29-41)

In interview, President Allende discusses role of science, technology, and scientists in Chilean development policy.

7748. Furnish, Dale B. Chilean antitrust law (The American Journal of Comparative Law [Berkeley, Calif.] 19:3, Summer 1971, p. 464-488)

Sketches post-1959 decline of antitrust law in the context of increased state control over economy. Useful contribution to literature on policy implementation.

7749. Galjart, B. F. Chili na Frei (NGIZ/IS, 25:6, maart 1971. p. 574-587)

Under President Eduardo Frei, agricultural reform definitely changed the Chilean countryside. Frei followed a middle-of-the-road policy towards foreign capital, which was encouraged, while at the same time conducting a "chileanization" of the copper mines which brought a 51 percent government ownership.

Growing inflation cost Frei part of his following. Under President Salvador Allende rapid nationalization of copper mines and banks was foreseen. Opposition of Christian Democrats remained strong in 1971. Author concludes that a further turn to the left will probably lead to serious economic difficulties. [H. J. Hoyer]

Gall, Norman. The agrarian revolt in Cautín. See item 1407.

7750. Garcés, Joan E. 1970 [i.e., Mil novecientos setenta]: la pugna política por la presidencia en Chile. Santiago, Editorial Universitaria, 1971. 127 p., tables (Col. Imagen de Chile, 13)

Two essays on party and voting behavior during 1960s with competent empirical analysis. Third essay explores symbolic patterns in campaign propaganda of principal candidates in 1969.

7751. García-Goyena, Juan. Chile, una experiencia nueva (CJ/RF, 879, abril 1971, p. 371-382)

Balanced journalistic assessment of Allende's first weeks in office.

7752. Gouré, León and Jaime Suchlicki. The Allende regime: actions and reactions (USIA/PC, 20:3, May/June 1971, p. 49-61)

Describes events leading up to the UP (Unidad Popular) electoral victory of 1970 and analyzes the reactions of China and the USSR. For a Spanish version of this article, see "El Gobierno de Allende: Acciones y Reacciones," in *Problemas Internacionales* (USIA, Washington, 20:3, mayo/junio 1971, p. 1-13).

7753. Gray, Richard B. and Frederick R. Kirwin. Presidential succession in Chile: 1817-1966 (UM/JIAS, 11:1, Jan. 1969, p. 144-159, bibl., tables)

Concise but very useful listing of all Presidents of Chile through Eduardo Frei. Obviously a reference work, not an analysis. [P. B. Taylor, Jr.]

Hamburg, Roger P. Soviet foreign policy, the Church, the Christian Democrats, and Chile. See item 8203.

7754. Holmberg, Mats. "Revolution med piroger och vin:" Ett reportage fran Salvador Allendes Chile. Stockholm, Bokförlaget PAN/Norstedts, 1971. 94 p.

Author is Latin American correspondent for the Swedish *Expressen*. He lived in Santiago de Chile during Aug. 1970-April 1971. This account of the Chilean "revolution" with "*empanadas* and wine" is based on his personal experiences. Narrative presents the revolution in a positive light although opponents' views are not neglected. [R. V. Shaw]

7755. Horne, Alistair. Commandante Pepe: letter from Chile (ENCOUNT, 37:1, July 1971, p. 33-40, illus.)

Reports interview with young *MIRista* (Movement of the Revolutionary Left) militant involved in land invasions in highland Chile. Interesting insights on complexity of first months of Allende administration.

7756. Imas Urrea, Jorge Renato. La social democracia. Santiago, Editorial Jurídica de Chile, 1969. 77 p.

General historical-theoretical essay on origins of democratic socialism and its points of contrast to orthodox marxism.

Inkeles, Alex. Participant citizenship in six developing countries. See item 7958.

7757. Jobet, Julio César. El Partido Socialista de Chile. t. 1/2. Santiago, Ediciones Prensa Latinoamericana, 1971. 2 v. (220, 268 p.) bibl. (Col. Doctrinas sociales)

Traces development of Chilean Socialist Party from origins in 1932 to electoral victory of Popular Unity in 1970. Author is PS activist and thus much of the effort is a defense and explanation of the PS and marxism. Provides useful detail on PS and contemporary Chilean politics.

Jordan, David C. Marxism in Chile: an interim view of its implications for U.S. Latin American policy. See item 8206.

7758. Joxe, Alain. Las fuerzas armadas en el sistema político chileno. Santiago, Editorial Universitaria, 1970. 176 p., tables (Col. Imagen de Chile, 8)

Critiques contributions by North American scholars on Latin American military and emphasizes economic dependency, class linkages, and professionalization of Chilean military to account for the nature of military participation in politics in that country. Provides comparative data on military expenditures in Chile and other Latin American nations as well as US military aid during 1960s. Solid interpretive contribution on comparative study of military in Latin America.

7759. Kaufman, Robert R. The politics of land reform in Chile, 1950-1970: public policy, political institutions, and social change. Cambridge, Mass., Harvard Univ. Press, 1972. 321 p., table.

Analyzes Chilean politics, particularly party and coalition behavior, from point of view of agrarian reform issue. Treatment of policy definition and adaptation by party leaders and followers is subtle and insightful. Author claims only a case study, but one finds here a satisfying account of an important political process. Solid contribution.

7760. Korteweg, P. G. J. Chili, Zuid Amerika's grote vraagteken (NGIZ/IS, 25:16, sept. 1971, p. 1541-1551)

Surveys thoughts from item 7741 where Allende advocates legal path to socialism. Nationalization in Chile, however, means a totally different thing from Venezuela's "capitalistic" nationalization. In 1973 elections will be held for parliament and author doubts whether Allende's "Unidad Popular" will have achieved enough progress to remain as the largest coalition. [H. J. Hoyer]

7761. Labarca Goddard, Eduardo. Chile al rojo: reportaje a una revolución que nace. Santiago, Ediciones de la Univ. Técnica del Estado, 1971. 398 p.

Detailed journalistic narrative of events surrounding elections of 1970 (assassination of Schneider, campaign violence, secret pacts and negotiations), which led to victory of Popular Front candidate Salvador Allende.

7762. Latinskaía Amerika. Akademia Nauk SSSR, Institut Latinskoi Ameriki (USSR Academy of Sciences, Latin American Institute). No. 2, March/April 1972- . Moskva.

Entire issue devoted to Chile under the Allende government. More interesting articles are: M. S. Nikitin, I. K. Shepemet'ev "Revoliutsiia i Problemy Ekonomicheskogo Razvitiia" (The Revolution and Problems of Economic Development) and I. N. Zorina "Narodnoe Edinstvo i Burzhyaznaia Demokratiia" (The Popular Front and the Bourgeois Democracy). [T. S. Cheston]

7763. Lechner, Norbert. La democracia en Chile. B.A., Ediciones Signos, 1970. 173 p., bibl., tables.

Translation of 1969 doctoral dissertation presented at Freidburg im Breisgau, FRG. Couched in terms of domination-dependency (drawing on André Gunder Frank), describes Chilean political history since independence in terms of class struggle in a process of gradual democratization. Well grounded in European, North American and Latin American literature.

7764. Lehmann, David. Peasant consciousness and agrarian reform in Chile (AES, 13:2, 1972, p. 296-325, table)

Probes interrelations among changes in structural (e.g., unionization) and political (e.g., party affiliation) factors and peasant perceptions of class, work, and society. Based on sample of 60 peasants in southern Chile, eschews standardized questionnaire for more flexible search for organizing constructs. Innovative and suggestive.

7765. ———. Political incorporation versus political stability: the case of the Chilean agrarian reform, 1965-70 (JDS, 7:4, July 1971, p. 365-395)

Sees even the small amount of land redistribution carried out under the Frei government as politically destabilizing; more change would have led more swiftly to greater instability. [B. Herrick]

7766. McCoy, Terry L. La reforma agraria chilena: un análisis político del cambio estructural (CLAPCS/AL, 13:2/3, abril/sept. 1970, p. 30-50, table)

Analyzes economic factors (e.g., inflation, land tenure patterns) as constraints on political decision-making in agrarian reform. Formulates generalizations based on Chilean case.

7767. MacHale, Tomas P. *ed.* Chile: a critical survey. Santiago, Institute of General Studies, 1972. 324 p., tables.

16 essays on politics, economics, Church, agriculture, education, and armed forces, by Chilean professionals and intellectuals critical of marxism and the Allende government.

7767a. Münster, Arno. Chile: friedlicher Weg? Historischer Bericht und politische Analyse. Berlin, FRG, Wagenbach, 1972. 198 p., bibl.

Author views Chile's history as a permanent class struggle furthered by foreign interventions. He judges the Chilean road to socialism as a constant interaction of reformist and revolutionary processes. [W. Grabendorff]

Mutchler, David E. The Church as a political factor in Latin America, with particular reference to Colombia and Chile. See item 7663.

7767b. Nohlen, Dieter. Chile: das sozialistische Experiment. Hamburg, FRG, Hoffmann und Campe, 1973. 432 p., bibl, tables.

Specialist on parliamentary problems in Latin America, author offers detailed analysis covering political process and socio-economic change in Chile, the "revolution in liberty" of Eduardo Frei, the significance of the 1970 elections and Allende's socialist experiment. His great wealth of information cannot hide his partisanship for the Christian Democrats in Chile. [W. Grabendorff]

7767c. ———. Sozio-ökonomischer Wandel und Verfassungsreform in Chile 1925-1972 (Verfassung und Recht in Übersee (6:1, 1973, p. 65-85)

Author traces constitutional development in Chile and its relation to socio-economic change. Stresses need for constitutional reform in the deposed Allende government while striving for socialist democracy. [W. Grabendorff]

7768. Nunn, Frederick M. A Latin American state within the state: the politics of the Chilean army, 1924-1927 (AAFH/TAM, 27:1, July 1970, p. 40-55)

Ties professionalization of Chilean military to attitudes and actions of General Ibáñez and other "progressive" military leaders during this pivotal period.

7769. Olavarría Bravo, Arturo. Chile bajo la Democracia Cristiana. v. 6, Sexto y último año: 3 de noviembre de 1969-3 de noviembre de 1970. Santiago, Editorial Salesiana, 1971. 401 p.

Detailed chronology of last year of Frei administration from university elections of 1969 to formation of Allende's first cabinet. Antimarxist point of view, critical of Frei as the "Chilean Kerensky."

7770. Parrish, Charles J.; Arpad J. von Lazar; and Jorge I. Tapia-Videla. Electoral procedures and political parties in Chile (RU/SCID [Political sociology, 074] 6:12, 1970/1971, p. 255-266, bibl., tables)

Analyzes impact of electoral procedures on congressional representation over period 1925-69. Suggests that electoral laws tended to favor middle-class parties and penalize splinter and leftist parties, particularly the Socialist. Indicates linkages between electoral outcomes and policymaking. Competent institutional analysis.

7771. Payró, Ana Lía; Laura Robles; Miguel Donoso Pareja; and Carlos Suárez. Chile: ¿cambio de gobierno o toma del poder?

México, Editorial Extemporáneos, 1971. 203 p., bibl., illus., tables (Col. A pleno sol, 4. Serie: teoría y práctica políticas)

Chapters on political parties, Church, literature, peasant movements, and economic policy by four Argentines obviously sympathetic to Allende regime.

7772. Petras, James. The transition to Socialism in Chile: perspectives and problems (MR, 23, Oct. 1971, p. 43-71, tables)

Succinct analysis of contemporary Chilean political situation. Describes factions within the governing Popular Unity coalition, nature of Chilean bureaucracy and military, and international factors in an assessment of strategic problems facing the regime. Optimistic on balance. See also item 7783.

—— and **Robert LaPorte, Jr.** Can we do business with radical nationalists? Chile: no. See item 8223.

7773. Portes, Alejandro. Leftist radicalism in Chile; a test of three hypotheses (CUNY/CP, 2:2, Jan. 1970, p. 251-274, tables)

"The effects on [leftist] radicalism of socio-economic position, status discrepancies, and other factors are only as strong as their effects on key subjective factors." Interesting secondary analysis of 1961 survey data.

Pratt, Raymond B. Community political organization and lower class politization in two Latin American cities. See item 7699.

7775. ——. Parties, neighborhood associations, and the politicization of the urban poor in Latin America: an exploratory analysis (MCPS/JPS, 15:3, Aug. 1971, p. 495-524, tables)

Based upon surveys taken in Santiago and Lima in 1965, explores linkages between membership in neighborhood associations, party affiliation, and knowledge about and sense of efficacy in political matters. Some problems of clarity in presentation and discussion of data.

7776. Quinzio, José Mario. La libertad de prensa en Chile (LNB/L, 16:190, sept. 1971, p. 33-42)

Vigorous response by Chile's ambassador to Panama to charges of media censorship by the Allende administration. Focuses on exercise of the Law of Abuses of Publicity.

7777. Ranitz-Haaften, E. H. de and **C. W. M. de Ranitz.** De Chileense landhervorming: een korte inleiding (NGIZ/IS, 25:6, maart 1971, p. 588-601)

Briefly describes origin, purposes and implementation of land reform (i.e., legislation, planning, expropriation, indemnization,*asentamiento* system—a three-year period of government ownership preceding a cooperative undertaking with individual titles, etc.). Discusses some field experiences on various *asentamientos*. Outlines effect of owning small piece of ground. Stresses inequality. [H. J. Hoyer]

7778. Ribeiro, Darcy. Nuevos caminos de la Revolución Latinoamericana (UCIEI/EI, 5:18, abril/junio 1972, p. 3-28)

Intreprets Chilean and Peruvian regimes as alternative models of social revolution in comparison with the Cuban. Suggests that Peruvian model may be more easily transferrable to other Latin American nations.

7779. Sanders, Thomas G. Allende's first months. Hanover, N.H., American Universities Field Staff Reports, 1971. 9 p. (West coast South America series, 28:2)

Overview sketch of April 1971 municipal elections, cabinet appointments, and domestic and foreign policies. Stresses distinctiveness of Chilean leftist-populist regime in contemporary Latin American context.

7780. Sigmund, Paul E. Chile: two years of Popular Unity (USIA/PC, 21, Nov/dec. 1972, p. 38-51, plates)

Contrasts Allende's comparatively successful 1971 with crises encountered in 1972 in implementing "socialist consumerism." Suggests that Allende will continue a legal or quasi-legal strategy.

7781. ——. Las corrientes electorales en Chile (USIA/PI, 19:1/2, enero/abril 1972, p. 9-17)

Challenges assumptions that Chilean voting patterns have shifted leftward markedly and reformism has failed in that country.

7782. Sinding, Steven W. The evolution of Chilean voting patterns: a re-examination of some old assumptions (SPSA/JP, 34:3, Aug. 1972, p. 774-796, tables)

Based on aggregate data from period 1920-60, tests 'Lerner hypothesis" and stability of party constituency. Reports rather surprising and interesting findings.

7782a. Sonntag, Heinz Rudolf. Revolution in Chile. Frankfurt, FRG, Fischer, 1972. 272 p., bibl.

Designed to give first-hand information about recent Chilean developments, the book comprises an interview with Allende and a couple of other prominent Unidad Popular leaders. It also contains the UP program and part of Allende's first message to the Congress. [W. Grabendorff]

7783. Sweezy, Paul M. Chile: advance or retreat? (MR, 23:8, Jan. 1972, p. 1-15)

Suggests that Chilean regime now must decide whether to consolidate gains in social reform or continue on to genuine social revolution. Emphasizes institutional and personal powers of the President in making the decision, but concludes that final outcome will be determined by the nature of the class struggle.

7784. Thome, Joseph T. Expropriation in Chile under the Frei agrarian reform (The American Journal of Comparative Law [Berkeley, Calif.] 19:3, Summer 1971, p. 489-513, tables)

Enumerates criteria for successful agrarian reform legislation. Focuses on legal and administrative obstacles to a "quick-taking procedure" under 1967 Chilean legislation. Useful case study of the role of law in policymaking.

7785. Urzúa Frademann, Paul. La demanda

campesina. Santiago, Univ. Católica de Chile, Vicerrectoria de Comunicaciones, 1969. 256 p., bibl., tables (Ediciones nueva universidad. Comunicaciones)

Reports on 1965 survey of about 700 campesinos in Central Valley of Chile from various occupational categories (*munifundistas, jornaleros, inquilinos,* etc.) to gauge present level of satisfaction and aspirations for reform. Useful addition to growing literature on Chilean agrarian reform.

7786. Urzúa Valenzuela, Germán. Evolución de la administración pública chilena, 1818-1968. Advertencia preliminar de Francisco Cumplido Cereceda. Santiago, Editorial Jurídica de Chile, 1970. 277 p., bibl., tables.

Product of a larger research project on public administration as a factor in Chilean development by the Institute for Political and Administrative Science of the Univ. of Chile. Outlines development of Chilean bureaucracy, public finance, personnel practices, and public services, with some emphasis on period 1925-68. Based in the main on primary sources. Somewhat legalistic but a quite valuable contribution.

7787. Valenzuela, Arturo. Political constraints and the prospects for socialism in Chile (PAPS, 30:4, 1972, p. 65-82)

Subtle and interesting development of thesis that "the same political practices and institutions which made [Allende's] election possible are now making it difficult for him to institute his basic program."

7788. Vitale, Luis. ¿Y después del 4, qué? perspectivas de Chile después de las elecciones presidenciales. Santiago, Editorial Prensa Latinoamericana, 1970. 98 p.

Marxist analysis of 1970 elections which calls for a "theoretical rearmament" of revolutionary left to defend socialist government from bourgeois counterattacks. Prescribes organization of workers and readiness to employ violence.

Wolpin, Miles D. Cuban foreign policy and Chilean politics. See item 8184.

7789. ———. La influencia internacional de la revolución cubana: Chile, 1958-1970 (CM/FI, 12:4, abril/junio 1972, p. 453-496)

Notes linkages between Cuban revolution and Chilean domestic politics, such as US reaction, Cuban news media, and visits by Chileans to observe Castro regime. Attempts to distinguish between international influence and domestic factors to account for Chilean voting behavior. Insightful in parts, but tends to ramble.

7790. ———. Revolutionary Cuba's impact upon Chilean politics (NGIZ/IS, 26:16, Sept. 1972, p. 1600-1619)

Indicates three developments in Chile which may be linked indirectly to the Cuban Revolution: 1) strengthening of radical reform organizations; 2) reform of certain socioeconomic institutions; and 3) decline in elite support for traditional parliamentary democratic institutions.

SOUTH AMERICA: EAST COAST

(VENEZUELA, BRAZIL, PARAGUAY, URUGUAY, ARGENTINA)

PHILIP B. TAYLOR, Jr.

Professor of Political Science
Director, Latin American Studies Center
University of Houston

IN AUGUST 1973 AN OFFICIAL UNITED STATES REPORT raised the question whether Brazil should be granted technical assistance and foreign aid in the future; after all, it was observed, Brazilian developmental achievements now have nearly removed the country from the "underdeveloped" list. While it could be argued by political scientists that the Brazilian political system is still severely defective by some development criteria, Brazilian social science scholarship is developing very rapidly. In the reported biennium Brazilian writers have taught lessons of concept, method and analysis to the world scholarly community. Cardoso, Jaguaribe, and Fernandes head the list, for example; and Brazil has inspired English language examination that is equally outstanding for its competence, as in the case of Schmitter and Schneider.

More important, the literature on Brazil is beginning to examine in much detail the many other aspects of the political system that a complex large country can justify: public administration, regional and state governmental problems, the roles and effects of interest groups, etc In effect, Brazil's intellectuals are proving their ability to develop excellence and contemporary interests despite the repression of an authoritarian regime.

The literature of other countries of this regional group is highlighted by occasional good pieces, but they are fewer in proportion. Uruguayan materials were clearly affected by the atmosphere of the country, as it slid almost fatalistically into military reaction for the first time in nearly a century. Equally, Argentina's auto-hypnosis with the twin tyrannies of peronismo and the armed forces predominated in the publications during this period. This is not to say that strong pieces have not been published; Díaz Araújo, Kirkpatrick, Marsal and Orona, to cite a few, produced exceptionally useful articles on the Argentine system. Astori, Calatayud, Rama and de Riz produced the most impressive work seen by this reviewer on Uruguay. On the other hand, Venezuelan literature was a good deal skimpier in quality than the foregoing, although Chen, Domingo A. Rangel and Rey contributed useful studies.

Despite these comments, on the whole the quality of Latin American scholarly and popular discussion of the region's political reality continues to rise, and the competitive offerings of United States writers also continues to improve. The training of all of these authors in more careful techniques of research and analysis in the social sciences is only one of the contributing causes. At least as important is rising Latin American recognition of its own need for well-trained and hopefully more objective examination and reporting. And last, there is the increasing respect generally granted scholars in the region (as contrasted with the *pensadores* and *intelectuales* of past generations), with accompanying concrete tokens of adequate university salaries, established research institutions or positions, and serious and competitive graduate students with their own strong research orientations.

VENEZUELA

Alexander, Robert J. The Communist Party of Venezuela. See *HLAS* 34:2522.

7791. Andueza, José Guillermo. El Congreso: estudio jurídico. Caracas, Ediciones del Congreso de la República, 1971. 94 p.

Very useful and serious study of the Venezuelan Congress. Writer has been involved in academic and political/administrative activities most of his adult life.

7792. Aportes a la historia del P.C.V. Maracaibo, Ven., n.p., 1971. 154 p. (Biblioteca de documentos históricos)

Written in 1951 by the Local Committee of the Communist Party in Maracaibo, this paper was intended to seek a reconciliation of an intra-party split in that year. Highly detailed and offers a running history of the party from its founding in 1931.

7793. Arellano Moreno, Antonio *ed.* Mensajes presidenciales. t. 1, 1830-1875; t. 2, 1876-1890; t. 3, 1891-1909; t. 4, 1910-1939. Recopilación, notas y estudio preliminar preparados por el doctor . . . Caracas, Presidencia de la República, 1970/1971. 4 v. (414, 422, 418, 423 p.)

Selection of major speeches and messages by Presidents of Venezuela, to Congress and to constituent bodies.

7794. Beltrán Prieto Figueroa, Luis. Sufragio y democracia. Caracas, Ediciones del Congreso de la República, 1971. 266 p., bibl.

Essays by an experienced political leader who played principal role in the 1967 splintering of the Acción Democrática party. Collection is substantially more legal and theoretical than partisan. Includes many documents.

7795. Blank, David Eugene. Politics in Venezuela: a country study. Boston, Mass., Little, Brown, 1973. 293 p. (The Little, Brown series in comparative politics)

Occasionally ethnocentric and often incorrect textbook. This usually prestigious series of national monographs has severe need of heavy editorial correction in this case, although the book has its useful points.

7796. Briceño-Iragorry, Mario. Pérez Jiménez, presidente: la autoelección de un déspota, 30 de noviembre de 1952. Caracas, Ediciones Centauro, 1971. 226 p.

Posthumous publication including Briceño's essay, "Sentido y Vigencia del 30 de Noviembre de 1952" (p. 19-83); and 14 documents of the period relating to Pérez Jiménez' palace golpe of 1952, in which votes were rigged to report his victory in the presidential election of that year.

7797. Burelli Rivas, Miguel Angel. Afirmación de Venezuela: itinerario de una inquietud. Caracas, Editorial Arte, 1971. 354 p.

Ruminations (i.e., editorial comment articles) by the conservative candidate for the presidency in the 1968 elections about virtually every subject. Burelli is a candidate again in 1973.

7798. Burggraaff, Winfield J. The military origins of Venezuela's 1945 revolution (UPR/CS, 11:3, Oct. 1971, p. 35-54)

Useful and quite unpretentious historical recounting of the coup that brought down the Medina government, placed Acción Democrática in power for the first time, and renewed the armed forces' tendency toward politicization. Based in part on interview information, but draws together available overt bibliography.

7799. ———. The Venezuelan armed forces in

politics, 1935-1959. Columbia, Mo., Univ. of Missouri Press, 1972. 241 p., bibl.

Useful extended discussion of "militaristic" phase in political behavior of soldiers. Concludes that 1940s and 1950s experiences, recounted in considerable detail, have laid the bases for a less politicized role.

7800. Caldera, Rafael. Cuenta ante el país: mensaje del Presidente de la República y exposiciones de los Ministros del Gabinete ante el Congreso Nacional, en el primer (segundo) año de gobierno. Caracas, Oficina Central de Información (OCI), 1970/1971. 2 v. (585, 513 p.) plates.

Customary annual volume.

7801. ———. Habla el Presidente: diálogo semanal con el pueblo venezolano. t. 1, 20 marzo 1969-5 marzo 1970; t. 2, 20 marzo 1970-5 marzo 1971; t. 3, 18 marzo 1971-2 marzo 1972. Caracas, Ediciones de la Presidencia de la República, 1970-1972. 3 v. (666, 686, 684 p.) plates.

Dr. Caldera has followed the habit of holding regular press conferences, with full live TV coverage. Three volumes consist of transcripts of these sessions from 20 March 1969 through 2 March 1972.

7802. Canal Ramírez, Gonzalo. Rafael Caldera, o capacitación del ciudadano: boceto para una biografía. Bogotá, Canal Ramírez-Antares, 1971. 291 p., plates.

Although a "traditional" kind of biography, the adulatory sort usually reserved for tyrants from whom volunteer biographer expects well-paid post, volume contains much information about Caldera.

7803. Carpio Castillo, Rubén. Acción Democrática, 1941-1971: bosquejo histórico de un partido. Caracas, Ediciones República, 1971. 132 p.

History of the party on its 30th anniversary. The tone is reportorial, and the obvious attempt is to cover all the significant events of the period—and the names of actors.

7804. Chacón Alfredo. La izquierda cultural venezolana, 1958-1968: ensayo y antología. Caracas, Editorial Domingo Fuentes, 1970. 431 p., tables.

Author and compiler is a sociology professor at Central Univ. of Caracas, as well as an intellectual leader of the left. His collection is a serious effort at representing the views of the left, and at definition of this position in his society. Large number of writers are represented in the collection, as well as anonymous or institutional spokesmen.

7805. Chen, J. Chi-Yi. Estrategia del desarrollo regional: caso de Venezuela. Caracas, Editorial Arte, 1967. 130 p., bibl., maps, tables.

Theoretical and practical argument in favor of national development by regions, with Venezuela the case in hand. Serious study, which sketches existing governmental planning and carries it to concrete suggestions originated by author.

7806. *Los Crímenes* de Pérez Jiménez. 1- Caracas, Ediciones Centauro. 1971- .

Monographic series consisting of individual volumes about victims of the dictatorship each containing biographical data, details of his anti-Pérez Jiménez action, and death. Three volumes seen so far:
León Droz Blanco: Teniente del Ejército Venezolano asesinado en Barranquilla, Colombia (159 p.)
Wilfredo Omaña: Capitán del Ejército Venezolano, asesinado en Caracas (134 p.)
Leonardo Ruiz Pineda: guerrillero de la libertad (150 p.)

7807. Figueroa Velásquez, Emilio. El barcelonazo: relato de un sobreviviente de uno de los mas bestiales crímenes cometidos por los adecos. Prólogo de Silvio Ruiz. Caracas, Ediciones Garrido, 1971. 229 p., plates.

In June 1961 a military rightist uprising occurred at the Barcelona barracks. Number of officers and men were killed in the barricks, and others captured. A participant reports.

Gall, Norman. Teodoro Petkoff: the crisis of the professional revolutionary. See item 7404.

7808. Ghioldi, Américo and others. Libertad de prensa y otros ensayos sobre periodismo. Prólogo de Miguel Acosta Saignes. Caracas, Univ. Central de Venezuela, Facultad de Humanidades y Educación, 1969. 483 p. (Ediciones del XX Aniversario de la Escuela de Periodismo)

Ten essays, previously published as monographs, on freedom of the press and journalism, by or about leading figures in the Venezuelan press. Not all the papers relate to Venezuela, and there is some interesting material on the history of press freedom in other countries as seen by the Venezuelan authors.

7809. López Borges, Nicanor *ed. and comp.* El asesinato de Delgado Chalbaud: análisis de un sumario. Introducción [de] Cipriano Heredia A. Caracas, Ediciones Centauro, 1971. 473 p.

Delgado, first chief of military government established in 1948, was killed in 1950. As a result, Marcos Pérez Jiménez assumed power and held it until 1958. Volume is an extraordinary collection of court documents of the investigation of the event.

7810. Lott, Leo B. Venezuela and Paraguay: political modernity and tradition in conflict. N.Y., Holt, Rinehart and Winston, 1972. 395 p., bibl., maps, tables (Modern comparative politics series)

College text of real substance makes use of nearly all contemporary tools for examination of political systems. Nevertheless, text retains awareness that it should also inform students and other readers.

Morales, Víctor Hugo. Del porteñazo al Perú. See item 7443.

7811. Naranjo, Yury. La revolución de la democracia. Caracas, n.p., 1972. 108 p.

Until Venezuelan youth become involved in restructuring society—through political ability and consciousness-raising,—the political system will be incompetent and corrupt. Political activist of much experience, in and out of political imprisonment, writes with much feeling.

7812. No hay término medio. Caracas, América Rebelde, 1972. 71 p. (Col. Documentos para la historia del movimiento revolucionario)

Collection of several short policy and propaganda statements by Bandera Roja, small leftist "party" with guerrilla links.

7813. Petkoff, Teodoro. ¿Socialismo para Venezuela? Caracas, Editorial Domingo Fuentes, 1970. 139 p. (Col. Estos días)

Young leader of the Partido Comunista de Venezuela looks rather soberly and critically at the needs and realities of the country. Underpinning of short piece is commitment to change. How can it be achieved in view of the idiosyncracies of the economy, the society and his own party?

7814. Powell, John Duncan. Peasant society and clientelist politics (APSA/R, 64:2, June 1970, p. 411-425, table)

Strong, comparative/theoretical paper based on author's earlier research in Venezuela but also on investigations conducted by others in Latin America, Europe, and Asia.

7815. ———. Venezuelan agrarian problems in comparative perspective (CSSH, 13:3, July 1971, p. 282-300, tables)

Relates Venezuelan process of agrarian reform to historical cases in other countries (e.g., Russia) and analyzes causes for the declining role of the peasantry in contemporary Venezuelan politics. Perceptive analysis and interpretation. [J. J. Bailey]

7816. Rangel, Domingo Alberto. La oligarquía del dinero. Caracas, Editorial Fuentes, 1971. 404 p.

Detailed examination by moderate leftist intellectual/politican of the role of Caracas fat cats in the national economy. Major contribution to study of country's power structure.

7817. ——— and others. Rómulo, el General Betancourt y otros escritos. Caracas, Ediciones Centauro, 1970. 142 p. (Centauro, 2)

Collection of commentaries of varied length and purpose by eight writers. Concludes with press-conference transcript dated Sept. 1970. Represented are Venezuelans: Domingo Alberto Rangel, Mariano Picón Salas, Luis Beltrán Prieto, Guillermo Feo Calcano, Ambrosio Oropeza; and foreigners: Diógenes de la Rosa, Luis Alberto Sánchez, and Arthur Schlesinger, Jr.

7818. Rey Martínez, Juan Carlos. El sistema de partidos venezolanos (Politeia [Caracas] 1, 1972, p. 175-230, tables)

Extended development of paradigm for comparative analysis of party systems is followed by quick overview of parties in Venezuela. Serious effort is made to show that elements therein have been systematized; that rules of the game have been agreed upon; and that the system is stabilizing. Deserves careful reading of both students and specialists.

7819. Reyes, Vitelio. Ustedes son los delincuentes o mi defensa en el tribunal de la historia. Madrid, Gráficas Egos, 1969. 480 p., plates.

Author was accused of "illicit enrichment" under Venezuelan law, and tried. This is a self-defense in substantial detail. Interesting volume offers view of a unique process (in Latin American terms), as well as many unsavory details of "how things are done," in such cases.

7820. Rivas Iturralde, Vladimiro. Las fuentes de información en el periodismo venezolano. Caracas, Estudio 70 Editores, 1971. 152 p., illus., tables.

Quantitative analysis of space assigned by source in three major newspapers of Caracas (*Nacional, Universal* and *Ultimas Noticias*) in a three month period of 1970. Method and sampling is explained carefully. Survey has much interesting and useful information concerning the city's press and the relative influence of private as against public groups and institutions.

7821. Sader Pérez, Rubén. Temas para un cambio de régimen político. Caracas, FECOMUN (Fondo Editorial Comuneros), 1971. 218 p.

Highly nationalist former President of Corporación Venezolana del Petróleo offers his thoughts on reforming his country's political system. His views are left/nationalist, and call for forceful action implemented by military participation, *à-la*-Peru, with which he makes some comparisons.

7822. Schuster F., Jorge F. Rural problem-solving policies in Venezuela, with special reference to the agrarian issue. Madison, Wis., Univ. of Wisconsin, Land Tenure Center, 1972. 116 p., tables (mimeo) (Research paper, 46)

". . . . essentially an abbreviated version of the author's Ph.D. thesis of the same title." Largely a historical recounting of policies concerning land use through 1960, when present agricultural policies were adopted. Final brief section sketches results in the 1960s.

7823. Semanario Copei. Organo oficial de la Democracia Cristiana. Partido Social Cristiano COPEI. Año 2, Nos. 77/78, 18/25, agosto 1971- . Caracas.

Tabloid-sized publication which first appeared in 1970.

7824. Silva Michelena, José A. The illusion of democracy in dependent nations. v. 3, The politics of change in Venezuela. Cambridge, Mass., The MIT Press, 1971. 312 p., bibl., tables.

Much of work is solid analysis, but much is ideological nonsense, an extension of tendencies marring earlier Bonilla volume (see *HLAS 33:8050*). Work is also designed to provide thorough explanation of subject as well as to be of didactic use. This is third volume in projected series drawing on data compiled in 1963 in an extraordinarily intensive and extensive behavioral study conducted by MIT and the Centro de Estudios del Desarrollo of the Univ. Central de Venezuela, Caracas. For previous volumes, see *HLAS 33:8050*.

7825. Taylor, Philip B., Jr. Analysis of the organization and legal machinery for population protection and resources management in Venezuela: 1960-1964 (*in* Condit, Doris M. and others. Population protection and resources management in internal defense operations: organization and legal machinery. Kensington, Md., American Institutes for Research, 1972, p. 1-88)

Venezuelan governmental and political tools in official resistance to operations by the Fuerzas Armadas de Liberación Nacional, during indicated period.

7826. ———. Thoughts on comparative effectiveness: leadership and the democratic left in Colombia and Venezuela. Buffalo, N.Y., State Univ. of New York, Council on International Studies, 1971. 42 p., table (mimeo) (Special studies, 2)

Revised and updated version of paper presented at the Conference on Political parties and the Search for Institutional Stability, Buffalo, N.Y., 1968.

7827. ——— ed. Venezuela: 1969, analysis of progress. Houston, Tex., Univ. of Houston, 1971. 266 p.

Papers prepared for conference held in Washington, Nov. 10-11, 1969:
Philip B. Taylor, Jr. "Successful Change in Venezuela?" p. 1-12
Gordon C. Ruscoe "The Efficacy of Venezuelan Education" p. 13-33
José Rafael Revenga "The Efficacy of Education in Venezuela" p. 34-54
John Duncan Powell "Venezuelan Agrarian Problems in Comparative Perspective" p. 55-73
J. Raúl Alegrett "The Venezuelan Agrarian Reform: Impact and Perspectives" p. 74-83
David Eugene Blank "Political Conflict and Industrial Planning in Venezuela" p. 84-106
Arturo Sosa "Structural Factors in Venezuelan Economic Development" p. 107-121
John R. Dinkelspiel "Technology and Tradition: Regional and Urban Development in the Guayana" p. 122-145
Antonio Morales Tucker "The Urban Development of Venezuela: the Case of Caracas" p. 146-167
John H. Lichtblau "United States Oil Import Policies and Venezuelan Petroleum Exports" p. 182-196
Humberto Peñaloza "The Political Framework of Venezuelan Oil: Changes and Opportunities" p. 196-215
Robert P. Clark, Jr. "Economic Integration and the Political Process: Linkage Politics in Venezuela" p. 216-236
Antonio Alamo B. "Economic Integration in Latin America and the Case of Venezuela" p. 237-248.

7828. Vallenilla Lanz, Laureano. Cartas de ausente. Caracas, Ediciones Garrido, 1971. 267 p.

Collected letters to correspondents in Caracas and elsewhere dated July 1966 to June 1968.

7829. Venezuela. Comisión Investigadora Contra el Enrique cimiento Ilícito. Los jerarcas impunes del perezjimenismo; Vallenilla, aristócrata del oprobio. Caracas, Ediciones Centauro, 1971. 153 p.

Contains large part of documentation offered by the Commission in its judgment against Laureano Vallenilla Lanz. Minister of Interior for Perez Jiménez.

7830. Zago, Angela. Aquí no ha pasado nada. Caracas, Síntesis Dosmil, 1972. 205 p., plates (Testimonios)

Recounting in first person, not without charms, of 18 months in the life of a guerrilla.

BRAZIL

Argentine-Brésil. See item 7922.

7831. Augusto, José. O Rio Grande do Norte no Senado da República. Natal, Bra., Imprensa Universitária, 1968. 100 p.

Biographical notes on eight men who have served for the state in the national Senate. Useful piece of historical material on the region.

7832. Balchman, Morris J. Eve in an Adamocracy: women and politics in Brazil. N.Y., New York Univ., Ibero-American Language and Area Center, 1973. 23 p., bibl. (Occasional papers, 5)

Preliminary report of lengthy behavioral study on women in politics in Brazil. Based on author's field work and published materials by others, it concludes that much "consciousness raising" will be necessary before Brazilian women are able to take an appropriate place in their society.

7833. Barata, Mário. Presença de Assis Chateaubriand na vida brasileira. Prefácio [de] Carlos Rizzini. São Paulo, Martins, 1971. 122 p.

Uncritical biography of man who dominated Brazilian news media for a generation before his death in 1968. [E. B. Burns]

7834. Bastos, Tocary A. and Thomas W. Walker. Partidos e fôrças políticas em Minas Gerais (UMG/RBEP, 31, maio 1971, p. 117-157, tables)

Study based on interviews with 73 legislators of Minas Gerais state. Questions dealt with personal experiences and backgrounds of respondents in education, status and party activity prior to 1964, as well as attitudes on issues. Tentative conclusions are reached concerning social structure, political mobility, behavior of the electorate, and contradictions between political behavior and values. Study is exploratory and very useful.

7835. Bonavides, Paulo. O planejamento e os organismos regionais como preparação a um federalismo das regiões: a experiência brasileira (DPB/RICS, 18, 1971, p. 363-396)

Brief survey of concept of regions for political and planning purposes in Brazilian history. Constitutional provisions are cited, and agencies established under the 1946 constitution are mentioned. Discussion emphasizes SUDENE as an example of means for rectifying current trend toward unitarism, in light of the ever-increasing concentration of power in Brasília.

7836. Brazil. Presidência da República. Metas e bases para a ação de govêrno. Brasília [?]1970. 1 v. (Unpaged), illus., tables.

Highly detailed report on national development planning for the 1970s, complete with literally hundreds of graphics.

7837. Brésil—l'évolution de la situation politique depuis 1967—les présidences Costa e Silva et Garrastazu Médici: l'écrasement des forces politiques traditionnelles; le développement des nouvelles oppositions; l'évolution du régime (FDD/NED, 3749/3750, 30 dec. 1970, p. 5-27, bibl.)

Reports political events, 1967-70, but offers little analysis. However, scholar/specialist will find much of factual value.

7838. Cardoso, Fernando Henrique. O modelo político brasileiro e outros ensaios. São Paulo, Difusão Européia do Livro, 1972. 211 p. (Corpo e alma do Brasil, 35)

Collection of nine papers presented at conferences, 1969-72, dealing with selected general problem areas and with problems of method of analysis. General topic theme is dependency which author applies in analysis of population, policy planning, participation, and industrialization.

7839. ———. Política e desenvolvimento em sociedades dependentes: ideologias do empresariado industrial argentino brasileiro. Rio, Zahar Editores, 1971. 221 p., bibl., tables (Biblioteca de ciências sociais)

Scholarly work based on both conceptual and empirical research. Initial portion examines past and present theory of dependency in the light of author's defined model, while latter discussion is based on substantial behavioral and attitudinal work.

7840. ———. El régimen político brasileño (ILARI/A, 25, julio 1972, p. 6-31)

Nature of regime and society that have emerged from the 1964 golpe have surprised nearly everyone. Is it restoration, fascism, or what? Based on effective use of conceptual analyses by other authors, article concludes that strong risks of evermore repressive government exist unless remedial action is taken. It should originate from within the regime as well as from society.

7841. Chilcote, Ronald H. Protest and resistance in Brazil and Portuguese Africa: a synthesis and classification (in Chilcote, Ronald H. ed. Protest and resistance in Angola and Brazil. Los Angeles, Calif., Univ. of California, African Studies Center [and] Latin American Studies Center, 1972, p. 243-302)

Bibliographic essay concludes author's edited volume which handles Brazil and Africa separately, the former in exhaustive detail. Short conclusion discusses trends and offers first-order hypotheses based on generalizations.

7842. Cintra, Antônio Octávio. Um estudo de modernidade, ideologia e envolvimento político (UMG/RBEP, 31, maio 1971, p. 53-89, tables)

This work and item 7875 are both based on data compiled in Belo Horizonte in 1967 for yet another study. However, this discussion is more extensive and draws upon a different set of dependent variables than item 7875.

7843. Convenção Nacional do Movimento Democrático Brasileiro, III, Brasília, 1967. Estatutos e programas aprovados pela . . . Brasília, 1970? 43 p.

Statutes, program, and listing of party's congressional representatives elected in 1966.

7844. Costa, Jorge Gustavo da. Planejamento governamental: a experiência brasileira. Rio, Fundação Getúlio Vargas, 1971. 569 p., bibl., tables (Biblioteca de administração pública, 16)

Exhaustive survey and analysis of planning experience in Brazil offers both history and theory. Little has been slighted: budgets nor political atmosphere.

7845. Delorenzo Neto, Antônio. Teoria das funções municipais. Osasco, Bra., Faculdade Municipal de Ciências Econômicas e Administrativas de Osasco, Instituto de Pesquisas, 1970. 90 p., tables (Cadernos de economia, 2)

Modest and useful effort to propose functional overhaul of municipal structure and operation, with special reference to São Paulo *municipio*. Author's involvement with subject extends back over two decades.

7846. Dias, Edmundo Fernandes. Sôbre representação política no Brasil (Cadernos da PUC [Pontifícia Univ. Católica, Rio] agôsto 1971, p. 135-164)

Critical analysis of an article by Simon Schwartzman published in *Dados* (Instituto Universitário de Pesquisas, Rio, 7, 1970) which offered a research design concerning political participation. This analysis provides reader with notion of quality of professional criticism in a specific instance.

Dulles, John W. F. Unrest in Brazil: political-military crises, 1955-1964. See *HLAS* 34:2892a.

Einaudi, Luigi R. and Alfred C. Stepan, III. Latin American institutional development: changing military perspectives in Peru and Brazil. See item 7685.

7847. Farris, George F. and Anthony D. Butterfield. Limites culturais às teorias de liderança: um teste empírico no Brasil (Revista de Administração Pública [Rio] 6:3, julho/set. 1972, p. 55-85, tables)

Application of leadership theory to 16 Brazilian finance firms. Is American-produced theory applicable to research in Brazil? Does it contribute towards an understanding of leadership utility and technique in Brazil? Authors answer in the affirmative. Highly technical and conceptual article.

7848. Ferreira Filho, Manoel Gonçalves. A

democracia possível. São Paulo, Edição Saraiva, 1972. 133 p.

Is democracy possible in Brazil? Slight piece is long on theory and short of application to Brazil. More political philosophizing than political science.

7849. Flores, Mario César. Formulação de uma política marítima: Estudo de Estado-Maior (Revista da Escola de Guerra Naval [Rio] 2, dez. 1971, p. 5-19, bibl., tables)

Short examination of policy making. Proposes organization of a Council on Maritime Policy, reporting to the President of the Republic.

7850. Franco Sobrinho, Manoel de Oliveira. História breve do constitucionalismo no Brasil. 2. ed., ampliada. Curitiba, Bra., n.p., 1970. 143 p.

Contains very useful legal information for the 1964-69 period. [E. B. Burns]

7850a. Füchtner, Hans. Die brasilianischen Arbotergewerkschaften, ihre Organisation und ihre politische Funktion. Frankfurt, FRG, Suhrkamp, 1972. 276 p., bibl.

Author divides his analysis of labor's organization and political role before the "Brazilian Revolution" of 1964 in three parts: labor in industry and labor laws and practice; agricultural labor movement and social conditions in Brazilian agriculture; labor in politics and the political system of Getúlio Vargas. Excellent bibliography. [W. Grabendorff]

7851. Greenfield, Sidney M. On monkeys, fish, and Brazilian agricultural development: some questions and suggestions (JDA, 5:4, July 1971, p. 507-516)

Questions and suggestions are pungent reminders that all technical assistance is relative to cultural reality.

7852. Ianni, Octavio. O colapso do populismo no Brasil. 2. ed., rev. Rio, Editôra Civilização Brasileira, 1971. 223 p., tables (Col. Retratos do Brasil, 70)

Serious and much-documented examination of Brazil's economy, and of its outputs for mass of workers and lower class. Ianni offers much detail on question of dependency, principally on the US. Also examines alternatives for the future.

7853. Jorge, J. G. de Araujo. Brasil com letra minúscula: retrato do Brasil, tamanho 3 × 4. Rio, Irmãos Pongetti Editores, n.d. 262 p., illus.

Suggests that if Brazil is less than it should be, in terms of political coherence or emotional or symbolic virtue, the fault lies with its leaders. Author is described as one who was harrassed and expelled by the Vargas regime. 45 short articles and several poems date from a 1950s undated volume.

7854. Lima, Alcides de Mendonça. As novidades da Constituição Federal de 1967: segundo a emenda no. 1, de 1969. São Paulo, Editôra Juriscredi, 1971. 289 p.

Legal study of new constitution, as amended to 1969. Briefly reports on political circumstances surrounding documents. Includes index.

7855. Lima Filho, Vivaldo Palma. O Amazonas no Senado Federal: actuação parlamentar do Senador . . . , 1° Fev. 1951-31 Jan. 1967. Brasília? Serviço Gráfico do Senado Federal, 1971? 2 v. (642, 664 p.) plate.

Participation of author in Senate debates is of historical value as representative of his state's interests.

7856. Lonaeus, Gunnar. Brasilien: politik och politiker efter 1945. Stockholm, Utrikespolitiska institute, 1968. 32 p., bibl. (Världs politikens dagsfragor, 1)

Concise introduction to political developments in Brazil from 1945-68. Short bibliography suggests further readings. [R. V. Shaw]

7857. McCann, Frank D. The military and change in Brazil (*in* Rippy, Merrill *ed.* Cultural change in Brazil. Muncie, Ind., Ball State Univ., p. 1-12)

Although concise and rather simplistic scanning of record of Brazilian armed forces in their political involvements, paper offers useful sketch of broader outlines of events.

7858. Machado, Luiz Toledo. Estudos brasileiros: a nação e as aspirações nacionais. São Paulo, Editôra Itamaraty, 1972. 337 p., maps, tables.

Text for secondary school students in Brazilian studies. Although it reminds one of a basic course in civics, it includes text of a variety of policy articles and laws since 1964 of interest to the specialist.

7859. Marighela, Carlos. For the liberation of Brazil. Translated by John Butt and Rosemary Sheed. Introduction by Richard Gott. Baltimore, Md., Penguin Books, 1971. 191 p.

Collection of writings by man who drew up blueprints for urban guerrilla warfare. [E. B. Burns]

7860. ———. Teoría y acción revolucionarias. México, Editorial Diógenes, 1971. 135 p.

Collection of short statements, publications and manuals concerning the guerrilla movement in Brazil by its late leader. For first edition, see *HLAS 33:7762* and for an English translation, see item 7859.

7861. Médici, Emílio Garrastazu. A verdadeira paz. Brasília? Presidência da República, Secretaria de Imprensa, 1971. 203 p.

Formal speeches and statements by the President of Brazil, April-Oct. 1970.

7862. Metodologia para o estabelecimento da política nacional: especificamente em relação à política segurança. Curitiba, Bra., Escola Superior de Guerra, Associação dos Diplomados [ADESG], Delegacia do Estado do Paraná, 1971. 22 p., tables (Ciclo de conferências sôbre segurança nacional e desenvolvimento)

Training manual dealing with national security: policies and means for its establishment. Consists of report of lecture presented by four-member team, visuals, excerpts from the constitution justifying recommendations, etc.

7863. O modêlo Brasil—MBRSL: manual de análise para experimentos (UMG/RBEP, 31, maio 1971, p. 207-224)

Working manual for discussion purposes and designed as a guide for computer-aided research. Prepared by the Political Science Dept. of the Univ. de Minas Gerais.

7864. Moreira, Marcílio Marques. Indicações para o projeto brasileiro. Rio, Edições Tempo Brasileiro, 1971. 218 p., tables (Biblioteca tempo universitario, 29)

Collection of previously published pieces by author, who has held a large number of responsible positions in economic areas and institutions, both in Brazil and abroad. Although in some respects a very personal volume, it is also innovative and useful.

7865. Muricy, Antônio Carlos da Silva. Palavras de um soldado. Rio, Imprensa do Exército, 1971. 342 p.

Collection of speeches and other personal statements by Gen. Muricy, Army Chief of Staff until 25 Nov. 1970.

7866. Núñez, Carlos. Brasil: satélite y gendarme. Montevideo, Aportes, 1969. 118 p. (Cuadernos de información política y económica, 5)

Predictable tract describing Brazil as US satellite and regional policeman. Author bases contention on 1967 general strategic planning document from Brazil's Escola Superior de Guerra. Granted the influence of US military advisors and techniques in Brazil, piece seems trite and more than a little dated. Still, it will evoke sympathetic response among some readers.

7867. Oliveira, José Xavier de. Usos e abusos de relações públicas. Apresentação [de] Orlando Figueiredo. Rio, Fundação Getúlio Vargas, Instituto de Documentação, Serviço de Publicações, 1971. 414 p., bibl., tables.

Text on the subject also constitutes lengthy warning. Contains much information concerning market and public of Brazil for the business and public-opinion-oriented student.

7868. Page, Joseph A. The revolution that never was: Northeast Brazil. N.Y., Grossman Publishers, 1972. 273 p.

Despite distinctly journalistic and often light-hearted approach, reinforced by first-person treatment and loaded vocabulary, volume has much merit and material cannot be discounted.

7869. Pearson, Neale J. Small farmer and rural worker characteristics in the emergence of Brazilian peasant pressure groups, 1955-1968 (*in* Rippy, Merrill *ed.* Cultural change in Brazil. Muncie, Ind., Ball State Univ., p. 65-100, tables)

Based on a detailed interview schedule applied to over 200 *campezinho* and rural-worker organization leaders, article deals with a variety of issues. Discusses leaders' characteristics, as well as the tactics and values of organizations. Examines question of whether or not *campezinhos* will be adequately represented in policy outputs and events.

7870. Pelaez, Carlos Manuel. A política econômica so President Vargas: Wirth e *The Politics of Brazilian development, 1930-1954* (IBE/RBE, 24:3, julho/set. 1970, p. 183-197, bibl., tables)

Critical analysis of recently-published monograph, which attempts to analyze Vargas' policies in commerce, steel and oil, over three discrete policy periods. Author concludes book errs seriously in both its methodology and conclusions, and offers his model, based on a large number of his published works.

7871. Pinheiro, Luís Adolfo Corrêa. A consciência nacionalista. Brasília, Coordenada, 1971. 110 p., bibl.

After brief theoretical review of concept of nationalism, author offers some thoughts on the subject in Brazilian practice.

7872. O processo revolucionário brasileiro. Brasília, Presidência da República, Assessoria Especial de Relações Públicas [AERP], 1969. 118 p., table.

Collection of 14 short essays by nine writers about the policies of the regime. Stature of the writers rescues this from oblivion.

7873. Quartim, João. Dictatorship and armed struggle in Brazil. London, NLB, 1971. 221 p., map, tables.

Why did armed struggle develop in Brazil, and where is it going? Essential work for students beginning work on the subject. Originally published in France.

7874. Reis, Arthur Cézar Ferreira. Como governei o Amazonas. Manaus, Bra., Secretaria de Imprensa e Divulgação, 1967. 224 p., tables.

Report of 30 months as state governor, with much statistical and policy data appended.

7875. Reis, Fábio Wanderley. Educação, economia e contestação política na América Latina (UMG/RBEP, 31, maio 1971, p. 9-52, tables)

Following a brief methodological hypothesis establishing introduction, study presents data on political attitudes of a sample of Belo Horizonte's population. Dependent variables include, principally (in several tables) leftism as correlated with education and economic status. Pt. 4 focuses on the Latin American region as a whole, with referrents such as violence, political stability and employment/educational opportunities. For a more extensive examination of the same data, see item 7842.

7877. Rodrigues, José Albertino. Sindicato e desenvolvimento no Brasil. Apresentação [de] Manuel Diégues Júnior. São Paulo, Difusão Européia do Livro, 1968. 215 p., bibl. (Corpo e alma do Brasil, 27)

Solid contribution to literature of labor movements in Brazil contains brief history of labor, some material on effects of its activity, and present role of unions.

7878. Roett, Riordan. Brazil: politics in a patrimonial society. Boston, Mass., Allyn & Bacon, 1972. 197 p., bibl., map, tables (The Allyn and Bacon series in Latin American politics)

Recent college textbook in new series with distinct and almost exclusive emphasis on politics. Cites from and draws upon all available literature, as of mid-1972. Useful introduction for beginning students, and a source of critical discussion for more advanced ones.

7879. Rolando, Stefono. Brasile: società e potere. Firenze, Italy, Nuova Italia Editrice, 1970. 133 p., tables.

Brief and popular introduction to Brazil for Italians. Appendix contains pieces by number of Brazilian writers and political activists, ranging from Furtado to Marighela.

7880. Rosenbaum, H. Jon and William G. Tyler. Policy-making for the Brazilian Amazon (UM/JIAS, 13:3/4, July/Oct. 1971, p. 416-433)

Overview and analysis of contemporary Amazonian developments. [E. B. Burns]

7881. ——— and ——— eds. Contemporary Brazil: issues in economic and political development. N.Y., Praeger, 1972. 460 p., tables (Praeger special studies in international economics and development)

Collection of relatively high-quality pieces in areas of politics, economics, and political economy. However, similar to item 7884 in that quality varies, with best articles devoted to development, foreign trade, agriculture and population migration.

7882. Rosenn, Keith S. The *jeito:* Brazil's institutional bypass of the formal legal system and its developmental implications (AJCL, 19:3, Summer 1971, p. 514-549)

Description and analysis of *jeito*, unique Brazilian problem-solving style. Highly useful descriptive introduction to a practice in legal sociology that can be used to one's advantage or disadvantage, at whatever level.

7883. Santos, Theobaldo Miranda. Organização social e política do Brasil: de acordo com a nova Constituição Brasileira de 1969. 12. ed., rev. e atualizada. São Paulo, Companhia Editora Nacional, 1972. 200 p., bibl.

Discusses "social and political organization" of Brazil within framework of last (new) constitution of 1969. [J. F. B. Dasilva]

7884. Saunders, John V. D. ed. Modern Brazil: new patterns and development. Gainesville, Fla., Univ. of Florida Press, 1971. 350 p., illus., maps, tables.

Brazilian and American authors contribute potpourri of papers of mixed quality. Those on economic and political culture are exceptional; those on politics, population, geography, and law are useful; but those on literature and the arts are hardly worth including.

7885. Schmitter, Philippe. Interest conflict and political change in Brazil. Stanford, Calif., Stanford Univ. Press, 1971. 499 p., bibl., tables.

Exceptional monographic study demonstrating that Brazil was controlled by an authoritarian political system before 1964, pointing to little change between then and now. However, this conclusion is not the announced goal of the study. Based on both traditional and behavioral analysis. Includes exhaustive bibliography on Brazil.

7886. Schneider, Ronald M. The political system of Brazil: emergence of a "modernizing" authoritarian regime, 1964-1970. N.Y., Columbia Univ. Press, 1971. 431 p., bibl.

Essentially a political history of period in question offers much detail and little analysis, except for introductory and concluding chapters. Nevertheless, a substantial contribution to knowledge of Brazil.

7887. Silva, Fernando A. Rezende da. A evolução das funções do govêrno e a expansão do setor público brasileiro (IPEA/PP, 1:2, dez. 1971, p. 235-282, tables)

In the period 1947-68 the public sector has grown in absolute terms by 455 percent and its contribution (both central government and public enterprises) has grown from 18 percent of GNP to 24.7 percent. Following a substantial introduction that includes data from the 40 years prior to 1947, author draws on hypotheses concerning growth patterns of public sectors. Modest model is offered to develop analysis and predictions for the future.

7888. Silva, Glauco Lessa de Abreu e. A ação do govêrno na administração de pessoal. Brasília, n.p., 1971. 43 p., tables.

Statement to the Committee on the Civil Service of the National Chamber of Deputies by the Director of the Dept. of Personnel Administration (DASP). Covers period June 1964-June 1969, in one set of data; and to the date of the testimony, Oct. 1971, in second set.

7889. Sua Boa Estratêia. Mercedes-Benz do Brasil, Divisão de Documentação, Depto. de Promoção de Vendas. Ano 4, No. 27, 1970- . São Paulo.

Special issue devoted entirely to army military academy, Academia Militar das Agulhas Negras. Presentation is factual though glamorous, as befits a publicity journal. Includes substantial amount of detail on the lore of the army, course work of cadets, military history, and much useful graphic material in color.

7890. Tabak, Fanny. Estudos de política local: a experiência do Brasil (FGV/R, 5:2, abr./junho 1971, p. 61-90)

In some respects, the real action in politics is at local rather than at national level. Since 1964 golpe, national political thought has progressed little, in part because of the politics of an artificial two-party system. Struggles between forces for change, and forces for conservatism, now dominate the very pluralistic and varied Brazilian local scene.

7891. Tejo, [Aurelio de] Limeira. Brasil potência frustrada: a contra-revolução do semicapitalismo. Pôrto Alegre, Bra., Editôra Leitura, 1968. 177 p.

Military government of 1964 was not the beginning of a revolution in any beneficial sense but merely a re-establishment of an outmoded quasi-capitalist system, deeply infected by anti-nationalist influences.

Valle, Alvaro. Estruturas políticas brasileiras. See *HLAS 34:3013a.*

7892. Young, Jordan M. *ed.* Brazil, 1954-64: end of a civilian cycle. N.Y., Facts on File, 1972. 197 p., map, table.

Detailed selective chronology of earlier years followed by more comprehensive and interpretive treatment of period 1959-64. Some emphasis on relations with the US appears, especially in the discussion of 1963.

PARAGUAY

7893. Franco, Carlos Hernán. Esquema del sistema represivo vigente en el Paraguay (UTIEH/C, 14, 1970, p. 125-138)

Descriptive analysis of adaptations of Western legal norms to facilitate authoritarian rule. [J. J. Bailey]

7894. Frutos, Juan Manuel. Aspectos de la tarea revolucionaria del coloradismo. Asunción Biblioteca Colorada, 1969. 94 p., illus., tables.

Evocative, propaganda-ladened piece, based on presentation at the Jornadas de Capacitación Política in Paraguarí city on 30-31 May 1969, dedicated to review and eulogy of Colorado Party's development in Paraguay and greatness of present administration. [J. R. Scobie]

7895. Hicks, Frederick. Interpersonal relationships and *caudillismo* in Paraguay (UM/JIAS, 13:1, Jan. 1971, p. 89-111)

Somewhat superficial review of relationship between Colorado and Liberal parties made by anthropologist on the basis of residence in Paraguay in early 1950's. Explores briefly, and with more success, the patron-client relationship as underpinnings for *caudillismo*. [J. R. Scobie]

7896. ———. Politics, power, and the role of the village priest in Paraguay (UM/JIAS, 9:2, April 1967, p. 273-282)

Brief and somewhat shallow study of how being the village priest may force upon him a leadership role. Material drawn from one village. However, author believes conditions fostering such a prestige role probably exist in other villages as well.

7897. Kharitonov, Vitalii Aleksandroviich. Paragvia: voenno-politseiskaia diktatura u politicheskaia bor'ba (Paraguay: the military political dictatorship and the political struggle). Moskva, Nauka, 1970. 179 p., tables.

Claims to be first Soviet or foreign research-monograph to analyze the contemporary political life of Paraguay from a Marxist-Leninist viewpoint. Perceives Stroessner regime as dictatorship supported by military, leaders of Colorado Party, *latifundistas*, and representatives of big capital tied to foreign markets and countries such as the US, West Germany, Argentina and Brazil. [T. S. Cheston]

7898. Lewis, Paul H. Leadership and conflict within the Febrerista Party of Paraguay (UM/JIAS, 9:2, April 1967, p. 283-295)

Short survey of history of the party leads to tentative conclusions that it has become oligarchic and will probably continue as such, provided it has the requisite degree of political freedom.

Lott, Leo B. Venezuela and Paraguay: political modernity and tradition in conflict. See item 7810.

7899. Nichols, Byron A. La cultura política del Paraguay (CPES/RPS, 8:20, enero/abril 1971, p. 133-158, tables)

Behavioral study of 269 respondents, largely discusses perceptions, recognitions, and participation. Markedly similar in scheme to work reported in Gabriel A. Almond and Sidney Verba, *The civic culture: political attitudes and democracy in five nations* (Princeton, N.J., Princeton Univ. Press, 1963, 562 p.).

7900. Stroessner, Alfredo. Mensaje de Navidad. Asunción, Presidencia de la República, Sub-Secretaría de Informaciones y Cultura, 1970. 11 p.

Defense of the order and progress of Paraguay in a world of tumult. [J. J. Bailey]

URUGUAY

7901. Astori, Danilo. Latifundio y crisis agraria en el Uruguay. Montevideo, Ediciones de La Banda Oriental, 1971. 99 p., tables (Latifundio y crisis agraria en el Uruguay, 4)

Useful and serious short study of present condition of ranching in Uruguay. First section is largely historical, while the second discribes present condition of stagnation in ranching and socioeconomic effects on the country. Conclusions offer some thoughts on the significance of the ranching pattern for Uruguay and its inherent dependence on large countries as markets.

7902. Benedetti, Mario. Crónicas del 71. Montevideo, Arca Editorial, 1972. 254 p., (Bolsilibros Arca, 88)

Essays on Uruguayan politics published during 1971 in *Marcha* of Montevideo (see item 7434). Author is at his best when writing from experience instead of emotion, i.e., from knowledge rather than from ideology.

7903. Benvenuto, Luis and others. Uruguay hoy. B.A., Siglo XXI Editores, 1971. 455 p., tables.

Five serious and critical essays concerning country's present crisis (as of 1971). Deserves serious attention of specialists as well as of generalists on Latin America.

7904. Calatayud Bosch, José. Grandeza y decadencia del Partido Nacional. Montevideo, Ediciones Liga Federal, 1971. 199 p.

Carefully researched history of the party by an active member, worth the attention of specialists.

7905. Corso, Eduardo J. El cristiano y el Frente Amplio. Montevideo, Talleres Gráficos Barreiro y Ramos, 1971. 70 p.

Can a Catholic collaborate with either marxism or a marxist? 19 editorial articles published in *El País* of Montevideo deal with the role of the Christian Democratic Party in the Uruguayan election of 1971, when it participated in the Frente Amplio.

7906. D'Elía, Germán and others. El Uruguay en la conciencia de la crisis. Montevideo, Univ. de la República, Depto. de Publicaciones, 1971. 324 p.

Collected and revised lectures from the 13th Summer Course program at Montevideo's Univ. de la República, 1970.

7907. Dueñas Ruiz, Oscar and **Mirna Rugnon de Dueñas**. Tupamaros: libertad o muerte. Bogotá, Ediciones Mundo Andino, 1971. 185 p.

Largely factual treatment of the movement includes many documents and declarations of Tupamaro origin. Includes number of partial (and partisan) biographies. Also reproduced the movement's policy declaration concerning public affairs should their political initiatives within the Frente Amplio succeed in the 1971 elections.

7908. Foland, Frances M. Uruguay's urban guerrillas (NL, 54:19, 4 Oct. 1971, p. 8-11, illus.)

Rather "popular" short piece, prior to the 1971 election, asks some useful questions about the Tupamaros and about middle-class discontent with the country's political party system. Piece engages in much free association (Tupamaros are similar in quality to revolutionary movements elsewhere), and suggests that if the to-be-elected regime (Bordaberry, as it turned out) continues Pacheco's indifference to the need for change, the system will fail.

7909. Gilio, María Esther. The Tupamaro guerrillas: the structure and strategy of the urban guerrilla movement. Translated by Anne Edmondson. Introduction by Robert J. Alexander. N.Y., Saturday Review Press, 1972. 204 p.

Annotated, able if somewhat free translation of Gilio's *La guerrilla tupamara* (see *HLAS 33:8039*). Introductory material has been added by the translator and Alexander.

7910. Guiral, Jesús C. Ideologías políticas y filosofía en el Uruguay. Montevideo, Editorial Nuestra Tierra, 1969. 68 p., bibl., illus., plates (Nuestra tierra, 9)

Fragmentary and highly provocative effort, by member of the teaching Faculty of Philosophy, Univ. de la República, Montevideo, to define philosophically and ideologically the position of Uruguay and Latin America. Also briefly surveys country's principal philosophers and academic community in this intellectual area.

7910a. Kerbusch, Ernst-J. Das uruguayische Regierungssystem: Der Zweite Colegiado, 1952-1967. Köln, FRG, Heymann, 1971. 212 p.

Constitutional analysis of Uruguay's experiences with a plural executive. Very thorough and well researched treatment of that period. [W. Grabendorff]

7911. McDonald, Ronald H. Electoral politics and Uruguayan political decay (IAMEA, 26:1, Summer 1972, p. 25-45, tables)

Using the concept of "decay" as contrary to the concept of "development," author seeks to identify some symptoms, evaluate consequences on national politics, and to indicate causes. Suggests that period 1968-72 witnessed substantial withdrawal of public support from the political system, which in preceding decades was so stabilized it became decadent. As a result violence was logical and systemic, rather than anomic. Consequently, capabilities of the older parties were not refreshed by the 1971 election.

Marcha. See item 7434.

7912. Mayans, Ernesto *ed.* Tupamaros: antología documental. Cuernavaca, Mex., Centro Intercultural de Documentación (CIDOC), 1971. 1 v. (Various pagings) bibl. (CIDOC: Cuaderno, 60)

In a lengthy and sympathetic introduction by compiler, study seeks to place Tupamaros in time and to examine how the theory of violence for political purposes applies to them. Collection consists of individual works, newspaper reports, commentaries and documents of the movement.

7913. Moss, Robert. Las guerrillas urbanas en el Uruguay (USIA/PC, 18:5, sept./oct. 1971, p. 14-41)

Implies future course of Uruguay internal affairs (as of summer 1971) in an exceptionally comprehensive and perceptive essay. Author leans heavily on published work of Brazilian Carlos Marighela for tactical asides, but sticks to main point that, in general and in their published statements, Latin America's urban guerrillas have been Leninist and violent rather than programmatic.

7914. Movimiento de Liberación Nacional: Tupamaros, *Uruguay.* Actas tupamaras. B.A., Schapire Editor, 1971. 248 p. (Col. Mira)

Small volume claims to be authorized statement of Tupamaro movement prepared by some of its members. Contains rather lengthy statements of movement's strategic and tactical doctrine, reports on a number of its "operaciones," and includes brief statement of future plans.

7915. Panizza, J. Luis. Tupamaros: libertad. N.Y., Ediciones Relámpago, 1971. 93 p., illus., map, plates.

Pencil-drawn maps of locations of specific Tupamaro actions, publicized in the US press, make up principal contribution of this rather low-key presentation. Also includes poor quality photographs.

7916. *Política Internacional.* No. 136, junio 1971- . B.A.

Available issue does not show organization responsible for publication, ideologically inclined towards the left, but not radical. Director is a Dr. Jorge Julio Greco. Articles altogether too brief to cite. Includes among others, text of Frente Amplio Manifesto in the Uruguay 1971 elections.

7917. Rama, Germán W. El club político. Montevideo, Arca, 1971. 137 p. (Bolsilibros Arca, 87)

Fruitful and critical reporting of interviews with leaders of party clubs in Uruguay, prepared by a study-team headed by one of the country's better young sociologists. He reflects, in his introduction that since the interviews were undertaken in 1967, and so much has happened since, it is hard to know if he is writing history of the sustained reality of the system.

7918. Riz, Liliana de. Ejército y política en Uruguay (ITT/RLS, 6:3, sept./dic. 1970, p. 420-442, tables)

There is increasing military intervention in politics in Uruguay. Politicization of the military dates largely from the breakdown of the *batllista*-inspired concept of coparticipation. This concept became possible by relative economic and social success of the national system. The latter's breakdown in the 1950s led to that of the former in the 1960s. Careful and preceptive short paper.

7919. Suárez, Carlos and Rubén Anaya Sarmiento. Los Tupamaros. México, Editorial Extemporáneos, 1971. 247 p. (Mini extemporáneos, 4)

Pocket-sized volume (3 1/2" × 3 1/2") pretends to offer some history to explain why the Tupamaros were essential for the country. Also includes details of their operations and views, and a collection of the now-standard documents of the movement.

Vázquez Fraco, Guillermo. El país que Batlle heredó. See *HLAS 34:2893*.

ARGENTINA

7920. Alende, Oscar Eduardo. Los que mueven las palancas. B.A., A. Peña Lillo, 1971. 192 p.

Critical comments concerning the Argentine government since 1966, by an experienced political writer and activist.

7921. Argentina. Consejo Nacional de Desarrollo. Secretaría. Lineamientos de un nuevo proyecto nacional: documento de trabajo. B.A., 1970. 127 l.

Argentine National Security Council and the National Council for Development attempt to provide what might be called an ideology of national development. It is concluded that only a competitive political system with a dominant party or a pluralistic party system can achieve the values and goals of Argentina. [C. N. Ronning]

7922. Argentine-Brésil (FDD/NED [Problèmes d'Amérique Latine, 24] 1972, p. 1-91, bibl., maps, tables)

Covers period Nov. 1970-Dec. 1971 and consists of two articles: Romain Gaignard, "L'Evolution de la Politique Argentine en 1970 et 1971, du Président Onganía à Président Lanusse;" and Yves Leloup, "Croissance Démographique, Urbanisation et Déséquilibres Régionaux au Brésil." The series entitled *Problèmes d'Amérique Latine*, appears four times annually and handles several countries, usually according to geographic region. Coverage usually very good, includes bibliographies, chronologies and team-prepared analyses of periods covered.

7923. Argentine: opération-massacre (Partisans [Paris] 68, nov./déc. 1972, p. 71-95)

Leftist/journalistic account of events and persons leading to the inexplicable massacre of Trelew, in Aug. 1972.

7924. Borón, Atilio Alberto. El estudio de la movilización política en América Latina: la movilización electoral en la Argentina y Chile (IDES/DE, 12:46, julio/sept. 1972, p. 211-243, tables)

Brief study contrasts process of political mobilization in both countries. Author largely confines his paper to historical events, as a first step toward establishment of a multi-phase hypothesis concerning the subject in the entire region. Substantial contribution to analysis and to research design building.

Büntig, Aldo J. and Carlos A. Bertone. Hechos, doctrinas sociales y liberación: ensayo de exposición sistemática del Magisterio Social de la Iglesia en su contexto sociológico e ideológico. See item 7373.

7925. El Burgués. Año 2, No. 28, 10 mayo 1972- . B.A.

Biweekly popular magazine with some political commentary on Argentine affairs.

7926. Cantón, Darío. Military interventions in Argentina: 1900-1966. 2. ed. B.A., Instituto Torcuato Di Tella, Centro de Investigaciones Sociales, 1968. 27p., tables.

Develops thesis that since beginning of this century, the Argentine army has taken into its hands "the control of the mobilization of the people, formerly in the hands of the oligarchy." By "mobilization," author means "political" or "electoral" mobilization. Originally, this study was a working paper delivered at the Conference on Armed Forces and Society, held by the International Sociological Association in London, 14-16 Sept. 1967. [C. N. Ronning]

7927. ———. La política de los militares argentinos: 1900-1971. B.A., Siglo XXI Editores, 1971. 161 p., bibl., tables.

Collection of four long essays, most of them previously published, spanning a period of several years in author's development and growing out of his residence at the Di Tella Institute for Social Science Research. For historian's comment, see *HLAS 34:2680*.

Carril, Bonifacio del. El problema político: proposición para su solución. See item 7377.

7928. Casal, Horacio Néstor. Los años 30. B.A., Centro Editor de América Latina, 1971. 110 p., illus. (La historia popular: vida y milagros de nuestro pueblo, 25)

Popular historical recounting of the overthrow of Yrigoyen in 1930, and of subsequent military regime. Emphasizes latter aspects of period.

7929. ———. Los negociados. B.A., Centro Editor de América Latina, 1971. 111 p., plates

(La historia popular: vida y milagros de nuestro pueblo, 42)

Famous—or, better said, infamous—examples of the use of political power to obtain control of resources. Somewhat sharper and more pointed piece than most in this series entitled "La Historia Popular," see *HLAS 34:2896*.

7930. ———. La revolución del 43. B.A., Centro Editor de América Latina, 1971. 114 p., plates (La historia popular: vida y milagros de nuestro pueblo, 38)

Overthrow of Castillo's conservative civilian government by the armed forces in a popular version.

7931. Castagno, Antonio. Tendencias y grupos en la realidad argentina. Prólogo [de] Carlos S. Fayt. B.A., EUDEBA, 1971. 52 p. (Informes y monografías de EUDEBA)

Endpaper note calls this a "topography of the political terrain." Series of very short chapters attempts to put into some sort of structure or grouping the country's multitude of parties and political groups. Major parties are also illustrated in organizational charts. Insert offers a comparative chart of policies of a number of parties on a list of selected issues. Interesting and suggestive effort.

7932. Ceresole, Norberto. Argentina y América Latina: doce ensayos políticos. B.A., Editorial Pleamar, 1972. 362 p., tables

Very prolific young peronist writer offers a dozen essays and articles. One of them is signed by Perón, while others are by Ceresole, most of them previously published. Discussion relates to Argentine internal affairs, but several passages detail peronist (read Ceresole's?) thoughts on international relations of Argentina and the world.

7933. ——— and others. Argentina: estado y liberación nacional. B.A., Organización Editorial, 1971. 207 p.

Five lengthy essays on power and unions and economic development in a dependent nation. Writers are all members of Movimiento Nacional, "the backbone of peronismo."

7934. Chandler, Charlotte. Conversation with Juan Perón. (Oui [Chicago, Ill.] 2:3, March 1973, p. 67-68, 88, 92, 94, 96, 98, plates)

Playboy's alter ego "interviews" Perón about himself, his purposes, and his continuing aspirations. The date of the publication is cued by his Nov. 1972 return to B.A. It is claimed that the published conversation is the result of several interviews over an extensive period of time. Useful summary of the man's own self-image, but does not offer new material despite its introductory claim.

Ciria, Alberto. ¿Una imagen de la Argentina? See *HLAS 34:2689*.

7935. ———. Perón y el justicialismo. B.A., Siglo XXI Editores, 1971. 193 p. (Col. Mímima, 43)

Pocket size suggests bowlderization. Instead, reader finds that this is a serious effort to examine and define this now-historic movement in its past and present context, with much comparative examination included. For historian's comment, see *HLAS 34:2689a*.

7936. ——— and others. New perspectives on modern Argentina. Bloomington, Ind., Indiana Univ., Latin American Studies Program, 1972. 94 p., tables (Latin American studies working papers)

Seven papers, by as many authors, drawn from a 1971 seminar on contemporary Argentina, held at Indiana Univ. Several writers are known and experienced academics: Alberto Ciria; Robert A. Potash; Eldon Kenworthy; Rubén E. Reina. Two are graduate students: Michael Dodson and A. Lawrence Stickell. One, George Oclander, is an undergraduate. Papers have much use for both specialists and general reader.

7937. Codovilla, Victorio. Trabajos escogidos. t. 1. B.A., Editorial Anteo, 1972. 301 p.

Selected collection of writings and reports by Codovilla, one of the earliest and longest workers from the Argentine Communist Party. First of two projected volumes.

Confirmado. See item 7387.

7938. Cooke, John William. Peronismo y revolución: el peronismo y el golpe de estado, informe a las bases. B.A., Ediciones Papiro, 1971. 236 p. (Col. Política)

Experienced peronist leader, deceased in the late 1960s, analyzes the military government that has run the country, under different leaders, since 1966. Important book.

Correa, Jorge. Los jerarcas sindicales. See item 7389.

7939. Crawley, Eduardo D. Subversión y seguridad: la cuestión de la guerra de guerrillas en el contexto argentino. Introducción y fichas geográficas de R. Zúñiga Berrude. B.A., Círculo Militar, 1970. 138 p., bibl., maps, tables (Col. Estrategia, 618)

Argentine officer gives thoughts on guerrilla possibilities in Argentina, and on their interdiction.

7940. Dana Montaño, Salvador M. Contribución al estudio del cambio del régimen representativo argentino: legislación electoral y de los partidos políticos. B.A., Ediciones Depalma, 1972. 102 p.

Traditional and legalistic examination of the legal provisions concerning political parties in Argentina. Draws comparisons between them and those of selected countries, as well as with theoretical works by a number of foreign and Argentine authors. Useful for a researcher in this restricted area.

7941. ———. La participación política y sus garantías: contribución al estudio de la representación popular, del régimen electoral, y el reordenamiento de los partidos políticos. B.A., Victor P. de Zavalía Editor, 1971. 255 p.

Legalistic and comparative study of subject including theoretical and illustrative material from other political systems, with much detail on Argentina's national and provincial governments.

7942. Delich, Francisco J. Tipos de acción y organización campesina en Argentina (CPES/RPS, 8:22, sept./dic. 1971, p. 109-131, tables)

Begins from premise that culture and environment of Argentine campesinos are so different from those of Peru or Mesoamerica that studies involving these areas are hardly relevant. Writer examines selected data for three provinces and sees distinct tendencies in each suggesting possibility for development of a "yeoman-farmer" type in some instances.

7943. Díaz Araujo, Enrique. La conspiración del '43; el GOU: una experiencia militarista en la Argentina. B.A., Ediciones La Bastilla, 1971. 341 p., tables.

Detailed study of military officers' political and professional organization, 1930-46. Detailed emphasis on the 1945 golpe through Perón's takeover as President in 1946.

7944. ———. El G.O.U. en la Revolución de 1943: una experiencia militarista en la Argentina. Mendoza, Arg., Univ. Nacional de Cuyo, Facultad de Ciencias Políticas y Sociales, Instituto de Ciencias Políticas, Centro de Investigaciones, 1970. 292 l. (Series cuadernos, 9)

Solidly researched thesis in political science. Despite title, work is not confined to the military material implied. Instead, it is rather broad-scale and seeks to examine the *ambiente* at the time of the 1943 golpe.

7945. Di Tella, Torcuato S. La búsqueda de la formula política argentina (IDES/DE, 11:42/44, julio 1971/marzo 1972, p. 317-325)

Argentina's political problems seem insoluble except through the application of exceptional talent over a period of 30 to 40 years. Further, not everything can be done through governmental initiative. Neither Chile nor Uruguay have solved their problems through civilian government any better, which raises the possibility of the need for military leadership. All three sharply differ from other Latin American countries in which military solutions have served well (Peru, Brazil, or Cuba). Though brief, this is a provocative and insightful article.

7946. Echagüe, Carlos M. Las grandes huelgas. B.A., Centro Editor de América Latina, 1971. 112 p., plates (La historia popular: vida y milagros de nuestro pueblo, 31)

Primer-like treatment of the "great strikes" of Argentina. Major portion deals with events to 1945, and some of this has substantial historical value.

7946a. Evers, Tilman Tönnies. Demokratie ohne Demokraten-Politische Entwickling und Wahlrecht in Argentinien (Verfassung und Recht in Übersee [Hamburg, FRG] 5:2. 1972, p. 117-143)

Historical survey of voting rights and voting patterns in Argentina, with special emphasis on its effect on the rise of Peronism. [W. Grabendorff]

7946b. ———. Militärregierung in Argentinien: das politische System der "Argentinischen Revolution". Hamburg, FRG. Alfred Metzner, 1972. 288 p., tables (Darstellungen zur Auswärtigen Politik, 12)

Excellent treatment of origins, political ideology and political institutions of the Argentine revolution of 1966. Author views it as an attempt to consolidate the status quo in the country. Argues that proven failure of this model of dependent capitalist development is probably the greatest success of the political experience since 1966. Resumés in Spanish and English. [W. Grabendorff]

7947. Falcoff, Mark. Raúl Scalabrini Ortiz: the making of an Argentine nationalist (HAHR, 52:1, Feb. 1972, p. 74-101)

Although essentially biographical, article sketches intellectual changes of period 1930-43 among middle-class intellectuals. Rejection by Scalabrini and others of 1930's "Conservative Restoration" led to the nationalism of 1943 which this analysis views primarily as a home-grown movement with anti-leftist and anti-British characteristics.

Fernández, Julio A. The political elite in Argentina. See *HLAS 34:2704a*.

7948. Ferrer, Gustavo. Los partidos políticos. B.A., Centro Editor de América Latina, 1971. 111 p., plates (La historia popular: vida y milagros de nuestro pueblo, 51)

Popular survey of parties in Argentina. Although lacking depth, it is a useful compendium. Viewpoint is suggested by opening chapter: "The Political Parties as a Problem".

7949. Folino, Norberto. Barceló y Ruggierito: patrones de Avellaneda. B.A., Centro Editor de América Latina, 1971. 112 p., plates, tables (La historia popular: vida y milagros de nuestro pueblo, 14)

Biographies of two famed and infamous politicans of Buenos Aires province, Alberto Barceló and Juan Ruggiero. Case studies of two conservative paternalistic politicans which offer much useful data for the researcher.

Freels, John W., Jr. Industrial trade association in Argentine politics: historical roots and current prospects. See *HLAS 34:2709a*.

7950. Frías, Pedro J. Federalismo y planeamiento en la Argentina (DPB/RICS, 18, 1971, p. 407-411)

National planning and development scheme was established in 1966. Is it constitutional? Does it infringe unnecessarily on provincial rights? Short and legalistic piece.

7951. Gambini, Hugo. El 17 [i.e., diecisiete] de octubre. B.A., Centro Editor de América Latina, 1971. 111 p., plates (La historia popular: vida y milagros de nuestro pueblo, 26)

Popular volume depicts Perón's return from imprisonment on Martín García island amid popular orchestration by the military regime.

7952. ———. El peronismo y la Iglesia. B.A.,

Centro Editor de América Latina, 1971. 113 p., tables (La historia popular: vida y milagros de nuestro pueblo, 48)

Pro-peronist account of Church-State relations during the Perón era, in the primer-like style, characteristic of this series (see *HLAS 34:2896*).

7953. García Costa, Víctor. El periodismo político. B.A., Centro Editor de América Latina, 1971. 107 p., facsims., plates (La historia popular: vida y milagros de nuestro pueblo, 79)

Short popular history of political journalism, with emphasis (but not exclusively so) on the Argentine practice of this art.

7954. García Flores, José I. Frondizi: estrategia del desarrollo argentino. Rosario, Arg., Escuela Salesiana del Colegio San José, 1967. 217 p.

Somewhat uncritical political biography of the former president.

7955. García Martínez, Luis. La revolución argentina y las contradicciones nacionales. B.A., Ediciones Argentina Contemporánea, 1970. 60 p., table.

Critical examination of economic policy and planning after 1966.

7956. Goldwert, Marvin. Democracy, militarism, and nationalism in Argentina, 1930-1966. Austin, Univ. of Texas Press, 1972. 253 p., bibl. (Latin American monographs, 25)

Essentially a history of the actions and self-perceived role of the armed forces in the period 1930-60, sketchily updated to 1966. Useful but hardly startling review of attitudes of soldiers who cherish views already described in detail by authors who have examined the traditional "Latin" military mind. For historian's comment, see *HLAS 34:2720a*.

7957. Graham-Yooll, Andrew *comp.* Tiempo de tragedia: cronología de la "Revolución Argentina." Prólogo de Miguel Gazzera y Rodolfo Terragno. B.A., Ediciones de la Flor, 1972. 133 p.

Chronology of period June 1966-Dec. 1971; also includes two short interpretive essays by indicated authors.

7958. Inkeles, Alex. Participant citizenship in six developing countries (APRS/R, 63:4, Dec. 1969, p. 1120-1141, tables)

Compares Argentina and Chile among a group also including India, Israel, Nigeria and East Pakistan. Computer-aided study seeks to test four questions (all employed in prior studies in developed countries) of those measures of behavior that appear to have been useful in reaching conclusions concerning participation in politics.

7959. Kirkpatrick, Jeane J. Leader and vanguard in mass society: a study of Peronist Argentina. Cambridge, Mass., The MIT Press, 1971. 262 p., map, tables (MIT studies in comparative politics)

Major study of mass political behavior based on survey data developed by author who mildly deplores fact that she did not keep her book as "tight" and neat as she hoped. For the inquirer into Argentine politics, this admission has its advantages.

7960. Laura, Guillermo Domingo. El capitalismo del pueblo. B.A., Editorial Humanitas, 1971. 99 p., tables.

Rather intriguing non-professional criticism suggests that "people's capitalism" as practiced in Argentina has had the effect of requiring individual Argentines, willy-nilly, to save their earnings so that the government could become rich for its own sake, rather than for the benefit of the public. Offers some contrasts with other countries of Latin America.

López, Alfredo. Historia del movimiento social y la clase obrera argentina. See *HLAS 34:2746*.

7961. Luna, Félix. De Perón a Lanusse: 1943-1973. B.A., Editorial Planeta Argentina, 1972. 223 p.

Serious and lucid effort to put into perspective events of the past 30 years. Argues that Argentina's role, fashioned in the 19th century, as a quasi-member of the British Empire/Commonwealth, dissolved only in the 1950s. Today, country seeks a new and autonomous position and value system. Enormous stresses of 30 years demonstrates stability underlying Argentine society, despite apparent political facetiousness.

Marianetti, Benito. Las luchas sociales en Mendoza. See *HLAS 34:2752a*.

7962. Marsal, Juan Francisco. Los ensayistas políticos argentinos del postperonismo (ILARI/A, 25, julio 1972, p. 45-82, tables)

"Liberating Revolution" of 1955 was a victory of the upper classes over the lower. By consistently precluding political participation of peronists, the victors largely achieved their purposes of control and distortion in distribution. Marsal briefly reports both on how essayists of the period viewed these phenomena as well as what was their class status. Quotes on selected topics and extensive bibliography are appended.

7963. Merkx, Gilbert W. Sectoral clashes and political change: the Argentine experience (LARR, 4:3, Fall 1969, p. 89-114, tables)

Employing Mamalakis thesis concerning sectoral clash as principal motivator of political and economic change, author examines the Argentine case. Regards the country's experience as the most appropriate in Latin America for application of the model, although its use in this paper is hardly rigorous.

7964. Mora y Araujo, Manuel and **Nilda Sito.** The position of Argentina in the system of international stratification (RU/SCID, 7:3, Fall 1972, p. 264-277, tables)

Brief comparison of Argentina with other societies along a series of scales. Methodology employs national social systems as if they were individual actors, and ranks them in terms of greater or lesser development. Argentina comes out well in some respects, but in others it is still underdeveloped in both institutional and policy terms.

7965. Morello, Augusto Mario; Antonio A. Troccoli; and Félix R. Loñ. Meditación sobre la democracia argentina. La Plata, Arg., Editora Platense, 1972. 196 p., bibl.

Thoughts and ruminations about the qualities of democracy, what they should be and what the Argentine experience has produced. Writers' view imbued with economic conservatism.

7966. Murmis, Miguel and Juan Carlos Portantiero. Estudios sobre los orígenes del peronismo. t. 1. B.A., Siglo XXI, Argentina Editores, 1971. 126 p., tables (Sociología y política)

Two short individual essays, previously published as working papers of the Di Tella Institute of Buenos Aires, discussing social and economic conditions of the period after 1929. First essay is "Crecimiento Industrial y Alianza de Clases en la Argentina: 1930-1940." Second, "El Movimiento Obrero en los Orígenes del Peronismo." V. 2 by other authors forthcoming. For historian's comment, see *HLAS 34:2762a*.

7967. Nadra, Fernando. Perón: hoy a ayer, 1971-1943. Prólogo [de] Vicente Alvariza. B.A., Editorial Polémica, 1972. 94 p., tables.

Current interpretation of Perón and peronismo by the Communist party of Argentina.

7968. Niekerk, A. E. van. De vicieuze cirkel van de Argentijnse politiek (NGIZ/IS, 27:6, maart 1973, p. 188-195)

Author holds that peronismo was a populist force of genuine legitimacy, since, up to that time, no other outlet appeared to speak for the mass. Can this force be integrated into the national political system under Lanusse or a successor government? Variable elements are examined. Interesting reading in light of the outcome of the election that occurred virtually on the date of article's publication.

7969. O'Donnell, Guillermo A. Modernización y golpes militares: teoría comparación y el caso argentino (IDES/DE, 12:47, oct./dic. 1972, p. 519-566, tables)

Detailed examination of military behavior, 1955-66, within a general statement of the social context of Argentina in that period. Consists of 12 propositions that will base a comparative and cross-national study of military-political behavior. Contribution of the armed forces to modernization is perceived as fundamentally affected by their desire to retain coherence.

7970. Orona, Juan V. La dictadura de Perón. B.A., Talleres Gráficos Zlotopioro, 1970. 374 p. (Col. Ensayos políticos militares, 4)

Fourth of an exhaustive five-volume series on military politics in Argentina by a retired army colonel. Recommended as a must for investigators of the phenomenon.

7971. ———. La revolución del 16 de septiembre. t. 5. B.A., n.p., 1970. 317 p. (Col. Ensayos políticos militares, 5)

One of a series on the history of the Argentine military in politics. Although title refers to military overthrow of Perón regime, text wanders into many other contemporary subjects. Useful appendix of documents, debates, etc.

7972. Pasini, Emilio. La presencia sindical en Argentina (ESC, 4:15/16, julio/dic. 1970, p. 121-134)

General history of growth of labor organization in Argentina, with almost exclusive emphasis on the Confederación General del Trabajo, organized in 1930. The CGT's differences with the peronista movement are exemplified by the article's lack of mention of Perón. Conclusions stress future importance of sindical action and partisan pressure.

7973. Pastorini, Juan Guido. Reforma agraria y reforma politica: la salida de la crisis argentina. B.A., Ediciones Libera, 1971. 413 p., bibl., tables.

Argentine agriculture is in crisis, but then so is its society, says writer. Agrarian reform plans of other countries cannot serve Argentines with satisfactory blueprints. Large number of itemized sections indicate steps to be undertaken, in both technical agricultural area and in national politics. Further, specific strategy and tactics are to be developed in order to reach these goals. Provocative book.

7974. Peña, Milciades. Masas, caudillos y élites: la independencia argentina de Yrigoyen a Perón. B.A., Ediciones Fichas, 1971. 133 p., bibl.

Posthumous publication of material written between 1955-57. While mostly a historical recounting of events, piece is also sharply critical and, in some degree, analytical, within a nationalist and moderate structure.

7975. ———. Peronismo: selección de documentos para la historia. B.A., Ediciones Fichas, 1972. 166 p.

Collection of over 100 statements by and about Perón and peronism, taken from public statements and the press in period 1943-55. Unfortunately, organization is chronological rather than topical.

7976. Perón, Juan Domingo. Conducción política. B.A., Editorial Freeland, 1971. 368 p.

Reprinting of a collection of lectures delivered in 1952 at the Escuela Superior Peronista, for labor leaders. Its republication has both tactical and historical interest.

7977. ———. Latinoamérica, ahora o nunca. Rosario, Arg., Ediciones del Río Paraná, 1968? 130 p. (Col. de estudios sociales)

Fragments of writing and statements by Perón on *justicialismo*, Latin American integration, and international relations of the Americas.

7978. Polémica en la Iglesia: documentos de obispos argentinos y sacerdotes para el Tercer Mundo, 1969-1970. Avellaneda, Arg., Ediciones Búsqueda, 1970. 125 p.

Collection of documents produced by the clash between the conservative hierarchy and the more radical priests of the Church in Argentina. Short introduction places much of the substance of the collection in perspective.

7979. Polino, Héctor T. Compendio de desatinos: 5 años de revolución Argentina. B.A., Artes Gráficas CARDEMAR, 1971. 177 p., plates.

Collection of previously-published newspaper articles by author, an investigative free-lance reporter in the capital. First third is composed of a few run-downs on crises and scandals at the national level, in "Washington-Merry-Go-Round" style. Balance treats, in more detail, municipal problems and scandals of the capital. Latter portion has some value for the specialist.

7980. Puiggrós, Rodolfo. Las izquierdas y el problema nacional. 2. ed. B.A., Carlos Pérez Editor, 1971. 194 p., tables (Col. Los porqués)

Revised edition of *HLAS 20:2228*, where author states the need to develop some sense of political history in Argentine youth. Covers primarily period prior to 1930. Additions by author are "manifiestos" directed against "fascists": Yrigoyen, Uriburu, Perón, and Onganía.

7981. ———. El peronismo: sus causas. 2. ed. Prólogo para la segunda edición [por] Juan Domingo Perón, 1971. 172 p. (Col. Los porqués)

Why did peronismo find such a large following in Argentina? Because of the gaps and vacua left in the political system by a traditional and unadaptable society. Distinguished by *el líder's* introduction. Useful standard piece, though party-line.

7982. Ramos, Jorge Abelardo. Revolución y contrarrevolución en la Argentina. 4. ed. v. 4, El sexto dominio: 1922-1943. B.A., Editorial Plus Ultra, 1972. 266 p.

Revision of major political history by active leftist. Forthcoming v. 5 will cover period 1943-72. General Lanusse's coming to power. Replete with names, events, details.

7983. Rauch, Enrique. Un juicio al proceso político argentino. B.A., Editorial Moharra, 1971. 179 p.

Argentine brigadier general offers short, and somewhat personal, interpretation of recent history. His view of his country's future includes the armed forces in the top spot, though he is a nationalist who rejects foreign influences, ideas and, especially, investments.

7984. Sánchez Sorondo, Marcelo. Libertades prestadas. B.A., A. Peña Lillo, 1970. 305 p., illus. (La Argentina del tiempo perdido)

Collection of author's newspaper commentaries from *Azul y Blanco*, written during Aramburu period, 1956-58. Lengthy notes section is substantial contribution, and some original pieces are useful for students of the period.

7985. Sburlati, Carlo. Peron e il giustizialismo. Roma, Giovanni Volpe Editore, 1971. 112 p., bibl. (Serie: Gialla, 1)

Peronista primer, notable principally for its publication in Italian. Material consists largely of small items, often of only a few lines, taken from peronista declarations or memoirs (in the case of Eva Perón).

Senen González, Santiago. Ejército y sindicatos: los 60 días de Lonardi. See *HLAS 34:2800*.

7986. ———. El sindicalismo después de Perón. B.A., Editorial Galerna, 1971. 164 p.

Collection of documents relating to the labor movement compiled and introduced by labor leader. For historian's comment, see *HLAS 34:2800a*.

7987. Sigal, Silvia. Crisis y conciencia obrera: la industria azucarera tucumana (ITT/RLS, 6:1, marzo 1970, p. 60-99, tables)

Study based on interview data with union members in 1968, two years after government seizure of seven mills. An economically depressed area, region had had protective treatment in the past. Article explores worker reaction to government promises, authoritarian practices, and to fear of unemployment due to incompleted conversion of the mills. Worker doubts and clear class rejection of entrepreneurial competence to achieve constructive developmental change of region led to a situation too complex for easy solutions. Careful article with serious attention to methodological and analytical techniques.

7988. Sindicato de Luz y Fuerza, Buenos Aires. Cien años contra el país. B.A., Editorial "2 de Octubre," 1970. 202 p. (Col. Cuadernos CEES)

Analysis of attitudes and history of *La Prensa*, the great Buenos Aires newspaper, prepared by an unidentified research team and sponsored by the city's Light and Power Union. *La Prensa* is depicted as the voice of dependency, imperialism, and the oligarchy, throughout its century of existence.

7989. Smith, Peter H. The social base of Peronism (HAHR, 52:1, Feb. 1972, p. 55-73, tables)

Mathematical analysis of the 1946 election, which placed Perón in the presidency of Argentina. Regression analysis is explained in some detail, and applied to available data for big cities, townships, and rural areas. Correlations are developed. Concludes that generalizations about the socio-economic characteristics of those who voted for Perón do not stand up. For historian's comment, see *HLAS 34:2803*.

7990. Suárez, Héctor V. Argentina: con las armas en la mano (PC, 48, enero 1971, p. 114-163)

Correspondent for Cuba's *Prensa Latina*, interviews representatives of four guerrilla movements in Argentina: Montoneros, Fuerzas Argentinas de Liberación, Fuerzas Armadas Peronistas, and Fuerzas Armadas Revolucionarias. Discusses recent events involving political violence. Radical left interpretations.

7991. Tarnopolsky, Samuel. Los prejuiciados de honrada conciencia. B.A., Editorial Candelabro, 1971. 124 p.

Discussion of antisemitism in Argentina.

7992. Urtubey, Rodolfo J. Del régimen a la revolución: formas políticas argentinas. B.A., Ediciones Theoría, 1972. 70 p. (Biblioteca de ensayistas contemporáneos)

Short essay argues that country's past regimes, which are barely sketched, were never adequate to national need. Those now available only serve as institutional cloaking for essential change. Thus, revolution is inevitable.

7993. Villar, Daniel. El cordobazo. B.A., Centro Editor de América Latina, 1971. 113 p., illus. (La historia popular: vida y milagros de nuestro pueblo, 32)

Popular version of student-worker uprising May 1969, in automotive city of central Argentina. First major protest against Onganía government implies much for students of Argentine politics, as well as for its activists of all partisan affiliations.

JOURNAL ABBREVIATIONS

AAA/AA	American Anthropologist. American Anthropological Association. Washington.
AAFH/TAM	The Americas. Inter-American Cultural Agency. Academy of American Franciscan History. Washington.
AAPSS/A	The Annals of the American Academy of Political and Social Science. Philadelphia, Pa.
AES	Archives Européennes de Sociologie. Paris.
AF/AUR	Air University Review. The professional journal of the United States Air Force. Maxwell Air Force Base, Ala.
AJC/C	Commentary. American Jewish Committee. N.Y.
AJCL	The American Journal of Comparative Law. American Association for the Comparative Study of Law. Univ. of California. Berkeley, Calif.
APS/PSQ	Political Science Quarterly. Columbia Univ. [and] The Academy of Political Science. N.Y.
APS/WA	World Affairs. The American Peace Society. Washington.
APSA/R	American Political Science Review. American Political Science Association. Columbus, Ohio.
BID/T	Temas del BID. Banco Interamericano de Desarrollo. Washington.
BUS	Boletín Uruguayo de Sociología. Montevideo.
CEDN/R	Revue de Défense Nationale. Comité d'Etudes de Défense Nationale. Paris.
CFR/FA	Foreign Affairs. An American quarterly review. Council on Foreign Relations, Inc. N.Y.
CIDG/O	Orbis. Bulletin International de documentation linguistique. Centre International de Dialectologie Générale. Louvain, Belgium.
CIDGO/O	See CIDG/O.
CJ/RF	Razón y Fe. Revista mensual hispano-americana de cultura. Los Padres de la Compañía de Jesús. Madrid.
CLAPCS/AL	América Latina. Centro Latino-Americano de Pesquisas em Ciências Sociais. Rio.
CM/FI	Foro Internacional. El Colegio de México. México.
CPES/RPS	Revista Paraguaya de Sociología. Centro Paraguayo de Estudios Sociológicos. Asunción.
CSSH	Comparative Studies in Society and History. Society for the Comparative Study of Society and History. The Hague.
CUA/AQ	Anthropological Quarterly. Catholic Univ. of America, Catholic Anthropological Conference. Washington.
CUH	Current History. A monthly magazine of world affairs. Norwalk, Conn.
CUNY/CP	Comparative Politics. The City Univ. of New York, Political Science Program. N.Y.
DPB/RICS	Revista del Instituto de Ciencias Sociales. Diputación Provincial de Barcelona. Barcelona, Spain.
ENCOUNT	Encounter. London.
ESC	Estudios Sindicales y Cooperativos. Instituto de Estudios Sindicales, Sociales y Cooperativos de Madrid. Madrid.
FDD/NED	Notes et Etudes Documentaires. Direction de la Documentation. Paris.
FGV/R	Revista de Ciência Política. Fundação Getúlio Vargas. Rio.
FNSP/RFSP	Revue Française de Science Politique. Foundation Nationale des Sciences Politiques, l'Association Française de Science Politique avec le concours du Centre National de la Recherche Scientifique. Paris.
FRBNY/MR	Monthly Review. Federal Reserve Bank of New York. N.Y.
HAHR	Hispanic American Historical Review. Conference on Latin American History of the American Historical Association. Duke Univ. Press. Durham, N.C.

IAMEA	Inter-American Economic Affairs. Washington.
IBE/RBE	Revista Brasileira de Economia. Fundação Getúlio Vargas, Instituto Brasileiro de Economia. Rio.
IBEAS/EA	Estudios Andinos. Instituto Boliviano de Estudio y Acción Social. La Paz.
IDES/DE	Desarrollo Económico. Instituto de Desarrollo Económico y Social. B.A.
IEP/RPS	Revista de Política Social. Instituto de Estudios Políticos. Madrid.
IESSC/C	Comunidades. Instituto de Estudios Sindicales, Sociales y Cooperativos, Centro de Prospección Social. Madrid.
IFSNC/CD	Community Development. International Federation of Settlements and Neighborhood Centres. Rome.
ILARI/A	Aportes. Instituto Latinoamericano de Relaciones Internacionales. Paris.
IPEA/PP	Pesquisa e Planejamento. Instituto de Planejamento Econômico e Social. Rio.
ISTMO	Istmo. Revista del Centro de América. México.
ITT/RLS	Revista Latinoamericana de Sociología. Instituto Torcuato di Tella, Centro de Sociología Comparada. B.A.
JDA	The Journal of Developing Areas. Western Illinois Univ. Press. Macomb, Ill.
JDS	The Journal of Development Studies. A quarterly journal devoted to economics, politics and social development. London.
JLAIS/CS	Cristianismo y Sociedad. Junta Latino Americana de Iglesia y Sociedad. Montevideo.
LARR	Latin American Research Review. Latin American Studies Association. Univ. of Texas Press. Austin, Tex.
LNB/L	Lotería. Lotería Nacional de Beneficencia. Panamá.
MCPS/JPS	Midwest Journal of Political Science. Wayne State Univ. Press *for the* Midwest Conference of Political Science. Detroit, Mich.
MDZED	Merkur. Deutsche Zeitschrift für Europäisches Denken. Deutsche Verlags-Anstalt. Stuttgart, Germany.
MR	Monthly Review. An independent Socialist magazine. N.Y.
NGIZ/IS	Internationale Spectator. Tijdschrift voor internationale politiek. Het Nederlandsch Genootschap voor Internationale Zaken. The Hague.
NL	The New Leader. American Labor Conference on International Affairs, Inc. East Stroudsburg, Pa.
PAPS	Proceedings of the Academy of Political Science. Colombia Univ., The Academy of Political Science. N.Y.
PC	Pensamiento Crítico. La Habana.
PQ	The Political Quarterly. London.
PUCIS/WP	World Politics. A quarterly journal of international relations. Princeton Univ., Center of International Studies. Princeton, N.J.
RU/SCID	Studies in Comparative International Development. Rutgers Univ. New Brunswick, N.J.
SID/IDR	International Development Review. The Society for International Development. Washington.
SPSA/JP	The Journal of Politics. The Southern Political Science Association *in cooperation with the* Univ. of Florida. Gainesville, Fla.
SSSR/LA	Latinskaia Amerika [América Latina]. Akademia Nauk SSSR, Institut Latinskoi Ameriki [Academia de Ciencias de la URSS, Instituto Latinoamericano]. Moskva [Moscú].
UCIEI/EI	Estudios Internacionales. Univ. de Chile, Instituto de Estudios Internacionales. Santiago.
UM/JIAS	Journal of Inter-American Studies and World Affairs. Univ. of Miami Press *for the* Center for Advanced International Studies. Coral Gables, Fla.
UMG/RBEP	Revista Brasileira de Estudos Políticos. Univ. de Minas Gerais. Belo Horizonte, Bra.
UNAM/RMS	Revista Mexicana de Sociología. Univ. Nacional Autónoma de México, Instituto de Investigaciones Sociales. México.
UND/RP	The Review of Politics. Univ. of Notre Dame. Notre Dame, Ind.

UNESCO/I	Impact of Science on Society. United Nations Educational, Scientific and Cultural Organization. Paris.
UP/O	Orbis. A quarterly journal of world affairs. Univ. of Pennsylvania, Foreign Policy Research Institute. Philadelphia, Pa.
UP/TM	Tiers Monde. Problèmes des pays sous-développés. Univ. de Paris, Institut d'Étude du Développement Économique et Social. Paris.
UPR/CS	Caribbean Studies. Univ. of Puerto Rico, Institute of Caribbean Studies. Río Piedras, P.R.
USIA/PC	Problems of Communism. United States Information Agency. Washington.
USIA/PI	Problemas Internacionales. United States Information Agency. Washington.
UTIEH/C	Caravelle. Cahiers du monde hispanique et lusobrésilien. Univ. de Toulouse, Institut d'Études Hispaniques, Hispano-Americaines et Luso-Brésiliennes. Toulouse, France.
UU/WPQ	Western Political Quarterly. The Western Political Science Association; Pacific Northwest Political Science Association; and Southern California Political Science Association. Univ. of Utah, Institute of Government. Salt Lake City, Utah.
WM	Westermann's Monatshefte. Georg Westermann Verlag. Braunschweig, Germany.
ZPKW/A	Aconcagua. Iberoamérica-Europa. Zeitschrift für Politik, Kultur und Wirtschaft für die Länder iberischer und deutscher Sprache. Vaduz, Lichtenstein.

International Relations

C. NEALE RONNING
Professor of Political Science
New School for Social Research

YALE H. FERGUSON
Associate Professor of Political Science
Rutgers University

GIVEN THE GROWING IMPORTANCE OF LATIN AMERICA in the field of International Relations as well as the increase in the number of publications on the subject, the *HLAS* has instituted in this volume a separate section on INTERNATIONAL RELATIONS, formerly part of the Government and Politics section. The new section will be divided into the following five sub-sections: General, Mexico, Central America, The Caribbean, and South America.

Although it is always difficult to say anything meaningful by way of an overview of numerous selections on different subjects, a few patterns worth noting do emerge from the items reviewed in this volume. Current materials strengthen the impression mentioned by reviewers of international relations in previous years, that the quality of social science research on Latin America is steadily improving—with perhaps the most dramatic advances being made in Latin America itself and in the United Kingdom, Europe, and Japan. One still encounters many examples of the excessively legalistic and/or strictly polemical writing that predominated in Latin America in the past, and a new brand of sensational journalism focusing on the United States "empire" has emerged in Europe, but more and more books and articles evidence greater insight, balance, and methodological sophistication. In particular, the "dependence" concept has spurred thought-provoking studies of the impact of foreign influence on domestic social structure and the relationship between domestic political change and foreign policy. Anyone interested in these matters should not overlook the excellent work being done by scholars at the Colegio de Mexico (item 8114) among others. What is needed now are further case studies of "dependence," which should, in turn, clarify both the central concept and some of the policy implications for governments.

Another feature of the literature is greater attention to the political and economic role of extra-hemispheric powers in Latin America, reflecting in part Latin America's declining "special relationship" with the United States in the era of the "low profile." Herbert Goldhamer's (item 8028) is a major, pioneering contribution in this regard. The Soviet Union's relations with Cuba and with the rest of Latin America understandably remain of interest, while several items consider the implications of the USSR's naval build-up. Several studies examine expanding trade and aid ties between Latin America and Europe and Japan.

Readers seeking materials offering a Latin American perspective should not overlook particularly analyses of recent shifts in Mexico's foreign policy (item 8114); Rafael Caldera's speeches on the "Latin American bloc" (item 8004); Miles Wolpin's examination of Cuban policies toward Chile (item 8184); and Roy Preiswerk's comprehensive collection of documents on the international relations of the Caribbean (item 8176). The abrupt changes in Bolivian foreign policy brought about by the coup of 1971 are evident in items 8190 and 8202. Recent aspects of Chile's policy are also worth noting (items 8188 and 8234).

Brazilians continue to show an interest in Brazil's role in world affairs, on the South American continent and in its special relationship to the United States (items 8193, 8197, 8208, 8210, 8212, 8215, 8217, 8232 and 8237). Argentines also analyze the special position of Argentina, particularly with respect to regional diplomacy (items 8189, 8195 and 8197). Regional efforts to meet regional problems seem to be attracting the attention of an increasing number of Latin American scholars and diplomats (see items 8200, 8211 and 8236). Regionalism is frequently perceived as a means of countering United States hegemony.

Studies of United States-Latin American policies reviewed here could be grouped under three categories: historical, recent crises, and policy analysis. Among those items of a historical nature, there appears to be renewed interest, especially, in the motivations for U.S. turn-of-the-century imperialism and on the U.S. response to the Mexican Revolution prior to the Good Neighbor. New materials on the Cuban Missile and 1965 Dominican crises lead one to the conclusion that most of the returns are now in on both cases, although key issues may never be resolved, at least not until currently classified documents are made public in their entirety. Items in the third category of policy analysis testify to the malaise in contemporary inter-American relations. Analysts seem much more able to specify what is wrong with existing policies than to develop compelling alternatives. Policy prescription is made increasingly difficult by writers' perceptions of the great diversity of political patterns in Latin American (an old theme that is receiving new emphasis) and also of the domestic political and bureaucratic constraints on U.S. policy.

GENERAL

7994. Alfaro, Ricardo J. Un siglo de la Doctrina Monroe (LNB/L, 16:184, marzo 1971, p. 19-29)

One of the more interesting and thoughtful discussions to come to this reviewer's attention in a long time. Concludes that the Monroe Doctrine has been a number of things and that many of "these things" have had little to do with the Doctrine itself. Should be read in connection with items 8140 and 8145. [C. N. Ronning]

7995. Alvarado Garaicoa, Teodoro. Derecho internacional marítimo. Guayaquil, Ecua., Academia de Guerra Naval, Depto. de Publicaciones, 1970. 322 p., bibl.

Distinguished Ecuadorean jurist summarizes international practice, national legislation and the efforts of international agencies relating to jurisdiction over various oceanic zones in time of peace and in time of war. Useful introduction to the problem. [C. N. Ronning]

7996. Alvarez Soberanis, Jaime. Origen y proyecciones de la cláusula de la nación más favorecida en el Tratado de Montevideo (UNAM/RFD, 21:81/82, enero/junio 1971, p. 5-22)

Most favored nation clause was included in the Montevideo Treaty (which created the Latin American Free Trade Area) in order to get authorization from GATT for a free trade area. Article discusses the problems and contradictions that have developed as a result of this. [C. N. Ronning]

7997. Ball, Mary Margaret. The OAS in transition. Durham, N.C., Duke Univ. Press, 1969. 721 p., bibl., illus., table.

Most complete and up-to-date book on the OAS. It is of the same high quality as the Thomas book (see *HLAS 27:3156*) but more detailed. Both legal and analytical in approach, the book is well written and covers all aspects of the organization. Basic documents and an extensive bibliography add to its usefulness. [C. N. Ronning]

7998. Bazarian, Jacob. Mito e realidade sobre a União Soviética: confissões de um brasileiro que viveu 16 anos na URSS. São Paulo, Gráfica São José, 1970. 90 p.

Author's dissatisfaction with Christianity, imperialism and inequality drove him to communism but after 14 years in the Soviet Union he is now even more dissatisfied with communism. What is supposed to be new about this is not clear except that the author now appears dissatisfied with dissatisfaction. [C. N. Ronning]

7999. Belov, A. N. and A. I. Sizonenko. Vneshiaia politika SSSR I strany Latinskoi Ameriki (The foreign policy of the USSR and the countries of Latin America) (SSSR/LA, 6, Nov./Dec. 1972, p. 35-45)

Discusses Soviet defense of Latin American interests in the UN Security Council (e.g., 1954 Guatemalan crisis; 1964 Pan-American disturbances; 1965 Dominican crisis). Mentions types of Soviet aid to Allende government. [T. S. Cheston]

8000. Binning, William C. The Nixon foreign aid policy for Latin America (IAMEA, 25:1, Summer 1971, p. 31-45, tables)

Article asks and answers the question: What, if anything, is Nixon doing about economic development in Latin America? It also explains why certain policies were selected relative to other possible alternatives. [C. N. Ronning]

8001. Bode, Kenneth A. An aspect of United States policy in Latin America: the Latin American diplomats' view (APS/PSQ, 85:3, Sept. 1970, p. 471-491, tables)
Good discussion of the dilemma and inconsistencies of US recognition policy in Latin America. [C. N. Ronning]

8002. Bronheim, David. Latin American diversity and United States foreign policy (PAPS, 30:4, 1972, p. 167-176)
Arguing for a US foreign policy of pragmatism, "but not a pragmatism devoid of ideals," Bronheim insists that a viable US posture vis-à-vis Latin America must be based upon recognition of the profound differences between individual countries in the area. He offers several good illustrations of these differences. [Y. Ferguson]

8003. Cable, James. Gunboat diplomacy: political applications of limited naval force. N.Y., Praeger *for the* Institute for Strategic Studies, 1971. 251 p., bibl., tables (Studies in international security, 16)
British diplomat examines "applications of limited naval force as one of the instruments of foreign policy" 1918-present. He observes that "gunboat diplomacy" has not been limited to wartime situations and maintains that it is far from an outmoded technique today, although he foresees its future use "only in a small minority of disputes." Not focused primarily on Latin America, the book is perhaps most notable for its chapter on "The Soviet Naval Enigma" and an annotated chronology of cases. [Y. Ferguson]

8004. Caldera, Rafael. El bloque latinoamericano. Prólogo por Gonzalo García Bustillos. 3. ed., aumentada. Caracas, Oficina Central de Información (OCI), 1970. 371 p.
Excellent collection of Caldera's speeches in two parts, 1959-62 and 1969-70, latter made as President of Venezuela. Reader will be struck by Caldera's obvious sincerity, humanism, and eloquence, and by the consistency of his thought over the years on such subjects as the virtues of democracy, need for Latin American integration and political unity, and goal of "international social justice." [Y. Ferguson]

8005. Campbell, Alexander Elmslie ed. Expansion and imperialism. N.Y., Harper & Row, 1970. 186 p., bibl. (Interpretations of American history)
Extremely well-chosen anthology of essays setting forth a variety of explanations for the overtly imperialistic era in US history that began in the 1890's. Each explanation offers a valuable perspective on the subject, and the essays taken together argue against any single-factor analysis. [Y. Ferguson]

Ceresole, Norberto. Argentina y América Latina: doce ensayos políticos. See item 7932.

Cermakian, Jean. A geografia da ajuda estrangeira à América Latina: problemas de fontes e de método. See item 6522.

8006. Chalmers, Douglas A. The demystification of development (PAPS, 30:4, 1972, p. 109-122)
Excellent essay which all students of comparative politics and inter-American relations should read—despite the fact that this reviewer disagrees with Chalmer's major thesis. Chalmers makes a distinction between "development" and "developmentalism," the latter a projection of Western experience into the future as "*the* historical process" to serve as a touchstone for policy. He rejects developmentalism, arguing that it suffers from "two kinds of problems": It ignores "those elements of Latin American culture which may be adaptable and useful to make social and economic change more rapid and less painful," as well as "the significant differences which have emerged among the social and political structures of various Latin American countries." Chalmers does not consider the possibility that what is needed is a more sophisticated developmentalism. [Y. Ferguson]

8007. Chew, Benjamin. A sketch of the politics, relations, and statistics of the Western World. N.Y., AMS Press, 1971. 200 p.
Apparently a reprint of a work first published in 1827. It is a detailed and interesting argument for an American (inter-American) confederation. It calls for an alliance, a central congress, a prohibition of war, a central military force, and other forms of mutual assistance. [C. N. Ronning]

8008. Clark, Paul Gordon. American aid for development, N.Y., Praeger Publishers *for the* Council on Foreign Relations, 1972. 231 p.
"Establishment" critique of the US foreign-aid program, written by former AID official under the auspices of the Council on Foreign Relations. Clark generally supports the Nixon Administration's proposals for "reform" of aid—including separation of development and security assistance—with two major exceptions: He argues for a considerable *expansion* of US development aid and maintenance of a large *national* program. Clark's presentation, accentuating the positive, might be more persuasive had he addressed himself directly to the question of how adoption of his recommendations would remedy past failures of US aid in the realms of political and social development. [Y. Ferguson]

8009. Dinerstein, Herbert. Soviet policy in Latin America (APSA/R, 61:1, March 1967, p. 80-90)
Soviet Union's post 1945 expectations of rapid gains in a decolonizing world were largely unfilled. US reaction precluded some gains while the unplanned gain of a communized Cuba also contributed to lessening Soviet control of the process. Author anticipates Soviet alternatives in view of several circumstances: the differential rate of change throughout the world, the Chinese alternative, and Castro's uncontrollable initiatives, among others. Finally, author describes and compares Soviet doctrines and policies in Latin America. [P. B. Taylor, Jr.]

8010. Dockery, Robert H. Report on the Eighth Special Meeting of the Inter-American Economic and Social Council (IAMEA, 24:3, Winter 1970, p. 71-79)
Outlines old and new themes that were prominent at the meeting. Concludes that "in at least one respect,

Latin American policy-makers are in a better position than their US counterparts: the Latin Americans know what they want." [C. N. Ronning]

8011. Duncan, W. Raymond. Soviet policy in Latin America since Khrushchev (CIDG/O, 15:2, Summer 1971, p. 643-669, tables)

Identifies and compares basic trends in Soviet policy toward Latin America on the one hand, and Africa and Asia on the other, since Khrushchev. Moscow's special connection with Cuba, the one "revolutionary" state in the Western Hemisphere receives separate treatment. [C. N. Ronning]

8012. Dunn, William N. The Scholar-Diplomat Seminar on Latin American Affairs: the promise and illusions of the State Department reform movement (LARR, 6:2, Summer 1971, p. 77-84)

Evaluation of five Scholar-Diplomat Seminars (academic and government participants) held in Washington during the 1969-70 academic year. Concludes that "there is ample justification to criticize vigorously some of the dominant beliefs associated with the . . . Seminars. But perhaps the . . . Seminars, by raising problems and issues and by generating conflict, will provide conditions for change." [C. N. Ronning]

8013. Edmonds, David C. The 200 miles fishing rights controversy: ecology or high tariffs? (IAMEA, 26:4, Spring 1973, p. 3-18, illus., tables)

Holds that high tariffs on fish products in Europe, the US and Japan have encouraged Latin Americans to claim exclusive fishing rights in the 200 mile zone partly as a bargaining point to force tariffs down and partly to protect themselves against fishermen from Europe, US and Japan whose products could enter their respective countries duty free. [C. N. Ronning]

8014. Einaudi, Luigi R. Conflict and cooperation among Latin American states (*in* Einaudi, Luigi R., *ed.* Latin America in the 1970s. Santa Monica, Calif., Rand Corporation *for the* U.S. Department of State, Office of External Research, 1972, p. 148-157 [R-1067-DOS])

Following upon an examination of various trends encouraging conflict and unity in contemporary Latin America, Einaudi offers some predictions. In his view it is unlikely that any one Latin American nation will achieve regional hegemony, rather that "subregional alliances based on specific economic and social interests will emerge." He also speculates that the OAS "may retain significance mainly as an instrument for the exposition of the differences among Latin American countries themselves and for the forging of a new regional consciousness. . . ." [Y. Ferguson]

8015. Espinoza García, Manuel. La política económica de los Estados Unidos hacia América Latina entre 1945 y 1961. La Habana, Casa de las Américas, 1971. 194 p., bibl., tables.

Critical review of US policy. Unfortunately there is little here that has not already been said elsewhere. Final chapter on "The Effects of the Economic Policy of the U.S. on Latin America since 1945" is perhaps the most useful. [C. N. Ronning]

Fals Borda, Orlando. Subversión y desarrollo: el caso de América Latina. See item 7395.

8016. Fann, K. T. and Donald C. Hodges *eds.* Readings in U.S. imperialism. Boston, Mass., Porter Sargent Publishers, 1971. 397 p., bibl. (An extending horizons book)

Several chapters relate to Latin America and are essentially Marxist interpretations. Quality of contributions varies considerably. [C. N. Ronning]

8017. Ferguson, Yale H. Reflections on the inter-American principle of nonintervention: a search for meaning in ambiguity (SPSA/JP, 32:3, Aug. 1970, p. 628-654)

Suggests "that if we would know what the inter-American principle of nonintervention forbids . . . we must turn to the hemisphere actors who are continually engaged in assessing this matter for themselves." [C. N. Ronning]

8018. ———. United States policy and political development in Latin America (RU/SCID, 7:2, Summer 1972, p. 156-180)

Starts with a statement of purpose about the future course of US policy in Latin America, somewhere between the temptation voiced by the President to accept and support the status quo, and previous role of manipulative leadership adopted by earlier US governments. Solution offered, of support for development via international entities, is less impressive than the critical examination of past cyclical swings in American policy. [P. B. Taylor, Jr.]

8019. ——— *ed.* Contemporary inter-American relations: a reader in theory and issues. Englewood Cliffs, N.J., Prentice-Hall, 1972. 543 p., tables.

Useful text for courses in international relations of the Western Hemisphere or as supplementary reading in a general international relations course. By prominent scholars in the field, the readings are organized conceptually in order to give analytical perspectives to the issues. First part of the book deals with actor systems, linkages, integration and issue areas. The issues are grouped under "security and peaceful settlement" and "modernization." [C. N. Ronning]

8020. Fernandes, Florestan. Patrones de dominación externa en América Latina (UNAM/RMS, 32:6, nov./dic. 1970, p. 1439-1459, tables)

Traces historical evolution of factors leading to foreign domination of Latin America. These factors are all related to capitalism and the fact that changes in capitalism have been too rapid for the Latin Americans to be able to react effectively. [C. N. Ronning]

8021. Ferrell, Robert H. *ed.* America as a world power, 1872-1945. Foreword [by] Richard B. Morris. N.Y., Harper & Row, 1971. 306 p.

Second in a three-volume series on American foreign policy. Three related themes are emphasized: empire, democracy and security. Several chapters are directly related to Latin America: "War with Spain," "The Colossus of the North," "Good Neighbor and Latin America." Others touch on the area and, most important, help place Latin American policy in perspective. [C. N. Ronning]

8022. **Fisher, Bart S.** The International Coffee Agreement: a study in coffee diplomacy. Forword by Isaiah Frank. N.Y., Praeger Publishers, 1972. 287 p., bibl., tables (Praeger special studies in international economics and development)

Useful discussion of a surprisingly little understood issue. While this is a general treatment of the issue there are numerous references to Latin American coffee producing countries. Very important for understanding a critical aspect of the foreign relations of Latin American countries. [C. N. Ronning]

8023. **Francis, Michael J.** La ayuda económica de Estados Unidos a América Latina como instrumento de control político (CM/FI, 12:4, abril/junio 1972, p. 433-452)

Undertakes to show how economic aid is used as an instrument of political control and that US aid policy is unstable and contradictory. Four case studies are presented: Colombia, Brazil, Peru and Chile. [C. N. Ronning]

Frutkin, Arnold W. and **Richard B. Griffin, Jr.** Space activity in Latin America. See item 7400.

8024. **Galtung, Johan.** A structural theory of imperialism (JPR, 2, 1971, p. 81-117, illus., tables)

"Briefly stated, imperialism is a system that splits up collectivities and relates some of the parts to each other in relations of harmony of interest, and other parts in relations of disharmony of interest or conflict of interest . . . Conflict of interest is a special case of conflict in general, defined as a situation where parties are pursuing incompatible goals." Illustrations of this are drawn from Latin America and other areas. [C. N. Ronning]

8025. **Gantenbein, James W.** *ed.* and *comp.* The evolution of our Latin-American policy: a documentary record. N.Y., Octagon Books, 1971. 979 p., tables.

Reprint of a book first published in 1950, see *HLAS* 16:2299. [C. N. Ronning]

8026. **Gelfand, Lawrence E.** *ed.* Essays on the history of American foreign relations. N.Y., Holt, Rinehart and Winston, 1972. 434 p., map (Essays in American history series)

General anthology with several selections of interest to Latin Americanists: revisionist articles on the Monroe Doctrine and the Mexican War; essays focusing on American imperialism, including its relationship to capitalist expansion and case studies of Cleveland's Venezuelan policy and of Dollar Diplomacy in Nicaragua (1909-13); and an essay comparing US responses to intelligence reports in the Pearl Harbor and Cuban Missile crises. [Y. Ferguson]

8027. **Glauert, Earl T.** and **Lester D. Langley** *eds.* The United States and Latin America. Reading, Mass., Addison-Wesley, 1971. 204 p.

Singularly unimaginative anthology of selections in three parts: the 19th century; 1900-45; 1945-present. [Y. Ferguson]

8028. **Goldhamer, Herbert.** The foreign powers in Latin America. Princeton, N.J., Princeton Univ. Press, 1972. 321 p., tables (A Rand Corporation research study).

Splendid study, pioneering in its emphasis on Latin American relations with countries other than the US and the Soviet Union—although there are valuable insights about US and USSR policies too. Analysis of countries' "interests" in Latin America, "instruments" through which influence is exercised, and "results" achieved. Closing "interpretations" chapter is particularly thought-provoking. See also item 8029. [Y. Ferguson]

8029. ———. The nonhemispheric powers in Latin America (*in* Einaudi, Luigi R., *ed.* Latin America in the 1970s. Santa Monica, Calif., Rand Corporation *for the* U.S. Department of State, Office of External Research, 1972, p. 158-172 [R-1067-DOS])

Goldhamer's essay may be regarded as an extension of his book on the same subject (item 8028). He comments that although it appears nonhemispheric powers may well play an increasingly significant role in Latin America, it is not yet clear which of them will in the long run benefit most from the erosion of US influence. Nevertheless, he ventures some "useful guesses" about the later 1970s. See also item 8028. [Y. Ferguson]

8030. **Goodsell, Charles T.** The politics of direct foreign investment (*in* Einaudi, Luigi R., *ed.* Latin American in the 1970s. Santa Monica, Calif., Rand Corporation *for the* U.S. Department of State, Office of External Research, 1972, p. 173-185 [R-1067-DOS])

Goodsell perceives two "very long-range" trends relating to foreign private investment in Latin America: "host" governments are becoming more restrictive, while "home" governments are becoming less supportive of investors abroad. (To illustrate the latter trend, Goodsell draws mainly on Johnson period examples, and he does not speak directly to the Nixon hard-line.) On the other hand, the "main contention" in the essay is that "a prime feature of contemporary foreign investment politics in Latin America is not regularity and uniformity but distinction and difference." [Y. Ferguson]

8031. **Grayson, George W.** El viaje de Castro a Chile, Perú y Ecuador (USIA/PI, 19:3, mayo/junio 1972, p. 1-14, plate)

Discusses domestic and international political factors in the invitations by Allende, Velasco Alvarado, and Velasco Ibarra and Castro's acceptance of the 1971 visit. Speculates on significance of the trip for inter-American relations. [J. J. Bailey]

8032. **Green, David.** The containment of Latin America: a history of the myths and realities of the Good Neighbor Policy. Chicago, Ill., Quadrangle Books, 1971. 368 p.

Over the long run, the Good Neighbor Policy was a failure. Taking up where the Roosevelt administration had left off, the Truman administration completed the building of an inter-American system which was intended to ratify US supervision and control of Latin American economic development. [C. N. Ronning]

8033. **Griffin, K. B.** and **J. L. Enos.** Foreign

assistance: objectives and consequences (UC/EDCC, 18:3, April 1970, p. 313-327)

"In general, foreign assistance has neither accelerated growth nor helped to foster democratic political regimes. If anything, aid may have retarded development . . ." Examples are drawn largely from Latin America. [C. N. Ronning]

Hanson, Simon G. The memoirs of Spruille Braden. See *HLAS 34:2730a.*

8034. Herrera, Felipe. Nacionalismo, regionalismo, internacionalismo: América Latinaen el contexto internacional. B.A., Banco Interamericano de Desarrollo (BID), Instituto para la Integración de América Latina (INTAL), 1970. 449 p.

Discussion of the problems concerning and of steps taken in the regional integration of Latin America. Emphasis is on economic aspects and the role of the Inter-American Development Bank is treated at length. [C. N. Ronning]

8035. Hirsch-Weber, Wolfgang. Lateinamerika: Abhängigkeit und Selbstbestimmung Opladen, FRG, Leske, 1972. 170 p., bibl. (Schriftenreihe des For-schungsinstituts der Deutschen Gesellschaft für Auswärtige Politik).

Historical analysis of Latin America's international relations focusing especially on inter-American relations. Quite insightful are the chapters on intra-Latin American relations and the various expressions of Latin American nationalisms. [W. Grabendorff]

8036. Huguet Ribe, José. Colaboración entre naciones o aniquilación: un estudio de los grandes problemas de nuestros tiempos. México, B. Costa Amic Editor, 1971. 316 p.

This work discusses most of the important contemporary issues in international relations, and it is included in this section as an example of non-European or "non-Great Power" opinion on important issues. Treatment is philosophical and sociological rather than legalistic. [C. N. Ronning]

8037. Ibarra Vega, Salvador. La lucha latinoamericana por las 200 millas de mar territorial (UNAM/BCRI, 18, mayo 1972, p. 44-48)

Very brief outline of major steps in development of present situation where at least ten Latin American states now claim one or another form of jurisdiction over coastal waters to a distance of 200 miles. [C. N. Ronning]

8038. Isasi, Elda *ed.* Testimonios sobre el expansionismo norteamericano. Montevideo, Univ. de la República, Facultad de Humanidades y Ciencias, Depto. de Historia Americana, 1971. 61 p. (Fuentes para la historia social y económica del Río de la Plata, 12)

Brief excerpts from the writings of three Argentine intellectuals (Joaquín V. González, Roque Sáenz Peña and Paul Groussac), all critical of the US on a variety of themes and apparently covering period 1880-1930. [C. N. Ronning]

8039. Johnson, Cecil. China and Latin America: new ties and tactics (USIA/PC, 21:4, July/Aug. 1972, p. 53-66, plates)

Discusses Chinese interests in Latin America, phases of their policy there and treats at some length relations with Cuba, Chile and Peru. Other Latin American countries are briefly discussed. [C. N. Ronning]

8040. Joxe, Alain. El conflicto chino-soviético en América Latina. Montevideo, ARCA, 1967. 78 p., bibl.

Interesting discussion of Soviet-Chinese dispute since 1962. Examines nature of the conflict and its manifestation in several countries. [C. N. Ronning]

8041. Julien, Claude. America's empire. Translated from the French by Renaud Bruce. N.Y., Pantheon Books, 1971. 442 p., bibl.

Half analysis, half propaganda, this book is perhaps less interesting in what it says than in the fact that its author is the foreign editor of *Le Monde*. Julien discusses the rise and contemporary structure of what he terms the American "empire without frontiers," an empire founded not on direct colonization but mainly on economic domination—control of "half the wealth available in the world." In the US, Julien argues, the empire is sustained by the "internal cohesion of the 'power elite' " and "the basic adherence of the entire population to the dogmas and blessings of the American way of life." Nevertheless, he foresees the imminent decline of the empire as a result of the "inevitable" revolt of "proletarian nations" abroad and growing dissatisfaction with the "consumer society" at home. [Y. Ferguson]

8042. Karnes, Thomas L. *ed.* Readings in the Latin American policy of the United States. Tucson, Ariz., Univ. of Arizona Press, 1972. 302 p., bibl.

Documentary collection spanning a century and a half, consisting of excerpts tied together with editorial commentary in semi-narrative form. Emphasis is on history, with less than ten percent of the book devoted to the post-1945 era. Analysis is minimal, but Karnes's wide-ranging materials do offer the reader indications of the thinking of US policy-makers in particular historical periods. [Y. Ferguson]

8043. Kaufman, Burton I. United States trade and Latin America: the Wilson years (OAH/JAH, 58:2, Sept. 1971, p. 342-363)

Excellent discussion of a highly important period in US-Latin American relations: ". . . the European struggle clearly ushered in a new era of commerce between the United States and Latin America . . . In contrast to $15 million of Latin American securities offered in 1915, $125 million were offered in 1920. During the same approximate period United States' percentage of all goods imported into South American grew from under 16 percent to almost 42 percent." [C. N. Ronning]

8044. Kaufman, Edy. Los Estados Unidos y la URSS en América Latina y en Europa Oriental (ILARI/A, 24, abril 1972, p. 137-162)

Thoughtful essay. Kaufman, a professor at the Hebrew

Univ. in Jerusalem: 1) cautions against viewing Latin America as part of the "Third World"; 2) compares Soviet Control of Eastern Europe with US hegemony in the Western Hemisphere; and 3) examines options for the super-powers in their relations with countries inside one another's zone of influence. [Y. Ferguson]

8045. Kimball, Warren F. Lend-Lease and the Open Door: the temptation of British opulence, 1937-1942 (APS/PSQ, 86:2, June 1971, p. 232-259)

Excellent discussion of US short term and long term objectives in negotiating lend-lease with Britain and the methods used to achieve them. [C. N. Ronning]

8046. Kulitzka, Dieter. Zu einigen Haupttendenzen der Entwicklung in Lateinamerika und den Beziehungen der Deutschen Demokratischen Republik mit den lateinamerikanischen Staaten (EAZ, 11:2, 1970, p. 223-231)

East German author quotes from Moscow Conference of June 1969 that "the scene for the struggle between socialism and capitalism is worldwide." In Latin America, the growing "progressive" forces are different but share common tendencies. Contradictions between US imperialism and Latin American states are sharpening. Even West Germany is developing a so-called new policy towards Latin America. In contrast to these old patterns, author asserts, relations between the socialist states and Latin American countries have developed significantly in recent years; e.g., the German Democratic Republic which today has numerous commercial, economic, and cultural connections with Latin America. [H. J. Hoyer]

8047. Lara Velado, Roberto. Latinoamérica en la encrucijada: América Latina y el problema mundial contemporáneo. San José, Editorial Universitaria Centroamericana (EDUCA), 1972. 236 p., bibl. (Col. Debate)

Salvadorean lawyer and politician gives a Social Christian analysis of Latin American problems and contrasts it with marxist, fascist and liberal analyses. Calls for social justice under a democratic regime. [C. N. Ronning]

8048. Latin America: the quest for change (NGIZ/IS, 25:7, 8 April 1971, p. 725-733)

Brief but useful review of the "revolutionary" situation in Latin America during 1970. Factors prompting as well as inhibiting revolutionary activity are outlined. [C. N. Ronning]

8049. Lavenère-Wanderley, Nelson Freire. Estratégia militar e desarmamento. Rio, Bloch Editôres, 1969. 352 p., bibl., tables (Biblioteca do Exército, 414: Col. General Benício, 89)

Brazilian general discusses the problem of disarmament on a global scale. Two chapters deal with the "denuclearization" of Latin America giving a historical and analytical account of what has been accomplished. Brazilian position is outlined briefly. [C. N. Ronning]

8050. Lazarev, Marklen Ivanovich. Voennye bazy SShA v Latinskoi Amerike: mezhdunarodnyi delikt (United States military bases in Latin America: an international offense). Introduction by B. I. Gvozdarev. Moskva, Akademiia Nauk SSSR, Institut Latinskoi Amerikii, 1970. 133 p., maps.

Specialist in international law presents first Soviet "over-all study of the subject, giving an all-round concrete-historical and international-law oriented analysis of the existence of these bases." Separate chapters are devoted to: Latin America in the network of US bases; the bases as a violation of the sovereignty of Latin American countries; as a threat to peace; and ways of eliminating them and converting them into ccommercial ports, with attention to the role of international law and interstate agreements. Sources are indicated in footnotes. [A. R. Navon]

8051. Levinson, Jerome I. After the Alliance for Progress: implications for inter-American relations (PAPS, 30:4, 1972, p. 177-190)

In this perceptive article Levinson discusses the breakdown of consensus in the wake of the failure of the Alliance as to the proper hemisphere role for the US, which he sees as part of a post-Vietnam debate over US foreign policies generally. Critical of the Nixon Administration's alignment with conservative forces and protection of corporations in Latin America, Levinson asserts that the "essential issue" for the future is "how the United States can live with a region in the throes of change." [Y. Ferguson]

8052. Lodge, George C. Engines of change: United States interest and revolution in Latin America. Introduction by Samuel P. Huntington. N.Y., Alfred A. Knopf, 1969. 411 p., map, tables.

Influential book by a former Republican politician, newspaperman, and government official, now a professor at Harvard's Graduate School of Business Administration. Lodge identifies potential sources of change ("engines of change") in the institutions and social forces of contemporary Latin America and argues that a commitment to social development ("revolution") should be the cornerstone of US policy toward the area. Spin-off of Lodge's study was the establishment by Congress in 1969 of the Inter-American Institute for Social Development (now the Inter-American Foundation, see item 8095). [Y. Ferguson]

8053. Lowenthal, Abraham F. Alliance rhetoric versus Latin American reality (CFR/FA, 48:3, April 1970, p. 494-508)

"The United States cannot disengage from Latin America. The Colossus of the North is bound to cast its shadow southward no matter what direction it chooses to face. The challenge of the 1970s, for the United States and for Latin America, should be not to abandon the Alliance, but to forge a real one." Author outlines several steps that should be taken with this objective in mind. [C. N. Ronning]

8054. Lubbock, Michael R. Canadá y América (PAU/AM, 23:2, feb. 1971, p. 2-8, plates)

Author sees a growing interest in Latin America on the part of Canada. For more on subject, see items 8058 and 8105. [C. N. Ronning]

Lynch, John. British policy and Spanish America: 1783-1808. See *HLAS 34:1363*.

8055. Mariz, Vasco. A ampliação do papel da

OEA [Organização dos Estados Americanos] na solução pacífica dos problemas continentais (UMG/RBEP, 32, julho 1971, p. 45-55)

Brazilian diplomat offers highly favorable account of the OAS, noting many areas where he believes the organization has expanded its activities. [C. N. Ronning]

8056. Michelini, Zelmar. Batllismo y anti-imperialismo. Montevideo, Ediciones de la Banda Oriental, 1971. 59 p. (Col. Conciencia popular, 2)

This critical review of the OAS and its antecedents has nothing to do with "batllismo." Only the administrations of Franklin D. Roosevelt and John F. Kennedy are evaluated favorably. [C. N. Ronning]

8057. Needler, Martin C. The United States and the Latin American revolution. Boston, Mass., Allyn and Bacon, 1972. 167 p. (The Allyn and Bacon series in Latin American politics)

Concise and perceptive analysis—one of the best in the literature—of US policies under Kennedy and Johnson, with a "preliminary assessment" of the Nixon policies. Skimpy on issues of aid and trade (the Alliance for Progress is compressed into an eight-page chapter!), Needler's book is nevertheless strong on the "political dimension of hemisphere relationships." Author urges policy-maker to abandon "narrow preoccupation" with private interests and "shibboleths about national security" and instead to perceive "the revolutionary forces in Latin America today" and to frame policies working "with these forces and not against them." [Y. Ferguson]

8058. Ogelsby, J. C. M. Relaciones canadiense-latinoamericanas pasadas, presentes y futuras (UCIEI/EI, 5:18, abril/junio 1972, p. 68-87)

Commerce, investment, communications, education (via missionaries) have long been the major objectives of Canadian contacts with Latin American countries. Author expects this pattern to continue. For more on subject, see items 8054 and 8105. [C. N. Ronning]

8059. Ojeda Gómez, Mario. ¿Hacia un nuevo aislacionismo de Estados Unidos? Posibles consecuencias para América Latina (CM/FI, 12:4, abril/junio 1972, p. 421-432)

Recent US policy toward Latin America suggests a general retreat and even the abandonment of Latin America. Yet geopolitical realities suggest that we are in a period of transition perhaps towards a new form of association on a different basis. [C. N. Ronning]

8060. Organization of American States. General Secretariat. American Convention of Human Rights: "Pact of San José, Costa Rica" signed at the Inter-American Specialized Conference on Human Rights. Washington, 1970. 22 p. (Treaty series, 36: OAS Official Records OEA/ser.A/16 [English])

8061. ———. ———. Inter-American treaties and conventions: signatures, ratifications, and deposits with explanatory notes. Washington, 1971. 242 p. (Treaty series, 9, rev. 1971)

Most complete source of information on signature ratification, etc., of inter-American treaties 1902-71. [C. N. Ronning]

8062. ———. ———. Special Consultative Committee on Security Against the Subversion of International Communism. The paths of international communism in the Americas: study prepared by the SCCS at its fifteenth regular meeting, 1971. Washington, 1971. 31 p. (OAS/Ser.L/X/II.28-English)

Principal thrust of this report is to show that "international communism" aims to establish communist states in the Americas by two means: "peaceful coexistence" and subversion. [C. N. Ronning]

8063. ———. Secretaría General. Informe de progreso de los programas y proyectos en ejecución por la Secretaría General en el ejercicio 1970/71 al 31 de marzo de 1971. Introdución [por] Galo Plaza. Washington, 1971. 1 v. (Various pagings) tables (OEA/Ser.D/VIII [español])

Comprehensive and detailed report on the nature, size and status of OAS projects in operation in 1970-71. Since it was done in conformity with a General Assembly resolution it is hoped that it will be brought up to date periodically. [C. N. Ronning]

8064. ———. Special Consultative Committee on Security Against the Subversive Action of International Communism. Analysis of the Second Congress of the Young Communist League (UJC) in Cuba [and] The policy of Communist China in Latin America. Washington, 1972. 47 p. (OAS Official Records OEA/Ser.L/X/II.32 English)

This committee seems to be roughly the inter-American equivalent of the US House Un-American Activities Committee—both in terms of its intellectual level and its purpose. It is useful as an indication of attitudes which apparently prevail within at least one of the agencies of the OAS. [C. N. Ronning]

8065. Ortega y Medina, Juan A. Historia de un resentimiento: raíz y razón de la doctrina histórico-teológica del "Manifest Destiny" (in Extremos de México: homenaje a don Daniel Cosío Villegas. México, El Colegio de México, Centro de Estudios Históricos, 1971, p. 411-460)

Author's intriguing thesis is that many aspects of the later doctrine of "Manifest Destiny" were part of an intellectual heritage derived from the first English explorers and colonists to come to the New World. [Y. Ferguson]

8066. Petras, James F. and **Robert LaPorte, Jr.** Modernization from above versus reform from below: U.S. policy toward Latin American agricultural development (JDS, 6:3, April 1970, p. 248-266)

Using the criteria of success proposed by the architects of US policy for agricultural development in Latin America—1) per capita agricultural production, 2) per capita food production and 3) agricultural imports

—authors conclude that US policy has been a dismal failure. [C. N. Ronning]

8067. Piñeyro, Pedro. El super capitalismo internacional: su dominio del mundo en el año 2000. B.A., The Author, 1970. 604 p.

Best thing about this book is its title! Long, rambling tract, self-published by an Argentine, purporting to analyze the rise of international capitalism and predicting its reduction of mankind to "a permanent state of materialistic despair" by the end of the century. The end is nigh. [Y. Ferguson]

8068. Plaza, Galo. A América Latina em transição: as relações com o mundo industrializado. Paris, Instituto Atlântico, 1971. 43 p., tables.

Text of an address by the Secretary General of the OAS presented to a private international organization, the Atlantic Institute (includes Japan) in late 1970. More notable than the substance of the speech—full title: "Latin America in Transition and the Industrialized Northern Hemisphere"—is the fact that it was made, as further evidence of increasing contacts between Latin America and extra-hemisphere developed countries. Appended are the Declaration of Buenos Aires (1970), the Latin American Consensus of Viña del Mar (1969), and selected tables. [Y. Ferguson]

8069. ———. Beyond the Alliance (OAS/AM, 23:5, May 1971, p. 2-4, plates)

Abridged version of address by Secretary General of the OAS to the first Regular Session of its General Assembly (1971). Although very brief and general, it does contain some interesting (and optimistic) observations on the Alliance for Progress and on changing concepts of international relations in Latin America. [C. N. Ronning]

8070. ———. Whatever happened to the Alliance for Progress? Washington, Organization for American States, 1971. 8 p.

In a speech delivered to the World Affairs Council (1971) the Secretary General of the OAS says that "the Alliance for Progress is very much alive. As a slogan, it may have lost some of its early appeal, but the concept of multilateral cooperation to achieve more rapid economic growth and greater social justice is as valid as ever." [C. N. Ronning]

Política Internacional. See item 8173.

8071. Quadros, Jânio. Os dois mundos das três Américas. São Paulo, Martins, 1972. 495 p., maps, tables.

Former President of Brazil presents his thought on the history, problems and prospects of Pan Americanism. The two worlds mentioned in the title are made up of the US on the one hand and Latin America on the other. The three Americas are Anglo-Saxon, Spanish and Portuguese (or Latin America might also be divided into the small elite associated with Anglo Saxon America and the numerous poor). The relationship between the two worlds is one of tension and distrust. For the moment there is coexistence but it is threatened by the growing complaints of ever-increasing new generations. [C. N. Ronning]

8072. Rangel, Vicente Marotta. A próxima conferência sobre direito do mar e seus antecedentes (Problemas Brasileiros [São Paulo] 10:109, set. 1972, p. 6-16, illus., map)

Brief but useful summary of steps taken by international institutions and special conferences with regard to question of national sovereignty over territorial waters and extent of the latter. [C. N. Ronning]

8073. Reis, Arthur Cézar Ferreira. As relações internacionais da América Latina nos séculos XIX e XX (CFC/RBC, 3:10, out./dez. 1971, p. 9-37, bibl.)

Good historical summary of the highlights in relations of Latin American states with one another, US and rest of the world. [C. N. Ronning]

8074. Relaciones comerciales de la URSS con Latinoamérica (Revista Panorama Industrial [La Paz] 1:1, enero 1972, p. 12-14, plate, table)

Superficial account of non-Cuban Latin American trade with the USSR from 1965. Views possible expansion of such trade very favorably. [J. M. Hunter]

8075. Rens, Jef. América Latina y la Organización Internacional del Trabajo: cuarenta años de colaboración, 1919-1959 (Revista Internacional del Trabajo [Geneva] 60:1, julio 1959, p. 1-29)

Brief but excellent historical survey of works of International Labor Organization in Latin America during past 40 years. Should be read in connection with item 8076. [C. N. Ronning]

8076. ———. La Organización Internacional del Trabajo y la cooperación técnica internacional (Revista Internacional del Trabajo [Geneva] 63:5, mayo 1961, p. 1-28)

Credits OIT with an important role in international technical cooperation. Also includes good statement on nature of international technical cooperation, perceived as creating bonds among peoples. [C. N. Ronning]

8077. *Revista Brasileira de Política Internacional.* Instituto Brasileiro de Relações Internacionais. Ano 12, No. 47/48, set./dez. 1969- . Rio.

Entire issue devoted to "the law of the sea." Several articles discuss Brazil's position and text of major Brazilian decrees are given in full. General problems relating to the "law of the sea" are also treated. [C. N. Ronning]

8078. ———. ———. Ano 13, No. 49/50, março/junho 1970- . Rio.

Entire issue devoted to UN. Since all of the articles are written by Brazilian diplomats and military figures it sheds much light on official attitude toward the UN and world issues in general. Also some articles discuss Brazil's position on specific issues. [C. N. Ronning]

8079. Ruda, José María. Latinoamérica en las Naciones Unidas (CM/FI, 11:2, oct./dic. 1970, p. 362-377)

Distinguished Argentine diplomat gives a highly laudatory account of Latin America's participation in the UN. [C. N. Ronning]

8080. Saxe-Fernández, John. Proyecciones

hemisféricas de la Pax Americana. Lima, Instituto de Estudios Peruanos, 1971. 195 p., bibl., tables (Col. América-problema, 4)

US military policy aims to consolidate the power of military elites in underdeveloped countries making them relatively passive tools for intervention in the political system. Role of the Latin American military has been one of nation-destroying rather than nation-building. [C. N. Ronning]

8081. **Selivanov, V. I.** Voennaia politika SShA v stranakh Latinskoi Amerikii (U.S. military policy in Latin America). Moskva, Nauka, Institut Latinskoi Amerikii, 1970. 163 p., tables.

Study of US military policies in Latin America designed to update previous Soviet works on subject. Focuses on new techniques used by US military in 1960's, i.e., "to preserve the colonial exploitation of the people" of Latin America. Emphasizes inter-American military cooperation. [T. S. Cheston]

8082. **Seminario de América Latina y España,** Madrid, 1969. Bases comunes para el incremento de relaciones comerciales, financieras y de cooperación técnica: informe final, documentos, intervenciones, sugerencias, comunicaciones, anejos, discursos. Madrid, Ediciones Mundo Hispánico, 1970. 711 p., tables.

Optimistic papers concerning possibilities for increased commercial, financial and technical cooperation between Spain and Latin America. Also urges steps towards economic integration. [C. N. Ronning]

8083. **Sloan, John W.** Three views of Latin America: President Nixon, Governor Rockefeller, and the Latin American consensus of Viña del Mar (CIDG/O, 14:4, Winter 1971, p. 934-950)

"We may have to agree... that the fundamental issue for inter-American relations is revolution—radical structural change in the political, economic and social systems of Latin America and the relationship of it to the U.S." The author concludes that the issue is ignored by Nixon, by Rockefeller and by the Latin Americans themselves in the consensus of Viña del Mar. [C. N. Ronning]

8084. **Small, Melvin.** The United States and the German "threat" to the hemisphere, 1905-1914 (AAFH/TAM, 28:3, Jan. 1972, p. 252-270)

Author finds that in politics as well as in economics the German threat was more imagined than real. [C. N. Ronning]

8085. **Smetherman, Bobbie B.** and **Robert M. Smetherman.** The CEP [i.e., Chile, Ecuador and Peru] claims, U.S. tuna fishing and inter-American relations (UP/O, 14:4, Winter 1971, p. 951-972, tables)

Good discussion of most recent episodes (to 1971), controversies and dilemmas in effort to reach agreement on CEP claims and US fishing interests in waters claimed by Chile, Ecuador and Peru. [C. N. Ronning]

8086. **Smith, Wayne S.** Soviet policy and ideological formulations for Latin America (CIDG/O, 15:4, Winter 1972, p. 1122-1146)

Concludes that: 1) the primary Soviet objective is not to "communize" Latin America but to undercut US influence there, 2) Moscow's efforts are cautious and opportunistic, and 3) Soviet efforts are not likely to play a significant role in determining outcome of events in Latin America. [C. N. Ronning]

8087. **Stevenson, John R.** and others. Conflicting approaches to the control and exploitation of the oceans (in Meeting of the American Society of International Law, LXV, Washington, 1971. Proceedings. Washington, American Society of International Law, 1971. p. 107-143)

Title is somewhat misleading since these are really discussions of problems raised by conflicting approaches to the control and exploitation of the oceans. As one discussant puts it, "what we have is a revolution in the law of the sea." Several contributors discuss the US response to that revolution. Proceedings also available in one issue of *American Journal of International Law* (65:4, Sept. 1971). [C. N. Ronning]

8088. **Stinson, Hugh B.** and **James D. Cochrane.** The movement for regional arms control in Latin America (UM/JIAS, 13:1, Jan. 1971, p. 1-17)

Most attention is given to the Treaty of Tlatelolco (the denuclearization treaty) but there is a brief discussion of a 1957 Costa Rican proposal and a 1959 Chilean proposal. Factors retarding general arms control and factors promoting denuclearization are discussed. [C. N. Ronning]

8089. **Tarazov, Konstantin Sergeeviich.** SShA i Latinskoi Amerikii. (The U.S.A. and Latin America). Moskva, Izdatel'stvo Politicheskoi Literatury, 1972. 359 p., bibl., map, tables.

One of numerous Soviet works on US policies toward Latin America but broader in scope and better researched than most. Perceives US "imperialism" as cause of Latin America's social, economic and political problems. Examines place of Latin America in US strategy and ways in which it uses region's human and economic resources and maintains control. [T. S. Cheston]

8090. **Torres Bodet, Jaime.** Memorias: el desierto internacional. v. 3. México, Editorial Porrúa, 1971. 442 p.

These Memorias cover period 1948-52 when Torres Bodet was director of UNESCO. Writing style is beautiful and subject matter should interest anyone in the area of international relations, conflict resolution or international organizations. [C. N. Ronning]

8091. **Union of Soviet Socialist Republics. Akademiia Nauk CCCP. Institut Latinskoi Ameriki.** Strany Latinskoi Ameriki sovremennykh mezhdunarodnykh otnosheni (Latin America in contemporary international relations). Moskva, Nauka, 1967. 511 p., bibl., map, tables.

Collective effort by associates of the Latin American

Institute of the Soviet Academy of Sciences to do a comprehensive study of the place of Latin America in contemporary international relations. Topics include: place of Latin America in the "capitalist" world; role of US and other great powers in the region; development of Latin American relations with the USSR and other east European countries; foreign policies of specific Latin American countries and the effect of internal politics on them and international organizations related to Latin America. Principal contributors are: G. K. Seleznev, B. I. Gvozdarev, A. N. Glinkin, A. S. Strelin, A. S. Sizonenko. V. A. Vatul'fan, E. G. Lapshev, IU. V. Godunskii, V. A. Gamutilo, V. N. Seliyanov, E. A. Kosarev, S. S. Sertin, A. A. Matlina, IU. M. Grigor'ian, A. S. Koval' skaia. [T. S. Cheston]

8092. United States. Congress. House of Representatives. Committee on Foreign Affairs. Foreign Assistance Act of 1972: hearing before the . . . March 14-23, 1972. Washington, GPO, 1972. 2 v. 402 p. (Continuous pagination) (92nd Congress, 2nd Session)

Contains important testimony with respect to size and rationale of our economic and military aid programs. Reasons for increasing our ceiling on military aid from $75 million to $100 million for 1971 and to $150 million for 1972 are given by Defense Secretary Laird. [C. N. Ronning]

8093. ———. ———. ———. ———. Foreign Assistance Act of 1972: report of the . . . Aug 1, 1972. Washington, GPO, 1972. 37 p. (92nd Congress, 2nd Session)

Summary of the major provisions of the 1972 aid bill, with commentary concerning the committee's views. [Y. Ferguson]

8094. ———. ———. ———. ———. Subcommittee on Inter-American Affairs. Fishing rights and United States-Latin American relations: hearing before the . . . Feb. 3, 1972. Washington, GPO, 1972. 127 p., tables (92nd Congress, 2d Session)

Contains basic documentary materials and statements of US policy on the question of fishing rights and territorial waters. Careful general analysis of the issue is provided by Virginia M. Hagen, Analyst in Latin American Affairs, Library of Congress (1971). [C. N. Ronning]

8095. ———. ———. ———. ———. ———. Inter-American Foundation: first year of operations. Washington, GPO, 1972. 15 p., tables (92nd Congress, 2d Session)

Gives a history and summary of activities of a foundation said to be a "non-profit government corporation dedicated to support the Latin American and Caribbean efforts to solve their own 'grass-roots' economic and social development problems." Also see item 8052. [C. N. Ronning]

8096. ———. ———. ———. ———. ———. New directions for the 1970's: pt. 2, Development assistance options for Latin America; hearings before the . . . February 18, July 12, 19, 26, 27 and August 4, 1971. Washington, GPO, 1971. 271 p., tables (92d Congress, 1st Session)

In addition to the rationale for US aid to Latin America, much statistical information is given. [C. N. Ronning]

8097. ———. ———. ———. ———. Subcommittee on International Organizations and Movements. Law of the sea and peaceful uses of the seabeds: hearings before the . . . April 10 and 11, 1972. Washington, GPO, 1972. 115 p. (92nd Congress, 2d Session)

Herein US positions on such issues as territorial waters and marine pollution, pending the UN Conference on the Law of the Sea. [Y. Ferguson]

8098. ———. ———. Senate. Committee on Foreign Relations. Additional Protocol II to the Latin American Nuclear Free Zone treaty. Washington, GPO, 1971. 46 p. (92d Congress, 2d Session)

Contains information not only on additional Protocol II but on the Latin American Nuclear Free Zone Treaty as well. US and many other governments' official attitudes vis-à-vis the Protocol are given; and, especially, the significance of Protocol II whereby nuclear-weapon states would undertake to respect the aims and provisions of the treaty. [C. N. Ronning]

8099. ———. Library of Congress. Congressional Research Service. Foreign Affairs Division. U.S. foreign policy for the 1970's: a comparative analysis of the President's 1972 foreign policy report to Congress. Washington, GOP, 1972. 96 p. (Committee on Foreign Affairs reprint)

Study prepared by the Library of Congress's Congressional Research Service, comparing the President's Report with those for 1970 and 1971 and with the 1972 reports of the Secretaries of State and Defense. Includes five pages on Latin America. [Y. Ferguson]

8100. Véliz, Claudio. Cambio y continuidad: el Pacto Andino en la historia contemporánea (UC/B, 108, dic. 1970, p. 3-9)

Only occassionally touching on Andean Pact, author mostly discusses "continuity and change" and, more particularly, the nature of Latin American societies. [C. N. Ronning]

8101. Veneroni, Horacio Luis. Estados Unidos y las fuerzas armadas de América Latina. B.A., Ediciones Periferia, 1971. 188 p., tables (Col. Estados Unidos y América Latina)

One of the more detailed discussions of US military power to appear in Spanish. US military policy in Latin America is seen as a part of a global policy of negemony. In the future we may expect more emphasis on the OAS as a military instrument and the building up of Latin American armed forces as well. [C. N. Ronning]

8102. Waller, Robert A. John Barrett: Pan-American promoter (LU/MAM, 53:3, July 1971, p. 170-189)

Summarizes programs, aspirations and basic beliefs of an active diplomat, journalist, author and, during the first two decades of this century, organizer in inter-American relations. [C. N. Ronning]

8103. Whitehead, Laurence. Aid to Latin America: problems and prospects (CU/JIA, 24:2, 1970, p. 181-202, tables)

Shows that "aid can be calculated in about as many ways as there are calculations." Much of what is often called "aid" should not be calculated as such. A number of recommendations are stated in order to make future aid more useful. [C. N. Ronning]

8104. Williams, Edward J. The political themes of inter-American relations. Belmont, Calif., Duxbury Press, 1971. 178 p., bibl.

Defines and describes major political controversies in inter-American relations, discusses points of contention between the two Americas and shows how each side has framed its position. It should be a useful introductory text for a course in international relations of the Western Hemisphere. [C. N. Ronning]

8105. Wood, Bernard M. La nueva política de Canadá hacia América Latina (CM/FI, 12:1, julio/sept. 1971, p. 27-45)

Article is largely an analysis of the Canadian government's report, *Foreign policy for Canadians.* "New policy" was intended to bring Canada into closer cooperation with rest of hemisphere. For more on subject, see items 8054 and 8058. [C. N. Ronning]

8106. Wood, Bryce. How wars end in Latin America (AAPSS/TA, 392, Nov. 1970, p. 40-50)

Until 1948 most wars in Latin America ended on the victors' terms although in some cases internationally mediated settlements cloaked the military decisions in decent guise. Since 1948 the OAS has prevented many disputes from developing into serious armed conflicts and has facilitated the termination of others. [C. N. Ronning]

8107. The world as seen from Moscow: Latin America; Mexico, Costa Rica, Panama, Cuba, Haiti, Dominican Republic, Venezuela, Colombia, Ecuador, Peru, Chile, Argentina, Uruguay, Paraguay (Report [The California Institute of International Studies, Stanford] 2:2, 1972, p. 87-96)

Brief notes on communist (Soviet) activities in Latin America and several individual countries. Useful only if followed regularly or for purposes of reference. [C. N. Ronning]

MEXICO

8108. Blasier, Cole. The United States and Mexico (JLAS, 2:4, Nov. 1972, p. 207-231)

Henry Lane Wilson's behavior is analyzed in terms of parallel plots: the interaction between Wilson and Madero, between Wilson and General Díaz and Huerta, and between Wilson and Washington. [C. N. Ronning]

8109. Braun, Elisabeth E. La XXI [i.e., Vigésima quinta] Sesión de la Asamblea General de las Naciones Unidas: actitudes y decisiones mexicanas (CM/FI, 12:2, oct./dic. 1971, p. 221-228)

Discusses Mexico's policy on a number of issues before the UN General Assembly in 1970 including the Middle East, non-proliferation of nuclear weapons, chemical and bacteriological warfare, territorial waters and interference with civil aviation. [C. N. Ronning]

8110. Butley, Robert W., Jr. Trade conflict: the Mexican-Canadian yarn war of 1969-70 (IAMEA, 25:1, Summer 1971, p. 21-30, tables)

Describes and analyzes how a trade conflict (over textiles) between Mexico and Canada very nearly disrupted what were otherwise cordial relations. The dispute is seen as a microcosm of conflicting trade policies being pursued by developed and developing nations. [C. N. Ronning]

8111. Casillas Mármol, Jacobo. El Mar de Cortés, bahía vital (UNAM/BCRI, 18, mayo 1972, p. 74-106, bibl.)

Legal notes on two entirely different matters: 1) Mexico's potential claim to the Sea of Cortés on the argument that it is a "vital bay"; and 2) international satellite communication systems, specifically INTELSAT. [Y. Ferguson]

8112. Craig, Richard B. The bracero program: interest groups and foreign policy. Austin, Tex., Univ. of Texas Press, 1971. 233 p., bibl., tables.

Study of US and Mexican domestic politics and foreign policy on issues of Mexican laborers in US over period 1942-65. Straightforward descriptive analysis of group processes in policy formation. [J. J. Bailey]

8113. Enjalbert, Claudine and **Henri Enjalbert.** Une frontière du développement: Méxique-États Unis (FDD/NED, 21:3822/3823, oct. 1971, p. 37-49, bibl., map)

Overview of the genesis and current status of the economic special relationship between the US and Mexico. [Y. Ferguson]

8114. *Foro Internacional.* El Colegio de México. Vol. 13, No. 2, oct./dic. 1972- México.

Issue devoted to "The Foreign Policy of Mexico: Reality and Perspectives." Sophisticated collection, it testifies to the contemporary progress of Latin American (in this case, Mexican) social science scholarship. The dependence theme is common to several essays. Table of contents:

Lorenzo Meyer "Cambio Político y Dependencia; México en el Siglo XX" p. 101-138
Olga Pellicer de Brody "Cambios Recientes en la Política Exterior Mexicana" p. 139-154
María del Rosario Green "Deuda Pública Externa y Dependencia: el Caso de México" p. 155-177
Blanca Torres "México en la Estructura del Comercio y la Cooperación Internacional de los Países Socialistas" p. 178-210
Luis Medina Peña "México y la Política Exterior Japonesa: Límites y Posibilidades" p. 211-231
Bernardo Sepúlveda Amor "Derecho del Mar: Apuntes Sobre el Sistema Legal Mexicano" p. 232-271
Rafael Segovia "Nacionalismo e Imagen del Mundo

Exterior en los Niños Mexicanos" (item 8328) p. 272-291
Ricardo Valero "La Política Exterior en la Coyuntura Actual de México" p. 292-310. [Y. Ferguson]

8115. García Robles, Alfonso. México en las Naciones Unidas. v. 1/2. México, UNAM, 1970. 2 v. (302, 254 p.) bibl. (Serie Estudios, 18/19)

These volumes are useful primarily as a documentary source on Mexico's position with respect to several important issues that have come before the UN General Assembly as put forth in numerous speeches by its delegate Alfonso García Robles. Speeches are presented with only very brief introductions and thus must stand by themselves. Among subjects covered are the territorial sea, disarmament, denuclearization, Latin America, apartheid and intervention. [C. N. Ronning]

8116. Gondi, Ovidio. Las batallas de papel en la casa de cristal; ONU: los años decisivos. México, B. Costa-Amic Editor, 1971. 325 p.

Commentaries on numerous questions before and relating to the UN by a Latin American (Austrian-Mexican) reporter between Feb. 1955 and Dec. 1960. They are highly interesting as a documentation of a Mexican's informed opinion on a wide variety of subjects. [C. N. Ronning]

8117. Koslow, Lawrence E. Mexico in the Organization of American States. Tempe, Ariz., Arizona State Univ., Center for Latin American Studies, 1969? 15 p., bibl.

Years following the UN conference at San Francisco (1945) "have brought some Mexican disillusionment with the UN, but they have brought even more Mexican disappointment with the goals and activities of the Organization of American States. Today the Mexican position in the OAS is perhaps the most negative of all Latin American nations, with the exception of Cuba, which has been suspended from the OAS." [C. N. Ronning]

8118. Levenstein, Harvey A. Labor organizations in the United States and Mexico: a history of their relations. Westport, Conn., Greenwood Publishing, 1971. 258 p.

Excellent academic study of the subject. [P. B. Taylor, Jr.]

8119. Merino Ramos, Raúl. La Organización Internacional del Trabajo y México (MSTPS/R [6. época] 16:2, abril/junio 1969, p. 139-145)

Mexico is mentioned once in the title and once in the article. Other than that it is a useful discussion of the background and of the activities of the International Labor Organization. [C. N. Ronning]

8120. Meyer, Lorenzo. La política de la Buena Vecindad: su teoría y práctica en el caso mexicano (in Extremos de México: homenaje a don Daniel Cosío Villegas. México, El Colegio de México, Centro de Estudios Históricos, 1971, p. 241-255)

Meyer reviews the strained relations between the US and Mexico in the Cárdenas period, especially regarding petroleum. Concludes that external pressures were primarily responsible for the shift to the right in Mexican politics which culminated in the election of Avila Camacho. [Y. Ferguson]

8121. Oizumi Alasaka, José Kouichi. Japón-México: intercambio comercial-diplomático entre el Japón y la Nueva España. México, Editorial Letras, 1971. 132 p., plates.

Written by a Japanese citizen educated in Mexico, who is now both a professor in Japan and an employee of the Banco de Comercio in Mexico City, this slim volume examines the initial commercial and diplomatic contacts between Mexico (New Spain) and Japan in the 16th and 17th centuries. An interesting historical footnote. [Y. Ferguson]

Pellicer de Brody, Olga. México y la Revolución cubana. See item 7531.

8122. Seara Vázquez, Modesto. Algunos errores al juzgar la política exterior de México (UNAM/BCRI, 16, marzo 1972, p. 1-6)

Discussion of application and meaning of the Estrada Doctrine in Mexican foreign policy. Author holds that Mexico's refusal to recognize the Franco government in Spain is not a violation of the doctrine. [C. N. Ronning]

8123. Smith, Robert Freeman. The United States and revolutionary nationalism in Mexico, 1916-1932. Chicago, Ill., The Univ. of Chicago Press, 1972. 288 p.

Scholarly account of what Smith terms "the first important challenge to the world order of the industrial-creditor, and capitalistic, nations made by an underdeveloped nation trying to assert control over its economy and reform its internal system." Smith discusses US responses to the Mexican Revolution, from its outset to the eve of the Cárdenas era. He points out that, not coincidentally, "the official and unofficial protests and denunciations of the reforms engendered by Mexican revolutionary nationalism . . . are identical to those used against Cuba since 1959." [Y. Ferguson]

8124. Tello, Manuel. Apuntes sobre el problema de la aprobación de los instrumentos internacionales por el Senado de la República (in Extremos de México: homenaje a don Daniel Cosío Villegas. México, El Colegio de México, Centro de Estudios Históricos, 1971, p. 511-529)

Legalistic analysis of the problem of Senatorial approval of executive agreements in the Mexican context. [Y. Ferguson]

8125. Ulloa, Berta. Sesenta días decisivos entre México y Estados Unidos (in Extremos de México: homenaje a don Daniel Cosío Villegas. México, El Colegio de México, Centro de Estudios Históricos, 1971, p. 531-558)

Drawing on primary sources, Ulloa recounts the events of the two months (July and Aug.) that followed the Niagara Falls conference of 1914. She maintains that Carranza's disdain for the US-ABC appeal for a provisional government established the basis for the traditional Mexican policy of opposition to foreign intervention in domestic affairs. [Y. Ferguson]

8126. United States. Congress. House of Representatives. Committee on Foreign Affairs. Subcommittee on Inter-American Affairs. United States-Mexican trade relations: hearing before the . . . Feb. 24, 1972. Washington, GPO, 1972. 65 p., tables (92nd Congress, 2d Session)

Executive officials survey in considerable detail the current status of US-Mexico trade. Valuable document for those interested in this subject. [Y. Ferguson]

CENTRAL AMERICA

8127. Agresión salvadoreña contra la República de Honduras. Tegucigalpa, Talleres Tipográficos Nacionales Ariston, 1969. 26 p., map, plates.

Pamphlet in the nature of an official Honduran brief on the 1969 "Soccer War." Contents include a speech by President Oswaldo López Arellano and excerpts from the reports of OAS observers about the acts of violence allegedly perpetrated by El Salvador's occupation troops in particular Honduran villages. [Y. Ferguson]

8128. Bauer Paiz, Alfonso. The "Third Government of the Revolution" and imperialism in Guatemala (SS, 34:2, Summer 1970, p. 146-165)

"In the period we have analyzed, with the exception of the revolutionary decade 1944-1954, the judgment of history must condemn all governments [of Guatemala] for their negligence and servility, and for delivering the country into the hands of the imperialists. Of all the governments the one which merits the gravest condemnation is the so-called Third Government of the Revolution because, in the name of a movement claiming to be nationalist and dedicated to vindicating patriotic interests, it has mocked the good faith of the people." [C. N. Ronning]

8129. Brooks, Joseph J. The impact of U.S. cotton policy on economic development: the cases of El Salvador and Nicaragua (PU/PIA, 5:1, 1967, p. 191-214, tables)

New US cotton policy is considered effective as a measure to reduce the world supply of cotton but at the expense of the marginal producer in such countries as El Salvador. But these producers may be comparatively more efficient then their highly subsidized counterparts in the US. [C. N. Ronning]

8130. Calvert, Peter. The last occasion on which Britain used coercion to settle a dispute with a non-colonial territory in the Caribbean: Guatemala and the powers, 1909-1913 (IAMEA, 25:3, Winter 1971, p. 57-75)

Interesting, and occasionally tongue-in-cheek, article on subject in the title. Britain's successful efforts to pressure the Guatemalan government of Estrada Cabrera into satisfying financial claims. [Y. Ferguson]

8131. Castillero Pimentel, Ernesto. Política exterior de Panamá. Panamá, Impresora Panamá, 1961. 84 p., bibl., plate.

Panamanian diplomat discusses a number of theoretical postulates concerning "small nation" foreign policy, especially with reference to Panama and outlines major objectives of Panamanian policy. Special attention is given to the Canal issue. [C. N. Ronning]

8132. Chumakova, Marina L'vovna. Organizatsiia Central' noamerikanskikh Gosudarstv (The Organization of Central American States) Moskva, Izdetel'stvo, Mezhdunarodnye Otnosheniia, 1970. 127 p., tables.

Study of the Organization of Central American States by a Soviet political scientist. Views the OCAS as a tool for the subtle maintenance of US economic and political power in Central America. Narrow in concept and lacking in originality. [T. S. Cheston]

8133. Conte Porras, J. Controversia de límites entre Panamá y Colombia (LNB/L, 16:193, dic. 1971, p. 49-61)

The full text of diplomatic exchanges and a protocol purporting to show that a revision of the border between Colombia and Panama is in order. The documents all dating from the 19th century are presented without comment. [C. N. Ronning]

8134. Ealy, Lawrence O. Yanqui politics and the Isthmian Canal. University Park, Pa., The Pennsylvania State Univ. Press, 1971. 192 p., bibl. (A Rider College publication)

Author sets out "to provide a comprehensive chronology of the political issues surrounding the Panama Canal without, however, delving into tedious detail of interest only to the most dedicated and specialized scholars," and this is a fair description of the book he has produced. Ealy's is a well-documented and sensible historical survey of the canal question through 1970, with a useful bibliography appended. [Y. Ferguson]

8135. Heere, W. P. De Centraal Amerikaanse samenwerking (NGIZ/IS, 25:6, maart 1971, p. 557-567)

Subsequent to the dissolution of the Federal Republic of the United States of Latin America in 1839, many attempts were undertaken to develop closer cooperation among the five Central American republics. Results did not become apparent until after World War II. A multi-lateral treaty on free trade and economic development was signed in 1958; a treaty for economic integration was agreed upon by El Salvador, Guatemala and Honduras in 1960; the principles of both treaties were embodied in a new five-power treaty which became effective in 1961. Between 1958-68, cooperation was successful and intra-Central American trade increased from 21 to 260 million dollars. [H. J. Hoyer]

8136. Kalugin, IU. Sal'vadorsko-Gonduras Konflikt (The Salvadoren-Honduras Conflict) (SSSR/LA, 2, 1969, p. 90-93)

Soviet comment on the then (1969) current Salvadorean-Honduran war. Regards US as fundamentally responsible for conflict and describes US tactics in Central America as "divide and conquer." For a fuller Soviet study of subject, see P. I. Nikolaev "Sal'vadorsko-Gon'duvasskaia Drama" (The Salvadorean-Honduran Drama) in *Latinskaia America* (Moskva, 6, 1970, p. 47-60). [T. S. Cheston]

8137. Lindo, Hugo. Cavilaciones sobre la

integración centroamericana (ESME/C, 42, oct./dic. 1966 [i.e., 1967] p. 11-20, illus.)

Attempts to integrate Central America have never reached the people and this is the main reason for failure. They have also emphasized one or another aspect of integration instead of trying to make it a harmonious whole. [C. N. Ronning]

8138. *Lotería.* Organo de la Lotería Nacional de Beneficencia. No. 191, oct. 1971- Panamá.

Panamanian's detailed account of the 1964 riots relating to US occupation of the Canal Zone. Most of the background treaties are printed in full. Large section on "International Opinions in 1964" is offered to show Latin American solidarity with Panama. Entire issue dedicated to topic. [C. N. Ronning]

8139. Mallin, Jay. Salvador-Honduras War, 1969: the "Soccer War" (AF/AUR, 21:3, March/April 1970, p. 87-92, map, plates)

Brief factual account of the so-called "Soccer War." Underlying causes are mentioned and it is concluded that such wars can happen again on a much larger scale. [C. N. Ronning]

8140. Miró, Rodrigo. Los esbozos biográficos del Dr. Ricardo J. Alfaro (LNB/L, 16:184, marzo 1971, p. 3-6)

Useful biographical data on Panama's most famous diplomat. Should be read in connection with item 8145. [C. N. Ronning]

8141. Moreno, José Vicente. Las Naciones Unidas en el ámbito centroamericano: guía de estudio. San Salvador, Ministerio de Educación, Dirección General de Cultura, Dirección de Publicaciones, 1970. 206 p., illus., plates, tables (Col. Estudios y documents, 2)

As suggested by the title, intended as a "study guide" to inform Central American students and teachers about the general and regional activities of the UN. A Central American version of *Everyman's United Nations.* [Y. Ferguson]

8142. Prats, Raymond. Le conflit Honduras-El Salvador: ses conséquences pour la Communauté Centraméricaine (FDD/NED, 21:3822/3823, oct. 1971, p. 8-36, map, tables)

Analysis of background, course, and impact upon Central American integration of 1969 war between El Salvador and Honduras. There are several appendices including documents and chronology of 1970-71 events. In sum, welcome addition to literature on a conflict that merits more attention than it has received thus far. [Y. Ferguson]

8143. Ricord, Humberto E. El nuevo canal según ellos y nosotros (LNB/L, 185, abril 1971, p. 5-14) '

Dispassionate and lucid discussion of US and Panamanian interests in the Canal within historical and contemporary context. [C. N. Ronning]

8144. Rodríguez Serrano, Felipe. El canal por Nicaragua: estudio de la negociación canalera y su proyección en la historia de Nicaragua. Managua, Editorial Alemana, 1968. 292 p.

Extensive collection of documents pertaining to the Nicaraguan canal question, 1913-39. [Y. Ferguson]

8145. Rosa, Diógenes de la. Alfaro, sujeto histórico (LNB/L, 16:184, marzo 1971, p. 7-18)

Address delivered in honor of Panama's most famous diplomat consists of his biographical sketch and much about Panama's foreign policy. Also see item 8140. [C. N. Ronning]

8146. Tierney, John J., Jr. U.S. intervention in Nicaragua, 1927-1933: lessons for today (CIDG/O, 14:4, Winter 1971, p. 1012-1028)

Tierney compares and contrasts Vietnam and Nicaraguan (1927-33) experiences, with emphasis on similarities. Interesting exercise. [Y. Ferguson]

8147. United States. Congress. House of Representatives. Committee on Foreign Affairs. Subcommittee on Inter-American Affairs. Panama Canal, 1971. Washington, GPO, 1971. 173 p. (92d Congress, 1st Session)

Contains little new information but the large number of statements submitted by congressmen provides insight as to congressional opinion. [C. N. Ronning]

8148. ———. ———. Senate. Committee on Foreign Relations. Subcommittee on Western Hemisphere Affairs. Guatemala and the Dominican Republic. Washington, GPO, 1971. 11 p. (92d Congress, 1st Session)

Summary of economic, military and police (public safety) aid to these two countries. Gives official rationale for and against such aid and a good indication of the material and advice involved. Summary of extent of guerrilla and "terrorist" activity is also included. [C. N. Ronning]

8149. Velásquez, Rolando and others. El Salvador y su diferendo con Honduras: nuestra lucha por los derechos humanos. San Salvador, Imprenta Nacional, 1970. 239 p., plates.

Strongly pro-Salvadorean account of the so-called "football war" between El Salvador and Honduras. Gives the Salvadorean point of view concerning background, causes, conduct and outcome of the conflict. [C. N. Ronning]

THE CARIBBEAN

8150. Allison, Graham T. Essence of decision: explaining the Cuban missile crisis. Boston, Mass., Little, Brown, 1971. 338 p.

Author gives factual account of what happened in the crisis, basic logic and assumptions used by most analysts who explained these events and offers alternate approaches or models for viewing the crisis. [C. N. Ronning]

8151. Atkins, George Pope and **Larman C. Wilson.** The United States and the Trujillo regime. New Brunswick, N.J., Rutgers Univ. Press, 1972. 245 p., bibl.

Well-documented study of US relations with the Dominican Republic, 1904 to mid-1960's, emphasizing the Trujillo years. It assesses, among other things, US responsibility for Trujillo's rise to power and long-standing dictatorship. Authors conclude that democracy cannot be imposed from outside, and they urge policy-makers to recognize limits of US power while favoring democracy in principle. [Y. Ferguson]

8152. Barrett, Raymond J. The United States and the Caribbean (AF/AUR, 22:4, May/June 1971, p. 44-51, illus., map)

Reasons for US present and future involvement and interest in the Caribbean are outlined briefly. [C. N. Ronning]

8153. Bekarevich, A. D. Kuba: vneshneekonomicheskie otnosheniia (Cuba: foreign economic relations). Moskva, Nauka, 1970. 219 p., bibl., tables.

Examination of basic aspects of Cuba's foreign economic relations. Account of "process of liberation of the Cuban economy from domination by foreign capital, establishment of state monopoly for foreign trade, and geographic orientation of the economy towards the socialist states." Bibliography of books and articles from 1960-70. Reviewed in *Latinskaîa Amerika* (4:2, 1970, p. 179-182). [A. R. Navon]

8154. ———. SSSR-Kuba: Leninskie printsipy proletarskgo internatsionalizma (USSR-Cuba: Leninist principles of proletarian internationalism) (SSSR/LA, 1, Jan./Feb. 1970, p. 20-31)

Review of Soviet aid to Cuba in the 1960s noting specific types and amounts, e.g.: 1964-65, the Soviets sent Cuba 750 combines for sugar-cane cutting and 250 mechanics and 12 engineers to assist with the harvest. Reviews Soviet aid in fishing, chemicals, electrification, meteorology, atomic reactors, and medical services. Also discusses Cuba indebtedness to USSR. [T. S. Cheston]

8155. Betancourt, Salvador Cisneros; Manuel Sanguily; Enrique José Varona; and **Juan Gualberto Gómez.** Antimperialismo y república. La Habana, Editorial de Ciencias Sociales, 1970. 151 p.

Interesting and useful collection of historical documents and essays dating, 1901-07. They all deal with the formative years of Cuban-US relations and with Cuban opposition to the establishment of US domination. Congressional opposition (speeches) to the Platt amendment, opposition to treaties, an analysis of the "Revolution of '95" and a sociological analysis of imperialism (written in 1905) are among the contributions. [C. N. Ronning]

8156. Bhola, Ranal and **Harold Breimyer.** Cuba-U.S. sugar policy and interim suppliers' dilemma (Business & Government Review [Univ. of Missouri, Columbia] 11:6, Nov./Dec. 1970, p. 3-9, tables)

US-Cuba sugar policy still remains a problem. Interim suppliers are now enjoying a bonanza but "one perplexing issue will be how to keep an opportunity alive for a democratic Cuba to resume supplying the US market." [C. N. Ronning]

8157. Cozean, Jon D. Profile of U.S. press coverage on Cuba: was Bay of Pigs necessary? (The Journal of International and Comparative Studies [Washington] 5:1, Winter 1972, p. 18-52, bibl., tables)

Based on his content analysis of US newspapers' treatment of Cuban news prior to the Bay of Pigs, Cozean concludes that they (even the *New York Times*) were overwhelmingly biased in grossly underestimating the degree of popular support for the Castro regime in Cuba. According to Cozean, more objective reporting by the press, including a refusal to suppress advance intelligence about plans for the invasion, probably could have saved the Kennedy Administration a costly mistake. [Y. Ferguson]

8158. Crassweller, Robert D. The Caribbean community: changing societies and U.S. policy. N.Y., Praeger Publishers *for the* Council on Foreign Relations, 1972. 470 p., bibl., map, tables.

Businessman's view of the contemporary Caribbean. The nature of the area and its problems, its diversity and possibilities are discussed as background to recent political history. Policy recommendations call for US assistance but not leadership in developing a Caribbean community. [C. N. Ronning]

8159. De Kadt, Emanuel ed. Patterns of foreign influence in the Caribbean. London, Oxford Univ. Press *for the* Royal Institute of International Affairs, 1972. 188 p., fold. map.

Collection of papers presented at a Chatham House Latin American Seminar in 1967-68, most updated "more than once" prior to publication. Useful anthology, except for Lincoln Gordon's lackluster analysis of US policies. Essays on Jamaica, Guyana, French Antilles, Dutch possessions, Cuba, and Guatemala. General emphasis: relationship between foreign influence and domestic social structure. [Y. Ferguson]

8160. Divine, Robert A. ed. The Cuban missile crisis. Chicago, Ill., Quadrangle Books, 1971. 248 p., bibl.

Well balanced anthology of writings on the crisis of 1962, including various interpretations of Soviet motivations and both sides of the continuing debate about Kennedy Administration actions. Of particular importance in the latter connection are the contributions of Hilsman and Steel and their "exchange of views." [Y. Ferguson]

Duvalier, François. Historie diplomatique: politique étrangère; géographie politique; politique fronterale. See *HLAS 34:2125.*

8161. Freidberg, Sidney. The measure of damages in claims against Cuba (IAMEA, 23:1, Summer 1969, p. 67-86, table)

Foreign Claims Settlement Commission has been set up to adjudicate claims by US nationals against the government of Cuba arising out of confiscatory actions by the Castro government. Article discusses issues and methods used in measuring values of confiscated properties. [C. N. Ronning]

Gardiner, C. Harvey. The Japanese and the Dominican Republic. See item 6644.

8162. Gettleman, Marvin E. John H. Finley y el Caribe 1900-1903: contribuciones a un consenso imperialista (UPR/RCS, 15:3, sept. 1971, p. 303-316)

Gettleman uses the writings of Princeton professor Finley to demonstrate the relationship between the notion of a "civilizing mission" and US imperialism at the turn of the century, a relationship which he believes has received too little attention. [Y. Ferguson]

8163. Glassner, Martin Ira. The foreign relations of Jamaica and Trinidad and Tobago (UPR/CS, 10:3, Oct. 1970, p. 116-153, bibl., tables)

Deals primarily with attempts to organize a West Indies Federation. Issues and problems are clearly stated and discussed in detail. [C. N. Ronning]

8164. González, Edward. The United States and Castro: breaking the deadlock (CFR/FA, 50:4, July 1972, p. 722-737)

Writing before the hijacking pact, González maintains that the time is right for the US to take the initiative in ending the boycott of Cuba and he advances possible guidelines for US policy in this regard. [Y. Ferguson]

8165. Gorokhov, Iurii Petrovich. Dominikanskaia respublika i amerikanskii imperializm (The Dominican Republic and American imperialism). Moskva, Akademiia Nauk SSSR, Institut Latinskoi Amerikii, 1970. 196 p.

Presents a "general characterization of the Trujillo dictatorship" (1930-61) and relationship of Dominican dictator with US ruling classes, analyzes political situation in country after his assassination up to uprising of Constitutionalists (24 April 1965) and particular traits of US foreign policy towards country during this period. Also examines US armed intervention begun 28 April 1965, and position of both OAS and UN during intervention. Footnotes. [A. R. Navon]

8166. Kahan, Jerome H. and Anne K. Long. The Cuban missile crisis: a study of its strategic context (APS/PSQ, 87:4, Dec. 1972, p. 564-590)

Considering both pros and cons, authors generally approve Kennedy Administration actions in the crisis. However, they maintain that US insistence on strategic superiority prior to the crisis may have "forced" the Soviets to redress the balance and that Kennedy might have done better to seek an early negotiated settlement based on a trade for US missiles in Turkey. [Y. Ferguson]

8167. Khronologiia vazheneishikh sobytii istorii sovetsko-Kubinskikh otnoshenii: 1960-70 (Chronicle of the most important events in the history of Soviet-Cuban relations: 1960-70) (SSSR/LA, 3, May/June 1970, p. 219-224)

Listing of important events and dates in Cuban-Soviet relations, 1960-70. [T. S. Cheston]

8168. Lestrade, Swinburne; Vaughan Lewis; Bernard Marshall; and Dwight Venner. Essays on Caribbean unity; the case for integration of the Windward and Leeward Islands (UWI/CQ, 18:2, June 1972, p. 5-57, map)

Several useful essays deriving from a 1971 lecture-study tour of the islands undertaken by four members of the Windward and Leeward Student Association at the Univ. of the West Indies. While arguing for integration, authors express skepticism as to whether local politicians and technocrats are really so disposed. Includes text and an analysis of the Grenada Declaration of 1971. [Y. Ferguson]

8169. Linton, Neville. Regional diplomacy of the Commonwealth Caribbean (CIIA/IJ, 26:2, Spring 1971, p. 401-417)

Commonwealth (English-speaking) Caribbean constitutes a subsystem wherein politics is not directly dependent upon cold war developments. There are no territorial issues among its members and a relatively equal balance of power prevails. This makes them unique among small states that have a regional relationship. [C. N. Ronning]

8170. Lowenthal, Abraham F. The Dominican intervention. Cambridge, Mass., Harvard Univ. Press, 1972. 246 p., bibl.

Important book, unquestionably one of the best on the 1965 intervention, which focuses on critical period between onset of the "pro-Bosch" coup of April 24 and the US decision of May 3 to deploy troops in such a fashion as to divide and seal off part of rebel forces in downtown Santo Domingo. Introductory chapters trace US-Dominican relations prior to 1965 and declining fortunes of the Reid Cabral regime that ended in civil war. Thought-provoking final chapter assesses relative merits of viewing US policy in the crisis from "liberal," "radical," and "bureaucratic" perspectives. Valuable discussion of public sources for study of crisis and a comprehensive bibliography are appended. Lowenthal's research includes 150 personal interviews and "virtually all the State Department's cable traffic between Santo Domingo and Washington from April through June 1965." [Y. Ferguson]

8171. ———. The United States and the Dominican Republic (*in* Spiegel, Steven L. and Kenneth N. Waltz *eds*. Conflict in world politics. Cambridge, Mass., Winthrop Publishers, 1971, p. 99-114)

Highly useful article is included in a section of the book entitled "Conflicts within Hegemony." Author finds that the Dominican intervention was far too costly for what is accomplished and "does not provide the United States with a manual for successful intervention." For a fuller treatment of subject see item 8170. [C. N. Ronning]

8172. Pellicer de Brody, Olga. Cuba y América Latina: ¿coexistencia pacífica o solidaridad revolucionaria? (CM/FI, 12:3, enero/marzo 1972, p. 297-307)

Excellent review of Cuba's policy toward Latin America and a discussion of the factors that have lead Cuban leaders to reconsider that policy. Although no radical changes are to be expected, the changes for peaceful coexistence appear to be good. [C. N. Ronning]

8173. *Política Internacional.* Ministerio de Relaciones Exteriores, Instituto de Política Internacional. Año 6, No. 21, 1. trimestre, 1968- . La Habana.

Contains articles on the codification of the principles of international law, disarmament and denuclearization and the crisis of the Near East. Articles are not only of interest so far as Cuban policy is concerned but also shed much light on contemporary Cuban policy is concerned but also shed much light on contemporary Cuban interpretation of international law. Contents: Fernando Alvarez Tabío "La Codificación de los Principios de Derecho Internacional" p. 7-26 Eloy G. Merino Brito "Desarme y Desnuclearización" p. 27-42 Luis Gómez-Wangüemert "La Crisis del Cercano Oriente" p. 43-78. [C. N. Ronning]

8174. ———.———, ———. No. 27, 1. semestre 1970- . La Habana.

Contains studies on Lenin's ideas on colonialism, internationalism, and the self-determination of peoples. They are of interest mainly as Cuban interpretations of Lenin's ideas. An essay on Lenin and Martí points to a number of similarities in the lives and activities of the two heroes. [C. N. Ronning]

8175. Preiswerk, Roy. The teaching of international relations in the Caribbean (UWI/CQ, 17:1, March 1971, p. 16-22)

Survey of current practice, as of 1969, with special attention to the Institute of International Relations at the Univ. of the West Indies, Trinidad. Preiswerk closes with a strong defense of academic independence, which he says is threatened by extra-university pressures for policy-oriented research. [Y. Ferguson]

8176. ——— ed. Documents on international relations in the Caribbean. Foreword by Jacques Freymond. Río Piedras, P.R., Univ. of Puerto Rico, Institute of Caribbean Studies, 1970. 853 p.

Invaluable documentary collection which belongs on the book shelf of anyone interested in the international relations of the Caribbean. Subheadings give some idea of the scope of this volume: 1) "The General Orientation of the Foreign Policies of West Indian States and Guyana;" 2) "Extra-Regional Economic Relations;" 3) "Regional Cooperation and Integration;" 4) "Status of Dependent Territories;" 5) "Defense;" and 6) "Conflicts and Disputes." [Y. Ferguson]

Santos, Ralph G. Brazilian foreign policy and the Dominican crisis: the impact of history and events. See item 8232.

8177. Theberge, James D. *ed.* Soviet seapower in the Caribbean: political and strategic implications. N.Y., Praeger Publishers *in cooperation with* Georgetown Univ., Center for Strategic and International Studies, 1972. 175 p., bibl., maps, tables (Praeger special studies in international politics and public affairs)

Highly useful collection of essays emanating from a research project sponsored by Georgetown Univ.'s Center for Strategic and International Studies. Though authors believe the Caribbean is still a low-priority region for the USSR, they note the steadily increasing Soviet naval presence in the area and its relationship to Soviet strategic doctrine and political influence. Essays on Soviet trade and on Soviet and Cuban oceanographic and fishing activities, especially, fill vacuums in the literature. Incidentally, authors disagree as to whether the Soviet naval buildup gained much impetus from the USSR's "humiliation" in the 1962 missile crisis. [Y. Ferguson]

8178. Torres Ramírez, Blanca. Las relaciones cubano-soviéticas: 1959-1968. México, El Colegio de México, Centro de Estudios Internacionales, 1971. 142 p., bibl., tables (Jornadas, 71)

Useful and factual analysis of Cuban-Soviet relations. Many Cuban primary sources are used and some Soviet sources in English translation. [C. N. Ronning]

8179. Tretiak, Daniel. Cuba and the Communist system: the politics of a Communist independent, 1967-1969 (CIDG/O, 14:3, Fall 1970, p. 740-764, tables)

Examination of Cuba's relations with the Soviet Union, China, and other Communist countries during a period of *rapprochement* between Moscow and Havana. The *rapprochement* aside, Tretiak includes some interesting "quantitative measures of Cuban non-cooperation with the Soviet Union" and stresses that sublimation of the "armed struggle" controversy should not be allowed to obscure basic differences between Cuban and Soviet attitudes on this question. [Y. Ferguson]

8180. Trivers, Howard. Three crises in American foreign affairs and a continuing revolution. Carbondale, Ill., Southern Illinois Univ. Press, 1972, 220 p.

Book emanating from lectures by a retired Foreign Service officer at Southern Illinois Univ. (1969-71). Includes essays on the Berlin Wall, the Cuba Missile Crisis, and the Vietnam War, and an essentially unrelated chapter on some of the implications for international cooperation inherent in the environmental problem. Trivers makes no attempt to compare the three crises systematically, though he is convinced that the Cuban confrontation derived in part from the "weak" US reaction to the Berlin Wall. He stresses initial miscalculations on both sides in the Cuban case, while generally approving the Kennedy response. [Y. Ferguson]

8181. United States. Congress. House of Representatives. Committee on Foreign Affairs. Subcommittee on Inter-American Affairs. Soviet Naval Activities in Cuba: pts. 1/2; hearings before the . . . September 30, October 13, November 19 and 24, 1970, September 28, 1971. Washington, GPO, 1971. 2 v. (91, 22 p.) map (91st Congress, 2d Session)

8182. ———. ———. **Senate. Committee on Foreign Relations.** United States policy towards Cuba: hearing before the . . . Sept. 16, 1971. Washington, GPO, 1971. 29 p. (92nd Congress, 1st Session on S.J. Res. 146, S.J. Res. 148 and S. Res. 160)

Statement by Robert A. Hurwitch, Deputy Assistant Secretary of State for Inter-American Affairs, in response to proposed Senate Resolutions recommending normalization of relations with Cuba. Despite Hurwitch's lack of candor, his statement and ensuing dialogue with Senator Fulbright are revealing of the formal and some of the underlying bases of the Nixon Administration's stance. The hearing took place before the negotiation of the hijacking pact. [Y. Ferguson]

Valdés, Nelson P. La diplomacia del azúcar: Cuba y Estados Unidos. See item 7607.

8183. Wilson, Larman C. La intervención de los Estados Unidos en el Caribe: la crisis de 1965 en la República Dominicana (IEP/RPI, 122, julio/agosto 1972, p. 37-82)

Reviewing events of 1965 crisis, Wilson concludes that the US intervention "was an illegitimate unilateral exercise of military force that cannot be justified in legal terms." [Y. Ferguson]

8184. Wolpin, Miles D. Cuban foreign policy and Chilean politics. Toronto, D.C. Heath, 1972. 414 p., bibl.

Major work of interest to students of Latin American and Chilean politics as well as inter-American relations. Wolpin assesses the "structural features of Chile's political system" that "effectively limited the transnational appeal of the Cuban Revolution." His principal explanation is the "*differential* 'openness' " of the system to "revolutionary Cuban and essentially conservative United States infusions." Wolpin also argues that the Allende experience does not invalidate the thesis that "principled socialist parties" will have little electoral success in parliamentary systems. As author stresses, this study highlights the distinctive quality of individual-country political systems, the external factor in Latin American politics, and the importance of "system maintenance" variables. There is a wealth of bibliographical information and appendices including "Attitudinal and Behavioral Data" and "U.S. Non-Governmental Organizations in Chile." [Y. Ferguson]

———. La influencia internacional de la revolución cubana: Chile, 1958-1970. See item 7789.

———. Revolutionary Cuba's impact upon Chilean politics. See item 7790.

SOUTH AMERICA

8185. Ascanio Jiménez, Agustín and others. Venezuela y sus fronteras en la hora cero. Caracas, Talleres de Comotip, 1972. 186 p., map.

Preface notes this is a publication in defense of the country's frontiers, by the Movimiento Bolivariano de Mérida. While largely focusing on border dispute with Colombia, there is a short paper on the Guayana claims as well. Tone is ultra-nationalist, severely and self-consciously legalistic. Also includes blunt admonition to President Caldera to quit waffling about borders. [P. B. Taylor, Jr.]

8186. Barclay, Glen St. John. Struggle for a continent: the diplomatic history of South America, 1917-1945. London, Whitefriars Press *for* Sidwick and Jackson, 1971. 213 p., bibl.

Survey of South American diplomacy covering 1917-45 with emphasis on Argentina-US relations. Author stresses extent to which Argentina achieved relative "independence" from the US by refusing to play by the rules, a process that he argues culminated in Argentina's exercise of "hegemony over a continent" during 1947-51 (the "great Gaucho Empire"). Book is marred by Barclay's tendency to overstatement and by the fact that he gives little attention to factors contributing to growing US hegemony, which ultimately brought Argentina back into the fold. [Y. Ferguson]

8187. Basílico, Ernesto. Los derechos de la Argentina en el Beagle. B.A., Centro Naval, Instituto de Publicaciones Navales, 1970. 89 p., fold. map (Col. Relaciones internacionales, 2)

Another book stating with "objectivity" the "truth" of the Argentine case. Presumably this has now been stated in as many ways as the Chilean case. Chief interest in this book is the fact that it constitutes a reply to a Chilean statement: Rafael Santibáñez Escobar, *Los derechos de Chile en el Beagle* (1969). [C. N. Ronning]

8188. Berguño B., Jorge. Relaciones internacionales (UCC/CE, dic. 1970, p. 14-26)

Chile's international relations are discussed within several contexts: her immediate neighbors, the Andean Group, the Pacific, the inter-American system, the Latin American system and the world community. [C. N. Ronning]

Blasier, Cole. The United States, Germany and the Bolivian revolutionaries: 1941-1946. See *HLAS 34:2828.*

8190. Bolivia. Ministerio de Información. Dirección General de Informaciones. Una política internacional digna e independiente. La Paz, 1971. 43 p.

Statements by several Bolivian officials of the government of Gen. Juan José Torres (overthrown 19 Aug. 1971) relating to Bolivian foreign relations. Each calls for revolutionary changes in Bolivia's traditional posture of dependence. In a speech to the OAS, the Minister of Foreign Relations states that either the OAS must become an instrument for the help and liberation of "our peoples" or we must accept its failure. For an interesting contrast see the speech given before the UN by a representative of the government which replaced the Torres administration. [C. N. Ronning]

8191. Brazil. Ministério das Relações Exteriores. Divisão de Documentação. Indice da coleção dos atos internacionais. pt. 1, Ordem numérica; pt. 2, Assuntos; pt. 3, Países. Introdução [por] Enio Flores de Lyra. Rio, Depósito de Impressos, 1968. 1 v. (Various pagings)

List of international treaties and other acts of which Brazil is a party. Materials are classified according to chronology, subject, and countries. Indicates whether the acts are still in force or terminated. Brought up to 1968. [C. N. Ronning]

8191a. Bunge, César A. El mundialismo: una doctrina para la Argentina del futuro. B.A., Emecé Editores, 1972. 223 p.

Author notes that in Jean François Revel's *Without Marx or Jesus* (Garden City, N.Y., Doubleday, 1971,

269 p.) it was argued that the "new revolution" is developing in the US. Although this might be true, Bunge also sees possibility of Argentina leading similar transformation. [C. N. Ronning]

8192. Burns, E. Bradford. Tradition and variation in Brazilian foreign policy (UM/JIAS, 9:2, April 1967, p. 195-212)

Short general survey of main outlines and personalities of Brazil's foreign policy. Author points out that as of 1966, there were two schools of thought: one which emphasized Brazil's best options toward the US and another inclined towards a greater nationalism in policy. Since 1964, the military government has opted for the more traditional sympathy toward the US. [P. B. Taylor, Jr.]

Carpio Castillo, Rubén. El Golfo de Venezuela: mar territorial y plataforma continental. See item 6961.

8193. Castro, J. A. de Araújo. O congelamento do poder mundial (UMG/RBEP, 33, jan. 1972, p. 7-30)

Brazilian diplomat discusses Brazil's foreign policy and relations with the US in the context of a changing world situation. Sees no conflict of interest between US and Brazil. [C. N. Ronning]

Conte Porras, J. Controversia de límites entre Panamá y Colombia. See item 8133.

8194. Ecuador. Instituto de Comercio Exterior e Integración. El Acuerdo de Cartagena y la apertura inmediata de mercados. Quito, 1971. 23 p., tables (Serie divulgación, 1)

Very brief discussion of the treaty for economic integration of the so-called Andean nations (Colombia, Bolivia, Chile, Ecuador and Peru). Also discusses its particular import for Ecuador. [C. N. Ronning]

8195. Estrategia. Instituto Argentino de Estudios Estratégicos y de las Relaciones Internacionales. Año 2, No. 9, sept. 1970/feb. 1971-   . B.A.

Articles on Argentine policy with respect to the Latin American denuclearization treaty:
"Nuestro Tema Central, Anexo: Tratado de No Proliferación" p. 56-64
Luis Garasino "El TNP: Realidades e Interrogantes" p. 65-74
José María Ruda "La Posición Argentina Frente al Tratado" p. 75-80
Roberto Ornstein "La Desnuclearización de América Latina" p. 81-92. [C. N. Ronning]

8196. Evans, Henry Clay, Jr. Chile and its relations with the United States. N.Y., Johnson Reprint, 1971. 243 p., bibl. (Reprints in government and political science)

Reprint of a book first published in 1927 (Durham, N.C., Duke Univ. Press). Still a valuable work for the period it covers (Independence to 1925). [C. N. Ronning]

8197. Ferrer Vieyra, Enrique. Cuenca del Plata: su incidencia en la política exterior Argentina (IEP/REP, 185, set./oct. 1972, p. 311-329, tables)

Sees necessity of close cooperation between Brazil and Argentina in a multinational plan to develop the Plata Basin. Discusses potential importance and scope of the undertaking in terms of national and international interests. [C. N. Ronning]

8198. Frías Alvarez, Ricardo. El puerto para Bolivia y la paz mundial. Prólogo [por] Eduardo Ocampo Moscoso. Cochabamba, Bol., Editorial Canelas, 1971. 158 p., map.

Retired military officer gives a detailed (though not entirely objective) account of Bolivia's loss of its seacoast and of its attempts to retain it. Especially useful as an example of the feelings of an informed patriotic Bolivian. [C. N. Ronning]

8199. García Della Costa, Fernando. El juez me robó dos islas. Introducción [por] Enrique González. B.A., Ediciones Almafuerte, 1970. 210 p., maps.

Sees something of a "plot" between England and Chile to provoke a war with Argentina. Both England and Chile have territorial ambitions. Interesting as a study in the development of "war scares." [C. N. Ronning]

Goebel, Julius. The struggle for the Falkland Islands. See *HLAS 34:2719a*.

Gouré, León and **Jaime Suchlicki.** The Allende regime: actions and reactions. See item 7752.

8200. Greño Velasco, José Enrique. Las políticas nacionales en el marco del tratado de la Cuenca del Plata (IEP/RPI, 121, mayo/junio 1972, p. 99-122)

Excellent discussion of issues and problems involved in multi-national attempts to develop the La Plata basin. [C. N. Ronning]

8201. Gueron, Carlos. La "Doctrina Betancourt" y el papel de la teoría en política exterior (Politeia [Caracas] 1, 1972, p. 231-243)

Interesting and thoughtful critique of Rómulo Betancourt's policy of non-recognition of dictatorial governments coming to power through a *coup d'etat*. Betancourt was President of Venezuela 1959-63. [C. N. Ronning]

8202. Gutiérrez Gutiérrez, Mario R. La palabra de Bolivia en la Asamblea de Naciones Unidas. La Paz, Ministerio de Información y Deportes, 1971. 31 p.

Of value only because it offers an interesting contrast with the views of the Bolivian government which preceded this one. See item 8190. [C. N. Ronning]

8203. Hamburg, Roger P. Soviet foreign policy, the Church, the Christian Democrats, and Chile (UM/JIAS, 11:4, Oct. 1969, p. 605-615)

Improvement of diplomatic and commercial relationships between the USSR and the government of Eduardo Frei appeared to suggest a changing Soviet assessment of the best approach to Latin America, and the reverse. A short progress report on research. [P. B. Taylor, Jr.]

Hanson, Simon G. The memoirs of Spruille Braden. See *HLAS 34:2730a.*

8204. Holguín Peláez, Hernando. Proyecciones de un límite marítimo entre Colombia y Venezuela: primer ensayo sobre el tema controversia de límites Colombia-Venezuela. Bogotá, Editores y Distribuidores Asociados, 1971. 123 p., bibl., maps.

Reviews arguments of both sides and rejects claim that the Gulf of Venezuela is an "internal sea" or "historic" Venezuelan gulf. Recommends a settlement. Also see items 8215-8216. [C. N. Ronning]

8205. Ianni, Constantino. Descolonização em marcha: economia e relações internacionais. Rio, Civilização Brasileira, 1972. 274 p., facsim. (Col. Perspectivas do homen, 91; Série Política internacional)

Brazilian journalist writes on a variety of subjects relating to Brazilian and Latin American foreign policy. Central theme is that of dependence and the struggle against it. Most of the articles were published in a São Paulo newspaper between 1950 and 1960 (the paper ceased publication in 1968). [C. N. Ronning]

8206. Jordan, David C. Marxism in Chile: an interim view of its implications for U.S. Latin American policy (UP/O, 15:1, Spring 1971, p. 315-337)

Examines possibility of emergence of a radical, leftist regime in Chile and implications of such in context of US-Soviet-Latin American relations. Rather pessimistic in tone. [J. J. Bailey]

8207. Korolev, Nikolaĭ Vasel'evrch. Strany IUzhnoĭ Ameriki i Rossia: 1890-1917 (South America and Russia: 1890-1917). Moskva, Izdatel'stvo Shtiintsa Kishinev, 1972. 180 p., tables.

Study of little known subject of Russian-South American relations during 1890-1917, based on Russian diplomatic and military archives. Covers trade and diplomacy and contains an interesting chapter on Russian immigrants to Latin America. For more on Russian-Latin American relations during the 19th century, see *HLAS 34:1294-1295, 1301, 1433.* [T. S. Cheston]

8208. Lafer, Celso. Una interpretación del sistema de las relaciones internacionales del Brasil (CM/FI, 9:3, enero/marzo 1969, p. 298-318)

Following a brief historical survey of Brazilian foreign policy, emphasis is placed on the period beginning in the early 1950's and ending with the Castelo Branco government. Global, regional and national factors affecting Brazil's policy are analyzed. Emphasis is placed on relations with the US. [C. N. Ronning]

8209. La Roche, Humberto J. El control jurisdiccional de la constitucionalidad en Venezuela y los Estados Unidos. Maracaibo, Ven., Univ. del Zulia, Facultad de Derecho, 1972. 278 p., bibl.

Comparison of judicial review in the US and Venezuela. Finds that although the concept is basically similar in the two countries, in practice there are differences due largely to cultural and historical factors. [C. N. Ronning]

8210. Lobo, Oswaldo Castro. O Brasil na presente conjuntura do comércio internacional (UMG/RBEP, 32, julho 1971, p. 57-81)

Brazilian diplomat, discusses positive and negative aspects of recent developments in Brazil's foreign trade pattern. Among other things he notes the continuing deterioration in terms of trade for exporters of primary products. On the positive side, Brazil's exports are becoming more varied. [C. N. Ronning]

8211. Lucchini, Adalberto P. Geopolítica del cono sur: la Cuenca del Plata. B.A., Juárez Editor, 1971. 301 p., bibl., maps.

Argentine engineer provides knowledgeable discussion of possibilities and importance to Argentina, Bolivia, Uruguay, Paraguay, and Brazil, of joint development of the Plata basin. [C. N. Ronning]

8212. Marini, Ruy Mauro. Brazilian sub-imperialism (MR, 23:9, Feb. 1972, p. 14-24)

Model of Brazilian sub-imperialism is: 1) continued exploitation of the masses, 2) transfer of income from poorest strata to middle and upper strata in order to guarantee a market for a high technology industry, 3) expansion of foreign markets, and 4) extension of military expenditures and involvement in foreign military ventures. [C. N. Ronning]

8213. Martín, Juan. La política exterior argentina (Documentos [Univ. Central de Venezuela, Instituto de Estudios Políticos, Caracas] 39, oct./dic. 1969, p. 120-128)

Statement to foreign press by Argentine Minister of Foreign Affairs (Dec. 1969?) outlining Argentine foreign policy objectives. Covers wide range of topics including regional cooperation, Argentine relations with Latin America and with rest of world. [C. N. Ronning]

8214. Méndez, Epifanio. Psicología del colonialismo: imperialismo yanqui-brasilero en el Paraguay. Prefacio [por] Osvaldo Chaves. B.A., Instituto Paraguayo de Cultura Pane Garay, 1971. 100 p., illus., tables.

Portion of this was presented at the Institute as a lecture on Paraguayan history. Bulk of the work is extended revision, and has very little to do with the "yanqui" part of the title, but rather with selected aspects of Paraguay's international economic relations, emphasizing its immediate neighbors. [P. B. Taylor, Jr.]

8215. Morales Paúl, Isidro. Caso del Golfo de Venezuela (ACPS/B, 32:50/51, julio/dic. 1972, p. 211-231, map)

Author first argues that Gulf of Venezuela is without question a "historic bay" belonging to Venezuela. He then goes on to evaluate several methods of determining extent of Colombian and Venezuelan jurisdiction at the entrance to the bay. Also see items 8204 and 8216. [C. N. Ronning]

8216. Moyano Bonilla, C. and E. Vásquez Rocha. Los Monjes y las bahías históricas ante el derecho internacional. Bogotá, Editorial Temis, 1971. 142 p., bibl.

Attempts to refute Venezuelan claim to sovereignty over Los Monjes islands and to the so-called Gulf of Venezuela. The first part contains an interesting discussion on the relationship between treaties and diplomatic notes since much of the discussion over Los Monjes relates to this. For more on the subject, see items 8204 and 8215. [C. N. Ronning]

8217. Odalia, Nilo. As relações externas do Brasil: 1945-1964 (FFCLM/EH, 5, 1966, p. 233-250)

Two decades between 1945-64 are seen as a period when Brazil tried to develop a measure of independence in her foreign policy. 1964 marked the end of this period and a return to a policy of dependence on the US. [C. N. Ronning]

8218. Organization of American States. Consejo Permanente. Acta de la sesión extraordinaria celebrada el 26 y 27 de enero de 1971 aprobada en la sesión del 11 de mayo de 1971. Washington, 1971. 90 p. (OEA/Ser. G. CP/ACTA 37/71, 26 y 27 enero 1971)

Contains statements and documents relative to Ecuador's charges of economic coercion on the part of the US (as a result of long standing dispute over fishing rights in waters claimed by Ecuador) and a call for a meeting of consultation under articles 59 and 19 of the OAS charter. [C. N. Ronning]

8219. Orrego Vicuña, Francisco. Chile y el derecho del mar: legislación y acuerdos internacionales, práctica y jurisprudencia sobre mar territorial, plataforma continental, pesca y navegación. Santiago, Editorial Andrés Bello, 1972. 399 p., tables.

Comprehensive collection of Chilean legislation and practice relating to the law of the seas, major international treaties, rulings of Chilean tribunals and related diplomatic practice. [C. N. Ronning]

8220. Parra Aranguren, Gonzalo. El tratamiento procesal del derecho extranjero en los países de la América del Sur (ACPS/B, 32:47, oct./dic. 1971, p. 41-72)

Article states classical doctrine on the application of foreign laws in South America, new developments, relevant treaties and the legislation of several South American countries. [C. N. Ronning]

8221. Pessoa, Mário. Politica internacional e trópico. Recife, Bra., Univ. Federal de Pernambuco, 1970. 44 p.

As best I understand these fuzzy arguments, book calls for Brazil to serve as leader of the "tropical" world. [E. B. Burns]

8222. Peterson, Harold F. La Argentina y los Estados Unidos: 1810-1960. B.A., Editorial EUDEBA, 1970. 694 p., bibl., map.

Spanish translation of *Argentina and the United States: 1810-1960*, published in 1964 (see *HLAS 28:1126*).

8223. Petras, James F. and Robert LaPorte, Jr. Can we do business with radical nationalists? Chile: no (Foreign Policy [N.Y.] 7, Summer 1972, p. 132-158, tables)

States that within the framework which locks US private interests and government in combat with Latin American economic nationalists, the possibility of short-term arrangements are feasible and probable, given the decline of US influence in the hemisphere and the rise of nationalist regimes in Latin America. [W. H. Agor]

Pinsky, Jaime. O Brasil nas relações internacionais, 1930-1945. See *HLAS 34:3002a*.

8224. La política exterior del gobierno de Ovando (Documentos [Univ. Central de Venezuela, Instituto de Estudios Políticos, Caracas], 39, oct./dic, 1969, p. 129-133)

Brief official statement of principles that have determined the foreign policy of Gen. Alfredo Ovando of Bolivia. Also includes text of decree expropriating Bolivian Gulf Oil Company. [C. N. Ronning]

8225. Quiroga Santa Cruz, Marcelo. Acta de transacción con Gulf: análisis del decreto de indemnización a Gulf. La Paz, Univ. Mayor de San Andrés, 1970. 54 p.

Article-by-article analysis and justification of the decree expropriating the Gulf Oil properties in Bolivia (1970). Full text of the decree is reproduced at end of analysis. [C. N. Ronning]

8226. Ribera Arteaga, Leonor. El proletariado nacional y latinoamericano y nuestra cuestión marítima. Sucre, Bol., Escuelas Gráficas Salesianas Sucre, 1971. 29 p.

Appeal to the peoples, or more precisely to the proletariat of the continent, for the return of Bolivia's maritime coast. [C. N. Ronning]

8227. Rodríguez, Luis A. La verdad sobre la agresión peruana. Quito, Editorial de Casa de la Cultura Ecuatoriana, 1966. 128 p.

Ecuadoran military officer charges Peruvian aggression in the loss of Ecuador's eastern territories. It was a military defeat and the lack of Ecuadorean military preparedness and capabilities explain it. Probably one of the best discussions of the military factors involved. [C. N. Ronning]

8228. Roett, Riordan. The politics of foreign aid in the Brazilian northeast. Nashville, Tenn., Vanderbilt Univ. Press, 1972. 202 p., bibl., facsim., map, tables.

Excellent and useful study: "The United States experience in Northeast Brazil indicates that foreign aid can have a deleterious effect on a developing region. By failing to recognize the purpose and program of the regional development and co-ordinating agency, the USAID weakened that agency." [C. N. Ronning]

8229. Rosenbaum, H. Jon. Brazil's foreign policy: developmentalism and beyond (UP/O, 16:1, Spring 1972, p. 58-84)

Surveys major features of Brazil's foreign policy during past ten years and then considers seven possible projections for the future. Concludes that a "neo-independent" projection is the most likely. [C. N. Ronning]

8230. Rosenberg, Emily S. Dollar diplomacy

under Wilson: an Ecuadorean case (IAMEA, 25:2, Autumn 1972, p. 47-53)

Brief but useful treatment of little-known episode in US diplomacy which provides a clear-cut example of the Wilson Administrations' use of wartime powers as a tool of economic diplomacy. [C. N. Ronning]

8231. Rout, Leslie B., Jr. Which way out? a study of the Guayana-Venezuela boundary dispute. East Lansing, Mich., Michigan State Univ., Latin American Studies Center, 1971. 130 p., map.

Useful survey of facts and issues involved in the long-lived (and now apparently quiescent) dispute. Author writes in first person about recent material, based on field visits to affected sites and people. Includes some basic documents. [P. B. Taylor, Jr.]

8232. Santos, Ralph G. Brazilian foreign policy and the Dominican crisis: the impact of history and events (AAFH/TAM, 29:1, July 1972, p. 62-77)

Santos explains that Brazilian support for the 1965 Dominican operation was both a "clear indication" that the Quadros-Goulart independent posture had been discarded by the new military regime in favor of realignment with the US and "an abrupt departure from one of the basic tenets of Brazilian foreign policy—nonintervention." [Y. Ferguson]

8233. Scott, Rebecca. Economic aid and imperialism in Bolivia (MR, 24:1, May 1972, p. 48-60)

US influence through its aid programs has been a conservative force in Bolivia, eventually cutting the revolution off from its people. US was able to distort and redirect the 1952 Bolivian Revolution because of the economic control which accompanied Bolivian dependence. [C. N. Ronning]

8234. Sepúlveda A., Alberto. La nueva política exterior de Chile (IEP/RPI, 121, mayo/junio 1972, p. 71-97)

Only last part of the article deals with Chile. Principles presently emphasized in Chilean policy are: 1) non-confrontation with the US, 2) Hispano-Americanism to balance inter-Americanism, and 3) realignment of Latin American blocs. [C. N. Ronning]

8235. Shchegolev, B. N. Real'nost' sovetsko-argentinskoi torgovli (The reality of Soviet-Argentine trade) (SSSR/LA, 3, May/June 1970, p. 69-81)

Interesting discussion of history and problems of Soviet-Argentine trade in the 1960s. Calls for improved trade relations between both countries. [T. S. Cheston]

8236. Siles, Luis Adolfo. Bolivia e Iberoamérica (IESSC/C, 4:11, mayo/agosto 1969, p. 7-32)

Author calls for a gigantic national and international effort to develop Bolivia's Oriente. [C. N. Ronning]

8237. Silva, Jorge de Carvalho e. O Brasil em frente aos grandes problemas políticos internacionais contemporâneos (UMG/RBEP, 32, julho 1971, p. 9-24)

Brazilian diplomat sees in the very complexity of world affairs the possibility for the increasing importance of Brazil. Aware of this, Brazil's diplomacy is striving to establish the country's status in proper accordance with its increasing power. [C. N. Ronning]

8238. Smith, Peter Seaborn. Bolivian oil and Brazilian economic nationalism (UM/JIAS, 13:2, April 1971, p. 166-181)

Discusses reasons for Brazil's failure to develop its oil concessions in Bolivia (granted under a 1938 treaty). "Perhaps the most important reason for the collapse of the effort was that Brazilian economic nationalism channeled massive amounts of capital . . . into Petrobrás. . . . It thus proved impossible to find sufficient funds to finance the Bolivian venture." [C. N. Ronning]

8239. Snyder, J. Richard. William S. Culbertson in Chile: opening the door to a good neighbor, 1928-1933 (IAMEA, 26:1, Summer 1972, p. 81-96)

"In Chile, between 1928 and 1933, Culbertson helped forge the diplomatic connection by which the policy of theoretical intervention under the blanket of the Monroe Doctrine gave way before the concept of a diplomatic Good Neighbor." [C. N. Ronning]

8240. Tulchin, Joseph S. The Argentine proposal for non-belligerency, April 1970 (UM/JIAS, 11:4, Oct. 1969, p. 571-604)

Argentina's 1940 proposal that the Americas assume a neutral attitude toward World War II long has been regarded as a pro-axis posture, in the light of official US reaction. Writer suggests a number of motivating elements misunderstood or rejected for not-entirely candid reasons by President Franklin Roosevelt's aids. Real significance of US-Argentina conflict in the 1940's will not be known until all records are available. For historian's comment, see *HLAS 32:2634*. [P. B. Taylor, Jr.]

8241. United States. Congress. Senate. Committee on Foreign Relations. Agreement with Brazil concerning shrimp. Washington, GPO, 1972. 10 p. (92d Congress, 2d Session. Executive Report, 92-37)

Contains summary (not text) of treaty provisions, brief statement of issues and statement by the Coordinator of Ocean Affairs, US Dept. of State, in favor of the treaty. [C. N. Ronning]

8242. Uruguay. Presidencia de la República. Secretaría. América Latina y la extensión del mar territorial: régimen jurídico. Montevideo, 1971. 440 p., bibl., fold. maps.

Most complete source of documentation on this subject known to this reviewer. National constitutional provisions, laws and decrees are reproduced as are international treaties to which Latin American states are parties. Separate section deals with Uruguay. For geographer's comment, see item 6608. [C. N. Ronning]

8243. Valdés Sotomayor, Gabriel. Conciencia latinoamericana y realidad internacional. Santiago, Editorial del Pacífico, 1970. 278 p.

Author's speeches before Chilean Senate and various international organizations. Typical of such speeches, they are usually inflated but they offer insights into a Chilean's views of Latin American relations with US and rest of the world. [C. N. Ronning]

8244. Valdez Franck, Arturo. Fase oculta en la historia de la Guerra con Chile: con la réplica armada del Perú contra el armamentismo chileno. Lima, Editorial Impulso, 1971? 16 p.

Claims to show that it was deceit (on the part of some Peruvians as well as Chileans) rather than military prowess on the part of Chile that accounted for the Peruvian defeat in the war that officially ended in 1890. [C. N. Ronning]

8245. Valois Arce, Daniel. Reseña histórica sobre los límites de Colombia y Venezuela. Medellín, Col., Editorial Bedout, 1970. 128 p., maps, plates.

Colombian writes a historical survey of boundary negotiations and settlements between Colombia and Venezuela. He does not try to say what is the correct solution to the present dispute. It must be settled by negotiation. [C. N. Ronning]

8246. Vázquez Carrizosa, Alfredo. Colombia y los problemas del mar. Bogotá, Imprenta Nacional, 1971. 296 p.

General discussion of law of the sea with special reference to Colombia's policy. Venezuelan-Colombian dispute is given considerable attention. Study, commissioned by the Center for Colombian Studies also outlines what Colombian policy ought to be. [C. N. Ronning]

Wolpin, Miles D. Cuban foreign policy and Chilean politics. See item 8184.

8247. Ygobone, Aquiles D. Soberanía argentina de las Islas Malvinas; Artártida Argentina; cuestiones fronterizas entre Argentina y Chile. B.A., Editorial Plus Ultra, 1971. 260 p., bibl., map.

Defends Argentina's claim to three territories in dispute. Although there is little new here, the fact that all three territorial disputes are treated in a single work makes it a convenient source. [C. N. Ronning]

JOURNAL ABBREVIATIONS

AAFH/TAM	The Americas. Inter-American Cultural History. Academy of American Franciscan History. Washington.
AAPSS/A	The Annals of the American Academy of Political and Social Science. Philadelphia, Pa.
AAPSS/TA	See AAPSS/A.
ACPS/B	Boletín de la Academia de Ciencias Políticas y Sociales. Caracas.
AF/AUR	Air University Review. The professional journal of the United States Air Force. Maxwell Air Force Base, Ala.
APS/PSQ	Political Science Quarterly. Columbia Univ. [and] The Academy of Political Science. N.Y.
APSA/R	American Political Science Review. American Political Science Association. Columbus, Ohio.
CFC/RBC	Revista Brasileira de Cultura. Ministério da Educação e Cultura, Conselho Federal de Cultura. Rio.
CFR/FA	Foreign Affairs. An American quarterly review. Council on Foreign Relations, Inc. N.Y.
CIDG/O	Orbis. Bulletin international de documentation linguistique. Centre International de Dialectologie Générale. Louvain, Belgium.
CIIA/IJ	International Journal. Canadian Institute of International Affairs. Toronto, Canada.
CM/FI	Foro Internacional. El Colegio de México. México.
CU/JIA	Journal of International Affairs. Columbia Univ., School of International Affairs. N.Y.
EAZ	Ethnographisch-Archäologische Zeitschrift. Deutscher Verlag Wissenschaften. Berlin, GDR.
ESMC/C	Cultura. Ministerio de Educación. San Salvador.
FDD/NED	Notes et Etudes Documentaires. Direction de la Documentation. Paris.
FFCLM/EH	Estudos Históricos. Faculdade de Filosofia, Ciências e Letras, Depto. de História. Marília, Bra.
IAMEA	Inter-American Economic Affairs. Washington.
IEP/REP	Revista de Estudios Políticos. Instituto de Estudios Políticos. Madrid.
IEP/RPI	Revista de Política Internacional. Instituto de Estudios Políticos. Madrid.
IESSC/C	Comunidades. Instituto de Estudios Sindicales, Sociales y Cooperativos, Centro de Prospección Social. Madrid.
ILARI/A	Aportes. Instituto Latinoamericano de Relaciones Internacionales. Paris.
JDS	The Journal of Development Studies. A quarterly journal devoted to economics, politics, and social development. London.

JLAS	Journal of Latin American Studies. Centers or institutes of Latin American studies at the Universities of Cambridge, Glasgow, Liverpool, London and Oxford. Cambridge Univ. Press. London.
JPR	Journal of Peace Research. Edited at the International Peace Research Institute. Universitetforlaget. Oslo.
LARR	Latin American Research Review. Latin American Studies Association. Univ. of Texas Press. Austin, Tex.
LNB/L	Lotería. Lotería Nacional de Beneficencia. Panamá.
LU/MAM	Mid-America. Loyola Univ. Chicago, Ill.
MR	Monthly Review. An independent Socialist magazine. N.Y.
MSTPS/R	Revista Mexicana del Trabajo. Secretaría del Trabajo y Previsión Social. México.
NGIZ/IS	Internationale Spectator. Tijdschrift voor internationale politiek. Het Nederlandsch Genootschap voor Internationale Zaken. The Hague.
OAH/JAH	The Journal of American History. [Formerly the Mississippi Valley Historical Review] Organization of American Historians [and] Indiana Univ. Bloomington, Ind.
OAS/AM	Américas. Organization of American States. Washington.
PAPS	Proceedings of the Academy of Political Science. Columbia Univ. [and] The Academy of Political Science. N.Y.
PAU/AM	See OAS/AM.
PU/PIA	Public and International Affairs. Princeton Univ., Woodrow Wilson School of Public and International Affairs. Princeton, N.J.
RU/SCID	Studies in Comparative International Development. Rutgers Univ. New Brunswick, N.J.
SPSA/JP	The Journal of Politics. The Southern Political Science Association *in cooperation with the* Univ. of Florida. Gainesville, Fla.
SS	Science and Society. An independent journal of Marxism. N.Y.
SSSR/LA	Latinskaia Amerika [América Latina]. Akademia Nauk SSSR, Institut Latinskoi Ameriki [Academia de Ciencias de la URSS, Instituto Latinoamericano]. Moskva [Moscú].
UC/B	Boletín de la Universidad de Chile. Santiago.
UC/EDCC	Economic Development and Cultural Change. Univ. of Chicago, Research Center in Economic Development and Cultural Change. Chicago, Ill.
UCC/CE	Cuadernos de Economía. Univ. Católica de Chile. Santiago.
UCIEI/EI	Estudios Internacionales. Univ. de Chile, Instituto de Estudios Internacionales. Santiago.
UM/JIAS	Journal of Inter-American Studies and World Affairs. Univ. of Miami Press *for the* Center for Advanced International Studies. Coral Gables, Fla.
UMG/RBEP	Revista Brasileira de Estudos Políticos. Univ. de Minas Gerais. Belo Horizonte, Bra.
UNAM/BCRI	Boletín del Centro de Relaciones Internacionales. Univ. Nacional Autónoma de México, Facultad de Ciencias Políticas y Sociales. México.
UNAM/RFD	Revista de la Facultad de Derecho. Univ. Nacional Autónoma de México. México.
UNAM/RMS	Revista Mexicana de Sociología. Univ. Nacional Autónoma de México, Instituto de Investigaciones Sociales. México.
UP/O	Orbis. A quarterly journal of world affairs. Univ. of Pennsylvania, Foreign Policy Research Institute. Philadelphia, Pa.
UPR/RCS	Revista de Ciencias Sociales. Univ. de Puerto Rico, Colegio de Ciencias Sociales. Río Piedras, P.R.
USIA/PC	Problems of Communism. United States Information Agency. Washington.
USIA/PI	Problemas Internacionales. United States Information Agency. Washington.
UWI/CQ	Caribbean Quarterly. Univ. of the West Indies. Mona, Jam.

Sociology

LATIN AMERICA
Except Brazil

PEDRO F. HERNANDEZ
Associate Professor of Sociology
Loyola University

QUENTIN JENKINS
Associate Professor of Sociology
Louisiana State University

ALTHOUGH SOCIOLOGICAL WORK IN LATIN AMERICA has revealed tendencies over the past three years which vary from region to region and sometimes from country to country, all regions and nations share one common feature, or the almost complete lack of theoretical contributions of originality or notoriety. With the last consideration in mind, the critical observer of sociological literature may emphasize the relevance of four major works: *Guatemala* by Guzmán Böckler and Herbert (item 8348); *El perfil de México en 1980,* the third in a most scholarly and comprehensive series of essays on projections of Mexican national reality (item 8313); and *Mexico's social alternatives (Disyuntivas sociales)* under the editorship of M. Wionczek (item 8336). All three of them attempt a holistic analysis of the respective national societies and all three contain theoretical papers of scope such as Martínez Ríos' (item 8313) or R. Medellin's (item 8338). The fourth by J. Marsal (item 8274) constitutes an exceptional landmark of theoretical relevance in Latin American sociology and although completed eight years ago, (translated in 1967), it was not reviewed in the *HLAS* until now.

Some other works of a theoretical nature, although of lesser scope, appear in Nun's *Middle class and the military* (item 8279), and also in Galjart's article on *Peasant mobilization* (item 8263).

Without question, the most noticeable trends in the scholarly output of Latin America are demography and bibliography, closely followed by studies of peasant problems, class structure and the labor force. Although they cannot be regarded as indicative of sociological trends, other important works reviewed here concern religious analysis as in the outstanding contribution by González Ramírez on the Mexican Church (item 8386) and human ecology in Central America by Pons (item 8352). In contrast with the past decade's output, sociological literature on economic development, the problem of dependency and the Alliance for Progress is conspicuously absent from the material reviewed.

Among demographic topics, migration, internal and differential in particular, together with family planning, rate highest in terms of volume. The Caribbean region has received particular attention; see, for instance, the works by Tidrick (item 8404), Tumin (item 8405), Calcerrada and Belcher (item 8406) all of them related to Puerto Rico; Saint-Louis (item 8401) on Haiti; Leridon (item 8387) on human fertility in Martinique, etc.

The contributions of the Mexican Institute for Social Studies (IMES) focusing on the specific area of birth control in Catholic Mexico deserve special mention: for instance, Brito (item 8299) and Elu de Lenero (item 8303).

Although the sociology of education is not well represented below, D. Barkin's *Mexican education and social class* constitutes a solid piece of research (item 8296).

The continuing efforts of CIDOC (founded by Dr. Ivan Illich), coupled with the dedication of people such as L. Olivos (item 8282) and the editorial work of the *Latin American Research Review* (University of Texas), has produced a wealth of bibliographies paving the way for scholarly work of greater depth and scope.

Unlike the past decade, we found less sociological work in the southern cone (Argentina, Uruguay and Chile), than in the Andean countries, the Caribbean and Central America, relatively speaking. The present review, however, does not include items presented at the last meetings of the Latin American Sociological Association (Mexico City, 1970); therefore, we are not as comprehensive as would be desired. Neither do we include bibliographic notes on the Third World Congress of Rural Sociology, which resulted in the establishment of the Latin American Association for Rural Sociology (ALASRU). In addition, more sociologically relevant work has been initiated in recent years at the Graduate School of the Mexican Agricultural University, Chapingo, Mexico.

The forthcoming Congress of the Latin American Sociological Association, in Costa Rica, (Summer 1974), plans to undertake the first comprehensive evaluation of the major national schools of sociology in the sub-continent. We look forward to the contributions that will be submitted to this most promising and ambitious meeting.

For the convenience of the reader, we have subdivided the material reviewed into the following categories and regions: General, Mexico, Central America, The Caribbean and South America. [P. S. H.]

GENERAL

8248. Adrados, Isabel. Orientação infantil. Petrópolis, Bra., Editora Vozes, 1971. 341 p.

Focuses on questions of counseling children on variety of problems from a psychological perspective. Written to help families and educators dealing with these problem children. [J. F. B. Dasilva]

8249. Andrea, Flávio Fortes d'. Desenvolvimento da personalidade: enfoque psicodinâmico. São Paulo, Difusão Européia do Livro [and] Editôra da Univ. de São Paulo, 1972. 185 p., bibl.

Discusses from a socio-psychological viewpoint the development of personality. A survey of some of the literature on the subject. [J. F. B. Dasilva]

8250. Azevedo, Marcello Casado d'. Teoria da informação: fundamentos biológicos, físicos e matemáticos; relações com a cultura de massas. Petrópolis, Bra., Editôra Vozes, 1971. 180 p., bibl., illus. (Col. Meios de comunicação social, 5)

Analysis of general information theory (biological, physical, and mathematical dimensions). Also includes uses and transformation of communication processes according to changes in structural characteristics of society, with particular focus on mass society. [J. F. B. Dasilva]

8251. Azevedo, Murillo Nunes de. A reconstrução humana: o outro lado da comunicação de massas. Rio, Civilização Brasileira, 1971. 161 p., plates (Col. Caminhos para uma vida melhor, 4)

Another study on the growing bibliography on mass communication. In this case the emphasis is on the potential use of communications in social reconstruction. [J. F. B. Dasilva]

8252. Baéz, Leovigildo. Papel de la sociología en el proceso del desarrollo socio-económico (Aula, [Santo Domingo] 1:1, abril/junio 1972, p. 58-67, bibl.)

Journalistic editorial on the topic, with seminal ideas of Hoselitz, Costa Pinto, Sunkel and Mendes de Almeida. [P. F. H.]

8253. Balção, Yolanda Ferreira and **Laerte Leite Cordeiro.** O comportamento humano no emprêsa: uma antologia. 2 ed. Rio, Fundação Getúlio Vargas, Instituto de Documentação, Serviço de Publicações, 1971. 464 p., bibl.

Selection of essays on human behavior in business; a study on human relations. [J. F. B. Dasilva]

8254. Bell, Wendell and **James A. Mau** eds. The sociology of the future: theory, cases and annotated bibliography. N.Y., Russell Sage Foundation, 1971. 464 p., bibl., illus.

Impressive list of contributors and titles of their essays on futurology give this book more than necessary credentials for serious consideration. Wisely spares methodological discussions and concentrates on plans and images (social) of envisioned future stages of industrialized socieities. [P. F. H.]

Boyd, Monica. Occupational mobility and fertility in metropolitan Latin America. See item 1732.

8255. Burstein, Paul. Social structure and individual political participation in five countries (UC/AJS, 77:6, May 1972, p. 1087-1110)

Sophisticated research (using complex causal statistical models) on political participation, mostly correlated to various forms or expressions of socio-economic status. As suspected, the application of same techniques and questions to citizens of five cultures as different as US, Great Britain, Germany, Italy and Mexico, leaves researcher with more questions than answers especially in terms of the reliability of indexes and the complexity and latency of unaccounted variables. [P. F. H.]

Cardoso, Fernando Henrique and **Francisco Corrêa Weffort** eds. América Latina: ensayos de interpretación sociológico-política. See item 7376.

8256. ———; ———; **Hugh M. Lacey;** and **José Arthur Giannotti.** Sôbre teoria e método em sociologia. São Paulo, Edições CEBRAP [and] Editôra Brasileira de Ciências, 1971. 153 p. (Estudos, 1)

Collection of essays by well known young scholars discussing theoretical and methodological issues in contemporary sociology. Continuation of earlier studies on the critical re-examination of theoretical categories. [J. F. B. Dasilva]

8257. Costa Pinto, L. A. Negros y blancos en América Latina (IESSC/C, 4:11, mayo/agosto 1969, p. 115-135)

Three-part analysis including methodological evaluation, history and most important features of present inter-ethnic relations. Negroes were found to aspire to a situation defined in the US as "separate but equal." [Q. J.]

8258. Davis, Stanley M. and **Louis Wolf Goodman** eds. Workers and managers in Latin America. Lexington, Mass., D.C. Heath, 1972. 308 p., tables.

Very interesting reader on topic of Latin American labor force. Relevant, felicitous and wide-ranging selection of essays (from the socio-cultural to the political). Authors among best representatives of Latin American scholarship from US and rest of the continent. [P. F. H.]

8259. Delgado, Oscar. La organización de los campesinos y el sistema político (ILARI/A, 25, julio 1972, p. 83-106)

The principal problem of the investigation was to determine the type of relationship that existed between peasant organizations, agrarian reform and participation *concientización* of the masses is a key issue in this article. [Q. J.]

8260. Egg, Ezequiel Ander. Metodología y práctica del desarrollo de la comunidad. Prólogo de Gabriel Ospina Restrepo. B.A., Editorial Humanitas, 1965. 246 p., bibl., illus., tables (Col. Desarrollo social, 1)

Handbook for social workers and practitioners engaged in current projects. Brief final summary of agencies (of development) and bibliography is not scholarly but useful. Mostly a practical guide about how to divide and classify groups, activities, steps in decision-making and techniques of evaluation. Some case studies (Ceyan H. Philippines, etc.) precede rest. Complemented by preliminary chapter on development (general examples in philosophy of the 1960's). [P. F. H.]

8261. Eiman, Armando. El camino de las drogas. Córdoba, Arg., Ediciones Grossi, 1970. 109 p., bibl.

History of psychedelic drugs intended to warn parents and teachers of signs of the drug problem and how to deal with it. Informal description. Addressed to the general public. [Ed.]

Frank, André Gunder. Dependencia económica, estructura de clase y política del subdesarrollo en Latinoamérica. See item 1804.

———. Lumpenbourgeoisie, lumpendevelopment: dependence, class and politics in Latin America. See item 1805.

8262. Frankman, Myron J. Urbanization and development in Latin America (ULIG/C, 15:35, sept. 1971, p. 344-350)

Sober, penetrating though journalistic summary of relevant literature on topic with special reference to how future politics can make urbanization meaningful in human development. [P. F. H.]

8263. Galjart, Benno. Movilización campesina en América Latina (Boletín de Estudios Latinoamericanos [Centro de Estudios y Documentación Latinoamericanos Amsterdam] 12, junio 1972, p. 2-19, tables)

Excellent article which divides the general term *campesino* into five categories and goes into explicit detail on how land-tenure and social organization are related. [Q. J.]

8264. García, Noel A. Resultados preliminares de encuesta sociológica realizada entre los estudiantes de quinto años de secundaria (RCPC, 21:102, marzo 1969, p. 2-11, tables)

Interesting questionnaire on socio-economic background with answers in raw form. Unfortunately, neither method of study nor validity of sample is accounted for. [P. F. H.]

8265. García Steve, Joel. Obediencia a la autoridad en dos situaciones: con y sin responsabilidad propia (UPR/RCS, 15:4, dic. 1971, p. 439-445, bibl., tables)

Account of a minor experiment on how dangers of blind obedience can be damaging to third parties conducted in a type of laboratory situation (24 students). Replicates other experiments and hypothesis (particularly of S. Milgram in *Journal of Abnormal and Social Psychology*, 67, 1963). [P. F. H.]

Gendell, Murray and **Guillermo Rossel U.** The

trends and patterns of the economic activity of women in Latin America during the 1950's. See item 1812.

8266. Germani, Gino. Etapas de la modernización en Latinoamérica (IDES/DE, 9:33, abril/junio 1969, p. 95-137, table)

Examined in detail effects of endogenous and exogenous forces on change in Latin America. Article is primarily concerned with the development of a typology of change, with some methodological overtones. Includes complex table. For English translation see *HLAS 33:7544*. [P. B. Taylor, Jr.]

8267. Graciarena, Jorge. Notas para una discusión sobre la sociología de los intelectuales en América Latina (CLAPCS/AL, 13:2/3, abril/set. 1970, p. 63-69)

Notes that intellectuals in Latin America are torn by such problems as commercialization of their production and bureaucratization of their activities in the context of an individualistic ethic. [Q. J.]

8268. Gräbener, Jürgen comp. Klassengesellschaft und Rassismus: zur Marginalisierung der Afroamerikaner in Lateinamerika. Düsseldorf, FRG, Bertelsmann Universitätsverlag, 1971. 342 p. (Interdisziplinäre Studien, 4)

Papers presented at a colloquium organized by the Zentrum für Interdisziplinäre Forschung, Univ. of Bielefeld, dealing, in an interdisciplinary format, with the marginalization of Afro-Latins. Following should be singled out especially: Harry Hoetink "Pluralism and Assimilation in the Caribbean;" Sidney Mintz "Afro-Americans in the Antilles;" Roger Bastide "Religion and Marginality of Afro-Americans;" Magnus Mörner "Historical Background of the Social Position of Afro-Americans;" and Alejo Carpentier "Cultural Integration of Afro-Latins." Other outstanding contributors include, Verena Martinez-Alier, Manfred Kossok, Florestan Fernandes, Berta Alicia Corro, and Christoph Schwarze, among others. These studies on race and class are quite important and of great interest to scholars in a variety of fields. [G. M. Dorn]

8269. Hasperué Becerra, Oscar. Cultura y violencia. Acapulco, Mex., Editorial Americana, 1971. 65 p. (Col. Textos de cultura, 15)

Literary and philosophical essay of poor quality though well written and with an interesting selection of classic texts on this vast topic. [P. F. H.]

8270. Huizer, Gerrit. "Resistance to change" and radical peasant mobilization: Foster and Erasmus reconsidered (SAA/HO, 29:4, Winter 1970, p. 303-313)

Stimulating criticism by Huizer of the "overall picture of peasants as static and resistant to change," a view he believes George M. Foster and Charles J. Erasmus hold. Article followed by "comments" of all three men. [Q. J.]

8271. Karadima, Oscar. La planificación económica y social: sus aspectos sociológicos (ILARI/A, 22, oct. 1971, p. 123-150, tables)

Many major planning efforts do not produce desired goals. This is often caused by planners' failure to consider the social realities of their target areas. A number of failures are mentioned briefly. Tables seek to support the hypothesis that Latin America is underdeveloped. Essentially a survey of author's other work; does not break new ground. [P. B. Taylor, Jr.]

8272. Labelle, Yvan. Recherches sociales et sociétés en Amérique Latine (ULIG/C, 15:35, sept. 1971, p. 351-360, table)

Incisive report on institutional and doctrinal aspects of Latin American sociology. Author visits major centers of research in half of the nations. Finds much to comment upon, and concludes by offering classificatory scheme of schools and tendencies according to best known Latin American scholars. [P. F. H.]

8273. Macedo, Gilberto de. Aculturação e doença: convergências psico-sócio-culturais em medicina psicossomática. Maceió, Bra., Depto. Estadual de Cultura, n.d. 337 p. (Estante de ciências sociais, 1)

Study of the sociology and social anthropology of health focusing on convergence of psychosomatic medicine and results of socio-cultural etiology of certain illnesses. [J. F. B. Dasilva]

8274. Marsal, Juan F. Cambio social en América Latina: crítica de algunas interpretaciones dominantes en las ciencias sociales. Prólogo de Wilbert E. Moore. Traducción de Floreal Mazia. B.A., Ediciones Solar, 1967. 255 p., bibl., tables (Biblioteca dimensión americana)

Revised and updated version of the author's *The image of a changing Latin America: a sociological criticism of some current American and Latin American models* (Princeton, 1965). Provides useful synthesis and critique of North- and Latin-American theorizing on social change; discusses the ideological bases of the theories presented in a sociology-of-knowledge perspective; covers extensive amounts of material; and contains a lengthy bibliography. Important book. [J. J. Bailey]

8275. Mendieta y Núñez, Lucio. Breve historia y definición de la sociología: la sociología y la investigación social. México, UNAM, Instituto de Investigaciones Sociales, 1971. 164 p.

Simple, unpretentious classnotes of an outstanding scholar offering most relevant insights into process of social thought culminating with formal sociology. Last three chapters deal most originally, with the problem of definition of sociology. [P. F. H.]

8276. ———. Sociología de la guerra (UNL/H, 11, 1970, p. 743-756)

Brief summary and appraisal of two important works on the sociology of war: P. A. Sorokin *Society, culture and personality* (N.Y., Harper, 1947, 742 p.) and Vicente Guerrero "Efectos Sociales de la Guerra" (*Jornadas*, El Colegio de México, 6, 2. semestre 1943, p. 9-105). [P. F. H.]

8277. ———. Sociología del poder. México, UNAM, Instituto de Investigaciones Sociales, 1969. 127 p.

Insightful summary of classic and modern doctrines

of political thought concerning nature and uses of power in national societies. Does not attempt to review contemporary sociological or political research of empirical nature. [P. F. H.]

8278. Moraes, Tancredo. Pela emancipação integral da mulher. Rio, Editôra Pongetti, 1971. 194 p.

One of a growing number of studies 'for' women's liberation discussing issues on their social, economic, and political life. Of general interest. [J. F. B. Dasilva]

8279. Nun, José. Clase y conflicto de clases (PC, 48, enero 1971, p. 164-205, illus., tables)

Nun challenges the "American" idea of militarism in Latin America. He sees a connection between the militares and the middle class. Nun disagrees with the "traditional" assumptions about the LA middle class 'behavior', especially in terms of political and social change. [I. G.]

8280. Oliveira, José Xavier de. Usos e abusos de relações públicas. Rio, Fundação Getúlio Vargas, Instituto de Documentação, Serviço de Publicações, 1971. 414 p., bibl.

Essays on public relations discussing, and criticizing, extraneous, and sometimes dominant role, assumed by public relations in modern enterprises. [J. F. B. Dasilva]

8281. Olivos, Luis. Políticas de población y desarrollo para el año 2000 (CM/DE, 3:3, 1969, p. 267-278)

Matter-of-fact presentation of demography of Latin America projected to year 2000 combined with a plea for rational planning in regard to those projections. [Q. J.]

8282. —— **and Oscar Delgado.** Bibliografía sobre la Iglesia y el cambio social en América Latina (ASLEP/A, 5, 1969, p. 52-109)

Most useful bibliography on this topic. Has two divisions: General and Latin America and three appendices: "History," "Articles in the Process of Publication," and "Camilo Torres." [Q. J.]

8283. Panesso Robledo, Antonio. Los lunáticos: el populismo en la cultura. Bogotá, Editorial Revista Colombiana, 1972. 147 p. (Populibro, 49)

Taking his text from Karl Jaspers, author finds that "popular culture" is a cheapened and bowlderized version that neither informs nor satisfies the mass, nor remains true to the values or content of the original. [P. B. Taylor, Jr.]

8284. Ribeiro, Darcy. El desafío de la marginalidad (UCIEI/EI, 4:16, enero/marzo 1971, p. 93-125, bibl., illus., table)

Article taken from book soon to be published by Mexico's Siglo XXI Editores in Ribeiro's series on Latin American Culture. Analyzes relationships among masses, class and power in Latin America and examines alternatives for the study of social stratification therein. [J. F. B. Dasilva]

8285. Sanders, Thomas G. The Church in Latin America (CRF/FA, 48:2, Jan. 1970, p. 285-299)

Major emphasis is placed on a rather optimistic analysis of role of the Roman Catholic Church in supporting "development" in Latin America. [Q. J.]

8286. Seminario del Desarrollo Regional y Urbano, *I, Caracas, 1970.* La ciudad y la región para el desarrollo urbano. Editado por Julio César Funes. Prólogo de Allan R. Brewer Carías. Caracas, Comisión de Administración Pública de Venezuela, 1972. 600 p., illus., tables.

Papers presented by 11 top scholars on the subject of regional and urban development:
José Ramón Lasuen "Tecnología y Desarrollo: Reflexiones sobre el Caso de América Latina" p. 1-66
Milton Santos "Los Dos Circuitos de la Economía Urbana en los Países Subdesarrollados" p. 67-100
Anthony y Elizabeth Leeds "El Mito de la Ruralidad Urbana: Experiencia Urbana, Trabajo y Valores de los 'Ranchos' de Río de Janeiro y Lima" p. 101-176
Paul Coulaud "Tamaño Optimo de Ciudad" p. 177-238
Milton Santos "Las Ciudades Incompletas de los Países Subdesarrollados" p. 239-272
Paul Coulaud "Notas Sobre Teoría de los Umbrales de Boleslaw Malisz" p. 273-312
Anthony Leeds "Las Variables Significativas que Determinan el Carácter de los Asentamientos no Regulados" p. 313-388
Eduardo Neira "El Concepto de Estrategia Aplicado al Desarrollo del Recóncavo de Bahía" p. 389-430
Eduardo Roche; Oswaldo Armitano; and Pedro Burguillos "Programa de Industrialización de la Región Alto Llano Occidental. Modelo para la Evaluación de la Compatibilidad y la Cronología de los Proyectos Industriales y sus Relaciones Intersectoriales" p. 431-500
José Ramón Lasuen "Venezuela: Un Análisis de los Cambios Geográficos en la Participación Industrial. 1941-1961" p. 501-568
Eduardo Neira "La Planificación Regional y Urbana en Tela de Juicio" p. 569-600.

Simkins, Paul D. Contributions by geographers to Latin American population studies. See item 6597.

8287. Souza, José Armando de. Inconsistência de "status" e comportamento político (UMG/RBEP, 31, maio 1971, p. 159-180, tables)

Challenges the uni-variance analytical investigation of status inconsistency (Benoit-Smullyan, Homans, Lensky). Argues that the application of the multiple analysis of variance test is more useful for this problem. [I. G.]

8288. Uricoechea, Fernando. Intelectuales y desarrollo en América Latina. B.A., Centro Editor de América Latina, 1969. 91 p., bibl. (Cuadernos Latinoamericanos)

Cynically and hopefully, a young Colombian sociologist examines the role of the intellectuals in the creation of Latin America's present status. Because the social sciences are in fact sciences of human values—the writer states—academics and intellectuals must meet their responsibilities. [P. B. Taylor, Jr.]

8289. Waisanen, F. B. and Hideya Kumata. Education, functional literacy, and participation in development (YU/IJCS, 13:1, March 1972, p. 21-35, tables)

With all the reservations, the concept demand, the authors used six major expressions of attitudinal and behavioral modernity (from level of satisfaction to authoritarianism). Authors controlled education and functional literacy in five countries in different stages of economic growth, namely US, Japan, Finland, Mexico and Costa Rica (around 1000 persons in each). Relationship between education and upper levels of modernity appears to be more conclusive than the one between the latter and functional literacy. [P. F. H.]

8290. Yaukey, David; Timm Thorsen; and Alvin T. Onaka. Marriage at an earlier than ideal age in six Latin American capital cities (LSE/PS, 26:2, July 1972, p. 263-272, tables)

Neither the effect of consensual vs. legal marriage or pregnancy at the time of marriage explained gap between actual age of marriage and perceived ideal age of marriage. [Q. J.]

8291. Youssef, Madia H. Differential labor participation of women in Latin American and Middle Eastern countries: the influence of family characteristics (SF, 51:2, Dec. 1972, p. 135-153, bibl., tables)

Well developed article which links relatively high job participation of non-agricultural females in Latin America to interaction of marital and fertility characteristics with other social organization variables. [Q. J.]

MEXICO

8292. Acheson, James M. Accounting concepts and economic opportunities in a Tarascan village: emic and etic views (SAA/HO, 31:1, Spring 1972, p. 83-92)

Sound anthropological study of cases in rural Michoacán (Mex.) describes influence of traditional accounting practices on long-range plans of people devoted to commerce and small-scale industry. Relevance of the case lies in applicability to other regions of rural world in which decision-making process could vitally affect community development practices. [P. F. H.]

8293. Adsuara Sevillano, Eduardo and others. La juventud en la sociedad contemporánea. México, Confederación Patronal de la República Mexicana, Arte y Cultura, 1970. 969 p.

Reader of generally very good essays on topics such as youth crisis, and university life in general in Mexico followed by edited tapes and conversations of a "forum" on contemporary Mexican youth. Authors are intellectuals and educators from six major countries of Europe and America. [P. F. H.]

8294. Aguirre Beltrán, Gonzalo. Oposición de raza y cultura en el pensamiento antropológico mexicano (UNAM/RMS, 31:1, enero/marzo 1969, p. 51-71)

From the Mexican positivists to José Vasconcelos *La raza cósmica* (París, Agencia Mundial de Librería, 1920?) and the contemporary formal anthropologists, the view of Aguirre covers more than 70 years of scholarly nationalistic thought which manages in the final analysis to be faithful first of all to the demands of scientific inquiry and refrains from proclaiming biological superiorities or "cosmic" destinies which have not yet been found admissible by scientific standards. [P. F. H.]

8295. Asociación Pro-Salud Maternal, *México.* Attitudes de femmes mexicaines face á la position du Pape sur contraception (IRFDH/DC, 47/48, mars/juin 1972, p. 92-95)

Interesting as an ethnographic document, this brief sample of opinions and attitudes lacks information on respondents social background. [P. F. H.]

8296. Barkin, David. L'enseignement et l'inégalité sociale au Mexique: point de vue d'un économiste (UP/TM, 13:49, jan./mars 1972, p. 17-40, bibl., tables)

Well documented study, prefaced by description of process of Mexican economic development, helps to unmask myths and slogans about higher education in Mexico and to disprove many theses which were formerly regarded as common doctrine. Mexican educational system is clearly incapable of fostering social mobility and developing political aims for advancing the hopes and potentials of the lower classes. This is also due to inability of the Mexican governments to create jobs. [P. F. H.]

8297. Betley, Brian J. Otomi Juez: an analysis of a political middleman (SAA/HO, 30:1, Spring 1971, p. 57-64)

Sound observations of an Otomi *juez* (in Hidalgo, Mex.) interpreted here according to principles of Thomas Schwartz cultural model. Culture is distributed among members of any society rather than shared by them: distributed in "a commonality of interests and differences." Result is a re-evaluation of the middleman in a particular Indian culture which disproves older thesis of his "marginality." [P. F. H.]

Blough, William J. Political attitudes of Mexican women: support for the political system among a newly enfranchised group. See item 7506.

8298. Brandes, Stanley H. Tzintzuntzan wedding: a study in cultural complexity (KAS/P, 39, Fall 1968, p. 30-53)

Relevance of this paper—which looks like a very interesting appendix to Foster's *Tzintzuntzan* (1967)—lies in combination of constant effort to make explicit all refinements of field techniques with respectful but most inquisitive powers of observation. Delightful study of mores and folkways in Tarascan life. [P. F. H.]

8299. Brito Velázquez, Enrique. ¿Quién escucha al Papa? Sondeo efectuado sobre las actitudes ante la Encíclica *Humanae Vitae.* México, Instituto Mexicano de Estudios Sociales, 1971. 199 p., tables.

Demographer and also a theologian by education, author rigorously explores range of reactions to Pope's Encyclica on Birth Control among Mexican Catholics. Sample of opinions is well stratified and the study is particularly relevant as the first of its kind in Mexico. [P. F. H.]

Browning, Harley L. and Jack P. Gibbs. Intraindustry division of labor: the states of Mexico. See item 1910.

8300. Covo, Milena E. Las instituciones de investigación social en la ciudad de México. México, UNAM, Instituto de Investigaciones Sociales, 1969. 145 p.

Most useful guide to social research and its institutional setting in Mexico, accompanied by complete catalog of scholarly research papers and books from various agencies surveyed. Each research agency is well described and documented but not evaluated. [P. F. H.]

8301. Coy, Peter E. B. Social anarchism: an atavistic ideology of the peasant (UM/JIAS, 14:1, Feb. 1972, p. 133-149)

Interesting but questionable analysis of Mexican *ejido* villages perceived as practicing de facto anarchism. [Q. J.]

———. A watershed in Mexican rural history: some thoughts on the reconciliation of conflicting interpretations. See *HLAS 34:1830*.

8302. Elu de Leñero, María del Carmen. ¿Hacia dónde va la mujer mexicana? Proyecciones a partir de los datos de una encuesta nacional. México, Instituto Mexicano de Estudios Sociales, 1969. 203 p., tables.

Based on very ambitious survey undertaken by IMES in 1956-67 (see *HLAS 31:8122*). Present study is only partial and merely descriptive account of it. Nevertheless, useful and necessary tool for further research both because of lack of such studies and relevance of topics discussed, e.g., "masculine," "feminine" stereotypes in Mexican context, question of family planning, Catholicism and political views. Concluding chapter supports view of radical break of old Mexican female stereotype of submission, isolation, ignorance, and uncontrolled fertility. Believes Mexican women are at dawn of new era. [P. F. H.]

8303. ——— ed. Mujeres que hablan: implicaciones psico-sociales en el uso de métodos anticonceptivos. México, Instituto Mexicano de Estudios Sociales, Instituto Nacional de la Nutrición, 1971. 214 p., tables.

Three Mexican female sociologists and one male senior researcher have authored this series of essays on most important variables concerning family planning from point of view of the Mexican housewife. Founded upon empirical research of high standards, the essays are preceded by good summary of literature on growth of Mexican population. [P. F. H.]

Fábrega, Horacio, Jr. Begging in a southeastern Mexican city. See item 1045.

8304. Fox, David J. Patterns of morbidity and mortality in Mexico City (AGS/GR, 62:2, April 1972, p. 151-185)

Scholarly inquiry into death certificates of city's districts. Includes careful description of housing units and their stratification within each district, in order to offer a good picture of the problem. In spite of unreliable indications of causes of death, author's research is excellent and indicative of trends previously undetected or unexplained. Violent deaths are not considered here. [P. F. H.]

8305. Fromm, Erich and Michael Maccoby. El carácter de los aldeanos (Revista de Psicoanálisis, Psiquiatría y Psicología [México] 16, sept./dic. 1970, p. 3-44, tables)

Very interesting attempt to define the socio-psychological traits of Mexican villagers. Three major types are identified: exploitive, receptive, and accumulative. [Q. J.]

González Casanova, Pablo. Democracy in Mexico. See *HLAS 34:1839*.

8306. González Ramírez, Manuel R. La Iglesia mexicana en cifras. México, Centro de Investigación y Acción Social (CIAS), 1969. 200 p., bibl., map, tables.

Already an indispensable tool for studies of Catholicism in Mexico, this book constitutes the most serious attempt at collecting Church statistics in Mexico. Author, a Jesuit sociologist, has the competence and the passion for accuracy which inspires confidence. Dependable work at the grass roots, in spite of the handicaps of Church figures and statistics in Mexico. [P. F. H.]

8307. González Salazar, Gloria. Subocupación y estructura de clases sociales en México. México, UNAM, Facultad de Ciencias Políticas y Sociales, 1972. 162 p., bibl., tables.

Study focuses on problem of underemployment in Mexico within a neo-Marxist frame of reference (regarding classes, their nature and dialectics). Emphasizes changes in social structures from a sociological viewpoint. Theoretically, it relies upon previous works, mostly by González Casanova (but also Stravenhagen and Gunder Frank) with very little of author's original input. Nevertheless, it is a very solid exploration of the phenomenon of poorer classes, and the manifestations of their underemployment vis-à-vis capital distribution and other economic variables. Does not deal with other characteristics of underemployment (subjective and objective) which are less economic in their expression. [P. F. H.]

8308. Langrod, Witold ed. El campo de México: organismos de desarrollo de la comunidad. Prefacio de Luis González R. México, Univ. Iberoamericana, 1969. 321 p.

Annotated catalog of major agencies of community development in Mexico. First introductory chapters (two, on development and its strategy) are original contributions which summarize valuable record of literature and first-hand experiences in rural Mexico. Rest are a presentation of most important agencies (governmental, academic, both research and action oriented) through which bulk of developmental projects has been carried out until now. [P. F. H.]

8309. López Cámara, Francisco. El desafío de la clase media. México, Editorial Joaquín Mortiz, 1971. 104 p. (Cuadernos de Joaquín Mortiz)

Five essays on the Mexican middle class are only preliminary explorations of an almost virgin field (see *Ensayos sobre las clases sociales en México*, México, Editorial Nuestro Tiempo, 1968). Author's approach is journalistic and sociological. Only attempts to detect major variables. For more on subject, see item 8322. [P. F. H.]

8310. Lowry, Dennis T. Broadcasting's expanding social role in Mexico (AEJ/JQ, 46:2, Summer 1969, p. 332-336)

Short, factual report on subject. [P. F. H.]

8311. Maccoby, Michael. Social change and social character in Mexico and the United States. Cuernavaca, Mex., Centro Intercultural de Documentación, 1970. 1 v. (Various pagings) (CIDOC: Cuaderno, 55)

Like some other Cuadernos of CIDOC, this volume is a reader of sorts: a collection of one person's essays. Topics are psycho-social, educational and psychoanalytic: many of them deal specifically with cross-cultural comparison at the national level. Of particular interest are articles presenting the psychological portrait of the contemporary *mexicano*. Texts in English and in Spanish. [P. F. H.]

8312. Martínez, Pedro Daniel. Ambiente sociocultural en la faja fronteriza mexicana (III/AI, 31:2, abril 1971, p. 311-322)

Author enumerates some of the mutual consequences of the contact of Mexicans and North Americans along both sides of the border. [Q. J.]

8313. Martínez Ríos, Jorge and others. El perfil de México en 1980. v. 3, Sociología, política, cultura. México, Siglo XXI Editores *por acuerdo especial con* UNAM, Instituto de Investigaciones Sociales, 1972. 624 p., tables.

Third and most voluminous part of a series which has already become a classic "reader" on Mexican socio-economic development. Scholarly work of last two decades—beginning with the last big reader: *50 li.e., Cincuenta] años de Revolución mexicana* in four volumes—is projected here in series of papers, all of them original and rigorously scientific. Demographic, economic, political, diplomatic and cultural perspectives emphasize the actual data as well as prognosis (after a critical evaluation). [P. F. H.]

Mebane, Donata and **Dale L. Johnson.** A comparison of the performance of Mexican boys and girls on Witkin's cognitive tasks. See item 6156.

8314. Mendieta y Núñez, Lucio. La cuestión racial en América (UNL/H, 13, 1972, p. 485-507, tables)

Scholarly review of literature on subject of Indian ancestry in Mexico accompanied by insights into process of Indian acculturation by distinguished sociologist. Examination of political effects of colonial, independent, and revolutionary epochs on this process is the most relevant part of this paper. [P. F. H.]

8315. México. Comisión Nacional de los Salarios Mínimos. Familias con salario mínimo: algunas características económicas, sociales y culturales. México, 1971. 552 p., tables.

Although this study does not utilize figures of last demographic census, its depth and other aspects are outstanding and its analyses are still valid and very relevant. Based on series of stratified samples which were carefully controlled under the supervision of 18 researchers. Range of questions (from life facts to political participation) will facilitate future research. [P. F. H.]

8316. Mitchell, James E. The emergence of a Mexican Church: the Associate Reformed Presbyterian Church of Mexico. Foreword [by] E. Gettys. South Pasadena, Calif., William Carey Library, 1970. 183 p., tables.

Brief portrayal of 90 years of history provides relevant insights into nature of Protestant Evangelism in Mexico as much as into future relation between this church and missionary non-Protestant societies. [P. F. H.]

8317. Morelos, José B. El problema demográfico de México (CM/DE, 3:3, 1969, p. 319-327)

One of the best organized and documented summaries of present facts and trends of Mexican demography. To be incorporated later into work on the image of contemporary Mexico, edited by economist Miguel Wionczeck and published (1972) by Mexico's Ministry of Education. [P. F. H.]

8318. Muñoz, Humberto; Orlandina de Oliveira; and **Claudio Stern.** Categorías de migrantes y nativos y algunas de sus características socioeconómicas: comparación entre las ciudades de Monterrey y México (CPES/RPS, 8:21, mayo/agosto, 1971, p. 40-59, tables)

Based upon previous work by Harley L. Browning and Waltraut Feindt *Migración y movilidad social en México* (UNAM, 1971), authors successfully complete a more systematic classification of migrant populations into two major industrial regions of Mexico. Cross-regional comparison of relevant socio-economic variables is an important contribution to the scholarly literature on migration. Also available in monographic form (UNAM, Instituto de Investigaciones Sociales, 1971, 22 p.). [P. F. H.]

8319. Navarro, Roberto. El MMPI [Minnesota Multiphasic Personality Inventory] (Español) aplicado a jóvenes mexicanos: influencias de sexo, edad y nivel de inteligencia (SIP/RIP, 5:3/4, 1971, p. 127-137, tables)

Highly technical but relevant article not only because of its standards but also because of its potentials for cross-cultural comparisons. Shows that among the 13 basic MMPI test scales, only scale five was significantly affected by intelligence levels among Mexican youth. [P. F. H.]

Needler, Martin C. Política y carácter nacional: el caso mejicano. See item 7526.

8320. Nelson, Cynthia. The waiting village: social change in rural Mexico. Foreword [by] May N. Díaz. Boston, Mass., Little, Brown, 1971. 160 p., bibl., maps, plates, tables (A Latin American case study)

The people of Erongarícuaro (Michoacán, Mex.) are the subject of this gifted anthropologist's observations. The result is a splendid monographic work of very high standards in which Ms. Nelson aptly describes the major structures of modern Tarascan life and also manages to subject her friends to a TAT test which has potentials for further comparisons and studies. [P. F. H.]

8321. Ocampo V., Tarsicio *comp.* México: los médicos y la socialización de la medicina, 1965; documentos y reacciones de prensa.

Cuernavaca, Mex., Centro Intercultural de Documentación, 1968. 1 v. (Various pagings) (CIDOC: Dossier, 18)

Several hundred documents and newspaper articles are reproduced (as an annotated bibliography). Exhaustive coverage of Mexican press, second semester 1965, after well-known "huelga médica." Volume is an indispensable tool for research on topic. [P. F. H.]

Plattner, Stuart. Occupation and marriage in a Mexican trading community. See item 1089.

8322. Pogolotti, Marcelo ed. La clase media en México. Prólogo y selección de . . . México, Editorial Diógenes, 1972. 311 p., bibl. (Antologías temáticas, 10)

From Fernández de Lizardi to Carlos Fuentes, this selection of narratives, folkloric descriptions, dailogues and brief references shows the passage of time and images of the Mexican middle classes in the country's literature. Anthology reveals a common liberal preference for the poorer classes and a tendency to ridicule the bourgeoisie and the old "hacendados." Shows gradual weakening of moral values among middle classes as well as growth of their influence. For more on subject, see item 8309. [P. F. H.]

8323. Porras Muñoz, Guillermo. Lo mexicano por dentro y por fuera (ISTMO, 75, julio/agosto 1971, p. 51-57, illus., plate)

Journalistic but interesting observations. [P. F. H.]

8324. Pozas, Ricardo and **Isabel H. de Pozas.** Los indios en las clases sociales de México. La Habana, Casa de las Américas, 1971. 110 p., tables (Estudios monográficos, 8)

Important summary of contemporary research on the situation of Indians in Mexico. Not always fully documented (e.g., education, health, family) but reveals acquaintance with recent literature on most subjects and fully accomplishes purposes of a brief scholarly review. Last chapter is particularly interesting and a path-breaking inquiry into nature of the Mexican Indian as a social concept. [P. F. H.]

8325. Quiroz Cuarón, Alfonso and **Raúl Quiroz Cuarón.** El costo social del delito en México: symposium sobre el costo social del crimen y la defensa social contra el mismo. México, Librería y Ediciones Botas, 1970. 205 p., tables.

Important because this is a virtually unexplored field. Scholarly piece of research full of relevant theoretical consideration (e.g., question of crime and its relation to socio-economic development) with a solid empirical base and appropriate methodology (even if it does not make use of factor analysis). [P. F. H.]

8326. Rodríguez Sala de Gómezgil, María Luisa. El estereotipo del mexicano: estudio psicosocial. México, UNAM, Instituto de Investigaciones Sociales, Biblioteca de Ensayos Sociológicos, 1965. 217 p., bibl. (Cuadernos de Sociología)

Mexican "stereotype" refers here to the psycho-social category as elaborated mainly by W. Lippman (public opinion) and Th. M. Newcomb (social psychology). Theoretical part of study lacks further exploration into original contributions of Weber (ideal type) and G. Simmel. Work is further development of scholarly efforts initiated by S. Ramos and J. Gómez Robleda, otherwise well known through their books about the definition and answer of the Mexican character. Here author conducted a scientific analysis of radio, TV programs inasmuch as they show—content and reaction to it—the typical image *del mexicano actual*. As is to be expected, such stereotype reflects wishes more than truths. [P. F. H.]

8327. Romanucci Schwartz, Lola. Conflict without violence and violence without conflict in a Mexican mestizo village (in Short, James F., Jr. and Marvin E. Wolfgang eds. Collective violence. Chicago, Ill., Aldine Atherton, 1972, p. 149-158)

Study explores cases in which violence is not the result of conflict in a mestizo *ejido* in Central Mexico. Offers penetrating observations and interesting remarks about town gossips and crime. However, study may be questionable from point of view of conceptual coherence and lack of theoretical insights into very nature of conflict and conflict resolution. [P. F. H.]

Ross, Stanley R. México: las tensiones del progreso. See item 1948.

8328. Segovia, Rafael. Nacionalismo e imagen del mundo exterior en los niños mexicanos (CM/FI, 13:2, oct./dic. 1972, p. 272-291, tables)

Inspired by the analysis of nationalistic symbols—referential as well as "condensed" or indirectly applicable —by Murray Edelman *The symbolic uses of politics* (Urbana, Ill., Univ. of Illinois, 1964). Segovia sampled 3,575 children (ages 10-15) in five different states and in Mexico City. Sample included private and public schools and was properly stratified according to parents' occupational categories. Among other things, study shows that poorer classes (the ones who say the least in the processes of public life) are the ones who best internalize the values and symbols of nationalism according to the ideals of the Mexican Revolutionary Governments. [P. F. H.]

8329. ———. La percepción de la influencia política por los niños mexicanos (in Extremos de México: homenaje a don Daniel Cosío Villegas. México, El Colegio de México, Centro de Estudios Históricos, 1971, p. 461-473, tables)

Partial results of a survey described in item 8328, presented here in relation to interest-groups and their perception as influential in the Mexican political process by 8th and 10th graders. Results show an impressive range of variation according to different occupational categories of parents, although extremes of influences (top: president; lowest: church) are shared by all children. [P. F. H.]

8330. Semo, Enrique. Zur Struktur der Arbeiterklasse und zu den neuen Entwicklungstendenzen in der herrschenden Klasse in Mexiko (EAZ, 11:2, 1970, p. 261-274, tables)

Excellent highlights of contemporary data and literature on problem of class structure and present trends of development (economic in particular) in Mexico. Also shows how social and economic factors create and maintain a gap between the financial and industrial bourgeoisie on the one side and the working class on the other, the latter ineffectual as a political pressure group. [P. F. H.]

8331. Solís Garza, Hernán. Los mexicanos del norte. México, Editorial Nuestro Tiempo, 1971. 140 p. (Col. Ensayos sobre el mexicano)

Four papers presented at the Medical School of Monterrey (Mex.) constitute backbone of work. Ch. 1 and 2 are an excellent summary of contemporary literature on *lo mexicano* and the psychology of the Mexican character (national). Next, an anthropological exploration of traits of the *norteños* and impact of the US border upon them. An interesting complement reviews images projected by Mexicans towards their US neighbors and other aspects of everyday life along the southern border-line of Texas. Points out conflict of personalities in the *norteño* character and shows many glimpses of extraordinary value (anecdotic as well as scientific). It is regrettable that author did not explore in depth political aspects of this *norteño* personality. [P. F. H.]

8332. Stoltman, Joseph P. and John M. Ball. Migration and the local economic factor in rural Mexico (SAA/HO, 30:1, Spring 1971, p. 47-56)

Intense relationship between general changes in population (in predominantly rural municipalities of Mexico) and changes due to migration have given many a researcher the hypothetical bases for the use of general statistics of population (census and vital) as a source of explanation for migration due to external factors (economic, mostly). This study of cases proves the shaky grounds of such hypothesis and points to the need for more refined studies of strict migratory nature, including the search for psycho-social variables. [P. F. H.]

Thompson, Richard A. Structural statistics and structural mechanics: the analysis of *compadrazgo*. See item 1108.

8333. Tucker, William P. Las élites mexicanas (ILARI/A, 13, julio 1969, p. 102-106)

Periodical comparisons between Mexican-US "who-is-who" confirm higher relevance of education and governmental functions among Mexican elites. [P. F. H.]

8334. Uribe Villegas, Oscar. Los elementos de la estadística social. México, UNAM, Instituto de Investigaciones Sociales, 1971. 362 p., bibl., fold. maps, tables.

One of the most clear and pedagogic textbooks on statistics—as applied to social sciences—available in Spanish. Author has been teaching subject for over a decade at UNAM's School of Political and Social Sciences. [P. F. H.]

8335. Viya, Miko. La televisión y yo: crónica de la televisión mexicana. México, B. Costa-Amic, 1970. 181 p.

Series of journalistic sketches and brief notes covering span of more than two decades of interesting Mexican T.V. Worthwhile material for those attempting sociological history of electronic communications in Mexico. [P. F. H.]

8336. Wionczek, Miguel S. and others. Disyuntivas sociales: presente y futuro de la sociedad mexicana, pt. 2. México, Secretaría de Educación Pública, 1971. 307 p., tables (Col. SepSetentas, 5)

Highly regarded study both as expression of self-criticism and summary of reliable information about Mexico today. Organization and publication attest to quality of applied social research in Mexico and to good will and frankness of many political figures in government. Interpretation of Mexico's economic growth, urbanization and demographic changes, consists of a series of insights into the country's societal dynamics and the handicaps of its educational system. The latter results in a tragic waste of human resources and increasing levels of technological servitude (from abroad). [P. F. H.]

8337. Wolf, Monika. Probleme des Indigenismus und der Minoritätenpolitik in Mexiko (EAZ, 11:2, 1970, p. 275-281)

Indigenismo was born in Mexico as an ideology of the bourgeoisie, after the Revolution (1910-17). Systematic efforts to integrate the Indians into the nation, though not yet accomplished, have encouraged the political participation of minorities as well as influenced many tendencies in Mexican anthropology. [P. F. H.]

8338. Zea, Leopoldo and others. Características de la cultura nacional. México, UNAM, Instituto de Investigaciones Sociales, 1969. 89 p.

Definition of what we could call "Mexican culture" proves to be a task as difficult as the definition of what is "Mexican." Zea and his collaborators take here an existential and phenomenological approach to the problem and discuss some of the major cultural patterns of every day life in Mexico (including a chapter on contemporary lexicon of the Mexicans) without pretending to be either exhaustive or absolutely scientific about the theme. The result, however, is highly provocative. For another, splendid exploration of the Mexican dilemma, see Octavio Paz' latest, item 7529. [P. F. H.]

CENTRAL AMERICA

8339. Adinolfi, Allen A. and Robert E. Klein. The value orientations of Guatemalan subsistence farmers: measurement and implications (JSP, 87, June 1972, p. 13-20, tables)

Combination of Harvard "Values Orientation Schedule" with a coping Effectiveness Index based upon C. Kluckhohn's ideas is tested in Guatemalan village. Surprisingly interesting results among ladino farmers (e.g., propensity for "doing" rather than "being," more oriented towards "present" vs. "future"). Offers limits for new interpretation of Mexican-Americans' value orientation. [P. F. H.]

8340. Alemán, Hugo Gilberto. La mano de obra en Centroamérica. San Salvador, Organización de Estados Centroaméricanos [ODECA], Secretaría General, 1970. 243 p., tables (Serie monografías técnicas)

In many important ways, this study complements the 1968 CSUCA (Consejo Superior de Universidades Centro-Americanas) *Report on human resources*. Uses more recent demographic data, explores ratios of educational supply and demand, and also deals in considerable extent (almost half of the book) with problems of labor force planning. However, use of bibliographic references is vague and citations incomplete. [P. F. H.]

8341. ———. Trabajadores y condiciones de trabajo en Centroamérica. San Salvador, Organización de Estados Centroaméricanos (ODECA), Secretaría General, 1971. 11 p.

Informative general review of problems but of no use for scholarly work. [P. F. H.]

8342. Amaro, Nelson. La estructura social de Guatemala (ILARI/A, 23, enero 1972, p. 160-168)

Thoughtful review of Richard N. Adams' *Crucifixion by power* (see *HLAS 33:1275*). Guatemalan by birth, scholar by education, Amaro looks at Adams' work with admiration and sympathy. However, his critical analysis of Adams' work is shallow. [P. F. H.]

8343. Ashcraft, Norman. Economic opportunities and patterns of work: the case of British Honduras (SAA/HO, 31:4, Winter 1972, p. 425-433)

Case studies in the anthropology of economics contribute relevant insights into the complex world of social structures and social change. Work clearly shows effects of imbalance and distress of social patterns which were established under a monoeconomy of forestry—formerly based upon slave-work—and are still operating through stifling people as well. New emphasis on commercial agriculture fails to provide cash income necessary in a market economy. As a consequence, there has emerged a new servitude to commercial endeavors which use cheap labor in slack farming periods. [P. F. H.]

8344. Campos Jiménez, Carlos María. Apuntes para el estudio de uno de los aspectos de la estratificación social en Costa Rica. San José? Caja Costarricense de Seguro Social, Depto. de Administración de Riesgos, 1964? 1 v. (Unpaged) tables.

Relevant, despite date of publication, because of data collected. At end of 1950's, structure of classes in Costa Rica (from the point of view of labor and income statistics) revealed traits which should be taken into consideration by contemporary researchers. [P. F. H.]

8345. Cifuentes Díaz, Carlos. La marihuana en Centroamérica. San Salvador, Organización de Estados Centroamericanos [ODECA], Secretaría General, Depto. de Salud, 1970. 118 p., bibl., plates (Serie de informes técnicos, 1)

First scholarly attempt to evaluate use of marihuana in Central America and Panama. Methodology is sound but very limited in scope. Unfortunately, some of the interviewing appears exaggerated, and not all data were tabulated. There are no attempts at statistical correlations among relevant variables (like education, age, etc.). Growing use of marihuana poses a challenge to Central America, but book responds merely by identifying it. [P. F. H.]

8346. Erdmenger la Fuente, Eugenia. Integración familiar y adaptación psicosocial: estudio en un grupo de adolescentes guatemaltecas. Guatemala, Univ. de San Carlos, Facultad de Humanidades, 1964. 165 p., bibl., tables.

Very limited study of social dependency and readaptation to new styles of family living. Conducted at private correctional girls school in poor neighborhood of Guatemala City. Psycho-social monograph of partial scope. Results are to be treated with some reservations. Nevertheless, valuable as an indicative document and preliminary exploration of adolescence. [P. F. H.]

8347. Gutiérrez Pimentel, Rodolfo. Alcohol y alcoholismo en Centroamérica. San Salvador, Organización de Estados Centroamericanos [ODECA], Secretaría General, Depto. de Salud, 1970. 110 p., tables (Serie de informes técnicos, 2)

Serious assessment of variables (persons, consumption, health problems) related to alcoholism as a sociological dimension. Based on official figures and interviews (selected) with health officers. Does not explore either attempts to know the patients' world or their socio-psychological aspects. [P. F. H.]

8348. Guzmán Böckler, Carlos and **Jean-Loup Herbert.** Guatemala: una interpretación histórico-social. México, Siglo XX Editores, 1970. 205 p., bibl., tables (Historia y arqueología)

Authors maintain thesis that cultural unity emerged from a remote past of tribal differences. Analysis, based on neo-Marxian premises, attempts to provide one of most comprehensive and ambitious descriptions of a national society under neo-colonial circumstances. Practically exhaustive use of historical sources but in a dialectical framework. Of particular relevance and offering new dimensions, chapter "Ecological Relations" (in colonial period) and "Modern New-Colonialism," both indispensable future references. [P. F. H.]

8349. ———; ———; and **Julio E. Quan R.** Las clases sociales y la lucha de clases en Guatemala (CPES/RPS, 8:20, enero/abril 1971, p. 36-58, table)

Scholarly essay later on incorporated into book, (see item 8348). Proposes one of most interesting and accomplished descriptions of social stratification of Guatemalan society. Its vigor and finesse are manifest in the elaboration of basic stratificational scheme and discussion of its empirical grounds. [P. F. H.]

8350. Instituto para el Desarrollo Económico y Social de América Central (IDESAC). El reto del desarrollo en Guatemala. Guatemala, Editorial Financiera Guatemalteca, 1970. 428 p., fold. map, maps, tables.

Despite some deficiencies this book remains best and most complete primer on Guatemalan socio-economic development. Only lacks topics of legal reforms and their consequences. Authors are sound scholars. [P. F. H.]

8351. Mayone Stycos, J. and **Parker G. Marden.** Honduras: fecundidad y evaluación de los programas de planificación familiar (Estudios de Planificación Familiar [N. Y.] 57, sept. 1970, p. 40-49, tables)

Carefully designed experiment of mass-media impact upon low-class barrios of Tegucigalpa. Substantiates claim and relevance of less costly but well engineered campaigns of family planning among the Latin American less privileged urban masses. Several data are useful for the purpose of non-cultural comparisons. [P. F. H.]

Olien, Michael D. The Negro in Costa Rica: the role of an ethnic minority in a developing society. See item 1195.

8352. Pons, Gabriel. Ecología humana en Centroamérica: un ensayo sobre la regionalización como instrumento de desarrollo. San Salvador, Secretaría General de la Organización de Estados Centroamericanos (ODECA), 1970. 247 p., maps, tables (Serie monografías técnicas)

Of little value for purposes of regional economic planning, but a very important and useful contribution as an economic and social geography textbook of Central America. Unfortunately, bibliographical sources (demographic in particular) are not always explicit. [P. F. H.]

8353. Ram, Bali. Net internal migration by marital status for Panama: females 1950-1960 (UWI/SES, 20:3, Sept. 1971, p. 319-332, bibl., tables)

Major objectives of paper: 1) to develop a methodology for estimating intercensal net migration (when age distribution by sex and marital status is available); and 2) to show differential net migration by marital status. Concerns itself only with females 15 years old and over. Single females appear to show out-migration in early stages and in-migration at later stages in almost all states of the nation. [P. F. H.]

8354. Sánchez Ruphuy, Rodrigo. El impacto de la comunicación en el desarrollo rural: una investigación en Costa Rica; un estudio adicional. San José, Programa Interamericano de Información Popular, 1968. 1 v. (Various pagings) tables.

14 rural communities in country's southern area provided field for study of impact of communications in the use and improvement of agriculture (new crops, soil conservations, etc.) and housing techniques. Communities involved showed more progress than others subject to a formal experimental control in use of techniques. [P. F. H.]

8355. Schwartz, Norman B. Relaciones entre padre e hijo y diversos niveles de educación en un pueblo guatemalteco (III/AI, 32:2, abril/junio 1972, p. 391-412, tables)

Among factors associated with levels of school, (primary) enrollment and educational objectives, the relation (trust, respect, parental interest) between parents and children appears to be crucial in the rural world of Guatemalan ladino communities. San Andrés case study proves helpful in assessing significance of this factor. [P. F. H.]

8356. Seelye, H. Ned and **Marilynn B. Brewer.** Ethnocentrism and acculturation of North Americans in Guatemala (JSP, 80, 1970, p. 147-155, bibl., tables)

Sumner's basic theses on ethnocentrism are applied here with scientific rigor. Useful comparison in acculturation and moderate but real contribution in terms of quantitative measurement. [P. F. H.]

8357. Snyder, Peter Z. and **Juan de Dios Rosales.** Cambios de adaptación en las tierras altas de Guatemala (III/AI, 32:2, abril/junio 1972, p. 423-436, bibl.)

Modern democratic procedures and other traits of industrialized societies require complicated process of adaptation which often fails because of the poor understanding of the cultural context of ancient structures. Study of cases based upon many techniques of observation is a good and scholarly document on social adaptation. [P. F. H.]

8358. Solien González, Nancie L. Creencias médicas de la población urbana de Guatemala (GIIN/GI, 6:4, dic. 1971, p. 169-175)

Anthropological study of cases among ladinos of recent migration into Guatemala City shows various degrees of changes in the practice and acceptance of folk medicine because of urban life. Nothing conclusive is to be drawn from a rather superficial study, but the report has interesting observations regarding the persistence of the *curanderos*. [P. F. H.]

8359. Teller, Charles H. Internal migration, socio-economic status and health: access to medical care in a Honduran city. Ithaca, N.Y., Cornell Univ., Latin American Studies Program, 1972. 302 p., bibl., tables (Dissertation series, 41)

Migration, assimilation into new communities and health care are closely related and critically important in the development of the rapidly growing Latin-American urban societies. This doctoral study is valuable and relevant, not only because of the lucid attempt to evaluate medical care in San Pedro Sula, but also because it detects many important variables. These are important factors in future planning of health care and health service delivery. [P. F. H.]

8360. Thomas, Robert N. The migration system of Guatemala City: spatial inputs (AAG/PG, 24:2, May 1972, p. 105-112, illus., map, tables)

Rigorous and dependable methodological treatment. Proves four hypotheses about migration which also could be applied to other capitals in Latin America. However, the case of Indians (who migrate less than the mestizos) limits study's ultimate goal. [P. F. H.]

Torres Rivas, Edelberto. Les problèmes sociaux du développement et de l'integration en Amérique Centrale. See item 1981.

8361. Volio Jiménez, Fernando. Apartheid: prototipo de discriminación racial. San Jośe, Univ. de Costa Rica, 1971. 225 p., bibl. (Serie Tesis de Grado, 19)

Ethical and political analysis of racial discrimination as typified by South-African society. Accurately portrays historical and legal aspects of UN debates. Of special interest are international legal pronouncements of a Latin nation (Costa Rica) on discrimination. [P. F. H.]

8362. Zavala de Aquino, Carolina. Estudio

sobre valores realizado en una muestra de mujeres guatemaltecas que solicitaron ingresar en la Universidad de San Carlos de Guatemala, en los años 1960-1963. Guatemala, Univ. de San Carlos de Guatemala, Facultad de Humanidades, Depto. de Psicología, 1966. 44 p., bibl., tables.

Brief monographic work, almost a class assignment. Questionable conceptual scheme and mediocre analysis of data. Interesting as a starting point for further exploration. [P. F. H.]

THE CARIBBEAN

Abraham-van der Mark, Eva E. Differences in the upbringing of boys and girls in Curaçao, correlated with differences in the degree of neurotic instability. See item 1119.

8363. Acosta, Maruja and **Jorge E. Hardoy.** Políticas urbanas y reforma urbana en Cuba. B.A., Instituto Torcuato Di Tella, Centro de Estudios Urbanos y Regionales, 1971. 1 v. (Various pagings) bibl., tables (Documento de trabajo)

Excellent and scholarly work on urban and agrarian policies in Cuba. Covers not only more specific aspects of laws and policies but also ecological, demographic and economic ones. Also includes analysis of agencies in charge of implementing appropriate policies which enhances the perspective. [P. F. H.]

8364. Beckford, George L. Peasant movements and agrarian problems in the West Indies: aspects of the present conflict between the plantation and the peasantry in the West Indies (UWI/CQ, 18:1, March 1972, p. 47-53)

Prevalence of plantation system, already ossified and obsolete, constitutes most serious block to the social and economic development of the peasantry. In a very real sense, they are still unable to break through these old institutional relations. [P. F. H.]

———. Plantation society: toward a general theory of Caribbean society. See item 1126.

8365. Belcher, John C. and **Pablo B. Vázquez-Calcerrada.** A cross-cultural approach to the social functions of housing (WRU/JMF, 34:4, Nov. 1972, p. 750-761, tables)

In the touchy area of cross-cultural comparisons, few items may be more difficult to discuss relevantly than those pertaining to family life. Three successive surveys of rural regions in Georgia, Puerto Rico and Santo Domingo (from 1965-67) are reported here in the simple language of the American corresponding percentages of desired items (like rooms, toilets, etc.). In such a taboo area, a number of concrete and quantified references are welcome and may lead to future and deeper studies. [P. F. H.]

Benoist, Jean. L'archipel inachevé: culture et société aux Antilles françaises. See item 1127.

8366. Betancourt Roa, Gilda. Revolución cubana y cambio social (BUS, 8:15/17, dic. 1969, p. 119-128)

While author's thesis (no social change is possible without revolution) appears unscientific, at least in its present expression, the bulk of paper emphasizes comprehensive attempt at planned social change, as envisioned by the Cuban Agrarian Reform. Theoretically irrelevant work but valuable exploration of subject. Paper presented at the IX Congreso Latinoamericano de Sociología. [P. F. H.]

8367. ——— and **Carlos Amat.** Cuba: un laboratorio para la investigación social (UH/U, 32:190, abril/junio 1968, p. 73-76)

Brief report of major areas of concern for sociological research in Castro's Cuba. Does not account for either results or detailed programs. Almost platitudinous. [P. F. H.]

8368. Buitrago Ortiz, Carlos. Estructura social y orientaciones valorativas en Esperanza, Puerto Rico y el Mediterráneo. Río Piedras, P.R., Editorial Edil, 1970. 145 p., bibl.

Good essay on cross-cultural comparisons of values and attitudes concerning family life, social solidarity and friendship. Based on strict methodological procedure and best anthropological techniques (from observations to content analysis and biographical, personal notes). Also relevant as an ethnographic document. [P. F. H.]

8369. Byrne, Joycelin. A note on the 1970 census of Barbados (UWI/SES, 20:4, Dec. 1971, p. 431-440, tables)

Valuable introduction to the 1970 census. Also interesting to the outsider as a brief glance at major demographic changes in the country. [P. F. H.]

8370. ———. Population growth in St. Vincent (UWI/SES, 18:2, June 1969, p. 152-188, tables)

Very valuable monographic work covering historical as well as purely demographic data (including projections of population growth). Executed and written with scientific accuracy but marred by lack of proper references (bibliographical) for the tables. [P. F. H.]

8371. Camarano, Chris. On Cuban women (SS, 35:1, Spring 1971, p. 48-58)

View of certain trends of what a sociologist could detect as a "women's liberation movement." Short article, half-pamphlet, half-journalistic account. Of limited interest. For more on the subject, see item 7577. [P. F. H.]

8372. Camejo, Acton. Racial discrimination in employment in the private sector in Trinidad and Tobago: a study of the business élite and the social structure (UWI/SES, 20:3, Sept. 1971, p. 294-318, bibl., tables)

A particular occupational sector, the business elites (executive, administrative and managerial) reveals a definite racial bias in Trinidad. This has been already conveyed by Harewood's 1960 census-data findings. Scholarly, this survey grouped 233 of country's most important firms. Concerned with local residents only. [P. F. H.]

8373. Cirino Gerena, Gabriel. El desarrollo del inventario puertorriqueño de intereses vocacionales (SIP/RIP, 5:1/2, 1971, p. 47-51, tables)

Abridged version of important Ph.D. dissertation focuses upon process and nature of Puerto Rican Inventory of Vocational Interests (inspired by Kuger's Inventory References). Although a few results are tabulated and cross-culturally compared (with US cases) no further analysis is presented. [P. F. H.]

Clarke, Colin G. Residential segregation and inter-marriage in San Fernando, Trinidad. See item 6658.

8374. Cofresí, Emilio. El control de la natalidad en Puerto Rico (UPR/RCS, 13:3, julio/sept. 1969, p. 379-385)

Paper delivered at 1968 Conference on "The Family in the Caribbean." Merely indicates major studies and findings of Hill, Styen, Back & Hatt, and others with light comments on subject. Lacks even elementary bibliographical references. [P. F. H.]

8375. Cordasco, Francesco and **Eugene Bucchioni.** The Puerto Rican community and its children on the mainland: a source book for teachers, social workers and other professionals. Metuchen, N.J., The Scarecrow Press, 1972. 465 p., tables.

Among best and most successful anthologies of social and humanistic readings on Puerto Rico today. US scholars like O. Lewis, J. M. Stycos, C. Senior and others, alternate with prominent Latin Americans and Puerto Rican intellectuals such as R. Pobléte, J. Silen, etc. End product provides a vision of sober analysis and concern in major areas of cultural life, particularly family and education. Superb and scholarly bibliography. Of great value for future research on Puerto Rico. [P. F. H.]

8376. Demas, William G. The new Caribbean man (UWI/CQ, 17:3/4, Sept./Dec. 1971, p. 7-14)

Commencement address with good insights into the new roles of emerging nations of the Caribbean, including some platitudinous exhortations. [P. F. H.]

8377. Dohen, Dorothy. Two studies of Puerto Rico: religion data; the background of consensual union. Cuernavaca, Mex., Centro Intercultural de Documentación, 1966. 155 p., bibl., maps, tables (CIDOC: Sondeos, 3)

Highly interesting, original and useful studies. Relevant tools for research on demographic and socio-religious problems. In particular, very well documented presentation of data on Puerto Rican religious situation. Complemented by series of maps plotting dimensional aspects of major variables affecting religious behavior. [P. F. H.]

8378. Ebanks, G. Edward. Social and demographic characteristics of family planning clients in Barbados (UWI/SES, 18:4, Dec. 1969, p. 391-401, tables)

Using a complex of good sources (from census to new samples) these papers show major traits of social stratification of the island's family planning program. [P. F. H.]

8379. Elkins, W. F. Hercules and the society of peoples of African origin (UPR/CS, 11:4, Jan. 1972, p. 47-59)

Historical monograph on emergence of the "Society of Peoples of African Origin" also gives many insights into the personality of the Rev. F. E. M. Hercules to which most West-Indian youth and labor movements owe a new sense of pride and militancy. [P. F. H.]

Espín, Vilma. O zhenskon dvishenii na Kube (The women's movement in Cuba). See item 7577.

8380. González, Justo L. The development of Christianity in the Latin Caribbean. Grand Rapids, Mich., William B. Eerdmans, 1969. 136 p., bibl.

Although not based on research of primary sources, this monographic essay constitutes a good summary of most scholarly historiography on the Catholic Church in the Caribbean. Incorporates many recent works not available in English. [P. F. H.]

González, Nancie L. Solien. The sociology of a dam. See item 1154.

8381. Hageman, Alice L. and **Philip E. Wheaton** eds. Religion in Cuba today: a new church in a new society. Foreword by Harvey Cox. N.Y., Association Press, 1971. 317 p., tables.

Covers first decade of Cuban Revolution. Consists of interviews, essays, pronouncements of Catholic and Protestant authorities in search for a unifying theological principle, namely a "theology of liberation" upon which other Latin Americans (particularly G. Gutiérrez) have elaborated more vigorously. Articles by Bündig and Arce are indispensable sources for any study of topic. Uneven but relevant compilation. [P. F. H.]

8382. Harewood, Jack. Racial discrimination in employment in Trinidad and Tobago—based on data from the 1960 census (UWI/SES, 20:3, Sept. 1971, p. 267-293, tables)

Solid piece of research, will prove valuable for purposes of comparison with last census data findings. Demonstrates that up to the 1960's, there existed a definite racial bias (occupational) favoring whites over other ethnic groups and blacks over descendants from Hindu groups. [P. F. H.]

8383. Hernández Alvarez, Lilia Inés de. Matrimonio en Puerto Rico: estudio sociodemográfico, 1910-1968. Río Piedras, P.R., Editorial Edil, 1971. 177 p., maps, tables.

Outstanding contribution to demographic literature of Puerto Rico. Depth and rigor of scholarly endeavor in the sampling procedures and its careful analysis make this study an indispensable reference. Among other findings: a diminishing trend of consensual union together with an increase in divorce rates. [P. F. H.]

Hicks, Frederick. Making a living during the dead season in sugar-producing regions of the Caribbean. See item 6625.

Kätsch, Siegfried; Elke-Maria Kätsch; and **Henry P. David.** Sosua-verheissenes land: eine dokumentation zu adaptions-problemen Deutsch-Jüdischer siedler in der Dominikanischen Republik. See item 1168.

Karner, Frances P. The Sephardics of Curaçao; a study of socio-cultural patterns in flux. See item 1169.

8384. La Fay, Howard and **Winfield Parks.** Carnival in Trinidad (NGS/NGM, 140:5, Nov. 1971, p. 693-701)

Wonderful window onto an exotic Caribbean world. Authors have summarized their work with this lyrical stance:
For the rhythm, a jingling tamborine,
For the soul, a smile.
Soon feet take wing on a street turned stage.
The moment is Carnival in Trinidad! [P. F. H.]

8385. Lanz, Gregorio. Machismo en la República Dominicana (Boletín Documental sobre la Mujer [Cuernavaca, Mex.] 2:2, 1972, p. 41-48)

Journalistic essay on the popular topic of male superiority in Latin-American cultures. National survey mentioned by author (1,319 high-school students interviewed) seems questionable and superficial. His observations on family life in Santo Domingo, however, are sober and penetrating. [P. F. H.]

8386. LaRuffa, Anthony L. San Cipriano: life in a Puerto Rican community. N.Y., Gordon and Breach Science Publishers, 1971. 149 p., maps, plates, tables.

Pleasant and vivid description and case study of a Puerto-Rican municipality in the humid alluvial region between Arecibo and Luquillo. Combines anthropological scholarship with a lively style. Of particular interest are three chapters devoted to religion, namely belief in the supernatural and an account of Protestant sects (Pentecostalism in particular). [P. F. H.]

Lengermann, Patricia Madoo. Working-class values in Trinidad and Tobago. See item 1175.

8387. Leridon, Henri. Les facteurs de la fécondité en Martinique (INED/P, 26:2, mars/avril 1971, p. 277-300, tables)

Given lack of dependable information on fecundity and other statistical evidence of the life cycle in French Antilles, this study constitutes a landmark. Rigorous and sophisticated work based on a randomly sampled group of 1540 women (ages 15 to 54), properly stratified according to most relevant categories (geographic and demographic). Results indicate lower fertility rates among urban, more educated and professionally employed couples as well as the decisive effect of new contraception practices. [P. F. H.]

Lewis, Lawrence A. The spatial properties of population mobility within Puerto Rico. See item 6655.

8388. Lloyd, Antony J. and **Elaine E. Robertson.** Social welfare in Trinidad and Tobago. Port of Spain? Antilles Research Associates, 1971. 95 p.

Descriptive rather than critical, but includes good bibliography on topic. [P. F. H.]

Lowenthal, David. West Indian societies. See item 1178.

—— and **Lambros Comitas** eds. Consequences of class and color: West Indian perspectives. See item 1180.

MacDonald, John Stuart and **Leatrice D. MacDonald.** Transformation of African and Indian family traditions in the southern Caribbean. See item 1181.

8389. Marshall, W. K. Peasant movements and agrarian problems in the West Indies: aspects of the development of the peasantry (UWI/CQ, 18:1, March 1972, p. 30-46)

Very good summary of peasant history in the West Indies up to 1930 (100 years from emancipation of slaves). Account of slow and painful evolution under very adverse conditions of exploitation (mainly by planters and local government) in spite of Crown's good intentions. Treatment of this social movement is elementary and lacks detailed sociological discussion. [P. F. H.]

Miller, Errol. Education and society in Jamaica. See item 1189.

8390. ——. Self and identity problems in Jamaica: the perspective of shame (UWI/CQ, 17:3/4, Sept./Dec. 1971, p. 15-35, bibl.)

New sense of worth to be promoted among Jamaican society depends on new frames of reference (social-structural) in the everyday life of the emerging nation. An application of the relevant psychosocial thesis on role behavior of D. R. Miller, H. M. Lynd and others, this paper contributes to the understanding of basic problems of deviance in Jamaica and discusses important considerations for the society's future. [P. F. H.]

8391. Montes, Segundo and **Luis Fernando Valero Iglesias.** Sexo y juventud: encuesta a jóvenes de El Salvador y Panamá. San Salvador, Univ. Centroamericana José Simeón Cañas, 1970. 165 p., bibl., tables.

Complex picture of sexual life, sexual initiation and sexual values and attitudes. Good study (structured interviews on a sample of 8th graders) of Salvadorian and Panamanian youth. Results clearly show impact of industrialization and urban life upon traditional setting of Catholic societies of Central America. [P. F. H.]

Nag, Moni. Patterns of mating behavior, emigration and contraceptives as factors affecting human fertility in Barbados. See item 1190.

Nas, P. J. M. Stratifikatie onderzoek in het Caribisch gebied. See item 1191.

8392. Nieves-Falcón, Luis. La opinión pública y las aspiraciones de los puertorriqueños. Río Piedras, P.R., Univ. de Puerto Rico, Centro de Investigaciones Sociales, 1972. 198 p., tables.

In spite of limitations one should use the questionnaires (especially lists of selected neighborhood problems as well as those of society as a whole) to examine this sample of 1300 adult Puerto Ricans. It covers wide spectrum of personalities and social strata. Findings range from opinions about barrio problems to political references and national definition vis-à-vis the US. Very informative image of Puerto Rico during the 1960s. [P. F. H.]

8393. ———. Puerto Rico: un caso de aplicación transcultural de las ciencias de la conducta (UPR/RCS, 15:3, sept. 1971, p. 349-361, table)

Simple description of university curricula in undergraduate schools' departments of social sciences. Reveals mixed blessings of burdening young minds with ideas and behaviors which are not a part of their national cultural heritage. [P. F. H.]

8394. Presser, Harriet B. Puerto Rico: el papel de la esterilización en el control de la fecundidad (Estudios de Planificación Familiar [Bogotá] 4:2, nov. 1968/dic. 1969, p. 196-205)

Following in the steps of R. Hill, P. K. Hatt, K. W. Back and J. M. Stycos, Ms. Presser utilizes a rigorous survey (Continuing Master Sample Survey for P.R.) with newly introduced questions (1965) especially related to societal and familial backgrounds of women who underwent sterilization. Findings (over one-third of all married women between 20 and 49 years in Puerto Rico have been sterilized) are revealing of marital behavior and other aspects of family life. [P. F. H.]

8395. Puerto Rico. Bureau of Economic and Social Analysis. Planning Board. Manpower report to the Governor: a report on a society in transition; an assessment of manpower requirements, utilization, and training needs to 1975. San Juan, P.R.? 1968? 130 p., tables.

Sound government agency report makes extensive use of best sources in field. Before publication, evaluations were refined and checked through various processes of multiple exposure. Necessary reference for any further study of Puerto Rican economics. [P. F. H.]

8396. Rajbansee, Joseph. Civil Service associations & unions in the Commonwealth Caribbean. Mona, Jam.? Univ. of the West Indies, Trade Union Education Institute, Dept. of Extra Mural Studies, n.d. 51 p., tables (T.U.E.I. occasional papers in industrial relations, 1)

Short description of unions and union organization in the region. Includes documentary appendix on collective bargaining and useful bibliography. [P. F. H.]

8397. Reimer, Everett W. Social planning: collected papers, 1957-68. Cuernavaca, Mex., Centro Intercultural de Documentación, 1968. 1 v. (Various pagings) plates (CIDOC: Cuaderno, 22)

Encompasses series of varied documents. An important study of Puerto Rico's labor force (demands and projections in view of accelerated development) offers valuable information and is executed with methodological rigor. Other interesting papers are: "The Puerto Rico Case," "The Education and the Alliance for Progress," and finally "Schools for What?" The latter seems to draw its inspiration from Ivan Illich (see *Developing society*, N.Y., Harper, 1970). [P. F. H.]

Reyes Ramírez, José Ricardo. Evaluación de los censos de población de El Salvador de 1950 y 1961 a nivel de los Departamentos según la declaración de la edad. See item 6687.

8398. Reynolds, Jack. Family planning dropouts in Trinidad report of a small study (UWI/SES, 20:2, June 1971, p. 176-187, tables)

Short study of cases indicates that women who quit family-planning programs also quit contraceptive practices. Conclusion of restricted value. [P. F. H.]

8399. Rogler, Lloyd H. A better life: notes from Puerto Rico (*in* Horowitz, Irving Louis and Mary Symons Strong eds. Sociological realities: a guide to the study of society. N.Y., Harper & Row, 1971, p. 310-313, bibl., plates)

Brief and journalistic but penetrating account of the revolution of expectations. Examines problem of housing within microcosm of a lower middle-class family. [P. F. H.]

Romer, R. A. Korsow: een sociologische verkenning van een Caraibische Maatschappij. See item 1204.

8400. Ronceray, Hubert de. Les premières expériences du Centre Haïtien D'Investigation en Sciences Sociales (IFH/C, 108, 2./3. trimestres 1968, p. 16-25)

Accomplished sociologist, successful administrator, and founder of Haitian Center of Social Sciences, author summarizes here the early stages, problems of recruitment, and policy-making of this institution which has survived its most difficult years. [P. F. H.]

8401. Saint-Louis, René. La présociologie haïtienne où Haïti et sa vocation nationale. Montréal, Canada, Editions Lémeac, 1970. 127 p.

Professeur à l'Univ. de Montréal, l'auteur interroge les faits sociaux et les classes depuis la période coloniale jusqu'à nos jours pour expliquer la structure sociale haïtienne. C'est une bonne approche des problèmes sociaux existant en Haïti. [M. A. Lubin]

Sanders, Andrew. Amerindians in Guyana: a minority group in a multi-ethnic society. See item 1206.

Seda, Eduardo. Social change and personality in a Puerto Rican agrarian reform community. See item 1207.

8402. Seda Bonilla, Eduardo. La condición urbana: San Juan, Puerto Rico (UPR/CS, 11:3, Oct. 1971, p. 5-18)

Overview of recent demographic data and observations on life-conditions in San Juan during past 50 years. [P. F. H.]

8403. Silén, Juan Angel. Hacia una visión

positiva del puertorriqueño. Río Piedras, P.R., Editorial Edil, 1970. 244 p., bibl.

Journalistic analysis of views of younger generations. Historical discussion of nationalism and its struggle for economic and political power leads to critical examination of effects of US dominance on Puerto Rican youth in "Una Generación Encajonada . . ." Perceives young generation as being on a dead-end-road, thus bound to become revolutionary. Includes good bibliography. [P. F. H.]

Staton, Howard R. Social determinants of housing policy in Puerto Rico: a case study of rapid urbanization. See item 1209.

8404. Tidrick, Kathryn. Need for achievement, social class, and intention to emigrate in Jamaican students (UWI/SES, 20:1, March 1971, p. 52-60, tables)

In contrast to bulk of migration studies of West Indies, this paper focuses on Jamaica's "brain-drain." Applies scores to major socio-economic characteristics and relates them to respondents' attitudes. [P. F. H.]

8405. Tumin, Melvin Marvin with **Arnold S. Feldman.** Social class and social change in Puerto Rico. 2. ed. Indianapolis, Ind., Bobbs-Merrill, 1971. 549 p., tables (A social science research study. Univ. of Puerto Rico, College of Social Sciences)

Second edition of this 1961 classic work, one of the few attempts at systematic empirical exploration of stratification and mobility at the national level. Brings about several pieces of analysis and more particularly, it adds a good set of consideration to section on "Theoretical Speculation" regarding persistent problems of class structure in the island. [P. F. H.]

8406. Vázquez Calcerrada, Pablo B. and **John C. Belcher.** La vivienda y el cambio social en un municipio en el sur de Puerto Rico (UPR/RCS, 15:1, marzo 1971, p. 5-59, tables)

Partial report of item 8365. Sound piece of research based on reliable techniques and accurate field-work reporting. This compensates for less-familiar (or less "Latin") elements in original questionnaire which was also used in US rural settings. Does not fully explore references to social change. [P. F. H.]

Walker, Malcolm T. Politics and the power structure: a rural community in the Dominican Republic. See item 1214.

8407. Yurchenco, Henrietta. ¡Hablamos! Puerto Ricans speak. Photographs by Julia Singer, N.Y., Praeger Publishers, 1971. 136 p., map, plates.

Tape-recorded views of 15 Puerto Ricans of different strata and backgrounds (from peasant to artists) on their culture, problems of cultural assimilation and independence. Candid and engrossing. Relevant ethnographic document. [P. F. H.]

8408. Zahn, Margaret A. and **John C. Ball.** Factors related to cure of opiate addiction among Puerto Rican addicts (ISDA/IJA, 7:2, Summer 1972, p. 237-245, tables)

Vigorous case study of 108 male addicts treated in Puerto Rico Lexington Hospital shows clear interrelations between crime and normal married life, plus employment vs. other situations. [P.F.H.]

SOUTH AMERICA

Acedo Mendoza, Carlos and **Sheila Olmos de Manzo.** El desarrollo de la comunidad. See item 2118.

8409. Aduriz, Joaquín. Así viven y así nacen: estudio psicosocial de los condicionamientos de fecundidad en los migrantes provincianos de Lima-Callao. Lima, Centro de Estudios y Promoción del Desarrollo, 1969. 57 p. (Cuadernos de DESCO, A-3)

Qualitative investigation of the psychological mechanisms underlying motivational aspects of fertility among provincial immigrants who settle in the cities of Lima and Callao. The story of Gregorio and Sofía transcribed in their own words, illustrates these mechanisms. [Asst. Ed.]

8410. Agulla, Juan Carlos. Soziale Strukturen und soziale Wandlungen in Argentinien. Mit einem Vorwort von Hanns-Albert Steger. Berlin, FRG, Colloquium Verlag, 1967. 137 p., tables. (Bibliotheca Ibero-Americana, 8)

Contains Agulla's lectures concerning social structure and change in Argentina, delivered when he participated as guest lecturer at the Univ. of Münster in the "Social Research Program for Latin America." [G. M. Dorn]

8411. Alers, J. Oscar. Interviewer effects on survey response in an Andean estate (YU/IJCS, 11:3, Sept. 1970, p. 208-219, tables)

Methodological question of particular interest (due to extensive use of structured interviews in contemporary research) was tested in the well known "Vicos Project" community in 1963. Shows that opinion survey and scaling of values are not very reliable when techniques of research applicable to industrial societies are put to work in different cultures. [P. F. H.]

8412. Argentina. Consejo Federal de Inversiones. Estudio y asesoramiento en desarrollo de comunidades y asistencia social en la Provincia de Santiago del Estero. B.A., 1972. 187 p., map, tables (Serie técnica, 8)

Presents medium and long-range recommendations to speed up community development and social welfare in Argentina's Santiago del Estero province. Based on tables reflecting serious planning, this is an illuminating study. [G. M. Dorn]

8413. ———. **Ministerio de Bienestar Social de la Nación, Dirección Nacional de Política Social.** Estudio de la estructura social de la región de desarrollo Patagonia. B.A., 1970. 1 v. (Unpaged) (Col. Documentos de trabajo, 1:2)

Succinct demographic, social, and economic sketch of developing Patagonia region which encompasses Chubut and Santa Cruz provinces, the Tierra del Fuego territory, the Antarctic portion claimed by Argentina,

8414. ———. **Secretaría de Estado de Trabajo. Dirección Nacional de Recursos Humanos. Oficina Nacional de la Mujer.** Evolución de la mujer en las profesiones liberales en Argentina: 1900-1965. B.A., 1970. 160 p., illus., tables (Serie A: La mujer económicamente activa)

Comprehensive and detailed study involving eight Argentine universities over 65-year period concerning degrees granted women in fields of: medicine, pharmacy, biochemistry, odontology, law, administration, economics, philosophy, education, mathematics, physics, engineering, architecture and agricultural sciences. Half the volume consists of tables and graphs. Concludes that most marked increase in degrees granted occurred during 1961-65. [Asst. Ed.]

8415. Arnove, Robert F. Student alienation: a Venezuelan study. Foreword by Kalman Silvert. N.Y., Praeger Publishers 1971. 209 p., bibl., illus., tables (Praeger studies in international economics and development)

Rigorous examination of the Univ. del Oriente emphasizes importance which family and social class have on student's future prospects. Study fills gap in an often overlooked area of Venezuela. Based on sound data compilations, which include some interesting parallels with US educational institutions. [Ed.]

8416. Arze, José Roberto. Acotaciones para una bibliografía selecta sobre sociología boliviana (RIB, 20:3, julio/sept. 1970, p. 294-308)

Partial annotated bibliography of some sociological books, articles and magazines published in Bolivia; few published elsewhere. For historian's comment, see *HLAS 34:2827*. [I. G.]

8417. Beltrán Cortes, Luis María. Temas colombianos: la metamorfosis del "chino de la calle;" la hidra de Lerna: reflexiones sobre el tema de la violencia. Bogotá, Editextos, 1969. 156 p., bibl., illus., map, tables.

Two studies by a Colombian psychiatrist, one on Bogotá's vagrant children, the other on the *violencia*. Roughly half the book is devoted to each. [Ed.]

Berry, Brian J. L. Relações entre o desenvolvimento econômico regional e o sistema urbano: o caso do Chile. See item 6858.

8418. Biolcati, Adriano Augusto. Best seller. B.A., Ediciones Algoritmo, 1972. 186 p.

Catty, off-the-cuff observations about the society that sometimes comes close to home. [Ed.]

8419. Bonaparte, Héctor M. Subdesarrollo dentro del subdesarrollo (ILARI/A, 20, abril 1971, p. 171-204, tables)

Case study of "underdevelopment" in Argentina. [Q. J.]

Bourque, Susan Carolyn. Cholification of the campesino: a study of three Peruvian peasant organizations in the process of societal change. See item 7678.

Bourricaud, François. Changements à Puno: étude de sociologie andine. See item 1358.

8420. El campesino tucumano: educación y cultura. Tucumán, Arg., Secretaría de Educación y Cultura, Centro de Documentación e Información Educativa, 1971. 93 p., fold. map., plates, tables (Serie estudios y documentos, 4)

Detailed monograph on the culture and education of Tucumán's peasants. Some topics discussed: "La Promoción de la Cultura en el Interior de Tucumán;" "Fundamentos Básicos para la Educación-Promoción;" and "Cursos de Promotores Culturales." Researchers emphasize importance of establishing close relationship with the campesinos and reproduce taped conversations between the two groups. Valuable study, filled with data. [Asst. Ed.]

Cardona Gutiérrez, Ramiro. Las invasiones de terrenos urbanos: elementos para un diagnóstico. See item 6901.

8421. Clausen, Arne. Una imagen del hombre argentino. Presentación de José Míguez Bonino. Cuernavaca, Mex., Centro Intercultural de Codumentación, 1969. 1 v. (Various pagings) bibl. (CIDOC: Sondeos, 50)

Philosophical discussion of the concept of the "Argentine man," from a social and historic perspective. Essays on the national ethos by Mallea, Martínez Estrada, Mafud and Murena. Also examines the influence of religion on the country's life. [Ed.]

8422. Colombia. Dirección General de Integración y Desarrollo de la Comunidad. Estudio de las condiciones socio-económicas de los Municipios de Túquerres, Sapuyes y Guachucal, Departamento de Nariño. [Preparado por] Humberto Triana y Antorveza, Jaime Pacheco Hernández y Aloys Keune. Bogotá, Imprenta Nacional, 1971. 135 p.

Study of socio-economic conditions in three Colombian *municipios* is based on published and unpublished literature, on cross-cultural samplings as well as in-depth analyses by trained sociologists of community organizations. Includes many recommendations for more effective implementation of local and provincial services. [G. M. Dorn]

8423. Conning, Arthur M. Rural community differentiation and the rate of rural-urban migration in Chile (RSS/RS, 36:3, Sept. 1971, p. 296-314, tables)

Roles or antifacts in rural communities which are part of the national institutions of a single society are defined as indicative of differentiation in these communities. In author's view, the greater the differentiation the greater the migration to urban areas. This hypothesis was more strongly supported when the move was for purposes of employment as contrasted to moves for educational purposes. [Q. J.]

Coppens, Walter and others. Pegoncito, estado de Aragua, Venezuela: un estudio de desarrollo rural local. See item 6964.

8424. Corsi, Carlos and **Luis Rueda Gómez.** Colonialismo demográfico: la controversia sobre el control oficial de la natalidad. Bogotá, Ediciones Paulinas, 1972. 238 p. (Col. Defendamos la vida, 1)

Birth control and abortion are viewed as immoral, egotistical, lustful and diabolical (to name just a few) schemes of capitalism to destroy the family. Colombian authors substantiate their views with extensive quotes and polemical prose availing themselves of sophistic arguments. Valuable for its "point of view." [Ed.]

8425. Cotler, Julio and **Giorgio Alberti.** Estructura social y reforma agraria (PEMN/R, 36, 1969/1970, p. 178-188)

Suggests that rural change in Peru requires the dispersal of local power and resocialization of all persons involved in the change situation. [Q. J.]

Crespi, Muriel. Changing power relations: the rise of peasant unions on traditional Ecuadorian haciendas. See item 1374.

8426. Dobyns, Henry F. Comunidades campesinas del Peru. Lima, Editorial Estudios Andinos, 1970. 239 p., bibl., tables (Investigaciones sociales. Serie: monográficas andinas, 6)

Looks at rural communities' view of themselves and their self reliance and how they are seen by researchers including the Vicos Project; development potential; courses of action; and community requirements. See *HLAS 31:2259*. [Ed.]

Doughty, Paul L. The social uses of alcoholic beverages in a Peruvian coastal mestizo community. See item 1385.

8427. Enns, Arno W. Man, milieu, and mission in Argentina: a close look at church growth. Foreword [by] Sante Uberto Barbieri. Grand Rapids, Mich., William B. Eerdmans Publishing Co., 1971, 258 p. bibl., map, tables.

Analysis rich in data and implications which have potential use for many but are presented primarily by an evangelist for evangelists. [Q. J.]

8428. Flinn, William L. and **James W. Converse.** Eight assumptions concerning rural-urban migration in Colombia: a three-shantytowns test (UW/LE, 46:4, Nov. 1970, p. 456-466)

Another illustration that many common-sense assumptions about rural-to-urban migration are questionable if not false. [Q. J.]

8429. Floria, Carlos Alberto. La mujer argentina y la política. B.A., Ministerio de Cultura y Educación, Centro Nacional de Documentación e Información Educativa, 1972. 27 p.

Valuable overview of the role of Argentine women in national politics, from Remedios San Martín to Eva Perón. Also analyzes writings of Argentine *pensadores* on subject. Concludes with in-depth analysis of women's voting patterns, political affiliations and impact. [Asst. Ed.]

Fundación Bariloche, *San Carlos de Bariloche, Arg.* **Departamento de Sociología.** Datos comparativos de las provincias argentinas. v. 1, Indicadores demográficos, económicos, políticos y sociales: 1947-1960. See item 6812.

8430. Gall, Norman. Births, abortion and the progress of Chile. Hanover, N.H., American Universities Field Staff Reports, 1972. 10 p. (West coast South America series, 19:2)

Another excellent report by Gall (see items 1407, 7403-7404 and 7580). Stresses that Chile has become Latin America's leader on matters of demographic and family-planning research and practice. It is no coincidence that the UN's Centro Latinoamericano de Demografia is in Santiago. Gall focuses on achievements and failures of Chile's population control programs. [Asst. Ed.]

8431. Giberti, Eva. Los argentinos y el amor. B.A., Editorial Merlin, 1970. 109 p. (Colección Tiempos modernos)

Excellent collection of essays psychologically interpretating Argentine men, written by a trained psychologist; deals with "costumbres o instituciones que van desde los piropos callejeros, las leyendas incriptas en los camiones, las despedidas de soltero, el levante y el cancherear y el hotel alojamiento y la Villa Cariño hasta las relaciones familiares, los medios masivos de comunicacion, la infidelidad y el adulterio y la correspondencia recibida en un popular programa televisivo." [J. R. Scobie]

8432. Goldar, Ernesto. La mala vida. B.A., Centro Editor de América Latina, 1971. 114 p., illus., plates (La historia popular. Vida y milagros de nuestro pueblo, 20)

Another in this paperback series on "Argentiniana" (see *HLAS 34:2896*). This one discusses the emergence of prostitution in Buenos Aires during the immigration flood at turn of century. Topics discussed: "Liberalismo y Mala Vida;" "Prostituta Criolla Versus Prostituta Importada;" "El Prostíbulo:" "Los Rufianes Polacos;" "El Maquereu y La Maison Française;" "El Cafiolo y la Prostituta Criolla;" and "Industrialización y Migración Interna: La Nueva Prostituta." [Asst. Ed.]

Grunig, James E. Communication and the economic decision-making processes of Colombian peasants. See item 2064.

8433. Guido, Francisco Alberto. La mujer en la vida sindical argentina. B.A., Ministerio de Cultura y Educación, Centro Nacional de Documentación e Información Educativa, 1972. 151.

Valuable exploration of the role of Argentine women in the country's labor movement. Concludes that very little serious research had been conducted on this topic and that, although it is obvious that women play a much more active part in the movement since the late 1940's and peronismo, few rigorous conclusions can be drawn. [Asst. Ed.]

8434 Heath, Dwight B. Peasants, revolution,

and drinking: interethnic drinking patterns in two Bolivian communities (SAA/HO, 30:2, Summer 1971, p. 179-186)

Exploration into social effects of drinking. Agrarian reform in Bolivia led to an increase in interethnic drinking in some cases, and reduced it in others. [Q. J.]

8435. Hicks, Frederick. Interpersonal relationships and *caudillismo* in Paraguay (UM/JIAS, 13:1, Jan. 1971, p. 89-111)

Basic idea suggests that certain types of "dyadic contracts" of the patron-client or colleague type relationships which exist in Paraguay have reinforced the consultative and unstable political system which has existed there for the past century. [Q. J.]

——. Politics, power, and the role of the village priest in Paraguay. See item 7896.

8436. Imaz, José Luis de. Los que mandan [Those who rule]. Translated and with an introduction by Carlos A. Astiz. Albany, N.Y., State Univ. of New York, 1970. 279 p.

English translation of important empirical sociological study first published in 1964 (see *HLAS 27: 4139* and *HLAS 29:6308*), which utilizes social backgrounds of political leaders, landowners, industrialists, military officers, and labor union leaders in examining the power structure of modern Argentina. Includes index. [J. R. Scobie]

8437. Informe nacional sobre desarrollo de comunidades, 1971. n.p., Ministerio de Bienestar Social, Subsecretaría de Promoción y Asistencia Social, 1971. 1 v. (Unpaged) tables.

Reports of government agencies directly charged with community development; other government agencies indirectly related with community development; and private institutions. [Ed.]

8438. Leeds, Anthony. The significant variables determining the character of squatter settlements. Austin, Tex., Univ. of Texas, Institute of Latin American Studies, 1971. 1 v. (Unpaged) bibl. (Offprint series, 105)

Paper attempts to synthesize vast amount of empirical material on analytic problem of squatter settlement. Although vastly different, Latin American squatter settlements share in: 1) illegality of land occupancy, 2) irregularity of origin, and 3) the need for attention from public authorities. Painstaking and complex analysis. Originally published in *América Latina* (Centro Latinoamericano de Pesquisas em Ciências Sociais, Rio, 12:3, julho/set. 1969, p. 44-86). [Asst. Ed.]

Lehmann, David. Peasant consciousness and agrarian reform in Chile. See item 7764.

Mafud, Julio. Argentina desde adentro. See *HLAS 34:2751a*.

8439. Martínez Paz, Fernando and others. La juventud argentina (UNC/R, 11:5 [2. serie] nov./dic. 1968, p. 685-1014, illus., plates, tables)

Compilation of 18 scholarly articles on the predicament and characteristics of Argentine youth. Some of the better known authors and scholars: Fernando Martínez Paz, Agustín Caeiro, José Luis de Imaz, Pedro José Frías, Noé Jitrik, Jorge Orgaz, Sergio Bagú and Carlos Alberto Floria. Valuable compilation. [Asst. Ed.]

8440. Mas García, A. Promoción profesional de trabajadores en el Paraguay; un desafío, una respuesta. Asunción, Centro de Promoción Profesional de Trabajadores (PPT), Escuela Politécnica Cirilo Duarte, 1972. 143 p., tables.

Beginning with a schematic view of Paraguay's socio-economic history, study then goes on to explore possibilities of improved professional training of Paraguayan workers. Based on questionnaires and on scientific exploration of the feasibility of local and national training programs. [G. M. Dorn]

8441. Meluk, Alfonso. Etiología de la delincuencia en Colombia. Bogotá, Ediciones Tercer Mundo, 1969. 169 p., bibl., (Col. El dedo en la herida, 31)

Purpose is to focus attention on causes of crime and to stimulate further research in this sociological phenomena. [Ed.]

Millones, Luis. Deporte y alienación en el Perú: el fútbol en los barrios limeños. See item 1446.

8442. Montaño Aragón, Mario. El hombre del suburbio: estudio de las áreas periféricas de Oruro. La Paz, Editorial Don Bosco, 1972. 254 p., tables.

Description of Bolivia's socio-cultural realities to be considered in any attempts to integrate people meaningfully, using Oruro as a model. Suburban is not fully urbanized nor de-ruralized. Author believes *marginality* is a criollo-Spanish concept and wonders whether it is the latter who are marginated rather than those they seek to acculturate. Praises Quichua and Aymara for successfully retaining their ethno cultural identity since the Conquest. [Ed.]

8443. Morales Gómez, Jorge. El fondo de renta en una comunidad tabacalera de Santander (ICA/RCA, 14, 1966/1969, p. 277-284, bibl., plate)

Case study of a Colombian "tobacco community" (harvest tobacco). Approach is from the point of view of superficial economics. [I. G.]

Parra Sandoval, Rodrigo *ed.* Dependencia externa y desarrollo político en Colombia. See item 7664.

8444. Pasquali, Antonio. El aparato singular: análisis de un día de TV en Caracas. Caracas, Univ. Central de Venezuela, Instituto de Investigaciones, Facultad de Ciencias Económicas y Sociales, 1967. 119 p., illus., plates, tables.

Analysis of the effect of TV on its audiences. The role of advertising, the media's "exaggerated liberalism," and the advisability of regulations are reviewed. Results are not favorable. [Ed.]

Patch, Richard W. Attitudes towards sex,

reproduction and contraception in Bolivia and Peru. See item 1463.

Peñaherrera de Costales, Piedad and **Alfredo Costales Samaniego.** Historia social del Ecuador. See *HLAS 34:2601.*

8445. Penfold, Anthony. Caracas: urban growth and transportation (Town Planning Review, 41, April 1970, p. 103-120, bibl., illus., maps)

It is expected that by 1974 underground rail transportation in Caracas will be functioning. Venezuela's Oficina Ministerial de Transporte has been analyzing the problem since its inception in 1964. After rail system is in operation, the Oficina will possibly implement its highway systems study. [Ed.]

8446. Pérez Sanín, Enrique. Parámetros demográficos: 1951-1964; proyecciones de población, 1965-1968. Bogotá, Ediciones Univ. de los Andes, 1970. 280 p., tables.

Attempts to quantify Colombia's regional birth, mortality and migration rates using 1951-64 intercensus period as base, to project estimate for the 1963-85 period. [Ed.]

8447. Piel, Jean. The place of the peasantry in the national life of Peru in the nineteenth century (PP, 46, Feb. 1970, p. 108-133, bibl., illus.)

Peru's population was largely rural until about 1950; yet, there has been no rigorous examination of its *campesinado*. Piel attempts here first systematic study of this neglected phenomenon. [Ed.]

8448. Pinto, Luiz de Aguiar Costa *ed.* Transición social en Colombia. Bogotá, Univ. Nacional de Colombia, Centro de Investigación para el Desarrollo (CID), 1970, 187 p., bibl., tables.

First study made by the CID designed to coordinate and link the university's role with that of transforming Colombian society and contributing to its progress. Includes works by seven graduate students in sociology under the direction of Professor Costa Pinto. [Ed.]

———. Voto y cambio social: el caso colombiano en el contexto latinoamericano. See item 7667.

8449. Portes, Alejandro. Political primitivism, differential socialization, and lower-class leftist radicalism (ASS/ASR, 36:5, Oct. 1971, p. 820-835, bibl., tables)

Challenges political primitivism theory of Lipset, Hornhauser and others and finds support in a socialization theory in this study of Chilean slum dwellers. [Q. J.]

8450. Preston, David A. New towns; a major change in the rural settlement pattern in Highland Bolivia (JLAS, 2:1, 1970, p. 1-27)

Describes formation of new towns in Bolivia, mostly made up of rural people who have decided to break with past life-styles. [Ed.]

Rama, Germán W. El club político. See item 7917.

———. Educación universitaria y movilidad social: reclutamiento de élites en Colombia. See item 6132.

8451. Ratier, Hugo E. Villeros y villas miseria. B.A., Centro Editor de América Latina, 1971. 113 p., illus. (La historia popular. Vida y milagros de nuestro pueblo, 60)

Excellent analysis and description of the socio-economic life in Buenos Aires' *villas miseria.* Accurately depicts higher living standards of rural migrants who swarm to *villas miseria,* as well as eventual hopelessness of their predicament. Well written study which will appeal to both specialist and generalist. [G. M. Dorn]

Rodríguez Pastor, Humberto. Caqui: estudio de una hacienda costeña. See item 1480.

8452. Roux, Gustavo I. de. Jaimundí: realidad social y análisis. Bogotá, Instituto de Doctrina y Estudios Sociales, Centro de Investigación y Acción Social, 1971. 31 l., tables (Documento de trabajo, 2)

Painstaking analysis of the labor of INCORA and the problem of agrarian reform in Jaimundí. Study concludes by asking question: What is the first objective of agrarian reform in Colombia? To seek an improvement for the peasant masses or to stimulate productivity of the landowners' farms? Is agrarian reform social action or the boostering of farm production? (p. 28) Author, an agricultural engineer, believes agrarian reform can satisfy both: help the economic development of the country (largely dependent on primary agricultural products) but also improve the social conditions of the rural folk. [Asst. Ed.]

8453. Quintero, Rodolfo. Prueba de la encuesta obrera de Marx entre trabajadores de Caracas. Caracas, Univ. Central de Venezuela, Instituto de Investigaciones Económicas y Sociales, 1969. 82 p., bibl. (Cuadernos del instituto. Serie sociología, 1)

Questionnaire prepared by Marx and first published in Paris by the *Revue Socialiste* in April 1880 distributed by students of labor sociology as a project during 1967 and 1968. [Ed.]

Santillán de Andrés, Selva E. Esquemas de la estructura socioeconómica de la provincia de Tucumán. See item 6830.

8454. Schwartz, Robert N. Peru: country in search of a nation. Los Angeles, Calif., Inter-American Pub. Co., 1970. 178 p., bibl., illus., maps.

Useful, up-to-date history written by sociologist/historian. Includes discussion of country's religious and economic past. Also examines dire consequences of 1970 earthquake. Offers valuable appendix entitled "Geography: Key to Culture," and excellent bibliography with many primary sources. [Ed.]

8455. Seminario Nacional de Planificación Familiar, *II, Asunción, 1969.* Población y planificación familiar en el Paraguay. Asunción, Centro Paraguayo de Estudios de Población, 1970. 161 p.

Twelve papers presented at the seminar. Principal conclusions are that a well informed population can best decide for itself how to plan a family. Realistic approach. [Ed.]

8456. Sierra García, Jaime. El proceso social: Colombia, realidad y destino. Medellín, Col., Univ. Autónoma Latinoamericana, 1968. 246 p.

Textbook type discussion of sociology with one chapter on Latin America and three on Colombia. [Ed.]

Smith, Margo Lane. Institutionalized servitude: the female domestic servant in Lima. See item 1492a.

8457. Solari Bosch, Osvaldo. Escuela de penados: crónica de la penitenciaría nacional. B.A., Editorial Plus Ultra, 1971. 220 p.

Social processes among prisoners in national penitentiary of Uruguay. [J. F. B. Dasilva]

8458. Stone, Carl. Social modernization and left wing voting in Chile (UWI/SES, 20:4, Dec. 1971, p. 335-361, tables)

Major conclusion of this study is that leftist voting in Chile is based on factors associated with a working class movement which is itself the product of social modernization. Also demonstrates how additions of religion to existing class cleavage produces a greater proliferation of partisan groups. [Q. J.]

8459. Televisión argentina: un enfoque nacional. B.A., Ediciones Proartel, 1971. 95 p.

Reviews early legislative history of Argentine television and emphasizes that it is only recently that Argentine TV has emerged from its infancy and entered a vigorous adolescent period of growth. Work centers on TV's role as most powerful means of communications and its importance as a global media. [G. M. Dorn]

Uzzell, John Douglas. Bound for places I'm not known to: adaptation of migrants and residence in four irregular settlements in Lima, Peru. See item 1498.

8460. Valdivia Ponce, Oscar. Migración interna a la metrópoli: contraste cultural, conflicto y desadaptación. Lima, Univ. Nacional Mayor de San Marcos, 1970. 467 p., bibl., tables.

Four year study intended primarily for the medical profession, social anthropologists, educators, and politicians to inform them of the whys and wherefores of rural to urban migrations. Study made in Lima, Callao and Pucaraos. [Ed.]

Vásquez, Mario C. Discriminación campesina en el Perú. See item 1501.

8461. Venezuela. Oficina de Estudios Socioeconómicos. Equipo Técnico. Mafafa vs. sistema: el consumo de drogas en la juventud venezolana. Caracas, 1972. 109 p.

Study of youthful drug addiction in Venezuela conducted under the auspices of Comisión Venezolana de Justicia y Paz as well as a broad ecumenical church group, resulting from growing national concern about the problem. This essay-style report of a technical study is intended for a wide public. Topics discussed include: faddism of drug culture as well as examination of each particular drug; international nature of phenomenon and its reliance on modern transportation; examination of the counter-culture; and psychological and social impacts on society. Lucid essay also provides an interesting drug vocabulary. [G. M. Dorn]

Whitten, Norman E., Jr. The ecology of race relations in northwest Ecuador. See item 1507.

Wright, Winthrop R. *Café con leche:* a brief look at race relations in twentieth century Venezuela. See *HLAS 34:2581.*

8462. Wiarda, Iêda Siqueira. Family planning activities in a democratic context: the case of Venezuela; context, scope, impact, activities, and prospects. Columbus, Ohio, The Ohio State Univ. 1970. 155 p., tables (Mershon Caribbean Seminar)

Preliminary report of extended study on subject involving discussion of materials obtained through interviews of active Venezuelan specialists. Extraordinarily useful document. [P. B. Taylor, Jr.]

8463. Zapata Gollán, Agustín. La urbanización hispanoamericana en el Río de la Plata; segunda época, No. 6, 1971. Santa Fe, Arg., Ministerio de Educación y Cultura, Dirección General de Cultura, Depto. de Estudios Etnográficos y Coloniales, 1973. 176 p., illus., map.

Chapters on urbanization in Spanish America; first settlements on the River Plate; Sante Fe; and Buenos Aires. Appendix includes early construction contracts and other documents and there are a number of early Latin American city maps. [Ed.]

BRAZIL

JOSE FABIO BARBOSA DASILVA

Associate Professor of Sociology
University of Notre Dame

IN HER RECENT ARTICLE ON THE DEVELOPMENT of sociological research in Brazil, Pereira de Queiroz (item 8529) rightfully indicates the positive results achieved: an extremely rapid growth of knowledge about the characteristics of Brazilian society based on substantive field research; a concomitant growth of trained field researchers demonstrating high quality technical ability in the collection and interpretation of research data; an increasing use of diversified research techniques attuned to the problems at hand and including not only a skill in their use but also ability to deal with complex techniques called for in specific research topics. All developments are based on a diversification and expansion of training in sociology at the undergraduate and graduate levels and with acceptable academic standards; and finally an expansion of research support by private and public institutions that have learned to depend upon their results for applied programs and planning. Her evaluation of the remaining negative aspects of such expansion also are worthy of mention. Basically, and in many instances, she views the present expansion as fragmentary, repetitive and leading to a multiplication of reports on data regarding partially isolated phenomena. This attests to an empirical orientation and a scientific attitude that imputes development and theoretical growth as an inductive product of empirical generalizations. But, instead of calling for a focus on "middle range" preoccupations à-la-Merton, she advocates a division of labor that would in a sense institutionalize roles regarding basic and technical investigations. Or, in other words, she anticipates a continuing need for the training of highly skilled research technicians, experienced in field work. But even more she stresses the need for capable sociologists able to go beyond the fragmentary stage of present research by formulating problems that would synthetize a large number of separate issues. Thus, theoretical expansion and scientific growth would be assured and specialists would be able to leap from the systematic study of a problem to its analysis at higher critical levels of synthesis and generalization.

Although one could well agree with much of her presentation, a reading of the titles included in this survey of Brazil's sociological literature in the past two years reveals trends similar to those indicated for Hispanic America in previous *HLAS*. There has been indeed an increasing diversification of research topics as well as techniques for data collection and interpretation, for example, the fashionable studies on the status of women. Simultaneously, there is a decrease in the funding of research for works on population. The question of modernization persists, having incorporated much fashionable socio-psychological emphasis. However, at least one study calls for the inclusion of structural variables. Studies on the question of race relations, and in particular on the explicit or covert discrimination against blacks and their resulting socio-economic marginality have also multiplied. Many of them have become repetitive in their opposition to the classical concepts of a "racially free society" expounded by Gilberto Freyre.

Of all these studies, the one that commands the most attention is Florestan Fernandes' (item 8490). The presentation of the issues involved is innovative and illuminating, especially his analysis of the phenomena of race relations and how it relates to the political economy. Fernandes introduces a critical perspective and also examines a variety of questions concerning theoretical integration. This paper has often been translated and is based on extensive prior research.

The return of many graduates of U.S. sociology programs to their country, has increased the number of joint publications involving American and Brazilian colleagues. (Unfortunately, we have yet to see an example of these cooperative efforts published in a "main stream" journal such as the *American Sociological Review*.) The American preoccupation with a "critical sociology," which has always been evident throughout the history of modern Brazilian sociology, continues unabated, in this country despite difficult structural conditions of academic work. This point is examined by Fernandes in item 8488, on the role of the universities, and also in the volume on critical theory by Cardoso, Weffort and others (item 7376). Considering that the possibilities are there, one hopes that the search will continue for a theoretical paradigm which will explore the contradictions peculiar to Brazilian society.

8464. Almeida, Mauro Lauria de. Comunicação de massa no Brasil. Belo Horizonte, Bra., Edições Júpiter, 1971. 144 p., bibl.

Another study on question of mass communication in Brazil: characteristics, procedures, impact regarding the formation of publics and opinions.

8465. Angelini, Arrigo Leonardo; José Fernando Bitencourt Lomonaco; and **Nelson Rosamilha.** Motivo de realização e desenvolvimento econômico (SIP/RIP, 4:1, marzo 1970, p. 33-41, tables)

Study aimed at the analysis of relationship between self realization, motive and economic development of a given region. Following procedures developed by McClelland, analyzes motivation of adolescents in that region. Finds that the greater the index of industrialization of a region the higher the level of achievement motivation among adolescents. Authors conclude by reaffirming the high degree of relationship between these two factors.

Azevedo, Thales de. As ciências sociais no Bahia: notas para su história. See item 6212.

8467. ———. As regras do namôro no Brasil: um padrão tradicional (CLAPCS/AL, 13:2/3, abril/set. 1970, p. 128-153)

Attempts to provide explicit description of rules and techniques of traditional courtship which persist among urban and rural Brazilian families. Couples now tend to deviate from traditional pattern established by their parents towards a free-choice norm. But, regardless of the emergence of these new forms of association oriented towards more immediate personal satisfaction, serious courtship is still directed towards marriage sanctioned by the couple's families.

Balchman, Morris J. Eve in a democracy: women and politics in Brazil. See item 7832.

8469. Bock, E. Wilbur and **Sugiyama Iutaka.** Social status, mobility and premarital pregnancy: the case of Brazil (WRU/JMF, 32:2, May 1970, p. 284-292, tables)

Based on a field research conducted within large framework of KAP studies. Results tend to support established relationships between status, mobility, and premarital pregnancy.

8470. Bonilha, José Fernando Martins. Organização social e educação escolarizada numa comunidade de imigrantes italianos. São Paulo, Faculdade de Filosofia, Ciências e Letras de Presidente Prudente, 1970. 294 p., bibl., fold. map, tables.

This investigation linking social organization and education in a community of Italian immigrants will be of interest to students of social integration and assimilation of European groups in Brazil.

8471. Brasília: nível e padrão de vida do comerciário; estrutura da emprêsa comercial. Rio, Serviço Social do Comércio, Depto. Nacional, 1969. 185 p., tables.

Results of research conducted in Brasília on levels and standards of living of persons working in the commercial sector as well as structure of this sector.

8472. Camargo, Cândido Procópio Ferreira de. Igreja e desenvolvimento. São Paulo, Editôra Brasileira de Ciencias [and] Centro Brasileiro de Análise e Planejamento [CEBRAP], 1971. 218 p., bibl., tables.

Discussion of role of the Church in the process of development, based on a study of social "conscientização" in the Northeast. Of interest is author's argument, based on research results, that there are structural limitations that limit the intended scope of such social-action programs.

8473. Carvalho, Rodrigues de. Aspéctos da influência africana na formação social do Brasil. Paraíba, Bra., Imprensa Universitária, 1967. 95 p.

Another contribution of author's research on Africa's influence in the development of Brazilian culture. Analyzes cultural survivals, cultural materials, and patterns such as those present in northern Brazil.

8474. Cascudo, Luís da Câmara. Sociologia do açúcar: pesquisa e dedução. Rio, Instituto do Açúcar e do Alcool, Divisão Administrativa, Serviço de Documentação, 1971. 478 p. (Col. Canavieira, 5)

Ethnography of Brazilian culture and its regional variations, particularly sugar, pervasive throughout the culture, especially in the Northeast. See also item 8501.

8475. Centro de Estudos e Ação Social, *Salvador, Bra.* Tóxicos: cultura, juventude, contestação. São Paulo, Edições Loyola, 1972. 63 p. (Cadernos de CEAS, 17)

Research report of the youth culture of Salvador (Bahia) discusses interrelations of life styles, use of toxics and political rebellion.

8476. Cintra, Antônio Octávio. Um estudo de modernidade, ideologia e envolvimento político (UMG/RBEP, 31, maio 1970, p. 53-89, tables)

Analysis of relationships between modernity and social participation among high-status migrant and non-migrant respondents. Concludes that universalist criteria are significant for political participation only among non-migrants whereas, among lower-status respondents, there was a relationship between modernism as well as leftism and political participation.

8477. Collier, Mario Elisa Dias. Notas sôbre Gilberto Freyre, inovador e renovador (CFC/RBC, 3:7, jan./março 1971, p. 77-83)

Commemorates 70th anniversary of Gilberto Freyre by tracing his efforts in introducing the study of sociology and social anthropology to Brazil. Also discusses development of his now well known theses on *Tropicalism, Lusotropicalism,* and *Tropicologism,* and their impact on several generations of Brazilian intellectuals.

8478. Costa, Pedro Veloso. Política nacional de saúde. Prefácio [por] Geraldo Barroso. Recife, Bra., Editôra de Pernambuco, 1971. 238 p.

Discusses national plan and program of public health, its recent development and transformations, and its future impact for Brazil's population and its process of economic development.

8479. Daly, Herman E. El problema de la población en el Nordeste del Brasil: sus dimensiones económicas e ideológicas (CM/DE, 3:3, 1969, p. 279-307)

Author believes that world-wide population problem is due not only to natioanlist mentality of countries but to ethnocentric orientations of race and class within them. However, he is hopeful that a policy for population control will be accepted in the Brazilian Northeast, an area which is entering a new developmental phase.

8480. Delorenzo Neto, Antônio. Sociologia aplicada à administração: sociologia das organizações. São Paulo, Editôra Atlas, 1972. 275 p., bibl., tables.

Examination of role of sociology in public administration. Discusses how study of complex organizations can be applied to government bureaucracies.

8481. Dias, Fernando Correia and **Oder José dos Santos.** Ipatinga: uma comunidade operária (UMG/RBEP, 33, jan. 1972, p. 119-149, tables)

Study of urban structure of Ipatinga, factory workers community near Belo Horizonte, Minas Gerais state. Includes discussion of economic, geographic, health, educational, and urban characteristics. Financed by county government for purposes of urban and economic planning.

8482. Diégues Júnior, Manuel. Estrutura social brasileira: aspectos do passado e transformações do presente (UMG/RBEP, 33, jan. 1972, p. 31-61)

Argues that many attributes regarded as characteristics of social disorganization in contemporary Brazilian society should better be viewed as typical of a process of social change. These features are particularly evident in the family, economic organization, occupations structure and differential value orientation between older and younger generations. Accordingly, much of the present conflicts and tensions reflect only the heterogeneity of today's social structure.

8483. ———. Etnias e culturas no Brasil. Rio, Editôra Paralelo *em convenio com o* Instituto Nacional do Livro/MEC, 1972. 183 p., bibl., map, plates.

Presentation, in a re-elaborated form and including new materials, of author's well-known areal classification of regions and cultures of Brazil.

8484. Faissol, Speridião. Migrações internas: um subsistema no processo de desenvolvimento (IBGE/R, 33:3, julho/set. 1971. p. 163-170)

Analysis of internal migration as a subsystem within the development process. It constitutes the most important vehicle for the structural transformation of a society such as Brazil. Such moves are also moves in the occupational structure and through such migration individuals are exposed to a wide spectrum of activities and go through the important changes of a society in the process of urbanization. In particular, migrants acquire new motivations and aspirations essential for a modern society.

8485. Faleiros, Vicente de Paula. Metodologia de diagnóstico social. Brasília, Coordenada Editôra de Brasília, 1971. 101 p., bibl., tables.

Discussion of technical approaches for analysis of social problems with special emphasis on measures for social welfare. Includes and discusses recent data on these issues.

8486. Fernandes, Florestran. Beyond poverty: the Negro and the mulatto in Brazil (SA/J, 58, 1969, p. 121-137, bibl., tables) English version of item 8489.

8487. ———. Comunidade e sociedade no Brasil: leituras básicas de introdução ao estudo macro-sociológico de Brasil. São Paulo, Editôra Nacional [and] Editôra da Univ. de São Paulo, 1972. 587 p., tables (Biblioteca universitária, série 2. Ciências sociais, 37)

Selection of readings on various social, political, and economic characteristics of Brazilian society at the macro-level.

8488. ———. Los dilemas de la reforma consentida (CPES/RPS, 6:16, set./oct. 1969, p. 32-62)

Discussion of relationships between higher education and structural demands of society within process of social change. Minimal problems related to the efficacious extension and use of material and human resources must be solved through partial and specific criteria. Moreover, it is necessary not to misunderstand short and long-term goals with their manipulation, propaganda, and set backs. Ultimate goal is to create a university able to operate by itself and accomplish aims required by an urban and industrial civilization. It must operate as a source of historical-critical consciousness and of inventive thought, thus becoming the center for a democratic revolution.

8489. ———. Más allá de la pobreza: el negro

y el mulato en Brasil (UNAM/RMS, 33:2, abril/junio 1971, p. 253-269, bibl., tables)

Innovative study of the status of blacks and mulattoes in the political economy of contemporary Brazil. Emphasizes structural elements in their situation: 1) the specifically social (or lack of a competitive order able to absorb, even partially, the various segments of the population into the occupational and social system of production); 2) the specifically ethnic (or persistence of a complex system of racial prejudice inherited from the past, reinforced by conditions of a dependent-capitalist society, and persisting through composite discriminatory attitudes and behaviour based on color). For English translation, see item 8486.

8490. ———. O negro no mundo dos brancos. São Paulo, Difusão Européia do Libro, 1972. 283 p., bibl., tables (Corpo e alma do Brasil, 36)

One of the most influential studies on race relations in Brazil by an author who has carried extensive and noted research on the topic. Focuses on Brazilian society's process of structural transformation and on the role of blacks in country's "white" order.

8491. ———. Sociedade de classes e subdesenvolvimento. 2. ed. rev. e ampliada. Rio, Zahar Editores, 1972. 267 p., bibl. (Biblioteca de Ciências Sociais)

Excellent study with an important theoretical contribution on the transformation of the class structure of Brazil at the stage of economic underdevelopment. Author's analysis of structural changes in the urban sector is particularly significant.

Fernandes, Liliana Laganá. Aspectos da organização do espaço no bairro rural dos Pires, município de Limeira, Estado de São Paulo. See item 7062.

8493. Fernandes Neto, Antônio. Comunicação e persuasão. São Paulo, Sugestões Literárias, 1971. 138 p., illus., plates.

Study of the potential and capability of mass communications to transmit information and to command as well as to persuade opinions in mass society.

8494. Fischlowitz, Estanislau. Valorização dos recursos humanos do Brasil. Préfacio [por] Evaristo de Moraes Filho. Rio, Fundação Getúlio Vargas, Instituto de Documentação, Serviço de Publicaciones, 1970. 426 p.

Examines possibilities for the reevaluation of human resources which are marginal to the process of change in Brazilian society.

8495. Flusser, Vilém. A consumidora consumida (IBJCD/C, 13:51, 3. trimestre 1972, p. 35-46, illus., plates)

Discussion of how the Brazilian woman is now beginning to redefine her status. Deep cultural factors have placed her in an ambivalent position halfway between self-affirmation and subordination. The persistence of this ambivalence helps explain the hesitancy of the women's liberation movement in Brazil.

8496. Fontenelle, L. F. Raposo. A comunidade no Brasil: um estudo tentativo para sua configuração (Revista de Ciências Sociais [Fortaleza, Bra.] 2:2, 2. semestre 1971, p. 5-14)

Presents survey of various approaches to the conceptualization of "community" in order to draw up a theoretical framework for a more advantageous study of the community in Brazil.

8497. Fontoura, Amaral. Organização social e política do Brasil. 2. ed. Rio, Editôra Aurora, 1972. 221 p., illus. (Biblioteca didática brasileira, série 4. Col. Moral e cívica, 4)

Sociological, historical and political analysis of the organization of Brazil, including an examination of how historical process has affected the transformation of the country's political structures.

8498. Forsberg, Sven. Brand över Brasilien. Stockholm, Förlaget Filadelfia, 1967. 175 p., plates.

Account of trip to Brazil by Swedish author who records success of Swedish Pentecostal Church in different cities. Attributes greater growth of Pentecostal Church, as compared to other Protestant denominations, to its appeal to poorest citizens to whom it extends spiritual, medical and economic help. [R. V. Shaw]

8499. Franco, Celso de Mello. A educação e o tránsito (AJC/C, 47:12, julho/set. 1971, p. 80-86, plates)

Speculations on factors determining how and why motorists and pedestrians react the way they do to traffic and traffic regulations. Author is chief of Detran, Rio's traffic control department. He see three basic components in traffic control: engineering, education, and enforcement. Article offers general comments on the philosophical and psychological aspects of traffic control, not solutions. [A. E. Toward]

8500. Freire, Paulo. Cambio. n.p., Editorial América-Latina, n.d. 114 p.

Author of program of "conscientização" discusses problem of socio-cultural change and its relationship with the transformation of cognition settings.

8501. Freyre, Gilberto. Açúcar: em tôrno da etnografia, da história e da sociologia do doce no Nordeste canavieiro do Brasil. 2. ed., aumentada. Brasília, Ministério da Indústria e do Comércio, Instituto do Açúcar e do Alcool, Divisão Administrativa, Serviço de Documentação, 1969. 286 p., illus. (Col. Canavieira, 2)

Well-known authority on the ethnography and "cultural anthropology" of the Northeast focuses on sugar: history and sociology of sweets from the Brazilian cuisine. See also item 8474.

8502. ———. A casa brasileira: tentativa de síntese de três diferentes abordagens, já realizadas pelo autor, de um assunto complexo; a antropológica, a histórica, a sociológica. Rio, Grifo Edições, 1971. 97 p. (Enciclopédia da vida brasileira, 1)

Sociology and history of the Brazilian home, from an

8503. Gans, Marjorie; José Pastore; and Eugene A. Wilkening. A mulher e a modernização da família brasileira (CRPE/PP, 12, out. 1970, p. 97-139, tables)

Explores factors related to process of modernization as experienced by men and women in a sample of 321 couples randomly selected from Brazilian urban areas. Investigation of sexual and marital-status correlates reveals that males score higher than females in the modernity scale. Author attributes this to cultural differences between sexes which assign a more passive role to women. Study constitutes inquiry into dimensions of modernity similar to those conducted by Joseph Kahl in Brazil and Mexico and by Smith and Inkeles in other countries. Article also available in Spanish as "La Mujer y la Modernización de la Familia Brasileña" (*Revista Latinoamericana de Sociología*, B.A., 6:3, sept./dic. 1970, p. 389-419, tables).

8504. Gnaccarini, José César A. Organização do trabalho e da família em grupos marginais rurais do estado de São Paulo (FGV/RAE, 11:1, março 1971, p. 75-94, illus., tables)

Offers sociological reconstruction of life-styles prevalent in rural-workers' neighborhoods in three counties of the Piracicaba sugar region, São Paulo state. Analyzes relations between traditional norms and land-ownership; division of labor and status differentiation; conflicting group interests and the combination of capitalist plantations with forms of industrial social organization in agriculture.

8505. Gouveia, Aparecida Joly. Origem étnica e situação socioeconômica dos estudantes matriculados em diferentes áreas de estudo nas universidades de São Paulo (CLAPCS/AL, 13:4, oct./dez. 1970, p. 38-50, bibl., tables)

Attempts to show how structural factors related to class (in the Weberian sense) and cultural factors (values presumably related to ethnic origin) affect chances of university-bound students and determine their choice of study. Data based on sample of 1860 students of various ethnic backgrounds entering three São Paulo universities in 1967. Analysis confirms hypothesis that socio-economic status of student's family determines his choice of a field of study.

8506. Gracia-Zamor, Jean-Claude. Social mobility of Negroes in Brazil (UM/JIAS, 12:2, April 1970, p. 242-254)

Discusses some of the historical factors which significantly affect the social mobility of Brazilian blacks. Also suggests how to cope with what author regards as a grave, though largely ignored, racial situation which could lead to a social crisis.

8507. Graham, Douglas H. Divergent and convergent regional economic growth and internal migration in Brazil: 1940-1960 (UC/EDCC, 18:3, April 1970, p. 362-382)

Study notes that available data on aggregate income and population indicate that in decade 1940-50 there was a widening divergence in income per capita among the states of Brazil. Such a pattern was associated with strong divergent growth between upper and lower groups of states. Nevertheless, data from 1950-60 indicates a slight convergence of income per-capita among states, and between upper and lower groups of states. It also seems that increasing rate of internal migration during this period was associated with the changes in income per-capita.

8508. Guareschi, Pedrinho Arcides. A marginalização social (Boletim do IESPE [Instituto de Estudos Sociais, Políticos e Econômicos, Pôrto Alegre, Bra.] 13 dez. 1970, p. 3-24, tables)

Author observes that any analysis of social and urban marginality must first take into account the process of intensive urbanization that displaces large numbers of ill-equipped migrants and concentrates them in *favelas*. Moreover, these marginal urban groups suffer from mal-integration, alienation, and exercise minimal social and political impact. Lack of effective measures on the part of high public administration officials further contributes to the persistent marginality of these groups.

8509. Guerra, C. Vianna. Pequeno inquérito sôbre o conhecimento de 100 palavras da língua portuguêsa aplicado a 361 estudantes (UFRJ/BIP, 19:1/6, jan./junho 1969, p. 9-13, bibl., tables)

Study attempts to develop Portuguese vocabulary scale similar to Raven's Mill Hill vocabulary test. Presents research results of 361 students' knowledge of 100 Portuguese words.

8510. Haller, Archibald O.; Donald Holsinger; and Helcio Ulhôa Saraiva. Variations in occupational prestige hierarchies: Brazilian data (UC/AJS, 77:5, March 1972, p. 941-956)

Authors hypothesize that occupational prestige hierarchy labeled "Euro-American urban" is characteristic of all or almost all contemporary societal structures. However, they indicate that the extension of such a system within these societies might not be complete. Thus, they emphasize intrasocietal differences and provide new data consistent with hypothesis that deviation is associated with isolation from "Euro-American urban" culture. Data was compiled in three Brazilian communities which vary on a scale of isolation. Results from the more isolated sectors were at variance with the common scale of occupational prestige.

Iutaka, S.; E. W. Bock; and W. G. Varnes. Factors affecting fertility of natives and migrants in urban Brazil. See item 1739.

8512. Kelly, Celso. Arte e comunicação. Rio, Livraria Agir Editôra *em convênio com o* Instituto Nacional do Livro, 1972. 196 p.

Collection of essays analyze the relations of art and communication or how symbolic forms influence social processes and human behavior.

8513. Kumasaka, Y. and H. Saito. Kachigumi: a collective delusion among the Japanese and their descendants in Brazil (Canadian Psychiatric Association Journal [Ottawa] 15:2, April 1970, p. 167-175)

Follow-up study of The Shindo-Remmei, a Japanese organization in Brazil, whose members refuse to believe that Japan lost World War II. As time went by, a majority came to accept the facts. However, a minority of fanatics or "victory-believers" still persists, having shut themselves off from other Japanese immigrants. Authors provide a chronology of this phenomenon and relate it to the Japanese process of acculturation in Brazil. For more on the Japanese in Brazil, see item 8516.

Lambert, Jacques. Os dois Brasil. See item 7092.

8515. Lodwick, Robert E. The significance of the Church-State relationship to an evangelic program in Brazil. Cuernavaca, Mex., Centro Intercultural de Documentación, 1969. 220 p. (CIDOC: Sondeos, 40)

Analysis of change in relationship between Catholic Church hierarchy and Brazilian political system. Evaluates effects which recent tensions, latent and open, between both could have on the development of evangelic churches.

8516. Maeyama, Takashi. Ancestor, emperor, and immigrant: religion and group identification of the Japanese in rural Brazil: 1908-1950 (UM/JIAS, 14:1, Feb. 1972, p. 151-182)

Study of changes in cults among Japanese immigrants in Brazil (e.g., ancestors, emperor, religious, etc.). Author believes changes have followed pattern of acculturation but have also been influenced by historical events such as Japan's defeat in World War II (see item 8513). This event led to a change from emperor-worship to ancestor-cult as well as to membership in religious movements. Author regards religion, ethnicity, and other factors as important in today's group identification.

8517. Marcondes, J. V. Freitas. Cassiano Ricardo: sociologia de brasilidade (Problemas Brasileiros [São Paulo] 8:89, jan. 1971, p. 26-40, illus.)

Author analyses three works by Ricardo as sources for study and contributions to Brazilian social history which emphasize a sociological perspective, in particular *A marcha para o oeste* (see *HLAS 6:3596a*).

8518. ———. Trabalho, lazer e educação (Problemas Brasileiros [São Paulo] 8:87, nov. 1970, p. 29-40)

Football! Author reminds listeners (the original was a speech) of great impact of Brazil's World Cup Victory in Mexico, 1970, then moves to discuss evolution of philosophical relationship between labor and leisure, beginning with Greeks and citing Freyre and several Brazilian constitutions in his review. Most interesting part of commentary is devoted to description of São Paulo Palace of Leisure or cultural center. Concludes with the point that leisure is as essential as labor for general welfare, especially in a developing nation like Brazil. [A. E. Toward]

8519. Melikian, L.; A. Ginsberg; D. Cüceloglu; and R. Lynn. Achievement motivation in Afghanistan, Brazil, Saudi Arabia and Turkey (JSP, 83:2, April 1971, p. 183-184, bibl., table)

Preliminary compilation of data on, and comparison of, levels of achievement-motivation in Brazil, Turkey, Saudi-Arabia, and Afghanistan. All differences among male students were statistically significant except for differences between Brazil/Turkey and Saudi-Arabia. Moreover, differences between male and female Afghan students were also significant.

8520. Melo, José Marques de. Comunicação, opinião, desenvolvimento. Petrópolis, Bra., Editôra Vozes, 1971. 114 p., bibl. (Col. MCS/4)

Author discusses communication, opinion formation, and process of development. Focuses on question of communication processes and on mode of "social" integration.

8521. Milanesi, Maria Lucila. O abôrto provocado: estudo retrospectivo em mulheres não-solteiras, de 15 a 49 anos, residentes no distrito de São Paulo, em 1965. São Paulo, Livraria Pioneira Editôra, 1970. 97 p., bibl., tables (Biblioteca pioneira de estudos brasileiros)

Field work on induced abortion among married women (15-59 years old) residents of a São Paulo *município* in 1965.

8522. Moschini, Felipe Nery. Maconha e maconheiros (Problemas Brasileiros [São Paulo] 8:89, jan. 1971, p. 3-20, illus., plate)

Historical examination of Brazilian legislation regarding use of narcotic substances, especially four laws promulgated during 1830-1969. Nevertheless, author concludes, use of narcotics persists throughout Brazilian society.

8523. Novaes, Paulo. Tecnologia e recursos humanos. Rio, Editôra Renes, 1972. 145 p. (Série problemas brasileiros)

Essays on the relation of technology to human resources with special reference to the process of development as exemplified by Brazil.

8524. Oliveira, Roberto Cardoso de. A sociologia do Brasil indígena: ensaios. Rio, Edições Tempo Brasileiro, 1972. 149 p. (Biblioteca tempo universitário, 31)

Study of development of a sociology of Brazilian Indian cultures which examines stages of relationships between them and other Brazilian groups, such as expanding pioneers who invade Indian territories. Also includes materials on process of de-tribalization and *acaboclisação* of Indian groups.

8525. Pereira, Nereu do Vale and others. Ensaios sôbre sociologia e desenvolvimento em Santa Catarina. Florianópolis, Bra., Editôra Empreendimentos Educacionais (EDEME), 1971. 123 p., maps, tables.

Essays on the development of Santa Catarina state emphasizing education and economic questions.

8526. Perlman, Janice E. Dimensoẽs de modernidade numa cidade em franco desenvolvimento: estudo do caso de Belo Horizonte (UMG/RBEP, 30, jan. 1971, p. 137-178)

Draws on material collected in 1965-66 by political-science and sociology teams of Univ. of Minas Gerais. Involves intensive mathematical analysis of responses to behavioral questions. Appendix offers methodological data. [P. B. Taylor, Jr.]

8527. Pires, José Herculano. Arigó: vida, mediunidade e martírio. 3. ed. rev. e atualizada. São Paulo, Edicel, 1970. 232 p., bibl.

Biography of late and well-known Brazilian spiritualist. Discusses background of his personal development, involvement with spiritualism and "possession," accession to role of curer and religious leader, and crises that he faced towards end of his life.

8528. Portela, Jarbas Moacir. Social aspects of transference and countertransference in the patient-psychiatrist relationship in an underdeveloped country: Brazil (IJSP, 17:3, Summer 1971, p. 177-188)

Describes psychiatrist-patient relationship in three contexts: private clinics, social-welfare services, and public hospitals. Shows that manifestations of transferential or counter-transferential events are largely conditioned by social-status of participants. Status determines social distance which, in turn, becomes an important variable in the psychiatrist/patient relationship.

8529. Queiroz, Maria Isaura Pereira de. Desenvolvimento, no Brasil, das pesquisas empíricas de sociologia: ontem e hoje (SBPC/CC, 24:6, junho 1972, p. 511-525, bibl, tables)

Historical essay on development of sociology in Brazil, which author divides into pre- and post-1960 periods. Development of this science has led to: a) growing knowledge of Brazilian society; b) increase in technically skilled researchers; c) differentiation of research techniques used, some of which are highly complex; and d) an expansion in the public and private financing available for sociological research as well as a broadening of interst in the application of its results.

Quirino, Tarcízio Rêgo. Educação e profissionalização na área rural do Nordeste. See item 6282.

8531. Riane, Philip. The Catholic Church in Brazil (UM/JIAS, 13:2, April 1971, p. 279-295)

Examination of effectiveness of the Catholic Church in forcing change in Brazil, a society still dominated by entrenched elites buttressed by conservatives in the armed forces. After the 1964 revolution, a series of confrontations in the 1970's led to a Church/State *modus vivendi*. However, a more politically active sector within the Church continues to agitate for social justice and reform. This remains unlikely, unless the Church effects a real change in the attitudes of rural and urban elites as well as among military leaders. Only such a change in attitude could lead to reforms. Volume includes Brazilian Church documents which, for the first time, legitimize radical reform.

8532. Ribeiro, Augusta Barbosa de Carvalho. Relações industrias e administração de pessoal. São Paulo, LTR Editôra, 1971. 474 p., bibl., tables.

Focusing on central-south Brazil, this study treats topics related to problems of industrial relations and personnel administration in bureaucracies and industrial enterprises.

8533. Ribeiro, René. Personality and the psychosexual adjustment of Afro-Brazilian cult members (SA/J, 58, 1969, p. 109-120)

Author believes data compiled indicates that membership in African-derived religions and/or attendance at their rituals in Recife, Bra., are not responsible for the sexual problems or homosexuality of certain individuals. In fact, author traces their deviant behavior to complex parent-child relationships as well as to other primary-group relationships which shaped the early sexuality and tension-releasing mechanisms of these individuals.

Riegelhaput, Joyce F. and Shepher Forman. Bodo was never Brazilian: economic integration and rural development among a contemporary peasantry. See *HLAS 34:2924*.

8535. Rocha, José Martinho da. Virgindade, sexo, família. Rio, Editôra Rio, 1972. 255 p., bibl., plates.

Analysis of the "virginity complex," within the process of transformation of cultural values and in relation to the family, as social entity.

8536. Rosamilha, Nelson. Psicologia da ansiedade infantil: contribuição para o estudo problema e da medida da ansiedade em crianças. São Paulo, Livraria Pioneira Editôra [and] Editôra da Univ. de São Paulo, 1971. 106 p., bibl., plates, tables (Biblioteca pioneira de ciências sociais)

Field project which attempts to develop an instrument for the psychological measurement of anxiety among children. Includes research results and discussion of materials with instruments.

8537. Rosen, Bernard C. Industrialization, personality and social mobility in Brazil (SAA/HO, 30:2, Summer 1971, p. 137-148)

Analysis of how inter-generational social mobility in Brazil is related to the achievement syndrome and industrialization, the degree of either constituting good predictors of social mobility. Both are positively related to it and together they account for more variety in social mobility than either does separately. Author suggests that further research on antecedents of social mobility should include variables from both the structural and psychological levels.

8538. ———— and **Anita L. La Raia.** Modernity in women: an index of social change in Brazil (WRU/JMF, 34:2, May 1972, p. 353-360, tables)

Examination of relation of industrialization to certain family-linked attitudes and behavior among women of five markedly different Brazilian communities, in the urban-rural-industrial continuum. Results established through a derived modernity scale indicated that, whereas modernity in women is inversely related to family size (both preferred and actual), it tends to increase with the rise of certain levels (educational, occupational, social, membership in voluntary associations).

8539. Salmen, Lawrence F. Housing alternatives for the *carioca* working class: a comparison between *favelas* and *casas de cômodos* (CLAPCS/AL, 13:4, oct./dez. 1970, p. 51-70)

Investigation of opinions of Rio's slum-dwellers as to the advantages and disadvantages to their present housing. In spite of superiority of *favelas* (shantytowns) to certain tenements, individuals living in them expressed lack of interest in moving to the *favelas*. Author attributed disinterest to lack of familiarity with *favelas* as well as to social stigma attached to their dwellers.

8540. Sánchez, Maria Angela D'Incao Maciel and Maria Conçeicão D'Incao e Mello. Introdução ao estudo do cooperativismo na Alta Sorocabana (Boletim [Faculdade de Filosofia, Ciências e Letras de Presidente Prudente, Depto. de Ciências Sociais, Bra.] 1970, p. 33-42, tables)

First in series of reports on cooperatives in the Sorocabana region of São Paulo, in which authors discuss theoretical framework of larger research project on the same subject which they conducted with the National Institute of Agricultural Development.

8541. Sanjek, Roger. Brazilian racial terms: some aspects of meaning and learning (AAA/AA, 73:5, Oct. 1971, p. 1126-1143, bibl.)

Following Harris' demand for more studies on quantitative ethnography, author presents results of a study of racial vocabulary in a Brazilian village. Uses quantitative procedures to show that, despite considerable ambiguity, a small portion of the considerable corpus of 116 terms forms the cognitive map of most informants and organizes the bulk of the domain. Data on how children acquire the vocabulary is used to demonstrate that skin, color and hair form are the primary variables.

8542. Saraiva, Terezinha. A mulher no processo de desenvolvimento (IBJCD/C, 13:51, 3. trimestre 1972, p. 72-73, tables)

Brief note on possible role of women in process of development while engaged in their own socio-cultural liberation.

8543. Schaden, Egon *comp.* Homem, cultura e sociedade no Brasil: seleções da *Revista de Antropología*. Petrópolis, Bra., Editôra Vozes, 1972. 450 p. (Col. Estudos brasileiros, 1)

Collection of studies on Brazil by several anthropologists and ethnologists. Volume's organization follows country's levels of cultural complexity (e.g., native culture, the *caipira*, groups in process of cultural change, etc.). Valuable compilation makes available, for first time, a number of previously inaccessible and significant studies.

8544. Schneider, Eliezer. A formação e as atribuções profisionais do psicólogo (UFRJ/BIP, 20:1/6, jan./junho 1970, p. 15-24)

Analysis of professional education of psychologists in Brazil raises questions regarding present system. Author argues for a requirement of post-graduate training to improve field's current professional standards.

Shirley, Robert W. The end of a tradition: culture change and development in the *município* of Cunha, São Paulo, Brazil. See *HLAS 34:3007*.

8546. Silva, Helvécio de Siqueira e. Estudos e pesquisas sôbre a infância e a juventude. Pt. 1, A infância e a juventude desajustadas; deliqüências contra o patrimônio particular e público: furtos. Belo Horizonte, Bra., Univ. Católica de Minas Gerais [and] Instituto de Orientação Juvenil, 1971. 227 p., bibl., maps, tables.

Research communication on childhood and youth focuses on maladjusted and delinquent children involved in criminal acts against public and private property.

Silveira, Isôlda Maciel da. Aspectos sócio-econômicos de Oriximiná, sede: nota prévia. See item 1318.

8548. Sodré, Muniz. A comunicação do grotesco: introdução a cultura de massa brasileira. Petrópolis, Bra., Editôra Vozes, 1971. 83 p., bibl.

Essay debates characteristics of mass communication processes and their results in contemporary Brazil.

8549. Souza, José Armando de. Inconsistência de "status" e comportamento político (UMG/RBEP, 31, maio 1970, p. 159-180, tables)

Critical evaluation of previous works on status-inconsistency theory. Presents some alternative techniques for solution of research problems found in the application of such theory and suggests other alternatives that may be used in dealing with these problems.

8550. Studart, Heloneida. Da mulher brasileira (IBJCD/C, 13:51, 3. trimestre 1972, p. 52-53)

Short note links women's liberation movement to global social effort to break constraints of underdevelopment. According to author, the interdependence of these movements emphasizes the former's importance in view of its possible impact on the establishment of a dynamic and progressive society.

8551. Tabak, Fanny. O status da mulher no Brasil: vitórias e preconceitos (Cadernos da PUC [Rio], agôsto 1971, p. 165-201)

Statistical analysis of status of women in Brazil reveals that: a) about one third of those economically active work in agriculture, cattle-raising, and forestry—production sectors where archaic methods predominate and lacking in modern technology; b) another third work in bureaucratic occupations where mechanization and automation are still limited; c) less than one fifth of the total are in the liberal arts professions; d) only two thirds of those 18-years or older vote and one out of every three votes the same as her husband. Thus, the majority of Brazilian working women have few technical skills, low educational training, little political participation and/or independence.

8552. Tosta Berlinck, Manoel. The structure of the Brazilian family in the city of São Paulo. Ithaca, N.Y., Cornell Univ., Latin American Studies Program, 1969. 201 p., bibl., tables (Dissertation series, 12)

Excellent research report with extensive analysis of

data on characteristics of the contemporary family in São Paulo, at various levels of city's social structure. Emphasizes social dimensions and interrelationship of factors.

8553. Trindade, Mário. Habitação e desenvolvimento. Petrópolis, Bra., Editôra Vozes, 1971. 268 p., tables.

Study of housing problem and its relation to developing societies. Emphasizes humanistic aspects of question and provides partial data on the Brazilian case.

8554. Walker, Neuma Aguiar. O modêlo de mudança usado pelas teorias de mobilização e de anomia (CLAPCS/AL, 13:2/3, abril/set. 1970, p. 90-116)

Comprehensive review of socio-political literature related to sociological concept of mobility particularly as related to populistic movements in Latin America. A formal model of social change is developed and modified as it appears not to be entirely satisfactory in explaining (particularly) occurrences in Brazil. [J. M. Hunter]

8555. Wilkening, A. Eugene and J. C. van Ess. Response stability in research among lower class respondents in rural Brazil (CLAPCS/AL, 13:4, oct/dez. 1970, p. 3-17, tables)

Follow-up interviews with a sample of 108 couples in central Brazil are used to determine stability of answers for 80 variables. Sample includes persons of low social status, little education and limited cultural exposure to metropolitan area of Brasília. Results indicate that answer-stability decreased when referring to: 1) personal and family characteristics; 2) aspects of present behavior; 3) aspects of past behavior; and 4) evaluative items. Factor analysis indicates that it is not possible to judge the stability of an answer beforehand, on the basis of the previously given answer.

JOURNAL ABBREVIATIONS

AAG/PG	Professional Geographer. Journal of the Association of American Geographers. Washington.
AEJ/JG	Journalism Quarterly. Association for Education in Journalism with the cooperation of the American Association of Schools, Depts. of Journalism [and] the Kappa Tau Alpha Society. Univ. of Minnesota. Minneapolis, Minn.
AGS/GR	The Geographical Review. American Geographical Society. N.Y.
AJC/C	Commentary. Published by the American Jewish Committee. N.Y.
ASLEP/A	Anuario de Sociología de los Pueblos Ibéricos. Organo de la Asociación de Sociólogos de Lengua Española y Portuguesa. Madrid.
ASS/ASR	American Sociological Review. American Sociological Society. Manasha, Wis.
BUS	Boletín Uruguayo de Sociología. Montevideo.
CFC/RBC	Revista Brasileira de Cultura. Ministério da Educação e Cultura, Conselho Federal de Cultura. Rio.
CLAPCS/AL	América Latina. Centro Latino-Americano de Pesquisas em Ciências Sociais. Rio.
CM/DE	Demografía y Economía. El Colegio de México. México.
CM/FI	Foro Internacional. El Colegio de México. México.
CPES/RPS	Revista Paraguaya de Sociología. Centro Paraguayo de Estudios Sociológicos. Asunción.
CRPE/PP	Pesquisa e Planejamento. Centro Regional Prof. Queiroz Filho. São Paulo.
EAZ	Ethongraphisch-Archäologische Zeitschrift. Deutscher Verlag Wissenschaften. Berlin, GDR.
GIIN/B	Boletín. Instituto Indigenista Nacional. Guatemala.
IBGE/R	Revista Brasileira de Geografia. Conselho Nacional de Geografia, Instituto Brasileira de Geografia e Estatística, Rio.
IBJCD/C	Coméntario. Instituto Brasileiro Judaico de Cultura e Divulgação. Rio.
ICA/RCA	Revista Colombiana de Antropología. Ministerio de Educación Nacional, Instituto Colombiano de Antropología. Bogotá.
IDES/DE	Desarrollo Económico. Instituto de Desarrollo Económico y Social. B.A.
IESSC/C	Comunidades. Instituto de Estudios Sindicales, Sociales y Cooperativos, Centro de Prospección Social. Madrid.
IFH/C	Conjonction. Revue franco-haïtienne. Bulletin de l'Institut Français d'Haïti. Port-au-Prince.
III/AI	América Indígena. Instituto Indigenista Interamericano. México.
IJSP	International Journal of Social Psychiatry. London.
ILARI/A	Aportes. Instituto Latinoamericano de Relaciones Internacionales. Paris.

INED/P	Population. Revue trimestrielle de l'Institut National d'Études Demographiques. Paris.
IRFDH/DC	Développement et Civilisations. Institut de Recherche et de Formation en vue du Développement Harmonisé. Paris.
ISDA/IJA	The International Journal of the Addictions. The Institute for the Study of Drug Addiction. N.Y.
ISTMO	Istmo. Revista del Centro de América. México.
JLAS	Journal of Latin American Studies. Centers or Institutes of Latin American studies at the Universities of Cambridge, Glasgow, Liverpool, London and Oxford. Cambridge University Press. London.
JSP	Journal of Social Psychology. The Journal Press. Provincetown, Mass.
KAS/P	Kroeber Anthropological Society Papers. Univ. of California. Berkeley, Calif.
LSE/PS	Population Studies. A journal of demography. London School of Economics, The Population Investigation Committee. London.
NGS/NGM	National Geographic Magazine. National Geographic Society. Washington.
PC	Pensamiento Crítico. La Habana.
PEMN/R	Revista del Museo Nacional. Casa de la Cultura del Perú, Museo Nacional de la Cultura Peruana. Lima.
PP	Past and Present. London.
RCPC	Revista Conservadora del Pensamiento Centroamericano. Managua.
RIB	Revista Interamericana de Bibliografía [Inter-American Review of Bibliography]. Organization of American States. Washington.
RSS/RS	Rural Sociology. Official organ of the Rural Sociological Society. New York State College of Agriculture. Ithaca, N.Y.
SA/J	Journal de la Société des Américanistes. Paris.
SAA/HO	Human Organization. Society for Applied Anthropology. N.Y.
SBPC/CC	Ciência e Cultura. Sociedade Brasileira para o Progresso da Ciência. São Paulo.
SF	Social Forces. *Published for the* Univ. of North Carolina Press *by the* Williams & Wilkins Co. Baltimore, Md.
SIP/RIP	Revista Interamericana de Psicología (Inter-American Journal of Psychology). Sociedad Interamericana de Psicología (Inter-American Society of Psychology). Austin, Tex.
SS	Science and Society. An independent journal of Marxism. N.Y.
UC/AJS	American Journal of Sociology. Univ. of Chicago. Chicago, Ill.
UC/EDCC	Economic Development and Cultural Change. Univ. of Chicago, Research Center in Economic Development and Cultural Change. Chicago, Ill.
UCIEI/EI	Estudios Internacionales. Revista del Instituto de Estudios Internacionales de la Univ. de Chile. Santiago.
UFRJ/BIP	Boletim do Instituto de Psicología. Revista de estudos psicológicos. Univ. Federal do Rio de Janeiro. Instituto de Psicología. Rio.
UH/U	Universidad de La Habana. La Habana.
ULIG/C	Cahiers de Géographie de Quebec. Univ. Laval, Institut de Géographie. Quebec, Canada.
UM/JIAS	Journal of Inter-American Studies and World Affairs. Univ. of Miami Press *for the* Center for Advanced International Studies. Coral Gables, Fla.
UMG/RBEP	Revista Brasileira de Estudos Políticos. Univ. de Minas Gerais. Belo Horizonte, Bra.
UNAM/RMS	Revista Mexicana de Sociología. Univ. Nacional Autónoma de México, Instituto de Investigaciones Sociales. México.
UNC/R	Revista de la Universidad Nacional de Córdoba. Córdoba, Arg.
UNL/H	Humanitas. Anuario del Centro de Estudios Humanísticos. Univ. de Nuevo León. Monterrey, Mex.
UP/TM	Tiers Monde. Problémes des pays sous-développés. Univ. de Paris, Institut d'Étude du Développement Économique et Social.
UPR/CS	Caribbean Studies. Univ. of Puerto Rico, Institute of Caribbean Studies. Río Piedras, P.R.

UPR/RCS	Revista de Ciencias Sociales. Univ. de Puerto Rico, Colegio de Ciencias Sociales. Río Piedras, P.R.
UW/LE	Land Economics. A quarterly journal of planning, housing and public utilities. Univ. of Wisconsin. Madison, Wis.
UWI/CQ	Caribbean Quarterly. Univ. of the West Indies. Mona, Jam.
UWI/SES	Social and Economic Studies. Univ. of the West Indies, Institute of Social and Economic Research. Mona, Jam.
WRU/JMF	Journal of Marriage and the Family. Western Reserve Univ. Cleveland, Ohio.
YU/IJCS	International Journal of Comparative Sociology. York Univ., Dept. of Sociology and Anthropology. Toronto, Canada.

Indices

Abbreviations and Acronyms *

* Except for journal acronyms which are listed at: a) the end of each major disciplinary section (e.g., Anthropology, Economics, etc.); and b) after each serial title in the *Title List of Journals Indexed*, p. 473.

ABC	Argentina, Brazil, Chile
ACAR	Associação de Crédito e Assistência Rural, Brazil
ADESG	Associação dos Diplomados de Escola Superior de Guerra, Brazil
AGI	Archivo General de Indias, Sevilla
AGN	Archivo General de la Nación
AID	Agency for International Development
Ala.	Alabama
ALALC	Asociación Latinoamericana de Libre Comercio
ANAPO	Alianza Nacional Popular, Colombia
APRA	Alianza Popular Revolucionaria Americana
Arg.	Argentina
Ariz.	Arizona
Ark.	Arkansas
AUFS	American Universities Field Staff Reports, Hanover, N.H.
Aug.	August, Augustan
B.A.	Buenos Aires
bibl.	bibliography
BID	Banco Interamericano de Desarrollo
Bol.	Bolivia
Bra.	Brazil
ca.	circa
C.A.	Centro América
CACM	Central American Common Market
CADE	Conferencia Anual de Ejecutivos de Empresas, Peru
CAEM	Centro de Altos Estudios Militares, Peru
Calif.	California
CARC	Centro de Arte y Comunicación
CEDAL	Centro de Estudios Democráticos de América Latina, Chile
CEDE	Centro de Estudios sobre Desarrollo Económico, Univ. de los Andes, *Bogotá*.
CELADE	Centro Latinoamericano de Demografía
CEMLA	Centro de Estudios Monetarios Latinoamericanos, México
CENDES	Centro de Estudios del Desarrollo, Venezuela
CEPADE	Centro Paraguayo de Estudios de Desarrollo Económico y Social
CEPAL	*See* ECLA.
cf.	compare
CGE	Confederación General Económica, Argentina
ch.	chapter
CHEAR	Council on Higher Education in the American Republics
cía.	compañía
CLASC	Confederación Latinoamericana Sindical Cristiana
CLE	Communidad Latinoamericana de Escritores, México
CNI	Confederação Nacional Industrial, Brazil
Co.	Colombia, company
Col.	colección, coleção, collection

469

COMCORDE	Comisión Coordinàdora para el Desarrollo Económico, Uruguay
comp.	compiler
Conn.	Connecticut
CORFO	Corporación de Fomento de la Producción
Corp.	corporation
C.R.	Costa Rica
CVG	Corporación Venezolana de Guyana
DANE	Departamento Nacional de Estadística, Colombia
Dec.	December, décembre
Del.	Delaware
dept.	department
depto.	departamento
dic.	diciembre
DNOCS	Departamento Nacional de Obras Contra as Sêcas, Brazil
ECLA	Economic Commission for Latin America
Ecua.	Ecuador
ed(s).	edition(s), edición(es), editor(s)
EDEME	Editôra Emprendimentos Educacionais Florianópolis, Brazil
e.g.	exempio gratia [for example]
El Sal.	El Salvador
ELN	Ejército de Liberación Nacional, Colombia
et al.	et alia [and others]
ETENE	Escritório Técnico de Estudios Econômicos do Nordeste, Brazil
ETEPE	Escritório Técnico de Planejamento, Brazil
EUDEBA	Editorial Universitaria de Buenos Aires
facsim.	facsimile
FAO	Food and Agriculture Organization of the United Nations
feb.	February, febrero
fev.	fevreiro, février
FGV	Fundação Getúlio Vargas
Fla.	Florida
fold. map	folded map
fols.	folios
FRG	Federal Republic of Germany
Ga.	Georgia
GAO	General Accounting Office, Washington
GATT	General Agreement on Tariffs and Trade
GDR	German Democratic Republic
Gen.	General
GPO	Government Printing Office
Guat.	Guatemala
HLAS	*Handbook of Latin American Studies*
Hond.	Honduras
IBBD	Instituto Brasileiro de Bibliografia e Documentação
IDB	Inter-American Development Bank
i.e.	id est [that is]
IEL	Instituto Euvaldo Lodi, Brazil
IERAC	Instituto Ecuatoriano de Reforma Agraria y Colonización
III	Instituto Indigenista Interamericano, Mexico
Ill.	Illinois
IIN	Instituto Indigenista Nacional, Guatemala
illus.	illustrations
IMES	Instituto Mexicano de Estudios Sociales
INAH	Instituto Nacional de Antropología e Historia, México
Inc.	incorporated
INCORA	Instituto Colombiano de Reforma Agraria
Ind.	Indiana
IPA	Instituto de Pastoral Andina, Univ. de San Antonio de Abad, Seminario de Antropología, Cuzco, Peru
IPEA	Instituto de Pesquisa Econômico-Social Aplicada, Brazil

IPES/GB	Instituto de Pesquisas e Estudos Sociais, Guanabara, Brazil
Jam.	Jamaica
jan.	January, janeiro, Janvier
JUCEPLAN	Junta Central de Planificación, Cuba
Jul.	Juli
Jun.	Juni
Kans.	Kansas
km.	kilometers, kilómetros
Ky.	Kentucky
La.	Louisiana
LARR	*Latin American Research Review*
LASA	Latin American Studies Association
m.	meters, metros
Mass.	Massachusetts
Md.	Maryland
MEC	Ministério de Educação e Cultura, Brazil
Mex.	Mexico
Mich.	Michigan
mimeo	mimeographed, mimeografiado
Minn.	Minnesota
MIR	Movimiento de Izquierda Revolucionaria, Chile
Miss.	Mississippi
MNR	Movimiento Nacionalista Revolucionario, Bolivia
Mo.	Missouri
MRL	Movimiento Revolucionario Liberal, Colombia
ms.	manuscript
N.C.	North Carolina
n.d.	no date
N. Dak.	North Dakota
Nebr.	Nebraska
Nev.	Nevada
n.f.	neue Folge
N.H.	New Hampshire
Nic.	Nicaragua
N. J.	New Jersey
N. Mex.	New Mexico
no.	number, número
NOSALF	Scandinavian Committee for Research in Latin America
Nov.	noviembre, November, novembre, novembro
n.p.	no place, no publisher
N.Y.	New York
OAS	Organization of American States
OEA	Organización de los Estados Americanos
oct.	October, octubre
Okla.	Oklahoma
Okt.	Oktober
out.	outubro
Oreg.	Oregon
ORIT	Organización Regional Interamericana del Trabajo
p.	page
Pa.	Pennsylvania
Pan.	Panama
Par.	Paraguay
PCV	Partido Comunista de Venezuela
PEMEX	Petróleos Mexicanos
PLANAVE	Engenharia e Planejamento Limitada, Brazil
PLANO	Planejamento e Assesoria Limitada, Brazil
PLN	Partido Liberación Nacional, Costa Rica
P.R.	Puerto Rico
PRI	Partido Revolucionario Institucional, Mexico

PROABRIL	Centro de Projetos Industriais, Brazil
prov.	province, provincia
PETROBRAS	Petróleo Brasileiro
PS	Partido Socialista, Chile
pseud.	pseudonym, pseudónimo
pt(s).	part(s), parte(s)
PUC	Pontifícia Universidade Católica, Rio
PURSC	Partido Unido de la Revolución Socialista de Cuba
R.D.	República Dominicana
rev.	revisada, revista, revised
R.I.	Rhode Island
Rio	Rio de Janeiro
SALALM	Seminar on the Acquisition of Latin American Library Materials
S.C.	South Carolina
SENAC	Serviço Nacional de Aprendizagem Comercial, Rio
SENAI	Serviço Nacional de Aprendizagem Industrial, São Paulo
SESI	Serviço Social da Industria, Brazil
S. Dak.	South Dakota
Sept.	September, septiembre, septembre
set.	setembre
SIL	Summer Institute of Linguistics
SNA	Sociedad Nacional de Agricultura, Chile
SPVEA	Superintendência do Plano de Valorização Econômica da Amazônia, Brazil
SUDAM	Superintendência do Desenvolvimento da Amazônia, Brazil
SUDENE	Superintendência do Desenvolvimento do Nordeste, Brazil
t.	tomo, tome
TAT	Thematic Apperception Test
Tenn.	Tennessee
Tex.	Texas
TNP	Tratado de No Proliferación
trans.	translator
UN	United Nations
UNAM	Universidad Nacional Autónoma de México
UNESCO	United Nations Educational, Scientific and Cultural Organization
Univ.	university, universidad, universidade, université, universität
UP	Unidad Popular, Chile
URD	Unidad Revolucionaria Democrática
Uru.	Uruguay
US	United States of America
USIA	United States Information Agency, Washington
USSR	Union of Soviet Socialist Republics, Unión de Repúblicas Soviéticas Socialistas
UTM	Universal Transverse Mercator
v.; vol.	volume, volumen
Va.	Virginia
Ven.	Venezuela
Vt.	Vermont
Wis.	Wisconsin
Wyo.	Wyoming

Title List Of Journals Indexed*

A.I.F.L.D. Review. American Institute for Free Labor Development. Washington. (AIFLD/R)

Abhandlungen und Berichte des Staatlichen Museums für Völkerkunde Dresden. Berlin.

Aconcagua. Iberoamérica-Europa. Zeitschrift für Politik, Kultur und Wirtschaft für die Länder iberischer und deutscher Sprache. Vaduz, Lichtenstein. (ZPKW/A)

Acta Amazônica. Instituto Nacional de Pesquisas da Amazonia. Manaus, Bra.

Acta Científica Venezolana. Asociación Venezolana para el Avance de la Ciencia. Caracas. (AVAC/ACV)

Acta Ethnographica. Academiae Scientiarum Hungaricae. Budapest. (ASH/AE)

Acta Geographica. Helsinki.

Actualidad Pastoral. B.A.

Air University Review. The professional journal of the United States Air Force. Maxwell Air Force Base, Ala. (AF/AUR)

Allpanchis Phuturinqa. Univ. de San Antonio de Abad, Seminario de Antropología, Instituto de Pastoral Andina. Cuzco, Peru. (IPA/AP)

América Indígena. Instituto Indigenista Interamericano. México. (III/AI)

América Latina. Centro Latino-Americano de Pesquisas em Ciências Sociais. Rio. (CLAPCS/AL)

American Anthropologist. American Anthropological Association. Washington. (AAA/AA)

American Antiquity. The Society for American Archaeology. Menasha, Wis. (SAA/AA)

The American Behavioral Scientist. N.Y. (ABS)

American Economic Review. American Economic Association. Evanston, Ill. (AEA/AER)

American Journal of Clinical Nutrition. American Society for Clinical Nutrition. N.Y. (ASCN/J)

The American Journal of Comparative Law.

American Association for the Comparative Study of Law. Univ. of California. Berkeley, Calif. (AJCL)

The American Journal of Economics and Sociology. N.Y. (AJES)

American Journal of Human Genetics. The American Society of Human Genetics. Baltimore, Md. (ASHG/J)

American Journal of International Law. American Society of International Law. Washington. (ASIL/J)

The American Journal of Medicine. N.Y.

American Journal of Physical Anthropology. American Association of Physical Anthropologists [and] The Wistar Institute of Anatomy and Biology. Philadelphia, Pa. (AJPA)

American Journal of Sociology. Univ. of Chicago. Chicago, Ill. (UC/AJS)

American Journal of Tropical Medicine and Hygiene. American Society of Tropical Medicine and Hygiene. Baltimore, Md. (ASTMH/J)

American Political Science Review. American Political Science Association. Columbus, Ohio. (APSA/R)

American Scientist. Burlington, Vt.

American Sociological Review. American Sociological Society. Manasha, Wis. (ASS/ASR)

The Americas. Inter-American Cultural Agency. Academy of American Franciscan History. Washington. (AAFH/TAM)

Américas. Organization of American States. Washington. (OAS/AM)

Anais do Museu de Antropologia. Florianópolis, Bra.

Anales de Antropología. Univ. Nacional Autónoma de México, Instituto de Investigaciones Históricas. México. (UNAM/AA)

Anales de Arqueología y Etnología. Univ. Nacional de Cuyo, Facultad de Filosofía y Letras. Mendoza, Arg. (UNC/AAE)

---

* Journals which have been included in the *Handbook* as individual items are listed alphabetically by title in the Author Index.

473

Anales de la Sociedad Científica Argentina. La Plata, Arg. (SCA/A)

Anales de la Sociedad Rural Argentina. Revista pastorial y agrícola. B.A. (SRA/A)

Anales de la Universidad de Cuenca. Cuenca, Ecua. (UC/A)

Anales del Instituto de Investigaciones Estéticas. Univ. Nacional Autónoma de México. México. (IIE/A)

Anales del Instituto de la Patagonia. Punta Arenas, Chile.

Anales del Instituto Nacional de Antropología e Historia. Secretaría de Educación Pública. México. (INAH/A)

Annals of Human Genetics (Annals of Eugenics). Univ. College, Galton Laboratory. London. (UCGL/AHG)

The Annals of the American Academy of Political and Social Science. Philadelphia, Pa. (AAPSS/A)

Annals of the Association of American Geographers. Lawrence, Kan. (AAG/A)

Annals of the New York Academy of Sciences. N.Y. (NYAS/A)

Annuaire International de l'Education. United Nations Educational, Scientific and Cultural Organization, Bureau International d'Education. Genève, Switzerland. (UNESCO/AIE)

Annual Review of Anthropology. Palo Alto, Calif.

Annual Review of Ecology and Systematics. Palo Alto, Calif.

Anthropological Journal of Canada. Anthropological Association of Canada. Quebec, Canada. (AAC/AJ)

Anthropological Linguistics. Archives of the languages of the world. Indiana Univ., Dept. of Anthropology. Bloomington, Ind. (IU/AL)

Anthropological Quarterly. Catholic Univ. of America, Catholic Anthropological Conference. Washington, (CUA/AQ)

Anthropos. International Review of Ethnology and Linguistics. Anthropos-Institut. Posieux, Switzerland. (AI/A)

Anthropos. International Zeitschrift für Völkerkunde, St. Augustine, FRG.

Antropológica. Sociedad de Ciencias Naturales La Salle. Caracas. (SCNLS/A)

Anuario. Univ. Central de Venezuela, Instituto de Antropología e Historia. Caracas. (IAH/A)

Anuario de Estudios Americanos. Consejo Superior de Investigaciones Científicas [and] Univ. de Sevilla, Escuela de Estudios Hispano-Americanos. Sevilla. (EEHA/AEA)

Anuario de Sociología de los Pueblos Ibéricos. Asociación de Sociólogos de Lengua Española y Portuguesa. Madrid. (ASLEP/A)

Aportes. Instituto Latinoamericano de Relaciones Internacionales. Paris. (ILARI/A)

Arbor. Revista general de investigación y cultura. Madrid. (ARBOR)

Archaeology. Archaeological Institute of America. N.Y. (AIA/A)

Archeologia. L'archeologie dans le monde et tout ce qui concerne les recherches historiques, artistiques et scientifiques sur terre et dans les mers. Paris. (ARCHEO)

Archiv für Völkerkunde. Museum für Völkerkunde in Wien und von Verein Freunde der Völkerkunde. Wien. (MVW/AV)

Archive for History of Exact Sciences. Berlin.

Archives Européennes de Sociologie. Paris. (AES)

Archivos del Folklore Boliviano. La Paz.

Archivos Latinoamericanos de Nutrición. Sociedad Latinoamericana de Nutrición. Caracas. (SLN/ALN)

Arqueología y Sociedad. Lima.

Arqueológicas. Instituto de Investigaciones Antropológicas. Museo Nacional de Antropología y Arqueología. Lima. (PIIA/A)

Arquivos Brasileiros de Psicologia Aplicada. Fundação Getúlio Vargas. Rio.

Arstryck. Etnografiska Museet. Göteborg, Sweden. (EM/A)

Artes de México. México. (ARMEX)

Aula. Santo Domingo.

Baessler-Archiv. Beiträge zur Völkerkunde. Museums für Völkerkunde. Berlin. (MV/BA)

Bibliografía Argentina de Artes y Letras. Secretaría de Estado de Hacienda, Fondo Nacional de las Artes. B.A. (FNA/BAAL)

Biennial Review of Anthropology. Stanford Univ. Press. Stanford, Calif.

Bijdragen tot de Taal-, Land- en Volkenkunde. Koninklijk Instituut voor Taal-, Land- en Volkenkunde. Leiden, The Netherlands. (KITLV/B)

Black Lines. Pittsburgh, Pa.

Boletim. Faculdade de Filosofia, Ciências e Letras de Presidente Prudente, Depto. de Ciências Sociais. Presidente Prudente, Bra. (PP/B)

Boletim Carioca de Geografia. Associação dos Geógrafos Brasileiros, Secção Regional do Rio de Janeiro. Rio. (AGB/BCG)

Boletim da Sociedade Brasileira de Geologia. Univ. de São Paulo, Instituto de Geociências e Astronomia. São Paulo. (SBG/B)

Boletim do IESPE. Instituto de Estudos Sociais, Políticos e Econômicos da PUCRGS. Pontifica Univ. Católica do Rio Grande do Sul. Pôrto Alegre, Bra.

Boletim do Instituto de Psicologia. Revista de estudos psicológicos. Univ. Federal do Rio

de Janeiro. Instituto de Psicología. Rio. (UFRJ/BIP)
Boletim do Instituto Histórico, Geográfico e Etnográfico Paranaense. Curitiba, Bra.
Boletim do Museu de Arte e História. Vitória, Bra.
Boletim do Museu Nacional. Univ. do Brasil, Oficina Gráfica. Rio. (BRMN/B)
Boletim do Museu Paraense Emílio Goeldi. Conselho Nacional de Pesquisas, Instituto Nacional de Pesquisas da Amazônia. Belém, Bra. (MPEG/B)
Boletim do Serviço de Museus. Govêrno do Estado da Guanabara, Rio.
Boletim Geográfico. Conselho Nacional de Geografia, Instituto Brasileiro de Geografia e Estatística. Rio. (IBGE/B)
Boletim Paulista de Geografia. Associação dos Geógrafos Brasileiros, Secção Regional de São Paulo. São Paulo. (AGB/BPG)
Boletín. Instituto Indigenista Nacional. Guatemala. (GIIN/B)
Boletín. Museo Arqueológico de la Serena. Santiago.
Boletín. Sociedad Venezolana de Espeleología. Caracas.
Boletín Bibliográfico de Antropología Americana. Instituto Panamericano de Geografía e Historia, Comisión de Historia. México. (BBAA)
Boletín de Estudios Geográficos. Univ. National de Cuyo, Instituto de Geografía. Mendoza, Arg. (UNCIG/B)
Boletín de Estudios Latinoamericanos. Centro de Estudios y Documentación Latino-Americanos. Amsterdam.
Boletín de Estudios Oaxaqueños. Centro de Estudios Regionales. Oaxaca, Mex. (CER/BEO)
Boletín de Higiene y Epidemiología. La Habana.
Boletín de la Academia Chilena de la Historia. Santiago. (ACH/B)
Boletín de la Academia de Ciencias Políticas y Sociales. Caracas. (ACPS/B)
Boletín de la Academia Nacional de Ciencias. Córdoba, Arg. (ANC/B)
Boletín de la Academia Nacional de Historia. Quito. (EANH/B)
Boletín de la Oficina Sanitaria Panamericana. Washington. (OSP/B)
Boletín de la Sociedad Geográfica de Colombia. Academia de Ciencias Geográficas. Bogotá. (SGC/B)
Boletín de la Universidad de Chile. Santiago. (UC/B)
Boletín de Población. Bogotá.
Boletín de Prehistoria de Chile. Univ. de Chile, Facultad de Filosofía y Educación, Depto. de Historia. Santiago. (UC/BPC)

Boletín del Centro de Relaciones Internacionales. Univ. Nacional Autónoma de México, Facultad de Ciencias Políticas y Sociales. México. (UNAM/BCRI)
Boletín del Instituto Nacional de Antropología e Historia. Secretaría de Educación Pública. México. (INAH/B)
Boletín del Museo del Hombre Dominicano. Instituto de Cultura Dominicana. Santo Domingo.
Boletín del Seminario de Arqueología. Pontificia Univ. Católica del Perú. Lima. (PUCP/BSA)
Boletín Documental sóbre la Mujer. Cuernavaca, Mex.
Boletín Histórico del Estado Mayor General del Ejército. Sección Historia y Archivo. Montevideo. (EMGE/BH)
Boletín Uruguayo de Sociología. Montevideo. (BUS)
Bollettino della Societá Geografica Italiana. Roma. (SGI/B)
British Journal of Sociology. *For the* London School of Economics and Political Science. London. (BJS)
Bulletin. Field Museum of Natural History. Chicago, Ill.
Bulletin. Société Suisse des Américanistes. Geneva. (SSA/B)
Bulletin de la Faculté des Lettres de Strasbourg (TILAS [Travaux de l'Institut d'Études Latino-Américaines de l'Université de Strasbourg] subseries). Univ. de Strasbourg. Strasbourg, France. (TILAS)
Bulletin de l'Association de Géographes Français. Paris. (AGF/B)
Bulletin de l'Institut International d'Administration Publique. Paris.
Bulletin for International Fiscal Documentation. International Bureau of Fiscal Documentation. Amsterdam.
Bulletin for Libraries. United Nations, Educational, Scientific and Cultural Organization. Paris. (UNESCO/BL)
Bulletin of the African Studies Association of the West Indies. Kingston.
Bulletin of the International Committee on Urgent Anthropological and Ethnological Research. Wien. (ICUAER/B)
Business and Government Review. Univ. of Missouri. Columbia, Mo.
CLA Journal. Morgan State College, College Language Association. Baltimore, Md. (CLA/J)
Cadernos da PUC. Pontificia Univ. Católica. Rio.
Cadernos Região e Educação. Centro Regional de Pesquisas Educacionais do Recife. Recife, Bra. (CRPER/CRE)
Cahiers de Géographie de Québec. Univ.

Laval, Institut de Géographie. Quebec, Canada. (ULIG/C)
Cahiers des Amériques Latines. Paris. (CDAL)
Les Cahiers d'Outre-Mer. Publiée par l'Institut de Géographie de la Faculté des Lettres de Bordeaux, par l'Institut de la France d'Outre-Mer, par la Société de Géographie de Bordeaux *avec le concours* du Centre National de la Recherche Scientifique et de la VI.ième Section de l'École Pratique des Hautes Études. Bordeaux, France. (SGB/COM)
The California Geographer. California Council of Geography Teachers. Long Beach, Calif. (CCGT/CG)
Canadian Geographer. Le Géographe Canadien. Canadian Association of Geographers. Toronto, Canada. (CAG/CG)
Canadian Geographical Journal. Royal Canadian Geographical Society. Ottawa, Canada. (RCGJ/CGJ)
Canadian Psychiatric Association Journal. Ottawa, Canada.
Canadian Review of Sociology and Anthropology. Alberta, Canada.
Caravelle. Cahiers du monde hispanique et luso-brésilien. Univ. de Toulouse. Institut d'Études Hispaniques, Hispano-Americaines et Luso-Brésiliennes. Toulouse, France. (UTIEH/C)
Caribbean Quarterly. Univ. of the West Indies. Mona, Jam. (UWI/CQ)
Caribbean Review. Hato Rey, P.R.
Caribbean Studies. Univ. of Puerto Rico, Institute of Caribbean Studies. Río Piedras, P.R. (UPR/CS)
Carta Mensal. Rio.
Cerámica de Cultura Maya et al. Temple Univ., Dept. of Anthropology. Philadelphia, Pa. (TU/CCM)
Chungara. Univ. del Norte. Arica, Chile.
Ciência e Cultura. Sociedade Brasileira para o Progresso da Ciência. São Paulo. (SBPC/CC)
Ciencia Interamericana. Organization of American States, Dept. of Scientific Affairs. Washington. (OAS/CI)
Ciencias Económicas. Córdoba, Arg.
Civilisations. International Institute of Differing Civilisations. Bruxelles. (IIDC/C)
Coméntario. Instituto Brasileiro Judaico de Cultura e Divulgação. Rio. (IBJCD/C)
Commentary. American Jewish Committee. N.Y. (AJC/C)
Community Development. International Federation of Settlements and Neighborhood Centres. Roma. (IFSNC/CD)
Comparative Education Review. Comparative Education Society. N.Y. (CES/CER)
Comparative Politics. The City Univ. of New York, Political Science Program. N.Y. (CUNY/CP)
Comparative Studies in Society and History. Society for the Comparative Study of Society and History. The Hague. (CSSH)
Comunicaciones Antropológicas del Museo de Historia Natural de Montevideo. Montevideo. (MHNM/CA)
Comunidades. Instituto de Estudios Sindicales, Sociales y Cooperativos, Centro de Prospección Social. Madrid. (IESSC/C)
Conjonction. Revue franco-haïtienne. Bulletin de l'Institut Français d'Haïti. Port-au-Prince. (IFH/C)
Contributions of the University of California Archaeological Research Facility. Berkeley, Calif. (UCARF/C)
Courrier. Paris.
Cristianismo y Sociedad. Junta Latino-Americana de Iglesia y Sociedad. Montevideo. (JLAIS/CS)
Cuadernos de Antropología. Univ. de San Marcos, Centro de Estudiantes de Antropología. Lima. (CEA/CA)
Cuadernos de Geografía de Colombia. Sociedad Geográfica de Colombia, Academia de Ciencias Geográficas. Bogotá. (SGC/CGC)
Cuadernos de Historia y Arqueología. Casa de la Cultura Ecuatoriana, Núcleo del Guayas. Guayaquil, Ecua. (CCE/CHA)
Cuadernos de Investigaciones Históricas y Antropológica. Museo Regional del Iquique. Chile.
Cuadernos Geográficos del Sur. Concepción, Chile.
Cuadernos Hispanoamericanos. Madrid. (CH)
Cultura. Ministerio de Educación. San Salvador. (ESME/C)
Cultura Universitaria. Univ. Central de Venezuela, Dirección de Cultura. Caracas. (UCV/CU)
Current Anthropology. Univ. of Chicago. Chicago, Ill. (UC/CA)
Current History. A monthly magazine of world affairs. Norwalk, Conn. (CUH)
De Economía. Revista de temas económicos. Consejo Económico Sindical Nacional. Madrid. (CESN/DE)
De Gids. Amsterdam.
Dédalo. Revista de arte e arqueologia. Univ. de São Paulo, Museu de Arte e Arqueologia. São Paulo. (USPMAA/D)
Demografía y Economía. El Colegio de México. México. (CM/DE)
Demography. Population Association of America. Chicago, Ill. (PAA/D)
Desarrollo Económico. Instituto de Desarrollo Económico y Social. B.A. (IDES/DE)
Desarrollo Rural en las Américas. Bogotá.
Developmental Medicine and Child Neurology. National Spastics Society. London.
Développement et Civilisations. Institut de

TITLE LIST OF JOURNALS INDEXED

Recherche et de Formation en vue du Développement Harmonisé. Paris. (IRFDH/DC)
Econométrica. Menasha, Wis.
Economía. Univ. de Los Andes, Facultad de Economía. Mérida, Ven. (ULAFE/E)
Economía Salvadoreña. Univ. de El Salvador, Instituto de Estudios Económicos. San Salvador. (UES/ES)
Economía y Ciencias Sociales. Univ. Central de Venezuela, Facultad de Economía. Caracas. (UCV/ECS)
Economic Bulletin for Latin America. United Nations, Economic Commission for Latin America. N.Y. (UNECLA/B)
Economic Development and Cultural Change. Univ. of Chicago, Research Center in Economic Development and Cultural Change. Chicago, Ill. (UC/EDCC)
Economic Geography. Clark Univ. Worcester, Mass. (CU/EG)
Económica. Univ. Nacional de La Plata, Facultad de Ciencias Económicas, Instituto de Investigaciones Económicas. La Plata, Arg. (UNLP/E)
Économie Appliquée. Archives de l'Institut de Science Économique Appliquée. Vendôme, France. (ISEA/EA)
Economies et Sociétés. Geneva.
Encounter. London. (ENCOUNT)
Die Erde. Zeitschrift der Gesellschaft für Erdkunde zu Berlin. Walter de Gruyter & Co. Berlin. (GEB/E)
Erdkunde. Archiv für Wissenschaftliche Geographie. Univ. Bonn, Geographisches Institut. Bonn. (UBGI/E)
Estadística. Journal of the Inter-American Statistical Institute. Washington. (IASI/E)
Estudios Andinos. Instituto Boliviano de Estudio Acción Social. La Paz. (IBEAS/EA)
Estudios de Arqueología. Museo Arqueológico de Cachi. Salta, Arg.
Estudios de Cultura Maya. Univ. Nacional Autónoma de México, Centro de Estudios Mayas. México. (CEM/ECM)
Estudios de Cultura Náhuatl. Univ. Nacional Autónoma de México, Instituto de Historia, Seminario de Cultura Náhuatl. México. (UNAM/ECN)
Estudios de Planificación Familiar. Bogotá.
Estudios Internacionales. Univ. de Chile, Instituto de Estudios Internacionales. Santiago. (UCIEI/EI)
Estudios Sindicales y Cooperativos. Instituto de Estudios Sindicales, Sociales y Cooperativos de Madrid. Madrid. (ESC)
Estudos Econômicos. Univ. de São Paulo, Instituto de Pesquisas Econômicas. São Paulo. (USP/EE)
Estudos Históricos. Faculdade de Filosofia, Ciências e Letras, Depto. de História. Marília, Bra. (FFCLM/EH)
Ethnica. Barcelona, Spain.
Ethnographisch-Archäologische Zeitschrift. Deutscher Verlag Wissenschaften. East Berlin. (EAZ)
Ethnology. Univ. of Pittsburgh. Pittsburgh, Pa. (UP/E)
Ethnos. Statens Etnografiska Museum. Stockholm. (SEM/E)
Etnia. Museo Etnográfico Municipal Dámasco Arce. Municipalidad de Olavarría. B.A. (MEMDA/E)
Etnologiska Studier. Etnografiska Museet. Göteborg, Sweden. (EM/ES)
Expedition. Bulletin of the University Museum of the Univ. of Pennsylvania. Philadelphia, Pa. (UMUP/E)
Explorers Journal. N.Y. (EJ)
Filosofía, Letras y Ciencias de la Educación. Univ. Central del Ecuador. Quito. (UCE/FLCE)
Finanzarchiv. Tübingen, FRG.
Florida Anthropological Society Publications. Gainesville, Fla.
Folk. Dansk Etnografisk Forening. København. (DEF/F)
Folklore Americano. Organización de los Estados Americanos, Instituto Panamericano de Geografía e Historia, Comisión de Historia, Comité Interamericano de Folklore. Lima. (CIF/FA)
Food Research Institute Studies. Stanford, Calif.
Foreign Affairs. An American quarterly review. Council on Foreign Relations, Inc. N.Y. (CFR/FA)
Foreign Policy. N.Y.
Foro Internacional. El Colegio de México. México. (CM/FI)
Geographica Helvetica. Schweizerische Zeitschrift für Länder- und Völkerkunde. Kümmerly & Frey, Geographischer Verlag. Bern, Switzerland. (GH)
The Geographical Journal. Royal Geographical Society. London. (RGS/GJ)
The Geographical Magazine. London. (GM)
The Geographical Review. American Geographical Society. N.Y. (AGS/GR)
Geographische Rundschau. Zeitschrift für Schulgeographie. Georg Westermann Verlag. Braunschweig, FRG. (GR)
Geologische Rundschau. Internationale Zeitschrift für Geologie. Geologische Vereinigung. Ferdinand Enke Verlag. Stuttgart, FRG. (GV/GR)
Geotimes. Washington.
Gerencia. Lima.
Government and Opposition. London.

Guatemala Indígena. Instituto Indigenista Nacional. Guatemala. (GIIN/GI)

Handbook of Middle American Indians. Univ. of Texas Press. Austin, Tex. (HMAI)

Hispanic American Historical Review. Conference on Latin American History of the American Historical Association. Duke Univ. Press. Durham, N.C. (HAHR)

Hombre y Cultura. Univ. Nacional, Centro de Investigaciones Antropológicas. Panamá. (UNCIA/HC)

L'Homme. Revue française d'anthropologie. l'École Pratique des Hautes Études, La Sorbonne. Paris. (EPHE/H)

Human Biology. A record of research. Wayne State Univ. Press. Detroit, Mich. (WSU/HB)

Human Heredity. Basel, Switzerland. (HH)

Human Organization. Society for Applied Anthropology. N.Y. (SAA/HO)

Humanitas. Univ. de Nuevo León, Centro de Estudios Humanísticos. Monterrey, Mex. (UNL/H)

Humanitas. Univ. Nacional de Tucumán, Facultad de Filosofía y Letras. Tucumán, Arg. (UNT/H)

Icach. Instituto de Ciencias y Artes de Chiapas. Tuxtla Gutiérrez, Mex. (ICACH)

Imago Mundi. N. Israel, Amsterdam. (IM)

Impact of Science on Society. United Nations Educational, Scientific and Cultural Organization. Paris. (UNESCO/I)

Indian Notes. Museum of the American Indian. N.Y.

Industrial Puerto Rico. San Juan.

Informaciones Geográficas. Univ. de Chile, Facultad de Filosofía y Educación, Instituto de Geografía. Santiago. (UCIG/IG)

Instituto de Antropología. Univ. Católica de Córdoba. Córdoba, Arg.

Inter-American Economic Affairs. Washington. (IAMEA)

International Development Review. The Society for International Development. Washington. (SID/IDR)

International Journal of American Linguistics. Indiana Univ. *under the auspices of* Linguistic Society of America, American Anthropological Association, *with the cooperation of* Joint Committee on American Native Languages. Baltimore, Md. (IU/IJAL)

International Journal of Comparative Sociology. York Univ., Dept. of Sociology and Anthropology. Toronto, Canada. (YU/IJCS)

International Journal of Social Psychiatry. London. (IJSP)

The International Journal of the Addictions. The Institute for the Study of Drug Addiction. N.Y. (ISDA/IJA)

International Labour Review. International Labour Office. Genève. (ILO/R)

International Review of Education. United Nations Educational, Scientific and Cultural Organization, Institute for Education. Hamburg, FRG. (UNESCO/IRE)

International Review of History and Political Science. Meerut, India.

International Social Science Journal. United Nations Educational, Scientific, and Cultural Organization. Paris. (UN/ISSJ)

Internationale Spectator. Tijdschrift voor internationale politiek. Het Nederlandsch Genootschap voor Internationale Zaken. The Hague. (NGIZ/IS)

Investigación Económica. Univ. Nacional Autónoma de México, Escuela Nacional de Economía. México. (UNAM/IE)

The Iowa Geographer. Cedar Falls, Iowa.

Istmo. Revista del Centro de América. México. (ISTMO)

Jahrbuch für Wirtschaftgeschichte. Deutsche Akademie der Wissenshaften zu Berlin. Berlin.

Journal de la Société des Américanistes. Paris. (SA/J)

Journal of American Folklore. American Folklore Society. Austin, Tex. (AFS/JAF)

Journal of Applied Physiology. Washington.

Journal of Comparative Administration. Beverly Hills, Calif.

The Journal of Developing Areas. Western Illinois Univ. Press. Macomb, Ill. (JDA)

Journal of Development Planning. United Nations. N.Y.

The Journal of Development Studies. A quarterly journal devoted to economics, politics and social development. London. (JDS)

Journal of Economic Issues. Univ. of Massachusetts. Amherst, Mass.

Journal of Geography. National Council of Geographic Education. Menasha, Wis. (NCGE/J)

Journal of Inter-American Studies and World Affairs. Univ. of Miami Press *for the* Center for Advanced International Studies. Coral Gables, Fla. (UM/JIAS)

Journal of International Affairs. Columbia Univ., School of International Affairs. N.Y. (CU/JIA)

The Journal of International and Comparative Studies. Washington.

Journal of Latin American Studies. Centers or institutes of Latin American studies at the Universities of Cambridge, Glasgow, Liverpool, London and Oxford. Cambridge Univ. Press. London. (JLAS)

The Journal of Law and Economics. Chicago, Ill.

Journal of Marriage and the Family. Western

TITLE LIST OF JOURNALS INDEXED

Reserve Univ. Cleveland, Ohio. (WRU/JMF)
Journal of Peace Research. Edited at the International Peace Research Institute. Universitetforlaget. Oslo. (JPR)
Journal of Political Economy. Univ. of Chicago. Chicago, Ill. (JPE)
The Journal of Politics. The Southern Political Science Association *in cooperation with the* Univ. of Florida. Gainesville, Fla. (SPSA/JP)
Journal of Social Psychology. The Journal Press. Provincetown, Mass. (JSP)
Journal of the Barbados Museum and Historical Society. Barbados, W.I. (BMHS/J)
The Journal of Tropical Geography. Univ. of Singapore [and] Univ. of Malaya, Depts. of Geography. Singapore. (USM/JTG)
Journalism Quarterly. Association for Education in Journalism *with the cooperation of the* American Association of Schools, Depts. of Journalism [and] the Kappa Tau Alpha Society. Univ. of Minnesota. Minneapolis, Minn. (AEJ/JQ)
Katunob. Southern State College. Magnolia, Ark. (SSC/K)
The Kiva. Journal of the Arizona Archaeological and Historical Society. Tucson, Ariz. (AAHS/K)
Kroeber Anthropological Society Papers. Univ. of California. Berkeley, Calif. (KAS/P)
LTC Newsletter. Univ. of Wisconsin, Land Tenure Center. Madison, Wis.
Lancet. London. (LANCET)
Land Economics. A quarterly journal of planning, housing and public utilities. Univ. of Wisconsin. Madison, Wis. (UW/LE)
Language. Journal of the Linguistic Society of America. Baltimore, Md. (LSA/L)
Language and Linguistics. Georgetown Univ., Washington.
Latin American Research Review. Latin American Studies Association. Univ. of Texas Press. Austin, Tex. (LARR)
Latinskaia Amerika [América Latina]. Akademia Nauk SSSR, Institut Latinskoi Ameriki [Academia de Ciencias de la URSS, Instituto Latinoamericano]. Moskva [Moscú]. (SSSR/LA)
Letras de Hoje. Pontifica Univ. Católica de Rio Grande do Sul. Pôrto Alegre, Bra.
El Libro y el Pueblo. Secretaría de Educación Pública, Depto. de Bibliotecas. México. (MSEP/LP)
Lingua. North-Holland Publishing Co. Amsterdam. (LINGUA)
Linguistics. An international review. Mouton. The Hague. (LING)

Lotería. Lotería Nacional de Beneficencia. Panamá. (LNB/L)
Man. The Royal Anthropological Institute. London. (RAI/M)
Mar y Pesca. La Habana.
The Masterkey. Southwest Museum. Los Angeles, Calif. (SM/M)
Memoria de la Sociedad de Ciencias Naturales La Salle. Caracas. (SCNLS/M)
Memórias do Instituto Oswaldo Cruz. Rio. (IOC/M)
Mensaje. Santiago.
Merkur. Deutsche Zeitschrift für Europäisches Denken. Deutsche Verlags-Anstalt. Stuttgart, FRG. (MDZED)
Mid-America. Loyola Univ. Chicago, Ill. (LU/MAM)
Midwest Journal of Political Science. Wayne State Univ. Press *for the* Midwest Conference of Political Science. Detroit, Mich. (MCPS/JPS)
Milbank Memorial Fund Quarterly. N.Y. (MMFQ)
Mitteilungen der Geographischen Gesellschaft in Hamburg. Hamburg, FGR. (HGG/M)
Monatsberichte der Deutschen Akademie der Wissenschaften zu Berlin. Berlin. (DAWB/M)
Monthly Review. Federal Reserve Bank of New York. N.Y. (FRBNY/MR)
Monthly Review. An independent Socialist magazine. N.Y. (MR)
National Geographic Magazine. National Geographic Society. Washington. (NGS/NGM)
National Tax Journal. National Tax Association [and] Fund for Public Policy Research. Washington. (NTA/NTJ)
Nationalmuseets Arbejdsmark. Copénhagen.
Natural History. American Museum of Natural History. N.Y. (AMNH/NH)
Nature. A weekly journal of science. Macmillan & Co. London. (NWJS)
Nature and Resources. United Nations Educational, Scientific and Cultural Organization. Paris. (UNESCO/NR)
Naturwissenschaftliche Rundschau. Stuttgart, FRG.
Ñawpa Pacha. Institute of Andean Studies. Berkeley, Calif. (IAS/ÑP)
Neues Jahrbuch für Geologie und Paläontologie, Monatschrift. Stuttgart, FGR.
The New Leader. American Labor Conference on International Affairs, Inc. East Stroudsburg, Pa. (NL)
New World Archaeological Foundation Papers. Provo, Utah.
Nieuwe West-Indische Gids. Martinus Nijhoff. The Hague. (NWIG)

Notes et Études Documentaires. Direction de la Documentation. Paris. (FDD/NED)
Noticiario Mensual. Museo Nacional de Historia Natural. Santiago.
Notícias. Conselho Nacional de Pesquisas, Instituto Brasileiro de Bibliografia e Documentação. Rio. (IBBD/N)
Objets et Mondes. Revue trimestrielle. Musée de l'Homme. Paris. (MH/OM)
Orbis. Bulletin international de documentation linguistique. Centre International de Dialectologie Générale. Louvain, Belgium. (CIDG/O)
Orbis. A quarterly journal of world affairs. Univ. of Pennsylvania, Foreign Policy Research Institute. Philadelphia, Pa. (UP/O)
Oui. Chicago, Ill.
Oxford Economic Papers. Oxford Univ. Press. London. (OUP/OEP)
Pacific Discovery. California Academy of Sciences. San Francisco, Calif. (CAS/PD)
Paideuma. Mitteilungen zur Kulturkunde. Deutsche Gesellschaft für Kulturmorphologie Frobenius Institut auf der Johann Wolfgang Goethe-Universität. Wiesbaden, FRG. (PMK)
Partisans. Paris.
Past and Present. London. (PP)
Pedagogía. Río Piedras, P.R.
Pensamiento Crítico. La Habana. (PC)
Pensamiento Político. México.
Pesquisa e Planejamento. Centro Regional Prof. Queiroz Filho. São Paulo. (CRPE/PP)
Pesquisa e Planejamento. Instituto de Planejamento Econômico e Social. Rio. (IPEA/PP)
Pesquisas. Instituto Anchietano de Pesquisas. Pôrto Alegre, Bra. (IAP/P)
Plerus. Univ. of Puerto Rico, Graduate School of Planning. Río Piedras, P.R.
Política. Caracas.
Política Internacional. Ministerio de Relaciones Exteriores, Instituto de Política Internacional. La Habana. (IPI/PI)
The Political Quarterly. London. (PQ)
Political Science Quarterly. Columbia Univ. [and] The Academy of Political Science. N.Y. (APS/PSQ)
Population. Revue trimestrielle de l'Institut National d'Études Demographiques. Paris. (INED/P)
Population Studies. A journal of demography. London School of Economics, The Population Investigation Committee. London. (LSE/PS)
Practical Anthropology. Terrytown, N.Y. (PRAN)
Problemas Brasileiros. São Paulo.
Problemas Internacionales. United States Information Agency. Washington. (USIA/PI)
Problems of Communism. United States Information Agency. Washington. (USIA/PC)
Proceedings of the Academy of Political Science. Columbia Univ. [and] The Academy of Political Science. N.Y. (PAPS)
Proceedings of the American Philosophical Society. Philadelphia, Pa. (APS/P)
Professional Geographer. Association of American Geographers. Washington. (AAG/PG)
Psychopathologie Africaine. Dakar, Senegal.
Public Affairs Bulletin. Arizona State Univ., Institute of Public Administration. Tempe, Ariz.
Public and International Affairs. Princeton Univ., Woodrow Wilson School of Public and International Affairs. Princeton, N. J. (PU/PIA)
Pumapunku. Instituto de Cultura Aymara. La Paz.
Quarterly Journal of Economics. Harvard Univ. Cambridge, Mass.
Quarterly Journal of the Library of Congress. Washington.
Quarterly Review. Bank of London and South America. London. (BLSAL/QR)
Race. Institute of Race Relations. London. (IRR/R)
Rassegna Italiana di Sociologia. Bologna.
Razón y Fe. Revista mensual hispanoamericana de cultura. Los Padres de la Compañía de Jesús. Madrid. (CJ/RF)
Los Recursos Naturales de la Provincia de Cautín. Santiago.
Das Reisewerk du Kulturelle Monatschrift. Zürich, Switzerland.
Relaciones de la Sociedad Argentina de Antropología. B.A.
Res Facultatis. Faculdade Estadual de Filosofia, Ciências e Letras de Paranaguá, Bra.
The Review of Income and Wealth. New Haven, Conn.
The Review of Politics. Univ. of Notre Dame. Notre Dame, Ind. (UND/RP)
Review of the Sciences. San Francisco, Calif.
Revista. Comisión Municipal de Cultura, Depto. de Antropología y Folklore. Concordia, Arg.
Revista Bancaria. Asociación de Banqueros de México. México. (ABM/RB)
Revista Brasileira de Economia. Fundação Getúlio Vargas, Instituto Brasileiro de Economia. Rio. (IBE/RBE)
Revista Brasileira de Estatística. Ministério do Planejamento e Coordenação Geral, Instituto Brasileiro de Geografia e Estatística. Rio. (IBGE/RBE)
Revista Brasileira de Estudos Pedagógicos.

TITLE LIST OF JOURNALS INDEXED

Instituto Nacional de Estudos Pedagógicos. Rio. (INEP/RBEP)

Revista Brasileira de Estudos Políticos. Univ. de Minas Gerais. Belo Horizonte, Bra. (UMG/RBEP)

Revista Brasileira de Geografia. Conselho Nacional de Geografia, Instituto Brasileiro de Geografia e Estatística. Rio. (IBGE/R)

Revista Cartográfica. Instituto Panamericano de Geografía e Historia, Comisión de Cartografía. B.A. (PAIGH/RC)

Revista Colombiana de Antropología. Ministerio de Educación Nacional, Instituto Colombiano de Antropología. Bogotá. (ICA/RCA)

Revista Conservadora del Pensamiento Centroamericano. Managua. (RCPC)

Revista da Escola de Guerra Naval. Rio.

Revista da Universidade Federal de Minas Gerais. Belo Horizonte, Bra. (UMG/R)

Revista de Administração de Empresas. Fundação Getúlio Vargas, Instituto de Documentação. São Paulo. (FGV/RAE)

Revista de Administración Pública. Univ. de Puerto Rico. Río Piedras, P.R.

Revista de Agricultura de Puerto Rico. San Juan.

Revista de Antropología. Casa de la Cultura Ecuatoriana, Núcleo del Azuay. Cuenca, Ecua. (CCE/RA)

Revista de Ciências Sociais. Fortaleza, Bra.

Revista de Ciencias Sociales. Univ. de Puerto Rico, Colegio de Ciencias Sociales. Río Piedras, P.R. (UPR/RCS)

Revista de Economía Latinoamericana. Banco Central de Venezuela. Caracas. (BCV/REL)

Revista de Economía y Estadística. Univ. Nacional de Córdoba, Facultad de Ciencias Económicas. Córdoba, Arg. (UNC/REE)

Revista de Estudios Agro-Sociales. Madrid.

Revista de História. Univ. de São Paulo, Faculdade de Filosofia, Ciências e Letras, Depto. de História [and] Sociedade de Estudos Históricos. São Paulo. (USP/RH)

Revista de la Academia Colombiana de Ciencias Exactas, Físicas y Naturales. Bogotá. (ACCEFN/R)

Revista de la Biblioteca Nacional José Martí. La Habana. (BNJM/R)

Revista de la Facultad de Ciencias Económicas y Comerciales. Univ. Nacional Mayor de San Marcos. Lima. (USM/RCEC)

Revista de la Facultad de Ciencias Económicas y Sociales. Univ. Central de Venezuela. Caracas.

Revista de la Facultad de Derecho. Univ. Nacional Autónoma de México. México. (UNAM/RFD)

Revista de la Facultad de Ingeniería Química. Santa Fe, Arg.

Revista de la Sociedad Interamericana de Planificación. Calí, Co.

Revista de la Sociedad Mexicana de Historia Natural. México. (SMHN/R)

Revista de la Universidad de Costa Rica. San José. (UCR/R)

Revista de la Universidad de Yucatán. Mérida, Mex. (UV/R)

Revista de la Universidad Nacional de Córdoba. Córdoba, Arg. (UNC/R)

Revista de Política Social. Instituto de Estudios Políticos. Madrid. (IEP/RPS)

Revista de Psicoanálisis, Psiquiatría y Psicología. México.

Revista de Saude Pública. São Paulo.

Revista de Trabajo. San Juan.

Revista del Ateneo Paraguayo: Suplemento Antropológico. Ateneo Paraguayo, Centro de Investigaciones Antropológicas. Asunción. (CIAAP/RS)

Revista del Instituto de Ciencias Sociales. Diputación Provincial de Barcelona. Barcelona, Spain. (DPB/RICS)

Revista del Museo de La Plata. Univ. Nacional de La Plata, Facultad de Ciencias Naturales y Museo. La Plata, Arg. (UNLPM/R)

Revista del Museo Nacional. Casa de la Cultura del Perú, Museo Nacional de la Cultura Peruana. Lima. (PEMN/R)

Revista do Arquivo Municipal. Prefeitura do Município de São Paulo, Depto. Municipal de Cultura. São Paulo. (AM/R)

Revista do Instituto de Estudos Brasileiros. Univ. de São Paulo, Instituto de Estudos Brasileiros. São Paulo. (USP/RIEB)

Revista do Instituto de Filosofia e Ciências Humanas. Recife, Bra.

Revista do Museu Paulista. São Paulo. (MP/R)

Revista Dominicana de Arqueología y Antropología. Univ. Autónoma de Santo Domingo, Facultad de Humanidades, Depto. de Historia y Antropología, Instituto de Investigaciones Antropológicas. Santo Domingo. (UASD/R)

Revista Española de Antropología Americana [Trabajos y Conferencias]. Univ. de Madrid, Facultad de Filosofia y Letras, Depto. de Antropología y Etnología de América. Madrid. (UM/REAA)

Revista Geográfica. Instituto Panamericano de Geografia e História, Comissão de Geografia. Rio. (PAIGH/G)

Revista Geográfica. Univ. de Los Andes. Mérida, Ven. (ULA/RG)

Revista Geográfica de Valparaíso. Univ. Católica de Valparaíso. Valparaíso, Chile. (UCV/RG)

Revista Interamericana de Bibliografía [Inter-American Review of Bibliography].

Organization of American States. Washington. (RIB)

Revista Interamericana de Psicología [Interamerican Journal of Psychology]. Sociedad Interamericana de Psicología (Interamerican Society of Psychology). Austin, Tex. (SIP/RIP)

Revista Internacional del Trabajo. Geneva.

Revista Jurídica de la Universidad de Puerto Rico. Univ. de Puerto Rico. Río Piedras, P.R. (UPR/RJ)

Revista Latinoamericana de Sociología. Instituto Torcuato di Tella, Centro de Sociología Comparada. B.A. (ITT/RLS)

Revista Mexicana de Sociología. Univ. Nacional Autónoma de México, Instituto de Investigaciones Sociales. México. (UNAM/RMS)

Revista Panorama Industrial. La Paz.

Revista Paraguaya de Sociología. Centro Paraguayo de Estudios Sociológicos. Asunción. (CPES/RPS)

Revista Paranaense de Desenvolvimento. Companhia de Desenvolvimento Econômico do Paraná (CODEPAR). Curitiba, Bra. (CDEP/R)

Revista Quitumbe. Pontifica Univ. Católica del Ecuador, Facultad de Pedagogía, Depto. de Historia y Geografía. Quito.

Revista Trimestral. Asociación Nacional de Industriales. Medellín, Co. (ANI/RT)

Revue de Défense Nationale. Comité d'Études de Défense Nationale. Paris. (CEDN/R)

Revue des Deux Mondes. Paris.

Revue d'Historie Moderne et Contemporaine. Paris.

Revue Française de Science Politique. Foundation Nationale des Sciences Politiques, l'Association Française de Science Politique avec le concours du Centre National de la Recherche Scientifique. Paris. (FNSP/RFSP)

Rivista di Agricoltura Subtropicale e Tropicale. Istituto Agronomico per l'Oltremare. Firenze, Italy. IAO/RAST)

Rotunda. Bulletin of the Royal Ontario Museum. Toronto, Canada.

Rural Sociology. Rural Sociological Society. New York State College of Agriculture. Ithaca, N.Y. (RSS/RS)

Saeculum. Jahrbuch für Universalgeschichte. München, FRG. (SJUG)

Saturday Review. N.Y.

Savacou. Caribbean Artists Movement. Kingston.

Science. American Association for the Advancement of Science. Washington. (AAAS/S)

Science and Society. An independent journal of Marxism. N.Y. (SS)

Social and Economic Studies. Univ. of the West Indies, Institute of Social and Economic Research. Mona, Jam. (UWI/SES)

Social Biology. N.Y.

Social Forces. Univ. of North Carolina Press by the Williams & Wilkins Co. Baltimore, Md. (SF)

Sociedad y Política. Lima.

Southwestern Journal of Anthropology. Univ. of New Mexico and the Laboratory of Anthropology, Santa Fe. Albuquerque, N. Mex. (UNM/SWJA)

Staatliche Museen Pressischer Kulturbesity. Berlin.

Studies in Comparative International Development. Rutgers Univ. New Brunswick, N.J. (RU/SCID)

Sudene. Boletim de Recursos Naturais. Superintendência do Desenvolvimento do Nordeste. Recife, Bra. (SUDENE)

Sugar y Azúcar. N.Y.

Temas del BID. Banco Interamericano de Desarrollo. Washington. (BID/T)

Tiers Monde. Problèmes des pays sous-développés. Univ. de Paris, Institut d'Étude du Développement Économique et Social. Paris. (UP/TM)

Tlalolcan Revista de fuentes para el conocimiento de las culturas indígenas de México. La Casa de Tlalolc con la colaboración del Instituto Nacional de Antropología. México. (CT/T)

Tribus. Veröffentlichungen des Linden-Museums. Museum für Länder- und Völkerkunde. Stuttgart, FRG. (MLV/T)

El Trimestre Económico. Fondo de Cultura Económica. México. (FCT/TE)

UFES Revista de Cultura. Univ. Federal Espíritu Santo. Vitória, Bra

Universidad de La Habana. La Habana. (UH/U)

Universitas. Univ. Federal da Bahia, Bra.

L'Universo. Istituto Geografico Militare. Firenze, Italy. (IGM/U)

Verfassung und Recht in Ubersee. Hamburg, FRG.

Visible Language. Cleveland Museum of Art. Cleveland, Ohio.

Weltwirschaftliches Archiv. Zeitschrift des Instituts für Weltwirtschaft an der Christians-Albrechts-Univ. Kiel. Kiel, FRG. (CAUK/WA)

Westermann's Monatshefte. Georg Westermann Verlag. Braunschweig, Germany. (WM)

Western Political Quarterly. The Western Political Science Association; Pacific Northwest Political Science Association; and Southern California Political Science Association.

Univ. of Utah, Institute of Government. Salt Lake City, Utah. (UU/WPQ)
Wissenschaftliche Zeitschrift der Universität Rostock, Gesellschafts- und sprachwissenschaftliche Reihe. Rostock, Germany. (UR/WZ)
World Affairs. The American Peace Society. Washington. (APS/WA)
World Politics. A quarterly journal of international relations. Princeton Univ., Center of International Studies. Princeton, N. J. (PUCIS/WP)
Zeitschrift für Archäologie und Urgeschichte. Berlin.
Zeitschrift für Ethnologie. Deutschen Gesellschaft für Völkerkunde. Braunschweig, FRG. (DGV/ZE)
Zeitschrift für Politik. Berlin.

Subject Index

Bibliography and General Works 1-143
Anthropology 500-1773
Economics 1774-2529
Education 6000-6315
Geography 6500-7353
Government and Politics 7354-7993
International Relations 7994-8247
Sociology 8248-8555

Abortion and Birth Control. *See* Family Planning.
Acción Democrática, Venezuela, 7794, 7798, 7803.
Accompong, Jamaica, 1143.
Aconcagua Valley, Chile, 6862.
Adaptation, *Cardiopulmonary,* 1710. *Humans,* 1708-9, 1711-3, 1715, 1718-9. *Mountain Sickness,* 1714. *Temperature Extremes,* 1711-2.
Adult Education, 6008, 6019, 6053, 6146.
Afroamerican Studies, 1122, 1131, 1138-9, 1141, 1152, 1159, 1163, 1173, 1177-81, 1195, 1198, 1200, 1201, 1208, 1210-2, 1215, 1218, 1244, 1253, 1398, 1486, 1754, 8268, 8379, 8473, 8486, 8489-90, 8506, 8533.
Agrarian Reform, *General,* 1784, 1810, 6500, 6506, 6511, 6519, 6534, 6555, 6566, 6588, 6589, 6615, 7357, 7390, 7406, 7416, 7449, 8259. *Argentina,* 7973. *Bolivia,* 1369, 2169, 6534, 6848, 7710. *Brazil,* 7019, 7023, 7026a, 7067, 7104, 7145, 7187. *Caribbean,* 2017. *Central America,* 6668. *Chile,* 1407, 2183, 2196, 2198, 2215-7, 2221-2, 2226, 2230, 2247, 6534, 6856, 6870, 7759, 7764-6, 7767, 7777, 7784-5. *Colombia,* 2055, 2074, 6534, 6916, 7642, 7647, 8452. *Dominican Republic,* 6642. *Ecuador,* 1344, 2098, 6937. *El Salvador,* 6688. *Guatemala,* 7557. *Mexico,* 1918-9, 1946, 6717, 6724, 6731, 6734, 6739, 6757. *Peru,* 1373, 2269, 2279, 2283, 2284, 2290-2, 2301, 6528, 6954, 6955, 8425. *Puerto Rico,* 1207, 2483, 2526. *Venezuela,* 2128, 6974, 6985, 7815, 7822.
Agriculture, *General,* 1872, 1988, 6501, 6511, 6521, 6544, 6549, 6589, 6590, 6607, 8066. *Andean Pact Nations,* 1887. *Argentina,* 2339, 2341, 2345, 2353, 2356, 2365-7, 2377, 2383, 2389, 2412, 6501, 6760, 6765, 6782, 6784, 6786, 6788, 6790-2, 6796, 6802, 6803, 6810, 6816, 6827, 6832, 6837. *Belize,* 1166, 6546. *Bolivia,* 2175, 6084, 6841, 6847. *Brazil,* 2413, 2414, 2428, 2441-2, 2446, 2466, 2476, 6501, 6546, 6765, 6992, 6999, 7003, 7004-5, 7010, 7014, 7017, 7026, 7026a, 7030, 7034, 7035, 7037, 7041, 7042, 7047, 7048, 7068, 7080, 7086, 7090, 7096, 7110, 7111, 7124, 7133, 7135, 7136, 7144-5, 7174, 7177, 7178, 7850a, 7851, 7869. *Cacau,* 6992, 7041, 7096. *Cattle,* 2156, 2306-7, 6765, 6784, 6837, 6912, 7030, 7048, 7136, 7145, 7148. *Census,* 2414, 6734. *Central America,* 1965, 1979, 6671. *Chile,* 2186, 2203, 2206, 2248-9, 6501, 7737. *Coffee,* 1811, 1879, 6932, 6979, 7086. *Colombia,* 2043, 2045-6, 2058, 6501, 6521, 6546, 6905, 6910, 6912, 6915, 6916, 6922. *Commercial,* 6549. *Commodities,* 6521, 6791. *Corn,* 2366, 7177. *Costa Rica,* 1971, 6678, 6683. *Cotton,* 2177, 6946, 8129. *Credit,* 2287, 2413, 6511, 7110. *Cuba,* 2001, 2019, 2034-5. *Dairy,* 2019, 2156, 2248-9, 2365. *Dominican Republic,* 6641, 6643. *Ecuador,* 2094, 6925, 6927, 6932, 6937, 6938. *Factor Markets,* 6511. *Green Revolution,* 1047, 6538, 6544, 7161. *Guatemala,* 1047, 6694. *Haciendas,* 1395, 1480, 1495. *Honduras,* 6699, 6701. *Horticulture,* 6635. *Indigenous Communal,* 6743. *Irrigation,* 1922, 2425, 6771, 6816, 6827, 7161. *Jamaica,* 2030, 6651. *Land Use,* 6566, 6590. *Legal Systems,* 2214, 6511, 7133. *Libraries,* 6512, 6521. *Manioc,* 1030, 7003, 7042. *Marketing,* 1976, 2466, 6511, 6521. *Mexico,* 1083, 1922, 1940, 1944, 1951, 6501, 6546, 6710, 6716, 6724, 6725, 6731, 6734, 6755. *Modernization,*

6560, 6615, 6621, 6663, 6669, 6683, 6713, 6717, 6791, 7003. *Nicaragua,* 7604. *Paraguay,* 2259, 6546. *Peru,* 1462, 6501, 6546, 6589, 6946. *Precolumbian,* 510, 519, 524, 530, 532, 537, 608, 621, 625, 701, 793a, 794, 890, 920, 941, 969, 981, 989. *Productivity,* 1781a, 6567, 6637, 6792, 6802. *Reference,* 6549, 6590, 6797. *Research,* 6511, 6549, 6560, 6590, 6651, 6669. *Soils,* 6647, 6790. *Puerto Rico,* 2488, 2494, 2497, 2499, 2503, 2508, 2511, 2516-8. *Sugar,* 1129, 1938, 1986, 1989, 1994, 1999, 2034-5, 2094, 2103, 2389, 2488, 2511, 2516-8. *Surinam,* 2105. *Tobacco,* 1961, 7080. *Tropical,* 6581, 6659. *Uruguay,* 2306-8, 2313, 6958, 7901. *Venezuela,* 2153, 2156, 6501, 6546, 6968, 6969, 6971, 6973, 6977, 6979, 6980, 6985. *West Indies,* 2028, 6624, 8389. *Wheat,* 6760, 6847.
La Aguada Culture, 779.
Akurio Indians, 1128.
Alagüilac Languages, 1519.
Alakaluf Indians, 1223, 1240, 1256, 1280.
Alcohol and Alcoholism, 1385, 8347, 8434, 8475.
Les Aldas, Peru, 946a.
Alfaro, Ricardo J., 8140, 8145.
Alianza Nacional Popular, Colombia, 7643.
Alianza para el Progreso. *See* Alliance for Progress.
Alianza Popular Revolucionaria Americana, Peru, 7682, 7697.
Alliance for Progress, 1848, 2117, 6519, 6588, 7472, 8051, 8053, 8069-70.
Altun Ha, Belize, 692-3.
Amazon River, 6565.
Amazônia, Brazil, 2419, 2464, 6994, 7009, 7027, 7029, 7032a, 7036, 7061, 7065, 7100, 7107, 7113, 7130, 7140-2, 7149, 7154, 7167, 7188, 7190, 7855, 7874, 7880.
Amparo, Ley de, 7505.
Ancestor Worship. *See* Religion.
Andean Pact Nations, 1776, 1796, 1825, 1836, 1846, 1885, 1893, 2044, 2077, 2083, 2096, 2149, 2151, 2154, 2257, 6050, 8100, 8194. *Agriculture,* 1887, 2043, 2045. *Foreign Investment Code,* 1856, 1900. *Trade Agreements,* 1774, 1822.
Andes, 6763, 6770, 6777, 6859, 6891, 6928, 6949.
Antarctic, 6762.
Anthropometric Studies, 1688, 1695, 1699, 1704, 1717, 1757, 1759, 1764.
Antiquities Traffic. *See* Illegal Antiquities Traffic.
Antitrust Laws, *Chile,* 7748, 7767.
Apalaí. *See* Carib Languages.
Apartheid. *See* Race and Race Relations.
Apinayé Indians, 1291, 1292, 1316, 1325. *See also* Gê Indians.
Araucanian Language, 1550, 1625.
Araucanians, 875, 1493.
Arawak Indians, 510, 751, 754.
Arawakan Languages, 1540, 1582, 1585, 1592-3, 1615, 1647-8.

Archaeology, *Lithic Material,* 503, 705, 759, 770, 773, 783, 784, 787-8, 791, 797, 799, 816, 837-8, 845, 852, 855, 883, 947, 955, 982, 1008, 1014. *Terminology and Classification,* 502, 503.
Architecture, *Mesoamerica,* 510, 540, 550, 566, 586, 615, 641, 688, 704, 713. *Caribbean,* 737. *South America,* 769a, 892, 954, 972, 1011.
Argentina and the UK, 2398-9.
Argentina and the US, 8222.
Argentina and the USSR, 8235.
Argentine Revolution, 1966, 7946b, 7955, 7957, 7979.
Arguedas, José María, 1502.
Arid Zones. *See* Ecology.
Armed Forces, *General,* 7367, 7401, 7416, 7426, 7448, 7466, 7496, 8049, 8080-1, 8101. *Argentina,* 7926-8, 7956, 7969, 7971, 7983. *Bolivia,* 7712-3. *Brazil,* 2454, 7100, 7685, 7857, 7866, 7889. *Chile,* 7758, 7768. *Costa Rica,* 7548. *Peru,* 7676, 7679, 7681, 7683, 7685, 7687, 7700a, 7702, 7705, 7707. *Uruguay,* 7918. *Venezuela,* 7798-9.
Art and Artifacts, *General Mesoamerica,* 510, 533, 544, 550, 554, 555, 557, 558, 560, 577, 591, 593, 594, 602, 613, 615, 617, 619-20, 627-30, 631, 642-6, 648, 653, 657, 660, 662-5, 665a, 669, 673, 677-80, 683-7, 692, 694, 700, 704, 705, 710, 715, 720, 723, 914, 1051. *General Caribbean,* 738, 739-42, 743, 748-9, 751, 753, 756-7. *General South America,* 762-3, 765-6, 772, 787, 793, 796, 820, 823, 827-8, 834-5, 840, 843, 845, 848-51, 853, 880, 897-8, 900-1, 903, 914-5, 921, 925, 927, 929-30, 933, 935, 939, 946, 949, 952, 953-5, 976, 981-3, 988, 995, 999, 1013a, 1014, 1016, 1021, 1027, 1029. *Brazil,* 1299. *Ceramics Caribbean,* 738, 742, 750-1, 754-5. *Ceramics Mesoamerica,* 510, 550, 607, 612, 628, 636-7, 643, 648, 651, 658, 668, 670, 674, 676-7, 680-2, 685, 691, 707-8, 711, 714-5, 717, 720, 1033. *Ceramics South America,* 763, 771, 772-3, 775-6, 779, 782, 788, 795, 805, 810, 815, 825, 829, 831, 833, 848, 853, 856-7, 859-60, 863, 865, 870, 873, 877, 890-1, 895-6, 898, 903, 915-6, 916a, 921, 925, 927-8, 938, 940, 946a, 952, 954, 960, 969, 972, 977, 996-8, 1002, 1012-3, 1016, 1021, 1023, 1027, 1346. *Codices,* 593, 624, 722, 724, 729, 731-3, 735. *Ecuador,* 1470. *Peru,* 1386. *Petroglyphs,* 640, 748, 754-6, 780, 809, 814, 817, 829, 838, 852, 872, 904, 1019. *Štelae,* 654, 698, 722-3, 727-8, 730. *Textiles (Precolumbian)* 798, 813, 865, 909, 978-80, 1009-10, 1052. *Textiles,* 798, 813, 865, 909, 978-80, 1009-10, 1052, 1313, 1415.
Astronomy, 567, 626, 721, 731-2, 913.
Asurini. *See* Tupí-Guaraní Language.
Atacama Desert, 6865.
Atavism, 8301.
Atlantic Ocean, 500, 6808.
Atomic Energy, 6665, 6787.

Aucayacu, Peru, 1458, 6954.
Automobile Industry, 1848, 2309.
Ayahuasca. *See* Hallucinogens.
Aymara Indians, 1339, 1364, 1368, 1419, 1425, 1447, 1453, 1493, 1496.
Ayoreo Indians, 1278.
Aztec Indians, 512, 576, 618, 1060, 1063, 1064.
Aztecs *Maps*, 7192.

Baja California, 6711.
Balance of Payments, 1972, 1975, 2078, 2146, 2152, 2324.
Bandera Roja (Venezuela), 7812.
Baniva Indians, 1268, 1315.
Banking and Commerce, *General*, 1823, 1838, 1842, 1844. *Argentina*, 2325-7, 2330, 2347-8, 2372. *Bolivia*, 2173. *Brazil*, 2426, 2429, 2462. *Caribbean*, 2032. *Chile*, 2193, 2201, 2225. *Colombia*, 2065, 2072-1, 2078. *Costa Rica*, 1971. *Dominican Republic*, 2002. *Ecuador*, 2097, 6931. *Mexico*, 1905, 1926. *Paraguay*, 2260. *Uruguay*, 2314. *Venezuela*, 2123, 2127, 2137-8, 2146-7.
Barasano. *See* Eastern Tucanoan Languages.
Barceló, Alberto, 7949.
El barcelonazo, Venezuela, 7807.
Bari Indians, 1324.
Barrientos, René, 7721.
Barter Systems, 1443. *See also* Money.
Batallas Rituales, 1417.
Batllismo, Uruguay, 8056.
Beagle Channel, 8187.
Begging. *See* Class Structure.
Behavioral Studies, 8253-4, 8289-91, 8393, 8465, 8512, 8526, 8528.
Belmopan, Belize, 6674.
Belo Horizonte, Brazil, 7151.
Bequia Island, West Indies, 1121, 6617.
Betancourt, Rómulo, 7817.
Birth Control. *See* Family Planning.
Black Power, 1177, 1196, 1486, 6622, 7621.
Blood Pressure, 1664.
Bogotá, 6921.
Bolivia and the US, 8233.
Bolivian Revolutions, 7716-20.
Book Industry, 2363.
Border Disputes. *See* Boundary Disputes.
Bororo Indians, 1246.
Bosch, Juan, 7614.
Boundary Disputes, *Argentina/Chile*, 8187. *Colombia/Panama*, 8133. *Colombia/Venezuela*, 8185, 8204, 8215-6, 8245-6. *Guyana/Venezuela*, 8231.
Bracero Program. *See* Labor.
Brain Drain, 2026, 2062.
Brasília, 7126.
Brazil and the US, 8193, 8228, 8241.
Buenos Aires, 6815.
Bureilli Rivas, Miguel Angel, 7797.
Burial Customs. *See* Religion.
Burnham, Forbes, 7632.

Burr Frieze, 953.

Ça-Ira, Haiti, 6648.
Caciques, 1101, 1109, 1330.
Cadastral Survey. *See* Taxation.
Calama River Basin, 6891.
Caldera, Rafael, 7800-2, 8004.
Calendrics, 550, 689, 721, 729, 734.
Callawaya Indians, 1464.
Camayura Indians, 1293.
Campa Indians, 510, 1248, 1327, 1333.
Camsa Language, 1562.
Canadian-Latin American Relations, 8054, 8058, 8105.
Canals, *Central America*, 6665, 6705, 6746, 8134, 8143, 8144.
Cancha-Cancha, Peru, 996.
Candelaria Culture, 767.
Canela Indians, 1247, 1281, 1315-6.
Capital Gains, 2500.
Capital Markets, 1842, 1844, 1852, 1859, 1886, 2024, 2038, 2042, 2240, 2265, 2330, 2424, 2445, 2462, 2471, 2505.
Capital/Output Ratios, 1793.
Capitalism, 1894, 2297, 7700, 8046.
Caracas, 6959.
Cárdenas, Lázaro, 7540.
Carib Indians, 510, 750-1, 754, 1258, 1279.
Carib Languages, 1568.
Caribbean Development Bank, 2007.
Caribbean Free Trade Area, 1993, 1995-6, 2007.
Caribbean Unity, 8168.
Carnivals, 2172, 8384.
Caste War, Yucatan, 1111.
Castelnau, Fracis, 6844.
Castro, Fidel, 7571, 7578, 7580, 7586, 7588, 7608, 8031, 8164.
Castro and Latin America, 1816.
Catalan Chico, Uruguay, 1013a.
Catholic Church, *General*, 7361, 7454, 7587, 7659, 8285. *Brazil*, 8515, 8531. *Doctrine and Reform*, 7373, 7375, 7378, 7380, 7393, 7403, 7421, 7435, 7479, 7486-7, 7490, 7744, 7663, 7675, 7978. *Education*, 7384. *Mexico*, 1909, 8306.
Caudillismo, 8435.
Caudillos and Caudillismo, 7895, 7974.
Cautín, Chile, 6872.
Cayapa Indians, 1321.
Ceará, Brazil, 7134.
Ceja de la selva, 917.
Central America and the UN, 8141.
Central American Common Market, 1954-5, 1956, 1962, 1964, 1972, 1975, 1977-9, 1981.
Centro Coordinator Cora-Huichol (CCCH), 1090.
Centro Coordinador Tzeltal-Tzotzil (CCTT), 1069.
Centro Latino-Americano de Demografia, 6572.
Cepalismo, 1779.
Ceramics. *See* Arts and Artifacts.

Chaac, Bajo el signo, 6736.
Chaco, Arg., 6813.
Chacobo Indians, 1308.
Chan Chan, Peru, 937, 953, 1001.
Chan Kom, 527.
Character and Personality Studies, 8305, 8311-2, 8326, 8346, 8355, 8421, 8435, 8436, 8442, 8499.
Chavin Culture, 914, 943, 946a, 957.
Checras, Peru, 1357.
Chibchas, 861, 1024, 1345, 1430.
Chichiriviche, Venezuela, 1018.
Chilca Canyon, Peru, 942.
Children, 8328-9.
Chile and Allende, 2188, 2234-5, 2237, 2241, 7729-32, 7734, 7738, 7741-2, 7751-2, 7760, 7762, 7767, 7779-80, 7782a, 7787.
Chile and the US, 2231, 8196, 8223, 8239.
Chile and the USSR, 8203.
Chile Hoy, 2202.
Chimu, 933, 937, 952.
Chinampa, 625.
Chinantecan Languages, 1642.
Chinchero, Cuzco, Peru, 910, 911, 996, 1392, 1476.
Chinese in Latin America, 1160.
Chiquitano Indians, 1309-10.
Chocó Indians, 1109, 1579, 1706.
El Chocón-Cerros Colorados, Arg., 6816, 2369, 2396.
Chol Indians, 605.
Cholification, 1402, 7678.
Chontal. *See* Hokan Language.
Chontal Indians, 590, 605, 719.
Christian Democratic Parties, 2207, 7477, 7746, 7749, 7767b, 7769, 7823, 7905, 8203.
Chromosome Imbalances, 1969.
Chubut, Arg., 6781, 6790.
Chumbivilcas, Peru, 976.
Church and Development, 8472.
Cienfuegos, Camilo, 7612.
Cinturão-verde, São Paulo, Brazil, 7161.
Cities. *See* Urbanization.
Class Structure, *General,* 1089, 1097, 1812, 7455, 8279. *Argentina,* 8410. *Begging,* 1045. *Brazil,* 7876, 7883, 8469-71, 8482, 8510, 8537, 8549. *Caribbean,* 1126-7, 1139, 1142, 1146, 1160, 1163-4, 1172-3, 1175, 1178, 1180, 1189, 1191, 1194, 1197, 1204, 1206, 1207, 1209, 1213, 1218. *Central America,* 1980. *Chile,* 7767a, 8458. *Colombia,* 7641. *Costa Rica,* 8344. *Education,* 1147, 1148, 1189, 8505. *Elites,* 8333. *Family,* 1083, 1084, 1089, 1104, 1108, 1117, 1281, 1322, 1330, 1365, 1456. *Guatemala,* 8342, 8349. *Haiti,* 8401. *Jamaica,* 8404. *Mexico,* 1080, 8307-9, 8322, 8324, 8330, 8336. *Peru,* 7698-9, 7701, 7706, 8425, 8447. *Precolumbian,* 543, 550, 561, 570, 941, 1032, 1064, 1067, 1068, 1449. *Puerto Rico,* 8368, 8405-6. *South America,* 1227, 1246, 1261, 1279, 1324-5, 1338, 1342, 1347, 1350, 1352, 1356, 1358, 1390, 1410, 1412, 1429, 1432, 1433, 1442, 1459-60, 1471, 1473, 1495, 1505, 1507. *Studies,* 8287.
Climate. *See* Ecology.
Coasa, Peru, 1448.
Coatlicue, 667.
Coba (Underworld argot), 1602.
Cocama. *See* Tupí-Guaraní Languages.
Codazzi, Agustín, 7193.
Codices. *See* Art.
Cofan Indians, 1300.
Coffee Commodity Agreement, 1811, 2438.
Coffee Diplomacy, 1811, 8022.
Colla Indians, 1399.
Colta, Indians of, 1445.
Columbus, Christopher, 500, 6702.
Comandante Pepe, Chile, 7755.
Communism, 7407a, 7549, 7572, 7579, 7604, 8062, 8107.
Communist Party, *Argentina,* 7937. *Chile,* 7382, 7740. *Cuba,* 8064. *Venezuela,* 7792, 7813.
Community Development, 2268, 2523, 8260, 8292, 8308, 8354, 8412-3, 8422, 8437-8, 8487, 8496, 8525-6, 8539.
Compadrazgo, 1053, 1108, 1418, 1422.
Confederación Cooperativa de la República Argentina, 6838.
Consejo Agrario Nacional, Arg., 6782.
Consejo Nacional de Desarrollo, Arg., 6783-4.
Consensus of Viña del Mar, 2244, 7481.
Constitutional History and Constitutionalism, *General,* 8209. *Brazil,* 7850, 7854. *Chile,* 7745, 7767c. *Uruguay,* 7910a.
Consumer Price Index, 1960, 2076, 2122, 2264.
Continental Drift, 6523, 6556, 6623.
Continental Shelf, *Brazil,* 7180. *Venezuela,* 6961.
Convention of Human Rights, 8060.
Copan, Honduras, 652.
Copper Industry, 2227, 2231.
Cora Indians, 1057-9, 1090.
Cordillera de la Costa, Chile, 6868.
El *cordobazo,* Argentina, 7993.
Corporación de Fomento de la Producción, Chile, 6867.
Corporativism. *See* Dictatorships.
Cortés, Hernán, 649, 6754.
Cosmology, 539, 1127, 1238, 1327, 1333, 1430, 1454, 1462.
Courtship, 8467.
Creole Culture, 1132.
Creole Languages, 1122, 1127.
Crime and Delinquency, 8325, 8327, 8441, 8457.
Cristero Rebellion, 1036.
Cross Cultural Studies, 8311-2, 8331, 8365, 8393.
Cruz, Ramón Ernesto, 7552-3.
Cruzob Indians, 605.
Cuba and Chile, 7789-90, 8184.

Cuba and Latin America, 8172.
Cuba and the US, 8153, 8155-7, 8161, 8164, 8180, 8182.
Cuba and the USSR, 8154, 8167, 8177-9, 8181.
Cuban Missile Crisis, 8150, 8160, 8166, 8180.
Cuban Revolution, 6636, 7565-6, 7568, 7578-9, 7581, 7583, 7590, 7594-5, 7601-3, 7610, 7611, 7789-90, 8366.
Cubeo. *See* Eastern Tucanoan Languages.
Cuchimilcos, 981.
Cueva del Toro, Venezuela, 1020.
Cuicuilco, Mexico, 661.
Cults, various. *See* Religion.
Cultural Development and Evolution, 504, 552, 556, 562, 562a, 608-9, 632, 651, 702, 707, 710, 745, 754, 761, 785, 822, 876, 885, 887-90, 893, 899, 922, 1037, 1054-6, 1078, 1111, 1140, 1161-2, 1203, 1383, 1389, 1403, 1419, 1421, 1424, 1429, 1432, 1467, 7458, 8266, 8283, 8313, 8320, 8343, 8348, 8357, 8366-8, 8390, 8399, 8403, 8406, 8407, 8448, 8488, 8491, 8494, 8500, 8501, 8504, 8510, 8543.
Culture and Population, Origin of, 509, 510, 1765.
Cupeño Language, 1558.
Curanderos, 1337, 1381, 1472, 1491-2, 1508.
Currency Convertibility, 1962.
Cuzco, Peru, 910, 911, 940, 6947.

Deception Island, 6759
Demography, *General*, 6517, 6519, 6520, 6533, 6535, 6536, 6542, 6545, 6548, 6551, 6555, 6572, 6594, 6612, 6614, 7198. *Amazon*, 6917. *Anthropology*, 1652. *Argentina*, 2331, 6783, 6792, 6812, 6839, 8413. *Belize*, 1126. *Bolivia*, 1275, 1463, 6842, 6853. *Brazil*, 6989, 7012, 7031, 7038, 7040, 7050, 7051, 7157, 7168, 7884, 7922, 8479. *Caribbean*, 8378. *Census*, 1431, 1444, 1469, 1668, 1968, 2261, 6572, 6619, 6680, 6687, 6719, 6734, 6824, 6839, 6901, 6930, 7012, 8369-70. *Central America*, 8352. *Chile*, 2254, 6870. *Colombia*, 2054, 6901, 6917. *Colonial*, 6864, 6889. *Dominican Republic*, 6643. *Ecuador*, 6930, 6937-8. *Guatemala*, 1076, 1097, 1982, 6691. *Human Adaptation*, 1708-19. *Indians*, 1082, 1109. *Mexico*, 1080, 1738, 1913-4, 6710, 6714, 6719-20, 6727-9, 6735-6, 6744, 8315, 8317-9, 8336. *Occupational Mobility*, 1732. *Panama*, 1055. *Paraguay*, 2261-2. *Peru*, 1421, 1458, 1463, 6945, 6957, 7695. *Political*, 587, 6517, 7661, 7875. *Population Studies*, 510, 841, 1055, 1197, 1380, 1414, 1449, 1487-8, 1490, 1498, 1503, 1735, 1753, 6537, 6545, 6550, 6551, 6564, 6572, 6583, 6594, 6603, 6605, 6614, 6655, 6680, 6697, 6719, 6727, 6728, 6773, 6828, 6842, 6930, 6947, 7145, 7157, 7168, 7462, 7485, 8281, 8446, 8481, 8484, 8507. *Population Structure*, 1731, 1762-3, 1765. *Precolumbian*, 504, 510, 548, 550, 568-9, 632, 671, 701, 707, 716, 917, 941, 973, 1071. *Puerto Rico*, 2501, 8383. *Reference*, 6585. *Research*, 6605, 6964. *Residential Patterns*, 6658, 6708. *Rural-urban Mobility*, 1487-8, 6606, 6719, 6832, 6853, 6858, 6870, 6945, 6957, 7388, 8318, 8332, 8423, 8428, 8460. *Studies*, 6597, 6650, 6691. *Surveys*, 6572.
Dengo, Omar, 6096.
Dependence and Dependency, 1790, 1804-5, 1807, 1814, 1820, 1860, 1881-3, 1894, 1911, 2005-6, 2020, 2118, 2140, 2148, 2187, 2246, 2371, 2391, 6021, 7414, 7456-7, 7466, 7471, 7473, 7542, 7743a, 7664, 7759, 7763, 7824, 7839, 7852, 7946b.
Dermatoglyphics. *See* Genetics.
Deschooling, 6036.
Desierto de Sechura, Peru, 6946.
Devaluation, 1996.
Diaguita Culture, 775, 886.
Dictatorships, 7496-8, 7600, 7619, 7873, 7893, 7897.
Disarmament, 8049, 8088, 8173.
Disease, *General*, 1680. *Brazil*, 7070. *Chagas*, 1660. *Diabetes*, 1673. *Intestinal*, 1670-1. *Liver*, 1667. *Malaria*, 1669. *Muyu-muyu*, 1366. *Nephritis*, 1676. *Panama*, 6709. *Tetanus*, 1659. *Venereal*, 1682.
Disturnell, John, 7203.
Dollar Diplomacy, 8230.
The Dominican Republic and the US, 8151, 8165, 8170-1, 8183.
Drug Problems, 8261, 8461, 8522. *See also* Hallucinogens.
Duvalier, François, 7618.

Early Man, 500, 505, 744, 745, 755-7, 824, 832, 842, 890, 929, 950-1, 992, 994, 1030, 1722, 6897.
East Indians in Latin America, 1151, 1192.
Eastern Tucanoan Languages, 1613, 1621, 1626, 1639-40, 1640a, 1641.
Echeverría, Luis, 7514-5.
Ecology and Conservation, *General*, 513, 6567, 6569, 6586, 6596, 6610, 6745. *Andes*, 1443, 6763. *Arid Zones*, 6860, 6865, 6882, 6884. *Brazil*, 7170-1, 7173. *Caribbean*, 6631. *Chile*, 6860. *Climate*, 6529, 6539, 6567, 6618, 6736, 6737, 6811, 6813, 6818, 6863, 6872, 6882, 6883, 6886, 6893-4, 6914, 6929, 6863, 7022, 7117-20, 7162-4, 7318, 7320. *Cultural*, 1351, 6530, 6539. *Demographic*, 6530, 6542. *Development*, 6531, 6536, 6542, 6906, 7158-9. *Ecosystems*, 510, 6596, 6793, 6851, 6854, 6914, 6922. *Environment*, 6542, 6555, 6590, 6652, 6745, 7167. *Erosion*, 6925. *Fish and Wildlife*, 6529, 6582, 6631, 6808, 6885. *Flood Control*, 6681. *Marine*, 6541, 6665, 6898, 6967. *Plants and Forests*, 6529, 6531, 6566, 6581, 6582, 6611, 6626, 6631, 6649, 6738, 6760, 6873, 6887, 6925, 6968, 6973, 7043, 7166, 7183. *Precolumbian*, 510, 747, 846, 876, 918, 936, 941, 1021. *Prob-

lems, 6529, 6539, 6541, 6566, 6581, 6587, 7158-9. *Research,* 6529. *Swidden Cultivation,* 1273, 6968. *Venezuela,* 6973, 6976-8

Econometric Model, 2469, 2492.

Economic Assistance, *General,* 1806, 1813 1824, 2286, 2484-5, 6522, 8030, 8033. *Netherlands,* 1992, 2031. *US,* 2168, 8023, 8092-3, 8096, 8103, 8148.

Economic Commission for Latin America, 1877, 6835.

Economic Development, *General,* 501a, 1794-5, 1800, 1804, 1806, 1809, 1817, 1819, 1826, 1837, 1839, 1841, 1846, 1855, 1857, 1860-1, 1865, 1869-71, 1879, 1882-3, 1888-9, 1892, 1902, 2117, 6015, 6562, 6567, 6599, 7415, 7418, 7420, 7442, 7452, 7457, 8006, 8286, 8288-8289. *Anegada,* 2036. *Argentina,* 2322-3, 2331-2, 2334, 2352-4, 2368, 2380-1, 2387-9, 2393, 2405-6, 2528, 6831, 7377, 7933, 7954-5, 7960, 8413, 8419. *Belize,* 1124, 1125. *Bolivia,* 1432, 2166, 2181. *Brazil,* 1778, 2415-6, 2419, 2421-2, 2424, 2430, 2432-5, 2441, 2444, 2447-50, 2455, 2459, 2467, 2477, 6998, 7009, 7011, 7013, 7026, 7026a, 7056, 7059, 7065, 7097, 7106, 7109, 7114, 7122, 7140, 7141-2, 7147, 7156, 7167, 7182, 7835, 7864, 7870, 7877, 7881, 7884, 7922. *Caribbean,* 1985, 2012, 2024, 6624. *Central America,* 1963-5. *Chile,* 2186, 2190-1, 2208-11, 2232-3, 2236, 2250-2, 6888, 7732, 7734, 7743a, 7767, 7773. *Colombia,* 2039, 2041, 2047, 2053-4, 2072, 2075, 2079, 6902, 6909, 6921, 7640. *Costa Rica,* 1971. *Cuba,* 1987, 1997, 2014, 7567, 7575-6, 7591. *Dominican Republic,* 1213, 1984, 2003. *Ecuador,* 2086, 2088, 2092, 2099, 2101-2, 6927, 6935, 6937. *Education,* 6015, 6038, 6272. *El Salvador,* 8129. *French Guiana,* 2109, 2111. *Guatemala,* 1967, 1970, 6693, 8350. *Guyana,* 2107-8, 6971. *Haiti,* 2008, 2021, 2025, 7618a. *Indians,* 1283, 7061. *Jamaica,* 2011, 2013. *Mexico,* 1911, 1914, 1915-6, 1921-3, 1927, 1932-3, 1937, 1939, 1940-1, 1945, 1948-50, 1952, 2528, 6749, 7511, 7516, 8296. *Multi-National Resources,* 6563-4, 6766, 6775. *Nicaragua,* 8129. *Peru,* 2267, 2272, 2277-8, 2281-2, 2285-6, 2294-5, 2303, 2305, 7684, 7691, 7697, 7703, 7426, 8454. *Precolumbian,* 510, 1031. *Puerto Rico,* 2482, 2486-7, 2505, 2509-10, 2512-3, 2528-9, 7627, 8395. *River Basins,* 6563, 6565. *Surinam,* 1149, 2106, 2112. *Trinidad and Tobago,* 2023, 2033, 7630. *Uruguay,* 2310, 2312, 2315-6, 2318-9. *Venezuela,* 2117-8, 2125-6, 2128-9, 2135, 2140, 2149-50, 2155, 2158.

Economic Integration, 1776-7, 1781, 1787-8, 1791-2, 1796, 1803, 1815, 1818, 1821, 1827, 1836, 1840, 1846, 1849, 1868, 1871-2, 1874, 1874a, 1884, 1954-5, 1956, 1958, 1971-2, 1985, 1993, 1995-6, 2020, 2024, 2037, 2059, 2083, 2085, 2100, 2144, 2178, 2258, 2276, 2342, 6525, 6567, 6775, 7355, 7428, 7492, 8007, 8135, 8137.

Ecosystems. *See* Ecology.

Ecuador and the US, 8230.

Education and Developing Countries, 6046, 6052, 6055, 6061, 6094-5, 6100-2, 6104, 6123, 6129, 6143-4, 6147, 6151, 6160, 6163, 6166-7, 6177, 6188, 6192-3, 6197-8, 6201, 6202, 6214, 6219-23, 6248-9, 6256, 6259, 6264, 6267, 6270, 6275, 6277, 6279, 6285, 6291, 6294, 6294-5, 6298.

Education and Social Change, 6057, 6077, 6085-7, 6097-8, 6108, 6114, 6127, 6132, 6152-4, 6159, 6168-71, 6174-5, 6179, 6194-5, 6198-200, 6203, 6205, 6230, 6245, 6282, 8470.

Education and Technology, 6263, 6292, 6296, 6300.

Education and Television, 6022, 6099, 6163, 6210, 6225, 6283, 6303.

Educational Counseling, 6148.

Educational Exchange, 6069, 6118.

Educational Programs, 6060, 6186, 6188.

Educational Systems, 6041, 6049, 6206-7.

Educators and Students, 6042, 6266.

Ejercito de Liberación Nacional, Colombia, 7636.

Ejidos, 1080, 8301, 8327.

Elections and Electoral Traditions, 7489, 7536, 7556, 7559, 7622, 7662, 7750, 7667-9, 7761, 7770, 7781-2, 7788, 7911, 7924, 7940-1, 7946a, 7965.

Electronics Industry, 2386.

Embera Indians, 1379.

Emerilon Indians, 1222.

Employment. *See* Labor.

Energy and Ecology, 6587.

Energy Sources, *General,* 1802, 6587, 7210. *Argentina,* 2396, 6525, 6764, 6817, 6835, 7231. *Bolivia,* 6525, 6850. *Brazil,* 6525, 7025, 7125. *Chile,* 6525. *Colombia,* 6525, 6902, 6907, 6908. *Ecuador,* 6525. *Guatemala,* 6695. *Mexico,* 7324. *Paraguay,* 6525, 6764. *Peru,* 1383, 6525. *Uruguay,* 6525. *Venezuela,* 2165, 6525, 6984.

Entrepreneurship, 2068.

Environment. *See* Ecology.

Environmental Crisis. *See* Ecology.

Erosion. *See* Ecology.

Eskimo Culture, 504.

Essequibo River, Guyana, 6940.

Ethnic Studies, 8257.

Ethnography, 515, 1038, 1059, 1062, 1063, 1065, 1075, 1082, 1115, 1150, 1173, 1254, 1271, 1317, 1396-7, 1409, 1431, 1441, 1548, 1555, 1646, 8295, 8474, 8501, 8541.

Ethnology, *Reference,* 1408.

European Common Market and Latin America, 1853.

Evolution, 6556.

Exchange Rate Systems, 2060.

Exogamy. *See* Marriage.

Explorers and Exploration, 6630, 7099.

External Financing. See Foreign Investment.

Falkland Islands, 6834, 8247.
Family Planning, 2462, 2504, 6603, 8295, 8299, 8303, 8351, 8374, 8378, 8387, 8394, 9398, 8424, 8430, 8455, 8462. See also Sex and Sexual Relations.
Family Relationships, 1053, 1143, 8552.
Febrerista Party, Paraguay, 7898.
Feria de Alacitas, Bolivia, 1465.
Fiallos, Mariano, 6101.
Finley, John H., 8162.
Fiscal Policy, Argentina, 2343, 2372, 2375, 2384, 2395. Brazil, 2433, 2471. Chile, 2197. Colombia, 2050, 2080. Ecuador, 2091. Mexico, 1952. Puerto Rico, 2481-2. Uruguay, 2311.
Fish and Wildlife. See Ecology and Fisheries and Fishing Industry.
Fish Meal, 6890.
Fisheries and Fishing Industry, Brazil, 7032-3, 7146, 7180-1, 7188. Caribbean, 1127. Chile, 6890. Cuba, 2022. Ecuador, 2096. Peru, 2302. Precolumbian, 536, 769, 890, 898a.
Fishing Rights, 8085, 8094.
Flood Control. See Ecology.
Flora and Fauna, Amazonia, 6571. Andes, 6761, 6776. Antarctic, 6523. Argentina, 1289, 6811, 6818, 6825. Belize, 6676. Bolivia, 6846. Brazil, 7066, 7101, 7170, 7172-3, 7186. Caribbean, 6626, 6631, 6649. Central America, 6571. Brazil, 6571. Chile, 6879. Colombia, 6918. Mexico, 6740. Precolumbian, 777, 967, 982, 1021. Venezuela, 6982-3.
Flow-of-Funds Analysis, 2063.
Folklore, General, 510, 1049, 1073, 1075, 1081, 1086, 1094, 1120, 1205, 1210, 1211, 1353, 1427-8, 1461, 1465, 1468, 1475, 1481, 1485, 1489, 1548, 1619-20. Guatemala, 8358. Haiti, 6646. Jamaica, 1143. Mexico, 8298. Puerto Rico, 8386. Trinidad, 1144, 8384.
Food Industry, 2359, 6546.
Food Marketing, 1963.
Food Supply. See Nutrition.
Foreign Aid. See Economic Assistance.
Foreign Investment, 1820, 1824, 1857, 1866, 1880, 1901, 1943, 2015, 2145, 2192, 2223, 2227, 2231, 2286, 2355, 2437, 2452-3, 2455-6, 2475, 2495-6.
Foreign Policy, Argentina, 8191a, 8213, 8240. Bolivia, 8190, 8198, 8202, 8224-6, 8236, 8238. Brazil, 8191, 8192, 8205, 8208, 8210, 8212, 8217, 8229, 8232, 8237-8. Chile, 8188, 8219, 8234. Colombia, 8133. Commonwealth Caribbean, 8169, 8175-6. Guatemala, 8130. Mexico, 8114, 8122. Panama, 8131, 8133-4, 8143. Paraguay, 8214. Venezuela, 8201.
Forests. See Ecology.
Fossils, Antarctic, 6523.
Fraile de Ocopa y Chiloé. See Juan Ignacio Molina.

Frei Montalvo, Eduardo, 2209, 7749, 7765, 7769, 7784.
Freyre, Gilberto, 6243, 8477.
Frondizi, Arturo, 7954.
Fuerzas Armadas de Liberación Nacional, Venezuela, 7825.
Fútbol, 1446.

Galapagos Islands, 6926.
The Galíndez Affair, 7616.
Games, Precolumbian. 601, 604, 711-2, 932, 1440.
Gamio, Manuel, 612.
Gê, 510.
Gê Indians, 1226, 1292.
General Agreement on Tariffs and Trade, 1875, 7996.
Genetics, 697, 1319, 1654, 1674, 1684, 1733, 1736-7, 1740, 1748-9, 1751-2, 1755-6, 1758, 1760-3, 1765, 1766-7, 1768-73.
Geography, Animal, 6508. Central America, 6559. Development Plans, 6524, 6540, 6542, 6562. Economic, 6536, 6540, 6610. Historical, 6592, 6617, 6620, 7123, 7191, 7202, 7204. Natural Resources, 2411, 6524, 6528, 6536, 6567, 6570, 6695, 6714, 6835, 6906, 7122. Physical, 6796, 7173. Political, 6591. Preston E. James, 6553, 6554. Reference, 6528, 6559, 6575, 6576-7, 6586, 6821. Regional, 6524, 6540, 6559, 6563, 6612. Research, 6562, 6591, 6597, 6598, 6602, 6606. South America, 6559. Vocabulary, 6799, 6900, 7085, 7121, 7207.
Geology, Andes, 6762, 6770, 6794-5, 6859. Argentina, 6805. Bolivia, 6843. Brazil, 6987, 6991, 7011, 7052, 7081, 7084, 7113, 7138. Chile, 6859, 6869, 6874, 6878, 6881, 6883, 6892, 6896-7. Colombia, 6919. Ecuador, 6934. Guyana, 6940. Maps, 7239, 7296. Mexico, 6712, 6722, 6758. Peru, 6948, 6949. Venezuela, 6962, 6966, 6972.
Geomorphology, 6586, 6670, 6685, 6686, 6851, 6862, 6866, 6875, 6884, 7015.
Geophysics, 6666.
Germany in Latin America, Brazil, 7091.
Glaciers, 504, 6762, 6875, 6876, 6880, 6924.
Goiás, Brazil, 7078.
Golfo de Venezuela, 6961.
Gondwanaland, 6523, 6843.
Good Neighbor Policy, 8032, 8120.
Goubaud Carrera, Antonio, 1093.
Gran Pajonal, 510.
Grammar. See Language.
Green Revolution. See Agriculture.
Gross National Product, 1848, 1972, 1983.
Growth Rates, 1800.
Guadeloupe, 6618, 6619.
Grupo de Oficiales Unidos (GOU), Argentina, 7943-4.
Guadalupe-Hidalgo, Treaty of, 7203.
Guahibo Indians, 510, 1286-7, 1297, 1322.

Guahibo Language, 1569.
Guajajara. *See* Tupí-Guaraní Languages.
Guajiro Indians, 1290, 1302-3, 1324, 1330-2, 1335.
Guamán Poma de Ayala, 931.
Guanajuato, Mexico, 6747.
Guanano. *See* Eastern Tucanoan Languages.
Guaporé, Brazil. *See* Rondônia.
Guaraní Indians, 1231.
Guaraní Languages, 1512, 1516, 1531-3, 1547, 1589, 1635.
Guaraquena. *See* Arawakan Languages.
Guarasug'wa Indians, 1311.
Guarayo Indians, 1275.
Guayakí. *See* Guaraní Languages.
Guayaqui Indians, 1264.
Guayas River Basin, 6935.
Guaycurú Language, 1631.
Guaymi Indians, 1109, 1117.
Guerilla Warfare and Movements, 7366, 7368, 7380, 7391, 7408, 7422, 7424, 7430, 7441, 7464-5, 7476, 7589, 7636, 7830, 7860, 7939, 7990, 8148.
Guevara, Ernesto "Che," 7405, 7582, 7584, 7593, 7714, 7726.
Guitarrero Cave, Peru, 909.
Gunboat Diplomacy, 8003.

Hallucinogens, 508, 534, 1235, 1243, 1329, 1249, 1250, 1252, 1272, 1288, 1300, 1329, 1662, 8345, 8408, 8475, 8522.
Headhunting, 985, 1272.
Health Care, 1663, 6000, 8359. *See also* Public Health.
Henequen, 6744.
Herskovits, Melville J., 1131, 1137.
Heyerdahl, Thor, 6541, 6662.
Highways, *General*, 6888. *Argentina*, 2328, 2361. *Brazil*, 2480, 7023, 7032a, 7125, 7130. *Central America*, 1956, 1978. *Colombia*, 2073, 6911. *Ecuador*, 6936. *Peru*, 7704.
Hindus, Surinam, 1123.
History, *Caribbean*, 1155, 1158, 1161-2. *Education*, 6054, 6064, 6070-1, 6072, 6095, 6097, 6134, 6141-2, 6174, 6181, 6196, 6212, 6236, 6240, 6254, 6262, 6273, 6304. *Indians*, 1088. *Precolumbian*, 550, 761a, 778, 781, 876, 880-1, 885, 899, 924, 943, 966, 1004-6, 1145, 1630.
Hokan Language, 1634.
Housing, *General*, 6518. *Argentina*, 2369, 6786, 6804, 6836. *Brazil*, 7016, 7028, 8539, 8553. *Chile*, 2229. *Colombia*, 6901, 6903. *Credit*, 6903. *Mexico*, 6710, 6716. *Puerto Rico*, 1209, 2523. *See also* Slums, Urbanization.
Huaca Corpus I, Fundo Pando, Peru, 933, 934-5.
Huaca de tres Palos, Peru, 926, 932, 935, 978.
Huaca Dieciocho, Peru, 915, 977.
Huaca Facho, Peru, 939, 952.

Huaca La Luz, Peru, 978.
Huaca Palomino, Peru, 928.
Huacas de Pando, Peru, 978-80, 990-1.
Huancavélica, Peru, 510, 922.
Huari Culture, 957-9, 1013.
Huarpa, Peru, 916.
Huascarán, Peru, 6547.
Huave Language, 1588.
Huayopampa, Peru, 1401, 1421.
Huayrapampa, Bolivia, 1418.
Huichol Indians, 1050, 1051, 1059, 1090, 1100.
Huitoto Muinane. *See* Huitotoan Language.
Huitotoan Language, 1574, 1590.
Human Adaptation. *See* Demography.
Human Biology, 1653-6, 1738, 1742, 1747, 1750.
Humboldt, Alexander von, 6502, 6509, 6510, 6552, 6558, 6561, 6580.
Hungary in Latin America, 1213.

Iatê Language, 1572.
Iconography, 543, 546, 560, 575, 579, 589, 594, 599, 614, 667, 706, 712, 721, 723.
Ijca Indians, 1430.
Illegal Antiquities Traffic, 544, 545, 580, 595-6, 606, 622, 862.
Illiteracy. *See* Literacy and Illiteracy.
Imbabura, Ecuador, 6928.
Imperialism, 1819, 2246, 8005, 8016, 8024, 8041, 8046, 8056, 8128, 8162.
Imperio Huari, 510.
Import Capacity, 1800.
Import Substitution, 1787, 1977, 2037, 2079, 2157, 2446, 2456.
Incas, 512, 527, 921, 924, 926, 972, 997, 1006, 1013, 1316.
Income Distribution, 1794, 2082, 2122, 2159-60, 2164, 2233, 2240, 2304, 2380, 2404, 2408, 2437a, 2449, 2455, 2502, 2528, 6555, 8315, 8507.
Indentured Servitude, 1129.
Indian Power, 1402.
Indians. *See* specific groups.
Indians and Integration, 523, 1058, 1069, 1078, 1221, 1257, 1259, 1267, 1304, 1479, 8324, 8524.
Indigenismo, 8337.
Industry and Industrialization, *General*, 1080, 2336. *Argentina*, 2320-1, 2333, 2343-4, 2351-2, 2357-8, 2359-60, 2364, 2382, 2386, 2392, 2397, 2402-3, 2410, 6800. *Brazil*, 2416, 2431, 2436-7, 2443, 2458, 2464, 2472-4. *Development*, 1861, 6690. *Mexico*, 1080, 6710. *Precolumbian*, 759. *Puerto Rico*, 2487, 2507. *Training*, 6033.
Infant Mortality 1668, 1746.
Infections, 1672.
Inflation, *Argentina*, 2375, 2384-8, 2390, 2395. *Brazil*, 2446. *Chile*, 2228, 2255, 7766. *Colombia*, 2060, 2078, 2081.
Information Exchange, 6014.
Inga. *See* Quechuan Languages.
Intellectuals, 7436, 7509, 7804, 8267, 8288.

Inter-American Development Bank, 1798, 1827, 1829-30, 1899.
Inter-American Economic and Social Council, 8010.
Inter-American Foundation, 8095.
Inter-American Treaties and Conventions, 8061.
Internal Planning and Regional Organizations, 7835-6, 7844.
International Bank for Reconstruction and Development, 1831a, 1832.
International Coffee Agreement, 8022.
International Congress of Americanists, XXXIX, 510.
International Disputes, 8106, 8226-7, 8247.
International Finance Corporation, 1831a.
International Law, 8050, 8077, 8087, 8097, 8220-1.
International Petroleum Company, Peru, 2289.
Interpopulational Differentiation, 510.
Iron and Steel Industry, *General,* 6593, 6800, 6844, 7011. *Argentina,* 2374. *Bolivia,* 2174. *Brazil,* 2452-3. *Venezuela,* 2133.
Islas Malvinas, 6834.
Isolationism, 8059.
Italy in Latin America, 6583, 6748, 7093.
Itza Indians, 605.

Jagan, Cheddi, 7633.
Japan in Latin America, *Argentina,* 6806. *Brazil,* 2463, 2479, 7087, 8513, 8516. *Dominican Republic,* 1213, 6644. *Mexico,* 8121.
The *jeito,* Brazil, 7882.
Jê Languages, 1514, 1542, 1546, 1557, 1627, 1644, 1751.
Jesus de Machaca, Bolivia, 1338.
Jews in Latin America, 1168, 1169, 1178.
Jívaro Indians, 527, 1245, 1272, 1293, 1300, 1312-13, 1321.
Jivaroan Languages, 1600.
Joint Venture Firms, 1845.
Juárez, Benito, 6718.
Judicial and Legal Matters, 7505, 7539, 7688, 7882.
Junta Nacional de Auxilio Escolar y Becas, Chile, 6109.
Juruna Indians, 1301.
Justicialismo. *See* Perón and Peronism.
Kaingáng Indians, 1334.
Kaiwa. *See* Tupí-Guaraní Languages.
Karisiri. *See* Monsters.
Kaxuyana Indians, 1260.
Kayabi Indians, 1269, 1270-1.
Kayapo Indians, 1226, 1292, 1293, 1316, 1325. *See also* Gê Indians.
Kekchian. *See* Maya Languages.
Kickapoo Indians, 1637.
Kidnaping, 7519.
Kinship, 535, 1108, 1117, 1269, 1272, 1276-7, 1285, 1301, 1316, 1323, 1339, 1352, 1361, 1362, 1375, 1391, 1394, 1410, 1422, 1442, 1504, 1548, 1616, 1745.
Kofan, 510.
Kotosh, Peru, 954, 960-1, 963.
Kraho Indians, 1292, 1295-6, 1315. *See also* Gê Indians.
Krikití Indians, 1281, 1292. *See also* Gê Indians.
Kukulcan, 553.
Kuna Indians, 1061, 1109.

Labor, *General,* 6555, 7398, 8075-6, 8258, 8263. *Argentina,* 2362, 2400, 2404, 6840, 7946, 7972, 7986-8. *Bolivia,* 2171, 7722-4. *Braceros,* 8112. *Brazil,* 2415, 2443, 2460, 7091, 7850a, 7877. *Caribbean,* 5525, 8372, 8382. *Central America,* 1962, 8340-1. *Chile,* 2199, 2218-20, 2253, 7733, 7735, 8458. *Colombia,* 2051-2, 2056-7, 2066-7. *Cuba,* 7592. *Dominican Republic,* 7617. *Ecuador,* 1374, 2088. *Employment,* 1083-4, 1137, 1785, 1799, 1858, 1930, 2009, 2041, 2051-2, 2054, 2066, 2125, 2135, 2378, 2493, 2524-5, 6555, 6594, 6604. *Guyana,* 2110. *International,* 8119. *Management,* 7501, 7839. *Mexico,* 1910, 1923, 1925, 1929-30, 8307. *Paraguay,* 8440. *Peru,* 2271, 2275, 2280, 2285, 2293. *Puerto Rico,* 2493, 2512, 2520-1, 2524-5. *Technology,* 2303, 2362, 2364-6, 2371, 2437, 8523. *Trinidad,* 1129. *Unions,* 1923, 7389, 7507, 7722-3, 7680, 7972, 8118-9, 8396. *Uruguay,* 2317. *Venezuela,* 8453. *Wages,* 2120, 2205, 7143.
Lacandon Indians, 573, 605, 1034, 1102.
Ladinos, 6697.
Lake Titicaca, 6845, 6852.
Lambayeque, Peru, 1508.
Land Development, 6846.
Land Reform. *See* Agrarian Reform.
Land Tenure. *See* Agrarian Reform.
Land Tenure (Indians), 1072.
Land Use, 6570.
Language, *Brazil,* 1545, 1548, 8509. *Comparative Studies,* 1586-7, 1601, 1603, 1624-5, 1643. *Grammar,* 1532, 1581, 1611. *Guatemala,* 1622. *The Guianas,* 1543. *Labor,* 6840. *Linguistics,* 1584. *Maps,* 1530. *Morphology,* 1588, 1635. *Morphonemics,* 1526, 1570. *Morphophonology,* 1552, 1579. *Panama,* 1564. *Phonemes,* 1567-9, 1572, 1575, 1582, 1594, 1612, 1613, 1635, 1638, 1640a. *Phonology,* 1528, 1537-9, 1556, 1562, 1566-8, 1579, 1596, 1599, 1605, 1610, 1615, 1626, 1633, 1640, 1640a, 1641, 1644. *Semantics,* 1526, 1577, 1616. *Semology,* 1636. *Uruguay,* 1612. *Vocabulary,* 1525. Languages listed individually.
Language Zones, 1523.
Latifundio, 510, 6999, 7129, 7901.
Latin America, 6553, 6591, 6593, 6612.
Latin American Free Trade Area, 1818, 1828, 1875, 8013.

Latin American Nuclear Free Zone, 8049, 8088, 8098, 8173, 8195.
Latin American Relations, 8014, 8017, 8019-20, 8028-30, 8031, 8034-35, 8051, 8068-71, 8073, 8102, 8104, 8106, 8159, 8163, 8186, 8243.
Latin American Studies, 6006-7, 6067-8.
Leeward Islands, 8168.
Legislatures, 7354, 7535, 7563, 7727, 7767b, 7791, 7831, 7855.
Leninism, 2018, 7382, 7425, 7715, 8174.
Lerma-Santiago River Basin, Mexico, 1939.
Lima, 6956.
Linear Programming Model, 1809, 1874.
Linguistics. *See* Language.
Literacy and Illiteracy, 6088, 6191.
Literature, *Precolumbian*, 550, 1102.
Llanos Occidentales, Venezuela 6973, 6976-6978.
Lleras Restrepo, Carlos, 7648, 7658.
López Michelsen, Alfonso, 7660.

Machiguenga Indians, 1233.
Machismo, 1096, 1446, 8385.
Machu Picchu, 514.
Macroeconomics, 1803, 2061, 2162.
Makiritare Indians. *See* Yekuana Indians.
Malargüe, Argentina, 1336-7.
Manifest Destiny, 8065, 8162.
Mantaro, Peru, 919.
Maps, *Agricultural*, 7230, 7232, 7256-8, 7284. *Amerindian Reservations*, 7304. *Archaeological*, 7217. *Atlases*, 7205, 7216, 7222, 7229, 7237, 7269, 7281, 7285, 7300, 7306, 7346. *Bathymetric*, 7213. *Demographic*, 7221, 7227, 7243-4, 7313. *Descriptions*, 7207-8. *Fisheries*, 7232. *Historical*, 7282, 7312, 7345. *Indexes*, 7193, 7195-6, 7198-7202, 7287, 7292, 7309, 7311, 7338, 7340, 7348, 7349, 7351. *Minerals*, 7233-5, 7344. *Orthographic Projection*, 7254-5. *Physical*, 7242, 7251-3. *Soils and Vegetation*, 7212, 7218, 7260, 7299, 7323, 7328. *Tectonic*, 7246. *Thematic*, 7215, 7266, 7285, 7315. *Transparencies*, 7211.
Mapuche Indians, 510, 1393, 1407, 1482, 1493.
Mar de Cortés, 8111.
Marginality, 1882-3, 2113-4, 2118, 8284, 8442, 8494, 8504, 8508.
Mariátegui, José Carlos, 7677, 7696.
Marine Biology, 6707.
Maritime Policy, 7849, 7995.
Marketing and Product Distribution, *General*, 6599, 6980. *Brazil*, 2451, 2480. *Indian Communities*, 1114, 1401, 1405, 1416. *Puerto Rico*, 2529.
Marriage, 1038, 1365, 1456, 1650, 8298, 8383.
Martinique, 6618, 6619.
Marxism, 2018, 7391, 7579, 7716, 7735a, 7738, 7739, 7742, 7746, 7905, 8206.
Mass Communications, 8250-1, 8310, 8464, 8493, 8512, 8520, 8548.
Mataco Languages, 1596.

Mato Grosso, Brazil, 7152, 7172, 7182, 7187.
Maxakalí Language, 1604.
Maya Languages, 1511, 1513, 1518, 1524, 1534, 1536, 1541, 1548-50, 1560, 1563, 1565-6, 1580, 1597, 1618, 1624-5, 1629, 1628-9.
Mayas, *Ancient*, 510, 514, 527, 558, 561, 586-7, 600, 611, 618, 621, 623, 677, 698, 716, 719-20, 722-3, 726-9, 731, 733-6, 1043, 1048, 1063, 1079, 1086, 6732. *Living*, 510, 1081, 1086, 1105, 1111-2, 6736.
Mayo Indians, 1103.
Meat and Meatpacking Industry, 2333, 2353.
Médici, Emílio Garrastazu, 7837, 7861.
Medicine, *Etiology and Medical Care*, 1170, 1437, 1485, 8273. *Folk*, 8350. *Hypoglycemia*, 1354. *Medical Practice*, 8321, 8544. *Missionaries*, 1212. *Popular*, 1457. *Precolumbian*, 534, 674, 1063, 1075, 1359.
Mendoza, Arg., 6823.
Mennonites, 6753, 7008.
Merchant Marines, 2409.
Mestizos and Mestizoization, 510, 1058, 1402, 1406, 1438, 1445, 1449, 1455, 1473, 1501, 1736, 1744, 8327.
Metalworking, 520, 522, 634, 860, 863, 865, 867, 920, 925, 935, 946, 1091, 2157.
Methodology, *Anthropology*, 578, 588, 973. *Archaeology*, 502-3, 525, 538, 597, 607, 691, 758, 760, 764, 884. *Demography*, 1743. *Economics*, 1782, 1787, 1792, 1828, 2200, 2211-2, 2351, 2360. *Education*, 6066, 6115, 6234, 6276. *Ethnology*, 1037, 1413, 1499, 1500. *Geography*, 6009, 6574, 6598, 7031, 7059-60, 7069, 7074, 7094. *Political Science*, 7365, 7439, 7474, 7478, 7482, 7545, 7651, 7661, 7842, 7847, 7862, 7964. *Sociology*, 8256-7, 8353, 8360. *See also* Research.
Mexican Revolution, 1080, 7512, 7525, 7541.
Mexico and Japan, 8121.
Mexico and the OAS, 8117.
Mexico and the UN, 8109, 8115-6.
Mexico and the US, 8108, 8113, 8123, 8125-6.
Mexico City, 1913, 1917.
Migration, *International*, 1974, 2406. *Puerto Rico*, 2501. *Seasonal*, 1336. *Trans-Oceanic*, 507, 511, 588, 1725.
Military and Militarism. *See* Armed Forces.
Milpa System, 1111.
Minifundismo, 1047, 1931, 2198.
Minimum Wage Law, 2502.
Mining, *General*, 1814, 6569. *Brazil*, 7024-5. *Chile*, 6855, 6877. *Colonial*, 501. *Peru*, 2296. *Precolumbian*, 501, 510, 681, 762, 890, 920. *Venezuela*, 6981.
Minnesota Multiphasic Personality Inventory, 8319.
Minorities, 6595.
Misiones, Arg., 6824.
Miskito Indians, 510, 1054, 1082.
Missile Crisis, Cuban, 7605.
Missionaries, 1232, 1259, 1411, 1447.

Mitla, Oaxaca, Mexico, 664.
Mixe-Zoquean Language, 1559.
Mochica Culture, 916a, 939, 956.
Moctezuma, 649.
Modern Man, 1656.
Molina, Juan Ignacio, 6871.
Mollusks, 551, 769, 822, 1223,
Moncada Fortress, Cuba, 7596.
Money, *Precolumbian,* 531, 616.
Money and Banking. *See* Banking and Commerce.
The Monroe Doctrine, 7994.
Monsters, 1436.
Monte Alban, Mexico, 510, 626, 717, 923.
Montevideo, Treaty of, 7996.
Mopán. *See* Maya Languages.
Morbidity and Mortality Patterns and Rates, 8304.
Morley, Sylvanus G., 541, 581.
Morphology. *See* Language.
Morphonemics. *See* Language.
Morphophonology. *See* Language.
Most Favored Nation Agreements, 1875, 7996.
Motilone Indians. *See* Bari Indians.
Moussy, Martín de, 7205.
Movimento Democrático Brasileiro, 7843.
Movimiento Nacional Revolucionario, Bolivia, 7708, 7716, 7719, 7725.
Muinane. *See* Huitotoan Language.
Multi-national Corporations, 1775, 1808, 1814, 1825, 1876, 1881, 1889, 2463, 7492.
Multi-National Resources. *See* Economic Development.
Munduruku. *See* Tupí Languages.
Muricy, Antônio Carlos da Silva, 7865.
Music, *General,* 1118, 1144, 1159. *Precolumbian,* 510, 564-5, 678, 695, 879.
Mythology, 510, 1035, 1051, 1063, 1094, 1231, 1236, 1268, 1276, 1302, 1311, 1327-8, 1353, 1426, 1430, 1450-2, 1461, 1481, 1591, 1630.

Nahuat Languages, 1046, 1064, 1518, 1561, 1571, 1611, 1650-1.
Nambikwara Indians, 1263.
Nambiquara. *See* Jê Languages.
Naqaq. *See* Monsters.
Nasserism, 7496, 7700a.
National Parks, *Argentina,* 6807. *Brazil,* 1271, 1328, 7171, 7186. *Central America,* 6660. *Costa Rica,* 6660. *Guatemala,* 6660. *Mexico,* 6660. *Nicaragua,* 6660.
National Party, Uruguay, 7904.
Nationalism, *General,* 1846, 7495, 7620, 7711, 7725, 7700, 7871, 7947, 7956, 8034. *Mexico,* 1924, 8328. *Peru,* 2297.
Natural Resources. *See* Geography.
Naupas, Peru, 948.
Nazcas, 514, 975, 985, 1002, 1013.
Negro in Latin America, 624, 8257.
Neolithic Revolution, 504.
Newspapers. *See* Press.

Nicaragua and the US, 8144, 8146.
Nitrate, 6857, 6890.
Noanama Indians, 1477.
Nóbrega, Manoel da, 6287.
Nomatsiguenga Language, 1645, 1648.
Northeast, Brazil, 2420, 2443, 2464, 2466, 2480, 6226, 7018, 7066, 7097, 7106, 7112, 7114, 7117, 7119, 7133, 7174, 7175-6, 7181, 7184, 7261, 7267, 7868, 8479, 8501.
Nutrition, *General,* 1680, 1687, 1697, 1705-6, 6010, 6532, 6538, 6544, 6550, 6555, 6573. *Argentina,* 1701. *Brazil,* 1678, 1683, 1698, 7026, 7128, 7139, 7160. *Chile,* 1700. *Costa Rica,* 1691. *Guatemala,* 1696, 1702. *Haiti,* 1685. *Honduras,* 1690. *Mexico,* 1703. *Precolumbian,* 536, 547, 585, 697, 984, 1223. *Puerto Rico,* 1689.

Oaxaca, Mexico, 6715.
Ocaina. *See* Huitotoan Language.
Occupational Mobility. *See* Demography.
Ocobamba, Peru, 1431.
Oil Industry. *See* Petroleum Industry.
Olivera, Mercedes, 1095.
Olmecs, 542, 543, 554, 557, 559, 560, 562a, 567, 575, 600, 620, 630, 635, 640, 647-8, 660, 665, 708.
Omacatl, 666.
Omagua Indians, 1293.
Ometeotl, 667.
Ona Indians, 1236, 1280, 1305.
Opinion Surveys, 8411.
Organization of American States, 1857, 6048, 7997, 8055-6, 8063, 8117, 8218.
Organization of Central American States, 1957, 8132.
Organization of Petroleum Exporting Countries, 1891, 2119.
Orinoco River, 6565.
Ornithology, 6706, 6723, 6726.
Oruro, Bolivia, 6857.
Otavalo Indians, 1506.
Otomi Indians, 1042, 1060.
Otomi Juez, 8297.
Otomí Language, 1556, 1636.
Oyampik Indians, 1222.
Oztoticpac Map, 7192.

Pachacamac, Peru, 962.
Padilla, Heberto, 7570.
El Paisaje, Peru, 986.
Paleoanthropology and Osteology, *Dental Practices and Traits,* 1723, 1726. *Femoral Characteristics,* 1720. *Skulls and Skeletal Remains,* 1721, 1724, 1728, 1730.
Palikur. *See* Arawakan Languages.
La Pampa (Prov.), Arg., 764-5, 6819, 6825, 6840.
Pan American Institute of Geography and History Reports, 6524, 6578.
Panajachel, 1106.
Panama Canal, 8134, 8138, 8147.

Panare Indians, 1254.
Papabuco Language, 1610.
Papago. *See* Uto-Aztecan Languages.
Papaloapan River Basin, 6714.
Paracas, Peru, 927.
Paraíba, Brazil, 7124.
Parana River Basin, 6764.
Parasites, *Trypanosome*, 1681.
Parintitín. *See* Tupí-Guaraní Languages.
Parties, Political. *See* Political Organization.
Patagonia, Arg., 2337, 6826.
Patamona Indians, 1241.
Payaguá Indians, 830.
Peasants, *General*, 1153, 1374, 6560, 6840, 8434. *Argentina*, 7942. *Bolivia*, 1363, 1378, 1418. *Brazil*, 7869. *Caribbean*, 8364, 8389. *Central America*, 1973, 1976. *Chile*, 2182, 2224, 7764, 7771, 7785. *Colombia*, 1388, 2064, 6905, 7644. *Cuba*, 7599. *Ecuador*, 1363, 1374, 7672. *Honduras*, 6699. *Mexico*, 1940, 1944, 7500, 7518, 7528a, 8301. *Organization*, 2182, 7416, 7500, 7599, 7644, 7646, 7672, 7678, 8259, 8270. *Peru*, 1395, 1435, 1444, 1501, 6951, 6954, 7678, 7703, 8447.
Peba-Yaguan Languages, 1605.
Peçanha, Nilo, 6269.
Pediatrics, 1665, 1686, 1692-3.
Pehuenche Indians, 1337.
Pentecostal Church, 8498.
Per Capita Income, 1848, 2000, 2122, 2159-60, 2164, 2206.
Pérez Jiménez, Marcos, 7796, 7806, 7809, 7829.
Perón and Peronismo, 7932-4, 7935, 7938, 7943-4, 7946a, 7951-2, 7959, 7961, 7962, 7966-8, 7970-1, 7975-7, 7981, 7985-6, 7989.
Peruvian Revolution, 2274, 2298, 2300, 7717, 7677, 7681, 7683, 7687, 7689-90, 7692, 7702, 7705, 7707, 7778.
Peten, Guatemala, 716, 6696.
Petkoff, Teodoro, 7404.
Petroleum Industry, *General*, 1783, 1891. *Bolivia*, 7709. *Brazil*, 2427, 2465. *Colombia*, 7670. *Curação*, 6639. *Peru*, 2289, 2298. *Teheran Agreement*, 1780. *Trinidad and Tobago*, 2023. *Venezuela*, 2119, 2130, 2134, 2141-3, 2148, 2153.
Pharmaceutical Industry, 2069.
Phonemes. *See* Language.
Phonology. *See* Language.
Photointerpretation, 655, 6567.
Plantations, 1126, 1786, 1904, 1988, 2503, 7564.
Plants and Forests. *See* Ecology, Flora and Fauna.
Policy Making. *See* Political Organization.
Political Development, 7763, 7921-2, 7945.
Political Ideologies and Philosophies, 7910.
Political Instability, 7445.
Political Integration, 7628-9.
Political Models, 7379, 7399, 7419, 7426, 7475, 7545, 7560, 7736, 7651, 7691, 7706, 7838, 7862, 7946b, 7963.

Political Organization, *Bolivia*, 2176. *Brazil*, 7883, 7885-6, 7890, 8476, 8497. *Caribbean*, 1143, 1148, 1179, 1193, 1194, 1202, 1214. *Indian Communities*, 1101, 1107, 1110, 1224, 1227, 1258, 1347, 1355-8, 1360, 1402, 1471, 1507. *Mesoamerica*, 587. *Mexico*, 7508-9. *Parties*, 7356, 7358, 7371, 7383, 7431, 7438, 7450, 7502, 7504, 7517, 7524, 7528, 7534, 7546, 7708, 7716, 7718-9, 7643, 7650, 7657a, 7666, 7771-2, 7775, 7818, 7826, 7834, 7917, 7948. *Power Structures and Policy Making*, 7381, 7493, 7526-7, 7529-31, 7690, 7692, 7783, 7816, 7834, 7846, 7885, 7896, 7920, 7929, 7931, 7962, 7973. *Puerto Rico*, 2515, 2519. *South America*, 1348-9, 1350, 1421, 1423, 1429.
Political Parties. *See* Political Organization.
Political Traditions 7728, 7896, 7899.
Politics and Armed Forces, 7417, 7739, 7671, 7681, 7683, 7685, 7687, 7705, 7707, 7821, 7858, 7918, 7926-8, 7956, 7969, 7971.
Pollution. *See* Ecology.
Population. *See* Demography, Urbanization.
Population Structure. *See* Demography.
Population Studies. *See* Demography.
Populism, 1860, 7852, 7968.
Porfiriato, 7512.
Post Industrial Societies, 1778.
Power Structures. *See* Political Organization.
Prebisch, Raúl, 1854, 1870, 1878.
Preferential Trade Agreements. *See* Tariffs and Protection.
Prehistory. *See* Early Man.
The Press, 7510, 7776, 7808, 7820, 7833, 7953, 8157.
Pressure Groups, 7543.
Price Stabilization. *See* Fiscal Policy.
Pricing Controls and Structures, 1787, 2354.
Private Enterprise, *Argentina*, 2329. *Bolivia*, 2170. *Brazil*, 2418, 2423.
Profit Sharing, 2400.
Proto Chibchan Languages, 1643.
Proto Guahiban Languages, 1520.
Proto-Yucatec. *See* Maya Languages.
Proyecto Andino de Estudios Arqueológicos, 912.
Psychology Studies, 1119, 1182-3, 1187, 8248-9, 8536.
Public Administration, 2163, 7423, 7494, 7513, 7522, 7532, 7562, 7786, 8480.
Public Finance, 2041, 2121, 2376, 7847.
Public Health, *General*, 1657, 1661, 6010, 6023, 6111. *Brazil*, 8478. *Honduras*, 8359. *Mexico*, 6744. *Puerto Rico*, 2514.
Public Opinion, 8392.
Public Relations, 7867, 8280.
Pucara Culture, 944, 976.
Puerto Rican Status, 7623, 7624-6.
Puerto Suárez, Bolivia, 6844.
Pulp and Paper Industry, 7000.

Q'ero, Peru, 1456, 1503-5.

Quechua Languages, 1515, 1528, 1544, 1554, 1573, 1576, 1598, 1607-9, 1617.
Quechua Indians, 1419, 1425, 1503-4.
Quetzalcoatl, 602, 690.
Quibdo, Colombia, 1486.
Quichean. *See* Maya Languages.
Quichua Indians, 1361.
Quimbaya, Cultura, 862-5.
Quipus, 913.
El Quishihuar (Arbol de Dios), 1468.

Race and Race Relations, 1122, 1131, 1138-9, 1141, 1151, 1152, 1155, 1160, 1177-80, 1184, 1194, 1196, 1206, 7630, 7635, 8294, 8314, 8361, 8372, 8382, 8541.
Radiosonde Observation, 6851, 7163.
Railroads, *Argentina*, 2328, 2350, 2398-9. *Chile*, 6857. *Mexico*, 1923. *Nicaragua*, 6703.
Ramkokamekra Indians. *See* Canela Indians.
Recife, Brazil, 7189.
Regional Planning. *See* Economic Development.
Regionalism, 8034.
Religion, *General*, 1044, 1081, 1085-6, 1112, 1230, 1241, 1244, 1258, 1310-1, 6547. *Ancestor Worship*, 1253, 1306. *Baptists*, 1133. *Batuque*, 1282. *Burial Customs*, 672, 766-7, 1353, 1420. *Candomblé*, 1244. *Caribbean*, 1142, 1167, 1171, 1173-4, 1183, 1186, 1198, 1208, 1215, 8377, 8380, 8381.
Catholicism, see Catholic Church. *Cult of Death*, 592, 610, 633. *Cult of Egun*, 1253, 1306. *Cult of Maria Lionza*, 1307. *Cult of Tezcatlipoca*, 624, 666. *Cult of Wamani*, 1394, 1400, 1476. *Cult of Xipe Totec*, 599, 645, 1063. *Hallelujah*, 1241. *Messianic*, 1314-5. *Pentecostalism*, 1396.
Precolumbian, 543, 550, 553, 559, 563, 578, 583, 592, 594, 599, 601, 638, 666, 677, 690, 694, 697, 704, 712, 714-5, 718-20, 722-3, 725, 733-4, 736, 755, 808, 811, 812-3, 821, 865-6, 915, 972, 981, 1013, 1016, 1039-40, 1050-1, 1057, 1060, 1063. *Protestantism*, 8316. *Quichua*, 1409. *Revivals*, 1133. *Political and Social Change*, 7392, 7427, 7429-30, 7432, 7978. *South America*, 1340, 1425, 1441, 1447, 1453-4, 1475, 8427, 8454. *Spiritualism and Spiritual Cults*, 1171, 1244, 1282, 8527.
Research, *Agriculture*, 6511, 6514. *Anthropology*, 517a, 518. *Geography*, 6505, 6515, 6526. *Social Sciences*, 1797, 8300. *Space*, 7400. *See also* Methodology.
Reventazon Basin, 6681.
Revolutionary Movements, 7360, 7362, 7364, 7410, 7412, 7440, 7443, 7470, 7471, 7487-8, 7609, 7637, 7778, 7811, 7894, 7946b, 7983, 7992, 8048, 8052, 8057.
Ricardo, Cassiano, 8517.
Río Bueno, Chile, 6854.
Rio de Janeiro, 7163-4.
Río Nechí, Colombia, 6922.

Río Negro, Arg., 6827.
Río Valdivia, Chile, 6854.
River Basins. *See* specific river.
River Plate Basin, 1867, 6565, 6766, 6767, 6771, 6774-5, 6817, 7428, 8197, 8200, 8211.
Rondon, O Projeto, 7137.
Rondônia, Brazil, 7153.
Ruggiero, Juan, 7949.
Rural Development, 1784-5, 8426, 8450.
Rural Education, 6047, 6098, 6145, 6157, 6168, 6173, 6191-2.
Rural-urban Mobility. *See* Demography.

Sáliva Indians, 1298.
San Agustín, Cultura, 869, 871.
San Cipriano, P. R., 8386.
San Ildefonso, Treaty of, 7204.
San Martín, Peru, 6950.
San Rafael, Arg., 6803.
Sánchez Hernández, Fidel, 7551.
Santa Cruz, Arg., 6828.
Santa Cruz, Bolivia, 6844.
Santamariana Culture, 767.
Santiago del Estero, Arg., 6804.
Santo Domingo de los Colorados, Ecuador, 6938.
Santos, Brazil, 7002, 7159.
São João da Boa Vista, Brazil, 6988.
São Paulo, 7028, 7082, 7093, 7094, 7095, 7098, 7157-8, 7160-1, 7166.
São Vincente, Brazil, 7159.
Satellite Triangulation, 6543.
Savings, 2081.
Scalabrini Ortiz, Raúl, 7947.
Science and Technology, *General*, 1863, 1890, 1901, 6011-2, 6014, 6026, 6051, 6158, 6161, 6177, 6187, 6247, 6281, 7413, 7469, 7747. *Argentina*, 2391. *Colombia*, 2048-9. *Mexico*, 1920. *Transfer*, 1850, 2048, 2095.
Sechín, Peru, 923.
Sectoral Elasticities, *Labor/Capital*, 2190, 2275, 2379.
Securities Market, 1844, 1912.
Seismology, 699, 1466, 6547, 6682.
Selk'nam Indians. *See* Ona Indians.
Selknam Language, 1595.
Selvas Occidentales, 774.
Semantics. *See* Language.
Semitism and Antisemitism, 7991.
Semology. *See* Language.
Sergipe, Brazil, 7162.
Seri Indians, 1074.
Serological Studies, 1658, 1660, 1666, 1767.
Serranía del Mutún, Bolivia, 6844.
Sex and Sexual Relations, *General*, 1331, 1337, 1463. *Caribbean*, 1150, 1167, 1190, 8391. *Precolumbian*, 667, 723, 1035, 1081. *South America*, 8409, 8431-2, 8469, 8534-5. *See also* Family Planning.
Shamanism. *See* Witchcraft.
Shavante Indians, 1292. *See also* Gê Indian.

Shell Middens, 769, 822, 826, 836-7, 842, 850-1, 902, 906, 936.
Sherente Indians, 1292. See also Gê Indians.
Shillacoto, Huánuco, Peru, 510, 961, 963.
Ship Building Industry, 2394.
Shuar. See Jivaroan Languages.
Shuar Indians. See Jívaro Indians.
Sierras de Acegua, Cerro Largo, Uruguay, 1014.
SINAMOS (Sistema Nacional de Apoyo a la Movilización Social), 7673.
Sindicalism, 1348-9, 1374. See also Labor.
Sino-Latin American Relations, 8039-40, 8064.
Sirionó Indians, 1293, 1316, 1616.
Slavery and Slave Trade, 1136, 1138, 1156-7, 1159, 2103.
Slums, *General*, 6518. *Argentina*, 6807, 8451. *Colombia*, 6901, 6921. *Peru*, 1251, 1371, 6952, 7674. See also Housing, Urbanization.
Snuff. See Hallucinogens.
Soccer. See Fútbol.
Soccer War, 7550, 8127, 8136, 8139, 8142, 8149.
Social Democratic Parties, 7369, 7544, 7756.
Social Development and Planning, 1830, 7411, 7453, 8252, 8271-2, 8274, 8282, 8375, 8397, 8400-1, 8458, 8485.
Social Mobility, 8537, 8554. See also Class Structure.
Social Organization and Politics, 8255.
Social Progress Trust Fund, 1830.
Social Security, 2185.
Social Status, 8469, 8549. See also Class Structure.
Socialism, 1805, 2189, 2215, 2239, 2241-3, 2252, 2256, 7452, 7572, 7576, 7598, 7606, 7708, 7730, 7735a, 7743-4, 7652-3, 7687, 7767a, 7772, 7780, 7787, 7814, 8046.
Socialist Parties, 7757.
Sociedad Mexicana de Geografía y Estadística, 6718.
Sociedad Nacional de Agricultura, Chile, 2196.
Sociology, *History*, 8275.
Sociology of Power, 8277.
Sociology of War, 8276.
South Georgia Islands, 6762.
Sovereignty, 7363.
Soviet-Latin American Relations, 7999, 8009, 8011, 8074, 8086, 8107, 8177.
Spain in Latin America, 1213.
Spanish-Latin American Relations, 8082.
Sports, 8518.
Squatters, 1371.
Squier, Ephraim George, 7197.
Statistics, 1789, 1802, 1873, 1877, 1991, 1994, 2029, 2065, 2124, 2407, 2439-40, 8334.
Students, *Activism*, 6162, 6183, 7460, 7483-4, 7517, 7520, 7523, 7533, 7537-8, 7547, 7558, 7608. *Alienation*, 8415. *Financial Assistance*, 6109, 6122. See also, Universities.

Subsistence Economies, 8339.
Subversion and Development, 7395, 7724, 7645, 7939, 8062.
Sugar Diplomacy, 7607, 8156.
Swidden Cultivation. See Ecology.

Tablada de Lurín, *Peru*, 927, 929-930, 941, 950-951, 987, 989-990, 1008
Taboo systems, 1247, 1276
Tairona Indians, 1024
El Tajín, 671
Támesis, *Colombia*, 1387
Tangor, *Peru*, 1443-1444
Tanoan languages, 1633
Tapajós Indians, 1293
Tapirape Indians, 1225
Taraco, *Peru*, 1438
Tarahumara. See Uto-Axtecan languages.
Tarahumara Indians, 1052, 1066-1068, 1087
Taraqueño Indians, 1438
Tarascans, 1031, 1039-1040, 6743, *Languages*, 1535, 1537-1538
Tariffs and trade protection, 1782, 1787, 1835, 1874a, 1896-1897, 2345, 8013
Tastil, *Salta, Arg.*, 769a
Tataltepec. See Zapotecan language.
Taurodontism, 6895
Taxation, *general*, 1843, 1848, *Argentina*, 2346, 2349, 2369-2370, 2408, *Brazil*, 7020, *Caribbean*, 2015, *Colombia*, 2046-2047, 2050, *Jamaica*, 1998, *Paraguay*, 2263, *Puerto Rico*, 2507, *reform*, 1801, 2080, *sales*, 1953, 2194, *Venezuela*, 2149, 2151
Teaching techniques, 6022, 6030, 6044, 6107, 6190
Tehuacan Valley, 585
Tehuantepec, Isthmus of, 1942
Tehuelche Indians, 1234
Television, 8335, 8444, 8459
Temuco, *Chile*, 6870
Tenochtitlan, 688, 7312
Teotihuacan, 510, 549, 574, 594, 676, 693, 696, 706, 708-710
Tepehuan Indians, 1059, 1087
Territorial waters, *general*, 6608, 8013, 8037, 8072, 8077, 8085, 8087, 8097, 8111, 8242, *Venezuela*, 6961
Terrorism, 7360, 7433, 7554-7555
Texcoco, *Mexico*, 691
Theater, *West Indies*, 1120
Third World, 1876, 1878, 6522, 6538, 6542, 7385, 7978
Tiahuanaco, *Bolivia*, 808, 810-811, 813-818, 820
Ticul, *Yucatan, Mex.*, 1108
Tikal, 535, 730
Timbira Indians, 1281
Tin industry, 2180
Tiquimani, *Bolivia*, 6849
Tiriyo Indians. See Trio Indians.

Tlaloc, 666
Tlatelolco, Treaty of, 8088, 8098. *See also* Disarmament and Latin American Nuclear Free Zone.
Tlatilco, 510, 670
Toba Indians, 1227
Toltecs, 549, 613, 686
Topa Inca Yupanqui, 910
Torre, Antonio de la, 6923
Torres, Camilo, 7430, 7587, 7636, 7649, 7654, 7656-7657, 8282
Torres Bodet, Jaime, 6150
Totonac Indians, 1063, *language*, 1583
Tourism, *general*, 1957, 6568, 6622, 6624, 6639, 6645, 6689, 6733, 6785, 6826, *Argentina*, 6785, 6826, *Mexico*, 1935, *Puerto Rico*, 2491, *Surinam*, 2104
Tourtellot and Sabloff Hypothesis, 538
Tovar, *Venezuela*, 6970
Trade, *agricultural*, 6501, 6544, 6546, 6641, *Argentina*, 2328, 2398, 6786, 6798, 6817, 6820, *Brazil*, 2430, 2436, 2456, 2460, 2472-2473, 2475, 7002, *Canada*, 8110, *Chile*, 2195, 2213, 2227, *Colombia*, 2059, *Curaçao*, 6638, *Dominican Republic*, 6644, *Ecuador*, 2085, 2087, 2089-2090, *exports and imports*, 1840, 1970, 1977, 1983, 2043-2044, 2079, *international*, 1840, 1862, 1874a, 1878, 1895, 1994, *Mexico*, 1907, 1921, 1932, 1934, 1947 *Panama*, 1966, *Paraguay*, 2266, *precolumbian*, 542, 549, 611, 616, 790, 890, *Puerto Rico*, 2490, 2522, *US-Latin American*, 1896, 8043, *Venezuela*, 2132, 6975, *Virgin Islands*, 2522
Transoceanic migration. *See* migration.
Transportation, *general*, 6540, 6661, 6705, *Argentina*, 2328, 2398, 6786, 6798, 6817, 6820, *Brazil*, 2480, 6993, 7071-7072, 7075, 7082, 7094-7095, 7158, *Colombia*, 2073, 6911, *Ecuador*, 6936, *Nicaragua*, 6703, *Paraguay*, 2266, *Peru*, 2272, *precolumbian*, 991, *Puerto Rico*, 2498, *Venezuela*, 6965, 8445
Travel, *general*, 6502, 6513, 6552, 6558, 6580, 6629, 6662, *Argentina*, 6513, 6833, *Barbados*, 6504, *Bolivia*, 6778, 6845, 6849, *Brazil*, 6513, 6778, 7070, 7089, 7105, 7190, *Central America*, 6661, 6702, *Chile*, 6779, *Colombia*, 6552, 6778, 6923, *Cuba*, 6552, 6636, *Dominican Republic*, 6645, *Ecuador*, 6778, 6933, *Jamaica*, 6504, *Mesoamerica*, 1079, *Mexico*, 6711, 6715, 6732, 6742, 6750-6751, 6754, *Paraguay*, 6778, *Peru*, 6778-6779, *precolumbian*, 6541, 6662, *South America*, 6768-6769, 6778, *Uruguay*, 6513, *Venezuela*, 6552, *West Indies*, 6504, 6552, 6620, 6622, 6627, 6629, 6631, 6633-6634
Treaties. *See* Name of treaty.
Trepanation, 514, 821, 1725, 1727
Trio Indians, 1202, 1259
Triticum timopheevi, Zhuk, 6760

Trotskyism, 7359
Trujillo, *Venezuela*, 1016
Trujillo Molina, Rafael Leonidas, 7614, 7616, 8165
Tucano. *See* Eastern Tucanoan languages.
Tucumán, *Arg.*, 6829-6830
Tukano Indians, 1315
Tumaco, culture, 866
Tupamaros, 7907, 7909, 7912-7915, 7917
Tupí language, 510, 1521, 1527, 1529
Tupiguarani Indians, 763, 830, 835, 844-846, 848, 857, *languages*, 1509-1510, 1552-1553, 1575, 1599, 1601
Tzeltal. *See* Maya Languages.
Tzeltal Indians, 1101
Tzibanche, *Mexico*, 659
Tzotzil. *See* Maya languages.
Tzotzil Indians, 1102

UN-Latin American relations, 8078-8079, 8202
UNCTAD, 1854, 2201
US and Germany in Latin America, 8084
US-Latin American relations, 1821, 1831, 1896, 1898, 8000-8003, 8005, 8008, 8015-8016, 8018, 8021, 8023, 8025-8028, 8032, 8038, 8041-8044, 8052-8053, 8057, 8066, 8080-8081, 8083, 8085, 8089, 8099, 8101, 8129, 8134, 8152, 8158
USSR in Latin America, 8044, 8207
United Fruit Company, 6672
United Kingdom and Latin America, 1895, 8199
United States Geological Survey-International Decade of Ocean Exploration, Yucatan, 6632,
Universities, *general*, 1817, 6017-6018, 6020, 6029, 6031, 6035, 6043, 6052, 6063, 6070, *Argentina*, 2401, 6074, 6076, *Autonomous*, 6032, 6185, *Bolivia*, 6089, 6091-6092, *Brazil*, 6215, 6224, 6227, 6229, 6231, 6243, 6252, 6302, 6306-6312, 6314-6315, 7876, *Catholic*, 6016, 6218, *Central America*, 8362, *Chile*, 6105, 6110, 6112-6113, 6119-6120, *Colombia*, 6124-6127, 6133, 6138, *Cuba*, 6198, *curricula*, 6004, 6026, *El Salvador*, 6103, *Guatemala*, 6093, *Mexico*, 6155, 6162, 6164, *Paraguay*, 6165, *Peru*, 6160, 6171, 6176, *planning*, 6000, 6002, 6075, *politics*, 6035, *reform*, 6027, 6031-6032, 6039-6040, 6043, 6058-6059, 6070, 6072, 6103, 6105, 6112, 6120, 6126, 6130-6131, 6171, 6184, 6286, *Venezuela*, 6183-6185, *Uruguay*, 6177, 6182
Urban guerrillas, 7368, 7447, 7468, 7859, 7908-7909, 7913, 7990
Urban planning and reform, 8363, 8442
Urbanization, *general*, 1873, 2115, 6518, 6524, 6545, 6548, 6557, 6562, 6564, 6570, 6593, 6603-6606, 6609, 6613, 6616, 6773, 7372, 7388, 7485, 8262, 8286, 8438, *Argentina*, 6786, 6793, 6803, 6829, 6839, 8463, *bibliography*, 6557, *Bolivia*, 6842, 8450, *Brazil*, 6548, 6553, 6603, 6990,

7040, 7044, 7046, 7050, 7055, 7058, 7062-7064, 7072-7074, 7076, 7094, 7102-7103, 7109, 7115-7116, 7158-7159, 7169, 7922, 8481, 8492, *Caribbean*, 1127, 6626, *CentralAmerica*, 6548, *Chile*, 6548, 6858, 6870, 6888, 7775, 8449, *Colombia*, 6518, 6603, 6910, 6920-6921, 7669, *Costa Rica*, 6548, *Dominican Republic*, 6640, *Ecuador*, 6548, *fertility and mortality studies*, 1732, 1739, 1741, 1746, *flood control*, 7045, *Guatemala*, 6606, 6697, 8360, *Honduras*, 6548, *Mexico*, 1080, 1114, 6548, 6710, 6719-6720, 6727-6729, 6733, 6747, 8336, *Panama*, 6707, *Peru*, 1384, 1421, 1435, 1490, 6548, 6945, 6947, 6951-6952, 6956, 7674, *precolumbian*, 510, 769a, 911, 918, 937, 945, *Puerto Rico*, 2489-2523, 8402, *research, traffic and transportation*, 7158, *Venezuela*, 1332, 2113-2115, 2131, 2139, 2161, 8445, *vocabulary*, 6579
Urcos, *Peru*, 1441
Uto-Aztecan languages, 1577-1578, 1614

Vale do Maxotó, *Brazil*, 2425
Valle de Cañete, *Peru*, 971, 1003
Valle de Catamayo, *Ecuador*, 6937
Valle del Cauca, *Colombia*, 859, 6907-6908, 6916, 7647.
Valle de Chancay, *Peru*, 1356, 7695
Valle de Chillón, *Peru*, 954
Valle de Chincha, *Peru*, 971
Valle de Cotzal, *Guatemala*, 623
Valle de Ica, *Peru*, 971, 985
Valle de Mexico, 549, 612, 625, 632, 661, 717
Valle de Moche, *Peru*, 982
Valle de Palcamayo, 510, 955
Valle de Pastos Chicos, *Jujuy, Arg.*, 510
Valle de Pisco, *Peru*, 971
Valle de Piura, *Peru*, 1007
Valle de Tehuacan, 585, 655, 703
Valle del Mantaro, 510, 970.
Valle del Rímac, *Peru*, 928.
Valliserrana, 744, 779.
Valparaíso, *Chile*, 6889.
Vargas, Getúlio, 7850a, 7870.
Vargem Grande, São Paulo, *Brazil*, 7161.
Vicos, *Peru*, 1382, 1387, 1494, 8411.
Vicús-Pabur, *Peru*, 925.
Violence, 7493, 8269.
La Violencia, 8417.
Vodoo, 1176, 1182, 1186, 6646.
Vocational Training, 2371, 2520-1, 6052a, 6090, 6106, 6149, 6163, 6241, 6284, 6313, 8373, 8440.

Waika Indians. *See* Yanomamo Indians.
Waiwai Indians, 1293.
Wamali Indians, 1005.
Warao Indians, 1322-24, 1335.
Warman, Arturo, 1095.

Water Resources, *Brazil*, 7018, 7108, 7162. *Guatemala*, 6695. *Mexico*, 6741.
Waurá Indians, 1317.
Wayana Indians, 1274.
Weapons, *Precolumbian*, 650, 663, 665a, 693, 751, 873, 1266.
Weather. *See* Ecology.
Welfare, 8388, 8412.
Whaling, 1121, 6617.
Windward Islands, 8168.
Wine Industry, 2345, 2388.
Witchcraft, 510, 1042-3, 1075, 1105, 1116, 1167, 1186, 1237, 1258, 1302, 1359, 1381, 1457, 1496.
Witkin's Cognitive Tasks, 6156.
Woman, 1199, 1812, 6125, 7506, 7577, 7832, 8278, 8291, 8295, 8302-3, 8353, 8362, 8371, 8414, 8429, 8433, 8495, 8503, 8521, 8538, 8542, 8550-1.
Wood and Panel Industry, 2344.
World Bank, 1832.
World Power, 7156, 7891.
Writing Systems, 541, 550, 722, 724-6, 734, 749, 956.

Xavante. *See* Jê Languages.
Xikrin Indians, 1232, 1262.
Xinca Language, 1517.
Xingu Indians, 1245, 1301, 1328.

Yagul Oaxaca, Mexico, 510, 664.
Yahgan Indians, 527, 1280, 1305.
Yamana Indians, 1223.
Yanomami Indians. *See* Yanomamo Indians.
Yanomamo Indians, 1235, 1255, 1283-5, 1319-20, 1322, 1335, 1768, 1770-2.
Yaqui. *See* Uto-Aztecan Languages.
Yaqui Indians, 1103.
Yaruro Indians, 1322.
Yaruro Language, 1594.
Ye'cuana Indians. *See* Yekuana Indians.
Yekuana Indians, 1224, 1242, 1324, 1335.
Yopará. *See* Guaraní Language.
Yoruba Indians, 1198, 1216, 1306.
Young Communist League, Cuba, 8064.
Youth and Society, 8293, 8439, 8475, 8546.
Yucatan, 536, 6732, 6736, 6744.
Yucatecan Indians, 605.
Yucuna. *See* Arawakan Languages.
Yuko Indians, 1265.
Yungas, Bolivia, 6853.
Yungay, Peru, 6547.

Zapotec Indians, 1072.
Zapotecan Language, 1606, 1610.
Zinacanteco Indians, 1112.
Zoque Indians, 1632.
Zoquean Language, 1632.

Author Index

Aaron, Waldo M., 1547
Abot, Jorge, 2320
Abraham-van der Mark, Eva E., 1119
Abrahams, Roger D., 1120
Abrales, Héctor, 2386
Abreu, Alcides, 6986
Abreu, Jayme, 6206
Abreu e Silva, Glauco Lessa de. *See* Silva, Glauco Lessa de Abreu e.
Abreu Sodré, Roberto Costa de. *See* Sodré, Roberto Costa de Abreu.
Acedo Mendoza, Carlos, 2113-2118
Acevedo Latorre, Eduardo, 7282
Acheson, James M., 1031, 8292
Ackermann, Fritz Louis, 6987
Acosta, Jorge R., 594
Acosta, Maruja, 8363
Acosta Hermoso, Eduardo Arturo, 2119
Acosta Solís, Misael, 6925
Acuerdos básicos para el comercio en el Grupo Andino, 1774
Adams, C. D., 6649, 6676
Adams, Dale W., 2413, 6500
Adams, John Edward, 1121, 6617
Adams, Nassau A., 1983
Adams, Richard E. W., 535, 623
Adams, Richard N., 76, 1032
Adamson, Alan H., 2103
Adie, Robert, 7500
Adinolfi, Allen A., 8339
Adovasio, James M., 909
Adrados, Isabel, 8248
Adsuara Sevillano, Eduardo, 8293
Aduriz, Joaquín, 8409
Affonso, Almino, 2182
Aftalión, Enrique R., 1775
Agor, Weston H., 7354-7355, 7727
Agostino, Vittorio, 1776
Agrait, Luis E., 7622
Agresión salvadoreña contra la República de Honduras, 8127
Agricultural trade of the Western Hemisphere: a statistical review, 6501
Agroplan-Planejamento Agrícola Limitada, *São Paulo*, 6988

Agudelo Villa, Hernando, 2039
Agüero Blanch, Vicente Orlando, 1336-1337
Aguiar Walker, Neuma. *See*. Walker, Neuma Aguiar.
Aguila, Juan Carlos, 8410
Aguilar, Flavio, 2155
Aguilar, Luis E., 7356, 7565, 7728
Aguilar León, Luis E. *See* Aguilar, Luis E.
Aguilera, Carmen, 624
Aguilera Dorantes, Mario, 6145
Aguilera L., Luis, 6966
Aguilera Peralta, Gabriel Edgardo, 7554-7555
Aguirre Beltrán, Gonzalo, 8294
Agulla, Juan Carlos, 7482a
Agundez Fernández, Antonio, 7357
Alacazar, Marco Antonio, 7501
Alagoas (state), *Bra*. Secretaria de Planejamento, 6989
Alaluf, David, 2183
Alamo B., Antonio, 7827
Albano Amora, Manuel. *See* Amora, Manuel Albano.
Alberti, Giorgio, 1421, 1424, 6168, 7695, 8425
Albó, Xavier, 1338-1340
Albores Guillén, Roberto, 7502
Albornoz, Orlando, 6000
Albuquerque, Roberto Cavalcanti de, 2443
Albuquerque, Marcos, 822-823
Albuquerque Lima, Afonso Augusto de. *See* Lima, Afonso Augusto de Albuquerque.
Alcina Franch, José, 500-501, 510, 895, 910-911
Alderman, Ralph H., 6677
Alegre, Marcos, 6990
Alegrett, J. Raúl, 7827
Aleixo, José Carlos Brandi, 1777
Alemán, Hugo Gilberto, 8340-8341
Alende, Oscar Eduardo, 7920
Aleong, Stanley, 1140
Alers, J. Oscar. *See* Alers, Oscar J.
Alers, Oscar J., 6945, 7695, 8411
Alexander, Robert J., 7358-7359
Alfaro, Gregorio, 6678
Alfaro, José Miguel, 1962
Alfaro, Ricardo J., 7994
Alfaro Palacios, Reinaldo, 6098

Aliaga de Vizcarra, Irma, 6841
Alisky, Marvin, 7673
Allemann, Fritz René, 7729
Allen, Robert Loring, 1897
Allende Gossens, Salvador, 7730-7732
Alleyne, Mervyn, 1122, 1180
Alleyne, Michael, 6188
Allison, Graham T., 8150
Allpanchis Phuturinqa, 1341
Allum, Desmond, 1179
Allwood Paredes, Juan, 1657
Almeida, Cândido Mendes de, 7374
Almeida, Fernando Bessa de, 6207
Almeida, Fernando Flávio Marques de, 6991, 7081, 7239
Almeida, Marco Aurelio Garcia de, 7409
Almeida, Mauro Lauria de, 8464
Almeida, Miguel Alvaro Ozório de, 1778
Almeida Brum, Hélio de. *See* Brum, Hélio de Almeida
Almeida Júnior, Antônio F. de, 6208
Altamirano Rúa, Teófilo, 510, 1342
Altenfelder Silva, Fernando. *See* Silva, Fernando Altenfelder.
Altimir, Oscar, 6781
Alvarado, Julio, 7708
Alvarado Garaicoa, Teodoro, 7995
Alvarez, Ricardo, 1219
Alvarez Soberanis, Jaime, 7996
Alvarez Tabío, Fernando, 8173
Alvaro Bobadilla, Pedro, 1984
Alves Cabral, Isnard. *See* Cabral, Isnard Alves.
Alves da Cunha, Raymundo Cyriaco. *See* Cunha, Raymundo Cyriaco Alves da.
Alves Pinheiro Filho, Arthur. *See* Pinheiro Filho, Arthur Alves.
Alves Santiago, Alberto. *See* Santiago, Alberto Alves.
Alvim, Marília Carvalho de Mello e, 824, 832, 1720
Alvim, Paulo de T., 6992
Amábile, Francisco Walter, 6993
Amadeo Vasconi, Thomas, 7409
Amador, Elmo da Silva, 7119-7120
Amaral, Maria Lúcia, 6209
Amaro, Nelson. *See* Amaro V., Nelson.
Amaro V., Nelson, 7566, 8342
Amat, Carlos, 8367
Amat Olazával, Hernán, 912
Amazônia: tipos e aspectos; excertos de *Tipos e aspectos do Brasil*, 6994
América Indígena, 1220, 1343
América Latina, 6001
América Latina en armas, 7360
American Management Association (firm), N.Y. Executive Compensation Service, 2120
American Universities Field Staff (firm), *Hanover, N.H.*, 1
Amersfoort, J. M. M. van, 1123
Amiran, David H. K., 6946

Amora, Manuel Albano, 6995
Ampuero Brito, Gonzalo, 872-873
Anais da Associação dos Geógrafos Brasileiros, 6996-6997
Anais da Comissão Nacional de Alimentação, 1683
Anales de la Universidad de Chile, 6105
Anaya Sarmiento, Rubén, 7919
Andean Indian Community Research and Development Project, 1344
Anderson, Michael B., 2184
Andic, Fuat, 1140, 1779, 1985, 2481-2482
Andic, Suphan, 1779, 1985, 2482
Andrade, Manuel Correia de Oliveira, 2414, 6998-7000
Andrea, Flávio Fortes d', 8249
Andreatta, Margarida Davina, 842
Andrews, David H., 510
Andrews, Frank M., 7674
Andritzky, Georg, 7001
Andronova, V.P., 7361
Andueza, José Guillermo, 7791
Añez Pedraza, David, 7709
Angelini, Arrigo Leonardo, 6210, 8465
Angell, Alan, 7733-7734
Anglade, Georges, 1140
Anglade, Mireille, 1140
Angulo, Jorge V., 594
Aninat, U. Eduardo, 2185
Antezana E., Luis, 7710-7711
Antonioletti, Rodrigo, 6854
Anuario Azucarero de Cuba, 1986
Anuario Bibliográfico Peruano: 1964-1966, 2
Anuario Bibliográfico: 1961, 3
Aparecida de Souza, Maria Adélia. *See* Souza, Maria Adélia Aparecida de.
Aparicio, Luis, 6002
Aportes a la historia del P.C.V., 7792
Apunen, Osmo, 7362
Apuntes Universitarios, 6093
Aracy Bezerra, Duarte. *See* Bezerra, Duarte Aracy.
Aranda, Sergio, 2186
Arango Cano, Jesús, 1345
Arango Londoño, Gilberto, 2040
Aráoz, Alberto, 2321
Araujo Filho, José Ribeiro de, 7002
Araújo Mesquita, Julio de. *See* Mesquita, Julio de Araújo.
Araújo Neto, Mário Diniz de, 7120
Arbeitsgemeinschaft Deutsche Lateinamerika-forschung, 65
Arce Cano, Gustavo, 1905
Archambault, Jean, 1127
Arciniega, Antonio, 1780
Arcoverde de Freitas, Celso, 1680
Ardissone, Elena, 4
Arellano Moreno, Antonio, 7793
Arenas, Jaime, 7636
Argentina. Consejo Agrario Nacional. Instituto

Geominero Argentino (INGEMAR), 6782
Argentina. Consejo Federal de Inversiones, 8412
Argentina. Consejo Nacional de Desarrollo. Instituto Nacional de Estadística y Censos, 6783-6784
Argentina. Consejo Nacional de Desarrollo. Secretaría, 7921
Argentina. Dirección Nacional del Turismo, 6785
Argentina. Fondo de Integración Territorial (FIT), 6786
Argentina. Ministerio de Bienestar Social de la Nación. Dirección Nacional de Política Social, 8413
Argentina. Presidencia de la Nación. Secretaría General, 2322, 6787
Argentina. Secretaría de Estado de Trabajo. Dirección Nacional de Recursos Humanos. Oficina Nacional de la Mujer, 8414
Argentine-Brésil, 7922
Argentine: opération-massacre, 7923
Argudín de Luna, Yolanda, 6003
Arias de Greiff, Jorge, 6502
Arias Sánchez, Oscar, 7543
Aristeguieta, Leandro, 6959
Ariza Macías, Jaime, 1684
Armando de Souza, José. *See* Souza, José Armando de.
Armas Alfonso, Alfredo, 66, 6960
Armero Sixto, Carlos, 6788
Armillas, Pedro, 625
Armitano, Oswaldo, 8286
Arnáiz Amigo, Aurora, 7363-7363a
Arnaud, Expedito, 1221-1222
Arnaud, Patricia M., 1223
Arnaudo, Aldo A., 2323, 2346, 2360
Arnold, Adlai F., 2259
Arnold, Dean E., 1346
Arnove, Robert F., 6183, 8415
Aronson, Mark D., 6709
Arquinio, José, 1347
Arquivos Brasileiros de Psicologia Aplicada, 6211
Arragoni, Gloria I., 780
Arrigazzi, Lucila, 6106-6107
Arrom, José Juan, 749, 755
Arrott, Margaret, 1033
Arroyave, Guillermo, 1702
Arthur D. Little, Inc. (firm), *Cambridge, Mass.*, 2104
Arvelo-Jiménez, Nelly, 1224
Arze, José Roberto, 8416
Asamblea Nacional Ordinaria del Partido Revolucionario Institucional, *VI, México, 1971*, 7504
Ascanio Jiménez, Agustín, 8185
Ascher, Marcia, 913
Ascher, Robert, 913
Aschmann, Homer, 6503, 6855

Ashcraft, Norman, 1124-1125, 8343
Asociación Colombiana de Universidades, *Bogotá.* Fondo Universitario Nacional. Comité de Planeación, 6123
Asociación Nacional Automobilística, *Mex.*, 7309
Asociación Pro-Salud Maternal, *México*, 8295
Aspectos de la enseñanza de la demografía en la universidad latinoamericana, 6004
Aspectos econômicos da mandioca, 7003
Associação de Crédito e Assistência Rural de Mato Grosso, (ACARMAT) *Cuiabá, Bra.*, 7004
Associação de Crédito e Asistência Rural do Espírito Santo (ACARES), *Vitória, Bra.*, 7005
Astica, Juan B., 6609
Astiz, Carlos Alberto, 7675-7676
Astiz, Lilia Veirano de Astiz, 7006, 7185
Astiz Astiz, Lilia Veirano de. *See* Astiz, Lilia Veirano de.
Astori, Danilo, 7901
Asturias, Miguel Angel, 82
Atkins, George Pope, 7671, 8151
Atkins, John, 6504
Atkinson, M. Jourdan, 510
Aubert, Michel Cl., 6939
Augelli, John P., 6505
Augustin, Donald, 1993
Augusto, José, 7831
Aus Politik und Zeitgeschichte, 7363b
Austral, Antonio Gerónimo, 502, 764-765
Automóvil Club Argentino, *Buenos Aires*, 7219-7220
Autoridades Brasileiras, 67
Avalos D., Beatrice, 6108
Aveni, Anthony F., 626
Avery, William P., 1781
Avila Salinas, Waldo, 807
Avramović, Dragoslav, 2041
Ayala Castañares, Agustín, 6670
Ayalaz, Alfredo, 7237
Ayearst, Morley, 1179
Azeredo Costa, Eduardo, 1658
Azevedo, Aroldo de, 7007
Azevedo, Fernando de, 68
Azevedo, J. B. C., 1744
Azevedo, Marcello Casado d', 8250
Azevedo, Murillo Nunes de, 8251
Azevedo, Thales de, 510, 6212, 8467
Azzarini, Mario, 2306
Babín, Maria Teresa, 6189
Bacchus, M. K., 6144
Bacha, Edmar L., 2415
Back, E. H., 1692-1693
Badner, Mino, 914
Baer, Donald E., 1953
Baer, Gerhard, 627
Baer, Phillip, 1034
Baer, Werner, 2416

AUTHOR INDEX

Baesa García, José, 6856
Báez, Leovigildo, 8252
Báez, Mauricio, 1781a
Baeza Flores, Alberto, 7369
Bagú, Sergio, 7409, 8439
Bagué Ramírez, Jaime, 2483
Baillon, Claude, 6710
Baird, D. M., 6926
Baja California norte: beginning the peninsular journey, 6711
Baker, Bonnie Lea, 1906
Baker, Charles Laurence, 6712
Baker, Paul T., 1652, 1708-1709, 1733
Baker, R. E., 6759
Baker, Richard D., 7505
Balán, Jorge, 6146
Balassa, Bela, 1782
Balboa, Manuel, 2324, 7374
Balção, Yolanda Ferreira, 8253
Balchman, Morris J., 7832, 8468
Baldus, Herbert, 1225
Balestrini C., César, 1783
Balhana, Altiva Pilatti, 7008, 7191
Ball, John C., 8408
Ball, John M., 8332
Ball, Joseph W., 536, 628
Ball, Mary Margaret, 7997
Ballance, R. H., 6713
Ballesteros, Juan, 6714
Ballesteros Guerrero, Carlos, 6927
Balow, Tom, 6673, 6698
Baltra-Cortés, Alberto, 2187
Bamberger, Joan, 1226
Bambirra, Vania, 7364
Banco Central de la República Argentina, *Buenos Aires*, 2325-2326
Banco Central de Reserva, *Lima*, 2267
Banco Central de Venezuela, *Caracas*, 2121-2124
Banco Central del Paraguay, *Asunción*, 2260
Banco da Amazônia (firm), *Manaus, Bra.*, 7009
Banco de Italia y Río de la Plata, *Buenos Aires*, 2327
Banco de la República, *Bogotá*, 2042
Banco do Nordeste do Brasil (firm), *Fortaleza, Bra.* Departamento de Estudos Econômicos do Nordeste (ETENE). Divisão de Agricultura, 7010
Banco Hipotecario de El Salvador, *San Salvador*, 21
Banco Nacional de Comercio Exterior, *México*, 1907
Baones, John M., 7677
Baquero, Rafael, 7640
Barata, Mário, 7833
Barba, Fernando E., 6789
Barbados. The Town and Country Development Planning Office, 7236
Barbosa, Getúlio V., 7011
Barbosa Vianna, A. J. *See* Vianna, A. J. Barbosa.

Bárcena, J. Roberto, 1721
Barclay, Glen St. John, 8186
Bardon, Alvaro, 2188
Bariteau, Claude, 1127
Barkin, David, 1987, 2189, 6147, 8296
Barneix, Atilio J., 7365
Barnes de Marshall, Katherine, 1348-1350, 6842
Barón Ferrufino, José René, 7549
Barraclough, Solon, 1784-1785, 6506
Barreto Coutinho Neto, Antônio. *See* Coutinho Neto, Antônio Barreto.
Barrett, Raymond J., 8152
Barrette, Christian, 1351
Barría S., Jorge, 7735
Barros, Ernani Thimóteo de, 7012
Barros, José Roberto Mendonça de, 2460
Barros, Roque Spencer Maciel de, 6213
Barros Cavalcanti, Mário de. *See* Cavalcanti, Mário de Barros.
Barros Coelho, Celso. *See* Coelho, Celso Barros.
Barroso, Luiz Pereira, 2465
Barth, Walter, 6843
Barthel, Thomas S., 721
Bartholomew, Doris, 1636
Bartolomé, Leopoldo J., 1227
Barzuna, Miguel, 1962
Bascom, William, 510
Bashilov, Vladimir Aleksandrovich, 758
Basílico, Ernesto, 8187
Bastide, Roger, 1140, 8268
Bastien, Rémy, 1140
Bastos, Tocary A., 7834
Bataillon, M. C., 6507
Bate P., Luis F., 503
Bateman, Alfredo D., 6900
Baudez, Claude F., 737
Baudouin, Renée Lescop, 7366
Bauer Paiz, Alfonso, 8128
Baumgartner, Jean-Pierre, 2328
Baumhardt, Gastão, 854
Bauver, Francés Vincent, 874
Bazant, Jan, 1909
Bazarian, Jacob, 7998
Bazin, M., 1704
Baztan R., Javier, 756
Beadle, George W., 537
Bear, J. C., 1656
Beaudoux-Kovats, Edith, 1127, 1136
Bechara, Evanildo, 102
Bechtol, Bruce E., 6690
Beck, Anamaria, 825-826
Becker, Itala Irene Basile, 839, 854
Becker, Marshall Joseph, 538
Becker, Rudolph L., 2105
Beckford, George L., 1126, 1786, 1988, 8364
Beckman, Jan D., 69
Becquelin, Pierre, 737
Bedregal, Guillermo, 7712
Beghin, Yvan, 1685

Behrman, Jere R., 2190-2191
Beirn, Russell, 6005
Bekarevich, A. D., 8153-8154
Beker G., Simon, 1667
Belcher, J., 2523
Belcher, John C., 8365, 8406
Belcore, Martha, 915
Bell, Betty, 550, 629
Bell, Harry H., 1787
Bell, Wendell, 8254
Bellizzia, Alirio, 7344
Belote, James, 1352
Belote, Linda, 1352
Belov, A. N., 7999
Beltrán Cortes, Luis María, 8417
Beltrán Prieto Figueroa, Luis, 7794, 7817
Benathar, Roberto Levy, 6214
Benavides Calle, Mario, 510, 916
Benbassat, Edgardo, 791
Bendor-Samuel, David, 1509-1510
Benedetti, Mario, 7902
Benevides Uchoa, Júlio. See Uchoa, Júlio Benevides.
Benn, Bernard W., 6190
Bennett, Charles F., 6508
Bennyhoff, James A., 661
Benoist, Jean, 1127, 1731
Benoit, Emile, 7367
Benoit, Pierre, 1140
Benson, Elizabeth P., 546, 630, 916a
Bentancourt L., Enrique, 2043
Benvenuto, Luis, 7903
Berberián, Eduardo E., 766-768
Berdichewsky S., Bernardo, 875-876
Berger, R., 1722
Berger, Rainer, 652
Berges, Roberto L., 6640
Berggren, Gretchen M., 1659
Berggren, Warren L., 1659
Bergholz W., Hans, 881
Bergmann, John F., 6790
Bergström Lourenço Filho, Manuel. See Lourenço Filho, Manuel Bergström.
Berguño B., Jorge, 8188
Berlinck, Manoel Tosta. See. Tosta Berlinck, Manoel.
Bermúdez, Luis A., 7637
Bermúdez, Oscar, 6857
Bernal V., Carlos, 2044
Bernal, Ignacio, 550, 631
Bernard, Jean-Pierre, 2166
Bernard, Philippe, 6215
Bernardes, Nilo, 7013
Bernardo, Robert M., 7567
Bernhard, Guillermo, 2307
Berrangé, Jevan P., 6940
Berrios, Héctor H., 6656
Berry, R. Albert, 2045-2046
Berry, Brian J. L., 6858
Bertholet, Christian Joseph Leonard, 2268

Bertone, Carlos A., 7373
Bertrand, Marie Andrée, 1141
Bérubé, Louis, 82
Besancenot, J.-P., 6618
Besil, Antonio C., 6791-6792
Bessa de Almeida, Fernando. See Almeida, Fernando Bessa de.
Best, Lloyd, 1179
Betancourt, Salvador Cisneros. See Cisneros Betancourt, Salvador.
Betancourt Roa, Gilda, 7568, 8366-8367
Betancur, Belisario, 7638
Betley, Brian J., 8297
Betting, Joelmir, 6216
Bettis, Lee, 2413
Betts, Vera, 1599
Beyer, John C., 2125
Bezerra, Duarte Aracy, 6272
Bhagwati, Jagdish N., 1806
Bhola, Ranal, 1989, 8156
Bibliografía Actual del Caribe [Current Caribbean Bibliography: Bibliographie Courante de la Caraïbe], 5-6
Bibliografia Brasileira de Educação, 60, 6217
Bibliografia das obras publicadas pelo Exmo. Prof. Dr. Giulo Davide Leoni, 18
Bibliografía literaria de la revista *Hoy*: 1931-1943, 61
Bibliografía Mexicana, 7
Bibliografía sobre servicio social, 22
Bibliografía Venezolana, 62
Bibliotecas 71, 8
Biermann, Kurt-R., 6509-6510
Bilkey, Warren J., 1990
Billard, Jules B., 6793
Binford, Lewis R., 748
Bingham, Marie Ballew, 23
Binning, William C., 8000
Biolcati, Adriano Augusto, 8418
Bird, Junius B., 946
Bird, Richard M., 2047
Biró de Stern, Ana, 1353
Birou, Alain, 63
Bischoff, Henning, 896
Bisschoff, W. V. A., 7139
Bitar, Sergio, 2192
Bitencourt Lomonaco, José Fernando. See Lomonaco, José Fernando Bitencourt.
Bitter, Maurice, 6646
Bizzarro, Salvatore, 70
Black, Robert J., 7368, 7485
Blaffer, Sarah C., 1035
Blair, Calvin, 76
Blair, Robert W., 1511
Blakemore, Harold, 71
Blanco, Flaliero, 7270
Blanco, Ricardo A., 1686
Blank, David Eugene, 7795, 7827
Blanksten, George I., 6006-6007

Blanton, Richard E., 632
Blase, Melvin G., 6511
Blasier, Cole, 7720, 8108
Blásquez Canales, Raúl García. *See* García-Blásquez, Raúl.
Blaut, James M., 1137
Blaut, Ruth P., 1137
Bledel, Rodolfo, 2329
Blomberg, Rolf, 72, 6928
Bloomgarden, Richard, 6715
Blough, William J., 7506
Bobbio, Emilio, 2270
Bock, E. Wilbur, 1739, 8469
Bodard, Lucien, 1228
Bode, Kenneth A., 8001
Bodenheimer, Susanne, 7544
Bodenheimer, Thomas S., 1687
Boehm, David Alfred, 6653
Boer, M. W. H. de, 1128
Boero de Izeta, Carlota, 6833
Boersner, Demetrio, 7369
Boggio, Ana, 6168a
Boghen, Dan, 1127
Boghen, Miriam, 1127
Boglár, Lajos, 1229-1230
Boizard, Ricardo, 7370
Boletim Bibliográfico, 64
Boletim Bibliográfico da Biblioteca Nacional, 9
Boletim da Biblioteca, 24
Boletim do IESPE, 6218
Boletín Bibliográfico, 25
Boletín Bibliográfico de COSEBI, 40
Boletín Bibliográfico de la Secretaría de Hacienda y Crédito Público, 73
Boletín Bibliográfico: lista de obras incorporadas, autores y materias, octubre-diciembre 1969, 26
Boletín de la Sociedad de Bibliotecarios de Puerto Rico, 41
Boletín del Museo del Hombre Dominicano, 748-749
Boletín Estadístico (BE), 1991
Boletín Mensual, 2193
Boletín para Bibliotecas Agrícolas, 74, 6512
Bolivia. Instituto Geográfico Militar, 7238
Bolivia. Ministerio de Educación, 6083
Bolivia. Ministerio de Información. Dirección General de Informaciones, 8190
Bolivia. Ministerio de Minas y Petróleo, 6844
Bolivia: agricultura, economía y política; a bibliography, 2167
Bolland, O. Nigel, 6191
Bollinger, Armin, 75
Bollinger, Klaus, 7424a
Bolsa de Comercio de Buenos Aires, 2330
Bolton, Ralph, 1354-1355
Bon, Espasandín, Mario, 2308
Bonachea, Rolando E., 7608
Bonaparte, Héctor M., 2331, 8419

Bonavia, Duccio, 510, 917-922, 995
Bonavides, Paulo, 7835
Bondeson, Wolmar E., 808
Bonfil, Alicia O. de, 1036
Bonifaz, Emilio, 897
Bonilha, José Fernando Martins, 8470
Bonilla Mayta, Heraclio, 1356
Bonino Nieves, Marco, 1455
Boodhoo, Ken, 1129
Borah, Woodrow, 510
Borde, Jean, 6859
Bordeaux, Edmond S., 539
Borhegyi, Stephan F. de, 633
Boris, Dieter, 7735a
Boris, Elisabeth, 7735a
Borón, Atilio Alberto, 7371, 7736, 7924
Borrello, Angel V., 6794-6795
Borrero Vintimilla, Antonio, 6929-6930
Bosch-Gimpera, Pedro, 504
Botana, Natalio, 7469
Botero G., Héctor, 2048
Bouchard, Paul, 82
Boudin, Max H., 1512
Bourque, Susan Carolyn, 1357, 1449, 7678
Bourricaud, François, 1358, 1402, 7679
Bowen, Emanuel, 7310
Bowen, W. Errol, 1130
Boyd, Monica, 1732
Brackenridge, Henry Marie, 6513
Bradbury, Robert W., 1788
Bradfield, Robert B., 1702
Bradfield, Stillman, 2271
Braghine, Alexandre Pavlovitch, 505
Braithwaite, Lloyd, 1136, 1180
Brand, Donald D., 76, 550, 571
Brand, W., 1992
Brandel, Catherine Terry, 1000
Brandes, Stanley H., 8298
Braniff, Beatriz, 540, 594
Brasil Netto, Thomás Pompeu de Souza, 2418
Brasil/Açúcar, 7014
Brathwaite, Edward Kamau, 1131-1132
Braun, Elisabeth E., 8109
Braun, Oscar P. G., 7015
Braun, Patrick, 1359
Bravo, Enrique R., 10
Bravo, Héctor Félix, 6072
Bray, Warwick, 634, 859
Brazil. Centro de Coordenação Industrial para o Plano Habitacional. Instituto de Desenvolvimento de Guanabara, 7016
Brazil. Companhia do Desenvolvimento do Planalto Central, 7248
Brazil. Congresso. Câmara dos Deputados. Comissão Especial do Polígono das Secas, 7017
Brazil. Departamento Nacional de Estradas de Rodagem, 7240
Brazil. Departamento Nacional de Obras Contra as Sêcas, 7018

Brazil. Embassy in the United States. Brazilian American Cultural Institute [BACI], 11
Brazil. Instituto Brasileiro de Geografia. Departamento de Cartografia, 7241-7244, 7249-7253
Brazil. Instituto Brasileiro de Reforma Agraria (IBRA), 7019-7020
Brazil. Marinha. Diretoria de Hidrografia e Navegação, 7022
Brazil. Ministério da Agricultura. Instituto Nacional de Colonização e Reforma Agraria (INCRA). Secretaria de Planejamento e Coordenação, 7023
Brazil. Ministério da Educação e Cultura. Conselho Federal de Educação, 6219-6220, 6222
Brazil. Ministério da Educação e Cultura. Instituto Nacional de Estudos Pedagógicos. Centro Brasileiro de Pesquisas Educacionais (MEC-INEP-CBPE), 6221
Brazil. Ministério das Minas e Energia. Departamento Nacional da Produção Mineral, 7024-7025
Brazil. Ministério das Relações das Relações Exteriores. Departamento de Administração, 77
Brazil. Ministério das Relações Exteriores. Divisão de Documentação, 8191
Brazil. Ministério do Interior Banco da Amazônia. Departamento de Estudos Econômicos, 2419
Brazil. Plano Decenal de Desenvolvimento Econômico e Social, 7026
Brazil. Presidência da República, 7836
Brazil. Superintendência do Desenvolvimento do Nordeste (SUDENE), 2420
Brazil: development for whom?, 2421
Brazil: land tenure conditions and socioeconomic development of the agricultural sector, 7026a
Brazil, the Medici administration: performance and prospects, 2422
Brasília: nível e padrão de vida do comerciário; estrutura da emprêsa comercial, 8471
Breimyer, Harold, 1989, 8156
Brésil—l'évolution de la situation politique depuis 1967—les présidences Costa e Silva et Garrastazu Médici: l'écrasement des forces politiques traditionnelles; le développement des nouvelles oppositions; l'évolution du régime, 7837
Brewer, Marilynn B., 8356
Briceño-Iragorry, Mario, 7796
Bricker, Victoria Reifler, 1513
Bridgman, A. R., 1477-1478
Bright, A. L., 860
Brinkman, W. L., 7027
Brisseau, J., 6947
Brisseau, Jeanine, 1360, 2272
Brisseau-Loaiza, Jeanine. See Brisseau, Jeanine.
British Honduras, 7276

Brito Velázquez, Enrique, 8299
Britto, Luiz Navarro de, 6223
Broadbent, Sylvia M., 861
Brochado, José Proenza, 854
Broder, Paulo, 2332
Brodovich, Boris Nikolaevich, 1789
Bromely, R. J., 78
Bronheim, David, 8002
Brooks, Joseph J., 8129
Brown, Jack, 1419
Brown, Lawrence, 6514
Brown, Marion R., 7737
Brown, William F., 6148
Browning, Harley L., 510, 1910
Browning, Hurley, 76
Brownrigg, Leslie Ann, 510, 1357, 1361, 1449
Broxson, Elmer, 39
Brugger, Karl, 7426a
Bruhns, Karen Olsen, 862-864
Brum, Hélio de Almeida, 6224
Brumbaugh, Robert, 510
Brunhouse, Robert L., 541
Brunn, Stanley D., 6515, 7372
Brunnschweiler, Dieter, 6516
Brush, Stephen B., 1362
Bucchioni, Eugene, 8375
Buck, Wilbur F., 6641
Buechler, Hans C., 1363-1364, 1435
Buechler, Judith Maria, 1364
Bueno Mendoza, Alberto, 923, 962
Buenos Aires (city), Arg. Oficina Regional de Desarrollo. Area Metropolitana, 7221
Buenos Aires (province), Arg. Asesoría Provincial de Desarrollo, 7222
Buenos Aires (province), Arg. Dirección de Geodesia, 7223
Buenos Aires (province), Arg. Ministerio de Asuntos Agrarios. Asesoría Ministerial de Desarrollo, 6796
Buenos Aires (province), Arg. Ministerio de Educación. Subsecretaría de Cultura, 6797
Bünstorf, Jurgen, 6798
Büntig, Aldo J., 7373
Bugarín, Antonio Alberto, 7224
Buitrago de Santiago, Zayda, 6656
Buitrago Ortiz, Carlos, 8368
Buitrón, Aníbal, 6008
Bullen, Adelaide K., 750
Bullen, Ripley P., 750
Bunge, César A., 8191a
Burchard, Roderick R., 1365
Burela, Alberto, 1366
Burela, Marta, 1366
Burelli Rivas, Miguel Angel, 7797
Burgess, Eunice, 1514
Burggraaff, Winfield J., 7798-7799
El Burgués, 7925
Burguillos, Pedro, 8286
Burke, Melvin, 2168-2170, 7720
Burnell, Elaine H., 7374

Burnham, Forbes, 7632
Burns, Donald H., 1515
Burns, E. Bradford, 8192
Burstein, Paul, 8255
Busto Duthurburu, José Antonio, 924
Butler, Gavan, 6615
Butler, Robert W., Jr., 8110
Butterfield, Anthony D., 7847
Buve, R. Th. J., 7507
Byrne, Joycelin, 8369-8370
Caballero Calderón, Eduardo, 7639
Cabero, Nora, 2194
Cabezas, Rodrigo, 2084
Cabezón, Pedro, 2195
Cable, James, 8003
Cabral, Isnard Alves, 1658
Caccia, Angela, 6845
Cadernos de Jornalismo e Comunicação, 6225
Cadernos Região e Educação, 6226
Cadogan, León, 1231, 1516
Caeiro, Agustín, 8439
Caffera, Rodolfo, 6760
Cafferata, Juan Daniel, 6799
Caggiano, María Amanda, 771, 773
Calandra, Horacio, 770, 772
Calatayud Bosch, José, 7904
Caldera, Rafael, 7800-7801, 8004
Calderón, Valentín, 827-828
Calello, Hugo, 1790
Calle Restrepo, Arturo, 6517
Calnek, Edward E., 510
Calvert, Peter, 8130
Calvo, Bernardino S., 79
Calvo, Gilberto, 6860
Camacho Peña, Alfonso, 7713
Câmara, Hélder, 7375
Câmara Barbachano, Fernando, 1037
Câmara Cascudo, Luís da. *See* Cascudo, Luís da Câmara.
Cámara de los Frigoríficos Regionales, *Buenos Aires*, 2333
Camarano, Chris, 8371
Camargo, Cândido Procópio Ferreira de, 8472
Camargo, Mario E., 1660
Camargo Pereira, José Severo de. *See* Pereira, José Severo de Camargo.
Cambron, Gérard, 82
Camejo, Acton, 8372
Camel V., Fayad, 1661
Cameron, William R., 900
Camisa, Zulma C., 6691
Camp, Roderic A., 7508
Campá Soler, Raúl, 925
Campbell, Alexander Elmslie, 8005
Campbell, Lyle, 1517-1519
Campbell B., Ramón, 510
El Campesino, 2196
El campesino tucumano: educación y cultura, 8420
Campos, Roberto de Oliveira, 2423

Campos Jiménez, Carlos María, 8344
Campusano, C., 1723
Canal Ramírez, Gonzalo, 7802
Canihuante, Gustavo, 7738
Canteiro, João Ruy, 7028
Cantídio, Walter de Moura, 6227
Cantón, Darío, 7926-7927
Capdeville Duarte, Aluízio. *See* Duarte, Aluízio Capdeville.
Capitanelli, Ricardo G., 6009
Cappalli, Richard B., 2484-2485
Cappeletti Vidal, Ricardo, 1954
Cardenal, Ernesto, 7569
Cárdenas, Martín, 6846
Cárdenas Martín, Mercedes, 926-930
Cardia, Nancy das Garças, 6274
Cardich, Augusto, 759, 931
Cardona Gutiérrez, Ramiro, 6518, 6901, 6921
Cardoso, Fernando H., 7376, 7482a, 7838-7840, 8256
Cardoso, Lamartine, 7029
Cardoso de Oliveira, Roberto. *See* Oliveira, Roberto Cardoso de.
Cardoso Montenegro, Abelardo. *See* Montenegro, Abelardo Cardoso.
Careaga, Gabriel, 7509
Caribbean Food and Nutrition Institute, 1680
CARIFTA Economist & Business Post, 1993
Carl, Beverly May, 2424
Carmona de la Peña, Fernando, 1911
Carneiro, José Fernando Domingues, 6228
Carneiro, José T. M., 2469
Carneiro Viana, José de Alencar. *See* Viana, José de Alencar Carneiro.
Carnoy, Martin, 1791-1792, 1821, 6192-6193
Caro Alvarez, José A., 748
Caron, Raymond, 1232
Carpenter, Allan, 6673, 6679, 6692, 6698
Carpentier, Alejo, 8268
Carpio Castillo, Rubén, 6961, 7803
Carr, W. I., 1180
Carranza R., Luis Felipe, 1038
Carrasco, Pedro, 550, 1039-1040
Carrasco Hermoza, Juan R., 1233
Carreño Silva, Luis, 6109
Carril, Bonifacio del, 7377
Carta da produção de Minas Gerais, 7030
Cartagena P., Aída, 755
Carter, George F., 506, 6716
Carter, William E., 1367-1369, 6519, 7720
Cartobrás (firm), *Rio*, 7245
Carvajal, Manuel, 6902
Carvajal, Rafael Tomás, 7378
Carvalho, Carlos Miguel Delgado de, 7031
Carvalho, J., 80
Carvalho, Joaquim Montezuma de, 6229
Carvalho, José Murilo de, 7379
Carvalho, Laerte Ramos de, 6228
Carvalho, Rodrigues de, 8473

Carvalho Ferreira, Carlos Mauricio de. *See* Ferreira, Carlos Mauricio de Carvalho.
Carvalho Ribeiro, Augusta Barbosa de. *See* Ribeiro, Augusta Barbosa de Carvalho.
Casado d'Azevedo, Marcello. *See* Azevedo, Marcello Casado d'.
Casal, Horacio Néstor, 7928-7930
Casamiquela, Rodolfo M., 6761, 6861
Casares, Vicente, 2365
Casas González, Antonio, 2126
Cascudo, Luís da Câmara, 8474
Casillas Mármol, Jacobo, 8111
Casimir, Jean, 1140, 6520
Caso, Alfonso, 550, 1041
Caso Bercht, Jorge, 1912
El caso Padilla, 7570
Castagno, Antonio, 7931
Castañeda, Rolando, 2486, 2502
Castaños Echazu, Arturo, 809
Castellanos, Edgar, 7482a
Castelnuovo, Elías, 7380
Castillero Pimentel, Ernesto, 8131
Castillo, Carlos Manuel, 7374
Castillo, Helia de, 1653
Castillo, Isidro, 6145
Castillo Ardiles, Hernán, 1370
Castillo Tejero, Noemí, 636
Castrillo Zeledón, Mario, 1955
Castro, Cláudio de Moura, 6230
Castro, Fidel, 7571-7572
Castro, J. A. de Araújo, 8193
Castro, Julio, 6124
Castro, Therezinha de, 7031
Castro Contreras, Jaime, 7680
Castro Corbat, Marcelo J., 2334
Castro Harrison, Jorge, 6169
Castro Hidalgo, Orlando, 7573
Castro Peixoto, Dídima de. *See* Peixoto, Dídima de Castro.
Catálogo bibliográfico de la Facultad de Humanidades y Educación, 1948-1968, 27
Catálogo colectivo de publicaciones periódicas en desarrollo económico y social, 2273
Catálogo de la colección cartográfica del Centro Documental, 28
Catálogo de publicaciones periódicas existencias, diciembre 1971, 29
Cataño, Gonzalo, 7640
Cato-David, Jorge, 1243
Cauas, Jorge, 2197
Cauwlaert, Isabel Haydée van, 6073
Cavalcanti, Mário de Barros, 7032a
Cavalcanti, Clóvis de Vasconcelos, 2425, 7032
Cavalcanti de Albuquerque, Roberto. *See* Albuquerque, Roberto Cavalcanti de.
Cavarozzi, Marcelo J., 7381, 7456
Cavedon, Ari Délcio, 7172
Caviedes, César, 6862-6863
Cazes, Georges, 6619

Ceará Pescas, S. A. (CEPESCA), *Fortaleza, Bra.*, 7033
Ceballos, Rita, 1234
Cehelsky, Marta, 7485
Celestino, Olinda, 1421
Centro de Estudos e Ação Social, *Salvador, Bra.*, 8475
Centro de Estudios Económicos del Sector Privado, *México*, 1913-1914
Centro de Industriales Siderúrgicos, *Buenos Aires*, 6800
Centro de Investigaciones Agrarias, *México*, 6717
Centro Internacional de Agricultura Tropical (CIAT), *Cali, Co.*, 6521
Cepeda Ulloa, Fernando, 7489a
Cerda, Carlos, 7382
Cereceda, Luz E., 6114
Ceresole, Norberto, 2274, 7681, 7932-7933
Cermakian, Jean, 6522
Ceron, Antônio Olívio, 7034
Cevallos Tovar, Walter, 6847
Cernuschi, Félix, 6177
Cervera, Felipe Justo, 2335
Cervera Andrade, Alejandro, 6010
Ceuppens, Henry D., 2261
Chacón, Alfredo, 7804
Chacon, Vamireh, 7482a
Chadwick, Robert, 550
Chagnon, Napolean A., 1235
Chahud, Carlos, 948
Chal Baud Zerpa, Reinaldo, 6184
Chalmers, Douglas, 7383, 8006
Chancy, Max, 1140
Chandler, Charlotte, 7934
Chaniotis, Byron N., 6709
Chapman, Anne M., 1236
Chapman, Florence Hantschke, 1724
Chara, Acir Diniz, 2426
Charles, Gérard Pierre, 1140
Charlton, Thomas H., 637, 696
Chase-Sardi, Miguel, 1237-1239
Chaves, Jonas Leite, 7035
Chaves, Maria Paula Ramos, 7036
Chaves, Milcíades, 2049
Chaves Camacho, Jorge, 6680
Chen, J. Chi-Yi, 7805
Chenery, Hollis B., 2487
Chevannes, Barry, 1133
Chew, Benjamin, 8007
Chiara, Vilma, 1317
Chilcote, Ronald H., 7841
Chile. Instituto de Capacitación e Investigación sobre Reforma Agraria. Instituto de Desarrollo Agropecuario, 2198
Chile. Instituto Nacional de Estadísticas, 2199
Chile. Oficina de Planificación Nacional (ODEPLAN), 2200-2201
Chile. Ministerio de Defensa Nacional. Instituto Geográfico Militar, 7281

Chile [e] Perú: democracia, marxismo, militarismo, 7739
Chile Hoy, 2202
Chile, Perú, Bolivia: documentos de tres procesos latinoamericanos, 7383a
Chilman, Walter J., 6705
Chin, H. E., 2106
Chiri, Osvaldo C., 769
Chirikos, Thomas N., 2171
Chivelekian, Juan C., 7225
Chmyz, Igor, 829-830
Chonchol, Jacques, 7374
Choudhry, Parimal, 2488
Christensen, Bodil, 1042
Christian, Diana R., 1520
Chrostowski, Marshall S., 510
Chu, David S. C., 2336
Chubut (province), *Arg*., 2337
Chumakova, Marina L'vovna, 8132
Church, Frank, 7374
Churchill, Anthony, 1956
CIDOC Informe: enero/junio 1970, 7384
Ciencia Interamericana, 6011
La ciencia y la tecnología al servicio de los pueblos de América: Programa Regional de Desarrollo Científico y Tecnológico de la OEA, 6012
Cifuentes Díaz, Carlos, 8345
Cigliano, Eduardo Mario, 769a-773, 1264
Cintra, Antônio Octávio, 7842, 8476
Ciria, Alberto, 7935-7936
Cirigliano, Gustavo F. J., 6074
Cirino Gerena, Gabriel, 8373
Ciski, Robert, 1134
Cisneros Betancourt, Salvador, 8155
Civeira Taboada, Miguel, 6718
Clague, Christopher K., 2275
Clair-Vasiliadis, Christos, 1240
Clan S. A. (firm), *Bra.*, 2427
Clapperton, Chalmers M., 6762, 6948
Clark, Colin, 1793
Clark, Paul Gordon, 8008
Clark, Peter B., 2212
Clark, Robert P., Jr., 7827
Clark, Ronald J., 6848
Clark, Sydney, 6620
Clarke, Colin G., 1137, 6658, 7628
Clarke, Edith, 1137
Clausen, Arne, 8421
Clermont, Norman, 1135
Cline, Howard F., 7192
Cline, William R., 1794, 2428
Clinton, Richard Lee, 7682
Clissold, Stephen, 7385
Cobbing, E. J., 6949
Cobean, Robert H., 542
Cobo, A., 1773
Cobo, Lesvia, 1747
Cochrane, James D., 1781, 8088
Codovilla, Victorio, 7937

Coe, Michael D., 530, 542-543, 594, 635, 722
Coelho, Celso Barros, 6231
Coelho, Francisco Ananias de Paula, 7037, 7173
Cofresí, Emilio, 8374
Coggins, Clemency, 544-545
Cogorno Ventura, Gilda, 932
Cohen, Lucy, 6125
Cohen, Martin A., 81
Colbert, Edwin H., 6523
Cole, John P., 7038
Cole, William E., 1795
Colegio de Economistas de Bolivia, *La Paz*, 2172
El Colegio de México. Centro de Estudios Económicos y Demográficos, 6719
Collier, David, 1371
Collier, Mario Elisa Dias, 8477
Collin-Delavaud, Claude, 1395, 1421
Collings, Dorothy, 42
Collins, B. A. N., 1179
Colombia. Comisión de Reforma Tributaria, 2050
Colombia. Departamento Administrativo Nacional de Estadística (DANE), 2051-2052
Colombia. Departamento Nacional de Planeación, 2053-2054
Colombia. Dirección General de Conservación, 7283
Colombia. Dirección General de Integración y Desarrollo de la Comunidad, 8422
Colombia. Federación Nacional de Cafeteros, 7284
Colombia. Instituto de Crédito Territorial. Departamento de Vivienda y Desarrollo Urbano, 6903
Colombia. Instituto Geográfico Agustín Codazzi, 7193, 7285-7289
Colombia. Instituto Geográfico Agustín Codazzi. Oficina de Estudios Geográficos, 6904
Colombia. Ministerio de Agricultura. Comité Evaluador de la Reforma Agraria, 2055
Colombia. Ministerio de Agricultura. Oficina de Planeamiento, Coordinación y Evaluación, 6905
Colombia. Ministerio de Minas y Petróleos. Instituto Nacional de Investigaciones Geológico-Mineras, 7290
Colombia. Ministerio de Trabajo y Seguridad Social. Servicio Nacional de Aprendizaje (SENA). División de Recursos Humanos, 2056-2057
Colombo, Oscar Juan Héctor, 6524
Coloquio de Comercialización Internacional, *Buenos Aires*, 2338
Colson, Audrey Butt, 1241
Comas, Juan, 507, 1653, 1725
Comercio Exterior, 1994
Comercio Exterior e Integración, 2085

Comisión de Integración Eléctrica Regional (CIER), *Montevideo,* 6525, 7210
Comitas, Lambros, 1136-1137, 1179-1180
Commonwealth Caribbean Regional Secretariat, *Georgetown,* 1995-1996
Comnéne, Raymond Alexis, 82
Companhia Agricola Imobiliária e Colonizadora (CAIC), *São Paulo,* 7039
Companhia do Desenvolvimento do Planalto Central (CODEPLAN), *Brasília,* 7040
Compton Advertising (firm), *San Francisco, Calif.,* 1957
Conant, Ralph W., 7485
Condarco Morales, Ramiro, 6763
Condoruma, Silvestre, 7364
Conference in Pre-Columbian Iconography, *Washington, 1970,* 546
Conference of Latin Americanist Geographers, *I, Muncie, Ind., 1969,* 6526
Conference of the Food and Agriculture Organization of the United Nations, *XVI, Roma, 1971,* 1997
Conference on the Western Hemisphere, *N.Y., 1970,* 7386
Conferencia Anual de Ejecutivos (CADE), *VIII-IX, Paracas, Perú, 1969-1970,* 2276-2277
Conferencia Consultiva de Ganaderos, *VII, Cúcuta, Co., 1971,* 2058
Confirmado, 7387
Congrès International de l'Université Laval sur les Problèmes Economiques, Sociaux, Culturels, Religieux et Politiques de l'Amérique Latine, *Québec, Canada, 1968,* 82
Congreso Centroamericano de Economistas, Contadores Públicos y Auditores, *II, San Salvador, 1965,* 1958
Congreso de la Emigración Española a Ultramar, *III, Madrid, 1965,* 6527
Congreso de los Consorcios Regionales de Experimentación Agrícola, *VI, Rosario, Arg., 1971,* 2339
Congreso Geológico Venezolano, *IV, Caracas, 1969,* 6962
Congreso Iberoamericano de Promoción Profesional de la Mano de Obra, *I, Madrid, 1967,* 6013
Congreso Internacional de Americanistas, *XXXIX, Lima, 1970. See* International Congress of Americanists, *XXXIX, Lima, 1970.*
Congresso Brasileiro do Cacau, *I, Itabuna, Bra., 1967,* 7041
Conjuntura Econômica, 2429
Conning, Arthur M., 8423
Conselho de Desenvolvimento de Extremo Sul (CODESUL), *Florianópolis, Bra.,* 7042-7043
Consiglieri, Isabella, 2469
Constituição da República Federativa do Brasil: emenda constitucional no. 1, de 17 de outubro de 1969, 6232

Consultoria e Planejamento de Hildráulica e Saneamento (firm), *São Paulo,* 7044
Conte Porras, J., 8133
Contreras, Agustín, 6963
Contreras, José del C., 738
Contreras S., Enrique, 6149
Convenção Nacional do Movimento Democrático Brasileiro, 7843
Converse, James W., 8428
Conway, Donna L., 1733
Cook, James M., 1235
Cook, Thomas, 7457
Cook de Leonard, Carmen, 550
Cooke, John William, 7938
Cooman, Maria Augusta de, 6273
Cooperativismo en El Salvador: legislación y doctrina, 1959
Cooperator, 2340
Coppens, Walter, 1242-1243, 6964
Corbacho Carrillo, Susana, 933-935
Cordasco, Francesco, 8375
Cordeiro, Laerte Leite, 8253
Cordera, Rolando, 7683
Cordero Miranda, Gregorio, 810
Córdoba G., J. Rodrigo, 6906
Córdova, César Ramón, 1408
Córdova, Federico de, 1796
Cornblit, Oscar, 1797
Cornehls, J. V., 1915-1916
Cornelius, Wayne A., 7388
Cornides, Albert, 837
Corona Núñez, José, 594
Corona Rentería, Alfonso, 6720
Corona S., Eduardo, 638
Coronelli, Vincenzo, 7352
Corporación Autónoma Regional del Cauca, *Cali. Co.,* 6907-6908
Corr, Edwin G., 7641
Corrada, Rafael, 2489
Corradini, Eugenio F., 2383
Côrrea, Arlindo Lopes, 6233-6234, 6259
Corrêa, Conceição G., 831
Correa, Gustavo, 1043
Correa, Jorge, 7389
Corrêa, R. Lobato, 7073
Corrêa Mascaro, Carlos, 6264
Correia Dias, Fernando. *See* Dias, Fernando Correia.
Corro, Berta Alicia, 8268
Corsi, Carlos, 8424
Corso, Eduardo J., 7905
Cortázar, Pedro Felipe, 6950
Cortés Conde, Roberto, 510
Cortés de Tadey, Mariluz, 2155
Corvalán Lepe, Luis, 7740
Coscia, Adolfo, 2341
Coser, Lewis A., 1150
Cosío, Carlos, 6084
Cosío Villegas, Daniel, 7510
Cosío Z., Gabriel, 1710

AUTHOR INDEX

Cosme Ramos, Dilson. *See* Ramos, Dilson Cosme.
Cossard-Binon, Giselle, 1244
Costa, Gerson Teixeira da, 7045
Costa, Jorge Gustavo da, 7844
Costa, Pedro Veloso, 8478
Costa, Roberto B. da, 6014
Costa, Ronaldo, 2430
Costa, Rubens Vaz de, 7046
Costa Filho, Miguel, 7047
Costa Lima, Haroldo José Sousa. *See* Lima, Haroldo José Sousa Costa.
Costa Pinto, L.A. *See* Pinto, Luiz de Aguiar Costa.
Costa Pinto, Luiz de Aguiar. *See* Pinto, Luiz de Aguiar Costa.
Costa Pinto, Sulamita B. de, 7458
Costa Villavicencio, Lázaro, 6528
Costa Rica. Instituto Geográfico Nacional, 7291
Costales Samaniego, Alfredo, 1372, 1468-1469, 2098
Cotler, Julio, 1373, 7695, 8425
Cotlow, Lewis, 1245
Coulaud, Paul, 8286
Coulthard, George R., 82
Council on International Educational Exchange, *N.Y.*, 83
Couriel, Alberto, 7456
Coutinho Neto, Antônio Barreto, 7045
Covo, Milena E., 1917, 8300
Cowart, Billy F., 6150
Coy, Peter E. B., 8301
Cozean, Jon D., 8157
Craig, Alan K., 510, 811, 936
Craig, Richard B., 8112
Crassweller, Robert D., 8158
Cravo Peixoto, Enaldo. *See* Peixoto, Enaldo Cravo.
Crawford, Michael H., 1654, 1738
Crawley, Eduardo D., 7939
Crazut, Rafael J., 2127
Crespi, Muriel, 1374, 7672
Crespo, Ana María, 686
Los Crímenes, 7806
A crise do ensino: coletânea de artigos de revista *El Correo* de la UNESCO, de abril de 1969 e janeiro de 1970, 6235
Crisis universitaria colombiana 1971: itinerario y documentos, 6126
Crispim, J., 1734
Crist, Raymond E., 6532
Crocker, J. Christopher, 1246
Crocker, William H., 1247
Crofts, Marjorie, 1521
Cross, Malcolm, 6194, 6203
Crosson, Pierre R., 2203
Crow, John Armstrong, 6721
Crowley, Daniel J., 1136
Crumrine, Lynne S., 1044
Crumrine, N. Ross, 510
Cruxent, José M., 755
Cruz, Ramón Ernesto, 7552-7553
Cruz, Waldemir B., 7108
Cruz López, David, 6196
Cruz Magnanini, Ruth Lopes da. *See* Magnanini, Ruth Lopes da Cruz.
Cserna, Zoltan de, 6722
Cüceloglu, D., 8519
Cuadernos de Antropología, 1522
Cuadernos de Economía, 2204
Cuadra, Héctor, 7511
Cuba. Fuerzas Armadas Revolucionarias. Dirección Política, 7574
Cuba. Instituto Cubano de Geodesia y Cartografía, 7292
Cuculiza, Pedro J., 961
Cuéllar, Oscar, 7390
Cuestionario para la delimitación de las zonas dialectales de México, 1523
Cueva Jaramillo, Juan, 898
Cuevillas, Fernando N. Arturo, 2342
Cummings, Richard L., 6236
Cumper, G. E., 1998
Cunha, Ernesto de Mello Salles, 832
Cunha, Maria Auxiliadora Versiani, 6237
Cunha, Raymundo Cyriaco Alves da, 84
Cunill G., Pedro, 6864
Currie, Lauchlin Bernard, 6909
Curitiba (city), *Bra.* Instituto de Pesquisa e Planejamento Urbano de Curitiba, 7271
Custred, Glynn, 1375
Dacal Moure, Ramón, 757
Dade, Philip L., 739-740
Dados preliminares gerais do censo agropecuário, região Sul: VIII recenseamento geral, 1970, 7048
Dagum, Camilo, 6015
Daino, Leonardo, 791
Dalle, Luis, 1376
Dalmasso, E., 6931
Daly, Herman E., 8479
Dam, Kenneth, 2490
Dana Montaño, Salvador M., 7940-7941
Danckwerts, Dankwart, 7482a
Dandler-Hanhart, Jorge Erwin, 1377-1378
D'Andrea, Héctor, 6764
d'Ans, André-Marcel, 510
D'Antoni, Héctor Luis, 774
Dantas, Humberto da Silveira, 7049
Da Rocha, F. J. *See* Rocha, F. J. da.
Dathorne, O. R., 1180
Dauelsberg, Percy, 877-878
Daugherty, Howard E., 6529
Daus, Federico A., 6801
Davenport, William A., 6663
David, Donald E., 7391
David, Henry P., 1168
David, L. Irby, 6723
David, Wilfred L., 2107-2108

Davidovich, Fany, 7050-7051
Dávila, Carlos, 1680
Dávila, Gerardo, 7512
Dávila, Mauro, 85
Dávila Ortiz, Alfonso, 7642
Davis, Emma Lou, 639
Davis, Harlan, 1848, 2413
Davis, Stanley. M., 8258
Davison, R. B., 1137
Day, Kent C., 937
Dean, Warren, 76, 2431
Deas, Malcolm, 7643
Debien, G., 1138
Debray, Régis, 7741-7742
DeCastro, Steve, 1999
De Kadt, Emanuel, 8159
Delaney, Patrick J. V., 7052
Delavaud, Claude Collin, 6951
Délcio Cavedon, Ari. *See* Cavedon, Ari Délcio.
De León, R. *See* León, R. de.
Deler, Jean-Paul, 6952
Delfino, Pedro, 6075
Delgado, Carlos, 1421
Delgado, Oscar,. 7644, 8259, 8282
Delgado Barreto, César, 82
Delgado de Carvalho, Carlos Miguel. *See* Carvalho, Carlos Miguel Delgado de.
D'Elía, Germán, 7906
Delich, Francisco José, 6802, 7942
Dell, Sidney, 1798
Della Valle, P. A., 2205
Delobelle, André, 6016
Delorenzo Neto, Antônio, 7845, 8480
Deluz, Ariane, 1379
Demas, William G., 1137, 8376
Denevan, William M., 510, 1248, 6530
Denis, Paul-Yves, 82, 6803
Denton, Charles F., 7532
Derring, Sandra, 1524
Desai, Sally M. P., 1693
El desarrollo económico y social del Ecuador: estructura, proceso y perspectivas, 2086
Desierto lunar en el norte de Chile, 6865
Despradel, Fidelio, 7613
Despres, Leo A., 1136
Dessau, Adalbert, 7424a
Devoto, Francisco C. H., 510
Devoto, Raúl A., 6076
Dew, Edward M., 7684
Diamand, Marcelo, 2343
Diarios de Bolivia: diarios de campaña de compañeros del Che no divulgados hasta ahora en nuestro idioma, 7714
Dias, Edmundo Fernandes, 7846
Dias, Fernando Correia, 8481
Dias, Ondemar, 833-834
Dias, Ondemar F., Jr., 835
Dias Collier, Mario Elisa. *See* Collier, Mario Elisa Dias.

Diatay B. de Menezes, Eduardo. *See* Menezes, Eduardo Diatay B. de.
Díaz, Hilda M., 16
Díaz, Lucía Stella. 2378
Díaz, Pío Pablo, 803
Díaz Araujo, Enrique, 7943-7944
Díaz Borbón, Rafael, 6127
Díaz Martínez, Antonio, 510, 1380
Díaz-Trechuelo Spínola, María Lourdes, 12
Díaz y de Ovando, Clementina, 6151
Dibble, Charles E., 550
Diccionario Porrúa de historia, biografía geografía de México, 86
Dicionário geográfico brasileiro, 7053
Dickenson, Joshua C., III, 6531-6532, 6659
Diégues Júnior, Manuel, 8482, 8483
Diehl, Richard A., 594, 696
Dietz, Robert S., 6623
DiLella, Eduardo F., 2344
Di Lullo, Orestes, 775, 6804
Dinerstein, Herbert, 8009
Diniz, José Alexandre Felizola, 7034
Diniz de Araújo Neto, Mário. *See* Araújo Neto, Mário Diniz de.
Dinkelspiel, John R., 7827
Dios Rosales, Juan de, 8357
Directorio jurídico biográfico mexicano: 1972, 87
Dirks, Robert, 1139
Di Tella, Torcuato S., 7945
Divine, Robert A., 8160
Divisão territorial do Brasil em grandes regiões e micro-regiões homogêneas, com suas nominatas, 7054
Dobkin de Ríos, Marlene, 1249-1252, 1381, 1662
Dobyns, Henry F., 1357, 1382, 1449, 8426
Dockery, Robert H., 8010
Documentación Bibliotecológica, 43
Dodson, Michael, 7936
Dohen, Dorothy, 8377
Dollfus, M. O., 6533
Domike, Arthur L., 1799
Domingo, W.A., 1179
Domingues Carneiro, José Fernando. *See* Carneiro, José Fernando Domingues.
Domínguez, Jorge I., 7575
Domínguez, Loreto M., 1800
Dominican Republic. Banco Central. Oficina Nacional de Estadística, 2000, 7294
Dominican Republic. Universidad Autónoma de Santo Domingo. Instituto Geográfico Universitario, 7295
Donnan, Christopher B., 938-939
Donnelly, John T., 2432
Donner, Donald D., 1729
Donner, R. W., 6941
Donoso Pareja, Miguel, 7771
Dória, Antônio Roberto Sampaio, 2438
Dorner, Peter, 6534, 6642
Dornstreich, Mark D., 547

Dos Santos, Deoscoredes M., 1253
Dos Santos, Juana Elbein, 1253
Dos Santos, Oder José, 8481
Dosser, Douglas, 1985
Dougherty, Bernard, 776
Doughty, Paul L., 1382-1385, 1435
Douyon, Emerson, 1140
Dovring, Folke, 1918, 6724
Dow, J. Kamal, 2059
Dozier, Craig L., 6535, 6725
Dozo, Salvador Ramón Manuel, 6536
Drekonja, Gerhard, 7392
Drenikoff, Iván, 7345
Dressel, Klaus, 7426a, 7489a
Driver, Edwin D., 6537
Drouet, Pierre, 6017
Drumond, Carlos, 1525
Duarte, Aluízio Capdeville, 7055
Duarte Pereira, Osny. *See* Pereira, Osny Duarte.
Dubelaar, C. N., 1141
Ducke, Erich, 7424a
Dueñas Ruiz, Oscar, 7907
Dufour, Jules, 6681
Duke, Keith S., 2491
Dumas, Benoit A., 7393
Dumond, D. E., 548-549
Dumont, Jean-Paul, 1254
Dumont, René, 6538, 7576
Duncan, W. Raymond, 8011
Dunham, Katherine, 1140, 1142-1143
Dunkerley, Harold B., 2060
Dunn, William N., 8012
Dupont-Gonin, Pierre, 2109
Dupuis, Jacques, 6638
Duque Corredor, Ramón José, 2128
Duque Gómez, Luis, 865-866
Durán, Eva Arcidiácono de, 6805
Durán T., Marco Antonio, 1919, 1946
Durate, Gerusa Maria, 836
Durbin, Marshall, 1526
Dussán de Reichel, Alicia, 867
Dutt, J. S., 1709
Dutta, M., 2492
Dutting, Dieter, 723
Dwyer, Edward, 940
Dyckerhoff, Ursula, 640
Dynastic republicanism to Haiti, 7618
Ealy, Lawrence O., 8134
Earle, Timothy K., 941
Easby, Elizabeth Kennedy, 751
Eaton, Jack D., 536, 641
Ebanks, G. Edward, 8378
Ebel, Roland H., 7394
Ebersole, Robert P., 1386
Echagüe, Carlos M., 7946
Echavarría Olózaga, Hernán, 2061
Echenique, Miguel, 2493
Echeverría, Roberto, 2206
Echeverría Bunster, Andrés, 2207

Echeverría Salvat, Oscar A., 2001
Eckhaus, Richard S., 2208
Economía, 2129
Económica, 2345-2346
Ecuador. Dirección General de Geología y Minas. Departamento de Cartografía, 7296
Ecuador. Instituto de Comercio Exterior e Integración, 8194
Ecuador. Instituto Nacional de Estadística, 2087
Ecuador. Junta Nacional de Planificación y Coordinación, 2088-2090, 2093
Ecuador. Ministerio de Agricultura y Ganadería, 6932
Ecuador. Ministerio de Finanzas, 2091
Ecuador. Ministerio de la Producción. Dirección General de Planificación, 2092
Edel, Matthew, 1387, 6714, 6910
Edelweiss, Frederico G., 1527
Eden, Michael J., 6965
Ediciones Ing. Behn, *Guadalajara, Mex.*, 7311
Ediger, Donald, 642
Editôra Presidente Limitada (firm), *Rio*, 7254-7255, 7272
Editorial Mapa (firm), *Buenos Aires*, 7226
Edmonds, David C., 8013
Educação. Ministério da Educação e Cultura, 6238
Educação. Orgão da Federação Nacional dos Estabelecimentos de Ensino, 6239
Edwards, D. T., 1137, 6621
Edwards, Ernest Preston, 6706, 6726
Edwards, Gertrud G., 2130
Edwards, Harold T., 7545
Edwards, Thomas L., 2209
Efron, Edith, 1180
Egg, Ezequiel Ander, 8260
Egloff, Schwaiger, 7426a
Ehrhardt, Wolfgang, 7735a
Eibl-Eibesfeldt, Irenäus, 1255
Eichler, Arturo, 6539
Eiman, Armando, 8261
Einaudi, Luigi R., 7685, 8014
Eisleb, Dieter, 643
Ekelund, Robert B., Jr., 1801
Ekholm, Gordon F., 550
El-Badry, M. A., 1735
Elder, J. D., 1144
Eletrificação do Paraná, 7056
Elkins, W. F., 8379
Ellis, Bengt, 6622, 6933
El Salvador. Instituto Geográfico Nacional, 7298
El Salvador. Ministerio de Economía. Dirección General de Estadística y Censos, 1960
El Salvador. Ministerio de Educación. Dirección General de Cultura, 6094-6095
Elson, Diane, 1879
Elu de Leñero, María del Carmen, 8302-8303

Emperaire, José, 1256
Enciso, Jorge, 644
Encontro Brasileiro sôbre Introdução ao Estudo da História, *I, Nova Friburgo, 1968,* 6240
La energía en América Latina, 1802
Engel, Frederic, 942
English, Burt H., 7546
English, William P., 7312
Enjalbert, Claudine, 8113
Enjalbert, Henri, 6727, 8113
Enne, Giuseppe, 6765
Enns, Arno W., 8427
Enos, J. L., 8033
Ensino técnico industrial em Minas Gerais, 6241
Epstein, Erwin H., 6170
Erb, H. H., 6806
Erdmenger la Fuente, Eugenia, 8346
Eriksen, Wolfgang, 6807
Erisman, H. Michael, 7457
Eritta, Elena, 510
Erk, Frank C., 6556
Escalante, Roberto, 724
Escalante, Rodolfo, 6808
Escalante, Rosendo, 594
Escardó, Florencio, 6809
Escobar, Alberto, 1528
Escobar, Gustavo, 2136
Escobar, María Elvira, 1388
Escobar Moscoso, Gabriel, 1389-1391, 1402
Escobar Sierra, Hugo, 7645
Esparza Torres, Héctor F., 7313-7314
Espejo Núñez, Julio, 943-944
Espín, Vilma, 7577
Espinal, Andrés Julio, 7614
Espinel Rivadeneira, Enrique, 2094
Espinet, Adrian, 1180
Espinet Colón, Gabriel R., 2494
Espinoza García, Manuel, 8015
Espinoza Soriano, Waldemar, 510, 945
Espinoza Uriarte, Humberto, 2278
Esser, Klaus, 7743-7743a
Esteva Fabregat, Claudio, 1392
Estrada, Alejandro, 510
Estrada, Raúl, 2095
Estrategia, 8195
Estrategia del desarrollo pesquero dentro del bloque andino, 2096
Estrella, Julio C., 2002
Estudios sobre la Economía Argentina, 2347
Eusse Hoyos, Gerardo, 2062
Evangelio, política y socialismos, 7744
Evans, Clifford, 755, 841
Evans, Henry Clay, Jr., 8196
Evans de la Cuadra, Enrique, 7745
Eveleth, Phyllis B., 1688
Evers, Tilman Tönnies, 7946a-7946b
Ewing, Maurice, 7213
La expansión de los centros universitarios de la Universidad de Chile, 6110
A experiência do Paraná, 88, 2434

Exposição da Imprensa Universitária, *I, São Paulo, 1972,* 13
Exposição lançamentos do ano 1969, 30
A extensão rural no Brasil, 7057
Eyre, L. Alan, 6650
Fabbrica Italiana Automobili Torino (FIAT), *Argentina.* Oficina de Estudios para la Colaboración Económica Internacional, 1803, 2309
Fábrega, Horacio, Jr., 1045, 1663
Fábregas Puig, Andrés, 1046
Fachin, R. C., 6242
Fagen, Richard R., 7578
Fairlie Fuentes, Enrique, 7686
Faissol, Speridião, 2435, 7038, 7058-7060, 7069, 8484
Fajnzylber, Fernando, 2436
Falcoff, Mark, 7947
Falcón de Gyves, Zaida, 6728-6729, 7315
Falegeau, Xavier, 6730
Faleiros, Vicente de Paula, 8485
Falk-Rønne, Arne, 1257
Falla, Ricardo, 1047
Fallaci, Oriana, 7426a
Fallas, Marco Antonio, 1961
Fals Borda, Orlando, 7395
Fann, K. T., 8016
Fanon, Frantz, 1179
Faron, Louis C., 1393
Farris, George F., 7847
Fastlicht, Samuel, 1726
Faust, Norma, 1529
Favre, Henri, 1048, 1394-1395, 1421
Federación Argentina de Cooperativas Agrarias, *Buenos Aires,* 6810
Fedor, Kenneth J., 1848
Feldman, Arnold S., 8405
Feldman, Ernesto V., 2348
Feldman, Lawrence H., 551, 683, 1530
Felizola Diniz, José Alexandre. *See* Diniz, José Alexandre Felizola.
Felstehausen, Herman, 6911
Feo Calcano, Guillermo, 7817
Ferguson, John Halcró, 6766
Ferguson, Yale H., 8017-8019
Ferkiss, Barbara, 7630
Ferkiss, Victor C., 7630
Fernandes, Eurico, 7061
Fernandes, Florestan, 7482a, 8020, 8268, 8486-8491
Fernandes, Liliana Laganá, 7062-7063
Fernandes, Neusa, 89
Fernandes de Sá, Paulo. *See* Sá, Paulo Fernandes de.
Fernandes Dias, Edmundo. *See* Dias, Edmundo Fernandes.
Fernandes Neto, Antônio, 8493
Fernandes Tavares, Denise. *See* Tavares, Denise Fernandes.
Fernández, Guido, 1962

Fernández, Jorge, 777
Fernández, Julio A., 7513
Fernández, Nelson A., 1689
Fernández del Valle, Agustín Basave, 6018
Fernández Guizzetti, Germán, 1531-1533
Fernández y Fernández, Ramón, 1946
Ferrari Leite, José. *See* Leite, José Ferrari.
Ferreira, Carlos Mauricio de Carvalho, 7064
Ferreira, Délia V., 6014
Ferreira, Evaldo Osório, 7246
Ferreira, Luis Pinto, 90
Ferreira, Osmar, 6228
Ferreira Balção, Yolanda. *See* Balção, Yolanda Ferreira.
Ferreira de Camargo, Cândido Procópio. *See*. Camargo, Cândido Procópio Ferreira de.
Ferreira Filho, Manoel Gonçalves, 7848
Ferreira Reis, Arthur Cézar. *See* Reis, Arthur Cézar Ferreira.
Ferreira Sana, Júlio F. *See* Sana, Júlio F. Ferreira.
Ferreira Sobral, Eduardo F., 7195
Ferrell, Robert H., 8021
Ferrer, Aldo, 7489a
Ferrer, Gustavo, 7948
Ferrer, Norberto C., 2349
Ferrer Vieyra, Enrique, 8197
Ferrero Calvo, César, 7646
Ferrocarriles argentinos: plan mediano plazo, 2350
Ferrocarriles, vapores: lo que va de ayer a hoy en Nicaragua, 6703
Fewkes, Jesse Walter, 1145
Ffrench-Davis, Ricardo, 7409, 2210
Fiallo, Fabio Rafael, 2003
Fidalgo, Francisco, 806, 6811
Figueira, José Joaquín, 1612
Figueiredo, Nuno Fidelino de, 2437
Figueiredo de Lima, Antônio. *See* Lima, Antônio Figueiredo de.
Figueroa, John J., 6195
Figueroa Velásquez, Emilio, 7807
Fillon, P., 6931
Finch, M. H. J., 2310
Fischlowitz, Estanislau, 8494
Fisher, Bart S., 8022
Fisher, William M., 1534
Fishlow, Albert, 2437a
Fitzgibbon, Russell H., 7396
Flannery, Kent V., 530, 552
Fleischhacker, H., 510
Fleischmann, Ulrich, 7618a
Fletcher, Alan Mark, 6942
Fletcher, L. P., 1146
Flieger, W., 1743
Flinn, William L., 8428
Flora, Cornelia Butler, 1396
Flora, Jan Leighton, 7647
Flores, Edmundo, 1946, 6731
Flores, Eusebio, 6866

Flores, Mario César, 7849
Flores García, Lorenza, 645
Flores Ochoa, Jorge A., 1397
Floria, Carlos Alberto, 8429, 8439
Floyd, Barry, 6651
Flusser, Vilém, 8495
Fock, Niels, 510, 1258
Folan, W. J., 553, 646
Foland, Frances M., 7065, 7908
Folino, Norberto, 7949
Fomenting improvements in food marketing in Costa Rica, 1963
Fonck, Carlos O'Brien, 6699
Foner, Nancy, 1147-1148
Fondo Ganadero de Santander, *Bucaramanga, Co.,* 6912
Forbes, Urias, 7629
Ford, John J., 6515
Forero, Manuel José, 6913
La formación de adultos y el desarrollo socioeconómico, 6019
Foro Internacional, 8114
Forsberg, Sven, 8498
Fortes d'Andrea, Flávio. *See* Andrea, Flávio Fortes d'.
Fossum, Egil, 7397
Foster, Dereck H. N., 91
Foster, George, 1049
Foster, Mary LeCron, 1535
Fougère, William, 1685
Foury, A. Paul, 7066
Fox, David J., 8304
Foxley, Alejandro, 2211-2213
França, G. E. de, 7177
France. Institut Géographique National, 7299, 7308
Francis, Michael J., 7398, 7746, 8023
Franco, Carlos de Mello, 8499
Franco, Carlos Hernán, 7893
Franco Sobrinho, Manoel de Oliveira, 7850
Frank, André Gunder, 1804-1805
Frank, Charles R., Jr., 1806
Franke, Richard, 1149
Frankman, Myron J., 8262
Franz, Carl, 92
Frederick, Kenneth D., 2438
Freeland, George L., 6623
Freez, Ray, 1536
Frei Montalva, Eduardo, 7399
Freidberg, Sidney, 8161
Freilich, Morris, 1150
Freire, Paulo, 8500
Freire-Maia, Newton, 1736, 1744
Freitas Marcondes, J. V. *See.* Marcondes, J. V. Freitas

Freitas Rachid, Cora Bastos de. *See* Rachid, Cora Bastos de Freitas.
Frente Nacional de Abogados para la Defensa de la Reforma Agraria, *Lima*, 2279
Freyre, Gilberto, 6243, 7067, 7482a, 8501, 8502
Freyre, Jorge F., 2495-2496
Frías, Ismael, 7687
Frías, Pedro J., 7950, 8439
Frías Alvarez, Ricardo, 8198
Friedemann, Nina S., 1398
Friedhelm, Merz, 7426a
Friedman, Arnold M., 946
Friedman, Bruno, 1920, 7747
Friedrich, Paul, 1537-1538
Frietahaler, William O., 1921
Frikel, Protásio, 1259-1260
Frisancho, A. Roberto, 1690-1691
Frites, Eulogio, 1399
Fromm, Erich, 8305
Frondizi, Risieri, 6020
Froude, James Anthony, 1136
Frutkin, Arnold W., 7400
Frutos, Juan Manuel, 7894
Fuchs, Helmuth, 1261
Füchtner, Hans, 7850a
Fuente, Beatriz de la, 554, 647
Fuente, Nicolás R. de la, 778-780
Fuentes Aguilar, Luis, 6755
Fuenzalida, Fernando, 1400-1402, 1421, 7695
Fuenzalida Faivovich, Edmundo, 6021
Fuenzalida V., Fernando. *See* Fuenzalida, Fernando.
Fuerst, René, 1262-1263
Fulchi, Gustavo Adolfo, 7401
Fundação Getúlio Vargas. Instituto Brasileiro de Economia. Centro de Estudos Agrícolas, 7068
Fundação IBGE, *Rio*, 2439-2440
Fundación Bariloche, *San Carlos de Bariloche, Arg.* Departamento de Sociología, 6812
Fundación de Investigaciones Económicas Latinoamericanas (FIEL), 2351-2352
Fundación de Investigaciones Económicas Latinoamericanas (FIEL), *Buenos Aires*, 2353-2355
Fundación e Instituto Miguel Lillo, *Tucumán, Arg.*, 31
Fundación de Cultura Universitaria, *Montevideo*, 2311
Fung Pineda, Rosa, 946a
Furley, Peter, 6674
Furnish, Dale B., 7688, 7748
Furst, Peter T., 508, 1050-1051, 1100, 1403
Furtado, Celso, 1807-1809, 2441-2442, 7482a
Furtak, Robert K., 7579
Gade, Daniel W., 510, 1404
Gaignard, Romain, 2131
Gakenheimer, Ralph A., 510
Galán, Miguel A., 7648
Galdo Pagaza, Raúl, 1405-1406

Galdós, Bertania, 1719
Galeano, Eduardo H., 2312, 7402, 7715
Galindo Pohl, Reynaldo, 1964
Galjart, B.F., 7749, 8263
Galjart, Benno. *See* Galjart, B.F.
Gall, Norman, 1407, 7403-7404, 7580, 8430
Gallinat, Walton C., 530
Gallo Mendoza, Guillermo, 2356
Gallovich, Eugenio, 6966
Gally, Héctor, 7649
Galmarini, Alfredo G., 6813
Galrao, María José, 7196
Galtung, Johan, 8024
Galvão, Marília Velloso, 7069
Gamarra, Moisés, 1327
Gambini, Hugo, 7951-7952
Gamboa, Emma, 6096
Gámez Solano, Uladislao, 6097
Gamio, Manuel, 571
Gancedo, Omar A., 1264
Gann, Thomas William Francis, 6732
Gans, Marjorie, 8503
Gantenbein, James W., 8025
Garaicoechea C., Manuel Felipe, 2132
Garasino, Luis, 8195
Garay, Luis G. B., 775, 6804
Garças Cardia, Nancy das. *See* Cardia, Nancy das Garças.
Garcés, Joan E., 7650-7651, 7750
García, Alicia I., 16
García, Antonio, 1810, 7652-7653
Garcia, Caio del Rio, 837, 858
García, Eduardo, 2211
García, Miguel Angel, 50, 6700
García, Noel A., 8264
García Barragán, Elisa, 6151
García-Blásquez, Raúl, 1408, 1431, 2269
García Bonnelly, Juan Ulises, 6643
García Cook, Angel, 702
García Cortés, Fernando, 6148
García Costa, Víctor, 7953
Garcia de Almeida, Marco Aurelio. *See* Almeida, Marco Aurelio Garcia de.
García de Miranda, Enriqueta, 7315
García del Pino, César, 752
García Della Costa, Fernando, 8199
García Firbeda, Miguel, 6536
García Flores, José I., 7954
García-Goyena, Juan, 7751
García Hassey, Eduardo, 6148
García Jiménez, Jesús, 6022
García Maldonado, Leopoldo, 6023
García Martínez, Luis, 7955
García-Passalacqua, Juan M., 7623
García Payón, José, 550
García Ramos, Domingo, 6152
García Robles, Alfonso, 8115
García Steve, Joel, 8265
Gardiner, C. Harvey, 6644
Gardner, George, 7070

Garn, Stanley M., 1690-1691
Garr, Thomas M., 1409
Garretón, Manuel, 2239
Garrido, Manuel I., 6767
Garrido Torres, José. *See* Torres, José Garrido.
Garvey, Marcus, 1180
Gasparini, Graziano, 510
Gates, G. Marilyn, 1922
Gates, Gary R., 1922
Gaurch, José M., 757
Gauthier, Howard L., 6540
Gavi, Philippe, 7405
Gavilán Estelat, Marcelino, 2214, 7406
Gay, Carlo T. E., 555, 648
Geer, Thomas, 1811
Geerdink, R. A., 1664
Gehlen, Iegle, 7071
Geiger, Pedro Pinchas, 7072-7073
Gelbard, José M., 2357
Gelfand, Lawrence E., 8026
Gelling, Peter S., 947
Gelsi Bidart, Adolfo, 6024
Gendell, Murray, 1812
Gendrop, Paul, 556-557
General Drafting Company (firm), *Convent Station, N.J.*, 7211, 7305
Genovés, Santiago, 6541
Geocarta (firm), *Rio*, 7526-7258
Geografía económica de Chile, 6867
Geomapas (firm), *São Paulo*, 7259
Geomapas Editôra de Mapas e Guias (firm), *São Paulo*, 7247
George, Pierre, 6542, 7074
Gerber, Mirtha Sonia, 510
Gerencia, 2280
Germani, Gino, 8266
Germidis, Dimitiros A., 1813
Gershowitz, H., 1737
Gerson Gradvohl, Roberto. *See* Gradvohl, Roberto Gerson.
Gettleman, Marvin E., 8162
Gevertz, Rachel, 6244
Ghioldi, Américo, 7808
Giacottino, Jean-Claude, 6624
Giannotti, José Arthur, 8256
Gibbs, Jack P., 1910
Giberti, Eva, 8431
Gibson, Charles, 550
Giffoni, O. Carneiro, 19
Gil, Federico G., 7407
Gil, Mario, 1923
Gil Arántegui, Malaquías, 6025
Gil-Bermejo García, Juana, 2497
Gil Huerta, Gorgonio, 574
Giliberto de Guevara, Ninfa, 6111
Gilio, María Esther, 7909
Gillette, Philip, 7467
Gillon, Hadassah, 6026
Gillon, Philip, 6026
Gilmore, Norman, 7075

Giménez-Carrazana, Manuel, 2173
Gimeno, José, 2215
Giner de los Ríos, Francisco, 6027
Ginsberg, A., 8519
Gioja, Rolando I., 7076
Giorgio, Alberti. *See* Alberti, Giorgio.
Girard, Victor, 1539
Girault, Christian A., 6733
Girvan, Norman, 1814
Givogri, Carlos A., 2358
Glanville, E.V., 1664
Glasgow, Roy Arthur, 1151
Glass, Bentley, 6556
Glassner, Martin Ira, 8163
Glauert, Earl T., 8027
Glazer, Myron, 6112
Glazer, Penina Migdal, 6112
Glean, Carlyle A., 1165
Glynn, Peter W., 6707, 6967
Gnaccarini, José César A., 8504
Godard, C., 1665
Goddard, D., 1410
Goddard, S. N. de, 1410
Godoy, Horacio H., 1815
Goes, Terezinha de Jesus M., 7077
Goes Ribeiro, M. N. *See* Ribeiro, M. N. Goes.
Goff, Nollie R., 6543
Goiás (state), *Bra.* Secretaria do Planejamento e Coordenação, 7078
Goicoechea, Helga Nilda, 6814
Goldar, Ernesto, 8432
Goldberg, Maria Amélia Azevédo, 6245
Goldenberg, Boris, 7363b, 7426a
Goldhamer, Herbert, 8028-8029
Goldwert, Marvin, 7956
Golte, Jürgen, 1401, 1421
Golubjatnikov, Rjurik, 1666
Gomes, Raymundo Pimentel, 7079
Gomes Pereira, Sonia. *See* Pereira, Sonia Gomes.
Gómez, Henry, 2133
Gómez, Juan Gualberto, 8155
Gómez, Sergio, 2216
Gómez Gómez, Antonio, 1265
Gómez P., Mario, 2213
Gómez Riveros, Armando, 2063
Gómez Tejera, Carmen, 6196
Gómez-Wanqüement, Luis, 8173
Gonçalves Schatzmayr, Herman. *See* Schatzmayr, Herman Gonçalves.
Gondi, Ovidio, 8116
Gondim, Maristella de Miranda Ribeiro, 6246
Góngora Perea, Amadeo, 7335
Gónima, Ester, 6128
Gonzaga de Oliveira, Luiz. *See* Oliveira, Luiz Gonzaga de.
Gonzáles Navarro, Moisés, 1924
Gonzáles Salazar, Gloria, 1925
González, Alberto Rex, 781-782, 1266
González, Alfonso, 1816, 2004, 6544

González, Carlos Hank, 7514-7515
González, Edward, 8164
González, Eugenio, 6113
González, Joaquín V., 8038
González, Justo L., 8380
González, Miguel H., 510
González, Nancie L. Solien de, 1152-1154, 8358
González, Ricardo Raúl, 6654
González-Bonorino, Félix, 6868
González Carbalho, José, 6815
González Carré, J. E., 948
González del Río Gil, Concepción, 949-951
González Fley, Carlos, 1965
González Náñez, Omar E., 1267-1268, 1540
González Navarro, Moisés, 6734
González Pedrero, Enrique, 6028
González Prieto, Pedro, 2359
González Quintero, Lauro, 675
González Ramírez, Manuel R., 8306
González Rul, Francisco, 649-650
González Salazar, Gloria, 8307
González Tejera, Efraín, 2498
González Villafañe, Edgardo, 2499
Goode, Judith Granich, 6545
Goodman, David E., 2443
Goodman, Louis Wolf, 8258
Goodrich, Carter, 7720
Goodsell, Charles T., 8030
Gorbachev, B. V., 7581
Gorenstein, Shirley, 651
Goring, Paul, 1411
Gorokhov, Iurii Petrovich, 8165
Gott, Richard, 7408
Goulart, Rina Norma Tosello, 2444
Gouré, León, 2005-2006, 7752
Goussault, Yves, 2217
Gouvêa, João Baptista Soares, 7096
Gouvêa Vieira, Jorge Hilário. *See* Vieira, Jorge Hilário Gouvêa.
Gouveia, Aparecida Joly, 8505
Grabendorff, Wolf, 7409
Grabert, Hellmut, 838
Gracia-Zamor, Jean-Claude, 8506
Graciarena, Jorge, 1817, 6029, 6077, 6247, 8267
Gradin, Carlos J., 783-784
Gradvohl, Roberto Gerson, 7080
Gräebener, Jürgen, 8268
Graham, Douglas H., 8507
Graham, John A., 558, 652, 711, 725-728
Graham-Yooll, Andrew, 7957
Gramberg, C. B. E., 1818
Granado G., U. M., 7297
Granthan-McGregor, S. M., 1692-1693
Grases, Pedro J., 1667
Graves, Theodore D., 1116
Gray, Richard B., 7753
Grayson, George W., 7689, 8031
Graziani, Giovanni, 1819
Greaves, Thomas C., 1412-1413
Green, David, 8032

Green, Harold G., 1647
Green, Judith Strupp, 1052
Green, María del Rosario, 1820
Greene, Lawrence S., 1694
Greene, Merle, 558
Greenfield, Sidney M., 7851
Greer, Thomas V., 1966
Grenier, Philippe, 6869
Greño Velasco, José Enrique, 8200
Griffin, Ernst, 6549
Griffin, Gillet G., 653
Griffin, K. B., 8033
Griffin, Margaret, 6849
Griffin, Richard B., Jr., 7400
Griffiths, B., 1926
Grigulevich, Iosif Romul'dovich, 7582-7583
Grimes, James L., 1541
Grimes, Joseph E., 1542-1543
Gromsen, Erdmann, 702
Grondín N., Marcelo, 1544
Groot, Silvia W. de, 1155
Grossman, Joel Warren, 952
Grote, Bernd, 7410
Groussac, Paul, 8038
Grove, David C., 559-560, 654
Grünberg, Friedl, 1269-1270
Grünberg, George, 1270-1271
Grunig, James E., 2064
Grunwald, Joseph, 1821
Grupe, Héctor J., 2360
Grupo Andino: Programa de Liberación; Arancel Externo Mínimo Común, 1822
Guadagni, Alieto, 2361
Guaraldi, Carlos, 1823
Guardia Romero, Jaime, 2174
Guareschi, Pedrinho Arcides, 8508
Guatemala. Consejo Nacional de Planificación Económica, 1967
Guatemala. Instituto Geográfico Nacional, 7300-7302
Guatemala. Ministerio de Economía. Dirección General de Estadística, 1968
Guatemala. Ministerio de Hacienda y Crédito Público. Dirección Tcnica del Presupuesto, 1969
Gudeman, Stephan, 1053
Gudschinsky, Sarah C., 1545-1548
Gueiros Leite, Eraldo. *See* Leite, Eraldo Gueiros.
Guerberoff, Simón G., 2362
Gueron, Carlos, 8201
Guerra, C. Vianna, 8509
Guerra, Hernando, 2076
Guerra Borges, Alfredo, 1970
Guerrero, Raúl, 6870
Guevara, Ernesto Che, 7584
Guía Roji (firm), *Mex.*, 7316-7317
Guía de escuelas y cursos de bibliotecología y documentación en América Latina, 45
Guide to Guadeloupe, 6645

Guido, Francisco Alberto, 8433
Guillén G., Oscar, 7216
Guillén Martínez, Fernando, 7411
Guillén Romo, Arturo, 1927
Guiral, Jesús C., 7910
Guliaev, Valerii Ivanovich, 561-562a
Gumerman, George J., 655
Gumucio, Mariano Baptista, 6085-6086
Gunckel, Hugo, 6871
Gunder Frank, André. See Frank, André Gunder.
Gusmão, Geraldo A., 7108
Gussinyer, Jordi, 656
Gustavo da Costa, Jorge. See Costa, Jorge Gustavo da.
Gutelman, Michel, 1928
Guterres Taveira, Carlos Cesar. See Taveira, Carlos Cesar Guterres.
Gutiérrez, Asir P., 6165
Gutiérrez, Carlos E., 2363
Gutiérrez, Carlos José, 7547
Gutiérrez de MacGregor, María Teresa, 6735
Gutiérrez-Girardot, Rafael, 7412
Gutiérrez Gutiérrez, Mario R., 8202
Gutiérrez Pérez, Francisco, 6030
Gutiérrez Pimentel, Rodolfo, 8347
Guyana. Lands Department. Cartographic Division, 7303-7304
Guyana. Ministry of Labour and Social Security. Manpower Research Division. Manpower Reporting Programme, 2110
Guyana Journal, 2007
La Guyane Française: le pays, ses problèmes economiques, 2111
Guzmán, Eulalia, 594
Guzmán Böckler, Carlos, 8348-8349
Guzmán Campos, Germán, 7654
Guzmán Peredo, Miguel, 563
Gúzman Velasco, Lucio, 6850
Gyarmati, Gabriel, 6114
Haberland, Wolfgang, 657, 741
Hacia la revolución cultural: escuelas populares de educación agropecuaria, 6087
Hadley, C. V. D., 1180
Häger, Olle, 7585
Hafer, Raymond Frederic, 1414
Hageman, Alice L., 8381
Haiti. Conseil National de Développement et de Planification, 2008
Halberstein, Robert A., 1738
Halkjaer, Eivor, 93
Hall, Douglas, 1136
Hall, Gwendolyn Midlo, 1156
Hall, Robert L., 1015
Haller, Archibald O., 8510
Halpap, Paul, 7424a
Halperin, Maurice, 7586
Hambleton, Hugues-Georges, 6546
Hamburg, Roger P., 8203
Hamilton, Patrick, 6948

Hammer, Olga, 715
Hammerly Dupuy, Daniel, 6547
Hammond, Norman, 564-565, 658
Hamour, Mukhtar, 2029
Hamp, Eric P., 1549-1550
Handler, Jerome S., 1137, 1157-1159
Hanna, J. Michael, 1711
Hansen, David, 1951
Hansen, Roger D., 7516
Harberger, Arnold C., 1824
Harburg, Ernest, 1015
Hardman-de-Bautista, M.J., 1551
Hardoy, Jorge Enrique, 510, 8363
Harewood, Jack, 2009, 8382
Harman, Nan, 1137
Harner, Michael J., 1272
Harrell, William A., 6248
Harrigan, Norwell, 2036
Harris, David R., 1273, 6968
Harris, Stuart A., 6682
Harris, Walter D., Jr., 6548
Harris, William G., 2134
Harrison, Carl H., 1552-1553
Harrison, Kelly M., 2529
Harrison, Peter D., 659
Harroy, Jean-Paul, 6660
Hartkopf, Herbert, 1415
Hartmann, Günter, 1274
Hartmann, Roswith, 510, 1416-1417, 1554
Hartung, Horst, 566
Harvey, Dodd L., 120
Harvey, Herbert R., 550
Hasperuá Becerra, Oscar, 8269
Hassan, M. F., 2135
Hastenrath, Stefan, 6851
Hasui, Yociteru, 7081
Haszard, Frank K., 2500
Hatch, Marion Popenoe, 567
Haussman, Fay, 6249
Haviland, William A., 568-570
Hawkes, Nigel, 6115
Heath, Dwight, B., 8434
Hébert, John, 7197-7198
Hedricks, Basil C., 571
Heere, W. P., 8135
Hegen, Edmund E., 6549
Heizer, Robert F., 660-661, 664-665a
Helbig, Karl, 6661
Helfeld, David M., 7374
Heller, Joyce de, 868
Helms, Mary W., 1054
Henne, Marilyn Hanson de, 1555
Henriques, Fernando, 1137
Hensey, Fritz G., 1556
Herbert, Jean-Loup, 8348-8349
Heredia-Durate, A., 1668
Hermosa Virreira, Walter, 1275
Hernández, Alejandro, 1055
Hernández, Roberto E., 7592
Hernández, Salvador, 7517, 7683

Hernández-Alvarez, José, 2501
Hernández Alvarez, Lilia Inés de, 8383
Hernández de Ospina, Bertha, 7655
Hernández Sánchez-Barba, Mario, 6031
Herranz M., Julián, 6969
Herrera, Amílcar Oscar, 7413
Herrera, Felipe, 8034
Herrera, Francisco, 1056
Herrera Fritot, René, 753, 757
Herrero, José A., 2486, 2502
Herrmann, Reimer, 6914
Herschel, Federico J., 2364-2365
Herskovits, Frances S., 1137
Herskovits, Melville, 1137
Herzfeld, Ana, 6032
Hess, Geraldo, 2445
Hester, Thomas Roy, 662-665a
Hey, Nigel, 6550
Heyden, Doris, 572, 666-667
Heyduk, Daniel, 1418
Heyerdahl, Thor, 6662
Hickman, John M., 1419
Hicks, David, 1557.
Hicks, Frederick, 6625, 7895-7896, 8435
Hidronor (firm), *Buenos Aires,* 6816
Higman, B. W., 1160
Higuera B., Tarcisio, 94
Hildner, Robert E., 7468
Hill, Jane H., 1558
Hinshaw, Robert, 1106
Hinton, Thomas B., 1057-1059
Hintzke, Werner, 7424a
Hirsch-Weber, Wolfgang, 8035
Historiografía y Bibliografía Americanistas, 14
Hjalmarsson, Helge, 812-813
Hjortsjö, Carl-Herman, 1727
Hobgood, John J., 1060
Hobsbawn, Eric J., 7690
Hochtief-Montreal-Deconsult (firm), *São Paulo,* 7082
Hochschule St. Gallen für Wirtschafts, und Sozialwissenschaften, *St. Gallen, Switzerland,* 2136
Hodara, Joseph, 7414
Hodges, Donald C., 8016
Hoege, Alfred, 7424a
Hoetink, Harmannus, 1161-1162
Hoetink, Harry, 8268
Holbrook, Sabra, 95
Holguín Peláez, Hernando, 8204
Holloman, Regina Evans, 1061
Holloway, Ralph L., 1655
Holm, Olaf, 898a
Holmberg, Mats, 7754
Holshouser, Judy, 510
Holsinger, Donald, 8510
Honduras. Instituto Nacional Agrario [INA], 6701
Hoogshagen, Searle, 1559
Hooker, James R., 7631
Hopkins, Nicholas A., 1560

Horcasitas, Fernando, 1062, 1561
Hori Robaina, Guillermo, 6033
Horne, Alistair, 7755
Hornman, Wim, 7656
Horowitz, Irving L., 7415
Horst, Oscar H., 6551
Horta Pôrto, Rubens d'Almada. *See* Pôrto, Rubens d'Almada Horta.
Houdaille, J., 1138
Houston, Margaret, 668
Houtart, François, 7587
How will multinational firms react to the Andean Pact's decision 24?, 1825
Howard, Agnes M., 571
Howard, Linda, 1562
Howell, Thomas A., 96
Hoy, Don R., 6549, 6693
Hoyt, Margaret A., 953
Hrdlicka, Ales, 571
Huanay Iturrizaga, Héctor, 1431
Huapaya Manco, Cirilo, 954
Huber, Holly, 1563
Huber, Klaus, 1956
Huddle, Donald L., 2446
Hueck, Hurt, 7212
Hütte, Bernd, 7424a
Huetz de Lemps, Christian, 2503
Huguet Ribe, José, 8036
Huizer, Gerrit, 7416, 7518, 8270
Humbert, Roger, 883
Humboldt, Alexander von, 6552
Hummelinck, P. Wagenaar, 6626
Huneeus C., Pablo, 2218
Hunnicutt, Benjamin Harris, 7083
Hunt, Christopher, 96
Hunt, Eva, 574
Hunte, George, 6627
Hurault, Jean, 1163
Hurtado de Mendoza, Luis, 510, 955
Hutchins, Robert M., 7374
Hyman, Elizabeth H., 7417
Ianni, Constantino, 8205
Ianni, Octavio, 2447, 7409, 7852
Ibáñez-Novión, Martín Alberto, 1420
Ibarra, Enrique, 2262
Ibarra Grasso, Dick Edgar, 509, 956
Ibarra Vega, Salvador, 8037
Ibérico Más, Luis, 510
Ibero-Amerikanska Institutet i Stockholm, 6034
Ichon, Alain, 742, 1063
Iglesias, Dolores, 7084
Iglesias, Enrique, 6178, 7418
Ikonicoff, Moïes, 1826, 6035
Illich, Ivan D., 6036
Imas Urrea, Jorge Renato, 7756
Imaz, José Luis de, 8436, 8439
Imazio, Alcira, 510
D'Incao e Mello, María Conçeicão. *See.* Mello, María Conçeicão D'Incao e.
D'Incao Maciel Sánchez, María Angela. *See* Sánchez, María Angela D'Incao Maciel.

Inclán, Raúl Suárez, 7037, 7173
Indice dos topônimos contidos na Carta do Brasil 1:1.000.000 do IBGE [Instituto Brasileiro de Geografia e Estatística], 7085
Indice general de la *Revista Conservadora del Pensamiento Centroamericano* por materias y autores: números 1 al 100, 97
Infante B., Ricardo, 2213
Información Financiera, 2065
Informaciones, 53
Informativo, 6250
Informativo LASPAU, 98
Informe estadístico acerca del alumnado de la Universidad de Chile en 1968 [and] 1969, 6116-6117
Informe nacional sobre desarrollo de comunidades, 1971, 8437
Ingham, John M., 1064, 1276
Inkeles, Alex, 7958
Instituto de Estudios Investigaciones [IDEI], *Buenos Aires,* 6817
Instituto de Estudios Peruanos, 1421
Instituto de Investigación de Recursos Naturales, *Santiago,* 6872
Instituto Euvaldo Lodi, *Rio,* 6251
Instituto Latinoamericano de Mercadero Agrícola, *Bogotá,* 6915
Instituto Lingüístico de Verano, *México,* 1564
Instituto para el Desarrollo Económico y Social de América Central (IDESAC), 8350
Integração universidade-indústria hoje: IEL-ADESG, 6252
Inter-American Development Bank, 1827-1830
Inter-American Economic Affairs, 1831
Inter-American Malaria Research Symposium, *1, San Salvador, 1971,* 1669
International Bank for Reconstruction and Development, 1831a, 1832
International Congress of Americanists, *XXXIX, Lima, 1970,* 510
International Labor Organization, *Geneva, 1929,* 2219-2220
Inventário cafeeiro: pesquisa com fotografias aéreas nas regiões cafeicultoras do Estado de São Paulo, a Este de 48° W., 7086
Irala Burgos, Jerónimo, 2144
Irala Burgos, Paul, 2144
Iribarren Charlin, Jorge, 879-881
Irigoyen Rosado, Renan, 6736
Isasi, Elda, 8038
Isaza, Rafael B., 2066
Isbell, Billie Jean, 510, 1422-1423
Isbell, William Harris, 510, 957-959
Isbister, John, 1930
Isidoor, 1164
Itzcovich, Samuel, 2348
Iutaka, Sugiyama, 1739, 8469,
Ivanoff, Pierre, 573
Ivie, Stanley D., 6153
Iwańska, Alicja, 1065
Izmui, Seiichi, 960-961

Jack, Robert F., 665-665a
Jackson, Frances L., 1565
Jacobs, Babette M., 6768
Jacobs, Charles R., 6768
Jacobs, H. P., 1180
Jätzold, Ralph, 6953
Jagan, Cheddi, 7633
Jaguaribe, Helio, 7374, 7419
Jamaica. Ministry of Finance and Planning. Town Planning Department, 2010, 7306
Jamaica. Ministry of Rural Land Development, 2011
Jamaica [National Electoral Board?], 7307
James, C. L. R., 1136, 1179-1180
James, Preston E., 6553-6554
Janvry, Alain de, 2366-2367
Japanese Cultural Association, *São Paulo,* 7087
Jaquette, Jane S., 7691-7692, 2281
Jaramillo, Francisco de Paula, 7657
Jaramillo, Luis Javier, 2048
Jaramillo Uribe, Félix, 7482a
Jaramillo Uribe, Jaime, 6037
Jáuregui O., Ernesto, 7318
Jefferson, Owen, 2012-2013
Jeffreys, M. D. W., 511
Jenkinson, Michael, 1066
Jiménez Borja, Arturo, 962
Jitrik, Noé, 8439
Jobet, Julio César, 7757
Johannessen, Carl L., 6663
John, Kenneth, 1179
Johnson, Ann S., 669
Johnson, Carl M., 1681
Johnson, Cecil, 8039
Johnson, Dale L., 6156
Johnson, Frederick, 574
Johnson, Irmgard Weitlaner, 550
Johnson, Karl M., 6709
Johnson, Kenneth F., 7556
Johnson, Richard L., 6940
Johnston, Francis E., 1695, 1740-1742
Joly Gouveia, Aparecida. *See.* Gouveia, Aparecida Joly.
Jones, David, 6675
Jones, David W., 1165
Jones, Grant D., 1166
Jones, John Maxwell, 6154
Jones, William I., 1931
Joralemon, Peter David, 575
Jordan, David C., 8206
Jorge, Eduardo F., 2368
Jorge, J. G. de Araujo, 7853
Jorgenson, Harold T., 6555
Jornadas de Finanzas Públicas, *II, Córdoba, Arg., 1969,* 2369-2370
Jornadas Forestales de la Asociación Chilena de Ingenieros Forestales, *V, Santiago, 1969,* 6873
Joworski, Helam, 6171
Joxe, Alain, 7758, 8040
Joxe, Alan. *See* Joxe, Alain.

Juárez Toledo, Luis Adolfo, 6098
Juarroz, Roberto, 99
Juliana, E., 1167
Julien, Claude, 8041
Junguito, Roberto, 2067
Jurema, Aderbal, 7088
Juricie T., Bogoslav, 1680
Justo, Liborio, 7716
Kadt, Emanuel De. See De Kadt, Emanuel.
Kätsch, Elke-Maria, 1168
Kätsch, Siegfried, 1168, 7482a
Kahan, Jerome H., 8166
Kahle, Günther, 7482a
Kahrer, Wilhelm, 6934
Kalinin, A. I., 7581
Kalugin, IU, 8136
Kampen, Anthony van, 7089
Kane, Robert S., 6769
Kano, Chiaki, 510, 961, 963
Kapelusz (firm), *Buenos Aires*, 7227
Kaplan, Joanna Overing, 1277
Kaplan, Marcos, 510, 1833, 7409, 7420
Kapp, Kit S., 7199-7201
Karadima, Oscar, 1834, 8271
Karen, Ruth, 6664
Karner, Frances P., 1169
Karnes, Thomas L., 8042
Katz, Friedrich, 512
Katz, Jorge, 2371
Katz, Sherman E., 1835
Katzin, Margaret Fisher, 1137
Kaufman, Burton I., 8043
Kaufman, Edy, 8044
Kaufman, Robert R., 2221, 7759
Kaufman, Terrence, 1566
Kearns, Kevin C., 1836, 6665
Keast, Allen, 6556
Keen, Benjamin, 576
Keith, Robert G., 1421
Kelemen, Pal, 577
Keller, Elza Coelho de Souza, 7090
Kellert, Susan, 1424
Kelley, Charles, 550
Kelley, David H., 964
Kelley, J. Charles, 571
Kellman, M. C., 6676
Kelly, Celso, 8512
Kelly, Isabel, 670
Kelly, William J., 2504
Kelly Owen, Nancy, 729
Kelm, Heinz, 1278
Kemper, Robert V., 6557
Kennedy, John G., 1067-1068
Kennedy, Paul P., 100
Kennedy, William J., 756
Kensinger, K. M., 1741
Kent, George O., 32
Kenworthy, Eldon, 7936
Kerbusch, Ernest-J., 7363b, 7657a, 7910a
Kern, Horst, 702

Key, Mary Ritchie, 1567
Keyfitz, Nathan, 1743
Kharitonov, Vitalii Aleksandroviich, 7897
Khronologiia vazheneishikh sobytii istorii sovetsko-Kubinskikh otnoshenii: 1960-70 (Chronicle of the most important events in the history of Soviet-Cuban relations: 1960-70), 8167
Killer, Peter, 6558
Klitgaard, Robert E., 2282
Kimball, Warren F., 8045
King, Kendall W., 1685
King, Richard G., 6155
King, Timothy, 1932
Kinsey, David C., 6005
Kirby, Anne V. T., 530
Kirby, Michael J., 530
Kirkner, George O., 965
Kirkpatrick, Jeane J., 7959
Kirwin, Frederick R., 7753
Klass, Morton, 1136
Klaus, Dieter, 6737
Klein, Herbert S., 7720
Klein, Robert E., 8339
Kline, David, 6155
Klineberg, Otto, 1100
Kloos, Peter, 1170, 1279
Kloppenburg, Boaventura, 7421
Knoerich, Eckart, 2175
Kobysh, Vitalii Iavanovich, 101
Koch, Conrad, 6970
Koch-Weser, Caio Kai, 7489a
Köhler, Ulrich, 1069
Koehn, Edward, 1568
Koehn, Sally, 1568
Körner, Siegfried, 7424a
Kohlhepp, Gerd, 7091
Kondo, Riena, 1569
Kondo, Victor, 1569
Korolev, Nikolai Vasel'evrch, 8207
Korteweg, P. G. J., 7760
Koslow, Lawrence E., 8117
Koss, Joan D., 1171
Kossok, Manfred, 7424a, 8268
Kovar, Anton, 696
Kovats-Beaudoux, Edith. See Beaudoux-Kovats, Edith.
Kowalewski, Z. Martin, 7422
Kracmar, John Z., 1837
Kratochwil, Germán, 7409, 7426a
Kreider, L. Emil, 6166
Kressin, Jan, 2283
Krieger, H., 1744
Krieger, Ronald A., 1933
Kroeker, Barbara J., 1570
Krotser, G. R., 671
Krotser, Paula H., 671
Krumwiede, Heinrich W., 7409, 7489a
Kubanek, Florian, 6874
Kubler, George, 578-579, 594

Kuczynski, Jürgen, 2014
Kulitzka, Dieter, 7424a, 8046
Kumasaka, Y., 8513
Kumata, Hideya, 8289
Kumate, Jesus, 1670
Kumm, Björn, 7717
Kunter, Kari, 1728
Kurland, Gerald, 7588
Kusch, Rodolfo, 1425
LTC Newsletter, 2222
Labarca Goddard, Eduardo, 7761
LaBelle, Thomas J., 6038
Labelle, Yvan, 82, 8272
Labelle-Robillard, Micheline, 1127
La Calandra, Angelo, 96
Lacerda, Carlos, 102
Lacerda, Roberto Mündell de, 6253
Lacey, Hugh M., 8256
Lacombe, Laura Jacobina, 6254
La Fay, Howard, 8384
Lafer, Celso, 2448, 8208
Lafon, Ciro René, 785
Laganá Fernandes, Liliana. *See* Fernandes, Liliana Laganá
Lalouel, Jean M., 1745
Lamarch Henríquez, Carlos M., 7615
Lambert, Jacques, 7092, 7423
Lamberg, Roberto F., 7424
Lamberg, Vera B. de, 7589
Laming-Emperaire, Annette, 882-883, 1280, 6818
Lampe, W. F. M., 1172
Land, Washington, 2465
Landívar U., Manuel Agustín, 1426-1428
Lands and peoples, 6559
Langacker, Ronald W., 1571
Lange, Frederick W., 743
Langebuch, Juergen Richard, 7093-7095
Langer, Marshall J., 2015
Langley, Lester D., 8027
Langoni, Carlos Geraldo, 2449
Langrod, Witold, 8308
Lanz, Gregorio, 8385
La Pampa (province). *Arg.* Ministerio de Economía y Asuntos Agrarios. Dirección General de Geodesia y Catastro, 6819
Lapenda, Geraldo, 1572
Lapidus de Sager, Nejama, 1573
Laplante, André, 1127
LaPorte, Robert, Jr., 7457, 8066, 8223
Lara Velado, Roberto, 8047
La Raia, Anita L., 8538
La Roche, Humberto J., 8209
Larose, Serge, 1127
Larraín, Horacio, 513
La Ruffa, Anthony L., 1173, 8386
Lascano, Marcelo Ramón, 2372
Laso, Luis Eduardo, 1838, 2097
La Souchère, Elena de, 7616
Lasswell, Harold D., 1382

Lasuen, José Ramón, 8286
Lateinamerika, 7424a
Lathrap, Donald W., 510
Latin America, 1839
Latin America: economic history and conditions; an annotated bibliography, 54
Latin America: the quest for change, 8048
Latin American studies in the universities of the United Kingdom: 1972-1973; no. 7, 103
Latinskaíã Amerika, 104, 7425-7426, 7762
Latortue, François, 1140
Latortue, Gérard R., 1140
Lau, Stephen F., 2223
Lauer, Wilhelm, 702, 6875
Laugénie, Claude, 6770, 6876
Laura, Guillermo Domingo, 7960
Lauria de Almeida, Mauro. *See*. Almeida, Mauro Lauria de.
Lavallée, Danièle, 883
Lave, Jean Carter, 1281
Lavenère-Wanderley, Nelson Freire, 8049
Lavretski, Grigalevich-Lavretski, 1174
Lazarev, Marklen Ivanovich, 8050
Lazure, Denise, 1140
Lazzarotto, Danilo, 839
Leach, Ilo, 1574
Leacock, Ruth, 1282
Leacock, Seth, 1282
Leander, Birgitta, 6738
Leaños Navarro, David, 6039
Leão, Antônio Carlos, 7096
Lechner, Norbert, 6040, 7428a, 7763
Lechtig, A., 1696
Ledesma, Elmo, 510
Lee, Thomas A., Jr., 672
Leeds, Anthony, 8286, 8438
Leeds, Elizabeth, 8286
Leemann, Albert, 6634, 6639
Lefebvre, Gilles, 1127
Lehmann, David, 7764-7765
Lehner, Gunthar, 7426a
Lehnertz, Jay, 510
Leicht, Raymond C., 673
Leitch, Adelaide, 6657
Leite, Eraldo Gueiros, 7097
Leite, José Ferrari, 7098
Leite Chaves, Jonas. *See* Chaves, Jonas Leite.
Leite Cordeiro, Laerte. *See* Cordeiro, Laerte Leite.
Lemle, Miriam, 1575
Lemos, Néstor, 510
Lemus García, Raúl, 6739
Lenhard, Rudolf, 6255
Lenkersdorf, Karl, 7427
Lengermann, Patricia Madoo, 1175
Lentnek, Barry, 6560
León, R. de, 1706
León Ossorio y Agüero, Adolfo, 7519
León-Portilla, Miguel, 550
León Tello, Pilar, 7202

Leonardo L., Carlos H., 1070
Leonardos, Othon Henry, 7099
Léons, Madeline Barbara, 1429, 7720
Leons, William, 7720
Le Quesne, Philip, 1235
Lerdo de Tejada, Miguel, 1934
Leridon, Henri, 8387
Leser, Walter Sidney Pereira, 1746
Lestrade, Swinburne, 8168
Létourneau, Georges, 1127
Levenstein, Harvey A., 8118
Levin, Lillian, 6197
Levin, Peter J., 7428
Levinsohn, Stephen H., 1576
Levinson, Jerome I., 8051
Levy, Fred D., Jr., 2450
Levy, Joseph Josy, 1127
Levy, Owen Lancelott, 105
Levy, Samuel, 6256
Levy Benathar, Roberto. *See* Benathar, Roberto Levy.
Lewis, B. R., 1016
Lewis, Gordon K., 106, 1179
Lewis, Lawrence A., 6655
Lewis, Paul H., 7898
Lewis, Vaughan, 8168
Lewis, W. Arthur, 1179
La ley de reforma agraria del Perú, 2284
Ley federal sobre monumentos y zonas arqueológicos, artísticos e históricos, 580
Library Bulletin, 33
Lichtblau, John H., 7827
Lichtensztejn, Samuel, 1840
Liebermann, Emil, 2174
Liebman, Arthur, 7520
Liljemark, Thomas, 813
Lima, Afonso Augusto de Albuquerque, 7100
Lima, Alcides de Mendonçã, 7854
Lima, Antônio Figueiredo de, 7045
Lima, Gelson Rangel, 7101
Lima, Haroldo José Sousa Costa, 7080
Lima, Maria Nayde dos Santos, 6257
Lima, Revira Lisboa de Moura, 6258
Lima Filho, Alberto de Oliveira, 2451
Lima Filho, Vivaldo Palma, 7855
Linares de Sapir, Olga, 1071
Lindenberg, Klaus, 7409
Lindenfeld, Jacqueline, 1577
Lindo, Hugo, 8137
Linton, Neville, 8169
Lionnet, Andrés, 1578
Lipman, Aaron, 2068
Lisa Enciclopédia Universal, 107
Lisker, Rubén, 1747, 1773
Lister, Florence C., 581
Lister, Robert H., 550, 581
Listov, Vadim Vadimovich, 7693
Little, Michael A., 1712
Litvak King, Jaime, 582
Litzler, Beverly N., 1072

Lizano Fait, Eduardo, 1962, 1971, 6683
Lizardi Ramos, César, 583
Lizot, Jacques, 1283-1285
Llano Cifuentes, Rafael, 7429
Llarena, David I., 2373
Llarena G., David, 2285
Llaumett P., Carlos, 6877
Lleras Restrepo, Carlos, 7658
Lloyd, Antony J., 8388
Lobato, E., 7177
Lobato Corrêa, R. *See* Corrêa, R. Lobato.
Lobo, Oswaldo Castro, 8210
Lodge, George C., 8052
Lodwick, Robert E., 8515
Loeb, G. F., 1841
Loetscher, Hugo, 7426a
Loewen, Jacob A., 1579
Loftin, Horace, 6706
Lofstrom, William Lee, 2176
Lohier, Gérard, 6647
Lomnitz, Cinna, 6878
Lomonaco, José Fernando Bitencourt, 8465
Loñ, Félix R., 7965
Lonaeus, Gunnar, 7856
Lonardi, Alberto G., 7213
Long, Anne K., 8166
Long, Edward, 1136
Long, Stanley Vernon, 869
Loomer, C. W., 6642
Lope Blanch, Juan M., 1580
Lopes, Juarez R. B., 6041
Lopes Côrrea, Arlindo. *See* Côrrea, Arlindo Lopes.
López, Alvaro, 2067
López, Francisco, 7659
López, José Eliseo, 6971
López, Timoleón, 2069
López Austin, Alfredo, 674
López Borges, Nicanor, 7809
López Cámara, Francisco, 8309
López de la Parra, Manuel, 1935
López de Nisvovich, Nancy, 510
López Michelsen, Alfonso, 7660
López Oliva, Enrique, 7430
López Rosado, Diego G., 1936
López Sánchez, José, 6561
Lora, Carmen, 6168a
Lorandi de Gieco, Ana María, 786
Lorenzo, José H., 675
Lorscheiter, Vendelino, 108
Losada, Benito Raúl, 2137
Losada, Rodrigo, 7661-7662
Loser, Claudio M., 2374
Lotería, 8138
Lott, Leo B., 7810
Loughlin, Lidia N. C. de, 6042
Louis-Jean, Antonio, 1176
Lounsbury, Floyd G., 1316, 1616
Lourdes Meneghezzi, Maria de. *See* Meneghezzi, Maria de Lourdes.

Lourenço Filho, Manuel Bergström, 6260
Loveman, Brian, 2224
Lovera, Delia Magda, 786
Low-Maus, Rodolfo, 6129
Lowe, Ivan, 1648
Lowenfeld, Andreas F., 2016
Lowenthal, Abraham F., 8053, 8170-8171
Lowenthal, David, 1136-1137, 1177-1180
Lowry, Dennis T., 8310
Loy, Jane M., 109
Lozada, Salvador María, 513a
Lozano, Eduardo, 34
Lubbock, Michael R., 8054
Lucchini, Adalberto P., 8211
Lucena Salmoral, Manuel, 1286-1287, 1430, 1581
Lüders, Rolf, 1842, 2225
Lüthers, Alberto, 6805
Luján Muñoz, Luis, 584, 1073
Lumbreras, Luis Gillermo, 884, 966-967
Luna, Félix, 7961
Luna Ballón, Milagro, 1431
Luna P., Nazario, 6088
Lutchman, Harold A., 7634
Luxardo, José D., 6820
Lynch, Louis, 110
Lynch, Thomas F., 909, 968
Lynn, R., 8519
Macapagal, Diosdado, 111
McAuliffe, Dennis, 510
McBride, Harold W., 676
McCann, Frank D., 7857
McClelland, Donald H., 1972
Maccoby, Michael, 8305, 8311
McCosker, John E., 6707
McCoy, Terry L., 2226, 7766
McCreery, Lawrence D., 1691
McCullagh, M. J., 7038
MacDonald, John Stuart, 1181
MacDonald, Leatrice D., 1181
MacDonald, Ronald H., 7431, 7911
MacDougall, T., 6740
McDowell, Jack, 112
Macedo, Gilberto de, 8273
McEwen, William J., 1432-1433
McGee, W. J., 1074
McGinn, Noel F., 6005, 6155
Machado, Brasil Pinheiro, 7191
Machado, Emilio A., 6771
Machado, Luiz Toledo, 7858
Machado, Renato Rodrigues, 7102
Machado de Souza, Edson. *See* Souza, Edson Machado de.
Machado Gómez, Alfredo, 2136, 2138
MacHale, Tomas P., 7767
Maciel de Barros, Roque Spencer. *See* Barros, Roque Spencer Maciel de.
McIntosh, Terry L., 6515
Macisco, John J., Jr., 6613
McKern, Sharon S., 514

Mackey, Carol J., 973
Macklin, B. June, 510
McLellan, Donna L., 1697
MacLeod, Murdo J., 7720
McMahan, Mike, 7319
MacMillan Education Limited (firm), *Kingston*, 7214
MacNeish, Richard S., 530, 574, 585
McNulty, Michael L., 6562
McReath, I., 6759
Maderey Rascón, Laura Elena, 6741
Madrazo, Carlos A., 7521
Madrazo, Guillermo B., 787
Madsen, Claudia, 1075
Madsen, William, 1075
Maduro, Otto, 7432
Maeder, Ernesto J. A., 6821
Maeyama, Takashi, 8516
Magelsdorf, Paul C., 530
O Magistério, 6261
Magnanini, Ruth Lopes da Cruz, 7103
Magrassi de Sá, Jayme. *See* Sá, Jayme Magrassi de.
Maia, Newton da Silva, 6262
Malavé Mata, Héctor, 2140
Maldonado, Rita Marinita, 2505
Maldonado Denis, Manuel, 7624
Maldonado-Koerdell, Manuel, 6666
Maldonado Moreleón, Victor Alfonso, 82
Maler, Teobert, 586
Mallin, Jay, 7433, 8139
Malloy, James M., 7590, 7718-7720
Malmgren, Harald B., 1806
Malo de Ramírez, Gloria, 1434
Malone, Michael D., 677
Maloney, Neil J., 6972
Malpica S. S., Carlos, 2286
Mamalakis, Markos, 510, 2227
Maneschi, Andrea, 1809
Manganotti, Donatella, 1288
Mangin, William, 1435
Manley, Michael, 7620
Manning, Peter K., 1663
Mansen, Richard, 1582
Mansfield, Charles, 1843, 2263
Mantel, Rolf R., 2375
Manya, Juan Antonio, 1436
Manzo Taylor, Francisco, 695
Mapas y Guías Eureka (firm), *Montevideo*, 7340
Maranca, Sílva, 840
Maranhão Nina, Afonso Celso. *See* Nina, Afonso Celso Maranhão.
Marasciulo, Edward, 6563
Marcano, Gaspar, 515
Marcellino, Alberto J., 768
Marcha, 7434
Marcondes, J. V. Freitas, 8517, 8518
Marcus, Joyce, 587
Marden, Luis, 6852
Marden, Parker G., 8351

Marett, Robert, 6742
Margain, Carlos R., 550
Margaín, Hugo B., 7522
Marighela, Carlos, 7859-7860
Marini, Ruy Mauro, 8212
Mariscal, Nicolás, 7435
Mariz, Vasco, 8055
Markham, Brent J., 6879
Markun, Patricia Maloney, 6667
Marques de Almeida, Fernando Flávio. *See* Almeida, Fernando Flávio Marques de.
Marques de Melo, José, *See* Melo, José Marques de.
Marques dos Santos, Fabiano. *See* Santos, Fabiano Marques dos.
Márquez, Javier, 1844
Márquez, Rubens Murillo, 6263
Márquez V., Marcela, 6099
Marquina, Ignacio, 594
Marroquín, Alejandro D., 516, 1076
Mars, Louis, 1182-1183
Marsal, Juan Francisco, 7436, 7962, 8274
Marschall, Wolfgang, 588, 1583
Marshall, Bernard, 8168
Marshall, Katherine Barnes de. *See* Barnes de Marshall, Katherine.
Marshall, O. R., 2017
Marshall, W. K., 8389
Martí, Samuel, 589, 678, 1042
Martín, Daniel Fernando, 2376
Martín, Eusebia Herminia, 1584
Martín, Juan, 8213
Martin, Kenneth L., 6046
Martin, Lawrence, 7203-7204
Martin, Leann, 1184
Martin, Tony, 1185
Martínez, Alberto, 2186
Martínez, Héctor, 1437-1439
Martínez, Juan Carlos, 2367
Martínez, Pedro Daniel, 8312
Martínez, Rufino, 113
Martínez-Alier, Verena, 8268
Martínez Bonati, Félix, 7482a
Martínez Caicedo, Alejandro, 6916
Martínez-Crovetto, Raúl, 510, 1289, 1440, 6822
Martínez del Río de Redo, Marita, 679
Martínez le Clainche, Roberto, 1937
Martínez Montero, Homero, 6772
Martínez Paz, Fernando, 8439
Martínez Ríos, Jorge, 8313
Martínez Sáez, Santiago, 7437
Martinho da Rocha, José. *See* Rocha, José Martinho de.
Martins Bonilha, Jose Fernando. *See* Bonilha, José Fernando Martins.
Martz, John D., 7438-7439
Marzal, Manuel María, 1441
Mas García, A., 8440
Mascaro, Carlos Corrêa, 6264
Mashbits, Iakov Grigor'evich, 6564

Mason, J. Alden, 571
Mata, Leonardo J., 1671-1672, 1696
Mata Mollejas, Luis, 2139
Mateo de Acousta, O., 1673
Matheny, Ray T., 590
Mato Grosso (state), *Bra.*, 7104
Matos Mar, José, 1395, 1402, 1421, 7482a, 7694-7695
Matos Mendieta, Ramiro, 510, 969-970
Matos Moctezuma, Eduardo, 591-593
Matos Romero, Manuel, 1290
Matta, Roberto da, 1291
Matteson, Esther, 1520, 1585-1587
Matthews, Dom Basil, 1137
Matthews, Herbert Lionel, 7440
Matthews, P. H., 1588
Mattioni, Mario, 754
Mattsson, Ake, 7105
Maturana Medina, Sergio, 1938, 6743
Mau, James A., 1180, 8254
Mauro, Frédéric, 510, 529
Mauro Marini, Ruy, 7364
Max, Alphonse, 7441
Maxwell, Nicole, 510
May, Jacques Meyer, 1697
May, Peter, 7424a
Mayans, Ernesto, 7912
Maybury-Lewis, David, 1292
Mayer, Enrique, 510, 1402, 1442-1444
Mayer-Oakes, William J., 900
Mayer Varela, Romanita, 1698
Maynard, Eileen, 1357, 1445
Mayone Stycos, J., 8351
Maza Zavala, Domingo Felipe, 2140
Mazo, Gabriel del, 6565
Mazzulla, Jorge, 2377
Mebane, Donata, 6156
Médici, Emílio Garrastazu, 7861
Medidas e propostas para o desenvolvimento do Nordeste e sua integração à economia nacional, 7106
Medina Peña, Luis, 8114
Medina Valdés, Gerardo, 7523
Medinaceli, Carlos, 6089
Meeker, Guy B., 1845
Meggers, Betty Jane, 517, 755, 841, 1293, 7107
Meighan, Clement W., 550, 680
Meirinho, Jali, 6265
Mejía, Medardo, 6702
Mejía Alarcón, Pedro Esteban, 2141
Mejía Palacio, Jorge, 2077
Meksika: politika, ekonomika, kul'tura (Mexico: politics, economics, culture), 114
Melatti, Julio Cezar, 1294-1296
Meldau, Elke, 1956
Meléndez, Jaime Santiago, 2506
Melia, Bartomeu, 1589
Meliknia, L., 8519
Melli, Oscar Ricardo, 7205
Mello, María Conceicão D'Incao e, 8540

Mello e Alvim, Marília Carvalho de. *See* Alvim, Marília Carvalho de Mello e.
Mello Franco, Carlos de. *See* Franco, Carlos de Mello.
Melo, José Marques de, 8520
Meluk, Alfonso, 8441
Melville, Marjorie, 7557
Melville, Thomas, 7557
Membreño, María B. de, 7550
Mena Soto, Joaquín, 6043
Mendes de Almeida, Cândido. *See* Almeida, Cândido Mendes de.
Méndez, Betty, 1653
Méndez, Epifanio, 8214
Méndez G., Juan Carlos, 2228
Méndez Rodríguez, Alfredo, 1077
Mendieta Alatorre, Angeles, 517a
Mendieta y Núñez, Lucio, 8275-8277, 8314
Mendonça, Rubens de, 20
Mendonça de Barros, José Roberto. *See* Barros, José Roberto Mendonça de.
Mendoza Angulo, José, 6185
Mendoza Berrueto, Eliseo, 1939
Mendoza (province), *Arg.* Dirección de Estadísticas e Investigaciones Económicas, 6823
Meneghezzi, Maria de Lourdes, 7084
Menéndez, Arturo, 6744
Meneses Olivar, Alvaro, 2070
Menezes, Eduardo Diatay B. de, 6266
Menezes, Maria José, 842
Menezes, Raimundo de, 55
Mensário do Arquivo Nacional, 56
Mente, Alberto, 7108
Mentz, Raúl Pedro, 2378
Mentz Ribeiro, Pedro Augusto. *See* Ribeiro, Pedro Augusto Mentz.
Menz, John A., 6566
Menzel, Dorothy, 971
Meredith, Howard V., 1699
Merino Brito, Eloy G., 8173
Merino Ramos, Raúl, 8119
Merkx, Gilbert W., 2379, 7963
Merrick, Thomas, 7485
Merrifield, William R., 1034
Merrill, Robert North, 2229
Mesa, Darío, 7640
Mesa-Lago, Carmelo, 2018, 7591-7592
Mesa Ospina, Jorge Ernesto, 2071
Mesa Redonda de la Sociedad Mexicana de Antropología *XI, México, 1966,* 594
Mesa Redonda sobre Plan de Transporte del Algodón, *Santa Cruz, Bol., 1971,* 2177
Mesa Redonda sobre Recursos Naturales, *II, México, 1969,* 6567
Mesas Redondas sobre Problemas de Ecología Humana de la Cuenca del Valle de México, *México, 1970,* 6745
Meseses, Ulpiano T. Bezerra de, 843
Mesquita, Julio de Araújo, 1658

Metodologia para o estabelecimento da política nacional: especificamente em relação à política segurança, 7862
Métraux, Alfred, 1186
Mexico. Comisión de Estudios del Territorio Nacional y Planeación, 7320-7323
Mexico. Comisión Federal de Electricidad, 7324
México. Comisión Nacional de los Salarios Mínimos, 8315
Mexico. Departamento de Turismo y Petróleos Mexicanos, 7325
Mexico. Dirección de Obras Públicas, 7326
Mexico. Dirección General de Estadística, 7327
Mexico. Secretaría de Educación Pública, 1078
Mexico. UNAM. Instituto de Geografía, 7328-7329
México: nuestra gran herencia, 115
Meyer, A., 1187
Meyer, Harvey K., 116
Meyer, Karl E., 595-596
Meyer, Lorenzo, 8114, 8120
Meyer, Richard L., 2230
Meyerhoff, Bárbara G., 1100
Michael, Henry N., 597
Michelini, Zelmar, 8056
Micklin, Michael, 7442
Midgett, Douglas, 1188
Mielche, Hakon, 1079
Mieres, Francisco, 2142
Mihaly, Z. M., 2507
Mihelic', Dusan, 6746
Mikesell, Raymond Frech, 2231, 2452-2453
Mikoiam, S. A., 7593
Milanesi, María Lucila, 8521
Milenky, Edward S., 1846-1847
Miliani, Domingo, 117
Milledge, James S., 1713, 1718
Miller, Arthur G., 594
Miller, Errol, 1189, 8390
Miller, Frank C., 1080
Miller, Fred, 2287
Millo, Clara, 594
Millon, René, 594
Millones, Luis, 1446
Mills, Charles, 7457
Minas Gerais (state), *Bra.* Conselho Estadual do Desenvolvimento, 7109-7110
Minas Gerais (state), *Bra.* Departamento Geográfico, 7260
Minas Gerais (state), *Bra.* Secretaria de Estado da Agricultura, 7111
Minería prehispánica en la Sierra de Querétaro, 681
Mings, Robert C., 6568
Minkel, Clarence W., 6569, 6668, 6677
Minor, Dorothy Hendrich de, 1590
Minor, Eugene E., 1590
Mintchev, Tzoni Velcov, 2019
Mintz, Sidney, 8268

Miranda Ribadeneira, Francisco, 6141
Miró, Rodrigo, 8140
Misiones (province), *Arg.* Dirección General de Estadística, 6078, 6824
Mitchell, Glen H., 2264
Mitchell, James E., 8316
Mitrani, Barbara, 7445
Moçoró: um centro regional do Oeste Potiguar, 7112
O modêlo Brasil—MBRSL: manual de análise para experimentos, 7863
Modiano, Nancy, 6157
Mönckeberg, Fernando, 1700
Moacir Portela, Jarbas. *See* Portela, Jarbas Moacir.
Moerman, Michael, 1137
Mörner, Magnus, 8268
Mogrovejo Terrazas, Gerardo, 814
Molina, Sergio, 2232
Molina Chocano, Guillermo, 1972a
Molina Piñeiro, Luis, 7482a, 7524
Momsen, Richard P., 6570
Momsen, Richard P., Jr., 6935
Monast, Jacques Emile, 1447
Monasterio, Maxımina, 6973, 6976-6978
Monbeig, Pierre, 82
Monge, Luis Alberto, 7369
Montaño Aragón, Mario, 8442
Monte Urraca, Manuel E. del, 749
Monteiro, Mário Ypiranga, 7113
Montemayor G., Felipe, 518
Montenegro, Abelardo Cardoso, 7045
Montero de Bascom, Berta, 510
Montes, Segundo, 8391
Montevideo (city), *Uru.* Intendencia Municipal de Montevideo, 7341
Montezuma de Carvalho, Joaquim. *See* Carvalho, Joaquim Montezuma de.
Montgomery, Evelyn Ina, 1448
Montiel Ortega, Leonardo, 2143
Montoya Rojas, Rodrigo, 2288
Montrie, Charles, 1848
Montuschi, Luisa, 2380-2381
Moor, Jay, 6747
Moore, O. Ernest, 2021
Moore, Russell Martin, 1849
Mora, Guillermina, 1747
Mora y Araujo, Manuel, 7964
Moraes, Tancredo, 8278
Morales, Emilio Felipe, 6172
Morales, Isidro, 2144
Morales, Pedro, 2022
Morales, Víctor Hugo, 7443
Morales Gómez, Jorge, 1398, 8443
Morales Otero, Pablo, 7625
Morales Paúl, Isidro, 8215
Morales Ruiz, Carlos, 755
Morales Tucker, Antonio, 7827
Morato Vargas, Rafael, 6850
Morbán L. Mañón, Fernando, 755

Moreira, Eidorfe, 15
Moreira, Marcílio Marques, 2454, 7864
Moreira, María Elena, 788
Morelli, Alex, 7444
Morello, Augusto Mario, 7965
Morelos, José B., 8317
Morena, Alberto, 1591
Moreno, Francisco José, 7445
Moreno, José Vicente, 8141
Moreno, María A., 6829
Moreno de Marval, M. J., 1679
Moreno Toscano, Alejandra, 510
Moretić, Yerko, 7696
Morey, Robert V., 1297-1298
Morey, Robert V., Jr., 510
Morgan, Robert P., 1850
Mori, Alberto, 6748
Moriarty, James Robert, 1016
Morley, Samuel A., 2455-2456
Morris, Craig, 510, 972
Morris, Earl W., 1449
Morris, Kerwyn L., 1179
Morse, Richard M., 510
Morse, Robert M., 7446
Morse, Wayne, 7374
Morton, Newton E., 1745, 1748, 1758
Moschini, Felipe Nery, 8522
Moseley, Michael E., 859, 953, 982
Moshinsky, Marcos, 6158
Mosley, M. Edward, 973
Mosonyi, Esteban Emilio, 1592-1594
Moss, Robert, 7447, 7913
Mostny, Grete, 885
Mota, Fernando de Oliveira, 7114
Mott, G. O., 7139
Motta, Fernando C. Prestes, 1851
Mountjoy, Joseph B., 682-683
Moura Cantídio, Walter de. *See* Cantídio, Walter de Moura.
Moura Castro, Cláudio de. *See* Castro, Cláudio de Moura.
Moura Lima, Revira Lisboa de. *See* Lima, Revira Lisboa de Moura.
Mourão, Noemia, 1299
Le mouvement éducatif dans 75 pays, rapports nationaux: Brésil, 6267
La movilización de recursos internos, 1852
Movimiento de Liberación Nacional: Tupamaros, *Uruguay*, 7914
Moyano Bonilla, C., 8216
Moyano Llerena, Carlos, 2382
Mulchansingh, Vernon C., 2023
Müller, Fritz Paul, 6635
Mueller, Hans J., 2145
Müller, Paul, 6571
Mündell de Lacerda, Roberto. *See* Lacerda, Roberto Mündell de.
Münster, Arno, 7767a
Mulcahy, David, 1134
Muller, Doris Maria, 7115

Muller, Florencia, 702
Mullor, Jorge B., 1701
Mulville, Frank, 6636
Muñoz, Humberto, 8318
Muñoz de Suárez, María Angeles, 6044
Muñoz G., Oscar, 2233
Murgueytio, Reinaldo, 6142
Muricy, Antônio Carlos da Silva, 7865
Murillo Marquez, Rubens. See Marquez, Rubens Murillo.
Murilo de Carvalho, José. See Carvalho, Jose Murilo de.
Murmis, Miguel, 7966
Murphy, Timothy D., 1083
Muscolo, Vicente, 2383
Musenek, Lúcia, 532
Museo de América, Madrid, 35
Mustapich, José María, 1853
Mutchler, David E., 7663
Muzanek, Hermínia, 532
Myers, George C., 6572
Myers, Robert G., 6045
Myers, Thomas P., 510, 974
Nadra, Fernando, 7967
Nag, Moni, 1190
Naipaul, V. S., 1179
Najlis, Elena, 1595-1596
Nammacher, Mark A., 1702
Nance, C. Roger, 598
Naranjo, Plutarco, 1300
Naranjo, Yury, 7811
Nas, P. J. M., 1191
Nash, June, 1081, 1450-1452
Nath, Dwarka, 1192
National Academy of Sciences. National Academy of Engineering, 2508
National Geographic Society, 7215
Natividade Filho, Osny, 7273
Naue, Guilherme, 844
Navarrete, Alfredo, 7525
Navarrete, Carlos, 684-686
Navarrete, Ifigenia N. de, 1940
Navarrete, Jorge Eduardo, 1941, 6749
Navarro, Roberto, 8319
Navarro de Britto, Luiz. See Britto, Luiz Navarro de.
Needler, Martin C., 7526-7528, 8057
Neel, James V., 1674, 1749, 1767, 1771
Neely, James A., 574, 655
Neira, Eduardo, 8286
Neira Avendaño, Máximo, 975
Nelson, Cynthia, 8320
Nelson, Joan M., 6773
Nelson, Lowry, 7594
Nelson, Michael, 6714, 7448
Nelson, Richard R., 2072
Nery Moschini, Felipe. See. Moschini, Felipe Nery.
Nettleford, Rex, 1180, 1193, 7564
Neves, Gervásio Rodrigo, 7116

Newbry, Burton C., 6046
Nicaraguan Private Enterprise, Managua, 7332
Nicholls, David, 1194, 7619
Nichols, Byron A., 7899
Nicholson, Henry B., 550, 594, 599
Nickel, Herbert J., 7528a
Niekerk, A. E. van, 7968
Niemeyer F., Hans, 886
Nietschmann, Bernard, 510, 1082, 6573
Nieves-Falcón, Luis, 8392-9393
Nimer, Edmon, 7117-7120
Nina, Afonso Celso Maranhão, 6268
Nitsch, Manfred, 7409
No hay término medio, 7812
Noguera, Eduardo, 550, 687-688
Nogues, Julio J., 2364-2365, 2386
Nohlen, Dieter, 7363b, 7767b-7767c
Nonoya Fieno, José, 7261
Nordeste brasileiro; catálogo da exposição, 118
Nordyke, Quentin, 1453
Norman, James, 6750
North, Lisa, 7697
North American Congress on Latin America, N.Y., 2234
Novaes, Paulo, 8523
Nuestro experimento en la educación universitaria, 6198
Nun, José, 8279
Nunes de Azevedo, Murillo Nunes. See Azevedo, Murillo Nunes de.
Núñez, Carlos, 7364, 7866
Núñez A., Lautaro, 887-890, 894
Núñez del Prado, Oscar, 1456
Núñez del Prado Béjar, Juan Víctor, 976, 1454-1455
Núñez Jiménez, Antonio, 757
Núñez Regueiro, Víctor A., 760, 789-790, 804
Nunley, Robert E., 6574
Nunn, Frederick M., 7768
Nutini, Hugo A., 1083
Nye, J. S., 1854
Obando, Isolina, 977
Oberem, Udo, 1554
Oblitas Poblete, Enrique, 1457
O'Brien, Patricia J., 519
Observaciones sobre la reforma universitaria, 6130
Ocampo V., Tarsicio, 2289, 8321
Ochoa de Masramón, Dora, 510
Ochoa Salas, Lorenzo, 689-690
Oclander, George, 7936
Octávio, José, 6269
Odalia, Nilo, 8217
Odell, Peter R., 1855
Odle, Maurice A., 2024
O'Donnell, Guillermo A., 7969
Ogelsby, J. C. M., 8058
Oizumi Adasaka, José Kouichi, 8121
Ojeda Gómez, Mario, 8059
Ojeda Olaechea, Alonso, 6974

Olavarría Bravo, Arturo, 7769
Olien, Michael D., 1195
Olivares, Reynaldo Börgel, 6880
Oliveira, Adélia Engrácia de, 1301
Oliveira, Cêurio de, 7121
Oliveira, Décio Rufino de, 7122
Oliveira, Guarino Alves d', 7123
Oliveira, José Xavier de, 7867, 8280
Oliveira, Luiz Gonzaga de, 7274
Oliveira, Roberto Cardoso de, 8524
Oliveira Andrade, Manuel Correia de. *See* Andrade, Manuel Correia de Oliveira.
Oliveira Campos, Roberto de. *See* Campos, Roberto de Oliveira.
Oliveira Lima Filho, Alberto de. *See* Lima Filho, Aberto de Oliveira.
Oliveira Mota, Fernando de. *See* Mota, Fernando de Oliveira.
Oliver, Covey T., 1856
Olivera de Bueno, Gloria, 978-980
Olivera de Vázquez, Mercedes, 1115
Olivos, Luis, 8281-8282
Olmos de Manzo, Sheila, 2118
Olsen, Edward, 946
Omskriven revolution: fakta och asikter om Kuba, 1959-1971, 7595
Onaka, Alvin T., 8290
O'Phelan G., Scarlett, 981
Ordóñez Chipín, Martín, 1084
Ordóñez P., Antonio, 7485
Ordóñez Ramírez, Enrique, 2073
Orellana González, René Arturo, 1973
Orellana Rodríguez, Mario, 891
Orellana Valeriano, Simeón, 510
Organización de los Estados Americanos. *See* Organization of American States.
Organization of American States. Comité Interamericano del Desarrollo Agrícola, 6694
Organization of American States. Consejo Permanente, 8218
Organization of American States. Department of Economic Affairs. Sectorial Studies Unit, 2074
Organization of American States. Department of Social Affairs, 6047
Organization of American States. General Secretariat, 119, 1857-1858, 8060-8061
Organization of American States. General Secretariat. Special Consultative Committee on Security Against the Subversion of International Communism, 8062
Organization of American States. Instituto Interamericano de Ciencias Agrícolas. Centro Interamericano de Documentación e Información Agrícola, 6575-6576
Organization of American States. Instituto Interamericano de Estadística, 6577
Organization of American States. Instituto Panamericano de Geografía e Historia, 6578-6579
Organization of American States. Inter-American Council for Education, Science, and Culture, *III, Panama, 1972,* 6048
Organization of American States. Secretaría General, 46, 8063
Organization of American States. Secretaría General. Departamento de Asuntos Económicos. Unidad de Recursos Naturales, 6774
Organization of American States. Special Consultative Committee on Security Against the Subversive Action of International Communism, 8064
Orgaz, Jorge, 8439
Orme, Jean-Claude de l', 1127
Ornstein, Roberto, 8195
Orona, Juan V., 7970-7971
Oropeza, Ambrosio, 7817
Orozco, Luis Enrique, 1085
Orrego Aravena, Reynaldo, 6825
Orrego Vicuña, Francisco, 8219
Orrico, José Alexandre Robatto, 7080
Ortega, Elpidio, 748-749, 755-756
Ortega, Francisco J., 2066, 2076
Ortega y Medina, Juan A., 8065
Ortiz de Salcedo, Margarita, 6167
Ortiz Troncoso, Omar R., 892
Ortiz Vergara, Pedro, 1458, 6954
Ortiz Wadgymar, Arturo, 1942
Ortuño, René, 2178
Ortúzar, Pelagia, 6114
Osorio Torres, Jorge, 2278
Ossa, Paul P., 982
Ossandon G., Jorge, 2235
Ostrovskii, Viktor, 6774a
Oszlak, Oscar, 2384, 7449
Otero, Mario H., 6179
Oteyza, José Andrés de, 1859
Owens, Gene M., 7450
Oxaal, Ivar, 1196
Ozório de Almeida, Miguel Alvaro. *See* Almeida, Miguel Alvaro Ozório de.
Pablo, Juan Carlos de, 2385
Pabón, Milton, 7626
Pacheco Cruz, Santiago, 1597
Paddock, John, 594
Padilla, H., 1703
Paes, Isolda Holmer, 6292
Page, Joseph A., 7868
Pages, Walter Hugo, 2313
Palacio Rudas, Alfonso, 7451
Palacios, Julián, 983
Palacios Mejía, Hugo, 2077
Palacios Roji G., Agustín, 7330
Palanca, Floreal, 791
Palavecino, Enrique, 761-761a
Palazzo, Pascual Santiago, 2328
Palerm, Angel, 6159
Palermo, Alfredo, 6270
Paliforíc, Ljubomir, 7452
Pallestrini, Luciana, 845-846
Palm, Edwin Walter, 510

Palomino Flores, Salvador, 510, 1459-1460
Panama. Contraloría General de la República. Dirección de Estadística y Censo, 1974
Panesso Robledo, Antonio, 8283
Panizza, J. Luis, 7915
Panorama de la economía venezolana en el período enero-setiembre de 1970, 2146
Panorama de la economía venezolana en el período julio-diciembre del año 1969, 2147
Panorama Económico, 2236
Panzone, Clemente, 2356
Paolucci, A. M., 1750
Papers on Olmec and Maya archaeology, 600
Papvero, Nelson, 6580
Pará (state), *Bra.* Secretaria de Estado de Educação. Departamento de Educação Primária, 6271
Paradis, Louise I., 654
Paraíba (state), *Bra.* Comissão Estadual de Planejamento Agrícola, 7124
Paraná (state), *Bra.* Departamento de Geografia, Terras e Colonizaçao. Divisão de Georgrafia, 7262
Paredes, Américo, 510
Paredes Candia, Antonio, 1461
Parker, Gary John, 1598
Parks, Winfield, 6793, 8384
Parmasad, K. V., 1179
Parra Aranguren, Gonzalo, 8220
Parra-Peña, Isidro, 1860
Parra Sandoval, Rodrigo, 7664
Parrish, Charles J., 7770
Parsons, James J., 6581
Parsons, Jeffrey R., 691-706
Parsons, Mary Hrones, 706
Partido Unido de la Revolución Socialista de Cuba (PURSC). Dirección Nacional. Comisión de Orientación Revolucionaria, 7596
Pasini, Emilio, 7972
Paskoff, Roland, 6881-6884
Pasquali, Antonio, 8444
Um passo de gigante em 4 anos: Rio Grande do Sul, 7125
Pastore, José, 8503
Pastorini, Juan Guido, 7973
Pasztori, Esther, 601
Patch, Richard W., 1462-1466
Pate, J. B., 7027
Patee, Richard, 82
Patiño, Víctor Manuel, 6582
Patten, George F., 6704
Patterson, Clair C., 520
Patterson, Orlando, 1136
Patterson, Thomas C., 521, 530, 984
Paula Faleiros, Vicente, de. *See* Faleiros, Vicente de Paula.
Paulston, Rolland G., 1467, 6173-6175, 6199-6200, 7698
Payne, Horace, 6669
Payne, Ruth, 6090

Payró, Ana Lía, 7771
Paz, Ida, 7453
Paz, Octavio, 7529
Paz Sánchez, Fernando, 1946
Pearson, Neale J., 7869
Pease, Helen, 1599
Pébayle, Raymond, 7126
Peçanha, Wolga, 6272
Pedersen, Asbjorn, 522
Pedersen, Owe, 6775
Peeters, Francisca, 6273
Péfaur, Jaime, 6885
Peixoto, Dídima de Castro, 7127
Peixoto, Enaldo Cravo, 7128
Peixoto, Vicente, 80
Pelaez, Carlos Manuel, 7870
Pelczar, Richard S., 6131
Pellicer de Brody, Olga, 7531, 8114, 8172
Pellizzaro, Siro M., 1600
Peluso Júnior, Victor Antônio, 7129
Peña, Félix, 7409
Pena, Heloisa F., 1751
Peña, Milcíades, 7974-7975
Peña A., Orlando, 6886
Peña Bravo, Raúl, 7721
Peña Goméz, Rosa María, 1675
Peñaherrera de Costales, Piedad, 1372, 1468-1469, 2098
Peñaloza, Dante, 1714
Peñaloza, Humberto, 7827
Pendergast, David M., 692-693, 1086
Penfold, Anthony, 8445
Penn, Raymond, 6642
Pennington, Campbell, 1087
Penteado Coelho, Vera, 975
Pereira, José Severo de Camargo, 6274
Pereira, Nereu do Vale, 8525
Pereira, Osny Duarte, 7130
Pereira, Sonia Gomes, 89
Pereira Barroso, Luiz. *See* Barroso, Luiz Pereira.
Pereira de Queiroz, María. *See.* Queiroz, María Isaura Pereira de.
Pereira de Queiroz Neto, José. *See* Queiroz, José Pereira de.
Perera, Miguel Angel, 1017-1020
Peres, Janise Pinto, 6275
Pérez, Humberto, 6100
Pérez, Javier, 7454
Pérez, José Antonio, 781-782, 793
Pérez Alba, Simón, 6176
Pérez Alfonso, Pablo Juan, 2148
Pérez Arbeláez, Enrique, 6917-6918
Pérez Calderón, José A., 1088
Pérez de Arce, Hermógenes, 2237
Pérez Duprat, Rodolfo, 6079
Pérez Dupuy, Henrique, 2149-2151
Pérez Luciani, Rodrigo, 2152
Pérez Olivares, Enrique, 6186
Pérez Ramírez, Gustavo, 7665
Pérez Sanín, Enrique, 8446

Perlman, Janice E., 8526
Perón, Juan Domingo, 7976-7977
Perota, Celso, 847-849
Perrin, Michel, 1302-1303
Perrotto, Beatriz, 510
Persson, Lars, 523, 1304
Peru. Ministerio de Agricultura. Dirección de Comunidades Campesinas, 2290-2292
Peru. Ministerio de Guerra. Institiuto Geográfico Militar, 7336
Peru. Ministerio de Trabajo. Dirección General del Empleo, 2293
Peru. Presidencia, 2294
Pesantez de Moscoso, Gloria, 1470
Pessango Espora, Mario A., 1305
Pessôa, Dirceu Murilo, 2425
Pessoa, Mário, 8221
Petersen, George, 920
Petersen, John H., 7558
Petersen G., Georg, 762
Peterson, Harold F., 8222
Petkoff, Teodoro, 7813
Petrahn, Renate, 7424a
Petras, James, 7455-7457, 7772, 8066, 8223
Petrecola, Alberto, 2386
Petróleo Brasileiro, S.A. (PETROBRAS), Rio. Departamento de Exploração e Produção, 7131
Pettzer, Ernesto, 2136
Peuser Jacobo (firm), Buenos Aires. Departamento de Cartografía, 7228
Pfromm Neto, Samuel, 6276
Phelps, Barry, 6922
Philibert, Jean-Marc, 1127
Philipson, J., 1601
Phillips, George W., 7674
Philpoyt, Stuart B., 1197
Phleger, Fred B., 6670
Piauí (state), Bra. Govêrno do Estado do . . . Coordenação do Desenvolvimento do Estado (CODESE), 6277
Piazza, Walter F., 7132
Picó, Rafael, 2509, 6656
Picón Salas, Mariano, 7817
Piel, Jean, 8447
Pilatti Balhana, Altiva. See Balhana, Altiva Pilatti.
Pilon-Lé, Lise, 1127
Pimenta Veloso, Henrique. See Veloso, Henrique Pimenta.
Pimentel Gomes, Raymundo. See Gomes, Raymundo Pimentel.
Pimstein C., Rainer, 6776
Pina, Hélio, 7133
Piña Chan, Román, 550, 602, 694, 901
Pina Peña, Plinio, 748-749, 755-756
Pinchas Geiger, Pedro. See Geiger, Pedro Pinchas.
Pincus, Joseph, 1975
Piñeyro, Pedro, 8067

Pinheiro, Luís Adolfo Corrêa, 7871
Pinheiro Filho, Arthur Alves, 7119-7120
Pinheiro Machado, Brasil. See Machado, Brasil Pinheiro.
Pino, Milton, 757
Pinto, Aníbal, 1861, 2238
Pinto, Edmundo G., 510, 1471
Pinto, Luiz de Aguiar Costa, 7458, 7666-7667, 8257, 8448
Pinto, Myrthes da Fonseca, 6278
Pinto-Cisternas, J., 1752-1753
Pinto Ferreira, Luis. See Ferreira, Luis Pinto.
Schmitt, Karl, 76
Pinto Peres, Janise. See Peres, Janise Pinto.
Piquet, Rosélia Perissé, 1862
Pires, José Herculano, 8527
Pires Pontes, Salvador. See Pontes, Salvador Pires
Pisano Valdés, Edmundo, 6887
Pitcher, W. S., 6949
Pizarro, Roberto, 2239
Plattner, Stuart, 1089
Plaza, Galo, 7459, 8068-8070
Podestá, Roberto, 1603
Pogolotti, Marcelo, 8322
Poitras, Guy E., 7532
Polémica en la Iglesia: documentos de obispos argentinos y sacerdotes para el Tercer Mundo, 1969-1970, 7978
Polidoro, Nicola, 6583
Polino, Héctor T., 7979
La política exterior del gobierno de Ovando, 8224
Política Internacional, 7916, 8173-8174
Pollak-Eltz, Angelina, 1198, 1306-1307
Pollard, Gordon C., 893
Pollock, Nancy J., 1199
Pomonti, Bernard, 2025
Pompeu Sobrinho, Thomaz, 7134
Ponce, Lautaro, 6118
Ponce García, Jaime, 7722
Ponce Sanginés, Carlos, 815-818
Poniatowska, Elena, 7533
Pons, Gabriel, 8352
Ponte, Alberto da, 7333-7334
Pontes, Salvador Pires, 6279
Poon-King, Theo, 1676
Popovich, Harold, 1604
Poppovic, Ana Maria, 6280
Porras Garcés, Pedro I., 902-906
Porras Muñoz, Guillermo, 8323
Portantiero, Juan Carlos, 7966
Portela, Jarbas Moacir, 8528
Porter, Nancy, 1140
Portes, Alejandro, 7773, 8449
Portnoy, Leopoldo, 1863
Pôrto, Rubens d'Almada Horta, 6228
Portocarrero, Felipe, 2295
Portorreal, Juan E., 6201
Post, Peter W., 1729

Potash, Robert A., 7936
Poveda Ramos, Gabriel, 2075
Powell, Andrew Foster, 2451
Powell, John Duncan, 7814-7815, 7827
Powelson, John P., 1864, 7460
Powhson, Paul S., 510
Powlison, Esther, 1605
Pozas, Isabel H. de, 8324
Pozas, Ricardo, 8324
Prada, Abner, 6178
Prado, J. Leal, 6281
Prado Júnior, Caio, 7135
Prats, Raymond, 8142
Pratt, Raymond B., 7699, 7775
Prebisch, Raúl, 1865
Precolumbian America, 603
Un predicamento del hombre: la población, 6584
Preiswerk, Roy, 8175-8176
Prem, Hanns J., 640
Premdas, Ralph R., 7635
Press, Irwin, 1472
Presser, Harriet B., 8394
Prestes Motta, Fernando C. *See* Motta, Fernando C. Prestes.
Preston, David A., 6853, 8450
Price, Barbara J., 510, 524
Price, Richard, 1200-1201
Price, Sally, 1201
Pride, Kitty, 1606
Pride, Leslie, 1606
Prieto, Rafael, 2076
Prieto Figueroa, Luis Beltrán. *See* Beltrán Prieto Figueroa, Luis.
Princeton University, *Princeton, N.J.* Office of Population Research, 6585
Los problemas del financiamiento externo del desarrollo, 1866
O processo revolucionário brasileiro, 7872
Proctor, Jesse Harris, Jr., 1179
Proenza Brochado, José. *See* Brochado, José Proenza.
Programa de desenvolvimento da pecuária de Corte, 7136
O projeto Rondon, 7137
Pronsato, Domingo, 6826
Proskouriakoff, Tatiana, 550
Prost, Marian D., 1308
Proulx, Donald A., 985
Proulx, Paul, 1607-1608
Proyecto de Estatuto Orgánico de la Universidad de Chile emanado del Congreso Universitario Transitorio, 6119
Psuty, Norbert P., 936, 6586
Puble, Hans-Jürgen, 7409
The Puerto Rican sugar industry: rehabilitation providing design for future, 2511
Puerto Rico. Bureau of Economic and Social Analysis. Planning Board, 8395
Puerto Rico. Junta de Planificación, 2510
Puiggrós, Rodolfo, 7980-7981

Pujadas, Leo, 2026
Pujol, Nicole, 1754
Puleston, Dennis E., 701
Pulgar Vidal, Javier, 986
Pulte, William, 1609
Purser, W. F. C., 2296
Quadri, Mario A., 1867
Quadros, Jânio, 8071
Quan R., Julio E., 8349
Quargnolo, Jorge, 7229-7232
Quartim, João, 7873
Quartino, Bernabé J., 6805
Queiroz, Maria Isaura Pereira de, 8529
Queiroz Neto, José Pereira de, 7138
Quijano, Aníbal, 2297
Quijano Obregón, Aníbal, 1473, 7700
Quinn, L. R., 7139
Quintanilla, Antonio, 1719
Quintero, Rodolfo, 6187, 8453
Quintín Lame, Manuel, 1474
Quinzio, José Mario, 7776
Quirarte, Jacinto, 604
Quirino, Tarcízio Rêgo, 6282-6283
Quiroga C., Luis, 2044
Quiroga Santa Cruz, Marcelo, 8225
Quirós Varela, Luis, 7456
Quiroz Cuarón, Alfonso, 8325
Quiroz Cuarón, Raúl, 8325
Rajbansee, Joseph, 8396
Rachid, Cora Bastos de Freitas, 6284
Raffino, Rodolfo A., 772-773, 793a-795
Raffo del Campo, José M., 6813
Raggi, Carlos M., 756
Ralph, Elizabeth K., 597
Ram, Bali, 8353
Rama, Carlos M., 7482a
Rama, Germán W., 6132-6133, 7668, 7917
Ramírez, Jesús Emilio, 6919
Ramírez, Juan Andrés, 1475
Ramírez, Sergio, 6101
Ramírez, Novoa, E., 2298
Ramírez Pérez, Miguel A., 2512-2515
Ramírez Tazza, Jesús, 510, 955
Ramírez Vázquez, Pedro, 631
Ramlot, Michel Jean Paul, 2387
Ramos, Dilson Cosme, 7075
Ramos, Jorge Abelardo, 7982
Ramos, Joseph R., 2240
Ramos, Manuel M., 6587
Ramos, Sergio, 2241
Ramos Chaves, Maria Paula. *See* Chaves, Maria Paula Ramos.
Ramos de Carvalho, Laerte. *See* Carvalho, Laerte Ramos de.
Ramos de Cox, Josefina, 987-991
Ramos Garza, Oscar, 1943
Ramphal, S. S., 1179
Rands, Robert L., 558
Rangel, Domingo Alberto, 2153, 7816-7817
Rangel, Vicente Marotta, 8072

Rangel Guerra, Alfonso, 6155
Rangel Lima, Gelson. *See* Lima, Gelson Rangel.
Ranis, Peter, 7461
Ranitz, C. W. M. de, 7777
Ranitz-Haaften, E. H. de, 7777
Raposo Fontenelle, L. F. *See.* Fontenelle, L. F. Raposo.
Ratier, Hugo E., 8451
Ratinoff, Luis, 7374, 7462
Rattner, Henrique, 2458
Rattray, Evelyn C., 594
Rauch, Enrique, 7983
Rauth, José Wilson, 850-851
Ravines, Eudocio, 6588
Ravines, Rogger, 510, 921-922, 992-995, 1476, 7694
Rawls, Joseph, 6777
Ray, Víctor, 6080
Las realizaciones de la nueva política económica del Brasil, 2459
Reca, Inés Cristina, 6120
Reed, Irving B., 120
Reed, Karen Barbara, 1090, 1403
La reforma agraria: realizaciones y proyectos, 6955
La reforma de la agricultura en Iberoamérica, 6589
Reforma do ensino no Estado da Guanabara: ensino de 1. e 2. graus, 6285
Reforma universitária: 1968-1969, 6286
Rêgo Quirino, Tarcízio. *See* Quirino, Tarcízio Rêgo.
Reiche Caal, Carlos Enrique, 1091
Reichel-Dolmatoff, Gerardo, 870-871
Reimer, Everett W., 6049, 8397
Reina, Rubén E., 7936
Reinoso Hermida, Gustavo, 907
Reipert, Herman José, 36
Reis, Arthur Cézar Ferreira, 6287, 7140-7141, 7874, 8073
Reis, Fábio Wanderley, 7463, 7875
Reis Velloso, João Paulo dos. *See* Velloso, João Paulo dos Reis.
Reiter, Udo, 7426a
Relaciones comerciales de la URSS con Latinoamérica, 8074
Rémy, Raoul, 6648
Rendón, Juan José, 1610
Renner, Richard R., 6134
Rennie, Drummond, 1715-1716
Rens, Jef, 8075-8076
Resources for the study of Latin America at Indiana University, 121
Restrepo Fernández, Iván, 1938, 1944
Reunión de Ministros de Educación de la Región Andina, *I, Bogotá, 1970*, 6050
Reunión Extraordinaria del Consejo Interamericano para la Educación, la Ciencia y la Cultura, *II, Washington, 1972*, 6051

Reunión Latinoamericana de Fitotecnia, *VIII, Bogotá, 1970*, 6590
Reunión Nacional para el Estudio del Desarrollo Industrial en México, *Naucalpán, Mex., 1970*, 1945
Revenga, José Rafael, 7827
Revilla C., Arcenio, 1445
Revista Brasileira de Estudos Pedagógicos, 6288-6289
Revista Brasileira de Política Internacional, 8077-8078
Revista Cámara de Comercio de Bogotá, 2077
Revista de Educación, 6081
Revista de la Academia Nacional de Ciencias Económicas, 2299
Revista de la Facultad de Ciencias Económicas, 2388
Revista de la Facultad de Derecho de México, 1946
Revista del Banco Nacional de Cuba, 2027
Revista del Centro de Estudios Educativos, 6160
Revista Dominicana de Arqueología y Antropología, 755-756
Revista Industrial do Amazonas, 7142
Revista Panorama Industrial, 2179
Rex González, Alberto. *See* González, Alberto Rex.
Rey Martínez, Juan Carlos, 7818
Reyes, Alvaro, 2067
Reyes, Vitelio, 7819
Reyes Ramírez, José Ricardo, 6687
Reyna, José Luis, 7534
Reynolds, Clark W., 1947
Reynolds, Jack, 8398
Rezende da Silva, Fernando A. *See* Silva, Fernando A. Rezende da.
Riane, Philip, 8531
Ribeiro, Augusta Barbosa de Carvalho, 8532
Ribeiro, Darcy, 6052, 7778, 8284
Ribeiro, Lidio, 6180
Ribeiro, M. N. Goes, 7027
Ribeiro, Pedro Augusto Mentz, 852
Ribeiro, René, 8533
Ribeiro, Sylvio Wanick, 7143-7144
Ribeiro de Araujo Filho, José. *See* Araujo Filho, José Ribeiro de.
Ribeiro Gondim, Maristella de Miranda. *See* Gondim, Maristella de Miranda Ribeiro.
Ribeiro Neto, Adolpho, 6290
Ribera Arteaga, Leonor, 8226
Ricaurte, Daniel Schlesinger, 2063
Ricci, Susana M., 7233-7235
Ricci, Teodoro Ricardo, 2389
Richardson, Bonham C., 2028, 6943
Richardson, C. Howard, 6591
Ricord, Humberto E., 8143
Riemens, H., 7464
Riese, Berthold von, 605, 730
Riester, Jürgen, 1309-1311

AUTHOR INDEX

Rife, David C., 1755
Rijckeghem, W. Van, 2390
Riley, Carroll L., 571
Rímoli, Renato O., 749
Rino, José Bautista, 1677
Rio Garcia, Caio del. *See* Garcia, Caio del Rio.
Rio Grande do Norte (state), *Bra.*, 6291
Rio Grande do Norte (state), *Bra.* Comissão Estadual de Planejamento Agrícola, 7145
Rio Grande do Sul (state), *Bra.* Grupo Executivo do Desenvolvimento da Indústria da Pesca (GEDIP), 7146-7147
Río Negro (province), *Arg.* Departamento Provincial de Agua, 6827
Riofrío, Gustavo, 6168a
Riollano, Arturo, 2516
Rios, José Arthur, 7867
Rippy, Merrill, 122
Ristow, Walter W., 7203-7204
Rivas Iturralde, Vladimiro, 7820
Rivera Brenes, Luis, 2517
Rivera Díaz, Mario, 872-873
Rivera Domínguez, Rafael, 1092
Rivera Dorado, Miguel, 510, 895, 996-998
Rivero de la Calle, Manuel, 755, 757
Rivière, Peter, 1202, 7148
Riz, Liliana de, 7918
Robalino Gonzaga, César Raúl, 2099
Robatto Orrico, José Alexandre. *See* Orrico, José Alexandre Robatto.
Roberts, C. Paul, 2029
Roberts, Derek F., 1656, 1756
Robertson, C. J., 6628
Robertson, Elaine, 8388
Robertson, Merle Greene, 606
Robinson, Carol, 1445
Robinson, D. J., 6592
Robinson, David J., 6975
Robinson, Harry, 6593
Robinson, J. W. L., 1477-1478
Robinson, Scott S., 510, 1445, 1479
Robirosa, Mario C., 6594
Robles, Laura, 7771
Robles Ortiz, Manuel, 695
Robson, J. R. K., 1704
Rocca, Carlos Antônio, 2460
Rocha, F. J. da, 1751, 1757
Rocha, José Marinho da, 8535
Roche, Eduardo, 8286
Rocque, Carlos, 7149
Rodgers, William B., 1203
Rodney, Walter, 7621
Rodrigues, Carlos, 7150
Rodrigues, David Márcio Santos, 7011, 7151
Rodrigues, José Albertino, 7877
Rodrigues Machado, Renato. *See* Machado, Renato Rodrigues.
Rodríguez, Amílcar A., 796-797
Rodríguez, D. W., 2030
Rodríguez, Domingo, 7344

Rodríguez, Humberto Angel, 6135
Rodríguez, José, 6888
Rodríguez, Luis A., 8227
Rodríguez Mariño, Tomás, 6920
Rodríguez Pastor, Humberto, 1480
Rodríguez Rouanet, Francisco, 1093-1094
Rodríguez Sala de Gomezgil, María Luisa, 6161, 8326
Rodríguez Serrano, Felipe, 8144
Roel, Virgilio, 2300
Roett, Riordan, 123, 7878, 8228
Rofman, Alejandro B., 510
Rogler, Lloyd H., 8399
Rohr, João Alfredo, 525, 853
Rohrbach, Paulo Carlos, 7275
Roig, Juan Miguel, 124
Roisenberg, I., 1758
Rojas, Manuel, 6751
Rojas R., Iván, 2154
Rojas Rodríguez, Marta Tania, 7465
Rolandi de Perrot, Diana Susana, 798
Rolando, Stefano, 7879
Romain, Jean-Baptiste, 1759
Romano Delgado, Agustín, 1095
Ramanova, Zinaida Ivanovna, 1868
Romanucci-Ross, Lola, 1096
Romanucci Schwartz, Lola, 8327
Romeo, Carlos, 2242
Romer, R. A., 1204
Romero Kolbeck, Gustavo, 7374
Romero Pittari, Salvador, 7723
Romero Rojas, Francisco José, 51
Roncada, M. J., 1678
Roncagliolo, Rafael, 6168a
Ronceray, Hubert de, 6202, 8400
Rondon, J. Lucídio N., 2461, 7152
Rondônia (territory), *Bra.* Ministério do Interior. Serviço de Geografia e Estatística, 7153
Roos, P. J., 6626
Roosevelt, Anna, 999
Roque Musalem, Alberto, 2078
Rosa, Diógenes de la, 7817, 8145
Rosamilha, Nelson, 8465, 8536
Rosário, Milton, 6992
Rosario Green, María del, 8114
Rose, Jean, 1611
Rosen, Bernard C., 8537, 8538
Rosenbaum, J. Jon, 7880-7881, 8229
Rosenberg, Emily S., 8230
Rosenn, Keith S., 7882
Rosenstein-Rodan, Paul N., 2208, 7374
Rosero, Magdalena, 1312
Ross, Patricia Fent, 6752
Ross, Stanley R., 1948
Rossel U., Guillermo, 1812
Rothhammer, Francisco, 1717, 1760-1761
Rotstein, Enrique, 2365
Rouquié, Alain, 7466
Rouse, Irving, 755

Rousseau, André, 7587
Rout, Leslie B., Jr., 8231
Roux, Gustavo I. de, 8452
Rowe, John Howland, 1000
Rox-Schulz, Heinz, 6778
Roy, E. Van, 1915-1916
Rubio Orbe, Gonzálo, 1097
Ruda, José María, 8079, 8195
Ruddle, Kenneth, 7467
Rudolph, Klaus, 7424a
Rueda Gómez, Luis, 8424
Rueda-Williamson, Roberto, 1680
Ruete, Silvia E., 768
Rufino de Oliveira, Décio. See Oliveira, Décio Rufino de.
Rugnon de Dueñas, Mirna, 7907
Ruiz, Leovigildo, 7597
Ruiz, María Angélica, 510, 1481
Ruiz-Esquide Jara, Mariano, 2243
Ruiz Franco, Arcadio, 1098
Ruscoe, Gordon C., 7827
Russe, Jean, 7724
Russell, Charles A., 7468
Ruth, James M., Jr., 6695
Sá, Jayme Magrassi de, 2462
Sá, Paulo Fernandes de, 2471
Saavedra, Alejandro, 1482
Sabat Pebet, Juan Carlos, 1612
Sábato, Jorge A., 2391, 7469
Sabloff, Jeremy A., 607, 616
Sabogal Wiesse, José R., 1483-1484
Sachs, Ignacy, 1869
Sader Pérez, Rubén, 7821
Sáenz Peña, Roque, 8038
Sáez Iglesias, Hernán, 7470
Saffir, A. J., 1706
St. Clair, David, 7154
Saint-Hilaire, Auguste de, 7155
Saint-Louis, René, 8401
Saint-Méry, Médéric-Louis-Elie Moreau de, 1136
Saint-Pierre, Madelene, 1127
Saito, H., 8513
Sakamoto, Jorge, 2392
Sal y Rosas, Federico, 510, 1485
Salaverry, José A., 2301
Salazar, Diego, 2067
Salazar L., Arturo, 6956
Salazar Quijada, Adolfo, 1205
Salcedo Cáceres, Epifanio, 6167
Salcedo Salazar, Guillermo, 2073
Salera, Virgil, 1870, 2463
Salgado, Germánico, 1871, 2100, 7374
Salinas, René, 6889
Salinas, Rolando, 6890
Salles Cunha, Ernesto de Mello. See Cunha, Ernesto de Mello Salles.
Salmen, Lawrence F., 8539
Salser, J. K., Jr., 1613
Salvador, Nélida, 4
Salvador Lara, Jorge, 907a

Salzano, Francisco M., 1751, 1757, 1762-1767
Samaniego R., Lorenzo Alberto, 1001
Sampaio Dória, Antônio Roberto. See Dória, Antônio Roberto Sampaio.
Samper, Armando, 1872
San Martín, Julio, 2155
Sana, Júlio F. Ferreira, 2443
Sánchez, Luis Alberto, 7817
Sánchez, Maria Angela D'Incao Maciel, 8540
Sánchez, Otto, 1679
Sánchez Baron, Ricardo, 6936
Sánchez Cárdenas, Carlos, 7535
Sánchez Cortés, José, 6743
Sánchez Hernández, Fidel, 7551
Sánchez Labrador, José, 1631
Sánchez Masi, Luis, 2265
Sánchez Román, Rodolfo, 1976
Sánchez Ruphuy, Rodrigo, 8354
Sánchez Sorondo, Marcelo, 7984
Sanders, Andrew, 1206
Sanders, Richard, 1795
Sanders, Thomas G., 1486-1488, 7779, 8285
Sanders, William T., 550, 608, 696, 1652
Sandner, Gerhard, 6708
Sandoval Rodríguez, Isaac, 7725
Sanguinetti de Bórmida, Amalia, 799
Sanjek, Roger, 8541
Sanoja, Mario, 1021, 1313
Sanquily, Manuel, 8155
Santa Ana, Julio de, 6178
Santa Cruz (province), Arg., 6828
Santa Catarina (state), Bra. Departamento Estadual de Geografia e Cartografia, 7263
Santa Fe (province), Arg., 2393
Santa María, Domingo, 2244
Santamarina, Estela B. de, 16, 6829
Santana, Jorge, 6974
Santana-Aguilar, Rómulo, 6891-6892
Sant'Anna, Flávia Maria, 6292
Santiago, Alberto Alves, 2464, 7156
Santillán de Andrés, Selva E., 6830
Santisteban Tello, Oscar, 510, 1489
Santoro de Ycaza, José, 7216
Santos, Fabiano Marques dos, 7151
Santos, Milton, 1873, 8286
Santos, Ralph G., 8232
Santos, Theobaldo Miranda, 7883
Santos, Theotonio dos, 7471
Santos A., Eduardo, 2101
Santos Lima, Maria Nayde dos. See Lima, Maria Nayde dos Santos.
Santos Rodrigues, David Marcio. See Rodrigues, David Marcio Santos.
São Paulo (state), Bra. Secretaria de Economia e Planejamento. Departamento de Estatística. Divisão de Estatísticas Demográficas, 7157, 7265
São Paulo (state), Bra. Secretaria de Economia e Planejamento. Grupo Executivo da Grande São Paulo (GEGRAN) [and] Secretaria de

Transportes. Assessoria Técnica de Coordenação e Planejamento (ATCP), 7158
São Paulo (state), *Bra.* Secretaria dos Serviços e Obras Públicas. Companhia de Saneamento da Baixada Santista, 7159
São Paulo yearbook 1972, 125
Saraiva, Hel cio Ulhôa, 8510
Saraiva, Terezinha, 8542
Sardón, José, 1780
Sarmiento, Guillermo, 6973, 6976-6978
Sasson, Lil Despradel, 7617
Sastre de Cabot, Josefa Margarita, 6082
Sater, William F., 6121
Saul, Frank, P., 697
Saunders, John, 126
Savloff, Guillermo, 6178
Sawatzky, Harry Leonard, 6753
Saxe-Fernandez, John, 7548
Saxton, Dean, 1614
Saxton, Lucille, 1614
Sanz de Santamaría, Carlos, 7472
Saunders, John V. D., 7884
Saxe-Fernández, John, 8080
Sburlati, Carlo, 7985
Scantimburgo, João de, 6293
Schaden, Egon, 1314-1315, 8543
Schaedel, Richard P., 510, 1490
Schatzmayr, Herman Gonçalves, 1658
Schauer, Stanley, 1615
Schauer, Junia, 1615
Schaumann, Ingeborg, 730
Schaw, Janet, 6629
Scheffler, Harold W., 1316, 1616
Schegel, Mary Luz, 799
Scheidenhelm, Kristin K., 743
Schell, Lois, 127
Schell, Rolfe, 127
Scheller, Ulf, 908
Scheone, Oswaldo, 2361
Schiavo-Campo, Salvatore, 1977
Schlenterther, Ursula, 1617
Schlesinger, Arthur, Jr., 7817
Schloz, Rudolf, 7363b
Schmitt, Ariete Alice, 830
Schmitt, Karl M., 7536
Schmitter, Philippe C., 7473-7475, 7885
Schmitz, Pedro Ignacio, 771, 839, 854
Schneider, Eliezer, 8544
Schneider, Hans, 6893-6894
Schneider, Ronald M., 7886
Schobinger, Juan, 800, 838
Schöndube B., Otto, 609-610, 631
Schoultz, Lars, 7669
Schubert, Carlos, 1027
Schulgovski, A. F., 7424a
Schulke, Flip, 6852
Schulman, Sam, 6603, 7485
Schultz, Harald, 1317
Schultz, T. Paul, 2072
Schulz Friedmann, Ramón P. C., 731

Schumann, Otto, 1618
Schump, Walter, 7476
Schuster, F., Jorge F., 7822
Schwartz, Norman B., 8355
Schwartz, Robert N., 8454
Schwartzbaum, Allan M., 6194, 6203
Schwarze, Christoph, 8268
Schwerin, Karl H., 510, 526
Schydlowsky, Daniel M., 1874-1874a
Scobie, James R., 510
Scott, Rebecca, 8233
Seabra, Manoel, 7160-7161
Seaga, Edward P. G., 1180
Seara Vázquez, Modesto, 8122
Seda Bonilla, Eduardo, 1207, 8402
Sedat, David W., 698
Seele, E., 702
Seelye, H. Ned, 8356
Segovia, Rafael, 8114, 8328-8329
Seibert, Paul, 7212
Sejourné, Laurette, 594
Selections from 1970, 1680
Selivanov, V. I., 8081
Selser, Jorge, 7369
Semanario Copei, 7823
Semenov, Sergeĭ Ivanovich, 7477
Seminar on the Acquisition of Latin American Library Materials, *XVI, Puebla, Mex., 1971,* 37
Seminario de América Latina y España, *Madrid, 1969,* 8082
Seminario de Introducción al Procesamiento de Datos Aplicados a la Bibliotecología y la Documentación, *Buenos Aires, 1971,* 47
Seminario de Professores de Ciencia Política, *I, Bogotá, 1969,* 7478
Seminario del Desarrollo Regional y Urbano, *I, Caracas, 1970,* 8286
Seminario Interamericano sobre la Integración de los Servicios de Información de Archivos, Bibliotecas y Centros de Documentación en América Latina y el Caribe (SI/ABCD), *Washington, 1972,* 48
Seminario Nacional de Planificación Familiar, *II, Asunción, 1969,* 8455
Seminario Regional Interamericano de Educación Profesional para Adolescentes y Jóvenes, *III, São Paulo, 1966,* 6053
Seminario sobre Actividades de Formación Cultural de los Adultos, *La Catalina, C. R., 1968,* 6053
Seminario sobre Industria de la Construcción Naval, *Buenos Aires, 1970,* 2394
Semo, Enrique, 8330
Senén González, Santiago, 7986
Senise, Paschoal E. Américo, 6294
Sepúlveda, César, 7537
Sepúlveda A., Alberto, 8234
Sepúlveda Amor, Bernardo, 1875, 8114
Sepúlveda Whittle, Tomás, 2266

Sergipe (state), *Bra.*, 7162
Serie Espelológica y Carsológica, 757
Serna Silva, Jairo, 2048
Serra, Adalberto B., 7163-7164
Serra, José, 7456-7457
Serrano, Antonio, 801
Serrano S., Carlos, 1730
Service, Elman R., 527
Serviços Aerofotogramétricos Cruzeiro do Sul (firm), *São Paulo,* 7265
Seton, Francis, 2245
Setti, Enrique de Jesús, 6829
Severin, Timothy, 6630
Sewell, William G., 1136
Sexton, James D., 1099
Seyferth, Giralda, 824, 1720
Sharer, Robert J., 698
Sharma, P. L., 2492
Sharon, Douglas C., 1491-1492
Shaw, Mary, 1619-1620
Shaw, Robert d'A., 1806
Shchegolev, B. N., 8235
Sheahan, John, 2079
Sheck, Ronald C., 6595
Sheets, Payson D., 699-700
Sheldon, Breiner, 635
Shell Compañía Argentina de Petróleo (firm), *Buenos Aires,* 6831
Shepard, Marietta Daniels, 49
Shibata, Sayuri, 7172
Shlemon, Roy J., 6922
Sideri, S., 1876
Siefer, Elisabeth, 128
Siemens, Alfred H., 701
Sierra García, Jaime, 8456
Sigal, Silvia, 7987
Sigmund, Paul E., 7479-7480, 7780-7781
Silén, Juan Angel, 8403
Siles, Luis Adolfo, 8236
Silla, Ousmane, 1140
Silva, Ady Raul da, 6295
Silva, Benedicto, 6296
Silva, Fernando A. Rezende da, 7887
Silva, Fernando Altenfelder, 855
Silva, Glauco Lessa de Abreu e, 7888
Silva, Helvécio de Siqueira e, 8546
Silva, Hilda da, 7165
Silva, Jorge de Carvalho e, 8237
Silva, Juan, 6973, 6976-6978
Silva, Luiz Octávio Souza e, 2465
Silva Amador, Elmo da. *See* Amador, Elmo da Silva.
Silva Galdames, Osvaldo, 528, 611
Silva Maia, Newton da. *See* Maia, Newton da Silva.
Silva Michelena, Héctor, 2140
Silva Michelena, José A., 7824
Silva Muricy, Antônio Carlos da. *See* Muricy, Antônio Carlos da Silva.
Silveira, Estanislau Kostka Pinto da, 6596
Silveira, Isôlda Maciel da, 1318

Silveira Dantas, Humberto da. *See* Dantas, Humberto da Silveira.
Silverman, Bertram, 7598
Silvert, Kalman H., 6054
Silvicultura em São Paulo, 7166
Sime, Francisco, 1714
Simkins, Paul D., 6597
Simmons, Alan B., 6921
Simões, Mário F., 831, 856-857
Simon, Kate, 129
Simone, Dante, 2395
Simone, José de, 6107
Simonelli, Jorge, 2396
Simoni-Abbat, Mireille, 529
Simposio del Proyecto Puebla-Tlaxcala, *I, Puebla, Mex., 1973,* 702
Simposio Internacional sobre Lagunas Costeras, UNAM-UNESCO, *México, 1967,* 6670
Simpósio sobre Poluição Ambiental, *I, Brasília, 1971,* 7167
Simpson, George Eaton, 1208
Sinaloa (state), *Mex.,* 7331
Sindicato de Luz y Fuerza, *Buenos Aires,* 7988
Sinding, Steven W., 7782
Sinopse preliminar do censo demográfico, Brasil: VIII recenseamento geral, 1970, 7168
Siqueira e Silva, Helvécio de. *See* Silva, Helvécio de Siqueira e.
Siri, Gabriel, 1978
Sirolli, Amadeo Rodolfo, 802
Sisson, Edward B., 703
Sito, Nilda, 6055, 7964
Sittón, Salomón Nahmad, 1100
Siverts, Henning, 1101
Sizonenko, A. I., 7999
Sjörgen, Bengt, 6631
Skupch, Pedro Rodolfo, 2397-2399
Slater, Charles, 2466
Slighton, Robert L., 2072
Sloan, John W., 7481, 7559, 8083
Small, Melvin, 8084
Smetherman, Bobbie B., 2302, 8085
Smetherman, Robert M., 2302, 8085
Smiley, Charles H., 732
Smith, A. Leydard, 704
Smith, Carlos J., 7482
Smith, Connie, 1621
Smith, Gordon W., 2455-2456
Smith, M. G., 1136-1137, 1180
Smith, Peter H., 7989
Smith, Peter Seaborn, 8238
Smith, Raymond T., 1137
Smith, Richard, 1621
Smith, Robert E., 607
Smith, Robert Freeman, 8123
Smith, T. Lynn, 7485
Smith, Thomas R., 7206
Smith, Wayne S., 8086
Snow, Dean R., 594
Snyder, J. Richard, 8239

AUTHOR INDEX

Snyder, Peter Z., 8357
Soares, José Teodoro, 2467
Soares, W. V., 7177
Soares Gouvêa, João Baptista. *See* Gouvêa, João Baptista Soares.
Sobrado, Miguel, 7422
Sociedad Rural Argentina, *Buenos Aires*. Instituto de Estudios Económicos, 6832
Sociedad y Desarrollo, 2246
Sociedade Comercial e Representações Gráficas Limitada (firm), *Curitiba, Bra.* 7266-7268
Soderstrom, R., 1704
Sodi M., Demetrio, 1102
Sodré, Muniz, 8548
Sodré, Roberto Costa de Abreu, 6297
Söderlund, Börje, 6754
Söderlund, Siv, 6754
Soja, Edward W., 6598
Sokolova, Z. I., 7599
Solano, Francisco de, 1622
Solari, Aldo, 7374
Solari Bosch, Osvaldo, 8457
Solari Yrigoyen, Hipólito, 2400
Solaun, Mauricio, 7489a, 7600
Solc, Vaclav, 1493
Solien de González, Nancie L. *See* González, Nancie L. Solien.
Solís Garza, Hernán, 8331
Solís M., Leopoldo, 1949
Solís Mimendi, Antonio, 7538
Solís Y., Néstor, 1445
Sommer, Juan, 2401
Sonntag, Heinz Rudolf, 7700a, 7782a
Sorensen, Soren C., 1713, 1718
Soria, Dante R., 767
Soruco, Felix, 6850
Sosa, Ademar, 6181
Sosa, Arturo, 7827
Soto Blanco, Ovidio, 6102
Soto Holguín, Alvaro, 510
Soto Jiménez, Roland A., 1979
Soto Mora, Consuelo, 6755
Sousa, Octavio E., 1681
Souza, Edson Machado de, 6234
Souza, José Armando de, 8287, 8549
Souza, Maria Adélia Aparecida de, 7169
Souza e Silva, Luiz Octávio. *See* Silva, Luiz Octávio Souza e.
Souza Keller, Elza Coelho de. *See* Keller, Elza Coelho de Souza.
Soza, José María, 6696
Spence, Michael W., 705-706, 710
Sper, Sheldon A., 1623
Spicer, Edward H., 1103
Spiegel, Erich, 2283
Spielbauer, Judith, 1002
Spielman, Richard S., 1319, 1717, 1768
Spinner, Julius, 6895
Spores, Ronald, 707
Spranz, Bodo, 702, 708-709

Springer, Hugh W., 1179
Spuhler, James N., 1769
Staff research in progress or recently completed in the humanities and the social sciences, 130
Stahl, John E., 2518
Stahle, Vera-Dagny, 510
Stanzick, Karl-Heinz, 7489a
Stark, Louisa R., 1624-1625
Statistical Bulletin for Latin America, 1877
Staton, Howard R., 1209
Stedman, John G., 1136
Steger, Hanns-Albert, 7482a
Stein, L., 1878
Stein, William W., 1494-1495
Steinberg, A. G., 1766
Steinhardt, Ricardo J. M., 6599
Steinmetz, Rolf, 839
Steinvorth Goetz, Inga, 1320
Stepan, Alfred C., III, 7685
Stephens, Richard H., 7701
Stephenson, Yvonne, 38
Sterlin, Carlo, 1140
Stern, Claudio, 8318
Stevens, Evelyn P., 7539
Stevenson, John R., 8087
Stevenson, Merritt R., 7216
Stewart, Robert, 744, 6707
Stickell, A. Lawrence, 7936
Stiefel, Jörg, 6896
Stillwell, H. Daniel, 6600
Stini, William A., 1705
Stinson, Hugh B., 8088
Stocker, Terrance L., 710
Stöhr, Walter B., 6601, 6775
Stolk, Anthonie, 1321
Stolte, Joel, 1626
Stolte, Nancy, 1626
Stoltman, Joseph P., 8332
Stone, Carl, 8458
Stone, Doris Z., 745
Stouse, P. A. D., Jr., 6602
Stout, Mickey, 1627
Stout, Ralph E., 6154
Strachan, Lloyd W., 2468
Strang, Harold Edgard, 7170-7172, 7186-7187
Strange, Ian J., 131
Strassmann, W. Paul, 2303
Strauss, Werner, 7424a
Streeten, Paul, 1879
Stresser-Péan, Guy, 550
Stroessner, Alfredo, 7900
Stross, Brian, 1628-1629
Struever, Stuart, 530
Stuart, George F., 7217
Studart, Heloneida, 8550
Studebaker, Beth Witt de, 1555
Student activism and higher education: an inter-American dialogue, 7483
Stug, David, 612
Stumer, Louis, 1003
Sturdevant, William D., 613

Stycos, J. Mayone, 7485
Sua Boa Estratêia, 7889
Suárez, Andrés, 7355, 7601
Suárez, Carlos, 7771, 7919
Suárez, Héctor V., 7990
Suárez, Macrino, 1880
Suárez, María Matilde, 1322-1323
Suárez de Asuaje, M. M., 1324
Suárez Huízar, J. Armando, 6044
Suárez Inclán, Raúl. See Inclán, Raúl Suárez.
Suárez Valles, Manuel, 7540
Suassuna, Ariano, 132
Subsídios para o estudo do ginásio polivalente, 6298
Suchl, Jan, 6596a
Suchlicki, Jaime, 120, 7484, 7602, 7752
Sullivan, Thelma D., 1630
Sundell, Jan-Olof, 7603
Sunkel, Osvaldo, 1881-1884
Surinam. Centraal Bureau Luchtkartering, 7337
Surinam. Stichting Planbureau, 2112
Susnik, Branislava, 1631
Sweeney, Edward A., 1706
Sweezy, Paul M., 7783
Swift, Jeannine, 2247
Switzer, Kenneth A., 1885
Szinyei-Merse, E., 1655
Szmuk, Peter Raphael, 763
Tabak, Fanny, 7890, 8551
Tabbush, Berta de, 6833
Tabío, Ernesto E., 757
Taborga, Huáscar, 6091-6092
Tabra Chávez, Emilio, 6056
Taddei, Antonio, 1013a-1014
Taggart, James M., 1104
Tahal Consulting Engineers, Rio. Sondotécnica Engenharia de Solos, 7174
Taintor, Mavis Bunker, 7609
Tamer, Alberto, 7175-7176
Tanaka, T., 7177
Tanzi, Vito, 2080
Tapia Videla, Jorge I., 7456, 7770
Tarasov, K.S. See Tarazov, Konstantin Sergeeviich.
Tarazov, Konstantin Sergeeviich, 6610b, 8089
Tarifa, José Roberto, 7178
Tarnopolsky, Samuel, 7991
Tarragó, Myriam N., 790, 803-804
Tarso Santos, Paulo de, 6057
Taveres, Denise Fernandes, 6299
Tavares, María C., 7456-7457
Taveira, Carlos Cesar Guterres, 7179
Tax, Sol, 1105-1106
Taxay, Don, 531
Taylor, John M., 1553
Taylor, Lester D., 2081
Taylor, Margaret Stewart, 6834
Taylor, Philip B., Jr., 6603, 7485, 7825-7827
Taylor, R. E., 683
Taylor, Roselyn G., 6604

Técnica Agroforestal (firm), Caracas, 2156
Téfel, Reinaldo Antonio, 1980
Teixeira, Anísio, 6300
Teixeira da Costa, Gerson. See Costa, Gerson Teixeira da.
Teixeira Vieira, Dorival. See Vieira, Dorival Teixeira.
Tejo, [Aurelio de] Limeira, 7891
Televisión argentina: un enfoque nacional, 8459
Teller, Charles H., 8359
Tello, Manuel, 8124
Temme, Mathilde, 6937
Tepfenhart, Mary A., 1766
Terada, Kazuo, 960
Terres Valdés, Pastor, 757
Tesh, Robert B., 6709
Texier, Jean Marie, 6979
Thebaud, Annie, 6301
Theberge, James D., 8177
Theses in Latin American studies at British universities in progress and completed: no. 7, 1972-1973, 57
Thesing, Josef, 7560
Theuns, H. L., 2031
Thomas, Clive Y., 1179, 1993, 2032
Thomas, J. J., 1136
Thomas, Norman D., 1107, 1632
Thomas, R. Brooke, 510
Thomas, Robert N., 6605-6606, 6697, 8360
Thomas de Cornides, Albert. See Cornides, Albert Thomas de.
Thome, Joseph, 6642, 7784
Thompson, Donald Enrique, 510, 1004-1006
Thompson, J. Eric S., 733-735
Thompson, Richard A., 1108
Thompson, Ruth, 1627
Thorn, Richard S., 7720
Thorsen, Timm, 8290
Thurber, Floyd, 736
Thurber, Valerie, 736
Tibón, Gutierre, 614
Tidrick, Gene, 1137
Tidrick, Kathryn, 8404
Tierney, John J., Jr., 8146
Tiller, Frank M., 6058
Tintner, Gerhard, 2469
Tirado, Irma G., 2519, 6204
Tirado, Manlio, 7512
Tobias, José Antônio, 6302
Tobriner, Stephen, 594
Togo, José, 795
Tolentino, Hugo, 6059
Tolstoy, Paul, 550, 1007
Tonni, Eduardo P., 806, 6811
Tooley, R. V., 7207-7208
Toro Agudelo, Hernán, 7640
Toro Sugrañes, José A., 133
Torre, Antonio de la, 6779, 6923
Torre López, Egidio, 1682
Torres, Blanca, 8114

Torres, José Garrido, 2470
Torres, Manuel, 6897
Torres Bodet, Jaime, 8090
Torres de Araúz, Reina, 746-747, 1109, 1707
Torres Montes, Luis, 594
Torres Neto, Pedro, 6303
Torres Ramírez, Blanca, 8178
Torres-Rivas, Edelberto, 1981, 7542,
Torres Sánchez, Isabel, 6060
Torruellas, Luz M., 2482, 2520-2521
Toscano, Salvador, 615
Tosello Goulart, Rina Norma. *See* Goulart, Rina Norma Tosello.
Tosta Berlinck, Manoel, 8552
Tourtellot, Gair, 616
Trager, Felicia Harben, 1633
A travers les livres et les revues: a la recherche d'un communisme sans larmes, 7604
Trejos Dittel, Eduardo, 6061
Trejos Quirós, Juan, 6684
Tretiak, Daniel, 8179
Trías, Vivian, 2314, 7702
Trinidad and Tobago. Government of . . ., 2033
Trinidad and Tobago. Survey Division, 7738-7339
Trindade, Mário, 8553
Trivers, Howard, 8180
Troccoli, Antonio A., 7965
Troike, Nancy P., 711
Troike, Rudolph C., 711
Trubek, David M., 2471
True, Delbert L., 894
Tschopik, Harry, 1496
Tucker, William P., 8333
Tuggle, H. David, 617, 712
Tulane University of Louisiana, *New Orleans, La.*, 134
Tulchin, Joseph S., 8240
Tullis, F. LaMond, 7703
Tumin, Melvin Marvin, 8405
Tun Wai, U., 1886
Turner, Frederick C., 7486
Turner, John C., 1435
Turner, Paul, 1634
Turner, Shirley, 1634
Turner, Terence S., 1325
Tutino, Saverio, 7605
Twining, Mary Arnold, 1210-1211
Tyler, William G., 2472-2473, 7880-7881
Uchôa, Dorath P., 858
Uchoa, Júlio Benevides, 6304
Uhía Pinilla, Agustín, 6062, 6136
Ulhôa Saraiva, Helcio. *See* Saraiva, Helcio Ulhôa.
Ulloa, Berta, 8125
Unión Industrial Argentina, *Buenos Aires*, 2402
Union of Soviet Socialist Republics, 7353, 8091
United Kingdom. Directorate of Overseas Surveys, 7280

United Kingdom. Ministry of Defense. Directorate of Military Survey, 7277-7279
United Kingdom. Overseas Development Administration, 7293
United Nations. Comisión Económica para la América Latina, 6835
United Nations. Economic Commission for Latin America (ECLA), 1887-1889, 2157, 2403, 2474
United Nations. Education, Scientific, and Cultural Organization (UNESCO), 58
United Nations. Food and Agriculture Organization (FAO), 2248-2249, 7218
United Nations Industrial Development Organization, *Wein*, 6607
United States. Board on Geographic Names, 7209
United States. Comptroller General, 7704
United States. Congress. House of Representatives. Committee on Foreign Affairs, 8092-8093
United States. Congress. House of Representatives. Committee on Foreign Affairs. Subcommittee on Inter-American Affairs, 8094-8096, 8126, 8147, 8181
United States. Congress. House of Representatives. Committee on Foreign Affairs. Subcommittee on International Organizations and Movements, 8097
United States. Congress. Senate. Committee on Foreign Relations, 8098, 8182, 8241
United States. Congress. Senate. Committee on Foreign Relations. Subcommittee on Western Hemisphere Affairs, 8148
United States. Department of Agriculture. Economic Research Service, 6958
United States. Federal Maritime Commission. Bureau of Domestic Regulation, 2522
United States. Library of Congress. Congressional Research Service. Foreign Affairs Division, 8099
La Universidad, 6688
La universidad ante la intervención de secundaria, 6182
Universidad Central de Venezuela, *Caracas*. Centro de Estudios del Desarrollo (CENDES), 2158
Universidad de Chile, *Santiago*, 2250-2252, 6122
Universidad de La Habana. Centro de Información Científica y Técnica. Centro de Investigaciones de la Caña, 2034
Universidad de La Habana. Equipos de Investigaciones Económicas, 2035
Universidad de la República, *Montevideo*. Facultad de Ciencias Económicas y de la Administración. Instituto de Economía, 2315-2316
Universidad de Los Andes, *Mérida, Ven*. Facultad de Economía, 2159-2161, 6980

Universidad Nacional de Buenos Aires. Instituto de Investigaciones de la Vivienda, 6836
Universidad Nacional de Colombia, *Bogotá.* Oficina de Planeación. División de Programación Económica, 6137
Universidad Nacional de Rosario, *Arg.* Facultad de Ciencias Económicas. Instituto de Economía Aplicada, 2404
Universidade Católica do Paraná, *Curitiba, Bra.,* 6305
Universidade de São Paulo. Instituto de Geografia, 7269
Universidade de São Paulo. Instituto Oceanográfico, 7180
Universidade do Estado de Guanabara, *Rio,* 6306-6307
Universidade Federal de Santa Catarina, *Florianópolis, Bra.,* 6308-6309
Universidade Federal do Ceará, *Fortaleza, Bra.,* 6310
Universidade Federal do Ceará, *Fortaleza, Bra.* Instituto de Pesquisas Econômicas, 7181
Universidade Federal do Rio Grande do Norte, *Natal, Bra.,* 6311
Universidade Federal do Rio Grande do Sul, *Pôrto Alegre, Bra.,* 6312
Universidades, 6063
Uratsuka, Josefa N., 532
Urban, Francis S., 6671, 6837
Uribe Villegas, Oscar, 8334
Uricoechea, Fernando, 8288
Urquidi, Victor L., 1890, 7485
Urquidi Barrau, Fernando, 819
Urquidi Morales, Arturo, 1497
Urrutia, J. J., 1671, 1696
Urtubey, Rodolfo J., 7992
Uruguay. Comisión Coordinadora para el Desarrollo Económico (COMCORDE). Secretaría Técnica, 2317
Uruguay. Ministerio de Defensa Nacional. Servicio Geográfico Militar, 7342
Uruguay. Ministerio de Transporte, Comunicaciones y Turismo, 7343
Uruguay. Presidencia de la Repúblic. Secretaría, 6608, 8242
Urzúa Frademann, Paul, 7785
Urzúa Valenzuela, Germán, 7786
Uschner, Manfred, 7424a
USSR. *See* Union of Soviet Socialists Republics.
Uzcátegui, Emilio, 6103
Uzzell, John Douglas, 1498
Vainstok, Arturo, 6838
Valdés, Nelson P., 7606-7608
Valdés Sotomayor, Gabriel, 8243
Valdez Franck, Arturo, 8244
Valdivia Ponce, Oscar, 8460
Valdivieso D., Ramón, 1680
Vale Pereira, Nereu do. *See* Pereira, Nereu do Vale.
Valenzuela, Arturo, 7787
Valero, Ricardo, 8114
Valero Iglesias, Luis Fernando, 8391
Valiente, Teresa, 1401, 1421
Valla, Víctor, 2475
Valladares, Licia de Prado, 6981
Valle Quiroga de Corcuera, Rosa del, 1008
Vallée, Lionel, 510, 1499-1500
Vallejo, César, 2082
Vallejo Arbeláez, Joaquín, 2083
Vallenilla Lanz, Laureano, 7828
Vallier, Ivan, 7487
Valois Arce, Daniel, 8245
Valverde, Orlando, 7182
van Ess, J. C., 8555
Van Horn, Lawrence, 1110
Van Meurs, A. P. H., 1891
Van Stan, Ina, 1009-1010
Vanek, Yaroslav, 1892
Vapñarsky, Cesar A., 6839
Varela, Hernani, 135
Vareschi, Volkmar, 6982-6983
Varese, Stefano, 1326-1327
Vargas, Luis A., 593
Vargas Arenas, Iraida, 1022
Varlack, Pearl, 2036
Varnes, W. G., 1739
Varona, Enrique José, 8155
Varsavsky, Oscar A., 2405
Vasconcelos Cavalcanti, Clóvis de. *See* Cavalcanti, Clóvis de Vasconcelos.
Vasconcelos Sobrinho, João de, 7183-7184
Vásquez, Emilio, 6064
Vásquez, Mario C., 1501-1502
Vásquez Rocha, E., 8216
Vásquez Varini, Felipe S., 2318
Vaughan, Denton R., 136
Vaz da Costa, Rubens. *See* Costa, Rubens Vaz da.
Vázquez Arroyo, Francisco, 1950
Vázquez Cacerrada, Pablo B. *See* Vázquez-Calcerrada, Pablo B.
Vázquez-Calcerrada, Pablo B., 2523, 8365, 8406
Vázquez Carrizosa, Alfredo, 8246
Vázquez Presedo, Vicente, 2381, 2406-2407
Vázquez-Viaña, Humberto, 7726
Vedder, John G., 6632
Vega, Bernardo, 756
Vega, Juan A., 2408
Veirano de Astiz, Lilia. *See* Astiz, Lilia Veirano de.
Vekemans, Roger, 7374, 7482a, 7488
Velasco Letelier, Eugenio, 6065
Velasco S., José Miguel, 2180
Velásquez, Rolando, 8149
Vélez O., Jorge, 6517
Véliz, Claudio, 1893, 8100
Velloso, João Paulo dos Reis, 6313
Velloso Galvão, Marília. *See* Galvão, Marília Velloso.
Veloso, Henrique Pimenta, 7171, 7186-7187

AUTHOR INDEX

Veloso Costa, Pedro. *See* Costa, Pedro Veloso.
Veloz Maggiolo, Marcio, 748-749, 755-756
Veneroni, Horacio Luis, 8101
Venezuela. Comisión del Plan Nacional de Aprovechamiento de los Recursos Hidráulicos, 2162
Venezuela. Comisión Investigadora Contra el Enriquecimiento Ilícito, 7829
Venezuela. Corporación Venezolana de Guayana, 6984
Venezuela. Dirección de Cartografía Nacional, 7346-7350
Venezuela. Dirección de Vialidad, 7351
Venezuela. Oficina Central de Información, 6985
Venezuela. Oficina de Estudios Socioeconómicos. Equipo Técnico, 8461
Venezuela. Presidencia. Comisión de Administración Pública, 2163
Venezuela. Presidencia. Oficina Central de Coordinación y Planificación, 2164
Venner, Dwight, 8168
Vera-Godoy, Hernán, 7746
Verez Peraza, Elena, 52
Veríssimo, José, 7188
Verner, Joel G., 7489, 7562-7563
Versiani Cunha, Maria Auxiliadora. *See* Cunha, Maria Auxiliadora Versiani.
Viacava, Carlos, 2476
Viana, José de Alencar Carneiro, 6314
Vianna, A. J. Barbosa, 7189
Vianna Guerra, C. *See* Guerra, C. Vianna.
Vieira, Dorival Teixeira, 2477
Vieira, Francisca Isabel Schurig, 2479
Vieira, Jorge Hilário Gouvêa, 2471
Viel, Benjamín, 7485
Viera, Eduardo, 2319
Vieragallo Quesney, José A., 7470
Vierteljahresberichte, 7489a
Vilá, María Electra, 2409
Vilches, Rubén A., 2524-2525
Villa Rojas, Alfonso, 1111
Villagra Caletti, Agustín, 550
Villagra de García, Sara Delicia, 1635
Villalba, Rodrigo, 2165
Villamil, José A., 1982
Villamizar V., Jaime, 2044
Villanueva, Benjamín, 6672
Villanueva, Javier, 2410
Villanueva, Víctor, 7705
Villar, Daniel, 7993
Villar Roces, Mario, 2526
Villarán, José Luis, 1401, 1421
Villarreal, Juan F., 6138
Villas Bôas, Aldo, 1680
Villas Boas, Cláudio, 1328
Villas Boas, Orlando, 1328
Villasis Terán, Enrique M., 137
Villegas, Jorge, 7670
Villegas V., Alberto, 6906

Villela, Annibal V., 2416
Villius, Hans, 7585
Viñas, Ismael, 1894
Violand de Ponce, Emma, 6090
Violich, Francis, 6609
Visser, J. D., 7706
Vitale, Luis, 7788
Vitalis, Hellmut Gnadt, 7490
Viteri A., Enrique, 6877
Viteri Gamboa, Julio, 896
Vivante, Armando, 805
Vivó, Paquita, 52a, 138
Viya, Miko, 8335
Vogt, Evon Zartman, 1112
Voigtlander, Katherine, 1636
Volio Jiménez, Fernando, 8361
Vollmar, Rainer, 6938
Volskii, Viktor V., 6066, 6610-6610b
von Brunn, Reinhard, 7489a
Von Lazar, Arpad, 7491-7492, 7770
von Schuler-Schömig, Immina, 533
Von Winning, Hasso, 713-715, 820
Voorhies, Barbara, 716
Voorhis, Paul H., 1637
Vries, Jan de, 1212
Wadhams, Peter, 6898
Wagenheim, Kal, 2527
Waggoner, Barbara Ashton, 6032, 6104
Waggoner, George R., 6032, 6104
Wagley, Charles, 139
Wagner, Erika, 1023-1027
Wagner, Philip L., 6611
Wainer, Judith Carson, 668
Waisanen, F.B., 8289
Waldmann, Peter, 7493
Walcott, Derek, 1180
Wald, Richard A., 1906
Walker, Malcolm T., 1213-1214
Walker, Neuma Aguiar, 8554
Walker, Thomas W., 7834
Walker Errasuriz, Francisco, 2253
Wall, David, 1895
Wallace, Alfred Russell, 7190
Wallace, Dwight T., 1011
Waller, Robert A., 8102
Walter, Hanf, 7426a
Walter, Heinz, 717
Walter, Ingo, 1896-1897
Walters, Alan, 1956
Walters, Elsa H., 6205
Walton, James, 1638
Walton, Janice, 1638
Waltz, Carolyn, 1640
Waltz, Nathan E., 1639-1640
Wanick Ribeiro, Sylvio. *See* Ribeiro, Sylvio Wanick.
Ward, Richard H., 1770
Warman, Arturo, 1113
Warner, Maureen, 1215-1216
Wassén, S. Henry, 140, 534, 821, 1329
Waterbury, Ronald, 1114

Waterhouse, Viola, 1640a
Watson, Lawrence C., 1330-1332
Weaver, F. Stirtin, 1898
Weaver, Jerry L., 7494
Weaver, Muriel Porter, 618
Webb, Kempton E., 6612
Webb, Richard, 2304
Webster, Steven S., 510, 1503-1506
Weckstein, R. S., 6757
Weeks, John R., 2254
Weeks, Morris, Jr., 6633
Weffort, Francisco, 7376, 8256
Weil, Thomas E., 6944
Weinkle, Julian, 2005-2006
Weiss, Gerald, 510, 1333
Weiss, Joseph S., 2480
Weisskoff, Richard, 2528
Weitkamp, Lowell R., 1767, 1771-1772
Weitlaner, Roberto J., 1115
Welch, Betty, 1641
Welch, Claude E., Jr., 7609
Weller, Robert H., 6613
Wells, Henry, 7627
Wences Reza, Rosalio, 6162
Wendler, Hans J., 7489a
Wesche, Marjorie Bingham, 1217
Wesche, Rolf, 6957
West, Birdie, 1641
West Indian Agricultural Economics Conference, *IV, Cave Hill, Barbados, 1969*, 2037
Westheim, Paul, 619
Westley, David O., 1642
Westphalen, Cecília Maria, 7191
Weyl, Richard, 6685-6686
Wheaton, Philip E., 8381
Wheeler, Alva, 1639, 1643
Whitaker, Arthur P., 7495
White, John, 1899
Whitehead, Laurence, 2181, 8103
Whitehead, Lawrence. *See* Whitehead, Laurence.
Whitehead, P. C., 1410
Whitten, Norman E., Jr., 1507
Whyte, William F., 1424, 7695
Wiarda, Howard J., 7496-7498
Wiarda, Ièda Siqueira, 8462
Wicke, Charles R., 620
Wiercinski, Andrzej, 510
Wiesemann, Ursula, 1334, 1644
Wilbert, Johannes, 1335
Wilgus, A. Curtis, 17
Wilken, Gene C., 621
Wilkening, Eugene A., 8503, 8555
Wilkerson, S. Jeffrey K., 718
Wilkie, James W., 7720
Willey, Gordon R., 530, 719-720
Williams, Aubrey W., Jr., 530
Williams, Edward J., 8104
Williams, Eric, 1179
Williams, Lawrence K., 1424, 7695

Williams, Lynden S., 6614
Williams, Miles W., 7662
Williams, R. J. Luke, 39
Williams, R. L., 2038
Williams, Stephen, 622
Wils, F. C. M., 7707
Wilson, Desmond P., Jr., 7610
Wilson, Jacques M. P., 6143
Wilson, Larman C., 8151, 8183
Wilson, Michael R., 6663
Wilson, Peter J., 1218
Winkelman, Don, 1951
Winsberg, Morton, 6840
Wionczek, Miguel S., 1821, 1900-1901, 8336
Wise, Mary Ruth, 1645-1648
Wish, John Reed, 2529
Witter, G. P., 6315
Wittfogel, Karl A., 574
Wöhlcke, Manfred, 7409
Wolf, Monika, 8337
Wolgemuth, Carl, 1650
Wolpin, Miles D., 6067-6068, 7789-7790, 8184
Womack, John, Jr., 7541
Wonsewer, Israel, 7374
Wood, Bernard M., 8105
Wood, Bryce, 6069, 8106
Wood, Walter A., 6924
Woodall, J. P., 1767
Woodbury, Richard B., 574
Woodhall, Maureen, 6140
Woods, Clyde M., 1116
Worcester, Donald E., 1902
The world as seen from Moscow: Latin America; Mexico, Costa Rica, Panama, Cuba, Haiti, Dominican Republic, Venezuela, Colombia, Ecuador, Peru, Chile, Argentina, Uruguay, Paraguay, 8107
Wormald Cruz, Alfredo, 6899
Worthington, E. B., 6652
Wright, Freeman J., 6070
Wyatt, R. G., 1672
Wylie, Kathryn H., 6637
Yáñez, Agustín, 6163
Yángüez B., Juan A., 869
Yarrow, Jorge M., 510, 1508
Yarza de la Torre, Esperanza, 6758
Yarza G., Alberto J., 1952
Yaukey, David, 8290
Yde, Jens, 1012
Yepes del Castillo, Ernesto, 2305
Yglesias, José, 7499, 7611
Ygobone, Aquiles D., 8247
Ynsfrán, Pablo Max, 141
Young, Jordan M., 7892
Young, Philip D., 1117
Young, Ruth C., 1903-1904
Youssef, Madia H., 8291
Ypiranga Monteiro, Mário. *See* Monteiro, Mário Ypiranga.
Yudelman, Montague, 6615

AUTHOR INDEX

Yurchenco, Henrietta, 8407
Yver, Raúl E., 2255
Zago, Angela, 7830
Zahl, Paul A., 6780
Zahn, Margaret A., 8408
Zambrano, A., 7344
Zammit, J. Ann, 2256
Zamora, Rita, 1906
Zanotti, Luis Jorge, 6071
Zapata, Antonio, 7364
Zapata, Juan Antonio, 2411
Zapata Gollán, Agustín, 8463
Zárate, Dora P. de, 510, 1118
Zavala, C., 1773
Zavala de Aquino, Carolina, 8362
Zavaleta Mercado, René, 7456
Zea, Leopoldo, 6164, 8338
Zeballos, Jorge, 1719
Zegers de Landa, Gerardo, 2257

Zeil, Werner, 6874
Zellers, Margaret, 6620
Zéndegui, Guillermo de, 6689
Zeni, Enrique R., 2412
Zepeda Henríquez, Eduardo, 142
Zetti, Jorge, 806, 6811
Zeuske, Max, 7424a
Ziehm, Elsa, 1651
Zimmer, Norbert, 143
Zorina, A. M., 7612
Zsilincsar, Walter, 6616
Zubatsky, David S., 59
Zubieta, Roberto, 2386
Zucchi de Romero, Alberta, 1028-1030
Zuidema, R. Tom, 1013
Zuleta, Estanislao, 7640
Zuvekas, Clarence, Jr., 2102
Zylberberg, J., 2258